THE BUILDINGS OF ENGLAND

FOUNDING EDITOR: NIKOLAUS PEVSNER

SOMERSET:
SOUTH AND WEST

JULIAN ORBACH
AND
NIKOLAUS PEVSNER

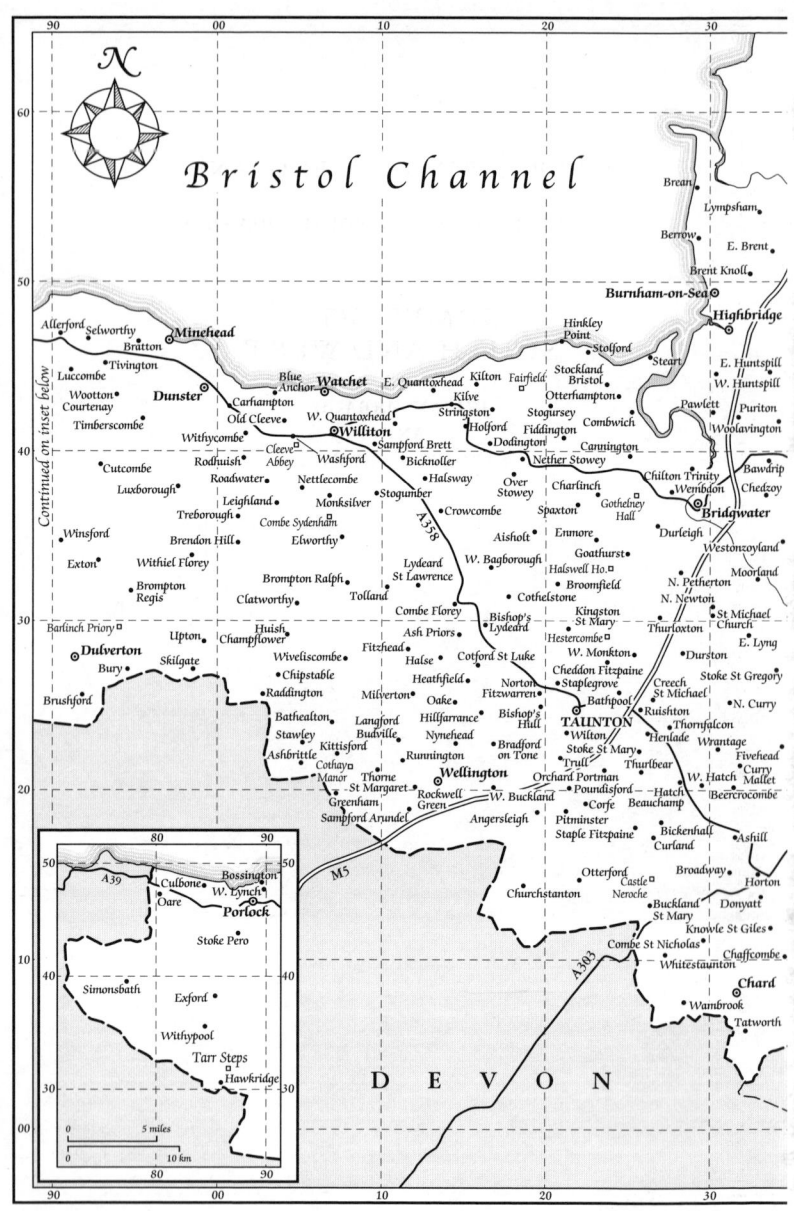

PEVSNER ARCHITECTURAL GUIDES

The Buildings of England series was created and largely written by Sir Nikolaus Pevsner (1902–83). First editions of the county volumes were published by Penguin Books between 1951 and 1974. The continuing programme of revisions and new volumes was supported between 1994 and 2011 by research financed through the Pevsner Books Trust. That responsibility has now been assumed by the Paul Mellon Centre for Studies in British Art.

Donations from

STACKS

helped support the *Buildings of England* series, 2006–14

Somerset: South and West

BY
JULIAN ORBACH
AND
NIKOLAUS PEVSNER

THE BUILDINGS OF ENGLAND

YALE UNIVERSITY PRESS
NEW HAVEN AND LONDON

YALE UNIVERSITY PRESS
NEW HAVEN AND LONDON

302 Temple Street, New Haven CT 06511
47 Bedford Square, London WC1B 3DP
www.pevsner.co.uk
www.lookingatbuildings.org.uk
www.yalebooks.co.uk
www.yalebooks.com

Published by Yale University Press 2014
2 4 6 8 10 9 7 5 3 1

ISBN 978 0 300 20740 8

Copyright © Nikolaus Pevsner, 1958
Copyright © Julian Orbach, 2014

Printed in China
through World Print
Set in Monotype Plantin

All rights reserved.
This book may not be reproduced
in whole or in part, in any form (beyond that
copying permitted by Sections 107 and 108 of the
U.S. Copyright Law and except by reviewers
for the public press), without written
permission from the publishers

The 1958 edition of
South and West Somerset
was dedicated
TO THE LEVERHULME TRUST

2014 dedication
TO KATE PAWSEY

CONTENTS

LIST OF TEXT FIGURES AND MAPS	x
PHOTOGRAPHIC ACKNOWLEDGEMENTS	xiv
MAP REFERENCES	xv
FOREWORD AND ACKNOWLEDGEMENTS	xvi
INTRODUCTION	1
GEOLOGY AND BUILDING MATERIALS, BY DESMOND DONOVAN AND HUGH PRUDDEN	2
THE PREHISTORIC AND ROMAN PERIODS, BY CHRIS WEBSTER	8
ANGLO-SAXON SOMERSET	14
ECCLESIASTICAL ARCHITECTURE AFTER 1066	16
MEDIEVAL SECULAR ARCHITECTURE	40
TUDOR AND STUART BUILDING, c. 1540–1700	45
LATE STUART AND GEORGIAN, c. 1700–1837	56
ARCHITECTURE 1837–1914	68
ARCHITECTURE AFTER c. 1914	82
FURTHER READING	86
GAZETTEER	91
GLOSSARY	725
INDEX OF ARCHITECTS, ARTISTS, PATRONS AND RESIDENTS	751
INDEX OF PLACES	771

LIST OF TEXT FIGURES AND MAPS

Every effort has been made to contact or trace all copyright holders. The publishers will be glad to make good any errors or omissions brought to our attention in future editions.

Geological map, drawn by Michael J. Sims	3
South Cadbury, Cadbury Castle, engraving after W. Stukeley (W. Stukeley, *Itinerarium Curiosum*, 1724)	13
Penselwood, St Michael, doorway, engraving by William Barnes, early C19	18
Somerset church towers	30–1
Somerset church window traceries	34
Kingston St Mary, St Mary, bench-ends, engraving (*Proceedings of the Somerset Archaeology and Natural History Society* vol. 18, 1872)	38
Bossington, cottage, drawing by J. Crowther (C. E. H. Chadwyck-Healey, *The History of the Part of West Somerset ...*, 1901)	50
Witham Friary, design for Witham Park, front elevation, engraving (C. Campbell, *Vitruvius Britannicus*, vol. II, 1717)	58
Taunton Castle, under alteration, engraving after C. Warre Bampfylde (J. Toulmin, *The History of Taunton, in the County of Somerset*, 1791)	60
Bridgwater, former Town Bridge, engraving, 1797	66
Taunton School, engraving, 1870, courtesy of the Somerset Archaeological and Natural History Society	79
Allerford, bridge and cottages, drawing by J. Crowther (C. E. H. Chadwyck-Healey, *The History of the Part of West Somerset ...*, 1901)	95
Bower Hinton, Parrett Works, bird's-eye view, engraving, c. 1865	126
Bridgwater, St Mary, engraving by T. Bonnor (J. Collinson, *The History and Antiquities of the County of Somerset*, 1791)	134
Brympton D'Evercy, Brympton House, from the south, engraving by J. Kip (J. Kip and L. Knyff, *Britannia Illustrata*, 1707)	164
Castle Cary, All Saints, before alteration, watercolour by J. Buckler, 1833, courtesy of the Somerset Archaeological and Natural History Society	182

LIST OF TEXT FIGURES AND MAPS

Castle Neroche, plan, courtesy of Lesley & Roy Adkins/ Dovecote Press	185
Chard, Fore Street, engraving (G. P. R. Pulman, *The Book of the Axe*, 1875)	190
Cleeve Abbey, plan, reproduced by permission of English Heritage	207
Cleeve Abbey, cloister, engraving by T. Bonnor (J. Collinson, *The History and Antiquities of the County of Somerset*, 1791)	210
Combe Sydenham, drawing by J. Crowther (C. E. H. Chadwyck-Healey, *The History of the Part of West Somerset …*, 1901)	218
Crewkerne Grammar School, engraving (*The Builder*, 28 August 1880)	236
Culbone, St Beuno, drawing by J. Crowther (C. E. H. Chadwyck-Healey, *The History of the Part of West Somerset …*, 1901)	247
Dillington House, before alteration, engraving (J. P. Neale, *Jones' Views of the Seats, Mansions, Castles etc. of Noblemen and Gentlemen in England, Wales, Scotland and Ireland*, 1829)	255
Dunster Castle, before alteration, watercolour by J. Buckler, 1839, © National Trust Images	270
Dunster Castle, ground-floor and first-floor plans, © National Trust Images	272
Dunster, Yarn Market, engraving (*The Builder*, 20 August 1892)	275
Enmore Castle, before alteration, engraving (J. P. Neale, *Jones' Views of the Seats, Mansions, Castles etc. of Noblemen and Gentlemen in England, Wales, Scotland and Ireland*, 1829)	296
Glastonbury Abbey, bird's-eye view, engraving after W. Stukeley (W. Stukeley, *Itinerarium Curiosum*, 1724)	306
Glastonbury Abbey, plan (after C.A. Ralegh Radford, *The Pictorial History of Glastonbury Abbey*, 1966)	309
Glastonbury Abbey, gatehouse, engraving by William Barnes, early C19	317
Halsway Manor, before alteration, engraving (*Proceedings of the Somerset Archaeology and Natural History Society* vol. 15, 1868–9)	338
Halswell House, engraving by T. Bonnor (J. Collinson, *The History and Antiquities of the County of Somerset*, 1791)	341
Hestercombe House, formal gardens, plan drawn by R. W. M. and J. M. Monks, Yale University Press, 1989	354
Hinton St George, Hinton House, before alteration, engraving by T. Bonnor (J. Collinson, *The History and Antiquities of the County of Somerset*, 1791)	362

Ilminster, St Mary, brass to Nicholas and
Dorothy Wadham †1609 and 1618, reproduced
courtesy of H. Martin Stuchfield — 376

Kingweston House, engraving (J. P. Neale,
*Jones' Views of the Seats, Mansions, Castles etc. of
Noblemen and Gentlemen in England, Wales, Scotland
and Ireland*, 1829) — 393

Langport, Cocklemoor Bridge, drawing by R. La Trobe-
Bateman, *c.* 2004 — 398

Lympsham, Manor House and church, engraving
by W. Willis, *c.* 1840, courtesy of the Somerset
Archaeological and Natural History Society — 415

Lytes Cary, ground-floor plan showing enlargement,
by C. E. Ponting (*Building News*, 2 July 1909) — 418

Marston Bigot, Marston House, engraving by
R. Parr (J. Badeslade and J. Rocque, *Vitruvius
Britannicus* vol. IV, 1739) — 423

Martock, The Treasurer's House, plan, drawn by
Margaret Wood, 1949 (M. Wood, *The English
Medieval House*, 1965) — 429

Meare, Manor Farm, engraving after A. Nesbitt
(*Proceedings of the Somerset Archaeology and
Natural History Society* vol. 9, 1859) — 433

Milverton, former market cross, engraving (C. Pooley,
*An Historical and Descriptive Account of the Old Stone
Crosses of Somerset*, 1877) — 447

Minehead, St Michael, rood screen, engraving
after E. B. Nevinson (*Architectural Association
sketchbook*, second series, vol. 4, 1882) — 450

Montacute House, ground-floor and first-floor plans,
© National Trust Images — 466

Montacute House, hall screen, engraving by Laing
(*The Builder*, 22 January 1848) — 468

Muchelney Abbey, plan (adapted from English
Heritage guidebook, *Muchelney Abbey*, 2011),
reproduced by permission of English Heritage — 472

Pendomer, St Roch, monument probably to
Sir John Dummer †1320, engraving
(*Proceedings of the Somerset Archaeological and
Natural History Society* vol. 17, 1871) — 517

Porlock, the Ship Inn, drawing by J. Crowther
(C. E. H. Chadwyck-Healey, *The History of the
Part of West Somerset ...*, 1901) — 528

Shapwick House, engraving by T. Bonnor
(J. Collinson, *The History and Antiquities of the
County of Somerset*, 1791) — 553

'Somerton Castle', drawing by J. C. Buckler, 1830,
courtesy of the Somerset Archaeological and
Natural History Society — 560

South Petherton, Manor House, before alteration,
engraving (W. H. H. Rogers, *Memorials of the West,
Historical and Descriptive*, 1888) — 568

Stoke Pero church, before restoration, drawing by
J. Crowther (C. E. H. Chadwyck-Healey, *The History
of the Part of West Somerset ...*, 1901) — 586

Stoke-sub-Hamdon, St Mary, interior, engraving
(*Proceedings of the Somerset Archaeology and
Natural History Society* vol. 3, 1853) — 590

Taunton Castle, plan (adapted by C. Webster after
original by H. St G. Gray, 1940–1) — 616

Taunton, Market House and New Market, drawing
by E. Turle, 1829, courtesy of the Somerset
Archaeological and Natural History Society — 623

West Bagborough, Triscombe House, drawing by
Ernest Newton (*Building News*, 28 July 1905) — 664

West Camel, Anglo-Saxon cross, engravings
(C. Pooley, *An Historical and Descriptive Account
of the Old Stone Crosses of Somerset*, 1877) — 668

West Pennard, churchyard cross, engraving
(C. Pooley, *An Historical and Descriptive
Account of the Old Stone Crosses of Somerset*, 1877) — 683

West Quantoxhead, St Audries, plan
(*The Architect*, 21 September 1872) — 685

Wincanton, St Peter and St Paul, before rebuilding,
drawing by J. Buckler, 1844, courtesy of the
Somerset Archaeological and Natural History Society — 694

Witham Friary, Witham Park, elevation, engraving by
T. White after J. Woolfe (J. Woolfe and J. Gandon,
Vitruvius Britannicus, vol. V, 1771) — 702

MAPS

South and West Somerset	ii–iii
Bridgwater	139
Glastonbury	322
Minehead	452
Taunton	608
Yeovil	719

PHOTOGRAPHIC ACKNOWLEDGEMENTS

The photographs were almost all taken by James O. Davies (© James O. Davies). We are grateful for permission to reproduce the remaining photographs from the sources below.

© English Heritage: 5, 15, 30

© Landmark Trust: 56

© National Trust Images: 28, 54, 59, 60, 63, 79, 81, 88

MAP REFERENCES

The numbers printed in italic type in the margin against the place names in the gazetteer of the book indicate the position of the place in question on the index map (pp. ii–iii), which is divided into sections by the 10-km. reference lines of the National Grid. The reference given here omits the two initial letters which in a full grid reference refer to the 100-km. squares into which the county is divided. The first two numbers indicate the *western* boundary, and the last two the *southern* boundary, of the 10-km. square in which the place in question is situated. For example, Aisholt (reference 1030) will be found in the 10-km. square bounded by grid lines 10 (on the *west*) and 20, and 30 (on the *south*) and 40; Yeovilton (reference 5020) in the square bounded by the grid lines 50 (on the *west*) and 60, and 20 (on the *south*) and 30.

The map contains all those places, whether towns, villages, or isolated buildings, which are the subject of separate entries in the text.

FOREWORD AND ACKNOWLEDGEMENTS

This new edition replaces Nikolaus Pevsner's *South and West Somerset* of 1958. The companion volume of 1958, *North Somerset and Bristol*, was revised by Andrew Foyle as *Somerset: North and Bristol* in 2011. (This northern volume incorporates much material from paperback *City Guides* to Bath and Bristol, published in 2003 and 2004.) The chief difference in scope from the old account concerns the division with the rest of Somerset, which now runs further N on the eastern side of the county, giving a roughly straight line beneath the Mendips from Brean on the coast just S of Weston-super-Mare to Woodlands on the Wiltshire boundary just S of Frome. The line passes to the S of, and does not include, the towns of Axbridge, Cheddar, Wells, Shepton Mallet and Frome. Included in this volume, but previously in the North Somerset and Bristol volume, are a group of entries for places S of that line: Batcombe, Chesterblade, Cloford, East Cranmore, Gare Hill, Henton, Marston Bigot, Milton Clevedon, Penselwood, South Brewham, Stavordale Priory, Trudoxhill, Wanstrow, Westcombe, West Cranmore, Witham Friary, Woodlands, and Wookey (but not Wookey Hole).

Pevsner's two volumes were based on his tours of the county in 1955. The research for Somerset was done in 1953 by Mrs Schilling and revised by Miss Mary Littlemore. His coverage of the rural parts of the county was hampered by the absence for Somerset of the lists of historic buildings then being compiled by the Ministry of Housing and Local Government. That he missed so few of the most important buildings is all the more impressive. Small flashes of Pevsner in action have survived, anecdote verging on myth, the car arriving, the man in a macintosh asking to see the staircase, being shown it, remarking, 'It is just as I thought' and turning to leave, declining offers of tea as there was not time. His visit to Fairfield is remembered for his single comment: 'This seems to be genuine.' It is humbling to have put four years into revising a work produced at such speed, but with such clarity of judgement. The text has been greatly expanded by the inclusion of those rural houses for which information was not available in 1955, of industrial and vernacular buildings, of Victorian and Edwardian buildings that in 1955 were at the nadir of academic or public interest, and of buildings erected since then.

A great number of people have helped in the research for this volume, but first of all I should thank all those in Somerset who made the county such a delight to work in and especially those in Langport who made the living in the county so easy. The list of organizations that helped begins with the staff of the Somerset Heritage Centre, under Tom Mayberry, including those of the County Record Office and erstwhile Local Studies Centre, especially David Bromwich. Thanks are also due to Bob Croft and Chris Webster of the County Archaeology Department, and to the Exmoor National Park archaeologist, Rob Wilson-North. Mary Siraut of the *Victoria County History* and her predecessor, Dr Robert Dunning, have been unfailingly helpful, always sharing research. The Somerset volumes of the VCH are among the best of the county series, and the generosity of the VCH in making both published volumes and work in progress available online is a shining example.

The Somerset Archaeological and Natural History Society welcomed me to its meetings, events and historic buildings committee. Much advice has come from historic buildings committee members and members alike, but especial thanks are due to Anthony Bruce, Mary Ewing, Alex Maxwell Findlater, Alan Hudson, John Page, Nigel Pearce, Neil Rushton, Chris Sidaway and Anita Sims of the committee. The help from the Somerset-based English Heritage officers, Jenny Chesher and Francis Kelly, has been unstinting. From the National Trust staff, thanks are due to the Holnicote estate office, the house managers at Dunster and Montacute and especially Del Wiggins at Barrington Court. The Somerset Vernacular Buildings Research Group encouraged me, made me welcome at their meetings and made information available. Thanks are especially due to John Dallimore, Denny Robbins and Dave Taylor. From the Somerset Industrial Archaeological Society, a great debt is owed to Brian Murless; from the Wessex Mills Group, the debt is to Stephen Bartlett; and to all the mill-owners, a most welcoming bunch of people.

Thanks should be given to those who contributed specialist sections to the book. The foreword to both Somerset volumes of 1958 thanked Mr D. T. Donovan of Bristol University for the 'geological remarks'. Fifty-six years later the same Desmond Donovan, now Emeritus Professor, has, with Hugh Prudden, recast the building materials introduction to cover the southern half of the county, a continuity unrivalled in the *Buildings of England* series. The building stones map has been drawn by Mike Simms. The archaeological entries and the introductory piece on archaeology in 1958 were provided by Jon Manchip White, who died in Knoxville, Tennessee, in 2013, after a later career in film and as a novelist. The archaeology entries have been revised by Chris Webster, who has written a new introduction to the archaeology.

There are those to whom the debt is general rather than specific, to the depth of their generosity as much as the breadth of their knowledge: the late Ian Constantinides, Fergus Dowding, Nick Durnan, Robert Dunning, Andrew Foyle, Peter Howell, Russell Lillford, Mark McDermott, Jerry Sampson, John Schofield, Mary Siraut and John Winstone. Joshua Schwieso wrote drafts for parishes between Crowcombe and Stogursey when the timetable risked being entirely lost, and discovered important things about Crowcombe Court. Stephen Croad generously passed on all his notes on Somerset country houses. John Foden convened a meeting of former architects in the County Architect's Department, to help me form a picture of that most important generator of modern buildings in the county. Malcolm Thurlby has twice broken visits from Canada to add his expertise to the question of Saxo-Norman overlap at Milborne Port and to Romanesque–Gothic overlap at Glastonbury. Brian and Moira Gittos have revised all the material on effigial monuments and on early medieval churches. Robin Downes was generous with his researches for the Corpus of Romanesque Sculpture. Nicholas Cooper helped with C16–C17 houses, especially Barrington Court and Brympton House. Geoffrey Fisher has contributed those attributions for sculpture marked (GF), as he has to so many other volumes of the series. Jeannie Hobhouse has given advice on paintings. David Hunt contributed generously on Second World War matters, Jeremy Gould and Diana Crighton on C20 architecture. Thanks are due to the many readers who contributed corrections to the 1958 text, notably George McHardy and David Palliser. An enormous debt is owed to Alan Brooks for being prepared to offer opinions on C19 stained glass unstintingly and for supplying references from his own research. Advice on stained glass has come also from Jim Cheshire, Peter Cormack and Martin Harrison. For geology, Desmond Donovan and Hugh Prudden must be joined by Eric Robinson in a trio who made the rocks of Somerset come to life.

The following were generous with their research on particular artists: James Bettley (T. G. Jackson), Matthew Craske (Henry Cheere), Peter Howell (J. F. Bentley), Paul Joyce (G. E. Street), Russell Lillford (Richard Carver), Tony Nicholson (C. E. Ponting) and Sarah Whittingham (George Oatley). I was greatly helped in particular places by people with special local knowledge: Simon Andrew (Crewkerne), Charles Bird (Hinton St George), John Bishton (Bruton), Roger Carter (Chard), Peter Cattermole (Bridgwater), Penny Cudmore (Norton-sub-Hamdon), Oliver Davies (Minehead), Caroline Gould (Street), William Hobson (Elworthy and the Smith-Escott family), Nancy Langmaid (Somerton), Tony Lock (Nynehead), Brian Luker (Wookey), David Martyn (Yeovil), Michael McGarvie (Marston Bigot), Carol Parker (Stoke-sub-Hamdon), Liz Randall (South Petherton), Pam Slocombe (Mark), Chris Smith (Langport), Duncan Stafford (West Quantoxhead), John Townson (Hatch Beauchamp) and David Worthy (the Quantocks).

I was welcomed by too many country house owners to name here, with unfailing generosity. Especial thanks are due to those who gave me the benefit of their own researches and knowledge: at Barford House, Donald Rice; at Cloford Manor, Richard Mawer; at Cothay Manor, Alastair and Mary Anne Robb; at Croydon House, John Prideaux; at Ditcheat Priory, Dermot Coleman; at Fairfield, Lady Gass; at Hadspen House, Niall Hobhouse; at Hinton House, Rupert Lewin; at Lympsham Manor, James Counsell; at Ven House, Jasper Conran; at Westholme

House, Mark Franklin; and at Whitestaunton Manor, Stuart Moore.

Last but not least I must thank those whose hospitality was especially generous, and those whose networks of acquaintance opened many a door to me: Delia and Peter Allen, Jane and Francis Blake, Hattie and Alex Findlater, Harriet Graham, Fleur and Francis Kelly, Philippa Lewis and Miles Thistlethwaite, Charlotte and the late David Mayou, Paddy and Judith O'Hagan, Yseult Ogilvie, Biddy Peppin and David Curtis, Pek Peppin and Will Vaughan, and Paul and Sophia Quinn who gave me a base for exploring West Somerset. Hermione Hobhouse introduced me to South Somerset in 1975 and was there to welcome me back in 2009.

This book could not have been produced without funding from the Paul Mellon Centre, or the support and patience of the team at Yale University Press. Sally Salvesen was the commissioning editor. Simon Bradley edited the book with care and precision. Phoebe Lowndes managed the editing and designed the inset, seeing the book through to publication with the assistance of Catherine Bankhurst and Alice Winborn, the latter especially responsible for the text figure illustrations. Judith Wardman compiled the indexes.

In the established Pevsner tradition, I take full responsibility for any inadvertent errors or omissions, and appeal to readers to draw them to our attention for future revision.

INTRODUCTION

The south of the county is our subject, politically the modern administrative county of Somerset minus the Mendip Hills which are included in the *Somerset: North and Bristol* volume, as is the entire area covered by the two unitary authorities, North Somerset, and Bath and North-East Somerset. Southern Somerset is a serene region, varied in mood more than most, yet always mild, if without the subtropical displays as you find them in Devon and Cornwall. Even Exmoor is greener and warmer than Dartmoor and Bodmin Moor. There are almost East Anglian stretches in the flat watery meadows and brick cottages of the Levels, yet one never feels the endlessness of the East Anglian expanses. The plain of Somerset cuts across the county in a SE direction. Much of the land here is below sea level, yet always in the background are hills, varying in scale from the Mendips behind the Levels of the River Axe to the Polden Hills dividing Sedgemoor from the Avalon Marshes, to the nameless ridge dividing West Sedgemoor from the Southern Levels. The hills rise to 1,700 ft (520 metres) with Dunkery Beacon in Exmoor towards the W end of the county, and to just over 1,000 ft (305 metres) in the Mendips along the northern edge of the plain. The Exmoor coastline W of Porlock, where the hills rise to 900 ft (275 metres) straight out of the sea, is the grandest piece of scenery that Somerset has to offer, and the only coastline comparable with that of Devon and Cornwall. After Minehead, the Bristol Channel narrows to become the Severn estuary, and rocks give way to low muddy cliffs full of fossils and alabaster and then to the muddy foreshores of Bridgwater Bay.

Across South Somerset, between Exmoor and the Mendips, are a variety of hills, mostly running E–W. Behind the coast at Watchet are the Brendon Hills, sloping to the S into Devon. Their level ridge connects Exmoor to the broad valley NW of Taunton. On the other side of this valley, the Quantocks run SE from the coast at West Quantoxhead to the Levels between Bridgwater and Taunton. The Quantocks have an especially scenic quality, self-contained, rising in wooded combes to a long bare ridge, 1,261 ft (384 metres) at the highest point. S of the Quantocks is the fertile Vale of Taunton Deane, some sixty square miles between Taunton and Wellington, through which runs the River Tone. From the vale, the Quantocks form a clear horizon on the N, the Blackdown Hills on the S, with the Brendon Hills less defined on the W. The Blackdown Hills roll S into Dorset. E of them, the Windwhistle ridge touches 778 ft (238 metres) between Chard and Crewkerne, declining to low hills before Yeovil. W of Yeovil, Ham Hill, although not high, forms a prominent edge to the Southern Levels. E of Yeovil, downs run N from Sherborne in Dorset to Castle Cary, most impressively above Corton Denham. These downs are bounded on the E by the low-lying Marshwood Vale. N of Castle Cary and Bruton, hills roll E from the Glastonbury Levels to the high wooded ridge along the Wiltshire boundary, crowned by Alfred's Tower.

Extremes in landscape are few outside the long majestic lines of Exmoor. Memorable are the sudden bumps and knolls rising from the watery Levels: Glastonbury Tor (the most famous), Brent Knoll and Burrow Mump. The landscape of the Levels is unforgettable, flat fields bordered by innumerable ditches, called rhynes, and drained by canalized rivers such as the Brue and stately man-made canals, such as the King's Sedgemoor Drain and the Huntspill River, running straight across the landscape. Along the roads and rhynes are willows, pollarded now for tidiness and maintenance rather than the osiers they once provided. The Levels are a country of brick, though that material never achieved the dominance that it did in East Anglia, because the fingers of hills mean that building stones are never far away. This is why there are no brick churches in Somerset, and there is no major use of brick before the late C17.

GEOLOGY AND BUILDING MATERIALS
BY DESMOND DONOVAN AND HUGH PRUDDEN

The rocks of South and West Somerset belong to geological systems from the Devonian to the Cretaceous. Cretaceous rocks are only found only in a small area in the S and E. The generalization that the older the rock, the higher the ground, holds fairly well. Exmoor, the Brendon Hills and the Quantock Hills, made up of Devonian and Carboniferous rocks, form the highest ground, as do the Mendip Hills just to the N of the area. The Permo-Triassic rocks are dominant in Taunton Deane and neighbouring areas. They generally give rise to reddish soils. Jurassic rocks occupy the largest area within South and West Somerset, at least if one includes the Levels where they are covered by Quaternary deposits of alluvium. Freestones were predominantly obtained from the Jurassic rocks, but other rocks were pressed into service locally for ashlar work.

Building stones

The DEVONIAN AND CARBONIFEROUS LIMESTONES of our area were certainly quarried from medieval times, largely for burning for lime and for dry-stone walling, and were not generally

GEOLOGY AND BUILDING MATERIALS

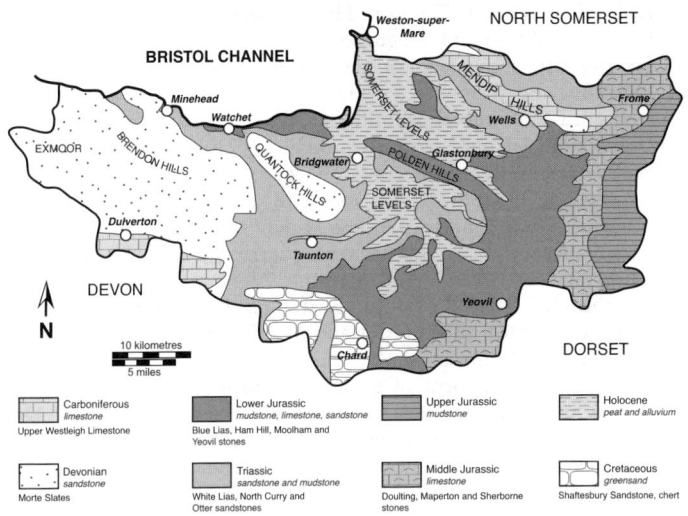

Geological map

suitable for window tracery and carved work. However, the grey UPPER WESTLEIGH LIMESTONE has been used in squared blocks around Wellington and in Taunton, where it was widely used in the late C19 (cf. St Andrew's church; Taunton School). The Upper Palaeozoic rocks of the Quantock Hills and the country to the W were mainly used for rubble masonry, though some slaty beds could be used for roofing. The Devonian HANGMAN GRIT sandstone was used in limited amounts, near the outcrop, as at Minehead and Porlock, where split purple and grey beach boulders are a distinctive feature. It is widely found on northern Exmoor and occurs in the northern Quantocks around Bicknoller. PICKWELL DOWN SANDSTONE makes a colourful building stone, especially in the Dulverton area, such as Dulverton church. The siltstones and fine sandstones of the ILFRACOMBE BEDS occur on Exmoor from Simonsbath to Withycombe, further E to Treborough, where they are interbedded with true slate, and in the middle Quantocks. The rather similar MORTE SLATES are widely found on southern Exmoor and in the Quantocks.

Permo-Triassic rocks underlie the area around Taunton and the Quantocks. They extend further E, where they are largely covered by Quaternary alluvium. The lower part of the sequence includes breccias and the Budleigh Salterton Pebble Beds, which contain pebbles of limestone quarried for lime burning and roadstone. The Permo-Triassic includes two important sandstones which were much quarried. The red OTTER SANDSTONE was used widely in and around Taunton and Wellington, all along the coast from Minehead to Bridgwater, and also up the valley from

Bishop's Lydeard to Williton. The best ashlar came from quarries between Williton and Stogumber. Ashlar from Williton was used for the C19 rebuilding of the tower of St Mary Magdalene, Taunton, and probably for the C15 tower at Bishop's Lydeard. Red sandstone tracery is found locally as a substitute for Jurassic stones from further E, as at Combe Florey church. A pale pinkish-buff variety of the Otter sandstone was widely used for dressings around the Quantocks, for example on Spaxton church. The other important sandstone, less widely used, was the greenish-grey NORTH CURRY SANDSTONE quarried at Knapp near North Curry and also W of Taunton around Norton Fitzwarren, where the church is a good example. It was used as ashlar on Queen's College, Taunton. Both Otter and North Curry sandstones were used for rubble masonry.

ALABASTER, a form of gypsum (hydrous calcium sulphate), occurs in veins, nodules and occasional slabs of Triassic age. Obtained from the cliffs between Watchet and Blue Anchor, it was used for church monuments in the C16 and C17. A short-lived attempt to quarry alabaster from the Triassic Blue Anchor formation was made far to the E, at Hurcott, near Somerton. Somerset alabaster has a more variegated and blotchy appearance than that from the East Midlands.

The Jurassic includes important limestones. Of these, the building stone most widely used in central Somerset was the BLUE LIAS, of latest Triassic and earliest Jurassic age. The Blue Lias formation consists of limestone beds, mostly less than 1 ft (30 cm.) thick, alternating with shales or mudstones of similar thickness. The limestones are generally fine-grained and the lower and upper surfaces more or less planar. Predominantly grey, they may vary from pale to dark, while the weathering along the joints produces a yellowish tinge on some faces. Although the formation is thin, its outcrop area is extensive, hence its ubiquitous, not to say monotonous use from the Polden Hills to Glastonbury, Street, Somerton, innumerable villages in central Somerset, and to the W of Taunton.* Blue Lias limestones could be got in large thin slabs, ideal for paving and ledger slabs in churches, both of which are found in buildings well outside the area of outcrop. Paving slabs are usually less than 3 ft (1 metre) in length, but slabs of 6 by 3 ft (2 by 1 metres) or more were used for ledger stones from the C16 onward. Often used for headstones in churchyards, they weather badly. There is localized use, around the quarries at Keinton Mandeville and Charlton Mackrell, of slabs as garden fences. The WHITE LIAS is found beneath the Blue Lias and occurs in similar thin beds, but weathers to a whitish colour. It was used fairly extensively around Langport and around Queen Camel, mostly in the C19. The church at Hambridge, 1842, is a notable example. WEDMORE STONE, a shelly limestone of similar geological age, was used very locally around Wedmore, notably on the church.

---

* Alec Clifton-Taylor found it 'one of the least attractive of English limestones'.

GEOLOGY AND BUILDING MATERIALS 5

Also used locally was the MARLSTONE (Marlstone Rock Bed in earlier Geological Survey publications), one of several limestones which owe their warm golden brown colour to hydrated iron oxides. Often there are conspicuous fossils. Also known as MOOLHAM STONE, it gives its character to a smallish area near the southern border of the county around Ilminster, used notably in Dowlish Wake church. Buildings in the Yeovil area, in particular Yeovil church, Preston Plucknett church and the adjacent Abbey Manor, are built of YEOVIL STONE, from a bed only a few feet thick, which forms the upper part of the Junction Bed (Barrington Beds) from Seavington St Michael eastwards to the Yeo valley. This is a rubbly, whitish, earthy limestone, a condensed conglomeratic deposit with crinoids, algal mats, bivalves, ammonites and other fossil shell debris. A similar stone is dominant in the Crewkerne area. To the W it gives way to Calcareous Grit of the Upper Greensand. In the E of the county, brown limestones from the FOREST MARBLE and CORNBRASH were used for rubble masonry, almost invariably in thin slabs which were all that could be extracted. Forest Marble is used on Holton and Pendomer churches.

The most important FREESTONES, architecturally, are found in the Lower and Middle Jurassic rocks. From medieval times they were used far beyond the areas where they were quarried. HAM HILL STONE is unique geologically, formed from a local shelly bank in the Bridport Sands, cropping out from Ham Hill itself, W of Yeovil, for about 6 m. to near Crewkerne. Unusually for a freestone, it is a coarse shell-fragment limestone showing conspicuous oblique current bedding. It contains softer bands ½–1 in. (1–2 cm.) thick, which weather out leaving grooves or vents. It is expensive to work but weathers well, to a rich golden brown colour, due to hydrated iron oxides. It is much used for rubble walling. In the surroundings of Ham Hill many buildings are wholly of Ham Hill stone. Parishes which could afford it, mainly near the quarries, built Perp towers completely faced with Ham ashlar – Ilminster, Martock, Norton-sub-Hamdon, Shepton Beauchamp. It was used over a much wider area for dressings – tracery, battlements and pinnacles – combined with local rubble masonry. Combined with Blue Lias in C15 and early C16 church towers to the NW of the quarries, such as Curry Rivel, East Lyng, Huish Episcopi, Isle Abbots and North Petherton, it makes a most attractive alliance. Ham Hill stone is found especially to the S and W of the quarries, where it had the advantage of being a closer source than Doulting, about 20 m. away to the NNE. In Taunton it is combined notably with red sandstone in the two rebuilt medieval church towers.

The outcrop of the INFERIOR OOLITE extends from N to S down the eastern part of Somerset, and supplies most of the limestone freestones in the central and eastern parts of the county. Dundry and Doulting freestones, along with that of Bath, have been used since Roman times, and quarried continuously since at least medieval times. DUNDRY STONE was quarried and used N of the region covered by this book, but is found in some buildings in the northernmost part of the area. Examples include Weare church tower, where it was used in alternate courses with Blue Lias, and a few places near the coast, where it was perhaps brought by water from Bristol. It is a fine-grained stone of pale yellowish colour. DOULTING STONE is the most commonly used freestone over a wide area of Somerset S of the Mendips. Medieval Doulting stone can be fine-grained, but later quarrying, especially in the C19, produced coarser varieties in which constituent grains can be seen. The rock is made up largely of disc-shaped or cylindrical skeletal elements of fossil crinoids, a minute dark spot marking a central canal. In contrast to the Bath freestones, it is not oolitic in texture. Fresh surfaces are pale yellow at best but tend to be a dull whitish colour, less attractive than Ham Hill and some of the Bath stones. Glastonbury Abbey was faced with Doulting stone, though Dundry was imported for some carved work. Perp church towers of villages which could afford it, such as Evercreech and Batcombe, were faced entirely with Doulting ashlar. Freestone dressings with coursed rubble (usually Blue Lias) for walls are standard for towers in central Somerset, such as Westonzoyland. Elsewhere there is a transition to towers of Lias with minimal freestone (Ansford, Babcary, Brent Knoll) and rarely, buildings of Blue Lias with hardly any freestone at all except window tracery (Bawdrip, though this is a C13 tower).

Of more limited importance is HADSPEN or CARY STONE, a local development in the Castle Cary area. Like the Upper Lias of Yeovil, but geologically younger, it is a yellow-brown colour with conspicuous fossils – belemnites, shells. It is responsible for the bright orange-yellow colour of many buildings in Castle Cary and neighbouring villages. As with Ham Hill stone, it is the colour that is attractive, for it is too irregular in texture to be properly classed as a freestone, though sometimes dressed to a smooth surface. Another iron-rich limestone in the Inferior Oolite was quarried in a small area SW of Wincanton, around Maperton. In MAPERTON STONE the iron is concentrated in meandering dark brown veins. It gives local character to a string of villages S of the A303 – Maperton, Blackford and Compton Pauncefoot. SHERBORNE STONE, a pale limestone like Doulting, and also from the Inferior Oolite, was quarried N of Sherborne (Dorset), in the extreme SE of Somerset. The proximity of the Ham Hill quarries limited its penetration into South Somerset.

The use of BATH STONE S of the Mendips was curtailed by the ready availability of Doulting stone until the C19, when it was produced on an industrial scale and exported widely, appearing as dressings on Victorian buildings all over the county. Its occurrence in earlier buildings often indicates later restoration. Curiously Bath stone was used in Anglo-Saxon times, probably from quarries near Bradford on Avon, occurring for example at Milborne Port church, but this use ceased for the rest of the medieval period.

The sandstones of the UPPER GREENSAND formation (LOWER CRETACEOUS) were used in the eastern and south-western parts of the area. The SHAFTESBURY SANDSTONE, a glauconitic sandstone with a greenish tinge, was used as freestone in the extreme E, for example Cucklington church tower. The CALCAREOUS GRIT, a creamy white calcareous sandstone with rounded quartz grains set in a matrix of fine quartz grains and shell fragments, was sourced from a number of pits in the Chard area, the best-known being at Snowdon Hill. It was used on Whitestaunton church and widely in the Blackdown Hills, notably on the Wellington Monument. Flints from the Chalk (Upper Cretaceous) were rarely used in Somerset, though flinty CHERT of Cretaceous origin was used extensively in and around the Blackdown Hills for rubble walling and squared for decorative effect, as on Chard School (1583), with freestone dressings. BEER STONE, a variety of the Middle Chalk mined at Beer, on the SE Devon coast, since Roman times, found its way into buildings in West Somerset and Devon in small quantities.

After the Second World War, ARTIFICIAL STONE, coloured to match Blue Lias limestone or Jurassic freestone, was widely used to face buildings in places where there was a desire or a requirement to harmonize with local materials. Quarrying of natural stone was then at a low ebb, from which it recovered in the late C20 and C21. An earlier artificial stone was Minster Stone, made at Ilminster from *c.* 1914 onwards.

Roofing materials

Apart from major churches, which used lead, medieval buildings were probably roofed with either stone tiles or thatch. There are also natural SLATES in the Ilfracombe Beds in the W, e.g. from Treborough where slates of roofing quality were obtained, used at Dunster Castle as early as 1426. The Treborough quarries were exploited on a relatively large scale by quarrymen from North Wales in the 1840s and worked profitably until 1910. Many small slate quarries existed in the outcrop from Exford to Withycombe. There is a certain amount of slate-hanging of walls in West Somerset, notably on The Nunnery, a medieval jettied house at Dunster, but this is hardly a Somerset style. Rocks thin-bedded enough to be used as stone tiles occur in the Jurassic, for example in the Forest Marble Formation, and examples of their use can be found in the eastern part of the area, including a few churches. Ham Hill was an important source of stone tiles, as can be seen at Montacute. The resulting tiles were not as thin as some well-known Jurassic stone tiles, for example the Stonesfield Slate of Oxfordshire, and the roofs were correspondingly heavy. THATCH still occurs fairly widely through the area, if less widely than in the past. Thatch was replaced by Welsh slates as the latter became available in the C19, though the popularity of CLAY pantiles in Somerset has happily limited their spread. Vernacular stone buildings are most commonly roofed with clay tiles, made in very large quantities at Bridgwater, and also in other localities.

Bricks

The earliest post-Roman use of BRICK has long been claimed for the Gray's Almshouses, Taunton, dated 1635, but the absence of contemporary brick buildings has undermined this dating, and it seems more probable that there was a late C17 refronting here. Brick appears fairly widely in the late C17, such as at Haydon House, near Stoke St Mary (*see* Henlade), and, dated 1698, at Huish Barton, Nettlecombe. By the early C18 it was chosen over stone to face important country houses, the bricks often being made on the site. Crowcombe Court, begun 1723, is faced with brick made locally from the Mercia Mudstone (Triassic). Ven House, Milborne Port, and Earnshill House, Hambridge, are of similar date. Brickyards exploited the alluvial deposits of the Somerset Levels, especially at Bridgwater. Brickmaking on an industrial scale began here in 1709, and spread to other sites in the Levels. Much of the output was exported. Bridgwater has been predominantly brick-built at least since the early C18, with Castle Street, begun 1723, particularly notable. The Bridgwater industry became extinct about 1965. Another important centre was near Wellington, where the brickworks at Poole worked Permo-Triassic mudstones. Begun in 1837, the pit here was over 50 acres in extent when it closed in 1996. In the C19 and early C20 there were around fifty other sites of brick- and tile-making in the area covered by this volume, some large, such as at Minehead, but many of them small, working Jurassic rocks in the E and S and the Permo-Triassic in the central area. In the eastern part of the area the silty upper part of the Charmouth Mudstone Formation (Lower Jurassic; also known as Pennard Sands) was dug for brick- and tile-making, for example at Evercreech Junction and at Glastonbury, where more recent buildings are largely of brick. Place names such as Brickyard Farm in Maperton parish suggest former activity on the Middle Jurassic outcrop.

THE PREHISTORIC AND ROMAN PERIODS
BY CHRIS WEBSTER

South Somerset in prehistory

Somerset has some of the most important archaeological sites in the country, but unfortunately most are not visible. This is certainly true of sites from the first half million years of human occupation when Somerset was dominated by an environment that fluctuated between glacial and temperate climates. During the cold periods the part of northern Europe that would become Britain was uninhabited, at times for tens of thousands of years. The earliest evidence for HUMAN ACTIVITY in Somerset comes from caves in the Mendip Hills to the N but there are also handaxes made from Greensand chert from Cotlake Hill and Norton Fitzwarren close to Taunton. While the material from caves can often be dated by the associated animal remains, finds of stone tools from open sites cannot. Work in other parts of the country suggests that most of these handaxes date from before 300,000 years ago, after which humans became increasingly rare and finally absent for about 120,000 years until about 60,000 years ago. When people returned, perhaps gradually following the spread of large mammals northwards as the climate warmed, they were a more modern species: *Homo neanderthalensis*. There is evidence which may suggest that a group of Neanderthal people hunted along the Mendip Hills, using some of the caves and probably hunting in the lowlands.

There is slightly more evidence from the UPPER PALAEOLITHIC (about 35,000 to 10,000 years ago) from Mendip cave sites, and it was during this period that the first modern humans (*Homo sapiens*) appeared, but habitation was still intermittent as the climate fluctuated rapidly. About 10,000 years ago the climate warmed rapidly, from sub-Arctic to temperate in perhaps as little as fifty years, and woodland gradually became established across southern Britain over the following millennium. Groups of people who had hunted reindeer on the North German plain adapted to the wider range of resources available in the woods and became more settled. Over seventy locations in Somerset have produced large numbers of the small flint flakes known as microliths that these MESOLITHIC people fixed on to tools of wood to form sharp edges. Settlement was still impermanent but certain locations may have been used seasonally, perhaps following the movement of animals. A recent excavation at Hawkcombe Head, close to a spring above Porlock, found the remains of fireplaces and the post-holes of wooden buildings. Radiocarbon dates have shown that the occupation dates to about 7800–7400 B.C. More formalized burial seems to have begun around this time in Mendip caves and also at an open site at Greylake, near Westonzoyland. The change in climate also saw rapid sea-level rise, bringing the sea close to Somerset for the first time and finally making Britain an island about 7,500 years ago.

Around 4000 B.C. this lifestyle of hunting wild animals and gathering natural resources was challenged by a new idea: farming. It is not clear exactly how the change occurred but for those who adopted the NEOLITHIC way of life the change was profound. Controlling domestic animals and caring for crops meant that land had to be cleared of forest and people had to remain in the same location. New foods, such as bread and cheese, were available; the use of pottery allowed new ways of cooking and storage; and with the newly introduced sheep came wool and woven clothes. This economic basis to society then remained fundamentally the same until the Industrial Revolution. Very few Neolithic settlements are known, perhaps suggesting that mobility was still important, but people expressed themselves by the communal construction of huge monuments: circles defined by earthwork banks (HENGES), linear monuments (CURSUS), again defined by earth banks, and large earthen mounds containing the remains of the dead (LONG BARROWS).

They also encircled hilltops with lines of banks and ditches, cut with regular gaps (CAUSEWAYED ENCLOSURES). Surviving examples of earth circles are known at Priddy (N)* on Mendip (dated to before 2870 B.C.) and a small causewayed enclosure has recently been discovered during work on a gas pipeline near South Petherton. Seven features that may be cursus are known from aerial photographs, several of them in the Westonzoyland/Chedzoy area, and there may well be a causewayed enclosure hidden by the later ramparts at Cadbury Castle. Long barrows are more common but again only a small number survive, predominantly on Mendip.

The construction and use of all these monuments was accompanied by rituals expressed in the deliberate placing of objects and materials in certain places, such as along the bottoms of the ditches. Burial also involved rituals, with only certain parts of certain bodies being placed in the long barrows, sometimes in chambers constructed of huge stones (megaliths), and the grave being opened periodically for new activity. Many of these monuments seem to be associated with unusual landscape features (such as the numerous swallet holes around the Priddy Circles) and several have evidence of Mesolithic activity preceding them. In other places, excavations sometimes uncover small pits that, again, appear to have had groups of objects deliberately buried within them.

The peatlands of central Somerset provide some of the most spectacular evidence from the Neolithic, but it must be remembered that this was in response to unusual environmental conditions often over short periods. The peat, which had been forming for about a millennium in very wet conditions, was crossed by wooden structures running between drier raised areas. The earliest, the Post Track, has been tree-ring-dated to 3838 B.C.; it was replaced by the more famous Sweet Track thirty-two years later. The Sweet Track was over 1¼ m. long, running between Westhay and Shapwick. Examination of the wood has shown that at the southern end, some timber was from re-grown woodland which had been cleared 100 years earlier, while at the northern end some was from mature forest with oak trees over 400 years old. These old trees were over 3 ft (1 metre) in diameter when they were felled using only stone axes. Numerous other trackways are known, continuing into the Bronze Age, with differing constructional techniques and following different routes as the environment changed.

Burials are rare from the Middle and Late Neolithic, but the beginning of the BRONZE AGE sees the widespread use of ROUND BARROWS (of earth) and CAIRNS (of stone), usually with a single primary inhumation or cremation burial. These mounds are very common in parts of Somerset (Mendip, the Quantocks and Exmoor) but very few have been excavated using modern techniques. Evidence for settlement continues to be rare in the Early

---

* (N) indicates places covered by the companion *Buildings of England* volume, *Somerset: North and Bristol*.

Bronze Age, but fragments of oval houses were recorded from the sand cliffs of Brean Down. The construction of monuments appears to continue into the Early Bronze Age with STONE ROWS, CIRCLES and other settings known from Exmoor. Unlike the better known sites on Dartmoor, the Exmoor examples are often formed of quite small rocks that can be hard to spot in the vegetation. Some appear only when the peat soil shrinks in dry conditions. None has been dated, but the use of small stones appears to be a deliberate local variation, as there are larger stones that could have been, and sometimes were, employed.

At the beginning of the MIDDLE BRONZE AGE settlement becomes more permanent (although only a handful of sites are known from Somerset) and the land began to be divided up into fields. These settlements appear to be small farms, but there may have been larger sites such as on the hill at Norton Fitzwarren. Some stone-built ROUND-HOUSES survive on Exmoor; none has been dated, but by analogy with Dartmoor they are likely to be from the later Bronze Age. Overall, the LATE BRONZE AGE is poorly understood, with much past work based on metalwork styles, several of which have been given Somerset names after important finds. Otherwise the evidence becomes difficult to interpret owing to a change away from burial with grave goods, and pottery becomes less distinctive to a particular period. Settlements are known from Brean Down sand cliff and at Cadbury Castle preceding the construction of the hillfort there.

Traditionally the study of the IRON AGE has concentrated on the obvious HILLFORTS. These are not common in Somerset, but Ham Hill and Cadbury Castle (South Cadbury) stand out, and have seen significant excavations. Geophysical survey at Ham Hill has shown that the interior appears to have been divided into smaller enclosures, some containing buildings, others storage pits. A similar plan has been seen at Norton Fitzwarren from aerial photographs of cropmarks. Similarly sized small enclosures are also known outside hillforts, often on sites just below the crests of low hills, leading to the name HILLSLOPE ENCLOSURES. Large numbers have been found from the air around the southern end of the Quantocks. This settlement type, of a few round-houses surrounded by a large bank and ditch, is also being found more often in the lowlands. Significant areas of the associated fields have also been discovered during large modern developments in places such as Podimore to the N of Yeovilton. The wetlands have preserved LAKE VILLAGE SETTLEMENTS at Glastonbury and Meare which, because of the survival of organic materials, provide some of the most comprehensive assemblages of Iron Age finds in the country. Against this it must again be remembered that these were sites in unusual environments, and are probably not typical. They also differ from each other: numerous round-houses were built on clay platforms on an artificial island at Glastonbury, but there are few indications of permanent settlement at Meare, where the site occupied two natural humps of raised bog. Meare has produced evidence for specialized weaving and is also one of very few sites of this period in Europe with evidence for glass-making, the products being found as far away as the north of Scotland.

Roman Somerset

Many Iron Age sites continued into the Roman period, and some new sites that were established appear identical in form, suggesting that for most of the population life continued much as before. There is almost no evidence in Somerset for the military conquest that Roman writers describe: only a few ROMAN FORTS are known for certain, and the so-called massacre deposit in the gateway at South Cadbury is now believed to date from twenty years after the invasion of the 40s A.D. There is evidence for the early exploitation of MINERAL RESOURCES by the military at Charterhouse on Mendip (N) and for large-scale Roman iron-working on Exmoor, and in the Brendon and Blackdown hills throughout the Roman period. Other large engineering work can be seen in the reclaiming of low-lying land from the sea in the Axe valley, N of Brent Knoll. The area to the S of this seems to have remained marshland and extensive areas were used for salt extraction.

The principal ROMAN ROADS ran down the eastern half of the county. The Fosse Way ran from Cirencester (Corinium) to Bath (Aquae Sulis), Ilchester (Lendiniae) and thence to Exeter (Isca Dumnoniorum). At Ilchester the road forked to Dorchester (Durnovaria).

The settlement at Ilchester appears to have started around a fort but in the later Roman period it became a WALLED TOWN with significant buildings, many with expensive mosaic floors. The notable concentration of VILLAS around it, many again with mosaics, suggests that Ilchester had some political importance, perhaps as the capital of a divided *Civitas Durotrigium*, the southern part being ruled from Dorchester (Dorset). Most of the villas are known only from antiquarian accounts, but recent excavations at Dinnington and Lopen have emphasized the high quality of the mosaics from the area. There are no villa remains on display in the county but the unique narrative mosaic from Low Ham, telling the story of Dido and Aeneas, is well displayed at the Museum of Somerset in Taunton. The small TOWN at Fosse Lane, Shepton Mallet (N), was only discovered in 1990 but has been extensively excavated. It was very different in character from Ilchester, with little evidence for a planned layout, few large buildings and no surrounding villas. This suggests that it had a commercial rather than a political function, in common with most of the smaller towns of Roman Britain.

Evidence from sites away from those traditionally studied has begun to show significant changes over the Roman period. In the C4, for instance, there appears to have been increased investment in the countryside. This is seen not only in the growth and architectural sophistication of villas but also in the construction of simple rectangular STONE BUILDINGS, replacing the Iron Age tradition of wooden round-houses. This type of structure is also seen in the settlement at Fosse Lane, while in Ilchester large town houses very like villas were built. It is likely that these changes were caused by alterations in the taxation and political systems of the later empire, which also saw the splitting of Britannia into two and then four smaller provinces. The exact locations of these are not known, but Somerset is believed to have lain within *Britannia Prima*, whose capital was almost certainly at Cirencester (Glos.).

The post-Roman period

The C4 saw episodes in which a military commander in Britain made a bid to be emperor and withdrew troops to the Continent to further his aims, so that what is now seen as the end of Roman Britain in A.D. 410 may have been little noticed at the time. The four provinces may have fared differently in the following century: there is increasing evidence that *Britannia Prima* survived as a political entity while provinces to the E fell under Anglo-Saxon control. Mediterranean pottery, found at sites close to the western coasts of Britain such as Cadbury Castle, may be explained by diplomatic attempts to reconstitute the empire, particularly under the Emperor Justinian (A.D. 527–65). Cadbury Castle was re-fortified at about this time, involving the construction of over 0.6 m. of walling around the earlier hillfort, and may have taken over the role of Ilchester in previous centuries. The amount of work involved indicates an authority able to access and organize a large workforce. Only part of the interior has been excavated, however, and the nature of the occupation, permanent or seasonal, high or low status, is not clear.

Although Ilchester may not have survived as an urban area, it seems that burial continued in the large roadside CEMETERIES around it. St Andrew's church at Northover (Ilchester) perhaps originated as a cemetery chapel or a shrine to an early saint. There is also a very large rural cemetery at Cannington and there are smaller ones at sites such as Stoneage Barton (Cothelstone), where Late Roman Christian burial practices continued for several centuries.

Somerset, and particularly Glastonbury, was at the heart of Arthurian legend from at least the C12. Glastonbury was the Vale

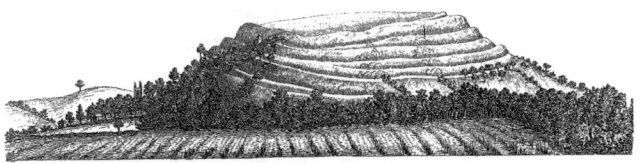

South Cadbury, Cadbury Castle.
Engraving after W. Stukeley, 1724

of Avalon, and the presumed bodies of Arthur and Guinevere, found in the abbey cemetery, were reburied in Glastonbury Abbey in 1278. It is powerful legend, but actual finds of Arthur's time, let alone related to Arthur, have been minimal even at Glastonbury. The re-fortification of Cadbury Castle has produced nothing to confirm the site's identification as King Arthur's Camelot made by Leland in the C16.* The best guess of the date of Arthur's death, around 515, falls only just within the period of the fortification of Cadbury.

The missionary activities of Celtic saints are attested in the Glastonbury foundation legends. These, involving in the C5 to C6 St Patrick and St David, are part of the tapestry of stories collected by William of Malmesbury that made Glastonbury 'the first church in the Kingdom of Britain, and the source and foundation of all religion'. Church dedications to Welsh saints such as Carantoc (Carhampton), Cyngar (Badgworth), Decuman (Watchet), and Dyfrig/Dubricius (Porlock) testify to traffic across the Bristol Channel. The single INSCRIBED STONE of the region, at Winsford on Exmoor, records the most potent name of ancient Britain, Caratacus. It dates from the late C6.

ANGLO-SAXON SOMERSET

The incorporation of the area into the expanding kingdom of Wessex appears to have happened in the later C7, traditionally after Cenwealh won a battle at Peonnan (possibly Penselwood) in 658. There is, however, little evidence that the incorporation was violent, and initially at least there seem to have been attempts to absorb the British church into the Saxon system. Under King Ine (c. 688–726) this seems to have changed, when Aldhelm, bishop of the new diocese of Sherborne, was ordered to expunge unorthodox practices and to found a system of MINSTER CHURCHES on new sites to replace British religious centres. Glastonbury appears to have been one product of this campaign, replacing the British site of Lantokay at Street. These minsters seem to have formed the nucleus around which later towns grew, such as Taunton and Yeovil, but the nature of the original foundations is extremely obscure. Place names such as Ilminster and Pitminster are clearly indicative. The best-known site is at Cheddar (N) where a sequence of halls and chapels, dating from at least the C9, has been excavated to the W of the parish church. It is not clear whether this site was a royal palace with adjacent minster or a minster site which included a royal hall.

---

* A much earlier identification may have been made by the Mappa Mundi of c. 1300 at Hereford, on which only two locations are marked in all of SW England, Glastonbury and 'Cadnan' (Cadbury), presumably because of contemporary interest in Arthur.

The most familiar story of King Alfred is located in Somerset: his refuge at Athelney (East Lyng) in 878 before his victory over the Danes, the subsequent baptism of Guthrum at Aller, and the peace signed at Wedmore. Apart from the discovery of the Alfred Jewel at North Petherton in 1693, finds relating to the king have been few. Excavation has revealed a little of Athelney Abbey, founded in 888, and a possible fort at the other end of the Isle of Athelney (*see* East Lyng). Nothing is known of Alfred's palace at Wedmore.

The Anglo-Saxon church, especially the monasteries, was reformed and revived in the C10 under St Dunstan, native of Baltonsborough, made Abbot of Glastonbury by King Edmund *c*. 943 and Archbishop of Canterbury in 960 by King Edgar. Viking raids in the C9 and C10 affected the county, and the system of defended settlements known as *burhs* was begun by Alfred. Of the thirty *burhs* across southern England named in the C10 Burghal Hideage, only five were in Somerset: Lyng, Langport and Watchet in the S, and Axbridge and Bath in the N. Lyng, the smallest, was probably just a fort. Two Late Saxon kings were buried at Glastonbury, Edward the Elder and Edmund Ironside.

The scarcity of visible ARCHITECTURAL REMAINS is surprising so near Wiltshire and Gloucestershire, both rich in Anglo-Saxon architecture. Hardly anything of national importance is to be seen, especially since the excavations at Glastonbury have not been left exposed. These excavations uncovered the small church built by King Ine with its side *porticus*, the C8 or C9 extensions to the W and E, and Dunstan's square addition further E, with its transept-like N and S *porticus* – a composite design which can never have possessed much monumentality. Excavation has revealed the C10 monastic church at Muchelney, a small nave with an apse that may have had a *porticus* each side. Very little has been found of the minster churches, presumably because they are beneath subsequent parish churches. The church at Milborne Port is the most significant survival, straddling the period of the Conquest. What is significant there is the scale of the Anglo-Saxon building, roughly the length of the present church, and far wider than the comparable church at Bradford on Avon (Wilts.). The chancel (and formerly also the W front) shows the blind arcading of Bradford on Avon. The combination with equally typical Norman motifs, such as shafted windows, seems here to be a case of 'Saxo-Norman overlap', a building programme altered after 1066. There is scant Anglo-Saxon masonry in the churches at Wilton (St George, Taunton) and East Coker. There is similarly little SCULPTURAL WORK, a few pieces of carved interlace, the best the piece of C9 cross-shaft at West Camel. Anglo-Saxon FONTS, if they remain, are indistinguishable from Norman ones. Aller has one in which Guthrum was reputedly baptized, but the bulbous bowl with a roll rim occurs elsewhere (Bratton Seymour, Drayton). The bowl from West Dowlish (*see* Dowlish Wake) has shallow arcading of extremely primitive form.

ECCLESIASTICAL ARCHITECTURE AFTER 1066

Monastic foundations

Norman lords founded several new MONASTERIES to join the existing ones of Bath (N), Athelney, Glastonbury and Muchelney. The first were Montacute Priory, a Cluniac house founded by William, Count of Mortain, *c*. 1078, and William de Mohun's Benedictine priory at Dunster, founded around 1090 as a cell of Bath. In the first decade of the C12 William de Falaise founded Stogursey Priory, a Benedictine cell of Lonlay, Normandy. The Augustinians had a priory at Taunton, founded in the 1120s by Bishop Giffard of Winchester. The Augustinians were also at Bruton Priory before 1135, Keynsham (N) after 1172, and at the small priories at Barlinch, founded *c*. 1174, Woodspring (N), founded at North Curry *c*. 1210, Stavordale, founded *c*. 1243, and Burtle, in existence by 1270. The Cistercians had their only Somerset abbey at Cleeve, founded in 1198 by the Earl of Lincoln with monks from Revesby (Lincs.). The Carthusians built their first priory in Britain at Witham Friary in the same decade, part of the royal penance for the murder of Becket. A second Carthusian house followed at Hinton Charterhouse (N) *c*. 1230. URBAN RELIGIOUS HOUSES included the Franciscan friary at Bridgwater founded *c*. 1230, and a Dominican friary at Ilchester before 1261. A house of the Knights Templar at Templecombe, founded *c*. 1185, was given to the Knights Hospitaller on the suppression of the Templars in 1312. A Benedictine dependent of St Sever, Calvados, at Yenston (Henstridge), has an obscure history; it was in existence in 1225, and was last mentioned in 1347.

Some small NUNNERIES existed: a Benedictine priory at Cannington, founded *c*. 1138 by Robert de Courcy; Minchin Buckland (Durston), founded before 1180, the only female house of the Order of St John of Jerusalem; and a nunnery called Whitehall at Ilchester, possibly Augustinian, founded before 1281. There were also HOSPITALS (as at Eastover, Bridgwater), and HOUSES OF CHANTRY PRIESTS of varying size, very small as at Porlock, larger at Ilminster, and on the scale of manor houses, as at Kilve and Stoke-sub-Hamdon. Most elusive of all are the CELLS of hermits or anchorites, attached to the walls of churches. Several are suggested (e.g. St Pancras Chapel, Roadwater). The life of Wulfric (†1125) of Haselbury Plucknett allows a glimpse of one of these structures, less ascetic than might be imagined: a cell with an altar, and a substantial outer room for his servant, the preparation of meals, and visitors.

Of all the medieval monasteries, Glastonbury was by far the greatest: the oldest, the largest and the richest, its landholdings the largest in a region dominated by ecclesiastical landowners, notably the Bishop of Wells and the Bishop of Winchester. Relations between the Glastonbury abbots and the bishops at Wells were difficult, and sometimes violent, as in the time of Bishop Savaric FitzGeldewin (1192–1205) when the see and the abbey were united.

Norman architecture and sculpture

For NORMAN ARCHITECTURE South Somerset is not a prime hunting ground before the Transitional period of the 1180s. Quantitatively, not qualitatively, there is no shortage. Of doorways especially there are over thirty and a few chancel arches remain (Ashill, Stoke-sub-Hamdon, Sutton Bingham, Sutton Montis). There are complete crossings under the towers of Milborne Port and Stogursey and complete arcades at Thurlbear and Stogursey. Nor are these things usually bare and utilitarian. The DOORWAYS show all the usual Norman motifs of abstract ornamentation, from simple chevron (Brent Knoll, Middle Chinnock) to bands of chevron (Aller, Huish Episcopi), lozenges formed by the meeting of chevrons (Enmore), lozenge trellis (Barton St David, Kingweston, Swell), ornamented bosses (Staple Fitzpaine), beading (Bratton Seymour), and so on. Norman decorative figure-work is almost absent and foliage is rare. Beakheads, the motif of a monster-head biting into a roll moulding, occur only at Pawlett and in the arch recently found immured within Castle House at Taunton Castle. The colonnettes of doorways and chancel arches are occasionally decorated: spiral fluting at Blackford (near Sparkford), chevron at Huish Episcopi and Stogursey, diapering at Stoke-sub-Hamdon.

Altogether the archaeological interest should not blind the student to the barbarity of much Norman work in minor churches. Take the SCULPTURE, mostly confined to the tympana. Geometrical motifs are spread over the tympanum at Middle Chinnock without any feeling for the demands of the semicircle. When it comes to figure-work, one must distinguish between a case like Langport – actually a lintel not a tympanum – where there is a civilizing, if distant, influence from France, and the raw, vigorous, Celtic decoration of Milborne Port, Penselwood and Stoke-sub-Hamdon. At Stoke-sub-Hamdon the sculptor has assembled the Tree of Life, the Lamb, small in one corner, and two Signs of the Zodiac, Sagittarius and Leo, much bigger below. At Penselwood, a lintel not a tympanum, a lion and lioness flank a Paschal Lamb in a roundel, the lamb supremely incompetently done, the lion with the vigour of a Chinese dragon. The two lions at Milborne Port are quite different from the Penselwood lions, affronted, but one with head turned to bite its tail while the other breathes a fleur-de-lys flame. Strange wolves and human heads appear at the corners of the nave at Chesterblade. Another sculptural oddity is the capitals of the crossing at Milborne Port, in crude bands, carved with foliage. At Stogursey the Early Norman crossing has simple arches, and the capitals are crude with little volutes, distantly classical foliage, and a variety of beasts.

In PLAN Milborne Port and Stogursey are ambitious churches. They have transepts and a tower over the crossing, the standard plan of the major Norman church, and this plan is still distinct at Dunster despite Perp rebuilding. Norman plans may underlie cruciform churches with crossing towers such as at Crewkerne, Ditcheat and Ilminster, but no trace survives. Crossing towers without transepts also occur, e.g. at Kingstone and Dowlish

Penselwood, St Michael, doorway.
Engraving by William Barnes, early C19

Wake, but again without actual Norman evidence. At Stogursey the original plan represents a type more usual in C11 Germany than in France, but not entirely absent in England either (Old Shoreham, Sussex): cruciform, with three apses, one to the chancel and two on the E sides of the transepts. The plan uncovered at Muchelney Abbey on the other hand was the standard French Romanesque plan, again with apsidal chapels to the transepts, but with an ambulatory around the apsed chancel and three semicircular apses radiating off it. Surviving Norman ARCADES are confined to the simple ones at Thurlbear, and those cut through the chancel walls at Stogursey in the late C12. These latter have the complex chevron of the Glastonbury Lady Chapel (*see* below). No W towers survive with identifiable Norman work. Norman VAULTING only appears in the late C12, in Transitional work (*see* below).

Two points of detail must find mention in passing. The first is the segmental arches found not infrequently in doorways (Ashill, Chesterblade, the so-called Guildhall at Milborne Port, and Wambrook). The second is chancel arches flanked by shallow arched recesses for side altars (Ashill, also Chewton Mendip and Compton Martin, both North Somerset).

FONTS of Norman date are numerous, but none is of outstanding merit. They are divisible between the plain bowl or tapered tub, with or without ornament, and more sophisticated designs. A discrete group are the square Purbeck marble fonts with shallow arcaded sides, part of a well-known export trade from Dorset. Examples are at Templecombe, Bruton, Brushford, Crewkerne, Milborne Port and West Buckland. Local imitations are found, in Ham stone: with naïve reliefs instead of the arcading at Isle Abbots; and with the arcading but also naïve beasts at East Pennard. Square fonts with scallops, double (Edington) or triple (Biddisham), develop to circular ones scalloped all round (Marston Magna, Whitestaunton), and at Withypool the all-round scalloping becomes a fluting, under a broad band of chevron. Arcading of a very rough sort appears on the bowl at Winsford, and interlaced arcading at West Camel. There are few examples of figure sculpture on Norman fonts, and these – the monsters mentioned at Isle Abbots and East Pennard, some small oval heads at Stogursey – are very crude.

The TRANSITIONAL STYLE spans the Norman and Early Gothic period, and is especially the style of the late C12, strongly represented in Somerset by the rebuildings at Glastonbury Abbey and Wells Cathedral (N). Among the motifs especially typical of this period are the three-dimensional chevron, the trumpet capital and the waterleaf capital. The pointed arch also occurs quite frequently in contexts which still look entirely Norman, and the idea should be given up that pointed and Gothic are the same. Of major buildings Malmesbury (Wilts.) used it in the 1160s, Worcester in the 1170s. Early pointed arches in Somerset are largely confined to Wells and Glastonbury. Waterleaf capitals barely occur in the county, but trumpet capitals do. The trumpet capital is a scalloped capital in which the scallop, instead of rising and widening with straight outlines, curves forward as it widens – like a cornucopia or indeed a trumpet. A good example is the capitals of the N arcade at Pilton, on octagonal piers and with pointed arches indicative of a date just after 1200. Trumpet capitals occur also in the chancel arch at East Lambrook. The more generous three-dimensional character of these capitals corresponds to the Transitional chevron, at 45 degrees to the wall or even turned straight towards us. Such three-dimensional chevron, typical of the West Country School (Somerset, Bristol, the Marches, extending to St Davids Cathedral in Wales and Christ Church Cathedral, Dublin), is notable in the arcades pierced through the chancel walls at Stogursey. These date from *c.* 1175–80. Wells Cathedral was rebuilt from *c.* 1175–6, and after the disastrous fire at Glastonbury in 1184 the Lady Chapel there was rebuilt by 1186.

In these buildings and in these years Somerset leaps to the forefront of architectural events in England. The transition from the trumpet capital to the naturalism of stiff-leaf foliage, the hallmark of the Early English style, can be followed at Wells and Glastonbury. The two forms are so much side by side that it seems that the carver who carved the leaves was supplied by the hewer with a trumpet capital to work into. The Glastonbury Lady Chapel seems still a Late Norman building, by contrast with Wells, with plenty of intersecting blank arcades inside and out and with round-arched windows. Inside, however, it has rib-vaults which show a clear understanding of Gothic principles and Gothic spirit. The preponderance of Norman motifs by contrast with the choir and transepts of the abbey church, begun at the same time, may be conscious antiquarianism, as the Lady Chapel replaced the *vetusta ecclesia*, the most hallowed part of the abbey. It may be that by the time of the fire it had a Romanesque character that the monks wished to preserve. The inspiration at Glastonbury and Wells was West Country work done under the influence of the Cistercians, especially at Malmesbury *c.* 1160–70 and Worcester *c.* 1175–85. Neither of these can be called Gothic without reservation: both used Gothic and Norman motifs indiscriminately. However, so many of the motifs at Glastonbury and Wells come straight from Worcester that some must be recorded here: three-dimensional chevron, trumpet capitals, keeled shafts, paterae in spandrels, a triforium instead of a gallery, continuous mouldings in the triforium.

Early English to Decorated

Stiff-leaf foliage is an English speciality. The richness and yet the architectural discipline of these foliage forms is the happiest symbol of the C13. French crocket capitals are less natural, French foliage capitals of the late C13 more natural. Neither quite achieves the classic balance of style and nature as the stiff-leaf capital. Stiff-leaf occurs at the Glastonbury Lady Chapel in the paterae or roundels, together with French crocket capitals. Wells was the first English building in which the pointed arch – as a Gothic motif – was accepted throughout and without exception. Wells was begun *c.* 1175 and the Great Church at Glastonbury after the fire of 1184. While Wells still stands in all its C13 glory, Glastonbury is in ruins, and its beauty is that of cliff-like fragments on the green turf and arches and windows with the light blue sky behind them.

At Glastonbury the system of elevation was still Anglo-Norman, but continuous mouldings of a West Country Gothic type frame arches with extravagant Late Norman chevron on slim shafts with stiff-leaf capitals. As at Wells there is a triforium, not a gallery, but here it is bound to the arch below by one tall wall arch under the clerestory, as had been done at Jedburgh and Oxford before, and not with the novel horizontality of Wells. So little survives of the Great Church at Glastonbury that much else about the strange and insecure relationship with the great works going on just up the road in Wells must remain obscure. Suffice it to say that with the continuance of Norman chevron and roll mouldings, Glastonbury also shows GOTHIC MOTIFS such as clustered and keeled shafts and stiff-leaf carving. At Glastonbury the use of Blue Lias for capitals, bases and shafts, notably in the

Lady Chapel, parallels Wells in the late C12. Such Blue Lias inserts appear in the Glastonbury galilee of the 1230s (but not in the chancel), and in doorways at Cleeve Abbey of the mid C13.

Although Wells stands just beyond the edge of the region covered by this volume, EARLY GOTHIC work s of the Mendips is disappointing. Contemporary with Glastonbury and Wells is the small church at Witham Friary, built probably for lay brothers of the Carthusian priory. Its regular quadripartite vaults rest on short corbelled shafts whose capitals are polygonal and quite plain. Otherwise of the early C13 there is relatively little. There are stiff-leaf capitals in doorways at Bridgwater and Wedmore, and in the E window at Ilchester. The E end of the church at Cleeve Abbey was completed in 1232, so the dormitory and refectory ranges must be contemporary or mid-C13. Plate tracery and double-chamfered arches characterize the work there. CHAMFERED ARCHES, single, double and triple, occur in so many Somerset churches that this particular C13 motif must be said to continue through the C14 and into the C15. Chamfered arcades datable from typically C13 circular piers occur at Chedzoy, East Coker and Kingston St Mary. Carved corbel heads identify as C13 the crossing arches at Bawdrip and South Petherton and the tower arch at Milverton. C13 and early C14 PIERS are nowhere of course as elaborate as at Wells and Glastonbury. Scale forbade that. Circular piers are typical; octagonal ones of the C13 are less common (Pilton), and more likely to date from the early C14 (Charlton Horethorne, Cudworth). The piers of the arcade at Huish Champflower, reputedly moved from Barlinch Priory, are a chamfered square with a pair of fat three-quarter-column shafts applied to each of the four main faces. The capitals are a kind of upright leaf. Quatrefoil piers develop in the late C13. Plain quatrefoil piers with round capitals are found at South Cadbury. Similar round capitals are on the inner N aisle of St Mary Magdalene, Taunton, and at Wilton church, Taunton, in both cases on slightly more complex piers, demi-shafts attached to a circular pier. A kind of crude quatrefoil pier, actually cruciform with chamfered angles, occurs at Cucklington.

Plain TOWERS of the C13 survive in some numbers, identified as early by lack of buttresses, or heavy buttresses set low (Porlock), or the absence of a w doorway (Trull). Placing on the side of the church rather than the W end also often identifies an early tower. Many C13 towers are hard to recognize, having been altered with Perp doors and windows and heightened with a Perp bell-stage. The small group of Somerset OCTAGONAL TOWERS, about a dozen, are identified as C13 by their lancet windows. Big square towers are broached to octagonal at Ilchester and Somerton; smaller octagonal towers similarly square at the base are at Bishop's Hull, Podimore and Weston Bampfylde; and there are octagonal crossing towers at Barrington, North Curry, South Petherton and Stoke St Gregory. The transition from square to octagon is done by squinches at Stoke St Gregory, Pitminster and Podimore, not a usual thing in England. Only Barton St David (apart from a lost tower at Keinton Mandeville) rises octagonal from the ground, and this may be C15, replacing a crossing tower. C13 W towers include the very massive one at Bridgwater, and among the notable C14 towers is Milverton, sheer, without any horizontal divisions and with diagonal buttresses. Halse is similarly undivided.

The lancet is the characteristic window form of the C13, as in all the octagonal towers. Early windows survive more commonly in chancels, because the maintenance and rebuilding of these fell to the clergy, and they therefore often escaped the Perp rebuildings of the rest. The fine five-light set of stepped lancets of the E window at Martock may be paralleled by the stepped three lights at Luccombe, Rimpton and Porlock. At Porlock a single large lancet adorns the tower. The three separate lancets at the E end of Dunster are reconstructed. Lancets continue right through the C13, the harmonious cusped single lancets of the S transept at Stoke-sub-Hamdon being a late example. PLATE TRACERY developed from the lancet in the mid C13, still accepting the wall as predominant, but cutting in separately two lancet lights and a circle or quatrefoil above. The three-light E window at Ilchester has two punched quatrefoils and an octofoil above the lancets, and a shafted reveal with a double roll moulding. Plate tracery remains in the S aisles at Middlezoy and Charlton Horethorne. BAR or GEOMETRICAL tracery made a two-light window one whole, the bars only a subdivision. The transition to bar tracery can be seen at Watchet, South Petherton, Sutton Bingham and Puckington, where delicate foiled tracery is inserted into the circles above, but as yet with no piercing of spandrels to make the transition from solid to veil. The chancel side windows at Isle Abbots are similar but more advanced, the quatrefoil tracery bolder, more proportionate to the circles. These date from the end of the C13. The N transept window of *c.* 1300 at Montacute, of three lancet lights, is gathered in one pointed frame under three cinquefoils, but the mullions are still relatively thick. The E window at Puckington is similar. One final form of *c.* 1300 deserves mention. Y-tracery is a form of two-light bar tracery that becomes intersecting tracery when three or more lights are involved (Brympton D'Evercy). Delicate mullions branch into Y-tracery in the chancel at Middlezoy, each lancet containing a trefoil above a lancet – a feature emanating from the Wells chapter house – and the apex a little quatrefoil. The N transept window at Somerton is similar, with frillier cusping. The E window at Middlezoy shows that no sooner had this stage been reached, than designers turned away from harmoniousness and regularity in pursuit of a new ideal of complexity, intricacy, perhaps even perversity. The four lights are two pairs, each light with a trefoil in the head, each pair with a quatrefoil, and the whole window with a septfoil, still regular but of a wiry complexity.

This is a harbinger of the new DECORATED style of the C14. The classic French scheme of lancet lights with foiled circles is abandoned for more wiry motifs: pointed cusping, pointed trefoils (as at Middlezoy) in the heads of the lancets, and also curved-sided (spheric) triangles instead of circles. These motifs

ECCLESIASTICAL ARCHITECTURE AFTER 1066

are introduced in France and England as early as the mid C13, but then new combinations appear, no longer of quite such simplicity and logicality. For instance where the early C13 had made a group of three or five isolated lancet windows, the late C13 preferred the three or five as lancet lights under one arch, as in the E window at Isle Abbots. The late C13 liked intersection, that is, confusion as to how the arches should be viewed. The foremost examples of freer variations are the Bishop's Chapel and the Lady Chapel at Wells, the first of c. 1285–90, the other of c. 1320.

From c. 1300 an outburst of inventiveness in tracery forms takes place everywhere in the county, masked of course by subsequent Perp rebuilding. Among the new forms are three-light windows with the outer lights taller to gain space for a somewhat squeezed-in circle, as at Whitelackington. Harmony is maintained here by inserting an elongated trefoil in the head of each outer light, giving an even row of cusped lancets below the complexities of the tracery. The circle is typically subdivided by three trefoils (differently on each transept). There is similar tracery in the S transept at Brympton D'Evercy, and at Charlton Horethorne. The transept windows at Barrington are cruder, with the circle simply sexfoiled. The E windows at Ditcheat and Meare dispense with levelling the heads of the main lights, at Ditcheat putting three trefoils within a spherical triangle above, and at Meare two cusped triangles within a spherical lozenge. A spherical triangle appears in the head of the two-light E window of the transept at Limington, built as a chantry chapel c. 1329, the finest single structure of the early C14 in South Somerset. The corresponding W window has a swirled circle in the head, introducing that vitality of curves characteristic of the Decorated Gothic, shown more dramatically in the N window. Here the middle lancet is pushed higher than the others and given an ogee point to divide a flowing head of two mouchettes under a quatrefoil (there is similar tracery at Bridgwater and Winsham). At Stocklinch Ottersey and Compton Dundon attempts at radiating tracery without flowing curves result in strange ungainly kite shapes in the one and a kind of four-leaf clover in the other. Flowing forms appear in the big five-light W window at Somerton, again with an ogee point to the central light. The ogee point, seen first at the Wells chapter house, becomes a feature of these more complex traceries, especially reticulation, as in the fish-net window heads of the mid C14 (Stoke-sub-Hamdon, West Camel). There is an odd use of reticulation in the very curvaceous N transept window at Charlton Mackrell, of five lights, where reticulation fills the top roundel, as it does the roundel inserted over the N door at Bridgwater. Stranger forms of flowing tracery at Bridgwater appear to be genuine, although entirely restored.

South Somerset has only one of the great spaces created by the Gothic of the early C14, and it is not a major church like Wells or Bristol, as the nave at Glastonbury has gone, but rather the Abbot's Kitchen there, built around 1330. The octagonal ribbed vault and four corner fireplaces have the qualities of the best engineering.

Other than this, the best interior spaces are the small transept-like chapels at Limington and Stoke-sub-Hamdon, the former vaulted with close-set transverse ribs. There are TOWER-VAULTS at Stoke-sub-Hamdon, late C12, and South Petherton, mid-C13. The surviving antechamber to the chapter house at Cleeve Abbey has a low mid-C13 vault. There are also VAULTED PORCHES: a pointed tunnel vault at East Chinnock, a quadripartite vault at Stoke-sub-Hamdon, and a pointed tunnel vault with diagonal and ridge ribs at South Petherton.

C13–C14 MONUMENTS are fairly widespread, especially effigies in tomb-recesses. These recesses often have exaggerated cusping, as at Pendomer, which has, exceptionally, stone figures supporting a kind of cornice above the recess. The earliest tomb-recesses are the row of three in Blue Lias at Curry Rivel of the 1280s, with low-relief decoration of stiff-leaf type. Ham stone effigies were produced in some quantity from the late C13 onwards, most of them dating from the C14. Brian and Moira Gittos have counted sixty, concentrated in the Levels and westward to Dunster and Porlock – reflecting the ease of water-borne transport – with a further seven in Dorset and Devon. The best group is at Limington, especially the knight, probably Sir Richard Gyvernay, *c*. 1330. All the effigies were of course painted. Colour survives on the late C14 monument to Sir Matthew de Stawell †1379 and his wife at Cothelstone. Effigies sited outside churches remain, but are extremely eroded. CROSS-SLABS also survive in some numbers, from the C13 to the early C16, with little variation in the incised foliate crosses. Their reuse as building stones at Barwick, Muchelney and elsewhere suggests that these were of lesser status.

C13 and C14 FONTS are not present in comparable numbers to those of the C12. Plain octagonal bowls give way to more modelled forms after 1250. The large quatrefoil bowl at Brent Knoll is both moulded and shaped, and there are octagonal fonts with emphatic horizontal mouldings at Kingsbury Episcopi, Meare and Westonzoyland. Reticulated tracery is curiously wrapped around the font at Stoke St Gregory. Sculpture on fonts is rare. The early C14 font at Pitminster has two panels carved in relief and a band of good foliage above the capitals of the base. By the mid C14 octagonal fonts with quatrefoil decoration in the panels are harbingers of the typical Perp font (for which *see* p. 37). They can sometimes surprise, as with the bold underside foliage at Castle Cary.

Perpendicular churches

The first signs of the transition to the PERPENDICULAR STYLE of the later C14 appear as a changing spirit in Dec details. At Wells the choir and E window of *c*. 1325–40 show the beginnings of this spirit of verticality, vertical mullions standing hard on arches or pushing up against arches. The earliest occurrence of the full-blown Perp in Somerset may be the remodelling of the chancel of Glastonbury Abbey by Abbot Walter Monington,

ECCLESIASTICAL ARCHITECTURE AFTER 1066

abbot 1342–74, which was under way after 1350, the roof being completed in 1365. Monington refaced the inside with Perp panelling above the original arcades, similar to the internal refacing of the s transept and choir at Gloucester, *c*. 1335–60. A fragment of this survives by the crossing piers.

The sw tower at Wells was built before 1386 by *William Wynford*, but the later Middle Ages throughout England saw a shift in significance away from cathedrals and abbeys. Somerset is one of the richest counties for large and worthwhile Perp PARISH CHURCHES, for the epoch was one of great prosperity based on wool. It seems that the Great Epoch, as it was named by A. K. Wickham in his *Churches of Somerset* (1952), began with a major work, the building of the church at Yeovil about 1375–80, tentatively attributed to *Wynford*, who may also have been involved at Wedmore shortly afterwards. Yeovil, a wholly new work, illustrates the one major development in PLANNING of churches, the preference for w towers over crossing towers. The latter half of the C15 and early C16 is the culmination of Somerset tower-building. With towers still under way at the Reformation e.g. at Batcombe and Ruishton, the Great Epoch can be said to have been brought to an untimely rather than a natural end. The ideal form of the completely new church, where no compromise was necessary with earlier work, is w tower, nave and aisles, chancel and chancel chapels – and every member of this simple assembly decked out as lavishly as possible. Even where an older church existed the finished result could be just this, with perhaps vestigial transepts remaining, incorporated into the aisles, as a hint of the predecessor, but all the detail Perp, as at Glastonbury St John. A church with a crossing tower tended to represent the continuity of an old plan, and the grandest of such churches (Crewkerne, Ilminster, Bath Abbey) would have an ornamented w front. That at Crewkerne with its twin turrets echoes the royal chapels of Windsor, Eton and Cambridge. More commonly the w front is functional, a large window over a door flanked by the windows of the aisles under lean-to roofs, with ornamented parapets at North Curry and Wedmore, plain at South Petherton.

The single tower (rather than the grouped towers of the C12–C13) was the greatest thrill for the late Middle Ages, not only in Somerset but in England, and much of Europe: take Strasbourg, take Ulm, take Antwerp. Even so, among all English counties, Somerset remains the tower county *par excellence*, and there is much to say about them. Somerset WEST TOWERS often dwarf the rest of the church, at Taunton St Mary Magdalene unforgettably so. The fine towers of West Somerset – Luccombe, Winsham, Watchet – are other cases in point. Where there is no clerestory, even the classic mid-Somerset towers of Huish Episcopi, Kingston St Mary and Isle Abbots can seem to overwhelm the church behind, and on a small church like Kingsdon the contrast can be startling. The towers as a rule are square in plan. Oblongs only occur where an earlier plan dictated a narrowed shape, typically central towers (cf. Kingstone). And the towers are as a rule towers, in the sense that they have no spires.

It seems that SPIRES fell out of fashion in the late C14. Bridgwater has the best of the four stone spires remaining in South Somerset (also Chiselborough, Compton Pauncefoot, East Brent). Sheer and unadorned, it was built by a Bristol mason, Nicholas Waleys, from 1367, just as the Perp style was reaching the county. The change can be pinpointed to the late C14, after the Wells SW tower was completed. Yeovil was never intended for one, but the crossing tower at Wedmore was, as also the contemporary W tower at Shepton Mallet (N); and spires were never intended for the C15 crossing towers of Ilminster and Crewkerne, nor for any of the major western towers.

The big events were in square-topped towers, and quite a number are strikingly tall. After the Wells crossing tower at 182 ft (55.5 metres) the next in height is the W tower of St Mary Magdalene, Taunton, an astonishing 163 ft (50 metres), a fraction higher for example than the crossing tower at Bath Abbey. Of the parish church towers the tallest include Glastonbury St John, 134 ft (41 metres), Taunton St James, 120 ft (36.6 metres), Westonzoyland, just over 100 ft (30.5 metres), and Yeovil, 92 ft (28 metres).*

Quite apart from great height, an immense amount of thought was expended on the details of towers. Masons must have been asked by parishioners on the strength of one tower to design another. Batcombe and Chewton Mendip (N) so resemble each other that they are certainly related, but it is hard to guess which came first; money was left for the one in 1539 and the other in 1541. The close familial resemblances between Huish Episcopi, Kingston St Mary and Isle Abbots, and less close ones between Watchet, Winsford and Luccombe, have been enough to suppose that the same mason or groups of masons were involved with each tower of the group. But the idea of a coherent band of tower builders moving from site to site has fallen from favour recently. Close similarities of buttress type, window tracery and tower arches are enough to suggest a common pool of experience, shared among masons. Distances were never great, and details could be mixed from several sites – window tracery from one, crown and pinnacles from another. Jerry Sampson's study of masons' marks tracks individual masons not just around Somerset but further afield. These similarities of detail have given impetus to cataloguing, chronology and identification of familial groups and even single architects. John Harvey's short article in the *Transactions of the Ancient Monuments Society*, 1982, remains the best corrective, using documentary sources to date a few towers, and using these for tentative art-historical conclusions. Jerry Sampson has pointed out that archaism is not unknown, as in the early C16 towers in the Vale of Taunton Deane which have triple-chamfered tower arches (e.g. Hillfarrance and West Buckland), the triple chamfer being a motif of the C13. There are no

---

*The tallest in North Somerset are Chewton Mendip, 126 ft (38.4 metres) and Wells St Cuthbert, 122 ft (37.2 metres).

identical twins among the fifty or so best towers; the fascination in moving from place to place is the individuality that comes out in each tower, in the proportions, the choice of buttress, tracery or pinnacle detail.

And there is colour, more considered on towers than on the often random stonework of the body of the church, which was often rendered. The stones of Somerset give a wonderfully varied palette: deep red and rich orange-brown (Williton and Ham) at Bishop's Lydeard and Taunton St Mary Magdalene; pink and orange-brown (Quantock sandstone and Ham) at North Petherton; blue-grey and orange-brown (Blue Lias and Ham) at Isle Abbots, Long Sutton and Huish Episcopi; the same with added buff (Doulting) at Westonzoyland; entirely orange-brown (Ham) at Montacute; or entirely buff (Doulting) at Glastonbury St John. At North Petherton and Taunton it can be seen that polychromy is entirely part of the design; at Bishop's Lydeard it seems more accidental, with tracery in both Ham stone and red sandstone.

Pevsner classified towers in three main areas, a northern group (in the North Somerset volume), a group S of the Mendips that included the great churches of the Levels and a third group in the Vale of Taunton. His second group included outliers at Shepton Mallet (N) and Bruton. The West Somerset towers were deemed of lesser interest. The similarities already mentioned between Chewton Mendip in the northern group and Batcombe, an outlier near Bruton, illustrate how quickly exceptions tear apart geographical groupings. Pevsner concentrated on the upper tower, above the roof-line, for similarities of bell-lights and crowns, seeing the lower tower, the buttresses, W door and W window as preparation for the primary display. John Harvey pointed out that it is precisely in the lower half that analysis should start, because the arch to the nave is the beginning of any tower, and the most reliable dating evidence. It might be added that after the tower arch, important dating indicators are the placing of the buttresses, followed by the typology of the W doorway (four-centred-arched being later than two-centred) and then the form and tracery of the W window. Moreover the upper stages, although the undeniable climax, are not necessarily of one design with the base, and even where the design is consistent the tower was quite possibly subject to minor alteration over the period of building. Perp bell-stages to older bases are commonplace.

The documented sequence begins with Yeovil, for which money for completion was left in 1382. It seems likely that the tower was built last, i.e. in the final decade of the C14. It has emphatic horizontal division into four stages. Buttresses are set back from the angles rather than diagonal to the angles as in earlier towers (and still at North Cadbury c. 1400, and regularly in western Somerset, e.g. Spaxton, 1434). But the Yeovil buttresses are notably large compared to later ones. The stair-tower is clasped prominently between the buttresses of the front NW corner, a position used also at Martock, Queen Camel and West Huntspill, but one that fades out in the C15. The top two stages have an equal large two-light window on each face without any vertical linking or emphasis of the bell-stage. The parapet is flat, without pinnacles. Wedmore, although a crossing tower, is similar in its horizontal divisions, buttresses and parapet, but the bell-lights are a trio, one functional between two blind ones, giving the bell-stage special prominence. Other giants of these stacked towers, i.e. those built-up without linking the tiers vertically, are the five stages of Queen Camel, and the four of West Monkton, Cannington and Chew Magna (N). All are relatively early (Cannington perhaps late C14, Queen Camel early C15, Chew Magna before 1440) and all are relatively plain, though they can achieve a calm nobility. Stacked designs continue through to the C16, as with the four stages of Taunton St Mary Magdalene and Westonzoyland, the number of stages a function of the money available, on which depended also the degree of decoration.

DECORATION and the hierarchic arrangement of decoration distinguish the late towers. A first degree of ornament is the multiplication of bell-lights, as at Wedmore, blank or with pierced baffles to allow the bells to sound. These pierced baffles, a feature so peculiar to Somerset that Wickham named it 'Somerset tracery', substitute a traceried stone veil for the louvres common elsewhere in Britain. Vertical *élan* in stacked or staged towers necessarily depends on the buttresses. The progression from Yeovil onward accentuates verticality by, for example, not continuing horizontal courses around the buttresses, by placing buttress set-offs at levels intermediate to the stages of the tower, and giving these set-offs ornamental finials. And the buttresses acquire a more dynamic relation with the parapet, which no longer rings the tower right around but is broken by corner pinnacles that may be the actual culmination of the buttresses or, if separate, continue the upward movement initiated with the buttresses.

The masterpieces of the late C15 and C16 are mostly in a circle of hardly more than a twenty-mile radius around Taunton: Taunton St Mary Magdalene (the grandest of them all), Bishop's Lydeard, Huish Episcopi, Isle Abbots, Kingsbury Episcopi, Kingston St Mary, North Petherton and Staple Fitzpaine. But the wider group sharing some features spreads across the county, with the exception of West Somerset. Towers with some features of the Taunton group include Bruton, Chedzoy, Donyatt, East Lyng, Hatch Beauchamp, Kingsdon, Langport, Long Sutton, Lympsham, Mark, Middlezoy, Ruishton, Taunton St James, West Cranmore, Wellington and Westonzoyland within the area covered by this book, and Leigh-on-Mendip and Chewton Mendip in North Somerset. Their achievement as works of art derives from the manipulation of standard elements: buttresses, windows, parapets and pinnacles. The grandest towers are late, Tudor in the sense of being built after 1485: Taunton St Mary Magdalene dating from *c.* 1488–1514, Long Sutton *c.* 1493, Isle Abbots and Westonzoyland *c.* 1500, North Petherton after 1500, Ruishton 1530–5, and Batcombe 1540.

Set-back rather than diagonal BUTTRESSES allow more play of shafts and pinnacles in the upper parts. The ingeniousness displayed can only be appreciated by going from one tower to the other. No two are quite the same in the way buttresses turn into diagonal shafts. The angle of the tower may be hidden or partially hidden by a diagonal plane laid from buttress to buttress, or by a square fillet, such that buttresses on the corner of a tower can appear to be set back. And shafts can be attached in relief to buttresses, detach themselves from the walls, change orientation from square-set to diagonal, until in the end the crown is reached. Pinnacles punctuate the rising buttresses in a half-hearted way at Bishop's Lydeard compared to the magnificently tall applied shafts of North Petherton. In both churches the buttresses do not rise to the crown but stop below the bell-stage to carry a free-standing pinnacle. These pinnacles, set back from each corner, dissolve the sharp outline of the bell-stage. Such is the format of Isle Abbots and Huish Episcopi. At Kingsbury Episcopi the buttresses end in thin diagonal shafts against the bell-stage, outer echoes of the identical shafts that divide the bell-lights. Huish Episcopi and Kingsbury Episcopi share with North Petherton the accentuation of the horizontal by bands of quatrefoils, but all three vary in the relation of bell-stage to crown. At North Petherton the shaft between the bell-lights continues through the battlements to become the intermediate pinnacle of the crown. On the other two (and elsewhere) bell-stage and crown are not united except that the tips of the dividing shafts of the bell-lights touch the underside of the cornice beneath the battlements.

The CROWN may have four, eight or twelve pinnacles, and the main angle pinnacles may be the final achievement of the buttress and shafts below, or be quite independent of them. However it was done, the crown made a splendid final flourish. It can be said that towers such as those of the Huish Episcopi group are rich without being top-heavy. BATTLEMENTS are enriched by being pierced and moulded, corner pinnacles are crocketed, and as at Huish Episcopi, supported by outriders corbelled out from the corners; quatrefoil bands and lively squatting animals and grotesques enliven the cornice. A small group of crowns emulate the great crossing tower of Gloucester Cathedral, risking overdoing what a parish church can do. But such a transparent crown with battlements and big square pinnacles all in openwork is magnificent still at Taunton St Mary Magdalene, and works on the great height of Glastonbury St John. Battlements are not particularly indicative of date; pierced cusped triangles appear early on the Wells Lady Chapel and pierced lozenges also early at Shepton Mallet (N), and both forms continue through, so that the cusped lozenges at Meare for instance are late C15. To which it may be added that the flat arcaded parapet of Yeovil reappears much later at Pilton, West Pennard and on the S transept at North Curry. John Harvey thought quatrefoil pierced parapets (Bruton, Martock etc.) were late C15 to early C16, and the evidence for the moment supports him.

These towers are a lesson in overall decoration, as the intermediate stages (between the W window and bell-stage) acquire

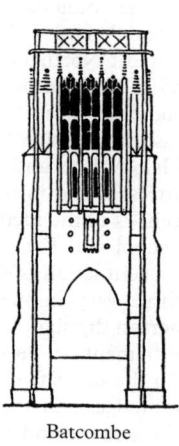
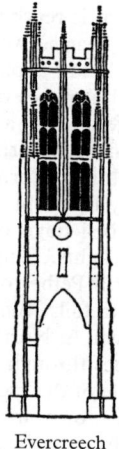

St Mary Magdalene   Batcombe   Evercreech
Taunton

windows, often blind, to break up the blank walling typical of multi-stage towers. From simply one window over another, the next stage is to have two over one, as at Isle Abbots (two two-lights over one two-light), Huish Episcopi (two two-lights over one three-light) or Kingsbury Episcopi (two two-lights over one four-light). If a stage is added, as at Bishop's Lydeard or Taunton St James, the lower stage can have the same window repeated. Opulence increases by increasing the bell-lights from two to three lights, and by lengthening the lights with transoms, until the system culminates in Taunton St Mary Magdalene. Here the three stages each have two large three-light windows all but filling each stage between the buttresses, and all transomed.

Less common but more individual than division in stages is the integration of the tower design vertically, in panels that link the bell-openings to blank panels below, known as the LONG PANEL MOTIF. This derives from Wynford's SW tower at Wells and was memorably echoed in the central tower there, c. 1440–50, a wonderful achievement of calm power, divided vertically into three long square-headed panels and horizontally by a lesser transom, so the whole upper structure is one. On the SW tower the verticality is less interrupted by the transom, here much narrower. The principle is the same in both – the descending mullion used in such a way that the upper tower is essentially ruled by

ECCLESIASTICAL ARCHITECTURE AFTER 1066 31

Huish Episcopi

North Petherton

Bishop's Lydeard

Somerset church towers

verticals. The progeny of the Wells towers is limited. Wells St Cuthbert (N) is the finest, begun, heraldry suggests, around 1390, the three-light bell-openings divided by a mullion so sheer that verticalism in the design of a tower could hardly go further. Evercreech, tentatively dated to the mid C15, follows the St Cuthbert tower in having two very long two-light panels divided by a central shaft, the top halves pierced and transomed, the lower half tall blank panels. Batcombe, 1540, follows the crossing tower in having three long two-light panels, although pointed not square-headed. Others ready to accept the principle of panelling the tower walls did not want to give up the normal staging. So the emphatic horizontal is retained at Ilminster, even though the lower half is fully panelled. Glastonbury St John is similar, if less rectilinear than Ilminster, where the bell-lights are in the square-headed panels. At Glastonbury the tall bell-lights have pointed heads, and the stage below is a grid of blind panelling. Ilminster is probably mid-C15, Glastonbury late C15.

There is also a small late C15 group that combines elements of the long panel with a staged tower in that the bell-light is extended downward into the stage below. The group consists of Crewkerne, Curry Rivel, Hinton St George, Shepton Beauchamp and Norton-sub-Hamdon. At Crewkerne and Shepton Beauchamp the horizontal division is accentuated as the string course between the tower stages aligns with the transom of the bell-light; on the others it does not. At Curry Rivel the string course is shifted up to align with the springing of the bell-window. Shepton Beauchamp is datable to after 1487 and Hinton St George was being built in 1494. Masons' marks are shared between all except Curry Rivel.

STAIR-TURRETS may be clasped by the buttresses at one corner of the front, which seems to be an early feature, as at Yeovil, or placed at the centre of the show front, as in a late C15 Vale of Taunton Deane group (Wellington, West Buckland, Hillfarrance and Bradford on Tone) with one outlier at Merriott. This placing is also found in Devon, as at Totnes. Most stair-towers are on the rear corner where the disruption to the bell-lights is least visible.

Not to be forgotten in the overall picture of Somerset Perp towers is SCULPTURAL DECORATION. Niches stud the towers, enriching the tiers below the bell-stage, and these were filled with sculpture. The quality is not in general high, but the survival of figures at East Brent, Isle Abbots, Kingsbury Episcopi and elsewhere indicates how rich the effect would have been, especially if the figures were painted, as traces of colour found at Isle Abbots suggest. Notable are the Crucifixion with six angels at Batcombe, very like the one at Chewton Mendip (N), the kneeling donors at Closworth, and the two reliefs at Minehead, God holding the Crucified Christ, and the Virgin and St Michael doing battle for souls. A different sculpture animates the crowns, namely gargoyles and squatting beasts, and these survive in far greater numbers than the overtly religious sculpture. Lively and surprisingly delicate, the beasts tend to perch a rump on the cornice and lean forward on two thin front legs. As with so many other features such decoration reaches its apogee in the late towers.

It remains to mention the church towers outside the regions of fine building stone, those of the Blackdown Hills, Quantocks, Brendon Hills and Exmoor. Fine detail is lacking, but the massive towers of three Quantock neighbours, Spaxton, 1434, Enmore, c. 1455, and Goathurst, C15, have a rugged grandeur. At Enmore the buttresses and stair-turret sprout pinnacles in emulation of the lowland churches. All three have diagonal buttresses, something of a Quantock feature (also at Bicknoller, Crowcombe and West Bagborough). Crowcombe is unusual in having had a spire. Diagonal buttresses and lack of ornament are features of towers further W into the Brendon Hills, as at Combe Florey, Huish Champflower and Brompton Ralph. Towards Exmoor are four fine tall towers, again sparing in ornament, closer to a Devon type, the verticals emphasized with set-back buttresses. These are Watchet, Minehead, Luccombe and Winsford. Diagonal buttresses typify church towers along the Devon boundary, e.g. West Buckland, Otterford and Runnington, though set-back buttresses occur at Chipstable and Kittisford. The best tower of the Blackdown Hills is Whitestaunton, of three stages with diagonal buttresses and with the stair-turret prominent on the S side.

TOWER ARCHES are a dating element to be used with caution. The survival or revival of double-chamfered or triple-chamfered arches has already been mentioned. The development sequence ought to be from shafted arches with big hollow mouldings in the C14, moving to wave mouldings in the early C15, and the diameter of the shafts reducing dramatically. Shafts are then omitted in favour of continuous mouldings, or mouldings interrupted by a

ECCLESIASTICAL ARCHITECTURE AFTER 1066   33

band capital. Finally panelled arches between thin shafts become the favourite of the late C15 and C16, as at Long Sutton, Martock, Muchelney, North Petherton, Taunton St Mary Magdalene and Westonzoyland. Fat shafts and a hollow at Aller probably date from before 1405, and at Spaxton from 1434. Fat shafts and a wave at Luccombe are C15 but as late as 1533 at Old Cleeve. Broad ogee and hollow mouldings at Dunster date from 1443, and the double wave at Minehead, although different, has similarities of capital that suggest the same mason, *John Marys*.

VAULTED TOWERS are relatively rare: star-vaults of the mid to late C15 at Enmore, Glastonbury St Benedict, Long Sutton and West Pennard, overlapping in date the first fan-vaults, which are at Taunton (both St Mary Magdalene and St James), Langport, North Petherton, Muchelney and Shepton Beauchamp, the last two datable to *c.* 1500. Fan-vaults were inserted under the crossing towers at Ditcheat and Wedmore, and there is one under the crossing at Ilminster. Several churches have late C15 to C16 VAULTED PORCHES: there are fan-vaults at Crewkerne, Curry Rivel, Isle Abbots and Kingston St Mary, tierceron star-vaults at Montacute, Muchelney and Taunton St Mary Magdalene, and lierne vaults at North Cadbury and Glastonbury St John. The curious vaulted porches at Lamyatt are perhaps early C16, untutored versions of vaults elsewhere. Ribbed tunnel vaults, an echo of the early C14 (cf. Limington), appear at Tintinhull, probably late C14, and oddly in the late C15–C16, at Norton-sub-Hamdon, Hinton St George and Odcombe, the latter two with Perp panelling between the ribs.

Porches bring us from the tower to the rest of the church. Large WINDOWS are the hallmark of the Perp, with variety achieved within the constraints of essentially binary composition. Windows are larger than those of the C13–C14, and occasionally of spectacular size where tracery all but fills the available space. Very large tower W windows and corresponding E windows are typical of the latest Perp. At Minehead, both end windows and one S window are tall, transomed, and of four lights. Ambitious churches could go up to five, six or seven lights. Glastonbury St John has a six-light W window and seven-light E window. Crewkerne has the greatest display, from the six-light aisle windows to the full-height glazing of the N transept in five- and six-light windows with transoms and four-centred heads. High Ham, Langport and Curry Rivel, late C15 to *c.* 1500, display the best of Late Perp tracery, delicate, complex, but, it has to be said, standardized. The use of TRACERY as another means of dating has the same pitfalls as using the towers. John Harvey's complicated sequence of 1983 is the most useful, but has too many categories to summarize here. The points that he draws out are that ogee heads (prefigured in the Wells cloister of *c.* 1420) replace pointed heads in the main lights only slowly, becoming the rule by the 1490s, and that four-centred heads to windows and depressed ogee heads to lights are a C16 feature.

The basic classes of tracery are best illustrated by taking the three-light window as a model. The lights are generally

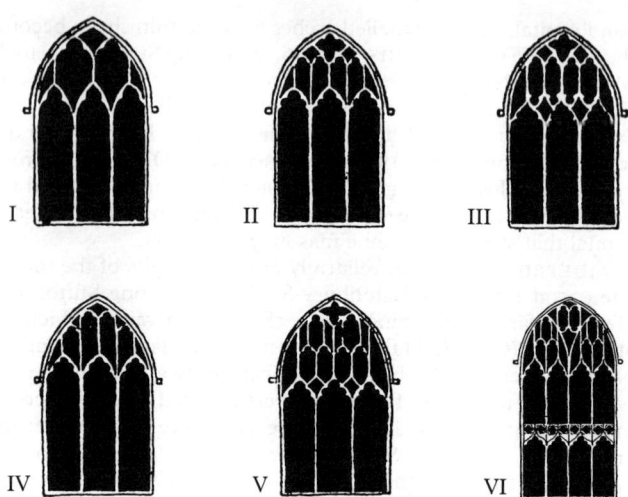

I Hinton St George II Merriott III East Pennard
IV Evercreech V Monksilver VI Luccombe

Somerset church window traceries

cinquefoil-cusped, occasionally trefoil-cusped, whether pointed- or ogee-headed. The tracery of the upper window develops from the reticulated tracery of the Dec, the reticulations no longer curved but straight-sided, roughly hexagonal except that the other four sides are slightly curved. Class I has large undivided tracery panels – the type of the Yeovil side windows, a late C14 and early C15 form – but late examples with ogee-headed main lights do appear, as at Bicknoller. Class II subdivides the tracery panels into three with a Y-mullion. This is the most typical Somerset form of the C15 (e.g. all the windows at Chard), the main lights usually pointed rather than ogee-headed. Ogee-headed examples appear at High Ham (1476) but are much more common with Class III windows, in which the Y in each tracery panel is split at the foot, and these are late C15 and early C16 (e.g. Alford, Stogumber).

Class IV is an exception to the general reticulation as the main mullions continue up to the window arch. These vertical mullions are termed 'supermullions', and the tracery consequently is set over each main light rather than in-between. There is a little group of supermullioned windows at Ashington, Mudford and Rimpton. North Cadbury, *c.* 1420, has windows of nearly this type except that the distinction of mullions and tracery is maintained by thinning the verticals as they pass through the tracery. There are supermullions with ogee-headed lights in the s aisle at Taunton St Mary Magdalene.

Class V is an enrichment of the Class III reticulation in which each large hexagon is subdivided into six with three elongated hexagons. This is the type of the best windows of *c.* 1500, including almost all those of Class VI (*see* below), like Curry Rivel, Langport and Selworthy. It appears always with ogee-headed lights. An earlier variant dividing the hexagon into five, and generally without ogee-headed main lights, is used for the largest windows at Yeovil and appears in the E window of St Mary Magdalene, Taunton.

Class VI is rather different, in that it relates not to the window head, but to square-headed lights either below a transom or free-standing. Examples date from after *c.* 1485. The lights are ogee-headed with a little trefoil or quatrefoil fitted into the spandrels. The type occurs in two separate areas, both around abbeys. Mid-Somerset examples emanate from Muchelney Abbey and include windows at Langport and Curry Rivel, the former parsonages at Aller and Walton, and the abbot's lodging at Muchelney. West Somerset examples emanate from the late C15 refectory at Cleeve Abbey. They include windows at Luccombe, Dunster, Minehead (dated 1529), Selworthy (dated 1538), and Timberscombe. An interesting variant are square-headed lights with strange shouldered tracery. These appear in West Somerset at Watchet, Bicknoller and Old Cleeve and far away under the transoms of the E and W windows at Glastonbury St John and the W window at Wellington. Both types appear one below the other in the hall window of Dovery Manor, Porlock.

The confidence of Somerset ecclesiastics and congregations just before the Reformation is well demonstrated in the enlargement and rebuilding of churches. The addition of AISLES seems to have been a particular feature, and often the gift of a single patron. Churches NW of Taunton demonstrate the phenomenon of 'show aisles' whose characteristic is an unusual elaboration of ashlar stonework, battlements and carved beasts. Often they are oriented to face the village, but not always. Examples are at Bicknoller, Bishop's Lydeard, Broomfield, Crowcombe, Lydeard St Lawrence, Spaxton and Stogumber. There is another group near Burnham: Brent Knoll, East Brent, Lympsham and Mark. Others are at Watchet and Brompton Regis in the W. All are late C15 or early C16, money being left for Broomfield in 1532–5.

The PIERS of Perp arcades are widely standardized. Two types make up the Somerset standard, both with four shafts in the main directions. One has four hollows in the diagonals and the other four-wave mouldings. Both are just as frequent in the other counties of the South West, and neither is missing in other parts of England. The four-hollow standard has its sources far back: the middle post of the N doorway at Wells, *c.* 1230, has this moulding, and the type continues right through the Perp period from Yeovil to Batcombe and beyond, the only dating feature being that the mouldings become more refined. The four-wave type seems to be commonly associated with the show aisles NW of Taunton (Bicknoller, Broomfield, Crowcombe and Stogumber), and is usually combined with a band capital right around the pier, rather than the round or polygonal capitals on the shafts of the four-hollow type. These band capitals are also a Devon feature.

They can be a particular pleasure in that they are carved with foliage, usually vine-trail, particularly good at Churchstanton. The band capital is not unknown on four-hollow piers (Timberscombe), nor are round or polygonal capitals unknown on four-wave piers (Brent Knoll, Old Cleeve). A peculiarity of four-hollow piers around Taunton is angel busts instead of capitals (Taunton St Mary Magdalene, Bishop's Hull, Bishop's Lydeard, Cheddon Fitzpaine, Combe Florey). More complex pier mouldings occur rarely. At Mark, the S arcade has shafts of ogee rather than round section. At Dunster the choir piers have a double-ogee moulding and band capitals. Memorably rustic is the arcade of oak at Kittisford, crudely attempting the standard four-hollow pier.

For naves and aisles TIMBER ROOFS rather than stone vaults were standard, and Somerset has produced some of the most beautiful of English timber roofs. The county did not accept the hammerbeam and double-hammerbeam roof, though the late C15 roof of the refectory at Cleeve Abbey makes a curious attempt at looking like one without being one. The main type is the panelled WAGON ROOF, a general SW English type in which the significant variations are in the moulding of the ribs, the carving of the bosses and the decoration of the wall-plates. Wagon roofs run through the whole Perp period. A West Somerset variant has carved rather than moulded framing (Watchet, Selworthy, Luccombe). Angels or wingless figures frequently decorate the wall-plate, as at Watchet and West Monkton. At Mark the wall-plate is ornamented with large heads. Different from the wagon roof and potentially much grander are LOW-PITCHED ROOFS with tie-beams and kingposts carrying flat panelled slopes. The degree of moulding is much greater and ornament may include tracery (dragons at Somerton) each side of the kingpost, angels against the kingpost, and angels ranged along the wall-plate. The panelled slopes are sub-panelled with bosses or carved leaves at the intersections, and the hundreds of panels may also be ornamented. The best are late in date: at Somerton and Westonzoyland (both c. 1500), and Martock (probably of 1513). Good ones are also at Taunton St Mary Magdalene, Queen Camel, West Camel, Bruton, and the N aisle at Brent Knoll. A simpler version at North Cadbury is of the 1420s. At Martock and Taunton the tie-beams stand on wall-shafts and these on stone canopied niches for statues. At Martock the remaining wall, that is the spandrels of the arcades, is given blind tracery, an integrated decoration of East Anglian type. Simpler panelled low-pitched roofs on cambered principal beams are at North Petherton, Stoke-sub-Hamdon and Wedmore. The N aisle ceiling at Mark has decorated panels. Easternmost panels were often sub-panelled and enriched when over an altar. The framed ceilings of the chancel and S chapel at Langport have exceptional undercut foliage along the wall-edge. One ceiling at Wedmore has painted decoration in the panels.

The CHANCEL is often the part which seems to have been cut short in size and display. Chancel rebuilding of less than equal magnificence can be seen at Bishop's Lydeard, and even at major

ECCLESIASTICAL ARCHITECTURE AFTER 1066

churches like Crewkerne and Taunton St Mary Magdalene the chancels do not rise to the quality of the other parts. Chancels were embellished with SCULPTURE, but this was even more damaged in the Reformation than less accessible exterior carving. The most interesting piece is the reredos from Wellington, of c. 1380, found broken under the church floor, and now in the Museum of Somerset, Taunton. Here we can see what a complete medieval reredos was like with figures not spoiled by Victorian sentimentality. The niches that flanked reredoses survive sometimes intact, as at North Cadbury. CHURCHYARD CROSSES survive in some numbers, many of Ham stone with the regional feature of carved figures on the cross-shafts (Bishop's Lydeard, Drayton), but these are generally eroded.

Late medieval sculpture survives largely in CHURCH MONUMENTS, but it is advisable to look at the monuments of the later Middle Ages as architecture rather than for sculpture of high quality. The Carent monument of 1463 at Henstridge with its canopy and surviving colour is striking, but unremarkable in carving and repetitive in detail. The contemporary Harington monument at Porlock, similarly canopied, is finer in detail, with alabaster effigies. The finest individual figure is probably John Camel †1487 at Glastonbury St John, of alabaster, with surviving colour. A single example of the cadaver effigy of the C15 is at North Curry. An incised alabaster slab at Dunster depicts Lady Elizabeth Luttrell †1493, the technique reminiscent of engraved brasses. The best BRASSES of the period are those to Sir William Wadham †1452 and his mother at Ilminster, and to Sir Giles Daubeney †1446 and his wife at South Petherton.

Late medieval FONTS are mostly octagonal with quatrefoils or rosettes in the panels, varying as to whether the panelling extends to the underside and the stem. One group (Horsington, Kilton (St Nicholas), Mark, Nettlecombe, Old Cleeve, Treborough, Watchet) has demi-angels under the bowl, analogous to those angel corbels that carry roof beams, but rarely carved with great skill. The best carving is at Minehead, where little figures sit on the lower moulding. This is late C14, as are Crowcombe, with charming relief figures in panels, and Nettlecombe, with reliefs of the Seven Sacraments, a theme hardly found outside East Anglia. Taunton St James is the most decorated, octagonal, with reliefs of saints in groups of three and the Crucifixion. The Crucifixion panel at Muchelney has an other-worldly quality, the figures globe-headed, the arms of the Christ eliding into branches. Stone PULPITS are few and plain: a C14 canted front with blind tracery at Baltonsborough, a C15 canted one at Holton, and a curved one at West Camel. More interesting is the base of a lost pulpit at Badgworth with the four Latin Fathers in relief.

WOODWORK of the late medieval period survives in some quantity, the finest in the SCREENS, although not of the quality or quantity of Devon and Cornwall or East Anglia. The best are a group of the Devon type with vaulted coving and bands of undercut foliage in the cornice. The tracery is four-light, subarched, with ogee-headed lights. These screens, closely related

Kingston St Mary, St Mary, bench-ends.
Engraving, 1872

through the use of a leaf-scroll or 'Aaron's rod' motif around the main openings, may be from the same workshop. The main set is in West Somerset, at Carhampton, Dunster, Minehead, Timberscombe and Withycombe. There are outliers at Bicknoller, Halse, Trull and Combe St Nicholas. Brushford has leaf-scroll borders but differs in detail; Bishop's Lydeard is very similar, but without the borders. Another type, also found in Devon, has supermullioned tracery where the middle mullion and sometimes the others run up to the main arch. Several mid-Somerset screens are of this type (Curry Rivel, High Ham, Kingsbury Episcopi, Long Sutton, Middlezoy and Queen Camel) though differing in detail. Norton Fitzwarren is the most remarkable of these supermullioned screens for the cheerfully rude figures inserted into the superbly undercut cornicing. Cruder screens with tracery in square-headed panels, i.e. not adapted for vaulted lofts, survive fairly widely, as at Culbone, Mark, Monksilver and Otterhampton, the latter with the lights gathered under a Tudor arch. Pawlett has a row of single ogee-headed lights each side. C16 Renaissance foliage appears at Pilton. Of timber PULPITS, that at Trull stands out as a sophisticated piece, with five statues, each under a crocketed gable rising in front of an angel. Long Sutton, much restored, has statuettes in a dense thicket of finials and crocketed gables, and Queen Camel is a simpler version. Pulpits at Bridgwater, Monksilver, East Lyng, North Petherton, Moorlinch and Combe Florey are assembled from traceried panels, Bridgwater's being particularly elaborate. The one at Broadway, well into the C16, has square panels with motifs, including the Crown of Thorns and Five Wounds, which survived Reformation iconoclasts by being plastered over.

BENCHES are preserved in such large numbers that they may be said to be a special characteristic of late medieval Somerset. None seem to be earlier than the C15, an expression of the growing importance of the sermon in services. Dated bench-ends tend to be C16 and span the period of the Reformation: Kingston St Mary 1522, Barwick 1533, Crowcombe 1534, Spaxton 1536, North Cadbury 1538, Milverton 1540, Trull 1560, and Spaxton 1561. The bulk of bench-ends are straight-topped; some rise to a finial, sometimes pentagonal (Alford, Badgworth, Brent Knoll, East Brent, North Cadbury), sometimes a split Y, sometimes the full fleur-de-lys or poppyhead. Poppyhead finials are more commonly on the front kneelers (Curry Rivel, Middlezoy, Othery). Typically bench-ends are ornamented with varieties of close tracery and plant motifs, developing from wiry intertwined plants to thick leaves with a hint of Renaissance acanthus. There are sometimes initials and monograms. The delight is the crude and lively relief carving. Religious iconography includes the Five Wounds (North Cadbury), emblems of the Passion (Trull), rosaries (Kingston St Mary), pelicans aplenty, Paschal Lambs, Evangelist symbols, and angels. There is a wealth of beasts, a devil at Charlton Mackrell, many green men, innumerable birds, and farm animals. People appear engaged in recognizable jobs (a fuller at Spaxton, a carpenter and spear-fisherman at East Lyng) or pastimes (a drinker at Milverton, a flute player at North Cadbury) and there are many profile heads, probably types rather than actual portraits. At Trull there is a whole little church procession over several bench-ends and at Brent Knoll the story of a wicked abbot depicted as the traditional fox and geese tale. At Milverton C16 frontals show the twelve Apostles.

A couple of wooden eagle LECTERNS survive, of a very minor order compared to the magnificent brass double-sided lectern made in the late C15 in the Meuse valley and bought for Yeovil in 1541, early spoil of the Reformation. Fragments of late medieval STAINED GLASS survive in quantity, but whole figures are rare and much reconstructed, as at East Brent and Langport. WALL PAINTINGS are mostly fragmentary and fairly routine where they do survive, apart from lovely faded paintings of *c.* 1300 at Sutton Bingham, including the Death and Coronation of the Virgin, mostly in red outline. There are large rustic St Christophers at Ditcheat and Wedmore. Somerset ENCAUSTIC TILES date from the C13 to the mid C14, tailing off with the Black Death. The pavement of the former refectory at Cleeve Abbey, datable by heraldry to after 1272, is among the most important in Britain. Pieces of pavement from Muchelney Abbey re-set in Muchelney church include two exceptional C13 roundel panels. Early C14 tiles can be found emanating from Cleeve, Muchelney and Glastonbury abbeys, the tiles at Watchet, Old Cleeve, Leighland and Timberscombe probably reused from Cleeve Abbey. The best medieval IRONWORK is the lively leaf-scroll on the door at Meare, long thought to be C14 but dated by Jane Geddes to the C15–C16.

The late C15 and C16 saw rebuilding of MONASTIC BUILDINGS on a considerable scale. At Cleeve the refectory was rebuilt for Abbot Juyner before 1487 as a first-floor hall with large transomed windows. The splendid roof is a cross between the wagon roof and the bayed roof, in that principal trusses on false hammerbeams subdivide the length. At Muchelney the work dates from 1500 and later: the fan-vaulted cloister, the refectory that would have had a wall of glazing as at Forde Abbey, Dorset, and the abbot's lodging, rebuilt with a new Great Chamber and fine fireplace. The s front of the house is curiously modern, with glazing given the maximum space in regularly disposed windows. At Glastonbury, Abbot Chinnock's cloisters have gone, and only the crypt under the Lady Chapel survives of Abbot Bere's work, which included the Edgar Chapel of *c.* 1500 at the E end of the Great Church. Stavordale Priory church was rebuilt in the early C15, as aisleless nave and chancel with timber roofs. What is special is the small chapel built after 1500 by Lord Zouche with one and a half bays of fan-vaulting. At Montacute Priory only the early C16 gatehouse range remains, but this is a fine thing, ashlar-faced, embattled, with an oriel over a vaulted throughway (tierceron vault), between stair-turrets. The gatehouse at Cleeve Abbey, by contrast, is a minor structure, just the throughway with a C16 chamber above. The gatehouse at Glastonbury, a much taller throughway with double-chamfered arches, is attached to a C13–C14 house, refronted in the C17. Of other monasteries too little is left for analysis. It is probable that the priory buildings at Dunster were rebuilt with the church in the mid to late C15. The Old Priory with its C15 roof is the only remnant, probably the prior's lodgings. Parts of Cannington Court remain from the nunnery there.

A feature of C15–C16 church life was the CHURCH HOUSE, generally an upper room over a bakehouse and brewhouse. The best surviving ones are the Court House at Martock, late C15, and the Church House at Crowcombe, 1515, the latter with a wind-braced roof. Medieval PARSONAGES were illustrated by John Buckler as they were demolished in the early C19, e.g. at Compton Dundon, East Coker and Pitney. Late medieval crosswings remain at Aller and West Camel, and a good wind-braced roof is hidden at Somerton. St Mary Magdalene's Hospital, Glastonbury, is a fascinating C13 complex consisting originally of a single infirmary hall with a chapel off the E end. Unroofed in the C16, the hall became two rows of ALMSHOUSES of which only one remains, within the high gabled walls of the original.

MEDIEVAL SECULAR ARCHITECTURE

South Somerset is poor in CASTLES, with nothing to equal Nunney and Farleigh Hungerford in the north. Norman barons established castles at Bridgwater, Castle Cary, Castle Neroche, Dunster, Montacute, Nether Stowey and Stogursey, and the Bishop of Winchester at Taunton. Castle Cary was demolished in the Matilda and Stephen wars of the C12. Others were kept up into the C15, Taunton enough so to be besieged in 1451, but most were dilapidated by the C16. Bridgwater, Taunton and

MEDIEVAL SECULAR ARCHITECTURE

Dunster saw action in the Civil War, and were slighted after it. A water gate survives of Bridgwater, and only earthworks of Castle Cary, Castle Neroche, Montacute and Nether Stowey. That leaves the charming but architecturally unremarkable moated site at Stogursey, and the lower ward of Dunster where the great Jacobean and Victorian house rides on C13 foundations, of which the lower half of the twin-towered gateway is the most obvious. At right angles to it is the outer gatehouse of 1419–21, modified with windows of the type found in local churches c. 1500. Of a different order is the castle at Taunton. Successive alteration, particularly the Georgian Gothic work to accommodate the justices for the assizes, has left architectural confusion, but the triangular courtyard still represents the inner ward, with its gatehouse intact, and Castle Bow, the gateway into the outer ward, remains under Georgian Gothic additions.

Of PRIVATE HOUSES the earliest Gothic remains are a doorway of c. 1225 at Court Farm, Wookey, a residence of the Bishops of Wells. The Treasurer of Wells owned the Treasurer's House at Martock, and the cross-wing is mid-C13, with a plate-traceried window to the solar and C13 wall painting of great rarity. A hall was being built in 1293–4, though the present building with its cinquefoiled rere-arches looks mid-C14 and the wind-braced roof C15. Reticulated tracery in the chapel at Lytes Cary dates it to the first half of the C14, but the house is later. While Somerset has a wealth of C15 houses of the standard plan of great hall between storeyed ends for the solar and kitchen, early examples tend to be altered. The roof of the cross-wing at North Cadbury Court, dated to c. 1300, survives where the hall has been replaced, and the hall roof dated to 1328 at the Court House (Long Sutton) is visible, although the hall is floored. Both roofs have base-cruck trusses carrying upper crucks and crown-posts. There are remnants of C14 halls at Bratton Court and Orchard Wyndham (Williton). At Bratton Court, a closed end truss has vertical posts that derive from aisled hall construction, although the hall itself was not aisled. No aisled halls survive.

C15 HALLS are found in considerable numbers, typically with arch-braced collar-trusses and wind-braced roof. Some roofs are distinguished by moulded principals and ornamented wind-braces and wall-plates. A particularly ornate example at Lytes Cary, mid-C15, has cusped wind-braces, quatrefoil piercing of the wall-plate and angels at the feet of the trusses. The damaged roof at Fairfield (dated 1508–28) has blind tracery decoration on the trusses, a feature of the late C15 refectory roof at Cleeve Abbey. The hall roof at Cothay Manor, 1485–8, is simpler, with wind-braces set to a V-pattern in each panel. Lytes Cary and Cothay are ground-floor halls in the earlier medieval tradition, and remain open to the roof. Most ground-floor halls were later floored over. Restored full-height halls are at Dodington Hall, Orchard Wyndham, Coker Court (East Coker) and West Coker Manor. Where inserted floors remain, roofs are visible upstairs, e.g. at the Old Manor and Old Priory, both at Dunster, and at Maunsel House (St Michael Church), this with especially frilly cusped wind-braces. The hall at Hymerford House (North Coker), a small-scale early C15 gentry house, is ceiled but still shows decorated wall-plates of an ornate roof. The best place to read the development of hall houses is at the Priest's House, Muchelney, where an open hall of *c.* 1308 between storeyed ends was given a tall transomed hall window in the late C15 and a fireplace in the early C16, and was floored over in the C17.

FIRST-FLOOR HALLS appear astonishingly prematurely in the 1320s at Manor Farm and the Fish House, Meare, both for the abbots of Glastonbury. They may have evolved from the C13 placing of the hall over an undercroft. They then disappear until the mid C15, at Whitestaunton Manor, dated to 1446–78, and Gothelney Hall. Whitestaunton has a decorated wall-plate and the most exuberant wind-bracing, cusped Y-tracery in three tiers. The Gothelney roof is simpler but still has tiers of cusped wind-braces. Cusped wind-braces are in the concealed roof of a small first-floor hall at The Chantry, Ilminster. The first-floor hall at Castle House, Taunton Castle, dated to 1483, once suggested as the Bishop of Winchester's apartment, is now thought to have been lodgings.

The families who built these houses were typically local gentry or professional men. John Stourton of Abbey Manor, Preston Plucknett, was a wealthy merchant, who endowed Stavordale Priory. Sir William Hody of Gothelney Hall was Chief Baron of the Exchequer, William Dodesham of Gurney Manor (Cannington) an M.P. Gentry families include the Sydenhams of Brympton D'Evercy, Combe Sydenham and Orchard Wyndham (Williton), the Luttrells of the Court House (East Quantoxhead) and Dunster, the Bluetts of Cothay Manor and Greenham Barton, Thomas Lyte of Lytes Cary, and the Maunsels of Maunsel House (St Michael Church). Some were long established like the Luttrells, Lytes and Maunsels, and also the Verneys of Fairfield. Coker Court and The Manor, West Coker, were lesser properties of the Courtenays, Earls of Devon.

Gentry houses typically have storeyed porches, entrance passages with wooden screens to the hall and service rooms, winding staircases in stair-turrets, generally on the rear, and stone fireplaces. Large lateral CHIMNEYS serving hall fireplaces are common, sometimes replacing open hearths. Turret chimneys of the late medieval sort are rare, and found serving the kitchen chimneys at Preston Plucknett and West Coker. PORCHES go in height from single-storey to three storeys and are occasionally vaulted, as at Preston Plucknett. CHAPELS occupy the porch room at Cothay and the Old Manor at Dunster. At Gothelney the chapel caps a stair-tower that probably originated as a storeyed porch. At Blackmore Farm (Cannington) the chapel is much larger, of full height at the end of a cross-wing. At Gurney Manor, William Dodesham squeezed in a chapel by the parlour beneath his new solar. Halls had ORIELS or hall-bays, of which there is a notable one at Coker Court. More often only the arch of the hall-bay remains, as at Orchard Wyndham and Brympton House. At Slough Court (Stoke St Gregory) and Beere Manor (Combwich) such arches show that oriels were not restricted to the larger houses. The two-storeyed canted bay on the solar cross-wing at the Manor House, South Petherton, is unusual both in position and in the degree of decoration. It was built for Lord Daubeney after 1487. An equivalent, not on a cross-wing but in line with the hall, is the highly decorated and battlemented bay on the parlour block at Brympton House, with its adjacent stair-turret, built after 1509.

FIREPLACES tend to be of stone before the C16. There is an exceptionally fine C14 fireplace with a canted stone hood on jowled jambs at Manor Farm, Meare. Plain jowled fireplaces survive at Monks House, Montacute, and Chimney Cottage, Kingsbury Episcopi. Flush fireplaces with traceried lintel panels occur at the Court House, Thornfalcon, with flowing ogee tracery of the early C15, at Abbey Manor, Preston Plucknett, with panels in a thick grid, 1420s, and at the Great Chamber at Muchelney, late C15, with fine quatrefoil tracery in the panels and vine-trail above. The round shafts of the jambs continue past the lintel to support the cornice or shelf, a form that occurs at The Tribunal, Glastonbury. At the Old Priory, Dunster, is an unusual arched fireplace with big quatrefoils in the spandrels. By 1500 broad moulded fireplaces are typical, square-headed or Tudor-arched.

WALL PAINTINGS of the late C15 and early C16 occur at Cothay, damaged by wax injection in the 1930s, the best a Madonna and Child. Some painted friezes at Cothay with texts on scrolls resemble work in the Old House, Milverton, a C15 property of the archdeacons of Taunton which was remodelled in the early C16. Beneath the Milverton frieze is the most significant discovery of modern times in Somerset, a huge painting of Henry VIII enthroned, dated to *c.* 1540, perhaps indicating that the hall was used as a courtroom.

WINDOWS range in size from two lights to as many as six, the hall windows generally the largest, but the solar may have windows of equal size. The early C14 hall at Manor Farm, Meare, and the mid-C15 hall at Hymerford House have pointed two-light windows, as does Coker Court, where a matching window lights the hall-bay. Pointed windows give way to square-headed windows at the abbot's lodging at Muchelney, cross-windows upstairs indicating the principal chamber. Windows at the Priest's House, Muchelney, and the Manor House, South Petherton, have similar quatrefoil spandrels to those of the abbot's lodging. Traceried heads and cusping fade to a Tudor type with simple arched or four-centred heads to the lights, as in the square-headed cross-windows at Cothay. Square-headed hall windows at Lytes Cary also have uncusped heads. Long horizontal mullioned windows appear on the storeyed parts of such houses. The early C16 parlour bay at Brympton has windows of 1–5–1 lights, the heads as at Lytes Cary. Plain six-light windows appear at Ivythorn Manor (Street), and, with a transom, at Swell Manor.

A few GATEHOUSES remain of courtyard arrangements. The barn-like entrances at Bratton Court and Holnicote House (Selworthy) probably had lodgings on either side. Each has a very similar room over the gateway, possibly a counting house. At Cothay the gate-tower is reconstructed, but the archway and surviving range date from *c.* 1400, before the house was rebuilt. At Naish Priory (North Coker) and West Bower Manor (Durleigh) gatehouses of greater elaboration remain from mansions that have gone. At Nash Priory there is an archway and an oriel over, and at West Bower a full turreted gatehouse with fine tracery in the two turrets. The Chantry at Brympton House, a detached range with first-floor rooms reached by an external stair-tower, may have been lodgings.

The hall-house type extends right through to relatively small VERNACULAR HOUSES, which are often very altered outside. The plan of the larger house is repeated in miniature: cross-passage between hall and kitchen generally, and a parlour beyond the hall in three-room-plan houses with a solar chamber above. Internal partitions are of timber. Heating was from an open hearth in the hall until fireplaces became common after 1500. The solar was often jettied over the hall partition, a feature that can survive when everything else is disguised. An example with the hall visible to full height is Lower Cockhill, Castle Cary, dated to 1435. Extraordinarily this relatively small house has a chapel, a timber-framed addition of *c.* 1500 over the porch. The walls have crudely painted patterning around the IHS symbol. Tree-ring dating has shown that timbers of great age survive in smaller houses, giving dates of 1267–99 at Higher Broughton (Stoke St Mary), 1305 at Bridge Farm (Butleigh), and 1315 at No. 14 Middle Street, Minehead. Bridge Farm has two-tier cruck trusses like the Glastonbury Abbey barns. Full cruck trusses are rare and C13–C14; base-cruck trusses tend to be C14, and from the C15 the jointed cruck is the dominant form, though arch-braced collar-trusses are also found.

The barns built for Glastonbury Abbey are outstanding among medieval FARM BUILDINGS. Four survive, at Glastonbury, Pilton, Doulting (N) and a small one at West Bradley. All have similar two-tier cruck roofs, although Doulting is late C13, Glastonbury and Pilton are mid-C14, and West Bradley is late C14 to early C15. Pilton, 120 ft (36.6 metres) long, and Glastonbury, 93 ft (28.3 metres), are magnificently large. Secular barns of note are the 114-ft (34.7-metre) early C15 one at Abbey Manor, Preston Plucknett, and the small cruck-framed example tree-ring-dated to 1285 at Castlebrook Farm, Compton Dundon. This has small and beautifully carved stone heads on the exterior. Of several medieval DOVECOTES, two at opposite ends of Somerset stand out for their corbelled stone-tile roofs, at Toomer Farm, Henstridge, and Blackford House Farm, Tivington. Other circular dovecotes are at Dunster Priory, in the churchyard at Norton-sub-Hamdon, and at Shapwick Manor. Medieval square or rectangular dovecotes are at Pilton Manor and at Witham Friary, the latter perhaps C13–C14. Highly unusual is the dovecote gable projecting from The Manor, West Coker.

The principal MEDIEVAL TOWNS of South Somerset were Taunton and Bridgwater, with smaller towns at Bruton,

Glastonbury, Minehead, Somerton and Yeovil. At Taunton, a row of timber-framed houses in Fore Street and the Grammar School of 1522 are the principal medieval survivors apart from the castle and churches. No. 15 Fore Street conceals behind a towering Elizabethan timber front a hall of 1323–4 with base-cruck trusses and crown-posts. The Grammar School has a good wind-braced roof of close-spaced trusses. Lost glory at Bridgwater is indicated by the ornate framed ceiling now in the Burrell Collection, Glasgow, from St Mary Street. The Blake Museum, Bridgwater, is a low C15–C16 house with cinquefoil-cusped lights to mullioned windows and a first-floor hall. First-floor living accommodation is typical of Bruton where timber-framed houses, variously disguised, line the High Street and alleys off it. The plan, a single room over a ground-floor shop, was sometimes doubled to include a throughway to a back yard. They are tree-ring-dated to the early to mid C15. A lone survivor in West Street, Somerton, and fragments in Glastonbury show that the type existed elsewhere. The Nunnery at Dunster, dated to 1453–89, is a similar but three-storeyed row, the jettied upper floors under later slate-hanging. The Tribunal at Glastonbury is a puzzle, a stone-fronted house of some status, probably a merchant's house, but the royal arms implies a formal use. The Priory at Bruton, with its carved corbels and heraldry, also had a formal use, perhaps as the courthouse of Bruton Priory. The Luttrell Arms, Dunster, originated as the residence and local administrative centre of the abbots of Cleeve. The rear wing has a decorated timber front unique in Somerset and a good wind-braced roof. The George and Pilgrim at Glastonbury was the abbey's *hospitium*, not a straightforward inn, but remains among the finest medieval hostelries in Britain, stone-fronted, with a notable gridded façade framing Late Gothic tracery of the Muchelney sort.

A few small BRIDGES are reliably medieval, as at Haselbury Plucknett and Bruton. The largest bridges, on the rivers of Exmoor, are very much rebuilt, but Barle Bridge, Dulverton, and Landacre Bridge, Withypool, are both probably medieval. The clapper bridge at Tarr Steps has been called prehistoric; current opinion inclines towards a medieval date, but evidence is lacking.

TUDOR AND STUART BUILDING, *c.* 1540–1700

Tudor churches and their furnishings

The Renaissance makes its appearance not very early, in certain forms in bench-ends of *c.* 1540–60 and gradually in church monuments. The destruction of the late 1530s and 1540s was sudden and brutal for the great monastic churches. Glastonbury Abbey was in ruins by 1547, and the abbey churches at Muchelney and Cleeve and priory churches at Taunton and Bridgwater probably also. Monastic buildings of Bruton Abbey, Barlinch Priory,

Witham Friary and Cannington Priory became private houses, as did the priory church at Stavordale, which saved that building when most monastic churches were lost. The church of Dunster Priory survived as the parish church. Iconoclasm was patchier in the parish churches, the statues for example on Isle Abbots removed at ground level, but not touched in the higher niches. There are post-Reformation dates on several parish churches, indicating some continuing work. At Wookey a chapel was added during the restitution of Mary's reign. The one significant C16 church is the private chapel at Low Ham, which opinion now tends to date to after 1588, for Sir Edward Hext. It is still Perp, but proportion and tracery detail are by now odd and provincial compared to work of the early C16.

Tudor CHURCH FURNISHINGS are few apart from the benches. The traceried Gothic SCREEN at High Ham, in the mode of late medieval screens but without the skill, is probably late C16. The linenfold PULPIT at Chedzoy may be mid-C16 and the fleshy arabesques at East Quantoxhead a little later. The stone pulpit at Wells (N) of *c.* 1545 is the first piece in which the RENAISSANCE is taken up in earnest, with plain broad pilasters and a big cornice, amazingly early, but understandable in the context of Bishop Knight's intimacy with the court of Henry VIII and the bishop's visits to Italy.

CHURCH MONUMENTS seem to be specially late in accepting pilasters and columns, acanthus and arabesques. The Speke monument at Whitelackington of *c.* 1550 or later, canopied with fan-vault and pendants, the Clerke tomb-chest at Wookey, *c.* 1555, and even the Wyndham tomb, *c.* 1574, at Watchet (formerly canopied), have no Italian details, though the Gothic is very tired on the Wyndham tomb. Renaissance ornament infects the Gothic on the double Paulet monument at Hinton St George, which is mid-C16. The monument at Bruton to Sir Maurice Berkeley †1581 is fully Renaissance, with a twin-arched canopy and Corinthian columns. It was probably designed by *William Arnold*, going by similarities to fireplaces at Montacute and Wayford Manor. To *Arnold* also should be credited the Thomas Phelips monument at Montacute, †1588 and †1598. An Ionic-pilastered arched canopy shelters Thomas Strode †1595 at Stoke-sub-Hamdon, and there is a splendid double-arched canopy with three pairs of Corinthian columns over Sir George Sydenham †1597 at Stogumber. Another monument type, impressive in its restraint, has no figures, just a tomb-chest and a sort of columned reredos, such as the alabaster memorial to Humphrey Walrond †1580 at Ilminster, or the Ham stone one to Robert Jennings †1593 at Curry Rivel.

Tudor and Jacobean houses

The best stonework in which the new Renaissance is taken notice of is on HOUSES, specifically the porch from Clifton Maybank in Dorset which was re-erected at Montacute. This must date from *c.* 1535, and it is eminently typical of that moment in that an

TUDOR AND STUART BUILDING, c. 1540–1700   47

essentially Gothic design is brightened up just by some putti and acanthus scrolls. Otherwise Renaissance motifs came very slowly, so that the transition in domestic architecture from Late Perp to Elizabethan, that is from Early to Later Tudor, is imperceptible. The additions of the 1530s at Lytes Cary are mullion-windowed with oriels over the porch and hall-bay. What is notable is that the S front is symmetrical about a two-storey battlemented bay window. In addition there is the earliest in Somerset of those ribbed plaster ceilings which one connects so firmly with Elizabethan and Jacobean architecture but which first evolved it seems in the 1520s and 1530s at the Court. If not of the 1530s, the ceiling must date from before 1558.

The key houses of the mid century are Poundisford Lodge and Poundisford Park, for which an earliest date is 1546. Both still have mullioned windows with depressed-arched heads to the lights. What is notable again is symmetry, present at Poundisford Park where both front and rear are a recession of five gables: outer cross-wings, then matching hall-bays and porches, and, innermost, the hall window (on the garden front) and hall chimney (entrance front). This scheme is writ much larger with far greater flair at Barrington Court in the 1550s. Here the Elizabethan E-plan is entirely present, seven-gabled with stair-turrets in the angles to the cross-wings. Renaissance detail is still absent, the skyline bristling with twisted finials, three to each gable and similarly twisted chimneys. Symmetry is so nearly complete that the slight difference between the two halves is barely apparent, but the hall windows are set slightly higher than those on the other side; the medieval hall and cross-passage plan still remains, but with a loss of logic, as shifting the cross-passage to the centre gives equal space to the hall and the minor rooms on the other side. This hybrid Renaissance and medieval planning characterizes Fairfield, c. 1580, where very tall gridded windows mark the hall, and Bishop's Hull Manor, 1586, where desire for symmetry has disguised the hall by evening out the window sizes. The great hall changes successively from being full-height open to the roof, as at Lytes Cary, to a two-storey room with a flat ceiling, as at Barrington, Poundisford Park, Rowland's (Ilton), Brympton House and Nettlecombe Court, to a low-ceilinged ground-floor room as at Bishop's Hull. The older plan with cross-passage and porch offset, but balanced for symmetry by the hall-bay, is still found at North Cadbury Court, 1586, Nettlecombe Court, 1599, and Newton Surmaville, 1608–12. Of the three, only Nettlecombe retains the two-storey hall and therefore the tall gridded windows. Depressed-arched window heads, still present at Barrington, are discarded in the full-blown Elizabethan style for mullion-and-transom windows without any arches.

Montacute, 1595–1601, the only Somerset Elizabethan house of the first rank nationally, follows these trends in having complete external symmetry, a central cross-passage and a ground-floor hall. Where it leaves all the others behind is in its external design, rejecting straight gables for Dutch curves, aligning classicizing sculptures in niches along the upper floor, and setting up minor rhythms in the two-storey bay windows and smaller curved gables that punctuate the parapet. *William Arnold* was probably the designer here, and also at Wayford Manor, *c.* 1602, where the shell-headed niches of Montacute reappear. Cothelstone Manor also left behind late C16 norms, but Civil War destruction has rendered much uncertain, even whether it was a two- or three-storey house. The charming and very personal details, particularly the strange baluster mullions, have no precise English parallels. By the time the Court House (East Quantoxhead) was remodelled *c.* 1614–29, gables had given way to flat parapets. The long-demolished mansion at Orchard Portman, a courtyard house eclipsing in scale anything left in the county, had flat parapets, probably from an early C17 remodelling. Dunster Castle as remodelled by *Arnold* after 1617 had flat battlements.

The Elizabethan and Jacobean taste for LANDSCAPE BUILDINGS finds its most dramatic expression in The Dovecote at Bruton, a giant cross-gabled viewing tower built for the Berkeleys, whose great house made of the remains of Bruton Abbey has entirely gone. Most fantastical is the forecourt at Montacute with its two ogee-domed pavilions and balustraded walls with little columned tempietti on top. The small gatehouses at Cothelstone and Cathanger (Fivehead) are really decorative features to the garden or forecourt, at Cothelstone a little play of stacked cubes, at Cathanger prettily banded in contrasting stones.

Elizabethan and Jacobean TOWN HOUSES are rare, despite the prosperity of Somerset towns. The towering timber-framed front of No. 15 Fore Street, Taunton, 1578, suggests the quality of what has gone. The plan and decorated plasterwork of a C16–C17 house survive behind a Victorian front at No. 18 Fore Street, Taunton. Chard School, of 1583, a house of the Symes of Poundisford, has a handsome front of well-dressed chert, two large dormer gables and a cross-gabled porch-tower. The much subdivided Nos. 7–11 Fore Street, Chard, was a larger Late Elizabethan house with two porch-towers. An early C17 barrel-vaulted courtroom survives behind, lit by a ten-light transomed window each side.

Tudor and Early Stuart interiors are notable for PLASTERWORK. The thin-ribbed ceilings of Lytes Cary are to be found all over Somerset, with decoration in the form of foliage and heraldry interspersed in the intersected shapes. At Poundisford Park and Nettlecombe Court the hall ceilings have large pendants; at Rowland's the hall ceiling is flat. At Poundisford Lodge the ceilings are barrel-vaulted, giving space for additional decoration in a tympanum each end. There is a barrel ceiling decorated in much broader ribs interspersed with symbols at the courtroom behind Fore Street, Chard. Strange and fantastical beasts in ceilings seem to be an early C17 phenomenon, at Wigborough Manor (Over Stratton), *c.* 1630, Hinton House, dated 1636, and Whitestaunton Manor. They may be by the same hand. One plasterer, *Robert Eaton* of Stogursey, is traceable via documents and then motifs. In the 1590s he worked at Combe Florey, Poundisford Lodge, West Coker Manor House and Montacute. Ornamental panels are the climax of Somerset plasterwork, often barbaric by contrast with the houses themselves, like the Skimmington ride at Montacute, and frequently adorned with strange caryatids, masks and bundles of fruit. Subjects are generally Old Testament (the Judgment of Solomon etc.), though New Testament at the Court House, East Quantoxhead. The Triumph of Time at Binham Grange (Old Cleeve) comes from Petrarch, and the classical Death of Actaeon is depicted at the Luttrell Arms, Dunster. The strange horse-legged mermaid at East Quantoxhead must come from a medieval bestiary. Such panels are also found in smaller houses, though these more typically have repetitive patterns made from moulds.

The stone FIREPLACES beneath these overmantels are mostly Tudor-arched. Barbaric figures similar to those in plasterwork, including American Indians, appear on the large stone chimneypiece at Dodington Hall, possibly of 1581. *William Arnold*'s chimneypieces at Montacute and Wayford are giant columned pieces with strapwork overmantels. More conventional is the columned chimneypiece at Barrington with heraldry, after 1623. There are arched stone SCREENS at Montacute and Coker Court, the former with elaborate strapwork cresting, the latter columned to match the hall fireplace. Jacobean domestic WOODWORK is richest in the carved overmantels and fireplace surrounds featuring caryatid figures, strapwork and heraldry. Barrington Court is filled with such woodwork imported in the early C20, and such trade in panelling and carving means that authenticity to the site is often impossible to prove. The arcaded overmantel with unusual *trompe l'œil* architecture at the Old Parsonage, Somerton, almost certainly comes from elsewhere in the town. The panelling in The Priory, Ditcheat, came from the parish church. STAIRCASES develop from stone spirals to stone ones in stair-towers, as at Montacute, to oak dog-leg and open-well stairs. The oak Jacobean stair with large finials and pendants on the newels has a wide currency in smaller gentry houses, e.g. Cloford Manor, 1633, continuing after the Restoration (Great House, Theale, 1670). At West Compton Manor, Pilton, rather flat carved balusters slope to the line of the stair. At the Court House, East Quantoxhead, 1620s, balusters, newels and pendants are variants on a fluted obelisk, the newels and balusters vertically symmetrical.

Smaller VERNACULAR HOUSES arrive by the early C17 at a three-room plan of kitchen, hall and parlour, with a cross-passage between hall and kitchen. Cross-passage partitions were panelled between broad chamfered uprights. The hall fireplace either backed on to the cross-passage, with a spiral stair next to it, or, particularly in West Somerset, was placed on the front or rear wall in a lateral chimney. Both positions derive from the way chimneys were inserted into earlier open halls. Framed ceilings of the C16 and early C17 give way to plain cross-beams. Windows are stone-mullioned with hoodmoulds in the areas of better stone, and oak-mullioned elsewhere. A locally notable feature is a two-storey canted bay under a gable, common around Martock. By contrast the front-wall gables of North Somerset are rare s of

Bossington, cottage.
Drawing by J. Crowther, 1901

the Mendips. Little C16–C17 TIMBER FRAMING survives. Some stone-cased rural houses show timbered end gables, evidence perhaps of re-clad timber frames.

Mention should be made of ALMSHOUSES, something of an early C17 type. Gray's Almshouses, Taunton, brick-fronted with tall chimneys, are probably a late C17 refronting and extension of almshouses founded in 1635. Inside is an early C17 chapel with a low ceiling painted with clouds. There are single-storey almshouses at Stogumber, *c.* 1600, and Somerton, 1626, here with paired niche seats in the front wall. Two-storey almshouses survive at Broadway, *c.* 1608, Ilton, 1634–6, East Coker, 1640, and Crewkerne, 1644, all mullion-windowed. Much grander is Sexey's Hospital, Bruton, 1626–8, around a courtyard like a miniature college, with its chapel and hall range. C16 SCHOOLS remain at King's School, Bruton, small and domestic, the schoolroom divided from the master's room by a cross-passage, and larger, at Ilminster, 1586, with transomed schoolroom windows.

The surviving MARKET CROSSES of South Somerset are the very large Yarn Market at Dunster of 1609, rebuilt in 1647, and the smaller cross at Somerton, 1673, both octagonal about a central core. Otherwise C17 civic buildings like market halls have been replaced. The Town Hall at Somerton, very altered, is probably late C17 in origin.

C17 churches and fittings

The only complete EARLY C17 CHURCH is the private chapel at Wyke Champflower, 1623–4. Gothic is reduced to plain mullioned windows in a plain rendered building with a bellcote. The interior arrangements are of interest in that a boarded tympanum such as is known from late medieval churches marks off the chancel, adorned not with religious motifs but with the royal arms between those of Wells and Canterbury. Like the chapel at Sexey's Hospital, Bruton (*see* above), the window lights have cusped heads to distinguish church from domestic, as does a window dated 1638 at Chapel Allerton. The 1637 date on the tower at Kilve seems credible for such a plain structure. The most interesting church embellishments of the early C17 are the PLASTER CEILINGS at Axbridge (N) and East Brent, of 1636 and 1637. They are ribbed in the Jacobean way but, like the church windows, have cusping for ecclesiastical effect. Gothic here becomes a decorative motif, as it certainly is by the time of the chapel at Kittisford, 1659, lit by mullioned windows with funny trefoiled heads, one under a classical cornice. The CEILING PAINTINGS at Muchelney with angels in low-cut Elizabethan dress amid cotton-wool clouds are probably early C17.

CHURCH FURNISHINGS of the first half of the C17 are a richer field. The revival of enthusiasm begun *c.* 1610 was encouraged by William Laud as Bishop of Bath and Wells (1626–8) on his way to the archbishopric of Canterbury (1633). His insistence on orderly ritual resulted in many new communion tables, pulpits, rails and screens, although dated examples run back before his time. In pulpits, benches, screens and the like the motifs are consistently the secular ones: broad blank arches, strapwork from the Netherlands, arabesques from France, etc. The PULPITS ring entertaining small changes on standard motifs. Some, such as Enmore, Wedmore and Lydeard St Lawrence, have ornament particularly thickly encrusted. At West Huntspill the pulpit (from Stogursey) includes panels of raised-letter text. Giant flowers appear in the arched panels (Chilton Trinity, Tintinhull and Mudford), sometimes Scottish thistles (Badgworth, Bishop's Lydeard and Wedmore). Angles can be pilasters (Brent Knoll) or long fern-like feathers (Sparkford and Witham Friary). At Ilchester the standard arches are given a *trompe l'œil* perspective. Dated pulpits run from Middlezoy, 1606, to North Newton, 1637. Slightly later pulpits dispense with the arched panels and have slim bulbous columns in pairs at the angles (Donyatt, Goathurst, Ilminster, Winsham) or bands of cabochon ornament (Luccombe, Minehead, Timberscombe, Watchet). Cabochon ornament of a different sort appears on the North Newton pulpit and the handsome Pitminster pulpit (from Frome). Pulpits at Stoke St Gregory and Thurloxton are carved with the female Virtues that more usually appear as caryatids on secular overmantels. At Stoke St Gregory, Faith, Hope and Charity are joined by Love. At Thurloxton, 1634, the same three are joined by Father Time and an Archangel holding the soul of Adam. The carving is naïve. An exceptional stone pulpit at Wyke Champflower is a riotous stone variation on the mid-C16 pulpit at Wells Cathedral, the pilasters full of strapwork and the cornice of scrolled foliage. There are also early C17 FONT COVERS, openwork of ogee scrolls (Rimpton), conical (Thurloxton) or ogee-domed (Raddington). The traceried ogee dome at Old Cleeve is C16. The only notable FONTS are later, of Watchet alabaster, at Williton, 1666, and Elworthy, late C17.

There are PEWS with ends still carved in the C15–C16 vein at West Coker, dated 1633. More Jacobean in style are the box pews with strapwork and little half-round shell finials at Ashington, Mudford and Chilthorne Domer. The C17 SCREENS at North Newton and Thurloxton are arcaded, the piers at North Newton with typical figures of Faith, Hope, Charity and the Virgin Mary. Thurloxton is simpler, the arches frilled. The arcaded screen to the Corporation Pew at Bridgwater is altogether richer, and barbaric, with monsters and dragons and spearheaded strapwork cresting. The tower screens at Bruton, dated 1620, and Curry Mallet are of equal richness, but in both cases may not be made for their present positions. The gallery at East Brent, 1635, on vine-wreathed columns, was originally a chancel screen. Columns of something similar remain at Spaxton. COMMUNION TABLES were part of Laudian re-fitting, typically with bulbous turned legs. The most outlandish is at Somerton, 1626, with carved legs showing e.g. Adam ploughing and Noah. The Minehead table has two angels on the front rail. Minehead has an early set of COMMANDMENT BOARDS dated 1634–7, consisting of eight arch-headed panels. The first ROYAL ARMS were set up in churches in the C16, the earliest in Somerset dated 1609.

Early C17 CHURCH MONUMENTS are large, colourful, and often coarsely carved. The monument to Sir John Popham †1607 at Wellington, a towering triumphal arch on Corinthian columns that ring the effigies, on a tomb-chest ringed with kneeling relations, is without modesty based on the monuments to Elizabeth I and Mary, Queen of Scots, in Westminster Abbey. The chequer-painted catafalque under a canopy to Sir John Sydenham †1625 at Brympton D'Evercy derives from Lord Hunsdon's memorial in Westminster Abbey. Crude, large and canopied is the Jennings memorial at Curry Rivel, father and son (†1625 and †1630) under a curved canopy with recumbent putti, all brightly painted. Rather finer, more classical, double effigies of Sir Nicholas Halswell †1633 and his wife at Goathurst lie under a double-arched canopy on panelled piers.

FUNERAL SCULPTURE is redeemed by the discovery of the potential of alabaster, found locally at Watchet. The best alabaster monument, to George Farewell †1609 at Bishop's Hull, is of Midlands alabaster. He reclines on one elbow under a coffered arch with his family on the tomb-chest. Watchet alabaster is used for the enormous Luttrell monument of 1613 at Dunster, three recumbent effigies and one kneeling, under a great corniced canopy on angle columns. Propped on one elbow in a columned aedicule of Somerset alabaster is Sir Francis Kingsmill of Ballybeg †1620 at Bridgwater. Good alabaster effigies include Sir John Stawell †1603 and his wife at Cothelstone, Humphrey Wyndham †1622 and his wife at Wiveliscombe, and the two John Colles monuments at Pitminster, the earlier †1608, picked out with

TUDOR AND STUART BUILDING, c. 1540–1700   53

colour, the other, †1627, notable for the four beautifully carved daughters on the tomb-chest. Of stone, without the fineness of alabaster, are Sir Edward Hext †1623 and his wife at Low Ham. Less grand than the recumbent effigies and canopied tombs are the wall monuments with kneeling figures, typically husband facing wife over a prayer-desk, such as William Brewer †1618 at Chard and John Pyne (1642) at Curry Mallet. Memorial BRASSES continue to be made, notably to Nicholas and Dorothy Wadham (†1609 and †1618), the founders of Wadham College, Oxford, at Ilminster. Their fine memorial in the form of an alabaster altar with columned reredos is attributed to *Nicholas Johnston*.

New schemes of composition belong to the 1630s – see the standing figure at Taunton St Mary Magdalene of Robert Gray †1638. The bust in an oval frame was a favourite with the London Court sculptors. The gilded bronze bust of William Godolphin †1636 in an oval of black marble at Bruton is just possibly by *Hubert Le Sueur* himself. Bills confirm that *Nicholas Stone* made the monument at Watchet to John Wyndham and his wife in 1634–7, a Tournai marble slab with low-relief portraits of shining brass. The London conceit of showing the deceased rising from the tomb in a shroud appears at Winsham, 1639, attributed to *Humphrey Moyer*. A series of brightly painted monuments with figures or three-quarter figures in niches may be the work of one local sculptor or workshop, probably in the Mendips as the memorials appear on both sides of the divide between the two *Buildings of England* Somerset volumes. The first is at Rodney Stoke (N), 1657, with two frontal demi-figures. John Somerset †1663 at Brent Knoll has three, with a cheerful Baroque frame of twisted columns and half-pediments. At Cloford, 1676, two figures gaze forward under paired arches. The Ayshe monument at South Petherton (†1657–77) has three kneeling figures facing sideways, with only the children behind looking outward, but the monumental broken-pedimented frame of Somerset alabaster suggests a different craftsman. Baroque aedicules with curved pediments appear at Shapwick †1657 and †1691, and Goathurst, mid-C17, the piled up detail showing why the style appealed to English artists used to the overcrowding of the Jacobean style.

The first Italian scagliola in Britain is on the Lord Poulett monument of *c*. 1668 at Hinton St George, made by *Baldassare Artima* and *Diacinto Cawcy*, a work so completely Baroque in its tapering pilasters, inlaid sarcophagus and angel hovering under a thick garland of flowers as to show how cautious were English designers of the time. There are no followers. No piece of sculpture in Somerset can rival those accidental arrivals, the twin angels by *Arnold Quellin* from *Grinling Gibbons*'s Whitehall Palace altarpiece of 1686 at Burnham, their fluid grace from another world, seemingly. Two lesser marble pieces deserve recognition. That to Sir William Wyndham †1683 at Watchet, attributed to *James Hardy*, has putti in front of a gadrooned grey marble sarcophagus under a scrolled pediment carrying a trio of urns. Static by comparison is that to the 1st and 2nd lords Stawell (†1689, †1692) at Low Ham, attributed to *William Stanton*, with marble curtains looped back to black-shafted columns.

Domestic architecture from 1630 to 1700

The restrained Palladian CLASSICISM introduced into Court circles by Inigo Jones had some impact in Somerset, with two houses of the 1630s and a third of the 1660s clearly influenced by it. The SW wing at Ashton Court (N) was remodelled in 1633–4 by Thomas Smyth, an M.P. involved in the committee for Inigo Jones's work at St Paul's Cathedral. Smyth's brother-in-law was Lord Poulett of Hinton House (Hinton St George), who refronted the S range there in *c*. 1634–6. Sir John Posthumus Sydenham, who refronted the S range at Brympton House after 1664 in imitation of the Hinton House range, was married to a Poulett. In these houses the façade was no longer treated as a surface to be decorated, the skyline was not punctuated by gables but given a balustrade, and the windows were made upright and were rhythmically placed, and crowned with the pediments that are the hallmark of Palladianism. Yet the work of the 1630s is not pure: there are irregularities in the spacing at Ashton Court and Hinton House that reflect an older building being remodelled, and Hinton House has a pierced parapet of late medieval type. At Brympton there is improvement in detail: regular window spacing, pediments alternately triangular and segmental, and balustraded parapet. Both Hinton and Brympton have large architraved cross-windows which remained the classical form until sash windows came in from Holland in the late C17.

These houses remained the exceptions. The usual domestic style was mullion-windowed and remained so for smaller houses well into the C18. The infiltration of classical and Baroque elements such as twisted columns and segmental pediments into details can barely be detected in buildings before the late C17. Breadstone House, Barton St David, dated 1692, and South Street Farm, South Petherton, 1700, are typical of larger farmhouses without a hint of Jonesian classicism.

The one late C17 COUNTRY HOUSE of metropolitan aspirations was Halswell House, rebuilt in 1689. Here the style of Wren is absorbed and given a higher pitch – a little provincially, similar to the way in which Sir William Wilson worked in the Midlands. *William Taylor* may have designed it. The centre or frontispiece in particular is much dramatized with arches, pillars in recession and military trophies. The other, very much smaller, late C17 country house espousing the new sash windows and steep hipped roofs is Nynehead Court of 1675. The sash windows with thick glazing bars and plain stone architraves with keystones are notably modern, and a curved-pedimented doorway appears inside. Although now rendered, Nynehead Court is of brick, and this was probably exposed. BRICKS, typically a late C17 feature of the county, are known to have been made in quantity for a

TUDOR AND STUART BUILDING, c. 1540–1700

lost hall at Hinton House in 1651–4. Brick show fronts appear at Croydon House (Timberscombe), late C17, and Petherton Park (North Petherton), c. 1700, becoming fairly common in the C18. Croydon Hall and Petherton Park have timber shell-hoods over the doorways, found on modest houses like Escott Farm, Rodhuish, by the early C18. The popular motif of North Somerset, the keyed oval window set upright in attic gables, is rare in South Somerset, where such gables are uncommon. Horizontal keyed ovals are at Cannington Court, c. 1714, and horizontal ovals without keys appear in early C18 pediments. ESTATE BUILDINGS range from the very large stables at Dunster Castle of the 1680s, among the most complete of their era remaining in Britain, to the tiny summerhouse at Poundisford Park in moulded brick.

In the second half of the C17 great changes took place in INTERIOR DECORATION, more evident than the changes in external architecture in South Somerset. The garlanded oval of Inigo Jones's PLASTERWORK appears early at Gaulden Manor, Tolland, encircling a naïve King David and his harp. But the central roundel has a Jacobean pendant and the surrounding frieze has beasts of the earlier school. Similar work is at Bournes (Wiveliscombe) and in a ceiling at Nettlecombe Court of 1641. Something quite other arrives in 1681 at Dunster Castle, the fully modelled flowers and fruit of the Jonesian style as established at Ham House, London, in the 1630s and introduced to the region at Forde Abbey, Dorset, in the 1650s. It is almost certain that the Dunster ceilings come from a metropolitan source and are by a London plasterer, *Edward Goudge*, who worked at Belton, Lincs., in 1685. Following the Dunster ceilings was work at Halswell (replaced in replica in the 1920s) and, more rustic, at Steyning Manor (Stogursey), the first of a series of West Somerset ceilings that relate to North Devon ceilings attributed to the *Abbott* family of Frithelstock.

Of equally superb craftsmanship is the STAIRCASE at Dunster, with gorgeously thick openwork foliage scrolls. Again the likely craftsman was one who operated from London, *Edward Pearce*. An earlier example of the style is at Forde Abbey, 1658. The typical staircase until the mid C17 had thickly carved Jacobean balusters or flat balusters (Langford Manor, Fivehead), sometimes pierced. Turned balusters of generous outline appear before 1650, as at Brympton House. There are openwork panels of wonderfully naïve type at the Great House, Theale, 1670, featuring dragons. All these staircases have very thick moulded handrails. Theale still has the towering openwork finials of the early C17, replaced at Dunster by vases of fruit.

VERNACULAR HOUSES of the late C17 and early C18 are still mullion-windowed, hoodmoulds giving way to continuous dripcourses and regularly aligned windows, as at Eason House, Barrington, 1715. Brick appears in the late C17 (Haydon, near Henlade), and is more common in the early C18, as at Ashford House, Ilton, 1703, and The Red House, Drayton, 1737. Thatch is still the dominant roofing material in this period.

LATE STUART AND GEORGIAN, c. 1700–1837

The development of towns

With the introduction of brick, Somerset towns begin to follow urban trends from elsewhere, although in only one case did London fashion touch a South Somerset town. That was when in the 1720s the Duke of Chandos decided to improve Bridgwater for his own profit. Otherwise Queen Anne and Early Georgian URBAN IMPROVEMENTS are restricted to a house here and there. The outer arms of the market places at Crewkerne and Somerton show town houses for the professional classes, and Wincanton High Street has several houses probably by *Nathaniel Ireson*, resident here as builder, architect and potter from 1726 to 1769. Ireson was the first professional architect to make his career in South Somerset. Castle Street, Bridgwater, begun 1723, involved the builders Chandos used in London, with a local man, *Benjamin Holloway*, as executant. The broad five-bay brick houses bear comparison with anything in contemporary Bristol or Bath, the architecture still Queen Anne, rather than the Palladian that John Wood introduced at Queen Square, Bath, a few years later. *Holloway*'s own house, The Lions, is less disciplined, in chequered brick with a two-storey ashlar centrepiece. Formal urban design next occurs much later at Taunton: the replanning of The Parade around the Market House of 1770–2, and Hammet Street, 1788, another uniform brick street of five-bay houses, focused in this case spectacularly on the church tower. At Bridgwater, Castle Street was intended to lead into a square once the ruins on the castle site had been cleared, but King Square was begun only in 1807 and never completed. Its tall plain brick houses are echoed in The Crescent, Taunton, begun in the same year, and also only partly achieved. Fire cleared the centres of Wincanton in 1707 and Minehead in 1791 without initiating any grand replanning.

Somerset TOWNS prospered in the early C18 thanks to textiles. Defoe in 1722 mentions that Taunton made serges and druggets, and that finer cloths, 'Spanish medleys', were made at Bruton, Castle Cary and Wincanton, while Wells and Glastonbury knitted stockings for the Spanish trade. The textile trade declined later in the century, with some exceptions: flax and hemp for sailcloth were produced in quantities around Crewkerne, a coarse cloth from Wiveliscombe clothed slaves in the West Indies, and silk manufacture prospered in Bruton, Evercreech, Taunton and elsewhere after the import of silk was banned in 1776. But a rich agricultural hinterland was as important, for livestock, dairy products and orchard fruit sold in the towns. There were PORTS at Bridgwater, Watchet and Minehead. Bridgwater had by far the largest trade, from quays along the Parrett. Watchet and Minehead were small harbours protected by a single pier before the C19. In the early C18 Minehead had some trade across the Atlantic. Surprisingly substantial business was done from Langport up the River Parrett, represented by one remaining Late Georgian warehouse there. RESORTS, whether for sea air or medicinal

LATE STUART AND GEORGIAN, c. 1700–1837

waters, were very restricted outside Bath. Minehead was recommended in the late C18, but its significant development is late C19. At Burnham-on-Sea, a sea-bathing spa, Daviesville, was started in the 1820s, but failed to prosper. The little pump room at Glastonbury, 1754, represents a brief mania for healing waters, and there are buildings of a rural spa at Horwood (Wincanton) of 1803–5.

Minor CIVIC BUILDINGS proliferated in the Georgian era. Simple single-storey covered MARKET BUILDINGS, as at Ilminster, have mostly gone. The two-storey market house with an open ground floor beneath a room for town business became common, with charming small-scale examples surviving at Langport (1733), Martock and Milborne Port. These market buildings became rather grander in the early C19 as TOWN HALLS, with a market beneath a civic hall and business rooms, as at Glastonbury, 1813–14, Wellington, 1832–3, and Chard, 1834–5. Chard, by *Richard Carver*, is much the grandest, with its two-storey classical portico. At Bridgwater the functions were separated, with a town hall in the sense of municipal offices by *Carver*, 1820–3, and a very proud domed and columned market hall, 1826–7 by *John Bowen*, at the focal point of the town. At Taunton the Market House of 1770–2 contained an assembly room upstairs and offices below, with markets in cruciform structures each side (since demolished). Unusual replacements for medieval MARKET CROSSES are the columns in front of the market houses at Ilchester and Martock. LOCK-UPS were included in town halls or built as little free-standing structures at Castle Cary (1779), Kingsbury Episcopi and Merriott. One piece of CIVIC SCULPTURE is the marble statue of Queen Anne at Minehead, almost certainly by *Francis Bird*, erected in 1719.

p. 190

98

p. 623

Domestic architecture and garden buildings

Georgian COUNTRY HOUSES are less common in South Somerset than in the environs of Bristol and Bath, because new money was less in evidence. The great Baroque house at Witham Friary, designed c. 1717 perhaps by *James Gibbs* for Sir William Wyndham of Orchard Wyndham, was apparently never begun, Wyndham contenting himself with altering the family seat instead. The typical country house of early C18 England, a three-storey block with the cornice below an attic storey and articulated with giant pilasters or quoin pilasters, has examples at Sandhill Park (Ash Priors), 1720, and Ven House (Milborne Port) and Crowcombe Court, both begun c. 1725. Both Ven and Crowcombe are of brick. Crowcombe, by *Thomas Parker*, a Dorset builder, has the curiosity of Borromini capitals with inturned volutes, as used by the Bastard family when rebuilding Blandford, Dorset, after 1731. Hazlegrove House, 1730–2, divided by superimposed pilasters in all three tiers, fits no category, having reputedly been based on a palazzo in Genoa by its amateur architect, *Humphrey Mildmay*. Redlynch of 1708 was extended from 1725, probably by *Nathaniel*

p. 58

89

Witham Friary, design for Witham Park, front elevation.
Engraving, 1717

Ireson. He designed the two large service blocks of 1740–6 which remain, the house having been demolished.

With Earnshill House (Hambridge), 1728–31, the PALLADIAN style reached the region. Earnshill is a large five-bay villa, pedimented with a *piano nobile*, of brick on a stone basement. Typical of mid-C18 English Palladianism is Hatch Court (Hatch Beauchamp), 1755, by *Thomas Prowse* M.P., a large square villa with corner towers in the manner of Colen Campbell and William Kent. Hatch Court is almost the twin of Hagley Hall, Worcs., designed by another gentleman amateur, Sanderson Miller, with help from Prowse. Hadspen House, remodelled *c.* 1747, is more conventional, pedimented across the centre three bays and with alternating pediments to the lower windows. The only Georgian country house on a grand scale is Marston House (Marston Bigot), a product of alterations for the Earls of Cork and Orrery. A house of the 1640s was remodelled in 1750–2 with sash windows and balustrades, the original showing in angle projections that were C17 stair-towers. This large eleven-bay house was extended by *Samuel Wyatt* in 1776, with lower wings, to an impressive twenty-seven bays, and *Jeffry Wyatt* (*Wyatville*) probably added the colonnade between the former stair-towers in 1820. Across the park the effect is magnificent; close to, the eye notices the lack of a centrepiece, indeed of a central doorway (reflecting the C17 arrangements).

Substantial LATE C18 HOUSES are few. *Robert Adam*'s house of the 1760s at Witham Friary for Alderman Beckford was demolished after Beckford's death in 1770. Cricket House (Cricket St Thomas), remodelled by *John Soane* for Viscount Bridport in 1786–8 and 1801–4, is confused by enlargement of the 1830s. Its astylar elevations with window architraves just incised are starkly simple, especially compared to the grand porticoes Soane had proposed for Hinton House. Kingweston House deserves mention for its remodelling in 1824–5 by *William Wilkins*, as a severe Blue Lias block distinguished by a pure Greek porch on one end.

Older fashions lasted longer on SMALLER C18 HOUSES. Cross-windows still appear on Roundhill Grange (Charlton Musgrove), an early brick house of 1701, and Tintinhull House, c. 1722. Horsington House, early C18, is a plain three-storey block, without the classical pediment and proportions of Tintinhull. It still has bolection-moulded window frames, as does Charlton House (Charlton Mackrell), 1726, which has a Baroque upswept string course and cornice. At Godminster Manor (Bruton), the refaced cross-wing has alternating pediments hinting at Palladianism, but also a bolection-moulded doorcase with a split curved pediment. Barford House (Enmore), fronted in red brick, has the curved window heads of Castle Street, Bridgwater, and moulded brick detail on the wings typical of the early C18, but was being built in 1751. Pilton Manor, refaced c. 1754, has an elementary Palladianism with a Venetian window. Westholme House (Pilton) of the 1760s is more sophisticated, a three-storey, five-bay house with cornice and parapet and central Venetian window, in an ashlar front that might have strayed from around Bath. The ashlar front of Hendford House, Yeovil, 1776, has a similar quality. Huntspill Court (West Huntspill), a brick house of c. 1765, shows post-Palladian sophistication, with two-storey canted bays under Diocletian windows, but Somerton Randle of the late 1780s is still cautiously Palladian. Pixton Park (Dulverton), 1803–5, is also conservative, stuccoed with ashlar Ionic pilasters to the upper floors. Refinement in detail is rare. Kilve Court, 1782–5, a three-storey, five-bay block, has a well-carved ashlar doorway, Venetian window and Diocletian window. Hill House (Otterhampton), also of the 1780s, has an ashlar tripartite doorcase neatly linked to a corniced window above, and bowed end walls. When building recommenced after the Napoleonic Wars the typical small country house was a deep-eaved villa, as provided by *Richard Carver* at Willett House and Hartrow Manor (both at Elworthy), c. 1815. But Carver was soon designing in Tudor Gothic styles, and the Georgian alternatives to classicism need to be considered.

Ancient lineage or the suggestion of it was high in the aspirations of Georgian landowners, and ancient English styles were best suited to expressing it. Mellifont Abbey (Wookey), if it dates from 1730 for Col. William Peirs M.P., represents both EARLY GEORGIAN GOTHIC and early antiquarianism in the reused medieval oriel and carvings. Peirs can be linked politically to the Pelhams, significant figures in the Gothic Revival, for whom William Kent worked. But the date cannot be fixed with certainty. The brick porch-tower with its strange rustication fits the 1730s. Peirs also built Bradley House (West Bradley), 1726, a tall square house with square bays set diagonally at each corner that looks like an Elizabethan conceit, and must reflect an antiquarian disposition. The CASTLE STYLE of Vanbrugh, all round arches and battlements, had a very large example in Enmore Castle, 1751–7, designed for himself by the *2nd Earl of Egmont*. Four-square around a courtyard, with regular towers and regular arched sash windows, it must have been magnificent, if mechanical. Only part of one side remains. A late example of the toy castle is Compton Castle (Compton Pauncefoot), 1821, by *John Finden*, complete with corner turrets and an entrance tower.

When in the late C18 the 4th Earl Poulett sought to remodel the Elizabethan Hinton House he was persuaded to demolish a great deal and fit the remainder with sash windows and battlements. The result as executed was so poor that the earl turned to *Soane* to redesign it as a classical mansion, before *James Wyatt* persuaded him that Tudor Gothic was more appropriate (and thereby ousted Soane). Wyatt re-clad the W front in a thin Tudor style *c.* 1801 and added Gothic interiors. A castellated *porte cochère* was added at the back in 1814 by *Jeffry Wyatt*. A late C18 wing at Pilton Manor uses stepped lancets of early medieval type, in contrast to the more usual pointed or Tudor-arched windows. When Sir Benjamin Hammet remodelled Taunton Castle for the justices after 1786 he gave their new rooms large pointed sash windows. These were echoed in two inns of 1816 that framed the castle forecourt, an effect unfortunately spoiled since. *Richard Carver's* Tudor style begins with Chapel Cleeve Manor (Old Cleeve), 1818–23, with a symmetrical front about a canted bay, the type of his classical villas. His largest new work, Knowle Hall (Bawdrip), 1829–33, is also symmetrical, with gables, but hardly convincing. His Tudor-style additions to houses are rarely inventive, the largest being at Maunsel House (St Michael Church), 1827–8, and St Audries (West Quantoxhead), after 1835. The most successful Tudor Revival work is the rebuilding of Dillington House in 1835–8 by *James Pennethorne*. He demolished most of the old house to impose a new symmetry about the battlemented porch-tower, but with greater appreciation of detail than Carver.

Taunton Castle, under alteration.
Engraving after C. Warre Bampfylde, 1791

Gothic or Tudor styles become common in the early C19 for LODGES and ESTATE BUILDINGS and appear for Picturesque effect in villages, as at the Rose and Crown inn, Huish Episcopi. The paired Gothic lodges to Dillington House are more formal than most, the two-storey lodges to Compton Castle rather larger. Not Gothic, more Picturesque vernacular, are the Acland estate cottages around Selworthy, with their conical chimneys and thatched roofs. The best group, Selworthy Green, 1828, invisibly incorporates old cottages with new work. There are classical lodges at Sandhill Park (Ash Priors), with a pedimented archway of c. 1815; at the demolished Cothelstone House of 1817–20; and at Walford House (West Monkton).

FOLLIES and landscape features were generally Gothic, but not always. Wilderness walks were laid out in the early to mid C18 at Orchard Wyndham, Redlynch and Hatch Court, ornamented with structures from ephemeral shelters to solidly built grottoes. *Stephen Switzer* worked at Marston Bigot, c. 1730, but little survives apart from terracing, and also a grotto and bathing pool of slightly later date. At Halswell in the 1750s Sir Charles Kemeys Tynte built a rotunda and a rockwork dam close to the house, and, further away, laid out Mill Wood with a sequence of ponds ornamented with grottoes, rockwork bridges and (originally) a druid's hut, finishing in 1764–5 with a classical temple by *Thomas Prowse*. Above Halswell, Robin Hood's Hut, 1765 by *Henry Keene*, was a Gothic seat or belvedere backed by a cottage where meals could be prepared. Tynte was a friend of Hoare of Stourhead (Wilts.) and Coplestone Bampfylde of Hestercombe. The landscape at Hestercombe echoes that at Halswell, but has more dramatic water effects. It had classical, rustic, Chinese and Gothic structures and a 'Turkish Tent'. *Richard Phelps* of Dunster may have been involved. He designed the rockwork bridges below Dunster Castle and the circular Gothic tower on Conygar Hill, Dunster, 1775, and also a Gothic bridge (1776) and folly ruin at Crowcombe Court. The towered Gothic gateway at Redlynch, 1754–5, may be by *Henry Flitcroft*. It is precisely contemporary with a Palladian tearoom for viewing the menagerie. Redlynch also had a Chinese seat and a temple.

Georgian FOLLY TOWERS are Palladian at Newton Surmaville, 1745, plain and circular at Montacute, 1760, Gothic and church-tower-like at Willett (Elworthy), c. 1774, and Gothic and circular at Inwood (Henstridge). The greatest of them all is Alfred's Tower at the edge of the Stourhead estate (South Brewham), 1769–72, by *Henry Flitcroft*. This is castellated and Gothic, of a monumental 131 ft (40 metres). The small folly tower at Chilton Polden of c. 1836 is attached to a mock church built to contain medieval fragments collected by the antiquary William Stradling. Higher than the towers are the COLUMNS that punctuate the landscape. *Capability Brown*'s Pynsent Column (Curry Rivel), 1766–7, on a pedestal, with a staircase within, rises 140 ft (43 metres) to the top of the urn. Slightly lower is the Hood Monument, 1831, by *H. E. Goodridge*, at Butleigh. The original Wellington Monument (Wellington), 1817, would have been a strange triangular shaft topped with a cast-iron statue, but was completed much later as an obelisk of 176 ft (53.6 metres).

Rockwork GROTTOS begin at Barwick House, of the 1770s. These imitate the grotto at Stourhead, especially the main Pantheon-domed chamber. In the park are also four high rockwork structures, a thin tower, an obelisk, an arch carrying a cylindrical turret, and a steep cone on a circular Gothic base. William Stradling had a grotto at Tower House, Chilton Polden, *c.* 1832, capped by a druid altar. Inside is a plunge bath. A plunge bath is hidden within the massive rockwork dam at Compton Castle, *c.* 1820–30. Shell grottos, or rather tearooms encrusted with shells, remain at Jordans (Broadway), 1828, and St Audries, of similar date.

Developments in country-house PLANS mostly occurred in the early C18. At Ven House a two-storey hall opened (before the alterations of the 1830s) to a stair hall of similar height, making the centre of the house just two rooms for display. At Crowcombe Court a large single-storey hall opens to the stair hall, while at Earnshill the staircases are on each side of the entrance hall, which opens to the saloon beyond. By the mid C18 the usual plan had a stair hall behind an entrance hall, with principal rooms to each side (Hatch Court).

The grandest INTERIORS are those of Ven House and Crowcombe Court. The hall at Ven is panelled to mid height, with pedimented Ionic frames to the opposed fireplaces. Ionic columns carry a gallery over the entry to the former stair hall. The ceiling exceptionally has an Italian painting surrounded by Rococo plant-trail plasterwork. At Crowcombe, PLASTERWORK becomes the main decoration, richly detailed in the manner of William Kent, with lush swags and a Palladian opening to the staircase. The interiors at Crowcombe were designed *c.* 1740 by *Nathaniel Ireson* who may have been responsible for the much smaller but similarly decorated stair hall at Shanks House (Cucklington). Coarse early C18 ceilings with especially thickly detailed foliage and perched cherubs, derived from the Dunster ceilings of the 1680s, occur at Fitzhead Court and Stockland Lovell (Fiddington), and at Nettlecombe Court, there dated to *c.* 1704. These are probably by the *Abbott* family of North Devon. Rococo plasterwork of the mid C18 with little Chinese figures covers the stair hall at Nettlecombe Court. One room at Ven has similar Chinoiserie in the ceiling. A Rococo ceiling at Hatch Court dates from the 1750s, and there is similar work in the older part of St Audries. Adamesque decoration of the 1780s appears on one ceiling at Nettlecombe, the great hall at Fairfield, and the saloon at Hill House (Otterhampton). It is eclipsed in quality by superbly detailed ceilings at Somerton Randle (Somerton), done probably after 1798 for John Pinney of Bristol, presumably by Bristol plasterers. There is Greek Revival plasterwork of the 1820s at Kingweston House and Bagborough House (West Bagborough). The Gothic plasterwork by *Richard Carver* at Chapel Cleeve Manor and St Audries has undercut vine-trail borders and an occasional pendant. His octagonal entrance hall

LATE STUART AND GEORGIAN, c. 1700–1837

at Chapel Cleeve is outdone by *Finden*'s octagonal stair hall at Compton Castle. *James Wyatt*'s entrance gallery and huge top-lit saloon at Hinton House have disappointing flat panelled ceilings. The Gothic doorcases there are of plaster coloured to imitate wood.

CHIMNEYPIECES follow changing Georgian taste. At Ven, the hall fireplaces have large scrolled pediments and eagles. At Crowcombe the Kentian female head appears between foliage scrolls, a motif much used later with scrolls simplified to drapery. A variant of the late 1760s at Coker Court (East Coker) has a lion mask between drapes of pelt complete with feet. Shanks House and Hazlegrove House have coloured marble pieces of the 1730s and 1740s, more ornate than elsewhere, in the Kentian taste. Mid- to late C18 chimneypieces ornamented with a carved plaque occur widely, at Earnshill House using startling red and yellow marbles. Fluting inlaid in such colours occurs in chimneypieces at Dunster Castle, 1770s, and Fairfield and Nettlecombe Court, 1780s. There are Neoclassical chimneypieces of exceptional delicacy at Somerton Randle, c. 1799, probably Bristol work. A sculptural early C19 chimneypiece at Dillington has naturalistic female supporters. Proto-Victorian is the curvaceous marble piece of the 1830s by *J. E. Carew* at Orchard Wyndham (Williton). A feature of relatively modest houses is the OVERMANTEL PAINTING, more rustic than refined, showing views, landscapes and hunting scenes (cf. Roobies Farmhouse, Fiddington). PAINTED ROOMS occur at Manor Farm, Charlton Mackrell, datable to after 1709, and The Dogs, Wincanton, with classical landscapes in grisaille.

Georgian STAIRCASES begin in timber with moulded or carved tread-ends. After the thick turned type (Orchard Wyndham) come twisted balusters (Crowcombe Court) or turned ones, generally a column on a squat baluster or vase (Edington House), sometimes alternating (Westholme, Pilton). Tread-ends are carved or moulded. Modest Chinese Chippendale balustrades appear at Mellifont Abbey (Wookey) and Bickham Manor (Timberscombe). None of these are exceptional. More impressive stone cantilevered stairs appear from the 1730s (Hazlegrove House). The open-well stair at Coker Court, 1766–70, has stonework as thin and precise as good engineering. The fine dividing stair at Hatch Court with delicate iron rails is probably of c. 1800, and the curving stair at Henlade House is similar. *Carver*'s curving cantilevered stairs at Chapel Cleeve Manor and Knowle Hall have iron Gothic railings.

VERNACULAR HOUSES remain mostly mullion-windowed until the late C18, when they were succeeded by Late Georgian sash windows or casements, depending on the status. Centralized plans predominate, as elsewhere in Britain. Smaller FARM BUILDINGS proliferate, such as granaries, stables, cowsheds, again as elsewhere. An unusual aisled BARN of the early C18 is at Higher Hill Farm, Butleigh. A significant regional type is the BANK BARN, a two-storey barn built into a slope, with barn access from the back and storage beneath, common in the Quantocks. Unusual shelter-sheds with columned fronts were erected for

William Pitt the Elder around Burton Pynsent (Curry Rivel). w of Taunton such shelter-sheds were two-storey LINHAYS, the upper floor a hayloft, fronted with tall round piers.

Georgian churches and monuments

Quite a number of CHURCHES were rebuilt and many more repaired in the C18, but the dislike of the Victorians for Georgian work has swept much away, including *Ireson*'s rebuilding of Wincanton (1748). Only the bell-stage remains of the 1738 rebuilding at Horsington. The tower of Woodlands church, 1712–14, built for the Longleat estate, has some ambition, combining classical angle pilasters and cornices with Gothic pinnacles and spire. Towers with typical Georgian Gothic Y-tracery are at Milton Clevedon (1790) and East Coker (1792–4). Redlynch, a plain estate chapel of 1750, is probably by *Ireson*. The chancel at Bruton was rebuilt in 1743, externally plain but with a lavishly plastered interior. The s transept at Goathurst was rebuilt in 1758 with pretty Georgian Gothic plasterwork, perhaps by *Henry Keene*. *Richard Carver* designed most of the Late Georgian Gothic churches in the area: Blackford (near Wedmore) 1823, Theale 1826–8, Sutton Mallet 1827, Wiveliscombe 1827–9, and Wellington (dem.) 1828–31. Carver was inventive with plans in a way that was impossible after 1840. Blackford is octagonal, and Theale and Wiveliscombe have curious square corner projections, more decorative than practical. Wiveliscombe, Carver's major work, shows symmetry on every face, in Perp Gothic, the tracery copied or indeed transplanted from the previous church. Carver's interventions in older churches could be brutal, as at Bishop's Hull, 1826, but he reused windows there too, and he reproduced Somerset Perp adeptly for the s aisle at Hatch Beauchamp, 1834.

South Somerset has a number of good early NONCONFORMIST CHAPELS. These include Long Sutton (Quaker, 1717), Ilminster (Unitarian, 1719), Taunton (Unitarian, 1721), Mid Lambrook (1729) and Crewkerne (Unitarian, 1733). Of these Long Sutton is the most charming and complete, hip-roofed with a simple interior. The Taunton interior – galleried on three sides with the ceiling carried on two giant square Corinthian piers – shows the wealth of urban Nonconformity. Mid Lambrook has the simple carpentry of rural chapels, crowded by the three-sided gallery. Crewkerne is gable-fronted, the pattern for later chapels like Bridgwater (Unitarian, 1788) with its barrel-vaulted 'nave' on tall stone columns. By contrast the original Octagon Chapel, Taunton, 1776–8 (now offices), shows the Wesleyan interest in centralized plans. Octagonal within a square is the ROMAN CATHOLIC chapel at Cannington Court, 1830–1 by *John Peniston*, on a grand scale because Cannington was briefly the seat of the bishop. The R.C. church at Taunton (now the Masonic Hall) of 1822 is grandly Ionic, of stucco.

Most CHURCH FITTINGS of the C18 have not survived, but the reredos at Bruton fortunately remains to show the scale of

LATE STUART AND GEORGIAN, c. 1700–1837

such things, the iconography startlingly Counter-Reformation. Remote Oare and Stawley have good rustic Late Georgian fittings. GALLERIES include a large classical W gallery at Selworthy, 1750, and early C18 galleries at Creech St Michael and Stocklinch, the latter still with the painted King David and his harp. There are paintings from a lost gallery at Glastonbury St John. A rare SCREEN of 1729 at Crowcombe was made by *Thomas Parker*, who designed Crowcombe Court. This goes with a pulpit. Panelled PULPITS of the 1740s–50s survive at Bradford on Tone, Carhampton, East Pennard, Kingston St Mary, Langport, Nettlecombe, Wellington and Woodlands, several by the same carpenter. Large and elaborate brass CANDELABRA, called at the time much more tellingly 'branches', were made in imitation of Dutch C17 pieces in Bristol and Bridgwater. There are examples at Stogursey (1732), Batcombe (1737), Lympsham (1744), Ilminster (1762), Stogumber and Old Cleeve (1770), Burnham (1773), Meare (1777) and Somerton (1782). The Bridgwater makers *John Bayley* and *Thomas Bayley* also made church weathercocks. Accidentally in Somerset are the very Gothic stone screen and pulpit carved for the Lord Mayor's Chapel, Bristol, in 1823 by *Thomas Clarke*: the screen is at Low Ham, and the pulpit at Muchelney. Accidental too is the enormous Deposition painting at Bridgwater, probably Italian, c. 1700, reputedly wartime booty.

CHURCH MONUMENTS of the C18 and early C19 are of course plentiful, the majority simple tablets. A particular Somerset type consists of Blue Lias slabs blackened and incised to imitate slate. Starting as ledger stones in the C17, these migrate to the walls, where the ornament acquires a rustic exuberance: skulls and bones in the early C18, bookplate engraving by the later C18 (Mary Mitchell †1756, Langport). In the first half of the C18 marble wall monuments tend be to individuals of higher status. Baroque cartouches (Combe St Nicholas †1714) give way to large pedimented plaques (Horsington †1713, Merriott †1732), with columns (Martock †1747) or pilasters (Charlton Musgrove †1730), rarely signed. Larger, more architectural works include the Harbin monument at Yeovil (1711). A giant pedimented aedicule frames a sarcophagus against an obelisk on the massive Phelips monument at Montacute (probably 1720s). A standing monument with carving of unusually high quality is that to Sir Thomas Wroth at Stogursey, attributed to *Henry Cheere*, c. 1737, in several colours of marble. A notably sculptural mid-C18 monument at Wedmore (†1755) has a bird drawing back a drape to reveal the inscription on the urn. Marble plaques proliferate in the late C18 and C19 from firms like *Paty*, *Tyley* and *Wood* in Bristol and *Ford*, *King* and *Reeves* in Bath, which is not to say that the quality is not high (especially by comparison with *Long* of Taunton, *Gibbs* of Axminster and others). Their works tend to generic themes: the draped urn, the urn with mourning females.

Portrait busts are rare before the second half of the C18. That of Elizabeth Morris †1699 at Ditcheat, in Somerset alabaster, deserves note. At Goathurst and Hinton St George, a sculptor of national note, *Rysbrack*, signs monuments with busts to Sir John Tynte †1742 and the 1st Earl Poulett †1743, the latter particularly fine. Also at Hinton are another portrait bust (†1747) and two relief portrait medallions (†1765 and †1785), these two set with angels against red obelisks. All three monuments are unsigned. At Goathurst, another leading sculptor, *Nollekens*, signs a handsome Neoclassical monument (†1785) with portrait medallion supported by an angel with cast-down torch. Neoclassical sculptors from London appear more commonly in the early C19, *Sir Richard Westmacott* most often. His relief at Marston Bigot (†1826) is nobly classical. His ostentatious Earl Nelson monument (†1835) at Cricket St Thomas stands opposite one to Viscount Bridport †1814 designed by *Soane*, Neoclassical too but more architectural. *Chantrey* is represented by relief portraits at Selworthy (†1828 and †1837) and a classical female in relief at Somerton (†1818). Notably good, but unsigned, is the mourning husband and child (†1826) at Whitelackington.

The most interesting early STAINED GLASS of the region is the E window of the 1690s at Low Ham, a brownish transparency derived from painting. Georgian glass is rare. An early C19 two-light window at Nynehead includes one figure from Reynolds's window at New College, Oxford.

Georgian transport

Transport developments opened up the county from the early C18. Turnpike Trusts improved the roads, leaving their characteristic TOLL HOUSES with polygonal ends or bay windows to give views in both directions. There are single-storey ones at Muchelney and Kingsbury Episcopi, *c.* 1824, and two-storey ones at Galhampton, South Cheriton and Aller. Snowdon Hill, Chard, 1838, is the most picturesque, conical-roofed in thatch. The single-arched BRIDGE over the Parrett at Burrowbridge, 1826, by *Philip Ilett*, was handsome before it lost one parapet. The important early iron bridge of 1794–8 at Bridgwater, made at Coalbrookdale, was replaced in 1883.

Bridgwater, former Town Bridge.
Engraving, 1797

LATE STUART AND GEORGIAN, c. 1700–1837

Several CANALS were attempted. The most ambitious was the Grand Western, intended to link the Bristol and English channels. As proposed in 1768–9, it was to join the Tone at Taunton with the Exe at Topsham. It was redesigned by *John Rennie*, and construction began in 1810–14 with a branch off the main route, to Tiverton, Devon. The canal to Topsham was never built, but the Tiverton branch was joined to Taunton in 1830–8 under *James Green*. Seven radically innovative perpendicular boat-lifts were used instead of locks to master the 262-ft (79.9-metre) rise between Taunton and the Devon boundary. The enormous masonry remains of the Nynehead lift are the most complete. There was also an inclined plane (inclines, like boat-lifts, worked by placing the vessels in water-filled caissons). The Bridgwater and Taunton Canal opened in 1827 from Taunton to the River Parrett below Bridgwater, and was extended in 1841 to the new Bridgwater Docks. This relatively simple canal across flat country is the only canal still in use, having been restored in 1994. The canal story extends into the Early Victorian period with the Parrett Navigation of 1836–41, which improved the river from Bridgwater to Langport and on up the River Ile. *William Gravatt* designed the handsome triple-arched bridge at Langport, and also the very short Westport Canal of 1840 which was meant to bring traffic closer to Ilminster. This was rendered useless when the Chard Canal opened in 1842, passing through Ilminster. Innovative designing by *Green*, engineer from 1831, gave the Chard Canal only one lock but four inclined planes, that at Wrantage climbing to the 1,800-ft (550-metre) long Crimson Hill Tunnel. The central span of the bridge at Long Load, widened in 1814, represents another improved river navigation, from Langport via the Yeo towards Ilchester. The Glastonbury Canal crossed the peat moors to Highbridge, opening in 1833, but was bedevilled by seepage.

Georgian industry

WATER MILLS for corn milling were ubiquitous. The best surviving early example is Rowland's Mill (Ilton), *c.* 1700. Little Norton Mill (Norton-sub-Hamdon), 1782, is on the tiny scale typical of many rural corn mills. Castle Mill, Dunster, was rebuilt in Gothic dress in 1779–82. Large structures evolved for corn milling too, three-storeyed at Orchard Mill, Williton, and on a factory scale at Thorney Mill (Muchelney), 1823. Two WINDMILLS remain of many: Ashton Mill (Chapel Allerton), *c.* 1770, and Stembridge Mill (High Ham), 1822. Late Georgian TEXTILE MILLS were concentrated along rivers for water power. The largest are at Tonedale near Wellington, where Thomas Fox replaced a corn mill with brick-built woollen mills in 1801–3. The early C19 crêpe mill at Dulverton originally produced blankets. Gant's Mill, Bruton, was an C18 woollen factory extended for silk manufacture in 1812. The Union Chapel, Bruton, began as an C18 silk factory. Lace factories moved to Chard after labour troubles in

Nottingham in 1819. The surviving mills, of 1825 and 1828–30, are up-to-date brick-built structures of five to six storeys with iron-framed roofs. Canvas, sailcloth and twine were made from flax and hemp grown around West Coker, with factories in Crewkerne and Merriott. Webbing, of wool or flax, was made at Crewkerne from 1789 and at Castle Cary from 1797. Of HEAVY INDUSTRY there was little. Until its wartime demolition there was one spectacular monument, the Duke of Chandos's 103-ft (31.4-metre) high kiln for glass-making, at Bridgwater, erected in 1725–6. The enterprise failed by 1733.

ARCHITECTURE 1837–1914

Local architects

Outside Bristol and Bath professional ARCHITECTS only emerge in numbers after 1800, and then most still term themselves indiscriminately architect, builder and surveyor. *Daniel Carver* of Bridgwater who designed Woolavington parsonage, 1807, was the father of *Richard Carver* (1792–1862), the first local architect to be London-trained, in the office of Jeffry Wyatt. Carver was the father-in-law of *Charles Edmund Giles*, 1822–81, and they were in practice together *c.* 1843–9. Giles's unpublished autobiography is seamed with hatred from that unhappy relationship. It also tells us much about provincial practice. Carver had a wide practice of small country houses, churches, schools, town halls and markets, as well as the work that came to him as County Surveyor from 1830. Giles had mostly church work, together with parsonages and schools, before he gave up through ill-health in the early 1870s.

Carver began his career in Bridgwater, 1813–30, before moving to Taunton. *Richard Down*, iron-founder, came to Bridgwater in the 1820s and worked as an architect, followed by his son *Edwin Down* (1806–80), who had an extensive commercial practice with chapel and church work, latterly with his son *Evan R. Down* (born 1850). *Basil Cottam* (1861–1911) joined the firm in 1885 and ran the Bridgwater office after the practice was joined with the Taunton practice of C. H. Samson. *Charles Knowles* (1806–86) practised in Bridgwater from the 1840s to the 1880s.

C. H. Samson (1838–1925) moved to Taunton in 1878 from Minehead. *F. W. Roberts* (1859–1932) set up in Taunton in 1892. Church work after Giles left fell to *John Houghton Spencer* (1844–1914), son of the vicar of Wilton. Taunton had three dynasties of builders who also designed: *Pollard, Shewbrooks* and *Spiller*. Yeovil had builders who also designed, but the first architect was *Thomas Stent, c.* 1844–56. *Charles Benson* was active from 1860, later with his son *C. B. Benson. Joseph Nicholson Johnston* (1860–1942), who trained in the London office of George & Peto, came to Yeovil in the 1880s. An earlier London-trained architect was *James Mountford Allen* (1809–83), son of the headmaster of Crewkerne Grammar School, and a pupil of Charles Fowler. He had work from *c.* 1847, establishing his office in Crewkerne in 1856.

Minehead's resident architects began with *Samson*, who worked for the Luttrell estate in the 1870s, with the London architect *J. P. St Aubyn*. From the 1890s *F. W. Roberts* had work in Minehead through the Luttrell estate. By 1900–10 there were three principal architects based in Minehead, *W. J. Tamlyn* (1870–1933), *A. L. Cox* (1870–1912) and *T. H. Andrew* (1859–1947). Wellington had its own architect in *Edwin Howard* (1846–1920), Borough Surveyor from 1873. *G. J. Skipper* of Norwich worked for the Clark family in Street in the 1880s; he was supplanted *c.* 1890 by W. S. Clark's nephew, *William Reynolds* (1864–1918), who was followed after 1906 by another relation, *S. T. Clothier* (1888–1933). Most smaller towns supported a builder who might also design. *Jesse Gane* (1798–1855) of Evercreech and *Maurice Davis* of Langport (fl. 1830–75) went much further, doing church work, and designing parsonages and schools.

Churches 1837–1914

Correct Gothic for ANGLICAN CHURCHES neatly coincides with *Benjamin Ferrey*'s appointment as Diocesan Architect in 1841, and the fading of *Richard Carver* as a church designer. *Ferrey*'s Hambridge, 1842, differs from *Carver*'s Taunton Holy Trinity, 1840–2, in having no galleries, and in the steep hammerbeam roof, which Ferrey used again at Moorland, 1843, and Henton, 1847. The major church of the 1840s was Bridgwater St John, 1843–6, by *John Brown* of Norwich. This is in the Gothic of Salisbury Cathedral, used a few years earlier by *G. P. Manners* at Bath (St Michael), and is tall and impressive inside under a hammerbeam roof. The exterior has the harsh crispness of Bath stone ashlar, decried by Pugin in favour of more random stonework. Neo-Norman was attempted without special success by *Manners* at Godney, 1838–9, and East Huntspill, 1839–40, by *Ferrey* at Corfe, 1842, and with much greater character at Marston Bigot, 1844–5, by *Edward Davis* of Bath, a pupil of Soane. *Ferrey* showed at West Lydford, 1843–4, that he could do competent Somerset Perp, and at Castle Cary, 1853–5, that he could competently enlarge a Perp church, adding his own tower and spire. At Buckland St Mary, 1853–63, he moved beyond careful imitation to a grandly scaled Dec Gothic with a High Victorian emphasis on mass over detail. The interior is enriched with the varied materials and colours of the era. *Carver* revived his church practice by taking *C. E. Giles* into partnership in 1843. Their Nether Stowey, 1849–51, shows that Giles understood the ideas of Pugin.

In 1853–6 *John Norton* of Bristol designed the estate church at West Quantoxhead with the same flat-topped tower as Ferrey's Buckland St Mary, but with intensified colour inside, using Babbacombe marble piers. Norton's subsequent church work includes the polychrome Highbridge, 1858–9, and heavy-handed restorations, notably the neo-Norman reworking of Stogursey, 1863–5. Norton, based in Bristol, illustrates a trend for architects with a more than regional practice to win commissions in the area. Of the leading London architects, *George Gilbert Scott* added a major work of his maturity at Taunton St John, 1858–63, a spired church with external polychromy and excellent internal carved detail. His restoration at Shapwick is not notable, but he and *Ferrey* oversaw the rebuilding of the tower of Taunton St Mary Magdalene, 1858–62, the major restoration work in South Somerset. *G. E. Street* is represented by new churches at Pitcombe, 1857–8, and Minehead St Andrew, 1877–80, both minor works. More notable are his restorations at Shepton Beauchamp, 1864–5, and Dunster, 1875–7. *William Butterfield* did one small church, at Gare Hill, 1857–8. *Arthur Blomfield* rebuilt Chilton Cantelo expensively in 1865, and re-created Odcombe around the medieval crossing tower in 1874. *William White* restored the late C12 church at Witham Friary in 1876, his forceful W end a welcome substitute for a weak early C19 tower. *J. L. Pearson* finished Woodlands church in 1879–81, modifying plans by *Giles*. *Henry Hall*, a less well-known London architect, rebuilt the nave at Milborne Port in 1867–9 and restored Montacute in 1870–1, expensively and ostentatiously. In total contrast, two small churches by *T. G. Jackson*, at Hornblotton, 1872–4, and Lottisham, 1876, illustrate the taste of the pupils of Scott and Street – the contemporaries of Norman Shaw – for a softer palette of materials and gently mixed period detail. Hornblotton, with its extraordinary red and white interior of sgraffito plasterwork, is the one Victorian church of national consequence in the region. The muscular Early French of William Burges appears at Yarlington by *J. Arthur Reeve*, a little-known London architect, 1877–8. *J. D. Sedding* rebuilt Wincanton, 1887–9, in a Somerset Perp, grandly scaled but without the personality of his more radical London works.

New churches, though not the major ones, still went to local men in the second half of the C19. *James Mountford Allen* of Crewkerne designed the well-finished estate church at Cricket Malherbie, 1851–5. *Giles* claims some twenty new churches in his career, not all in Somerset. Kingweston, 1851–5, built under the eyes of leading Ecclesiologists, emerges with credit. Bathealton, 1853–4 and Long Load, 1854–6, are small and decent. Chapel Allerton, 1858–60, shows High Victorian spirit in its polychrome columns and Isle Brewers, 1861, has personality, with its porch-tower turning octagonal. Three new churches by obscure architects display the angular spiky detail of the 1860s: Stockland Bristol, 1865–70, by *Oswald Arthur* of Plymouth; Combwich, 1868–70, by *Charles Knowles* of Bridgwater; and Corton Denham, 1869–70, by *James Baker Green* of Blandford. *John Houghton Spencer* of Taunton designed two churches with startling brick interiors at Taunton St Andrew, 1879–81, and Rockwell Green, 1888–90, but new churches become rare in the late C19 and early C20. Unusually expensive, in full Somerset Perp, is Yeovil St

Michael, 1895–7, by *J. Nicholson Johnston*. *Bligh Bond*'s rebuilding of Stowell in 1913 added a discreet low nave and chancel to an existing tower.

CHURCH RESTORATION was dominated by the Diocesan Architects, *Ferrey* into the 1870s, then *J. D. Sedding* until 1891, and then *Edmund Buckle*, moving progressively from restoration to repair. Otherwise local architects had the bulk of general repair work, which was rarely done with notable sensitivity. *Mountford Allen* restored churches from the late 1840s. *C. E. Giles* was prolific from the late 1840s, claiming to have repaired forty-two churches and 'restored' seventeen more by the early 1870s. *Houghton Spencer* restored without particular personality. Standing out for the quality of workmanship was the restoration of West Huntspill after a fire in 1878 by *Price & Wooler* of Weston-super-Mare. A few restorations by outsiders stand out for fine fittings: by *Street* at Shepton Beauchamp and Dunster, *John Oldrid Scott* at North Curry, 1881–4, and *S. S. Stallwood* of Reading at Chedzoy, 1884–5. *Sedding* restored carefully but not conservatively. Ernest Gimson, a Sedding pupil, wrote while on holiday at Bossington: 'It is poor old JD who is (or was) responsible for the spoiling all the churches (i.e. around Porlock)...Thank goodness they were done after my time with him.' Sedding's former partner, *Henry Wilson*, restored Norton-sub-Hamdon after a fire in 1894, introducing outstanding fittings. Sedding's nephew, *Edmund H. Sedding*, did interesting early C20 work at Weare, Lympsham and Pawlett. The restoration of Chillington, 1909–10 by *W. D. Caröe*, was transformative of a plain building.

CHURCH FURNISHINGS of the C19 and early C20 are of course prolific. It is worth isolating a few churches where the *tout ensemble* of stained glass, tiles, pews, rails, pulpit, font, etc. works as a utility. For the 1840s, there are Taunton Holy Trinity, still with its galleries on three sides, and Marston Bigot with neo-Norman fittings, unusual glass by *Eleanor Boyle* and imported Continental C15–C16 glass. For the 1850s, Cricket Malherbie with its *Minton* tile floors, towering font cover and glass by *O'Connor*; Buckland St Mary with its wonderful glass by *Clayton & Bell*, stencilled decoration, tiled floors, and carving by *Earp* and *Forsyth*; and West Quantoxhead with its carving by *Farmer*, glass by *O'Connor*, tiles by *Minton*, and brass rails by *Hardman*. For the 1860s, Taunton St John for the carved detail and the glowing glass by *Hardman*, and Corton Denham, for the carving and for the glass by *Capronnier*. For the 1870s, Hornblotton, for the sgraffito, the lovely inlaid pews and pulpit, the Cosmati-style mosaic floors, the reredos tiles and stained glass by *Powell's*; and the chancel at Stogumber by *J. D. Sedding*, with its Morris-like stencilled decoration, tiles and carved stone reredos. For the 1880s, North Curry for the ironwork, woodwork, and the glass by *Burlison & Grylls*. For the 1890s, Taunton St Andrew for the glass by *Lavers & Westlake*. For the early C20, the chancel refitting at Weare by *E. H. Sedding*, with marble and alabaster rails and lavish woodwork. Crossing the decades are Lympsham and Nynehead, transformed into family shrines: Lympsham full of portraits and heraldry of the Stephensons, Nynehead full of monuments to the Sanfords, and enriched with Italian art.

Individual pieces worth seeking out may also be listed by decade. For the 1830s and 1840s the E window by *Willement* at Lytes Cary, the *Minton* tile floors at Charlton Mackrell, and the glass by *Ména* of Paris (1842–65) at West Pennard. For the 1850s, the window by *Pugin* at Butleigh and the unsigned chancel S window at Milverton. For the 1860s the glowing E window at Fiddington, probably by *Lavers & Barraud*, the unusual grisailles by *Mary Miles* at Isle Brewers, the NE window at Aller by *Clayton & Bell*, the enormous W window at Taunton St Mary Magdalene by *Alexander Gibbs*, the *Hardman* glass at Yeovil, and the beautifully drawn glass at Chilton Cantelo by *R. T. Bayne*. For glass at the limits of good taste, the lurid Crucifixion at West Cranmore by *Thomas Baillie*, and similar E window at Dulverton. Also of the 1860s, the carved reredoses at Cloford by *Woodyer*, and at Taunton St Mary Magdalene by *Street*. For the 1870s, the early glass by the *Morris* company at Over Stowey, the E window at Hambridge, the Annunciation by *Hardman* at Butleigh, and the powerfully drawn W window at Langport by *H. A. Kennedy*; also the brass-railed pulpit at Montacute by *Henry Hall*, and furnishings at Dunster by *Street*, including the lovely painted reredos by *Clayton & Bell*. For the 1880s, the E window at Goathurst by *Lavers, Barraud & Westlake*, and windows by *Kempe* at Badgworth, Horsington, Minehead St Andrew, and Ashcott. Also the wrought-iron pulpits at Horsington and Norton-sub-Hamdon, the latter probably by *Blomfield*. For the 1890s, *Henry Wilson*'s wrought-iron screen at Taunton St John; the reredos at Cannington, with tile-mosaic panels by *Powell's*, and similar tilework at Cutcombe; and the windows by *Burne-Jones* for *Morris* at Brushford and West Buckland, and the window at North Petherton by *Kempe*. For the first decades of the C20, the wondrous font at Norton-sub-Hamdon by *Wilson*; the glass by *Henry Holiday* at Minehead St Michael, Old Cleeve and Yeovil St John, and the E window at Milborne Port by *W. B. Reynolds*; the tile-mosaic by *Powell's* at Queen Camel; the marble and mosaic pulpit at Wilton by *Dudley Forsyth*; and the iron and brass lectern at Old Cleeve by *Ramsden & Carr*.

Stained glass by *Alice Erskine* at Bradford on Tone, Halse, Stowell and Wiveliscombe, by *Margaret Chilton* at Pilton, and *Mary Hutchinson* at Minehead St Michael, marks the emergence of women designers within the Arts and Crafts movement. C20 Arts and Crafts woodwork made by local classes features at Selworthy, the reredos with embossed leather panels, and at Horsington, the sinuous tower screen. Conventional but impressive are the screens at North Petherton by *Charles Baker King*.

The growing preference for commemoration in stained glass and brass means that Victorian CHURCH MONUMENTS worth seeking out are rare. Still Neoclassical and of quality are the marble child at Goathurst, 1838, by *Christopher Moore*, the seated female in relief at Milverton, 1845, by *Patrick Macdowell*, a standing female at Hinton St George, 1857, by *E. J. Physick*, and above

ARCHITECTURE 1837–1914

all, the kneeling angel at Nynehead, 1840, by *Aristodemo Costoli* of Florence. Gothic monuments proliferate without being memorable. Madalina Lance and her infant breaking through the lid of their tomb at Buckland St Mary, by *Forsyth*, c. 1860, remain memorable for the wrong reasons, as does the ascending soul to Viscountess Bridport †1884 at Cricket St Thomas. The monument to Speke the explorer †1864 at Dowlish Wake has an arch of African animals supporting his bust, over a severe dark marble sarcophagus. The white marble St George outside Cricket St Thomas is Edwardian work of quality, by *Alfred Drury*, c. 1904.

ROMAN CATHOLIC CHURCHES of the period are Gothic. Most are by *Father A. J. C. Scoles*, son of an architect and parish priest in Bridgwater and Yeovil. He designed Bridgwater, 1881–2, Yeovil, 1897–9, Minehead, 1896–1900, and Wincanton, 1907–8, and also convents in Burnham and Wincanton, 1888–90, and presbyteries at Yeovil and Minehead. His well-detailed interiors stand comparison with Anglican contemporaries. So does the tall clerestoried interior of the R.C. church at Taunton, 1858–60, by *Benjamin Bucknall*, whose tower faces down the street in an echo of St Mary Magdalene. The Franciscan convent at Taunton with its chapel and cloister by *C. F. Hansom* has been subdivided into flats. The Convent of Perpetual Adoration, Taunton, 1871 by *J. F. Bentley*, is now offices, but the top-floor chapel retains lovely stained glass designed by *Bentley*. The convent chapel at Burnham is also subdivided and the top-floor chapel of the convent at Minehead, by *A. L. Cox*, 1910, has been stripped of fittings.

NONCONFORMIST CHAPELS have closed in large numbers, especially the small village chapels, and few remain unaltered. Examples are at North Curry, 1825 and 1833, Burrowbridge, 1836, Curry Rivel, 1840, and Churchinford (Churchstanton), 1846. In the towns, early C19 BAPTIST CHAPELS remain at Minehead, 1831, and Wellington, 1833, the latter by *Carver*, both stuccoed, Italianate, with arched windows and deep-eaved roofs. Those at Bridgwater, 1837 (by *Edwin Down*), Chard, 1842, and Burnham, 1843, are more classical, that at Bridgwater with a recessed Ionic portico. A pedimented front was added to Crewkerne chapel as late as 1880. Baptist chapels at Yeovil and Taunton were refronted in 1866–8 and 1870 in Italian round-arched style. Montacute chapel, 1879, by *Morgan H. Davies*, is Italian Gothic with a rose window.

Congregationalists and Methodists tended more to the Gothic. Of the CONGREGATIONAL CHURCHES, Dulverton, 1831, is plainest stuccoed Gothic, and Taunton, 1843 by *James Pollard*, is more church-like, in lancet Gothic style with an aisled interior. Wellington, 1860–1 by *Samuel Pollard*, and South Petherton, 1862–3, have more elaborate traceried windows, but still symmetrical gable fronts. Stoke-sub-Hamdon, by *R. C. Bennett* of Weymouth, 1865–6, is more audacious, with a spire and little flying buttresses. North Petherton, 1869, Merriott, 1878, and Yeovil, 1878 (by *T. Lewis Banks*), show the round-arched Italian or Lombard style then popular across Nonconformity. METHODIST CHAPELS tend to be Gothic after 1850, following the denominational handbook on church building. Bridgwater, 1816, is plain Late Georgian, refronted in 1860. Castle Cary, 1838–9, has similar arched windows but its odd octagonal angles hint at change. Ilchester, 1851–61, and Glastonbury, 1866, are Gothic, but plain. *Alexander Lauder* of Barnstaple began his sweep of Methodist building committees in the late 1860s. His bold and eccentric Gothic chapels are at Yeovil, 1869–70, Burnham, 1878–80, South Petherton, 1881–2, Martock, 1886, Ilminster, 1887, and a small one at Kingsbury Episcopi, 1900. There were a few other large Gothic chapels. Taunton was rebuilt by the local builder *Samuel Shewbrooks* in 1868–9, keeping the gable front of 1846 by *James Wilson* of Bath. Watchet, 1870–1, rejected Lauder for a local builder, and Williton, 1883, was by a national Methodist architect, *Robert Curwen*. Minehead went to *Foster & Wood* of Bristol for their chapel of 1875–6, which became an aisle to an impressive apsed addition of 1885–6 by the same architects. The Free Perp popular around 1900 appears late, at Bridgwater, 1911, Wincanton, 1916–17, and Porlock, 1927.

Two QUAKER MEETING HOUSES deserve mention: at Wellington, 1845, with a plain pedimented front, and at Street, 1850, by *J. F. Cotterell* of Bath, a stately hip-roofed building with a cupola and columned porch. Chapels of BIBLE CHRISTIANS are generally small, as at Brent Knoll, 1837, and Pilton, 1839. There is quite a large Gothic chapel of the AGAPEMONITES at Spaxton, 1846, and one for MORAVIANS at Baltonsborough, 1852. SUNDAY SCHOOL ROOMS of the urban chapels can be very large, as for the Congregationalists at South Petherton, 1882, and the Methodists at Street, 1895–6. The schoolrooms at the Unitarian chapel, Taunton, 1886, in Norman Shaw style, are unusually cheerful.

CEMETERIES proliferated after the Act of 1855 which permitted municipally financed burial grounds. Their buildings – chapels for Anglicans and Nonconformists and entrance lodges – display some of the oddest Gothic of the era, as at North Petherton, 1856 by *Charles Knowles*, Yeovil, 1860 by *R. H. Shout*, and Crewkerne, 1874 by *George Nattress*.

Victorian domestic architecture

The Tudor Gothic introduced for COUNTRY HOUSES in the Late Georgian period remained almost the only style for the Early Victorian period. *Carver*'s remodelling of St Audries (West Quantoxhead) continued in the 1840s with a grand top-lit oak staircase. Smaller Tudor Gothic houses are Norton Manor (Norton Fitzwarren) in diapered brick, 1842–3 by *Henry Roberts* of London; Monty's Court (Norton Fitzwarren), c. 1840–5 by *Carver*; and West Coker Hall, 1839–44. Quantock Lodge (Over Stowey), by *Henry Clutton*, 1857–60, for Lord Taunton, is the only large new Victorian country house. The style is C16, loosely asymmetrical on the front, symmetrical on the rear. Smaller and rather bleak is the Manor House, Brent Knoll, 1862–4, by *Norton*, whose new great hall and entrance tower to St Audries, 1870–2, is his major domestic work in the region. Abbotsfield (Wiveliscombe), by *Owen Jones*, of 1870–3, is strangely mixed in style; North Perrott Manor, 1878, is neo-Jacobean, freely handled. Otherwise Victorian country house work was largely re-casing of older houses. Cranmore Hall (East Cranmore) added Jacobean features to a C17 house, 1847–9 and 1868–9, both times by *T. H. Wyatt*. Barwick House was re-cased in a rich neo-Jacobean by *R. H. Shout* of Yeovil, 1858, and Chilton House (Chilton Cantelo) was given milder Jacobean dress *c.* 1865. Elizabethan mullion-and-transom windows of 1877 by *F. C. Penrose* disguise the Late Georgian Alford House. *T. G. Jackson* rebuilt Thorne House (Thorne Coffin), 1878–88, in his own 'Northern Renaissance' Jacobean style. None of these are major works. *Salvin*'s remodelling of Dunster Castle, 1867–72, was the most expensive Victorian work, creating a romantic silhouette, although the detail can be pedestrian. The brutal remodelling of Hestercombe, 1872–5, partly by *Henry Hall*, changed a medieval to C18 house into something amorphous with a tall pavilion-roofed tower to one side and an extremely large but coarse stair hall. A better stair hall at Marston House (Marston Bigot), 1857, by *C. E. Davis*, is reminiscent of a theatre or opera house.

Amid the many ESTATE BUILDINGS, the stables and main lodge at Quantock Lodge stand out, the one for its delightful conical roof, the other for the colours of the stone. At St Audries there are Gothic lodges of 1850 by *Norton*, a home farm of 1855, and a small gasworks. The thatched gatehouse-cum-lodge to Ashley Combe (Porlock) is Picturesque. In general Victorian lodges are gabled, Gothic to Tudor. The South Lodge at Hestercombe, 1890s, is larger and better detailed than most. At Inwood (Henstridge) there is a large late C19 stable court for a hunting squire. The best group of ESTATE COTTAGES is at Chilton Cantelo, of red brick patterned with black, 1867. Lympsham is the best ESTATE VILLAGE, with a very large and Gothic village-hall-cum-school, and numerous farmhouses and cottages provided by Prebendary Stephenson in the 1860s–70s.

Smaller houses not connected with landed estates were built by industrialists. Millfield, 1889, Domestic Revival by *G. J. Skipper*, was built for W. S. Clark, shoe manufacturer. Cleveland, a colourful house of stone, brick and timber by *Foster & Wood*, 1877, was built at Minehead for the owner of a chemical works, and the Scots Baronial Elgin Tower, of 1887, nearby was for a retired Scottish confectioner. Rosary House, Bridgwater, of the 1860s, Florida House, Castle Cary, 1887, by *Charles Bell*, and Merriott Court, 1891, by *Charles Kirk*, were all built for industrialists. The houses of the Fox family of Tonedale Mills, Wellington, are unremarkable despite the involvement of *Alfred Waterhouse* in two of them. Small country houses were not only built for industrialists. The delightfully Georgian Gothic Lympsham Manor, of the 1820s and 1840s, was for the Stephenson rectors and squires. Stockland Manor (Stockland Bristol), 1860, and The Priory, Ditcheat, remodelled 1864–8, were also for landowning parsons. Moorlands, Merriott, 1852 by *G. G. Scott*, a spiky Gothic villa with a tower, was for a local farming family. New Place, Porlock, 1890–2 by *Edmund Buckle*, a characterful reworking of the standard gabled and mullioned type, was for the barrister proprietor of *The Engineer* journal.

The story is similar for EARLY C20 HOUSES. Most new ones were built as holiday or retirement houses. Edwardian Free Style is represented by Barrow Court (Galhampton), a butterfly-plan brick house by *E. Turner Powell*, 1910–12, for an heir to Kelly's Post Office Directories. Large additions to Carver's Chapel Cleeve Manor (Old Cleeve), 1912–14 by *F. W. Roberts*, were financed by South Wales steel. They are notable for the plasterwork by *George Bankart* and lavish neo-Jacobean woodwork. Substantial houses for hunting or holidays surround Porlock and Dulverton, of which the largest are Lynch House (West Lynch), 1911–13, by *C. H. B. Quennell*, and Hele Manor (Brushford) by *Horace Farquharson*, 1912. Farquharson also designed the smaller Woolston Grange (Sampford Brett), 1911. Lillycombe (Culbone), 1912, a large roughcast villa in the Voysey style, was designed by the *Countess of Lovelace* with assistance from *C. F. A. Voysey*. Her addition to Worthy Manor (Porlock), 1911–14, is also in the manner of Voysey. One work for a major landed estate, and the one Edwardian work of national significance, was *Lutyens*'s formal gardens and orangery at Hestercombe, 1906–8. Here he exhibits the shift in his work from the Free Style to a classical 'Grand Manner'. Edwardian adaptation of older houses could be careful and conservative, like *T. E. Collcutt*'s Stavordale Priory, 1904–5, *Temple Moore*'s work at Coker Court (East Coker), 1900–2, and *Maurice Webb*'s library at the Manor House, West Coker. *C. E. Ponting*'s large additions at Lytes Cary, 1907–12, left the old house apparently untouched, with a new historicist W front. Arts and Crafts COTTAGES of interest include some in Voysey style by *Lady Lovelace* at Bratton and the small houses by *Violet Morris* for the Agapemonite community at Spaxton.

Plain hip-roofed Regency PARSONAGES continued to be built into the 1840s (Elworthy, *c.* 1838, Hinton St George, 1839, Ilchester, 1842) and Marston Bigot is in a stripped Italianate style, 1836–9 by *Edward Davis* of Bath. But the trend was towards neomedieval styles. There is an early gabled example at Walton, 1821, and a large brick Tudoresque one at Buckland St Mary, 1833. The parsonage at Babcary, 1840–1, reputedly by *Scott & Moffatt*, spreads impressively, with two-storey mullioned bay windows. The typical Victorian parsonage tended towards compact asymmetrical designs, an early example being at Castle Cary, 1845, by *James Davis* of Frome. Compact asymmetrical designs of some scale can be seen at Pendomer, 1857 by *J. M. Allen*, High Ham, 1863 by *John Norton*, Milborne Port, 1871 by *Henry Hall*, Shepton Beauchamp, 1874 by *Richard Drew*, and Dunster, 1875 by *St Aubyn*. High Ham is particularly good, with understated polychromy. Shepton Beauchamp is unusual, having been designed for a community of priests, with its own chapel.

Victorian expansion of the TOWNS started slowly. Taunton has a stuccoed terrace of the 1840s on the western edge and brick artisan housing around Holy Trinity church. Minehead has two short stuccoed terraces of the 1850s, and Burnham some seafront terraces of the 1840s, which were followed by the two quarter-round crescents of c. 1860 that mark the acme of Burnham's ambitions. Park Street, Taunton, has Gothic work by *C. E. Giles* with *Henry Davis*, builder. It includes a colourful terrace displaying the county's building stones and a brick house of 1857 displaying Davis's minute stone-carving. *Richard Carver* developed Haines Hill, Taunton, 1846–7, as a small middle-class suburb of stuccoed villas in three styles. Also at Taunton, a small suburb of brick terraces, Elm Grove, was begun in 1880, and large semi-detached brick villas of the 1860s–80s were built along Trull Road and South Road. Bridgwater has purple stone villas of the 1870s–80s, and more cheerful brick villas and terraces of the 1890s, mostly by *Basil Cottam*. Wellesley Park, Wellington, a small suburb of large brick villas, was begun in 1887 by the local architect, *Edwin Howard*, who also did villas on Station Road. The Park, Yeovil, was another small middle-class suburb, of the 1880s–90s, with villas mostly by *J. N. Johnston*. Minehead's expansion into a resort town dates mostly from after 1900. It began with semi-detached stone villas of the 1890s between the centre and the sea. After 1900 the palette is more mixed, roughcast, brick and half-timber, and more cheerful. Most of the houses are by three local architects, *Tamlyn*, *Cox* and *Andrew*, with *Roberts* of Taunton. Kildare Lodge, however, of 1905–6 by *Barry Parker* (*Parker & Unwin*), is a major Arts and Crafts work, radical in its avoidance of picturesque gables in favour of a single roof over white roughcast walls. At Porlock, The Hunting Lodge, 1905, by the painter, *John Lomas*, also roughcast, shows novelty in its square plan about a central hall. Edwardian villas are found in smaller numbers at Burnham-on-Sea.

The most interesting INDUSTRIAL HOUSING is at Street. In the late 1880s William S. Clark and Helen Clark commissioned picturesque terraces from *G. J. Skipper*, before passing the work in 1890 to a relation, *William Reynolds*. Street is not laid out as a company town, as was done by other Quaker manufacturers, but taken as a whole, with the public buildings, Street has importance in the history of town planning. An idiosyncratic row, Cumnock Terrace above Castle Cary, 1877, of relatively large houses with carved detail, was built for managers and senior employees of the Boyd horsehair factory.

Public and commercial buildings

CIVIC BUILDINGS of the period include a large classical Town Hall at Yeovil, 1847, that was destroyed by fire in 1935. Taunton built a Greek Doric Corn Exchange in 1853 (dem.). Bridgwater added a public hall behind its Town Hall in 1865, and a Corn Exchange within its market hall, 1875, both by *Charles Knowles*. The largest Victorian public building was the expensive SHIRE HALL at Taunton, by *W. B. Moffatt*, 1855–8, built for the Assize

Courts. Despite the size the building is disappointing, Moffatt's Gothic not having progressed in step with that of his former partner, G. G. Scott. The Shire Hall was sited opposite the COUNTY PRISON, moved to Taunton in 1842 when the notoriously bad gaol at Ilchester was demolished. The new prison, by *Carver*, was on the workhouse plan of an octagonal central tower overlooking courtyards. The core and two wings remain. There are very Gothic POLICE STATIONS at Wincanton, 1856 by *R. H. Shout*, and at Williton and Dunster, 1858 by *John Norton*, these two with central towers. By contrast, the County Court at Bridgwater, 1859, probably by *Edwin Down*, was Regency classical. Most of the WORKHOUSES were built shortly after the 1835 Poor Law Act. Williton, 1837–40, by *Scott & Moffatt*, remains almost intact, as does the small one at Dulverton, the last one built, in 1855, by *Edward Ashworth*. Others that remain in fragmentary form, at Bridgwater, Taunton and Yeovil, were of lesser interest. Two significant MILITARY BUILDINGS were products of national programmes. Brean Down Fort, 1864–7, was one of the Palmerston forts built to counter naval attack from the France of Napoleon III. Jellalabad Barracks, Taunton, 1879–81, was built under the Cardwell reforms that produced similar keep-like gatehouses at Reading, Devizes and Brecon.

At the turn of the century municipal buildings in Taunton were laid out along the new Corporation Street in front of the former Grammar School, which had become the municipal offices in 1885. These were the Technical Institute, 1898, the Library, 1904, and College of Art, 1907. A lesser municipal group on Leigh Road, Street, was largely the gift of the Clark family. The Gothic Crispin Hall, 1885, by *Skipper*, was joined by the Vestry Room and police station in 1887 and Technical School in 1899. The Town Hall at Minehead, a Gothic design by *St Aubyn*, 1889, was a private promotion, but the town itself built the pretty Market House, 1902, by *W. J. Tamlyn*. Competitions for the LIBRARIES in Taunton, 1904, and Bridgwater, 1905, resulted in good buildings by obscure architects, *Little & Goodson* and *E. G. Page* respectively. Another good early C20 public building is the MAGISTRATES' COURT at Bridgwater, 1911–12 by *Francis Parr*, Borough Surveyor. Of PUBLIC PARKS, only Vivary Park, Taunton, 1894–5, was on any great scale, with festive iron gates and a fountain from *Macfarlane* of Glasgow. CIVIC SCULPTURE is limited to the fine Admiral Blake at Bridgwater, by *F. W. Pomeroy*, 1900.

SCHOOLS are very much a Victorian building type, their planning, construction and sanitation a matter of debate right through the era. First it is worth considering the PUBLIC SCHOOLS built for the private education of middle-class children. There are three in Taunton, all with large Gothic or Tudor Gothic buildings spreading from a central entrance tower, the pattern established by *James Wilson* at Cheltenham in 1840. *Wilson* designed Queen's College for the Methodists, 1846–7. King's College, 1867–9 by *C. E. Giles*, was an Anglican foundation that grew out of the old Grammar School, and Taunton School, 1867–70, was Congregationalist, with buildings by a Congregationalist architect, *Joseph*

Taunton School.
Engraving, 1870

James. This last, oddly, has the most ecclesiastical chapel, of 1906–7 by *Frank Wills*. The over-ambitious chapel at King's College, begun in 1903, faltered for lack of money. King's School at Bruton, a C16 foundation revived in the C19, has a small schoolroom of 1836 and Gothic buildings of 1872. Crewkerne Grammar School moved to new Gothic buildings (with a central tower) by *Giles & Gough* of London in 1880. Money from the Sexey charity built two TRADE SCHOOLS, at Bruton and Blackford (near Wedmore), 1891 and 1899, for the practical education of poorer children. The buildings are smaller, of Board School type, by *G. J. Skipper*.

PRIMARY SCHOOLS were largely the province of the Church of England and usually Gothic, beginning with the simplest churchyard rooms, but becoming more elaborate with grants from the National School Society (Ilchester, 1837, Mudford, 1847). The most striking schools are those paid for by landowners or other benefactors. Such are Charlton Mackrell, with its tiled interior, 1853 by *C. E. Giles*, Marston Bigot, 1857 by *C. E. Davis*, and West Quantoxhead, 1856–7 by *Norton*. Especially lavish were Stogursey, 1860–1, also by *Norton*, and Milborne Port, 1863–4, and Queen Camel, 1872, both by *Henry Hall*. BRITISH SCHOOLS were non-denominational, and the largest example significantly was built at Street, 1858–9. BOARD SCHOOLS, set up after the 1870 Act, were also non-denominational, but their buildings tended to be by architects connected with the church, perhaps because of the dominance of church people on the boards. So Langport, 1876, is by *Hall*, who also built Board Schools at Castle Cary and North Cadbury. The tiny School Board at Meare, however, appointed a local builder-architect, *Joseph Day*, for its buildings at Meare and Godney.

Victorian COMMERCIAL BUILDINGS were mostly slotted into older town fabric, like the brick buildings of the 1890s in Bridgwater by *Basil Cottam*. Only at Minehead are there consistent rows, in plain stucco in the 1870s, in grander stone for The Parade in the 1890s. The strongest architectural statements were the BANKS. Stuckey's Bank, founded in Langport in the 1770s, covered the county. It had handsome Late Georgian-style premises in Crewkerne, 1838, and Glastonbury, 1846. Its bank at Wellington, 1864, was heavily Italianate, and that at Minehead, 1869–70 by *St Aubyn*, was Gothic. Just before the end of its independence Stuckey's built notable branches by *George Oatley* at Minehead, 1901–3, and Bridgwater, 1904. The Wiltshire & Dorset Bank built an Italian palazzo at Yeovil, 1856, by *Thomas Stent*, and chose Gothic at Glastonbury, 1885, by the bank's own architect, *G. M. Silley*. This was to harmonize with the adjacent George and Pilgrim inn. No. 4 Fore Street, Taunton, Ruskinian Gothic of *c*. 1860, may have been built for the Wiltshire & Dorset Bank, which later moved to an Italian palazzo at No. 7. The headquarters building of the Fox, Fowler Bank at Wellington is richly Italianate, 1885, by *Edwin Howard*, rivalling the Stuckey's branch nearby. Notable at Yeovil are the Capital & Counties Bank, in Northern Renaissance style, 1897–9, by *J. Nicholson Johnston*, and the Midland Bank, 1914, by *T. B. Whinney*, the bank's own architect.

Transport and industry

The railways rapidly closed the CANALS. Both the Glastonbury and Chard canals were purchased and partially infilled for railways. The new Bridgwater Docks, opened in 1841, revived shipping into Bridgwater more than they revived the Bridgwater and Taunton Canal, of which the dock basin was the new terminus. The first of the passenger RAILWAYS, *Brunel's* Bristol & Exeter Railway, came through Somerset in 1842–3. From it extended branches to Yeovil and Chard, 1849–53 and 1866, the West Somerset Railway to Watchet, 1857–62 (extended to Minehead 1872–4), and the Devon & Somerset Railway to Wiveliscombe and Barnstaple, 1871–3. Another Great Western subsidiary (the Wiltshire, Somerset & Weymouth Railway) passed through the E of the county from Frome to Yeovil, 1850–6, and on to Weymouth. This had a branch (the East Somerset Railway) to Shepton Mallet and Wells, 1858–62. Separate from the Great Western was the London & South Western Railway passing through Crewkerne to Exeter, 1860, with a branch to Yeovil (1861). The Somerset Central Railway from Glastonbury to Highbridge, 1853–4, was extended at each end, to Burnham and Wells (1859), and southward into Dorset, becoming the Somerset & Dorset Railway in 1862. It joined the Bristol and English channels from Burnham to Poole, but never made much of the potential traffic from Wales to France. A branch from Evercreech to Bath opened in 1874.

ARCHITECTURE 1837–1914

The Great Western Railway improved its main line to London by means of a cut-off from Taunton to Castle Cary, opened in 1906.

Steam railway preservation has meticulously restored the STATIONS of the West Somerset Railway, from Bishop's Lydeard to Minehead. Surviving in alternative use are Ilminster, Hatch Beauchamp and Chard on the Chard branch. On the lines still open, Bridgwater remains of the original Bristol & Exeter stations, 1842, as do the battered station and hotel at Taunton, and the Yeovil & Exeter (later London & South Western) station at Crewkerne, 1860, probably by *William Tite*. The most striking engineering works are the viaduct at Langport and the skew bridge beyond Somerton, both on the Great Western's Castle Cary line. The West Somerset Mineral Railway from the Brendon Hills to Watchet harbour (1857–64) was built to carry iron ore. At Brendon Hill is the winding station for the long incline that was the line's major feature.

The most impressive of the region's INDUSTRIAL BUILDINGS is Fox Brothers' five-storey mill at Tonedale, Wellington, 1861–71. There are large mill groups at Dowlish Ford (Ilminster), Castle Cary and Crewkerne. A three-storey factory at Castle Cary, 1851, produced cloth from horsehair. Leather industries began with tanneries, of which one survives, roofless, at Yeovil, 1853. Tanning was the beginning of Clark's shoe manufacture at Street, the works there, largely late C19 with a clock tower by *Skipper* (1887), enfold the original factory of 1829. Nearby at Glastonbury, the Clark, Son & Morland sheepskin works have largely been cleared, but Baily & Co.'s tannery and glove works remain, disused. Factory buildings from the leather glove industry remain in Yeovil and Stoke-sub-Hamdon. The engineering works and iron foundries of the area primarily served farming and water mills. A remarkable small rural factory, the Parrett Works at Bower Hinton, 1855, combined engineering and a flax mill for rope and sailcloth manufacture. No other works of the period survive so complete. Rope-walks for twisting twine survive here, and there are two at West Coker. The Nautilus Works, Yeovil, 1902, which made fire-grates and oil engines, was the ancestor of the Westland Works, set up in 1915 to make aircraft. Paper was made at Watchet and Creech St Michael: at the latter there are purpose-built brick buildings of 1885–7. The very extensive brick and tile production at Bridgwater has left very little apart from one bottle kiln, now part of a museum to the industry. The dock basin at Bridgwater has a large warehouse of 1840–1, extended in 1868. Small warehouses survive at the terminus of the Westport Canal (Hambridge), 1836–40.

DRAINAGE on the Levels was steam-powered from the 1830s. ENGINE HOUSES of that date remain at Westonzoyland and Saltmoor (Burrowbridge). One pioneering structure is Castle House, Bridgwater, 1851, a house for and possibly by *John Board*, cement-maker, of varied concrete building techniques: mass concrete walling, some very early reinforcing, and pre-cast applied decoration in the Tudor style.

ARCHITECTURE AFTER c. 1914

From the 1910s to the 1930s

The first authorities to build rural COUNCIL HOUSING under the Housing Act of 1909 were Street, 1911–12, by *S. T. Clothier*, and Yeovil Rural District, with building at Montacute, 1912, and at Martock and West Coker, 1914, all by *Petter & Warren*. The Housing Act of 1919 spurred building everywhere. Council house types of the 1920s include hip-roofed pairs and rows in Yeovil and surrounding villages by *Petter & Warren*, the brick Newtown estate at Bridgwater by *Samson & Colthurst*, the formally planned Newtown at Glastonbury by *Harold Alves*, and Severalls Park at Crewkerne. Later, and on a much larger scale, Halcon, Taunton, 1935, was laid out to a concentric plan. An unusual experimental council house type was developed by *Petter & Warren* from the wartime Nissen hut. Eight pairs under curved corrugated-iron roofs were built: a prototype in Yeovil, three in Barwick, and four at West Camel, all in 1925–8, before the design was rejected as more expensive than conventional houses.

COUNTRY HOUSES, at risk with the break up of landed estates, suffered few major losses. Montacute was bought for the National Trust in 1931; the Acland-Hood family abandoned St Audries to return to Fairfield in 1925; and the Cely-Trevilians left Midelney Place (Curry Rivel) for their original house, Midelney Manor (Drayton), in 1926. Against the trend was the restoration of Barrington Court by Col. Lyle as tenant of the National Trust, with all the appurtenances of a great house, gardens, cottages, farm buildings, provided by *J. E. Forbes*, 1922–5. *Hubert Lidbetter* restored Gerbestone Manor (West Buckland) in 1925 and *Harold Brakspear* Cothay Manor, in 1926–7. New houses tended to be for holiday or retirement, like Periton Mead (Minehead), 1920–2, a Cotswold-type manor house by *P. Morley Horder*. Holiday houses in the Quantocks included two by *Charles Holden* or his firm at Holford and Bicknoller, 1920s, and one by *Norman Jewson* at Kilve, 1937. *Eric Francis* designed in picturesque thatch or Cape Dutch (as *Stone & Francis*) at Wootton Courtenay and Porlock. His best house, 1930, for himself, at West Monkton, is in simplified Early Georgian style. Seaside villas continued to be built in Minehead, refreshed by roughcast and Delabole-slate cottages by *Edwin Gunn*. *Stone & Francis* probably designed the little group of MODERNIST HOUSES at Highlands, Taunton, 1930. The single outstanding Modernist house of the region was Pen Pits (Penselwood) for the composer Arthur Bliss, 1934–5, by *Peter Harland*.

CIVIC BUILDINGS of the era, schools, police stations, etc., were largely designed by the Architect's Department of Somerset County Council, under *A. J. Toomer*. Formal Neo-Georgian SCHOOLS, as at Minehead (1926–9), gave way to formally planned but minimally Georgian schools by the late 1930s (Ansford, Huish Episcopi, etc.). The Clark family promoted a school at Street, 1928, on the through-ventilated plan developed for Derbyshire schools, and *Toomer* imitated the Street school at

Bruton, 1929–32. Magistrates' courts and police stations were built in a modern-classical style at Minehead and Yeovil, 1936–8. There was no Modernism at the new County Offices, Taunton, 1932–5, by *Vincent Harris*, a specialist in civic Neo-Georgian, nor at the Municipal Offices, Yeovil, 1926–8, by *Petter & Warren*, also Neo-Georgian. The Post Office of 1932 opposite the Municipal Buildings was Neo-Georgian too, by *H.E. Seccombe* of the *Office of Works*, who also designed the neo-medieval Post Office thought appropriate for Glastonbury, 1938. Modernism crept in with swimming pools: the Lido at Minehead has gone, but the outdoor pool of 1936–7 at Street survives, with miniature white buildings. Building for PUBLIC SCHOOLS remained traditional: the Gothic Memorial Hall at King's Bruton, 1919–24 by *A. J. Pictor*, the neo-Tudor Science Building at Taunton School by *Vincent Harris*, 1923–5, the Neo-Georgian hall, 1924, and Perp chapel, 1928–31, at Wellington School, both by *C. H. Biddulph-Pinchard*, and the Early Georgian-style chapel at Heatherton (Bradford on Tone) by *H. S. W. Stone*, 1928.

INDUSTRIAL BUILDINGS such as the More Light Building for the Clarks at Street, 1933, and the surviving concrete building for Morlands at Glastonbury could be radical in a way still not permitted in COMMERCIAL BUILDINGS, where a few weakly *moderne* buildings nod to the new age. Typically it is a cinema that embraces the Art Deco style with confidence, the former Gaumont, at Taunton, 1932, by *W. Benslyn*.

New CHURCHES of the period include St Andrew, Yeovil, 1934, by *Petter & Warren*, mullion-windowed externally, plaster-vaulted inside, and the large Gothic R.C. church at Glastonbury, 1939–40, by *J. H. H. Willman*. Lutyens's chapel at Brushford, 1924–6, is the most significant ecclesiastical building, with its severe exterior and sombre interior lit by narrow windows. FURNISHINGS include the excellent screen at Westonzoyland, 1935–6 by *W. D. Caröe*, which brings unity to the great late medieval interior, without copying medieval work. *W. H. Randoll Blacking* made a harmonious unity of West Lynch, 1930, with limed oak fittings. He added the screen at Bruton, 1938, that mediates between the medieval and Georgian, and installed the lovely painted triptych by *Christopher Webb* at Porlock, 1931. *Ninian Comper*'s refitting of Bishop's Lydeard and West Bagborough, 1923–35, brought unity through colour to those late medieval interiors. *Martin Travers* made fittings at Drayton, 1935–7, and at Wyke Champflower, 1943, and stained glass at Nettlecombe, 1935. There is much STAINED GLASS of the Comper school, with clear backgrounds: by *Comper* himself, by *Christopher Webb*, and a window by *F. C. Eden* at Tintinhull. *Caröe* designed two pretty lychgates, at Cheddon Fitzpaine, 1921, and North Curry, 1930, as well as churchyard crosses, several as WAR MEMORIALS. The most notable inter-war sculpture is the bronze war memorial group at Bridgwater, 1924 by *John Angel*, a late masterpiece of the New Sculpture. *F. B. Bond*'s Celtic-cross war memorial at Glastonbury is carefully detailed. A simpler Celtic cross by *Roberts & Willman* stands large on the North Hill, Minehead.

Architecture after 1945

South Somerset TOWNS were not particularly war-damaged and post-war road building was less damaging here than elsewhere. *Thomas Sharp*'s plan of 1946 for a box of new roads around central Taunton was only partly implemented, using existing roads. Bridgwater and Yeovil gained inner ring roads or relief roads in the 1960s that separated centre from suburb but preserved the amenities of the centres. By-passes for Street and Glastonbury were built to the advantage of the centres. Old buildings suffered most in Yeovil, where the authorities pursued a modern image for the town, but the centre of Taunton was also battered by random commercial rebuilding, beginning before the war. Bridgwater town centre remains the most intact of the three large towns.

Post-war COUNCIL HOUSING was extensive, especially in Taunton, Bridgwater and Yeovil, but notable estates are few. Quarry Close estate at Minehead, by *Gunn & Fry*, 1944–6, responds well to its hillside setting. Bridgwater has the single point block of the region, of eleven storeys, 1963–5. The *County Architect's Department* designed SECONDARY SCHOOLS through the 1950s, with variations on flat-roofed classroom blocks around a school hall. Wiveliscombe, 1953, built around a community hall-cum-theatre, stands out, and Richard Huish College, Taunton, 1961–3, is a good example of the rest. The Art School at Taunton, 1972, uniquely for the area, displays the Brutalist aesthetic of that time, a tough building, well adapted for teaching art. Bridgwater College, 1979–83, has strongly modelled brick elevations, while Bishop Fox School, Taunton, 1993–4, shows the picturesque planning of the 1990s, with neo-Victorian coloured brickwork. Schools of the 1950s reached the end of their lives around 2010: there have been two replacements so far at Bridgwater, 2012, one by *NVB* of Frome, the other by *Scott Brownrigg*. PUBLIC SCHOOLS at last began to commission modern buildings. Millfield School (Street) led with a library, 1977–80, and arts block, 1990–2, both by *J. & C. Gould*, a theatre block, 1994–5 by *Neville Conder*, dining hall, 2000–1, and music school, 2005–6, both by *DKA*, amid many other new buildings. Notable also is the library at King's College, Taunton, 2010–11, by *Mitchell Taylor*. At Bruton, King's School, Sexey's School and Bruton School for Girls are all greatly expanded, as is Wellington School, the architectural quality variable.

Other PUBLIC BUILDINGS include the extension to the County Offices at Taunton, 1962–9, won in competition by *Goodwin & Tatum*. The Divisional Police Headquarters, Yeovil, 1973, a sturdy square-plan block clad in pre-cast panels, are by the *County Architect's Department*. Postmodern contextualism appears in later buildings by the department, such as Yeovil Library, 1986–7, which hints at the classical of the adjacent Municipal Offices, and the neo-Victorian Magistrates' Courts, Taunton, 1992. Since the 1990s public buildings have been commissioned from outside architects, e.g. the additions to Somerset

College, Taunton (by *LHC Architects*) and to Yeovil College (by *ADP*), the police headquarters, Bridgwater (by *Ryder Architecture*), and the addition to Musgrove Park Hospital, Taunton (by *BDP*). Community hospitals have been built at Glastonbury, South Petherton and Minehead, the latter two by *DKA*. Doctors' surgeries are of a scale not seen before, including a notable one at Dulverton, 2009, by *Guy Greenfield*. Buildings for the arts include two performance spaces at Heathfield School (West Monkton) by *Kensington Taylor*, 2000 and 2006–8, the conference centre at Dillington House by *Niall Phillips Architects*, 2006–9, and the conversion of Durslade Farm (Bruton) by *Benjamin & Beauchamp*, 2013–14.

New CHURCHES were rare. *Eric Francis*'s St Teresa (R.C.) at Taunton, 1958–60, and *Caroe & Partners*' Holy Trinity, Bridgwater, 1960–1, both have character, brick-clad, but neither especially modern, especially by contrast with the Taunton Deane Crematorium chapel (Bishop's Hull), 1962–3, by *Potter & Hare*, with its wall of glass to the garden.

Modern INDUSTRIAL BUILDINGS have tended to be large sheds, of which the distribution centres for Morrison (Bawdrip), 2010–12, and Clark's (Street), 2005, are the largest in the area. The nuclear power stations at Hinkley Point, 1957–75, to external designs by *Frederick Gibberd*, are by far the largest buildings in the county, both due for replacement. The design for the third power station is evolving.

A few late C20 HOUSES should be mentioned, notably a small group at Glastonbury by *A.J. Hepworth*, 1956, one at Street by *Ray Moxley*, 1961, and one at Somerton by *Stout & Litchfield*, 1972; but distrust of the new was the norm, so the tally of good late C20 houses is miserably small. Two C21 houses at Norton-sub-Hamdon show local practices able to be modern: a two-level house, 2003, by *Boon Brown*, and a plate-glass and grass-roofed one by *Orme Architecture*, 2010–11, but the first is sunken to invisibility. Invisibility is also the effect at Upper Crannel Farm, Glastonbury, 2006–11, by *Richard Paxton* of London, where two houses are within standard agricultural sheds. Temple Cross House, Godney, 2010–11, by *Nigel Begg*, imitates in form the hoop-topped barn previously on the site. Are these answers to the *genius loci* or well-founded caution? At Shatwell, Hadspen, a layered glass-and-timber stair-tower, 2005, by *Charlotte Skene Catling*, leaves an Edwardian cottage looking unaltered to the casual passer-by. Three small groups of housing association cottages in West Somerset, 1987–92 by *Percy Thomas Partnership*, are contextual without being imitative. Most private housing estates tend to bland traditionalism, but Icon at Street, 2007–9 by *Feilden Clegg Bradley Studios*, stands out, a mixed development in a modern idiom, large enough to show intelligent planning and landscaping.

South Somerset in the C21 is, as far as buildings go, in better condition than for many years: churches have been repaired with National Lottery money, country houses renewed with private money from the City of London, and urban money has left hardly any old cottages unrestored. There has been loss of texture, grain and character in this wholesale renovation, but houses that were threatened even in the 1960s and 1970s are unlikely to go now. The casualties of the recent financial crisis have been schemes to renovate or convert large, complicated industrial structures like the Tonedale Mills at Wellington, and these remain of concern.

FURTHER READING

Somerset is well provided with COUNTY HISTORIES, beginning with Thomas Gerard's entertaining and partial *The Particular Description of the County of Somerset*, 1633. The value of the Rev. John Collinson's *History and Antiquities of the County of Somerset*, 3 vols, 1791, is much enhanced by the recent publication of the preliminary notes collected in the 1780s by Edmund Rack. These have been edited by Mark McDermott and Sue Berry as *Edmund Rack's Survey of Somerset*, 2011. William Phelps, *The History and Antiquities of Somersetshire*, 1836, covering mainly prehistory and ecclesiastical history, is notable for early plans of hillforts and barrows. Histories of more restricted areas are J. Savage, *History of the Hundred of Carhampton*, 1830, C. Chadwyck-Healey, *The History of the West Part of Somerset*, 1901, and John Batten, *Historical and Topographical Collections Relating to the Early History of Parts of South Somerset*, 1894. A modern history of a part of the region is *The Vale of Taunton Past*, by Tom Mayberry, 1998.

The indispensable *Victoria County History* is the pinnacle of historical research for the county. Volumes I and II on general and ecclesiastical history came out in 1906 and 1911. Coverage of the parishes of the county began in 1974 with vol. III for Langport, Somerton and surrounding parishes, and has now reached vol. XI, all covering parishes within this volume. The *Proceedings of the Somerset Archaeological and Natural History Society* (*PSANHS*), begun in 1849, are among the best of the archaeological journals in the country. Its older volumes include catalogues of the monumental brasses and monumental effigies of the county. Within its more recent volumes are the reports of discoveries made by the Somerset Vernacular Buildings Research Group. *Somerset and Dorset Notes and Queries* has a reputation for turning up unexpected information. The Historic Environment Records kept online by Somerset and Exmoor are the first place to look for archaeology and increasingly other material such as records of C20 military structures. The British Newspaper Archive has Somerset newspapers searchable online.

For GEOLOGY, the maps and guides published by the British Geological Society include *The Geology of the Country around Taunton and the Quantock Hills*, 1985, by E. A. Edmonds and G. W. Green. Peter Hardy, *The Geology of Somerset*, 2003, and R. A. Edwards, *Exmoor Geology*, 2000, are good popular guides, to which must be added Hugh Prudden's *Geology and Landscape of Taunton Deane*, 2001, and his pamphlets, *Ham Hill: The Rocks* and *Quarries*, 1995, and *Geology and Landscape around Yeovil*, 2005. A summary by Hugh Prudden of the building stones of Somerset appears in the *PSANHS* 146, 2003. Richard Durnan, *Ham Hill: Portrait of a Building Stone*, 2006, is a study of the stone and its distribution as a building material.

Introductory and general works on ARCHAEOLOGY include M. Aston and I. Burrow, *The Archaeology of Somerset*, 1982, L. and R. Adkins, *A Field Guide to Somerset Archaeology*, 1992, Chris Webster (ed.), *Somerset Archaeology*, 2000, a useful collection of essays, and C. Webster and T. Mayberry (eds), *The Archaeology of Somerset*, 2007. Hillforts are listed in I. Burrow, *Hillforts and Hill-top Settlements in Somerset*, 1981. The South Cadbury excavations of 1966–70 are covered in L. Alcock, *South Cadbury that is Camelot*, 1972, and those on Brean Down, 1983–7, in M. Bell, *Brean Down Excavations*, 1990. For the ROMAN period the general introduction is P. Leach, *Roman Somerset*, 2001. S. R. Cosh and D. S. Neal, *The Roman Mosaics of Britain: South-West Britain*, 2007, illustrates all the mosaics found in the county for which records survive. Broadly the same buildings are covered by K. Branigan, *The Roman Villa in South West England*, 1972. The *English Heritage Book of Glastonbury*, 1993, on the archaeology of Glastonbury, was the work of Philip Rahtz, pre-eminent among the archaeologists involved on that most dug-over of sites, and covers the prehistoric tracks, lake villages and ecclesiastical sites.

The beginnings of TOWNS are covered in J. Haslam (ed.), *Anglo-Saxon Towns in Southern England*, 1984, and M. Aston and R. Leech, *Historic Towns in Somerset*, 1977. The works of the late Mick Aston, notably on medieval settlements and landscapes, are scattered through *PSANHS* and many other publications and are always worth seeking out. Town and village histories are covered with greater or lesser scholarship in the numerous *The Book of...* volumes. The older ones, on *Taunton* (1977) and *Wellington* (1981) by Robin Bush, on *Street* by Michael McGarvie, and *Yeovil* by Leslie Brooke (1978), are especially good. Notably useful later volumes are those for *Carhampton* and *Minehead* by Hilary Binding, *Marston Bigot* by Michael McGarvie, and *St Audries and West Quantoxhead* by Duncan Stafford. Older local histories include *The History of Taunton*, by Joshua Toulmin, 1791, revised by J. Savage, 1822, the *Book of the Axe* (Crewkerne and Chard), 1875, by G. Pulman, and the *History of Wincanton*, 1903, by G. Sweetman. *From Portreeve to Mayor*, L. C. Hayward's history of Yeovil, 1987, remains relevant, as does Robin Bush, *Jeboult's Taunton*, 1983, on Victorian Taunton. For the villages, Robin Bush, *Somerset: the Complete Guide*, 1994, is an indispensable gazetteer, enhanced by Julian Comrie's photographs. There are many village histories, most of which have something to offer. Of more than usual interest are *Witham Friary, Church and Parish*, 1989, by Michael McGarvie, and *Mark, a Somerset Moorland Village*, 1999, by Pamela Slocombe.

The medieval PARISH CHURCHES were visited in the C19 by Sir Stephen Glynne of Hawarden. His notes, accompanied by early C19 drawings by John Buckler, John Chessell Buckler and

W. W. Wheatley from the SANHS collections, have been published as *Sir Stephen Glynne's Church Notes for Somerset*, 1994, ed. M. McGarvie. No other English county can have so useful a volume, illustrating in words and pictures the churches just before Victorian restoration. Pevsner admired greatly A. K. Wickham's *Churches of Somerset*, 1952, more an elegant essay than a detailed enquiry, but still very much worth seeking out. John Harvey, the great expert on English Perpendicular, published articles in the *Transactions of the Ancient Monuments Society* on dating Somerset tracery (vol. 27, 1983) and on dating Somerset church towers (vol. 26, 1982). His *The Perpendicular Style 1330–1485*, 1978, remains the essential national overview. Adrian Webb (ed.), *Ancient Church Fonts of Somerset*, 2013, reprints Harvey Pridham's illustrations of all the medieval fonts. Christopher Woodforde, *Stained Glass in Somerset 1250–1830*, 1946, describes all the pre-Victorian glass. A. B. Connor, *Monumental Brasses in Somerset*, 1970, is collected from articles by Connor in *PSANHS*, 1931–53. In *PSANHS* also are Fryer's descriptions of the monumental effigies. Brian and Moira Gittos catalogued the effigies and incised slabs made of Ham Hill stone in the *Journal of the British Archaeological Association* 165, 2012. Barbara Lowe, *Decorated Medieval Floor Tiles of Somerset*, 2003, is a complete catalogue. P. Poyntz Wright, *The Rural Benchends of Somerset*, 1983, *Hunky Punks: a Study in Somerset Stone Carving*, 1982, and *Parish Church Towers of Somerset*, 1981, are useful for comparative photographs. Poyntz-Wright's dating thesis for the church towers was rejected by John Harvey (*see* above). Church guides are very variable in quality. John Bishton, *St Mary the Virgin, Bruton*, 2011, is a book-length history. A useful little booklet is N. V. Allen, *Churches and Chapels of Exmoor*, 1974. Robert Dunning's *Christianity in Somerset*, 1976, and *Somerset Monasteries*, 2001, outline Christian and monastic history.

The online catalogue of the collection at Lambeth Palace of drawings for the Incorporated Church Building Society, *churchplansonline.org*, is indispensable for CHURCH RESTORATIONS, as is the collection of faculty plans at the Somerset Heritage Centre. For ROMAN CATHOLIC churches, J. A. Harding, *The Diocese of Clifton, 1850–2000*, 1999, is worthwhile, though occasionally missing crucial details concerning architects. For CHAPELS, Christopher Stell, *An Inventory of Nonconformist Chapels and Meeting-houses in South-west England*, 1991, is the best survey, though not exhaustive. For CHURCH MONUMENTS, Ingrid Roscoe, *A Biographical Dictionary of Sculpture in Britain 1660–1851*, 2009, greatly adds to Rupert Gunnis's pioneering work. For STAINED GLASS, Martin Harrison, *Victorian Stained Glass*, 1980, is the best general survey. For individual glassmakers much remains unpublished, but A. G. Sewter, *The Stained Glass of William Morris and His Circle*, 2 vols, 1974–5, and Philip Collins (ed.), *The Corpus of Kempe Stained Glass in the United Kingdom and Ireland*, 2000, cover those two firms. Hugh Playfair's *Jewels of Somerset*, 2012, illustrates stained glass after 1830 with colour photographs of stunning quality by Chris Akroyd. For

TILES, Lynne Pearson's *Tile Gazetteer*, 2005, has a Somerset section. Robert Dunning, *Somerset Churches and Chapels*, 2007, tells the recent story of rescue from neglect.

For material on VERNACULAR BUILDINGS the Somerset Vernacular Buildings Research Group (SVBRG) is unrivalled. Originating in the pioneer work of Commander E. H. D. Williams, Ron Gilson, Clare Austin, Mark McDermott and John and Jane Penoyre, the group was founded in 1979. Records of thousands of individual buildings, almost all with measured plans, have been deposited in the Somerset Heritage Centre. The publications associated with the group are invaluable: the Penoyres' *Decorative Plasterwork in the Houses of Somerset 1500–1700*, 1994, Jane Penoyre, *Traditional Houses of Somerset*, 2005, and John and Pamela McCann, *The Dovecotes of Historical Somerset*, 2003. The SVBRG's published parish surveys cover some dozen villages in exemplary detail, from *West Chinnock*, 1980, to *Stogursey*, 2010. The work of the group has exposed the weakness of the Statutory Lists of protected buildings compiled by the Department of the Environment during the 1980s, especially for building interiors, and therefore dating. But the lists remain of value. More time and space were allocated for subsequent revisions of selected urban lists, including those for Bridgwater, Chard, Crewkerne, Ilminster and Minehead.

Coverage of SECULAR BUILDING TYPES is patchy. For CASTLES, see *Somerset Castles*, 1995, by Robert Dunning. For MEDIEVAL HOUSES, Margaret Wood's overview, *The English Mediaeval House*, 1965, has been supplemented by Anthony Emery, *Greater Medieval Houses of England and Wales, 1300–1500*, of which vol. III, 2006, includes Somerset. Robert Dunning's *Some Somerset Country Houses*, 1991, needs to be read with his *Somerset Families*, 2002, for an overview of COUNTRY HOUSES and their owners. GARDEN BUILDINGS and follies are covered in James Bond, *Somerset Parks and Gardens*, 1998, T. Mowl and M. Mako, *Historic Gardens of Somerset*, 2010, and Jonathan Holt, *Somerset Follies*, 2007.

For INDIVIDUAL ARCHITECTS, Sir Howard Colvin's *Biographical Dictionary of British Architects, 1660–1840*, 4th edn, 2008, is the bedrock, supplemented for later architects by the RIBA *Directory of British Architects 1830–1914*, 2001. Russell Lillford, *Notes on Some Architects and Surveyors Working in Somerset between 1820 and 1939*, 2009, is invaluable. On individual architects, F. Bligh Bond's career in architecture, archaeology and spiritualism is told in *The Rediscovery of Glastonbury*, 2007, by Tim Hopkinson-Ball. *W. D. Caröe* has a biography by Jennifer Freeman, 1991, and *Sir George Oatley* is very fully treated by Sarah Whittingham, 2011. For Samson & Cottam and their successors see *A Somerset Architects' Practice in the 19th and 20th Centuries*, 2007, by H. A. Derek Gibson, a partner in the practice. The series *Bath History* (from 1986) includes articles on Edward and C. E. Davis.

For INDUSTRY and TRANSPORT the county has the Somerset Industrial Archaeological Society (SIAS), whose *Bulletins* go back to 1975 and whose *Surveys* cover various industries and subjects.

The overview is Peter Stanier, *Somerset in the Age of Steam*, 2003, and the SIAS gazetteer of sites is published as *Somerset's Industrial Heritage*, 1996, ed. Derek Warren. Stanier's bibliography cannot be surpassed. A few more recent works are: Mary Miles, *Perfectly Pure*, 2006, a directory and gazeteer of all the breweries; Mike Williams, *Textile Mills of South West England*, 2013, and C. A. Buchanan, *From Field to Factory*, 2008, on the flax and hemp industry.

GAZETTEER

ABBOTSFIELD see WIVELISCOMBE

AISHOLT

A beautiful remote fold of the Quantocks.

ALL SAINTS. Plain two-stage W tower of reddish rubble. No W doorway, sometimes an early feature, but the wave-moulded tower arch is late C14. Square NE stair-turret. The porch and gabled S aisle are late C15, the S doorway probably reused. C15 oak DOOR. Two-bay arcade of four-centred arches on standard four-hollow piers. Long tunnel SQUINT. Georgian plaster still covers the aisle and nave barrel roofs. Early C14 red sandstone chancel arch, double-chamfered, the inner chamfer on octagonal responds with plain capitals. – FONT. Octagonal, retooled. Bowl-shaped below, so probably C12–C13. – ORGAN. By *Samuel Parsons* of London, *c.* 1820. STAINED GLASS E window, 1896, comically stiff. Medieval fragments in the W window.

In the valley, the thatched OLD SCHOOLHOUSE, C17, home of Sir Henry Newbolt 1927–38. AISHOLT HOUSE was the rectory that Coleridge visited. Late C18, three-storeyed, with leaded casements.

LOWER AISHOLT FARMHOUSE, ¾ m. SE. Red rubble stone, with rear wings. C16 fireplace and framed ceiling.

HAWKRIDGE RESERVOIR, 1 m. ENE. Created in 1962, landscaped by *S. Colwyn Foulkes*.

ALCOMBE see MINEHEAD

ALFORD

The church stands in a fine position away from the village and against the grounds of Alford House, which extend to the River Brue.

ALL SAINTS. An uncommonly complete example of a small Perp church, not substantially restored or freshened up, and still with its screen and benches. Modest W tower with pyramid roof behind a parapet. Embattled three-bay nave with large gargoyles and S porch. Two-bay chancel. The windows have cusped ogee lights and tiny headstops. Heads also at the chancel corners. C15 porch roof. The chancel roof is Somerset timberwork at its best, on a small scale. Unusually steep, perhaps replicating an earlier roof pitch. Moulded tie-beams and intermediate angels on short columns on stone corbels – four angels and two large earlier heads. The shafted chancel arch looks C14 rather than C15. Mosaic FLOOR and marble-panelled E wall by *T. G. Jackson*, 1876–8. – FONT. Re-tooled C13, octagonal. – ROOD SCREEN. A curious C15 design in nine unequal bays and three tiers: net-like ogee tracery, a transom band of narrow lights, and pendants suggesting a lower arcade. – PULPIT. 1625. Narrow, profusely ornamented, with monogram initials. – BENCHES. An excellent C16 set with pentagonal finials. Plain tracery and vigorous motifs: dragon, pelican, Paschal Lamb, and green man. – STALLS. Later C19. Reliefs of the Evangelists. – STAINED GLASS. A composite figure of Mary Magdalene from fragments of C15 glass introduced in the C19, rearranged in the 1930s. Chancel side windows, 1860s, probably by *O'Connor*. One, softer, by *Powell's*, 1899. – MONUMENT. John Thring †1830. Grecian, by *Tyley*.

Restored medieval CHURCHYARD CROSS. Two massive Thring tombs, *c.* 1891 and *c.* 1874.

ALFORD HOUSE. A remodelling by *F. C. Penrose* in 1877 of a Georgian Gothic house built for John Thring after 1807. Penrose's style is C16, between French and English, with steep hipped roofs behind parapets and mullion-and-transom windows. Blue Lias and ashlar. On the S side the original canted centre carries a high French roof, while the W side has, confusingly, twin porch-towers with pyramid roofs. Edwardian interiors.

In the village, the OLD RECTORY has C17 mullioned windows. The OLD POST OFFICE, with veranda, *c.* 1865, was built as a museum for the Thring ichthyosaurus. ALFORD FARMHOUSE has distinctive chequering of Lias and Cary stone, apparently C17, and PARSONAGE FARM, in three parts, grey, ochre, and grey, is partly C16 with a wind-braced roof.

BOLTER'S BRIDGE, ¾ m. NNE. Medieval four-arched packhorse bridge over the Alham.

CLANVILLE MANOR FARM, 1 m. WNW. Dated 1743, but of the early C19, for the Stourhead estate. Hip-roofed with an arched window over a pedimented false door. Large BARN with full-height doors and throughway.

ALFOXTON PARK see HOLFORD

ALHAMPTON

1 m. S of Ditcheat

CHURCH. 1892. Corrugated iron, painted green and red.
HOUSES. Blue Lias and ochre Cary stone are equally displayed, mixed in several mullion-windowed farmhouses, notably CORNER HOUSE, which has C17 plasterwork. Tree and bird friezes downstairs and an overmantel dated 1624 upstairs.

ALLER

The church and Aller Court are isolated on a small rise above Aller Moor.

ST ANDREW. An important Anglo-Saxon site, where Alfred reputedly witnessed the baptism of Guthrum in 878. Late Norman S doorway with an arch of heavy chevron on colonnettes and a crocketed ogee C14 niche. The most puzzling feature of the church is the Perp W tower of *c.* 1400, because it stands on three arches, carried on free-standing piers to the E and on responds to the W. There is no western arch, which makes it unlikely that Sir Peter Courtenay †1405 (whose arms are on the W window) intended this as the crossing of an enlarged church. The N and S arches open to narrow lean-to spaces of no obvious function, but which are carefully detailed with panelled quadrant vaults. The piers are of standard four-hollow design, broadly treated with large simple capitals. There is a similarly puzzling tower at Woolavington. The upper parts are later, the junction visible inside on the nave W wall where the buttresses are started high up on angel brackets. Octagonal NW stair-turret, with spirelet. N aisle added by *John Norton*, 1861–2, overwhelmingly Victorian with botanical capitals. – FONTS. Rimmed bulbous bowl, probably C11–C12, but traditionally the Guthrum font. The other, dated 1663, is octagonal with simple Jacobean motifs, on a spiral stem. – PULPIT. 1610, daintily detailed with Ionic balusters and arched panels. – REREDOS. 1887, by *J. D. Sedding*. – STAINED GLASS. By *Joseph Bell* the E window, 1855, the W, 1861, and two N aisle windows, 1866–8. Much finer the N aisle E, *c.* 1861, by *Clayton & Bell*, lovely deep blues. – MONUMENTS. An eroded cross-legged knight (N aisle) may be Sir John of Aller, *c.* 1272. – A knight in full armour in a many-cusped C14 chancel recess may be Sir John of Clevedon, *c.* 1373. – Reginald Botreaux †1420. A rare medieval wall slab, pale Lias, with lightly incised lettering and heraldry. – Rachel Foster †1637 and Rachel Northover

†1639. Alabaster-framed tablets with heraldry in misunderstood scroll pediments.

ALLER COURT. 1812. Three-storeyed, badly modernized. C17 windows in the rear wing and C15 two-light cusped windows in an outbuilding remain from the 'ancient castle-like place' mentioned in 1633. The tall BARN has a good late medieval wind-braced roof on arch-braced trusses.

On the tiny triangular green, the OLD POUND INN, early C19, of White Lias, and MANOR HOUSE, *c.* 1800, mansard-roofed, brick, with ashlar eaves.

OLD RECTORY, below Beer Road. A late C15 parlour block remains; the rest remodelled for Emmanuel College, Cambridge, *c.* 1855. The N end has a gabled stair-and-garderobe tower beside a large six-light window of Muchelney type (ogee-headed lights, quatrefoil spandrels). The two-light pointed window above retains some C15 stained glass. Moulded framed ceiling, pointed archway into a small E room. Remnants of a wind-braced roof.

TOLL HOUSE, 1 m. SSE. 1828. Two-storeyed, brick, Gothic.

SOWY RIVER, 1 m. S. Artificial, built in 1969–72 to take excess water from the River Parrett to the King's Sedgemoor Drain.

ALLERFORD

1½ m. W of Selworthy

The view of the PACKHORSE BRIDGE of two shallow arches and a pair of C16–C17 COTTAGES is as familiar as any in Somerset. The prettiness is partly C19, the circular chimney on the cottages typical of Holnicote estate improvement (cf. Selworthy). The cottages were thatched, as was most of Allerford. HILLSIDE stands well on the slope behind, yellow-washed, thatched, with lateral chimney and hip-roofed storeyed porch. In the village, the thatched SCHOOL (now museum) of 1821 barely differs from the cottages. By the A39, ALLERFORD HOUSE is Georgian on a C17 core. CROSS LANE HOUSE has roof timbers dated to 1544.

ANGERSLEIGH

ST MICHAEL. Small and rendered. C14 battlemented W tower, with buttresses and stair-turret to the lower stage. Dec two-light bell-openings. The rest has Perp straight-headed windows, the nave embattled. Victorian interior of 1855 with family pew on the N. – WOODWORK. C16 style, made after 1901 by a class led by *A. E. Eastwood* of Leigh Court. – FONT. C12. Bulbous bowl with rough centre band. – STAINED GLASS. Mostly

ANGERSLEIGH · ANSFORD

Allerford, bridge and cottages.
Drawing by J. Crowther, 1901

1865–70 by *Lavers & Barraud*. Nave S by *Ward & Hughes*. Silvery E window by *Kempe & Co.*, 1914.
LEIGH COURT. Rebuilt after a fire in 1837, for a wealthy rector, perhaps by *Carver*. Hip-roofed five-bay front with pedimented central bay. Elegant ashlar details, especially the half-inset octagonal porch with unfluted Ionic columns. Canted bay on the S. Cantilevered stone staircase with iron serpent balusters, screened by columns, Ionic below, Corinthian above.
LEIGH FARMHOUSE. Spreading roughcast farmhouse originating as a late medieval hall house.
LOWTON MANOR. Mid-Georgian, three bays with pedimented doorway. Once stuccoed; now iron-rich cornerstones are exposed. Large hip-roofed C18 OUTBUILDINGS, the N one exceptionally long with a broad throughway.

ANSFORD

ST ANDREW. Simple Perp W tower, the rest by *C. E. Giles*, 1861, in Cary stone. – FONT. Re-tooled C12 bowl. – PULPIT. C17. With intricate panels and angle feathers (cf. Sparkford).

– STAINED GLASS. Colourful E window, 1862. W window, 1935, by *Cuthbert Atchley*. – MONUMENTS. Rev. Samuel Woodforde †1766. – Marble cartouche, 1772, by *John Ford Jun*. Latin inscription by the diarist Parson Woodforde.

ANSFORD SCHOOL 1936–40, by *A. J. Toomer*, County Architect. Modern Georgian like Huish Episcopi etc. LEISURE CENTRE, 1998, by *Boon Brown*.

THE OLD PARSONAGE (Parson Woodforde's birthplace in 1740) has C17 timber-mullioned windows. Further S are the former RECTORY, later C18 with pedimented doorway, and Georgian Gothic STABLE; the former ANSFORD INN, C17 and early C18; and ANSFORD HOUSE, late C18, with a well detailed Roman Doric doorcase.

ASH

HOLY TRINITY. 1840–1 by *Sampson Kempthorne*. Bare lancet style, followed in the chancel of 1887 by *J. N. Johnston* and the W tower of 1919 by *C. B. Benson*. Early C19 chamber ORGAN.

On the main road, ASH HOUSE, hip-roofed, with five-bay fronts, alike in detail except that the S front has sash windows, and the W one, unevenly spaced, has stone cross-windows of *c*. 1710. Mid-C18 staircase. BRITANNIA, Back Street, reuses a C17 bay with corbelled gable from the Britannia Inn, Yeovil, demolished 1969. On Burrough Street several of the Ham stone farmhouses typical of the Martock area: MANOR FARM-HOUSE, early C17 with a framed ceiling; THE GRANGE, with flatter late C17 mullions; and BOLEYN HOUSE, C17 but with Regency tripartite sashes. Early C18 staircase.

Good farmsteads also in the hamlets of WITCOMBE and MILTON. At Milton, COURTFIELD HOUSE was a chapel licensed in 1287. Pointed N doorway and small W lancet. C15 framed ceiling.

ASHBRITTLE

ST JOHN BAPTIST. The medieval church was encased in 1862–6 in heavily embossed Westleigh stone, reminiscent of railway engineering, with new tower top and chancel. By *William Cottrell*, mason, for the Rev. C. P. Quicke, squire and rector. But the church has considerable interest. The large six-light S window with sub-arched tracery traditionally came from Barlinch Priory. The N aisle is C15–C16, with depressed pointed arches to the arcade and chancel N arch, on slim piers of four-wave type with leaf-band capitals. Wagon roof. Reused leaf-band capitals in the porch. – PULPIT. 1845. Large, ashlar. From Holy Trinity, Barnstaple, Devon. – STALLS. 1903, from Wellington church. – STAINED GLASS. Pictorial E window by

Wailes, c. 1870. Chancel s windows by *Toms*, 1860s. Nave s, 1869, with pretty Morris-style quarries. Two NE windows, 1882–3, Kempe-style, with roundel portraits.

In the churchyard, an immensely old yew and restored C15 CROSS.

By the green, the former SCHOOL, 1875, and GREYWELLS HOUSE, Victorian crazed rubble, for the Quicke estate.

OLD RECTORY, ½ m. WSW. 1827, by *William Burgess* of Exeter. Substantial, deep-eaved, with a central canted bay.

ASHCOTT 4030

ALL SAINTS. Later C15 W tower with the initials of Abbot Selwood of Glastonbury, the top stage and SE stair-turret rebuilt, apparently accurately, in 1857. The rest was rebuilt and widened northward in 1831 by *J. B. Beard*. The latticed parapet (like Selwood's work at Meare) was copied reusing some grotesques. Beard's bleak interior was refashioned as far as possible in 1889–90 by *Edward Dampier* of Colchester. – FONT. Early Norman. Plain bowl, re-tooled. – PULPIT. 1831, reusing C15–C16 panels and a C17 moulding. – BENCH-ENDS. Four, C15–C16, traceried. Also C17 ones with a concentric arched pattern. – ROYAL ARMS. Hanoverian. – STAINED GLASS. Chancel s, 1889, and E window, 1898, both by *Kempe*. Is it delusion to find the earlier window more intense and concentrated? – MONUMENTS. Part of a medieval grave-slab built into a porch bench. Several charming incised Lias plaques: Whitehead family, two of 1711–12, one with skull and poppies; Sarah Jones, with winged cherub head, signed *J. Baily*, Woolavington, 1782, 'Life how short. Death how long!'; Henry Pain †1793, prettily bordered oval.

On the main road is ASHCOTT HOUSE, raised and refaced in the early C19. Stuccoed, five bays, with overhanging eaves, Venetian centre window and paired-columned porch. Battlemented wings. To the W, ETONHURST, c. 1865, red brick and stone, three-storeyed with deep eaves. Probably by *Edwin Down*, who designed the STABLES, 1869. To the E, LOCKHILL HALL, ashlar-fronted, has Early Victorian detail: thin giant pilasters and an over-arched Venetian screen to the doorway in a curved recess.

ASHFORD see CHARLINCH

ASHFORD see ILTON

ASHILL 3010

ST MARY. Not large, of notably mixed stones. Perp W tower with patches of Blue Lias. Four-centred-arched W window of after

1500, an earlier pointed one visible within. Polygonal NE stair-turret. C15–C16 square-headed nave windows with quatrefoil spandrels (cf. Muchelney Abbey), but on the N side a late C13 three-light with cinquefoiled rere-arch. Both N and S doorways are Norman, with segmental arches, octagonal shafts, and varied capitals, one S one of delicate foliage. The S arch has chevron, as does the much-restored chancel arch, between plain blank arches. These and exterior stonework may indicate chapels to a narrow chancel, rebuilt to full width in the C14 (cf. the Dec side windows and shafted reveal to the Perp E window). Two C14 cusped tomb-recesses (nave N). The larger, earlier one has bold forked cusping, a niche above and fleur-de-lys finial. Both house EFFIGIES, the larger possibly Maud de Moulton †1293, low-relief, holding a heart, with angels at her pillow. In the other, a stiff knight of *c.* 1380. The nave roof is C15, the wall-plates with thirty shields showing original colour. Chancel restored 1862 by *Ewan Christian*, porches and tower arch by *J. D. Sedding*, 1882. – FONT. Perp. Octagonal, with shields etc. in sexfoils. Panelled stem. – PULPIT. Early C17, panelled, with scrolled creatures in the frieze (cf. Beercrocombe). – BENCHES. C16. Solid baulk ends. – MONUMENT. William Speke †1686. Ornate Lias floor slab.

The OLD RECTORY is mostly picturesque Gothic of 1840–1 by *William Patch* of Ilminster. Formerly thatched. But the low centre has an early C16 moulded framed ceiling. The S addition has concave corners. These intrude into a parlour with Gothic plasterwork. Just N, ASHILL FARMHOUSE, C16–C17, long and colourwashed, attached to OLD ASHILL HOUSE, Late Georgian, stuccoed, with formal if inelegant dressings of Ham stone.

WOOD COURT, ¾ m. W. Remodelled in 1840 in enthusiastic Gothic, reusing medieval pieces. Five bays with off-centre storeyed porch. Perp three-light ecclesiastical windows below, first-floor cross-windows, and mullioned dormers with reused finials. At right angles, a false chapel with reused gargoyles and finials.

THICKTHORN HOUSE, 1 m. SE. Mostly brick, the front range Late Georgian, the rear externally early C18 but with C16 framed ceilings.

ROWLAND'S. *See* Ilton.

ASHINGTON

ST VINCENT. Small and very pretty. C13 nave and chancel with one of the distinctive C15–C16 lantern bellcotes found also at Brympton D'Evercy and Chilthorne Domer, here gabled rather than pyramid-roofed. The supporting buttress blocks a C13 W lancet. In the nave E gable, a Crucifixion relief. C13 chancel lancets with trefoiled rere-arches, the triple E lancets of the restoration in 1878. The bellcote may be slightly later than the Perp remodelling of the nave. Large windows with supermullions; continuously moulded chancel arch. Roofs of 1878. Oak C14 S DOOR with a strip of tracery. – FONT. C13. Shallow octagon, coved below. – FURNISHINGS. A notable early C17 set similar to those at Mudford (q.v.), including BOX PEWS with shell-tops and arabesques, the two larger ones for the manor and rectory. Attached to the rectory pew are a balustraded reader's DESK and PULPIT with strapwork and big encircled flowers, back (dated 1637) and tester. – STAINED GLASS. C15 fragments. Chancel windows, 1878. – MONUMENTS. Sir John St Barbe †1723. Well-carved aedicule with scroll-footed pilasters. By the same hand as the Humphrey Sydenham monument at Dulverton.

MANOR HOUSE. A reduction of a large manor house of the St Barbes, known from an early C19 engraving. Ham stone and stone tiles. A late C15* hall house was remodelled in the early C16 to a triple-gabled E-plan, early for the type. Of the three, only the l. gable survives with a large two-storeyed canted bay window. The central storeyed porch has been removed and the doorway moved, and the r. gable demolished entirely. The canted bay window looks Elizabethan, under a corbelled gable of the local early C17 type (cf. Martock and Bower Hinton). The present entrance is inserted to the l. of where the porch would have been, reusing (badly) a shafted C15 doorway. The original C15 cross-passage doorways survive, the front one visible only from inside. Further testimony of the C15 are a SW diagonal buttress, and windows with cusped ogee lights above the rear door and on the W end. The rear NW wing is early C16. Its windows have shaped heads to the lights. The rear wall has twin chimneys serving two fireplaces on each floor. Reused elements in the wing probably came from the C15 front range. A ground-floor fireplace lintel has late medieval tracery on the back; some tie-beams are reused from a moulded framed ceiling, and the NW stair-tower with its spiral stairs may have been moved from the W end of the front range. In the front range, two Tudor-arched fireplaces: one with a deep corniced lintel of *c.* 1500, the other moved in the C19. The location of the earlier hall fireplace may be marked by the moulded jamb of the doorway to the C16 staircase in the angle to the NW wing. Quatrefoil plaques from the demolished porch are reset on a C19 OUTBUILDING.

ASH PRIORS

HOLY TRINITY. Red sandstone with an undivided W tower for which money was given in 1438–9. Diagonal buttresses, ashlar

---

* Jerry Sampson has found masons' marks matching those in Shepton Beauchamp church tower, of *c.* 1500.

battlements and square higher stair-turret. Two-light bell-openings with pierced baffles. W doorway and window of 1874. Double-chamfered tower arch. Gabled aisles, the N aisle Perp with three-light windows and rood-stair projection. Humble two-bay arcade of four hollow piers with relatively fat shafts. S aisle of 1833. Perp chancel arch on corbels over older chamfered jambs. The chancel N arch is cut through older wall, a shafted arch to each face. Roofs of 1874 by *J. H. Spencer*, who lengthened the chancel and added the porch. – FONT. Octagonal, C15–C16, with shallow overall ornament (cf. Bishop's Lydeard). – PULPIT and REREDOS. 1874. Ornate stone and marble. – STAINED GLASS. E window †1890, gloomy colours. Chancel N, 1874, and NE, 1891, by *Clayton & Bell*. SW, 1911, by *Powell's*.

SE of the church, COURT HOUSE, chequered brick with wooden cross-windows, built in 1725 for John Winter. Stuccoed Gothick STABLES, 1808, with ogee-arched openings. Large GRANARY on sandstone monoliths behind. Thatched COTTAGES beyond dated 1632.

THE PRIORY, ¼ m. W. The site is associated with Taunton Priory. The front with Tudor-style veranda and storeyed central porch was remodelled around 1830 for the Winter family, but the four-centred doorway is credibly Tudor, dated 1529. At the back, a narrow stair-turret and rear wing with C16 beams.

SANDHILL PARK, 1 m. NE. The hospital here closed in 1991, and was sold for restoration with development in the grounds. The restoration was never begun and the house burnt in 2011. The shell remains, hopefully not irredeemable, for it is strikingly monumental. Built in 1720 for John Periam. Three storeys, seven by five bays, of red sandstone ashlar with Bath stone dressings. Of that Queen Anne type with attic windows above the cornice and quoin pilasters at the main angles, originally finished with parapet statues. Shouldered architraves, the central first-floor one each side and the tall corniced W doorway with devil-mask keystones. The S doorway was similar, replaced when the handsome three-bay portico was added *c.* 1815 for the Lethbridge family. Paired Tuscan columns, triglyph frieze and centre pediment. Presumably then the E side was refaced and the large canted bay added. An impressive array in distant views is created by square three-bay, two-storey additions at both rear corners, faced in Bath stone. The NW one with an arcaded orangery behind is early C19, the NE one probably of 1889–90. The entrance hall had fine Rococo plasterwork.

Stately Neoclassical NORTH LODGE, *c.* 1815, ashlar, three bays, with pedimented arch over the drive. Two early C19 estate follies in red sandstone: BALLIFANTS FARMHOUSE, in the park, with a battlemented tower one end, and, facing the lane to the S, GREENWAY HOUSE, cottages refronted with gables and central turret.

ATHELNEY see EAST LYNG

BABCARY

HOLY CROSS. Blue Lias. Sturdy three-stage Perp W tower with big diagonal buttresses and square NE stair-turret. The tower arch seems to indicate an Early Perp date: on fat shafts with polygonal capitals ornamented with thin vertical leaves. Perp nave, S porch and chancel, stone-tiled. N aisle by *Ferrey & Son*, 1876. Their roofs and arcade dominate inside. C15 chancel arch with marks of a lost screen. – PISCINA. Ogee, C14. The finial has the strange spearhead points of the aumbry at Lovington. – FONT. Perp. Octagonal with leaves in quatrefoils. Panelled underside and stem. – PULPIT. 1632. With typical arches and flat scroll decoration. – MEMORIAL. Elizabeth Hext †1636. Incised slab. – STAINED GLASS. E window by *Clayton & Bell*, 1905.

By the churchyard N wall, a C14 GRAVE-SLAB with two eroded heads.

SE of the church, CHURCH FARM is Late Georgian, hip-roofed, in Lias with a little Ham stone. YEW TREE FARMHOUSE has a C16 rear wing with framed ceiling and Tudor-arched fireplace. The RED LION, C17–C18, faces W with twin thatched gables.

OLD RECTORY, ½ m. NW. 1840–1, reputedly by *Scott & Moffatt*. Large, asymmetrical Tudor-to-Elizabethan with ashlar bay windows. Early for the type.

BUSH FARM, ½ m. W. Late Georgian, hip-roofed, with chamfered corners and Gothic windows.

STANDERWICK FARM, Higher Foddington. Mid-C16, with Tudor-arched lights to mullion windows. Moulded framed ceiling and carved fireplace. Altered low late C15 N range. Traces of a moat.

BADGWORTH

ST CONGAR. Dedicated to Cyngar, the C5 Welsh saint who founded an abbey at Congresbury (N).* Four-stage W tower of Blue Lias. Angle buttresses only to the lower two stages, which are C14, cf. the continuous double-ogee and quadrant mouldings of the tower arch. Perp bell-stage (as late as 1575 if a date under the openwork parapet is related) with corner pinnacles. The NE stair-turret turns octagonal. Depressed-arched

---

* (N) indicates places covered by the companion *Buildings of England* volume, *Somerset: North and Bristol*.

w doorway, probably of 1704, the date in a blind third-stage window. Nave, short roughcast N aisle, and chancel, mostly early C14. Chancel rebuilt in 1864 with fancy tracery. Original chancel arch, double-chamfered with a continuous moulding; also the large tomb-recess (heavily restored). This has a cusped ogee arch with crockets and a finial; one fine original headstop. Also C14 the nave S doorway with quadrant mouldings. Oak DOOR with reticulated tracery. The two large corbels, a king and a queen, must have carried a porch gallery. But the porch is later as are the large Perp nave S windows, the second with IH and SAV inscribed in the stops. The N aisle takes us again to the early C14, with Dec two-light end windows (the W one blocked) and W doorway, all with cinquefoiled rere-arches, unusual in a doorhead. Perp flat-headed N window. The two-bay double-chamfered arcade is so crude that Pevsner could not accept it as medieval, but it is harder to accept his suggestion of the C17. The central pier is a cluster of polygonal shafts carrying a single heavy banded capital and the respond capitals are similar without the abaci. Arch-braced roof trusses. Nave roof, 1956, by *Alban Caröe*. Under the tower, wooden vault ribs on twelve little heads and four corner corbels. Early C19?

FURNISHINGS. FONT. C13. Plain bowl on a quatrefoil stem. – PULPIT. Early C17, large, densely ornamented, as at Wedmore (q.v.). Square panels below blank arches, each filled with a plant, notably the thistle. But it stands on a stone foot which is clearly Perp from a previous pulpit. None of the other surviving Perp pulpits in Somerset have a foot decorated in the costly way in which it is done here, with low-relief figures of the four Latin Fathers. The sculptural quality is indifferent. – BENCHES. Plain C16, the ends with thin finials, like Weare. – RAILS. Mid-C19, timber pierced like doilies. – STAINED GLASS. E window by *Kempe*, 1886. Crucifixion, in deep colours set off by pale gold quarries. More conventional W window, 1879, also by *Kempe*. – MONUMENTS. In the chancel floor, two medieval Lias slabs with foliate crosses, one with a lettered border to Jon de Hamtone, alive in 1312.

In the churchyard, a WAR MEMORIAL CROSS and some early C18 CHEST TOMBS. Lias panels between floral-ornamented ashlar piers.

By the church, the stuccoed early C19 former RECTORY. Downhill to the W, BADGWORTH GRANGE is Late Georgian, three bays, with a parapet.

BADGWORTH COURT, ¾ m. SE. Early and Late Georgian. Stripped of stucco, revealing a mix of brick and stone. Early Georgian five-bay S front with parapet and three-bay pediment. In 1820 a parallel rear range was added with twin bow-fronted projections. Also added was a pedimented brick piece to the E end with a stone Roman Doric four-column porch. A square-domed lantern lights the stair hall. Tuscan columns screen an open-well staircase with finely turned balusters and carved tread-ends.

BALTONSBOROUGH

St Dunstan. Dunstan was reputedly born at Baltonsborough in 909. All Perp. Plain rendered battlemented tower with a pyramid roof. The very large WEATHER VANE of scrolly ironwork is the best feature, of 1837 by a local blacksmith. Stone-tiled nave and chancel, restored in 1848. Ashlar-fronted porch with early C19 ironwork and a lantern. Traceried inner DOOR, C15, with original knocker. Panelled nave wagon roof, sub-panelled at the E end. Original bosses. The tower arch and chancel arch have two quadrant mouldings. The fleuron wall-plate and angels of the chancel roof are probably original. SEDILIA in the SE window, with two shields in cusped panels from a later monument. Ogee-cusped PISCINA with original colour, blue, white and red. – FONT. Perp with quatrefoils and one big rose in the panels. Flat C17 COVER. – PULPIT. Later C14 stone canted front, with heavy ogee blind tracery. – BENCHES. C16, moulded but not carved. Hinged on to one is a stool on Jacobean legs. – SCREENS. Late C19. On the tower screen are reused C17 rails. – REREDOS. 1870s, Gothic, with relief scenes and a malachite cross. – STAINED GLASS. E window, c. 1850, patterned, with roundels. Nave window (1892) by *Lavers & Westlake*, as are probably two others.

The base of the CHURCHYARD CROSS is medieval, the rest of after 1877. The GATEWAY to the field is a pretty feature, a pointed arch under an oval plaque dated 1820 or 1826. THE PARISH HOUSE (Landmark Trust) on the N is the church house of c. 1529, altered. Two little gables. Large ground-floor fireplace and long upper room divided by a C17 partition, under an economical wind-braced roof.

Three substantial Victorian buildings just outside the village. St Anne's, ¾ m. SE, was an Anglican convent school founded by the Neville-Grenvilles of Butleigh in the 1860s. Rear wing with a first-floor chapel reached by an octagonal stair-tower. Towards Ham Street, Orchard Neville, for the Neville-Grenvilles, c. 1850, C16 style with paired gables. Hillside House to the N, 1868, for William Austin, is more emphatically Victorian, asymmetrical, with shouldered gables. The Gothic former Moravian Chapel, near Orchard Neville, 1852, with a manse of 1858–9, was founded in opposition to the High Anglicanism of the Neville-Grenvilles.

Gatehouse, 1 m. W. Named for the Gatehouse family, here from 1698. The long thatched house is C15, enlarged in the C16 and C17. Mullioned windows of both C16 reserved-chamfer and C17 ovolo-moulded types. The E front, between unequal cross-wings, has an Elizabethan porch with Ionic pilasters, fluted frieze and steep pediment, to the r. of a three-light mullion-and-transom hall window. Similar rear window, and crude pedimented porch on Tuscan columns dated 1637. Moulded framed hall ceiling. The pedimented fireplace with Ionic pilasters has the knotted initials of Richard and Alice Walton, married in 1548.

BARFORD HOUSE see ENMORE

BARLINCH PRIORY

On the E bank of the Exe, NW of Dulverton.

ST NICHOLAS PRIORY at Barlinch or Barlynch was founded by William de Say for Augustinian canons in the time of Henry II. Its recorded history is slight. It had nine canons in 1524 and was dissolved before 1537. The position in the narrow valley is eminently picturesque but the ruins are too scanty to allow a mental reconstruction. W of the farmhouse is the most substantial fragment, a WALL with two broad plain buttresses on the S and two large window openings entirely robbed of ashlar; also two projections at the W end. This may be the S wall of the church, or the S side of a cloister court as at Cleeve. The attractive FARMHOUSE, in line with this, probably incorporates medieval work, but what is visible is late C16, with a large lateral chimney, extended E at a slight angle in the C17. C19 FARM BUILDINGS on three sides of the rear farmyard. In the S gable of the E range is re-set one fragment of tracery, enough to show that Barlinch shared the fine late C15 to C16 work of the churches to the W of Cleeve Abbey.* In the N wall, facing N, is a blocked four-centred arch. A further substantial WALL, a high two storeys without openings, is parallel to the N, behind the cottage called Barlynch. FISHPOND to the W, next to a leat.

BARRINGTON

ST MARY. A picturesque sight with its group of N transept, porch and octagonal crossing tower. Essentially C13, certainly the lower stage of the tower with its small lancets (the top with two-light bell-openings is C15) and the transepts with their corbel tables. The transept gable windows have roll-moulded late C13 tracery of three cusped lights, the outer lights under pointed trefoils which flank a large sexfoiled circle. Shafted reveals inside. The nave has plain parapets and Perp windows but the W wall is clearly earlier. Perp N porch with crocketed ogee terminal to the doorway and shafts of unfinished panelling above. Modest Perp chancel. S aisle, 1860–1, by *J. M. Allen*. Inside, the tower has double-chamfered arches without capitals, and squinches carry the octagon. Enormous Purbeck floor slab. Two broad squints. Renewed late C13 PISCINA in the S transept. Victorian roofs and arcade. – FONT. 1860. Also a

---

*The N aisle stonework at Huish Champflower is said to have come from Barlinch.

misshapen small octagon on a thin octagonal stem, undatable. – PULPIT. C19, wood. Medieval to C17 motifs. – STAINED GLASS. E window, 1874, designed by *J. F. Bentley*, the architect. Late Gothic-style Crucifixion. Side windows by *Kempe*, 1896–7. – MONUMENTS. Thomas Royse †1749. Incised Lias, notable for the vivid original colour. – John Royse †1767, incised with Father Time and scroll borders. – Francis Webb †1815, 'The Friend of Mankind'.

An extremely attractive VILLAGE of ochre stone cottages, many of them thatched. The church is halfway along the village street. A good number of houses are of C15–C16 origin. Going E, ROSE COTTAGE has a C16 timber-framed W end. THE KNAPP, roughcast, C15 originally, has a C16 framed ceiling. GLEBE HOUSE, 1710, ashlar-fronted, has mullioned gables. BUDDS FARMHOUSE, long and low, is C16–C17, and VICTORIA FARMHOUSE is an altered C15–C16 hall house. At the far end of the street, EASON HOUSE has a long front of ovolo-mullioned windows under conjoined hoodmoulds, dated as late as 1715. It faces the Gothic SCHOOL, 1848. W from the church, POUND COTTAGE, small and thatched, C17, stands in front of THE CROSS, late C16, now three cottages. Gothic former METHODIST CHAPEL, 1859. ALLENBURY COTTAGE was a C15 hall house. Further out, THE PRIORY looks Late Victorian, with shaped gables and mullion-and-transom windows. It conceals two former open halls at right angles, not originally joined. Arch-braced cruck trusses and crossed windbraces. C16 framed ceiling.

BARRINGTON COURT (National Trust). The Daubeney family were here from the C13, in a house recorded as having a gatehouse, chapel etc. It has been tempting to attribute the present house to the extravagant Henry Daubeney, created Earl of Bridgwater in 1538 and disgraced in 1541. But the evidence points to building in 1552–9 for William Clifton (†1564), a London cloth merchant, whose son was knighted, and grandson ennobled as Lord Clifton, a sequence as indicative as the Daubeneys' decline. The house is of exceptional architectural interest, and extremely attractive with its warm Ham stone walls covered with lichen and its skyline of gables with fantastically twisted finials and chimneys. It is of two main storeys with a third in the gables, the porch of three storeys with a fourth in the gable. It faces S, unusual among Tudor houses. The most remarkable thing is the almost complete symmetry of the front, on the E-plan generally considered an Elizabethan creation. Such symmetry is in line with Renaissance ideals even where, as here, it appears without Italian motifs. There are significant deviations: to the r. of the porch two four-light windows mark the great hall, whereas to the l. there is just one, and the stair-towers in the angles differ slightly, the l. one being wider to allow for the main staircase. The windows are mullioned and hoodmoulded with four-centred-arched lights. The principal ones have transoms. The porch and the fronts of the wings are strengthened by thin diagonal buttresses. The array of spiral finials is a link with earlier C16 houses like Brympton D'Evercy, Somerset, and Clifton Maybank, Mapperton, and Melbury, all in Dorset, where such pedestals carry heraldic beasts.

The rear of the house became the entrance front in the early C20 (the current entrance is on the E side). This N side is only fragmentarily symmetrical, the ends having gables of identical size and the centre a smaller dormer gable. But the l. gable has a garderobe projection and the intervening ranges have chimney-breasts neither evenly placed nor of equal size.

The interior is of interest mainly thanks to brought-in rather than original fittings, for Barrington Court was derelict before becoming the first country house acquired by the National Trust. A benefactor, Julia Woodward, gave £10,000 for the purchase in 1905, but the Trust at that time could barely afford repairs. Fortunately Col. Arthur Lyle of the Renfrew sugar-refining family, war-wounded and in search of somewhere to install his collection of C15–C17 woodwork, saw the house in 1915 and leased it from the Trust in 1920. Lyle was allowed free hand in re-creating the house. What was done between 1922 and 1925 by Lyle and his Scots architect *Edwin Forbes* (of *Forbes & Tate*) went far beyond repair, amounting to the creation of an idealized country-house estate: an image of seigneurial order, perhaps, after wartime chaos. In this respect the work to the house and its environs should not be separated from the working farm, productive gardens, staff cottages, and large houses for the farmer and agent.

The PLAN of the house is the one still current at Montacute in the 1590s, with a screens passage dividing the hall from buttery and service rooms. The wings contained the parlour (SE) and kitchen (SW). Unlike at Montacute, the principal staircase was on the service side, reached by a passage behind the buttery. Now to Col. Lyle's alterations. Frustratingly the provenance of his woodwork remains obscure, and much is skilful reproduction. The new STAIR HALL in the NE corner is roofed with a heavy C15–C16 moulded framed ceiling with bosses and deeply coved sides, said to come from Hereford or East Anglia. The oak staircase is based on at least one C17 newel from Scotland. Baronial electrolier by *Singer* of Frome, 1925. The garderobe of the removed first-floor chamber remains on the N wall. The GREAT HALL, while still to the medieval double height, is already flat-ceilinged. The lateral fireplace and close-studded minstrels' gallery are original. Much else is imported or new: rope-moulded ceiling beams and carved gallery beam from Italy, C16–C17 linenfold panelling, C15–C16 'parchemin' door panels. The SCREENS PASSAGE has a lovely N door by *Forbes* and a new Gothic arch to the BUTTERY, a convincing Jacobean room, although even the stone fireplace is imported, as are the Jacobean overmantel and panelling with typical blind arches and strapwork pilasters. Much of the woodwork is modern, to match the imported material. Forbes designed the cage-stair to the minstrels' gallery and porch-chamber, both rooms linenfold-panelled. The SMALL DINING ROOM is the most intense of Lyle's apartments. The early C16 screen of blind and glazed traceried panels allegedly formed the outer wall of an unidentified house at King's Lynn, Norfolk, whence also the honeycomb ceiling of wooden ribs in star patterns. Linenfold panelling with profile heads, largely modern. The CORRIDOR behind is panelled with (mostly modern) strapwork pilasters carrying squat figures. At the E end an original washing recess. At the W, late C17 imported carving over the door to the KITCHEN, which has a massive stone fireplace. One window sill here has C18 ashlar cream-scalders. The cage-stair in the SW stair-tower is Forbes's most delightful creation, its skeletal uprights subtly twisted. The SE LIBRARY has bland large-field panelling.

Upstairs, the SW BEDROOM has an original Tudor-arched fireplace beneath rustic plasterwork of the Judgment of Solomon in a cartouche framed by columns. William Strode, Shepton Mallet clothier, owned the house after 1623, and the plasterwork probably dates from his time. Of this period also the Jacobean corridor arch, and the elaborate painted stone fireplace in the GREAT CHAMBER, SE. This has columns, a fluted frieze, and a band of what may be carnations, under an overmantel with blocked pilasters and Strode heraldry. Over the S porch, a fielded-panelled room of c. 1700. Staircase of 1998 by *Philip Hughes* in the second stair-turret. Spectacular full-length LONG GALLERY in the attic, again with imported woodwork including charmingly crudely inlaid pilasters, one dated 1679.

W of the Court, and uncomfortably close, was a three-sided courtyard of brick farm buildings initialled WS (for William Strode). This was converted by *Forbes* into private apartments in 1922–5, renamed STRODE HOUSE. A rainwater head is dated 1674, but the only reliable detail is the handsome seven-bay S front of the early to mid C18. Ham stone paired depressed-arched doorways under a pedimented window, between three-bay former stables, each with a pedimented doorway between arched windows and three similar windows above. The W front is entirely Forbes's, with arched French windows and square windows above in a 1–3–1–3–1 rhythm. A new N service range closes the courtyard, which Forbes narrowed with lean-to corridors around an Italianate pool. The quality of the new work impresses. New and old are mixed, and the character is that Edwardian favourite, the age of Wren. The principal S room, the WREN ROOM, is lined with fine late C17 panelling supposedly from 'Wren's house in London'. Lush foliage carving frames a green marble bolection-moulded chimneypiece and its overmantel panel. It is all too good to be true. More panelling, rather simpler, in the 'William-and-Mary Room', SW, and 'Early Wren Room', E. The DINING ROOM, W, is Italian in response to two handsome C15–C16 hooded fireplaces, reportedly found by Col. Lyle being used as wartime barricades in an Italian railway station. Good C20 carved animal keystones around the walls. Conventional E staircase, but the S service stair has the intricacy of Forbes's staircases in the Court. In the paved COURTYARD, a rectangular island in a rectangular pool with C18 lead water-spouting cherubs on dolphins at the corners. On the N wall, a waterspout in a shell niche fills a Baroque stone basin. The surrounding architecture is comfortably English, with wooden cross-windows beneath sweeping tiled roofs.

Forbes's GARDEN plan of 1917 plan shows three enclosed gardens roughly within farmyard walls W and NW of Strode House, moated to the W and N. These were made with advice from *Gertrude Jekyll*.* The present low walls and bridged moat of the N forecourt were part of a large-scale layout of ancillary roads and buildings that *Forbes* designed in an English vernacular seen through French Beaux-Arts eyes. The drive runs directly N to a green in front of picturesque but formally symmetrical thatched COTTAGES. On the way it crosses a precisely axial drive terminated by hip-roofed mullioned houses, BEACHAMS to the E, for the agent, facing distantly COURT FARMHOUSE, for the farmer. Towards the farmhouse, on the S side, are garden and farm buildings, two large near-symmetrical groups separated by another drive running S. Both are in a relaxed vernacular style of sweeping tile roofs over walls of local marlstone. The four-gabled GARDEN BUILDINGS (gardeners' court, recessed garages, and laundry court) back on to a very large KITCHEN GARDEN. Notable in the garden are Ham stone gateways with excellent ironwork, and, at the SE corner, a charming gambrel-roofed SQUASH COURT. The second group, the FARM BUILDINGS, have stone central and outer gables, the latter with half-hipped overhangs. Linking these are tiled roofs over colonnades of concrete, a notable but relaxed modernity. Model farmyard behind. The boarded and thatched TEAROOMS were intended for Col. Lyle's model trains but used as kennels.

BARTON ST DAVID

ST DAVID. The tower in the angle between N transept and chancel is octagonal from the foot, an East English feature, now unique in Somerset.† It seems entirely Perp, rendered, with small Ham stone windows, but the church is much older, perhaps originally with a crossing tower. Norman N doorway with one order of columns and, in the arch, a lattice with pellets (cf. Kingweston). Medieval oak DOOR. The small

---

* Not done were parterres S and E of the Court and a more elaborate N forecourt.
† There was another at Keinton Mandeville.

transept arches must be C13, single-chamfered on shafts with plain moulded capitals. Matching chancel arch from *T. G. Jackson*'s restoration of 1872. His cusped chancel lancets with cinquefoiled rere-arches reproduce work of *c.* 1300. E window of three stepped lancets. Diminutive N transept between porch and tower with a C17 window. A long-demolished S transept was replaced on a much larger scale in 1894 by *E. Buckle*. Squint from tower to chancel. – PULPIT. C17, panelled, with simple guilloche moulding. – PAINTING. C18. King David with harp.

CHURCHYARD CROSS. C15. Eroded figure on the shaft, possibly St David.

LOWER CHURCH FARMHOUSE has a regular front with C17 mullioned windows, but is older. Framed ceiling and smoke-blackened trusses. HIGHER CHURCH FARMHOUSE is L-plan with C18 sash windows. To the E, a small Gothic SCHOOL, 1864, and at the SE edge, PEACOCK HOUSE, the former vicarage, 1853–4 by *C. E. Giles*.

MANOR HOUSE, Silver Street, ½ m. N. A substantial mullion-windowed house with uneven cross-wings. The small E wing is C16, to a main range remodelled in the C17 when the larger W wing was added. C17 mast stair about a massive post with solid oak treads, removed at the lower level. Moulded fireplaces in the W wing: C17 below, of C16 reserved-chamfer type above. This moulding also appears in one rear window, suggesting some reuse of parts.

BREADSTONE HOUSE, Silver Street. Dated 1692, yet showing nothing essentially beyond the Jacobean conventions. Symmetrical with ovolo-moulded mullioned windows and two tall dormer gables, these more typical of North Somerset.

TOOTLE BRIDGE, 1 m. NE. Spanning the River Brue, which is not large, on three tight arches with cutwaters.

BARWICK

In folded country cut by deep sandy hollow ways.

ST MARY MAGDALENE. C13 transeptal N tower, unbuttressed, with small paired cusped lancet bell-openings and parapet. The rest was remodelled in the C15.* The show side is the N aisle, with three-light windows enriched by buttresses, beasts and battlements. In 1489 the Abbess of Syon Abbey gave 40 shillings towards building what was probably this aisle. The S aisle was embattled at the same time, but the arcade is older and was gained by cutting through a yet older wall. Single-chamfered piers and arches, with crude caps on the inner faces

---

* At least six consecration crosses on the exterior. B. and M. Gittos.

only; C13 perhaps. The caps relate to the capitals of the round chancel arch. But the chancel is of 1885, by *Wilson, Willcox & Ames*, apart from the doorway from the tower, the arch of which is made from parts of a C14 grave-slab with foliated cross. – FONT. Circular, Norman. Broad flutes above a cable moulding. – BENCH-ENDS. Lively set, one dated 1533, probably by the same carver as those at East Lyng and those dated 1536 at Spaxton. One man shoots a bird, another climbs a tree; other motifs include a fox and goose, dogs hunting a rabbit, some charming birds and fabulous beasts. A few foliage motifs suggest the Renaissance. – STALLS. Made up of fragments, with some panels from a screen. – WALL PAINTING. Feet of a large standing figure (S aisle S). – PULPIT. Two tiers, blank arches below strapwork panels. Graffito date 1619. – MONUMENTS. Thomas Syme †1681, marble cartouche. – John Newman †1799, marble with fluted columns, by the same hand as the Newman memorial at Yeovil.

Down from the church, CHURCH COTTAGES, 1811, with Y-tracery windows, built as a schoolroom, and a hip-roofed former RECTORY, 1908. At the bottom, BARWICK FARMHOUSE underwent an unusually colourful late C18 refronting: buff brick, red brick dressings, and Ham stone for the windows and door. Pedimented centre. In the lower village, SCHOOL COTTAGES, a row with a gabled cottage each end, contemporary with the adjoining Gothic SCHOOL, 1840. Opposite, a three-storey FLAX MILL, *c*. 1810. COURT HOUSE, ¼ m. E, is of *c*. 1700, hip-roofed with characteristic bolection-moulded door and oval window. A nice rhythm of single and two-light mullioned windows in seven bays. At the S edge of the village are three pairs of the hoop-roofed COUNCIL HOUSES, 1928, designed by *Petter & Warren* (*see* Introduction, p. 82).

BARWICK HOUSE, ½ m. N. Neo-Jacobean in contrasted Yeovil and Ham stone, a remodelling of 1858 by *R. H. Shout* of the late C18 house of the Newmans. This was pedimented with Venetian windows to the centre and the pavilions. Shout added a storey topped with two pedimented features, raised the pavilions and introduced fancy Jacobean ornament. Most fanciful are the projection that masks the r. pavilion and the conservatory with splendidly barbaric strapwork. The cantilevered stone staircase inside is probably original.

What is extraordinary at Barwick is the PARK created by John Newman *c*. 1770–90. Its small serpentine lake issues from a semi-subterranean rockwork GROTTO, closely derived from the one at Stourhead, Wilts. The antechamber is domed and arched four ways – to the entrance, to the lake, to a dark vaulted pool to the r., and ahead to a broad Pantheon chamber lit from an oculus, with pairs of statue niches and a circular pool. Exotically named FOLLIES adorn the surrounding bowl of hills, at the compass points. JACK THE TREACLE EATER, E, is a rockwork arch carrying a cylindrical turret with short spire crowned by Mercury (his finger suggests the name). The ROSE TOWER, W, is a wonderfully slim spire with ball finial on a visually inadequate rockwork Gothic 'umbrella'. To the N the FISH TOWER, a thin rockwork cylinder with an ashlar cap ornamented with almost Art Nouveau plant tracery. Named for a fish vane, now gone. It was originally one of a pair. Finally, 1 m. S, a vertiginous rockwork OBELISK, leaning above the A37. Octagonal early C19 LODGE with Y-tracery.

KEY FARMHOUSE, ½ m. SSW. Late C17 hip-roofed E front with irregularly disposed mullioned windows. The house is older. At the N end a hip-roofed storeyed porch with Tudor-arched entry.

BATCOMBE

ST MARY. The tower is the dominating motif from any distance, not especially high at 87 ft (26.5 metres) but broad and very ornate. Money and stone were left for its construction in 1539, making it one of the last Somerset towers, with Chedzoy and Chewton Mendip (N). Of Doulting ashlar, it is without pinnacles and was apparently designed so. The effect is thus concentrated on the bell-stage. Angle buttresses with a square fillet between and a diagonal fillet to the main walls. The square fillet ends in a little pinnacle, above which the angle turns diagonal, between the detached panelled pinnacles which cap the buttresses. The buttresses have attached panelled pinnacles that finish level with the fillet finial. W doorway with a dragon and a hound in the spandrels and a splayed hoodmould, under a string course with headless angels, the middle angel carrying the Crown of Thorns. Four-light sub-arched W window. Above is a bare-legged Christ in a crudely canopied niche, flanked by hovering angels (as at Chewton Mendip), the top pair censing, the middle pair with Passion implements, the bottom pair carrying grave-cloths. The splendid bell-stage has no fewer than three tall two-light openings each with two transoms. The bottom panels are blank; those above have pierced baffles. Four diagonal shafts divide the openings, capped by finials below the parapet, which is pierced with cusped lozenges. Two canopied niches on the second tier of the S side. Polygonal NE stair-turret. Tall panelled tower arch with a band of angels for capitals. Fine fan-vault on corner shafts.

Aisle and clerestory parapets with pierced quatrefoils and pinnacles. The S aisle has two large flat-headed windows with cusped ogee lights, perhaps re-set from an earlier S wall. The N aisle has windows matching those of the clerestory and a polygonal rood-stair turret at the E end. The aisles slightly overlap the tower, but a date for these after 1540 seems improbable. Stone-tiled S porch dated 1629 with the initials of James Bisse, the doorway perhaps reused, but the pinnacled buttresses and stretched hoodmould certainly C17. Low and insignificant chancel with a domestic Elizabethan E window of three lights with a transom. Four-bay arcades of pointed arches on standard four-hollow piers. In the N aisle two low cusped ogee-headed C14 tomb-recesses. Good moulded and framed aisle ceilings, the N one on angel corbels. Nave roof of 1732 (once plastered), above original angel corbels. C19 chancel roof. Fragmentary black-letter text in the SE corner.

FURNISHINGS. FONT. 1844, copying a Perp original. Panels of alternating foliage and shields. The stem must have been older, with angle shafts. Also a large broken octagonal FONT from Spargrove chapel (dem. 1560), with Perp quatrefoils and a heavy base moulding. – CARVING. Eroded small Crucifixion, formerly a gable finial. – COMMUNION RAIL. Jacobean, with symmetrical balusters. – ROYAL ARMS. 1773. Lively and large, over the chancel arch originally between matching COMMANDMENT BOARDS. – CANDELABRA. 1737. Brass, one tier. – STAINED GLASS. C15 fragments in the chancel S window. E window by *A. K. Nicholson*, 1930. Three by *Heaton, Butler & Bayne*: SE and S, 1908, not inserted until 1929 because of disapproval of the divorced state of Captain Ernst (depicted as an elderly St George); NE, 1911. Two N windows by *Sally Pollitzer*, 2001 and 2010. – MONUMENTS. Archdeacon Philip Bisse †1613. Small brass, he kneeling at a prie-dieu. – James Bisse †1640 and family (death dates 1593–1681). Three panels under heraldry between coarse strapwork scrolls. – Mary Coward †1773. Signed *Ford*. Coloured marble in three tiers. The woman seated by an urn is stiff by comparison with the Ford monuments in Castle Cary and Ditcheat, so is probably by *John Ford Jun*. – Thomas Coward †1800, by *King*. Draped urn against an obelisk. – Amy Coward †1812. Draped urn above an oval plaque. By *Reeves & Son*.

N of the churchyard the former SCHOOL, 1842, probably by *Jesse Gane*. Tudor Gothic, with a parallel range of 1888. Nearby, the JUBILEE HALL, 2002.

W of the church is CHURCH FARM, late C16, L-plan, with reserved-chamfer mullioned windows in a formal front. Opposite is the former METHODIST CHAPEL, Gothic, 1868. Set into the hillside below, a radically modern HOUSE, 2012–13, by *Michael Brierley* of *NVB Architects*. Oval plan with a two-storey faceted glass front and sedum roof. BOX BUSH FARM is late C16, mullion-windowed, the chimney backing on the cross-passage. TRUNCHEON HOUSE was the police station. Mid-C19, 1–3–1 bays, the outer bays lower. ROCKWELL HOUSE has a colourwashed front with C17 mullioned windows embellished with very pretty cast-iron Gothic casements. Rear wings have disappeared within a hip-roofed five-bay Georgian garden front. Bracketed eaves rising in a pedimental central gable. BOORD'S HOUSE faces up the street. Thatched, early C17, with later windows. Mid-C19 N addition.

E of the church, BATCOMBE HOUSE, well set in hillside gardens, was the rectory, of 1788 by *John Gane*. Ashlar-fronted, of six bays, giving an uncomfortable pedimented two-bay centre with central pedimented doorway. Dormers in a mansard roof. Lofted STABLES with cupola, C18 and 1849. On the front the caduceus monogram of Dr Philip Bisse †1613. Kale Street continues E, with terraced cottages dated 1827 facing ELM HOUSE, a narrow house with late C18 architraves. All were associated with a silk mill.

SAITE FARM, ½ m. SE. A long late C17 mullion-windowed front of five plus two bays. Over the doorway a plaque with the Bisse arms. Buckler drew the house with a gabled dormer above this.

LOWER ALHAM FARM, 1 m. NW. Mid-C17, for James Ashe, clothier. Three-bay front of three-light mullion-and-transom windows.

ALHAM MILL, Higher Alham. A long two-storey range with pedimented doorway, converted in the C18 from an earlier mill. Outbuilding with Georgian Gothic paired windows.

SPARGROVE MANOR. *See* Westcombe.

BATHEALTON

ST BARTHOLOMEW. Rebuilt 1853–4 by *C. E. Giles*. Red sandstone, neatly detailed Dec, with W tower and N aisle. – FONT. Typically minute carving by *Henry Davis*. – STAINED GLASS. By *John Toms*. – MONUMENTS. Edward Sharpe †1673. Early C18 engraved brass. – Webber family, *c.* 1785. Pedimented beneath an obelisk, quite elegant.

BATHEALTON COURT. A mid-C19 enlargement for Archdeacon Moysey of an early C18 house. Tall front of 2–3–2 bays with hipped roofs, pedimented dormers, and balustraded pavilions. (Bolection-moulded stair-hall ceiling with shells and putti, over a staircase with twisted balusters.)

RIDGE FARMHOUSE, 1 m. N. C16–C17 with two panelled partitions, one under a carved cornice.

THE CASTLES, 1½ m. WNW. Prehistoric earthwork. The irregular oval, 230 by 140 yds (210 by 130 metres), has a steep E bank with an entrance. Elsewhere the builders used the scarp of the hill.

BATHPOOL

NE of Taunton, on the canal to Bridgwater.

ALL SAINTS. Now a house. 1897–8, chancel 1901. – STAINED GLASS. E window, 1903, by *Heaton, Butler & Bayne*.

Brick CANAL BRIDGES here and at HYDE, to the E, the latter prettily overlooked by the thatched C17 HYDE FARMHOUSE.

HYDE COTTAGE, just S, derelict, had early C17 plasterwork. Long brick BARN dated 1733 at REXHILL FARM.

BAWDRIP

ST MICHAEL. A C13–C14 cruciform church, of Blue Lias. The tall crossing tower rests on arches of *c.* 1300. It has cusped lancets and blind two-light Dec windows of the early C14 on alternate faces. The plain battlemented bell-stage with small cusped openings is rebuilt. Inside, the crossing is most impressive, on low double- and triple-chamfered arches of Ham stone on plain Lias piers. The E and S arches rest on small heads carrying stiff-leaf corbels, the W and N arches on larger heads of great perfection. An odd feature of the interior is the exposed staircase climbing the wall above the E arch of the nave to connect the staircase in the angle between nave and N transept with the upper storey of the tower. This must be part of the wholesale restoration of 1864–7 by *C. E. Giles*, during which the roofs were raised (lower roof-lines visible inside both transepts, and also corbel heads for ridge-beams). The tracery is all renewed but, if copied, indicates a C14 date. All four arms are wider than the tower. C14 S transept PISCINA with an ogee arch terminating in exaggerated spike topped by a bishop's head. The N transept was the de Bradney chantry from 1330. The restored tomb-recess is mid-C14 with openwork cusping, the points carved as heads. The Ham stone EFFIGY of a knight may be Stephen de Bradney †1375. – STAINED GLASS. Chancel, early C20, by *Hardman*. S transept, *c.* 1855. – MONUMENT. Knott family, early C19. Draped urn on a curved-fronted pedestal.

Little in the village. To the NE, facing the embankment of the former Somerset & Dorset Railway, TUDOR COURT FARMHOUSE, 1532, is modernized. C16–C17 framed ceilings and rare painted decoration: floral trail, texts, and figures including the Prodigal Son. Further out, BARKERS FARMHOUSE, dated 1705 in a plaster wreath, and KINGS FARMHOUSE, 1650, roughcast with E cross-wing.

KNOWLE HALL, 1 m. NW. 1829–33, for Benjamin Greenhill, by *Richard Carver*, probably his largest country house. Blue Lias, Tudor-style, still with Georgian symmetry and uncertain period detail. Seven bays and three gables, the windows close-spaced with hoodmoulds. Triple Tudor arches screen a curving cantilevered staircase.

BRADNEY HOUSE, 1 m. SW. Hip-roofed Lias villa dated 1837. Typical deep eaves.

HORSEY MANOR FARM, 1½ m. W. Long and rendered. Early C19 sash windows disguise a medieval to C17 house with two good framed C16 ceilings. Horsey was a medieval village.

MORRISON DISTRIBUTION CENTRE, 2 m. W, by the motorway. 2010–12, by *DLA* of Wakefield. Vast flat-roofed complex clad in long panels of varied greens, inspired it is said by woven willow. Surprisingly it works as camouflage.

BAYFORD see WINCANTON

BEERCROCOMBE

3020

ST JAMES, isolated E of the village. Rendered Perp W tower with polygonal SE turret. A small two-light window below the W bell-light and the double-chamfered tower arch on two frog-footed monsters suggest early C14 origins. The nave has Perp S windows and one C13 N lancet. Remnant of a late C14 N tomb-recess, just the jambs. Rere-arches of the S windows on angels. The panelled roof looks C17. Nave restored in 1897 by *J. H. Spencer*. Chancel rebuilt 1876. – PULPIT. early C17, with fish-like scrolled creatures in the frieze (cf. Ashill). – BENCHES. Plain C16. – TOWER SCREEN. Reused tracery from a rood screen. – ROYAL ARMS. 1762, overpainting 1660. – ORGAN. early C19, domestic. – STAINED GLASS. E window, *c.* 1855.
By the church, the gabled RECTORY, by *Spencer*, 1893–4, and, just E, the derelict CHARD CANAL, 1842.

BERROW

2050

Continuous coastal development N from Burnham.

ST MARY. Against the dunes. Of Blue Lias. The three-stage W tower has diagonal buttresses and Perp two-light bell-openings with pierced baffles. Heavy battlements and higher square NE turret. The S aisle is Perp, embattled with three-light windows. But the church is C13: see the double-chamfered chancel arch, the inner order on moulded round capitals on short corbelled shafts. The chancel S doorway is C13 too, with a continuous roll moulding. The chancel windows are renewed or new (restorations by *G. P. Manners* in 1843–4 and *J. H. Spencer* in 1885). The E window with intersecting tracery and ballflower arch, if reliable, is early C14. Inside, curved Georgian nave ceiling and low five-bay arcade on standard Perp four-hollow piers. Defaced niche, N, with lacy frill to a curved arch, probably C16. – FONT. C14–C15, very like that at Brean. Octagonal, with paired fleurons above thick ribs curving in to the stem. Also a C13 bowl of unusual quatrefoil shape. From where? – CROSS-HEAD. C15–C16, with the Crucifixion on one side, the Virgin on the other, between praying figures. – BEAM. From a lost W gallery. Inscription of 1637. – PULPIT. Early C17. The usual short blank arches in two tiers, the angles treated as big fluted pilasters. – READERS' DESKS. C20, made up of panels similar to those on the pulpit, one dated 1631. – ROYAL ARMS. 1667. – STAINED GLASS. E window, 1890, colourful and pictorial. Two excellent Arts and Crafts windows by *Arnold Robinson*, with subtle colours on opaque glass, SE of 1913, N war memorial, 1921. W window, 1970, by *Geoffrey Robinson*. Much more attractive his clear glazing of the chancel, 1974. – MONUMENT. Rev. Joseph Durston †1770. White and grey marble, open pediment with egg-shaped urns.

In the churchyard, two badly eroded C14 EFFIGIES of a civilian and lady.

Inland from the church a few of the brick Late Georgian houses typical of this part of the county. The largest, MANOR HOUSE (Manor Close), has later C19 fenestration. The OLD RECTORY and MARSH FARMHOUSE have parapets, stone window heads and cornices.

BICKENHALL

The church is isolated W of the village, where the medieval churchyard survives.

ST PAUL (village hall). 1848–9, by *P. C. Hardwick*. Minimal lancet Gothic.*

BICKNOLLER

ST GEORGE. All Perp. The red sandstone tower, with diagonal buttresses, battlements and two-light bell-openings, is late C14; from the triple-wave tower arch. Higher square NE stair-turret. Like others in this valley, the church was enlarged with an ornate Late Perp aisle, here on the N side. The original short nave and chancel are of variegated local stones, the S side embellished when the N addition was made with a high porch and battlements pierced with quatrefoils. The porch has a gable parapet and lively corner animals. One flat-headed four-light nave S window has the strange stilted cusping found at Watchet. The chancel was given a similar gable parapet to the porch, with a canopied niche. Both of its S windows have supermullions and finely detailed tracery, presumably C16. The five-light E window has uncusped top lights as in the N aisle. Blocking at the foot of each light decorated externally with a quatrefoil containing a shield or rosette was no doubt because of a former reredos.

---

* Perp font in the Museum of Somerset, other pieces at Staple Fitzpaine.

The N aisle is of red ashlar with three-light windows of Ham stone between the buttresses. Battlements with pierced quatrefoils and high gable parapets. The piers of the five-bay arcade are of the four-wave section with well-carved capitals of the Devon type, i.e. in bands with foliage. The chancel arch, like the tower arch, is C14, and of red sandstone, in contrast to the arcade. On each side of the chancel is a shelf under a broad four-centred arch with traceried spandrels, one perhaps an Easter Sepulchre, but what of the other? Barrel roofs from the restoration by *J. D. Sedding*, 1871–2; some nave bosses reused.

FURNISHINGS. FONT. 1872. A copy of the C15 one. – SCREEN. C15–C16, said to have come from Huish Champflower in 1726. Of the same workshop as Carhampton, Minehead and Dunster, with four-light sub-arched tracery, rib-vaulted coving with tracery in the panels, and undercut foliage bands above. The leaf-scroll borders to the openings, a common feature of the group, are also seen at Halse and Combe St Nicholas. – BENCHES. Early C16, straight-headed and excellently detailed. Most have close tracery and typical wiry plants with flowers and fruit, but no Renaissance detail. Two sets are differentiated by width, and a third by broad leaf-scroll borders (cf. Trull). Five of 1932, with saints and local scenes. – PILLAR PISCINA. The sole evidence of a Norman church. With a cable moulding. – FITTINGS. A good set of 1930 by *W. H. Randoll Blacking*, dark-stained with linenfold panels: pulpit, organ and screens, stalls, and rails. – STAINED GLASS. In the chancel, mid-C20 glass, typically on clear backgrounds. E window, 1946 by *Christopher Webb*; less good than his N window, 1931, with particularly refined drawing. One S window, 1936 by *Martin Travers*, has great charm. The other, 1919, thick with detail, shows what Webb and Travers reacted against. W window by *Margaret Rope*, 1952. Medieval fragments in the chancel. – MONUMENT. John Sweeting †1688. Painted pilaster-framed oval with rustic angels on the pediment scrolls.

In the churchyard a tall CROSS on a C14–C15 stepped base, the top renewed.

The core of the village is roughly square N of the church, which may represent a medieval layout. In Church Lane, OLD COURT, long with many iron casements, is C17, to a lobby-entry plan. No. 4, probably C16, is roughcast, with undulating thatch and a lateral chimney. A diversion S, on Trendle Lane, finds WAYVILLE FARM, long, roughcast, with C16 lateral chimneys. Windows and flat chimney tops from an Arts and Crafts enlargement of 1904 by *Charles Greswell*, engineer, for himself. C16 cross-passage partitions. Arts and Crafts staircase with tapering newels under moulded caps. Returning N, HARCOMBES is thatched, C17–C18. Dashwoods Lane descends W past COMBE COTTAGE, late C17, thatched. GATCHELLS, limewashed, contains a C15 hall.

GREAT HILLCROFT, Hill Lane, against the hillside. 1925–6 by *Charles Holden*. A larger version of Willoughby Cleeve, Holford (q.v.). Similar severe outline, here in the local hard red sandstone, under a long roof of graded slates, slightly bellcast at the eaves. The gables slate-hung. Matching rear wing, the brick chimney linked by an arch to one on the main range. Simple small-scale interiors.

FORD, ¼ m. sw. c16, thatched and whitewashed, with a particularly imposing lateral chimney.

TRENDLE RING, ½ m. E. A Late Bronze Age or Early Iron Age earthwork enclosure on the steep Quantock side. There is almost no flat ground for settlement within the ring, but the site was clearly important, as another earthwork further up the hill signals its location to those approaching from the E.

WOOLSTON. *See* Sampford Brett.

BIDDISHAM

Down a secluded lane in the levels of the River Axe.

ST JOHN BAPTIST. The leaning lower stage of the small W tower, unbuttressed, and with an unmoulded tower arch, may be C13. More probably it is minimal work of the C14–C15. The bell-stage of 1878 corrects the lean, to comic effect. The rest was heavily restored in 1863. S DOOR with Jacobean low-relief decoration. – FONT. Square, Norman, with three scallops each side, on the E with rosettes or leaves. – PULPIT. C17, with narrow panels, lozenges below arches. – STAINED GLASS. Good E window, *c.* 1870, Crucifixion, on deep blue. – CHURCHYARD CROSS. Late C14 base and tapered shaft.

By the church, in grey Mendip stone, the former SCHOOL, 1859, with triple lancets, more sternly Gothic than usual, and the former RECTORY, 1858, free of period detail, a hip-roofed front on a steep-roofed rear. Both by *Valpy & Gibbs* of London. MANOR FARMHOUSE has a seven-bay ground floor with drip-course, and five-bay upper floor inconsistently aligned. C17, remodelled in the C18.

BISHOP'S HULL

ST PETER AND ST PAUL. Remarkable N porch-tower of four stages, the top three octagonal (cf. Podimore). It dates in its lower parts from the C13: see the doorway with continuous double-chamfer and the small lancets of the second stage. Blank stage above. Perp battlemented top with two-light bell-openings. NW vestry with reused C13 two-light window. The rest was brutally treated in 1826 by *Richard Carver*, who demolished the nave and S aisle to make the barn-like nave which the age favoured. Broad stuccoed W front with Tudor-arched wooden windows, and triple-arched porch (rebuilt 1956). But the chancel and its flanking chapels, datable to 1523–30, are surprisingly intact, and Carver reused two three-light Perp s windows with nice cusping and a moulded W doorway. His nave is broad and light, with a WEST GALLERY (side galleries went in 1923) and some BOX PEWS. The SE chapel and chancel have not particularly well formed four-centred Perp arches. Better is the arch between them, shafted with simple capitals, and better again are the two to the NE chapel, with angel capitals as at St Mary Magdalene, Taunton. Panelled Perp roofs. In the NE chapel two grotesque CORBEL HEADS, perhaps C14, and two angel corbels, one dated 1530. The SE chapel became a family pew, hence the fireplace.

FURNISHINGS. FONT. C15, from St Mary Magdalene, Taunton. Heavy, octagonal, with quatrefoils. – PULPIT. Reusing C16 plant-trail panels from the rood screen. – BENCH-ENDS. Several C16 examples with the leaf-scroll border characteristic of *Simon Werman* (*see* Trull). Tracery or plant-trail decoration; the keys of St Peter also depicted.* – STAINED GLASS. Medieval fragments in several windows. E window, *c.* 1860, unsophisticated. – MONUMENTS. George Farewell †1609. Very lavish, of Derbyshire alabaster. In gown and ruff, he reclines on one elbow under a coffered arch on squat piers. Broad strapwork surrounds the back inscription. On the tomb-chest, his wife under an arch with kneeling children l. and r., these carved exceptionally beautifully. – Sir George Farewell †1647 and wife †1660, rustic classical with little cherubs recumbent on a curved pediment. – Mary Farewell †1697. Even more rustic classical, with out-turned pediment scrolls. Beneath is a small niche of 1676 with two girls and an infant piled rather on top of each other; the children of Edmund Fowell. – Rev. James Upton †1749. Rococo cartouche on a drape. – William Crotch †1847, composer.

CONGREGATIONAL CHAPEL. 1718, remodelled 1883. Stuccoed, with fancy Victorian wooden tracery to ogee-headed windows.

TAUNTON DEANE CREMATORIUM, Wellington New Road. 1962–3, by *Potter & Hare*. In well-planted grounds. Luminous chapel, glass-walled towards an enclosed garden, with a prow-like stone front cut by full-height glazed slots. Tall slim piers carry a folded timber ceiling. The slots have blue-green STAINED GLASS by *Geoffrey Clarke*, who made the ALTAR FITTINGS. Separate circular MEMORIAL CHAPEL, stone, lit from under the eaves.

MANOR HOUSE, NE of the church. Grand E-plan Elizabethan house, the four-storey gabled porch dated 1586, with the Farewell arms above an arch flanked by good fluted Ionic columns. Elaborately carved and panelled door. The mullion-and-transom windows, an early occurrence of ovolo moulding, are disposed with complete symmetry. *J. H. Spencer* in 1901 found

---

* Two bench-ends in the Museum of Somerset depict a night watchman, and Christ stepping from the tomb, with the Pelican below; cf. Hatch Beauchamp.

evidence that the porch was an addition, but the dates must be very close. Altered interiors.

The village street winds uphill from the church past cottages of 1912 and the C18 OLD INN. LAUREL HOUSE, roughcast with thick early C18 glazing bars, adjoins the chapel (*see above*). Opposite, two Georgian brick houses, BRAMDEAN, late C18, with parapet, and BISHOP'S HULL HOUSE, slightly earlier, five bays, double-pile. NE of the church, the Manor House (*see above*) and HAYDON HOUSE, dated 1666, roughcast. Netherclay runs N from the church past NETHERCLAY HOUSE. Late Georgian, stuccoed, with an ashlar three-bay columned porch. On the River Tone beyond is BRIDGE MILL, painted brick, *c.* 1800.

LONGALLER MILL, ¾ m. NW. Roughcast brick, 1823. Re-equipped in 2010 with an undershot wheel.

BARR HOUSE, 1 m. WNW. Victorian rendered fronts under bracketed eaves, but the rear is early C18 brick with a hip-roofed stair between rear wings. C18 brick BARN and cottage.

UPCOTT, 1 m. WSW. UPCOTT MANOR is early C18, brick, 2–3–2 bays, with ashlar channelled pilasters, cornice and pilastered doorcase. Stone hall chimneypiece with bold consoles; panelled room with Corinthian pilasters. UPCOTT HOUSE, a long C17–C18 brick farmhouse, has a short Late Georgian rendered front with parapet.

RUMWELL, 1 m. SW. RUMWELL PARK, 1855, is Italianate, with shallow outer gables and heavily framed ashlar windows. RUMWELL HALL, 1805–10, may have been altered in the mid C19. Three-storeyed, stuccoed and hip-roofed with tripartite sash windows. Elegant four-column pedimented porch. On the lane running N, an early C19 TERRACE with Georgian Gothic windows.

BISHOP'S LYDEARD

ST MARY. The splendid four-stage W tower is one of the best of an outstanding group of Somerset towers built around 1500. Taunton St James, Isle Abbots, Kingston St Mary and Staple Fitzpaine share the ascending hierarchy of decoration. Red sandstone ashlar with Ham stone. Angle buttresses carry three tiers of attached pinnacles and large diagonally set finials against the bell-stage, a counterpoint set up by smaller finials in the corner fillets. Tall first stage, the W door in a square-headed frame beneath a broad transomed five-light window. Both second and third stages have a two-light window on each side, and canopied statue niches add ornament to the prominent E and S faces of the third stage. Then the bell-stage blossoms with paired three-light openings, each with a transom and pierced baffles between a trio of slim pinnacles. Long-legged beasts support the crown, which has corner and

BISHOP'S LYDEARD

intermediate pinnacles rising through pierced battlements (quatrefoils and arcaded merlons). Tiny pinnacles around the NE stair-turret complete the array. The tall tower arch is wave-moulded, not panelled as one would expect at this date. The contemporary S aisle and chapel are also faced in red ashlar, embattled, with battlemented large porch and polygonal rood turret. The modest chancel, which projects one bay further, was rebuilt in 1859–60 by *C. E. Giles*, who also rebuilt the N aisle, adding the NE chapel.

The interior is a wonderful unity of architecture and woodwork enhanced by colour judiciously applied by *Ninian Comper* from 1923. Four-bay arcades of standard four-hollow piers with round caps to the shafts. The N arcade is much lower than the S, which could indicate an earlier arcade reshaped to conform. Broad chancel arch of similar section. Wagon nave roof with lozenge bosses and a panelled CELURE over the screen, the panels with diagonal crosses, the bosses including heraldry and initials IB. *Comper* coloured the celure and bosses, the C15 screen, C16 bench-ends, and the C17 pulpit, and these are a prelude to his own work in the chancel, startlingly gold. He whitened the Victorian roof to enhance his E window, which is set in a gilded reveal painted with seraphim, the effect Byzantine. Above, shining gold, hangs a great square CANOPY painted with a radiating Pentecostal dove. This overhangs an 'English' altar, with curtains on blue and gold RIDDEL-POSTS carrying gilded angels. On the N, a beautifully lettered board, like a hatchment, is the WAR MEMORIAL. Behind the screen, L-plan STALLS and kneelers.

OTHER FITTINGS. FONT. Octagonal, with unusual shallow geometric patterning. C14? – ROOD SCREEN. Remarkably complete, early C16, across both nave and S aisle. Four-light pointed tracery, sub-arched, with ogee-headed lights, under a ribbed coving with numerous bosses. The layered cornice has fine undercut friezes and a rare inscription band (the Creed). *Comper* added the rood figures in 1948. – PULPIT. Early C17. More intense than usual, the arched panels larger, framing giant thistles or flowers, the upper panels with winged cherub heads. – BENCH-ENDS. An extensive early C16 set. Square ends with predominantly tracery and wiry twisted plants, no Renaissance touches. Scattered images include a windmill, a ship, a pelican, a stag, rabbits, a green man, and the Five Wounds. Good frontals and dorsals. – STAINED GLASS. E window, 1924, and SE, 1938, by *Comper*; lucid drawing in clear colours. The sequence to Comper illustrated by two N windows by *Powell's*, 1899 and 1903, in muted Arts and Crafts colours, contrasting with numerous windows in the dominant blues and reds of the 1860s by various makers, the SW one possibly by *Alexander Gibbs*. In the vestry, some good medieval fragments. – MONUMENTS. Nicholas Grobham †1585 and wife †1594. Brass with kneeling figures. A cherub blows bubbles. – John Periam †1753 and Elizabeth Periam †1767. Yellow and white, obelisk on sarcophagus. – Emma Peachy †1809. Draped urn with verse by W. L. Bowles. – Slocombe family to 1811. Two women by an urn, a copy of one by *Thomas King* in Langford Budville. – Harriett Lethbridge †1826. Hope and her anchor, also a scythe and flowers, already Victorian motifs.

Unusual C15 CHURCHYARD CROSS. The panels of the octagonal base have eroded Apostles in pairs and Christ (twice). On the shaft, a canopied John the Baptist. Another cross, the MARKET CROSS, moved here in the C19, is a sorry pile. Detached eroded head with figures.

One long winding village street. N from the churchyard are ALMSHOUSES built by Sir Richard Grobham in 1616, extended 1854. Tudor-arched doorways and original armorial panel. Poor C20 windows. Beyond is the former CONGREGATIONAL CHAPEL, early C19, with cast-iron latticed lancets. Returning S, down a lane is the former VICARAGE, 1914–15 by *H. C. Benson* of London (killed 1915). Red sandstone with coved eaves and leaded windows, the style of *c.* 1700. The thatched OLD FORGE is an altered C15 hall house, with jointed crucks. SCHOOL of 1872, with arched windows in triplets, and a gabled piece set back at each end. Some distance S, WARRE HOUSE is late C17 with a Regency addition, all thatched. No. 44, on the corner of Mill Lane, is C16–C17, thatched, with lateral rear chimney. Down Mill Lane, BISHOP'S LYDEARD MILL, early C19, the mill and roughcast house under one hipped roof. Restored in 2003, the machinery turned by a 13-ft (4-metre) wheel. On Gore Square are FARRINGDON, thatched, C16–C17, and the LETHBRIDGE ARMS, roughcast with Regency sash windows. Behind is an impressive early C19 FIVES WALL, brick-faced with diagonal buttresses and curved top.

LYDEARD HOUSE, West Street. A fine show across the fields behind handsome balustraded walls. Built *c.* 1740 for John Coles, attorney, in contrasting red sandstone and Bath stone; 2–1–2 bays, divided by quoins, the narrow centre with a rusticated oval in the pediment. The architraves are corniced above, pedimented below. Early C19 porch on paired Ionic columns. Plain rear range of 1787–8 continued W in the C19 to link to an C18 storeyed archway to the stable yard. Good cobbled paving.

LYNCHFIELD HOUSE (Dunkirk Memorial House), ¼ m. SW. Three-bay stuccoed villa of *c.* 1800. Large almshouse-style courtyard in brick with tall chimneys, 1993–4, for the British Legion.

STATION, ½ m. SW. 1862, for the West Somerset Railway. Small sandstone station, brick engine shed and two bargeboarded stone houses.

WATTS HOUSE (Cedar Falls), ½ m. NW. 1829–32, for Charles Winter. A square villa in red sandstone with ashlar columned porch and timber eaves cornice. Greatly extended behind and to the r. after 1902 by *F. W. Roberts* in matching style. Two panelled Edwardian rooms, one neo-Jacobean with animals in the plasterwork, the other with vine-trail plastered beams.

SANDHILL PARK. *See* Ash Priors.

BLACKFORD
3 m. E of Sparkford

ST MICHAEL. Humble W tower with Perp bell-stage and C17–C18 battlements. The base is C14 with double-chamfered tower arch on bold corbels, a grotesque and a female. Otherwise Perp windows, renewed in 1880. Norman S doorway with chevron arch on colonnettes with scalloped capitals and decorated shafts, one with chevron, the other with spiral fluting. Outer arch of small lozenges. On the E impost is incised WM10.IMP. Perp moulded chancel arch, triple-shafted. NE rood stair. Corbels for the rood beam. – FONT. Massive C12 tub. Double ring at the rim, single one below. – SCREEN. 1917, by *F. Bligh Bond*. – PULPIT. C17, narrow, with reeded panels rather than the usual arched ones. – SCULPTURE. From a C15 alabaster reredos, torsos of St Michael and Christ Crucified. – STAINED GLASS. E window, 2002, by *John Hayward*. The Good Shepherd in grey on green, yellow and blue. C15 shields in the chancel.

Village largely of local Maperton stone. E of the church, the former RECTORY, hip-roofed, 1830s, and then two farmhouses amid handsome outbuildings, WEST HALL of 1883 and EAST HALL, rebuilt in 1670, formally symmetrical with ovolo-moulded mullioned windows. Staircase with thick rail. On Chapel Lane, NW, CHAPEL COTTAGE, thatched, the E half C15 with four-centred-arched doorway and rear stair-turret.

BLACKFORD
2 m. W of Wedmore

HOLY TRINITY. 1823, by *Richard Carver*. One of the more interesting Georgian Gothic experiments in the county. A stuccoed octagon with an ogee-capped cupola, Y-traceried windows with four-centred heads, an ashlar porch, and short transepts. Chancel rebuilt by *P. H. Thomas*, 1921. Octagonal ribbed ceiling. Carver's fittings are dismantled apart from one GALLERY.

HUGH SEXEY SCHOOL, Wedmore Road. 1897–9, founded as a trade school from Sexey's School, Bruton. Similar buildings, perhaps like the Bruton school by *George Skipper*; slightly Jacobean, with a pedimented centrepiece and lantern.

Opposite the church, a small hip-roofed SCHOOLROOM, 1817–18, with patterned glazing. Up Church Street, YEW TREE HOUSE is C17, with a Regency shop window and SW addition of *c.* 1830. Towards Wedmore, a very Gothic former BOARD SCHOOL, 1877–9. Towards Mark, WEST END FARM possibly encases a medieval hall.

TOTNEY FARM, 1 m. WSW. Blue Lias farmhouse of *c.* 1830. Three storeys, with hoodmoulded windows.

BLACKMORE FARM see CANNINGTON

BLUE ANCHOR

A very modest seaside resort developed behind the small STATION of 1872 on the Minehead Railway. Brick platform building and SIGNAL BOX of 1904. On the beach, an INFANTRY POST, 1940, one of the early coastal defences, hastily built of rough concrete.

MARSHWOOD FARM, ¼ m. S. Probably built by George Luttrell for his son in the early C17. Long and whitewashed with Georgian leaded windows, apart from the storeyed porch, which has Ham stone-mullioned windows over a Jacobean arched doorway. In the porch are re-set two former overmantels. Coarse strapwork encloses Old Testament figures in C17 dress. One scene shows Abraham and Isaac in a small octagonal panel; the other, an elongated oval, shows Naboth being stoned while Ahab ploughs the stolen vineyard. This complex scene resembles most nearly the Triumph of Time at Binham Grange, Old Cleeve (q.v.). In the back parlour another overmantel with the Luttrell arms between two naked male half-figures holding halberds. Barrel ceilings upstairs, the end lunettes decorated with floral scroll. In one lunette are small figures of deer and a central naked male, in the other, a fish in an oval panel. In this second room is an overmantel with heraldry of a Luttrell–Popham wedding of 1621 between small female figures holding ribands that tie bundles of fruit to the strapwork background. The detail is typical of *Robert Eaton* of Stogursey.

BOSSINGTON

METHODIST CHAPEL. 1894–5 by *Foster & Wood*. Pretty, and cheap at £244. An Arts and Crafts sensitivity shows in the varied colours: sandstones against brick-faced buttresses, and red tile roof. The roof is hipped over a vestry with off-centre circular chimney. Tiny pyramidal lantern.

Bossington, memorably set under Bossington Hill, was part of the Holnicote estate (*see* Selworthy), with C16–C17 COTTAGES typically altered by raising roofs and giving the lateral chimneys circular stacks. KITNORS, in the middle, is the least altered, long, yellow-washed, with a bread oven on the lateral chimney. Several more lateral chimneys down the street. The other way, towards the sea, passes a six-bay LINHAY next to Nos. 3–4, yellow-washed and thatched with two Holnicote chimneys at one end. Finally, LOWER HOUSE is C16–C17, thatched, L-plan. On Bossington Beach, two boulder-studded PILLBOXES, as at Porlock Weir, and a large C19 LIMEKILN.

BOWER HINTON

A linear village of C19 terraces interspersed with substantial C17 Ham stone houses typical of Martock, from which it continues without a division.

UNITED REFORMED CHURCH. Congregational chapel of 1791. Hip-roofed with large pointed windows, each with stone mullions and transom. End gallery on iron columns. Gothic schoolroom, 1866–8.

The lower village, HURST, is particularly rich in C17 houses. HURSTBOW BRIDGE has been rebuilt, preserving cast-iron panels of 1848 from *Murch*'s foundry, Bridgwater. On the l. are HURST HOUSE, with C18 mullioned windows in architraves, HURST LODGE, with C17 mullions and continuous dripcourse, and ORCHARD HOUSE, Late Georgian brick, but inside a C16 moulded framed ceiling and medieval roof. Opposite, Nos. 9–11 have one of the showy C17 canted bays under corbelled gables typical of this region. HURST BARTON was raised and extended in the mid C18. Jointed crucks, a C16 fireplace and framed ceiling, and mid-C18 chimneypieces show the evolution. Three-storey early C19 WOOL STORE behind. More mullion-windowed houses before GOGSPOOL HOUSE, which has a similar (but grander) corbelled and gabled bay to that at Nos. 9–11. Opposite, HURST MANOR, dated 1828, has arched windows to both floors and a parapet.

BOWER HINTON rises gently past the chapel (*see* above). THE HOLLIES is of two C17 phases, the l. earlier, with heavy chamfered beams. Down Middle Street, HIRSTS FARMHOUSE, thatched, has a particularly handsome C17 ashlar front with canted bay. At the top of Back Lane, BROAD HINTON FARMHOUSE has early C17 dormer gables. Heavily moulded sixteen panel ceiling. A smoke-blackened cruck (removed) indicated beginnings as a medieval hall house. OUTBUILDING with C19 cast-iron windows. Higher Street returns past HINTON HOUSE, a sharply detailed ashlar Regency villa, and HIGHER BARTON, long and mullion-windowed. Back on the main road, BOWER HOUSE has another gabled canted bay, dated 1632 on a plaster panel upstairs. Winged female demi-figures and dragons.

PARRETT WORKS, 1 m. W. A remarkably advanced industrial complex of 1855, combining flax-processing and engineering. The four-storey flax mill was of partial fireproof construction, because George Parsons's previous mill had burnt in 1854. Iron columns and beams, iron roof structure, and iron winding stair encased in a brick cylinder. The side range above the waterwheel faced PARRETT HOUSE, where Parsons lived, so was embellished with C18 cornicing and mullioned windows from Hele Manor, South Petherton, then being demolished. On the roof was a water tank for fire-fighting, the water dispersed down the shaft of the winding stairs. Exceptionally wide (10-ft 6-in.; 3.2-metre) breast-shot waterwheel. Italianate chimney

Bower Hinton, Parrett Works, bird's-eye view.
Engraving, c. 1865

behind, added for steam-powered looms in 1865. Other buildings were finishing sheds, engineering workshops, and a long twine-walk. Complex water management involving the diversion of the River Parrett. Parsons's enterprise failed in 1868.

BRADFORD ON TONE

On a bluff above a narrow C14 BRIDGE, of two double-chamfered pointed arches.

ST GILES. Perp W tower with stair-turret placed centrally on the show side (cf. Wellington and West Buckland). Diagonal buttresses up to heavy diagonal pinnacles. Simple two-light bell-openings with transoms. The tall triple-chamfered tower arch is probably Perp (cf. West Buckland). Perp embattled aisles and chapels. But the three-bay arcades are of c. 1300, double-chamfered on circular piers, as are the broad chamfered chancel arch and chancel S lancet. The chapels match externally but have different arches to the chancel, the S with Devon leaf-scroll band capitals, the N with standard Somerset detail. Roofs of 1858–9. – FONTS. One Victorian. Also a shallow octagonal bowl (cut down?) on a tapered stem and spurred C13 base. – PULPIT. C18, from St Mary Magdalene, Taunton. Richly carved, like the Kingston St Mary pulpit of 1742. – STAINED GLASS. E window, 1850, by *Joseph Bell*. Crucifixion on deep blues. Crude W window by *John Toms*, 1859. N windows, 1967 by *Gerald Coles*, to Hugh Easton, stained-glass designer, and 1913 by *Alice Erskine*, strangely naïve Arts and Crafts (cf.

Stowell). – MONUMENTS. Knight wearing a pointed bascinet, possibly Sir John de Merriet †1391. – William Adair †1844. Gothic brass. – Josiah Easton †1848, engineer. – Easton's CHEST TOMB outside is appropriately indestructible: Welsh slate on cast iron.

Opposite the church, the former VICARAGE, good red brick Gothic, 1871–3. To the E, BRADFORD COURT, later C19, stone, with neo-Jacobean cresting on the porch and bay windows. Down Back Lane, RISDONS was a C15–C16 hall house. Oak-mullioned windows and dormer bargeboards from a remodelling in 1617.

HEATHERTON PARK, ¾ m. SSW. Built *c.* 1770 but remodelled *c.* 1830–40 for Alexander Adair. Two hip-roofed three-storey blocks joined at the corner. Rendered, with corniced first-floor architraves and channelled ground floor. Detached former CHAPEL by *H. S. W. Stone*, 1928, from when one of the Woodard schools (cf. King's College, Taunton) was here. Early C18 style, five arched windows, a steep hipped roof and cupola. A plain late C18 brick LODGE spans the drive.

BRATTON

1 m. WSW of Minehead

9040

BRATTON COURT. A remarkable survival of much of a C14–C15 manor house of the de Bratton family. Stone and roughcast buildings enclose a farmyard. Along the N side is a C15 gatehouse range, 105 ft (32 metres) long. The early C14 former hall is on the W side, its cross-wing at the S end given a high-status early to mid-C15 addition running E, overlooking the yard. The rest of the S side is an C18 linhay. A C16 barn fills the E side.

The C14 HOUSE is not square to the yard. It has a C16 lateral chimney and C19 casement windows. The large, two-bay hall, 37.5 by 24.5 ft and 28 ft high (11.4 by 7.5 by 8.5 metres), was to the N of the cross-passage. The feet of massive trusses can still be seen. What is not obvious is that the end trusses were of the early aisle-truss type, i.e. with posts to the ground. The middle truss was a base cruck and there were arch-braced intermediate trusses and wind-braces. Monolith lintel to the C16 fireplace. C16 partition with peaked-head doorway to the service end. The cross-wing, of equal height, contained a solar, heated by a lateral chimney, over an undercroft. It has a six-bay roof of close-spaced arch-braced collar-trusses, largely concealed, apart from some vertical wall-pieces with rounded ends. The undercroft has massive timbers – an axial beam on an octagonal post with braces on four sides – overscaled surely for a parlour.* C16–C17 W extension projecting outward from

---

* There is a similar post in the C14 gatehouse range at Dartington Hall, Devon.

the courtyard. Two C16–C17 first-floor oak door frames remain in the dividing wall, as well as a lateral chimney.

The finest work is in the C15 eastward addition. Oak square-headed windows randomly disposed on two floors, with or without transom, all different (perhaps reused), and with delicate tracery. The upper room has a handsome three-bay roof of arch-braced jointed crucks with wind-braces carried through two tiers and partly cusped. Evidence of an eastern partition makes the building's identification as a chapel doubtful.* A low pointed E doorway to an outside stair (replaced by the linhay) and rear lateral chimney suggest that it served as a courtroom.

The GATEHOUSE RANGE has a throughway as at Holnicote (*see* Selworthy), with oak lintels and tall oak doors of horizontal bars dovetailed to the uprights, and a chamber above of high status. Two-bay roof of chamfered arch-braced jointed crucks with shield stops. Lime-plaster floor. Notable C15 cylindrical chimney with a conical cap. The roofs on each side are also of jointed crucks, but left rough. The E range was probably always agricultural. The W range has oak first-floor windows with cinquefoiled heads lighting a single unheated chamber, perhaps lodgings, reached by the same stairs as the gate chamber. The W end wall appears to be reused from an earlier building. Window of rough oak mullions. The BARN has jointed crucks and a gabled porch. Massive buttressing on the rear wall.

In the valley are roughcast C16–C17 cottages, some altered in the early C20 by *Mary, Countess of Lovelace* (*see* Porlock). By the ford, ALICE COTTAGE, thatched, has a prominent lateral chimney, as does STEPS COTTAGE further up, with an altered upper floor. FORGE COTTAGE has Lady Lovelace's typical gabled chimneys and WENTWORTH COTTAGES, a four-gable pair with tall tapering chimneys, are entirely by Lady Lovelace, c. 1909.

BRATTON SEYMOUR

ST NICHOLAS. Low Perp W tower with small pinnacles, but the massive lean-to stair-tower and plain chamfered tower arch much older. Indeed the much-rebuilt nave (altered 1837 by a *Mr Davies*) has C12 fragments in the wall, reused latticed voussoirs in the porch, and an arched S doorhead of double chevron with pellets separating the two, on chevron imposts. A restored Dec S window and E window of cusped intersecting tracery in the chancel may be trustworthy as C14, likewise the almost triangular chancel arch. – FONT. C11–C12. Bulbous rimmed bowl on a squat ringed base.

---

* An oratory is recorded in 1317.

BRATTON HOUSE. Begun in 1868 for *Charles Penruddocke* to his own design, with *James Soppitt* of Shaftesbury. Cross-wing dated 1888. Steep-gabled with tall brick chimneys. Behind, a suggestion of the Abbot's Kitchen at Glastonbury.

BREAN

A long coastal strip, with far more caravans than houses.

ST BRIDGET. A rare dedication in Somerset. The church looks appropriately Celtic with its low proportions and gabled S tower, rebuilt after lightning damage in 1729. The lower part may be C13 (see the cusped W lancet), as may the rest of the church, but everything is over-restored. Chancel of 1883 by *Price & Wooler*. Two C14 corbel heads on the nave E wall. C13 trefoiled PISCINA on a scalloped corbel. – FONT. Perp, octagonal, with paired fleurons and curved panelled underside (cf. Berrow). – PULPIT. 1620. The middle panels have large foliage rather than the usual blank arches. Fluted angles. – REREDOS. 1883. Dumfries sandstone. – BENCHES. 1883. Based on one C15 original in the porch.

MANOR HOUSE. Later C18, typical of the region. Brick with parapet, and stone open-pedimented doorcase.

BREAN DOWN, 1½ m. N. The limestone ridge jutting into the Bristol Channel has remains from many periods. Along the S side an accumulation of sand covers successive BRONZE AGE SETTLEMENTS containing some of the best-preserved houses in Europe. On top, a substantial Late Iron Age BANK cuts off the E end, presumably indicating a settlement, but this area has been much disturbed by military use. Recent MILITARY REMAINS are visible near the top of the steps including a large concrete arrow that guided aircraft to the bombing ranges in Bridgwater Bay. On the first hill a ROMAN TEMPLE was excavated, dated to the C4. A small successor building may have been a Christian church (cf. Lamyatt). Beyond this, the summit shows evidence of cultivation. Low BANKS define small fields, with small MOUNDS, mainly stone clearance but some burial mounds. Nothing remains of works begun in 1864 for a transatlantic port linked to the Bristol & Exeter Railway, destroyed by storm. At the W end is BREAN DOWN FORT of 1864–7, one of the Palmerston forts built against the perceived threat from Napoleon III, by *Lt Robert Veitch*, to the overall design of *Lt-Col Jervois*. With those on Steep Holm, Flat Holm, and Lavernock Point (Glamorgan), it defended the Bristol approaches. It had single-storey barrack blocks for fifty men and officers, an underground magazine and cliff-edge gun sites. Much of this survives, damaged in 1900 by a magazine explosion. Rearmed in the Second World War, with concrete gun-emplacements, and a searchlight on the furthest rock.

BRENDON HILL

Haematite was discovered in 1838 on top of the Brendon Hills. Proposals for a tramroad eventually resulted in the eleven-mile West Somerset Mineral Railway built in 1857–64, linking mines along the ridge with a steep descent to Watchet for shipment to the Ebbw Vale ironworks. The engineers were Welsh, *Rice Hopkins* (†1857), succeeded by *Morgan Morgans*. Miners were housed at the top, next to the great embankment where the line crossed the road. The VILLAGE has gone apart from the former Temperance Hotel, and, behind it, the hip-roofed STATION built when the line opened to passengers in 1865. BEULAH CHAPEL, 1861, stands alone further E, roughcast with pointed windows. The embankment is the summit of a spectacular INCLINE from Combe Row, up which trucks were pulled by cable: 3,320 ft (1,010 metres) long, engineered to an even 1 in 4 gradient, it cost £44,800. Beneath the twin tracks at the top was the winding house back-to-back with a two-storey house. The present front walls are mid-C20, the originals blown out in 1917. To the E, overlooking the incline, the stuccoed HILL HOUSE, built for Morgan Morgans in 1860–1.

After the station, the line turned W to serve several mines along the ridge. Near BURROW FARM an impressively large ENGINE HOUSE survives, with circular chimney. Re-erected here in 1878, having been built in 1866 at the Langham Hill Mine further W. The enterprise failed against cheaper ore from Spain, and the last mine closed in 1883.

BRENT KNOLL

Brent Knoll soars suddenly out of the plain to a height of nearly 450 ft (137 metres). Tradition has it that the Devil threw a shovelful of earth down at this spot while he was digging Cheddar Gorge, and imaginative history has sited Arthur's *Mons Badonicus* here. An impressive IRON AGE CAMP commands the whole district. There is evidence of Roman activity and the defences may have been improved in post-Roman times. A battle against invading Danes in 847 may be commemorated by Battleborough to the E. The village, on the S slope, was called South Brent until the C19.

ST MICHAEL. Of Blue Lias, quite large, in a hillside churchyard. Predominantly Perp, with important earlier survivals. Norman S doorway with chevron at right angles to the wall in the outer arch and jambs. Roll-moulded inner arch on thin nook-shafts. The opening was made pointed at a later date, reusing Norman lozenge-pattern stones on the inside. The S porch and S transept are next in order of date. They are early C14, from the triple-chamfered porch doorway with one order of shafts, and in the transept the ogee-headed w lancet and the three-light s window with cusped intersecting tracery, both with cinquefoiled rere-arches.

Perp four-stage w tower with set-back buttresses, a parapet pierced with quatrefoils in lozenges, thin pinnacles, and an octagonal NE stair-turret. Good squatting beast grotesques. W doorway with shield spandrels, flanked by niches. Renewed five-light w window, two-light window on each face on the third stage, and triple bell-openings of similar detail, the outer ones blind. Tower arch on responds of a broadly treated four-hollow section, the fat shafts suggesting a date *c.* 1400. Showy late C15 N aisle, as at East Brent. Six bays, with pinnacled buttresses and a pierced parapet like that of the tower. Octagonal rood-stair turret in the angle to the chancel. Tall thin arcade with piers of four-wave moulding, and a very good panelled aisle roof of the richest Somerset type. Spread-winged angels above a wall-plate with fleurons. Each panel sub-panelled, and each of these sub-panels differently ornamented. Stone angel corbels, and a single angel low in the NE corner, its shield showing the Five Wounds. Wagon roof in the nave with C19 boarding, but largely original, carried on fourteen stone heads on the s wall. Low triple-chamfered arch to the s transept, infilled with C19 stone tracery. Cusped ogee PISCINA on the s wall. Broad C15 shaft-and-hollow chancel arch. The chancel is rebuilt with an incongruous queenpost roof. Victorian TILES on the sanctuary floor and E wall.

FURNISHINGS. BENCHES. C15–C16, and most interesting, for iconographical reasons. They have poppyhead ends of the pentagonal type. But in addition to the usual tracery and representations of the Pelican, Paschal Lamb, and signs of the Evangelists, three show the fable of Reynard the Fox, with a polemical meaning which must have been patent at the time to everybody who saw it. On the first the fox is seen disguised as a mitred abbot. He is paid respect to by three monks in cowls who have the heads of swine. At the foot two monkeys roast a pig on a spit. On the second the fox is stripped and foot-cuffed, and below he is put into the stocks, guarded by a monkey. His mitre hangs on the wall. On the third he is hung by the triumphant geese. What does this imply? A general hatred for monasteries, and Glastonbury in particular, to which the parish belonged? Or a topical reference which escapes us? Whatever the immediate meaning, the outspokenness of the statement remains memorable. – FONT. Highly unusual. C13–C14, a wavy quatrefoil in plan, with flat cardinal faces and strong upper and lower mouldings. Shaft-and-hollow stem and quatrefoil base. – PULPIT. 1637. Quite richly carved, with the familiar short blank arches in two tiers. Fluted Ionic angle pilasters. – PILLAR PISCINA. On a spiral-ornamented Norman column, with scalloped capital on a cable moulding. – ROYAL ARMS. Charles II. – TOWER SCREEN. Late C19, carrying the organ. – STAINED GLASS. E window, with unusual pale colouring, 1892, by *Wailes & Strang*. NW, 1973, by *James*

Crombie. – MONUMENT. John Somerset †1663. He is in the centre of this big and naïve monument, a three-quarter figure in an oval niche, with military trophies, between his wives, sweet figures, also in oval niches, the younger one with a large and becoming hat. Two reliefs below. In one, three family members kneel, among them a swaddled infant with skull. In the other Somerset rises in his shroud from his tomb, summoned by the trumpeting angel. The Bridges monument at Keynsham (N) has similar twisted columns, carrying here a broken curved pediment with heraldry. Half of a scrolled pediment and a skull over each wife. The Rodney monuments at Rodney Stoke and the Prowse monument at Axbridge (both N) were probably made by the same workshop.

CHURCHYARD CROSS. 1921, by *W. D. Caröe*, 1921. Good sculpted head.

METHODIST CHURCH, Brent Street. 1837. Originally Bible Christian. Short lateral façade with cornice and arched windows.

Below the church, a large brick former VICARAGE, 1842, by *G. P. Manners*, Tudor-Elizabethan style. *Manners* also designed the grey stone Gothic SCHOOL, 1861, on Brent Street. NW past the chapel, IVY HALL is late C18, brick, with full-height canted bays flanking a good open-pedimented Ionic doorcase. Further on, OLD MANOR HOUSE, stuccoed and hip-roofed, early C19, backs on to WEST CROFT FARMHOUSE, early C18, brick with the gable copings and curved window heads typical of this region.

MANOR HOUSE, E of the church. 1862–4, by *John Norton*. Gaunt grey Mendip limestone, laid as crazed rubble, with Doulting Stone dressings. Gabled, asymmetrical, the r. side with a full-height canted bay. Cramped staircase in the central projection.

BALL'S COPSE HOUSE, ½ m. NW. 1903, by *Samson & Cottam* for William Holt, brewer. Pink rock-faced Draycott Conglomerate, like Temple Meads Station, Bristol, but the upper floor of grey Mendip stone, as if the supply ran out. Mullion-and-transom windows.

BATTLEBOROUGH FARMHOUSE, I m. SE. C16–C17, in roughcast Gothic dress of 1830.

BRIDGWATER

A relatively late foundation at the uppermost crossing point of the tidal River Parrett. Charters of 1200 allowed William Brewer a castle, borough and markets. Prosperous in medieval times as a wool-exporting port, the town included a suburb, Eastover, across the bridge from early on. Beyond Eastover was St John's Hospital and beyond the W gate a Franciscan friary with a church of 1445. The castle declined in the C14 and was replaced by a

C17 mansion, ruined when Bridgwater was stormed by Parliament in 1645. In the 1720s the Duke of Chandos attempted an urban and industrial revival, building a new street, the finest of its era outside London, between the ruined mansion and the river. Much of the town is post-Civil War, but enough survives to show that timber framing on stone preceded brick, the stone being red sandstone from Wembdon or Blue Lias from the Polden Hills. From the later C17 locally made brick was the characteristic material of Bridgwater, initially a pinkish buff colour, later red. Houses of the early C18 have segmental-arched windows, the Late Georgian houses have gauged brick window heads, parapets, and mansard roofs, and those of the early C19 ashlar window heads and overhanging eaves. Contrasted coloured bricks typify the later C19. The making of bricks, roofing tiles and scouring bricks, along with iron-founding, dominated C19–C20 industry. The heart of the town was the port, along riverside quays until the docks opened in 1841, the year the railway arrived. Trade was both coastal and inland, by canal and navigable river. The port and the traditional industries declined before 1939, and the docks eventually closed to river traffic. The town had some success in attracting C20 industries, notably British Cellophane in 1935, resulting, after the Second World War, in large housing estates: Sydenham on the E, and Westfield with its tower block.

CHURCHES

ST MARY. A large and spreading church. Its Ham stone spire is tall and exceedingly elegant, without any fussy dormers. Exceptional in a county of towers, it rises to 187 ft (57 metres) on an earlier tower, of *c.* 1300, which is by contrast massive and of Wembdon stone. Big diagonal buttresses, small cusped lancets mid-height N and S, and small two-light later C14 bell-openings with pierced baffles. Similar two-light W window over a C15 doorway with large leaves in the spandrels. Square SE stair-turret. Tower arch of three continuous chamfers. The battlements of Ham stone are probably contemporary with the spire, begun in 1367, unfinished in 1385. The masons named are *Nicholas Waleys* of Bristol and *John Betere*.

The spreading plan represents a profusion of medieval chantries, indicative of a prosperous town church. In addition to the aisles and chancel chapels, there is an outer layer of porches and transepts made solid by infilling the intermediate bay on both N and S sides. Large windows of three, four and five lights. Wembdon stone in the older, eastern parts; the rest is of Blue Lias, the S side refaced in the heavy-handed restoration of 1849–51 by *W. H. Brakspear* of Manchester. Of this date the nave clerestory, the frilly parapets (previously the aisles and chapels had battlements), and most of the window tracery. The N side is the earliest, C13 with mid-C14 Dec work more florid and inventive than the Dec style usually is in Somerset. Especially inventive the traceried tympanum of the outer N doorway and the round window above with its cusped Star-of-David

p. 134

Bridgwater, St Mary.
Engraving by T. Bonnor, 1791

tracery.* Victorian statue niche each side. The doorway has C13 stiff-leaf capitals on short shafts resting on corbel heads (possibly twin popes). Stiff-leaf also to smaller, outer capitals on slim shafts and to leaf sprays in the outer moulding of the big pointed arch. In the C14 Dec tracery was inserted as a tympanum in the doorhead, a roundel with reticulated tracery between small trefoils, above a segmental-pointed arch of undercut vine-trail emerging from the ears of green men. Elaborately traceried Dec five-light windows in the intermediate bay and N transept. But clasping buttresses and a crypt show that the transept is of c. 1300. The small single-chamfered crypt doorway is set between tomb-recesses each under a seven-cusped arch. Extremely eroded effigies. The two bays of the aisle W of the porch are externally Perp, of squared Blue Lias (but with older Dec tomb-recesses inside). The S side is all refaced, but the oculus above the porch with double-cusped quatrefoil tracery is as shown by Buckler. If the window tracery

---

* A similar oculus is on the Bishop of Winchester's palace, Southwark.

(flowing SW and reticulated S) is credible, the aisle is early C14 and the transept C15. The chancel chapels and chancel have tall Perp windows (work recorded in the 1420s) inserted in older masonry. E window by *Brakspear*. NE vestry by *Samson & Cottam*, 1902.

Inside are Perp arcades of six bays with piers of standard four-hollow section and little circular capitals to the shafts – an uninspired treatment. The clerestory windows, angel corbels and hammerbeam roof are *Brakspear*'s. The sixth arch, to each transept, is wider. The plain chancel arch piers may belong to the pre-Perp building, with a Perp arch dying in. The transepts are separated from the chapels to their W by arcades running N–S, that on the N three-bay and entirely C19, that on the S two-bay, nearly matching the nave arcades. The upper storeys of the porches open into the church, a remarkable feature, if original, but entirely remodelled by Brakspear apart from a moulded framed ceiling in the S chamber. In the N porch Brakspear inserted a broken Perp FONT, apparently from the site of St John's Hospital, Eastover. In the N aisle are two C13–C14 tomb-recesses, one with open cusping, the other cusped and sub-cusped. The S tomb-recesses are Victorian. Good early C15 framed ceilings in the S aisle and transept, the latter with Christ enthroned on the central boss. In the N aisle, C15 angel corbels hold painted shields. The pointed barrel roof of the chancel with its frilly principal braces is Brakspear's but includes many early C15 bosses including an elephant-and-castle. One names William Patehull †1422. Brakspear's climax is lost, his E end ornament swept away and his giant window hidden by the painting he disliked (*see* below). Encaustic TILES of 1878.

FURNISHINGS. CHANCEL SCREENS. The side screens are the reused rood screen, documented to 1415–20. Close-tra-ceried four-light sections, in two tiers, the upper lights cusped top and bottom. – CORPORATION PEW. A splendid Jacobean SCREEN encloses the S transept. Originally it faced the rood screen and was three-sided with a central entry. Reconstructed here as a sixteen-bay length with two doorways. Dado panels of superimposed Jacobean arches between rusticated columns under a frieze of grotesque masks and fish-tailed beasts. Above is a lacy arcade with pierced spandrels on thin ornamented columns. In the cornice are fish-tailed creatures between troll-like creatures, the whole crested in open strapwork and obelisks. The Jacobean-style benches are mostly C19. – SE CHAPEL. Re-fitted in 1920 by *Caröe*. – FONT. Good C14. Octagonal, with quatrefoils, the underside coved with linked roses, on a stem gently splayed to a moulded base. – PULPIT. A fine Perp oak piece. Octagonal, of unusual size, with traceried panels in two tiers. – COMMUNION TABLE. C17, triple-arched on bulbous legs. – PEWS. By *Brakspear*. – ROYAL ARMS. 1712. – ORGAN. 1871, by *Henry Willis*. – SEDILIA. Three medieval oak stalls, once with misericords. Traceried ends. – TABLE. Pierced trac-eried C15 octagon, roughly vaulted beneath; actually a very rare hanging canopy, or pyx-shrine (cf. Milton Abbey, Dorset). – PAINTING. Covering the E window. The Descent from the Cross, a very large emotional Baroque work of quality, given c. 1775 by Anne Poulett M.P. (cf. Hinton St George). Admired by Reynolds, it has been called Spanish, French or Italian. Pevsner thought it Bolognese, second half of the C17; recent opinion has tended to Rome and c. 1700. – STAINED GLASS. S transept S, 1852; SE chapel, 1885, by *Clayton & Bell*. Nave S first, 1926, by *H. Wilkinson*. – MONUMENTS. In the nave S recesses, medieval cross-slabs, one unusually of Purbeck marble. Sir Francis Kingsmill of Ballybeg †1620. Grand wall monument of Watchet alabaster. Semi-reclining effigy in armour in front of two kneeling sons, Henry †1621 and Francis †1640, framed by a broken pediment on black-shafted Corinthian columns. – John Phelps †1782. By *Paty & Sons*, with their usual competent good taste. – John Evered †1785. Large obelisk memorial with urn. – Anderdon family, 1788. Incised Lias, elaborate, and, unusually, Gothic. – John Dunning †1821. By *Reeves* of Bath. Large, Grecian, with sarcophagus and fasces.

CHURCHYARD. Two cast-iron Gothic GATEWAYS from *Edward Murch*'s Bridgwater Iron Foundry, one dated 1831. Also two contemporary cast-iron GRAVE-SLABS.

ST JOHN BAPTIST, Blake Place, Eastover. 1843–6, by *John Brown*, surveyor of Norwich Cathedral. Neo-E.E., with nothing of the leanness of the Commissioners' churches. It cost the Rev. Moore Capes some £9,000. He became a Catholic before it was consecrated. In composition and proportion it is far from the spirit of the C13; the smooth Bath stone and Salisbury Cathedral detail resemble George Manners's St Michael, Bath, of 1834–7. Octagonal vestry. Rather underscaled tower; a broach spire was intended. Impressively high interior with massive hammerbeam roofs, the chancel roof with angels. Contemporary FITTINGS: font, pulpit, gabled reredos and sedilia. Poppyhead PEWS. – STAINED GLASS. Attractive patterned glass of 1899 and dull E window, 1916, all by *Dudley Forsyth*.

ST FRANCIS, Saxon Green, Sydenham. 1959–60, by *Stone & Partners*. Brick-clad steel portal frame. Chancel, 1984, tile-hung tower with short copper spire, 1987, by the same.

ALL SAINTS, Westonzoyland Road (disused). 1881–2. Red sandstone with triple-lancet E window.

HOLY TRINITY, Hamp Street. 1960–1, by *Caroe & Partners*. A neat design in buff brick with a transverse-roofed W bellcote on full-height buttresses. Broad nave arches; parabolic chancel arch. Delicate oak SCREEN, typical of the firm. – FONT. Inverted cone.

ST JOSEPH (R.C.), King Street. 1881–2, by *Fr Alexander Scoles*, architect, and parish priest here. Red brick with triple-lancet E window. Extended in 1981 by *Terence Moody*, the S door re-set at the W end. Well detailed interior with tall chancel arch and N arcade on octagonal piers. Arcaded E wall and spired tabernacle.

NE ALTAR by *Scoles* in memory of his father, the architect J. J. Scoles. – STAINED GLASS. Probably all by *Hardman*.

BAPTIST CHURCH, St Mary Street. 1837, by *Edwin Down*. Soberly classical as Nonconformity could be. Pedimented ashlar front with giant unfluted Ionic columns *in antis*. Interior nicely re-fitted in 1901 by *Samson & Cottam*, the galleries given inset cast-iron panels. Platform pulpit above the total-immersion baptistery.

METHODIST CHURCH, King Street (disused). 1816, by *Thomas Hutchings*. Quite large. Red brick with arched windows on two floors, the parapet ramped to an open pediment. Triple-arched porch added by *Hutchings* in 1860, when the chapel was lengthened and the manse added behind. Curved late C19 gallery fronted in looped ironwork by *James Culverwell*, iron-founder.

METHODIST CHURCH, Monmouth Street, Eastover. 1911, by *W. H. Dinsley* of Chorley. Brick and stone, in the free Perp favoured by Methodists after 1900.

QUAKER MEETING HOUSE, Friarn Street. Founded 1722, rebuilt 1801. Domestic brick front. Meeting room divided by a wooden screen.

CHRIST CHURCH UNITARIAN CHAPEL, Dampiet Street. Originally Presbyterian of 1688. Rebuilt in 1788 on the original footprint. Tall brick façade with open pediment and stone-framed windows, the central one Venetian. The fine large timber shell-hood is from the original chapel, which Defoe had praised. Surprising basilican interior, tunnel-vaulted in plaster on four tall ashlar colmns with fluted necks. Flat aisle ceilings. Large Venetian end window. Panelled rear GALLERY on columns with fluted necks. – BOX PEWS.

WESTFIELD CHURCH (United Reformed), West Street. 1965–6, by *Ralph Nicholls*. Brick, with broad open pediments on the cardinal faces and concrete grid windows in the narrow diagonals. It replaces a Gothic Congregational chapel in Fore Street by *Edwin Down*, 1862.

PUBLIC BUILDINGS

TOWN HALL, High Street. 1820–3, by *Richard Carver*. A nicely restrained classical front in stucco, three storeys, 2–5–2 bays, the first-floor windows arched. Panelled giant pilasters to the upper floors of the centre; two pillared porches. Hall behind of 1865, by *Charles Knowles*, of brick on Wembdon sandstone. Galleried inside, the cast-iron front of a looped design with flowers, by *James Culverwell*, iron-founder. *Carver* built houses to the E, 1824–7; the first pair was refronted as municipal offices, 1950.

MARKET HALL, Cornhill. Right at the centre of the town and just right in scale and formality for a town of proud traditions. 1826–7, by *John Bowen*, an engineer returned from India. The pivot of its triangular site is a rotunda of two concentric rings of columns. A more-than-semicircular outer colonnade of unfluted Ionic columns carries a deep cornice and panelled parapet, while an inner ring of Tuscan columns carries the panelled ashlar drum to a rather Continental shallow dome capped by a tall glazed lantern. Low wings end in pavilions with Ionic columns *in antis*, and the side ranges run back with pedimented Ionic market entrances. The rotunda was neatly glazed behind the columns in 2006, by *Smith Gamblin*. The open market behind was roofed and partly infilled with a top-lit Corn Exchange, by *Charles Knowles*, 1875. Romanesque detail inside. In the market, a TILE PANEL by *Philippa Threlfall*, 1976.

LIBRARY, Blake Gardens. 1905–6, a competition victory by *E. Godfrey Page*. Freely classical in an Arts and Crafts way, the corner rotunda echoing that of the Market Hall. Octagonal hall lit by lunettes under a copper-clad dome with a cupola. Barrel-vaulted reading rooms with canted bays. Extension, 1970.

MAGISTRATES' COURT, Mount Street. 1911–12, by *Francis Parr*, Borough Surveyor. Like the library, a demonstration of the ease with which the early C20 could use period motifs without pretension. Ashlar segmental-pedimented doorway. Adjacent POLICE STATION, 1965–6, by *Somerset County Architects*. Exposed steel frame, replacing a concrete one that failed.

REGIONAL POLICE HEADQUARTERS, Express Park. 2012–14 by *Ryder Architecture* of Newcastle. Much glass, the entrance taller than the three- and two-storey ranges each side.

BRIDGWATER INFIRMARY, Salmon Parade. Founded 1813. Italianate front of 1876, in brick and stone with columned porch.

RAILWAY STATION, St John Street. 1842. Designed in the office of *Brunel* for the Bristol & Exeter Railway. Stuccoed, single-storeyed, with top-lit booking hall. *Brunel* designed two successive pioneering bridges over the Parrett, some distance S, at SOMERSET BRIDGE. An extremely shallow masonry arch of 1839–43 failed and was replaced in laminated timber (replaced in steel in 1904).

BRIDGWATER COLLEGE, Sydenham. 1977–83, by *Somerset County Architects*, project architect *Jeff Davey*. Forceful buildings in dark red brick, single- and two-storeyed, the dominant motif a chamfering of the corners. Entrance clasped by asymmetrical windowless stair-towers. Additions by the *Shirley-Smith, Gibson & Rigler* firm, later *Smith Gamblin*: Derek Gibson Building, 1996; Media and Business, 2002; St Mark's, 2004–5; Health and Fitness, 2007–8, the later ones with overhanging eaves.

BLAKE MUSEUM, Blake Street. *See* Perambulation 3.

SOMERSET BRICK AND TILE MUSEUM, East Quay. The remnant of the Barham Bros brickworks, established 1857. One brick pinnacle-kiln and replica drying-shed.

SCHOOLS. A proposal to replace all four secondary schools was reduced to two, built in 2011–13, ROBERT BLAKE, by *NVB Architects*, and CHILTON TRINITY, by *Scott Brownrigg*. Both of similar plan of short wings from a central hub, the triangular interstices conceived as part of the teaching spaces. The replacement of HAYGROVE (Boys' Grammar School, 1937) and EAST BRIDGWATER (Sydenham Secondary, 1957–61, by *Somerset County Architects*) has been suspended. Of the County Council designed schools the best survivor may be HAMP JUNIOR, 1950–2 (project architect *Guy Ward*), sculptural in a late Thirties manner, single-storey with a curved brick tower by the entry.

YMCA, Friarn Avenue. 2010, by *Smith Gamblin*. A large canal-side activity centre of angular forms, the upper floor clad in deep red or mottled brown, the parts split by a glass corridor. Separate grid-fronted accommodation block.

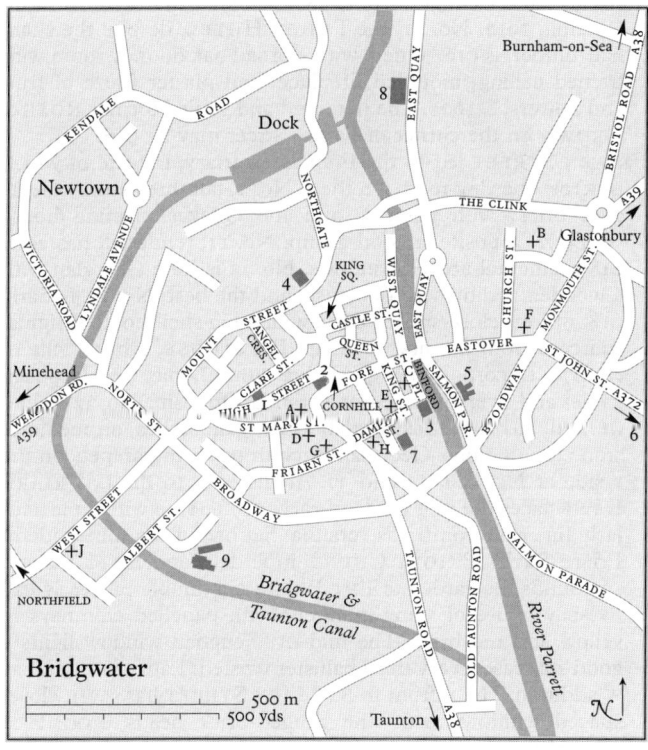

A	St Mary	1	Town Hall
B	St John	2	Market Hall
C	St Joseph (R.C.)	3	Library
D	Baptist church	4	Magistrates' Court
E	Methodist church (disused)	5	Bridgwater Infirmary
F	Methodist church	6	Railway station
G	Quaker meeting house	7	Blake Museum
H	Christ Church Unitarian Chapel	8	Brick and Tile Museum
J	Westfield Church	9	YMCA

PERAMBULATIONS

1. St Mary Street, Friarn Street and High Street

Facing the churchyard on ST MARY STREET, the OLD VICARAGE is a C15 hall house with later cross wing. The parlour has C17 panelling and a shell alcove. Late Georgian brick buildings on each side refronting C16 structures. Going E, the Baptist church (p. 137) is recessed before No. 41, an Early Georgian six-bay house with segment-headed first-floor windows. MARYCOURT (the Carnival Inn), beneath a great deal of reused C17 woodwork, is genuine late C16, the upper floor jettied, with three six-light mullion-and-transom windows of oak. Opposite, Nos. 34–38, low, with a gabled cross-wing, are altered C17. No. 40, later C18, was of quality, the three-storey four-bay front of ashlar, and corniced. All painted, and the ground floor lost.* Back on the S side, the broad gable at No. 25 fronted the Bijou Cinema, 1912. No. 21, the TUDOR HOTEL, despite the sham half-timber, is C16, jettied, with a broad oak door. W room with framed ceiling, moulded fireplace, and plaster frieze of fruit and flowers, *c.* 1600. The rendered and gabled former ROSE & CROWN on the corner of Friarn Street may be C16.

FRIARN STREET led to the Franciscan friary, the site of which is across the ring road. On the r. No. 2, tall three-storey Georgian brick, with parapet, and the Quaker meeting house (p. 137). Opposite, a good group: No. 11, rendered, has early C18 segmental-arched windows, No. 13 is Late Georgian with a wooden pedimented doorcase, and the best, No. 15, is Early C18, of four close-spaced bays, with a big shell-hood. Original staircase from the first floor up. IVY HOUSE, a brick villa of *c.* 1870 (incorporating an earlier house), has neo-Jacobean gables and a very Gothic iron veranda. Opposite, No. 32, gable-fronted, has C17 brickwork and Georgian sashes, on medieval stone foundations. Georgian brick fronts with parapets on the S side at Nos. 29, 35 and 37. At the end, to the l., FRIARN LAWN faces the ring road, an early C19 terrace with a particularly fine cast-iron trellis veranda. Set back from the N side of Friarn Street, PRIORY COURT, infill development of *c.* 2000, surrounds the garden of THE PRIORY, a double-pile early C18 five-bay house of some grandeur with panelled chimneys in yellow and red brick. The mid-C18 Venetian window lights a good staircase, every third baluster twisted. Late C18 three-bay W addition. The N front to ST MARY STREET has seven close-spaced windows with fine gauged-brick heads divided by stuccoed strips, probably altered pilasters. Curved-pediment doorway. Back E towards the church, St Mary Street has minor C18 houses to SILVER STREET, where No. 6 is C16 in rubble stone, horribly altered. Oak Tudor doorway. Returning W past The Priory, St Mary Street joins High Street, which runs

---

*The fine late C15 panelled ceiling in the Burrell Collection, Glasgow, came from No. 50, demolished 1932.

between ancient market places at Penel Orlieu (w) and Cornhill (E). In PENEL ORLIEU, two former cinemas: the battered hulk of the ODEON, by *Cecil Howitt*, 1936, a smaller version of his Odeon, Weston super Mare, and the PALACE, 1916 by *Samson & Colthurst*, with stucco classical detail and a square dome.

HIGH STREET runs E, broad and straight, with Georgian and later buildings, some refronting older work, few of especial note. On the N, No. 62, painted brick, keeps a pointed doorway dated 1563 and fireplace from a gabled house recorded *c*. 1845. At No. 73, a rounded mid-C19 front fills the acute junction with St Mary Street. Before the Town Hall (p. 137) a shaped Blue Lias pier remains from a jettied medieval house. No. 34, a broad three-bay house by *Richard Carver*, 1824–7, with finely gauged window heads, screens an early C16 first-floor hall with jointed crucks above a moulded framed ceiling. On the S, the low THREE LIONS, a Late Georgian refronting. It adjoins Nos. 23–27, two double-gabled buildings of 1892 by *Basil Cottam*, framing a pedimented later C18 front, with a draper's shop of *c*. 1875, the name gilded on glass. Late Georgian to Early Victorian fronts continue E to the Market Hall (p. 137), the GOLDEN BALL altered with an Edwardian pub front and cheerful oriel. On the N side, the MANSION HOUSE was a C16 church house, refronted after 1801. Painted brick with panels above the upper windows. Older stonework in the end wall. Behind is a diminutive late C18 house with steep mansard roof. Crude concrete columns mark the Angel Place Shopping Centre (*see* p. 145). Before Cornhill, BARCLAYS BANK, 1822, is stuccoed, but old photographs show a brick front like No. 14 adjoining. This was pierced for THE AVENUE, a charming glazed arcade through to Clare Street, of 1927, by *Samson & Colthurst*. The granite columns on Clare Street came from the dismantled High Street shopfront.

2. *Cornhill, Fore Street, the Quays, Castle Street, King Square*

CORNHILL is Bridgwater's hub, a fine civic space with one side filled by the Market Hall (p. 137). On the N side is the former ROYAL CLARENCE HOTEL of 1824–5, stuccoed, seven bays, with a heavy porch of paired Ionic columns. The cast-iron town crest came from the 1790s Town Bridge (*see* below). Shops replace the lower windows. Curved SE corner. The NAT WEST BANK, 1904, by *George Oatley* for Stuckey's Bank, peeps an ashlar concave corner to Cornhill. The brick sides have Ionic colonnades and garlanded lower windows in the Anglo-Baroque style. S of the Market Hall, Nos. 6–7, a late C18 five-bay brick front with parapet and Venetian window, and two Bath stone four-storey commercial buildings in sober Italian High Renaissance style, as if they stood somewhere in the City of London. Nos. 8–9 are dated 1856; Nos. 10–11 of 1870. The E side is spoilt apart from No. 23, ashlar, with Grecian detail.

Facing down FORE STREET, the ROBERT BLAKE statue, 1900, by *F. W. Pomeroy*, a lively work, the Admiral life-size in bronze, pointing. Pedestal by *Basil Cottam* with bronze reliefs by *Pomeroy*. The pedestrianized street runs E to the Town Bridge. Some battered Late Georgian and Early Victorian buildings, the best the curved corner to George Street. On the N, COURT STREET runs up to the Grecian ashlar former COUNTY COURT, of as late as 1859, perhaps by *Edwin Down*. Five bays and two storeys. Segmental-headed ground-floor openings in segmental-headed arches. On the first floor an attached three-bay Ionic portico *in antis* between pilastered outer bays with tall tripartite windows. Opposite, CASTLE HOUSE, 1851, a sadly derelict pioneer house demonstrating the versatility of *John Board*'s experimental concrete. Neo-Tudor with cast friezes and battlements, mass-concrete rusticated first floor. Concrete staircase and rail, the structure tensioned by iron ties. Back at the foot of FORE STREET, Nos. 4–6, 1898, by *Cottam*, the best of his commercial buildings, has terracotta oriels, pediments, and a central chimney ornamented with serpent heads. No. 2, painted brick of 1795, curves to West Quay.

It is with the river and the quays that Bridgwater displays its individual character, a character curiously East Anglian with the brick houses and muddy tidal river. The TOWN BRIDGE is no longer that of cast iron made at Coalbrookdale in 1794–8 (*Thomas Gregory*, engineer, with *James Parry* of Cardiff, architect). This was replaced in iron in 1883, by *G. B. Laffan*, Borough Engineer, with *Richard Else*, consultant. The quays are a minor edition of Wisbech, Cambs., minor indeed in terms of good architecture. The best group is on West Quay. A glance first across the river. EAST QUAY has a pleasantly mixed short row with a curved brick corner to Eastover. The one house of note, No. 4, Early Georgian, clearly relates to the Castle Street houses across the river (*see* below), although stuccoed. Doorway with a heavy Gibbs surround, and segment-headed windows. SALMON PARADE, on the other side of Eastover, has a modest early C19 brick row before the Infirmary (p. 138) and then a low stuccoed deep-eaved row of three mid-C19 houses. For Binford Place, the SW quay, *see* Perambulation 3.

Now to WEST QUAY. The FOUNTAIN INN, tall, early C18 with a massive lateral chimney, has a stuccoed gable front altered *c.* 1900. FISHERMAN'S WHARF, 1911, was the Oddfellows Hall, inventive in red brick, with four large curved-headed oriel windows in imitation stone breaking the eaves. Next a five-bay Early Georgian brick house, with windows like No. 4 East Quay. No. 6, stuccoed, with a parapet ramped over the attic window, was the King's Arms, perhaps refronting an early C18 gabled warehouse. Nos. 7–9 was a Late Georgian four-to-five-storey brick warehouse. Then narrow Early Georgian fronts frame Castle Street (*see* below) before Nos. 11–12, damaged early C18, with Ham stone for quoins and first-floor window heads. Squeezed in the alley beyond is the WATERGATE of Bridgwater Castle, possibly of 1201–5. The wall is 12 ft (3.7

metres) thick with three segmental arches in pale stone, the inner arch double-chamfered. A length of possible curtain wall is exposed beyond the next house.

Further on is the best house of Bridgwater, THE LIONS, an ambitious if compact waterfront mansion built for himself before 1731 by *Benjamin Holloway*, the builder employed by the Duke of Chandos on Castle Street. In a robust provincial Baroque taste, far from correct in its motifs. Five bays, two storeys on a basement, of chequered yellow and red brick with an ashlar centrepiece and ashlar channelled outer pilasters. It fronts a small forecourt between pyramid-roofed pavilions with Venetian doorways to the street and ashlar corners (originally carrying urns). A balustrade connects the pavilions, the gate-piers with rather Chinese lions. The entrance, up broad stone steps, has attached Doric columns and a triglyph frieze with monograms. The window above is arched and flanked by fluted pilasters with corbels instead of capitals carrying an open segmental pediment breaking the parapet. The parapet replaces an elaborate panelled one with urns on corner piers and a centrepiece with blind oval and pineapple urns. Bolection-moulded curved-headed window surrounds with keystones and ashlar aprons. Contemporary staircase and two good panelled rooms, one with Ionic pilasters, the other with shell alcoves. Roughcast rear. Brick Late Georgian NW addition with stone architraves. Ballroom with Neoclassical cornice inside. By the road bridge of 1988, BLACK BRIDGE, 1869–71, was built for a branch railway to the docks. The central span was retractable.

We return now to CASTLE STREET. If The Lions is the best house at Bridgwater, this is the best street, indeed one of the finest Early Georgian streets outside London. It was projected by the Duke of Chandos in 1721 and begun in 1723. It is not quite certain who designed the houses. The Duke's surveyors and masons on his mansion at Canons (Middlesex) and urban developments in Mayfair, London, *Thomas Fort* and *Edward Shepherd*, appear in the story, but the designer of at least four, and possibly all, is *Holloway* of The Lions. The Duke called him 'a very great knave' but 'a good workman and the only one thereabouts'. The street begins humbly with three-storey houses squeezed narrowly between the West Quay buildings. Chandos's houses are of brick with painted stone quoins and the delightful motif of parapets curving up as the street rises. Ten three-storey houses, six on the N, four on the S, each of a generous five bays with segment-headed windows in bolection-moulded architraves. Varied doorways on the N: Ionic pilasters (No. 6), Ionic pilasters outside an arched Gibbs surround (No. 10), Corinthian pilasters (No. 14), and fluted Roman Doric piers set diagonally (No. 16), carrying a triglyph frieze with the same monograms as The Lions. Panelled rooms and closed-string staircases. The S side doorways are simpler. Nos. 11–13 was the first arts centre in England, 1946, with theatre by *Ralph Edwards*. It hosted the 1947 MARS international conference on architecture, attended by Gropius, Le Corbusier and Maxwell Fry. No. 15 is later C18. Parallel to the N, four artisan houses of 1726–8 in CHANDOS STREET.

Castle Street led up to Bridgwater Castle. The ruin shown in engravings was a mansion of 1635–7 for Henry Harvey, assumed to be on the site of the castle keep. Chandos intended to clear the ruin but this did not happen until after 1800. Typical Bridgwater curved corners frame the entrance to KING SQUARE, which should have completed this outstanding piece of urban planning; but only two-and-a-bit sides were built, of tall plain houses with parapets and mansard roofs. The S side, begun 1807, has pedimented doorways, the E, 1820s, arched doorways and iron balconies. The N side had only two houses (originally with tent-roofed balconies), of 1850, until completed for the Bridgwater Building Society, 1962 (except that the undersized MASONIC HALL, by *Cottam*, 1911, had intervened). *Thomas Hutchings*, who built the two N houses, may have designed them all. In the square is the bronze WAR MEMORIAL of 1924 by *John Angel*, whose subsequent career was in America. Something of a masterpiece of the New Sculpture movement, in the spirit of Alfred Gilbert. The programme is worth savouring: Civilization, seated, extends the Orb of the World on which dance the Four Corners of the Earth, connected by the Band of Brotherhood. On her lap the Book of Law is upheld by crouching child-angels. Under her feet writhe Strife, Bloodshed, Corruption and Despair. On the back are Labour, Motherhood and Education. Such a scheme, inconceivable even a few years later, was already out of date by comparison with memorials by Jagger or Goscombe John. On the W side of the square, minor Edwardian buildings include ST MARY'S HALL, 1902, by *Samson & Cottam*. Around the corner heading S, No. 24 pre-dates the square: vernacular, C17–C18 in painted brick. Opposite are Nos. 13–15 YORK BUILDINGS, tall, L-shaped Late Georgian. On York Buildings, MALDON HOUSE, late C18, mansard-roofed, and CORNHILL CHAMBERS, *c.* 1905, an office building in the manner of Voysey, brick with unmoulded grid windows and central oriel. It faces the NatWest Bank (*see* Cornhill).

3. South of Fore Street: Binford Place, Dampiet Street, Blake Street

From the Town Bridge, BINFORD PLACE, the SW quay, runs S, dismally redeveloped in 1966. Nos. 8–9, a tall Late Georgian brick pair, remain next to the R.C. church (p. 136). The library (p. 138) stands at the entrance to BLAKE GARDENS. In these a curious brick SUMMERHOUSE with plastered dome. Behind the library, on KING STREET, is the former Methodist church (p. 137). Adjoining to the r., the impressive former chapel SCHOOLS, 1923, by *Samson & Colthurst*. Neo-Georgian brick between ashlar curved-pedimented doorways. Next, BRENT

HOUSE is early C19, oddly undomestic: its high ground floor and low upper one resemble country-house stables. Tall recessed-arched doorways alternate with windows. Domestic rear with a trellis veranda. Behind the chapel, DAMPIET STREET runs up to St Mary Street. Mixed C18–C19 houses and the Unitarian chapel (p. 137) on the l. On BLAKE STREET, No. 3, tall, bare Late Georgian brick, was extended for the former School of Art (1898 and 1908 by *Basil Cottam*). Inside have been found remnants of an even taller C16–C17 stone house with mullion-and-transom windows and stair-tower. The adjoining BLAKE MUSEUM, C15–C16 timber-framed over stone, probably became the service wing. Damaged stone-mullion windows. The one complete window, inside, has cinquefoil-cusped lights. Framed ceilings below a first-floor hall with jointed crucks and curved wall-braces. No. 6, opposite, is Late Georgian, three-storeyed. Back on Dampiet Street, the overbearing late C20 TELEPHONE EXCHANGE hides a decent Neo-Georgian predecessor of 1936 in GEORGE STREET. The Late Georgian block adjoining, with a throughway, is a remnant of the GEORGE INN, the principal coaching inn. George Street runs through to Fore Street.

4. North of the centre: Angel Crescent, Northgate, Bridgwater Docks

The Avenue arcade (*see* Perambulation 1) leads to ANGEL CRESCENT, a development of 1816: an elegant shallow crescent between end houses. It faces the ANGEL PLACE SHOPPING CENTRE, 1986, inevitably overwhelming despite busy modelling of the long brown brick front, curved back in answer to the crescent. MOUNT STREET to the N is lost to traffic and car parking. To the W the former GRAMMAR SCHOOL remains, an early C19 single-storey brick schoolroom with arched windows. Brick addition with little entrance tower of 1904, by *Cottam*. Neo-Georgian REGISTRY OFFICE of 1937. Going E are the Magistrates' Court (p. 138) and the large BRIDGWATER HOUSE, offices of 1962 behind the replica façade in King Square. NORTHGATE runs up to the docks. On the W side was the WORKHOUSE of 1837, to *Sampson Kempthorne*'s hexagonal plan (cf. Yeovil and Taunton). Only the hospital range, 1847–8 by *Edwin Down*, remains at the back of the site. On the E side is the base of the giant GLASS KILN of 1725–6, built by the Duke of Chandos to compete with Bristol glassmakers. The enterprise failed by 1733. An astonishing 103 ft (31.4 metres) high, it survived until 1943. Just E, in VALETTA PLACE, a pretty pair of early C19 houses with curved corners and cast-iron nameplate.

BRIDGWATER DOCKS were created in 1837–41 by *Thomas Maddicks*, engineer, for the Bridgwater and Taunton Canal, which since 1827 had joined the River Parrett at Huntworth, S of the town. The canal was extended around Bridgwater to a new

floating basin, with a canal lock at the NW and a complicated
E exit to the river. A lock with iron BASCULE BRIDGE (replaced
1907) opens into a tidal basin with parallel locks to the river.
There was an underwater sluicing system for silt, such as
Brunel had just introduced at Bristol. On the s side, a large
brick four-storey WAREHOUSE in five sections each with
central loading doors, the r. three of 1840–1, the other two of
1868. Modern housing otherwise around the basin, added
since the 1980s restoration, and a late C19 OIL-CAKE MILL at
the NW corner. Opposite the river exit, the former DOCK-
MASTER'S OFFICE, 1840s, brick, hip-roofed, the wings since
raised by a storey.

OUTER AREAS

East of the river: Eastover and Sydenham

Eastover was a medieval suburb, but Eastover the street has
nothing of note. CHURCH STREET runs N with houses in
Wembdon stone with bargeboards, 1884, by *Edwin Down*. On
BLAKE PLACE, an almshouse-like mid-C19 group faces St
John's church (p. 136). MONMOUTH STREET, part of the ring
road, keeps some minor early C19 terraced houses. At the N
end is No. 68, stuccoed Tudor of the 1840s, gable-fronted with
pretty glazing. It faces No. 43, a minimally Tudor toll house. E
of Monmouth Street are low brick terraces of the 1840s, the
railway era, as far as the railway station (p. 138). This marked
the E edge of the town until the huge post-war SYDENHAM
ESTATE was built, cut N–S by the grandiose double-width
PARKWAY (spoilt by pylons down the central reservation).
Housing began with concrete mansard-roofed Cornish Units
at the N end but is mostly brick of 1955–65. Nothing, not even
the secondary school, 1957–61, meets the scale of Parkway; the
group of shops with flats above is unremarkable. Colourful,
economical YOUTH CENTRE on the E, 1997–8, by *Gareth
Hoskins* of *Penoyre & Prasad* of London, the social space with
full-height glazed quadrant. Set back to the W is Bridgwater
College (p. 138).

SYDENHAM MANOR, Bath Road. British Cellophane made it
the centrepiece of their factory in 1937, the factory buildings
cleared in 2013. An early C16 house of the Percevals, greatly
enlarged after sale in 1613 to William Bull of Shapwick. Blue
Lias. The earlier house, incorporated at the back, has lozenge
hoodmould stops typical of the early C16. A similar hoodmould
to a reused doorway (with the Perceval arms) on the C17 N
range, in a storeyed porch to the l. of a large chimney-breast.
Paired diagonal chimneystacks. Gabled stair-tower behind in
the angle of the W front, an open court formed by a S cross-
wing matching the N range. Interiors much reworked by the
architect *Philip Sturdy*, owner 1921–35, including the staircase.
Some C17 fireplaces.

South of the centre: Taunton Road

TAUNTON ROAD continues St Mary Street southward. Before the ring road, the red brick Gothic former VICARAGE, 1878–80, by *Down & Son*, adjoins the churchyard of the demolished Holy Trinity (1839–40, by *Carver*). On the far side, late C19 brick villas, the first villa distinguished by a square cluster of chimneys linked by arches, a Vanbrugh motif unexpected in this context. Opposite, Nos. 17–55, gabled semi-detached houses in red-and-yellow brick. Beyond the canal a painted brick TOLL HOUSE, after 1829, one end rounded. The HOPE INN, 1930, is extravagantly half-timbered, in the manner of inter-war roadhouses.* Ashleigh Avenue leads W into Hamp Street, with the church (p. 136) and schools (p. 139).

West of the centre: West Street, Durleigh Road and Wembdon Road

WEST STREET was redeveloped after the Second World War with the only point-block council housing in the region. WESTFIELD HOUSE, 1963–5, eleven storeys, is surrounded by five- and four-storey blocks. Opposite Westfield church (p. 137), a survivor, Nos. 118–122, externally C18–C19, but No. 118 has C16 timbers and a screen. On DURLEIGH ROAD, villas of *c.* 1900 on the N side, mostly by *Cottam*. On the S, two roughcast Arts and Crafts houses of considerably greater interest. No. 3, L-plan, has cottage casements under tilework arches and a porch in the angle with Voysey-style sloping buttress. This is of *c.* 1906 by *Parker & Unwin*, then working on Letchworth Garden City.† Can the much more complex No. 5 be theirs also? Rear roof swept over stepped stair windows. To the garden, the l. gable has a canted bay with ornamented leadwork between narrow bands of casement windows. Further out, beyond Haygrove School (p. 139), is ROSARY HOUSE, a heavyweight Victorian villa of the 1860s. Of Wembdon stone, with Jacobean shaped gables and Gothic windows and porch. Not undisciplined, for everything rotates around a tower with an indescribable pavilion roof, but indigestible.

Returning towards Westfield Church, NORTHFIELD runs N, with bargeboarded villas of Wembdon stone, probably by *Edwin Down*, 1880s. On WEMBDON ROAD, late C19 gabled terraces of brick, of which the best are Nos. 71–93, 1890s, with pretty cusped bargeboards and fretted verandas. The CEMETERY of 1851 has lost its buildings, but the columned MEMORIAL to James Cook, 1912, by *W. B. Colthurst*, deserves a look. Prim angel in front. Prominent at the far end, the Italianate tower of THE QUANTOCK, a hefty red sandstone villa of the 1830s.

---

* Contemporary arterial road pubs are West India House, Durleigh Road, and New Market Inn, Bristol Road.

† Mervyn Miller says that the design is by *Raymond Unwin*, who was related to the Sully family of Bridgwater.

North and north-west of the centre: Newtown

The canal defines the NW edge of the centre. To its N, NEWTOWN was the first large area of council housing. Well-designed, by *Samson & Colthurst*, 1926, in red brick groups with arched windows in the outer gables. The spine is KENDALE ROAD. S of it by the canal a *rond-point* at COLERIDGE GREEN. Down the canal to the SW, council houses give way to coloured brick late C19 gabled terraces in LYNDALE AVENUE, VICTORIA ROAD, ALEXANDRA ROAD and NORTH STREET, where the MALT SHOVEL pub, 1904, cheerfully assembles Domestic Revival motifs. Most of this is by *Basil Cottam*. Off Victoria Road, the COMMUNITY CENTRE, 2005–8, an irregular courtyard surrounded by community rooms, medical centre, café and pharmacy, in monopitch-roofed red brick. N of the docks, up CHILTON STREET, a hipped-roofed FLOUR MILL of 1845, of red sandstone, steam-powered from the outset.

BROADWAY

ST ALDHELM AND ST EADBURGA. Perp W tower in squared marlstone; diagonal buttresses and NE stair-turret. The rest is cruciform: C13–C14 chancel and transepts, C15 nave. Refined Perp three-light nave windows, and porch against the S transept. Three C13 stepped lancets to the chancel E, and a small S two-light cut from a C13–C14 incised grave-slab. Three-light transept windows with cusped rere-arches: elegantly ogee-cusped lancets on the S transept E and uncusped intersecting tracery on the N transept N. Contrasting transept arches: double-chamfered N, Perp S. No chancel arch. Panelled C15 roofs, that in the chancel with cusped ribs. – FONT. Octagonal, C14–C15. Each face has a small figure in a pointed frame between slim cusped panels with shields. – PULPIT. Oak, early C16, with numerous square panels, the one with the Crown of Thorns and Five Wounds reportedly saved by being plastered over at the Reformation. – STAINED GLASS. W window, 1863. Three by *Wippell & Co.*, 1923–35. – MONUMENTS. Rev. William Fewtrell †1777. With urn. – Rev. John Fewtrell †1819. Curved-fronted, by *Tyley*.

CHURCHYARD CROSS. C14–C15. On the shaft male saints, one over the other, under an ogee canopy.

EVERY'S ALMSHOUSES are a two-storey row of seven dwellings, in Ham stone, *c.* 1608. Mullioned windows, Tudor-arched doorways. Along the main street, thatched C16–C17 houses amid modern infill. The former MEETING HOUSE, 1739, has arched windows with mullions and transom, as at Mid Lambrook, under a broad gable added 1870.

JORDANS, ½ m. E. The classical house built for William Speke in 1796 has gone. A thatched Gothic TEAROOM of 1828 survives. Square, gable-fronted, enclosing a circular chamber lined in ammonites and rockwork, corniced in coral under a dome star-patterned in seashells. Coloured-glass lantern. Sheep vertebrae for flooring. Three lozenge-shaped front windows had medieval glass. The narrow-side chambers housed caged canaries. An exuberant *cottage orné* at SHRUBBERY FARM, N, is contemporary. Thatched umbrella roof on posts.

BROMPTON RALPH

ST MARY. Quite a big plain tower, roughcast, three-stage, with diagonal sandstone buttresses up to the battlements and small two-light Perp bell-openings with pierced baffles. Square NE stair-turret. Tall slightly chamfered tower arch. The rest was reputedly rebuilt in 1738 but looks Perp, much as in Buckler's drawing of 1841. N aisle of 1847 by *J. P. Harrison* of Oxford; chancel rebuilt in 1880–2 by *Henry Parsons* of Misterton. The square-headed C16 nave S window of four lights and the band of quatrefoils below a chancel S window are reliable. Victorian roofs, arcade and chancel arch. – FONT. Perp, octagonal, with crude low-relief motifs, plants, a green man, and a chalice with two flagons. One underside panel was started but abandoned. – ROOD SCREEN. Re-created by *Bligh Bond* in 1913 from fragments taken to Hartrow Manor (Elworthy) by the rector. Eight narrow square-headed bays, each with pointed three-light tracery, cusped with intersecting arches, similar to Elworthy. Some original colour. The loft is entirely Bond's. – BENCHES. C16, straight-headed, mostly plain, one with unfinished foliage like the carving on the font. – PULPIT. Early C19, panelled. – COMMUNION RAIL. Important, because dated: 1677. The balusters turned and quite sturdy, but already of a certain elegance in outline. – REREDOS. Reused Jacobean arcaded panels. – STAINED GLASS. E window, 1908. Chancel S, 1852, by *John Toms*. – MONUMENT. Rev. Thomas Camplin †1780. Draped urn on a grey oval. By *Thomas King*.

Churchyard MEMORIAL to the Rev. W. Sweet-Escott †1913. Based on Pembrokeshire Celtic crosses.

The village runs SW to a small triangular green by the former CONGREGATIONAL CHAPEL, 1840, hip-roofed, whitewashed, with narrow lancets. NW from the church, former RECTORY, 1862–4 by *William Slater*, with arrays of arched windows.

MANOR FARMHOUSE, ¾ m. SSE. Faced in early brickwork. The original range is late C17 with a dentilled string course and segmental ground-floor arches with keystones over casement windows. In the corner, a door with a shell-hood, added with the SW range. This contains a staircase of *c.* 1720. Twisted balusters, carved tread-ends, the treads and dado panels decorated with inlay.

BROMPTON REGIS

Previously known as King's Brompton. The village wraps around three sides of the large churchyard.

ST MARY. Mostly Perp. The base of the plain W tower could be older – see the low diagonal buttresses. Two-light bell-openings with pierced baffles. Square NE stair-turret to below the bell-stage. The N aisle is one of those showy Late Perp additions with large traceried windows and a rood stair. The rest was much restored in 1852–3 by *C. E. Giles*. Spacious, light interior with a five-bay N arcade on piers of the four-wave type with well-carved vine leaf on banded capitals. Perp double arch from the chancel to the aisle. The S transept, so Victorian outside, has a C14–C15 moulded arch on corbel heads. Squint from here and a cusped squint from the N aisle. – PULPIT. 1625. With a lozenge in each panel and some typical Jacobean arches. – ROYAL ARMS. Victorian, cast-iron. – STAINED GLASS. Good E window by *Kempe*, 1896.

WIMBLEBALL LAKE. A large reservoir for Tiverton, formed in 1979 by damming the headwaters of the River Haddeo. Impressive concrete DAM, 1974–8, 161 ft (49 metres) high, fronted by raking buttresses. *Rofe, Kennard & Lapworth*, engineers; landscaping by *Sylvia Crowe*.

BROOMFIELD

ST MARY AND ALL SAINTS. Two-stage W tower in the local rubble with red sandstone diagonal buttresses and moulded W doorway. Perp two-light bell-openings, one similar window below on the S, and three-light W window. Square higher NE stair-turret. Tower arch of two chamfers dying in to the sides, an early type, but here C15. The chancel has a prettily cusped early C14 S doorway, but is otherwise remodelled with the nave and S porch. The work seems coeval with the early C16 N aisle, but work is recorded before 1443 (*see* below). The aisle, for which money was left in 1532–5, is another of those show aisles added to Somerset churches just before the Reformation (e.g. Spaxton, Lydeard St Lawrence). Lias buttresses, originally contrasting with rendered walls, and Ham stone ornament. Four-centred-arched windows with vertical mullions, good squatting beasts on the cornice, rich embattled parapet with quatrefoil-pierced merlons, and gable parapets. In the S porch a large ogee-headed STOUP with trefoiled spandrels. Four-bay Ham stone arcade of four-centred arches on piers of four-wave section. Leaf-band capitals of Devon type, all different, one with the Instruments of the Passion on shields, one with a green man. The chancel arch is of similar section to the arcade, but with a small capital only to the shaft. Leaf bands also on the capitals of the narrow chancel N arch. Shafted aisle window reveals. Wagon roofs to the nave and aisle, tree-ring-dated to 1507–39, with bosses, the wall-plate undercut and ornamented with numerous little angels.

FONT. Octagonal, Perp. The usual quatrefoil panels, outlined in fat rolls. Underside and stem panels. – BENCHES. A very complete mid-C16 set, square-headed, with tracery, wiry plants and more fleshy foliage, all with the leaf-scroll border associated with *Simon Werman* (cf. Trull); and indeed he signs one. – ROYAL ARMS. 1715. – STAINED GLASS. In the chancel S windows C15–C16 fragments: architectural canopies, two angels commending two kneeling figures, an inscription to Alice Reskymer (prioress of Buckland Priory, Durston, in 1457), angels' heads, etc. Fragments in other window heads. E window by *Morris & Co.*, 1913, using *Burne-Jones* figures. – MONUMENTS. Brass to Richard Silverton †1443 (tower floor), chaplain, holding a chalice. The head is missing. The inscription records that he 'sumptuously repaired and magnificently decorated' the church. – Two monuments with draped urns by Bath firms, John Jeane †1790, by *King*, and Elizabeth Jeane, *c.* 1810, by *Reeves*, more Greek.

In the churchyard a C15 CROSS, the shaft with pinnacled shafts suggested at the angles and moulded octagonal cap. The unusually ornate CHEST TOMB to Andrew Crosse †1653 has naked demi-figures and Jacobean ornament.

The churchyard opens W to a square green bordering the Fyne Court estate. FYNE COURT COTTAGES on the N, the former Parsonage Farm, have brickwork of *c.* 1700 to the lower walls.

FYNE COURT (National Trust). The house of the Crosse family burnt in 1894 leaving only two endpieces, the five-bay music room at the W end of the S façade, and a lofted piece from the N end of the E front. Also some modest outbuildings. The main house had a Georgian character from alterations before 1800. The music room was rebuilt in 1849 for the pioneer scientist Andrew Crosse (†1855) whose electrical experiments were carried out here. Above the house, an unromantic FOLLY, two brick turrets, frames the outlet from a canal laid out by *Crosse* after 1805.

BROOMFIELD HALL, 2 m. NNE. High three-storey, five-bay brick front of 1803. The bracketed eaves and cast-iron porch columns look like alterations.

BRUSHFORD

ST NICHOLAS. C15 W tower with diagonal buttresses, the top stage rebuilt in 1887 by *C. H. Samson*. Roughcast nave with finely traceried early C16 S windows; copies on the N by *Samson*.

The major architectural interest is the NE chapel to Aubrey Herbert of Pixton Park by *Sir Edwin Lutyens*, 1924–6. Primitive in feeling, with extremely narrow arched windows linked by flush ashlar bands. Cross-shaped E window; the only decoration, three raised squares around it, was intended for heraldry. C15–C16 roofs, mostly plastered over, and plain plastered chancel arch. The Herbert Chapel is separated by a flat-headed opening under which is the tomb, the soffit treated like a rood loft with deep cove and traceried panels with painted heraldry. The chapel is mysterious, the narrow windows glowing pink-orange under a cradling rafter roof. Trio of E windows under segmental arches, the geometries of the central cross more striking from inside.

FURNISHINGS. FONT. Square, Norman, of Purbeck marble (cf. Milborne Port, Templecombe). Typical shallow arches each side. Base of 1890. – ROOD SCREEN. Late C15, five bays. The leaf-scroll borders suggest the Carhampton–Minehead group, but other detail differs, especially the intermediate shafts. Missing tracery. Good loft with ribbed and traceried coving and cornice of four intricate layers. In the r. bay a PULPIT of reused traceried panels. – WEST GALLERY. 1906. – BENCHES. In the chapel. C16, cut down. – STAINED GLASS. Nave N first, by *Burne-Jones* for *Morris & Co.*, 1892. The scenes below the three single figures are particularly fine. Three colourful windows by *Powell's*: nave S, 1891 (design by *Holiday*), E, 1898, nave N second, 1899. Chancel S, 1925, with an early C16 French Virgin Mary and two Flemish C16 pieces. – MONUMENTS. Aubrey Herbert M.P. †1923. By *Cecil de B. Howard*, a Canadian-born American based in Paris. Herbert, the reputed model for John Buchan's hero Sandy Arbuthnot, and twice offered the throne of Albania, is depicted in riding clothes recumbent on his cavalry cloak and rolled mat. Slats of black marble raise the catafalque slightly over the tomb-chest, a classic Lutyens design, with deep coves stopped against flush plaques. – Elizabeth Howard †1929. Brass lettered by *Eric Gill*, 1931. – Mary Herbert †1970. Brass lettered by *Denis Tegetmeier*.

At the E end of the village is the former DULVERTON STATION, 1873, with goods shed, of the Devon & Somerset Railway. Also the large former CARNARVON ARMS HOTEL, 1873–4, promoted for hunting visitors by Lord Carnarvon of Pixton Park (Dulverton). Three storeys with gabled cross-wings, the l. one slightly later.

COMBE, ¾ m. NW. Late medieval to early C17 house of the Sydenhams, much altered. Of U-plan (a storeyed porch has been removed). Most of the oak mullion windows date from 1926–7. (Fifteen-panel framed ceiling beneath a first-floor hall with wind-braced roof. Parlour with linenfold panelling, plaster frieze of cherubs and festoons, and ribbed ceiling.)

HELE MANOR, Exebridge. Large Georgian-style hunting lodge by *Horace Farquharson*, begun 1912, for Harry Heathcoat Amory. Relaxed in an Edwardian way, of rubble stone under hipped roofs with swept eaves. On the garden front canted bays and a loggia. Panelled entrance hall and stair hall. Contemporary ESTATE COTTAGES: a hip-roofed pair at the entrance, a row of three by the stables uphill to the W.

EXE BRIDGE, Exebridge. C18. Three broad round arches, rising to the middle. Repaired in 1829 by *John Stone*.

BRUTON

A small town, essentially comprising one street above the River Brue, but of far from average architectural interest. The narrow level ground S of the river was an ecclesiastical site from the C7, probably an Anglo-Saxon minster, then an Augustinian priory, from which came the parish church and the C16 school.

ST MARY. One of the proudest churches of the county: clerestoried nave, aisles, dominant W tower, and a N porch-tower that would on its own dignify any small Somerset church. The building history is confused by the disappearance of Bruton Abbey, of which too little is known. It was an Augustinian priory founded by William de Mohun before 1135, and an abbey from 1511. The abbey church may have been the parish church, but documentary evidence of its unroofing after 1539 suggests not. Monastic buildings SW of the parish church became the great house of the Berkeleys called Bruton Abbey, demolished in 1786. Illustrations show a courtyard house, the formal S front with twin polygonal turrets. There were two late C7 churches, founded by King Ine and St Aldhelm, the latter becoming the church of the priory. Of Norman work all that survives is a broken font, a chevroned double capital (Bruton Museum) perhaps from a cloister, and some fragments in the wall behind the organ.

The earliest part of the present church is the six-cell vaulted CRYPT partly below the chancel. This looks early C14 – it has plain chamfered ribs dying into two octagonal piers – and is of Hadspen stone, not used elsewhere in the church. Its position implies an earlier church that has been entirely replaced, for everything else apart from the C18 chancel is Perp.

The church is externally unified, all of Doulting stone. There is an apparent sequence from an early C15 nave with aisles and N tower to a late C15 W tower, concluding with the clerestory and nave roof *c.* 1510. But inconsistencies suggest a more complex story in which older parts were modified to match C15 additions. Both aisles have three-light window tracery with a high transom not found elsewhere in SW England, but the windows differ in width on each side and do not align, so one aisle was possibly modified to match the other. The S aisle and clerestory have pierced parapets, while the N aisle has battlements datable to the early C16 from the emblems of the founders of King's School.* The N TOWER seems to be an elaborated porch, such as existed on much larger scale at Glastonbury Abbey. Perp detail: diagonal buttresses, two-light bell-openings and a square SW turret. The five-bay clerestory of uncommonly wide four-light windows stands over arcades of shafted piers of standard four-hollow section. The conjoined capitals suggest the early C15. The arches have a slightly flattened curve.

Splendid late C15 W TOWER, 102 ft (31 metres) high, ashlar-faced in four well-proportioned stages. Set-back buttresses connected by a diagonal across the angle relate it to three groups of Somerset towers – around Shepton Mallet, around Langport, and around Westonzoyland – a relationship confirmed by their similar bell-stages. The buttresses carry tall shafts set diagonally, crowned by pinnacles quite detached from the wall, and the main diagonal is continued into the tower pinnacles, also set diagonally. W doorway with leaf spandrels under a tall six-light W window (transomed with ogee-headed lights) with three canopied niches stepped above. Canopied niches to the third stage, on shafts with angels and linked by the extended sill of a two-light window. Three tall two-light bell-openings with transoms and latticed baffles, separated by pinnacled shafts. The battlements are richly pierced: merlons with diagonal crosses over a band of quatrefoils with shields above encircled quatrefoils. On the N side the arrangement is modified for a polygonal stair-turret. The tower arch inside has an imposing continuous triple wave moulding. The fan-vault is Georgian plaster.

The NAVE has a lovely roof of the best Somerset type, richly detailed, panelled and sub-panelled, on tie-beams with king-posts flanked by tracery (two quatrefoils and a mouchette each side). There are braces above the tie-beams that replicate intermediate trusses, but more elegantly done than at Martock, the pieces here shallow-arched rather than horizontal. The intermediate trusses have a pendant, and rise from wall-plate angels. Angels also face out from the main tie-beams, which are arch-braced from wall-shafts linked laterally by carved spandrels. As at Martock the wall-shafts rest on stone angel corbels above canopied niches, and there are angels at two levels below the niches. Panelled aisle roofs enriched at the E: the N with original colour marking the site of a medieval altar, the S with enriched panels against the arcade, marking perhaps an important tomb. Both aisles have recesses apparently for stairs, but the rood stair is at the chancel arch. Cusped S piscina. In the restoration by *Slater & Carpenter* in 1868–78 the chancel arch was found (and rebuilt) beneath 'modern wood and plaster', i.e. C18 work – for the chancel was rebuilt in 1743, probably by *Nathaniel Ireson*, for Sir Charles Berkeley.

---

* The monogram of Abbot Gilbert of Bruton, the shield of Bishop Fitzjames of London, and the monogram and punning beer-barrel of Abbot Bere of Glastonbury.

This C18 CHANCEL is externally bald, with a blank E wall under a pediment with the Berkeley arms. Pierced parapets and buttresses between rudimentary Gothic windows enclosing two arched lights and a circle. The interior is not Gothic at all and exceedingly handsome in white, blue and gold, as restored by *Alan Rome*, 1964. A groined plaster vault of laurel-leaf ribs and encircled acanthus roses rests on a deep cornice on exuberant corbels with cherub heads (the second S by *Ernst Blensdorf*, 1964), all brilliantly gilded. The E wall has a giant Corinthian tripartite composition of Counter-Reformation splendour. A pediment on columns frames a large gadrooned panel with the IHS motif in a sunburst, over a panel with a smoking thurible between cornucopiae. Between the outer pilasters the Crown of Thorns and Sacred Heart nestle amid lively Rococo scroll. Some detail (the gadrooned frame) relates clearly to *Ireson*, but unspecified work to the chancel is recorded in 1770 for John, last Lord Berkeley. Stone paving in three colours; black marble steps, rebated in concave curves. Plaster-vaulted C18 N vestry.

FURNISHINGS. FONT. 1847, with openwork ogee cover. The remaining pieces of a square C12 font of Purbeck marble indicates a very handsome work with seven-bay arcading and well-carved fluted capitals. – SCREEN. 1938, by *W. H. Randoll Blacking*. Large oak arcade on Corinthian columns with Rood figures above, a clever transition between disparate spaces. – TOWER SCREEN. Dated 1620 on an affixed panel, but was it intended for a church? The carving is intense, not of strapwork but rich foliage scrolls and classical beasts, quite without classical restraint. Reused medieval lower panels. – ALTAR RAILS. Early C18. Delicate alternately twisted balusters, between Ionic newels. STALLS C18, panelled. – BENCH-ENDS. C17, with shell-tops, and many C19 copies. – NE CHAPEL furnished 1920 by *Harold Rogers*. Painted reredos. Reused C15 pieces in the communion rail. – ROYAL ARMS. Charles II. Large, carved and painted. – SCULPTURE. Crucifixion, 1969, a powerful Expressionist piece in sycamore by *Ernst Blensdorf*, a German refugee living in Bruton from 1942. – ORGAN. early C19 Gothic case. – STAINED GLASS. Chancel, C16–C17 armorial roundels. W window, 1877, numerous figures, by *Clayton & Bell*. S aisle W, 1888, by the *Royal Windsor Stained Glass Works*. Moses leads to the Promised Land, a gift of descendants of the Ames family who founded Williamsburg. S third, †1854, bright figure panels on patterned quarries. N fourth, signed *W. F. Dixon*, c. 1884, subtle colours.

MONUMENTS. Eroded Perp tomb-chest with big quatrefoils (nave). – Sir Maurice Berkeley †1581 and two wives †1559 and 1585 (chancel recess). Probably by *William Arnold*. Three effigies on a tomb-chest with strapwork panels. Corinthian columns frame two arches with naïve Renaissance nudes in the spandrels. He, armoured, lies between matching wives in a chamber with obelisks, strapwork cartouches and strapwork ceiling. – William Godolphin †1636. Exotic. Gilded bronze bust in a black marble oval under an unorthodox curved pediment. Of the school of *Hubert Le Sueur*. – William, Lord Stratton, †1741. Compact, well-detailed, with broken pediment and flaming urn. – Captain William Berkeley. 1749, by *Peter Scheemakers*. Military trophies and urn. – John Donne †1782. Three-colour marble with urn. – Anna Hoskyns-Abrahall †1837, Gothic, by *Osmond*.

KING'S SCHOOL. In its original form, housed just outside the abbey precinct, the school was small, as most C16 schools were. Bishop Fitzjames of London founded it in 1519, perhaps stimulated by Colet's foundation of St Paul's School in 1510. It was re-founded in the name of Edward VI in 1550. The C16 school, OLD HOUSE, has an entirely domestic front, roughcast, with Tudor-arched lights to mullioned windows and a pedimented C18 doorway. Just two lower rooms divided by a passage. Plank partition r. to the schoolroom; moulded framed ceiling to the parlour, l. The master presumably lived above. Very early on a rear wing was added, with a schoolroom under a dormitory. Four-centred-headed doorways. The N end windows and bellcote are C19. Modest C18 W and NW additions for the master, the W with a Venetian window. Having declined to just one boy in 1811, the school revived under the Rev. John Hoskyns-Abrahall from 1826. He built the hip-roofed BIG SCHOOLROOM to the E in 1834. Not large, with a dormitory reached by a diminutive embattled NW stair-tower. Lobby of reused Jacobean woodwork. Behind are a stone early C19 FIVES WALL and a three-storey DORMITORY by *Ronald Vallis*, 1982, glazed in vertical strips. By the river, an early C19 brick Gothick GAZEBO. PLOX HOUSE, at right angles to the road, is dated 1687. Roughcast with Georgian sashes and paired rear gables, a good C17 staircase in one. NEW HOUSE to the W, 1870–2, typical Victorian collegiate Gothic, with a storeyed porch, was extended W in 1878 and 1913. Dining hall behind by *Vallis*, 1975.

Across the road, a campus began grandly with the Gothic MEMORIAL HALL of 1919–24 by *Arthur Pictor*. Seven-bay hall with open timber roof, between library and classroom wings. Each hall panel bears a name, of some 120 dead. More recent, and more modest, buildings on the other two sides of the courtyard: the RECEPTION BUILDING, S, 2006–8 by *Acanthus Clews Architects*, with drum-shaped offices for the headmaster and bursar, the flat-roofed SPORTS HALL AND THEATRE, SE, 1979, by *Severnside Architects* (relief sculpture by *John Robinson*), and BLACKFORD HOUSE, E, 1960, by *Vallis*. The HOBHOUSE BUILDING, SE, of 1999, by *Mancon Project Management*, houses *Ernst Blensdorf*'s monumental woodcarving, Abraham's Sacrifice, 1951.

SEXEY'S SCHOOL, Cole Road. 1891–2, by *George Skipper* of Norwich. Double-gabled with a timber lantern, showing nothing of Skipper's Art Nouveau. To the NE, two large yellow brick buildings, 1998 and 2008–9, by *Charles Evans* of *Lawray Architects*, before CLIFF HOUSE, three-storeyed, stuccoed, of

c. 1820, with columned porch. Extended in 1929 and in 2003, the latter by *Evans*. sw of Skipper's building, COOMBE HOUSE, 1983, by *Alan Dickens* of *Somerset County Architects*, overhangs the deep combe. Beyond the combe, buildings of similar date, and MACMILLAN HOUSE, 2011, by *Timothy MacBean*, a boarding house in buff brick with central glazed gable.

PRIMARY SCHOOL, Higher Backway. 1929–32, by *A. J. Toomer*, County Architect. Roughcast courtyard school with the veranda classrooms pioneered in Derbyshire schools (cf. Hindhayes School, Street).

SEXEY'S HOSPITAL, High Street. Founded under the will of Hugh Sexey †1619. Like a small Oxford college. Plain two-storey Tudor-style ranges to the street, but within are two quadrangles, the w quadrangle of 1626–8 and the E C19, its w range being the fourth side of the first court. This has residences N and w, and a collegiate range on the s comprising the chapel and two Visitors' rooms beneath the master's apartment. The residences have mullion windows and Tudor-arched doorways. A remodelling of 1882 made upper doors reached by galleries, of which one remains. The s range has three-light windows with cusped-headed lights, the centre light wider and taller (cf. Leweston church, Dorset, 1616), under stepped hoodmoulds. One window to the chapel, l., two to each floor to the r., the upper ones in dormer gables. Three doorways (original doors): for the chapel, for the two Visitors' rooms, under a festooned late C17 niche with Sexey's bust signed by *William Stanton*, and to the committee room (blocked). The E and s chapel windows are three-light Perp, possibly reused. The CHAPEL, almost square under a plastered barrel ceiling, has C17 panelled stalls on three sides, desk and pulpit on the fourth. Schoolboy graffiti from the C17 onward. A good C17 screen with Ionic columns (plank panelling above) divides the Visitors' room from the committee room. Basement kitchen and refectory, opening on to vegetable gardens with a pyramid-roofed SUMMERHOUSE. The E range, between the two courts, is of c. 1805, three-storeyed with parapet. Good neo-Tudor for the date, the windows two-light and flat-headed except on the top floor where they are arched. The E court behind has a s range of 1854 facing outward with dormer gables and stepped ground-floor windows (copying those of the chapel range), and a longer N range of 1882 backing on to the High Street, plain neo-Tudor.

THE DOVECOTE, Park Wall. Stark on the hilltop to the s. The large four-gabled tower was probably built in the late C16 as a prospect tower for the Berkeleys of Bruton Abbey, although the windows are small. The nesting boxes are C18 insertions. An early view shows it approached by an avenue of trees.

PERAMBULATION. The long street is cut towards the E end by the ascending road from the church, the crossing of that warped kind that old towns evolve when a market place has been infilled. Narrow passages (bartons) drop down towards the river. Houses are of limestone rubble, some fronted in

Doulting ashlar, some plastered, and a significant number are timber-framed, indicating an extended linear settlement already by the C15.

W of the church is the high thirteen-bay ABBEY WALL, divided by strong ashlar buttresses. The purpose of such a wall, some way from both abbey and great house, is uncertain. A doorway under one buttress suggests embellishment perhaps by the Berkeleys, whose stables it screened. These were replaced by the stately VICARAGE, 1822, of 1–3–1 bays with cornice and parapet. Opposite, the CHURCH SCHOOL, 1851, by *James Davis* of Frome, with complicated tracery. Behind is the narrow C16 BOW BRIDGE, a steep single arch with Bishop Fitzjames's crest. Beyond is King's School (*see* p. 156). Over the river from the church, PATWELL HOUSE, painted ashlar of the 1860s, with pilasters and a teardrop fanlight. BELL HOUSE, at right angles, mirrors the details. PATWELL STREET climbs to the central crossing. No. 9 is C15, jettied timber over stone. No. 7, with Georgian sash windows, has C16 fireplaces. Nos. 3–5 was the Old Bull inn, with central throughway.

The staggered central crossing is a much-encroached market square where stood a vaulted market cross of *c.* 1535. A Tudor-style LIBRARY, by *Pictor*, 1913, faces W down HIGH STREET. On the S side, BRUTON HOUSE, a later C18 refronting with central Venetian window (pediment of 1985), looks across at No. 1, ashlar-fronted Late Georgian with a double-bowed shopfront. Both sides of High Street are continuously terraced, on medieval burgage plots. On the N side, No. 3 has undisciplined late C18 detail: festoons, arched doorway uncomfortably under a columned pediment. It had a balustraded parapet. Nothing hints that this refronts a C15 house. A C16 jettied timber-framed range encloses the back courtyard, and behind that is a hip-roofed Georgian Gothic stable. No. 5 has a pedimented doorcase. No. 13 was the King's Arms, the throughway (disguised by 1890s infill) dividing two late medieval ranges, the E one over a barrel vault. No. 15 was Stuckey's Bank, 1892, by *C. & C. B. Benson*, double-gabled, coarsely detailed. No. 17 has a Late Georgian front of painted stone with parapet. No. 23, with two Venetian windows of different builds, echoes two narrow burgage plots. Roughcast Late Georgian fronts at No. 27, narrow, with bowed Regency window, and HAMILTON HOUSE, double-fronted with pedimented doorway. No. 31 is medieval: the gabled cross-wing has a fine arch-braced roof of *c.* 1400, while the eastern roof has been tree-ring-dated to 1453. A cellar beam yielded the exceptionally early date of 1294–8. No. 35 has a moulded framed C16 ceiling. The MASONIC HALL was the Market Hall, its double arches infilled in 1875 for an infants' school. Tall ashlar gable dated 1684, 1642 date behind. Late Georgian roughcast on SAXON HOUSE disguises two medieval houses. The E half was gabled; its upper parlour has a moulded fireplace and a beam prettily painted in a three-colour zigzag with tiny fleurs-de-lys at the points. In the W half, chamfered beams and a C16 fireplace.

On the S side, after Bruton House, a pleasantly varied group before Nos. 16–20, a C15 commercial row with some close-studded timbers. Wind-braced roof tree-ring-dated to 1453. The very complete jettied and close-studded house behind No. 24 is tree-ring-dated to 1430. BRUTON MUSEUM occupies a coach works of 1893. The former UNION CHAPEL (Congregational) occupies a tall late C18 silk mill, whose L-plan encloses the chapel added in 1836. The front was remodelled, probably in 1836, as two storeys (No. 30 shows the original three) with typical Y-tracery windows, combined with a classical cornice and pilasters. The centrepiece looks later. Luminous interior with galleries on thin Gothic columns, well converted to a restaurant in 2009 by *Mackenzie Wheeler*. BERKELEY HOUSE is stuccoed, with a fluted late C18 Doric doorway, but irregular spacing of the five bays shows that it is a refronting. Open-well Late Georgian staircase. THE PRIORY was possibly the priory courthouse. Jettied timber frame over stone. Three stone corbels (unicorn, green man, lions), support priory heraldry including the rebus of John Henton, prior 1448–98. Framed ceilings. E room panelled in the mid C18 with an overmantel landscape showing Glastonbury Tor. Nos. 38–40 are three-storeyed, ashlar-fronted, mid-C19. Then nothing exceptional until Sexey's Hospital (p. 157). No. 72, just beyond, is early C17, of some quality, perhaps built for the hospital. Mullioned windows and the base of a central oriel. Fine corniced stone fireplaces, the E room panelled with a Jacobean arcaded overmantel.

High Street drops to the much-altered C17 TOWN MILL. Down Mill Lane, THE BOARD HALL, 2012–13, timber-framed with a double-curve roof, by the owner, *Mark Pickthall*, with *Roger Gallannaugh*. An altered mill at No. 8. At West End, the MILL ON THE BRUE has a bow-ended meeting hall, 2005, by *Roger Gallannaugh*. Steel-framed, with deep eaves sheltering balcony access. Behind the METHODIST CHAPEL (1848, later C19 detail), WEST END HOUSE has a Late Georgian brick front. Above, in its own grounds, PROSPECT HOUSE is late C18, hip-roofed, three-storeyed. ST CATHERINE'S HILL climbs N from High Street. TOLBURY HOUSE, framed by tall hip-roofed cross-wings, seems to be a remodelling of *c.* 1830 (date 1835 on the boundary wall). HIGHER BACKWAY returns E past the primary school (p. 157) and the PROVENDER MILL, mid-C20, with tall hoist tower. Reclad in black metal in a hard-edged conversion by *Stanley Merer*, 1999. Top-floor apartment for the artist Victor Burgin, by *Paul Fineberg*, 2007. Minimal metal stairs and gallery appropriate to the exposed steel roof structure. Back on the central crossroads, the late C18 BLUE BALL INN has plain assembly rooms behind. QUAPERLAKE STREET runs E. GROVE HOUSE on the N side is later C18, detached. On the S a row with Georgian pedimented doorways refronts older work, apparent from C17 mullions on No. 11. THE GLEN, with a Doric doorcase, has C15–C16 origins. Incorporated in the rear range are C16 carved stone shells from the Berkeley mansion. VINEY'S YARD was a late C18 silk mill.

GANT'S MILL, ¾ m. WSW. A beautiful industrial site with tall stone buildings. The three-storey E half was perhaps built as a stocking mill in 1740, the four-storey W half added for silk manufacture by the French entrepreneur Theophilus Perceval, c. 1812. This has close-spaced windows for maximum light. Floors altered when converted to corn-milling c. 1850. A S projection of 1883 covers the medieval mill. A mid-C19 wheel was supplemented by steam (1883), then replaced by a 20-in. (50-cm.) Armfield turbine (1888), which remains. A hip-roofed cottage, c. 1800, and miller's house with mid-C19 front complete the group.

SHEEPHOUSE FARMHOUSE, 1 m. ENE. Compact early C18 hip-roofed house with stone cross-windows. Over the railway, the dry RESERVOIR protects Bruton from flash flood water. 1984 by *Rendel, Palmer & Tritton*, modified 2008.

DURSLADE FARM, ¼ m. SE. Late C18 model farmstead, the house of c. 1768 with Lord Berkeley's arms. Gothick rear wing and stable with loft roundels; barn and granary around a large farmyard, converted to an ARTS CENTRE for Hauser & Wirth, 2013–14, by *Benjamin & Beauchamp* with new galleries behind by *Luis Laplace* of Paris. These, around a small polygonal court, are sober in buff brick with colonnades of square concrete piers. Meadow GARDEN behind by *Piet Oudolf*. Shop and café interiors with recycled materials by *Björn & Oddur Roth*. Farmhouse with neo-Cubist murals by *Guillermo Kuitca* of Buenos Aires.

GODMINSTER MANOR, 1¼ m. S. The C15 to C18 house, restored c. 1910 by *Pictor*, was badly repaired after a fire in 1924. Its character derives from a reworking in 1999–2006 by *Donald Insall Associates* for Richard Hollingbery, a contemporary equivalent of Edwardian transformations as at Lytes Cary. Rear additions are replaced with a tall mullion-windowed piece, restoring a visual unity of gables, octagonal chimneys and stone-tiled roofs. The C15 S range was refashioned with a storeyed porch and seven-light window marking the great hall, which gained a new wind-braced roof. Original large W fireplace with traceried spandrels. The C16 cross-wing has a framed ceiling and pretty seven-bay W façade of the early C18. Rendered, with ashlar angles, cornice and parapet, alternating ground-floor pediments and bolection-moulded doorcase. Large square DOVECOTE restored in 1923, the four gables and cross-gabled timber crown copied from photographs. Narrow brick C18 GRANARY. A truncated BARN has been restored to length, with an oak rafter roof.

BRYMPTON D'EVERCY

Still unaffected by the westward expansion of Yeovil, the ensemble of Brympton House with its forecourt, the Chantry House,

BRYMPTON D'EVERCY

and the church, is of exquisite beauty, one of the most perfect the county has to offer. The stone used is from Ham Hill, and its lovely colour can nowhere be seen to greater advantage.

St Andrew. Low, rambling and extremely attractive. The w end has a picturesque heavy bellcote like a big lantern, as at Chilthorne Domer and Ashington. This is late C15, as is the w window. The church was cruciform until the N transept was subsumed into three-bay NE chapel c. 1460. Late C13 trefoiled s doorway and arch into the s transept. The transept has a Late Geometrical s window of c. 1300 of rare delicacy, three small trefoils and three even smaller within the roundel head, and a w window with intersecting tracery (moved in the 1890s from the opposite wall). The N transept has large late C14 w and N three-light windows, the tracery heads cusped ovals. The chancel has simple Perp tracery of c. 1400, flush with the wall. The NE chapel, called the 'new Ile' in the will of Walter Sydenham †1469, has contrastingly rich deep-set Perp three-light windows, and typical plinth, buttresses, and battlements, the battlements extended over the N transept.

A wonderfully disparate interior is let down only by the roofs of 1897 by *C. B. Benson*. No chancel arch; very different arches to each transept and to the NE chapel. Squints from both transepts. The s transept has a narrow trefoiled C13 arch on corbels, delicate nook-shafts to the s window, and a trefoiled piscina. The N transept has a narrow rounded arch, undatable, and early C14 cinquefoiled piscina. The crudely carved opening to the NE chapel is probably an altered niche, triangular-headed, cusped, with crocketed cresting and a dove on one pier. The C15 panelled ceiling came from the s transept. The chapel is better finished, the mid-C15 ceiling with good bosses including the Stourton arms and a deer in a thicket. Broad panelled arch into the chancel, and twin-canopied E wall niches.

FURNISHINGS. FONT. Large, late C13 octagonal bowl with rough cinquefoil-cusped panels, on a thick octagonal base with angle shafts. – PULPIT. Early C17. Arched panels and arabesque panels. – SCREEN. Stone, which is rare in Somerset but found in north Dorset (Nether Compton, Bradford Abbas, Thornford). Reconstructed since Wheatley drew it in 1847. The stone bench and pointed openings in pairs are C19; only the doorway, with green-man spandrels, and the wooden cresting are reliable. The beam is painted blue and red, with embossed fleurons and heraldry, this indicating a date before 1434. – CANDELABRA. Three, two-tier, C18. – Lord's Prayer and Creed BOARDS, 1700. – STAINED GLASS. C14–C16 fragments in three windows: NE chapel N, W window, and S transept s. s transept w, by *Powell's*, 1902. – MONUMENTS. Small slab with raised cross (s transept N wall). – Large early C14 Purbeck floor slab with lettered border, and two Ham stone cross-inscribed slabs (N transept). – Purbeck base of a C15 canopied tomb (NE chapel), inscribed to Sir John Posthumus Sydenham

†1696. – Four effigies, outside until *c.* 1850, then recarved by *J. E. Carew*. In the N transept an early C14 priest and a lady wearing a kerchief and wimple, *c.* 1325. Both are under canopies like fireplace lintels, cusped, with carved reliefs. The one over the priest is C15, with the Adoration of the Magi and the Annunciation in the spandrels. The other is by *Carew*. – NE chapel. A knight, *c.* 1275 or a little later, cross-legged with mail coif, much restored. – A lady, *c.* 1440, uncommonly large, with horned head-dress. – Sir John Sydenham †1625. A flamboyant painted tomb covered in family heraldry. No effigy but a chequered slab with sloping sides (cf. Lord Hunsdon, Westminster Abbey) on a large tomb-chest with shields over low open arches. A skull in each partly conceals a gruesome floor of fictive bones, an extreme *memento mori*. The imagery comes from Sydenham's funeral sermon, 1626, 'Nature's overthrow and Death's triumph'. Corinthian columns support a canopy with enormous strapwork heraldry between Sydenham rams. – Robert Young †1790. Well-carved draped urn. – Jane, Countess of Westmorland †1857, florid Gothic.

In the churchyard, the circular stepped base of a CHURCHYARD CROSS and notably good CHEST TOMBS, one with Perp quatrefoils. A chalice on the W end indicates a priest.

BRYMPTON HOUSE. The property was given in 1434 by John Stourton of Preston Plucknett to his daughter, who was married to John Sydenham. It remained with the Sydenhams (also of Combe Sydenham) until the 1690s, by which time it had its present form, illustrated in a setting of enclosed gardens in the Kip engraving of 1707. The Sydenhams were followed by Thomas Penny (†1730) who made significant alterations inside and out, and then by Francis Fane M.P. The alterations for the Fanes, Earls of Westmorland after 1762, are ill recorded, but Buckler's 1827 view shows that the front was regularized before 1845. The rearrangement of the gardens is credited to Lady Georgiana Fane (†1874). The C15 house probably had two courts divided by a great hall. The most significant medieval survival is the Chantry, the detached range on the S side of the outer court, possibly lodgings. What there is of the C15 in the main house is disguised by Tudor to Elizabethan work which gives the W front its character. The whole extremely picturesque group is completed by the Clock Tower (an early C18 summerhouse), the church to the S and the stables to the N. And there is the particular glory of Brympton, the palatial ten-bay S front added in the 1660s.

The WEST FRONT makes an admirable group but consists of multiple layers, late C15, early and mid-C16, early C18, and C19. Under a single broad hipped roof (probably C18) are gathered the hall, a parlour block to the N and the solar cross-wing to the S. A stepped buttress marks the NW corner of the original service end, rebuilt as a grand Tudor parlour block, perhaps the apartment documented as reserved for his own use by John Sydenham II in 1534. This consists of a broad full-height canted bay with battlements over a quatrefoil frieze.

A large transomed upper window indicates the principal chamber. The lights, arranged 1–5–1, have uncusped curved heads. Below this window, a broad band of cusped lozenges in squares flank exuberantly carved arms of Henry VIII. In the lozenges are shields with royal devices. Below the band, ground-floor mullioned lights are set high in the wall, above a basement window. To the r., against the hall, is an octagonal stair-turret with similar battlements and a narrower band, of pointed quatrefoils in lozenges. Slightly later in the C16 the great hall was floored and given a new front wall slightly forward of the old, uncomfortably joined to the parlour-block stair-turret. Three bays and two high storeys, with two large double-transom mullioned windows to the hall, central porch, and three large cross-windows above. Behind the flat parapet are marks of three gables, which presumably carried the twisted finials with heraldic beasts now on each end. Similar finials at Barrington Court and Montacute are of the 1540s and 1550s. The regularity is deceptive. Buckler's drawing does not show the large ground-floor r. window, but a small pointed doorway with window above, and he shows the remarkable central PORCH as an oriel bay. It does indeed appear to be an early C16 oriel, moved here in 1722. A cage of stone and glass, it has battlements, quatrefoil frieze, and five-light transomed windows on three sides, with single lights in the chamfered angles. The ogee Gothic doorway was there by 1845. The solar cross-wing to the r. has a low gable and a C17–C18 curved-pedimented first-floor window. Buckler drew a tall blocked four-centred archway below this.

The REAR COURT has a C17 character. The KITCHEN on the E side is a high hall lit by full-height double-transom windows. On the back wall, a polygonal stair-turret with bellcote. The S range contains the staircase of the 1660s, serving the parallel main S range. One corniced doorway is of this period. But the four gables and stone cross-windows must be early C17, even if some windows have been re-set to the line of the staircase. There is C15–C16 work in the cellar: heavy corbelled beams and a moulded E doorway. Buildings on the N side have gone.

Now the SOUTH RANGE. Set back to the W is the side of the C15 cross-wing, battlemented and buttressed. Four windows below, three above, tall early C18 sashes in hoodmoulded frames of C15–C16 type. The S range may have a front of the 1660s, but is C16–C17, dated from three chimney gables in the valley to the stair hall, and a fragment of plaster (*see* below). It presumably continued the line of the cross-wing before the range was reconstructed with a façade forward of the old line. This grand façade is one of three in Somerset, with Ashton Court (Bristol) and Hinton House (Hinton St George), that show the evolution of a Carolean classical style from the excesses of the Jacobean. In terms of proportion it is the best of the three. This is not the pure classicism of Inigo Jones, but a more provincial strand leading to such buildings as the Old Ashmolean, Oxford, 1679–83. Ashton Court, of 1633–4,

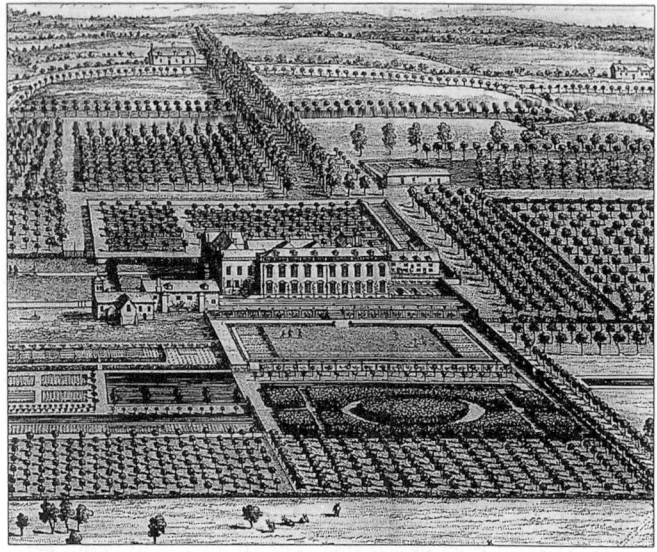

Brympton D'Evercy, Brympton House, from the south. Engraving by J. Kip, 1707

introduced alternating pediments on the ground floor and corniced upper windows, but still had Jacobean shell niches and pierced parapet. Hinton House, *c.* 1634–6, is much bolder with very much broader windows in pedimented architraves, but is not a complete work of architecture in that its irregular window spacing shows older work refaced and the pierced parapet is Perp Gothic. Brympton resembles Hinton in the scale of the windows, but their bolection-moulded surrounds point to a post-Restoration date. Sir John Posthumus Sydenham came of age in 1663 and married Elizabeth Poulett in 1664, giving a connection to Hinton. Their arms are on a rainwater head, so a commencement between 1664 and her death in 1669 seems likely. Ten broad windows are closely spaced on each floor, each with stone cross-mullions, under alternating pediments. Top balustrade with urns on piers. There is no centrepiece, and no doorway; joists in the E end wall suggest that the range should have been longer. One extra bay would have balanced the alternating pediments. This was intended as a great suite of State Rooms, but the construction exhausted the Sydenham wealth, the interiors being unfinished when Sir John died in 1696.

INTERIORS. The porch opens into the HALL which has a plain plaster ceiling. The four-centred-arched N doorways formerly entered the service range from a lost cross-passage. The dais was at the other end, indicated by a Perp SE archway, formerly the hall oriel. This now opens into the STAIR HALL, a long room with the STAIRCASE rising in an extremely extended fashion across the N wall. Thick turned balusters, thick rails, and pedestal finials, 1660s, renewed in the C19. A Georgian doorway by the hall archway enters the CROSS-WING on the S end, which has two good panelled rooms. Large raised-field panelling and modillion cornices. The eastern room has applied drops and festoons of fruit and flowers. All this must be of c. 1720–40. The STATE ROOMS of the 1660s are five in sequence, each with a thick C17 cornice with bay-leaf frieze. But they cannot have been fitted up until the early C18, possibly after the sale to Francis Fane in 1731. Four are linked by double doors, and the fifth was a closet. The first and largest has a ceiling oval of bay leaf, painted panelling, and a three-colour marble fireplace. The second, also fully panelled, has a pedimented frieze with festoons and female head over a marble bolection-moulded fireplace. The third and fourth have panelled dados and fabric wall hangings. Both have grander chimneypieces with marble fireplaces beneath pedimented picture panels. The fourth was the State Bedroom, its woodwork walnut rather than pine, the overmantel Baroque with a scrolled pediment. The single-bay fifth room is panelled and corniced. N of the passage, the KITCHEN has a large chamfered stone fireplace. C20 plaster barrel vault.

On the FIRST FLOOR, the two rooms of the solar cross-wing have early C18 marble chimneypieces, but the S windows have Perp reveals, one shafted for an oriel. Between this and the principal S rooms is a cupboard retaining a plaster frieze with fish-tailed dragons similar to those at Montacute. This indicates that the S range existed c. 1600, as is confirmed by the attic fireplaces. The large rooms over the State Rooms are plain, with some C18 cornices, the five eastern bays never even partitioned. E of the kitchen is THE FARMHOUSE, a two-storey almost-detached range with late C17 mullioned windows, but the irregular alignment suggests older origins. A gabled stair-tower towards the l. has spiral stairs and a bolection-moulded doorway dated 1722.

The FORECOURT that contributes so much to the setting is the product of centuries, beginning with the church and the Chantry. The CHANTRY was probably originally lodgings, indicated by garderobe towers on the back, removed after 1837. Three upper chambers, lit by cross-windows with cusped-headed top-lights, are reached by a polygonal embattled stair-turret with similar two-light upper windows. The stairs open to a lobby partitioned from the E chamber. This has a C15 fireplace with a frieze of large quatrefoils, and C16–C17 plasterwork. Thin-rib ceiling with curved and straight ribs and a pendant. Frieze of floral scroll. A timber-framed partition with two Tudor-arched doorways divides this from a narrow two-bay room open to the roof. Three tiers of wind-bracing. Another partition divides this room from the five-bay main room, here with two tiers of cusped wind-braces. On the front wall a fireplace, on the back wall blocked garderobe doorways. The ground floor was also heated. Framed ceiling in the E room.

In the main room, the curved back of a lost N staircase and blocked garderobes.

The CLOCK TOWER opposite the Chantry is a folly of 1723. The archway with block rustication of *c.* 1600 may be reused from a lost porch to the main house. The upper storey with rear ladder access contains the clock mechanism, with a bell in a strange gridded bellcote, like the one on the stair-turret behind the kitchen. Further on are single-storey STABLES with hip-roofed wings, not shown by Kip, but with cross-windows, so of the early C18. The FORECOURT WALL with balustrades and urns looks late C17 but is later C19, for Lady Georgiana Fane, as also the balustraded S TERRACE with its cube sundial. The TEMPLE there is C20, composed of pieces of *Thomas Stent*'s Yeovil Town Hall of 1847–9, burnt 1935.

RAILWAY BRIDGES, ¾ m. N. Two elegant stone arches over the A3088 originally spanned the line to Yeovil, built 1847–53 for the Bristol & Exeter Railway. *Francis Fox,* engineer, under *Brunel.*

BUCKLAND ST MARY

2010

ST MARY. 1853–63, by *Benjamin Ferrey.* A noble incongruity, far too large for a small, scattered congregation. Erected by the Rev. John Lance in memory of his wife who died in childbirth (*see* below). It reputedly cost £20,000. In a Dec style not at all *du pays*, in chert and Ham stone, with a substantial SW tower. Everything is done with the utmost care, each part separately articulated, uncluttered with extraneous decoration. The tower had a pyramid roof. Lavish flowing tracery. Rib-vaults to both porch and tower. Impressively high clerestoried nave, under a hammerbeam roof on naturalistic foliage corbels. Between the corbels are niches with Apostles carved by *Thomas Earp.* Naturalistic capitals also to the arcades and chancel arch. The chancel is more intense and more colourful: Purbeck-shafted chancel arch with low marble and alabaster screen, stone side screens, encaustic floor tiles, and diapered wall surfaces coloured red-brown and blue-green to shimmering effect. The roof is stencilled (by *A. Stansell*), carried on stone musician angels. Tub SEDILIA copying, in richer materials, those at Isle Abbots (q.v.). – REREDOS. 1888, by *James Forsyth.* A white marble Pietà with angels against stark red marble, framed in alabaster. – PULPIT. By *Forsyth, c.* 1860. Large and elaborate with much marble shafting. – FONT. Given, with its enormous spired Gothic cover, by the builder *Henry Davis.* Williton red conglomerate with marble plaques. Base columns of Quantock marble and Watchet alabaster. – ORGAN. By *William Sweetland*, 1863. – STAINED GLASS. Chancel, 1857, by *O'Connor*, stiff and glaring compared to the lovely W window (Last Judgment, based on the C15 window at Fairford, Glos.) and tower window

(Crossing the Red Sea), both by *Clayton & Bell*, 1859. N transept N, 1857 by *Powell's*, strangely murky. Two (SE and NW) by *Kempe & Co.*, 1914. – MONUMENT. Madalina Lance †1839. Positioned as a founder's tomb. She and her baby break through the lid of her tomb. Coarsely dramatic. Of *c.* 1860, by *Forsyth*.

The CHURCHYARD CROSS has a medieval base and shaft, with tabernacle head of 1888. LYCHGATE, *c.* 1860, Puginian carpentry under a funny hipped roof with gablets.

Above the church, BUCKLAND HOUSE, built for Lance in 1832. A large Tudor-style rectory in buff brick. The Gothic SCHOOL may be by *Ferrey*, 1851, extended 1883.

BURNHAM-ON-SEA

On a spacious curve of Bridgwater Bay. The town's origins as a resort go back to the 1820s, but it developed slowly and modestly compared to Weston or Clevedon.

ST ANDREW. Of Blue Lias. The large and notably leaning W tower is a landmark to mariners. Late C14 or early C15, with set-back buttresses, battlements, a higher stair-turret, and no pinnacles. Two-light bell-openings. The W window and door are inserted. Tower arch with the large-scale mouldings to the piers and the banded moulded capital found at Dunster and Minehead. Perp nave and chancel, much restored in 1875–9 by *Ewan Christian*, but with evidence of the early C14 in the S transept. The N transept was removed in 1838 for an embattled five-bay aisle by *Richard Carver*. This has piers of standard Perp section, but excessively flat four-centred arches and a GALLERY squeezed in under them. Similar chancel arch, but a medieval rood stair to the N. The S transept must be early C14 despite the Perp shafted arch, from the two big cinquefoiled TOMB-RECESSES under the cinquefoiled two-light window.

What the church must be visited for is, however, not its architecture, but the remains of the WHITEHALL ALTAR, commissioned in 1686 by James II for his short-lived Roman Catholic chapel in Whitehall Palace. The chapel was splendid and the altar especially so. It was designed by *Wren* and had two tiers of columns set in a curve, some 40 ft (12 metres) high and 33 ft (10 metres) wide. The sculpture included four large figures (now utterly eroded in College Garden, Westminster Abbey) and the two large kneeling angels and several small pieces with cherubs, all here. Commissioned from *Grinling Gibbons*, the angels were carved by *Arnold Quellin* (†1686) whose carving is more vigorous than Gibbons's generally dull work in this medium. The two were paid £1,875. Dismantled after the 1688 Revolution, the altar escaped the Whitehall fire of 1698. It was re-erected by Wren in Westminster Abbey in

1706, a Protestant text replacing the original Annunciation altarpiece by Gennari. In 1820 it was dismantled. The pieces here were saved by Bishop King of Rochester, vicar of Burnham.

The engraving of the altarpiece when at Westminster disagrees with the surviving description, and the one drawing of the altarpiece when at Whitehall disagrees again. It is clear, however, that the ANGELS stood high on the outermost corners, with their arms swept downward and inward towards the altar. Angels worshipping the sacrament are characteristic of French and Flemish Baroque altars. These two are noble figures, rhetorical and yet in attitude and expression not too melodramatic. Raised on stone pedestals by *John Bucknall* in 2010. *Gibbons*'s contribution was the many cherubs. Four RELIEFS in the reredos: two praying cherubs, one censing cherub, and one carrying a chalice and flagon. The former pair were over the outer doors and the latter pair over the inner niches. In the N aisle, three small cherubs displaying a Bible. They crowned the whole edifice (as re-erected in the abbey), just above the PANEL now under the tower, which has ten delightful cherubs' heads surrounding the Lord's name in Hebrew.

OTHER FURNISHINGS. PULPIT. Painted green. Typical Jacobean, but is any of it original? One tier of blank arches and one of oblong panels within panels. – FONT. 1883. Marble. – CHANDELIER. 1773. Of three tiers, by *Thomas Bayley* of Bridgwater. – TRANSEPT SCREEN. 1921, by *G. H. Fellowes Prynne*. – STAINED GLASS. S window, three plaques, two C15, one dated 1618. E window, 1876, by *Clayton & Bell*. W window, 1878. Chancel S, 1918, by *A. J. Davies*. Arts and Crafts opaque colours. – MONUMENT. Reed family, *c.* 1859. Very Gothic, identical to the one at East Brent signed *Casentini*.

ST ANDREW, Edithmead. 1910. A tiny corrugated-iron chapel complete with spired lantern.

OUR LADY AND THE ENGLISH MARTYRS (R.C.), Highbridge Road. 1966–7 by *Peter Ware*. The most interesting post-war church of the region. Uncompromising exterior (compromised a little by an added porch): an oval of pale rock-faced stone under a close-fitting copper roof with lantern, the wall openings vertical slots. The interior is changed; the altar originally faced the entrance. STAINED GLASS by *Michael Lassen* re-set around the new altar.

BAPTIST CHAPEL, College Street. 1843, by *Edwin Down*. Brick, Late Georgian style, with pediment.

METHODIST CHAPEL, College Street. 1878–80, by *Alexander Lauder*. Grey limestone with an outsize traceried window. Was No. 34, brick, Gothic, with a tower, the manse?

PIER. The 'shortest pier in England', 1911–14. Just an iron-roofed pavilion of quite festive outline, on concrete legs.

LIGHTHOUSES. 1832, by *Joseph Nelson*. The HIGH LIGHT (disused) in Berrow Road has a 120-ft (37-metre) rendered tower between the pair of pyramid-roofed cottages that frequently accompany Trinity House lights (cf. Happisburgh, Norfolk). On the beach, the LOW LIGHT is of weatherboarded timber, on twelve legs. Aligned, the two indicated the entrance to the Parrett.

PERAMBULATION. The era in which the resort began is indicated by street names close to the church: Regent, Princess, Victoria. Behind the church, TREGUNTER, a stuccoed villa of 1841–3, and BRUNSWICK TERRACE, 1838–41, four stuccoed houses, the entrances raised above a basement. The broad ESPLANADE dates from the 1850s, the present concrete SEA WALL from the 1980s. Development of the seafront began N of the church after 1820 when the curate, the Rev. David Davies, established a spa called Daviesville. Typically, everything was stuccoed. MARINE HOUSE, two-storeyed with later bay windows, was Davies's house, to which he attached a lighthouse in 1820. The lighthouse dues were so profitable that it cost Trinity House £13,500 to buy them out in 1829. The tower was then truncated; only the round base remains. STEART HOUSE, 1830, the former bath house, is the best building, with parapet and large sash windows. Of the 1830s also Nos. 46–48, with four canted bays, and No. 50, with two rounded ones. The Esplanade finishes on a different scale with CATHERINE TERRACE, *c.* 1859, and JULIA TERRACE, *c.* 1865, Burnham's attempt to emulate Weston-super-Mare. George Reed, Burnham entrepreneur, built them and named them for his daughters. Two short quadrant-curved terraces, the former ashlar-faced, the latter stuccoed. Catherine Terrace is undoubtedly ambitious, Italianate, seven houses, the middle and ends accented with pedimented attics. Julia Terrace is decidedly cheaper. The length of the Esplanade was established in 1857–8 by Reed, who promoted a jetty ½ m. S for ships from Wales to connect with the new Somerset Central Railway and a hotel to serve the traffic. S from the church little is intact after the attrition of climate and poor-quality alteration. KINVER TERRACE, 1842–3, by *James Wilson*, has lost balustrades at both levels. The ROYAL CLARENCE HOTEL, *c.* 1825, had a first-floor veranda of panelled piers. ROYAL TERRACE and BEACH TERRACE, stuccoed, 1840s, were always plain. Nos. 11–14, of stone with Jacobean gables, mark a different style, and indeed are dated 1897. Finally the REED'S ARMS, 1858, Reed's florid Italianate railway hotel, faces his JETTY. The station was across Pier Street.

High Street, parallel to the seafront, is very modest. The commercial centre was COLLEGE STREET, running back from the Esplanade across High Street. The seaward end was built up in stucco on one side in the 1840s, facing the Baptist chapel. The inland end is late C19, with the Methodist chapel. A detour S down OXFORD STREET finds the former R.C. PRIORY, 1888–90, by *Father A. J. C. Scoles* for the La Retraite sisters. Their chapel, brick with triple lancets, and a big triple-gabled boarding school flank The Rookery, a stuccoed early C19 villa. Going N, then W on PRINCESS STREET, are the former MARKET HALL, 1869, by *Edwin Down*, round-arched Italianate in brick and stone, the LIBRARY, 1985, by *Somerset County Architects*, and a former INFANTS' SCHOOL, 1913, by *Samson & Colthurst*.

Late Victorian and Edwardian villas begin N of the church, along BERROW ROAD, too infilled for coherence now. Before the lighthouse (*see* p. 168), ELLEN'S COTTAGES, 1868, single-storey Gothic almshouses, facing over a lawn to a Gothic roadside arch. On RECTORY ROAD, to the E, the OLD RECTORY, brick Tudor Gothic, and the better Edwardian houses, roughcast with half-timber, notably Nos. 19 and 40.

BURROWBRIDGE

The feature conspicuous here for miles is BURROW MUMP, a natural eminence traditionally identified as King Alfred's camp. If there was a fort, it was replaced by a cruciform church dedicated, as was usual for churches on hills, to St Michael. An engraving of 1774 shows it with a crossing tower. The present ruined CHURCH, so effective from afar, is of 1793–6, an incomplete replacement rather than the folly it resembles. W tower and boxy nave with typical Y-tracery. A few reused carvings on the tower.

ST MICHAEL. 1836–8, by *Richard Carver*. A simple lancet job in Blue Lias with shallow gable and bellcote. Original W gallery. *J. H. Spencer* created a chancel in 1888 by inserting a triple-arched wall.

Behind the church is the former VICARAGE, by *Carver*, 1836, white render with paired brick chimneys, without the affectation of more expensive Tudor Gothic. The handsome BRIDGE, 1826, by *Philip Ilett* of Taunton (*John Stone* of Yarcombe, Devon, builder), spans the Parrett in a 68-ft (20.7-metre) elliptical arch, outlined in Ham stone. Up the E bank is EBENEZER BAPTIST CHAPEL, 1836, hip-roofed red brick, with Georgian Gothic windows, charmingly simple. On the W bank, further out, SALTMOOR HOUSE, given a five-bay brick front around 1810. Flanking outbuildings disguised with pediments increase the display.

Seen from the Mump, the pre-drainage landscape of islands in the marsh becomes clear, as also the Herculean task of controlling the water. High banks contain the Parrett and Tone rivers. The causeway to Othery originated as the C13 BURROW WALL that contained the River Cary, until this was redirected to the King's Sedgemoor Drain in 1791–5. The seven-mile SOWY RIVER, 1969–72, is a relief channel from the Parrett to the Drain. All around Burrowbridge are PUMPING STATIONS. On the E bank, hidden in an industrial yard, the modest brick Allermoor station, 1869, with its original *Easton & Amos* pumping engine. On the W bank, the Saltmoor station, 1837, has the engine and attendant's house under one hipped roof. S towards Langport is the small Stanmoor station, 1941, and, beyond Stathe the large West Sedgemoor station of 1944, both in the hip-roofed modern Georgian adopted by the Somerset River Board.

BURTLE

3040

Site of a small Augustinian priory of which nothing remains visible.

St Philip and St James. 1838–9 by *Richard Carver*. Typical of the date, of squared Blue Lias, the little bell-turret embattled with a spirelet. Simple interior with curved plaster ceilings and deep WEST GALLERY. Over the N door, the foundation PLAQUE, all in black letter, important words in black-letter capitals, very pretty, and quite illegible. – FONT. Small, the lid painted to resemble a stone finial. – STAINED GLASS. E window, 1864. Figures on startlingly bright blue.

Adjoining, plain former SCHOOL, 1839.

BURTLE FARM, ¼ m. w. Regency hip-roofed farmhouse. Tightly curved staircase to a top-lit landing. Large attached BARNS and pyramid-roofed CIDER HOUSE.

BURTON PYNSENT see CURRY RIVEL

BURY

9020

On the River Haddeo, E of Dulverton.

The picturesque BRIDGE is probably medieval, two pointed arches and two rounded, with cutwaters. Narrow cobbled pathway. To the N, CHURCH HOUSE was a mid-C19 church-cum-schoolroom, with bellcote.

TOWER, Louisa Gate, 1 m. NNW. An early C19 eyecatcher from Pixton Park (Dulverton), decaying in woodland. Circular, with battlements and remants of roughcast.

BURY CASTLE, ½ m. E. On the promontory between the Haddeo and Exe rivers, a late prehistoric enclosure about 100 yds (90 metres) across, adapted to a C12–C13 castle by the Besil family, who added a small motte at the S.

BUTLEIGH

5030

St Leonard. Cruciform with stone-tiled roofs. The nave, crossing tower and low chancel are early C14, but the character is

C19. Transepts were added in 1850–1 by *J. C. Buckler & Son* (son and grandson of the topographical artist). The N transept adjoins a large private chapel of 1828–30 by *Edward Blore*, and *E. B. Lamb* added a low N aisle in 1859, with gabled windows. The porch has reused, possibly Anglo-Saxon, column shafts, polygonal on the outer face and cylindrical to the inner. The embattled tower has no buttresses. It stands on low arches with C14 mouldings: three hollows for the arches, changing to a broad wave and a chamfer on the piers. The N and S arches are Victorian but the vault, with ribs and ridge ribs on corbels, seems genuine. The bell-stage is Late Perp. The windows are mostly Dec, renewed. The cinquefoil-cusped rere-arches are recorded before the Victorian work, even in the E window. Large four-centred-arched W window of six lights with a transom, echoing the greater Tudor churches. The panelled reveal inside reaches to the floor. Earlier roll-moulded doorway beneath. Hammerbeam nave roof of 1844. *Lamb*'s aisle has naturalistic carving around the piers and remarkably odd roof carpentry (cf. the wishbone bracing at each end). A heraldic Tree of Jesse surrounds *Blore*'s very large N window and the transom is elaborated into canopies. C19 barrel roof in the chancel.

FURNISHINGS. FONT. Perp, octagonal, panelled with quatrefoils alternating with reliefs: the lamb and cross, the lamb and flag and two eagles. Panelled stem, as at Baltonsborough and Wedmore (qq.v.). – STALLS. 1851. With misericords. – STAINED GLASS. Medieval figures in the W tracery. Nave S by *Hardman*, a lovely Annunciation against a lattice of blue and gold, 1872, and three saints under canopies, 1850–1, designed by *A. W. N. Pugin*. E window, 1851, by an amateur. Canopied figures, as with Pugin, but disjointed colour, the faces sweetly naïve. S transept S, 1853, by *Ward & Nixon*. – MONUMENTS. Three kneeling figures from the dismantled tomb of Thomas Simcocks, 1624. – Richard Helyar †1683. Lias floor slab with heraldry. – Vice-Admiral Sir Samuel Hood †1814 and his brothers. Octagonal panelled shafts frame an ornate Gothic panel (with verse encomium by Southey) bordered in foliage with dolphins for crockets. Shipwreck relief signed *Lucius Gahagan*, Bath. – Lord Hood of Avalon †1901. Brass by *Barkentin & Krall*.

In the churchyard, the scroll-topped CHEST TOMB to the Periam and Hood families, *c.* 1860. A version of the sarcophagus of Scipio Barbatus in Rome (another in Glastonbury cemetery, q.v.).

BUTLEIGH COURT, by the church. Large neo-Tudor mansion of 1845–51 by *John Chessell Buckler* for the Rev. George Neville-Grenville, Dean of Windsor. Eastlake's *Gothic Revival*, 1872, says that 'the elevations are varied in design, and embellished with buttresses, turrets, battlements, and other features suited to the style'. What is impressive is the control of square-topped elements under a skyline of splendidly tall stone chimneys. The house was restored from ruin after 1977; a rear ballroom was demolished. Some extremely elaborate Gothic fireplaces inside. COURT LODGE, by *E. B. Lamb*, 1856, has a pyramid-roofed turret, the pointed-arched throughway now blocked. NW of the house is an impressive C19 cedar avenue.

Below the church, the OLD VICARAGE, 1928 by *W. D. Caröe*, hip-roofed vernacular Georgian. Across the road is its larger predecessor, BUTLEIGH HOUSE, by *F. C. Penrose*, 1846, gabled and mullion-windowed, between older parts. The enlargement was for a scion of Butleigh Court. HIGH STREET runs SE with attractive Blue Lias cottages, mostly C16–C17 in origin. No. 17, thatched, was the Post Office, with a diminutive C19 gable-end shopfront and oriel. No. 18, dated 1699, adjoins the SCHOOL of 1846, with boarded lantern. CORNER HOUSE, with a lateral chimney, is mostly C18–C19, on a late C16 core. BRIDGE FARM conceals a remarkably early medieval hall with two-tier cruck trusses (cf. Abbey Farm, Glastonbury) and two-tier wind-bracing, tree-ring-dated to 1305. The rear wing was storeyed from the outset, as shown by a four-centred-arched first-floor doorway from the hall. Nearby is a moulded laver (piscina). Later C15 moulded and framed ceiling in the l. room. PERRIAMS, dated 1635, has typical mullioned windows and two eaves gables, but inside is a good late C15 moulded fireplace with slim shafts up to the rounded ends of the cornice (cf. The Tribunal, Glastonbury). Moulded framed ceiling. At the top, HIGHER ROCKE'S FARM is rather grander, with an early C17 storeyed porch and arched doorway. C16 moulded fireplace in the plainer bay l. of the porch. Opposite the other, NW, end of High Street are two farmhouses, LOWER ROCKE'S with a Late Georgian front and C17 rear (weathervane dated 1673), and OLD FARM with mullions of both the C16 reserved-chamfer and C17 ovolo-moulded types.

BUTLEIGH CROSS, 1 m. S. Base of a C15 wayside cross, the shaft and tabernacle-head a war memorial addition of 1920. To the W, LOWER HILL FARM is three-storeyed, Late Georgian. At HIGHER HILL FARM, a five-bay early C18 farmhouse overlooks a large C18 BARN. Its roof sweeps low around two cart entries because the interior is aisled.

BUTLEIGH WOOTTON, 1 m. NW. WOOTTON HOUSE was built in 1722 for James Perriam. His granddaughter erected the Hood Monument (*see below*) to her brother-in-law, one of three Hood admirals of the Napoleonic Wars. Five bays with an ashlar parapet, between single-bay hip-roofed wings of 1763. Ashlar quarter-columns in the junctions. Pretty early C19 iron trellis veranda. Single-storey NW range with wooden cross-windows of *c*. 1700, but 1649 datestone inside. Interiors altered after 1901. Nearby, No. 22, C17, embellished in the early C19 with a rounded thatched end on veranda posts. WOOTTON HILL FARMHOUSE, ½ m. E, is C16, long and plain between cross-wings. Some mullioned windows at the back and an off-centre stair-tower with an eagle plaque, reused medieval. Moulded framed ceiling.

HOOD MONUMENT, Windmill Hill. 1831, by *H. E. Goodridge* of Bath. To Vice-Admiral Sir Samuel Hood †1814, 'an officer of the highest distinction amongst the illustrious men who rendered their own age the brightest period in the naval history of their country'. On a pedestal, a towering Tuscan column carries a drum with wreathed oval openings under a splendid naval crown. The sight line to Glastonbury Tor oversails Wootton House.

NEW DITCH, Combe Hill. An earthwork of uncertain date that cuts the Polden ridge with a ditch to the E. It can be traced for ½ m. Less impressive than the analogous Ponter's Ball, Glastonbury, it may mark a boundary.

CADBURY CASTLE see SOUTH CADBURY

CANNINGTON

A large village NW of Bridgwater, the church tower a landmark.

ST MARY. The church is not the church of Cannington Priory, a house of Benedictine nuns, founded c. 1138 by Robert de Courcy of Stogursey, as Leland says that their church was 'hard anexid to the est of the paroch chirch'. Such a twin arrangement of monastic and parish churches existed at Muchelney, and possibly at Bruton (qq.v.). Cannington Court (see p. 176), almost touching the N side of the church, apparently replaces priory buildings. Cannington church is distinctive for its tall proportions and unified outline. One large roof covers the nave, aisles and chancel, and the W tower is exceptionally tall. All Perp, but more complicated than at first sight. A composite C12 pier with a strong attached shaft remains in the NE vestry. If it is *in situ*, the Norman church was not in line with the present church. But the present tower is not in line with the rest of the building either, so a phased rebuilding is indicated. Indeed the tower is late C14, the rest late C15. The entire church is of red sandstone, with local buff sandstone facing on the tower buttresses, whereas Bath stone is used for the buttresses elsewhere and for the battlements and gable parapets. The tower is of four stages, and stark by Somerset standards. Set-back buttresses, battlements, but no pinnacles. For decoration there are seven undersized niches, two each side of the squat W doorway (eroded leaf scroll on one moulding) and three around the head of the four-light W window. Transomed two-light bell-openings. Polygonal SE stair-turret. WEATHERCOCK of 1758, by *Bayley & Street* of Bridgwater. The niches have statues, the topmost C19, then two of the early C20, by *Virginia Venning*, the lower ones 1965–70 by *Tom Preater*. Another small niche low in the SW corner.

The rest of the church has tall Perp windows like a college chapel, three-light apart from the impressively large five-light

CANNINGTON

E window. All have cusped ogee lights in two tiers, those below the transom with the spandrel quatrefoils found at Muchelney and Cleeve abbeys from the late C15. The roof sweeps down over embattled five-bay aisles that stop one bay short of the E end, and partly embrace the tower. Good gargoyles. Rood-stair turret on the N. Tall gabled S porch with panelled and shafted doorway. Consecration crosses all round the exterior. A single high unified interior of great dignity. The panelled wagon roof, carried on extremely tall five-bay arcades, runs right through uninterrupted, with very many bosses and many shield-bearing angels along the wall-plates. Panelled lean-to aisle roofs. The piers are of standard four-hollow section and the shafts have thin capitals. The tower arch is lower than the arcades and the line of an earlier nave roof proves that the tower existed before the nave. The red sandstone of the walls is exposed, certainly not in accordance with the original state. In the chancel, a C15 ogee cusped PISCINA, and Victorian SEDILIA from the restoration of 1885–6, by *Evan Down*.

FURNISHINGS. FONT. C15, octagonal, with pointed quatrefoils, and large Tudor roses beneath. Tall C19 COVER. – SCREEN. Late C15, much reconstructed. Three sections across the nave and both aisles. Sub-arched four-light tracery and dado panels as in the Dunster-Carhampton group. No loft; cornice of 1885. – IRONWORK. Above the N stalls, an exquisite wrought-iron screen from a lost Clifford tomb of the 1730s, the scrollwork very refined. Clifford arms and entwined initials. – PULPIT. With reused pairs of long C15 panels with crocketed ogee tracery and plant-scroll. – REREDOS. 1893. Vaulted and marble-shafted, inset with *opus sectile* tile panels by *Powell's*. The donors, the Pleydell-Bouveries of Brymore, appear amid the saints on the r. Lovely blue-green tile-mosaic dado. – COMMUNION TABLE (SE chapel). C17, with frilled arches and cherubs. Marked 'Poenitenti dabitur' (To the penitent it will be granted). – PEWS. Two carved Jacobean frontals. – WOODCARVING. Several naturalistic pieces by *Tom Preater*, including the large dramatic ROOD, 1983, and the 'Cannington Girl', 1998, based on the skull of a girl found in the post-Roman cemetery by Cannington Hill. – PLAQUE. Early C19 painted plaster altarpiece from the R.C. chapel in Cannington Court, showing the Lamb of God. – ROYAL ARMS. Charles II. – STAINED GLASS. E window, 1874, perhaps by *Wailes & Strang*. Colourful crowded scenes. W window, 1893, by *Powell's*. Sombre Arts and Crafts colours. Fourth S window, 1888, by *Kempe*. Intensely detailed and richly coloured. SE window, 1862. Fourth N, 1926, by *J. C. Bewsey*. – BRASSES. Lettered fragments to Joan Dodesham †1472. – MONUMENTS. Amy St Barbe †1621. Black plaque between marble Corinthian columns set diagonally. – Elizabeth Poole †1819. Draped urn and horizontal fluting, typical of *King* of Bath.

CONGREGATIONAL CHAPEL, High Street. 1869, by *Habershon & Brock* of London. Gothic in Blue Lias. The two piers had sharp octagonal points.

CEMETERY, High Street. 1867. A wildly overdone gateway, the arch with a giant traceried head like the Bridgwater church doorway. Brash enough to be by *Charles Knowles*.

CANNINGTON COURT. On the site of buildings of the nunnery, but no specific structure can be identified with certainty. The property was granted in 1538 to Edward Rogers, whose descendants remained until 1672 when it passed to the 1st Baron Clifford of Chudleigh, whence the important Roman Catholic history. The Cliffords maintained a priest here until 1768, and services were held thereafter. Leased to French Benedictine nuns from 1807, the house became the seat of Bishop Collingridge of the Western District from 1812 until 1829 (his successor purchased Prior Park, Bath). The chapel, of 1830–1, served the area until 1921. The nuns left for Colwich, Staffs., in 1836. Another order came from 1863–7, then the Industrial School for Catholic Boys, 1868–1919, before the Somerset Farm Institute (Cannington College) until 2010. Restored as a training centre for EDF Energy, 2013–14.

The house runs out from the N wall of the church enclosing two courtyards, a small square S one now filled in by the chapel of 1831, and a larger N one, irregular because the N range is at an angle. None of this equates with a cloister. The S courtyard may not have been enclosed on its E side originally and the N court was not entirely enclosed until the early C18. Medieval fragments are scattered throughout the buildings, whose dominant character is Elizabethan. Of red sandstone rubble with Ham stone dressings, replacing soft local buff sandstone. The long W façade has first-floor mullion-and-transom windows with reserved-chamfer mouldings, of four lights except for a two-light each side of the central storeyed porch. Square-headed entry between thin fluted columns carrying entablature blocks under a cornice, rather etiolated. Four-light window above. A blocked pointed doorway indicates that the range to the r. is medieval. Originally of eleven bays, the front was extended N by one bay and an attic storey with parapet added, perhaps in 1714, from a dated rainwater head in the courtyard. The attic is of brick, but Ham stone over the porch. Bolection-moulded keyed ovals at each end and to the porch. Two of these ovals are blind, because the attic is false over the porch and the whole r. half. Segment-headed mullioned windows, real or blind, between the ovals. The W end of the N range has bolection-moulded sash windows, indicating that this corner of the courtyard was completed at the same date.

Inside the courtyard, the E range, behind an early C20 single-storey addition, contained a first-floor hall identifiable by two long Elizabethan double-transomed windows. It may be a successor to the nunnery refectory as the ornate doorway to their l. is C15–C16, four-centred, shafted, with carved spandrels. It was reached presumably by outside steps. Two relieving arches on the back of this range and four-centred-arched doorways on both N and S ranges are C15–C16. So medieval work is identifiable on three sides of the court. The S side conceals a medieval roof of chamfered arched-braced trusses, another first-floor hall, perhaps a dormitory. The trusses are not ornate. C16 stair-turret in the SE corner. Large Late Georgian sash windows replace the rear windows of the hall. The short S end of the house, against the church, is very rough, with two undatable rounded stair-towers, inferior to the Elizabethan work, but without any medieval feature. This S range was certainly Elizabethan, as mullion-and-transom windows were blocked presumably when the chapel was built in the courtyard in 1830–1, by *John Peniston* of Salisbury. The large chapel E window, tripartite under a lunette, appears off-centre in a roughcast four-bay three-storeyed E range of 1830–1.

The interiors have been spoilt by C19 and C20 institutional use. The S half of the W front range has early C18 first-floor panelled rooms. In the corridor behind is a good C15–C16 fireplace with shields in cusped quatrefoils and initials CHC and ALP, the latter possibly Alianor Poynings, prioress 1461–9. Similar C18 panelling in the W end of the N range. Only the inserted CHAPEL astonishes, a great top-lit domed octagon with altar recess to the E and deep gallery to the W. Each side is framed by giant pilasters with remarkably fine Composite capitals. The diagonal sides are narrow, with niches. Modillion cornice, panelled dome and glazed octagonal lantern. In the altar recess, a coffered ceiling with swirled acanthus leaves. Over the gallery a panelled plaster vault.

PERAMBULATION. Large walled GARDENS N and E of Cannington Court probably represent the priory precinct. The W front of the house is sunk below the level of a car park (to be restored as a garden). Low buildings of the college on two sides, 1920s on the N, 1938 on the NW corner, and 1956 on the W. Sunk at the original level on the S side is the PRIORY BARN, much rebuilt, but the buttressed back wall to Church Street is medieval. Church Street frames the church tower. S of the churchyard, a large Victorian former VICARAGE, 1879, on Brook Lane. This opens to a green with two pretty BRIDGES over the Cannington Brook. Mill Lane, which continues Church Street westward, has a section of C16 walling and a Tudor doorway. Church Street itself turns N towards High Street, passing BOWLING GREEN, modern-traditional council houses of the 1950s. A little rock-faced stone and storeyed porches on fat round piers. On High Street, the ROGERS ALMSHOUSES, founded 1672 but much rebuilt. Rubble stone, seven bays, two storeys. Going W, RED HOUSE is late C18, of fine red sandstone with limestone quoins, voussoirs and pedimented doorway, and the ROSE AND CROWN is dated 1638 inside. Beyond are the chapel and cemetery (*see* pp. 175–6). Returning E, CANNINGTON HOUSE, early C18, faces impressively down High Street, formerly the main road from Minehead. Five bays, of fine red ashlar with pedimented Gibbsian doorway, quoins, cornice, and a high parapet divided by vertical strips, further raised over the centre. Fore Street continues E along the buttressed precinct WALL, possibly late C15. THE PRIORY is late C18, brick, with a central Venetian window, echoed blind in the parapet. Good corniced doorcase. East Street runs out to Gurney Manor (below) past a C17 oak-mullioned and thatched house at No. 32, with canted bay, while the precinct wall curves s into Brook Street to the VILLAGE HALL, 1905, by *Basil Cottam*. Terracotta windows. Opposite, the hip-roofed single-storey SCHOOL of 1829.

GURNEY MANOR, Gurney Street (Landmark Trust). A singularly complete late medieval courtyard house, mostly mid- to late C15, for William Dodesham M.P. †1480. The pale yellow lime render dates from the careful restoration by *Peter Bird* of *Caroe & Partners*, 1984–90. The N range began as a C14 hall between storeyed ends. Dodesham added the storeyed porch with good four-centred-arched moulded doorways. Across the E end and enclosing the courtyard behind is a long early C15 BARN. The almost-detached building at the NW corner may have been a kitchen, raised and remodelled by Dodesham. The hipped W end of the N range is a C17–C18 alteration of a solar end abandoned for Dodesham's more splendid solar block parallel behind. This has an E gable to the courtyard, and an altered W gable, with three storeys of C16 mullioned windows, from when the solar was ceiled. Beneath the solar is a parlour, with a spiral staircase and tiny chapel to the E. On the S side, a two-light parlour window, transomed with cinquefoil-cusped upper lights, a lateral chimney, and a narrow cusped single light to the chapel, which has a flat-headed three-light E window. Dodesham also added the detached S range with kitchen beneath a first-floor chamber of some quality, indicated by similar cinquefoil-cusped transomed windows on the W and S. The small courtyard so formed is an intimate space of rare beauty, crossed by a timber-framed walkway, or PENTICE, to shelter food being carried to the hall.

The rooms of the N range are the most altered. A screen of 1990 re-creates the cross-passage. The hall was floored over in the early C16. Plain W fireplace. Dodesham's work is characterized by moulded stone doorways. One opens S from the hall into a lobby with four similar doorways: to the former W parlour (which Dodesham enlarged southward), to the new parlour, to the stairs and to the chapel. The CHAPEL has a small but ornate PISCINA, cusped and crocketed with finials. Restored boarded ceiling with original IHS boss. In the PARLOUR a framed ceiling and square-headed S fireplace. The stone spiral STAIRS to the solar emerge under a thin-rib plaster ceiling inserted before 1600, with an attic stair, when the solar was ceiled. The handsome SOLAR roof, restored to view by removal of the attic, is three-bay with arch-braced collar-trusses and two tiers of wind-braces. Fireplace like that below. Carved HEAD of a king, c. 1300, found during the works. Solid baulk stairs to a gallery (remnant of the attic). A bridge links the solar to the KITCHEN CHAMBERS, two first-floor rooms with a similar roof to the solar, but without wind-braces. Square-headed W fireplace, like that in the solar, served by a little octagonal chimney. C17 NE garderobe. The KITCHEN, reached from the courtyard has a large curved stone E fireplace and small S one, apparently never used. Unheated W room.

BRYMORE, ¾ m. W. Of the house where John Pym, the parliamentarian, was born in 1585, a C15–C16 storeyed porch survives. Red sandstone with Ham stone battlements, two carved, one with heraldry. Moulded pointed-arched doorway under a cross-window of cusped ogee lights. Inside, a mural stair at each corner. The rest is C19. On the site of the cross-passage is a single-storey corridor along the E side of an unadorned roughcast three-storey block built for Sir Philip Hales †1824. Regency cornices inside. The service range E of the passage was raised by a storey and given a Gothic bay window by *Cottam* in 1892.

CANNINGTON GRANGE, ½ m. SSE. Red sandstone Jacobethan, built for J. R. Poole in the 1860s, probably by *Charles Knowles*. Mullion-and-transom windows, gabled centrepiece, with little Jacobean features on the porch and parapets. Service range with a tower-like rear feature under a truncated-pyramid roof.

BLACKMORE FARM, 1 m. SW. A fortunate survival of a late C15 manor house, different in plan from Gurney Manor, comprising not a courtyard but a hall between cross-wings. Sir Thomas Tremayle bought the manor in 1476 and his house was built by 1490 (roof tree-ring-dated 1486). In the C16 the hall was floored across, a new staircase added, and a cross-wing placed at the service end, but thereafter the house was barely altered. Rubble stone, originally rendered, with dressings of soft pale sandstone except where Ham stone indicates later work. The windows are mostly straight-headed, of two or three lights with ogee heads, some with transoms. The E front has a storeyed porch with moulded four-centred-arched doorways. At the N end projects the remarkable chapel wing marked by a long three-light E window and a long cusped single light on each side. In the angle with the main range is the C16 staircase, once battlemented. On the rear W wall the hall chimney is to the r. of two mullion-and-transom windows, one two-light to the hall (a second removed) and one three-light to the parlour. Mullioned two-light first-floor windows. All have ogee-headed lights, so early rather than late C16. The C16 S cross-wing has a garderobe tower on the S side. 57

The cross-passage has gone, so that one directly enters the HALL, a low room with a framed ceiling. Huge monolith lintel to the lateral W fireplace. Two S doorways to the service end, one to the former kitchen, the other to a spiral staircase in a rear-wall lean-to. There would have been a dais oriel at the N end of the E wall, replaced by the C16 stair hall (with C19 stair). The moulded Tudor arch of the oriel is visible from the stair hall. Moulded doorways lead from the stair hall into the N parlour and NE chapel wing. Similar doorways upstairs. The PARLOUR has an original lime-ash floor and chamfered N fireplace. The SOLAR above has a matching fireplace, and a fine two-bay open roof of moulded arch-braced jointed crucks with three tiers of wind-braces. The roof continues for three bays over the hall, but this is largely enclosed. The chapel wing is particularly interesting. The ground floor has an ante-room, then a bay with a framed ceiling opens to the double-height CHAPEL. This bay was screened, perhaps as a family pew, from the mortices in the beam. The chapel is higher than it is long. Two fine vaulted niches flank the tall E window. Cusped ogee piscina. The ceiling was once framed – see the marks on the W beam. The first-floor CHAPEL CHAMBER, over the ante-room and ceiled bay, was of importance, to judge by the mullion-and-transom side windows. Moulded framed ceiling. The timber-framed wall above the chapel screen once had a window to the chapel. Opposite, a partition closes the chamber, with two four-centred-arched doorways. It screens attic stairs and a NW garderobe. The attic has plain jointed-cruck trusses, showing that the chamber was always ceiled.

CHILTON TRIVETT, 1 m. E of Blackmore Farm. Victorian exterior, but plasterwork upstairs of 1662, with initials of Francis Cridland on strapwork. Old-fashioned for the date, as is the central ceiling pendant.

CANNINGTON CAMP. Cannington Hill, NW of the village. Identified tenuously as Cynwit Castle, mentioned by Asser as where Saxons under Odda defeated Danish sea-raiders under Ubbe in 878. It has been much quarried but is crowned by the earthworks of an Iron Age hillfort which may have continued in occupation into the post-Roman period. An extensive cemetery was discovered on a hill to the E and partly excavated before the site was obliterated. Burials dated from the C4 to the C9.

BEERE MANOR. See Combwich.

CARHAMPTON

ST JOHN THE BAPTIST. Perp, of more interest inside than out, as over-restored in 1862–3 by *C. E. Giles*, and the tower was replaced in 1870 by *J. P. St Aubyn*. It has three-light bell-openings and a crocketed spirelet on the stair-turret. The previous tower was short, rendered, with a weatherboarded gabled top. Perp nave and chancel without division and a C15–C16 S aisle of equal length. This has restored three-light window tracery and buttresses added by *Giles*, who seems to have removed the Dec N windows mentioned by Glynne in 1855. Six-bay arcade of four-centred arches on piers of four-wave section. Small circular capitals to the aisle, polygonal ones to the two slightly taller arches to the SE chapel. Broad nave wagon roof and narrow aisle one, both of 1862–3, with reused bosses and some carved wall-plate in the aisle. In the chapel an ogee PISCINA with quatrefoil spandrels.

FURNISHINGS. SCREEN. The outstanding feature of the church, oddly with no associated rood stair. Late C15, in ten and a half bays. Four-light tracery divided by sub-arches into twice two lights. The leaf-scroll border to each opening identifies the same workshop that made the screens at Minehead, Dunster, Withycombe etc. Ribbed and panelled coving. Five carved friezes in the front cornice, three including a text from the Te Deum on the back. But the distinguishing feature of the Carhampton screen is the fact that it has been repainted in such a way as to represent the original appearance of all these screens. We may like the dark wood and the flickering highlights on it, but the C15 and C16 never saw them like that. They were coloured all over in red, blue, green, white and gold, and this painting, done in 1862 by *Alfred Stansell* of Taunton, restores a very pleasing, cheerful harmony. – FONT. Heavy as only the 1860s could be. The prettily painted round COVER looks medieval. – PULPIT. Early to mid-C18. Handsome, like those at Kingston St Mary and Nettlecombe, but more sparingly carved. – TOWER SCREEN. 1937, by *W. H. Randoll Blacking*. Well-detailed linenfold. – STAINED GLASS. E window, 1907, by *E. R. Suffling*. – MONUMENTS. Sarah Trevelyan †1677. Various colours of local alabaster. Twin Ionic columns. – Richard and Alfred Escott †1755 and 1763. Brass with a long text, handsome lettering, and elegantly drawn scrolls around the heraldry. Unusually it is signed: *C. Sherborn*, Gutter Lane, London.

Remains of a CHURCHYARD CROSS, circular C14 base on octagonal steps. There were once two churches: the older, dedicated to St Carantoc, may have been nearby, as the churchyard once extended significantly eastward. C6 Mediterranean pottery and other excavated evidence suggest an early monastic settlement.

On the main road, the BUTCHERS ARMS, with a metal inn sign by *Rachel Reckitt*, 1950s (cf. Rodhuish, Roadwater), and a cobbled floor inside dated 1658. Some C16–C17 thatched cottages along the main road: one on the S (Stoneybridge/The Nook) has oak mullion windows and a tiny stair light by the door. On the parallel lane to the S, LAUREL COTTAGE has a lateral chimney with a circular shaft. Smoke-blackened jointed-cruck trusses of a C15 hall, the partition and framed ceiling inserted in the C16.

ALLER FARMHOUSE, ½ m. SW. Medieval hall house altered *c.* 1600, with a large lateral stack to the r. of a gabled porch. Heavy oak doorway. Two cruck trusses survive, with windbraces. Good moulded framed ceiling.

CASTLE CARY

6030

Named for a short-lived Norman castle. The town developed in the C19 from specialist weaving industries – horsehair, webbing and linen. The plan is attractively irregular. From the triangular

Castle Cary, All Saints, before alteration.
Watercolour by J. Buckler, 1833

Market Place, High Street rises with the better houses and Fore Street descends with the shops. Mixed materials: ochre-coloured Cary limestone, both rubble and ashlar, C19 stucco, and brick, both Georgian and Victorian.

ALL SAINTS. Large Perp church on a hill to the S. *Benjamin Ferrey* extended the nave and added the 129-ft (39.3-metre) tower and spire in 1853–5, correctly C15 and absolutely Victorian. The old tower had a spire, unusual for Somerset, but Ferrey's is far more florid. C15 S porch with a niche between upper windows and a lierne vault (cf. North Cadbury). Clerestoried nave with aisles, the arcades on standard C15 shaft-and-hollow piers. Roofs by *Ferrey*, the chancel entirely his. – FONT. Octagonal, C14. Small paired pointed quatrefoils, and large and beautiful leaf scroll on the underside. – PULPIT. C19 version of the Queen Camel and Long Sutton pulpits. – STAINED GLASS. E window, 1855, figures in tiers by *O'Connor*, also the chancel S. W window, 1864 by *Powell's*. Small scenes in lovely colours. – MONUMENT. John Russ †1758, by *John Ford Sen.* (vestry). An amply draped female, her elbow on an urn.

METHODIST CHAPEL, North Street. 1838–9 by *Abraham Bryant*. Georgian arched windows and fanlight, but octagonal angles with bottle-teat finials. It had a columned porch.

MARKET HOUSE. 1855, by *F. C. Penrose*. An excellent centrepiece for a growing town, the more successful for being large for the cramped Market Place. Gothic, but by no means conventional.

Tuscan columns support a superstructure of Cary stone on which an arcade is suggested by pointed-arched panels with small mezzanine openings. Sparse upper windows and a rich N oriel light the assembly room. Butchers' shambles behind.

CASTLE, behind The Triangle, accessible by footpath from the Market Place. The Norman castle of the Lovels was demolished in the mid C12, the Lovels having supported Matilda. The motte remains against a hillside, with the dimensions of a square keep unreliably marked out. Earthworks continue westward under housing and Manor Farm, for which a medieval house of the Lovels was demolished in the 1820s. Excavation uncovered a Roman limekiln.

PERAMBULATION. Opposite the Market House, the thatched GEORGE INN, dated 1673. It was stuccoed and given Late Georgian sash windows, the stucco since removed.* The quintuple keystones of MARTIN'S, painted brick, mid-C18, suggest *Nathaniel Ireson*. Behind the Market House on the W is Bailey Hill, where the POST OFFICE occupies a good five-bay house of 1767 with pediment and Venetian window. A domed circular LOCK-UP of 1779 (*William Clark* builder) crowns the hill, overlooked by BAILEY HOUSE, with Victorian bargeboards, and SILK HOUSE, the late C19 warehouse of a horsehair cloth factory. Going downhill, SW, LONDON HOUSE, externally C18, has a C17 fireplace and winding stair. At the foot, Woodcock Street shows Victorian coloured brick on the former CONSTITUTIONAL CLUB, 1896, but is otherwise of Cary stone; DELAWARE HOUSE has C17 mullions. Lower Woodcock Street drops S to The Triangle. Here the granite WAR MEMORIAL cross, 1920, rises from the former horsepond (near to the source of the River Cary). Opposite, TRIANGLE HOUSE and the HORSEPOND INN are modest Late Georgian. Fore Street returns NE to the Market Place in an attractive mixture of heights and materials, No. 1 at the top dated 1804.

From here High Street climbs NE. The tall six-bay OLD BANK HOUSE is Late Georgian, with Victorian stonework for Stuckey's Bank. Replacement premises by *C. & C. B. Benson*, 1891, adjoin; now NATWEST. Ashlar with unexpected Middle European curves in familiar details. Opposite, a mixed row with Victorian shopfronts climbs to the curving stucco of PITHER'S YARD, a late C19 furniture works. HIGHFIELD HOUSE, with wings of Cary stone and a splayed centrepiece with good Roman Doric doorcase, has C17 origins – see one mullioned end window. BEECHFIELD, opposite, is mid-C18, with an oval light in the steep pediment. OCHILTREE HOUSE, red brick, five-bay, *c.* 1820–5, was bought by John Boyd, who built his three-storey thirteen-bay HORSEHAIR FACTORY behind in 1851. Opposite, COPPINS, 1946–8, by *W. A. Golding*, red brick, flat-roofed, the windowless end interestingly composed. High Street becomes North Street before the Methodist chapel

---

* Some Romanesque stones on the exterior may come from the castle. B. and M. Gittos.

(*see* above). Beyond is the finest Georgian house, THE PINES, named for the stone pineapples. Later C18 brick front with parapet and ashlar dressings, the doorcase particularly handsome with fluted columns and triglyphs. Staircase with delicate balusters. On the main road at the top, CUMNOCK TERRACE was industrial housing built for John Boyd, 1877. Two houses at each end, for managers, flank eight workers' cottages, the managers' houses given stone dragons and half-timber.

Returning now to The Triangle, Park Street runs s to the PRIMARY SCHOOL, made up of the gaunt National School, 1840 by *Abraham Bryant*, with a pedimented first-floor teacher's apartment of 1844, and a separate triple-gabled school by *Henry Hall*, 1876. On the hill to the w are the church (*see* p. 182) and the former VICARAGE, 1845–6, by *James Davis* of Frome, showing Puginian asymmetry early for Somerset. Above the rock bluff is SOUTH CARY, a C17 suburb. SOUTH COTTAGE has C17 mullions but an early C19 roof and canted s end. Then a brick-dressed former CHEESE STORE, *c.* 1900. Opposite, terraced houses conceal the former CONGREGATIONAL CHAPEL, 1816, brick with Y-tracery. Further on, an unspoilt row of late C18 workers' cottages; one is larger with a pedimented doorcase. At the upper end, SOUTH CARY HOUSE, late C18, five bays.

Returning again to The Triangle, Station Road runs w. Up Victoria Road is FLORIDA HOUSE, a quintessential industrialist's villa: by *Charles Bell*, 1887, for J. S. Donne, twine manufacturer. Each front has an offset gable, around a square-domed belvedere tower. Northern Renaissance detail. On Station Road, FOURHOUSE STEPS, hip-roofed cottages with stone Y-tracery windows. These may be the poorhouse of 1831, adapted. Charles Donne moved to the HIGHER FLAX MILLS on Torbay Road in 1818. The five three-storey buildings are later, the largest, of eleven bays, dated 1870.

LOWER COCKHILL FARMHOUSE, 1 m. SW. A exceptionally complete small hall house with a roof of wind-braced jointed crucks, tree-ring-dated to 1435. Two-bay hall reopened in an exemplary restoration, a storeyed bay on each side, and an added N bay, added perhaps at the same time as the timber-framed gable jettied over the doorway. The gable marks an exceptional oratory of *c.* 1500 with moulded beams (traces of red and white colour) intersecting at an exquisite Tudor rose. Two walls are covered in painted patterns with the IHS motif central, crudely done, but a rare and moving survival.* C18 farmhouse to the l. To the r., a small C15 BARN with three massive crucks, a C17–C18 STABLE, and an unusual hip-roofed BEE-HOUSE.

---

* James Ayres suggests a post-Reformation recusant use, from the crudity of the decoration and from the spyholes in the side walls.

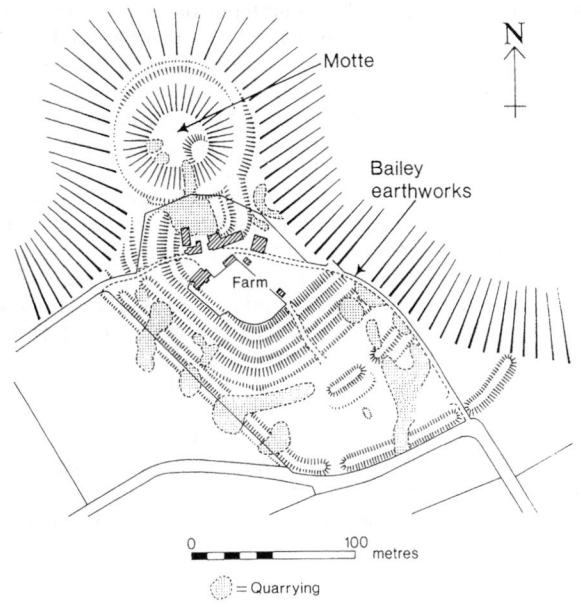

Castle Neroche.
Plan

CASTLE NEROCHE

An enormous DEFENSIVE WORK on the crest of the Blackdown Hills, of obscure history. Adapted from Iron Age earthworks by Robert, Count of Mortain, shortly after 1066, its Norman use was short. Briefly reused in the wars between Stephen and Matilda. Excavations produced Early Norman pottery in a French style but made locally, and a little Iron Age material. Triple banks curve SW to enclose the hillfort, protected by the sheer escarpment on the NE. The bailey of the C11 castle was at the N end, roughly on the site of the modern farmyard. Beyond this an enormous ditch announces the motte, scarped from a natural promontory. Earthworks downhill beyond the motte may indicate a second bailey.

CATCOTT

ST PETER. Blue Lias, with a short battlemented tower refaced in the C19. Its lower stage could be C13–C14, from the tiny paired lancets and double-chamfered tower arch. Perp nave, raised in the later C19 to incorporate C17 gallery windows. C13 chancel N lancet. Lovely pre-Victorian interior. White barrel-roofed nave with C17 TEXTS: the Lord's Prayer in a frame of wavy scrolls, and two from Titus, 2: 2–6: aged men admonished to exhort young men to be sober-minded, and aged women to teach young women to be sober, chaste and 'keepers at home', a message undermined by far from homely naked figures. Early C19 the WEST GALLERY with pierced flat balusters, and the N side family pew, now vestries. Good C15 chancel wagon roof with fleuron wall-plate and carved bosses. – Heavy plain BENCHES (the S ones with extendable planks for extra seats). – C17 PULPIT and DESK (lowered in 1928). – COMMUNION RAIL. C17, with vertically symmetrical balusters. – FONT. C13. Octagonal, on a round shaft with half-shafts. C17 COVER. – ROYAL ARMS. 1792.

SW of the church, on a small green, the WAR MEMORIAL, 1921, has a tabernacle head with carvings of servicemen. DIAL HOUSE, just SW, long and low, was a late medieval hall house, floored *c.* 1600 and the rear wing added. Two framed ceilings and a fireplace initialled ID.

CHAFFCOMBE

ST MICHAEL. Good Perp W tower of grey local stone (Calcareous Grit) with set-back buttresses continued as diagonal shafts to small pinnacles on the battlements. Higher octagonal stair-turret. The rest rebuilt in 1857–9 by *J. M. Allen*. Perp-style N arcade and chancel arch. – FONT. Much-scraped C12 bowl. – REREDOS. 1889. Gilded triptych installed with STAINED GLASS by *Hardman* above. S window, 1919, by *Powell's*. N aisle, 1859, by *Philip Palmer*, old-fashioned.

Churchyard MEMORIAL to Vincent Harris †1971, architect. Elemental stone post, designed by *Arthur Bailey*.

Behind the church, a large gabled stone RECTORY, 1886, by *J. P. Moore* of Gloucester. Below, on a small green, a good WAR MEMORIAL cross. The OLD RECTORY, W, has oak mullions, jointed crucks and a large C15–C16 moulded fireplace. A similar fireplace in a first-floor room at COURT FARMHOUSE, to the S, lit by a fine ogee-traceried window with hoodmould shields. The house is medieval, much reduced.

AVISHAYS HOUSE, ¾ m. S. Attractively grouped under a sheltering hill. Dated 1745 and 1756, but the E range facing the hill is late C17 with long mullion windows, parapet and Tudor-arched doorway. Early C18 shell-hood, added perhaps with the NE wing and the two hip-roofed stable pavilions opposite. These have pedimented doorways between cross-windows. Mid-C18 seven-bay W range with ashlar parapet, pediment and architraves. Below the hill, a hexagonal C18 SUMMERHOUSE, plastered inside, with niches. It once overlooked a water garden. The FOLLY above was a C19 water tower transformed by *Philip Jebb*, 1985, with a timber cupola housing a carillion clock from Highclere Castle.

CHAPEL ALLERTON

ALLERTON CHURCH. The chief interest is the rebuilding by *C. E. Giles* in 1858–60, indicated by the nave E bellcote, based on that at Biddestone (Wilts.). The church was late C13 – see the nave S lancet with trefoiled rere-arch and the single-chamfered S doorway. The flat-headed S window, of three lights with cusped pointed heads and spandrel roses and leaves, looks typical Late Perp, but minor oddities confirm the actual date, 1638. Giles added the N aisle and refashioned the interior, which shows him already influenced by G. E. Street. Round arcade columns, each with a top block of purple marble, under ballflower and nailhead capitals. Chancel arch on corbelled shafts with grape and wheat capitals. Draycott marble step to the tiled sanctuary. – REREDOS of red marble and alabaster. – FONTS. Norman, circular, with a C17 COVER. Giles's font has intricate naturalistic carving by *Henry Davis*. – STAINED GLASS. S window, 1921, by *Morris & Co.* – C15 CHURCHYARD CROSS, with restored head.

ASHTON WINDMILL, ½ m. E. The last intact windmill in SW England. Built *c.* 1770, re-fitted in 1900 with machinery from Moorlinch. Cylindrical whitewashed tower with restored cap, once thatched, like Stembridge Mill, High Ham (q.v.).

CHAPEL CLEEVE *see* OLD CLEEVE

CHARD

A market town on the Exeter road, its broad main street obstructed until 1834 by C17 market and shambles buildings. The church site to the S probably represents the original settlement. Chard was known for cloth-making from the C16, and for lace (plain net rather than fancy) from 1821 when industrial trouble in Nottingham brought factories to rural Somerset.

ST MARY THE VIRGIN. A long, low church, quite stately, without flights of fancy, the product of an unusually unified Perp rebuilding. One Norman fragment in the chancel S wall. Low W tower with set-back buttresses up to the bell-stage, and two-light bell-openings with pierced baffles. Octagonal NE stair-turret. Six-bay aisled nave with N and S porches and large transepts, leaving one bay of the chancel projecting. The whole church is battlemented and evenly buttressed, with diagonal shafts and pinnacles above each buttress. Three-light windows generally, four-light for each transept, five-light E window, all with standard Perp tracery. Octagonal stair-turret against the N transept. The nave is additionally lit by C17 dormers with obelisks. The porches are of even height with the aisles, with set-back buttresses, and shafted doorways. The N porch, with a crocketed ogee doorhead and a canopied statue niche, was embellished by *J. D. Sedding* in 1882. The niche is original. The interior is not high. Arcades on standard four-hollow piers, reaching right up to the C16 plaster cornice under the shallow wagon roof. The tower and N transept arches are of the same type; the S transept arches are panelled. Defaced niche in each transept,* a new pair in the chancel. – FONT. Octagonal, C15, with large crude quatrefoils. – PULPIT. 1884, by *Sedding*. Oak drum on a stone stem. – ROYAL ARMS. Hanoverian. High relief. – STAINED GLASS. Much by *Drake & Son*: nave windows, 1896–1913, perhaps the chancel N, 1880, and large E window, 1907. N transept E, 1884, by *W. C. Taylor*. – MONUMENTS. William Brewer †1618, physician. He faces his wife at a prie-dieu backed by eleven little adult offspring, all in black. Columned alabaster frame with curved broken pediment carrying semi-recumbent angels and a wreathed skull. – John Eveleigh †1767 and Humphrey Ash †1767. Two good marble memorials by *James Osborne* of Bristol. – George Warry †1782, urn and fulsome encomium. He 'really seems too good to be buried' wrote George Pulman. – Elizabeth Fry †1787. Elegant oval, by *Thomas Paty & Sons*.

Outside, an interestingly spartan WAR MEMORIAL cross. The Grecian MONUMENT to Rev. John Gunn †1832 was moved here from outside the demolished Congregational church. Cast-iron Gothic GATES, 1842. To the W, the two-storey Gothic CHURCH ROOM was the National School, 1827.

GOOD SHEPHERD (Furnham), East Street. 1872–3. *Maurice Davis* was involved, possibly not as architect. Angular, the long steep roof flared over low aisles, the bellcote acutely gabled. Unexpectedly rich High Church interior: arcades on paired marble shafts with foliage capitals, red marble octagonal FONT on green colonnettes, and high triple-gabled crocketed REREDOS of 1902, framing paintings. The circular PULPIT with marble panels came from Cuddesdon church, Oxon, and is by *G. E. Street*. Neat pyramid-roofed RECTORY, 1970s.

ENGLISH MARTYRS (R.C.), Fore Street. 1925–6, by *Sir Frank Wills*. Extremely old-fashioned lancet Gothic. Scissor-truss roof and a gallery.

BAPTIST CHAPEL, Holyrood Street. 1842. Grecian ashlar front with elongated pilasters and pediment. Just one cast-iron

---

* Two defaced BUSTS of Purbeck marble in the N transept may come from these niches.

arched window over the doorway. Panelled gallery on iron columns. A giant arch frames an early platform pulpit on two wine-glass stems.

METHODIST CHAPEL, Fore Street. 1894–5, by *Robert Curwen*, chapel specialist. Red brick with large five-light window between Gothic porches. Attractive apsed interior all in pitch pine, including the arcades and the Gothic screening to the clerestory lights.

TOWN HALL, Fore Street. 1834–5, by *Richard Carver*. It projects into the wide street with an impressive two-storey Bath stone portico of Tuscan columns, the outer ones paired, and the lower ones also paired in depth, all under a broad pediment. Square wooden clock turret carrying a cupola. Handsome first-floor council chamber with segmental-arched end bays. Iron-roofed CORN EXCHANGE behind, 1883, by *Henry Williams* of Bristol. Adapted as a public hall, 2002.

CHARD SCHOOL, Fore Street. Dated 1583, and faced with squared chert. Symmetrical, with a gabled dormer over four- and six-light windows on each side of a three-storey cross-gabled porch. Despite a fire in 1727, moulded beams, some timber framing and Tudor-arched fireplaces survive. In the rear wing a timber winding stair. William Symes of Poundisford gave the house to found a grammar school in 1671. Low thatched SCHOOLROOM behind; the crudely traceried E window looks earlier, perhaps indicating a domestic chapel. MONMOUTH HOUSE, adjoining, is later C18, stuccoed, with swept parapet. Adamesque doorcase, also bucrania friezes inside. W addition, *c.* 1870, with sumptuous ballroom plasterwork. Buildings to the NE of 1960–2, late works of *Vincent Harris*, in brown brick. The HALL, like an Arts and Crafts barn, with a sweeping roof and hip-roofed throughway, faces a strange composition, five-bay flat-roofed classrooms framed by much taller three-bay gabled residential blocks, the classrooms with a thin bellcote and arcaded ground floor.

CEMETERY, Combe Road. 1857–8, by *J. M. Allen*. Twin Dec chapels linked by a stone-vaulted *porte cochère*, all in Ham stone. To the NE, the MOORE MAUSOLEUM, *c.* 1914, in grimy marble, pyramid-roofed with an upward-pointing angel. Marble-lined interior with stained-glass Nativity by *Moore (A.L.) & Son*. Granite Celtic CROSS to T. Loader Brown †1899, by *Harry Hems*. Obelisk to John Stringfellow †1883, whose steam-powered aeroplane flew in 1848. Iron rails with adoring doves.

PERAMBULATION. From the central crossroads FORE STREET runs downhill. Its S side was rebuilt *c.* 1970 almost as far as the Town Hall (above). On the N side, NATWEST BANK, ashlar, with Soanean incised angle piers, is an unusually early bank building, built either for the Crewkerne & Chard Bank around 1821, or for Stuckey's Bank in 1829. Then the most interesting group in Chard, Nos. 7–11, the so-called COURT HOUSE, picturesquely uneven but a single Late Elizabethan house in origin, much subdivided. Two storeys and attic. The front in early illustrations had three gables, three two-storey

Chard, Fore Street.
Engraving, 1875

canted bays and two porch-towers, one three-storeyed between l. and centre, the other two-storeyed at the extreme r. Beyond this was a lower building. The porches remain, cross-gabled with Tudor-arched lights in mullion windows; the rest is much refaced, the ground floors lost to shops. No. 7 is faced in squared chert, Nos. 9–11 and the porches in Ham stone. The rear parts are all squared chert and much more credible. Nos. 9 and 11 have conjoined rear wings linked to buildings across their respective back courtyards. Behind No. 9 is a splendid COURTROOM, lit by a ten-light transomed window (still with four-centred heads to the lights) front and back, over a through passage with heavy oak partitioning. The room, 30 by 20 ft (9 by 6 metres), has a complete scheme of decorated plasterwork, to the tunnel vault, tympana, frieze and overmantel, with the strange animals that appear locally (at Whitestaunton Manor and Wigborough Manor, Over Stratton). In the vault, flat ribs intersect in patterns interspersed with flowers, sun and moon and stars, also beasts. The overmantel has a phoenix crest on strapwork between etiolated female terms in profile, and the tympanum above has a wolf badge in free scrolls that mutate into duck-heads disgorging plants. The E tympanum has two figures (Justice and Religion) between three small scenes in strapwork surrounds: the Judgment of Solomon, the Fiery Furnace, and Daniel in the Lions' Den, naïve and charming. Thin-rib plaster ceilings of *c.* 1600 survive on the first floor of No. 7, which has spiral stairs in a rear projection, on the ground floor of No. 9, and in two first-floor rooms of No. 11. The house was owned in the C16 by the Cogan family; little more is known.

Opposite the Town Hall, the PHOENIX HOTEL (formerly George Hotel), roughcast, with a heavy Greek porch, badly treated. LLOYDS BANK was built as the Chard Hotel in 1829, a grand three-storey, seven-bay Bath stone front. Arcaded and central tripartite windows mark first-floor public rooms. An upright brick box fronts the former CERDIC CINEMA, 1937, by *E. Holding*. ESSEX HOUSE, with a Venetian window, was refronted in 1866. It has exceptionally rare Baroque wall painting of *c*. 1740 in the SW upper room. Hagar and her child, resembling a Catholic Madonna and Child, between painted pilasters; angels over the doors. Further down are Chard School and Furnham church (above), and, on the S side, the R.C. and Methodist churches (above). On the S side, the earlier METHODIST CHAPEL, 1848, survives in a terraced row. Cast-iron Gothic windows; original galleries. Nos. 30–32, deep-eaved villas of *c*. 1850, display deeply channelled ashlar, one Ham stone, the other the grey Snowdon Hill stone.

HIGH STREET continues Fore Street uphill. SCULPTURE by *Neville Gabie*, 1991, three boulders, one natural, two of iron, representing industrial progress. The pavement watercourse is on a watershed between the English and Bristol channels. On the N side, THE CHOUGHS, early C17, with one of the corbelled gables on a canted bay typical of the Martock area. HARVEY'S HOSPITAL, 1843–9, by *Richard Carver*, two-storey neo-Tudor almshouses in Ham stone, with clustered chimneys and iron windows. Black-letter inscriptions in the gables and parapet. A parallel range behind. Further up, mixed vernacular thatch and Late Georgian stucco and Ham stone. On the N side, a mullion-windowed thatched row, now CHARD MUSEUM. Mostly of chert, the r. part, formerly the New Inn, with C16 lateral fireplace. W of town, on Snowdon Hill, a Picturesque thatched TOLL HOUSE, 1838.

Returning to the central crossroads, COMBE STREET runs N. HOPE TERRACE, *c*. 1820–30, an urban three-storey terrace of ten brick houses, was promoted by the Rev. John Gunn to relieve unemployment. The concrete mass opposite was a SECURE STORE, 1938, for the Westminster Bank. S from the crossroads is HOLYROOD STREET. On the E side, the Baptist chapel (above). The brick and terracotta former MACHINE WORKSHOPS, *c*. 1902, now shops, were associated with HOLYROOD MILL, 1828–30, behind. One of two impressive early C19 lace factories in Chard, both five-storeyed and of brick. Ten bays of large straight-headed windows. Fireproof construction – iron columns and girders, shallow brick arches, and roof on curved cast-iron trusses. No. 36 shows Victorian colour, red-and-white brick between giant pilasters. LAW CHAMBERS conceals C16 beams under Victorian stucco. Nos. 58–64 are C16 under Georgian stucco. Down MILL LANE is the larger of the lace mills, BODEN MILL, 1825. Eleven bays, extended to fifteen, with segment-headed windows. Similar fireproof construction to Holyrood Mill, the roof more spectacular in that it is wider and iron purlins and rafters are visible. Just W, a triple-arched pedimented GATEWAY dated 1901 and the BODEN INSTITUTE, 1892. By *John Wills* of Derby, of brick, with a large oriel and Norman–Transitional doorway. At the foot of Holyrood Street is the parish church (above). CHARD MANOR FARMHOUSE, S of the churchyard, has a seven-bay roughcast early C18 front with pedimented doorcase, cornice and parapet. Open-well staircase under Rococo plasterwork. Traces of a C15 hall with lateral fireplace.

NE Chard has a few things of interest. The basin of the CHARD CANAL, 1842, is obliterated, but CHARD JOINT STATION survives behind on Great Western Road. Brick and stone, 1866, elongated because the Great Western and London & South Western railways required separate offices. Typical GWR flat canopies; the overall roof covering the tracks was a GWR speciality of which few survive. CHARD RESERVOIR, NE, fed the canal. On the Crewkerne road, OAKLANDS, a late C19 industrialist's villa, for Col. J.W. Gifford of Holyrood Mill, who had an observatory here.

HORNSBURY MILL, 1½ m. N. Early C19 three-storeyed mill, with mullioned windows. Machinery of *c.* 1870; an 18-ft (5.5-metre) overshot waterwheel inside.

CHARLINCH

ST MARY. Deconsecrated. The tower is of 1863, the top apparently added later still. There is evidence of a Norman cruciform church, the S transept being rebuilt as a parallel S chapel in the late C15, the N transept removed. Plain Norman S doorway of pale stone. One order of colonnettes with square abaci carrying a segmental arch. Tiny heads in the corners of the hoodmould are the only decoration. Otherwise Perp and later external detail. The chancel arch is Norman at least in its responds. Double-chamfered arch renewed in 1887. – FONT. Norman. Circular with broad flat flutes. – STAINED GLASS. S chapel E window, four C15 figures in the tracery.

The former RECTORY has a three-storey hip-roofed front of 1807 facing the spectacular view. Red sandstone, originally rendered. Arched centre window, timber bay windows. The earlier rectory behind is externally later C17, with mullioned windows, but contains a C14–C15 three-bay hall with arch-braced cruck trusses.

ASHFORD, ½ m. N. Gothic PUMPING STATION of 1879 by *Thomas Nicholson* of Hereford, for the Bridgwater water supply. The screen walling of the TREATMENT WORKS, 1991–2, by *Graham Carruthers Partnership*, echoes the Victorian brickwork. ASHFORD HOUSE, N of the main road, is hip-roofed, stuccoed, of *c.* 1830.

GOTHELNEY HALL. See p. 332.

CHARLTON ADAM

A village of Lias stone, still quarried here.

CHARLTON ADAM

St Peter and St Paul. The external appearance is Perp. Three-stage tower with deep-set w window and small two-light bell-openings. Wave-moulded tower and chancel arches and the similar s doorway point to the late C14. s porch attached to a gabled C16 chapel. Two sharply pointed cusped niches in the porch are reused C14 window heads, and the nave corbels, two big roses and two heads also look C14. The chancel arch stops high for a lost screen wall. The C16 Strangways Chapel on the s side has elliptical arches to nave and chancel, the latter reached by an added diagonal passage. – FONT. C12, of swollen profile, as at Kingsdon. – PULPIT. Jacobean, panelled. – PEWS. Neat, square-ended, from the restoration by *J. D. Sedding*, 1890–2. – STALLS. Neat, neo-Jacobean, early C20. – PAINTINGS. Virgin and two saints, Venetian, C16, originally in the Zouche collection at Parham, Sussex. The altarpiece and Crucifixion are 1920s copies of Italian works by *Mrs Neville* of The Abbey. – MONUMENTS. Strangways Chapel. Thomas Basket †1592. A pediment on squat columns frames the inscription in a strapwork cartouche. – Giles Strangways †1677. A more rustic pedimented columned frame to a Lias plaque, delightfully incised.

The Abbey. The irregular mullion-windowed house NE of the church was the medieval rectory owned by Bruton Priory. Rebuilt in the late C16, it declined until restored in 1902–5 for Claude Neville of Butleigh Court. A hipped roof running N–S marks the core from which three gables project E, stepped back successively N to S. No entrance façade, but on the W are a three-storey stair-block with thin octagonal chimneys and an Edwardian porch. The core may be a C15 hall with two cross-wings (joined in the C16). Buttresses on the s wall, also to the stair-block, suggesting that this too may be C15. Both ends of the core have cross-windows indicating Elizabethan principal rooms upstairs. The hipped C18 roof replaces gables. Other early features are a pointed doorway on the N of the N cross-wing (now internal), and, on the stair-block, a two-light window with a panelled mullion and a first-floor relieving arch unrelated to the C16 fenestration. Both lower rooms have large Tudor-arched fireplaces. The s room has panelling of *c.* 1600, present before 1902 but not apparently made for the room. Carved top panels correspond with the deep bracketed frieze of the overmantel, too deep for the three pairs of thin columns beneath. The N cross-wing has a heavy oak pointed-arched attic doorway, possibly C15, and the s cross-wing has a plaster barrel ceiling on C15 wall-plates. A plaster barrel ceiling also to the stair-block, which has remnants of a C16 stair-rail and an arched first-floor doorway into the main range.

The village is on a square of roads around The Abbey grounds. On the corner of Broad Street, a Gothic SCHOOL of 1865. Just s, Jasmine Cottage is C16: oak cross-passage door, plank partitions, and a framed ceiling.

Cary Fitzpaine, 1 m. SE. Hip-roofed square villa of *c.* 1830 with a veranda.

CHARLTON HORETHORNE

Around an unusually spacious green below Manor Farmhouse.

St Peter and St Paul. Of local limestone with stone-tiled roofs. A rewarding, substantially C14 church with a Perp W tower of some ambition. Set-back buttresses formerly had tiny pinnacles. Two-light bell-openings with latticed baffles, ashlar battlements, and corner pinnacles. Square NE stair-turret. Statue niche above the W window. Tall tower arch without capitals. The rest, nave with gabled aisles, and chancel, has evidence of the C12–C13 in the S aisle, but is mostly C14, restored in 1863 by *William Slater*. The S aisle has one early C13 plate-traceried window and two C13 eastern windows with sharply pointed cusped lights. The reticulated chancel E window and two-light side windows, if reliable, are early C14 Dec, as also the good N aisle E window with spherical triangles encircled in the head. Small bellcote on the N aisle. Early C14 N arcade of double-chamfered arches on low octagonal piers. Capitals ornamented with ballflower, but the responds are carved heads, an exquisite king and queen. The S arcade is *Slater*'s, with Edward and Alexandra as responds. The S aisle has cusped rere-arches and a low early C14 ogee-headed tomb-recess with double cusping. The N aisle seems to have been of especial status, with twin large tomb-recesses, cusped, with ogee heads carrying florid finials. In the NE corner are fine statue niches, one ogee and C14, the other early C15. Remains of original colouring. Both are on ornate corbels, the former with dense foliage, the latter especially good, a woman's head with exceedingly horned head-dress, and two tiny heads. The adjacent window has tiny leaves in the rere-arch. Also a cusped Piscina. Panelled C15 nave and S aisle roofs. Chancel arch, roof and reredos by *Slater*. – Font. C12. Cylinder with a ring. – Furnishings. By *Slater*; the woodwork, including the pulpit, with carved roundels. – Tower railings. Cast-iron Gothic. – Stained Glass. By *Clayton & Bell* the fine E window and S two-light, 1871, also the very Gothic adjacent single light, 1863, and NE heraldic glass. Possibly also the N aisle N, 1869. – Monument. John Wright †1726. Grey and white with Baroque tapering pilasters and curved pediment.

Lychgate, 1881. The foliage brackets represent Death and Resurrection.

Mid-C19 estate cottages opposite the church, two pairs and a row with the school, 1851, quietly incorporated at the end. The former rectory, 1841, by *Maurice Davis*, is square and pyramid-roofed. On the green, early C18 gatepiers front Manor Farmhouse, a handsome symmetrically arranged five-bay house of *c.* 1620 with mullion-and-transom windows. Storeyed porch with an arched doorway between shell niches and a shallow gable. Double-gabled ends, the E with a circular stair-turret. In the farmyard, a large C18 barn with hip-roofed porches, and timber-framed granary. Down a lane SE, the former Blackmore Vale HUNT KENNELS show the scale on which such things were done, c. 1860. N of the green, MONKS PLACE is C17 with an off-centre storeyed porch. On Gunville Lane, CHARLTON HORETHORNE HOUSE, 1759, has bead-moulded mullioned windows in five bays, and a large later C19 addition.

CHARLTON MACKRELL

5020

The church, rectory and school are at West Charlton, separated from the modern village and Charlton House by the railway.

ST MARY. A handsome cruciform church with crossing tower. So much restored in 1847 by *C. E. Giles* that it has a Victorian character, although broadly consonant with Buckler's 1834 view. The crossing piers, of typical Perp four-hollow section, are treated so broadly that a C14 date is possible. The tower has standard C15 two-light bell-openings and a SW stair-turret with C19 spirelet. The N transept, the Lyte Chapel, is of Ham stone, with a fine and fanciful N window of c. 1330–40. Five lights with a large circle at the top divided perversely by means of reticulation. Flowing tracery of a simple kind in the two-light side parts. Ballflower rere-arch. The rest of the tracery has an earlier character than the Perp shown by Buckler. N vestry, 1861, probably by *Giles*.

TILES by *Minton* in the porch hint at the rich Early Victorian interior created for Archdeacon Brymer. *Minton* tiles also in the crossing and choir, the former honouring Brymer's bishop, the latter with emblems of the Passion. The chancel roof has over-scaled hammerbeam angels and the N transept has a good trefoil-cusped roof. Original squints from the transepts. Stone REREDOS and Commandment panels, 1847. – FONTS. Two. One Ham stone, C12, the bowl rimmed as at Aller. The other, 1847, excessively detailed Perp under an equally enthusiastic spired cover. – RAILS. Good C19, with brass scrolls. – BENCH-ENDS. Early C16, with blind tracery. One uniquely shows the devil Tittivilus who noted down sins. Also some poppyhead ends. – STAINED GLASS. Chancel N, signed *Joseph Bell*, 1854. N transept N, 1860, small scenes and saints.* – MONUMENTS. Rev. W. Dodd †1766 and wife †1778. Matching open-pedimented plaques. – Mary Pyne †1770, large draped urn. – Harriot Brymer †1827, mourning female.

CHURCHYARD CROSS, C15, on high octagonal steps, the base with posts at the diagonal sides. Tabernacle head of 1923. Under a yew NE, a featureless lump, formerly a Purbeck marble double effigy (the only double one known), reputedly William le Lyt, c. 1286, and wife.

* The painterly early C19 glass in the W window noted by Pevsner has gone.

SCHOOL, opposite. By *Giles*, 1853. A good Puginian Gothic group of house and schoolroom. The classrooms surprisingly are lined in *Minton* tiles between lettered bands giving Archdeacon Brymer's preferments. Also useful admonishments, e.g. (for the infants) 'lying lips are abomination to the Lord'. Below the church, THE COURT is the rectory of *c*. 1510, rebuilt *c*. 1790 on the old foundations. Georgian Gothic of the simplest kind. The three-storey, five-bay S front has sash windows but battlements and an ashlar Gothick porch (two-bay to disguise the asymmetry of the screens passage). Inside, a very pretty Gothick hall with tripartite screen opening to a curving cantilevered staircase with iron rail.

Further W, at WEST CHARLTON, some thatched and some C19 estate cottages. The OLD COTTAGE has an E room with large early C16 mullioned windows, a massive chimney and framed ceiling. Plank partitions.

MANOR FARM, Mill Lane. The manor house of Charlton Adam (q.v.). The long early C18 front with parapet but no particular features disguises an older house indicated by the lateral chimney. It may have been a medieval hall but the beams and roof point to the C16. In the remodelling of *c*. 1710–20 for the Strangways family, a panelled dining room was created, the panels attractively painted with imaginary landscapes amidst which the Charlton churches and Glastonbury Tor are recognizable. One panel celebrates the timber Eddystone lighthouse of 1709. Tudor-arched fireplace in the lateral chimney. Early C19 rear staircase. The upper E room has early C18 arches flanking a panelled overmantel. Big L-plan OUTBUILDINGS, a hip-roofed lofted C18 range screening a C16 barn. Also a boarded C19 GRANARY.

CHARLTON HOUSE, ½ m. N. Built in 1726 by Thomas Lyte for his son-in-law, the rector of St Martin-in-the-Fields, Westminster. The house has an urban formality that must have been more striking when only a narrow forecourt separated it from the road. Substantial double pile of seven bays in a lively and colourful Baroque rare in the region. Blue Lias, but orange Ham stone for the dressings: quoins, bolection-moulded surrounds and cornices. The cornices on each floor are ramped at the ends and the parapet coping is additionally ramped in the centre and broken forward over Lias apron panels for further distraction. The hipped roof was restored in an exemplary repair by *Paul Richold* of *Architecton*, 2009–10. The house had been altered *c*. 1809, when the narrow lights flanking the centre became niches and the columned porch and single-bay l. wing were added (the mullion-and-transom kitchen window presumably reused). The corresponding r. wing is late C19, reusing early C18 cornices and windows. The rear has old-fashioned drip-courses. Staircase with balusters in threes, scrolled tread-ends and Corinthian column newels. Behind, a tall gabled DOVECOTE may also be early C18.

WELHAM STUDIOS, ¾ m. W. 2008–9, by *Mark Merer*, sculptor, for himself. On a rectangular plan; prow-like gables rise at opposite corners from a green-roofed saddle. Varnished pine exterior cladding on structural insulated panels.

GREEN DOWN, ½ m. NW. Above the railway, a barrel-vaulted POWDER STORE, 1903, built to store the explosives that blasted the cutting.

CHARLTON MUSGROVE

7020

The church is near Wincanton racecourse, 1½ m. SSW of the modern village.

ST STEPHEN. Limestone with stone-tiled roofs. Perp W tower with two-light bell-openings and a good cresting of gargoyles, battlements and pinnacles, like South Cadbury. Battlemented NE stair-turret. Moulded shafted tower arch. Renewed C12 S doorway, and a Dec two-light window and early C13 small triple lancet window on the chancel S. C16 nave roof with cambered tie-beams, nicely coloured in the restoration of 1884. The corbelled wall-plate over the S door may indicate a lost S tower. Low pointed chancel arch, remodelled with Perp panelling. Perp niche adjoining. – FONT. Small, octagonal. C13 with C19 motifs. – FURNISHINGS. Much woodwork of 1884, muddled in design. – ROYAL ARMS. 1660. – STAINED GLASS. E and S windows, 1938, by *Powell's*. – MONUMENTS. Thomas Penny †1730. Handsome pedimented aedicule with scrolled sides. – Leir family, squires and parsons: a crude late C17 steep pediment on columns, and two Victorian Gothic memorials.

ST JOHN, Barrow Lane. 1877–8 by *C. E. Davis* of Bath. Muscular Victorian on a small scale, with colander rose window, spirelet and apse. Striking brick interior with stone transverse arches.

Opposite the old church, CHARLTON HOUSE, c. 1810, was bizarrely given a neo-Jacobean porch in 1903 (by *W. J. Willcox*) copied from Manor Farmhouse, Charlton Horethorne (q.v.). THE COACH HOUSE, ½ m. NE, neo-Regency, 2004, replaces a rectory of 1805 by *Harcourt Masters*. The STABLES survive. In the village, SOMERLEA FARM has an altered C17 farmhouse in front of an extremely long C19 MALTINGS offering an almost windowless, formally symmetrical, front to the fields.

ROUNDHILL GRANGE, ½ m. W of the village. A notably early brick house of 1701. Five bays with stone cross-windows, quoins and band. Bolection-moulded and curved pedimented doorcase. Extended S by one bay in 1775 and N by three bays c. 1900. Cornice and hipped roof of 1832. Some imported high-quality marquetry may be Dutch, c. 1700.

SHALFORD, SW of the village. Two hip-roofed early C19 farmhouses at SHALFORD FARM and LOWER SHALFORD, the latter added to an earlier house.

STAVORDALE PRIORY. *See* p. 575.

CHEDDON FITZPAINE

ST MARY. The thin unbuttressed W tower is C13, off-centre and skewed to the nave. Simple lancets and narrow paired cusped bell-lights above. Renewed pierced parapet. Perp S aisle and porch with pierced quatrefoil parapets. N aisle of 1860–1 by *Edward Ashworth*. The tower arch has Perp detail in a C13 opening. Broad Perp nave roof. Three-bay S arcade of four-centred arches on standard four-hollow piers with angel capitals (cf. St Mary Magdalene, Taunton). – PULPIT. Said to be medieval; if so, utterly retooled. Octagonal, of Ham stone with quatrefoils in bands, on a wine-glass stem. – BENCHES. C16. Straight-headed in unusually broad leaf-scroll frames: tracery, flowers, also a double-headed eagle. – STAINED GLASS. E window and chancel S, 1861, by *Joseph Bell*. Nave S, c. 1855, probably by *Lavers & Barraud*, from Bishop's Lydeard, and 1996, by *Mark Angus*. Strong colours, the leading overlaid.

Churchyard CROSS, 1935 on a medieval round base, by *W. D. Caröe*, by whom also probably the LYCHGATE, 1921. It is very Welsh, tunnel-vaulted in slaty stone with an interlaced cross. A foliate cross on the coffin-rest.

Pleasant village street of C17–C19 cottages. To the NW, former RECTORY, 1854–5, by *Ashworth*, asymmetrical between outer gables.

HESTERCOMBE. See p. 353.

CHEDZOY

Imperceptibly elevated above King's Sedgemoor.

ST MARY. A large Blue Lias church of great interest. Handsome Perp W tower for which money was left as late as 1539, similar to the tower at Ruishton of 1533. Four stages, with set-back buttresses cheerfully banded in Ham stone. These end in diagonal shafts which are missing their finials. Ham stone bell-stage with squatting beasts on the cornice, battlements with quatrefoils and small corner pinnacles. Polygonal NE stair-tower. W doorway with spandrel leaves under a large sub-arched four-light window, two-light windows on the third stage, and paired two-light bell-openings between three thin shafts with pinnacles.

The rest, clerestoried aisled nave with S porch, transepts, and lower chancel, is externally mostly Perp, remodelled from a substantial cruciform C13 church. The five-bay arcades with circular piers, simple moulded capitals and double-chamfered arches are clearly C13 work. The eastern arches open into the transepts. The S transept has matching W and E arches; the latter, blocked, but visible externally, was to a lost C13 SE chapel of considerable width. The chapel two-bay arcade, of chamfered arches on a circular pier with four attached shafts, remains visible outside in the chancel wall. Small blocked C13 lancet in the transept W wall. The aisles and S porch are C13, the N one slightly narrower. Double-chamfered S doorway and single-chamfered N doorway. One Dec two-light S window. The chancel, much rebuilt in 1884–5, has C13 pointed trefoiled rere-arches to both N lancets and the two-light S window. Perp work of the C15–C16 includes the E window, the nave clerestory with flat-headed three-light windows, the rather refined N aisle windows, flat-headed with ogee lights, and the parapets of the aisles, porch and transepts. The S transept is raised to cover one clerestory window, so one of the last works to be done, unless the 1579 date on the porch (with initials RF between HP and RB) represents rebuilding. Two good DOORS, the S door Elizabethan with lozenges in square panels, the N door C13–C14 with lovely scrolled iron straps. Five CONSECRATION CROSSES.

The tower arch is panelled and shafted. The arch from the N aisle to the transept is curious, the respond apparently C13 but the arch ornamented with vine-trail and the spandrels with well-carved leaves, probably early C16. Above is a defaced Calvary, indicating perhaps an important chantry chapel. In the S aisle, a cusped PISCINA. Plain but good nave roof of eleven bays with moulded cambered tie-beams, restored 1905. The chancel was expensively re-fitted in 1884–5 by *S. S. Stallwood* of Reading: panelled wagon roof ornamented with stars, marble steps, encaustic and coloured TILES by *Carter, Johnson & Co.*, brass CORONAE, oak STALLS, and a stone REREDOS with eroding paintings let into alabaster. C13 two-bay SEDILIA with pointed trefoiled arches on column shafts and a half bay to the r., suggesting alteration.

OTHER FURNISHINGS. FONT. C13. Octagonal, curved below. C12 shaft and moulded base. – PULPIT. With tall linenfold panels, perhaps Early Elizabethan. – SCREEN. 1884; remarkably delicate for the date. Above it hangs a good Victorian gilded CROSS. – BENCHES. A particularly large set, also with frontals. Broad coarse tracery and bold motifs including wiry leaf stems. Also a Lamb of God, a crowned M for Mary, dated 1559, and initials in Renaissance wreaths (W with a serpent, TB). – ORGAN SEAT. Reused panelling dated 1620. Typical blank arches in two tiers. – LECTERN. 1618. The stand is a big baluster. – HATCHMENT. Stradling family. – TOWER RAILS. Reused altar rails of 1637. – STAINED GLASS. Chancel, 1884, by *Gibbs & Howard*. The rest by *Powell's*, 1906–27, the quality declining over the period. – MONUMENTS. Brass, possibly Richard Sydenham †1499, a 4-ft 3-in. (1.3-metre) figure, bare-headed in armour. – Two striking mid-C18 memorials, inlaid in coloured marble, by *Prince Hoare* of Bath. – Stradling family, † to 1786. Long Lias slab imitating slate, with broken pediment. Motto in Welsh.

On Front Street, the hipped-roofed stuccoed RECTORY was given unconvincing Tudor dress by *Charles Knowles*, 1848.

Cantilevered staircase. Neat brick VILLAGE HALL, 1914, by *Samson & Colthurst*.

CHESTERBLADE

ST MARY. Ungainly but interesting. Small nave with outsize S porch and undersized chancel. The nave is Norman, from the carved corner corbels: an ass and human head SE, two human heads and a wolf's head NE. Transitional S doorway, late C12, with a stilted segmental arch on colonnettes with carved capitals, of a leaf-and-grape design and a grotesque face. Hood-mould with pellets and small animal-head stops. Perp niche above, with a C19 statue. Porch of *c.* 1300 with big double-chamfered doorway. Late Perp N window. W window of 1840 under a curious Georgian Gothic bellcote. Crude S parapet, perhaps of 1767, when the chancel was rebuilt. Marks of a much larger chancel. E window, 1911, by *Bligh Bond*. The nave roof, on tie-beams dated 1663, was found above plaster in 1925. – FONT. Norman, tapered. Once it had a cable moulding low down. – CHANCEL PANELLING. Reused Jacobean pieces. – STAINED GLASS. E window, 1913, by *Martin Travers*. Nativity, particularly sweetly drawn.

CHURCHYARD CROSS. C15.

CYPRESS HOUSE, an early C19 three-storey ashlar front, faces down the approach from the S. CHESTERBLADE HOUSE has C18 beaded mullions.

SMALL DOWN CAMP, ½ m. SE. An Iron Age hillfort with two lines of defences that surround an elongated knoll. Within, on the crest of the hill, is an earlier barrow cemetery with up to fourteen Bronze Age burial mounds in a line.

CHILLINGTON

ST JAMES. Small. Perp nave with bellcote and S porch, older chancel. Mullioned N windows of *c.* 1600. The interest comes from work in 1909–10 by *Caröe & Passmore*, who added the S transept and N vestry and gave the interior character with sturdy roof timbers and two-bay asymmetrical S arcade. C15 panelled chancel arch. – FONT. 1909. – PULPIT. 1909. Like a lectern. – RAILS. Cast-iron Gothic. 1842. – FRAGMENT. Fluted C12 capital on a modern column.

The church stands in a raised churchyard between SHEEPHOUSE FARMHOUSE, long, with C18 mullions, and MANOR FARM, with an C18 timber-framed BARN, unusual in the region. MANOR HOUSE has a stuccoed Late Georgian front.

CHILTHORNE DOMER

ST MARY. The character comes from a C15 remodelling of the nave with a heavy lantern-like bellcote (cf. Ashington and Brympton D'Evercy), raised battlemented walls and gables, and two large Perp S windows. The nave is C14. Dec N windows and S porch with unribbed, pointed, tunnel vault (cf. East Chinnock). Double-chamfered S doorway. There is no W window. The chancel may be a little earlier from the S lancet with cinquefoiled rere-arch. Double-chamfered chancel arch on large expressive corbel heads of mid-C14 type. A three-light Geometric window of *c.* 1300 was reused on the vestry in the restoration of 1883 by *Carpenter & Ingelow*. Nave roof on tie-beams with queenposts. – FONT. Octagonal, Perp, with shields in quatrefoils. – PULPIT. 1624. Complete with back and tester. Arched panels and lozenges. – PEWS. early C17, with shell-tops and knob finials. – REREDOS. 1884. Oak, with canopied reliefs, every surface carved, patterned or notched. – STAINED GLASS. By *Powell's*, 1897–1924. – MONUMENTS. Ham stone effigy of a knight with mail, surcoat and shield, *c.* 1330, his feet on a crouching man. Related to the knight at Pendomer (q.v.). – Elizabeth Lyte Browne †1794. A dove pecks at a draped urn.

Late Georgian OLD RECTORY with parapet. CASTLE COTTAGES, originally a C17 pair, were rebuilt in the early C19 with a hipped roof. The interest is a central double chimney inside entirely of wattle-and-daub. HOME FARM has C18 square mullions and an early C19 hip-roofed S wing. The BARN, unusually, is timber-framed. MANOR HOUSE has C17 mullions and a Victorian S wing. Early C18 panelled room. Six-seater C18 PRIVY in the garden, for four adults and two children.

CHILTON CANTELO

ST JAMES. Impressive Perp W tower with set-back buttresses pinnacled at the bell-stage. Ashlar battlements with small corner pinnacles and middle ones on corbels. Polygonal NE stair-turret. The large three-light bell-openings are, unusually, four-centred-arched, with transoms and pierced baffles. Quatrefoil frieze below (cf. Mudford). Panelled tower arch. The rest was expensively rebuilt in 1865 by *Arthur Blomfield* for the Rev. Charles Goodford, Provost of Eton. Without the robustness of Blomfield's early urban churches, this is a replacement to the original plan, but typically Dec in detail rather than the original Perp. Ashlar-lined with elaborate roofs, the chancel with shafted arch and shafted windows with cusped rere-arches. Blomfield's FURNISHINGS include the door ironwork, marble and encaustic tile floors, mosaic reredos, oak screen and pulpit. – FONT. C12 tapered bowl, the base with incised spurs. – SEDILIA. Two fine C13 thrones. – PISCINAE. Three reused, one with late C13 cinquefoiled head. – STAINED GLASS. Chancel and s transept by *R. T. Bayne* of *Heaton, Butler & Bayne*, 1866, among the best of the era. Deep colours, stylized drapery and ethereal faces. The lovely w window, Pre-Raphaelite processions on a pale background, was apparently exhibited in Paris in 1864.

CHILTON HOUSE. The Goodford house was remodelled *c.* 1865 perhaps by *Blomfield*. Neo-Jacobean N front added to a square hip-roofed house of *c.* 1700 with cross-windows, all renewed. SE wing by *John Pinch*, 1840s. Service court with an arcaded coachhouse and Italianate bell-turret. The Gothic LODGE, 1866, shows flair with its miniature stair-tower and clustered chimneys.

Opposite the church, HIGHER FARMHOUSE, T-plan, 1826, by *John Pinch*. The thatched C17 OLD RECTORY is the predecessor of CYPRESS HOUSE, further E, tall and hip-roofed, in White Lias. Of 1857, by *Thomas Bellamy*. At Lower Chilton, LOWER FARM, 1792, a brick Goodford estate farmhouse, double-pile with stone mullions, and large brick BARN. Twelve distinctive ESTATE COTTAGES, 1867, in four cruciform blocks, red brick banded in black.

HINTON FARM, 1 m. S. C17 farmhouse refronted for the Goodford estate in the 1860s. Opposite is a splendid brick BARN of 1780 with no fewer than four hipped projections. Mullion windows mark the MILL inserted in 1800–4 by *William Smith*, the geologist. An engineering *tour de force*. Coal miners tunnelled beneath the medieval MOATED SITE to the SE to a huge ashlar wheel pit inside the building and then back to the river. The 20-ft (4.1-metre) wheel (replaced with an Armfield turbine in 1893) powered a pioneering threshing machine.

CHILTON POLDEN

ST EDWARD. Rebuilt 1888–9, by *E. H. Edwards* of Bristol. Of Blue Lias, with a bellcote and embattled N aisle. Edwards kept the C14 chancel arch, pieces of C15 wall-plate, and the plain octagonal C13 FONT. – MONUMENTS. Three Lias plaques behind the organ, †1727–58, with wonderfully rustic foliage and angels. – Rev. R. Hole †1776. Draped urn against an obelisk, by *James Allen* of Bristol.

In the churchyard, a small stuccoed SCHOOLROOM of 1840. N of the church, SEALEY'S FARMHOUSE, C17–C18 with small-paned casements. Further W, CHILTON HOUSE, early C19, with a delicate cast-iron veranda, and WEST HOUSE, 1858, angular Tudor with double gables.

TOWER HOUSE, ¼ m. E. Late Georgian, stuccoed, with cornice and Greek Doric porch. The arms of William Stradling, antiquary, owner from 1832, are inserted in the fanlight. He created the miniature picturesque GARDEN. By a pond with rock-faced bridge, a delightful GROTTO crowned by a stone-slab 'altar'. Two vaulted chambers lined with tufa. One has a natural spring and a bath, the other, lit from a bizarre cone, has a poem to Childe Harold, by William Lisle Bowles, beneath a niche that once held a bust of Byron. In a grove at the end of the garden, a MONUMENT, apparently a reused medieval square crocketed pinnacle with canopied saint on one face. At the corner of a field to the NE, a FOLLY made from the porch of the large late medieval house in Somerton called Somerton Castle, demolished in 1842. The shafted doorway remains, and part of the blind window above, four-centred, four-light and transomed, is original. Both have leaf spandrels. The diagonal buttresses are copies. The battlements have fallen, as has the barrel vault.

CHILTON PRIORY, ½ m. S, on the main road. Built *c.* 1836 for William Stradling as a museum for medieval and other fragments, possibly by *William Halliday* (*see* Othery), the wood-carver, who acted as caretaker. Resembling a stunted church, it has a battlemented tower, short nave (the 'refectory') with S porch, and a battlemented 'chancel' (the 'oratory'). The tower has a plaster-vaulted viewing chamber. Medieval pinnacles from Langport church are on the ground nearby. The stair-turret top came from Shepton Mallet church (N), the porch door from Stogursey, and the quatrefoil above it from a house in Westonzoyland. Wooden traceried chancel window. Inside are turned baluster rails from the church at St Michael Church, 1635, a C15–C16 fireplace with heraldry in quatrefoils and Welsh mottoes (added by Stradling), and various medieval corbels. In the E window some lovely medieval stained glass fragments. W of the tower, POCOCK'S CELL, a tunnel-vaulted grotto with niches of the 1830s. The large castellated house just N is by *Bligh Bond*, 1909–10 and 1918, in stripped Edwardian manner: sheer walls, flush mullion windows and shallow crenellation.

CHILTON TRINITY

Still rural, on the edge of Bridgwater.

HOLY TRINITY. Red sandstone three-stage Perp tower with diagonal buttresses and octagonal NE turret. The rest, of mixed local stones, has C15–C16 detail but earlier origins from the low plastered chancel arch.* – FONT. Perp. Octagonal, with quatrefoils. C17 COVER. – PULPIT. Reached from the rood stair. Early C17, narrow and especially pretty, in tiers of arched panels each with a large flower. – MONUMENTS. Two corniced later C18 Lias plaques, one painted.
Circular base of a C13 CHURCHYARD CROSS.

---

* A C12 two-cell structure may underlie the building. *PSANHS* 136, 1992.

CHIPSTABLE

ALL SAINTS. Rebuilt in 1869 by *Benjamin Ferrey*, in careful Geometrical style, keeping the three-stage Perp W tower. Set-back buttresses, battlements and polygonal SE stair-turret. Panelled tower arch. Ferrey kept two capitals of the four-bay arcade, with busts of angels on all four sides, their wings touching, rather coarser than those of the Taunton area. – BENCH-ENDS. A large collection of *c.* 1540, square-headed, with Renaissance detail (cf. Milverton). Some heads in lozenge panels, a holy-water sprinkler, a huntsman and the Poulett arms. – Victorian FONT and strongly modelled PULPIT. – STAINED GLASS. Mostly *Clayton & Bell*, 1885–1905, the E window particularly good.

WATERROW, 1 m. SW. Stuccoed CHAPEL of 1890. Impressive stone piers remain ¾ m. S from the lattice-girder VIADUCT of the Devon & Somerset Railway, 1871–2. On a hilltop NW, TROWELL FARM, externally unremarkable, conceals a C15–C16 partition with linenfold panels, unique in the county. The Abbot of Muchelney's cook owned the house.

CHISELBOROUGH

ST PETER AND ST PAUL. Very disparate parts: a plain C13 tower with a C15 spire between a large ashlar E.E. nave of 1842 (by *E. L. Bracebridge* of London) and a late C17 chancel. The tower is unbuttressed and resembles that at Barwick, with small lancet bell-lights and plain parapet. Crossing arches within, but no other evidence of transepts. The spire, a rare thing in Somerset, has a distinctly swollen outline and a band of pointed quatrefoils. The mullion-windowed chancel resembles a Nonconformist meeting house and the nave a Commissioners' church. Five nave bays of large lancets and buttresses, and two porches, for symmetry not utility. Light, high interior without arcades or galleries. Three of the tower arches are double-chamfered starting almost from the ground without capitals. The western arch was rebuilt Norman, 1911–12, by *F. Bligh Bond*, on evidence found in the walling, mainly a capital and two shaft bases. The star-vault under the crossing rests on moulded corbels that look C14 but may be later, if the vault was added with the spire. The chancel, now a vestry, has two corbels in the exterior E wall, one clearly Romanesque. – FONT. Octagonal, C13–C14, the ornament added since Pridham drew it in 1898. – PULPIT. 1842. Painted and grained. It originally stood higher. – ROYAL ARMS. On canvas. 1820.

E of the church are COURT HOUSE, thatched, C17, raised in the C18, and the CATHEAD INN, early C17 with a stepped dripcourse over the ground-floor windows. At the centre is a Gothic former SCHOOL, 1870. In a terraced row to the E, STRAPP FARMHOUSE has a Tudor-arched doorway dated

1576 but later windows. Up North Street, GAWLERS COTTAGE, thatched, with a gable-entry plan and C16 framed ceiling and partitions. At the top, MANOR FARM, 1861, by *R. H. Shout*, was a model farm for Lord Ilchester. The house is hip-roofed with fancy gablets and fancy cast-iron windows. The farm buildings all converted.

CHISELBOROUGH HOUSE, ½ m. W. A large, slightly Tudor rectory of *c*. 1845–50, double-gabled on the S.

CHURCHINFORD see CHURCHSTANTON

CHURCHSTANTON

Transferred from Devon in 1896. The church is isolated; the village is at Churchinford.

ST PETER AND ST PAUL. Predominantly Perp, but the plain unbuttressed W tower in its lower parts looks *c*. 1300 – see the mouldings of the W doorway and the lancet above. C13–C14 double-chamfered nave N doorway, otherwise fine three-light Perp nave and S aisle windows in white Calcareous Gritstone, the reveals shafted. The arcade, also of white stone, is uncommonly ornate, more Devon than Somerset. Piers with four shafts and in the diagonals a wave moulding, set asymmetrically, as there is an additional ogee moulding against the N and S shafts. Instead of capitals, bands of particularly varied leaf and flower scroll. Finely moulded arches. A matching fifth arch runs parallel to a C14 chancel S arch with simple shafts. The resulting broad pier has a trefoiled squint cut through. Simple plastered chancel and tower arches. – FONT. C13. Ham stone, square with spurred corners, like the plinth of a churchyard cross. Norman Purbeck marble base, of a round pillar and detached shafts. C17 balustered RAIL around. – PULPIT. Early C17, with arabesque panels, more repetitive than usual. – WEST GALLERY. 1830, on thin iron columns. The front reuses twenty-six C16 BENCH-ENDS of remarkable invention, including varieties of close tracery, wiry entwined plant forms, and some figures. Scrolled borders typical of the Taunton area. – BOX PEWS. 1830. – ROYAL ARMS. 1813. – STAINED GLASS. Medieval fragments in N windows. E window, 1935, by *Wippell & Co*.

CHURCHINFORD, 2 m. SE. Six roads join at the YORK INN, partly C17 with both stone and wooden mullions. To the N, a little BAPTIST CHAPEL, 1846, with stuccoed lateral front and pointed windows. Down Moor Lane, FAIRHOUSE FARM is C14–C15, thatched, the lateral S chimney added with a C16 framed ceiling. C17 N wing.

CULMHEAD, 1 m. NE. Former aerodrome of 1941. Perimeter earth-sheltered blast-pens, each protecting two fighters from bombing attack.

CLAPTON see WAYFORD

CLATWORTHY

ST MARY. Roughcast and plain. Especially simple the w tower with diagonal buttresses and battlements. Mostly Perp. On the s side, a large porch with a good wagon roof, one finely traceried window, and a rood stair. The chancel doorway with a monolithic arched head in red sandstone may be Norman. Victorian roofs and furnishings of 1865. – FONT. Norman bowl with two rings above a splayed stem. – PULPIT. 1819, on a wine-glass stem. Reached from the vestry via a wall arch. – ORGAN CASE. Pretty, simple Late Georgian Gothic. – STAINED GLASS. E window, 1865, striking if amateurish, with slabs of blue sky. By *John Toms*, who made the Ten Commandment tablets, 1854. Chancel s windows, 1865, by *Warrington*. – MONUMENT. Hay family to 1771, coloured marbles, by *Thomas King*. CHURCHYARD CROSS. C15, with broken shaft.

CLATWORTHY CASTLE, ½ m. NW. The earthworks of a large Iron Age hillfort in woods above the reservoir. Its form is a rough triangle about 260 by 420 yds (238 by 384 metres). The bank still rises 15 ft (4.6 metres) above the ditch.

CLATWORTHY RESERVOIR. Formed to supply Taunton by damming the headwaters of the River Tone. Curving concrete DAM, 1957–9, by *Rofe & Raffety*, rising to 90 ft (27 metres). Landscaping by *S. Colwyn Foulkes*. When the water level is low, evidence of Roman iron smelting can be found on the shore.

CLEEVE ABBEY
Washford

Cleeve Abbey was founded in 1198 by William de Roumare, Earl of Lincoln, for Cistercians. It was colonized from Revesby, Lincs., which his grandfather had founded in 1142. First known as Vallis Florida, from the riverside setting, a typical Cistercian site, with watercourses that were managed for mills on both sides of the Washford River. Although the church has gone, so much remains of the monastic buildings as to give an unrivalled experience of life in a small Cistercian house just before the Reformation. The monastic buildings erected during the C13 survive in large part or can be traced, although the most remarkable work at Cleeve dates from a revival under Abbot Juyner (1437–87) when the refectory was sumptuously rebuilt. After the Dissolution the remaining buildings were sold and became a tenanted farm owned by the Botelers of Binham Grange (Old Cleeve). In the late C17 a farmhouse was added at the SW corner. George Luttrell of Dunster Castle began excavation in the 1870s. After

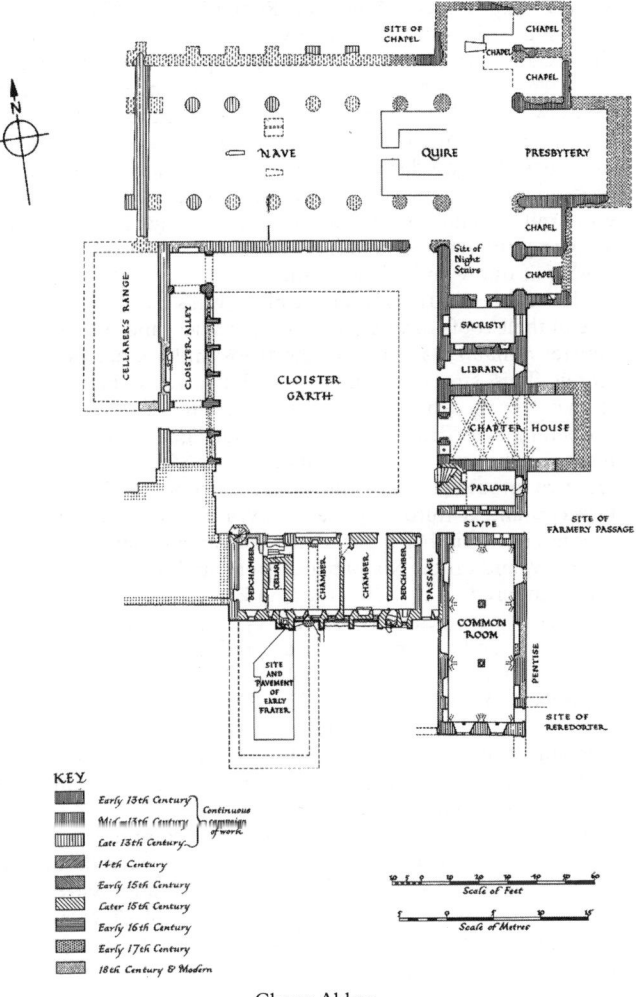

Cleeve Abbey.
Plan

acquisition by the state in 1951, accretions within the ruins were removed and the buildings restored.

The CHURCH, dedicated to St Mary, has to be traced from exposed foundations to the N of the remaining buildings. It was of the standard Cistercian plan, nave and aisles (of six bays) with circular piers, transepts with two straight-headed eastern chapels, probably a crossing tower on multiple chamfered piers, and a straight-headed chancel. Fontenay, the earliest surviving house in France, was similar, and this constitutes the basic plan for Cistercian houses of some ambition about

1135–75 (e.g. Tintern, Mon. and Roche, Yorks.). The windows were simple lancets, and there were clerestory lancets above the arcades and transepts. The eastern parts were finished by 1232 when oak was given for choir stalls, and the nave and aisles by the end of the C13. Only the s wall of the s aisle stands. Of pale sandstone, originally rendered, as were all the other buildings. As it bordered on the cloister, the windows were set high. These have gone but for all but some sills. The s transept end wall remains insofar as it forms the gable-end of the adjoining monastic buildings. Fragments of encaustic tile paving at the W end of the s aisle.

Now to the CLOISTER. The lean-to walks have gone but the line of their roofs can be seen on three sides, and on the W the cloister remains, as rebuilt in the 1530s under a narrow upper storey. This storey remains over the l. three bays, but is shown over the whole range in an engraving of 1790. The four r. openings are Tudor-arched, with four-light tracery of ogee-headed lights and vertical mullions. In the l. three bays there are two moulded four-centred arches, one to the through passage, and a third is replaced by a window. The through passage has a timber s partition with carved spandrels to the doorway, and on the N a panelled stone archway on five close-set chamfered shafts. Fleurons and a tiny grotesque mask between minimal capitals. Of the C13 cloister only the internal NW corner arches survive, four-centred, triple-chamfered, the inner order dying in. The sloping wall above the arch shows the line of the N cloister roof. The small trefoil-headed alcove in the N wall is a rare Collation Seat, from which extracts from Cassian's *Collationes Patrum* would be read before Compline. At the eastern end one jamb survives of the doorway into the s aisle, chamfered with an inset shaft.

The E and S monastic ranges remain as complete as in any British monastery. The mid-C13 EAST RANGE extends considerably beyond the s one, the whole line most impressive when seen from outside the cloister. The small single-chamfered first-floor lancets light the dormitory (*see below*). Beneath are a series of mostly small chambers. The SACRISTY, unmarked from the cloister, opens from the s transept. Narrow and barrel-vaulted, with wall-recesses for lockers, and a piscina. Very unusual is the large round E window, originally traceried. This room and the other chambers of the E range were plastered, whitewashed and decorated in red linear patterns, surprising given the austerity of the Cistercians. Principally the decoration was of masonry lines imitating ashlar, both on the walls and the vault, enhanced with a running scroll between wavy lines as transverse ribs and along the apex. A scrolled plant design in the piscina recess. Damaged tile pavement. The first doorway (narrowed in the C15) opens to a similar narrower barrel-vaulted room that was the LIBRARY. Fictive masonry decoration around the E lancet. Then, on a larger scale, follows the CHAPTER HOUSE, of which only the undercroft vestibule is complete. The plate-traceried two-light windows l. and r. of the entrance confirm the mid-C13 date. Double-chamfered doorway with a continuous moulding. Two bays of quadripartite vaulting, segmental-arched and exceptionally low for the width. Chamfered ribs rise from corbels on short shafts. The chapter house itself was a higher square chamber projecting E, with a pointed rib-vault on similar corbels. The western arch survives, on corbels with Blue Lias shafts, above a heavy triple-chamfered arch to the vestibule. Stubs of the side walls. A large stone slab indicates the position of the lectern. Next follows the winding stone DAY STAIR to the dormitory, inserted in the C15 to replace stairs formerly within the S range. The doorway is reused C13, the use of Blue Lias for capitals and bases typical of Wells at this period.

The DORMITORY is preserved exceptionally complete. It stretches the whole length of the upper floor, 137 ft (42 metres), lit by ten lancets towards the cloister and two groups of three on the opposite wall, divided by the doorway to a former chamber over the chapter house. Lancets spaced more widely in the S end of the room. Segmental-pointed rere-arches. The window seats have C14 tiles datable from the arms of Bishops Drokensford of Wells (1309–29) and Grandisson of Exeter (1327–69). The heraldry also includes local families: Beauchamp, De Mohun, Montagu and Ralegh. The tiles were probably reused here in the C15 when the dormitory was divided into wooden cubicles. In the floor a broken Purbeck marble grave-slab. The roof looks C16–C17 (much restored in 1961). The hipped S end replaces a gable with three lancets. At the N end is the doorway to the night stair into the church, and a corner door to a lost chamber over the transept SE chapel, perhaps the treasury. In the SE corner, a doorway opened to the REREDORTER or latrines. The frame shows that, exceptionally in medieval buildings, the door pivoted centrally, allowing entrance and exit to either side of the pivot. The latrines were on the upper floor of a demolished narrow range running out to the E, of which the water channel is clearly defined. This range formed the S side of a small cloister that had the infirmary on the E, a covered passage on the N and a lean-to walk on the W.

The dormitory stairs partly block a narrow ground-floor PARLOUR, with two E lancets and a plastered barrel vault. The numerous 'daisy-wheel' compass patterns in the plaster, graffiti rather than decorative, are found elsewhere in the abbey. Adjoining the parlour is the SLYPE or passage to the infirmary. Three sets of twin locker recesses in the side walls. Beyond the slype, under the S end of the dormitory is the large DAY ROOM or warming room. The groined vault of three by two bays on two round columns is re-created in concrete, on original column bases. Two handsome S windows have two layers of two-light plate tracery, the inner layer complete, with trefoiled lights on a Blue Lias column shaft and a quatrefoil above. The outer layer shows remains of quatrefoil heads. In the E wall is a tall doorway, formerly a two-light window. Also evidence of a hooded fireplace.

Cleeve Abbey, cloister.
Engraving by T. Bonnor, 1791

The SOUTH RANGE was C13, slightly later than the E range, but only part of the ground floor shows this; the rest was rebuilt in the C15. The C13 doorway in the angle, now to a through passage, probably served the original day stairs. C13 also the central doorway, with chamfered inner order and finely moulded outer arch. Blue Lias bases and capitals, as on the dormitory doorway. C13 broad arched laver or washing place to its l. These relate to the demolished OLD REFECTORY, which was on the ground floor and projected at right angles, the arrangement found also at Rievaulx and Fountains (Yorks.) and Hailes (Glos.). Within the foundations is the late C13 tiled floor, one of the largest known, excavated in 1876–7. The Cleeve TILES are among the most important groups in Britain. The nave, chapter house, sacristy, and both old and new refectories were paved, though only the old refectory pavement survives substantially. Laid out in bordered diagonal squares, the tiles depict mostly heraldry. The larger tiles at the dais end show the arms of England, Cornwall and de Clare. Edmund of Cornwall, nephew of Henry III, married Margaret de Clare in 1272. Among the smaller tiles is the double-headed eagle used by Edmund's father, Richard, as King of the Romans from 1257. The tiles probably come from Gloucestershire, where there are similar tiles at Richard's foundation at Hailes Abbey.*

The S side of the monastic buildings would have had three projecting ranges, all gable-ended: the dormitory, SE, the refectory, central, projecting even further, and the S end of the W range protruding slightly. Abbot Juyner (1437–87) demolished

---

*Tiles elsewhere at Cleeve Abbey include the famous late C13 design, on two double-length tiles, depicting Richard I jousting with Saladin.

the old refectory and placed the new one on an upper floor parallel with the cloister. He subdivided the bulk of the ground floor (previously the ante-room to the refectory and the day room) into two suites of rooms for senior monks or corrodians (wealthy pensioners) with the new refectory staircase inside the old doorway. Each suite had a living room, narrow bedroom and a garderobe; the latter are visible externally on the S, one beneath the refectory chimney, the other just r. of the stair window. The ceilings are moulded and framed, and the living rooms have moulded fireplaces.

The NEW REFECTORY has five large, regularly spaced three-light windows to the cloister and four to the S, with a chimney covering the site of the pulpit and pulpit stair. On this side are buttresses, of which the alternate ones were chimneys to the ground-floor fireplaces, with a pair of head corbels at eaves level. A parapet above has gone. The windows are finely detailed, with crisp cusping to ogee-headed lights. Those on the S side are longer, with tracery also below a transom. Their lower lights have quatrefoils in the spandrels, a feature found in the environs of Cleeve Abbey and those of Muchelney Abbey far to the E. Excellent headstops to the hoodmoulds. W of the refectory was an apartment of two storeys above the stairs, lit by transomed square-headed windows with quatrefoil spandrels, three on the rear (one without the transom) and one to the top floor facing the cloister. A stone hood to the l. of this window sheltered the refectory bell. A ruined winding stair to the r. gave private access, suggesting a high-status apartment, perhaps for the abbot. Access to the first floor is currently from the farmhouse to the W, which probably replaces further rooms of this apartment.

Entering from the W, the passage to the refectory has a timber partition with faint graffiti: 'Thomas' and a caricature monk's head. Behind the partition are the refectory stairs and the narrow PAINTED CHAMBER opening W off the stairs. This was perhaps an office or counting house. A large C15 painting on the E wall, crudely done,* illustrates a tale from the *Gesta Romanorum*. On a double-arched bridge over a river full of fish an old man prays, menaced by a lion and a dragon on the parapet, but protected by a little angel each side of his head. To either side, much larger, are saints Catherine and Margaret. The second-floor chamber shares a roof with the refectory, similar in structure but simplified. Traces of wall painting including Passion symbols. The C17 FARMHOUSE extends W over the site of the C13 kitchen in the SW corner of the cloister. It may be that the abbot's lodgings extended into the C16 range over the W cloister. In the surviving piece, the fireplace lintel is a C13 grave-slab with an incised foliate cross.

Now the REFECTORY itself, one of the finest rooms in Somerset, light and lofty, under one of the county's best medieval roofs, tree-ring-dated to the 1460s. This is not strictly a wagon

---

* But the under-drawing is good. F. Kelly.

roof, although panelled with moulded horizontals, because it has distinct principal trusses and sub-principals. Angels with shields support both, but to emphasize the principals these angels are larger, and horizontal, like hammerbeams. All rest on arched brackets on stone corbels, carved with angels under the principals, and shields under the sub-principals. A green man on one s bracket. Carved vine-trail on the wall-plates. Blind cusped arcading ornaments the principals, which have large ridge bosses; all the other intersections have smaller bosses. By these means a clear articulation is introduced in a roofing system which otherwise tends to be a little uniform. The panels appear never to have been boarded, though boarding was intended. Nor has any sign of colour been found. On the s wall are mural stairs to the lost pulpit which would have been above the inserted fireplace. A very large E wall painting of the Crucifixion has disappeared. Richly moulded w doorway to the stairs.

The PRECINCT was walled and moated on the E and N. The C13 GATEHOUSE at the NW corner was rebuilt by Abbot Dovell (1507–37) with a new upper floor. Large pointed archway at each end with continuous double chamfers, but no separate entry for pedestrians. Piers and springers for a two-bay C13 vault inside, and three broad side openings, blocked probably because the vault began to fail. The C16 floor has gone, revealing a restored wind-braced roof and a latrine in the NE corner. Buttresses flanking the entrances were added with the C16 upper storey, those on the s decorated with reused beasts. A straight-headed four-light upper window at each end. On the s end Dovell's arms are beneath the window. Above, between niches, is a Crucifixion in high relief under a canopy, the cross depicted as a tree. Over the N arch is inscribed 'Porta pate(n)s esto (n)ulli claudar(is) hon(e)st(o)' ('Gate be opened, shut to no honest person'). In the gable is a clumsier niche under a low-relief Virgin and Child in Ham stone. This may come from the coastal chapel near Blue Anchor which was destroyed by landslip in 1452 (cf. Chapel Cleeve, Old Cleeve). Ruinous lean-to structures on each side were a porter's lodge (SE) and an almonry (NW).

CLOFORD

ST MARY. w tower with battlements and pinnacles. Diagonal buttresses to the lower stage. Simple two-light bell-openings with pierced baffles, but all different; indeed the N one with transom and tiny quatrefoil looks C13, surely reused. So was the tower rebuilt after the Reformation? Early C18 Horner arms on the w side. The rest is Victorian, the nave rebuilt in 1856, the chancel in 1867–9, by *Henry Woodyer*. This has personality. The s windows are a set of three, and then one slightly higher. S porch dated 1887. Characterful interior with a low screen wall and iron gates, wrought-iron candle-brackets on the pews, and oil lamps. Marble-shafted chancel windows. – FONT. C11–C12. Crude, tapered with a roll moulding. – REREDOS. 1869 by *Woodyer*. Stone and alabaster, beautifully carved, with censing angels, lilies and a cross studded with marble balls. – STAINED GLASS. E window, 1869, faded. – MONUMENTS. Maures Horner †1621. Damaged tomb-chest without effigy. – Sir George Horner †1676 and wife. Memorably painted, mostly black-and-white. Rustic three-quarter figures face stolidly forward under a double arch contained in an open-pedimented aedicule. Black columns flanked by scrolly volutes and garlands. Similar monuments at Rodney Stoke (N), Brent Knoll and Axbridge (qq.v.).

Above the church, the OLD SCHOOLHOUSE, late C16, tall and narrow with a front gable, formerly the vicarage. The low C17 range with cross-wing became the school in the C19. The next vicarage was CLOFORD HOUSE, white, with a variety of stone windows in the hard-edged Gothic of the 1860s. Was *Woodyer* involved?

CLOFORD MANOR, across the stream to the E. A particularly attractive group around the house of the Horners (cf. Mells, N). Dated 1633, for Sir George Horner, but a house is recorded as being enlarged *c.* 1585. The whole was reduced *c.* 1720. Derelict by the late C20, it was carefully repaired in 1999–2004 by *Philip Hughes Associates* for Richard Mawer. Two parts, hall and parlour blocks. The latter is taller, with first-floor chambers emphasized by mullion-and-transom windows. The mullions, of a semicircular section without the usual fillet, are unknown elsewhere in Somerset. High blank attic, low ground floor, the parlour window lengthened later. The lower S block, replacing the C16 hall, has a porch with a typical Jacobean arched doorway, and large central mullion-and-transom window of eight lights (reduced to six and lengthened). Four small first-floor mullioned windows. Earlier rubble masonry shows on the l. corner. The cross-passage doorways match the porch, and the hall has a finely moulded rear-wall fireplace. The rooms above were unheated. In the N block, a broad dog-leg staircase with moulded finials on square newels, and timber framing instead of balusters. The parlour has a larger version of the hall fireplace and finely moulded oak doorways, one into a small NE closet. This closet is replicated above, and the two first-floor chambers have good fireplaces. Behind are fragments of the C16 house: a portion of walling inside the SW range, and possibly the narrow W outbuilding.

Enclosing the forecourt, a roofless C17 L-plan STABLE, and long, lofted seven-bay LODGING RANGE with varied two-light mullion windows, some reused. Roof tree-ring-dated *c.* 1700.

POSTLEBURY FARM, Cloford Common. A long farmhouse with an almost-detached block at right angles. C16 reserved chamfer mullions, the doorhead ornamented with a bar and lozenge.

CLOSWORTH

ALL SAINTS. Handsome Perp W tower with diagonal buttresses. Long transomed two-light bell-openings with pierced baffles, gargoyles, battlements and pinnacles. Higher polygonal NE stair-turret. To the sides on the lowest stage, defaced canopied niches. In the third stage on the W side, an undamaged one with, each side of the canopy, a kneeling figure in relief, and on the S side are three praying figures, perhaps donors and their children, their costume early C16. Panelled tower arch. C14 N porch with a stone-slab roof over a transverse-ribbed pointed tunnel vault (cf. Norton-sub-Hamdon). The rest looks Perp but was rebuilt in 1875 by *J. M. Allen*. No aisles. Nave roof on Victorian naturalistic corbels, as is the chancel arch. One N lancet dates the chancel to the C13. – FONT. C15, octagonal, with quatrefoil panels, tapered below. – PULPIT. C17, with tall blank arches and lozenges. – STAINED GLASS. E window, bright, 1860s, probably by *O'Connor*.

In the churchyard, the shaft of a C15 CROSS. Just E, the CHEST TOMB of Thomas Purdue †1711, bell-founder, with a bell on the E end.

S of the church, the former SCHOOL, 1871. On the larger road, the OLD RECTORY has a datestone of 1606 and C16 mullioned windows, also C19 roofs and sash windows.

COMBE FLOREY

ST PETER AND ST PAUL. Red sandstone, including the tracery. Mostly Perp. Three-stage W tower in ashlar with diagonal buttresses, battlements and pinnacles. Polygonal NE stair-tower. Two-light bell-lights and second-stage windows. Perp nave with a rood-stair projection. Chancel rebuilt in 1864–5. The N aisle has the earliest work, of *c.* 1300, but also bald early C19 pointed windows and pointed E doorway. A blocked W lancet shows the original form. All six N windows have cinquefoiled rere-arches, but the reliability is questionable as the last two replace a C15 door and window, from an enlargement indicated by the Perp aisle E window. Three-bay Perp arcade, the eastern arch much distorted. Piers of standard four-hollow section but handsome capitals with angel busts, typical of the Taunton area. Tall tower arch with similar angels. C15 panelled chancel N arch. Lavish chancel FITTINGS of 1865: absurd marble pole ALTAR RAIL, marble-shafted ALTAR and REREDOS, the sides with fairground glass inserts, and marble-topped tub SEDILIA, based on Isle Abbots (q.v.). – FONT. C13, octagonal, with a most unusual lower edge of cusped trefoils. – PULPIT. A good survival. Oak, C15, with ogee crocketed tracery in narrow panels bordered in leaf scroll. – BENCHES. C16, some complete.

COMBE FLOREY

Straight-headed ends. The front group have leaf borders and plant motifs as at Trull, the rear group plain borders and close tracery. – SCREENS. 1916 and 1925. – STAINED GLASS. E window, c. 1865 to Sydney Smith, rector. Probably by *Clayton & Bell*. Chancel s windows, 1866, signed *Warrington*. Nave s, 1905, by *Powell's*. – MONUMENTS. Maud de Merriet. Late C13 unmoulded cinquefoiled recess, in Blue Lias with incised ornament. A lettered strip records in French the burial of her heart and that she was a nun at Cannington. The base stone is hollowed for the heart casket. – Cross-legged knight and two ladies, possibly Sir John de Meriet †1327 and wives †1300 and 1344. He in old-fashioned chain-mail and surcoat lies beside near-identical wives, except that the later one is in Ham stone. – Several brasses to the Fraunceis family: lettered strip to Nicholas †1480; animated 12-in. (30-cm.) figure of Florence with two daughters, and a lettered strip referring to John †1485, whose brass has vanished. Nicholas †1526, depicted in armour, 28 in. (71 cm.) long, in a nicely incised Lias slab. – Philippa Fraunceis †1745. Big curved pedimented marble memorial, oddly never inscribed. – Rev. Alexander Malet †1773. Red and white marble with urn.

Restored C15 CHURCHYARD CROSS. Above and outside the churchyard, the burial plot of Evelyn Waugh †1966, a Roman Catholic.

w of the church, the GATEHOUSE of 1591 to the Elizabethan mansion of John Fraunceis demolished after the Civil War. Red sandstone, of two tall storeys (alleged improbably to have been reduced from four) between low wings. Asymmetrical, the gable roughly central, a four-light mullion-and-transom window to the l. over the moulded segmental-pointed archway, and a small mullioned window on each floor to the r., next to a gabled garderobe turret. Lavish chamber plasterwork by *Robert Eaton* of Stogursey, 1593. Thin-rib ceiling, scrolled frieze and an overmantel with the Fraunceis arms. Splendidly mantled helm on strapwork with much high-relief fruit, between demi-caryatid pairs (male and female) carrying overflowing baskets.

COMBE FLOREY HOUSE was built on a new site above the old one in 1730 for William Fraunceis. U-plan, the severe five-bay s front of good red ashlar. Basement and two storeys, with Bath stone cornice, architraves (those below with Gibbsian rustication and multiple keystones) and a fine Gibbsian pedimented doorway up a double flight of balustraded steps. Corniced hall with rebated curved corners, and open-well staircase with twisted balusters.

The village runs up the combe, turning sw to the former RECTORY, dated 1742. Stuccoed, five-bay, and hip-roofed. Giant pilasters frame the centre. Extended in 1829 for Sydney Smith who was incumbent here 1829–45, if only rarely resident. Pretty trellis porch. E from the church and gatehouse is the OLD MANOR HOUSE, late C16 to c. 1700. Roughcast, with

a porch chamber on bulbous oak columns and a rubble stone
E cross-wing with cross-windows of *c.* 1700. Much early C17
plasterwork. The hall ceiling has a large Tudor rose and floral
corner sprays or angel heads in each panel. Bolection-moulded
fireplace of *c.* 1700. The panelled rear room is a little later. The
porch chamber is completely decorated, with fluted Ionic pilasters, a scrolled floral frieze, and a lozenge plaque opposite a
square divided in five with animal motifs (stag's head, pig,
wyvern, lion, bird). In the W room a plaque with a lion and
fleurs-de-lys. On the Taunton road, the OLD FORGE, and,
under the railway bridge, SHOLERS, were both late C15 hall
houses with jointed-cruck trusses. N of the village, the FARMERS
ARMS, long and thatched with heavy oak doorway, was a hall
house of similar date.

COMBE WOOD TOWER, 1 m. NW. Built *c.* 1790 by John Winter,
perhaps to rival Willett Tower, Elworthy, though less architectural. Roughcast, with five storeys of small pointed windows.
The rear has angle piers and pointed panels on a central
chimney-breast. On the roadside nearer the village, a large
triple-arched LIMEKILN.

COMBE ST NICHOLAS

ST NICHOLAS. Long and relatively low, externally mostly Perp.
W tower, embattled nave, the aisles and chancel chapels embattled too, with octagonal rood-stair towers. In 1862–3 *William
White* extended the aisles W of the porches and rebuilt the S
porch. There is evidence of a Norman nave: one W end pier,
and one jamb of the N doorway, external before White extended
the aisle. Two orders; both capitals remain, one scalloped, the
other with a ribbon emerging from a mouth, and one column
shaft. Local white Calcareous Grit, by contrast to the Ham
stone arcades. Of *c.* 1300 the lower part of the tower, with
renewed cusped lancets and low doorway to the nave with
triple chamfers dying into splayed jambs. Also the roll-moulded
chancel PISCINA. Otherwise the chancel has C14 ogee-traceried side windows with rere-arches. Standard Perp the plain
upper part of the tower and the polygonal SE stair-turret.
Standard Perp too the arcades (on piers of four-hollow section)
and taller chancel arch. The chapels have C15 panelled arches
to the chancel and depressed four-centred arches to the aisles.
Gaunt roofs of 1862–3. The architect's perspective shows that
there were economies. – FONTS. Plain C12 bowl. Also a narrow
Perp font with quatrefoils, chamfered beneath. – SCREEN. Re-
created in 1921 by *Caröe* from two fragments of a full-width
C15–C16 screen. Five bays, with fan coving, delicate four-light
ogee tracery, very much of the West Somerset group (Carhampton, Dunster, Minehead). – PAINTING. King David.

Later C18, from the former gallery. – STAINED GLASS. E window, 1870, by *O'Connor.* – MONUMENTS. John Bone †1714. Fine Baroque cartouche. – Rev. Joel Smith †1758 and Bonner family, 1757. By the same hand, from the striking use of colour, notably red marble.

METHODIST CHURCH. 1890–1, by *Robert Curwen.* Free Gothic. Extended with a double transept, 1896.

On the village green, TITHE COTTAGE, rendered, late C16. The former VICARAGE has a barrack-like Victorian rear and gloomy Italianate tower, added to a Late Georgian stuccoed house with shallow-bowed centre. Down Frog Lane, WHITEHALL is of *c.* 1500, enlarged *c.* 1600. Moulded framed hall ceiling. Wind-braced roof. Its BARN looks Georgian Gothic but has C16 jointed crucks. Towards Wadeford, COMBE HILL FARM-HOUSE, chequered stone and chert, dated 1664. At Wadeford, THE MANOR, also chequered, is early C17, with a gabled cross-wing. To the S, WADEFORD HOUSE, with Early Victorian mullioned bays, faces a small stone-columned ROTUNDA brought in 1804 from Burton Pynsent (Curry Rivel), one of the garden temples that *William Pitt the Elder* reputedly designed *c.* 1767–70. It had a shallow dome. A ROMAN VILLA with seven mosaic floors was excavated nearby in 1810 and 1854.

CLAYHANGER, 1 m. E. Hamlet of C16–C17 houses. FOUR GABLES is a thatched *cottage orné* of *c.* 1840, all acute angles.

COMBE SYDENHAM
Stogumber

In a steep-sided valley S of Monksilver. The medieval HOUSE of the Sydenhams was rebuilt in 1580 for Sir George Sydenham, probably enlarged to surround a rear courtyard. There was work in the early C17 and after Civil War damage. Sir John Posthumus Sydenham sold to George Musgrave in 1693. By the early C19 the courtyard had been reduced by removal of the N and E ranges. The W range was re-fitted for George Notley, owner from 1793. Pink-washed roughcast, extremely picturesque thanks to the four-storey stair-tower rising in the angle behind the two surviving ranges. The six-bay S front is on the site of the medieval hall. It has Late Georgian leaded casement windows and a handsome ashlar two-storey porch in the fifth bay, dated 1580 on an ornate heraldic plaque. Shallow gable with ball finials on the shoulders, four-light mullion-and-transom window above an arched entrance in a square-headed frame with Renaissance busts in the spandrels. Thin Ionic pilasters on each side carry a cornice. Cross-vault inside, and a moulded arched doorway with heraldic beasts in the spandrels. A two-storey rear stair projection is in line

Combe Sydenham.
Drawing by J. Crowther, 1901

with the porch. The eight-bay W range is probably Elizabethan but alteration has rendered its early history obscure. On the upper floor l. are three very large Elizabethan four-light windows each with three transoms. The next four bays have Georgian sash windows, and there is an Elizabethan stone cross-window in the last bay, to the r. of a lateral chimney. Shallow buttresses to the ground floor and stone cross-windows with cinquefoil-cusped lights. The massive stair-tower in the angle, part of the 1580 work, has a shouldered gable to each face with sash windows. Blocked two-light mullion windows on the E mark the line of the original stair. Chimneys on the SE and NW corners.

(The cross-passage leads to a Late Georgian staircase, presumably replacing an earlier one on this site. Two Tudor-arched openings to the service end, E of the cross-passage. The medieval hall, W of the passage, was ceiled in the Elizabethan remodelling. Large Tudor-arched fireplace with moulded jambs. Behind this a stone newel stair. In one of the W range rooms an Elizabethan plaster frieze. Above is a first-floor hall or great chamber with a late C20 plaster barrel ceiling in Elizabethan style.*)

To the S is a GATEHOUSE range, pre-dating Sir George Sydenham's works, probably early C16 but very much altered. Three-storey gatehouse with a renewed four-light mullion window on each floor above. Rear NW stair-turret. Two-storey ranges each side, that to the l. ruinous, that to the r. with Georgian leaded casements.

---

* Description of the house is partial as access was not permitted.

COMBWICH

On the estuary of the River Parrett, an important crossing point from Saxon times until the C19. The character of the landscape is East Anglian, even Dutch.

ST PETER. By *Charles Knowles*, 1868–70. Blue Lias with red sandstone bands. The s porch-tower is such as only the 1860s could design. Square, broached to octagonal, then eight steep gables around the spire. Dec detail. Cruciform interior with big open roofs on naturalistic corbels. Similar carving to thick gabled arcading in the polygonal apse. Complicated marble-shafted PULPIT. Contemporary STAINED GLASS.

The village is too much infilled to have kept its character. By the ANCHOR INN (refronted in seaside-modern style), a brick FIVES WALL. TOWER HOUSE, 1879, is Victorian black-and-white, topped by a belvedere with cast-iron rails.

BEERE MANOR, 1¼ m. WSW. A C15 hall house, altered in the C16, with a storeyed porch and storeyed hall-bay. Rendered in grey cement. Late Georgian porch doorway, C15–C16 doorway within. The shafted doorway into the hall is made up from two damaged doorways in the same wall. The hall has dais arches to the oriel and rear stair-tower. Heavy late C17 stair. Fielded-panelled parlour, the cove painted with naïve acanthus and the monogram of Edmund Bowyer, datable before 1707. A painted overmantel panel shows the house with the porch and hall-bay each a storey higher, but is unreliable. Intriguingly, the roof timbers show that the roof was hipped before the painting was made, but hipped roofs are exceptional before the late C17. Five-bay early C18 STABLE.

COMPTON DUNDON

Two villages: Compton under the escarpment, Dundon between two hills that break w into the flat moors.

ST ANDREW, Dundon. In a sloping churchyard with an enormous yew. Remarkable early C14 chancel with an original treatment of the five-light E window. The head bisected diagonally to a kind of cusped four-leaf clover. Quatrefoil roundel above. Two-light side windows, one re-set in the vestry. Double-chamfered chancel arch closed by a stone screen-base thick enough for an E shelf-recess. Bold triple SEDILIA, the cusped ogee heads with finials, presumably later than the window they cross. Plain Lias W tower, embattled with pyramid roof; Perp in detail, but the S stair projection must be earlier. The tower arch is C14, double-chamfered on moulded capitals, the jambs hollowed. Perp porch. Nave windows with standard Perp tracery, one S window more elaborate. Two N projections, one for the rood and pulpit stair, the other, NW, implying a rebuilding to correct a different alignment. C15 panelled porch and nave ceilings, chancel ceiling of 1901 by *Edmund Buckle*. – FONT. C14–C15, octagonal. Cover by *Caröe*, 1936. – PULPIT. 1628. Tucked extremely prettily into a recess off the rood stair. Much decorative woodwork including cornice and balustraded screen. The enlarged opening cuts the adjacent window arch, stopped now on a fat stone Ionic volute. – BENCHES. Early C17 rear set with simple moulded ends, the frontals with Jacobean finials. Matching front ones by *Buckle*, also the attractive L-plan STALLS with canopied front seats for child choristers. – STAINED GLASS. C15 fragments in the nave tracery, including two female heads. – E window to the Rev. T. W. Harrison †1871, he whiskered among the saints, his relations among the angels. – MEMORIALS. Incised Lias floor slabs with pilastered borders, †1637 and 1640. – Richard Hasell †1819, amateur archaeologist. Good Gothic for the date. – On an outside wall, Katherine Coombe †1729, rustic Baroque frame with flowers.

A gabled stone VICARAGE, 1867, by *Ewan Christian*, overlooks the church at the N end of Dundon village. The three-bay OLD RECTORY looks C17 but has C16 roof-trusses. Behind the early C19 MIDDLE FARMHOUSE is LOCKYERS, thatched, C15–C17, the central gable with an early C17 stone oriel. Framed ceiling; haunched first-floor fireplace. Timber-framed accommodation block, 2012–13, by *O2i Design* of Langport. BADGER'S COTTAGE, thatched, is originally late medieval, attractively set between thatched barns. SWISS COTTAGE faces N, mid-C19 Italianate, like a rural railway station, the two-storey part with a deeply overhanging hipped roof.

On the main road, CASTLEBROOK BARN survives from an important medieval house. Thatched, with, on the external corners, exquisite C13 carved stone heads, another in the E gable. Arch-braced cruck roof trusses tree-ring-dated to as early as 1285. Compton village lines a lane running NE towards the Hood Monument (Butleigh). On the E side, KERRIS, thatched, C15–C16, has a cobbled cross-passage and oak Tudor-arched doorway within. On the W, OLD FARMHOUSE has a tiny ogee stair light and C17 ground-floor mullions. WILLEY'S FARMHOUSE is C16, refronted in the early C19, between a C17 barn and C19 stables. At the top TRAYS FARM, with a late C14 cross-wing. S end buttresses, long pointed N window, and a small circular E window with mouchettes. The hall was replaced by the present farmhouse.

DUNDON CAMP. Dundon Hill rises nearly 300 ft (91 metres), crowned by a very large Iron Age hillfort. Ramparts survive up to 8 ft (2.4 metres) high, quarried away on the E. At the S end is a mound 20 ft (6 metres) high, DUNDON BEACON, of unknown date or purpose. It appears to be later than the ramparts and could perhaps be a Norman motte, but when it was excavated in the 1830s a crouched burial of Bronze Age type was found.

LITTLETON, 1 m. S. MANOR HOUSE has a C17 canted bay with corbelled gable, typical of the Martock area.

COMPTON DURVILLE see SOUTH PETHERTON

COMPTON PAUNCEFOOT

6020

ST MARY. Perp, of ochre Maperton limestone. Sir Walter Pauncefoot left ten marks in 1485 for building the church and £20 for 'the making of myne ile there'. The plain W tower is slightly earlier. Diagonal buttresses, two-light bell-openings, and, relatively rare in Somerset, a stone spire, with a band of ornament. Otherwise notably unified, with separately gabled aisles (the N one of 1864) and chancel. High plinths and deep-set windows; leaf spandrels to the S porch doorway. Three-bay arcades with standard piers of four hollows. The tower arch, shafted with moulded caps, pre-dates the panelled chancel arch. Cusped squint. In the S aisle, E bay, below the S window, a frieze of quatrefoils with Pauncefoot shields and inscription to Anne Whyting †1535. Victorian painted ceilings, angels over the chancel. – FONT. C12. Plain, octagonal. – STAINED GLASS. Five colourful windows by *J.-B. Capronnier* of Brussels, 1865–77, illustrating how different was Continental glass, painterly in a post-Renaissance way. W window by *Kempe*, 1896, delicate Late Gothic. Two chancel windows by *Hugh Easton*, 1948. – MONUMENTS. Under the tower, Hunt family, 1698. Columns with drapes. – Large Hunt memorial of 1830, replacing the SW window. – In the churchyard, two medieval stone COFFINS.

A spacious green E of the churchyard. The late C18 ashlar-fronted MANOR HOUSE, N, has a Roman Doric columned porch. Small brick C19 dovecote behind. Converted HOME FARM buildings, NE, of 1852. To the S, the OLD RECTORY was handsomely remodelled *c.* 1745 by the addition of a centrepiece with parapet. Windows still with a centre mullion; broken-pediment doorcase. C17 mullions behind. The village curves SW from the bargeboarded former SCHOOL, 1858, to THE CRESCENT, built for J. H. Hunt *c.* 1820 (the 1808 date is not reliable). Similar to Lord Anglesey's crescent near Milborne Port (q.v.), but three-storeyed. The third floor was a single workshop. Five porches of 1874.

COMPTON CASTLE, ½ m. SSE. The orange stone Gothic castle and its Romantic landscape were created for J. H. Hunt from 1821 by *John Finden* of London. The toy fort, in the manner of Robert Smirke, has a square central tower, tall Gothic porch and round angle turrets, all battlemented. In the early C20 *C. H. Biddulph-Pinchard* embellished it by raising the two bay windows to two storeys, adding bay windows to the sides, and castellating the rear. The interior revolves around a theatrical octagonal stair hall in the Gothic of Wyatt and Fonthill, with a shallow ribbed vault (partly glazed). An octagonal arcade of ashlar, with buttresses whose finials are the newels of the landing, is broken on the W side for the stair, which divides at a traceried window. The five satellite rooms have some original ceilings and detail, but apart from the plain E hall and the Gothic panelled NE room are mostly Edwardian. The SE room is Gothic with a monumental chimneypiece, probably Continental C15, ogee-hooded. The S and N rooms are generically Queen Anne, the S room with painted panelling, the N one panelled in finely carved limed oak, with a Jacobethan ceiling to suggest unhurried evolution. One bedroom has an original plaster vault.

Long Gothic STABLES behind, between gabled coachhouses, the central clock tower with a battlemented octagonal top.

GARDENS. A rounded lawn in front of the house is fringed with slim TOWERS, four round ones and two square. The prospect widens to woods beyond a lake fed by cascades from a succession of ponds, a designed landscape of considerable sophistication. At the upper end of the lake, the GROTTO, a spectacular wall of naturalistic rockwork in three levels of galleries with one natural and one pumped cascade. Deep within is a rock-ceilinged pool of impenetrable gloom. By the house, a neo-Elizabethan storeyed LOGGIA overlooks an early C20 sunken garden. WINDSOR LODGE nearby and SHERBORNE LODGE across the park, of the 1820s, are castellated, two-storeyed, with angle turrets.

CORFE

ST NICHOLAS. Neo-Norman by *Benjamin Ferrey*, 1842, archaeological for the date. The robust W front and pyramid-roofed NW tower are of 1858 by *C. E. Giles*, who removed a C13 W tower. Ferrey replaced a Norman church, of which two superbly characterful C12 CORBEL HEADS survive. Also the fine FONT with interlaced arcading and large palmette. – ROYAL ARMS. George III. – STAINED GLASS. E window, *c.* 1850. W window, 1858, by *Clutterbuck*. – MONUMENTS. Clifton Wheat †1807. Fine draped urn on a pedestal. – Sir Frederick Cooper †1840. Grecian, going Victorian, by *Humphrey Hopper*.

CHURCH COTTAGES are C17, picturesquely thatched, with early C19 Gothic windows.

BARTON GRANGE. The big three-storey stuccoed block with plain parapets remains from the mid-C16 courtyard mansion of Humphrey Colles. Reduced *c.* 1800–20 to an L-plan and then in 1931 to the single remaining range. This has tall four-light mullion windows front and back, with Tudor-arched lights and a big plain stair projection with C16 doorway. The end wall was the l. bay of the demolished front range. It has a Georgian cornice and the top half of a corniced upper window that looks late C17. Early C18 panelled first-floor room.

BROOK FARMHOUSE, ¼ m. S. Thatched with C16–C17 oak windows. Fireplaces with monolith Lias jambs. Plaster frieze upstairs of birds and fruit.

HAYNE, 2 m. S. Enlarged *c.* 1920 in the stripped-down manner of the period, with flush mullioned windows and flat parapets. The rear is early to mid-C16, much remodelled, with a hip-roofed storeyed porch. Moulded four-centred-arched doorway, with hunting scenes in the spandrels. The relief above, of a deer, in local white stone, is late medieval, in a C16 Ham stone frame with twisted columns.

CORTON DENHAM

6020

ST ANDREW. 1869–70, by *James Baker Green* of Blandford, for the Portman family. Expensive ashlar in idiosyncratic Perp. Tower of three stages, acutely gabled S porch, polygonal chancel with a blind-traceried parapet. Ashlar-lined interior, the display increasing eastward with naturalistic and angel corbels. – FONT. Small and overdone. – PULPIT. Covered in stone foliage. – STAINED GLASS. Chancel, 1870, by *J.-B. Capronnier* of Brussels (cf. Compton Pauncefoot). Painterly in an un-English way, the colours eerily glowing. Another by him, NW, *c.* 1880. Two by *Hardman, c.* 1905.

CHURCH FARM to the N is mid-C19 for the Portman estate, the farmhouse hip-roofed, the buildings around a yard, with a rear waterwheel. Below the church, the OLD BAKERY, 1869, has the fancy later Portman estate detail with bargeboards and contrasted colour. CORTON DENHAM HOUSE was the rectory, large, late C18, ashlar, with cornice and parapet. Extended amply behind in 1819 by *Evan Owen* of Sherborne. Victorian STABLES with a clock turret; brick GRANARY on stone arches. On the drive, battered C14–C15 CROSS with traces of a shaft figure.

COSSINGTON

3040

ST MARY. Blue Lias. Nave, chancel, and three-stage Perp tower with battlements and polygonal NE stair-turret. Four-centred-arched W window over a doorway with carved spandrels. Perp nave, the porch doorway C14. Perp niche over the S door, both C14. The low chancel has C13 rere-arches to paired C19 S lancets and a blocked N lancet. Also a cinquefoil-cusped tomb-recess of *c.* 1300. C15–C16 wagon roofs. Unusually the nave has an E window above the chancel. – FONT. Narrow octagon with quatrefoils on a tapering stem. – STAINED GLASS. E window, 1840s, with symbols and heraldry amid patterned glass. –

MONUMENTS. John Brent †1524 and wife. Two good 2-ft 9-in. (84-cm.) brasses, he in armour. – John Brent †1691. Cartouche with urn and skull. – Catherine Hobbs †1829. Signed *Henry Wood*. – Edmund Broderip †1847. Tudor Gothic. The church is on the lawn of COSSINGTON MANOR, stuccoed and bargeboarded, *c.* 1835, for Edmund Broderip, probably by *Richard Carver*. E of the village, COSSINGTON GRANGE, for the Graham family. A deep-eaved early C19 villa with a five-bay front, overwhelmed by additions of 1860–3 by *Charles Knowles*, principally a hefty Jacobethan tower with truncated pyramid roof.

MOON COTTAGE, ½ m. S on the A39. Prettily thatched toll house with stone Y-tracery.

COTFORD ST LUKE

A dormitory village built around an asylum, not unsuccessfully, for Victorian asylums were superbly built in generously planted grounds. TONE VALE HOSPITAL (the Second County of Somerset & City of Bath Pauper Lunatic Asylum), of 1892–7, by *Giles, Gough & Trollope*, closed in 1995. Its monumental Baronial-Jacobean tower, floating over the curled roads of suburban housing, crowns an administration block flanked by infirmaries and backed by a huge recreation hall. Red sandstone with Ham stone. It overlooks playing fields like a grand public school.

Scattered through the village are the large cruciform Late Gothic CHAPEL with a flèche and complicated hammerbeam roofs, the manorial SUPERINTENDENT'S HOUSE, and the entrance LODGE. By the playing fields, a neat roughcast PRIMARY SCHOOL, 2003, by *Somerset County Architects*.

COTHAY MANOR

Cothay is one of the most perfect smaller English manor houses of the late C15. It is not large, looks warm and comfortable in its mixture of roughcast and reddish sandstone, and has all the picturesque informality of plan and elevation which the Renaissance was so anxious to get rid of. The house of the de Cothay family was sold to the Bluetts in 1457 and rebuilt in 1485–8 by Richard Bluett. The series of late C15 wall paintings discovered at Cothay in the C20 are among the earliest remaining in English houses. William Every added a dining-room wing around 1609, then very little changed until the restoration of 1926–7 by *Harold Brakspear* for Reginald Cooper, friend and colleague of Harold Nicolson of Sissinghurst, Kent. A range was added in 1938 to a C17 barn to close the N side of the forecourt, for Sir Francis Cook.

The house is approached through a GATEHOUSE RANGE that differs in its red sandstone dressings from the house itself and dates from just after 1400. The principal feature, the entrance tower, is by *Brakspear* apart from the double-chamfered rear arch. Brakspear also added a hexagonal top to the winding stair within the attached two-storey N range. If there was a balancing S range it had gone by the C19. The N range is two-storeyed, of two bays, buttressed on the E. On the W side, a red sandstone doorway and two small single-light upper windows. The chimney-breast suggests that it was heated from the outset, probably lodgings.

The HOUSE faces E towards the gatehouse. It has crosswings at each end, and the gabled storeyed porch is on the inside of the l. gable. The r. cross-wing, hall and porch are all buttressed. The Ham stone-mullioned windows have an almost round head to each light, uncusped, the hall marked by two tall and transomed two-light windows, set high. An identical window on the first floor of the r. cross-wing marks the great chamber or solar. The oak mullion-and-transom window below is Elizabethan. In the l. cross-wing the kitchen window has similar rounded heads to the lights but the first-floor window with hoodmould looks C16–C17. The porch has a pointed, moulded and shafted arch and moulded four-centred doorway within. C15 door. The tall window above lights a small chapel.

The rear of the house is less regular owing to the addition of the early C17 wing where the back door from the cross-passage had been, immediately adjacent to the hall chimney-breast. One window, like those on the E front, remains visible squeezed between the chimney-breast and the N cross-wing, which has another such window lighting the solar, beneath a pretty roundel of three mouchettes. This is surely C14 and reused. On the N side wall, the solar chimney-breast and staircase form a single projection. The early C17 wing is attached to the inside of the S cross-wing, and projects slightly further. The cross-wing has, on its S wall, a corbelled first-floor chimney-breast and the massive kitchen chimney. A tail of outbuildings runs attractively S and returns E to enclose the service yard.

The INTERIOR is wholly timber-framed within the outer walls. The hall screen, a simple plank-and-muntin structure with two openings, carries a jettied gallery leading to the chapel. Of simple square timber framing, it was apparently closed in from the beginning, with only a three-light mullioned window opening to the hall. The HALL itself is a splendid apartment under a strong roof of seven close-spaced bays. Moulded arched-braced collar-trusses rest on small but fine shield-bearing figures. Three tiers of reversed curved windbraces. Broad moulded stone W fireplace. Wall paintings once covered both the long walls; the only discernible fragment shows geese hanging Reynard the Fox. The windows have bosses on the mullion pierced for shutter-rods (cf. the Treasurer's House, Martock). At the dais end, two ogee-headed doorways and early C17 panelling with painted graining, an early example. Behind the dais are the parlour (NE) and an unheated store room (NW). The PARLOUR has a good moulded ceiling, a fireplace similar to that in the hall, and more painted-grained panelling (imitating walnut). Fragment of painted frieze of *c.* 1500. The spiral stair on the N wall rises to the large and stately SOLAR. This has a roof like that of the hall but with the trusses unmoulded and more widely spaced. Three tiers of wind-braces. Evidence of a partition in line with the staircase. Painted flower-trail decoration, *c.* 2000, by *Arabella Arkwright* (*née* Robb). The E window mullion is pierced for shutter rods, as in the hall. To the N, a stair-hall addition of 1938 contains an early C18 staircase of column-on-vase balusters, from somewhere in Somerset. The early C17 DINING ROOM behind the hall has a Tudor-arched fireplace with tiny six-point roundels in the spandrels. Jacobean panelling with typically rich fireplace decoration: tapered pilasters with Ionic capitals, strapwork shelf, and high overmantel with four female Virtues flanking framed cartouches with the Every family arms, all under a deep and lavish cornice. The plaster ceiling is in three panels framed in vine-trail and with tiny heads in each corner.

Three doorways open S from the screens passage, to the buttery, the kitchen, and the central one originally to a spiral staircase, replaced by a straight one in the C17. Three upper chambers in the S cross-wing, two with C15 wall paintings. In the centre, r. of the stairs, the PRIEST'S ROOM with a square-headed S fireplace. On the W wall are painted drapery and a standing figure of the Virgin within a large roundel, with the sun and moon and some architecture behind, also the arms of Richard Bluett.* The paint overlaps the framing. On the plaster it has suffered from *E. W. Tristram*'s 1930s restoration. The large SE GUEST CHAMBER has a moulded ceiling and broad chamfered stone fireplace. A painted frieze of ribbon scroll (as at the Old House, Milverton) has damaged inscriptions in English apparently referring to a betrothal. A figure l. of the fireplace in civilian dress of *c.* 1500 may be a Bluett portrait. On the E wall are two scenes: on the l. the Virgin stands before a lily pot as a tiny Christ Child is beamed towards her down rays from the hand of God, i.e. the Immaculate Conception. To the r. a female saint, possibly St Margaret of Antioch, before a kneeling figure. A tiny squint looks N to the chapel altar. The CHAPEL has a two-bay roof of arch-braced trusses. Low in the door jamb is one side of a square-headed mullion window that had its external face looking into the hall. This is inexplicable unless this is the W wall of an earlier hall that was sited on the courtyard. The third, SW, room has heavy intersecting beams with big scroll stops, the crossing point far from central.

---

* Alastair Robb points out that there are signs that the shield is added.

The framework of the compartment GARDENS dates from the 1920s; they were restored and extended by Alastair and Mary Anne Robb after 1993. The E forecourt curves into a sheet of water. On the other side, yew hedges with tall cylindrical accents frame the lawn, which drops to a square parterre with circular fountain basin. The lawn bisects a long narrow yew walk with turret-like accents. In the spaces behind are small yew-enclosed gardens.

COTHELSTONE

ST THOMAS OF CANTERBURY. Immediately behind Cothelstone Manor. Red sandstone. Mostly Perp. Two-stage W tower with diagonal buttresses, square-headed bell-lights and square NE stair-turret. The curious top is because the battlements have been raised for a top chamber, some time before 1820. Double-chamfered tower arch, dying into the jambs. Nave, chancel and S chapel, all much renewed in 1855 and 1863–4. The chapel is earlier than the rest. C13 arcade of two double-chamfered arches on a circular pier, the W respond a moulded corbel of *c.* 1200. – FONT. Late C15. Octagonal deep bowl with big square quatrefoils over frilly cusped arches. Original colour, stencilled fleurs-de-lys on red. Traceried stem. – PULPIT and READING DESK. C19, reusing Jacobean pieces with Stawell heraldry. – BENCHES. C16 and good C19 copies. Straight-headed, with the wiry plant forms of Bishop's Lydeard (q.v.). Motifs include Stawell heraldry, the Five Wounds, a lily vase, and a green man. STAINED GLASS. E window, 1919, by *Comper*. Chancel S, 1864, probably by *Lavers & Barraud*. Four small C15 saints in the heads of the chapel S windows, one pair over blue-winged angels by *Powell's*, 1900. SE window, 1864, in an unusual Flemish C16 style. W window, 1865, by *Clayton & Bell*. – MONUMENTS. Effigies on a panelled tomb-chest, probably Sir Matthew de Stawell †1379 and wife, he in armour, she with angels by her head and squirrels under her feet, her gown still a lovely blue. – Sir John Stawell †1603 and wife. Well-carved effigies of Watchet alabaster, on a shaped tomb-chest, the canopy missing. – Two matching later C17 wall-plaques to successive Sir John Stawells †1603 and 1662. Corinthian columns and broken pediments.

COTHELSTONE MANOR. Cothelstone is easier to like than to understand. The house is not large and consists of a centre between projecting wings. In front of the house the gatehouse survives, and the two together, in their red sandstone ashlar, form an enchanting whole. The aesthetic appeal is not lowered by the fact that much of the house is reconstruction of 1855–6 for E. J. Esdaile, by *Joseph Clarke* of London. The great house of the Stawells was sacked in the Civil War and the remnant reinstated as a farmhouse in 1681, the heirs having chosen to start again at Low Ham (q.v.). The hall fireplace is dated 1681. But it is the exterior of house and gatehouse that is so fascinating. Whoever designed them had a passion for baluster shapes. They occur primarily as window mullions, best described as a cylinder joining two cannons, but there are also elongated cannon forms on pedestals. These frame the doorway, and much larger versions are attached to the ground floor of the forecourt, one each to the centre and the projecting wings. All are in Bath stone. They are without parallel. The outline, big gables to the wings and dormer gables to the centre, is of 1856. The r. wing is wholly Victorian. The original house may have been a storey higher with balustraded parapets, as the present scale is small for a house said to have had six courtyards.

The first courtyard is closed by the cubic toy-fort GATE-HOUSE, with a castellated tower over the arched throughway. Toward the house the centre is faced in buff sandstone whereas the side blocks are red. Also two-storeyed, these are lower and broader, with parapets. Each contains a first-floor chamber with Tudor-arched fireplace and three-light windows. On the side blocks the plinth steps over strange three-light windows whose central light is a shell-headed niche. Niches appear also within the archway. These of course echo Montacute. The outer face is similar but with a four-light chamber window on each side and plainer red stone tower with a blind recess.

As to the date, two successive Sir John Stawells are possible builders. The first inherited as a child in 1540 and died in 1603. The second, inheriting also as a child, lived to see the house ruined after 1642. So is this Elizabethan or Carolean fantasy? The temptation is strong to ascribe it to the Carolean Sir John, as romantic historicism, but baluster forms appear in mid-C16 woodwork, e.g. the screen at Poundisford Park, and a gatehouse as garden feature with shell niches occurs at Cathanger, Fivehead, *c.* 1600, so a late C16 date seems more likely.*

CHURCH COTTAGES, between the house and the church, were possibly C14–C15 lodgings. Blocked pointed doorway and jointed-cruck roof. Garden TERRACES on the slope above the house bear witness to Elizabethan grandeur, exemplified by the fine Ham stone LOGGIA. Square, of three arches each side, with rustication in cabochons and cabochons also between the frieze triglyphs; typical of the 1590s. It may have overlooked a bowling green. The stonework is fire-reddened, the pyramid roof probably post-Civil War. Also overlooking the terraces, an Elizabethan BANQUETING HALL, two-storeyed, with high parapet. Two ashlar canted bays with baluster mullions. The lower rooms once had carved panelling and moulded ceilings.

---

* Gerard calls the house ancient in 1633, but he may be referring to the family, the Stawells having been here from the Conquest.

The outer SE forecourt once had another gatehouse. The present triple-arched GATEWAY from the road was apparently one arch spanning the road, moved here in 1855 with side arches from elsewhere. In the farmyard on the slope above, a big BARN, 1851–3, by *George Pollard*, raised on twin two-bay basement arcades of shallow brick arches. But the columns and responds surprisingly are Norman. The big scalloped capitals look C19, but the shafts and responds are surely reused.

To the E, the former SCHOOL, 1873–4, echoes the house with Cothelstone mullions and flat parapets, the teacher's house tower-like on the corner. W of the road is ST AGNES' WELL in a restored medieval chamber.

COTHELSTONE HOUSE, ¼ m. W. Demolished in 1967, it was a sophisticated Grecian design of 1817–20 by *Harcourt Masters* of Bath, assisted by *G. P. Manners*, for E. J. Esdaile, set in a landscaped park. The neat LODGE survives, bowed on three sides, the pedimented doorcase curved to fit. At Terhill is the converted COACHHOUSE, two ranges at right angles, faced in North Curry sandstone. Arched entries and centre pediment to the coachhouse, S; giant arched centrepiece to the stables, W. A narrow BRIDGE of 1838 spans the sunken lane, to walled gardens. To the N are outbuildings on the lane to MANOR COTTAGE, an L-plan, C16–C17 farmhouse with good plasterwork. Downstairs a big mid-C17 bay-leaf ceiling oval and an overmantel with unidentified heraldry between thin gowned figures of Hope and Wisdom. An overmantel upstairs shows Samson, in breeches, slaughtering Philistines, on strapwork between strange Ionic pilasters.

The PARK overlies the park of Terhill House, demolished by Esdaile. Gothic structures marked on a map of 1778 include the surviving double-arched GROTTO once adorned with animal skulls and a strange horned figure. The Terhill park was 'thick with statues of gods and goddesses'; only a naked headless STATUE remains, below the top road.

YEA COTTAGE, Cushuish, 1 m. SE. Thatched and rendered. A plaster overmantel with the arms of the Butchers' Company and initials of Robert Yea, Exeter butcher, is dated 1674. Flanking half-men on Ionic tapered pedestals, also plant-scroll with little grotesques. The motifs are entirely Jacobean.

COTHELSTONE HILL. Several Bronze Age barrows, one of which was the site for a folly tower of 1779, rebuilt 1832. Only foundations remain.

COXLEY

CHRIST CHURCH. 1839–40, by *Richard Carver*. Lancet Gothic in Blue Lias. WEST GALLERY. Chancel re-fitted *c.* 1884 with good encaustic TILES. – ROYAL ARMS. Cast-iron, 1839, from Godney.

CREECH ST MICHAEL

ST MICHAEL. An uncommonly interesting church. The sturdy N tower is late C13 to the penultimate stage, which has plate-traceried windows in panels with corbel tables. The battlemented top stage and very short polygonal stair-tower are Perp. Broad Perp nave and chancel with good ogee tracery, Perp N aisle and S transept. Handsome W front: the four-light window is flanked by niches, and above is a larger niche with headless figure. Below the niches are green-man corbels. The W doorway has fleshy leaf spandrels and headstops in C15 hats. However, the S doorway with an order of colonnettes and a double-chamfered arch is C13, probably reused. C15 DOOR. Impressively broad nave with a panelled wagon roof on deeply undercut carved wall-plates. The tower has fine sturdy late C13 double-chamfered arches on powerful triple shafts, opening E and also S, so there were then already a NE chapel and nave. Springers for an intended (or lost) vault. The W arch is Perp, matching the two-bay N arcade with capital rosettes. The narrow NE chapel has a matching C13 arch to the nave, but is otherwise Perp. Four-centred panelled arch to the chancel.* Similar S transept arch, panelled between thin shafts, with two niches one above the other on the E jamb. The designer had a special liking for niches – others are in the broad chancel arch and N aisle E respond. An earlier niche in a NE chapel window. Simple wagon roofs in the chancel and NE chapel. The plain chancel PISCINA looks C13 but is one with a Perp window reveal. In the S transept, plasterwork of *c.* 1700: ceiling oval with laurel and palm branches, heraldic cartouche on the W wall.

FURNISHINGS. FONT. C14. Octagonal with heavy quatrefoils and fleshy underside leaves. – SCREEN. C16. The bottom only, two large panels and two bands of quatrefoils each side. – WEST GALLERY. Early C18. Panel-fronted with prettily carved ROYAL ARMS between strips of rustic flowers. Elsewhere, painted ROYAL ARMS of 1636. – PULPIT. Typical C17 arched panels, remade in the C19. – BENCH-ENDS. A few scattered, some made up into a reader's desk dated 1634. The leaf-scroll borders are typically C16 (cf. Trull). Traceried bits in the stalls. – PAINTED TEXTS. Late C17, in the nave. – STAINED GLASS. E window by *A. L. Moore*, 1907. – MONUMENTS. Robert Cuffe †1595. Reused C15 altar with painted heraldry on the large quatrefoils. Undersized Elizabethan aedicule above, of fluted Corinthian columns and entablature with lion masks carrying the same heraldry. – John and Mary Keyt, †1732 and 1757. Coloured marbles, with a fine completely asymmetrical Rococo surround for the coat of arms. – Thomas Exon †1792. Smoking urn, by *Jones & Co.* of Bristol.

Behind the church, off Bull Lane, COURT BARTON was an important Elizabethan house, shown by large mullion-and-

---

* A three-light window above it may represent a lost gallery for watching over holy relics. B. and M. Gittos.

transom windows in the end wall with Tudor-arched lights, but reduced and altered. S of the village is the TONE BRIDGE, stone, triple-arched: widened in iron, 1848, by *Murch* of Bridgwater. Along the N bank, on Mill Lane, MILL HOUSE. Late Georgian, three-storeyed, in red brick, with a four-storey MILL at right angles. Beyond the derelict Chard Canal, 1842, are large red brick former PAPER MILLS, 1885–7. In the village is a CANAL BRIDGE over the Bridgwater and Taunton Canal, 1823–6.

CHARLTON, 1½ m. E. CHARLTON MANOR is of brick of three periods. The seven-bay front is a late C18 remodelling with a pedimented doorcase, but the r. end shows early C18 brickwork, as does the rear stair gable. Closed-string staircase. The rear wing is the original five-bay house of *c.* 1700, with timber cross-windows under segmental blind arches. Beyond is the CANAL with a typical brick BRIDGE, and a little SW the tall hip-roofed brick ENGINE HOUSE, 1826–7, by *James Hollinsworth*, that pumped water from the river to the canal. It had a high chimney.

HAM, ¾ m. E, was a wharf on the River Tone. At the E end, across a suspension bridge of 1969, COALHARBOUR. An externally plain house with confident rustic plasterwork in low-ceilinged rooms. One ground-floor room has a framed ceiling covered in moulded plaster; the other has a Jonesian oval panel of the Sacrifice of Isaac within two borders, of leaf scroll and bay leaf. Spandrel panels outlined in broad bands of leaf scroll. The style is mid-C17, like the oval ceilings at Gaulden Manor (Tolland), Bournes (Wiveliscombe) and Poundisford Park (qq.v.), but the date 1679 is on the overmantel, with the arms of the Merchant Adventurers of London and Bobbett family initials. Upstairs, a ceiling of four thin-rib stars divided by vine-trail, a frieze of opposed dragons facing stubby balusters, and an overmantel with a triple arcade framing flowers (cf. Ashe Farm house, Thornfalcon). This all looks early C17.

CREWKERNE

4000

An Anglo-Saxon minster town that prospered as a market town in the C15–C16. Most of the secular buildings are Late Georgian to Victorian, testimony to prosperity from textiles. By the late C18 this included sailcloth and webbing from flax, for which the first factory was built in 1789.

ST BARTHOLOMEW. Close to the centre, yet overlooking fields. The large parish church of a prosperous town, late C15 to early C16, but preserving traces of an earlier cruciform church. This is most evident in the different proportions of the E end, based on those of a C14 chancel. From the E the church appears low and spreading, below its dominant crossing tower, but from the W the surprise is the nave, with its tall clerestory and front flanked by polygonal turrets, like the front of Bath Abbey or a Tudor royal chapel. Total length 167 ft (51 metres), the height of the tower 80 ft (24 metres), and of the nave 50 ft (15 metres). Total width across the transepts 146 ft (44.5 metres).

The sequence of rebuilding begins with the chancel, remodelled in the early C15 with perhaps the E wall of the S transept. In the late C15 the transepts were widened westward and the nave replaced by one with aisles. The unfinished parapet of the S aisle suggests that a church like Yeovil was intended, presumably with a W tower. In the event the turreted W front was chosen, emulating royal building projects. The nave clerestory followed from this decision, and the existing tower was remodelled, *c.* 1480–1500, by analogy with similar towers. Finally in the early C16 came the NE additions: a N chancel chapel, a splendidly lit chapel extending the transept northward, and a square chapel in the angle between. The height of the aisles is maintained in the N transept, but not matched in the chancel, S transept or NE chapels. Certain inelegant junctions suggest that everything was intended to be brought to the greater height, but was not; the older chancel governed the height of the chancel chapel, where the chancel N windows were reused.

The whole church is embattled, with plenty of gargoyles, long-legged beasts, musicians on the porch, and a festive array of finials (lost from the W turrets, porch and N transept). The windows are very large: of four lights in the chancel, five in the E window and S transept S, six in the aisles (a lavishness unparalleled in English parish churches) and seven in the W window. Their traceries deserve inspection to see the variety possible within Late Perp. The W window, narrow for its height, is composed of two-light side arches and three-light centre, the three heads at the same level between supermullions, running straight up to the main arch. The source of these supermullions is Gloucester; the even heads appear at New College, Oxford. The S transept S window displays the same vertical mullions and ogee-headed lights. Pointed four-light windows terminate the aisles, with ogee tracery above and below the transom, the lights grouped in sub-arches. The aisle side windows, also pointed, also group their lights in sub-arches but the lights are not ogee-headed, indicating an earlier phase. The enormous windows of the N transept N chapel, five-light at the sides and six-light at the N, and transomed, fill the available space, more glass than wall. The curved three-centred heads are indicative of the Tudor era. Supermullions and ogee-headed lights here also.

The turreted W front also makes Crewkerne exceptional among parish churches; only Yatton (N) and St Mary, Beverley (Yorkshire East Riding), comparable. The ornate W doorway under a crocketed ogee gable with large spandrel quatrefoils emulates the S doorway at King's College Chapel, Cambridge. There are diagonally set shafts with finials, and outer canopied niches beneath demi-figures of a king and a bishop. The aisles are only three bays long, but the bays are wide. In fact nave and aisles form a square with aisles and nave of equal widths. The two-light clerestory windows, five in number, do not correspond to the arcades and are separated by diagonal shafts that do not continue through the battlements (as they do on the aisles), evidence of two changes of design. The S porch is tall, with a high fan-vault on corner shafts. Its doorway has diagonal shafts with finials. Above is a canopied niche between tiered cusped panels under flat gables. Large niche for a statue between the SE buttresses of the S transept, unusual for both scale and position. The N transept N chapel, embellished with quatrefoil friezes below the windows (a feature of later Somerset towers), is further emphasized by a processional doorway on the W.

The tower has set-back buttresses to the top stage, continued as diagonal shafts through the battlements to coupled corner pinnacles. The bell-openings are of two lights and very long, descending into the stage below with an embattled transom ranging with the string course between the stages. Tracery below the transom with tiny spandrel quatrefoils; conventional tracery in the head (pierced baffles from the restoration by *J. D. Sedding*, 1887–9). All this compares with the towers of Hinton St George, Shepton Beauchamp and Norton-sub-Hamdon. Hexagonal SE stair-turret ringed with finials.

The most felicitous effect of the INTERIOR is the picturesque grouping of chapel behind chapel in the NE corner, as seen through the nave arches. These have tall, very thin piers of an original design combining the two standard Somerset types. There are four shafts, but in the diagonals are especially deep hollows flanked by wave mouldings. Small round capitals. The arches are pointed. The clerestory has wall shafts to large stone angels carrying the roof, these also used decoratively on the nave E wall. The depressed wagon roof has uncommonly massive ridge and transverse beams. Lean-to aisle roofs on triple wall-shafts with rosettes in the capitals. The massive crossing piers, too heavy for their Perp detail, show that the tower survives from the earlier church. There is indeed a blocked C13 window in an upper chamber. The crossing arches have broad ogee mouldings and fat shafts. The E piers have vigorous C15 corbels for a rood loft, including a green man. Small grotesque heads higher up for a rood beam. The wooden fan-vault under the tower (1904 by *Howard Gaye*) rests on the beginnings of a medieval vault possibly destroyed by fire.

In the chancel, an arcade of two four-centred N arches repeats the nave pier section. Two doorways in the E wall once opened into a sacristy (cf. Ilminster, Langport, Kingsbury Episcopi). One has boars in the spandrels, the other angels. On the S, an acutely pointed early C14 PISCINA and a re-set mullion (moved from the S transept) with fine C15 St Michael figure. The roof, on angel corbels, is again unusual – thin braced trusses alternate with heavy tie-beams. Four-centred arches also characterize the rebuilt N transept: a panelled relieving arch against the tower, arches E and N framing a sort of antechamber to the NE and N chapels, meeting on an impressive eight-shafted NE pier. Over this antechamber and the N chapel is a rich C16 panelled ceiling; another over the small NE chapel. The magnificently lit N chapel is called the Woolminston Chapel after the seat of the Merefields, but nothing positively identifies them as its patrons. Stone benches N and W.

FURNISHINGS. FONT. Square, Norman, of the Purbeck marble type, all the detail recut. – Two WEST GALLERIES, 1809–11, by *John Kempshed*, the central section removed. – BENCH-ENDS. 1893. Carved with plants or tracery by *Francis Nicholls*. His portrait on one marked 'emigravit 1900'. – REREDOS. 1902, designed by *Howard Gaye*. Last Supper carved by *Harry Hems*. Ham stone. – ROYAL ARMS. George III. – STAINED GLASS. E window, 1897. Chancel S, 1958, by *Christopher Webb*. Circular on clear glass. Two chancel and two NE chapel windows of interestingly muted colours, 1920s, by *Percy Bacon*. NE window, 1880, colourful, by *Alexander Gibbs & Co*. N aisle, *c.* 1900 by *Hardman*, a lush Nativity. W window, Tree of Jesse, 1930, by *A. K. Nicholson*. – MONUMENTS. Chancel S, Thomas Golde †1525. Brass with small kneeling knight, the religious words of the inscription brutally gouged out. – NE chapel: Sweet family, 1683, two little embossed brass cartouches. – Elizabeth Wyke †1615. With acrostic rhyme. – N transept chapel, John Merefield †1666. Large, still Jacobean. Twin plaques between columns with fluted entablature. – N aisle W, Adam Martin †1678 and Bridget Thomas †1723. Small brasses, one with heraldry, the other with tiny skeleton and American Indian.

In the churchyard, WAR MEMORIAL CROSS, 1921, by *Bligh Bond*. Celtic, with interlace ornament. – S of the tower, a Purbeck marble coffin-lid of *c.* 1200.

BAPTIST CHURCH, North Street. Hip-roofed chapel of *c.* 1820–30, the pedimented frontispiece of tall arched windows between pilasters added 1880. Altered galleries of 1830. – MANSE, *c.* 1825, probably by *John Patch*, local builder-architect.

METHODIST CHAPEL, South Street. 1874. Dec Gothic, with a plain tower and spire on one of the wings. Now also the R.C. church.

UNITARIAN CHAPEL, Hermitage Street. 1733. Arched cross-mullioned windows (cf. meeting houses at Broadway and Mid Lambrook) and a lunette under a three-sided gable. Interior of 1900. – STAINED GLASS. S window *c.* 1920, 'Journey of Life' by *Margaret Blake*, subsequently minister here, a remarkable talent. Small scenes in heavy leading and restricted colours. – MONUMENTS. Rev. William Blake †1799, with urn. – Grace Joliffe †1810. Coloured marble, Greek, in a Gothic frame, by *Gibbs* of Axminster. – Three-storey MANSE, 1812.

WADHAM SCHOOL, Mount Pleasant. 1971, by *Jeff Davey* of *Somerset County Architects*. To a campus plan of linked two-storey cubes. Curved-roofed SPORTS CENTRE, 2004–5, by *Poynton Bradbury Wynter Cole* of St Ives.

ASHLANDS PRIMARY SCHOOL, North Street. 1877, by *J. M. Allen*. Very Gothic, banded both in colour and texture. Enlarged in 1896.

CEMETERY, Mount Pleasant. 1874, by *George Nattress*. Twin chapels linked by a hefty Early French spired tower serving as a *porte cochère*. Substantial LODGE.

RAILWAY STATION, Misterton. 1860, for the Yeovil & Exeter Railway, probably by *William Tite*. Tudor Gothic, stone. The three-storey stationmaster's house looms over the single-storey station (similar to Sherborne, Dorset).

AQUA CENTRE, Henhayes. 1996–7, by *Andy Couling* of *Feilden Clegg Design*. Brick with monopitch roofs on laminated beams.

PERAMBULATION. The large MARKET SQUARE is filled by a large TOWN HALL, horribly mixed in style after a recasting in 1900 by *C. B. Benson*. The plain hip-roofed building of 1742 and 1836 is discernible from the w. Mixed Late Georgian to Victorian fronts around the square in Ham stone and the pale pitted local stone, a combination typical of Crewkerne. On the w side, No. 5, 1867, Italianate, formerly the Wiltshire & Dorset Bank. No. 6 was the Nag's Head, Italianate with, inexplicably, Gothic lower windows. Nos. 7–11, Late Georgian, 1–3–1 bays, is remarkably elegantly proportioned. There was an iron balcony. No. 13 is much older, with a C15–C16 framed ceiling, thin, with carved leaf scroll. The cellar beneath is hard to date. Four by two bays with plastered shallow groin-vaults on stone columns, with half-column responds on a rubble dado. It is suggested as C12, but the proportions are surely C18. The KINGS ARMS, plain Georgian, was 'newly erected' in 1782. Across the N end of the square, CORNHILL HOUSE, elegant three-storey Regency, the broad centre with a shallow tripartite bow window on to a balcony. On the s side, the GEORGE HOTEL was the principal coaching inn. Ham stone, *c.* 1770. Three storeys, 2–1–2 bays, with an open pediment on paired consoles. LLOYDS BANK, low, apparently mid-Georgian, was built as late as 1832. Then Nos. 31–33, 1885, domineering Victorian with fancy gables.

EAST STREET was the London road. On the s side, No. 2 (Crewkerne Museum) has a mid-Georgian pedimented doorcase and older rear. The WHITE HART has C15–C16 mullion windows with Tudor lights and a massive haunched fireplace. No. 6, *c.* 1860, by *J. M. Allen*, with emphatic rustication, was built as a solicitor's office. No. 10, at right angles, has a late medieval N end. Framed ceiling beneath a fine jointed-cruck roof, the wall-plate with quatrefoils and mouchettes. No. 12, mid-C19, has an unusually robust Italianate character. Deep-eaved, receding in three stages, the two-bay centre with an open pediment on heavy quoins. Notable cast-iron railings. Opposite are Late Georgian fronts at No. 9, three-storey with an unmoulded Venetian window, No. 13, two-storey with triple sashes, and No. 15, three-storey with triple sashes in the centre. No. 11 intrudes: the neo-Tudor Post Office of 1902. The best Late Georgian front is MEREFIELD HOUSE, 1810–11, with an

Crewkerne Grammar School.
Engraving, 1880

inset Greek Doric porch. A longer history is shown by datestones of 1661 and 1683 and an excellent wrought-iron GATE with late C17 Merefield heraldry. This could pre-date the rare early garden, terraced up to a stuccoed Baroque SUMMER-HOUSE with a steep Dutch gable. Panelled inside, with shell niches and a little plaster dome in a square with exquisite spandrel roses. On the s side, Nos. 16–20, mullion-windowed, include a C15 hall at No. 18 with C16 moulded framed ceiling. No. 31A, Late Georgian, three-storeyed, was the Greyhound Inn, probably by *John Patch*. TOWNSEND HOUSE has C17 mullions and a lateral chimney. Further up is the former GRAMMAR SCHOOL. Now flats. 1876–80, by *Giles & Gough* of London. Tudor style, three-storeyed, rising to four for the central gabled tower. A big Perp five-light window, r., balanced by the headmaster's house, l. Beyond are the cemetery and Wadham School (pp. 235, 234).

w of Market Square is CHURCH STREET, formerly part of the medieval market, broad and gently rising. Three good five-bay Early Georgian houses on the s side, with pedimented doorcases. No. 3 has fielded panelling and a staircase of three balusters per tread. No. 9, ashlar-faced with a Venetian window, has a good staircase. No. 20, opposite, has a crisply detailed Regency front of 1815. Just beyond is the churchyard. N of the churchyard, facing ABBEY STREET, is the former GRAMMAR SCHOOL of 1636 by *Edward Bettscomb*. The five-bay front has much-restored stonework with a gabled porch between big mullion-and-transom windows. Master's house of 1827 attached. Continuing w, THE ABBEY, a Tudor Gothic villa of 1846, has as its stair window a C15–C16 two-light window with traceried square head, reused from a clergy house on the site. No. 28, ashlar, five-bay, early C19, overlooks the small valley of Pople's Well. THE GROVE was the rectory, plain, three-storeyed and hip-roofed, *c*. 1840, between additions by *J. M.*

Allen, 1863 and 1882. NW, in its own grounds, BINCOMBE HOUSE, 1855, a stately pedimented villa with similar deep eaves and quoins to No. 12 East Street. Abbey Street returns E to Market Square past No. 26, three-storeyed, by *John Patch*, 1828, built as a school, and No. 20 with *Patch*'s typical arched doorway. On the S side, No. 3, also by *Patch*, arched-windowed Early Victorian, stands between buildings of a former SHIRT FACTORY. To the r., red brick, 1880s, well-lit to a deep square plan, to the l., stone, pilastered and arcaded, *c.* 1870. Beyond is a plain early C19 warehouse.

MARKET STREET runs S from the Market Square. NATWEST BANK, 1838, originally Stuckey's Bank, is proud commercial architecture for a small town, ashlar, three-storeyed, with rusticated ground-floor arcade and short balustrade on the skyline. Several Late Georgian fronts, also No. 17, handsome, five-bay, mid-Georgian, like the Church Street group. At the S end roads to Dorchester, Lyme Regis and Chard divide. The Dorchester road is SOUTH STREET. On the r. THE ELMS, ashlar Late Georgian with parapet, but earlier interiors, and No. 20 with C17 mullioned windows and C18 upper floor. Before the Methodist chapel (p. 234) was Christ Church (1854 by *J. M. Allen*), demolished. The road had a C19 industrial character with factories and terraced housing. On the N side, LINEN YARD was the girth-web manufactory of Robert Bird, with later C19 buildings running back. The twenty cottages of SOUTH STREET TERRACE, 1864, housed Bird's workers. Towards the station, VINEY BRIDGE MILLS made sailcloth and webbing from 1789. C19 buildings line a narrow yard, with curved-headed cast-iron windows. Reused Late Georgian pedimented doorway with unorthodox cylindrical entablature blocks.

The Lyme road is HERMITAGE STREET. C18 to C19 cottages in rows, the late C18 ROYAL OAK in keeping with coachhouse and stable under the one roof. HERMITAGE TERRACE, 1879, by contrast, is of stuccoed, seaside type. On the E side, the Unitarian chapel and manse (*see* p. 234). At the top, SEVERALLS PARK, 1920, a formally planned council estate, centred on the strange WAR MEMORIAL by *Hubert Worthington*, a diminutive soldier on a granite dolmen. The houses are spoilt. A return N down MIDDLE PATH passes the brick COTTAGE HOSPITAL, 1904, and SOUTHFIELD HOUSE, 1838, by *John Patch*, before joining the Chard road, WEST STREET. Pretty neo-Jacobean ALMSHOUSES here, 1897, by *George Vialls*, who presumably altered the parent CHUBB'S ALMSHOUSES of 1644 just behind in Court Barton. Two-storeyed, mullion-windowed, once with three gables.* Further out on West Street is a Tudor-style NATIONAL SCHOOL, 1847, by *J. M. Allen*. GOULDSBROOK TERRACE was cut NE through to Church Street in 1841. Nos. 7–11 have *John Patch* detail. The RECTORY is deep-eaved Early Victorian.

---

*The DAVIS ALMSHOUSES of 1707, which Pevsner admired, have gone.

Finally NORTH STREET runs out from Market Square past the Baptist church and Ashlands School (p. 235). Further out, the former MALTHOUSE of the Crewkerne United Brewery, 1881, by *G. R. Crickmay*. Brick with polychrome arcading.

CRICKET MALHERBIE

ST MARY MAGDALENE. 1851–5 by *J. M. Allen*. Quintessential Victorian estate church, with spired NW tower, fancy Dec tracery, and ornate parapets. It is all well done, if not especially Somerset. Lord Beaverbrook gave the two statues in the W end niches, 1947. Model interior with family pew in the N transept and chancel appropriately richer, with heavily moulded arch, Minton FLOOR TILES and embossed WALL TILES. – FONT. Covered in fleurons under an enormous wooden spire. – STAINED GLASS. Mostly by *O'Connor*. – MONUMENT. Stephen Pitt †1848. Cusped and crocketed founder's tomb.

CRICKET COURT. Said to have been built after 1811 for *Stephen Pitt* to his own design, but not marked on the 1843 tithe map. 1811 seems a more appealing date than *c*. 1845, the house being Greek, if treated with untutored freedom. Ham stone against cream stucco, with an attic over a *piano nobile* raised on a high basement. E front of four bays, of which three are symmetrical about a heavy Doric portico, approached up grandiose balustraded steps. Greco-Egyptian doorway with tapering sides. Windows with triglyph friezes. Pedimented attic windows open on to a cornice that is railed like a nautical walkway. Angle quoins with floating capitals. The eight-light basement windows may come from the previous house, although the lodge has identical mullions. On the other fronts uncut flint is added to the palette, and the elements jostle for place: a central bow on the W side, another, offset, on the N. On the S side another storey is incorporated, with difficulty.

The interior has a theatrical vitality, and shows breathtaking nonchalance with classical rules. The oval-domed hall has two Ionic columns facing just one on the opposite wall, this between arches whose capitals retreat into the wall. On each side wall, blind arches flank a doorway whose lintel links Ionic volutes in one painfully stretched capital. A sinuous passage, mysteriously top-lit, leads to a dark stair which turns to reveal vistas of interlocking secondary stairs. Circular domed first-floor library.

Outside, a vaulted basement beneath the N terrace opens to a sunken oval, reputedly a bear-pit. Disused drives intersect strangely: a causeway from the N crosses a sunken E approach on a rusticated arch. Sunken woodland paths to the SW emerge through a mock-medieval terrace.

MANOR FARM has brick gatepiers with obelisks by a brick-ended barn, apparently C18, but also not on the 1843 map. The farmhouse has mullioned C18 windows to the front, earlier ones on the double-gabled E end. At the other end of the village, a thatched Georgian Gothic former RECTORY.

CRICKET ST THOMAS

No village, because it was removed for the park of Cricket House in the 1830s.

ST THOMAS, E of Cricket House. Rebuilt in 1820, subsequently thoroughly Victorianized. Squared chert with Perp windows and funny cross-gabled w bell-turret with a little spike. Victorian interior with Perp arches. – FONT. 1881. Of chestnut wood brought from Bronte, Sicily. – STAINED GLASS. Colourful w window, 1860. s transept, *c.* 1868. E and s, 1904–5, by *Powell's*. – MONUMENTS. Two grand ones in the chancel. Viscount Bridport †1814. Designed by *John Soane*, carved by *Thomas Grundy*, 1816. Inventive Neoclassical. A heavy unfluted Ionic aedicule, the pediment top-heavy with massive acroterial scrolls, stands on a broad sarcophagus with serpentine fluting and armorial plaques. – Rev. William Nelson †1835, Horatio Nelson's brother, Earl Nelson and Duke of Bronte. By *Sir Richard Westmacott*. Reclining, he watches an angel carry two grandchildren heavenward. – s transept. Mary Hood †1786. Spiral-fluted urn, by *Soane*, 1787. – Viscountess Bridport †1831. Charming mother and children by *Lucius Gahagan*. – Viscountess Bridport †1884. Etiolated ascending soul. – Nave. Alexander Hood †1877. Supremely Victorian winged infant's head framed in lily-of-the-valley. Signed *F. Williamson, Esher*. – Rosa Evans †1922. Oval with cherubs. – Jane Hall †1953. C19 plaque (from the house) with cherub orchestra.

The startling white St Michael outside holding an Art Nouveau bronze sword is the MONUMENT to Viscount Bridport †1904, by *Alfred Drury*.

CRICKET HOUSE. Rebuilt for Admiral Alexander Hood, Viscount Bridport, by *John Soane* in two phases, 1786–8 and 1801–4, and remodelled in similar style by an unknown hand probably after Lady Bridport died in 1831. The result is a surprisingly unified four-square house, faced in Ham stone. Soane altered an existing, possibly H-plan, house, giving it a plain three-bay w façade, since removed. In 1801–4 he infilled the centre of the s side as a drawing room and doubled the house northward with new w and N fronts. After 1831 the entrance was changed from w to N, with a new hall and central stair hall, and the w front given a centrepiece to match Soane's s front. A colonnade was stretched around both s and w fronts, of columned porticoes between pilastered conservatories. So externally the s front is Soane (apart from the colonnade), notably the three-bay centrepiece with chamfered angles, panelled piers, and window architraves reduced to incised lines. The outline of the N front is his, but not the entrance and portico. All three corner conservatories were removed by *George Oatley* in 1898.

The interiors have little of Soane, sadly, for his library was a wonderful shallow-domed space. The ashlar-lined entrance hall with shallow arcading and the square central stair hall, grand enough for a national museum, are much in Soane's manner as is the cantilevered imperial staircase with iron balustrades. A lantern of 1931 replaces a much broader Soanean dome with glazed lunettes. Various marble chimneypieces brought in since 1898.

Nondescript late C20 hotel additions E of the house and in the walled garden, before a large BARN of *c.* 1800 with ellipticalarched entries. This faces a triangular two-storey brick GRANARY with its angles shaved to give six faces. Each face has superimposed arched openings. It looks like *Soane*'s work. In the garden W of the house, a nine-bay ORANGERY, glazed between Ham stone pilasters, of the 1830s. Below, a modern GROTTO, 2010, by *Kate Gould*. The beautifully planted PARK was landscaped in the 1830s, the stream dammed and widened. On a hillside NNE a belvedere of 1795, the ADMIRAL'S SEAT, with reused C16 pieces: the doorway, blocked window and datestone 1595. LODGES and COTTAGES of the 1830s. LONGMOOR COTTAGE to the S was originally a pair of cottages by *Clough Williams-Ellis*, 1906.

CROWCOMBE

HOLY GHOST. Red sandstone three-stage C14 and C15 tower with reticulated tracery in the W window, and two-light Perp bell-openings with a transom. On the stage below, a similar, narrower, blind window on the S and E. The NE stair-turret shows two periods, the broad base being probably late C14. Corresponding tower arch with double-ogee mouldings. A stone spire nearly 80 ft (24 metres) high was destroyed by lightning in 1724, its collapse damaging the chancel. Plain nave and chancel of variegated local sandstones. The nave two-light N window is C14, the E window Perp. The S aisle, in pink Quantock sandstone, is among the most sumptuous of the Late Perp aisles so notable in this valley (Bishop's Lydeard, Bicknoller, etc.). High gable parapets at each end and on the twostorey porch in the second bay. This has a stair-turret in the re-entrant angle. Finely traceried three-light transomed windows between buttresses. Ogee lights, the lower ones with the quatrefoil spandrels familiar from Muchelney and Cleeve abbeys. Cornice grotesques (a bagpiper on the SW corner), battlements with quatrefoils in the merlons, and pinnacles. The date is probably just before 1534 (dated benches). The porch has a similar upper window and a fine fan-vault with pendant. N chapel of 1655 for the Carews of Crowcombe Court, with its own W porch and three-light straight-headed windows, entirely Late Gothic, apart from the heraldic cartouche on the porch. The arcade piers are very tall and shafted with a four-wave moulding, and foliage capitals that look like awkward sections of the Devon type bands of foliage. On the pier opposite the door are small Crucifixion symbols. The SE chapel has similar arches to the chancel and aisle. The chancel arch is C14–C15, wave-moulded with bolder shafts on the N, the S jamb cut away for the C16 arcade. The arch to the Carew Chapel matches the nave arcades, although the capitals are uncarved. It looks earlier than 1655. Nave and chancel roofs of 1869–70, keeping the wall-plate and the bosses. The Carew Chapel has early C18 panelled GATES and dado, painted heraldry, and nine large HATCHMENTS.

OTHER FURNISHINGS. FONT. Octagonal, Early Perp, unusually rich, the underside cusped between pendants. In the panels are reliefs: Christ showing his wounds, two kneeling donors (one perhaps a prioress of Studley Priory, Oxon, which held the advowson), the Annunciation, St Anne teaching the Virgin to read, the Virgin crowned, and two bishops. C17 COVER. – SCREENS and PULPIT. 1729, by *Thomas Parker* (cf. Crowcombe Court). Thin delicate screens with panelled piers and beautifully carved pierced foliage in the segmental head of each section. The pulpit has bordered panels under well-carved flowers. – BENCHES. One of the best sets in the county, the bench-ends square-headed, with close finely detailed tracery. One dated 1534. Both Late Gothic wiry plants and fleshy Renaissance foliage appear. Amid the detail, a green man, little naked men fighting a two-headed dragon, a mermaid, mermen with clubs, and Biccombe family arms and initials. – CHANDELIER. 1973, by *James Horrobin*. Extended wrought-iron tendrils. – REREDOS. After 1876. Intensely carved (by *Harry Hems*) with Arts and Crafts vine-leaf columns and angels. Is it by *J. D. Sedding*? Colourful *opus sectile* tile panels each side, by *Powell's*, 1888–9. – STAINED GLASS. E window, 1877, by *Clayton & Bell*. Nave N, 1870, by 'a man at Inverness'. Carew Chapel: E window, 1878, by a Shrewsbury maker, and N window, 1888, lush and colourful, by *J. W. Brown* of *Powell's*.

MONUMENTS. Farthing family, † to 1727. Coloured marbles with foliage drop each side. – Carew family. By the same maker, with pilasters and heraldry. – Thomas Carew †1766. By *William Tyler*, an expensive piece with a large putto garlanding an urn, against an obelisk. – Rev. Henry Lockett †1778. By *Robins* of Bath. On a grey ground, the usual female by an urn. – James Bernard †1811. By *Sir Richard Westmacott*. Grecian, between Doric quarter-columns, a fine figure of Charity to one side. – Robert Trollope. *Opus sectile* Renaissance knight, 1910, by *Powell's*, after Pinturicchio. By *Powell's* also the feebler war memorial, 1920.

CHURCHYARD CROSS. C14–C15. On the shaft a canopied figure of a bishop. Slim figures at right angles are St John the Baptist and a female, possibly a prioress of Studley. Nearby is the top 8-ft (2.4-metre) length of the SPIRE, re-erected here after capping the stair-turret for two centuries.

Outside the churchyard, a small green with a good Tuscan column WAR MEMORIAL, 1920. Next to this, the very attractive CHURCH HOUSE of 1515. Two storeys. Two moulded Early Tudor doorways below, for the brewery and bakehouse, and another up steps at the end, for the church room. Plain mullioned windows. Fine roof of arch-braced collar-trusses and tiered wind-braces. The massive beam upstairs at the N end formerly supported a smoke-hood downstairs. The OLD RECTORY, rendered with C19 bargeboards, incorporates in the l. half the original medieval house. Beyond the gates to Crowcombe Court (see below), a C15–C16 VILLAGE CROSS with a thin shaft and cross-head indicates that Crowcombe had a market, established c. 1230. The long red sandstone CAREW ARMS, formerly rendered, has Late Georgian leaded iron casements. Further on, several of the rendered houses and cottages are of cob: CAREW COTTAGES, thatched, C16–C17, particularly picturesque. CROWCOMBE HOUSE is Late Georgian, stuccoed, hip-roofed behind a low parapet.

CROWCOMBE COURT. Begun in 1723 for Thomas Carew, then aged twenty-one. The house, of brick with Ham stone dressings, is the finest of its date in Somerset outside the Bath area. The main building has been attributed to *Nathaniel Ireson* of Wincanton, who took over in 1734 after his predecessor, *Thomas Parker*, of Gittisham, Dorset, had been dismissed for theft. It has been claimed that only the stable court had been built by then, but the investigation into Parker's work after his dismissal mentions fireplaces, flooring and wainscotting, showing that the house was complete and being fitted out. Parker was charged with stealing a hoard of coins worth £900, found in the demolition of the previous house, and accused of refusing to hand over his plans to Ireson. For an otherwise unknown architect, Parker's design is ambitious, in a Queen Anne style such as used by Francis Smith of Warwick.

The S façade is of seven bays and three storeys, raised on a half-basement. Like the N front, this front is made asymmetrical by a narrow extra bay that relates to the W front. The centre three bays project a little and have giant Corinthian pilasters on the lower storeys, carrying a modillion cornice. The outer bays have channelled pilasters and a simpler cornice. The windows have stone architraves. Above the cornice is an attic of square windows, typical of houses of around 1700, but here there is a three-bay pediment into the base of which breaks a central Venetian window, a lively though not correct composition. The central windows and doorway are arched, the doorway with a scrolled pediment rather awkwardly on brackets. The window above it has foliage volutes down its sides and those to each side of it are lugged – all characteristic Early

Georgian motifs. The outer ground-floor windows have been lengthened, presumably by *E. M. Barry c.* 1870 when he redecorated rooms on the E front. To the l., the ground drops and a pedimented two-storey block comes forward, its upper room level with the ground floor of the house. It has a Venetian window between plain windows, and angle pilasters, above a broad arched carriageway with Gibbsian rustication between pedestrian arches.

The five-bay E front has no pediment, just brick angle pilasters with ashlar capitals. These are notable for having inward-turned volutes, a Borromini device that appears roughly simultaneously in the Bastards' work at Blandford in Dorset. Pedimented doorway with Gibbs surround. The windows of the main floors have stone architraves and the first-floor windows have brick aprons. Attic as on the S front but without ashlar angle piers. The N front has elements of both S and E sides, seven bays with a centre pediment, but channelled piers to the centre and brick ones with Borromini capitals to the outside. First-floor brick aprons, and a Venetian window to both the attic and the first floor (lighting the staircase), above a pedimented doorway.

The five-bay W front, owing to the fall of the site, is a full four storeys. Its being brought forward of the S and N façades surely represents an error by Parker who could not link the wings of the stable court except by a passage across the W front. He therefore provided instead a whole façade, replicating the E front on a basement arcade of channelled brickwork. This arcading continues as the basement of two-storey quadrants linking to the stable ranges. Each quadrant arcade is enriched with an ashlar centrepiece of pilasters with vermiculated blocks carrying a pediment broken to frame the window above. The long STABLE COURT has matching eleven-bay ranges with hipped roofs and octagonal ogee-domed lanterns, the S one dated 1723, so definitely by *Parker*. These ranges have mostly wooden cross-windows rather than the sash windows of the house. The N range contained the kitchens.

Sumptuous INTERIORS of *c.* 1740. Square ENTRANCE HALL with two pedimented doorways on each side wall, those towards the rear false. The plasterwork is more Palladian than Baroque, in the manner of William Kent. Over the doors are lively cartouches with eagles and acanthus foliage draped with festoons. Between the r. doors is a fine fireplace with panelled piers and a central female head under a great broken-pedimented overmantel with enriched pulvinated frieze and side scrolls. Excellent ceiling in rectilinear panels around a deep-set centre with rebated quadrant corners. On the other walls plaster-framed panels, and in the back wall a magnificent Palladian opening to the stair hall, of Ionic columns and pilasters paired in depth, the arch soffit panelled. A great drape above, gathered at the keystone. The STAIRCASE is of the square open-well type, wooden, with delicately twisted balusters and panelled and decorated tread-ends. The very rich plasterwork on the walls survived the fire in 1963 that destroyed the ceiling. Pedimented landing doorcase and answering aedicules flanked by Rococo ornament. A festoon of fruit held by cherubs drapes the Venetian window. The DRAWING ROOM on the E front was redecorated in a Kentian manner by *E. M. Barry*, c. 1870. Characteristically more sober, the festoons confined to the main frieze, and ornament to the panels of the pilasters. The grey marble fireplace is especially stately. The DINING ROOM to the W has a very restrained plaster ceiling and fielded panelling. Fine Kentian chimneypiece of coloured marble with a gilded female head in the central plaque of the wooden surround. The floorboards have painted patterns in white, including heraldry, imitating inlay – a very rare survival. At the top of the house, the two Venetian attic windows are at the ends of a high central gallery running across the house, an echo of Elizabethan and Jacobean long galleries.

Up the combe behind the house, a brick ICE HOUSE and a picturesque GOTHIC BRIDGE of red sandstone and flint. This was built in 1776 by *George Rawle* of Dunster to designs by the Dunster artist *Richard Phelps*. By *Phelps* also the nearby CONVENT, a collapsing Gothic ruin that supposedly incorporates fragments from a medieval chapel at Halsway Manor (q.v.). Further up were an arch and a grotto. All this was done for James Bernard, who built the folly tower at Willett (Elworthy).

CROWCOMBE HEATHFIELD STATION, 2 m. s. 1862. Small, red sandstone, for the West Somerset Railway.

CUCKLINGTON

ST LAWRENCE. S porch-tower faced in squared Greensand, not high but sturdy. Small Perp two-light bell-openings with pierced baffles, and battlements. The pretty cupola may date from repairs commemorated on a plaque of 1703. The church was restored in 1880 by *G. R. Crickmay*, the E.E. chancel entirely renewed. E window of three stepped lancets. Chapel of St Barbara, E of the tower, Late Perp, with its own s doorway. Perp N aisle with parapet. The N arcade of two unequal bays may be late C13 from the double-chamfered arches carried down without imposts to a cruciform pier with chamfered angles. *Crickmay* opened the arch from the chancel to the N chapel, and added narrow arches each side of the shafted Perp opening to the S chapel. In the chapel, a reused C14 corbel and a squint. – FONT. C12, circular, with unusually fine fluting. Ogee COVER, c. 1700. – PULPIT, 1880, and REREDOS, 1890, of that highly finished conventional woodcarving produced in Austria and Belgium, here by *François Vermeylen* of Louvain. The livelier STALLS with emblematic plants were carved by the rector's sister, *Caroline Phelips*, for *Crickmay*. – ROYAL ARMS.

CUCKLINGTON

1660, with the favoured Stuart text (cf. Low Ham): 'Fear God: Honour the King and meddle not with them that are given to change'. – STAINED GLASS. Fragment of a small C15 figure of St Barbara in the E window of her chapel. E window, 1874, by *Clayton & Bell*, strong colours. – MONUMENTS. Robert and Nicholas Watts †1716 and 1729, similar, ungainly, in coloured marbles.

On the church path, CHURCH HOUSE, C18, whitewashed and hip-roofed, formerly the poorhouse. CHURCH FARMHOUSE, dated 1637, has Georgian sashes. The road continues past Babwell, or St Barbara's well, in a utilitarian trough, to HOMER'S FARMHOUSE, C16, thatched. Opposite is the drive to CUCKLINGTON HOUSE, a large, stuccoed rectory of the 1820s overlooking a huge view. Terrace, conservatory and landscaping by *Michael Balston*, 2000.

SHANKS HOUSE, 1 m. S. A remarkable house of different periods. Called newly constructed in 1566, but the early C17 and C18 are most prominent, the latter work either of after 1729 for Elizabeth Watts or after 1747 for the Rev. Nathaniel Dalton. The N range with off-centre storeyed porch could be Elizabethan, but was remodelled with hipped roofs, sash windows and curved pediment in the early C18 when the hip-roofed E range was added. This is a perfectly symmetrical five-bay composition, ashlar, with pedimented doorcase, architraves and dentil cornice. Stair projection behind. The W range has late C16 reserved-chamfer mullioned windows. The N end was a C16 service range – see the blocked E doorway; altered to coachhouses after 1800. The S end was extended for kitchens, with a bellcote.

The house has unusually good Early Georgian interiors, especially the NE room and stair hall. The former is panelled, with Corinthian pilasters framing a Baroque chimneypiece in purple, dark green and white marble. Scrolled open-pedimented overmantel with a plaque of astronomical cherubs and a female head above. Concentric ceiling plasterwork, the outer ring of ribboned fruit and flowers. Fruit baskets and sprays in the spandrels. The stair hall has large plaster frames for portraits, flanked by lively plasterwork: urns above festoons ending in circular wreaths. The first-floor band with profile heads suggests *Nathaniel Ireson* – see his similar work at Crowcombe Court. Broad staircase with slim balusters, column newels and tread-ends with both floral scrolls and panels. C16–C17 chamfered beams in the W range. In the NW coachhouse range a square-domed Regency business room. In the N forecourt an opulent fruit basket shouldered by cherubs, from a gatepier at Basildon Park, Berks., a stone copy, 1842, of Van Nost's original on the Flowerpot Gate, Hampton Court, 1700.

MARSH COURT, 2 m. SW. Long stone C17 mullion-windowed front with hoodmoulds. Dated 1661 on a plaster overmantel.

CLAPTON FARMHOUSE, 1 m. N. Dated 1615. Off-centre storeyed porch. Early C18 mullion windows except on the W end, where reserved-chamfer mullions remain. Forecourt piers of *c.* 1700.

CUDWORTH

ST MICHAEL. Isolated on the side of the Windwhistle ridge. No tower. Nave, chancel and gabled N aisle. The aisle has the earliest detail. Norman N doorway of pale Calcareous Grit. One order of columns, capitals with scrolly foliage, roll-moulded arch. In the tympanum are reused pieces, saltire crosses framing anthemion, so the doorway may have been moved. Also at the E end of the N aisle a tiny Norman window in a round-headed recess beneath a good late C13 window with plate tracery of three lights with a quatrefoil and two cusped spherical triangles. Cusped and shafted reveal. Two C13 N lancets and a pair, all with rere-arches. Chancel windows of the same date, or a little later. The E window has intersected tracery, the N and S sides each have a lancet and a two-light Dec window. The nave shows a Perp remodelling, partly refaced in Ham stone with two three-light windows. Earlier masonry is revealed where the S porch has been removed. Harmonious interior, restored by *Edmund Buckle*, 1904. No chancel arch. The three-bay arcade has early C14 double-chamfered arches on octagonal piers. Cusped PISCINA with shelf. C13 corbel head (aisle) and C12 abacus with saltire crosses (set in chancel wall). C15 nave roof. – FONT. C12. Massive drum with saltire-cross rim and middle cable moulding. Cable on the base. – PULPIT. C17. Arched upper panels. Fluted frieze. – STALLS. 1904. Quirky angular bench-ends. – MONUMENT. Sarah Smyth †1684. The Latin inscription records Flemish ancestors expelled by the Duke of Alva.

Base of a medieval CHURCHYARD CROSS. Behind the churchyard, a large MOATED SITE and marks of a DESERTED VILLAGE to the E. Opposite is the former PREBENDAL HOUSE, mullion-windowed, three bays, 1630s.

WARE FARMHOUSE, ½ m. E. Externally Georgian, but with late medieval jointed crucks and a C16 framed ceiling.

CULBONE

ST BEUNO. Approachable only by footpath, the solitude of the tiny church is delightful. Whether with its total length of 35 ft (10.7 metres) it is indeed the smallest medieval church of England or not, the church is rightly famous. Equally delightful are its shape and surface, with the little slate spire (of *c.* 1810) riding on the nave roof and the remains of whitewash on the

Culbone, St Beuno.
Drawing by J. Crowther, 1901

rubble walls. Dedicated to the C7 saint associated with Gwynedd. Nave, large S porch, and chancel, this with Norman herringbone masonry and a tiny Norman N two-light, the arched lights divided by a low-relief pilaster under a grotesque face. Perp E window renewed with insensitive correctness in 1927–8. In the nave a Perp two-light N window of wood and a tiny, possibly Norman, light set low. Plank S DOOR with rustic scrolled ironwork. Charming whitewashed interior, with late C15 wagon roof to the nave and plastered pointed chancel arch. – FONT. C12 bowl with heavy rings at the top of the stem. – ROOD SCREEN. C15–C16, from the foliage-scroll framing, but very crude. Three square-headed bays and no loft. Four-light tracery, each light with a stilted and cusped arched head under a quatrefoiled circle. One dado panel has original linenfold. – FAMILY PEW. Simple C17. – BENCHES. Square-headed, plain, probably C16. Reused linenfold to the front N pew. – REREDOS. By *Voysey*, 1928, for Lady Lovelace (*see* Porlock). Painted wood, neo-Gothic rather than in the earlier Voysey style.

In the churchyard wall, a MEMORIAL to the 2nd Earl of Lovelace †1906, probably by *Voysey*. Three panels with typical Voysey lettering.

Only two cottages. CULBONE COTTAGE, just N, 1860s, has brick dressings and fancy brick chimneys of the 1st Earl of Lovelace's time (*see* Porlock). CULBONE LODGE, by the bridge, an almost windowless tower with deep-eaved pyramid roof, is probably of the 1860s. The through arch on the back, battered chimney and sw wing are presumably by *Lady Lovelace*.

On the open hill above are several farmhouses. ASH FARM-HOUSE, probably where the 'man from Porlock' interrupted Coleridge during his writing of *Kubla Khan*, is altered C16, a possible longhouse, with lateral chimneys. PARSONAGE FARMHOUSE, very pretty, has chimneys clearly by *Lady Lovelace*, but is C16 – see the lateral chimney. Reused three-light mullioned window of *c.* 1500.

LILLYCOMBE, 2 m. WSW, overlooking Exmoor . Built by *Lady Lovelace* in 1912 for the Exmoor historian Edward MacDermott. She was assisted by *Voysey*, but the design is bolder and coarser than his compositions. Voysey's roughcast walls, roofs of thick slates and emphatic chimneys are here, but he would not have made the hipped roof so dominant, punctuated by an off-centre ridge chimney and a soaring octagonal W one. Simple casement windows. Two gables project asymmetrically on the front, and at the back an entrance wing is pushed out, the gable oddly higher and wider than the roof behind. Hip-roofed STABLE COTTAGE to the E with hipped dormers. A later, pyramid-roofed BUNGALOW completes the sequence.

CURLAND

ALL SAINTS. Isolated below Castle Neroche. Rebuilt in 1856 by *Benjamin Ferrey*. Now a house. Small, just a nave with bellcote, carefully detailed.

CURRY MALLET

ST JAMES. Perp, except for the chancel masonry – the chamfered plinth and double-chamfered S doorway typical of *c.* 1300. Proud W tower of Blue Lias with Ham stone, the angles and set-back buttresses banded blue and brown. The buttresses carry diagonal shafts (also banded), stopped at the cornice with delicate beasts below the battlements. Polygonal NE stair-turret topped with ashlar panelling and battlements. Deeply moulded W doorway under a very large four-light window with ogee lights above and below the transom. Two-light bell-openings with pierced baffles. C15–C16 N aisle with Ham stone battlements and Perp panel tracery. Similar nave S window. The double-chamfered porch arch looks early C14. The S doorway inside has a Perp hoodmould on big curly stops. The porch itself was altered to lean against the Mallet Chapel. This is also C15–C16, of two bays. The chancel has C17 side windows and a C19 E window.

Panelled Perp tower and chancel arches, also the broad four-centred arch to the Mallet Chapel. The N arcade is of three bays with piers of standard section with shafts and four hollows. There is, however, one remarkable thing about them: both shafts and hollows are far more pronounced than usual and the capitals are in style decidedly C14, and not too late at that. N aisle with framed ceiling and ogee PISCINA. Plaster barrel ceilings to the nave and chancel. In the chapel, a handsome large angel bracket for an image, between the S windows.

FURNISHINGS. FONT. Octagonal Perp with shields in cusped panels. – TOWER SCREEN. Above a good war memorial screen of 1949 is the top of a most elaborate screen, made c. 1640 for Thomas Pyne and placed in the church in 1926. Its intervening history is obscure. Of robust and illiterate workmanship. Tripartite. The lower tier has the Pyne arms between the Crucifixion and Nativity. Four figures act as caryatids, carrying those flower baskets made popular by Floris in Antwerp. The caryatids are not just decorative maidens, but represent St Paul, the Magdalen, the Virgin, and St Peter, who should not have been degraded to such a function. Above an undercut leaf cornice, four little standing figures separate arched panels with tiny openwork scenes: Adam and Eve, the Expulsion, and Aaron and Hur sustaining Moses' arm (it had to be raised until Joshua defeated Amalek). What can have been the message? – Other C17 WOODWORK includes reused balustered arcading on the S chapel screen wall, BENCHES with small shell tops, some chancel PANELLING, and a READING DESK dated 1633. – STAINED GLASS. C15 kneeling saint in the NE window, and fragments in the SE window. E window, 1877, by *Layers, Barraud & Westlake*, rich and sweet. – MONUMENTS. Large plain medieval tomb-chest with an unrelated serene small C13–C14 effigy, a boy perhaps, on top. – John Pyne. 1642. A sumptuous piece in coloured marbles and Somerset alabaster. He faces his wife across a prie-dieu, framed by giant columns and a broken pediment. – Ralph Mighill †1633. All that remains is the somewhat ludicrous painted demi-figure of the bearded divine. – Nameless early C17 alabaster and marble memorial of good quality, similar to the Pyne monument. Columns and broken pediment frame a lady kneeling at a prie-dieu, above two reclining small daughters. Walsh of Cathanger (*see* Fivehead) heraldry.

MANOR HOUSE, ¾ m. NNW. Picturesque and irregular, with twisted C16 chimneys modestly reminiscent of those at Barrington Court. The main N range, reduced by a storey since the 1840s, is of carefully worked Lias. C16 mullion windows with arched lights and a stair-turret for a stone spiral stair. The moulded E doorway of the turret opens now into a slightly later kitchen range, C16–C17, with a similar window and the Pyne arms. In the main house C17 panelling with the Pyne arms and a moulded C16 fireplace on each floor. In the kitchen, a C17 plaster ribbon frieze. Low SE range with chamfered C16–C17 beams. The long s building, perhaps a former barn, has a high late C14 wind-braced cruck roof.

Near the Manor House, WEAVER'S MEAD, much renewed, has a C16–C17 partition. At ASH TREE HOUSE, of L-plan with C19 casements, nothing external indicates the C15 full cruck inside the door, nor the moulded hall bressumer. The adjoining cottages conceal a C16 moulded framed ceiling in CHESTNUT COTTAGE and early C17 detail in HULLS PLACE. HEADWELL HOUSE, beyond, has a C16 cruck. NW from the Manor House, LAVENDER COTTAGE, late C16, and the OLD BAKERY, with early C16 jointed crucks and C17 framed ceiling.

CURRY RIVEL

ST ANDREW. Although essentially a Perp church and a very good one, the building contains rich work of the late C13 only visible inside, confined to the NE chapel. The Perp work is of Blue Lias with a great deal of Ham stone. The 96-ft (29-metre) W tower must be given priority, although it had to be rebuilt in 1860–1 (by *C. E. Giles*). It is a dominating piece, with Ham stone angles and facing of the set-back buttresses. The buttresses continue as diagonal shafts through the bell-stage and battlements, originally to pinnacles. Higher octagonal NE stair-turret. Unusually tall lower and upper stages with a narrow one between. The lower stage is blank to the S. W doorway with traceried spandrels beneath a five-light window. Middle stage with flat-headed two-light windows, then a quatrefoil frieze under dramatically elongated single two-light bell-openings. These have ogee tracery above and below transoms. Pierced baffles. A string course continuing the hoodmoulds divides the bell-stage. Statue niche above, only on the S. The Ham stone battlements have a central diagonal shaft, so should have three pinnacles each side. The tower resembles Hinton St George and Norton-sub-Hamdon which retain pinnacles and Shepton Beauchamp which does not, and is early C16, to judge by the panelled tower arch and high fan-vault within.

After the tower the S aisle ought to be examined. It is a joy to the eye, battlemented with many beasts in the cornice, and with big, richly cusped four-light transomed windows, one to the l. and two to the r. of a storeyed porch. The windows fill the bays, between buttresses with shafts for pinnacles, as on the tower. They have the wonderfully rich tracery of Langport, transomed with lower lights of the Muchelney type, with quatrefoil spandrels. The porch has slightly cambered battlements, similar buttresses, and beasts, but a bagpiper in the centre, above a three-light window with fine polygonal hoodmould stops. In the quatrefoil frieze below, the portcullis of Lady Margaret, mother of Henry VII, and feathers of Prince Arthur, suggest a date *c.* 1500. The hooded STOUP resembles that at Muchelney. Inside, a fan-vault like those at Isle Abbots and North Curry, but the centre is a diagonal square with quatrefoils rather than the usual rose. The S transept, really a chancel chapel, has Ham stone battlements and dressings. S window as on the aisle, but the E window is shorter, with a quatrefoil in the foot of each light. Ashlar chancel S wall with one similar window, but the E wall is Lias. The chancel supposedly was shortened in the C18; if so, both the five-light window (with tracery matching the W window) and the buttresses were reused. The NE chapel is twice the length of the S one, equal to the chancel and with a matching E wall. Otherwise it is rendered, with Perp ashlar battlements and buttresses as elsewhere, but the windows more modest with vertical mullions. Nothing external suggests that this chapel is C13.

Inside, the arcades are tall and fragile with piers of standard four-hollow type. The chancel arch and chapel arches match: one arch from the chancel to the S, two to the N. Bearded heads support each end of the nave roof ridge (roof replaced 1861). Two much larger heads are tower corbels at the W end. The aisles have shallow-pitched panelled and sub-panelled ceilings with rosette bosses. Thin framed C15–C16 chancel roof. S wall SEDILIA, a long seat with quatrefoil frieze, and recess with linenfold DOOR.

Now the NE chapel. Here a most uncommon arrangement – a series of late C13 tomb-recesses along the N wall, six in all, of which three are treated as a group, a large one between smaller ones. All three have trefoiled arches on short shafts, under Lias gables flatly decorated with a kind of debased stiff-leaf. To the l. is another similar small recess and to the r. are two of Ham stone, a little later – one cusped with ballflower points. The EFFIGIES are all damaged. Under the large arch lies a cross-legged knight of the late C13 or early C14 with the Urtiaco arms. Unusually the chain-mail was modelled in gesso. The small effigies (3 ft to 3 ft 6 in.; 91–107 cm.) l. and r. tally in date, as does a small female effigy displaced to the SE corner. The shafted cusped PISCINA tallies too, as do the windows, despite inserted Perp tracery. The reveals show the original appearance; fine cusping of the N arches, and the E window shafted with small dogtooth decoration in the capitals and ballflower in the arch. Large E corbel (originally two) for statues. Traces of a C13 W opening. Also two INCISED SLABS: one in the first arch, to a priest, C14, just the face over a foliate cross; and a full figure on the floor below, also a priest, early C14, found beneath the nave N door in 2003.

FURNISHINGS. SCREENS. C15. Originally right across; only those to the chapels remain. They are interesting, in higher relief than usual. The four-light sections are separated by strong shafts placed in front of and detached from the posts. They carry a ribbed coving with bosses and vine-trail cornice. A strong mullion in each section runs into the apex of the arch, and each light has a pierced square halfway down. – BENCHES. C15–C16 frontals with poppyheads and flat tracery panels.

Bench-ends generally with three-tier tracery, but two profile heads and some other devices. – FONT. Octagonal. Victorian or possibly retooled C15. – PULPIT. 1863, by *Giles*. Marble-shafted. – STALLS and ORGAN CASE. 1956, by *Stephen Dykes Bower*. Gothic.   ROYAL ARMS. Charles II. – HATCHMENT. Hester Pitt, Countess of Chatham †1803. – STAINED GLASS. Many C15–C16 pieces, some assembled as four saints in a N aisle window. In the E window, heraldic pieces and a C13 quatrefoil roundel from Canterbury Cathedral. W window, 1865. Very gay colours and beefy Renaissance forms in the Holbein fashion, utterly unexpected. The designer was *Francis Penrose*, exploring alternatives to Gothic as Surveyor to St Paul's Cathedral. – S chapel E, 1913, by *Kempe & Co*. Chancel S, engraved panes by *Laurence Whistler*, 1987. – MONUMENTS. NE chapel. Robert Jennings †1593. Plain, well detailed 'reredos' of two Composite columns and cornice framing inscriptions, on an Ionic-pilastered chest. – Marmaduke and Robert Jennings †1625 and †1630. A splendid if rustic work, brightly painted. The two bearded men in half-armour repose on a tomb-chest with kneeling family along each side and babies at each end, several to a bed. The thin canopy arch is coffered with roses and crowned with heraldry between rather silly recumbent nude putti. Iron railings with spears and fleurs-de-lys. – Raphe Trevilian †1628. The front of a C16–C17 chest tomb, oddly inscribed inside. – In the S chapel, four particularly beautifully incised C18 Lias slabs to the Powell family. – In the chancel, Rev. James Sedgwick †1834. Greek draped altar, by *M. W. Johnson*.

In the churchyard, three Celtic Revival CROSSES to the Barringtons of Hurd's Hill, Langport, *c.* 1916. – Georgian Gothic SCHOOLROOM, 1828.

CONGREGATIONAL CHAPEL, Wiltown Road. 1840. Hip-roofed, simple Gothic. The adjoining cottage was the manse.

On the rectangular green outside the church are MANOR FARMHOUSE, Victorian, and THE COTTAGE, thatched, later C17. To the S, the SCHOOL, 1876 by *J. M. Allen*, faces the VILLAGE HALL, 1907 by *P. R. Berry*, brick and stone, freely styled. WATER STREET runs W to THE YEWS, early C18, of banded Lias with Ham stone details. Five bays with cornice and parapet, now under C19 eaves. Further out on water street, HEALE HOUSE began as a four-bay mullion-windowed house of 1620, for Samuel Powell. Handsome seven-bay W range added in 1725, of banded Lias with Ham stone curved-headed windows. Across the field NW, a gabled C17 DOVECOTE and HEALE WOLD, the predecessor house. Its low rear wing is a C15 hall with one cruck truss. Inserted Elizabethan fireplace and cheerfully random plasterwork including fish-tailed beasts (cf. Somerton church). Front range with early C18 staircase. S down HEALE LANE, by the footpath on the r. to the Pynsent Column (*see* below), STONELEY HOUSE, an early C19 White Lias villa raised by a storey in 2006 by *John Wratten*. The main road returns E with little of note apart from HILLARDS

FARMHOUSE with C17 mullions, extended in Ham stone. Early CIDER HOUSE behind.

Wiltown Road runs s past the chapel (*see* above). MIDDLE-THORPE HOUSE, despite the early C19 refronting, dates from the C16. C17 partitions; early C18 closed-string stair and panelled room. WILTOWN has farms interspersed with C19 villas. The roadside end of LITTLE WILTOWN, banded in Ham stone, is early C16 with a moulded framed ceiling and stone fireplace on each floor, the rest early C17. WILTOWN PLACE is a Victorian brick villa and WILTOWN HOUSE an early C19 hip-roofed one. WILTOWN HOME FARM, long, with casement windows, has a C16 framed ceiling. Attractive half-hip-roofed roadside BARN of 1797. Up Back Lane, MONKSCOMBE HOUSE is C16–C17 with rear cross-wing and framed ceiling.

On the main road E of the centre, DOMUS, built for himself by *Derek Seward*, 1968–72. Fitted to a very narrow site. Grey imitation stone (required by the planners), neatly varied. Rainwater is carried down in painted columns of concrete pipe. Just beyond, a late C19 LODGE spans the drive to MIDELNEY PLACE, a country house of 1863–6 by *J. P. St Aubyn* for the Trevilians of Midelney (Drayton). Gabled and mullion-windowed, of White Lias with Ham stone. Two fronts in counterpoint, a gabled porch between dormer gables on the entrance, a dormer gable between gabled cross-wings on the back. Neat near-symmetry enlivens both.

BURTON PYNSENT, 1 m. WSW. Burton was a C16–C17 mansion of the Jennings family. Their heiress married Sir William Pynsent of Urchfont, Wilts., who left his estates in 1765 to William Pitt as a token of esteem for the Prime Minister and distaste for his own relations. Pitt became Earl of Chatham and Viscount Pitt of Burton Pynsent in 1766. He sold the Wiltshire estate to spend extravagantly in 1765–7, adding to the house, creating gardens and rebuilding farms, but fell ill in 1768, and did little more before he died in 1778. After his widow died in 1803 the mansion was demolished, apart from Pitt's addition. The only known view shows an irregular N front of some fourteen bays with the addition at right angles on the W end. This was possibly to *Pitt*'s own design, built by *John Ford Sen.*, builder (and sculptor) of Bath. Brick, of 2–3–2 bays; two storeys with a basement under the N end. Ashlar quoins, cornice and pediment. Derelict by the 1830s, it was remodelled in 1909–10 for Sarah Crossley, sister of *Harold Peto*, who designed terraced gardens for her and presumably the door hood, cupola, and a Dutch-gabled W entrance, which was removed in the 1960s.*

The PYNSENT COLUMN on the steep bluff to the NE was erected by Pitt in 1766–7 to his benefactor, for some £2,000. Designed by *Capability Brown*, it is a sublimely monumental Bath stone Tuscan column rising 140 ft (43 metres) on its high

---

* One of Pitt's garden temples is re-erected at Wadeford House, Combe St Nicholas (q.v.).

pedestal. The top was a viewing platform outside a domed chamber with crowning urn. Brown first proposed a statue of Gratitude, on the model of the Grenville Column at Stowe, Bucks.

BURTON FARM, across the main road, was one of Pitt's three model farms, here with hip-roofed brick BARN and distinctly Mediterranean colonnaded cattle shelters. MOORTOWN FARM, 1 m. SSE, and BURTON DAIRY FARM, ½ m. N, are the others, the former with C16–C18 farmhouse and particularly beautiful colonnades.

WICK, 1 m. NE. A lost medieval chapelry. WICK FARM with mullioned windows is dated 1661 inside. WICK MANOR, with wings enclosing a little forecourt, began as a C15 hall house. At WICKMOOR COTTAGE, 1 m. WNW, a good surviving WITHY BOILER, for preparing basket willow, early C20. Brick tank and short chimney.

CUTCOMBE

ST JOHN. Plain two-stage W tower, limewashed yellow. Possibly C13 from the chamfered W doorway and unmoulded tower arch. Frilly cusped two-light W window, C14–C15. Perp N aisle and NE chapel, the plastered chamfered-arched N arcade undatable, but medieval. *C. E. Giles* added the S aisle and SE chapel in 1862. Very Victorian S arcade with florid naturalistic capitals on octagonal red sandstone shafts, echoed on the chancel arch. – FONT. C12 Purbeck marble base and central shaft, the rest of 1862. – PULPIT. 1862. Stone with relief scenes. The similar REREDOS was displaced to the SE chapel by one in tile and alabaster by *Powell's*, 1896. Typical matt blues and reds. – STAINED GLASS. By *Clayton & Bell* the E window, 1896, and, unexpectedly, the SE window, 1913, a Renaissance St Michael, after Guido Reni.

CHURCHYARD CROSS. C15, renewed 1898.

W of the church, stuccoed, hip-roofed former VICARAGE by *Richard Carver*, 1833. Towards Wheddon Cross, THE BEECHES, 1988–9, a neat cottage-style housing association development, by *Neil Embleton* of *Percy Thomas Partnership*. Two terraces at right angles. SCHOOL with half-hipped roofs, and similar teacher's house, by *Edward Aston* of London, 1875–6.

DILLINGTON HOUSE
Ilminster

Ham stone Tudor Revival house beautifully set in parkland, rebuilt in 1835–8 by *James Pennethorne* for John Lee Lee.

Dillington House, before alteration.
Engraving, 1829

Symmetrical with multiple gables (iron-spike finials) and octagonal chimneys. A C15 house was probably rebuilt for the Bonvilles after 1522 and altered for the Spekes after 1599. It had a N cross-wing and a hall with C15–C16 storeyed porch. Pennethorne altered the cross-wing and rebuilt the rest echoing the previous house, but with a longer front and a balancing S cross-wing. His porch reuses the shafted doorway, quatrefoil frieze, and battlements from the old one. It is central between large transomed windows and there are false stair gables in the angles. The garden fronts each have a similar centrepiece; an iron-roofed conservatory, S, and a dining-room bay, E. Tudor Revival interiors. The hall ends in triple-arched stone screens. The stair, N, has Georgian balusters reportedly from a Vaughan-Lee house in Wales. The library and drawing room in the S cross-wing have vine-trail cornices. Gothic chimneypieces, apart from that in the drawing room, with semi-clothed classical females. In the N cross-wing C16 partitions remain, and one room has C17 panelling from Barrington Court, badly reassembled. Fine first-floor marble chimneypiece with female head and drape, mid-C18.

Somerset County Council has maintained the house since 1949 and has restored the GARDENS with creative use of modern sculpture. The N edge of the upper lawn covers cellars and a deep ovoid brick ICE HOUSE. On the lower lawn, a C16 twisted finial from Barrington Court. Low-walled W forecourt with broad cast-iron gates. On the slope SE, a squat OBELISK with Butler arms, from Martock. Dated 1790, but the pedestal emblems of mortality look earlier.

The STABLE COURT, NW, 1875, by *George Nattress*, has a grandly over-scaled pedimented arch and eclectic detail, including convincingly Georgian courtyard doorways. C16 fireplace inside inscribed JH 1723. In the main room, converted to a theatre, a lively stained-glass window, The Circus, 1993, by *Patrick Reyntiens*. THE PHEASANTRY behind was a late C18 lofted cartshed, with dove holes.

THE HYDE, just N, a conference centre of 2006–9 by *Niall Phillips Architects* (*Tim Rolt* and *Dan Talkes*), is the best recent building of the region. A dramatic play of oblong volumes, meeting-rooms above a refectory, and residential wing at right angles, enclosing a sunken court with oblong pools. A stark black-boarded box floats over a glass-walled base, one end oversailing the old walled garden. Minimal glazing on the S, plate glass on the N. The residential wing has window bays looking outward over fields.

On the W drive, the thatched Gothic WEST LODGE, *c.* 1830, has a three-sided front similar to the lodges in Ilminster (q.v.). The E drive passes a mid-C19 pyramid-roofed DAIRY HOUSE to reach the Home Farm, well converted to offices called EAGLEWOOD PARK, 2005–8, by *Llewellyn Harker*. Very large BARN of the 1860s, the upper floor brick with ventilation slots. Mill attached behind. On the disused S drive to Ilminster are Second World War DEFENCES of the Ilminster 'anti-tank island': pillboxes, tank obstacles and settings for a removable road block.

DINNINGTON

ST NICHOLAS. Small, mostly of 1863 by *J. M. Allen*, but Perp chancel and porch arches, and a reused chancel S window with ogee tracery arched in a square frame (cf. Ilchester). – FONT. Cable-ringed. C12, horribly redone. – ROYAL ARMS. Hanoverian.

PARSONAGE FARMHOUSE contains the hall of a C14–C15 priest's house with jointed crucks.

ROMAN VILLA, ½ m. N. A courtyard villa excavated in 2002–7 contained remnants of several mosaics. One, at least, was of extremely high quality with figured scenes executed using very small tesserae. The design could not be restored but one part appeared to show Daphne and Apollo, from Ovid's *Metamorphoses*.

DITCHEAT

ST MARY MAGDALENE. A large cruciform church with crossing tower, in a large churchyard. Unified by Perp ashlar battlements and pinnacles, but of two main periods, the very late C13 and the late C15. The quality of detail derives from the connection to Glastonbury Abbey. The best part is the chancel, lofty outside, light inside. The late C13 contributed the plan and the main windows. Those on each side are of two lights still with trefoils, but the E window of three lights has at its top a spherical triangle fitted with three unencircled trefoils. Inside, the rere-arches have fine openwork cinquefoil cusping (similar to Manor Farm at Meare, the former abbot's hall), which in the E window seems to cut quite dazzlingly into the tracery. The chancel was heightened and given a clerestory (as at Pilton) between 1473 and 1491, from the shields on the battlements of the rector John Gunthorpe, Dean of Wells †1498, Bishop Stillington †1491 and Abbot Selwood †1493. Four-centred-arched upper windows with vertical mullions.

The base and first external stage of the crossing tower are from the earlier of the two periods. The heavy crossing arches have continuous double-chamfered mouldings, and the first stage has lancets of *c.* 1300. Above everything is Perp, the two-light bell-openings, battlements, corner pinnacles and polygonal NW stair-turret. On the W side are two niches for statues, the statues still in position. Of around 1300 is also the heavy S porch with double-chamfered arch and diagonal buttresses. Above, under a late C15 niche and battlements, is a tiny two-light window. The Perp remodelling of the rest of the church was thoroughgoing, including the nave clerestory, the aisle window tracery, and ashlar battlements with pinnacles and good gargoyle heads. The clerestory windows match those of the chancel. Indications of an earlier church are in the masonry, in the relative narrowness of the nave, and the crease of a steeper nave roof on the tower.

The four-bay arcades have standard four-hollow piers. Good Somerset roofs in the nave and transepts, with tie-beam trusses and tracery each side of short kingposts. Wooden angels on the wall-plate. The stone angels of the nave display Passion emblems. On one shield, two naked figures may represent souls of patrons of the work. Some original colour to the nave eastern bay. In the N aisle a narrow C15 oak DOOR. The crossing was given a fan-vault in the early C16. Two squint passages from the transepts. In the chancel the sill course drops under the SEDILE and rises over an ogee-cusped PISCINA. A cinquefoil-cusped PISCINA in the S transept.

FURNISHINGS. FONT. C14, plain octagonal bowl, coved beneath. – REREDOS. Victorian. – PULPIT and READER'S DESK. Possibly made from an early C17 Hopton family pew. Rich ornament within the convention of arched panels and deep scrolled friezes. Swollen Ionic balusters. – HERALDRY. Robert Hopton †1638, father of the Royalist commander. Wooden, dated 1610, but the gadrooned frame and lush carving look late C17. – WALL PAINTING. A St Christopher of *c.* 1500, found and repainted in 1931. Of rustic quality, the saint very large, on red with scrolled texts. In the background a church and a windmill; fish around his feet. – SCULPTURE. C15 tabernacle head of the churchyard cross, with the Crucifixion, and narrow figures on each side. – ROYAL ARMS. Hanoverian. –

STAINED GLASS. Medieval fragments in the S transept (two angels), N aisle, and chancel windows. Good E window, *c.* 1910, by *A. J. Dix.* – MONUMENTS. C14 effigy of a priest in relief under a somewhat capriciously shaped ogee canopy. – Dawe family. Four good Lias floor slabs, †1694–1772, with double panels and heraldry. – Elizabeth Morris †1699. Alabaster and marble, to the wife of the diarist Dr Claver Morris, inscribed in Latin. Her bust above is of quality, one breast bared, hair trailing, under a curved cornice draped with flowers and fruit. – Hannam family, to 1759. Painted wood, with a small painted skull. – Philip Day †1763, by *John Ford Sen.* of Bath. Coloured marble, over a weeping woman slumped by an urn, the drapery particularly well formed.

In the churchyard, the CROSS with a pillar sundial is mostly of 1955. On the S side, a small Tudor-style SCHOOLROOM, 1851.

Behind the church is the MANOR HOUSE of the Hoptons. They had larger houses at Evercreech and Witham Friary, so the history here is obscure. The long, near-symmetrical W front has early C17 two-light ovolo-moulded mullion windows and a central storeyed porch. Four bays to the l., five to the r., each part with a single big eaves gable. At the rear are paired gables to each side, both inner ones containing staircases, a type of much grander houses. Does it represent here twin units, beginning with a hall and cross-wing at the S end? The inner l. stair-tower is clearly added. Between the gables a battlemented two-storey addition. (Inside are a C17 carved chimneypiece with painted overmantel, some ornamental plasterwork, and a good C17 staircase with square newels, pendants, and carved baluster panels. Panelled first-floor room.) On an early C19 stable, some reused corbels of birds and fish on scrolls, probably C17. The WALLED GARDEN has three curved recesses for fruit trees and a brick hexagonal SUMMERHOUSE with Georgian Gothic windows. The brick MANOR LODGE is Late Georgian, hip-roofed and two-storeyed, with a canted front and pointed windows. S of the church, the brick MANOR HOUSE INN has a similar Late Georgian S half with parapet and pointed windows. The PRIMARY SCHOOL, just W, occupies an ashlar-fronted Late Georgian house. Brick schoolroom of 1875 behind.

THE PRIORY, at the SW edge of the village, originated as the rectorial house built by Dean Gunthorpe of Wells about 1473. This was moated. The Leir family, parsons in succession from 1699 to 1917, enlarged and altered it, and in 1864–8 rebuilt the main S range and W cross-wing with Jacobean gables, Gothic windows, and much antiquarian heraldry. Old walls were kept, and a roof of *c.* 1700, but the medieval fragments in the E gable are inserted. Part of the parallel rear range is later C15, marked externally by mullioned windows and inside by a narrow first-floor room, traditionally called the chapel, with wind-braced roof. An early C19 service range runs N, with unmoulded mullions and a (reused) datestone of 1663 on the porch. Interiors largely of the 1860s, with a great deal of reused C17 woodwork.

The church in 1855 (according to Sir Stephen Glynne) had a 'curious post-Reformation screen ... having round arches and double doors' and the chancel 'wainscoting and stalls of the same date'. This, one must assume, is what lines the cross-passage and forms the overmantel of the E room dated 1630. On the drive, an early C19 hip-roofed GRANARY on an arcaded stone base. ABBEY FARM was the home farm. Farmhouse of about 1840, in Blue Lias, with a deep-eaved hipped roof, and BARN of 1739 with an early C19 horse-engine house attached to the front.

RINGWELL HOUSE, ¼ m. NW. Mid-C19 Italianate villa built for the Leir family. Probably by *Wilson & Fuller* of Bath.

WRAXALL, 1¼ m. W. HILL FARMHOUSE. The only remarkable thing about it is that it is dated 1671 and yet still possesses the gables and whole apparatus of the Jacobean style. It should be noted that both the fenestration and the gables are symmetrical.

DODINGTON

ALL SAINTS. Battlemented red sandstone W tower with a square NE stair-turret and Perp wave-moulded W doorway. The disproportionately tall bell-stage may be C17. Arched single bell-openings at different levels. Roughcast short nave and chancel with Late Perp flat-headed windows. The large N porch is contemporary, with two eroded shields above the arch, original roof and a STOUP like a miniature font. SE chapel of 1610, the E window Victorian. The nave roof with bosses (including the Dodington arms) and the shafted chancel arch are Perp. Jacobean round arch to the chapel, with parallel ribs on three shafts. – FONT. Retooled Perp, with quatrefoils. C17 COVER. – STAINED GLASS. E window, remnants of a C15 Crucifixion, expressive heads of Christ and Mary.

CHURCHYARD CROSS. C14–C15 shaft and base.

DODINGTON HALL. Later C15 manor house of the Dodingtons, enlarged in 1581. The porch and service end were rebuilt *c.* 1857 for the Fairfield estate. The picturesque N front is sober Victorian to the l. with a lateral chimney and storeyed porch, replacing one drawn by Buckler in 1840. The roughcast two-bay piece to the r., dated 1581, obscures the great hall. Elizabethan mullion-and-transom windows. The cross-passage runs beneath a minstrels' gallery at the E end of the great hall. It is all impressive, if very much rearranged in the C19. Roof of three tiers of ornamental wind-bracing between arch-braced principals, the sub-principals and their collars given a serpentine wave. Enough early timber survives to suggest that the detail is correct. The stone angel corbels may be brought in. The tall S windows are Elizabethan, but the N dais arch is Late Perp, shafted with foliage on round capitals. At the dais end is a wonderful stone Elizabethan fireplace, moved from an upper room. Armless man-beasts in leaf tunics, with lion feet, support Ionic capitals, and the overmantel has naked men (American Indians perhaps) supporting the cornice. There are also sphinxes and heraldry. The dais arch enters the Elizabethan addition, two ground-floor rooms with moulded and framed ceilings, the NW one with a plaster frieze of foliage scroll with fruit, fleurs-de-lys and heraldry (this mostly C20). Mid-C18 pine chimneypiece with female head and drapery. The NE room upstairs, with a slightly cambered framed ceiling, is suggested as a chapel. Simple early C17 SW staircase.

DODINGTON HOUSE. Former rectory, 1832, by *Richard Down*. Three-bay front with deep eaves and prettily patterned glazing.

CASTLE OF COMFORT INN, 1 m. S on the A39. First-floor ceiling plasterwork dated 1655, the Dodington arms on the overmantel.

GLEBE SHAFT ENGINE HOUSE, ½ m. SW. Ruinous Cornish engine house of 1820–1, built for a copper mine exploited from the late C18.

DONYATT

ST MARY. Of moderate size, but designed with some ambition. All Perp, in marlstone. W tower with set-back buttresses and battlements (missing pinnacles). NE stair-tower starting square, then octagonal to a ring of carved heads that carried pinnacles to a lost spirelet. Four-light W window with sub-arched ogee tracery, two-light bell-openings with transom and pierced baffles. One similar two-light window on the stage below. By the W door a reused carved-head stoup. Aisled nave with clerestory, chancel of equal height with single-bay side chapels, and S porch, all embattled except the N aisle. Flat-headed clerestory windows, late C15. The chancel is embellished with beasts and projects by one bay with tall three-light side windows and four-light E window, all transomed. Harmonious interior, let down only by the C19–C20 roofs. Arcades of four bays of standard four-hollow section (capitals differing slightly N and S). Similar chancel arch and side arches to the chapels but with linked capitals of roughly carved foliage. Panelled tower arch. – PULPIT. Early C17, with panels and paired, ill-understood Ionic colonnettes; cf. Winsham and Aller. – BENCH-ENDS. C16, incorporated into C19 pews. Plant forms, a horse, a plough and harrow; several initialled for Cuffe, beneath a glove. – TOWER SCREEN. Mostly C19, some C15 bits. – STAINED GLASS. E window, 1873. – MONUMENT. Bridget Campbell †1750. Marble, draped cherub head below.

DUNSTER ALMSHOUSES, E of the church. 1624. Two-storey range of six. Mullioned windows, Tudor-arched doorways. Beyond the river, the disused Chard railway is crossed on a rock-faced stone BRIDGE, 1865–6. Remains of the 1940 STOP-LINE along the railway: various types of pillbox, tank obstacles (cubes and posts), also concrete supports for removable 'gates' across the line and bridge. W of the church, Gothic former SCHOOL, 1871–2. Along the main road, thatched cottages in yellow marlstone. At the N end, the OLD RECTORY, thatched, with C18 casements but a C16 lateral chimney. The countryside to the W of Donyatt, around the significantly named Crock Street, was an important area for pottery production in the C18, with quantities exported to the American colonies.

SEA, 1 m. SSE. LONGCROFT, rendered and thatched, of long-house type, is C15–C16. Jointed crucks, chamfered framed ceiling and timber partition. To the SW, SEA MILLS FARM-HOUSE, the remnant of a mansion of the Walrond family. C16 triple-gabled marlstone front, the three- and four-light windows with arched lights. Corbels for thatched pentices. In line are an early C19 cottage and mill with an internal waterwheel of c. 1860. Opposite, a granary with C16 fragments, a rear doorway and window.

DOWLISH WAKE

3010

The village is almost all of the Moolham marlstone quarried nearby.

ST ANDREW. Nave, chancel and crossing tower but no transepts, an early plan (cf. Winsham). In 1861–2 *Benjamin Ferrey* reworked everything apart from the tower and NE (Speke) chapel of 1528. Steep roofs replaced low battlemented ones and the Dec tracery is all new. Tall plain tower, rectangular in plan, buttressed on the narrow sides, with battlements and hexagonal NE stair-tower. The lower part is datable to c. 1300 from the tower arches, double-chamfered W and E, single-chamfered to the sides. An off-centre lancet looks N into the chapel. Unusually elaborate niche on the S wall, canopied and C15. – FONT and PULPIT. 1862. Much-carved with serpentine shafts. A rough bowl FONT from West Dowlish church (demolished before 1575) is perhaps C11. Ham stone with shallow arcading terminated in triangles. – STAINED GLASS. Mostly 1862, by *Thomas Wells* of Pimlico. Chapel window, 1865, by *O'Connor*. Tower S, 1866. – MONUMENTS (Speke Chapel). Three effigies, recarved in the C19: Isabella Wake †1359, a thin female in a C14 recess with large open cusps ended in carved heads. – John Speke †1442 and wife, he in plate armour, on a tomb-chest with weepers that look all C19. – George Speke †1528. Brass from a table tomb. Small figure in armour: 'edificavit hanc partem ecclesie de novo'. – John Hanning Speke †1864. The explorer. A splendid sarcophagus of dark marble before an arch with African fauna, surmounted by his bust.

Just W, former SCHOOL, 1840, minimally Gothic. The adjacent MANOR HOUSE has parallel ranges. The short S one has C15–C16 buttresses, but the attached double-chamfered archway could be C14. The long N roof is late C15, arch-braced with tiered wind-braces, partly smoke-blackened. Back-to-back C16 moulded fireplaces. Moulded framed ceiling upstairs. Several mullion-windowed village houses, e.g. the DOWER HOUSE dated 1664, facing down the street. Further E, MILL HOUSE is an altered C15 hall house. Beyond the picturesque five-arch PACKHORSE BRIDGE, C17, a hip-roofed CIDER MILL with fragmentary C16 jointed cruck. NW of this, the OLD PARSONAGE, C16 with lateral chimney. HIGHER FARMHOUSE, S, unusually tall with end-wall attic windows, is late C16. Central back-to-back fireplaces and solid-tread stair.

OXENFORD HOUSE, 1 m. W. Early C17, extended, the end wall of 1727 a combination of up-to-date rustication and old-fashioned mullions. Panelled early C18 room. In the older range, an early C17 painted text.

MOOLHAM, 1 m. WNW. Source of the Ilminster marlstone. MOOLHAM MILL is three-storeyed, early C19. Waterwheel, 1851. The house is late C17, with early C18 addition.

DRAYTON

ST CATHERINE. Lias and Ham stone. Low embattled Perp W tower with higher NE stair-turret and two-light bell-openings. C19 openwork iron spirelet with large weathercock. The body of the church is Perp with battlemented N aisle, much reworked by *Maurice Davis*, 1855, and *Edmund Buckle*, 1896. Four-bay N arcade of four-centred arches on standard piers (four hollows). Wave-and-hollow-moulded tower arch; panelled chancel arch with ogee niches facing one another. Framed aisle ceiling with bosses, sub-panelled over the altar. – FONT. C12 bulbous bowl ringed at the rim and base. – FURNISHINGS. An unusual C19–C20 selection connected with the Cely-Trevilians of Midelney. High-class Arts and Crafts woodwork of 1897, made by *Charles Trask* (cf. Norton-sub-Hamdon), perhaps designed by *Henry Wilson*. Arcaded PULPIT on swollen columns, the angles with vivid winged Evangelist symbols, LECTERN on a slender bulbous shaft, and remarkable TOWER SCREEN with tracery and frieze of plant forms, apparently bluebells. By an unknown hand, the panelled STALLS, *c.* 1910, and ORGAN CASE, 1915, with little obelisks. Chancel and Lady Chapel fittings by *Martin Travers* in his thin stage-decoration manner, 1935–7: ROOD or Crucifix on an iron bar (supporting figures in the arch niches, 1947) and chancel CHANDELIER. Better, the iron NE SCREEN and chancel RAILS. – STAINED GLASS. E window, 1894, by *Ward & Hughes*. NE, 1936, by *Travers*, Virgin and C20 scenes on clear ground. N window, 1976, by *Brian*

Thomas, in gold, blue and grey, a Baroque palette. – MONU-
MENTS. John Trevillian †1749. Curved, over heraldry.

CHURCHYARD CROSS. C14 tapered shaft with an elongated figure under an ogee canopy: St Michael, with sword raised, standing on a dragon. Two tiny donor figures beneath. C17 ball finial.

DRAYTON COURT, w of the church, was the vicarage. Late Georgian, with Ham stone quoins and windows. Pedimented end-wall doorway. Down School Street, DRAYTON MANOR, Georgian brick, refronted in the early C19 with parapet and ungainly stone window heads. E of the church, the DRAYTON ARMS, hip-roofed, *c*. 1840, and DUCK COTTAGE, thatched, with wooden mullion-and-transom windows. BRICK HOUSE is emphatically brick. Late Georgian, three-storeyed, with a pedimented stone doorcase. The l. wing encases a C15 hall. PALFREYS opposite has C16 jointed crucks and a framed ceiling. THE OLD COURTHOUSE is late C17 with mullioned windows regularly arranged under drip-courses. THE RED HOUSE, brick, dated 1737, still has mullioned windows.

MIDELNEY MANOR, 1 m. s. Low in the moor beyond the River Isle, the buildings line the E side of the lane without pomp. The house is Elizabethan, built by two brothers Trevilian, reputedly one half for each. The halves were apparently unconnected inside until 1926, but the story may be fanciful as the r. half has the polite rooms, the l. the kitchens. Facing over a shallow forecourt between cross-wings, the Lias front has mullion windows with hoodmoulds, gabled dormers to the l. half only, and a door in each corner. The roadside gable-ends are faced in Ham stone. Alterations datable to 1731 (rainwater head) include a suite with staircase and three fielded-panelled rooms in the r. half, the rooms retaining C16 framed ceilings and fireplaces. In one, a comic overmantel shows Sunday hunting watched by a devil in churchwarden's garb. Restored when the family returned from Midelney Place (Curry Rivel) in 1926, by *H. Fletcher*. Behind the l. house a rare early C18 FALCONRY MEWS, small, brick, with stone oval openings. Similar brick to the L-plan C18 COACHHOUSE.

DULVERTON

Market town in the Barle valley, the administrative centre for Exmoor. It had a cloth industry into the C19 and became a centre for hunting and fishing after the railway reached Brushford in 1873.

ALL SAINTS. Except for the W tower, rebuilt in 1852–5 by *Edward Ashworth* of Exeter. Plain tower with possibly C13 lower stage: diagonal buttresses and single-chamfered W doorway. C15 top stage with paired lancet bell-lights and battlements. Square NE stair-turret. The rest is a reasonable essay in the local Perp, based on the predecessor, which had similar tracery and battlements. Triple-gabled E end. Broad interior with three roofs on six-bay arcades. – SCREENS. 1902 and later. – ROYAL ARMS. 1774. – STAINED GLASS. E window, 1864. Startlingly coloured Crucifixion. MONUMENTS. Rev. Robert Kingsford †1700. Draped cartouche with cherubs, brightly painted. – Humphrey Sydenham †1757. Corniced, on scroll-footed pilasters. The same hand made the St Barbe monument at Ashington, which Sydenham erected.

LYCHGATE, 1907. Good Arts and Crafts carved oak.

ST STANISLAUS (R.C.), High Street. 1955, by *Albert Richardson*, then President of the RIBA, a friend of Mrs Herbert of Pixton Park (*see* below). Small and brick with a little rose window at each end. Flat-roofed deep-eaved porch. Simple interior. – ROOD. By *Eric Gill*. – STAINED GLASS. Rose windows by *Buckfast Abbey*. Windows on the l. by *Chinks Grylls*, 1980s. The third contains an earlier panel, of the Virgin Mary, by *Evie Hone*.

EXMOOR HOUSE, Bridge Street. Exmoor National Park Offices. The workhouse of 1855, by *Ashworth*, in a lovely riverside site, is smaller and much less grim than normal. Two-storeyed with a square cupola, and a single wing behind.

SCHOOLS, Fisher's Mead. The Middle School, 1956–8, was the smallest of the county secondary schools. Curtain-walled to the s with a gabled centre. Also by *Somerset County Architects* the hip-roofed PRIMARY SCHOOL, 1999. Timber-framed NURSERY by *Louise Crossman*, 2004–5, with a sedum roof.

EXMOOR MEDICAL CENTRE, Fisher's Mead. 2009 by *Guy Greenfield* of London. One of the best modern buildings of the region. The green copper roof floating above white curved wall suggests (in different materials) Le Corbusier at Ronchamp, and Coventry Cathedral is echoed in the staggered side wall with glazing recessed between the piers. Glass-fronted two-storey waiting room on the other side.

PERAMBULATION. Dulverton is a pretty little town, with the churchyard on the slope above the main street. The architecture is homely, stucco, roughcast and stone with some brick, little of before 1700. The market place runs down from Bank Square by the churchyard to Fore Street. On BANK SQUARE, BANK CHAMBERS, stuccoed, C19, with first-floor pilasters. The LION HOTEL, also stuccoed, Late Georgian, was given an over-large half-timbered gable *c.* 1900. FORE STREET still feels like a market square, the TOWN HALL of 1866 replacing a market house of 1760. Plain seven-bay stone front with arched ground-floor openings. It was theatrically improved in 1927 by *Albert Richardson*. He added a broad stone arch on the pavement carrying steps rising from both sides to a short bridge across to the first-floor entrance, with a good neo-Regency wrought-iron porch. Fore Street curves s to the foot of High Street, opposite the former LAMB HOTEL. Plain three-storeyed, stuccoed, mid-C19. Two-storey houses run w towards the bridge. On the s, set back, the R.C. church (*see* above). Down CHAPEL STREET, a former CRÊPE MILL, a fine rational early C19 design (a date of 1814 is mentioned). Five broad bays of windows recessed between stone piers, under a hipped roof. The windows are six-light casements in the outer bays, four-light in the middle three, with plain plaster between the levels. Just beyond is the CONGREGATIONAL CHURCH of 1831, stuccoed with three front lancets. Three-sided gallery inside. BRIDGE STREET continues High Street to the river, past the drive to Exmoor House (*see* above). BARLE BRIDGE is medieval, repaired in 1684, widened in 1816–19 by *John Stone*. Five arches.

Returning to the foot of Fore Street, HIGH STREET runs E behind the market place. Off to the S, THE GREENWAY, a long five-bay hip-roofed house of *c.* 1800, incorporating an older house (lateral chimney on the back). SYDENHAM HOUSE, altered and part of a terraced row, has a massive lateral chimney marking a C16 house of the Sydenhams. CHURCH LANE returns to the church past a terrace of five whitewashed Late Georgian cottages, with straight hoods on brackets over the doorways. From the churchyard, LADY STREET runs N past No. 20, a former police station of 1902, the top-floor courtroom marked by church-like windows, and the former BIBLE CHRISTIAN CHAPEL, red and white brick, 1902, by *S. Deering* of Tiverton.

VICARAGE HILL, the continuation of High Street, passes WRENEATON, 1889, well-detailed in brick and half-timber with Ham stone-mullioned windows, some removed for a car showroom. Further out, WOODLANDS and WOODLIVING, two long C16 houses backing on to Jury Road, each with three lateral chimneys. Woodliving has jointed crucks and plank partitions. Further on, Amory Road leads down to the schools and medical centre (*see* above).

PIXTON PARK, 1 m. SE. Classical villa of some size, built in 1803–5 by the otherwise unknown *Hassell* of Exeter for Lord Porchester, later 2nd Earl of Carnarvon, who had married the Acland heiress. Identical N and S fronts of five bays and three storeys. Stuccoed with ashlar giant Ionic pilasters on the upper floors, at the outer angles and the angles of the pedimented three-bay centre. The ground floors have niches between the three centre windows. Enlarged in 1870, probably by *T. H. Wyatt*, with a single-storey top-lit hall along the E side (replacing a *porte cochère*) and service buildings beyond. A mansard-roofed piece was added on the other side, and the staircase was moved from a central hall to the principal N room, and the two connected by a triple arcade. Otherwise the interiors are of 1803–5, with cornices and panelled mahogany doors. Large pedimented STABLE COURT with a pyramid-roofed lantern. To the NE, the slate-hung JURY LODGES, each with a lunette over an arched recess in the end gable, may be of the 1830s.

NORTHMOOR, 1 m. NW. Large and rambling stone house begun in 1859 by John Locke who is said to have added a piece with every new child (there were eight). Ultimately shapeless. Bought by Sir Frederick Wills, the tobacco tycoon, for whom estate buildings were added by *Frank Wills*, notably KENNEL FARM, 1907, to the E.

HIGHERCOMBE, 2 m. N. A hunting lodge built on to an existing farmhouse, probably after 1785 for Sir Thomas Dyke Acland. Three bays with pedimented centre and stone quoins. Subsequently almost entirely slate-hung, including the chimneys.

HOLLAM, ½ m. NE. Transformation of a Victorian gabled mansion of the 1860s to a Neo-Georgian five-bay house with veranda between lower hip-roofed wings. Perhaps by *Oswald Milne*, who made plans in 1954 for curtailment more drastic than what was ultimately done.

IRON AGE CAMPS. There are three defended enclosures above the River Barle: OLDBERRY CASTLE across the river to the W of Dulverton and BREWERS CASTLE and MOUNSEY CASTLE on opposite sides, 2 m. NW. Oldberry Castle is much damaged by ploughing. The embankments of the other two are small and not at all eleborate.

COMBE. *See* Brushford.

TARR STEPS. *See* p. 606.

DUNSTER

The little town nestling between the Castle Tor and Grabbist Hill is unsurpassed in Somerset among towns of its size. The view as one enters the High Street from the N is perfect, a wide market place descending past the polygonal Yarn Market straight towards the wooded hill crowned by the red stone castle. Behind one's back is Conygar Hill with its tower. The town is Norman, founded with the castle and priory, called a borough by 1197, its history tied up for six hundred years with the Luttrell family of the Castle.

ST GEORGE. The Benedictine priory of Dunster began as a cell of Bath. Founded by William de Mohun before 1100, it was not organized into a priory until around 1330, when a prior and four monks are mentioned. The Norman church was substantial, although little survives. Its nave and crossing were on the footprint of the present church, as shown by a heavily restored W portal and the W face of the crossing piers. The portal is of two orders, only one column being original. The face of each crossing pier is stepped, with a tall angle shaft. One capital is scalloped, the other has a volute and a strange figure with large head and floating legs.* Also at the adjacent end of the S arcade is a Norman chamfered pier and base. Next in date comes the C13 chancel, although all the detail, especially the three big stepped E lancets, is of 1875–7 by *G. E.*

---

* The shafts are far apart for an arch but Buckler drew one in 1842, roll-moulded, probably his invention as it is otherwise unmentioned.

Street, based on evidence found. Also C13 the top of the eastern archway in the s transept (*see* below).

The big cruciform red sandstone church is otherwise Perp of *c*. 1450–1500. The date of rebuilding the crossing tower is known, as the contract of 1443 survives between the parishioners (not the monks) and *John Marys* of Stogursey. It stipulates that the tower up to its 'batylment and pynacles', with three 'french botras' (buttresses) and 'gargylles', should be put up in three years. For some windows a 'patern' (i.e. design) made by the 'advyce of *Richard Pope*, Fre Mason' is mentioned. The tower is without the exuberant ornament of so many Somerset towers but striking in its bulk and strength. The buttresses are diagonal, with pronounced offsets. A square NW stair-turret rises a little higher than the battlements. Three stages of two-light openings, the bell-openings larger, with a transom.

The s aisle was finished just before 1500, the N aisle just after. The w front has, above the Norman doorway, a four-light window with a transom and that refined tracery of *c*. 1500 that emanated from Cleeve Abbey, with little quatrefoils in the spandrels of ogee-headed lights. The s aisle, as the show side, has ashlar battlements and a rood-stair turret. This must correspond to the rood screen, i.e. after 1498. Embattled s porch with a straight-sided doorhead, repeated for the doorway within and a w doorway on the N transept. The battlements of the sw corner are inscribed 'God Save the king 1624'. The N aisle starts further E because of the former priory buildings (*see* p. 269). Transepts of even size, the s transept embellished, like the aisle, with buttresses and pinnacles. Also a niche each side of the big transomed four-light s window.

The s arcade inside is of six bays; the N arcade has only four. The piers have the standard four-hollow section with polygonal capitals to the shafts, but the E responds have bands of carved foliage instead. Strong Perp crossing piers with broad ogee and hollow mouldings, and moulded banded capitals with fleurons (similar to the tower arch at Minehead). The arch from the s transept to the SE chapel is C13, shown by the roll mouldings and carved heads between the capitals. The shafts bend outward like hoses to allow for an inexplicably wider arch. If this is Late Perp adjustment it is entirely without Late Perp detail. Chancel chapels of two bays with four-centred arches on piers with double-ogee mouldings and banded capitals. The SE chapel is the Luttrell Chapel. The chancel retains the separation of a monastic choir and indeed was separately owned by the Luttrells until 1990. Here *Street* is most apparent, replacing a Perp E window with his great shafted lancets. SEDILIA and PISCINA in similar style. On the s side a crocketed ogee TOMB-RECESS of *c*. 1330, much restored, with an effigy of a lady (*see* p. 269). The pointed arch has big cinquefoil open cusping, on each cusp a head. Flanking piers with crocketed finials. On the N, a much-restored later C15 TOMB in the position of a founder's tomb (with earlier effigies – *see* p. 269). Tomb-chest with shields in quatrefoils under canopy with complicated cusping, angels on the two major points. Big leaves in the spandrels and an ornate pierced cresting. Behind is a small chapel with medieval floor TILES, de Clare and Beauchamp heraldry prominent.

Street's restoration was thorough and expensive, costing around £11,000. He furnished the crossing and the two bays between crossing and screen as a chancel, with handsome STALLS with fleur-de-lys finials and ogee-arcaded frontal, parclose SCREENS, and an encaustic TILE PAVEMENT. The paving is even richer in the private Luttrell parts, the choir and SE chapel. It was for the choir that *Clayton & Bell* made the painted triptych REREDOS now in the chancel, a notable piece by any standards, bright with gold leaf, Italian Late Gothic in style, but framed without Gothic fancy. The arched top follows the starburst behind the resurrected Christ. By *Street* also the FURNISHINGS of the choir, the stone nave PULPIT, and the PEWS, these with bench-ends by *Harry Hems* copied from medieval examples. Street also restored the late medieval wagon roofs with good bosses, including carved heads. The nave roof is impressively wide. The crossing tower and S aisle have framed ceilings.

OTHER FURNISHINGS. FONT. Perp, octagonal, with quatrefoils containing alternate shields and rosettes, the shields with Passion implements and the Five Wounds. Tall Victorian openwork COVER. Also a damaged C12 FONT with a raised ring. – SCREEN. Erected to delineate the chancel of the parish church, the outcome of a quarrel between monastery and town in 1498. A splendid specimen, worthy of the best in Devon: 54 ft (16.5 metres) long, right across the nave and aisles from the S rood stair. Fourteen four-light sections each subdivided into two, with delicate cusped ogee lights and much cusping in the tracery heads. This is typical of the workshop responsible for screens at Carhampton, Minehead, Timberscombe, etc.; indeed the leaf scroll that outlines each section is its signature. The loft is complete with ribbed and panelled coving and layers of finely carved cornices. Dado panels of blind two-light tracery under crocketed finials. – SCREEN to SE chapel. Early C15, and very good. 3–4–3 lights, not gathered but each squareheaded light enclosing delicate two-light tracery with a crocketed finial, over a pair of quatrefoils. Uncommonly broad frieze of beautifully carved vine-trail, and a band of pierced work over the dado. Dado panels similar to the main screen. – SCREEN to NE chapel. Made of reused pieces, a beam with a broad frieze of vine-trail, and the tracery of the square-headed openings. – SCULPTURE (NE chapel). C15 cross-head with relief Virgin and Child and kneeling donor. – PULPIT (N transept). Plain C17–C18. – ROYAL ARMS. 1660. – CANDELABRA. 1740, by *Francis Billo* of Bristol. Three-tiered, hanging from very big ornamental ironwork. – PAINTING. The Brazen Serpent, by *Sir James Thornhill*, altar painting of the chapel he added to the castle in 1723 (*see* p. 271). – CHESTS. Three, one dug-out *c.* 1150, one *c.* 1250 and a third with sloping desk top *c.* 1450.

– STAINED GLASS. By *Clayton & Bell*, 1876, the SE, SW and first S windows, and the E window, this in an earlier Gothic style to accord with Street's lancets. – MONUMENTS. Lady wearing a wimple (chancel S recess), *c.* 1320, effigy in Ham stone. – Adam de Cheddar, prior *c.* 1345–55 (S transept). Cross-slab with foliated cross. – Damaged alabaster effigies of a knight and lady, probably Sir Hugh Luttrell †1428 and wife †1435 (chancel N). – Lady Elizabeth Luttrell †1493 (SE chapel). Large incised slab of white alabaster, depicted with angels at her pillow. – John Wyther †1497 and wife (nave W). Brass, 2-in. (51-cm.) figures and inscription in English. – Thomas Luttrell †1571 and George Luttrell †1629 (SE chapel). Very large Jacobean monument set up in 1613 by George Luttrell after the death of his wife. Not of special skill or elaboration but notable for its scale and use of Watchet alabaster. It commemorates his parents, his wife and himself. As the only one living, he kneels; the others are recumbent. The whole is treated as one theatrical composition, under a heavy cornice supported by an Ionic column on each corner and a large central bracket. Freestanding heraldry on top. On the tomb-chest two scrolled plaques, George's left blank. – Anne Luttrell †1731 (SE chapel). By *Michael Sidnell* of Bristol. Baroque cartouche squarely in an Ionic aedicule.

Base of a large C15 CHURCHYARD CROSS.

PRIORY BUILDINGS. On the N side of the church. The wall abutting the N transept has the beginnings of a plinth, perhaps of the cloister, but very little remains – no indication of chapter house, refectory or dormitory. However, the OLD PRIORY, on the N side of the blank part of the nave extending beyond the W end, may have been the prior's house. It is L-shaped, with mostly C17–C18 oak-mullioned windows, but both ranges are late medieval, the E–W one presumably pre-dating the N aisle of *c.* 1503. This range has a good wind-braced six-bay roof of arch-braced trusses, at least three bays over the hall. Smoke-blackening found above the plaster indicates that the roof pre-dates the handsome late C15 fireplace on the ground-floor S wall. This has an unusual arched head and traceried spandrels with quatrefoils. Next to it a three-light window with cinquefoil-cusped ogee lights. The window should extend upward if it lit a full-height hall that was later floored over, but slate-hanging hides any external sign. The range at right angles is altered. The tall brick lateral chimney is inserted, as also the wooden cross-window in the S gable. Remains of large medieval arch-braced trusses. The lovely sequence of walled GARDENS N and E of the church dates from when the house became a Luttrell farmhouse. The lane called Priory Green crosses the former farmyard under two early C19 red sandstone arches to pass between the monastic dovecote and barn. The DOVECOTE is circular with a small late medieval pointed oak doorway. A potence or revolving ladder to collect from the nesting boxes survives inside. The TITHE BARN post-dates the priory, perhaps C16 with an C18–C19 roof. Restored as a community hall in 2006–7 by *Chris Mitchell* of Williton. In Conduit Lane, on the way up Grabbist Hill, is ST LEONARD'S WELL. The plain stone chamber is probably C16, but the supply for the priory came from here.

DUNSTER CASTLE (National Trust). Owned by the de Mohuns until 1376, when it was sold to the Luttrells. They remained owners until 1976. The Mohun castle, on the tor above the present house, was well enough defended in 1138 for King Stephen to be deterred from attack by its towers, walls, rampart and outworks. In decay when Leland saw it in 1542, the upper castle was finally levelled as a bowling green in 1727. The surviving CASTLE is the lower ward below to the N, high above the town and the River Avill. This was defended by a curtain wall with rounded towers facing W and N, a twin-towered gatehouse facing NE, and a length facing SE with two D-plan towers and a small rounded one between. Against this side were probably the C13 keep, great hall and kitchen, replaced by the present house. The gatehouse and much else was rebuilt in the mid C13 by Reynold de Mohun. His GATEWAY survives between the bases of drum towers. Big double-chamfered archway, the segmental-pointed head almost straight-sided. The great doors with iron bands are probably early C15. The r. tower was partly incorporated in a grand new GATEHOUSE built at right angles in 1419–21. This is a three-storey battlemented oblong with a polygonal SE turret. The tunnel-vaulted throughway has finely moulded arches. The mullion-and-transom windows, hardly defensive, are early C16 insertions, of the local type with quatrefoil spandrels. In 1764–5 the gatehouse was remodelled when the courtyard was raised by 18 ft (5.5 metres). The battlements were made even and the courtyard end remodelled with polygonal towers, one standing on

Dunster Castle, before alteration.
Watercolour by J. Buckler, 1839

the base of the C13 gateway tower. The towers frame a reused early C16 arched doorway with oak door. This opens into the top floor, remodelled as the Tenants' Hall in 1871–2. Previously two rooms, as shown by two C15 fireplaces.

The living quarters of the medieval castle, against the SE curtain of the lower ward, are the basis of the present house. Reconstructed for George Luttrell who inherited in 1571. Some work was done before the major rebuilding by *William Arnold*, the architect of Wadham College, Oxford, and probably of Montacute. Arnold's contract in 1617 was to supply plans and elevations and oversee the work of a house 'to be sett up and built within the castle of Dunster'. Remodelled again in 1867–72 by *Anthony Salvin*, the present house is Victorianized Jacobean. But the outline of both towers of the SE front is medieval, the larger r. tower perhaps the keep or the new tower mentioned in 1284, and portions of chamfered plinth are probably C13. *Arnold*'s house was well recorded and can be envisaged fairly easily. Its courtyard front was to the E-plan favoured by Elizabethan designers, embattled, with three taller embattled accents: the central porch-tower and stair-turrets in the angles to the two-bay outer wings. The windows were transomed, mostly two-light, some three-light, and ornament was confined to the doorway. The stair-turrets had chamfered inner angles, and all the angles were marked with buff ashlar quoins. Above the vertiginous SE slope the rear had an even row of battlements between rounded outer towers, the r. tower containing the main staircase. There was little of the virtuosity shown at Montacute. The rounded central turret was replaced in 1723 by a Baroque chapel by *Sir James Thornhill*, shown in C18 views gleaming white, in Portland stone, against the red castle.

The present variety derives from *Salvin*, who unbalanced the symmetries with typically booming Victorian statements. He added a massive square 'keep' for the kitchen and service rooms, obscuring the outer l. wing and stair-tower, and altered the parapets of the centre to achieve a raking ascent to the r. stair-tower. On the opposite side he added a four-storey tower on the site of Thornhill's chapel. Estimated at £35,000, Salvin's scheme was cut down by nearly £10,000, without apparent ill effect, save for a certain baldness in the porch-tower. And, if coarse from close up, Salvin's piled-up centrepiece on the other side makes picturesque sense from a distance.

The porch opens to an OUTER HALL created by *Salvin*. neo-Jacobean plaster ceiling in panels, coved uncomfortably on two sides. Twin archways open to the much lower INNER HALL, *Arnold*'s Great Hall. The thin-rib ceiling with pendants is genuine. Massive fireplace by Salvin under a heraldic panel dated 1589. While little is left of Arnold's interiors, Salvin happily left untouched most of the alterations made by Col. Francis Luttrell after he came of age and married profitably in 1680. These are the glory of the castle. It is suggested that the

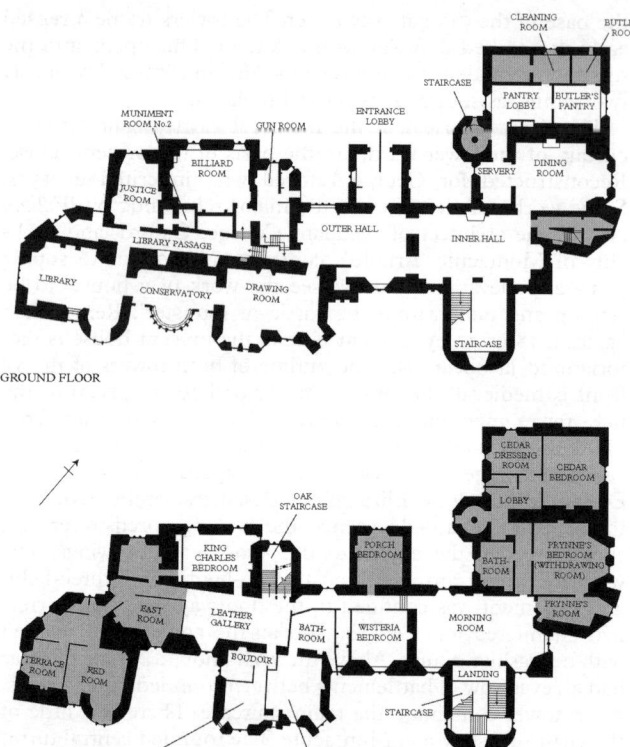

Dunster Castle.
Ground-floor and first-floor plans

architect *William Winde* was involved, and craftsmen associated with him. The type of decoration at Dunster, prefigured at Ham House, London, in 1637–8, appears in the West Country at Forde Abbey in the 1650s, and becomes general after the Restoration, e.g. at Eltham Lodge, London, *c.* 1665, Sudbury, Derbys., 1675, and Belton, Lincs., 1685–8. The plasterwork here is attributed to *Edward Goudge*, who worked for Winde at Belton. Rich three-dimensional plaster appears in Devon in 1680 at the Exeter Custom House, the work of *John Abbott Jun.*, who may have worked at several North Devon houses. Similar work is found in Somerset, at Halswell House, 1689, Nettlecombe Court, 1704, and Stockland Lovell (Fiddington). But the lack of concordant detail prevents the Dunster ceilings being attributed to a Devon or Somerset craftsman.

The DINING ROOM, in the wing obscured by Salvin's kitchen tower, was given large-field panelling and one of the most gorgeous plaster ceilings in SW England. A square with half-round aprons is bordered in a rope of leaves, fruit and flowers of miraculous artistry. Around it are concave-sided panels with Liliputian figures, barely visible in rich acanthus foliage, and in square corner panels cherubs are variously occupied in roundels. In four semicircles around the edge are scrolls inscribed 'Anno Dommini Christi MDCLXXXI'. Frieze of festoons and foliage with heraldry. Good marble chimneypiece with consoles. The only window, at one end, was Venetian, removed by Salvin. Plasterwork of equal richness in the panelled SERVERY in the former stair-tower. Coved cornice of scallop shells and plant sprays. Centre panel with a three-dimensional winged cherubs' heads in the corners and a border of lush festoons dropping from lion masks. Of the same date is the spacious STAIRCASE in the rounded eastern tower of the SE front, reached through two of Salvin's arches from the inner hall. The type of staircase – square with an open well – and the type of carving, continuous instead of balusters, appears in England at Ham House. The staircase here is a virtuoso piece probably by *Edward Pearce* who did the similar staircase at Sudbury Hall, Derbys. Each of the four rails is a single piece of elm 9 in. (23 cm.) thick, carved with an intense rolling scroll of acanthus and flowers among which cherubs with their dogs hunt stags and foxes. The top landing has a military trophy and tiny cannons, and on the back an eagle between lion and unicorn. Elsewhere is a collection of coins carved with such precision as to identify a Charles II shilling issued in 1683–4. Fruit and flowers in the panels of the newels, which are topped with vases of carved flowers, as appear at Ham House, Eltham and Sudbury. The ceiling again is wonderfully done. A curved-ended rectangular panel is bordered with splendid acanthus scrolled around a rope of flowers, and there scallop shells nest amid roses in the end panels, and tiny hunters appear amid acanthus scroll in the side strips.

Twin Neoclassical doorways on the landing, with hunting-trophy plaques in fluted friezes, are contemporary with the MORNING ROOM over the Inner Hall, created in 1772–3. Good marble chimneypiece with flutings inlaid in yellow. The oak leaves and feathers commemorate Charles II (*see* below). Of similar date the short corridor, NE, and PRYNNE'S BEDROOM, with Rococo ceiling ornament. Victorian bedrooms over the Outer Hall and in Salvin's drawing-room tower, the Wisteria Room with a reused Adam-style wooden chimneypiece. To the SW, the LEATHER GALLERY remains from a Long Gallery which probably extended to the end. Altered in 1704 and by Salvin, it lacks shape. The extraordinary WALL HANGINGS brought in after 1704 illustrate the story of Antony and Cleopatra in brightly coloured leather. The costumes are later C17, the backgrounds exotic Baroque. The figures look Spanish or Portuguese but the hangings are suggested as Dutch. KING CHARLES' BEDROOM in the NW pavilion, over the former kitchen, was where the future Charles II slept in

1645. Plaster overmantel of 1620, moved from elsewhere, of the type known from George Luttrell's alterations to Court House, East Quantoxhead (q.v.), and the Luttrell Arms in Dunster (*see* p. 276). Strapwork, fruit, putti and naked caryatids around a small Judgment of Paris.

In the adjoining stair-turret, the OAK STAIRCASE is mostly Georgian (C17 balusters to the attic flights). It descends to the former kitchen, with a huge elliptical-arched fireplace. *Salvin* made it a BILLIARD ROOM, with woodwork of the 1680s discarded from the Inner Hall. Two large Corinthian columns with entablatures from the triple-arched screen to the stairway, and the two scroll-pedimented Baroque doorways. A passage leads to the LIBRARY by *Salvin*, partly within the SW medieval tower. Jacobean-cum-Rococo ceiling plasterwork, the pink frieze and dark marble chimneypiece surprisingly concordant with the blue embossed wallpaper patterned with hoopoes. A CONSERVATORY by *Salvin* with a *Minton* tile pavement links the SW tower to Salvin's central tower. Here the large DRAWING ROOM, again Jacobean, going Rococo in the plasterwork, but the walls were given Neo-Georgian panels in the 1930s. The fine chimneypiece is surely of the 1770s, white marble with red flutings and jasper-ware medallions. Two levels of basement SERVICE ROOMS run back from under the stair hall to the C13 gateway, arranged by *Salvin*, excavating behind the medieval wall. The octagonal turret on his kitchen tower gives access from the basement kitchen to the dining room.

Below the gatehouse is one of the best surviving early STABLES in Britain, built just after 1680. Two large ranges at right angles with hipped roofs and wooden cross-windows. The seven-bay front has little hipped dormers breaking the eaves and a lateral chimney. A passage runs through to the rear range, and both ranges have original stalls and cobbled floors, the stalls divided by stout posts with moulded finials. Below the stables is the HOME FARM. Two yards, with a brick hip-roofed GRANARY and late C19 KENNELS in the first. The second has a converted hip-roofed HAY BARN on square piers, and a LINHAY with round piers attached to an altered FARMHOUSE dated 1749. In the adjacent garden, a BEE WALL with two levels of recesses.

GARDENS. The forecourt is the lower ward as levelled in 1765, burying the back of the rounded TOWER on the N. The tor is shown bare in Buck's view of 1733 with a low brick wall around the new bowling green and octagonal brick SUMMERHOUSE of 1727. Now planted, the bowling green remains with the summerhouse. This has one reused C15 two-light window (other windows are blocked), a moulded oak doorway, and a tall wrought-iron weather vane. Beneath the lawn, a brick-vaulted RESERVOIR of 1870. The gardens below the castle were laid out by Henry Fownes (Luttrell) who married Margaret Luttrell in 1747. Two ornamental bridges of 1775 cross the river. The LAWNS BRIDGE is triple-arched with rockwork trim and a Palladian pedimental centrepiece. The LOVERS' BRIDGE

Dunster, Yarn Market.
Engraving, 1892

is more picturesque, undulating, with two single arches separated by an island. Much rockwork ornament. The painter *Richard Phelps* probably designed both, and also the simple Gothic of the CASTLE MILL and GATEWAY, 1779–82. The mill is roughcast with quatrefoils and pointed windows in the cross-wings, the gateway pointed under a kind of bellcote. Two overshot waterwheels on the mill, served by a long leat behind. Over the river, to the S, a DEER PARK created in 1755, and to the E, THE LAWNS, an early C20 polo-ground.

CONYGAR TOWER, Conygar Hill. Though distant from the castle, this is part of the later C18 landscape improvements, built in 1775 for Henry Fownes Luttrell by *Richard Phelps*. It is tall, circular, embattled, and has pointed windows to each of the three stages. Nothing remains of floors within. More than the castle it is the beacon of Dunster for miles around. On the approach from the W are THE ARCHES, a Gothic screen wall with archway and ruined towers, by *Phelps*.

PERAMBULATION

The HIGH STREET, so well aligned on the castle but related so oddly to the incoming roads, may be deliberate medieval planning, replacing an earlier settlement along West Street. The street descends and narrows from a wide N end, wide enough for the octagonal YARN MARKET, a market cross built by

George Luttrell in 1609 and repaired in 1647 after Civil War damage. The largest such structure in Somerset, it has a central stone core radiating strong beams to support the octagonal slated roof ringed by gabled dormers. Beneath them a pentice runs all around, shading the square-headed openings. Pentices curiously are a feature of Dunster's High Street shops and houses up to the late C19.

The LUTTRELL ARMS at the N end is by far the most important house, the Dunster residence of the abbots of Cleeve, then a Luttrell property, and the Ship Inn by 1651. Three-storey, three-bay red sandstone front with windows and eaves cornice probably of 1777. But the storeyed porch is early C16 with a moulded Tudor-arched doorway and two-light flat-headed window above. The inner doorway looks slightly earlier, pointed in a square-headed frame with spandrel ornament. Lower three-storey Late Georgian addition to the N, curving into Dunster Steep. The front range was altered inside by George Luttrell after 1622. Panelled partition to the parlour, which has C17 plasterwork, a fruit-and-flower frieze and ornament in each ceiling panel. Upstairs a remarkable overmantel showing the death of Actaeon, rather dwarfed by the strapwork oval surrounded by typical cherubs and fruit. Conventionally dressed female caryatids part a skirt to display a leg.* Cresting of lions with royal heraldry and obelisks, flanking a gabled frame to a male demi-figure, with hands on the cornice; perhaps Luttrell himself. Another overmantel has heraldry from Luttrell's marriage of 1622. The early C19 stair is lit by an early C18 window. Two rear wings, the NE one of *c.* 1500 has exceptionally for Somerset a highly decorated oak S front in two storeys. Stone E end wall. On the ground floor two pairs of long two-light windows with cusped-headed lights and spandrels. Between the floors is panelling similar to that of church screens, twice five panels with crocketed finials over tracery. The top floor again has twice two pairs of cusped-headed lights, save that the four outer ones are blank. One panel retains the tracery of the middle tier. The ground floor has heavy moulded beams and deep-chamfered joists. Upstairs, a good roof of moulded arch-braced trusses with two tiers of big cusped wind-braces.

High Street is lined with rendered houses, structurally often older within, medieval to C17. Opposite the Luttrell Arms, the YARN MARKET HOTEL occupies two buildings, No. 33 Victorian and twin-gabled, No. 31 apparently Late Georgian, three-storeyed, but with C16–C17 beams. Nos. 25–29, three-storeyed but much higher, are Early Victorian. Nos. 19–23 are C17, two-storeyed, as is No. 15, the Post Office, on the far side of the MEMORIAL HALL of 1921. No. 13, with irregularly spaced Late Georgian sashes, is partly C16. On the E side the upper end is Georgian to Victorian with nicely varied roof-lines. Nos. 26–28, dated 1825, were built as the butchers' shambles.

---

*The same caryatids appear at No. 18 Fore Street, Taunton.

No. 16 has a later C17 oak doorway outlined in running scroll.
Nos. 12–14, long and low, are earlier than the oak mullions
suggest – see the massive C15–C16 pointed oak doorway. No. 6
is charmingly small, with C17 oak mullions. Opposite, the
DUNSTER CASTLE HOTEL has a Georgian front of close-
spaced curved-headed sash windows, seven above, larger
windows below, and an open-pediment door hood. No. 3
introduces Late Georgian red brick, a small front with corniced parapet. CASTLE HILL continues High Street towards
the castle. HIGH HOUSE, three-storeyed, stuccoed, Late Georgian, faces Nos. 2–4, C17, white-rendered with oak mullions.
No. 6 shows Victorian timber to the High Street, but is C17.
KEEPER'S HOUSE beyond is thatched, with C17 oak mullions
and doorway.

Before Castle Hill, CHURCH STREET runs W, narrow and con-
gested. Called New Street in 1380, it replaced the steeper route
via Castle Hill. On the r. THE NUNNERY, a late medieval row
of three houses on a scale exceptional in the region, tree-ring-
dated to 1453–89. Three storeys and six bays. Stone ground
floor with piers indicating former shopfronts under two jettied
timber storeys, both slate-hung, the slates curved over a
ground-floor pentice. The slate-hanging is perhaps C18 but
very striking. On the E end are two original ogee-headed single
lights. Winding stairs at the rear begin in stone and continue
in solid timber treads. A lower stuccoed row follows; heavy oak
doorway to No. 14. Further on is the churchyard. The church
itself lies back and does not form part of the street sequence.
The timber-framed CHURCH COTTAGE administers a jolt.
There was a C15 house here which *Street* rebuilt in 1877
to a Home Counties timber-framed appearance with red tiles
and fancy rear chimneys. Much of the ground-floor front
framing looks genuine however. In the churchyard wall a
deep double-chamfered segmental-pointed RECESS must
be medieval, perhaps for a water-trough. A stuccoed early C19
row overlooks the churchyard. No. 22, on the end, has an
original shopfront. Nos. 26–28 beyond have a C16–C17 lateral
chimney.

WEST STREET continues SW. On the corner, the former METH-
ODIST CHURCH of 1878, with a rather Flemish Baroque front
in red sandstone by *Samuel Shewbrooks* of Taunton. A pedimented porch has gone. Along the street, vernacular C17–C18
fronts are mixed with more formal Late Georgian to Early
Victorian work, but older detail is concealed. SPEARS CROSS,
with C17 oak mullions, may be partly C15; Nos. 6–8, HATHA-
WAYS, with C18 leaded casements, may be C16, as also the
STAG'S HEAD, behind an early C19 stuccoed front. EXMOOR
HOUSE has Early Victorian bracketed eaves and segment-
headed sash windows. Beyond Mill Lane No. 29, thatched,
with a lateral chimney and circular stack. At the end, PARK
STREET runs S to the river. Pretty thatched cottages before the
serpentine approach to the narrow, twin-arched GALLOX
BRIDGE. Another thatched pair the other side.

ST GEORGE'S STREET, NW from top of West Street, was the old road to Minehead. On the l. the large red sandstone PRIMARY SCHOOL, 1871, by *J. P. St Aubyn*, the teacher's house to one side. Further on are a C17 thatched row, Nos. 15–19 and VINE COTTAGES, dated 1833. At the top end is the BUTTER CROSS, the C14–C15 market cross formerly at the lower end of the High Street, moved here in the C19. Opposite the school, PRIORY GREEN runs NE through the priory precinct (*see* p. 269). Set back further on, PRIORY COURT, large and stone-mullioned, was the vicarage of 1875, by *St Aubyn*. PRIORY THATCH is earlier C20, picturesque. Behind it, NORTHANGER, 1923, by *J. J. Taylor* of London, a large Arts and Crafts vernacular house, roughcast with a stone storeyed porch, tall stone chimneys and graded slate roofs. Priory Green curves E to THE BALL, a triangular green at the head of the High Street with a C19 cottage row. From here DUNSTER STEEP runs E to the A39. On the r. Victorian coachhouses behind the Luttrell Arms. On the slope above, reached from the car park, is an exceptionally rare Georgian POTTERY KILN, set up by Bristol potters in 1759 for Henry Fownes Luttrell. Whitewashed, circular, with a corbelled domed roof, open at the apex. A brick internal vault is pierced for air flow.

DUNSTER MARSH, ½ m. NNE. By the A39, the very Gothic former POLICE STATION, 1858, by *John Norton*. Similar to that at Williton, with a porch-tower and cross-wings, but elaborated with stair-turrets in the angles. On Marsh Street, No. 1 is thatched and pink-washed, C17 with C18 leaded casements. Nos. 15–17 have C16 lateral chimneys, one each side. Due N is DUNSTER STATION on the Minehead Railway, 1872–4. Contemporary GOODS SHED. Beyond, at Lower Marsh Farm, is THE OLD MANOR, C15, built for the Lotys family. The great hall is to the r. of the two-storey porch, the solar cross-wing to the l. The porch was added slightly later. In its upper storey a chapel, marked by a tall two-light pointed window and a square-headed one on the N side. Massive oak pointed-arched doorway inside. The hall has been floored over. Wind-braced roof on arch-braced trusses. The pantry and buttery were beneath the solar, which also has an arch-braced and wind-braced roof. The chapel has a handsome little wagon roof with carved wall-plate and bosses. Also a statue niche and an ogee-headed piscina. Sea Lane leads to DUNSTER BEACH, the medieval port at the mouth of the Avill. By the beach a pebble-clad PILLBOX of 1940.

BATS CASTLE, 1 m. S. A defended Iron Age enclosure on the top of a 692-ft (211-metre) hill. Roughly circular, enclosing 3.5 acres within a double stony bank. An unusual feature is the two entrances, opposite each other on the E and W. There is a wonderful view over the Bristol Channel. To the SE a zigzag bank crosses the ridge and is probably entries to defend this easiest approach or for display, where the main enclosure is least visible. To the NE is BLACK BALL CAMP, an oval hillslope enclosure with a single bank and ditch.

DURLEIGH

ST HUGH. Quite small, of red sandstone. The tower is unbuttressed, early C14 (see the Dec W window), the upper stage with battlemented sides and saddleback roof added in the C15. Late C13 to early C14 two-light nave windows, the S one with quatrefoil head. N rood-stair projection. The chancel masonry and proportions of the small N and S windows indicate a Norman date. Disappointing interior, heavily restored in 1882. The tower arch and chancel arch are moulded without capitals. – FONT. Perp. Octagonal with square quatrefoils.

Behind the church is DURLEIGH FARMHOUSE, early C18, hip-roofed with a symmetrical E front. DURLEIGH RESERVOIR, 1936–8, supplied the British Cellophane plant outside Bridgwater. By *E. A. Sandford Fawcett*, engineer. TREATMENT WORKS of brick, with central tower, by *R. A. Watson*, Borough Engineer. New works of 1993–5 by *Graham Carruthers Partnership*. A certain classicism in the roofs and cornices.

WEST BOWER MANOR, ½ m. WNW. An impressive survival, especially beautiful when seen across the reservoir, of the C14–C15 gatehouse of a manor house of the Coker family (Seymour after 1489). The centrepiece now of a red sandstone farmhouse, the gatehouse is rendered with dressings of buff sandstone and Ham stone. Twin polygonal turrets frame a broad shafted four-centred archway beneath a flat-headed two-light window, under corbels of lost machicolated battlements. Each turret is handsomely lit by five pointed two-light windows at first-floor level, with transoms, blind tracery heads and linked hoodmoulds. A string course above, with gargoyles, was probably beneath battlements, replaced by polygonal slate roofs. Moulded doorways within the archway, one to each turret. Lovely lantern-like turret rooms, the r. one with bits of original glass. Spiral stair in the l. turret. The farmhouse has Late Georgian casements and one C16 two-light mullioned window at the back.

REXWORTHY FARM, 1½ m. W. A medieval MOAT tightly surrounds the farmhouse on three sides.

DURSTON

ST JOHN BAPTIST. Late Perp W tower with set-back buttresses and square-headed triple bell-lights. Panelled tower arch. The rest was rebuilt in 1853 by *Charles Knowles*. Cruciform ashlar-lined interior with dark woodwork, the bench-ends in Somerset C16 style. Commandments on the E wall in large Gothic frames. – COMMUNION TABLE. 1635, on sturdy baluster legs. Enlarged 1894. – STAINED GLASS. Chancel, by *Alfred O. Hemming*, 1894.

LODGE HOUSE, N of the church. An important if much-restored C14 house consisting of a hall with storeyed porch and W cross-wing. Two tall pointed Perp windows, one marking a chapel over the porch, the other the solar in the cross-wing. Both are of two lights with transom but the simple tracery differs. The porch has an uncommonly broad archway. Spiral staircase in the angle between porch and cross-wing. The hall range has Victorian half-dormers over two moulded four-centred arches. These must be reused in this position. Smoke-blackened roof of common rafters, rare in Somerset. In the chapel a Perp wagon-roof.

BUCKLAND FARM, Lower Durston. The site of Minchin Buckland Preceptory, the only medieval house for sisters of the Order of St John. BUCKLAND HOUSE is three-storeyed and hip-roofed, c. 1800, to the N, but two-storeyed, deep-eaved, to the S, c. 1840. Long formal C18 walled garden. The big BARN incorporates medieval masonry.

OUTWOOD, 1 m. E. Two of *Brunel*'s flying BRIDGES, 1841–2, cross the Bristol & Exeter main line. The former RAILWAY HOTEL, 1853, brick, is a relic of Durston Junction Station, where the Yeovil branch of 1847–53 joined.

EARNSHILL HOUSE see HAMBRIDGE

EAST BRENT

ST MARY. The church has one of the few spires in Somerset, rising to 140 ft (43 metres). It stands on a tall slim Blue Lias tower of five stages. Angle buttresses to the top of the third stage. There is a rough architectural scheme to the W face, all the detail early C15 Perp. The pointed-arched doorway and window above are of the same width. Above the window a framing course of the same width steps up and over a niche whose canopy is linked vertically to a similar niche in the third stage, and this to another above. It is all rather thin, and the two-light bell-openings are small, without enrichment. Parapet pierced with trefoils in triangles, square corner pinnacles, and at last the spire. It has a collar with blank arcading that does not disturb the vigorous outline. The niche STATUES survive more completely than anywhere else in the county: the Virgin and Child, God the Father holding the Crucified Christ, and Christ crowning the Virgin, more charming than skilled. On the sides of the tower, two tiers of two-light windows instead of the niches. Double-chamfered tower arch, the chamfers dying into the sides, perhaps indicating that a C14 tower was raised; this also suggested by the NE stair-turret changing from square to octagonal.

Proud late C15 N aisle of five bays with tall three-light windows, buttresses and pinnacles, and a pierced parapet with quatrefoils in lozenges, very similar to Brent Knoll. Rood-stair turret in the angle to the chancel. The S side has a large late C13 porch against a short Perp two-bay aisle. The porch has angle buttresses, chamfered with little cusped stops. Tall doorway of three orders, the inner two on polygonal shafts with big (renewed) leaf capitals. Chamfered inner arch, roll mouldings to the middle one, uninterrupted outer chamfer. Good C15 traceried S DOOR with original iron ring-plate. The chancel was much rebuilt in the mid C19.

As for the interior, the first and lasting impression is the NAVE CEILING of 1637, a piece of early Gothic Revival, presumably by *George Drayton* who made the similar ceiling at Axbridge (N). Panels of typical Jacobean plasterwork, thin-rib shapes with three pendants, but these standard elements richly cusped to make them Gothic. The high S rood-loft window pre-dates the ceiling as do the stone corbel heads. The arcades are Perp. The five-bay N arcade has tall, slim shafted piers with four-wave mouldings. The S arcade is much lower, of only two bays, with a pier of four-hollow type, rather broadly done, probably late C14. The chancel arch accords with the N arcade. Otherwise the chancel is elaborately Victorian, embellished for Archdeacon Denison, vicar 1845–95.* Roof stencil-decorated in Puginian style. Tiled floors and E wall, the latter probably by *Minton*. Can the PISCINA, behind three small arches, and twin SEDILIA with prettily crested back be original? N aisle roof replaced in 1890, copying the aisle roof at Brent Knoll. In the aisle, a restored Perp niche, with a vaulted polygonal canopy. In the S chapel a plastered ceiling.

FURNISHINGS. BENCHES. Late C15. With pentagonal finials, as at Brent Knoll, but thinner. Coarse tracery and wiry plant forms, also a pelican, a lamb, the Annunciation and the signs of the Evangelists. On one the arms of Glastonbury Abbey, and on another the initials of John Selwood, abbot 1456–93, who had a house at East Brent. – LECTERN. C15, one of twenty-one wooden medieval lecterns in England. The eagle is portrayed launching off the big heavy baluster stem. – FONT. C19 copy of the Perp original, now at Rowberrow (N). – PULPIT. Reached through the wall. 1634. Two tiers of short blank arches, rather richer than usual, between three patterned rows. Big scrolls support the book-rest. – WEST GALLERY. 1635. Standing on vine-decorated columns (two similar at Spaxton). Moved in 1824 from the chancel arch and the projecting middle section added. C17 stairs behind. – ROYAL ARMS. George IV. – STAINED GLASS. NE window. Nine crowded scenes in early C15 style, similar to e.g. Crudwell, Wilts. Woodforde suggests that this is a copy of 1852 reusing some original pieces. In the adjoining N aisle window three large figures of saints, reliably C15. Only yellow used as a colour. This arrangement of large figures was continued in the C19 in the other

---

* Denison's wall paintings in the porch, c. 1873, have gone.

aisle windows, by *Joseph Bell*. Jumbled medieval fragments in a chancel N window. The colourful E window, 1858, by *O'Connor*, replaced the present W window, thin medievalizing figures, by *Bell*, 1852. *Bell*'s also the NW window, *c.* 1850. Three chancel S windows of *c.* 1845–60, the third a striking blue-on-gold and grisaille window by *Mary Miles* (cf. Isle Brewers). Chancel N, 1939, by *Martin Travers*. Cherubs and butterflies. – EFFIGIES. Two priests. That in the N aisle, late C14, eroded. That in the S chapel later C14, on a tomb-chest. A Perp niche in each window reveal above. – MONUMENT. Reed children, *c.* 1859, signed *Casentini & Co.* of Lambeth. Big and Gothic. There is an identical monument in Burnham church.

In the churchyard, C15 CROSS, refashioned in 1895 with too many bits; an eroded C15 EFFIGY of a civilian, and a gargantuan ridge-backed block of limestone, a MONUMENT to the Rev. W. T. Law †1844.

Behind the churchyard, brick SCHOOL, 1841, probably by *Richard Carver*, who designed the roughcast former VICARAGE (Rossholme), 1837–8, both Tudorish with a central gable. By the main road, the simple Gothic METHODIST CHAPEL, 1871, and WAR MEMORIAL, 1921. Stone cross with four statues (three servicemen and a merchant seaman), stiffly done, but moving.

EAST CHINNOCK

ST MARY. Good, typical Perp three-stage W tower of Ham stone with an octagonal SW turret. Double-chamfered tower arch. The nave and N aisle were thrown together as a flat-ceilinged box with Georgian Gothic windows in 1835–7 by *Henry Perry* of Crewkerne, leaving the chancel off-centre. Perp S windows and a hollow-moulded chancel arch. The barrel-vaulted S porch of *c.* 1300 and double-chamfered doorway within also survived. C14 ogee-cusped PISCINA. C14. – FONT. C13. Octagonal, on a water-holding base. – STAINED GLASS. The principal interest of the church. Almost all the windows were given over twenty-six years from 1962 by *Günther Anton* of Stuttgart, prisoner-of-war here 1945–8. Simple drawing style, the shapes outlined in the lead; clear glass contrasted with startling colour.

On the main road are two prominent Victorian accents, the double-gabled PORTMAN ARMS and the Gothic SCHOOL, 1877, by *Samuel Shewbrooks* of Taunton. Also DAWES FARMHOUSE, with early C17 ovolo mullions. W of the school, the OLD RECTORY, *c.* 1700, and THE PINNACLES, ashlar-fronted, thatched, behind obelisk gatepiers. BARROWS FARMHOUSE, 1887, shows contrasted stone and brickwork, typical of the Portman estate. Finally, WESTON HOUSE, a substantial house of 1637, for the Portman steward, has ovolo-moulded mullions and a rear stair gable.

EAST COKER

St Michael. Until 1791 this was cruciform, but the crossing tower became unsafe after bells were inserted in 1772. The new tower N of the chancel is of 1792–4 by *Joseph Radford* of Chard. *Henry Linscombe*, Yeovil marble-cutter, was also paid for a plan. Ham stone ashlar, with Y-tracery and arcaded parapet. The nave remarkably could be Anglo-Saxon, evidenced by long-and-short W cornerstones and narrow proportions. Perp aisles and transepts, battlemented on the N. S transept altered in the C17. Chancel rebuilt in 1711, with later C19 tracery. N arcade with standard Perp shafted piers, but the three-bay S arcade is mid-C13 inserted in earlier walling. Double-chamfered arches on circular piers with big moulded capitals, the responds on delicately fluted corbels. Traceried C15 N DOOR. Perp panelled eastern arches to both aisles. The transept arches at the former crossing have pilasters of 1792. The chancel arch was similar but is now Gothic, redone with the roofs in 1862–3. Colourful E WALL TILES, 1882. – FONT. C12. Circular, with one cable moulding. – ROYAL ARMS. 1660, with the exhortation against change. The date altered to 1690 in support of William and Mary. – WAR MEMORIAL. 1919. Corinthian-columned, C17 style. – S TRANSEPT ALTAR. C19, reusing Continental C17 carved panels. – STAINED GLASS. C15 and C17 fragments in the S transept. E window 1866. W window 1885, probably by *Hardman*. Three windows of 1920–3 by *Powell's*. Most significant is the N aisle window, 1936, by *Leonard Walker*, in streaked Tiffany colours, to the Eliots who emigrated to Salem, Massachusetts, *c.* 1660. They were ancestors of T. S. Eliot †1965, whose ashes are buried here. One of his *Four Quartets* is 'East Coker' – MONUMENTS. A particularly fine if battered later C13 effigy of a lady in Purbeck marble. Also an eroded early C14 civilian (under the altar) in Ham stone. – William Dampier, the C17 explorer, 1908, by *Singer* of Frome. Good portrait roundel in copper. – Outside, E of the porch, a slab of *c.* 1300, with incised female figure, set on a stone coffin.

Coker Court. An uncommonly interesting and rewarding house, of four periods: the C15 hall of the Courtenays, altered for Archdeacon Helyar after 1616, with an E range of 1766–70, designed according to Helyar family tradition by *William Chambers*, but built by *Joseph Dixon* of London, and finally restored with new SW ranges of 1900–2 by *Temple Moore*, among the best of Late Victorian architects. The HALL has large two-light transomed Perp windows on both sides. The entrance is from the N, and here the porch and big bay window project, strengthened by diagonal buttresses. Their windows match those of the hall. The single bay to the r. of the porch, the former service end, was restored in 1900–2 with a new W gable. Then also the gable of the big bay window was reinstated. The cross-passage is enclosed by a heavy, soberly detailed Jacobean stone screen with coupled Roman Doric columns and a triglyph frieze with lozenges. The two arches are studded. Matching coupled columns to the fireplace. w of the screens passage are three doorways formerly to pantry, kitchen and buttery. The hall roof is largely of 1900–2, though said to be restoration after a Georgian ceiling was removed. The ceiling of the hall-bay is of 1900–2.

The C18 E RANGE presumably replaced a C15 cross-wing. Soberly detailed, of 2–3–2 bays and hip-roofed, it is stuccoed with minimal stone dressings. Centre pediment with a tripartite lunette. Similar lunette over a Venetian window on the N end. This arrangement is repeated on the hip-roofed STAIR HALL, projecting into the rear courtyard. Superbly minimal cantilevered stone staircase of the thinnest ashlar, the iron balustrade rising uninterrupted around the square hall. Three well-proportioned FRONT ROOMS with modillion cornices and excellent fireplaces: in the N room green-and-white marble with a sunburst female mask; in the central saloon, white marble with female busts over consoles, and, in the lintel, a lion mask and pelt; in the S room, Adam-style timber around red-and-green marble. Over the saloon fireplace a timber Corinthian aedicule with broken pediment. Similar pedimented aedicules in the CONSERVATORY, S, and as the overmantel in the NE BEDROOM. This room has C20 *trompe l'œil* panelling and grisaille figures. Two other BEDROOMS were in the Chinese taste. The S room is prettily painted with flowering trees and has a green lacquered door. The wallpaper of the SE room has gone; a lacquered door and some pelmets remain.

Behind the r. gable, *Moore's* notably sympathetic short range encloses the W side of the courtyard. His service wing then runs W, divided by buttresses. The rear S side has gables in balanced asymmetry. – ICE HOUSE in the field to the W.

Below the church, the HELYAR ALMSHOUSES of 1640, completed in 1660. For eleven women and one 'broken-down tradesman'. A long two-storey row of twelve in mirrored pairs, with mullioned windows and dormer gables. Stuccoed hip-roofed VICARAGE, to the W, of 1835, by *Thomas Churchouse* of Yeovil. The village street runs E. ESTATE COTTAGE is late C17, still mullion-windowed, the dripmould stepped over the door. An arched panel links the two windows each side. The stuccoed and hip-roofed HELYAR ARMS is dated 1834 but has C16 beams. To the l., CHAPEL COTTAGE has picturesque C19 Y-traceried wooden windows. It was two C17 cottages joined in 1713. Jointed-cruck trusses. Similar jointed crucks in two pairs of COTTAGES before SLADE'S FARMHOUSE, thatched, C17, with a long front of mullioned windows. TOWNSEND FARMHOUSE has twin C17 dormer gables. The ashlar front of BUBSPOOL HOUSE has both C17 mullions and Georgian sashes, but the N end shows a damaged C15 pointed-arched transomed window and there is a C15 first-floor doorway within. The service range has two early doorways, C15 and C16, and a stone newel stair.

DARVOLE FARMHOUSE, 1¼ m. E. Formal late C16 rendered and thatched house with stone mullions and dripmould.

EAST CRANMORE

ST JAMES. Now a house. 1845–6, by *T. H. Wyatt*. A typical Victorian estate church, not large but full of detail. S porch-tower with broached spire, set against a S transept. C13 to early C14 style. Mostly lancets, with a stepped E triplet. Large ballflowers under the spire, which has small lucarnes.*

CRANMORE HALL (All Hallows School). Externally Victorian of 1847–8 by *T. H. Wyatt* for J. M. Paget, with neo-Jacobean gables framing the W front. But a C17 house remains, represented by the five centre bays. It was square, three-storeyed, with cross-windows and mullioned attic windows, under a hipped roof of 1830, and dated 1658 and 1661. Low ceilings mark the original part. The former hall keeps a painted timber screen with strapwork heraldry above. The panelling and timber chimneypiece with columns are partly original. C17 carved panels and a stone fireplace are reused elsewhere. The Early Victorian work becomes more cheerful on the E front, with a SE corner tower and a stair-tower with a rather Austrian ogee dome. *Wyatt* returned in 1868–9 to add to this E front a stone veranda in Northern Renaissance style, continued in front of a new E range: billiard room and vinery, finished with a seven-bay ORANGERY. The billiard room has a festive iron-crested roof and lavish marble-columned neo-Jacobean interior. SW of the house, a pyramid-roofed SUMMERHOUSE with angle pilasters of 1763. To the NW, a cruciform C17 service building with ovolo mullions and a Victorian cupola. HOME FARM, just E, a model farm of the 1860s, much rebuilt in 1893. On the lane W, WESTERN FARM, 1791, ashlar-fronted with pedimented doorway, with old-fashioned mullioned windows. WEST LODGE, 1866, Tudor-style, is perhaps by *Wyatt*. C18 rusticated GATEPIERS.

CRANMORE TOWER, 1 m. N. Prominent on the ridge. An Italianate folly by *Wyatt*, 1863–5. 148 ft (45 metres) tall and slim in proportion. Continuous balcony halfway up and a balcony under paired arched belvedere windows on each face. Luncheon room at the foot.

TOLL HOUSE, on the A361. Georgian Gothic of the 1820s.

EAST HUNTSPILL

ALL SAINTS. 1839–40, by *G. P. Manners* of Bath. Neo-Norman, of Blue Lias. Nave, chancel and S porch, raised to a bell-tower in 1957. Neo-Norman fittings. – STAINED GLASS. W window, 1888, by *W. H. Constable*. Chancel S, Late Georgian heraldic glass. Nave E roundel, 1967.

---

* A window by *Morris & Co.*, 1905, is now at Doulting (N).

Several C18 brick farmhouses with the raised gables of East Anglia, notably along New Road. HACKNEY FARM has curved-headed cross-windows and a stair gable on a catslide roof. (Good plasterwork and staircase.)

GOLD CORNER PUMPING STATION, 2 m. ESE. 1941–2. It spans the Huntspill River which supplied water to the Puriton explosives works. Brick, cinema-modern, by *Leonard Mew* of *Somerset County Architects*, astonishingly architectural for wartime.

EAST LAMBROOK

ST JAMES. Nave, chancel and Victorian bellcote. Varied exterior: intersected E window tracery of *c.* 1300, C14 and C15 flat-headed two-light S windows, long nave windows of *c.* 1700, Late Georgian gallery stairs and Victorian porch. Chapel-like early C19 interior with high pews and WEST GALLERY. But the distorted chancel arch is of *c.* 1190, double-chamfered with Transitional trumpet-scallop capitals. These rest on short shafts which stand on stiff-leaf corbels. Cinquefoiled E window rere-arch. – FONT. Perp. Heavily retooled. – PULPIT. Early C17, very plain, set high. – ROYAL ARMS. 1780.

EAST LAMBROOK MANOR. The lateral chimney indicates a remodelled late C14–C15 hall, and a Perp two-light E window with cusped pointed lights and transom marks the solar. Both have wind-braced roofs. The parlour has a framed ceiling encased in moulded plaster, and early C17 panelling. Moulded C16 hall fireplace. Alterations, notably mullioned windows, of 1937, for Margery Fish, who created the GARDENS. Substantial three-storeyed hip-roofed MALTHOUSE, early C19.

Several substantial farmhouses. LAMBROOK HOUSE, to the S, is in two halves, Late Georgian windows, W, and C17 mullions, E. The W half has a C15 roof with cusped wind-braces. In the E half, the kitchen window sill has a set of C18 ashlar cream-scalders, as at Barrington Court. PITTARDS FARMHOUSE, mid-C17, has a mid-C18 canted end bay, still with mullioned windows, but the top ones in a charming Venetian-window arrangement. Pyramidal thatched C18 HAY BARN on tall octagonal stone piers. W of the manor are BAKERS FARMHOUSE, with a C16 lateral chimney, EAST LAMBROOK FARMHOUSE with a long C17 ashlar front, earlier than the 1680 sundial, and GLEBE HOUSE, Georgian Gothic in brick, possibly as late as 1840.

SOUTHAY FARMHOUSE, ½ m. NNE. Mullion-windowed with dormer gables. C16–C17 moulded and framed ceiling. The C18 end-wall plaque refers to a family dispute.

GAWSBRIDGE MILL, 1 m. NE. Big three-storeyed early C19 mill with an internal waterwheel. Late Georgian hip-roofed mill house.

EAST LYDFORD

ST MARY. Disused and boarded-up (2012). It replaced a small CHURCH of which walls remain ½ m. NNE, near the River Brue. 1864–6 by *Benjamin Ferrey*, a memorial to Louisa, wife of the Rev. J. J. Moss. Blue Lias with roofs of both plain and stone tiles. Nave, porch, chancel and tower against the nave NE corner. Late C13 style, lancets and Geometrical tracery, going in the E window beyond neo-1300. Good naturalistic carving, notably the chancel eaves. The tower starts square and turns octagonal for a bell-stage with eight recessed long lancets under an ashlar spire with gabled lucarnes. Mrs Moss is commemorated in a columned external N recess carved with swallows. Ashlar-lined interior with much similar carving. Chancel arch on short, thick-set coupled columns with marble shafts. The foliage of the capitals envelops the Signs of the Evangelists, the plinth foliage a tiny head of Mrs Moss and clasped hands. – FONT. 1866. Bowl banded with lilies; lily capitals beneath. – STALLS. Bench-ends carved with squirrels.* – STAINED GLASS. E window by *Kempe*, 1879. Boarded over.†

EAST LYNG

Site of an Anglo-Saxon fortified *burh* on raised ground W of the Isle of Athelney.

ST BARTHOLOMEW. The tower, as usual, is what counts most. Perp of the more elaborate C15–C16 type, like Middlezoy or Westonzoyland. Blue Lias and Ham stone. Angle buttresses connected by a diagonal fillet rise to diagonally set pinnacles. W doorway with traceried spandrels. W window of four lights, sub-arched. Above this a two-light window with pierced baffles, then a pair of two-light bell-openings also with pierced baffles, flanked by typical thin diagonal shafts and pinnacles. Battlements with quatrefoils and angle pinnacles. Polygonal SE stair-tower to the lower stage only. The tower arch is panelled. Chancel and aisleless nave with opposed porches. Two-light windows with rere-arches in the nave as well as the chancel, C14 Dec to Perp. Simply chamfered doorways. N rood-stair projection. Roofs much restored in 1905 by *Samson & Cottam*. Chancel arch stepped on the W, probably for a boarded tympanum. Big early C14 SEDILE with a monolithic head with cusped ogee arch, the points exaggerated, crockets barely sketched. – FONT. C12. Bowl with roll moulding below. – SCREEN. C16. Just the plain panelled base. – PULPIT. C15–C16.

---

* A Jacobean pulpit and C15 alabaster sculpture have gone.
† Pevsner noted that the design derived from Dürer of *c.* 1510–25.

Finely carved traceried panels between leaf-scroll uprights. –
BENCHES. C16. Square-headed with many more graphic motifs
than usual: wrestlers, a miller on horseback, a carpenter with
an adze, pole-vaulters, a married couple, fox and goose, a green
man, and mythical beasts, one carrying a backward-facing
child. – DESK. Reused traceried panels. – STALLS. Reused
pieces of large-scale open tracery. – PAINTINGS. Large figures
of Moses and Aaron, naïvely painted, late C17, Aaron in exotic
priestly robes. – STAINED GLASS. E window by *O'Connor*, 1870.
Medieval fragments, chancel N.

A main road village, with only the ROSE AND CROWN notable.
Early C19 rendered front, but inside a C16 nine-panel framed
ceiling and a central fireplace with continuous moulding. Cuts
Road runs along the medieval BALTMOOR WALL, built for
flood control in 1374–5 between Lyng and Athelney.

ATHELNEY. The former island is marvellously evocative, even
if there is little to show for its illustrious history. Here Alfred
took refuge from the Danes in 879, as commemorated by the
MONUMENT erected in 1801. A tall corniced base with marble
plaque carries a scroll-sided pedestal with roundel relief of
Alfred beneath a stubby obelisk. It marks the site of the abbey
founded by Alfred in 888, of which nothing is visible. Described
as a square with four apses, Alfred's church was replaced by a
cruciform one with cloister to the S, and was rebuilt in the C15.
The neat brick Late Georgian FARMHOUSE stands parallel to
the cloister alignment, possibly on medieval foundations.
Alfred's fort (on an Iron Age site) was further W, opposite East
Lyng. To the S, by the River Tone, CURRYMOOR PUMPING
STATION, 1954–5, in the brick Georgian-modern style
espoused by the River Board. A circular annexe shelters the
Easton & Amos engine of the previous station, 1864.

LYNG COURT, West Lyng. Substantial brick farmhouse of 1808.
To the E an altered C15 TITHE BARN of Athelney Abbey. Preserved are diagonal buttresses, ventilation loops and the chamfered jambs of the fine W arch. Within the porch, a blocked
four-centred-arched S doorway and one original roof truss.

EAST PENNARD

ALL SAINTS. Site of an Anglo-Saxon minster church. After the
finery of so many Somerset towers and parapets East Pennard
is refreshingly blunt. Plain parapets, a W tower with a parapet,
not even battlements, let alone pinnacles. And the walls beautifully unscraped. The church is mostly Perp, except for the
lower stage of the tower, which is unbuttressed and had no W
door before 1740, when the W window lost its tracery. Short
plain Perp bell-stage. Aisled nave with clerestory and S porch,
all with parapets, and a chancel. Perp panel tracery with cusped
ogee lights to three-light aisle windows, two-light chancel

windows and the four-light E window. Small flat-headed clerestory windows. The tall four-bay arcades have standard piers (four hollows) and round capitals but double-chamfered arches. By contrast the otherwise similar chancel arch has a standard Perp arch moulding. So the arcade arches are reused. Good Somerset nave roof with framed panels and carved bosses, on tie-beam trusses which are arch-braced from stone angels holding shields. The easternmost truss is coloured, and remarkably, above the tie-beam, are painted two censing angels, connected presumably with 'barbarous paintings on wood' (Glynne) that once filled the chancel arch. Aisle roofs on angel corbels. Victorian chancel roof. C14 cusped ogee PISCINA.

FURNISHINGS. FONT. Late C12, square, and remarkable. Each side has shallow blank arcading over a boldly carved monster, with human head in a pixie hat, bird body and leaf-scroll tail. Base with devil-mask spurs. – WEST GALLERY. 1842. The front panels are fourteen narrow medieval panels from a screen, with refined, sometimes Flamboyant, tracery. The wider central panel reuses two bench-ends, with a pelican and a Crown of Thorns. – PULPIT. Early to mid-C18, panelled, with fine carving of leaves, flowers and fruit in the Gibbons tradition. – BOX PEWS. In the aisles. Georgian to Early Victorian. – STALLS and READING DESKS. Made up of pieces, the stalls of Jacobean panelling, the desks each faced with a large mid-C18 cherub head amid garlands, from a Georgian reredos. – REREDOS. Late C19, colourful mosaic and marble. – SCREEN. 1889. – CHANDELIER. 1798. Smaller and fussier than usual. – STAINED GLASS. In the E window, heraldic panels of c. 1845 in a patchwork of C15 glass. Three colourful windows of 1857–8 may be by *Horwood Bros*. – MONUMENTS. Henry Martin †1751. Clumsy Baroque with columns and urn. – Judith Martin †1764. Coloured marbles with an urn in a broken pediment. – Two good examples of the work of *Thomas King*: Gerard Martin †1789, with the usual standing woman by an urn, on a large pink oval with drooping leaves over the top; and prettier still, Sarah Berkeley Napier †1799, on a grey Gothic background with similar drooping leaves, a plaque with roses and urn.

In the churchyard, C15 CROSS. Spired tabernacle head of 1920, by *Thomas Falconer*.

The church is approached between the neat walls and hedges of the gardens of PENNARD HOUSE. The C17–C18 house of the Martins was encased in 1815 for Gerard Berkeley Napier, in unpainted stucco with ashlar eaves, cornices and plinths. Plain three-storey N front of four bays, with a five-bay colonnade of paired Roman Doric columns, between wings with two-storey canted bays. Similar canted bays at the centre of the E side and the r. of the S front. The latter adjoins a three-storey front of refaced C17–C18 work, with close-spaced tall first-floor sash-windows. Early C19 interiors. Pretty early C19 STABLES to the NW, with short coachhouse wings ending in Diocletian windows. E of the drive, the five-bay early C18 former SCHOOL, large for the period. Single-storey on a basement, with flush stone cross-windows. From the church, a stone-paved path runs W to THE GARDENS, mid-C19 estate cottages in four twin-gabled pairs. E of the church is the substantial former RECTORY, 1841, mullion-windowed and gabled, by *Jesse Gane* of Evercreech. The lane drops S to the stream. On the rise beyond, BATCH FARM, thatched, C16–C17, with mullions, dormer gables, and good doorways with carved spandrels and rosettes. Beyond is a picturesquely composed former BOARD SCHOOL, 1877, by *C. & J. Wainwright* of Shepton Mallet.

HOME FARM, ½ m. W. Long farmhouse with moulded four-centred-arched doorway. Part of a late C15 hall roof survives with an arched-braced truss and two-tier wind-bracing, the top braces in pairs. C16 first-floor fireplace. Early C19 FARM BUILDINGS around an open court.

HEMBRIDGE MILL, I m. SW. Small-scale, mostly C18, but one C17 mullioned window to the house. Mill at right angles with early C19 machinery.

PENNARD HILL FARMHOUSE, I m. NW. Five-bay front with ovolo-mullioned windows but a corniced bolection-moulded doorway, *c.* 1700. Relieving arches over this doorway and the two windows to the l. indicate two phases.

HUXHAM, I m. S. ASH FARM is C17, refronted, HUXHAM FARM is typical three-bay Late Georgian, and LOWER HUXHAM FARM, despite C17 mullions, has a C15–C16 four-centred-arched stone doorway between the cross-passage and hall. Large stone fireplace.

EAST QUANTOXHEAD

Among the prettiest of Somerset estate villages. Thatched cottages and farm buildings below the church and big house on a hillock overlooking the coast.

ST MARY. In the shadow of Court House. Blue Lias with mixed sandstones. Two-stage Perp W tower with diagonal buttresses, battlements, and higher NE stair-turret. But the double-chamfered tower arch on half-octagonal shafts with coved capitals can hardly be later than the mid C14. Perp nave and chancel, restored in 1860. Red sandstone four-centred-arched S doorway. Interior stripped of plaster, the main interest the woodwork and Luttrell tomb. C15 nave wagon roof. – FONT. Red sandstone, Early Perp. Narrow octagonal bowl with square quatrefoils. Panelled stem. – ROOD SCREEN. Five bays, late C15, of square-headed sections without mullions. Head tracery of deformed oval quatrefoils above flattened ogee arches. Posts with attached diagonal shafts; dado with blind tracery. The rood-stair position shows that there was a loft. Attached is a

C17 READING DESK with typical motifs. – PULPIT. Polygonal, C16, with long panels and angles ornamented with lush arabesque foliage. – VESTRY SCREEN. C17 domestic, perhaps from Court House, with a four-centred doorway. – BENCHES. An excellent C15–C16 set with close tracery, wiry plants and occasional birds. Also six-pointed stars, Luttrell arms, and strange monograms beneath a crowned Tudor rose supported by bizarre beasts. – COMMUNION RAIL. C17. Vertically symmetrical balusters and carved rail. – STAINED GLASS. E window by *Kempe*, 1891, much better than the chancel s, by *Kempe & Co.*, 1912. Medieval fragments in the w window including the Trinity shield. – MONUMENT. Hugh Luttrell †1522 and Andrew Luttrell †1535. A fine Tudor Gothic canopied tomb. Panelled chest with shields under segmental cusped arches. Single alabaster slab with a border inscribed in English. Tudor-arched canopy, panelled inside. Twin ogee-headed lights at the w end, just one at the E. Cornice and heraldry between two bands of cresting carrying small finials between larger angle pinnacles.

CHURCHYARD CROSS. C15 base and truncated shaft.

COURT HOUSE. Owned by the Luttrell family since 1232. A medieval courtyard house probably underlies most of the present one, which was largely rebuilt for George Luttrell †1629. It remained little altered as the family removed to Dunster Castle from the late C17 until 1888. The house is of blue-grey Lias, probably once rendered, of two storeys. The E front is the last built, in 1628–9, to the typical Elizabethan–Jacobean E-plan except that the SE wing is omitted. Otherwise all is regular, and plain, with flat parapets and large mullion-and-transom windows. Four-light window on each side of the porch, which has a three light window over the arched doorway and heraldry of 1628. The NE wing has similar four-light windows on the s side and E end. There are similar windows on the long N face, but the NW end is late C16, remodelled, as is suggested by the uneven bay spacing. Set back where the SE wing should project is a corner with battlements facing s and a moulded pointed-arched doorway facing E. This was the porch-tower of the medieval house, although its corner position hardly relates to any conventional medieval plan. Its relatively small scale is shown by its battlements being of a height with the parapet of the adjoining s range. The tower has early C17 mullioned windows on the s. The s range, added before 1614, is much rougher than the E front, with wooden mullion-and-transom windows. The wall appears to have become unstable as the chamber windows were infilled shortly after completion.

Behind the E range, a polygonal stair-tower fronts into a narrow enclosed courtyard, Cock Court (so named for a former cock-pit). This stair-tower has early C17 windows matching those on the SE corner tower. The stairs, with solid oak winding treads, gave access to the s range but were soon superseded when the E range was rebuilt and a new stair hall added, filling the N half of the courtyard. An early C16 piece remains at the W end of the N range, with oak-mullioned N windows and garderobe turret. And there are sufficient remnants at the W end of the S range and W side of Cock Court to suggest that the 1614 work was remodelling: a truncated wall with a little oriel, a cross-passage with red sandstone doorways.

The E range has a moulded Tudor-arched doorway into a lobby with Tudor-arched doorways framing round-arched doors, two into the hall to the N, one to the parlour to the S. The doors fold ingeniously when opened. An unusual feature of the hall is the four-light N window at the dais end behind the high table. Off the hall is the long NE withdrawing room. This range also contains the NW kitchen, which opened to the courtyard before the stair-block was added parallel to the S. This has an open-well staircase with vigorous Jacobean detail: vertically symmetrical tapered and fluted balusters, writ larger for the newels, and halved for large obelisk finials. Three doorways in the N wall of the stair hall show that the kitchen pre-dates the stair-block: two are C17, one is older, four-centred. The parlour incorporates pre-1628 fragments: a blocked Tudor-arched S doorway and another early doorway into the S range. This has ground-floor service rooms: a second kitchen and a bakehouse, both with large fireplaces.

Aesthetically the outstanding feature of the house is the plasterwork over the fireplaces. The seven overmantels include two with heraldry, four scenes from the Life of Christ* and one strangely mythological. All but one are on strapwork with plump fruit and lion-mask ornament, and five have caryatid supporters, including three sets of Virtues carrying baskets of fruit on their heads. These motifs, found at Montacute, Poundisford Lodge and West Coker Manor, suggest the plasterer *Robert Eaton* of Stogursey. The hall overmantel, dated 1629, with the Luttrell arms between armoured soldiers, differs in lacking the strapwork, but the mechanical fretwork of the fireplace frieze is replicated on four others. The biblical scenes are Christ blessing the Children (downstairs NE), and a possible Last Days sequence upstairs, identified as the Approach to Gethsemane (or Entry to Jerusalem), Agony in the Garden, and Deposition. The supporters seem to be unrelated, indeed the Deposition is between American Indian demi-figures. Exceptions to the biblical theme are in the two upstairs S rooms abandoned because of structural failure. Here the fireplaces have lion-mask friezes. One overmantel has heraldry of 1614, the other, in an oval panel, an over-taxed attempt to mythologize a naked female. Her upright top half holds a mirror and a book, and has horse's front legs, winged. A huge tail loops around her impossibly attached bottom half. The masks here sprout buffalo horns to add to the strangeness.

Below the house and church, a very long BARN, partly thatched, with a C19 horse-engine house on the N and shelter-sheds on

---

* New Testament scenes are rare in post-Reformation iconography.

the S. The stone-walled MILL POND and thatched MILL HOUSE, rebuilt 1729, stand at the top end of the village. The pretty thatched COTTAGES running S are externally C18, probably older. Nos. 33–39 end in particularly undulating roofs. Nos. 43–45 are altered late medieval. VILLAGE HALL, 1913, by F. W. Roberts.

EDINGTON

ST GEORGE. 1878–9, by *Down & Son*. Conventional Perp, in Blue Lias, with a W bellcote. – FONT. Norman, unusual, the two big scallops each side with a kind of drapery beneath, over a cable moulding. Squat stem on a spurred base. – CHAMBER ORGAN. By *Henry Bryceson*, c. 1840. – STAINED GLASS. By *Clayton & Bell*, 1880–1900.

Downhill from the church, BURNT HOUSE FARMHOUSE, c. 1700, five bays with wooden cross-windows. Good panelled room. Uphill, GREAT HOUSE, a mid-C19 hip-roofed villa with a trellis porch. W of the church, the late C19 brick SCHOOLROOM has reused two-light Gothic windows and a 1772 datestone.

EDINGTON HOUSE, Broadmead Lane. Of three parts, all in Blue Lias. The handsome S range is of c. 1765–70, for Richard Field. Three bays, with parapet and urns, the outer bays defined by quoins and pediments, the centre narrow, perhaps because an older house was refaced. Pedimented door hood. Narrow dog-leg stair with fluted column newels. A W additon of c. 1821 contains the drawing room, with good cornice, beneath a square-domed bedroom. C17 rear range, remodelled c. 1810. Pyramid-roofed C18 SUMMERHOUSE with ramped parapet.

ROMAN SALT WORKINGS. On the moors to the N of the village, indicated by low mounds in the fields. This area appears to have been left marshy, whereas further N the land was drained at this period. A villa is recorded near Lakehouse Farm.

ELWORTHY

ST MARTIN (Churches Conservation Trust). In a sloping churchyard with an enormous yew. Small. The plain battlemented W tower is probably late C17 or C18. Outside stairs to the ringing chamber. The porch and nave wagon roof are C15, the rest much rebuilt in 1846 by *William Shewbrooks* of Taunton. Buckler in 1839 shows different windows. – FONT. Alabaster, like Williton, late C17. – PULPIT. C19, with C17 panels. – SCREEN. C19, reusing two-light Perp tracery. The text 'O Lord prepare our (he)arts to praye Anno 1632' was formerly over the N door. – STALLS. C19. Medieval-style ends. – COMMUNION RAIL. Late C17 turned balusters. – STAINED GLASS. Two medieval St Johns in the nave N lancet. E window, c. 1846. Symbols on clear glass, with coloured borders.

Substantial hip-roofed OLD RECTORY, c. 1838, roughcast with three-bay fronts. ELWORTHY FARMHOUSE, long and rendered, is altered late medieval. First-floor plaster overmantel of a shrub with acorn-like fruit, dated 1686.

HARTROW MANOR, 1 m. E. Stuccoed deep-eaved villa of c. 1815 for the Rev. Thomas Sweet-Escott, built with Willett House (*see below*) on the Escott estate, presumably by *Richard Carver*. Five-bay S front, the centre subsequently brought forward over a colonnade. Four-bay E side. Curving staircase. The curiosity of Hartrow is Sweet-Escott's medievalism, in strange contrast to his new house. Attached to the W of the house, part of the C16–C17 predecessor survives between Romantic Gothic additions.* To the SW, a steep-roofed great hall, of variegated stones, has quartz boulders in the footings, a circular lateral chimney and a lozenge pattern of quartz in the front gable. The NW addition has herringbone masonry and stubby circular chimneys. Much reused medieval material: a yard archway with massive eroded jambs and capitals, and a similar shaft inside the hall, which has some reused Norman corbels. Miniature gatehouse to the stable yard. Conventional Late Georgian hip-roofed COACHHOUSE, the S end glazed as a conservatory.

WILLETT HOUSE, 2 m. ESE. A classical villa in a handsome park, also built c. 1815, for Lt-Gen. Daniel Blommart, brother-in-law of Sweet-Escott of Hartrow. By *Richard Carver*. Yellow-washed with deep eaves and an inset Greek Doric porch. Ashlar canted bay on the E end. Good plasterwork, a curved ceiling over the dividing stair, lit by a large oval window introduced in the restoration by *Louise Crossman*, 2008. One sumptuous marble chimneypiece with inlaid fluting. Small rear courtyard created from miscellaneous outbuildings, and a sedum-roofed SWIMMING POOL below, all by Louise Crossman. The pool building has a classical formality, with circular piers and flared brise-soleil eaves. Formal gardens by *Arabella Lennox-Boyd*.

WILLETT TOWER, Willett Hill. A folly like a large church tower, built c. 1774 at the expense of local gentry, principally Mr Bernard of Crowcombe. Tall brick pointed archways and diagonal buttresses to the lower stage, two tiers of paired windows above, battlements, and a false corner stair-turret. Screen wall with a long Gothic window.

ELWORTHY BARROWS, 1¼ m. SW, on the ridge. Not burial mounds but the earthworks of an Iron Age hillfort about 200 yds across. Its importance lies in the fact that it appears to be unfinished, providing evidence of construction techniques.

---

*These are said to date from c. 1817 and post-date the new house, but the VCH dates the new house to c. 1830.

ENMORE

ST MICHAEL. Fine Perp three-stage tower with dressings of the local pale sandstone. A crane hired in Bridgwater in 1455 may give a date. Broad diagonal buttresses ending in tall pinnacles. The battlements and the polygonal SE stair-turret are pinnacled as well. Two-light bell-openings with pierced baffles. Renewed four-light W window over a moulded pointed-arched doorway. Statue niche on the S side. Tall tower arch of broad wave mouldings, and a handsome star-vault. The rest was virtually rebuilt in 1873 by *Benjamin Ferrey*, who added the N aisle. The chancel was C13–C14. Ferrey copied the E window of three stepped cusped lights with foiled circles above. Late Norman S doorway of *c.* 1180–90. The shafts, slightly keeled and with water-holding bases, have capitals of trumpet type, the l. one with small stiff-leaves appearing in the openings. The arch has bold gaping chevrons. Ferrey kept the panelled C15–C16 chancel arch. – FONT. C12–C13. Octagonal, with an inset band over a broad tapering stem. – PULPIT. C17, uncommonly rich. Two tiers of arched panels, but it is the friezes and angle panels that are special, with writhing scroll and carnival masks. – REREDOS. 1873. Good stiff-leaf carving and an alabaster cross. – STAINED GLASS. E window, 1873. – MONUMENTS. James Jeanes †1759. High quality, in contrasted marbles, still Baroque. Draped urn under an open pediment. – John Guy †1788, by *Wood* of Bristol. Three ovals depend from a cornice with draped urn.

C15 CHURCHYARD CROSS on a stepped base, the socket decorated with shields, the shaft with square angle shafts.

Behind the church is Enmore Castle (*see* below). Opposite, CASTLE FARMHOUSE, L-plan, roughcast, with shaped Dutch gables, rare in Somerset. The small arched windows resemble those on the castle, i.e. mid-C18. On the main road, at the E end, CASTLE HOUSE was the Castle Inn. The five-bay front has thick glazing bars and a projecting three-storey pedimented centrepiece, probably mid-C18, though the mansard roofs point to a slightly later date. Arcaded screen walls each side, to grand overall effect. At the W end, the SCHOOL, 1846–8, replaces the very first National School in England, established in 1810 by the Rev. John Poole.

ENMORE CASTLE. *John Perceval, 2nd Earl of Egmont*, designed for himself a very large castellated mansion, built 1751–7, of red sandstone, four-square around a courtyard. It had square corner towers and intermediate round towers, except on the E side where there was a twin-towered gatehouse. This had a functioning drawbridge over the vast dry moat, broad enough for carriage access to vaulted stables buried in the revetment. The detail was designed for economy through repetition, with arched sash windows. This strand of the castle revival, running from Vanbrugh at Blackheath through to Adam at Culzean, withered in the face of the revived Gothic. Most of the house was demolished in 1835. Part of the W range was reconstructed

Enmore Castle, before alteration.
Engraving, 1829

as a still substantial house with deep-eaved hipped roofs. The round W tower, once central, remains with one bay to the l. and four to the r., instead of five each side, and there are no battlements. The taller three-storey E front is on the site of Egmont's principal range but not recognizably his, although it reuses his arched windows. Italianate hip-roofed square towers frame a centre with two-storey loggia on square ashlar piers. Slight asymmetries suggest the ghost of Egmont's house.* The PARK with a large lake was extended over part of the village, including the RECTORY, which the 3rd Earl rebuilt a mile E in 1803.

BARFORD HOUSE, ¾ m. NW. Turned from a farmhouse into a small country house in the mid C18 (work in progress in 1751), for James Jeanes. Handsome red brick five-bay front with Bath stone quoins, cornice, and old-fashioned curved-headed architraves. A later C18 attic storey screens the loft. The remarkable feature is the pair of quadrant wings with blind arcading, ending in little two-bay pavilions with pilasters supporting pediments against parapets. Apart from stone window architraves the detail is all in moulded brick, a rarity in Somerset. Again they look old-fashioned for the mid C18. The chimneys are disguised as cupolas, with vanes dated 1666 and 1775. At the rear projects a late C18 two-storey bow. Some fielded panelling inside, and a late C18 yellow-and-white marble chimneypiece in the room with the bow. Mid-C18 WALLED GARDEN with quadrant corners and twin pedimented SUMMERHOUSES let into the back wall.

TIRELANDS, ½ m. S. Altered C15 hall house, with a gabled SW corner projection that may have been a prospect tower. Good C16 framed ceiling.

---

* An Egmont staircase is at Cruwys Morchard, Devon.

EVERCREECH

ST PETER. The fame of the church is its W tower, deemed by some one of the most perfect in Somerset. Of three stages, in Doulting ashlar, it belongs to the type of the Wells Cathedral towers, exemplified also at St Cuthbert in Wells, and at Wrington (N), in which an impression of extreme height is obtained by continuing tall twin two-light bell-openings downward in twin two-light blank panels. The effect is of three tiers divided by transoms, the panels of the upper two tiers pierced for the bells, the lower tier longer. What is particularly special here is the arrangement of buttresses, pinnacles and crown. Each setback buttress carries, from the base of the top stage, twin shafts rising to finials at sill level of the bell-openings. Between them, set diagonally, a shaft rises right up to become one of the outriders of the intricate corner pinnacles. Stout, diagonally set main pinnacles with crockets are ringed by outriders not only on the angles (the aforementioned shafts) but also diagonally set on each face, and thus square to the main lines of the tower. This would imply no fewer than eight outriders, but there are only five as those not required for show are omitted. There is also a small intermediate pinnacle on each side, capping a continuous diagonal shaft that divides the whole top stage. The battlements themselves are pierced with quatrefoils. The second stage has blind two-light windows N and S and a canopied niche on the W, above a big sub-arched four-light W window, over a generously moulded four-centred doorway with traceried spandrels. The tower plinth lifts over the doorway. The SE stair-turret is kept low and minimal, so as not to intrude on the lines of the design. The date would seem to be mid-C15.

The church seems low behind all this. It is, however, treated ornately too: ashlar-faced aisles and Blue Lias clerestory, all with pierced quatrefoil parapets and pinnacles. The S aisle dates from 1843, a creditable copy by *Jesse Gane* of Evercreech, even down to the crouching beasts under the parapet. Chancel of Blue Lias, with pierced ashlar N parapet, and plain E and S parapets with pinnacles. The chancel is the earliest part, the E window with reticulated tracery, but the two N windows are Late Perp.

Internally the effect of the church is curiously cosy, thanks to Gothic gallery fronts by *Jesse Gane* squeezed balcony-like into the arcade arches. Those on the N are of 1825–35 (carried on an iron column cut into the back of each arcade pier) and those on the S came with the aisle in 1843. There is also good C15 work. The tower arch is uncommonly elaborate with four shafts, the outer ones set back, and three sets of panels between. The arcade is standard Somerset Perp with rather short four-hollow piers. On two N piers are angel brackets for images (originally on all the piers). Big three-light clerestory windows. The roof is Somerset at its best, and the bright C19 colouring helps to give something of the original effect. Tie-beams with fleurons, big leaf bosses, and angels leaning forward from short kingposts. Angels on the wall-plates between the trusses. Arched braces off stone angel corbels. Perp chancel arch. The chancel has a good Victorian encaustic TILE FLOOR and a coved plaster ceiling, probably early C19, from the panels with little leaves at the intersections.

FURNISHINGS. FONT. 1840s, with too many Perp motifs. – PULPIT. Stone, 1840s. – TOWER GALLERY. Mid-C19; traceried panels. – Elaborate Gothic REREDOS, c. 1875, infilled with mosaic. – CANDELABRA. Two, of brass, one dated 1761. – STAINED GLASS. E window, probably by *O'Connor*, later 1850s. – MONUMENTS. Rev. James Dugdale †1660. Elegant mid-C18 curved-fronted plaque under a broken pediment. – Joseph Barker. 1715, by *James Paty Sen.* With side scrolls; a cherub head and festoon below. – Rev. William Rodbard †1777. Open-pedimented, in coloured marbles, by *T. Paty & Sons*. – Cozens family, 1782. Corniced grey and white.

The churchyard occupies most of a modest square, with the C15 VILLAGE CROSS outside to the W, remarkably complete on four high steps. It stands in front of C18 COTTAGES with two pedimented doorways and THE LONG HOUSE, with C17 mullions and Georgian sashes. More C18 COTTAGES on the N side. On the E side, PRIORY COTTAGE, with mullioned windows, has Elizabethan plasterwork: fleurs-de-lys and initials downstairs, a Tudor rose, crown, and the initials ER upstairs. On the S side, a two-storey Tudor-style former SCHOOL, 1842, and CHURCH HOUSE, the bleak former vicarage, 1852, by *Jesse Gane*. High Street curves NW and then runs N without special architecture apart from EVERCREECH HOUSE, a confusion of pieces. The three-bay early C19 cube, with ashlar angles, cornice and low parapet, was a ballroom added to the corner of a much lower house built in 1777 for William Rodbard. Plain S side and, originally, two rear projections with canted ends. The gap between was filled in the early C19 with a third canted bay, making a strange array, as all three have plain Venetian windows. A double-height stair hall was inserted after 1876 (said, without evidence, to be by *T. G. Jackson*). Handsome woodwork: columns and carved consoles under a gallery with balustrading matching the staircase. Further N, on the r., are buildings of a CREAMERY established in 1891 behind BATT'S HOUSE, a stone-mullioned farmhouse of the C18. Down Queen's Road are SILK FACTORIES: Ward's on the S, two-storeyed, is early C19, Kemp's, on the N, is three-storeyed, c. 1860. SW, down Weymouth Road, the former BREWERS ARMS, with an ashlar Late Georgian three-storey front. A cottage dated 1676 adjoins the Gothic former METHODIST CHAPEL, 1872. On the Bruton road, E, opposite the CEMETERY of 1893, is THE KENNELS, a Georgian Gothic cottage with a long pointed window under a shaped gable, attached to monopitch-roofed kennels with C17 arched doorway.

STONEY STRATTON, ½ m. NNE. A hamlet around an irregular square of fields with a number of good houses. On the NW corner, CROSSWAYS has a C16 Tudor-arched doorway. On the NE corner, STRATTON HOUSE is ashlar-fronted Late Georgian, with paired outer sash windows and pedimented doorway. Down the E side, farmhouses facing over a pretty stream: ROCK FARM and HOME FARM, Late Georgian, and OLD PARSONAGE FARM, C17, with C18 mullioned windows. PARSONAGE HOUSE has an early C19 front and an older rear wing.

PECKING MILL, ½ m. SW. A Georgian mill treated with some dignity. Five-bay two-storey centre, with a one-bay pediment which looks rather like a gable and has a finial. Venetian window in the pediment, plainly framed, as are the other windows. Pedimented doorway.

EVERCREECH PARK, I m. SW. Site of a mansion of the Hoptons built in 1609–17 and demolished for the present farmhouse c. 1840.*

EVERCREECH JUNCTION, 1½ m. SW. Here the extension to Bath left the earlier Somerset & Dorset Railway from Highbridge to Bruton. House and single-storey former STATION of 1861–2. Just E, CUTTERNE MILL, on the River Alham, a Late Georgian house and mill in line: the house, of some elegance with ashlar window surrounds and pedimented doorway. A large stone fireplace on the end wall to the mill looks C17, improbable in this context. Mill machinery and internal 12-ft (3.7-metre) wheel of 1862.

EXFORD

ST MARY MAGDALENE. Originally St Salvyn. Plain three-stage C15 W tower with diagonal buttresses right up to the battlements, small bell-openings and a square NE stair-turret. The purplish stone is banded in grey slate. Angel- and devil-stops around the W window. Tall tower arch with a continuous hollow chamfer. The rest was much rebuilt in 1868–71 by *C. E. Giles*, of whom the E window and REREDOS are typical. The S aisle was added after 1534, when George Elsworth, blacksmith, left £3 towards 'the makyng of an yled'. The aisle and matching N windows, all renewed, are flat-headed, of the graceful design with quatrefoil spandrels to ogee-headed lights, found at Exton and elsewhere. The three-light pointed-arched E window of the aisle is specially elegant, also as at Exton. Four-bay S arcade. Piers of standard four-wave section, banded capitals with shields and good vine-leaf carving. Victorian roofs carried right through. – FONT. Octagonal, Perp, with quatrefoil panels and foliage motifs. Stem panels each containing a cusped bow-curve, randomly affronted or back-to-back. – ROOD SCREEN. Remnants of the C15–C16 screen from West Quantoxhead

---

* Buckler in 1822 illustrated a splendid three-storey porch-tower and a ribbed plaster hall ceiling with pendants.

church, demolished in 1853, were the basis of a new seven-and-a-half-bay screen of 1928–9. The original detail shows that it was of the local type of Minehead, Dunster, Carhampton, etc., with four-light sections, each arch subdivided in two, and bordered in leaf scroll. Ribbed and panelled coving beneath four richly carved foliage friezes. Giles's low stone SCREEN is now by the font. – PULPIT. 1929. With painted carved heraldry in wreaths. – STALLS. Reputedly from Queens' College, Cambridge, but they do not resemble the set from there by Bodley, 1858, now at Little Eversden, Cambs. – ORGAN. Victorian, from a private house. Gothic case with Renaissance-style painted panels. – STAINED GLASS. E window by *Clayton & Bell*, c. 1871. s aisle, two windows, 1937, by *Reginald Bell*, finely drawn on clear backgrounds, Comper-style.

In the village two hotels testify to the growth of Exmoor tourism c. 1900: the WHITE HORSE, overlooking the three-arched bridge, and the CROWN overlooking the green. Between them a former METHODIST CHAPEL, stuccoed, of 1838.

STONE FARMHOUSE, Stone. Built for Sir Thomas Dyke Acland, 7th Bt, in his role as Warden of Exmoor Forest after 1767. A Palladian design, ambitious for Exmoor. Hip-roofed, stuccoed with ample ashlar dressings: heavy quoins, band, eaves cornice, architraves. A Venetian window on each floor flanks a taller canted centre with quoins, ashlar attic with little lunettes, and an arched first-floor window over an arched doorway.

ROAD CASTLE, 1 m. SE. An almost square defended Iron Age enclosure with a 13-ft (4-metre) high bank with a ditch on three sides. To the N the slope has been scarped to form the fourth side. There are traces of stonework at places in the bank.

EXTON

ST PETER. Herringbone masonry found in the footings of the SW corner indicates a Norman date. The very plain and horribly cemented W tower with buttresses only at the foot may be C13. Low, slightly chamfered tower arch. Chancel of 1878. The nave S wall and the N aisle N wall have the handsome flat-headed early C16 windows, with quatrefoils in the spandrels of ogee-headed lights, found at Exford, Timberscombe, Porlock, etc. Conventional but elegant tracery to the pointed-arched E window of the aisle. In the s porch a chequered floor of end-on slates (cf. Watchet). Attractive interior under broad wagon roofs. Three-bay arcade on piers of standard four-hollow section with round capitals. – FONT. Perp. Octagonal with foliage in large quatrefoils. Large plain shields in the underside panels and on the base. – REREDOS. 1878, by *Powell's*. Matt tiles and unattractive mosaic. – Some medieval TILES re-set on the NE wall and chancel steps. – STAINED GLASS. E window, 1886, by *Lavers, Barraud & Westlake*. – MONUMENT. Rose

Pearse †1712 and Robert 'againe Joyned to his Amiable spouse March the 1. 1732'. Painted, the border rich with Death, Father Time, skull and bones, also flowers and angels in low-necked dresses.

Restored C15 CHURCHYARD CROSS.

On the hillside, RED DOOR FARMHOUSE is C16–C17 with a lateral chimney. The large gabled EXTON HOUSE, just above, was the rectory, 1871, by *Edward Ashworth*. At BRIDGETOWN in the valley, the MILL, gable-ended to the road, has mid-C19 machinery and a breast-shot wheel.

FAIRFIELD
2 m. w of Stogursey

The handsome white house in parkland has descended uninterrupted from *c.* 1200. William Verney was licensed in 1473 to enclose it within a rectangular circuit of walls with seven towers. Three towers were still apparent on an early C18 map, to the E of the house. The NE tower on excavation proved to be narrow, decorative rather than defensive, but the array must have made a fine show. Robert Verney (†1547) 'built a fair gatehouse of hewn stone, a fair chapple and four chambers with a new buttery in so much that a fairer dwelling was not in these parts'. The gatehouse and chapel have gone, but his first-floor hall and solar are now the western cross-wing. A range to the W known from C18 views was probably late medieval. Elizabeth Verney married William Palmer in 1571 and rebuilt the house before 1589 to its present typically Elizabethan E-plan with a central four-storeyed porch-tower. It is uncertain how far the medieval house extended eastward from the W cross-wing. The only evidence is a broad four-centred archway in the W wall of the central cross-passage, a position that does not relate to any typical medieval plan, but the archway is not obviously reused. Staircases were added in each cross-wing after 1700. The major remodelling was begun in 1781 by John Acland (Sir John Palmer-Acland, Bt, from 1818). Little subsequent alteration: Sir John's heir, Sir Peregrine (†1871), built St Audries (West Quantoxhead) to which his daughter Isabella moved on her marriage in 1849, and St Audries was the principal residence until her grandson the 2nd Baron St Audries returned to Fairfield in 1925.

The near-symmetrical s front is dated 1589 on the heraldry over the porch. Early C18 paintings show gabled cross-wings, a gabled central porch-tower and gabled garderobe turrets symmetrically between. John Acland removed the garderobes and the gables, substituting a cornice and parapet all around, with hipped roofs. The porch-tower was lowered a storey and given a pyramidal roof within parapets. It is all very tidy, with grids of mullion-and-transom windows. How much of this smoothness is Georgian is uncertain; underneath the lime render are indications of hoodmoulds and a plinth hacked back. The windows are in canted bays to the ends of the cross-wings, and regularly spaced elsewhere, save that, to the r. of the porch, two very large full-height windows light the Great Hall. These resemble the fenestration at Parham, Sussex, built from 1578 by Sir Thomas Palmer, a relation of William Palmer. Very many lights are false and some whole windows are blind. The cross-wings run back as service wings, the roofless NE one a former brewhouse. Between the rear wings is a late C18 kitchen.

Since the C18 the main entrance has been in the E cross-wing, into a full-height STAIR HALL. Good open-well staircase of *c.* 1700. Thick ramped rail on fat turned balusters. Medieval and later heraldic stained glass. The cornice dates from the 1780s, as does the decoration of the SE DRAWING ROOM. An anthemion frieze and Corinthian-columned yellow-and-white marble chimneypiece here. The GREAT HALL is a splendidly tall room with an exceptionally deeply coved Late Georgian ceiling, the plasterwork unremarkable Adam-style, but the scale impressive. It must supplant a flat Elizabethan ceiling, perhaps with pendants. Large plain grey-and-yellow marble chimneypiece. Now comes the CROSS-PASSAGE, with on the W wall the large Perp archway already mentioned. No rebate for a door. Two pretty square bays with circular-pattern ceilings of the 1780s, one in the porch, one just inside, on pilasters with simple anthemion ornament. The BOOK ROOM, W of the passage, has a simple marble and wood late C18 chimneypiece. In the W cross-wing a closed-string STAIRCASE of the early C18 with turned balusters. First-floor rooms of late C18 character. The damaged western attic roof, tree-ring-dated 1508–28, suggests a first-floor hall and solar in line. The hall-bays are more closely spaced, with principal trusses handsomely adorned with blind tracery. One section of wind-bracing remains, in opposed tiers making a concave lozenge. At the solar end the trusses are more widely spaced without blind tracery.

The kitchen backs on to an attractive rear courtyard closed by a plain single-storey STABLE. A brick cross-gabled DOVECOTE was added above the throughway in the early C19. Two potences (revolving ladders) inside. The slightly skewed alignment of the stables may relate to the medieval walled enclosure. Behind are a large C18 hip-roofed GRANARY and a thatched C17 BARN. The PARK was landscaped before 1791, removing a short canal in front made for Thomas Palmer (†1734). C18–C19 WALLED GARDENS to the NW, a stone dated 1778 in one.

FIDDINGTON

ST MARTIN. Rendered Perp W tower with Blue Lias diagonal buttresses and battlements. Polygonal NE stair-tower. Over-restored in 1860–1 by *John Norton*, who added the N aisle. But the nave has herringbone masonry and on the SE corner, an CII–CI2 SHEILA-NA-GIG, exceptional in Somerset. Low relief, carved with unskilled enthusiasm. Globe head, one arm upraised, and spread legs. C15–C16 roofs and shafted tower arch, C14 double-chamfered chancel arch. – FONT. Perp, octagonal with quatrefoils, the underside panels continued down the stem. – BENCHES. Some C16 ends with leaf-scroll borders (cf. Trull) and wiry plants. – PULPIT. Early C17. Typical arched panels below single flowers. – STAINED GLASS. Excellent E window, *c*. 1860, probably by *Lavers & Barraud*. Crucifixion against a glowing blue. N window, 1879, by *Lavers, Barraud & Westlake*.

CHURCHYARD CROSS, C15, with the ghost of a canopied figure.

ROOBIES FARMHOUSE, ½ m. W. Later C17. Early C18 panelled room with charming overmantel showing a stag hunt against an idealized local landscape, centred on a great house a little like Fairfield. Timber-framed C17 BARN, rare in this region.

BONSON MILL, ¾ m. E. Mostly early C19 despite a 1739 datestone. Roughcast three-bay house and long rubble-stone mill.

STOCKLAND LOVELL, I m. NE. Externally Victorian, but structurally a five-bay medieval house, the jointed-cruck roof tree-ring-dated to 1404. Inserted fireplace and plastered framed ceiling in the hall. Two C17 rear wings, the E one with a splendid early C18 plaster ceiling. A giant floral ring within a ring of husks, surrounded in foliage, all done with considerable naturalism (cf. Fitzhead Court and Nettlecombe Court). Kitchen, W wing, with curing-chamber and ovens.

FITZHEAD

ST JAMES. Red sandstone. Only the W tower is medieval. Perp, two-stage, with diagonal buttresses, battlements and square SE stair-turret. Chamfered tower arch. Nave and chancel of 1849, N aisle of 1881 when the chancel was re-windowed. Inside, a row of little C15 stone heads, some plain C16 PEWS, and the C15–C16 SCREEN. This was moved to the tower and horribly widened before being reinstated. Two unaltered bays each side with four-light sub-arched tracery. Ribbed coving with traceried cells; cornice restored 1907. – STAINED GLASS. E window, 1863, symbols on red or blue. N aisle, good set of 1882. – MONUMENT. Cannon family to 1762. White and grey marble.

In the churchyard, a C15 CROSS with eroded canopied saint. Tabernacle head of 1908. Small medieval TITHE BARN, rebuilt 1908 as the parish hall. Opposite the church, gabled RECTORY, 1865, by *Benjamin Ferrey*.

FITZHEAD COURT, in the village, is C16, a long rendered front between cross-wings. Georgian Gothick sash windows, probably inserted for Lord Somerville (†1819). Good early C18 room with notably exuberant ceiling of high-relief plasterwork: floral wreaths, shells, and in the cove, cherubs supporting Cannon family heraldry. Similar to work at Nettlecombe Court, perhaps by the Devon plasterer *John Abbott Jun.*

WEST FITZHEAD, ½ m. w. ILEX HOUSE, for Lord Ashburton's agent, is large, stuccoed and bargeboarded, *c.* 1840; probably by *Richard Carver*. WASHER'S FARMHOUSE, with a stair projection at one end, is C16–C17. Two framed ceilings, one moulded nine-panel, the other four-panel, plastered, with C18 laurel wreaths.

FIVEHEAD

ST MARTIN. Late Perp w tower of eroding Blue Lias. Diagonal buttresses, battlements, pinnacles. Two tiers of openings in the top stage, two-light bell-openings over three-light windows, all with pierced baffles. Polygonal NE stair-turret. w doorway with leaf spandrels; large five-light w window with panel tracery below the transom. Perp nave and two-bay s chapel, lengthened to an aisle in 1864 by *C. E. Giles*. Late Perp square-headed chancel s windows, with a high transom, but two N lancets are late C13, one cinquefoiled inside. Standard Perp tower arch, chancel arch and arcade (only two bays original), shafted with four hollows. NE rood stair. One rood-loft corbel is reused C12, with saltire-cross decoration. – FONT. Norman. Circular bowl with saltire-cross rim and cable moulding at the bottom. – PULPIT. Oak, High Victorian. – TOWER SCREEN. 1953, by *Philip Sturdy*. Good, with swan-head arm-rests. – STAINED GLASS. E window, 1901. – MONUMENT. Jane Seymour †*c.* 1565, daughter-in-law of Somerset, the Lord Protector. The 3-ft 6-in. (107-cm.) brass figure is a palimpsest of older brasses including one late C14 Flemish one inscribed in Spanish, and one dated 1428.

BAPTIST CHAPEL. 1866. White Lias. Still essentially Georgian Gothic.

LANGFORD MANOR, ¼ m. E. A substantial C16–C17 house of Blue Lias with mullioned windows, some transomed. E-plan on both sides. Broad gabled cross-wings projecting further than the storeyed s porch. The three rear gables are more evenly sized, so the cross-wings are not of a piece. The s cross-wings and probably the porch are early C17, which fits with the flat balusters of the sw staircase, but the main roof has early C16 arch-braced trusses.

CATHANGER MANOR, ¾ m. W. The remnant of a C16 house rebuilt for John Walsh, lawyer. Once three-sided. Two ranges remain, C16 and early C19. The N range, dated 1559, has in the western half deep-set mullion windows marking a first-floor hall reached by a polygonal stair-tower. The hall is stripped out apart from a moulded C16 fireplace. C18 roof. The stuccoed E range has Late Georgian triple sash windows, but a plinth and string course on the S end are C16. A garden wall with plinth and moulded doorway indicates the lost S range.

Facing the E range is a GATEHOUSE small enough to be a garden pavilion (cf. Cothelstone). Gabled, thatched, of banded Blue Lias and marlstone, it dates from *c.* 1600 and has Montacute-type shell niches flanking the archway. Mullioned window above. The outer face lacks the niches. At the courtyard corners are banded stone gables of otherwise plain outbuildings, the NW one a very large DOVECOTE (some 1,200 nesting boxes, originally more), the SW one a BARN with jointed-cruck trusses.

GALHAMPTON

s of Castle Cary

CHURCH. 1876. Gothic former Congregational chapel.
On the main road, FOXCOMBE FARMHOUSE with C17 ovolo mullions, and a canted-fronted TOLL HOUSE decorated with ammonites.
MANOR HOUSE, ½ m. SE. 1723. Hip-roofed with two matching fronts poised between C17 and C18 sensibilities. The walls are gridded in raised strips and the windows mullioned but architraved, and there is a good cornice. Baluster staircase.
BARROW COURT, 1 m. SW. 1910–12, by *E. Turner Powell*, for Captain Kelly, of *Kelly's Directories*. An Arts and Crafts house to the butterfly plan, of warm handmade brick with oak mullion-and-transom windows, more Sussex than Somerset. Sweeping roofs and clustered chimneys. Canted wings frame a shouldered gable on rusticated piers. In the hall, exuberant plasterwork in C17 style and a branching oak stair.

GARE HILL

Poised on a saddle of hill near the Wiltshire boundary.

ST MICHAEL. Now a house. 1857–8, by *William Butterfield*, for the Earl of Cork and Orrery. Approached under a gabled archway. Nave and chancel under a single red-tiled roof with an octagonal W bellcote on a central buttress. Neat Early Dec tracery. Butterfield's individual roof structures survive, but mostly hidden. – STAINED GLASS. By *Horwood Bros*, 1858, the E window especially good, designed by *Butterfield*.
Butterfield designed two COTTAGE PAIRS below, 1857–8, the hipped half-dormers characteristic. Stone with brick dressings, both now partly roughcast, and Corner House extended.

Butterfield may also have designed the gabled stone PARSON-AGE, further along, and small OLD SCHOOLHOUSE (teacher's house), just below, both *c.* 1862.

GAULDEN MANOR *see* TOLLAND

GERBESTONE MANOR *see* WEST BUCKLAND

GLASTONBURY

Glastonbury Abbey was founded on an eminence above the meres, according to legend by Joseph of Arimathea, who landed at Glastonbury bringing the Holy Grail with him. He had been sent out by St Philip, Christ's disciple, to evangelize Britain, and built an oratory of wattle and sand, the ancestor of the venerable *vetusta ecclesia*. Legend also identifies Glastonbury with Avalon and makes it the burial place of King Arthur. With these traditions Glastonbury can in fairness be called the most famous of Britain's monasteries. The abbey church at the Reformation was among the largest of the Christian world, its destruction among the greatest losses. Glastonbury town grew up outside the four-square walls of the precinct, principally on the N and W. It retains more medieval work than is immediately apparent in the typical market-town streets with their buildings of Blue Lias, Doulting ashlar and brick. The town has spread over the backdrop hills, to unfortunate effect in distant views. Glastonbury's early C20 reincarnation as a centre for Arthurian lore, and late C20 redirection to accommodate most spiritual persuasions, has given the town a distinct personality, but no especial architecture.

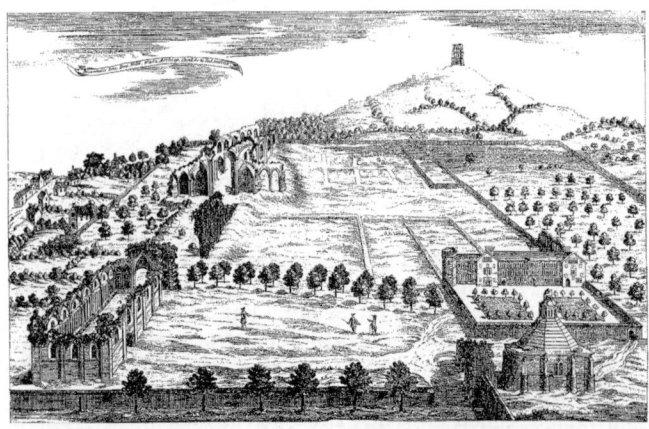

Glastonbury Abbey, bird's-eye view.
Engraving after W. Stukeley, 1724

GLASTONBURY ABBEY

William of Malmesbury's early C12 history, much interpolated in the surviving version, gives an account acceptable in broad outline. The first church, the *vetusta ecclesia*, on the site of the present Lady Chapel, was a timber building dedicated to the Virgin Mary and hallowed by association with the saints of the C5–C6. That sanctity was enhanced by the burial of saints in a walled cemetery to the S and by the collection of relics, including important ones from Northumbria. A holy well was just outside the S wall of the church. The sanctity of the site was respected by the Anglo-Saxons and in 712–19 King Ine built a second church, dedicated to Saints Peter and Paul, just E of the original. Pottery evidence shows occupation of the site from the C3 or even C4 B.C. through Roman times. Fragments of Eastern Mediterranean pottery of c. 450–600 are scant evidence for the period of St Patrick, St David and King Arthur. We are on surer ground for the C7–C10 with the close-packed cemetery and artefacts from a ditch defining the E side of the monastic enclosure dated to the early C7. Also later documents refer to a land grant by King Cenwealh c. 650. The earliest archaeological evidence for glass-making in Anglo-Saxon Britain, c. 680, has been obtained by radiocarbon-dating of material found in the 1950s.

The *vetusta ecclesia* is lost to archaeology under the Lady Chapel. The ANGLO-SAXON CHURCH, beneath the W end of the nave of the main abbey church, has however been excavated, although nothing remains visible. It started intriguingly with a tomb, a narrow space with steps down probably pre-dating Ine's church. It was just outside Ine's chancel but was filled in when Dunstan, abbot 940–60, added what may have been an eastern tower. This church of Ine and Dunstan comprised a narrow nave and chancel, widened with small square chambers (porticus) on each side. After Dunstan's additions it was roughly square. Of Ine's time was a small W courtyard or atrium connecting to the back of the *vetusta ecclesia*. William of Malmesbury records two 'pyramids' outside, 18 and 26 ft (5.5 and 7.9 metres) high, carved with figures and names. These were probably C9–C10 commemorative stone pillars. The nave of the *vetusta ecclesia* (according to a lost C14–C15 plaque) was 60 ft by 26 ft (18.3 by 7.9 metres), substantial indeed, longer apparently than the church of Ine and Dunstan. There were also small timber oratories within the cemetery. Dunstan built a separate stone chapel that may have served as some kind of gatehouse, W of the original church. The three churches were in a typical Anglo-Saxon linear arrangement. King Edgar made generous gifts towards Dunstan's works and was buried here in 975. Other Saxon kings buried at Glastonbury were Edmund (†946) and Edmund Ironside (†1016).

After the Norman Conquest the oldest church (unusually) was kept, because of the sanctity of the site, and a new one begun under the first Norman abbot, Turstin (1078–96). The church of Ine and Dunstan disappeared under the nave of a larger Norman church built under Abbot Herlewin (1100–18), dissatisfied with

Turstin's beginnings. This was completed with a cloister and ancillary buildings by Henry of Blois (1126–71), the most powerful of Glastonbury's abbots, Bishop of Winchester, papal legate, and brother of King Stephen. These were of some splendour to judge from surviving fragments including superbly carved Blue Lias capitals. All this was burnt in the disastrous fire of 1184. Immediately a new *vetusta ecclesia* and a new abbey church were begun in axis with each other and carried on simultaneously, promoted by Henry II. The former, the church of St Mary, later known as the Lady Chapel, was built so rapidly that it was consecrated in 1186; the latter, the church of St Peter and St Paul, more slowly, indeed the ruined nave was patched to remain in use for thirty years. The style of the Lady Chapel was Romanesque, probably in homage to predecessor buildings, although clearly the architect understood well the Early Gothic style being introduced at Wells from 1180. Early Gothic appears within the chapel and is the style of the abbey church, or Great Church, itself.

The Great Church took the whole medieval period to complete. The death of Henry II in 1189 curtailed royal support. Fortunately in 1191 when funds were most needed, the grave of Arthur and Guinevere in the old cemetery was revealed, enhancing an already shining appeal to pilgrims. Abbot de Sully (1189–93) was granted the right to the mitre (bringing independence from episcopal interference) but immediately Glastonbury was embroiled in conflict with the bishops. For twenty years, 1199–1219, the abbey was subsumed into a bishopric of Bath and Glastonbury. Nevertheless work continued through this period. The choir and transepts were built first, the monks taking possession at Christmas 1213. The outline of the nave was then set out, and in the 1220s or 1230s a Galilee or narthex was built between the Lady Chapel and the W end of the great church. The nave was probably complete in time for the transfer of the remains of Arthur and Guinevere in the presence of Edward I and Eleanor in 1278, though not yet vaulted. A very large ceremonial N porch, a substantial tower, was the principal entrance. Under Abbot Fromond (1303–22) the crossing tower was completed and the E part of the nave vaulted. Under Abbot de Sodbury (1323–34) the nave vault was completed. Under Abbot Monington (1342–74) the choir was lengthened to six bays, refaced inside, and a retro-choir was added. The contract for the roof is dated 1364. Abbot Chinnock (1375–1420) rebuilt the cloisters and monastic buildings. Under Abbot Bere (1493–1524) an eastern chapel was erected for the remains of King Edgar, flying buttresses were added to the choir, and strainer arches, as at Wells, were placed under the side arches of the crossing, indicative of structural problems. Also, to accommodate the cult of Joseph of Arimathea, a crypt was placed under the Lady Chapel with access to the holy well just outside the chapel. By then the Lady Chapel, the prime focus of pilgrimage to Glastonbury, had taken in the whole of the Galilee, so that its high altar was at the foot of the steps to the Great Church. Finally, under Abbot Whiting (1525–39) the

Edgar Chapel was completed such that the whole church, from here to the end of the Lady Chapel, was some 580 ft (177 metres) long (nave, chancel and retrochoir *c.* 375 ft (114 metres)), the longest in England (Canterbury 547 ft (167 metres), Wells 415 ft (126.5 metres)).

The abbey ruins passed into private hands until 1908 when they were purchased for the Church of England and repaired by *W. D. Caröe*. The story of the excavation and presentation of the site is one of the messier stories of British archaeology. Underfunded and bedevilled by changes of direction, a great deal that was dug was never recorded. The excavations of 1908–22 under *Frederick Bligh Bond* began well, but came to a controversial end over Bond's use of spirit guides to direct his work. After him, the foundations of the Anglo-Saxon church were found. Post-war excavations under C. A. Ralegh Radford, 1951–64, were never adequately published, and many of Radford's conclusions, particularly on the Anglo-Saxon site, have proved ill-founded. All

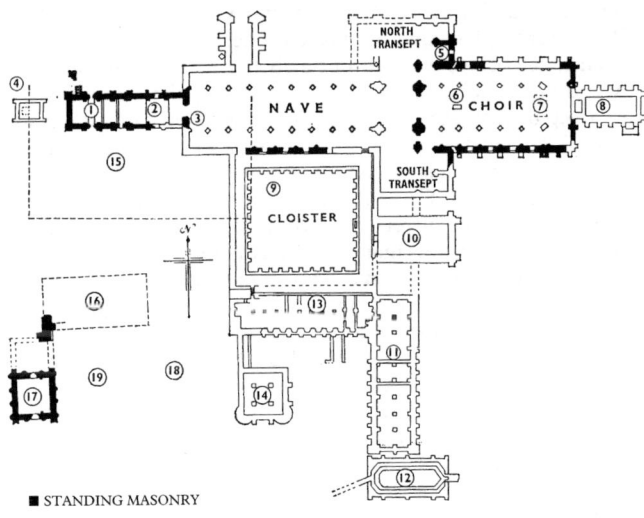

■ STANDING MASONRY

1. Lady Chapel
2. Galilee
3. Position of Ine's Church
4. St Dunstan's Chapel
5. Chapel of St Thomas Becket
6. King Arthur's Shrine
7. High Altar
8. Edgar Chapel
9. Position of Bell Tower
10. Chapter House
11. East Range (Dormitory on Upper Floor)
12. Latrine
13. Vault under Refectory
14. Monks' Kitchen
15. Position of Ancient Cemetery
16. Abbot's Hall
17. Abbot's Kitchen
18. Position of East Range of Abbot's House
19. Garden

Glastonbury Abbey.
Plan, 1966

the excavation material from 1904 to 1979 is being re-examined to ascertain which reported discoveries can still be called reliable. The presentation of the actual site, however, under the Glastonbury Abbey Trust, has greatly improved since Pevsner saw it in the 1950s.

Entrance and Lady Chapel

The site is entered through the VISITOR CENTRE of 1989–93 by *Beech Tyldesley*. Here are gathered excavated fragments, and the model of the abbey at the Reformation is displayed. Among the fragments are Blue Lias pieces probably from the mid-C12 cloister of Henry of Blois, of exceptional refinement, especially considering the intractable material. Also displayed are a selection of encaustic TILES and some EFFIGIES, the most complete being an early C13 abbot under a cinquefoiled gabled canopy, perhaps Abbot de St Vigor (†1223); the C15 Othery cope, embroidered with the Assumption and six-winged seraphim; and *Eric Gill*'s Virgin and Child, 1928, from the R.C. church preceding the present one.

The entrance brings one appropriately to the Lady Chapel at the w end of the abbey church, which replaced the *vetusta ecclesia* in 1184–6. Just w is the footprint of St Dunstan's detached chapel, and just N, a piece of masonry from an unidentified structure. The most complete surviving part of the abbey church, the LADY CHAPEL stands as a four-bay oblong with pronounced angle turrets. Its decorative motifs and the relation of them to plain wall make it a Norman building, but unlike any other, more akin to an ornamented casket. It may echo the *vetusta ecclesia*, perhaps in the corner towers, though its Late Norman antecedents include similar angle turrets at Gloucester, Hereford, Worcester and St Davids cathedrals, and intersected arcading and shafted buttresses at Malmesbury Abbey. The enriched chevron emanates from Gloucester and Hereford of the 1120s, through the Bristol Abbey gatehouse to Worcester after 1175 and St Davids after 1182. Surprisingly, and unlike any of these buildings, the roof was hipped.

The corner towers have angle shafts to eaves level, and two still carry pyramid-roofed turrets with close-spaced intersecting arcading. The top pyramids once carried lanterns on eight colonnettes which must have made a brave show. Piers divide the sides, the angle shafts slightly keeled and already with Gothic leaf capitals, showing the co-existence of Late Norman and Early Gothic that is so much a feature of the abbey. The piers rise only to two-thirds height, ending in upturned scallop capitals that are the bases of missing shafts up to the corbel cornice. These shafts separated four big arched windows. The w end has a stepped triplet of similar windows (with inserted tracery of *c.* 1500). Between the lower piers on all three sides is intersected arcading, the missing shafts having been set into concave recesses. The ornament is typical Latest Norman chevron and similar motifs. The simple chevron of the lower arcading is placed at an angle of 45 degrees. The upper windows each have one order of much richer chevron carried on shafts (missing) between two continuous roll mouldings. This chevron is of that inventive pipework familiar from the English Marches and St Davids Cathedral. Notable on the lower arcading and on the windows is that the remaining capitals, bases and securing middle rings are of Blue Lias, as presumably were the missing shafts, a striking use of contrasted materials comparable e.g. with the use of Purbeck marble in the eastern arm at Canterbury. The capitals have Early Gothic stiff-leaf foliage and the bases are of the water-holding type.

The round-arched and gabled N and S DOORWAYS, although eroded, contain sculpture of high quality. In general disposition the doorways are in the Anglo-Norman and more specifically West Country traditions. Malmesbury of c. 1165 in particular ought to be compared, where the figures are also small, set in foliage trails and medallions, and the arches unbroken. Of the five orders within each arch the two with narrative scenes are on columned shafts, whereas the other three are unbroken. The narratives are in the second and fourth, between three orders of particularly lovely foliage inhabited by men, birds and beasts. On the N doorway the inner order is uncarved. On the S, the jambs of the inner order are uncarved and all of the second and fourth, that is the narrative scenes, except two medallions of the second, the creation of Eve and the Fall. Both inner orders were repaired by *Caröe* in 1908–9 so the extent of carving is uncertain. On the N side the carving relates to the Nativity. In the second order, amid foliage, are the Annunciation, Visitation, Nativity, and the Magi before Herod. In the fourth order the depiction is more formal, in nineteen pointed-oval medallions, the scenes spread across several. The first four show the Magi (one in each) and the seated Virgin. The next three show the Magi riding, then three show them (individually) in bed, then five show the Massacre, with Herod on his throne, three individual soldiers (in chain-mail) and mourning mothers. Finally three show Joseph's Dream, an ass, and Joseph carrying a bundle. Amid the foliage of the third order, a woman, perhaps St Bridget, can be recognized, milking.

Pevsner thought the style of the sculpture entirely Gothic, entirely French, and hardly possible before c. 1230, a date supported by the armour depicted. Malcolm Thurlby* thought it likely that it was of 1184–9, arguing that the complexity of the foliage made it necessarily carved *ex situ* and therefore of a date with the building. This is challenged by the S portal medallions being incomplete, and clearly being worked *in situ*. John of Glastonbury states that work stopped in 1189 when Henry II died. It seems likely that the S doorway marks the moment the workmen left.

11

---

* *Antiquaries Journal* 75, 1995, 107–70.

Now to the roofless interior. The floor was raised for a crypt introduced by Abbot Bere *c.* 1500, the vault since collapsed. The lower walls have the intersecting arcading of the exterior, here enriched by small paterae or roundels of Early Gothic stiff-leaf foliage, under the heads and in the spandrels. There are traces of colour in the paterae and arch-heads, and Early Gothic trefoil arches were painted into each panel. The upper windows are, as on the outside, chevron-arched, on column shafts between continuous rolls. A similar roll borders the pointed-arched panel in which each window is set. These panels indicate the essential thing about the Lady Chapel, that it was vaulted, and the vaults are fully understood Gothic. Not only were they rib-vaults – there are after all plenty of Norman rib-vaults including some in Somerset and including also the new building which was stylistically the most important for Glastonbury, the w end of Worcester Cathedral of *c.* 1175–80 – but here they were consistently pointed. The ribs had a double roll moulding, but the transverse arches had the rich chevron of the window heads. The vaults spring from Blue Lias capitals whose missing shafts were set into concave recesses in piers that correspond to the external buttresses.

As antecedents for the combination of Late Norman and Early Gothic, Malmesbury and Worcester seem indeed the immediate premises, always subject of course to the possibility of others having been destroyed. Malmesbury in the 1160s has pointed arches in a Norman setting, Worcester in the 1170s a combination of pointed and round, and in addition nibbed shafts and chevron at right angles to the wall, just like Glastonbury; moreover at Worcester the aisles are rib-vaulted, and the decorative motif of paterae occurs consistently. Malcolm Thurlby points out that the fragments of Keynsham Abbey (N), built *c.* 1167, provide an antecedent geographically closer. And there are keeled shafts and paterae in the nave at Wells.

At the E end a great pointed arch with triple transverse ribs on Lias shafts (missing) opens into the GALILEE, built to the same height as the chapel in the 1220s or 1230s, from evidence of masons' marks. It would appear that a screen replaced the Lady Chapel E wall, and another screen crossed the Galilee at the foot of steps up to the W doorway of the great church, so the Galilee was not a processional way but more of an ante-chapel. Of three bays, it echoes the Lady Chapel in having windows set high in large pointed panels of a rib-vault. Below the windows inside is tall trefoiled blank arcading, formerly on Lias shafts with shaft-rings. On the outside the bays are defined by buttresses with shallow niches for statues, originally in two tiers and on all three faces, suggesting the type of overall figure sculpture of the W front of Wells Cathedral. The elegant pointed-arched N doorway has two orders of shafts and a trefoiled tympanum. The pointed windows were remade probably in the C15 when the upper buttresses were altered.

Around 1500 Abbot Bere built a CRYPT beneath the Lady Chapel as a chapel to Joseph of Arimathea. This extended under two bays of the Galilee. The vault under the Lady Chapel has gone, the surviving detail clearly Perp, but one bay under the Galilee survives. Here the vault, of very thick round ribs in pairs on short paired wall-shafts, is not Perp but C12–C13. The oblong bay has longitudinal and transverse ridge-ribs, the short transverse rib dividing clumsily to meet the diagonal ribs from the corners. The explanation for this vault is still unclear. It may be old-fashioned work of the 1230s; more probably it is reused from elsewhere in 1500. From the Lady Chapel crypt access was made to the holy well originally reached from the churchyard on the S. Renamed ST JOSEPH'S WELL, it was a key element in the cult. The circular basin is set off-centre beneath an arch of C12 chevron, with another chevron arch within the recess.

The abbey church

The ABBEY CHURCH was begun in the same year as St Mary's Chapel, i.e. 1184. Work here also halted in 1189, but resumed such that enough of the eastern parts was complete for the monks to use by 1213. The church was dedicated under Abbot Fromond (1303–22) although the nave vault was only completed around 1330. The plan is laid out in the grass, and easy to understand. The nave is accompanied by aisles and had nine bays. On the S side was the cloister, and on the N side the porch-tower of an internal depth equal to that of two bays of the nave. Crossing, and transepts with, unusually, eastern aisles before twin E chapels. Aisled choir of five bays and straight-ended aisled retrochoir of two bays, and then the aisleless Edgar Chapel of 87-ft (26.5 metre) length. What survives, apart from the plan, is something of the outer walls of the C14 retrochoir and the late C12 chancel aisles, mostly on the S; a large and tall fragment of the eastern crossing piers and adjoining transept E chapels; a three-bay stretch of outer wall of the S nave aisle; and a substantial portion of the W front, with the doorway into the Galilee.

The CHANCEL has the same mixture of Norman and Gothic as the Lady Chapel, though the proportion between the two is now reversed. Here is still the old chevron, but the capitals are crocketed and the arches pointed with a Gothic purpose. The shafted windows also are pointed. Chevron appears only in the window heads, between plain chamfers, and does not occur in the aisle vaulting, where the ribs are roll-moulded on triple wall-shafts. This is similar to the W end of Worcester (c. 1175–80). The Blue Lias shafting so prominent in the Lady Chapel does not appear at all here, suggesting a different master mason. The wall-shafts rise from a continuous bench and the windows are set in broad pointed panels outlined in a roll moulding matching the vaulting ribs. The broken fifth bay marks the end of the C13 work. The RETROCHOIR added by Abbot Monington (1342–74) preserved the same composition at least for the aisles, even to the chevron arches,* although the wall-shaft bases give away the later date. He added two bays. The narrow blank S aisle bay corresponded to the piers between the high altar and ambulatory. Monington also vaulted or re-vaulted the chancel at a higher level (the chancel height was c. 90 ft (27.4 metres)) and relined the walls. Of the way in which he proceeded the blank panelling just E of the NE crossing pier is evidence. There remain five tiers of small blank-arched single-light panels. So one has to assume an arrangement based on that of the Gloucester choir, and indeed the choir at Wells as reworked in 1333–7, whereby the new style was put as a veneer on the late C12 or early C13 walls, and new higher and probably wider clerestory windows were made part of that grid. As an early case of the Perp style in Somerset this choir must be remembered. Only foundations remain of Abbot Bere's oblong Edgar Chapel of c. 1500.

Only the E piers of the CROSSING survive. They have soaring paired shafts right up to a pointed transverse arch. The E side of the TRANSEPTS is most helpful in reconstructing the original appearance of the upper parts of the church of 1184 etc. The elevation consists of arcade, triforium and clerestory, with a wall passage in front of the clerestory windows. The piers of the arcade consist of a large number of shafts grouped towards the transept so as to carry with a central triple shaft the transverse arch and ribs of the high vault, with further shafts for the moulded arcade arches, and with one shaft between these two groups to carry a wall arch taller than the arcade and lower than the high vault. This wall arch frames arcade and triforium together – a peculiarity of some early C12 churches in England and Scotland, of which Jedburgh and Oxford are the most familiar examples, whereas Tewkesbury and Romsey are the examples nearest to Glastonbury. The small arches of the grouped triforium – three to each bay – are trefoiled and not pointed, and above, under each wall arch, was a lozenge-shaped patera. Gathered under each high vault arch was a stepped triplet of pointed clerestory windows, the tall centre light shafted with three shaft-rings and the side lights with two orders of shafts, also with shaft-rings. Square paterae above the side lights. The arches of the three levels each have one order of chevron decoration. The details of capitals, etc., are clearly early C13. The chevron achieves the richness of the Lady Chapel in the arches from the transept E aisles into the square eastern chapels, best preserved on the N transept. A huge wall-monument with pinnacles once filled the N wall of the NE chapel.

The NAVE continued this system, but from fragments found it is certain that, when the triforium stage was reached, the C13 was over. There was ballflower decoration in the triforium arches. All that remains *in situ* is the outer S aisle wall, and here the C13 design was kept for five bays. Then there is clearly a

---

* Reusing stonework presumably from the original E wall. J. Sampson.

break in the treatment of the vaulting springers, and it is assumed that it marks the period of Abbot de Sodbury, i.e. the second quarter of the C14. The windows revert to round heads inside but are pointed outside, suggesting that continuity with the Romanesque was of greater importance here than in the earlier choir. Was this in homage to the Lady Chapel? Part of a S doorway to the cloister remains at the W end, with two orders of chevron on colonnettes, between three plain orders. Only one of the three surviving aisle windows has chevron inside, and none outside. The exterior is blank to sill height for the lost cloister. Broad nook-shafted piers between the windows above. These piers have stubs of flying buttresses added when the cloister was rebuilt *c.* 1400. The nave W wall has, to each side of the portal, trefoiled recesses of the same kind as in the Galilee outside. The portal itself is not high to the interior, and is covered by a depressed pointed arch of English C13–C14 type. But externally, to the Galilee, the WEST PORTAL is a stately, finely moulded arch on four orders of shafts (reverting here to the Blue Lias consonant with the Galilee ornament). In front of the tympanum was an arcaded screen with foiled or cusped heads, the centre arch trefoiled, those on each side with two rising foils or lobes each.

Monastic buildings

The Glastonbury community was generally of forty to fifty monks. Foundations remain of their CLOISTER, which was about 135 ft (41 metres) square. On its E side was an oblong CHAPTER HOUSE, built under abbots Monington and Chinnock. Chinnock was buried here in 1420. He rebuilt most of the monastic buildings, including the cloisters, refectory and dormitory. On the S side, the outline of an undercroft with a row of central supports indicates the REFECTORY. Of the W side almost nothing remains. S of the W end of the refectory was a detached, square MONKS' KITCHEN, very large, with curved projections at the SW and SE angles and four central supports. The E range was continued southward beyond the refectory by the DORMITORY, also with an undercroft with middle supports. The nine-bay undercroft was subdivided into three rooms. S of the dormitory are visible the remains of the drains of the REREDORTER or lavatories.

SW of the cloister were the abbot's quarters, recorded as having a Great Hall completed under Abbot Breynton (1334–42) and chapel completed under Monington. Abbot Breynton probably also built the detached kitchen. Stukeley's drawing of 1723 shows the abbot's lodging as a long two-storey range facing W towards the kitchen. This had just been demolished but his view roughly accords with a description of 1712 of a ten-bay range with projecting gables. All that remains of the abbot's quarters are the kitchen and some broken wall running northward to the remaining corner of the ABBOT'S HALL, just part of a fine rib-vault of the porch and a vaulted mural staircase.

The ABBOT'S KITCHEN, one of the best-preserved medieval kitchens in Europe, is unsurpassed in Britain. Others are at the bishop's palaces of Durham and Chichester. It was built with the Abbot's Hall in the 1330s by Abbot de Sodbury. Marks of masons who worked on the choir extension at Wells 1333–7 and at Ottery St Mary, Devon after 1337, which to Jerry Sampson suggests the involvement of *William Joy* as master mason. The kitchen is square in plan, with fireplaces fitting the four corners so as to result in an octagonal interior. Three-stage stone octagonal roof, the main part carrying a large tall lantern of Early Perp character with panelled transomed two-light sides, each with small windows above the transom, and shallow battlements. A further octagonal roof carries a much smaller lantern, also with two-light sides, crowned by a little octagonal cap. The external square is of three bays, divided by heavy curved buttresses that elide into the walls and change above a mid-height string course to chamfered buttresses with set-offs. The central bay has a two-light window at the upper level, simple and square-headed over the N and S doors, pointed and with cusped ogee-headed lights to the E and W. Cornice all around, with gargoyles E and W, waterspouts N and S. On the S side rough masonry and corbels show that a structure was attached. The N doorway has a stark unmoulded curved surround, the S one a pointed arch behind a segmental arch. Soaring octagonal ribbed vault with vents around a circular top opening. The four corner fireplaces have slightly chamfered broad segmental-pointed arches under hoodmoulds. S of the kitchen were FISHPONDS associated with a mill on the SW corner of the precinct.

Around the whole site is the PRECINCT WALL, highest along the N side, perhaps the back wall of lodgings. Here once was the Great Gate to the abbey. Behind the visitor centre and against this wall were ST PATRICK'S ALMSHOUSES, refounded by Abbot Bere *c.* 1512. Rebuilt as a plain Late Georgian row, they were demolished as late as 1960. The simple early C16 CHAPEL survives, restored and limewashed in 2003. A narrow moulded doorway on each side wall. Windowless N and W walls, the latter with Tudor roses and the abbey arms on shields. Flat-headed four-light S window. The bellcote and E window are Victorian replacements. Inside, a simple plastered barrel ceiling and charming painted scenes and ornament by *Fleur Kelly*, based on late medieval examples (as done in the re-erected church at St Fagans Museum, Glamorgan). – STAINED GLASS. S window. Medieval and later fragments including a pair of heads at a prison window. E window by *Wayne Ricketts*, 2003. The pedestrian GATEWAY to the precinct survives behind the abbey gatehouse. It has a Tudor rose shield over a scroll (dated 1512 in an engraving of 1817).

The ABBEY GATEHOUSE to the Market Square was the secondary entrance, depicted in 1752 as a substantial house

Glastonbury Abbey, gatehouse.
Engraving by William Barnes, early C19

attached to a pointed archway with machicolated battlements. The archway was infilled before the C19 as part of the Red Lion Inn. The battlements disappeared for a tiled roof by the later C19. Reopened in 1908–9 by *W. D. Caröe*, the arches front and back are segmental-pointed and double-chamfered, probably C14. The entrance for pedestrians, shown round-arched in 1752, may have been remodelled. It is now pointed and double-chamfered and opens to a vaulted passageway under the r. bay of the adjacent house. This is of two storeys, refronted in 1639. It has a broad battlemented canted bay with ovolo-moulded mullion-and-transom windows on each floor, two-light in the sides, twice three-light in the front. A cornice with little modillions extends over similar two-light windows on each side at first-floor level. Another on the l. below replaces an archway there in 1752. Rear wing with C17 windows in the E gable. The house is medieval – see the heavy chamfered beams in the front room side and a low, roughly vaulted undercroft behind. Upstairs, a C16 fireplace on the front S wall, and a chamfered screen to the rear room which has plasterwork of *c.* 1600 in a framed ceiling. (Collected stonework includes a good C15 fireplace lintel from the High Street, with three relief panels.)

CHURCHES AND MAJOR BUILDINGS

ST JOHN BAPTIST, High Street. A C15 church, rebuilt, with a few hardly noticeable exceptions, from the 1420s to *c.* 1500. The C12–C13 church was cruciform with a crossing tower. Of this there remains only a cinquefoiled rere-arch to the S transept W window, of *c.* 1300. The church was called new in 1428–9 but the unified interior suggests a coherent rebuilding beginning when the crossing tower was removed around 1465. The master mason *William Smyth* was involved, but on what part is not known. The blocked chancel side windows may be early C15, also the lower storey of the porch. The masonry of the transepts is earlier still. These were opened into the nave and aisles when the nave arcades, clerestory, and roofs were built in the later C15. The remodelling of the chancel and chancel chapels is a little later, and finally came the tower and upper storey of the porch.

The tower is the second tallest of any Somerset parish church at 134 ft (41 metres) high, of Doulting stone. It deserves close study. It has set-back buttresses with pinnacled shafts above the first set-off and then shafts again against the bell-stage. The W doorway is uncommonly large, and the plinth is carried over it in a big square frame. It has quatrefoils with the Lamb and Eagle in the spandrels, and leaf sprays in one hollow of the arch. Canopied niches on each side are repeated taller on each side of the six-light W window. The display on the N and S sides starts with two tiers of two canopied niches, divided by a band with angels, and, on the N, squeezed by the big polygonal base of the stair-tower. Between them and up the centre of each side and from the apex of the W window rise triangular shafts (cf. North Petherton) going right through two tall stages to end in the intermediate pinnacles of the crown. The next two stages are one composition, both very tall. The lower one is covered with twin two-light panelling with two transoms, and the vertical lines of this are then taken up at the bell-stage by twin four-light bell-openings with two transoms. On top of this stands the filigree crown that reached here from Gloucester via Bristol, Dundry and Taunton. The Taunton tower was built between 1488 and 1514. The battlements are completely pierced by arcading in two tiers, and between square angle turrets also pierced in two tiers, each with a pierced and crocketed spirelet between corner finials. In addition a little outrider stands free of each turret corner, corbelled out on a gargoyle. The intermediate pinnacles are also accompanied by junior and outrider pinnacles. The scale of the tower prevents all this exuberance making the crown top-heavy.

The rest of the church is proudly Perp, if without the especial display of Crewkerne or Ilminster. The nave appears tall – 'lightsome' is the word used by Leland for it – from the long seven-bay embattled clerestory that sails above. This is embattled, as are the elements of the show S side, the aisle and porch ashlar-faced. Eastern bellcote; pinnacles on the porch and transept, which both have a shaped central merlon. The porch is two-storeyed; the lower storey, with a lierne vault, dates from before 1428, the upper from shortly before 1500, with statue niches (statues, 1931, by *Herbert Read*) on each side of a small four-centred four-light window. The S transept has a large sub-arched four-light S window (similar to the N transept N) and a broad four-centred five-light E window with a transom, of the late C15 and akin to the windows of the SE chapel. Then the chancel projects by one bay. Its seven-light E window has exceedingly refined tracery, similar to the tower W window. Their curious tracery below the transom, a kind of shouldered arch, is unknown locally, but a cruder form occurs in West Somerset, at Watchet and Old Cleeve. There are traces of the preceding chancel in the masonry and the jamb of a blocked s window (and a blocked N one inside). On the N, the transept and NE chapel are embattled, but not the aisle. Octagonal stair-turrets clasp the transept. The NE chapel matches the SE one except in the E window tracery, a net of mouchette and vesica forms cusped like a briar rose. This was replaced in 1897. Does it copy a predecessor?

The arcades and aisles march right across the transepts and continue as chancel arcades and chapels the other side of the chancel arch. Seven bays to the nave and two to the lower chancel arcades. All the piers are of standard four-hollow section, the shafts with little round capitals sparingly decorated with rosettes. Between the clerestory windows shafts on angel busts carry a typical Somerset roof of *c.* 1495–1500, not particularly ornate and mostly renewed. The chancel ceiling is from *George Gilbert Scott*'s restoration of 1856–7. The chapels have moulded panelled ceilings, oddly adrift from the stone angel corbels. The broad chancel arch springs from the last nave pier and the two arches beyond are lower and four-centred. Four-centred also the arches from these chapels into the aisles. The transepts are effectively reduced to single-bay projections from the aisles. The tower arch is of course very tall, and panelled, and there is a fan-vault.

FURNISHINGS. FONT and COVER. 1856–7 by *Scott*, who also designed the stone PULPIT and the STALLS (currently in the N aisle). – SCREENS. To the SE and NE chapels, 1913 by *Bligh Bond*, and 1931 by *Herbert Read*. *Bond* also designed the NW organ screen in 1926, and the rather more robust S transept screen, 1929. This was made up with four headpieces from a C15 screen, retrieved from the museum or found built into Northload Street houses. Three two-light openings, the lights with ogee-cusped heads and blind upper tracery carved with a rose, Paschal Lamb, pelican, or St George. – ROYAL ARMS. Charles II. Free-standing, with lively animal supporters. – VESTMENTS. Pall and Gremial (lap-cloth) of Abbot Whiting †1539. The pall, with the Assumption and floral sprays, must have been a fine piece originally. The gremial is small with an extremely pretty spray of Tudor roses. – PAINTINGS. S transept, Crucifixion, with the Virgin and St John between figures representing Church and Synagogue, attributed to *Konrad Witz*. Early C15, much restored. Brought from Pepinster near Liège, but probably from Basel, where two panels in the museum are from the same altarpiece. Original linenfold reused in the setting, 1919. Also seven late C18 painted panels of King David etc. from the former W gallery. S aisle W, C18 copy of Caravaggio's *Madonna dei Parafrenieri* in the Borghese Gallery. – SCULPTURE. Resurrected Christ, 1942–4, and Virgin and Child, 1948, two powerful Expressionist works in wood by *Ernst Blensdorf* (*see* Bruton). Also a small Italian C15 marble relief of the Nativity (S aisle), bought in Sicily. – STAINED

GLASS. Chancel N and S, C15 glass, on the N reassembled to give the impression of a complete window. The kneeling figures at the foot especially handsome. On the S, a patchwork. E window, 1879, large and busy, by *Lavers, Barraud & Westlake*, by whom probably also the chapel E windows, 1880 and 1897, and SE chapel S, 1895. N transept N, 1935, by *A. J. Davies*, still entirely Arts and Crafts. S transept S, 1867, by *Clayton & Bell*. – MONUMENTS. In the chancel N and S, similar tomb-chests of Richard Atwell †1476 and Jane Atwell †1485. He was a wealthy cloth merchant and no doubt helped to pay for the church. Matrices of lost brass effigies. The chests have small figures between the usual panels with shields. – John Camel †1487. Fine alabaster effigy in civilian dress (Camel was an attorney), his pillow held by angels. Tomb-chest with angels and camels. Much original colour. – Tomb-chest (N transept), large, C15. Eroded because it was outside, moved from the abbey to the churchyard here. Quatrefoils with shields on the sides. – Capt. John Dyer †1670. Brass, with engraved laurel border and skulls. – Mary Trent †1753. Pedimented against an obelisk.

ST BENEDICT, Benedict Street. Dedicated originally to Saint Beon (Benignus) of Meare. Rebuilt *c.* 1500 by Abbot Bere, whose initials are over the N porch and on a nave corbel inside. The W tower is the best feature, ashlar-fronted and with an ashlar bell-stage. Three tall stages with set-back buttresses, battlements, and paired tall two-light bell-openings. These have a transom and pierced baffles, one shaft between, ending in a pinnacle, and outer shafts on the buttresses, these carried up as outriders to big square corner pinnacles. The W window is flanked by niches. Polygonal SE stair-turret. Inside, the tower has a good star-vault and a panelled tower-arch between thin shafts.

The rest was over-tidied in 1885 by *J. D. Sedding*, who added the S aisle and transept and refaced a SE chapel of 1862 by *Benjamin Ferrey*. The N side, although also refaced, is as drawn by Buckler in 1825, with battlemented aisle, porch and clerestory. Large three-light aisle windows and flat-headed clerestory windows. The four-bay arcades have four-centred arches on four-hollow piers with polygonal capitals, the S arcade of 1885. Angel corbels carry shields with abbey and Bere emblems. In the N aisle an older image bracket with foliage. Over the chancel arch, an older spandrel panel of the Crucifixion. Also earlier is a C13–C14 PISCINA, half-octagonal between small candle-brackets, under a trefoil-headed arch with rolled-leaf crockets. – FONT. Perp, octagonal, with tapered sides and cusped panels. – STAINED GLASS. E window, 1865, Crucifixion against a black sky. W window, 1959, by *Powell's*. – MONUMENTS. Sir Henry Gould †1711. Lias slab with heraldry. – Ann Emery †1743. Rustic Baroque with big flowers. A similar memorial is at Compton Dundon (q.v.).

ST MARGARET'S CHAPEL, Magdalene Street. See Perambulation.

GLASTONBURY: CHURCHES AND MAJOR BUILDINGS

ST MICHAEL. *See* Glastonbury Tor, p. 328.

ST MARY (R.C.), Magdalene Street. 1939–40, by *J. H. H. Willman* of Taunton. Rock-faced stone with lancets. A giant recess frames a triple lancet over the entrance. The sides are gabled. Concrete transverse arches over the nave; short transepts and lower chancel. – REREDOS. Our Lady of Glastonbury, 1955, by *Philip Lindsey Clark*. Painted wood, based on an image from the abbey seal. Tapestry panels on each side by *Brother Louis Barlow* of Prinknash, 1965, made by *Edinburgh Weavers*.

UNITED REFORMED CHURCH, High Street. Congregational chapel of 1814. Quite a proud ashlar front, corniced with a bowed centre. Minimal Venetian window over curved double doors with an intricate fanlight. Unfortunately in 1898 'Florentine' stone tracery was introduced and a heavy porch added, on thick columns. Late C19 gallery with cast-iron panels.

METHODIST CHURCH, Lambrook Street. 1866. Gothic, in Blue Lias, probably by *Frederick Merrick*, its builder. Schoolroom behind of 1873.

CEMETERY, Wells Road. 1855. Gothic lodge and barrel-vaulted archway and twin chapels on the slope. – Scroll-topped CHEST TOMB to the Rev. W. Allnutt †1879. Copied from the sarcophagus of Scipio Barbatus, Rome, like the Periam–Hood tomb at Butleigh.

TOWN HALL, Market Place. 1813–14, by *Joseph Beard* of Somerton. By contrast to the picturesque abbey gatehouse (p. 316), the Town Hall presents a well-behaved ashlar classical front to the square. Five bays, two storeys, with a rusticated ground-floor arcade (originally open) and a three-bay pediment. Rear hall of 1930.

ABBEY FARM (Somerset Rural Life Museum), Bere Lane. Outside the SE corner of the abbey precinct. The splendid BARN is 93 ft (28.3 metres) long, of seven bays with a central porch each side, the roof tree-ring-dated to the mid C14. The porch gables have coped shoulders, a flat-headed two-light window under a deep hoodmould, and an apex quatrefoil with an Evangelist emblem (St Mark and St Luke). The doorways are double-chamfered and four-centred. Pointed-arched side doors. On the N porch, dog-like creatures bestride the gable shoulders. Buttresses and vent-loops to the barn flanks. The gable-ends are monumental with angle buttresses and a great mid-buttress up to an Evangelist plaque (St John and St Matthew) under an apex hoodmoulded window, a curved-sided triangle infilled with three cusped similar triangles. Finials of an abbot and the Virgin, and carved heads at the gable feet. The magnificent interior has two-tier cruck trusses, i.e. base crucks support small apex crucks to give greater width, here 26 ft (8 metres). Similar roofs appear in the other Glastonbury barns at Doulting (N; tree-ring-dated 1290), Pilton and West Bradley. The base-cruck collars are arch-braced and cranked, and carry a longitudinal square beam on each side, not quite a purlin, more an echo of the wall-plate of an aisled barn, here carrying the intermediate trusses. Two tiers

322 GLASTONBURY

of wind-braces. Large stone FARMHOUSE of 1894 for James Austin of Abbey House.

WEST MENDIP HOSPITAL, Old Wells Road. 2004–5 by *Devereux Architects* of London. Single-storey brick flanks to a two-storey spine, irritatingly split at the entrance gable. More attractive curving single-storey wards behind, opening to gardens.

PERAMBULATIONS

1. The centre

Two principal streets along the N and W sides of the abbey precinct meet at the MARKET PLACE. The MARKET CROSS is a

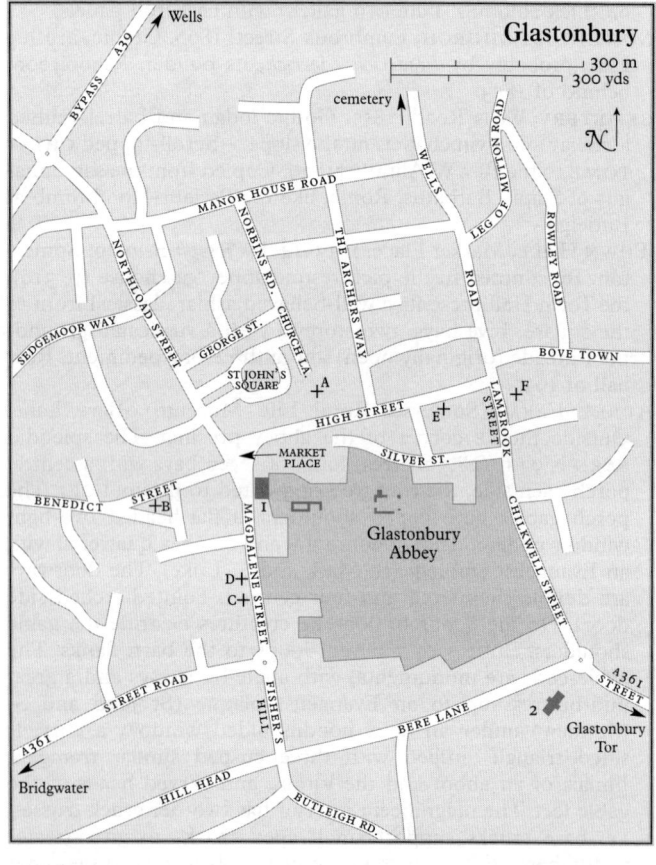

A St John
B St Benedict
C Magdalene Almshouses and chapel
D St Mary (R.C.)
E United Reformed church
F Methodist church

1 Town Hall
2 Abbey Farm

kind of Perp Eleanor Cross, by *Benjamin Ferrey*, 1846, that looks right in the small square. It replaced a covered structure of 1604, like that at Somerton. On the N side, on the corner of Northload Street, Nos. 1–2 are late medieval with a jettied first floor and two corbels, a dancing couple on one, a grotesque on the other. No. 3, although refronted, is also medieval. The three-storey CROWN INN, roughcast, with square bays, is an early C19 refacing of a C15–C16 inn. In 1812 the r. half was still gabled and jettied. The ashlar-fronted NATWEST BANK looks Late Georgian but was rebuilt as late as 1846 for Stuckey's Bank. Ground floor *c.* 1900. On the E side, No. 6 is tall and thin, brick, of *c.* 1800. No. 7 is late medieval with a broad bargeboarded gable jettied over the ground floor. A dragon beam inside at the NW corner. No. 8, behind a low Georgian front of painted brick, is also late medieval. Heavy square joists; moulded beams at the back. No. 9, much larger, in red brick, is dated 1892. Then follow the abbey gatehouse (p. 316) and Town Hall (p. 321). The W side has mixed terraces with late C19 corners to Benedict Street. No. 12 retains a C16 framed ceiling. This mixed terrace continues as MAGDALENE STREET. Opposite, two early C19 brick houses intrude into the abbey grounds, No. 3 and ABBOTS LEIGH. Between them, and much more intrusive, is the abbey car park, tidied since Pevsner railed at its ugliness, but still a disappointing first and indeed only view of the abbey church from the town. Opposite, down Heritage Court, are the brick AUSTIN ALMSHOUSES, 1887, by *Joseph Spire* of Glastonbury. Two-storeyed, Gothic, softened with a veranda roof over four square bays. Back on Magdalene Street, SOMERSET HOUSE is early to mid-C19, five bays, with ashlar cornice and giant pilasters, clumsily handled especially in the centre where the pilasters are shortened for a Tuscan porch. NAISH HOUSE, *c.* 1800, is much prettier, five bays, of Blue Lias with ashlar doorway, sill course, cornice and parapet. The doorway is Venetian, the fanlight and side-lights with fancy glazing. MAGDALENE HOUSE and PRIORY HOUSE, apart from the lower r. piece, are successful if dour neo-Regency of 1926 for a R.C. convent. After the R.C. church (p. 321), COPPER BEECH is ashlar-fronted, Late Georgian, three storeys. The former PUMP ROOM beyond opened in 1754, after a mania in 1751 brought ten thousand people a month to try the health-giving water issuing at the Chain Gate opposite. The pump room adapts one end of a C17 building, but to some effect. Two Georgian three-bay fronts at right angles, each with an ashlar entablature and parapet. On the entrance side, pilasters on pedestals divide the bays, the centre bay with pediment and arched doorway. To the road, blank windows and a rusticated blank arch.

Down an alley are the MAGDALENE ALMSHOUSES, founded around 1284 as a hospital for men. It comprised a large C13–C14 hall as at St Mary's Hospital, Chichester, West Sussex, with an eastern chapel of slightly earlier date. Within the hall were probably timber cells. The great E gable with a bellcote and part of the W gable survive, but in the C16 the hall was unroofed and two rows of two-storey stone almshouses built within. The s range was demolished in 1958. Off-centre C13 doorway into the CHAPEL OF ST MARGARET, between sweetly small windows of three ogee-headed lights. The chapel side windows are Late Perp but an E lancet and plain trefoil-headed piscina are C13. C19 barrel ceiling. On the opposite side of Magdalene Street, ABBEY GRANGE, with a painted ashlar five-bay front, is possibly early C18, with C19 windows. CHAIN GATE, the site of a medieval mill, was just s.

Returning to the Market Place, two older streets run outward, with relatively little of interest. On BENEDICT STREET, running W, No. 4 is jettied, late medieval. By St Benedict's church (p. 320), the SCHOOL of 1875 and detached teacher's house facing a very plain former VICARAGE, of 1882, by *Ewan Christian*. On the N side, loosely planned around a courtyard is the former POLICE HEADQUARTERS of 1861, located here because Glastonbury was central to the county. Barrack range with gabled centre and ends, a house on the W side with an ashlar gabled centrepiece, both plain, and the courthouse on the E. This is livelier, with a roundel window and curved pediment over the entry. On NORTHLOAD STREET, running N off Market Place, No. 5 is the best jettied C15–C16 front left in Glastonbury. Plastered timber-framed upper floor over Lias stone with a C17 mullioned window. Moulded framed ceiling. Further out, No. 56, red brick, of three bays and three storeys with ashlar quoins and architraves. It looks mid-C18, but the projecting centre has Victorian yellow brick corners. ALBERT BUILDINGS behind, of 1870 by *Frederick Merrick*, artisan housing in red brick with a parapet.

Back at the Market Place, we turn now to the HIGH STREET, running E. It is a typical principal street of a prosperous market town, except that there are very significant medieval survivals. First of all the GEORGE AND PILGRIM HOTEL, originally the pilgrims' inn or *hospitium* of the abbey, of *c.* 1475, among the most sumptuous of surviving pre-Reformation English inns. Stone-faced, embattled and incidentally three-storeyed, in itself something exceptional, with a first floor taller than the others. The throughway arch is placed asymmetrically, with to the l. a three-storey canted bay of 1–2–1 lights flanked by a single light on either side, and to the r. two similar lights on each floor. The lights are straight-headed lights with ogee arches and the spandrel filled by small quatrefoils in circles, a favourite C15–C16 Somerset motif (e.g. Muchelney and Cleeve abbeys). On the top floor there are transoms, below which the lights have blind cusped four-centred heads. Above the throughway are three panels with the arms of the abbey and Edward IV under a three-light window with cusped four-centred heads to each light. Above that the attic three-light window has similar heads, blind tracery below the transom, and a narrow statue niche each side. All that has been described is set in a vertical grid divided by strong horizontals and thus appears well-ordered, in spite of its lack of uniformity. Renewed battlements. Moulded-framed ceiling and heavy timbered partition to the front room. NE newel staircase. Next door, LLOYDS BANK, the Wiltshire & Dorset Bank of 1885, by *G. M. Silley*, the bank architect, sets out to outdo the George, notably in having almost complete symmetry. The quality of the undercut frieze with foliage and animals deserves respect. Nos. 5–7 have three-storey ashlar fronts, one heavily Victorian, the other still Late Georgian in its relative simplicity.

The TRIBUNAL is the other medieval highlight of the street, but its story is more obscure. Long identified as the abbey courthouse known to have been in the High Street, it now seems that this is a C15 merchant's house. But its two-storey stone front of *c.* 1500, splendid for a merchant, has the royal arms, indicating an official use. This front replaces a timber frame, set between stone side walls, one of which is visible to the r. A four-centred-arched doorway, beneath the arms and a Tudor rose, stands to the l. of four contiguous two-light windows. Above, two-light windows flank a canted oriel of 1–4–1 lights. All the lights have four-centred heads. There is a clumsiness in the masonry on each side of the oriel, as if the façade were reused, but if so, when and from where? The front room and smaller rear room on each floor are divided by a narrow stair hall with a winding stair. Moulded framed ceilings, four-centred-arched stone doorways, and stone fireplaces. Linenfold panels under the front windows. The rear fireplace has thin shafts supporting rounded cornice ends. C16–C17 thin-rib plasterwork in the ceiling panels of this room. Upstairs the front range has a renewed wind-braced roof of C15 type. The much-restored detached KITCHEN has a broad stone fireplace and a moulded framed ceiling. Pieces of broken carving found in the walls suggest that the kitchen was built after the Dissolution.

The S side of the High Street begins Late Georgian at Nos. 2–4, painted ashlar, of two then three storeys. Nos. 6–10, three-storeyed, in painted brick, are mid- to late C18, rustic Georgian, No. 8 formally symmetrical, the centre with quoins and pediment. Behind are utilitarian ASSEMBLY ROOMS of 1864. Opposite, after the Tribunal, No. 11, painted ashlar, with cornice and parapet, *c.* 1840. Of the same height the single-storey HSBC BANK, 1922–3, a Neo-Georgian refronting in brick and stone with giant arched windows. Nos. 15–17 have C18 brick fronts to C15–C16 houses, a moulded framed ceiling in No. 15. Long second-floor windows on the Late Victorian No. 19 indicate a photographer's studio. BARCLAYS BANK, ashlar-faced neo-Tudor of as late as 1957, refronts a Post Office of 1897. On the corner to the churchyard, No. 23, Late Georgian, with ashlar angles and cornice, faces the VESTRY HALL of 1865, a strong Gothic statement with its high ashlar gable front and large oriel. Outside St John's church (p. 317), a large Celtic cross WAR MEMORIAL, 1919, by *Bligh Bond*. Behind the church EASTER COTTAGE, roughcast, C17, with early C19

Gothic windows, and ST JOHN'S SCHOOL, 1863–5, Gothic, symmetrical about a central gable. Rather coarse, given that *G. G. Scott* designed it, but *Frederick Merrick* reputedly simplified the design.

Beyond the churchyard, No. 27 is ashlar-fronted, mid-C19. No. 29 was a significant early C18 house. A handsome doorcase with a pineapple urn in the broken pediment remains in an otherwise altered front. The panelled hall with fluted pilasters should announce the stair hall, but the staircase went to the Victoria and Albert Museum (where it was never displayed) in the 1920s, and the space is ceiled over. No. 31, four narrow stuccoed bays with a parapet, is also early C18, to judge by a little surviving panelling; the front early C19. Opposite are Georgian brick fronts to No. 36, three-storeyed, and Nos. 38–40, two-storeyed, refronting earlier houses. No. 48 may be C17, low and rendered. Next the hefty Jacobean-style AVALON CLUB, 1897, in rock-faced conglomerate. Opposite, down ARCHER'S WAY, the LIBRARY occupies part of ORCHARD COURT, offices of 2006, by *Stone & Partners*, brick, deep-eaved, with a cutaway corner entry. Beyond is NEWTOWN, brick council housing of 1920, by *Harold Alves*, to a cruciform layout.

Back on High Street, the POST OFFICE dominates the upper end with its neo-Tudor ashlar front of 1938, by *H. E. Seccombe* of the *Office of Works*. Early C19 stuccoed fronts at Nos. 41–43, at No. 43 (BECKETS INN) fronting a C16 building. The low cottages at Nos. 51–63 are also partly C16. On the S side, Nos. 64–66, last-gasp Georgian, ashlar façades with pilasters and parapets, on brick gable-ends. These must be of around 1837 as they frame the entry to Victoria Buildings. Further up, the United Reformed church (p. 321), and Nos. 78–80, an ashlar-fronted three-storey pair of *c.* 1830, the ground floors originally in mirror image. At the top NW corner, the HEALTH CENTRE, 1970, fits in well. Brick, with monopitch roofs, by *John Foden* and *P. C. Cooke* of *Somerset County Architects*.

2. *Chilkwell Street to the Tor*

SUMMER HOUSE, an ashlar-fronted mid-C19 villa, faces down High Street, next to the Methodist church (p. 321) in LAMBROOK STREET. Further on, the former VICARAGE, 1819, by *Hugh Adams* of Glastonbury, set back. Stuccoed, with a hipped overhanging roof and open-pediment doorway. Opposite, at right angles to each other, are KYLEMORE, a narrow two-storey brick Georgian house, and the former METHODIST CHAPEL of 1825, ashlar-fronted with arched windows. CHILKWELL STREET continues S along the eastern PRECINCT WALL of the abbey which is pierced by a convincingly medieval gateway with plaques front and back. The plaques are C15–C16 (Abbot Bere's pelican and initials) but the gateway is early C19. It serves ABBEY HOUSE, a large Tudor Gothic villa of 1825–30 by *John Buckler* for John Fry Reeves, owner of the abbey ruins. Buckler (the topographical artist) is advanced in his asymmetrical elevations, if not in the smooth ashlar facing. Near-symmetrical front with a boxy oriel over the porch. At the back, the main gable is off-centre, aligned on the ruins. Gothic plaster cornices and iron stair-rail. On the E side of the street are early C19 suburban villas. No. 5, painted ashlar with cornice and parapet, stands on the corner of the former drive to CHALICE HILL HOUSE, the grandest villa, of 1830 for Richard Periam Prat, promoter of the Glastonbury Canal. Stucco with ashlar for the cornice, parapet, panelled angle piers and columned porch. Rich plasterwork, and stained glass in the stair window, grisaille figures of the Seasons. CHALICE LEAZE, small and stuccoed, has a two-storey wrought-iron veranda. BLENHEIM HOUSE is hip-roofed with windows in curved-headed recesses.

Chilkwell Street turns SE towards Frome opposite the abbey barn (p. 321). Minor C16–C17 houses amid terraces on both sides. Further out, LITTLE ST MICHAEL, a Georgian front banded in Lias and Ham stone, marks the entrance to C20 gardens around the CHALICE WELL. The principal spring supplying the abbey was rediscovered in the mid C18 for its health-giving properties, and revived in the early C20 as a place of pilgrimage. The medieval well-house, wholly buried in silt, is capped by a lid with Celtic ironwork by *Bligh Bond*, 1919. On WELL-HOUSE LANE, beyond the footpath to Glastonbury Tor (p. 328), a RESERVOIR of 1872 has been adapted to a water shrine, its triple tunnel vaults on stone arcades gloomily illuminated by candles.

3. Bove Town

From the top of the High Street WELLS ROAD runs N with little of special interest. On the l., CHINDIT HOUSE by the builder *John Merrick* for himself, 1903, mostly Gothic but with a curved-pedimented front doorway. BOVE TOWN, climbing E, was the older approach from Wells. On the N side, THE HOLLIES, three storeys, early C19, and JACOBY COTTAGE, the pilgrimage chapel of St Katharine recorded in 1260, a cottage by 1503. C15 flat-headed three-light S window with cusped lights and a blocked four-centred E window. There were originally three of these 'slipper' chapels at Glastonbury. At the top, No. 104, a former farmhouse, thatched, with early C17 stone mullions. Extended at both ends. Beyond, on WICK HOLLOW, Nos. 8, 10 and 14 overlook Bushy Combe. Built for Morland family members (*see* Northover, below) in 1956 by *A. J. Hepworth*, the Morland company architect. Two-storeyed, starkly modern, the fronts a rectangular casing to timber and glass. No. 8 was much the most expensive, in Bath stone, the rear wall with quasi-mullion windows and a shelter on thin posts. Extended to the l. in 1972 by *Hepworth*.

OUTLYING BUILDINGS

NORTHOVER, 1 m. SW. An early industrial area, with mills served by the Mill Stream from the River Brue. The MORLAND SITE housed two important firms making sheepskin rugs, gloves, etc.: Clark, Son & Morland and A. Baily & Co. The Morland site is mostly cleared. The prominent surviving FACTORY building is of the 1930s, by *Harold Alves*, remarkably minimal for the date, a little piece of the Bauhaus. Two concrete floors on mushroom piers under a sawtooth roof. No perimeter structure, just small-paned metal glazing. To the S, the RED BRICK BUILDING, a late C19 sawtooth-roofed group, restored for community use by *Orme Architecture*, 2011–12. The Baily & Co. FACTORY on the W edge remains largely intact, if derelict. The three-storey front buildings of 1890–6 were the glove factory and boiler house, marked by a tall chimney. Behind were the tannery and offices of 1867, extended S *c.* 1880, and behind the offices are three-tier boarded drying sheds. S of the Red Brick Building, the small stone NORTHOVER MILL has C16–C17 mullioned windows. Just W, NORTHOVER MILL HOUSE is Late Georgian, mansard-roofed, with ashlar pilasters, parapet, and columned porch. A footpath runs N to BECKERY ISLAND, a pretty hillock behind the sewage works, the site of an outlying medieval chapel. Excavation revealed two phases of chapel, priest's house and small cemetery, C10–C11 and late C13.

GLASTONBURY TOR, 1 m. E. An unforgettable image, the single battlemented tower on its 520-ft (158-metre) conical hill, visible across much of Somerset. The terraces on the hillside appear not to be natural or caused by ploughing. They may represent Neolithic activity but they are not, as also suggested, a maze, as they do not join up. Excavation on the top has shown occupation from the prehistoric period onwards, with Early Christian use in the C6 indicated by the presence of Mediterranean pottery. The remains of at least two subsequent medieval churches were uncovered and the head of a C10–C11 Anglo-Saxon wheel-head cross. A Norman church dedicated to St Michael (typical for hilltop sites, e.g. St Michael's Mount etc.) was destroyed by earthquake in 1275. As rebuilt by Abbot de Sodbury (1323–34) the church was narrow and aisleless, with a W tower. In 1539 Abbot Whiting, his treasurer and a monk were executed outside the church. By the C18 the tower alone survived, and only just, the NE stair-turret having collapsed.

The three-stage TOWER stands massively, with small openings, clasped by full-height ashlar angle buttresses. The tower looks early to mid-C14 apart from the bell-stage and tower arch which are C15. The W face has all the embellishment. First a narrow copiously moulded doorway beneath panels of St Bridget milking and St Michael holding scales. Then the middle stage has five niches around a small two-light window of cusped Y-tracery, the outer niches linked vertically. The niches have nodding ogee heads and side shafts. Only the top

r. one preserves substantial sculpture, a fine headless cleric. The bell-stage has a single Perp two-light opening on each side between canopied niches, and a single carved plaque, of an eagle. Plain embattled parapet. The sides have similar bell-lights and Y-tracery windows, but also a narrow cusped lancet in the lower stage. The tower arch is much later than the w door, panelled between continuous roll mouldings. There was a ribbed vault, of roll-moulded ribs on column shafts. One large head corbel of the s arcade is preserved.

NORWOOD PARK FARM, Wick Lane, 1½ m. E. A manor house of the abbots of Glastonbury. A porch and N wing of 1910 project from a cross-wing, whose E gable has diagonal buttresses and a battlemented two-storey square bay with the monogram of Abbot Selwood (1456–93). The square-headed two-light Perp windows are renewed. Lateral N chimney. The rear gable has set-back buttresses and a similar first-floor two-light window.

EDGARLEY HOUSE (Millfield Preparatory School), 1 m. ESE. An outsized addition of 1882, by *Frederick Huish*, builder from Street, to a modest C16–C18 farmhouse, of which the cross-wing retains a C16 moulded framed ceiling. The addition, for Albert Porch, has high bargeboarded bays, both canted and square, studded with carved plaques, some genuinely medieval. The Porch family inherited the abbey ruins from J. F. Reeves. In the full-height stair hall, a fireplace with C15 Evangelist symbols. A first-floor oriel displays medieval and C16 stained glass. Many more stone fragments are incorporated in the HERMITAGE, an octagonal summerhouse of the 1830s. The assembly is a copious jumble of Romanesque chevron, Early Gothic stiff-leaf and Perp mouldings, with some carved fragments. Also two windows displaying the Muchelney tracery (as on the George and Pilgrim Hotel). On one external panel, a lovely medieval version of the Roman eagle. SCHOOL BUILDINGS (by *HBS* of Highbridge) include a gambrel-roofed dining hall, 1980s, and a music school with large arched windows to the concert hall, 1990–1. Classroom block, 2000, by *DKA* of Bath. Boarding houses, 2004. Colossal stone HEAD of Meyer, the founding headmaster, by *Seyed Edalatpur* (similar head outside the Meyer Theatre, Millfield School, Street). At the entrance, double-gabled ESTATE COTTAGES, 1882, and CHAPEL, 1897, with spired lantern, both built by Porch.

UPPER CRANNEL FARM, 2 m. N. 2006–11, by *Richard Paxton* of London. Two standard agricultural open sheds were erected some distance apart, at right angles, one to contain the house, raised on a basement, and reached by an earth ramp. The other is mostly barn but with a guest apartment similarly raised. The steel uprights remain forward of the inserted structures, so the aesthetic is agricultural, with a classical formality. From the back, the house is a glass box, while the front and guest apartment are boarded.

GLASTONBURY LAKE VILLAGE, 1 m. NNW. Glastonbury Lake Village was built on an artificial island in a swamp, *c*. 200 B.C.

Originally there were five or six round wooden houses but the site expanded to about fifteen, perhaps housing a population of 200. Rising water levels appear to have led to the abandonment of the village *c.* 50 B.C. and the subsequent waterlogging allowed the preservation of many objects made from organic materials. These included personal items such as beads, brooches, tweezers and dice. Most food, and other material, was brought to the village by boat but fish could be caught locally. The site is significantly different from the other 'lake villages' at Meare as it appears to have been a permanent settlement. It survives as a bumpy field, the bumps formed by the clay floors of the houses that were built up over the years.

PONTER'S BALL, 2 m. E. A linear earthwork crossing the ridge linking Glastonbury to the higher ground to the E. Various purposes and dates have been suggested but excavation suggested that it may post-date the C12, and was therefore constructed as a boundary marker by the abbey.

GOATHURST

ST EDWARD. Massive plain W tower of exceedingly thin purplish siltstones. Diagonal buttresses to halfway up the bell-stage, narrow flat-headed two-light Perp bell-openings with pierced baffles. Plain battlements and higher square SE stair-turret. Perp W window uncomfortably over a C15–C16 door. The heavy tower arch mouldings dying into side piers look older but the tower is surely C15. Perp nave, S porch, S transept and chancel, the tracery restored in 1884 by *J. H. Spencer*. The S transept became the Halswell family pew and the NE chapel was built by Sir Nicholas Halswell after 1559 for their monuments, the especial feature of this church. Perp nave barrel ceiling. Moulded arch to the S transept. This was remodelled in 1758, probably by *Henry Keene*, with a pointed barrel ceiling of Gothick plasterwork in quatrefoils over a heraldic frieze. In the chancel a cusped PISCINA and plain aumbry recess.

FURNISHINGS. FONT. Perp, retooled. Octagonal with quatrefoil panels, panelled beneath. – PULPIT. Early C17. Instead of the usual blind arches, arabesque panels between paired fluted bulbous columns. Big TESTER of *c.* 1700, an inlaid star beneath, little flaming urns on top. – ROYAL ARMS. 1707. – HATCHMENTS. Nine in the tower. – PANELLING. C18, from a W gallery. Eight painted panels showing King David, the Evangelists, etc. – BENCHES. Reused C17 carved panels from the old box pews. – STAINED GLASS. Chancel, 1884, by *Lavers, Barraud & Westlake*, the E window especially fine. W window, 1885, probably *Clayton & Bell*. – MONUMENTS. NE chapel. Sir Nicholas Halswell †1633 and wife. Tomb-chest with recumbent effigies. Six sons kneel on the long side, three daughters on the short side. The effigies are well done, illuminated by the W window. Original paint shows through buff Georgian stone colour. The canopy has two sturdy arches to the side and one to the end, on panelled piers, each with a heraldic cartouche above. The cornice, inset with plaques to the children, carries heraldry leaning out between strapwork finials. – Halswell family, c. 1650. Also repainted in stone colour. Big Baroque aedicule with Corinthian columns and curved pediment broken for a heraldic cartouche. Outside the columns, female figures (Hope and Religion) in corner niches, and on the outer cornice, cherubs carrying emblems of mortality. These motifs are more characteristic of the early C17. – Isabella Cooper, 1838, by the Irish sculptor *Christopher Moore*. Marble sleeping three-year-old, following Thomas Banks's celebrated Penelope Boothby (1793) at Ashbourne, Derbys. It deserves better siting. – Nave. Rev. Sir John Tynte †1742. By *Rysbrack*. In two tones of marble, with scrolled sides, carried on heavy consoles framing a pretty Rococo cartouche. On top an excellent portrait bust. – Sir Charles Kemeys Tynte †1785. By *Joseph Nollekens*. On a fine fluted sarcophagus, a classical female extinguishes a torch, leaning disconsolate on a pedestal with Sir Charles's portrait. – Lt Milborne Kemeys Tynte †1845. Military accoutrements. By *W. Spence* of Liverpool.

Churchyard MONUMENT to John Wilton †1725, a curious combination of table tomb and obelisk. Lush curved-ended tomb with flying cherubs and theatrical drapes, the obelisk a tapering Corinthian pillar with floral drops beneath athletic cherubs. Base of an urn on top. Also the base of a C15 CHURCHYARD CROSS.

By the churchyard, Georgian Gothic ALMSHOUSES, 1780. Red sandstone, seven bays, with Ham stone ogee-headed doorway and Y-tracery windows. NE of the church, PAULET HOUSE was the manor house, then the rectory. Externally Victorian stucco by *Charles Knowles*, 1872, but the NE room with Georgian porch hides a C15 hall, the arch-braced roof itself hidden by a C17 tunnel vault. Buncombe and Paulett heraldry at each end relates to a marriage in 1650. On the main street, the Halswell House LODGE, c. 1825, rustic, thatched. Older cottages E of the SCHOOL of 1876, notably OLD COBB, an altered C15 hall house.

HALSWELL HOUSE. See p. 339.

SHERWOOD, ½ m. SE. Around an attractive courtyard. Rendered C16–C17 house with Georgian windows. The brick range at right angles was remodelled for the Halswell steward with Regency drawing room and estate office. Chimneypiece with festoons and pineapple.

HUNTSTILE FARMHOUSE, ¾ m. SE. Manor house of the Brodripp family, here from 1571. Roughcast, the parlour cross-wing with a big lateral chimney and projection for a spiral stair. Cross-passage with good moulded oak doors of late C16 type. Similar doors within, also Tudor-arched fireplaces and some early C17 panelling. C19 GRANARY on staddle-stones.

GODNEY

HOLY TRINITY. 1838–9, by *G. P. Manners*. Neo-Norman with bellcote, replacing a building 'restored to its antient use' in 1737. Thoroughly Norman nave, the W front with flat intersecting arches below the windows. Apsed chancel, 1903–4, by *E. Buckle*. – PULPIT. 1903. Arts and Crafts. – STAINED GLASS. A C15 angel of St Matthew, and (W windows) C16 heraldry from Lillington, Dorset. – SCULPTURE. Two C15 reliefs, Agnus Dei and Eagle, the latter very like one on the tower on Glastonbury Tor. – MONUMENT. Bowen children, 1782. Lias with painted heraldry.

At Higher Godney, a polychrome brick former SCHOOL, 1875, by *Joseph Day* of Glastonbury. At Lower Godney, two houses by *Wilf Burton* exemplify the hand-built ethos of the later C20: OAK HOUSE, traditional timber frame, glazed to the S, 1995, for himself, and ROUNDHOUSE, 1999, boarded timber frame around an octagonal core, opening out with glass to the S. TEMPLE CROSS HOUSE, 2011–12, by *Nigel Begg* with the owner *Sally Strachey*, echoes the outline of a curved-roofed barn with lean-to previously on the site. Boarded timber frame with a spine wall for thermal mass.

GOTHELNEY HALL
1 m. E of Charlinch

An impressive manor house of the late C14 and *c.* 1470. Owned by the Malet family from the C13 and from the early C15 by the Hodys. Sir John Hody †1441–2 was Lord Chief Justice; Sir Alexander forfeited Gothelney in 1455 as a Lancastrian, reversed in 1483 for Sir William (†1524), Chief Baron of the Exchequer. It survived as a farmhouse, repaired from 2007 by *Marius Barran*. The house comprises two halls one above the other with a four-storey chamber block to the S, behind a tall stair-tower capped with a battlemented oratory. A lower range to the S appears to contain yet another hall but is altered.

Most of the datable features are late C15, overlaid on something earlier of roughly equal footprint. A two-storey C19 addition against the ground-floor hall with a battlemented storeyed porch was already present in 1845. Some Ham stone details are reused. The windows of the upper hall are altered to the front but at the back are late C15, two long two-light windows with double transoms and blind tracery in the top lights. Also a corbelled chimney-breast. The addition of the upper hall is marked by a horizontal external course. The front stair-tower was raised to serve this hall, and the oratory, marked by a Perp three-light window, was then added on top. The oratory is reached by a narrow stair corbelled out from the SW corner of the stair-tower. The lower hall, and lower part of the stair-tower and chamber block, are perhaps late C14 from the pointed-arched N doorway into the tower (now within the C19 addition) and the pointed-arched doorway to the l. of the tower. The chamber block was served by a rear stair-tower, raised to serve the solar added with the upper hall. The front stair-tower may have originated as a storeyed porch with an upper chamber reached from the chamber block (the blocked doorway survives). The staircase is C19, but with a C15 moulded and framed ceiling above and a C15 oak doorway to the upper hall, ornamented with fleurons and an IM monogram. A precipitous mural stair climbs to the oratory, which had a sexpartite ribbed roof of which six angel corbels remain. A square window allowed a view from the solar.

The outstanding feature of Gothelney is the roof over both hall and solar, of arch-braced collar trusses with three tiers of cusped wind-braces. Alternate hall trusses are carried on shafts finished with shield-bearing angels, these visible below an inserted floor. The four-centred head of what must have been an eastern oriel window remains, decorated with fleurons. The lower hall was unheated unless a relieving arch on the W wall marks a lost fireplace. In the early C19 a fireplace was inserted against a remodelled cross-passage. The massive crossed beams should be inserted with the upper hall. The thin-rib plaster decoration is probably C19, different from the genuine C17 ceiling S of the inserted chimney. The N parlour has a good C17 curvilinear thin-rib ceiling, with bosses and foliage. The room above had a garderobe, the tower formerly being on the N wall.

The lower S range has a first-floor C14–C15 ogee-headed single light on both front and rear walls, not enough to prove that this was another hall (the jointed-cruck roof is C16–C17) but enough to show a significant domestic building. The big range enclosing the N side of the courtyard had two broad C15–C16 first-floor halls, perhaps lodgings, with jointed-cruck trusses. Smoke-blackening in the roof of the unaltered E hall must pre-date the enclosed smoke-bay. Good oak doorways front and back.

GREENHAM

0010

ST PETER. 1860, by *Henry Davis*, C. E. Giles's preferred builder, which explains why it looks like a work of Giles. Lancets, canted apse, thin octagonal NW tower with candle-snuffer spire. Single roof inside like an upturned boat. – STAINED GLASS. Apse windows, 1860, by *Lavers & Barraud*. – ROYAL ARMS. 2008. – MONUMENTS. Admiral Kelly †1936. Lettering by *Eric Gill*. By *Gill* also two other plaques, and the CROSS outside to Lady Kelly †1937.

GREENHAM BARTON. A manor house of about the size of nearby Cothay (q.v.), but less completely preserved. Like

Cothay (and Holcombe Court nearby in Devon) it belonged to the Bluetts. It was probably rebuilt after 1403 and was altered in the later C16. It seems to have had four ranges enclosing a courtyard with a porch-tower on the W front. Two ranges survive, this W range, with the principal rooms, and the kitchen range, N. On the S is only a single pointed archway, and on the E nothing. Here there may have been an earlier hall (Vivian-Neal in 1934 refers to a C13 hall and chapel both recently lost). Restoration for Harold Fry in 1927–9 confuses the evidence.

The porch-tower has early C14 detail: diagonal buttresses, triple-chamfered outer arch, and double-chamfered inner doorway. The tracery of the two-light upper window dates from 1927–9, when a gable was replaced with a parapet. To the r. of the porch-tower, the hall, with two large transomed five-light windows, clearly C16. The parlour window beyond and round SW corner turret are of 1927–9. On the rear, the cross-passage doorway, a projection for the gallery stair, the hall chimney and another large hall window. The transomed window beyond, to the parlour, is perhaps late C16. The N service end is much rebuilt. Inside, N of the cross-passage, Commander Williams found evidence of posts of an aisled truss, suggesting that the C13 hall may have been here. The partition to the S is of 1927–9, reused, under a reused bressumer. The convincing high-ceilinged C16–C17 hall is mostly restoration. The ceiling with pendants and double ribs, similar to that at Red Lodge, Bristol, is by *Lewis Smallcorn* of Bath. Original moulded E fireplace and two pointed S doorways. The thin-rib parlour ceiling may also be reproduction. Reused four-centred-arched doorway to the stair-turret. The thin-rib ceiling of the solar looks new.* The NE kitchen range has a small pointed C14 S doorway and two square-headed Perp windows above (one a C20 copy). Rough SE stair projection.

GREENHAM HALL. Tudor Gothic house of 1848 for Thomas Clarke. Typically rotated about a slim octagonal corner turret, such that both main faces have an off-centre principal gable. Twisted finials and chimneys copied from Barrington Court.

GREINTON

ST MICHAEL. Blue Lias, refaced in 1852–3 by *David Mackintosh* of Exeter. Two-stage Perp tower with diagonal buttresses, battlements, and octagonal SE stair-turret. Broad four-centred tower arch. The rest also mostly Perp. E window with quatrefoil

---

* It is not clear what if any of the plasterwork is original. Vivian-Neal refers to 'reproduction and restoration' by Smallcorn.

panels below. N rood-stair projection. C15–C16 panelled nave roof. Moulded chancel arch (much distorted). The chancel S lancets replicate C13 originals. The narrow, chamfered N and S doorways could be C13. Traceried C15 DOORS. – BENCH-ENDS. Several with typical C16 tracery. Another dated 1621, with Jacobean arch. – SCREEN. 1850s. – STAINED GLASS. 1850s, by *Beer* of Exeter.

In the churchyard, N of the church, a medieval grave-slab with three crosses incised.

GREINTON HOUSE, 1852 by *Mackintosh*, was the rectory. Surprisingly large, gabled, with an ornate Bath stone oriel. Matching former SCHOOL of 1850. MANOR FARMHOUSE, with ovolo-moulded mullions and drip-course, is dated 1696.

GURNEY MANOR see CANNINGTON

HADSPEN

Village of colourful Hadspen stone, which is still quarried here. NETTLECOMBE FARMHOUSE, early C19, has iron lattice glazing. HADSPEN VALLEY HOUSE, just S, of almost orange ashlar, is an early C19 hip-roofed villa with pedimented doorcase. PRIDDLES HILL HOUSE, dated 1688, has a cross-wing and reserved-chamfer mullions typical of a century earlier. Beyond, in a pretty group of dependent buildings, HADSPEN FARMHOUSE has similar mullions, here surely early C17, and an off-centre storeyed porch. W of the village, HONEYWICK is a charming early C18 miniature. Two-colour front with corniced architraves below and alternating pediments above.

HADSPEN HOUSE, 1 m. S. A three-storey house of 1687–90 was rebuilt as two storeys *c.* 1747 (date on the stable weathervane) and altered after the sale in 1785 to Henry Hobhouse. Work for the Hobhouses is recorded in 1786–7 and 1828. A rear range was added in 1886 by *Waller, Son & Wood* of Gloucester. There was early C20 work by *Arthur Pictor*. For all this a harmonious mid-C18 front faces the park, of 1–3–1 bays with parapets and pedimented centre in ochre stone with Doulting stone dressings. Alternating ground-floor pediments and columned Doric porch. The house of 1687 is incorporated evidenced by the thick spine wall. It may have been the basis of the C18 exterior if the cross-windows now on the stable are reused from the ground floor of the house. The dimensions are similar. Four-bay W side, with enclosed porch and canted bay added in 1886. Altered interiors, some Late Georgian. Victorian panelled billiard room, NW. The NE garden room has an C18 stone stair salvaged from Redlynch, demolished in 1913. The best room is inserted into the centre, 2000, for Niall Hobhouse, by *Ptolemy Dean*. It has a Soaneian dome, and is lit from a slot in the rear wall. This is hung with architectural fragments, as at Soane's London house.

Mid-C18 STABLES, W, with a pediment stretched over five bays, between single-bay coachhouses. Stone cross-windows perhaps reused (*see above*). Beyond, a low cartshed, with brick columns, shelters the ESTATE OFFICE. Hip-roofed early C19 two-storey COACHHOUSE opposite, with a pleasing syncopation of mullioned windows. Behind is another yard around a charming stone GRANARY. On the N side are plain stables (perhaps of 1687) at the back of LAUNDRY COTTAGE, hip-roofed, early C19. On the main road, a canted-ended early C19 LODGE.

A double avenue of elms formerly extended to the SW horizon, re-created in the late C20 as a swathe through plantation. Below the WALLED GARDEN, a minimal downhill range of KENNELS was modified in 1999 by *Cedric Price*. The roof is stepped four times, allowing light to enter at the breaks. Nearby, a brick early C19 GARDENER'S COTTAGE, with reused mullions, by a former water garden.

SHATWELL FARM, ¾ m. S of Hadspen House. Later C18 square farmhouse with a hipped roof. Paired sashes and pedimented doorway on both façades. Contemporary outbuildings. In the farmyard below are several interesting structures for Niall Hobhouse. An OFFICE and STORE, 2013–14, by *Hugh Strange*, of thick insulated timber panels under a single corrugated roof, dropped behind the wall of low C19 shed. To the N, a large COWSHED by *Stephen Taylor Architects*, 2012, a large agricultural shed given Roman grandeur with a colonnade of cylindrical piers of ochre aggregate. Across the lane, THE DAIRY HOUSE, a cottage of 1902, modified in 2005 for Niall Hobhouse by *Charlotte Skene Catling*. New rear stair-tower, the lower part glazed with a black slab pathway passing right through. Upper layers of rough-barked oak slab and slab glass, a transparent reminiscence of weatherboarding.

HALSE

ST JAMES. Red sandstone. Plain undifferentiated W tower with a diagonal NW buttress, battlements and narrow Dec bell-openings. The polygonal N stair-tower reaches halfway up, and the low SW buttresses and the lack of a W door indicate an earlier base, perhaps C13. Slightly chamfered tower arch. Broad nave with Perp windows including a rood light. The S doorway could be Norman from the plain arch inside. C16 porch, the side walls filled with tracery, perhaps reused. This may be contemporary with the showy N aisle, rebuilt *c.* 1546 by *John Harris*, mason. Deep-set flat-headed N windows, polygonal stair-turret and fine traceried end windows. The chancel, presumably raised in the C15, shows older masonry. Three-bay

N arcade on C14–C15 piers of four-hollow section with banded capitals of almost abstract striations. The bases and double-hollow arches belong to an earlier arcade. Between the arches are a quatrefoil panel with a rose and a roundel with a green man in delicate foliage of c. 1300. Similar to the arcade, the hollow-moulded arch on the chancel N side, double-depth, and its E shafts, but the two W corbel-capitals are of c. 1300. A plaster roundel dated 1758 above the tower arch relates to the plastering of the broad nave wagon roof, since removed. The roof is ceiled at the E end. No chancel arch, just a rood beam on angels added in the restoration of 1900 by *C. E. Ponting*. He also replaced the chancel roof.

FURNISHINGS. FONT. Norman. Tapering tub with closely interlaced arches, the rim cut down. Moulded base. – ROOD SCREEN. C15–C16, much repaired in 1900. Five bays. Finicky four-light tracery with little shields in the upper tracery. Ribbed coving, traceried cells, densely carved undercut cornice. Very like the Combe St Nicholas screen, and of a group with those at Carhampton and Dunster. N screen of 1903 by *Ponting*. – PAINTINGS. Two large panels of the Annunciation, of good quality. Italian, late C16, typically Mannerist, probably Bolognese. – WALL PAINTINGS. Superimposed black-letter texts, C16–C17. E wall, 1900 by *Susan Smith*. Horrible. – BENCH-ENDS. A robust set of 1900, designed by *Grace Smith*, depicting the Creation and the rise of the arts and crafts, carved by a local group under the Smith sisters. – PULPIT. 1897, traceried oak, by *W. J. Giles* of Wellington. – CHANCEL FITTINGS by *Ponting*, 1900, including the black-and-white floor. – SCULPTURE. In the porch, base of a churchyard cross shaft with small kneeling figures. – STAINED GLASS. E window, Flemish roundels from a C16 set commemorating Johane van Hoyssen of Bruges and other pieces given by the Rev. John Sanford of Nynehead (q.v.). Late Georgian heraldry in the tracery. NW window, 1919, by *Alice Erskine*. Arts and Crafts opaque glass in striking blues, the Communion of Saints. Delightful grisaille children below.

HALSE MANOR. Mid-C18 five-bay front with quoin pilasters to the angles and pedimented central bay. Lunette in the pediment. Bay windows and porch of after 1902. Added outer bays with parapets. Open-well staircase with slim turned balusters.

A long, closely built main street of varied houses, some thatched. Set back on the r. is a cruciform former MALTHOUSE of 1768.

STOFORD HOUSE, 1 m. NE. A C15 hall house floored c. 1608 (tree-ring-dated stair). Cross-passage with heavy oak doorway to the hall, with early C17 plaster motifs in the ceiling panels and also a frieze. The kitchen has a drying kiln and curing chamber flanking the fireplace under one bressumer. Jointed-cruck trusses. Outbuilding with similar bressumer and framed ceiling.

HALSE WATER, ¼ m. S of Stoford House. Thatched, C16–C17. Plaster motifs in a framed ceiling.

Halsway Manor, before alteration.
Engraving, 1869

HALSWAY

NW of Crowcombe

HALSWAY MANOR (National Centre for Traditional Song and Dance). The long, picturesque Tudor Gothic display on the hillside is a C15 and C16 house of the Stradlings thoroughly rebuilt by *J. D. Sedding* after 1875 for the Rowcliffe family. The new parts are in red sandstone ashlar and Ham stone. The original was roughcast and charmingly varied, attracting painters in the 1860s, notably J. W. North and Fred Walker. A chapel is recorded in 1415.* The house had, as now, three battlemented projections. The battlemented late C15 hall had a storeyed porch on the l. and a larger oriel on the r. A cross-wing with a later canted bay adjoined the oriel. Then followed a range of equal length with a lateral chimney, ending with another C15 storeyed porch. This suggests, highly unusually, two halls, but the evidence is too confused to tell if the r. range ever contained one.

Sedding made the oriel into the main entry, reusing a C15 doorway with leaf spandrels. He inserted three conventional Gothic windows to the hall and removed the l. porch. Beyond this he added a large twin-gabled block with gables and parapets of Ham stone. A two-storey square bay window reuses the battlements of the demolished porch. On the r. range Sedding removed the cross-wing gable, took out the adjacent medieval pointed doorway (re-set now at the back), altered the windows, added battlements, and put a new cross-wing behind the r. porch. This porch is the best survivor. Moulded shafted arch and red sandstone battlements with finials and gargoyles.

---

* Fragments incorporated in the C18 Crowcombe Court folly.

Moulded pointed doorway inside. Inside, the wagon-roofed Great Hall retains little that is original. The interiors are filled with C16–C17 panelling imported after 1924 for William Mitchell, a director of Wills Tobacco. In the hall, the panelling with pilasters is late C16 from Cock's House, Quayside, Newcastle, and the C16–C17 wooden chimneypiece and overmantel come from Albright Hussey, Shropshire. Two medieval stained-glass roundels. The sitting-room ceiling was raised to accommodate panelling from Standish Hall, Lancs., with arabesque pilasters and an overmantel. The ribbed plaster ceiling seems to be copied from Haddon Hall, Derbys. The library beyond is the best room, with some marquetry to the imported C17 panelling and a lush curved thick-rib plaster ceiling, the tympana also thickly decorated. A library ceiling, presumably this one, was called 'restored' in 1908 and the panelling 'newly installed', so not for Mitchell.

Plain two-storey STABLES were given Domestic Revival half-timber gablets and a cupola *c.* 1880. On the lane below, a WELL-HEAD reuses a Perp doorway from the house. Nearby is an eroded yale, emblem of Cardinal Beaufort, whose daughter married Sir Edward Stradling †1453.

THORNCOMBE HOUSE, ½ m. NW. Early C19 stucco refacing of a five-bay house of 1744. Tall C18 OUTBUILDINGS including an L-plan hip-roofed barn and a tall linhay with circular rubble piers.

MIDDLE HALSWAY FARM, ¼ m. SE. Altered in the C19 but with a C16 framed ceiling. Half-hipped cob-walled BARN with C16–C17 jointed crucks.

HALSWELL HOUSE
Goathurst

The park at Halswell slopes down from the Quantocks, the park of equal interest to the great house at its centre. The house was built in 1689 by Sir Halswell Tynte in front of the C16 house of the Halswells. *William Taylor* may be the architect. A letter of 1683 mentions his having to be at 'Sir Haswell's'. It is the most important house of its date in the county, a massive three-storeyed block of Ham stone, seven bays by five bays, with a parapet interrupted by balustrades. The N front has projecting two-bay wings with segment-headed windows in flat surrounds to the two main floors and square attic windows. In the recessed centre, tall arched windows in architraves finished in little flat cornices flank a rich Baroque centrepiece of the doorway and window above it. The two are connected and rather crowded in their motifs. The doorway is set back in a big coved niche, *à la* France and Wren's St Mary-le-Bow. Trophies in the spandrels. This is framed by rusticated pillars, one stepped forward, the outer one stepped back, with a quarter-column in the angle, its entablature on the original plane. The window above is square-headed, in an eared architrave, the ears over panels with hanging garlands. Outside this, panelled pilasters carry a big open pediment with splendid garlanded heraldry, and outer half-pilasters develop at the foot into volutes. Again square attic windows. The end walls were altered by *Francis Cartwright* in 1754, the W end probably rebuilt as three bays, with a big first-floor corniced architrave in stone above an arched doorway in rusticated stonework. Small canted bay window each side. The E end has five close-spaced bays under a balustraded parapet, the first-floor windows in stone corniced architraves, the central one pedimented. Rusticated arcaded ground floor. The barrack-like back with corniced mullion or mullion-and-transom windows towers over the courtyard of the earlier house. The N range of the old house was incorporated, as can be seen from inside. The E and S ranges of the earlier house remain, of two storeys and attic, without particular embellishment. Three gables on the E range, the l. one projecting. Off-centre doorway with rusticated oak door of *c*. 1600. Brick early C19 addition against the r. gable, for a new staircase. The S range has a near-central stair gable. Much was tidied in the 1920s, old photographs showing especially the outside E face of the E range re-windowed and the SE corner entirely rebuilt. The W side is closed by a screen wall of 1754 with a rusticated doorway matching that on the W end of the main house. The screen wall meets an extension to the S range with a hipped roofed over a lunette and Venetian window.

The interiors of the front block are replicas of 1924–6 (after fire) by *Thomas Vickery* of London. While the woodwork detail is unconvincing – see the big open-well staircase with twisted balusters – the plasterwork is excellent, reproducing what was lost. Three ceilings all at the E end. In the drawing room, NE, a deep coved Rococo ceiling of mid-C18 type. Intertwined branches and thin naturalistic trails. Upstairs two ceilings akin to the rich ceilings of the 1680s at Dunster Castle. The stair hall has a giant wreathed circle with palm-frond spandrels, and a coved cornice with putti supporting cartouches. In the NE chamber, a circle bordered in high-relief flowers is within a square frame curved out to enclose cartouches amid palm fronds with tiny cherubs. Cherub heads and festoons of flowers in the cornice. Chinoiserie wallpaper, also of the 1920s. Some imported marble fireplaces, the best, mid-C18 with a female mask and drapes, in the central hall. Low rooms at the back, from the previous house. An early C17 overmantel upstairs shows Daniel in the lion's den between large figures of Hope and Mercy. Narrow open-well staircase with ball finials, mostly replica. The interiors of the E and S ranges are in poor condition (2013). In the E range the kitchen is marked by a large stone fireplace with keystone. Moulded Tudor arched S doorway, and another the other side of the passage from the E doorway. Also roof trusses of C16 type with cranked collars. Jointed crucks in the S range.

Halswell House.
Engraving by T. Bonnor, 1791

To the SW is an irregular sloping yard with a handsome C18 brick WALL on the lower E side. Blind arches between giant rusticated gatepiers. It may have screened a riding school. Behind it now is a very large circular DOVECOTE, rendered over stone, cob and brick, remodelled in the C18 under a bell-shaped roof. At the SE corner, the OLD FARMHOUSE, converted from low C18 outbuildings with shaped gables to mansard-roofed cross-wings. On the upper W side, the former STABLES are a stone castellated gatehouse between brick ranges with outer cross wings. The gatehouse dates from 1750, relatively early medievalism. Late C17 brickwork to each side and in the r. cross-wing. At the back, long Gothic windows to make a show of the approach from the W. On the N side, a plain brick castellated COACHHOUSE of three bays, C18.

Closer to the house, a stepped PYRAMID on a pedestal covers the water supply. Erected 'in honour of a pure nymph', to a niece (†1744) of Sir Charles Kemeys Tynte, owner 1740–85, and creator of the extraordinary LANDSCAPE here. The pyramid evokes the Mausoleum of Halicarnassus. Sir Charles, friend of Coplestone Bampfylde of Hestercombe and Henry Hoare of Stourhead, rivalled them in embellishing his estate. If he had an overall scheme this is hard to see: the references range from biblical to classical, medieval and ancient British. Little remains of the formal gardens that preceded Sir Charles's day. On the E lawn a straight canal has been naturalized. Its badly decayed DAM, one with the ha-ha, is similar to a design in *Thomas Wright*'s *Grottos* of 1758, but may date from 1754. Five bays divided by rockwork piers, all but the centre bay lined with squared Lias. Water emerged high up from the central arched recess, falling across a plaque into a circular pool, and from low down in the open-pedimented outer bays.

Niches in the intermediate bays. On the adjacent wooded hill, a Doric ROTUNDA of 1755. Eight columns carry a well-carved frieze of triglyphs and bucrania. The shallow dome has collapsed. The large ICE HOUSE underneath is improbably said to be of later date, 1767. On the hillside above stands ROBIN HOOD'S HUT (Landmark Trust), 1765, a fascinating piece of Georgian romanticism, the name evoking ancient freedoms (cf. Hoare's Alfred's Tower, South Brewham). A thatched cottage, containing a 'hermit's room', kitchen and china room, backs on to a sophisticated Gothic 'umbrello', a half-recessed octagonal belvedere overlooking the Bristol Channel. Ogee Gothick arches beneath a blind attic. An ogee-headed window each side. The design by *Henry Keene* derives from Batty Langley's Gothic pattern-book of 1741. Restored by *Peter Bird* of *Caroe & Partners*, 1997–9, for the Somerset Building Preservation Trust, the umbrello entirely reconstructed.

Sir Charles also landscaped MILL WOOD, a shallow valley well W of the house. On the path to it was a memorial of 1765 to his favourite horse, a garlanded horse's skull on a big sarcophagus, all on a high pedestal. The work at Mill Wood began in the mid 1750s. The trees have all gone, leaving a descending chain of small lakes ornamented with picturesque features. At the upper end, a sunken passage passes two damaged features, a bust of Shakespeare on a brick plinth and an ashlar altar with obelisk top inscribed 'Passenger prepare for change', to emerge at the GROTTO, a platform overhung with laurels and backed by three cave-like recesses. A stream emerges from the E recess into a little octagonal basin, under a plaque recalling Moses drawing water from the rock. In the W recess are slate picnic shelves. Originally the path ran through woods past an octagonal rustic shelter, or Druid's Temple, of 1756, based on a design by *Wright*, before regaining the water at the lower end of the top pond. Trees and temple are gone. At the end of the pond, the STONE BRIDGE of 1755 forms the dam. A large ashlar hemispherical niche faces across the pond, the arch and flanking piers with intermittent whorled rustication, more marine than icicle. Ramped sides crested in marine ornament, originally ending in female demi-figures each emerging from water reed with a floral shoulder-strap. The r. side only intact (2012). Two ponds further down, another dam carries the rubble jamb of an ARCH that stood over a statue of Neptune. Gothic niche in the spandrel. Between the lowest ponds, a FOOTBRIDGE of three shallow arches, missing its parapet. From here appears the climax, the TEMPLE OF HARMONY, NW of the lowest pond. A perfect Ionic temple in Bath stone, of 1764–5 by *Thomas Prowse*, based on Palladio's version of the Temple of Fortuna Virilis, Rome. A portico two bays deep fronts a windowless temple with half-columns between rusticated walling. The rear is rusticated with only capitals and bases to indicate where pilasters should be. Illuminated only through the tall doorway, the interior contains the impressive altarpiece commemorating Prowse (†1767), by *Robert Adam*. A statue of Terpsichore (original by *John Walsh* in the Museum of Somerset, replaced in terracotta by *Philip Thomason*) stands in a tall aedicule of part-fluted columns with Palmyra capitals. On the pedestal a spiral-fluted plaque. Adam's ornament for the flanking walls and tympanum was not done. It would have replaced plasterwork by *Thomas Stocking* with Rococo scrolls, already passing out of fashion. Restored for the Somerset Building Preservation Trust by *Caroe & Partners*, 1997–8.

At the head of the same valley, at Patcombe, the TEMPLE OF PAN. A hip-roofed brick pavilion of 1771, by *John Johnson*, housing the estate bailiff. N front with a curved Tuscan portico on the ground floor (the answering recess making an oval) between sash windows in arched recesses. An attic oval breaks the eaves under a gablet. Blind three-bay W wall with panels over arched recesses.* ARCH BARN beyond is a converted late C18 bank barn, the basement arcade echoed in blind arcading (now windows) above.

HAMBRIDGE

ST JAMES. 1842, by *Benjamin Ferrey*. Thin W tower, nave and chancel of hard White Lias. Side additions to match, 1870. – STAINED GLASS. E window, 1870, lovely colours. – Well-detailed CHURCHYARD CROSS to Charles Grueber †1894, the founding vicar. The SCHOOL, 1844, and GLEBE COTTAGE complete a little Gothic group.

N of the church, Grueber's large VICARAGE, *c.* 1855, enlarged 1866, asymmetric and deep-eaved. N of the River Isle, the comically narrow MILL, *c.* 1860, built for Lang's Brewery. Four storeys, the upper two with a boarded overhang on iron brackets. Earlier brick mill house.

EARNSHILL HOUSE. A substantial Palladian villa of brick and Bath stone, 1728–31. Built for Francis Eyles M.P., who was impeached over the South Sea scandal. The date and metropolitan connection suggest an architect in the Palladian inner circle. A near cube with matching pedimented fronts to the N and S of 1–3–1 bays, the *piano nobile* and attic raised on a stone basement. Stone outer quoins, cornice, plain architraves and pedimented Ionic doorways, the S doorway up branching ashlar stairs. Richard Combe, owner from 1758, added overlarge service wings framing the forecourt. Much of the interior is taken by the hall on the front and saloon on the back. Twin dog-leg staircases with alternate twisted balusters rise from the basement, open on each side of the hall, the main flights cantilevered. Beautifully proportioned saloon with a deep coved ceiling and modillion cornice. Festoons over the pedimented doorway and a sumptuous coloured marble chimneypiece with dazzling urn in red streaked with yellow. Dining room to the

---

* A late C18 watercolour shows this as one end of a model farm of three pavilions linked by arcades, the central pavilion pedimented. It is improbable that the rest was built.

w; panelled parlour and library to the E. Two more coloured marble fireplaces, with delicate reliefs: ploughing and water-carrying in the parlour, a boar at bay in the dining room.

WESTPORT, 1 m. s. The short WESTPORT CANAL of 1836–40, 2¼ m. long, terminated here, completing *William Gravatt*'s Parrett Navigation towards Ilminster via the Parrett and Isle rivers. BRIDGES remain, and the terminal WHARF with a pedimented three-storey WAREHOUSE and pyramid-roofed TIMBER STORE of arcaded brick over Blue Lias stables. THE LAURELS was the canal manager's house.

HAM HILL
Stoke-sub-Hamdon

A tremendous fortified settlement, the largest HILLFORT in Britain, visible for many miles around. Altogether it covers an area of 200 acres, and the defensive rampart is over 3 m. in circumference. The settlement was shown by excavation to have been in continuous occupation from Neolithic times up to and beyond the Roman epoch. The period of occupation cannot be less than twenty-five centuries, and may well be longer. The evidence for post-Roman use apart from quarrying is modest: the boss of a Saxon shield, a small medieval village in Witcombe, the evocative valley s of the narrow eastern neck of the plateau, and a manorial rabbit warren. Quarrying was the principal activity from the C12 onwards.

The great ramparts are of Iron Age construction, built between 600 and 100 B.C., and the hillfort was a principal settlement of the Durotriges until conquered by the Romans around A.D. 55. The interior was divided into smaller enclosures by banks and ditches, some containing circular wooden houses, but there were also areas where pits had been dug for grain storage. The outer ramparts are most prominent on the northern spur that juts out over Stoke-sub-Hamdon village. This was strategically the primary part of the fort and its probable entry was at the SE corner, at the head of the combe running up from Stoke church to the Prince of Wales Inn. An entry to the whole plateau was at Bateman's Barn on the narrow neck, 1 m. SE.

Stone-quarrying has massively disturbed the archaeology especially on the northern spur, where the Roman fort would have been. A rectangular earthwork identified as Roman cannot be so certainly labelled, and the 'amphitheatre' depression on the eastern spur is more probably connected with cattle fairs held intermittently from medieval times to the C19. Some distance away, a Late Roman VILLA above Warren Covert on the eastern escarpment seems to have been a farmstead. Some nineteen rooms in a linear plan. Significantly it was partly of Ham stone and it may be that quarrying was the principal Roman activity on the hill, for the town at Ilchester

The principal visible feature of the hill is the spoil of stone quarrying that has shaped the northern spur into a dune-like undulation, with deeper quarry holes to the S. The quarries were along the western edge and at their peak in the later C19. Stone tiles were produced from the top of the relatively thin beds. The stone lies as a raised cap of shelly debris over Yeovil Sands, these sands very visible in the deep hollow ways that run down from the hill.

WAR MEMORIAL. 1923. Ham stone obelisk on a pedestal, prominent above Stoke-sub-Hamdon.

SCULPTURE. The Timestones by *Eve Body*, 1999. A large circular stone is pierced to let the Midsummer sunrise illuminate a tall stone behind.

HARDINGTON MANDEVILLE

ST MARY THE VIRGIN. Low W tower with Perp bell-stage, but the unbuttressed lower stage with square SW stair-turret is much earlier. Double-chamfered C14 tower arch with moulded capitals. The rest is of 1863–4 by *George Pearce* of Haselbury Plucknett who added a N aisle. Complicated roof timbers. Sumptuous neo-Norman transept arch based on the chancel arch at Stoke-sub-Hamdon, designed and made by the *Rev. John Hancock* of Haselbury. Four original voussoirs and three original capitals. On the chancel N wall, a C10–C11 beak-headed monster, more Scandinavian than English. Did the Rev. Hancock find it here or import it? – FONT. C12. Circular, a band of lozenges at the rim, recut below – PULPIT. C17. Typical arched panels below strapwork panels, with long angle feathers (cf. Sparkford). – REREDOS. 1864. Stone, with Pelican and Evangelist symbols. – STAINED GLASS. E window, 1883.

By the church, the former SCHOOL, 1860, and C19 MANOR FARM. The village street is much infilled. GRASS HILL, thatched, began as a C15 hall house. W of the church, HARDINGTON HOUSE was the rectory, built after 1823. Stuccoed, two parallel hip-roofed ranges, the back one a storey higher.

HASELBURY PLUCKNETT

ST MICHAEL. Perp W tower with diagonal buttresses and two-light bell-openings. Polygonal SE turret. The rest by *Sampson Kempthorne*, 1839, broad, aisleless and battlemented, the Perp windows rather good (or reused). Kempthorne kept the Perp chancel arch and adjoining C12–C13 arch to the NE chapel, double-chamfered on paired capitals with upright leaves. Missing shafts. Kempthorne replaced the chapel itself, which was on the site of a well-attested anchorite's cell, of Wulfric †1125. The arch to the chancel is a copy. Broad, bleak nave, the w gallery replaced by a heavy Gothic insertion of 1998. – FONT. C12 bowl, ringed above and below. BENCH-ENDS. Rustic scenes carved by the *Rev. John Hancock, c.* 1870. – STAINED GLASS. E window, 1872. Nave S, Art Nouveau patterns, 1908. – MONUMENTS. William Hoskins †1768. Showy, in contrasted marbles with festoons and sarcophagus. – Martha Best †1834. Greek, by *Humphrey Hopper*.

The VILLAGE grew with C19 sailcloth and webbing manufacture. W of the church is MANOR FARM, 1840s, for the Portman estate. Three-storeyed stuccoed hip-roofed farmhouse backing on to a big three-sided farmyard. The village street descends N from a small triangular green overlooked by HASELBURY HOUSE. Regency to Victorian Gothic detail, but originating as a C15 hall house. The angled SE wing may have been a detached kitchen. Just E, the OLD VICARAGE, late C17, five bays, with mullioned windows and drip-course. C16 chamfered framed ceilings. On Swan Hill, W, GENTLEMAN'S ROW, an unusual row of three mid-C18 houses with framed mullioned windows and channelled pilasters. Downhill, the thatched centrepiece of OAK HOUSE is the end of an early C16 house.* On the E, a small SCHOOL, 1858, with bellcote on the central porch, and JARED GEAR COTTAGES, single-storey almshouses of *c.* 1870. Further on, BROOK FARMHOUSE is early C16, with a fifteen-panel moulded framed ceiling. THATCHCOMBE and THE OLD HOUSE were C15–C16 hall houses. LEAZE FARMHOUSE, 1888, is typical Portman estate, two-colour, with deep-eaved pyramid roof. The estate BRICKYARD on the Yeovil road is marked by polychrome brick cottages, 1889.

HASELBURY MILL, ¾ m. w. Two mills, early and late C19, both mullion-windowed, the latter a storey taller. On the lawn, a very large version of a Glastonbury Abbey TITHE BARN (for wedding receptions), 2007–9, by *Robert Wheelwright* of Bridport. Just s, HASELBURY BRIDGE. Small, C15. Two low segmental-pointed double-chamfered arches.

HATCH BEAUCHAMP

ST JOHN BAPTIST. In the grounds of Hatch Court, between the house and Home Farm. Blue Lias. Good Perp w tower, with diagonal buttresses. Three-light bell-opening each side, with ogee-headed lights and pierced baffles. Pierced battlements, quatrefoils in the parapet, lancets in the merlons. The large corner pinnacles have small outriders, the outer ones on thin

---

* Passages inside suggest that the s side was a timber-framed gallery, perhaps that of an inn. Somerset Vernacular Building Research Group.

detached shafts carried up from the buttresses. Also intermediate pinnacles and pinnacles around the stair-turret spirelet. Four-light w window. A fan-vault was intended. The rest is Perp, aisled, with four-centred-arched windows, the mullions carried up to the arch-head. The N aisle is early C15, the windows with leaf-carved spandrels inside, the arcade of four-centred arches. Low piers of shaft-and-wave type with leaf-band capitals; narrow eastern arch. The aisle was reputedly extended in 1825 as a family pew but the E window is convincingly Perp. s aisle, porch, and transept (vestry) of 1834 by *Richard Carver*, the arcade a creditable copy. Carver reused the s doorway, dated 1530, and probably also the windows, with panelled reveals. Large chancel s window of 1899. C15 roofs, picked out in colour in the restoration of 1867 by *George Gilbert Scott*, who replaced the chancel arch.

FURNISHINGS. FONT. Perp, octagonal with quatrefoils. – PULPIT and REREDOS. 1867. Caen stone. – PANELLING. NW corner. The dismantled C17 pulpit. – BENCH-ENDS. An excellent C16 set with the leaf-scroll borders associated with *Simon Werman* (cf. Trull). Apart from the usual large plants and close tracery, noteworthy carvings include Christ stepping from the tomb, the pelican beneath (cf. Bishop's Hull), a kneeling man, St George and the dragon, St John the Baptist, a cock-fight. Few hints of the Renaissance. C19 copies by *Samuel Blackmore*, local carpenter. – PAINTING. Large C17 Deposition of Christ, perhaps Flemish, once the altarpiece. – STAINED GLASS. Medieval pieces in the N window heads. Much Victorian glass: E window by *Lavers & Barraud c.* 1867; colourful W and SW windows by *Alexander Gibbs c.* 1875; NW, 1845, by *William Wailes*; NE chapel set of 1875–80, perhaps by *Joseph Bell*; chancel s, 1899, by *Burlison & Grylls*, to John Chard V.C., hero of Rorke's Drift.

Churchyard OBELISK to John Symes †1798, said, improbably, to be the medieval cross re-carved.

BAPTIST CHAPEL. Stuccoed double gable, the chapel of 1783 and hall of 1883. Only the arched mullion-and-transom windows on one side are typically C18. Panelled gallery of 1825.

HATCH COURT. A great medieval house, seat of the Beauchamps and Seymours, was in ruins by 1633. It stood probably W of the church. The new house is to the s, overlooking parkland. Dated 1755, it was built for John Collins, heir to Ilminster clothiers, to designs by *Thomas Prowse*, M.P. and amateur architect. Prowse was a friend of that other gentleman amateur Sanderson Miller, and both were involved at the similar Hagley Hall, Worcs., 1754–60. *John Sanderson* worked up their plans at Hagley, and Prowse's for Wicken church, Northants, and Kimberley Hall, Norfolk, so probably did the same here. A fine square stone mansion in the Palladian style, two-storeyed with the four square corner towers made popular by Colen Campbell and William Kent. The s front departs from convention with an arcaded loggia of five arches known as the 'piazza'. It has ornamented plaster groin-vaulting. Balustraded upper floor. E and W sides with canted balustraded bays. The principal ground-floor windows are emphasized by pedimented architraves and balustraded aprons. At the back is a pyramid-roofed kitchen, originally detached, with clock turret (bell dated 1757). There were major alterations inside and out around 1800. The typical Palladian square first-floor windows were enlarged, the ground-floor windows lengthened and steps added to the side bays. Before 1820 arcaded quadrant-curved wings were added running back from the rear towers to rectangular two-bay ends. Restored 2007–11 for Philip Gibbs by *Donald Insall Associates*, who fenestrated the blind E quadrant and placed a swimming pool in a service court under a large oval lantern.

The interiors are mostly of *c*. 1800. An Ionic screen separates the hall from an elegant cantilevered dividing staircase to a curved gallery. Delicate iron rails with cast ornament. Vaulted three-bay Ionic-columned recess at the back of the landing. Both side rooms have early C19 cornices and chimneypieces but the W one keeps an original Rococo ceiling, almost certainly Bristol work. The head of Apollo in a sunburst is the centrepiece, flowers and ribbons breaking the outlines of the framing panels. In the bay a nesting crane, superbly modelled. Behind each side room is a narrow room made curved-ended with early C19 glazed corner cupboards.

Early C19 rendered STABLE COURT, N. N of the church, the HOME FARM (now Belmont) has converted C18 buildings and a polygonal HORSE-ENGINE HOUSE with granary above. At the SW corner of the PARK an octagonal ashlar SUMMER-HOUSE, 2009, by *Andrew Stone* (with *Philip Gibbs*, the owner), in Georgian Gothic style. Ogee-headed sashes and battlements. Around the N perimeter in 1761 were a Gothic shell temple, a hermitage with cascade, a summerhouse and a grotto, all now gone.*

On the village crossroads, the three-storey HATCH INN indicates that this was once the main road to Chard. Just E, LLOYD COTTAGE, a stuccoed hip-roofed former Methodist chapel, *c*. 1855, entirely Georgian Gothic. Opposite the inn, BEAUCHAMP HOUSE, *c*. 1800. Substantial roughcast front with cornice and parapet, the Corinthian doorcase particularly good, in an arched recess. At the back a bow-fronted centrepiece rises a storey higher. Going SW, PERRIS is a C15 hall house with inserted framed ceilings. BUTTLES LODGE, a mid-C19 cruciform lodge to Hatch Park, has pediments and a columned loggia facing W. SE from the crossroads, Station Road passes the former STATION of the GWR Chard line, 1863–6. Brick and stone with the deep-eaved hipped roof typical of Brunel's office. GOODS SHED beyond. Further out, THE CLOSE, a large rectory of *c*. 1835, triple-gabled in squared Lias, in the mild Tudor of *Carver*.

---

* *Lutyens* designed hip-roofed lodges and gates, 1926, not built.

Hatch Park, NW of the village. Burnt in 1942. It was stuccoed with columned verandas, of c. 1825, with a top storey of 1890. An open-ended stable court survives. The replacement house, by *H. S. W. Stone*, 1952, is modest Neo-Georgian.

HAWKRIDGE

Indeed on a ridge, above the River Barle, about 960 ft (290 metres) above sea level.

St Giles. Norman doorway with one order of colonnettes, the capitals with elementary upright volutes on stalks. Chamfered imposts. Roll-moulded outer arch with chevron ornament in the hoodmould. Inner piers carry a segmental arch. Plain two-stage W tower with battlements and square higher stair-turret. The narrow single bell-openings (paired on the S) are more probably primitive than really ancient. The plain pointed tower arch is equally undatable. Ungainly W window from the restoration of 1877 by *John Cock* of South Molton. His also the over-large S windows. But the small three-light E window with cusped intersecting tracery and part of the chancel masonry are C14. – FONT. Large Norman monolith of eroded grey sandstone. A cable moulding above broad fluting on the bowl. Squat stem and base. – TOWER SCREEN. C17, plank and muntin. – ROYAL ARMS. 1877. – ORGAN. Early to mid-C19, by *J. W. Walker*, in a pretty Gothic case. – MONUMENT. C13 coffin-lid with foliated cross. Inscription on the top and along the chamfered edge, in French, the name William decipherable.

Tarr Steps. See p. 606.

HAZLEGROVE HOUSE
Sparkford

Granted in 1558 to Sir Walter Mildmay, Chancellor of the Exchequer, but Hazlegrove was not his principal seat. His modest C16 house remains behind the hip-roofed three-storey house of 1730–2 built for Carew Hervey Mildmay. Seven-bay ashlar S front and plain three-bay NE range. Carew's brother *Humphrey Mildmay* is said to have designed the front based on a palace in Genoa, but the model cannot be identified. The 2-3-2-bay front has the palazzo-like eschewal of vertical accents but lacks the emphatic horizontals apart from the modillion cornice. Much low-relief detail: bands and sill courses, windows linked vertically, superimposed pilasters. Openings are corniced below and pedimented on the first floor, plate glass replacing small panes. Blue Lias NE block with ashlar window surrounds. Extensive buildings around, from 1962 for the preparatory school of King's School, Bruton.

Three principal rooms in the S front and one in the NE range. *John Bastard* of Blandford signed a bill mainly for woodwork in 1732–3: some £64 for wainscot and carving in the 'Great Parleur'. The principal panelled room was the NE dining room, lost in America since its sale to William Randolph Hearst in 1929. Photographs suggest that the panelling was late C17, possibly from Mildmay's house at Newington Green, London. There was thick acanthus carving to cornice, doorcases and wall panels and exuberant Rococo scrolled ornament of *c.* 1740 over a marble chimneypiece said to have cost £1,000. The present early C18 marble chimneypiece was upstairs. The three front rooms – central hall, study to the l. and drawing room r. – have painted large-field panelling, the hall with acanthus cornice and columned doorcase. Good marble chimneypieces in the hall and drawing room. The former has exaggerated grey console jambs under lion masks, the latter a thick floral frieze with a child's head in a sunburst. Stone stair against the rear wall with wrought-iron lyre balustrade and Venetian window. Behind the NE block is the earlier house, much lower with uneven N gables. The parlour ceiling is framed, with C16 thin-rib plasterwork in the panels, with pretty flower and pomegranate motifs.

The dogs on the early C18 DOG GATES to the S are the Hervey crest. Handsome ashlar piers with scrolled abutments. They were formerly closer in. A map of 1795 shows the lawn to the W terminated at a hexagonal 'bastion' over the 'kennel-ground'. In Sparkford, separated by the by-pass, is the ENTRANCE ARCH to the disused drive. Elliptical, between broad pilasters with stretched Ionic capitals. It is of *c.* 1690 and comes from Lord Stawell's mansion at Low Ham (q.v.). Howard Colvin, noting its un-English character, attributed it to *Jacques Rousseau*, a Huguenot refugee. Bisected into barn entries, it was re-assembled here in 1872 by *Henry Hall*, whose LODGE is coincidentally French. Its steep roof was copied from a house of Napoleon III in Normandy or Sedan, family tradition carelessly notes.

HEATHFIELD

ST JOHN BAPTIST. Small, red sandstone. Plain tower with parapet. Diagonal buttresses. Perp bell-lights. Double-chamfered tower arch. The rest over-restored in 1869–70 by *Edward Ashworth*. Renewed Dec E window. Perp S porch attached to a rebuilt S chapel. C15–C16 wagon roofs and four-centred S arch. – PULPIT. 1841, reusing good C16 traceried panels. – STAINED GLASS. E window, 1869, probably by *Warrington*. – MONUMENT. Margaret Hadley. Colourful Jacobean. She faces her husband across a prayer-desk under an arch. Outer columns carry figures.

CHURCHYARD CROSS. C15, the shaft with a headless figure of the Baptist under a canopy. Angel corbel below.

OLD RECTORY, 1 m. NW. Rebuilt by *James Wilson*, 1854, with acute bargeboarded gables and a funny corner spirelet. LODGE, 1859, by *Wilson*.

HENLADE
Ruishton

HENLADE HOUSE (Mount Somerset Hotel). Substantial stuccoed villa of the Anderdon family, *c.* 1805–10. 2–1–2 bays with cornice, parapet and outer pilasters. Large, later, Ionic porch. Good octagonal domed entrance hall; curving cantilevered stone staircase beyond. Gothic STABLES, with pyramid-roofed tower, and LODGES, in brick, by *J. H. Spencer*, 1871–2.

In the village, MUSGRAVE HOUSE, externally nondescript, was a C14–C15 hall house with jointed crucks. Inserted framed ceiling cased in C17 vine-trail plaster, and broad early C16 moulded stone fireplace.

HAYDON HOUSE, 1 m. W. Notable for early (late C17) brickwork. Buff coloured and used decoratively with panels and nogged strings. Visible on the house (refronted in stucco *c.* 1830–40) but especially on the tall lofted OUTBUILDING. Similar brickwork on HAYDON FARMHOUSE, NW, which has a panelled plaster ceiling with stars.

HENLEY MANOR *see* MISTERTON

HENSTRIDGE

ST NICHOLAS. Mostly of 1872–3 by *J. M. Allen*, the W tower rebuilt larger by *Edmund Buckle*, 1900. Perp fragments remain inside, and a late C14 NE chapel with double-chamfered W arch and S arcade. C15 corner SHRINE, or Easter sepulchre, of Purbeck marble. A single octagonal shaft supports a canopy, ogee-arched on both sides, with fleurons, square quatrefoils and cresting. Vaulted within, with crocketed panels on the E wall. – FONT. Octagonal, C15, retooled. – RAILS. 1904, brass. – STAINED GLASS. Chancel, 1875. – MONUMENTS. NE chapel. William Carent †1476 and Margaret †1463. Spectacular if coarsely detailed canopied monument of 1463 still with much original colour. Defaced effigies under a canopy, depressed-arched, much cusped and elaborately panelled inside. Spandrels with cocooned angels, cornice with shields. On the tomb-chest, slim figures in elementary niches, eleven N, six S, flanking an offering recess. Attached doorway with cresting. – Rev. Baptist Isaac †1772. Curved-headed, two-colour marble.

Churchyard TOMB of T. Merthyr Guest †1904. Railed, with bronze heraldry. – Base and shaft of a C15 CHURCHYARD CROSS.

E of the church, the altered mid-C18 former VICARAGE and Georgian Gothic SEXTON'S COTTAGE. HENSTRIDGE HOUSE is of the 1830s, stuccoed with a large hip-roofed glass lantern. The cornice raises an eyebrow over a tall arched recess. The s side overlooks the village square. CROSS HOUSE, on the E side, is early C18, long, hip-roofed, with a heavy staircase. On the High Street two former CHAPELS, both of 1899, the Methodist with old-fashioned four-centred-arched windows, the Congregational more animated, with triple lancets. MANOR FARMHOUSE has C17 mullioned windows. N from the square, POND FARM has an unusual early C18 front. Two giant recesses frame Baroque doorways and roundels, not a domestic composition. PRIMARY SCHOOL, 1872, by *Henry Hall*.

INWOOD, 1 m. N. 1881, for Thomas Merthyr Guest, of the Merthyr Tydfil ironworks family. He may have designed the thinly Scottish Baronial house and the huge detached TOWER nearby. The house is grey rendered, the tower red brick with Venetian belvedere windows. Guest collected and incorporated architectural salvage: wrought-iron window guards, iron railings, and stonework, including the porches. In the gardens, the TURKISH TENT, a splendid copper-roofed, onion-domed pavilion, of unknown provenance. In the walled garden two reused stone aedicules, one sheltering a bronze LAOCOÖN STATUE that belonged to William Beckford. Large STABLES (Guest was a renowned huntsman). Circular Georgian Gothic FOLLY TOWER, adapted as a water tower, hence the reinforcing buttresses. Opulent wrought-iron GATES to the A30, S; lesser ones to the W and E drives.

YENSTON, 1½ m. N. Yenston Priory, founded from St Sever, Normandy, is recorded *c.* 1225–1350. It stood near MONMOUTH HOUSE, C17, with mullioned windows. Early C18 panelled room. Damaged twin pavilions remain from a formal C18 garden.

TOOMER FARM, 1 m. W. Site of the Carent mansion. C15 fragments over the farmhouse door. The BARN was a house, see the C16–C17 string courses and blocked windows. Circular late medieval DOVECOTE, roofed in corbelled stone tiles.*

HENTON

CHRIST CHURCH. 1847, by *Benjamin Ferrey*. Nave, chancel and bellcote. Late C13 style Geometrical tracery. Tall hammerbeam nave roof. – REREDOS. 1876. Inset with tiles. – STAINED GLASS. E window, 1905, by *A. O. Hemming*.

BLEADNEY MILL, ½ m. W. The mill with overshot wheel may be C17, raised with a drying loft for a paper mill after 1784.

---

* Similar dovecote at Tivington, near Minehead.

HESTERCOMBE
2½ m. NNE of Taunton

The famous gardens designed by *Edwin Lutyens* in 1904 for Edward Portman and planted by *Gertrude Jekyll* have since 1995 been supplemented by a landscape created after 1750 by *Coplestone Warre Bampfylde*, retrieved from forestry by the Hestercombe Trust.

HESTERCOMBE HOUSE. The medieval and C17 house of the Warres underlies the present one and can be discerned despite two C18 refrontings and the 1st Viscount Portman's drastic remodelling in 1872–5. Before 1872 the W front looked Georgian, with large sash windows in Bath stone architraves and projecting hip-roofed wings, but with longer windows and buttresses marking the medieval great hall. Refaced in brick, 1730–2, the house was faced again in distinctive purple Hestercombe diorite, presumably by *Bampfylde* in the late C18. Lord Portman bought Hestercombe to give the family a seat in their home county (*see* Orchard Portman). *Henry Hall* made plans, rejected for a cheaper scheme by *James Baker Green* who died after work began. *Hall*, recalled to make something of the wreck, wanted to replace Green's feeble attic gables and add an enormous bowed garden-front projection, but was held in check. His additions, in debased 'free Renaissance' style, are principally the centrepiece, with *porte cochère* and the terrible pavilion-roofed N tower (for the water tank). The rendered garden front, essentially a pedimented C18 SW range and C17 SE block with two narrow gabled turrets, was spoilt by Green, who added the attics.

Inside the impressive, if stylistically incoherent, stair hall is Hall's work. Marble columns, neo-Jacobean imperial staircase and coved neo-Rococo ceiling with lantern. The southern front room retains large-field panelling and a chimneypiece of pinkish 'Plymouth' marble of the 1720s. The Victorian N room sadly replaced a Great Hall with C17 barrel vault and gallery. The medieval hall was longer, for in a corridor beyond is amazingly a late C13 roll-moulded chamfered archway, presumably to an eastern oriel. The NW room has an inventive inlaid chimneypiece possibly by *Bampfylde*. In the SW room, a Corinthian-columned screen and a plaster ceiling of *c.* 1700 with typical thick oak-leaf border and lush floral scroll in the spandrels.

Hip-roofed STABLES of *c.* 1680 with fine armorial cartouche. Probably built as an orangery, perhaps by *William Taylor*; reduced in width in 1878. Oak cross-mullions from repairs by *Architecton*, 2005, who added the glass roof to the courtyard behind. Courtyard W range of 1878, N and E ranges of 1895, also the COTTAGE, NW.

FORMAL GARDENS. *Lutyens*'s largest single garden design. Below the balustraded upper TERRACE of 1875–7 he excavated the parterre or Great Plat. The descent is managed via side additions to the terrace and steps down to raised walks. Green

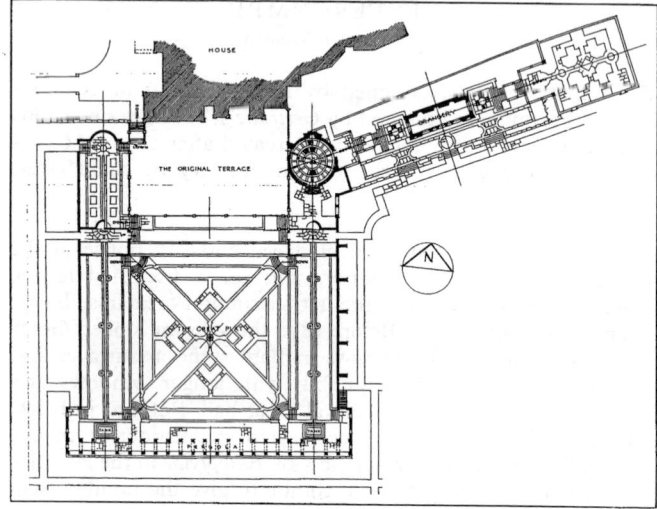

Hestercombe House, formal gardens.
Plan drawn by R. W. M. and J. M. Monks, 1989

lawn contrasts with silver-grey paving in geometric patterns. Narrow, rather Moorish watercourses characterize the layout, the first in the ROSE GARDEN, W of the terrace. E of the terrace is the ROTUNDA, a circular space to manage changes of direction. A round pool within high walls of local Morte slate with highlights of Ham stone: an open-pediment niche and circular dishes, echoing Montacute. Balustrades overlook the raised walks from high terraces, at the base of which hemispherical recesses frame circular pools. From these pools narrow channels bisect the raised walks, running straight to vanish over the far ends. Paving borders each channel, looped occasionally around tiny flanking circular pools. At the far end is a lower terrace with a 230-ft (70-metre) PERGOLA, overlooking fields below. The raised walks and lower terrace frame the GREAT PLAT itself. Its lawns form a diagonal cross within a square, the triangles and borders planted. All this is formal, relieved by the planting. By contrast, the E opening from the Rotunda reveals a terrace overlooking a natural garden. Broad steps drop to Lutyens's grand ORANGERY of 1906–8, in his individual interpretation of late Wren or Vanbrugh. Ham stone ashlar interspersed with slate; red pantiles and white woodwork complete the sensuous colour. On each end, fat festoons drop from deep open pediments to the keystone of a tall arched doorway. Corner pilasters are strikingly rusticated in slate. These pilasters are repeated on the main front, framing outer bays with ashlar niches. In the centre are three more tall arches (here French windows), separated by two broad piers pierced for doorways, setting a Palladian theme within the Roman rhythm. Spandrel dishes above the doorways. Barrel-roofed white interior punctuated by stone basins and fireplace. Matching steps rise E to an intricately paved DUTCH GARDEN on a vaulted terrace. A Chinese door in a rusticated N doorway here allows a glimpse of Bampfylde's landscape. Lutyens altered the C18 WATER MILL and BARN to the E, whose pantiled roofs make a rustic backdrop to the gardens.

LANDSCAPE. *Coplestone Bampfylde*, friend of the like-minded landscapers, Henry Hoare of Stourhead (Wilts.) and Sir Charles Kemeys Tynte of Halswell, enhanced the steep combe with picturesque structures and water features to create views reminiscent of Claude or Poussin. A pear-shaped LAKE fed by a prettily modified stream contrasts with the GREAT CASCADE, a very natural-looking waterfall on one side, of 1762–5. Lord Palmerston in 1787 called the cascade 'a most romantick and beautiful object ... one of the best Things of the Mind I have seen in the territory of any private Person'. The structures have mostly been reconstructed since 1995 from photographs, foundations, or contemporary accounts. On the W, a large brick OCTAGONAL SUMMERHOUSE and four-post CHINESE SEAT. In the valley, a thatched RUSTIC SEAT. On the E, the TEMPLE ARBOUR on a high crag, a replica reusing the original columns of *c.* 1775. The nearby FRIENDSHIP URN (original now in the stables), 1786, honours Hoare and Kemeys Tynte. The design is from *Coade*'s catalogue. The thatched, bark-lined WITCH HOUSE is re-created from photographs. Bampfylde probably designed the rose-coloured MAUSOLEUM, *c.* 1755, a garden chamber with appropriate verse by Pope: 'Happy the man who to the Shade retires...'. Rusticated arch, outer piers and crowning obelisk with urns. It resembles a lost grotto by William Kent at Stowe. Above the combe, a GOTHIC ALCOVE overlooking the vale, modern, based on a sketch by Bampfylde.

The Portman ESTATE BUILDINGS at Hestercombe include late C19 stone and brick farmhouses at HESTERCOMBE FARM, E of the mill, and COMBE HOUSE, above the car parks, both with picturesque minor touches. Well-designed stone houses at MIDDLE LODGE and KIRKLANDS along the lane to the S are, like the grander SOUTH LODGE near Cheddon Fitzpaine, probably of the 1st Viscount Portman's time, after 1894. The tougher GOTTON LODGE, to the E, is dated 1889.

HEWISH

1½ m. SW of Crewkerne

CHURCH OF THE GOOD SHEPHERD. 1868. Built as school-cum-chapel.

WOOLMINSTONE HOUSE, ¾ m. SW. Mullion-windowed with cross-wing dated 1617 and the Merefield arms.

HIGHBRIDGE

Named for a bridge over the River Brue. Diverted to the New Cut in 1802–4, the old river became the Glastonbury Canal in 1833, waterless now. The town grew with railway workshops of the Somerset & Dorset Railway, now cleared, and has little architectural character.

ST JOHN EVANGELIST. 1856–8 by *John Norton*, the s aisle completed in 1882. Blue Lias, banded in red sandstone. Lancet Gothic, triple-roofed, with a truncated NW tower, once with cross-gabled bell-stage and tiled spire. Interesting wide interior. Short polished marble columns set two deep, with big crocket capitals, carrying tall arches. – FONT. Hefty High Victorian. Square, with mosaic quatrefoils. – STAINED GLASS. Triple E lancet, 1860, rich blues and reds. Triple w lancet, 1909, by *Kempe & Co.*, numerous finely drawn scenes.

Flanking the church, the former VICARAGE, 1860, and SCHOOL, 1863, both by *Norton*, and similarly banded. Just w, CHURCHFIELDS SCHOOL, by *Somerset County Architects*, 2011–12. On Old Burnham Road, HUISH, a large mid-C18 brick farmhouse. In the commercial centre, only the brick Gothic NATWEST BANK, 1877, originally Stuckey's Bank, stands out.

HIGH HAM

ST ANDREW. Unremarkable w tower, early C14 below with diagonal buttresses, C15 above. Two-light bell-openings with pierced baffles and plain battlements. On one s battlement a statue of the Virgin and Child. The rest, however, has considerable grandeur, rebuilt traditionally in one year, 1476, the nave for Abbot Selwood of Glastonbury, Sir Amyas Paulet and others. The chancel may have come slightly later, at the expense of the rector. Embattled clerestory and aisles with plenty of big gargoyles and finely traceried three-light windows. The large s porch is exactly central, with side battlements and canopied niche. But it must be older – see the banded stonework on the sides and ogee-canopied stoup. The C15 panelled roof with angels on stone angel corbels heralds the outstanding roofs within. C15 DOOR with blank tracery. The aisle E windows may be C17 insertions. The chancel, although steep-roofed, seems to be all late C15 and shows symmetry also, of three bays with the centre blank. The windows are particularly fine, with extra cusping and hoodmoulds. Notably good the five-light E window. The battlements are richer too, with pinnacles and finer gargoyles, including a musician and an ape.

Inside, C14 tower arch of two strong continuous wave mouldings, the early roof-line visible above. Excellent nave roof of cambered tie-beams on slight arched braces from stone angel corbels. Fleurons and leaf bosses on the beams, short kingposts above, and angels on the wall-plate. Similar aisle roofs, all three sub-panelled in the eastern bays. Arcades of five bays on tall thin piers of the standard four-hollow type. Deep chancel arch with shafts and cusped panelling. The chancel roof is similar but steeper, allowing more play of the kingposts, and fully panelled. Remnants of canopied niches, and a cusped PISCINA. – ROOD SCREEN. An outstandingly good one of *c.* 1500. Tall, five bays, of four-light sections. Centre mullions reaching up to the arch and sub-arches with thin panel tracery. Fan-vaulted coving on both sides, the panels traceried. Cornices with two bands, of vine and leaf. Against the nave wall above, a beam with fleurons. – FONT. C12 bowl with cable moulding beneath. Retooled. Ogee cover, 1934, by *F. E. Howard.* – PULPIT. 1868, from the restoration by *Foster & Wood.* – LECTERN. Adjustable, of C17 turned bits, but surely C19. – BENCHES. Kneelers with poppyheads, the bench-ends traceried, an alphabet of forms current *c.* 1500. – SCULPTURE. N aisle E, plaster head of Christ, 1959, by *T. B. Huxley-Jones.* – STAINED GLASS. E window, 1890, and S aisle E, *c.* 1891, by *Ward & Hughes.* N aisle E, 1868, bright-coloured, by *Alexander Gibbs.* In the tracery of the chancel E and SW windows some lovely C15 figures. – MONUMENTS. Brass inscription, from a floor slab, to John Dyer †1499, rector from 1459, 'qui hanc cancellā de novo fieri fecit'. – Rev. Charles Morgan †1772. Coloured marbles.

In the churchyard, war memorial CROSS, *c.* 1920, well done. Gothic cast-iron railings by *R. Dyke* of Langport.

The church is just off the pretty village green. SCHOOL HOUSE, facing S over the green, was the school built by the Rev. Andreas Schaell in 1598, two storeyed with hollow-moulded mullions. The r. bay, with ovolo-moulded mullions, is added. Opposite is the large OLD RECTORY, 1863, by *John Norton*, very good High Victorian Gothic. Determinedly asymmetrical with varied window forms, the elements in careful control. The W front typically balances a steep-roofed polygonal bay against a gable. Typical too the subtle polychromy and patterned tile roofs. Gothic fireplaces beyond period precedent, with coloured marble insets. Further S, SOUTH END HOUSE, a mid-C19 hip-roofed villa, opposite the drive to HAM COURT, of 1906, White Lias with red tile roofs and Ham stone-mullioned windows. The playful Edwardian way shows in the varied roofs, a little pyramid roof accentuating the entrance. E of the green, the PRIMARY SCHOOL, 1988 by *Somerset County Architects*, echoes the Edwardian style in mullioned windows and tile roofs. One reused doorway from Norton's school of 1865. Friendly detached classroom, timber-clad under monopitch sedum roofs, 2006, by *ARCO2* of Bodmin. N of the green, MANOR FARMHOUSE is C16, much repaired. E-plan with Tudor-arched lights to mullioned windows, and central porch. Opposite, THE GRANGE, 1830s, a hip-roofed villa in White Lias with columned porch.

STEMBRIDGE TOWER MILL (National Trust), ½ m. SE. Windmill of 1822. Tower of bulging profile in Lias stone with the last thatched cap in England. Restored, but not to working order.

HENLEY, ¾ m. N. WINDSOR FARM has a moulded framed C16 ceiling and jointed-cruck trusses, also found at HENLEY FARMHOUSE, a late medieval hall house. ZION CONGREGATIONAL CHAPEL, 1841, is hip-roofed, of Blue Lias.

HILLFARRANCE

HOLY CROSS. The interest of the church is its W tower. Sturdy, relatively plain, of sandstone, the lower stage red, the upper two stages and diagonal buttresses buff-coloured. Quatrefoil-pierced parapet without finials, so the outline is very square. Polygonal N stair-turret set centrally on the show front, as at Wellington, West Buckland, and in parts of Devon. The tower is datable from a bequest of 1509 from John Peryn of Wellington. The parapet bears his initials. Small two-light bell-openings with pierced baffles. Tall tower arch, triple-chamfered, two chamfers dying into the sides. The rest is externally Perp, much restored by *C. E. Giles*, 1857, but the chamfered chancel arch without capitals must be earlier. Nave wagon roof. The S transept, traditionally built by William de Verney († 1333) (*see* Stogursey), looks late C14. Typical Perp arch, on double shafts on the W and an ungainly angel corbel on the E. – FONT and stone PULPIT, 1857. – BENCH-ENDS. Straight-topped, with flowers, leaves, etc., and also such Renaissance elements as heads in profile.

HINKLEY POINT
2 m. N of Stogursey

Three coastal nuclear reactor buildings visible from all across the Bristol Channel. HINKLEY POINT A was built in 1957–65 to the then standard Magnox design. The twin reactors were housed in two cubes designed by *Frederick Gibberd*. Shut down in 1999, for clearance within a hundred years. *Gibberd* also designed HINKLEY POINT B, 1967–75, the largest structure in Somerset. Grey superimposed oblongs. The broader lower piece with broached corners and a narrow window band carries a high shoebox clerestory. Two Advanced Gas Reactors were designed to generate 870 MW. Massive squat chimney behind. Scheduled to close in 2016. In 2012 site work began on HINKLEY POINT C, twin reactors each generating 1600 MW, to be built by EDF Energy to their European Pressurised

Reactor design, the prototype then building at Flamanville, France. *YRM* were appointed architects in 2009, their design handed over to *Grimshaw Architects* in 2013.

WICK BARROW. Near the main entrance. Also known as the Pixies' Mound. Excavation in 1907 found a circular dry-stone walled structure, possibly Neolithic, containing disturbed human bones. Early Bronze Age burials had been added in the sides of the mound and the disturbance to the central area appeared to date to the Late Roman period.

HINTON ST GEORGE

4010

A particularly stately village of golden stone, along a broad main street, with the church off to the NW and great house to the SW.

ST GEORGE. A good Perp church. Thomas Marsh, rector, left £4 in 1494 towards completing the tower. This resembles Shepton Beauchamp and Norton-sub-Hamdon in having long, transomed two-light bell-openings that reach through the two upper stages. Ogee tracery above and below the transom, with pierced baffles. Set-back buttresses up to the fourth stage, continued as diagonal shafts to end in subsidiary pinnacles accompanying the major corner pinnacles. These are set diagonally, giving a cluster of three at each corner. Also intermediate pinnacles on the minor scale. Diagonal main pinnacles and battlements pierced with shields in quatrefoils, as at Kingston St Mary and Isle Abbots. SE octagonal turret ringed with pinnacles. Statue niches on the S, second stage, and E third stage.

So much for the tower. The church itself has a S aisle and porch, N transept, and chancel chapels. Plain parapets (replaced in 1814), except the embattled S porch and SW angle. The porch, with a niche over the entrance and good grotesques, is tunnel-vaulted with transverse ribs and Perp panelling. The tracery of the western end is uncusped, possibly replaced. Other windows are standard Perp. Notably more refined the four-light sub-arched tracery of the SE chapel. The chancel is much rebuilt, the five-light E window 1883, the roof probably 1814. In that year the N transept was converted to a Poulett family pew and their adjoining mortuary chapel rebuilt by *Jeffry Wyatt (Wyatville)*.

The S arcade is of three bays with standard four-hollow piers. A narrow eastern arch curved to meet the chancel arch perhaps fossilizes some kind of access to a S transept. Chancel arch of the same section, N transept arch too. But the NE and SE chapels open to the chancel in later panelled arches, as does the tower to the nave. The nave roof is panelled C15–C16 with no tie-beams or collar-beams or braces, just principals with a little cusping. Angels along the wall-plate. Matching lean-to aisle roof. Pointed chancel vault, painted to resemble stone,

1814. W gallery front of 1848 with ROYAL ARMS in bronzed *Coade* stone, 1812. The Poulett pew, raised over the family vault, still has some of the upholstered furniture that made it 'rather a drawing-room than a place of worship'. – FONT. Circular, Late Norman, the lower scallops linked by Transitional leaf scroll. Recarved c. 1520 with quatrefoil panels displaying the Poulett arms. Recut stem. – PULPIT. 1913. – MODEL of the church on a Gothic traceried stand, 1844. – STAINED GLASS. Good E window, 1883, by *Clayton & Bell*. Theirs also the SE window, 1916, and S aisle first, 1915. Chancel side windows, delicate quarries, 1922, by *J. C. Bewsey*. N transept, crude and bright, 1858, by *Charles Gibbs*. S aisle third, c. 1961, by *A. E. Buss*.

MONUMENTS. An uncommonly rich selection, mostly to the Pouletts. Chronologically they follow each other thus. Anastaise de St Quentin, eroded Purbeck marble slab (by the font). – Knight in plate armour on a traceried tomb-chest (nave N), probably John Denebaud †1429. – John Chudderle and wife (next to the previous). Late C15 brasses recovered in 1949 from Grove Park, Warwicks. 18-in. (46-cm.) figures, half-turned, he in armour. – Sir Amyas Paulet †1537 and his son Sir Hugh †1573 (Poulett Chapel N). The two monuments in ornate recesses are nearly identical and must have been made for Sir Hugh, perhaps in the 1550s, as the date of his death is missing from the inscription. Signs of clumsy reassembly. Two pairs of recumbent, stiff, rather archaic effigies. Each monument has a row of little headless figures, kneeling at lecterns, above a panelled tomb-chest with the Poulett arms in quatrefoils. Four-centred-arched canopies panelled in the Perp style, but the scrolls and shields in the spandrels, the foliate cresting, and the back walls have exuberant Early Renaissance decoration, especially lively around the Poulett arms with their wild-men supporters. Renaissance candelabra balusters flank both recesses. – Sir Amyas Poulet †1588 (Poulett Chapel W). Brought from St Martin-in-the-Fields, Westminster, in 1728. Reclining alabaster effigy, the head on a rolled mat. Very like Lord Southampton at Titchfield, Hants, so probably by *Gerard Johnson* (GF). Inscriptions in old French ('Passant arreste. Ioy voy l'honneur d'Angleterre...'), Latin, and English ('Never shall cease to spread wise Poulet's Fame...', this reputedly written by Queen Elizabeth). Sir Amyas was the final warder of Mary Queen of Scots. Heavy entablature on two unfluted Ionic marble columns. These are C16 (also the heraldry on the back wall) but the entablature dates from the removal and forms the plinth for a superimposed pedimented memorial to Bernard Hutchins †1733. Black sarcophagus between coupled pilasters. – Adam Martin †1597 (S aisle). Brass of his family (eleven named children), c. 1590, above an alabaster-framed plaque* with emblems of age (spectacles, crutches) and death. – Sir

---

* Similar design to Lady Poulett †1602 at Sampford Peverell, Devon.

Anthony Poulett †1600 and wife †1601 (Poulett Chapel S). Large. Two effigies, kneeling children against the long sides of the tomb-chest. Four-centred coffered arch between columns, crowned by obelisks and heraldry (twenty-five quarterings).

John, Baron Poulett, †1649 (Poulett Chapel E). This is in many ways the most remarkable monument in the church. It is so unrestrainedly Baroque that it can only be the work of foreigners. Adam Bowett has convincingly attributed it to the Italians *Baldassare Artima* and *Diacinto Cawcy*. It can be dated to after 1667 from heraldry, and Cosimo de' Medici (Cosimo III of Tuscany from 1670) saw it complete in 1669. The monument is not of stone but of plaster marbled in scagliola, the first example of the technique in Britain, rich and coarse. Sarcophagus on a harpy and two lions, with the Poulett wild man and wild woman each side. The sarcophagus has scagliola scrolls and lush acanthus foliage on top, from which Fame (once with trumpets) rises from a platform of skulls. Theatrical backdrop drape with a thick festoon hanging from the corners. The whole is framed in crazily over-sized tapering Ionic pillars marbled in alarming colours under an encrusted entablature, from the arch of which recording angels extend a wreath over the Poulett arms. Flaming outer urns.

John, 1st Earl Poulett, †1743 (Poulett pew E). By *Rysbrack*. Plain large classical base and free-standing bust of telling features. Detached cartouche. There is missing superstructure. – Bridget, Countess Poulett, †1747 (Poulett pew W). Bust against obelisk background. The elegant pedestal in coloured marbles looks later C18. – Rebecca Poulett †1765 (nave N). On an obelisk background, a large flying putto holds her portrait medallion. – Anne Poulett M.P. †1785 (adjoining). Similar obelisk with two elegant classical females (Wisdom and Faith) by an urn. His portrait (he was named after Queen Anne) above. – Nathaniel Lloyd †1774 (over pulpit). Festooned urn. – John Helliar †1792 (S aisle). Brass plate, marble obelisk with urn. – Vere, 3rd Earl Poulett, †1788 (Poulett pew E). Greek, with flanking female figures. 1819, by *Sir Richard Westmacott*. – John, 4th Earl Poulett, †1819 (nave N). Greek, probably also by *Westmacott*. – Thomas Beagly †1826 (nave W). Draped urn, by *Tyley*. – Children of the 5th Earl, after 1857 (Poulett pew W). Large standing mourning female. By *E. J. Physick*. – Family of the 6th Earl, c. 1865 (above pulpit). Pedimented. By *William Theed*. – William, 6th Earl Poulett, †1899 (S aisle). Ponderous Greek, with portrait roundel. By *C. Smith & Son*.

By the churchyard, the former RECTORY, 1839–41, by *Maurice Davis*, minimal classical, with ashlar pilaster strips. Church Street intersects with High Street and West Street at the large VILLAGE CROSS of c. 1400, the best surviving in the county. On high steps, with elongated figure on the shaft, probably St John the Baptist. C18 sundial top. On West Street, three close-spaced thatched farmhouses. TETTS FARMHOUSE has early C17 mullions and C18 casements, the buttress on the end wall perhaps C16. Framed ceiling and jointed crucks. MANOR

House Farmhouse, mullion-windowed, but formal with a pedimented doorway, was remodelled in the mid C18. Old Farm, C16 originally, has a low mullion-windowed front with lateral chimney.

The School, 1850, in orange ashlar, has long mullioned windows and an acute corner bellcote on the teacher's house. Oldway Lodge, presumably another farmhouse, has a C16 chamfered framed ceiling.

On High Street, The Priory, a long front with four dormer gables and central lateral chimney, the detail mostly C17. But a mid-C14 hall was enveloped in a C15 rebuilding, its roof surviving in the first-floor chapel at the E end. Roof of arch-braced trusses with a crown-post over the middle collar, and wind-braces. Further E, Fosseway, thatched, late C16, with back-to-back fireplaces. On the N side, Brown's Farmhouse, much restored, has a porch room carried on just two columns. Dated 1713. The Poulett Arms has a formal ashlar Late Georgian front with sashes. Behind, a fives wall of *c.* 1800. Parallel to the S, in Gas Lane, the Poulett Almshouses, 1872. Single-storeyed, three-sided courtyard. Quite plain. At the W end is the stable court of Hinton House (*see below*). Abbey Street returns to the cross past Abbey House, thatched and mullioned, late C17.

Hinton House. An uncommonly interesting house in certain respects but disappointing as a whole, lacking overall shape. This it retained as late as the 1780s when engraved for Collinson. The house of the Denebauds came to William Paulet *c.* 1430 and his family's steady rise can be followed in their funeral monuments. The medieval hall was swallowed by Elizabethan rebuilding. In the Collinson view, an Elizabethan three-storey centrepiece faced W in a deep forecourt, flanked by

Hinton St George, Hinton House, before alteration.
Engraving by T. Bonnor, 1791

three-storey crenellated wings ending in taller crenellated corner towers. From these, crenellated wings ran out at right angles, remodelled from C17 outbuildings. The impression was of the forecourt of a great house whose principal court would have been behind. Now the W front consists of the centre, rebuilt in Georgian Gothic, and the northern of the two L-plan wings with its corner tower, still crenellated, but with only two visible storeys as, extraordinarily, the ground level has been raised a full storey's height. One most curious feature, a cobbled surface modelling of the ashlar on the northern range was noted in 1662, then said to have been done 'in a dear year on purpose to imploy the more poor people thereupon'. It was copied in the late C18 on the outer NW arm and on the S face of the stable court.

Architecturally the most important piece at Hinton House is the SOUTH RANGE of c. 1634–6, remarkably early for Serlian classicism, hence occasionally attributed to Inigo Jones. Hinton though is contemporary with Thomas Smyth's new work at Ashton Court, Bristol, of 1633–4 (Smyth was Lord Poulett's brother-in-law), which comes from the orbit of Bristol masons, and which, like Hinton, has elements incongruous with the most up-to-date classicism of the Court. The front is of nine bays, two tall storeys of very large pedimented windows with (later) wooden cross-mullioned glazing. By comparison with the similar range at Brympton D'Evercy (built after 1660) the architrave detail is very good, but there are clumsy things (the 3–1–5 bay spacing) and incongruous things (the quatrefoil-pierced parapet). These and the moulded plinth suggest that the range is a remodelled Tudor one. The family made expensive additions during the Commonwealth but these are hard to reconcile with any surviving feature. By 1664 there were forty-seven hearths. In the early C18 the S range was doubled in depth to add a chapel and staircase.

The recasting of the house, a disastrous sequence for the 4th Earl from 1788, was initially under an otherwise unknown surveyor named *Felton*. Sweeping away the SW ranges and raising the ground level were huge works in themselves, but Felton also rebuilt the centre block as a high two-storey range on vaulted basements. The remaining forecourt arm became private accommodation, its ground floor a basement, and the arm running N from the corner tower was altered to match. There seems to have been an intention of reconfiguring the house with the S range as the centrepiece between set-back ranges, the NW one the old forecourt arm, and the NE one the S side of a large stable court added in 1792–3. This has cobbled walling and a corner tower matching the forecourt arm. But the composition does not work: the wings are too far back, the S front is compromised by the side of Felton's tall W block rearing up on the l., and changing ground levels have left the S range unhappily sunk, its E end semi-submerged.

Felton's W block was of 1–3–1 bays, battlemented, with canted centre and pedimented windows, decidedly old-fashioned.

Behind an octagonal entrance hall was a very high saloon. The basements were at ground-floor level of the 1636 range, resulting in unbearably inconvenient circulation. The earl then consulted *John Soane* who in 1796–7, presumably despairing of the muddle, proposed refronting Felton's new block and raising the 1636 S front to equal height, both with giant columned centrepieces. This hugely expensive scheme, Soane complained, was sunk by *James Wyatt* suggesting to the earl that no man of taste would classicize an ancient seat. So the W front is by *James Wyatt*, c. 1801. Hardly complicated given that it refaces Felton's work, it has giant square-headed windows and mildly Tudor detail: glazing (brass glazing-bars), buttresses and corner turrets. Wyatt remodelled inside in Gothic but could do nothing for the disparate levels and mercifully ignored the S range. Between 1804 and Wyatt's death in 1813, the inconvenience of keeping the entrance on the W was remedied by the complicated expedient of a 132-ft (40-metre) long corridor within the W range of Felton's stable court, beginning at a castellated *porte cochère* (by *Jeffry Wyatt*, 1814) and ending at a cruciform Gothic corridor disguising the muddled link to the Saloon. Under the *porte cochère* (now enclosed) are reused early C16 armorial panels. The stable court, originally three-sided, was given a N range (rainwater heads dated 1805–14) to replace the lost accommodation.

INTERIORS. *James Wyatt* enlarged Felton's octagonal entrance hall to a high longitudinal gallery swelling to half-octagonal in the centre. Gothic dado and ceiling in plaster imitating timber. Two tall Gothic doorways enter the Saloon, a vast, disappointing room with flat Gothic ceiling panels around a big lantern light. Panelling from Henley Manor (Misterton) introduced c. 1913 (also in the S range). Beneath are impressive brick-vaulted basements. The central bedroom has a fireplace cunningly beneath the window sill. Subdivision as flats has broken up *Wyatt*'s long entrance corridor and cruciform Gothic hall. His top-lit secondary stair (1804) and plain library remain, not Gothic at all. In the S range are three rooms: dining room, ante-room and very large withdrawing room. The latter two have plain C18 cornicing, probably from a refurbishment for an expected visit by Queen Anne. The former retains a wonderfully rich plaster ceiling dated 1636, the centre lost for an early C18 oval. Complex ribs frame an abundance of plants and creatures, domestic, exotic (dodo, turkey, lobster), and mythical (harpy, mermaid). Two principal figures, a full-bellied mermaid(?) with apples labelled 'Eternitas' and a naked man against stars, 'Homo Microcosmus', suggesting a programme. 'Homo Microcosmos' was an image in Henry Peacham's *Minerva Britannia*, but Peacham is more complicated than the cheerful riot here. Similar beasts at Whitestaunton Manor, Whitestaunton, and Weston Farm, Wambrook (qq.v.), suggest a Somerset workshop, but the greater sophistication may point to the Devon plasterers, *John Abbott Sen.* (†1635)

Glastonbury Tor, from the E (p. 328)
King's Sedgemoor Drain (p. 2)

3. Somerton, Market Place and Town Hall (p. 559)
4. East Quantoxhead, mill pond and church (p. 290)
5. Ham Hill, hillfort, Iron Age (p. 344)
6. Winsford, Caratacus stone, probably late c6 (p. 699)

7. Milborne Port, St John, chancel s wall, C11 (p. 439)
8. Milborne Port, St John, s doorway tympanum, C11 (p. 440)
9. Stoke-sub-Hamdon, St Mary, N doorway tympanum, C11–C12 (p. 589)
10. Thurlbear, St Thomas, N arcade, C11–C12 (p. 637)
11. Glastonbury Abbey, Lady Chapel, s doorway, late C12, detail (p. 311)

7	10
8	11
9	

12. Glastonbury Abbey, Lady Chapel, 1184–6 (p. 310)
13. Glastonbury Abbey, crossing, late C12 (p. 314)
14. Witham Friary, St Mary, St John Baptist and All Saints, late C12, interior (p. 701)
15. Cleeve Abbey, chapter house vestibule, mid-C13 (p. 208)

12	14
13	15

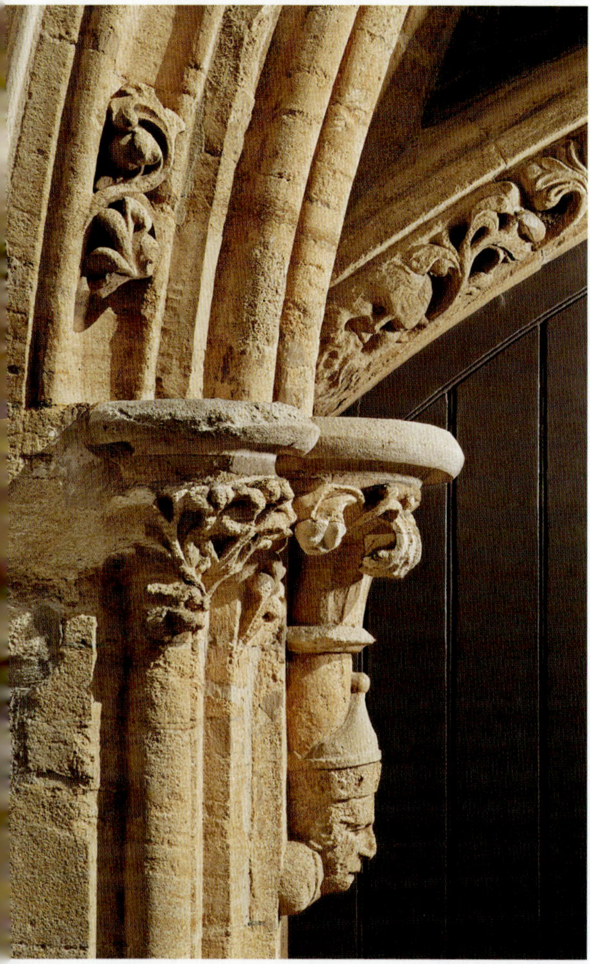

16. Bawdrip, St Michael, corbel head, c. 1300 (p. 114)
17. Bridgwater, St Mary, detail of N doorway, C13 and C14 (p. 133)
18. Stocklinch Ottersey, St Mary, s transept window, c. 1300 (p. 578)

19. Meare, Fish House, early C14 (p. 434)
20. Glastonbury, Abbey Farm, barn, mid-C14 (p. 321)
21. Withycombe, St Nicholas, effigy, early C14 (p. 703)
22. Meare, St Mary and All Saints, s door ironwork, late medieval (p. 432)

| 19 | 21 |
| 20 | 22 |

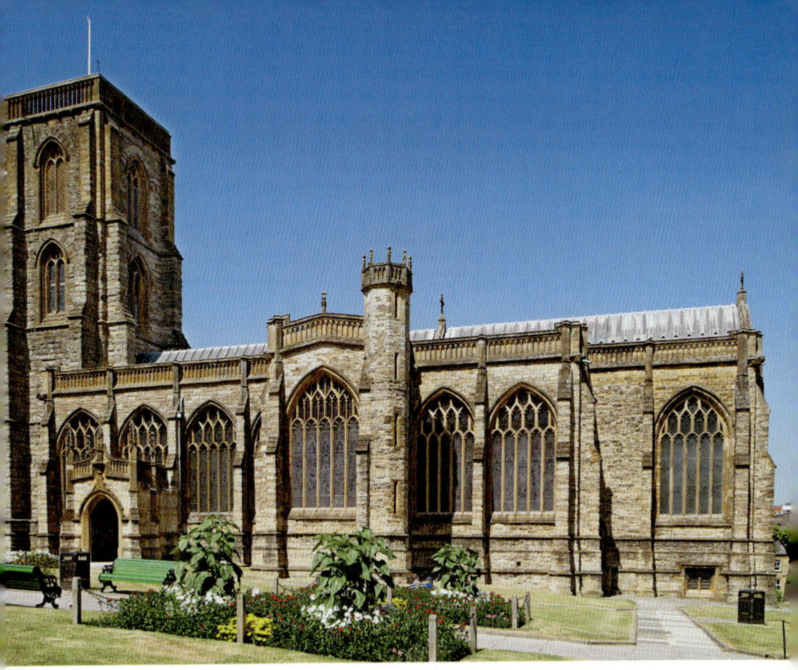

23. Glastonbury Abbey, Abbot's Kitchen, early C14 (p. 316)
24. Wedmore, St Mary, mostly late C14 (p. 654)
25. Yeovil, St John, late C14, from the S (p. 715)
26. Yeovil, St John, interior, looking E (p. 716)

23 | 25
24 | 26

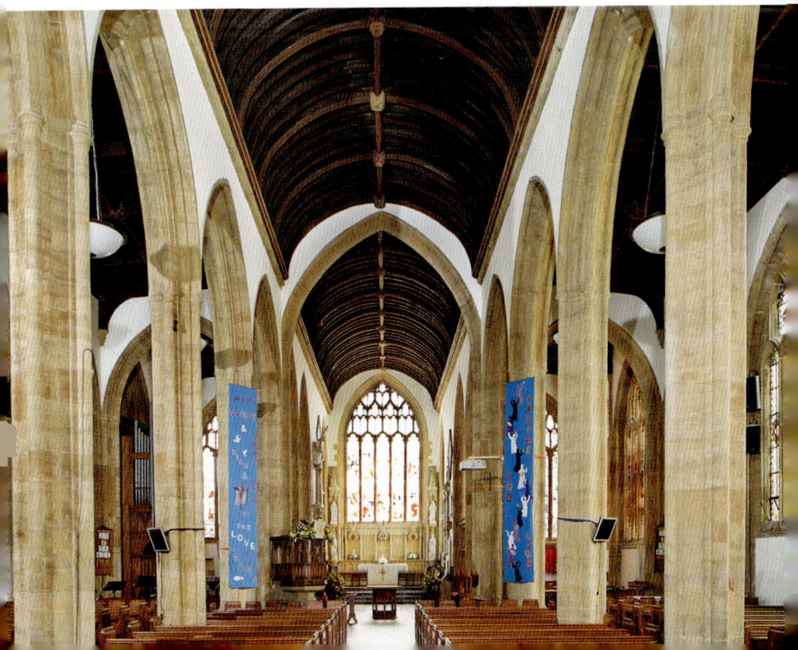

27. Durleigh, West Bower Manor, C14–C15 (p. 279)
28. Muchelney, The Priest's House, C14–C15 (p. 476)
29. Muchelney Abbey, fireplace in the Great Chamber, early C16 (p. 474)
30. Cleeve Abbey, refectory range from the s, late C13 and late C15 (p. 211)

27	29
28	30

31. Montacute Priory, gatehouse, early C16 (p. 462)
32. Stavordale Priory, Jesus Chapel, early C16, detail of vault (p. 575)

3. Crewkerne, St Bartholomew, C15–C16, from the SW (p. 231)
4. Ilminster, St Mary, late C15, from the NE (p. 375)

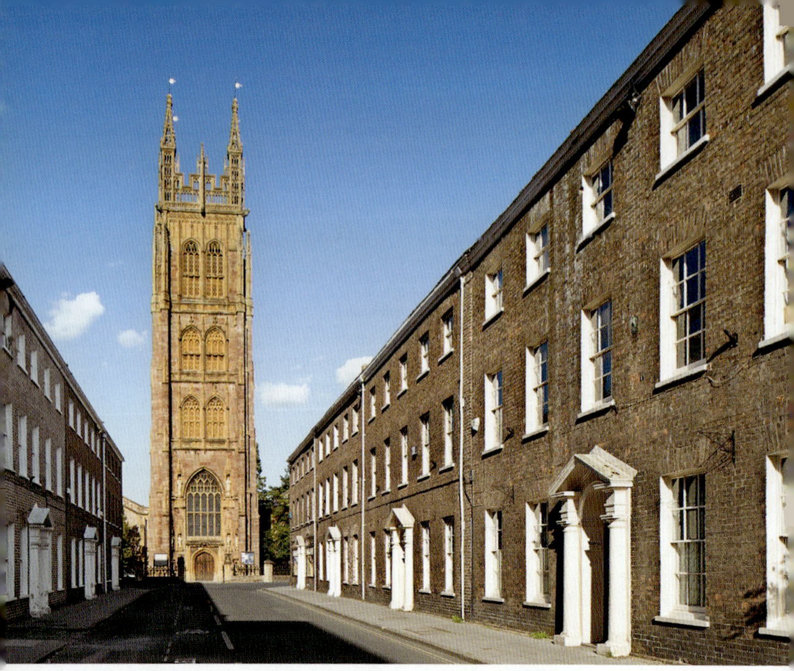

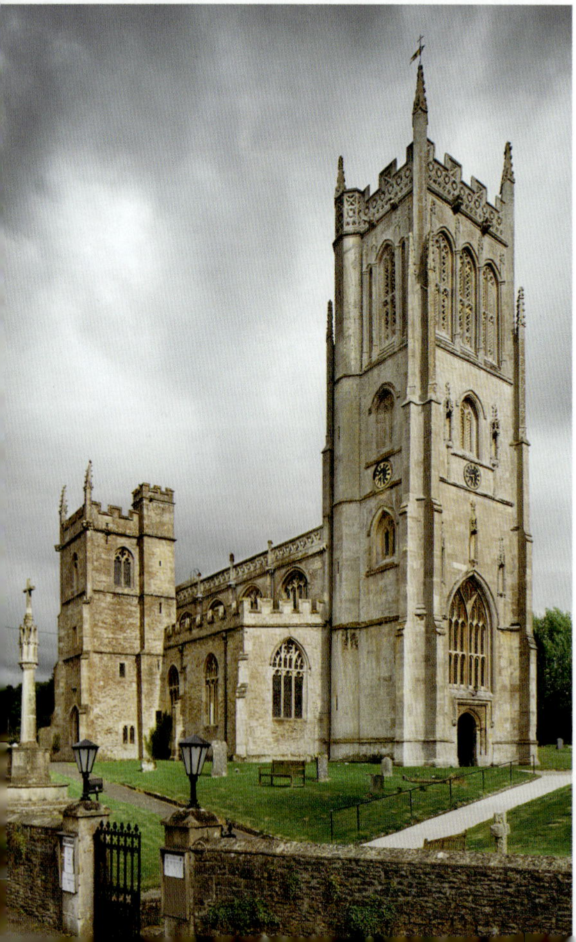

35. Taunton, St Mary Magdalene, W tower, C15–C16, with Hammet Street 1788 (p. 608)
36. Bruton, St Mary, C15 to early C16, from the NW (p. 153)
37. Westonzoyland, St Mary, rebuilt *c.* 1500, from the SE (p. 679)
38. Glastonbury, St John, W tower, late C15 (p. 318)

35 | 37
36 | 38

39. Martock, All Saints, nave interior looking E, C15 and early C16 (p. 427)
40. Churchstanton, St Peter and St Paul, nave capital, C15 or early C16 (p. 205)

41. Westonzoyland, St Mary, nave interior looking E, c. 1500 (p. 680)
42. Somerton, St Michael, nave roof, c. 1500, detail (p. 558)

43. Crowcombe, Holy Ghost, font, early C15, with C17 cover (p. 241)
44. Muchelney, St Peter and St Paul, font, C15 (p. 475)
45. Brent Knoll, St Michael, bench end, C15–C16, detail (p. 131)
46. Hatch Beauchamp, St John, bench-end, early C16, detail (p. 347)
47. Bishop's Lydeard, St Mary, bench frontal, early C16, detail (p. 121)

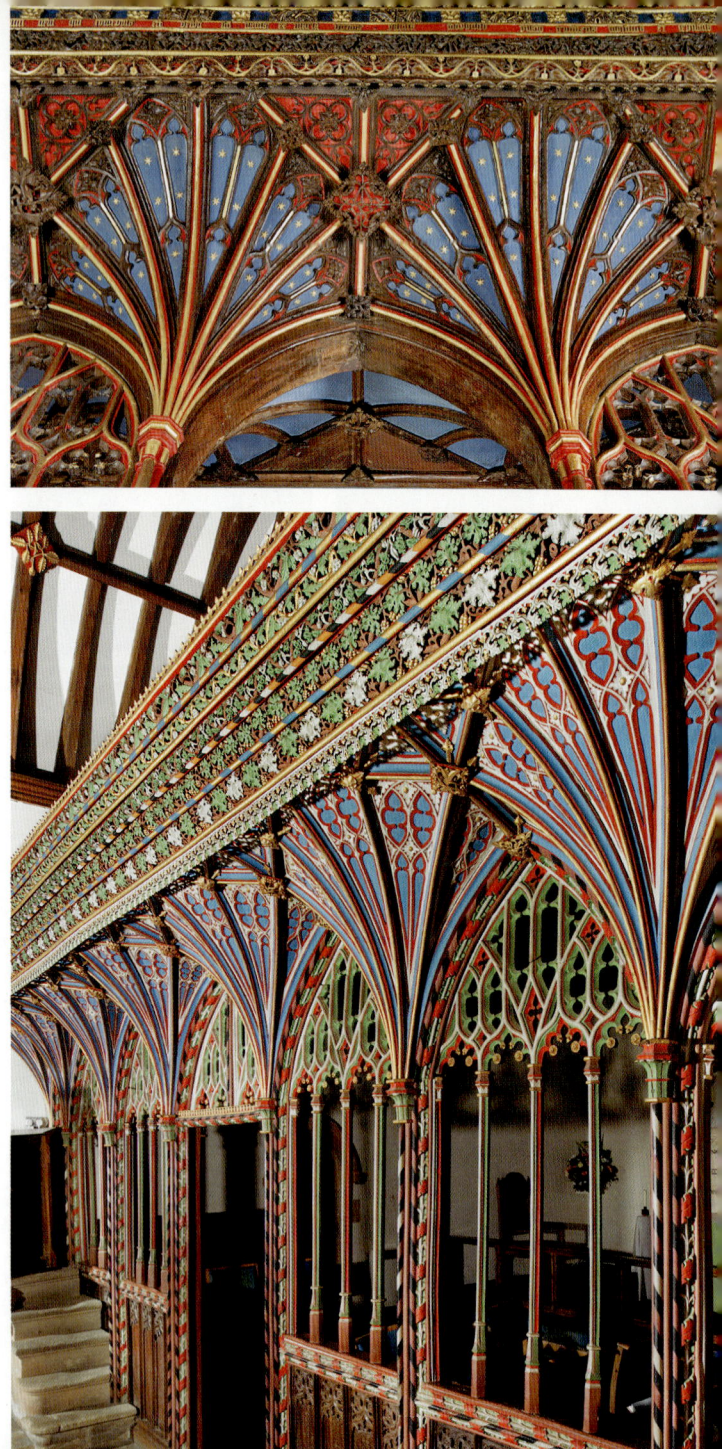

48. Bishop's Lydeard, St Mary, screen, early C16, detail of coving (p. 121)
49. Carhampton, St John, screen, C15–C16 (p. 180)
50. Norton Fitzwarren, All Saints, screen, early C16, detail of friezes (p. 499)
51. Trull, All Saints, pulpit, c. 1500 (p. 644)

48	50
49	51

52. Porlock, St Dubricius, tomb of Sir John Harington and wife, *c.* 1460 (p. 527)
53. Glastonbury, St John, effigy of John Camel †1487, detail (p. 320)
54. Lytes Cary, Great Hall, mid-c15 and 1520s (p. 418)

55. Glastonbury, George and Pilgrim inn, *c.* 1475 (p. 324)
56. Cannington, Gurney Manor, from the W, mostly mid- to late C15 (p. 178)
57. Cannington, Blackmore Farm, *c.* 1486 (p. 179)
58. Brympton D'Evercy, Brympton House, W front, mainly early C16 and mid-C16 (p. 162)
59. Barrington Court, S front, probably 1552–9 (p. 105)

55	58
56	59
57	

60. Montacute House, w front centrepiece from Clifton Maybank, *c.* 1546 (p. 465)
61. Milverton, The Old House, dais painting of Henry VIII, 1540s (p. 446)
62. Fairfield, main 1580s, altered 1781, s front (p. 301)
63. North Cadbury Court, 1586–9, N front (p. 488)
64. Montacute House, *c.* 1595–1601, E front (p. 464)

60	62
	63
61	64

65. Bruton, Sexey's Hospital, 1626–8 (p. 157)
66. Hinton St George, Hinton House, s range, *c.* 1634–6 (p. 363)
67. Nettlecombe Court, Great Hall ceiling, *c.* 1600, detail (p. 482)
68. Old Cleeve, Binham Grange, overmantel, *c.* 1624 (p. 509)
69. East Brent, St Mary, nave ceiling, attributed to George Drayton, 1637 (p. 281)

65	67
66	68
	69

70. Muchelney, St Peter and St Paul, nave ceiling paintings, probably early C17 (p. 475)
71. Low Ham church, E window, early C17 (p. 408)
72. Somerton, St Michael, communion table, 1626, detail (p. 558)
73. Stoke St Gregory, St Gregory, pulpit, early C17 (p. 587)
74. Bridgwater, St Mary, Corporation Pew, early C17 (p. 135)

5. Bruton, St Mary, monument to Sir Maurice Berkeley †1581 and wives, detail of effigies (p. 155)
6. Wellington, St John, monument to Sir John Popham †1607 and wife (p. 659)
7. Pitminster, St Mary and St Andrew, monument to John Colles †1627 and wife (p. 524)
8. Watchet, St Decuman, monument to Sir John and Lady Wyndham, by Nicholas Stone, 1634–7 (p. 651)

79. Dunster Castle, dining-room ceiling, 1681, detail (p. 273)
80. Halswell House, probably by William Taylor, 1689, N front (p. 339)
81. Dunster Castle, staircase, c. 1685, carving probably by Edward Pearce (p. 273)

2. Hinton St George, St George, monument to John, Baron Poulett, by Baldassare Artima and Diacinto Cawcy, *c.* 1668 (p. 361)
3. Burnham-on-Sea, St Andrew, angel from the chapel at Whitehall Palace, by Arnold Quellin, 1686 (p. 167)
4. Yeovil, St John, Harbin family monument, 1711 (p. 717)

82 | 83 84

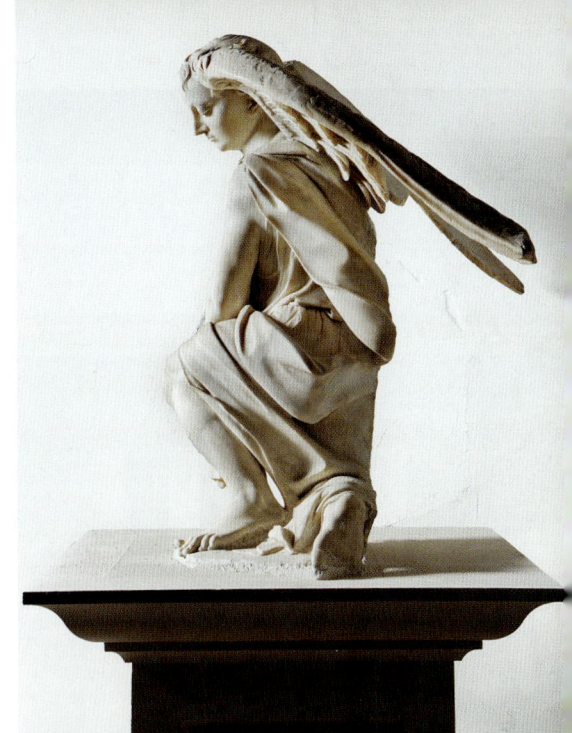

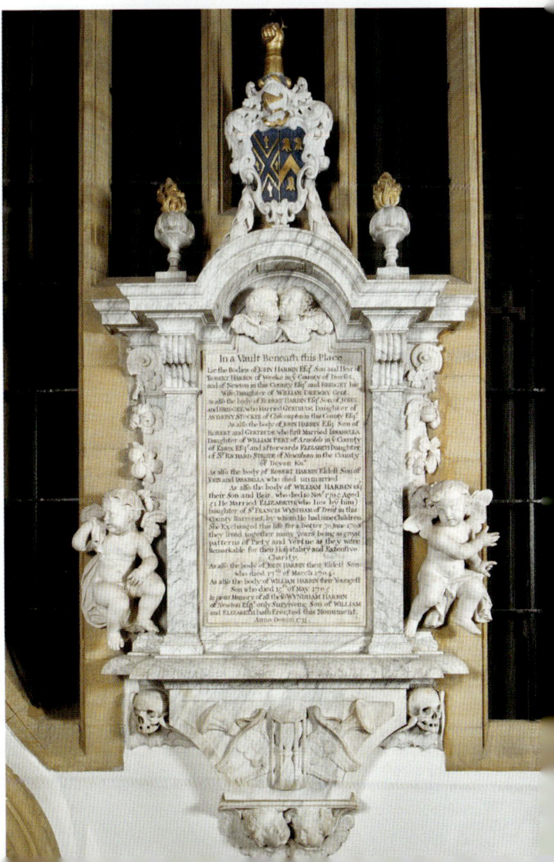

85. Long Sutton, Friends' meeting house, 1717 (p. 405)
86. Bridgwater, Castle Street, begun 1723 (p. 143)
87. Bruton, St Mary, chancel, 1743, interior (p. 155)

88. Tintinhull House, w front, *c.* 1722 (p. 640)
89. Crowcombe Court, by Thomas Parker, begun 1723, s front (p. 242)
90. Crowcombe Court, entrance hall, by Nathaniel Ireson, *c.* 1740 (p. 243)

1. Hatch Beauchamp, Hatch Court, by Thomas Prowse, 1755, S front (p. 347)
2. Taunton Castle, medieval, remodelled after 1786 (p. 618)
3. South Brewham, Alfred's Tower, by Henry Flitcroft, 1769–72 (p. 564)

94. Curry Rivel, Pynsent Column, by Capability Brown, 1766–7 (p. 253)
95. Halswell House, Temple of Harmony by Thomas Prowse, 1764–5 (p. 342)
96. Blackford, Holy Trinity, by Richard Carver, 1823 (p. 123)
97. Cricket St Thomas, St Thomas, monument to 1st Earl Nelson †1835, by Sir Richard Westmacott (p. 239)

94	96
95	97

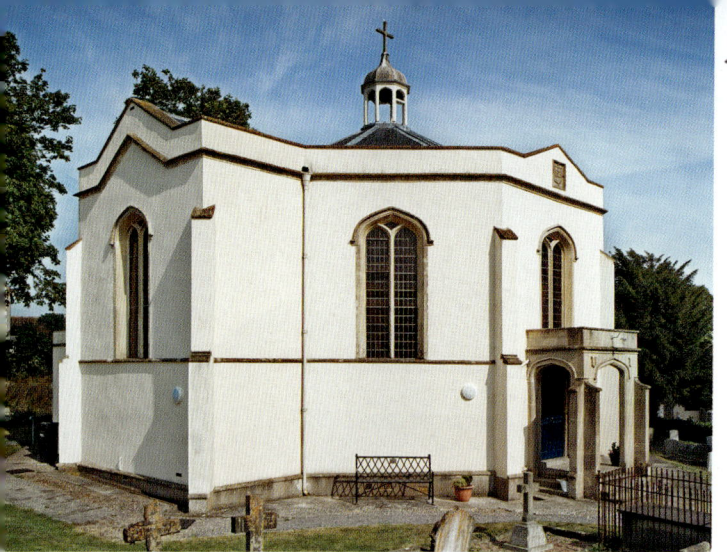

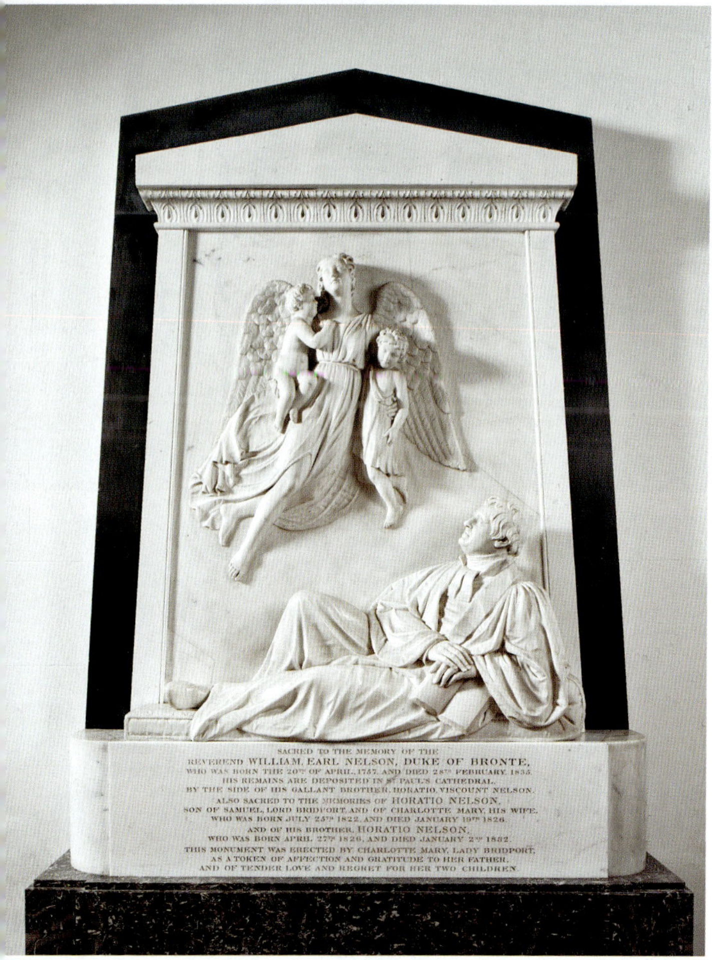
SACRED TO THE MEMORY OF THE
REVEREND WILLIAM, EARL NELSON, DUKE OF BRONTE,
WHO WAS BORN THE 20TH OF APRIL, 1757, AND DIED 28TH FEBRUARY, 1835.
HIS REMAINS ARE DEPOSITED IN ST PAUL'S CATHEDRAL,
BY THE SIDE OF HIS GALLANT BROTHER, HORATIO, VISCOUNT NELSON.
ALSO SACRED TO THE MEMORIES OF HORATIO NELSON,
SON OF SAMUEL, LORD BRIDPORT, AND OF CHARLOTTE MARY, HIS WIFE,
WHO WAS BORN JULY 25TH 1822, AND DIED JANUARY 19TH 1826.
AND OF HIS BROTHER, HORATIO NELSON,
WHO WAS BORN APRIL 27TH 1826, AND DIED JANUARY 2ND 1832.
THIS MONUMENT WAS ERECTED BY CHARLOTTE MARY, LADY BRIDPORT,
AS A TOKEN OF AFFECTION AND GRATITUDE TO HER FATHER,
AND OF TENDER LOVE AND REGRET FOR HER TWO CHILDREN.

98. Bridgwater, Market Hall, by John Bowen, 1826–7 (p. 137)
99. Dillington House, by James Pennethorne, 1835–8 (p. 254)
100. Selworthy Green, cottages, remodelled 1828 (p. 550)

101. West Quantoxhead, St Etheldreda, by John Norton, 1853–6 (p. 683)
102. Hornblotton, St Peter, by T. G. Jackson, 1872–4 (p. 366)
103. Nynehead, All Saints, monument to Henrietta Sanford, by Aristodemo Costoli, 1840 (p. 504)
104. Hornblotton, St Peter, by T. G. Jackson, 1872–4, interior looking E (p. 367)

101	103
102	104

105 106 | 108
107 | 109

105. Nynehead, All Saints, chancel s window, stained glass, Hope, early C19 (p. 504)
106. Chilton Cantelo, St James, s transept E window, stained glass by R. T. Bayne, 1866, detail (p. 202)
107. Langport, All Saints, w window, stained glass by H. A. Kennedy, 1877 (p. 398)
108. Bridgwater, Baptist church, by Edwin Down, 1837 (p. 137)
109. South Petherton, Coke Memorial Methodist Church, by Alexander Lauder, 1881–2 (p. 568)

110. Williton, former workhouse, by Scott & Moffatt, 1837–40 (p. 691)
111. Castle Cary, Market House, by F. C. Penrose, 1855 (p. 182)
112. Taunton, Queen's College, by James Wilson, 1846–7 (p. 621)
113. Dunster Castle, remodelled by Anthony Salvin, 1867–72 (p. 270)
114. Street, Cobden Terrace, Wilfrid Road, by G. J. Skipper, 1889 (p. 598)

115. Chard, Boden Mill, iron roof, 1825 (p. 191)
116. Langport, Great Bow Bridge, by William Gravatt, 1839–41 (p. 399)
117. Bower Hinton, Parrett Works, 1855 (p. 125)
118. Wellington, Tonedale Mill, lower mill, 1861–71 (p. 662)

115 | 117
116 | 118

119. Norton-sub-Hamdon, St Mary, font, by Henry Wilson, 1894 (p. 501)
120. Porlock, New Place, leather frieze, by Anne Baker, 1897 (p. 529)
121. Hestercombe, orangery, by Edwin Lutyens, 1906–8 (p. 354)
122. Minehead, Kildare Lodge, by Barry Parker, 1905–6 (p. 457)

123. Brushford, St Nicholas, Herbert Chapel, by Sir Edwin Lutyens, 1924–6, interior (p. 152)
124. West Camel, Nos. 1–8 Howell Hill, by Petter & Warren, 1928 (p. 668)
125. Taunton, County Offices, by E. Vincent Harris, 1932–5 (p. 619)

126. Taunton, Somerset College, Art School, by Peter Hirst and Derek Rutherford (Somerset County Architects), 1972 (p. 620)
127. Dillington House, The Hyde conference centre, by Tim Rolt and Dan Talkes (Niall Phillips Architects), 2006–9 (p. 256)

and his son, *Richard Abbott*. Behind these rooms are the early C18 oak staircase (thick rails and bulbous balusters) and an altered room that was the chapel.

Sunken S GARDEN with enclosing walls of 1913. The very large PARK is now farmland. A Portland stone STATUE of Diana (1704), originally amid woods, now stands W of the house on a later C18 round pedestal. 1 m. W, on a steep wooded ridge, KEEPER'S LODGE is an early C17 banqueting house, pyramid-roofed, roughcast with stone mullions. Moulded first-floor fireplace. It stands square in a square yard with square corner pavilions. Lord Poulett's Walton Castle, Clevedon (N), *c.* 1620, has a similar layout.

HOLFORD

ST MARY. Small, red sandstone, with plain gabled W tower whose slightly stepped outline looks post-medieval. One flat-headed C16 nave S window. N windows of 1842–4. Interior altered 1876–9 by *John Norton*. His are the roofs, inlaid marble REREDOS and massive square FONT of coloured marbles. A possibly medieval font, retooled, supports the oak PULPIT of 1896. – BENCH-ENDS. Some C17, imitating C15–C16 tracery in elaborate scrolls.

CHURCHYARD CROSS. C14–C15, the shaft with an eroded headless relief.

Opposite is the former RECTORY, 1833, by *Richard Down*, stuccoed, with deep-eaved hipped roofs. The village winds prettily up Holford Combe. At the top end, COMBE HOUSE, C16–C17 originally, the lower end raised and refronted around 1820, when a tannery was established here. A 26-ft (8-metre) waterwheel of 1892 breaks through the roofs of the upper outbuildings. Up the parallel Hodder's Combe, the pyramid-roofed octagonal ROUNDHOUSE was reportedly an early C19 game-larder for Alfoxton Park. Behind is WILLOUGHBY CLEEVE, an excellent Arts and Crafts house of 1921, by *Adams, Holden & Pearson* for G. Falk of Wills Tobacco. It resembles Holden's slightly later house at Bicknoller in the unbroken roof of small slates, bell-cast at the eaves, and the slate-hung gables, here over walls of Cotswold limestone. Two slate-hung gabled chimneys, one axial to the ridge. Leaded casement windows. Simple oak staircase, inscribed in Greek.

ALFOXTON PARK, ¾ m. W. The early C18 house that William and Dorothy Wordsworth leased from the St Albyn family in 1797–8, the wonderful year of the *Lyrical Ballads*. Seven bays with a three-bay pediment and pedimented porch. There were cross-windows before it was modernized in 1806–10 with sash windows and deep-eaved roofs. The interior is mostly early C19, including the staircase.

WOODLANDS, E of the main road. WOODLANDS FARMHOUSE is a hip-roofed, roughcast, five-bay house of *c.* 1740 with curved-headed windows. Good staircase with column newels. The older rear wing has a C17 overmantel upstairs with strapwork enclosing the Five Wounds of Christ, astonishingly Roman Catholic. Just E, WOODLANDS HOUSE, square, roughcast, and hip-roofed, looks early C19, but a 'modern brick mansion' is mentioned in 1792. Long lofted STABLE behind.

HOLNICOTE HOUSE see SELWORTHY

HOLTON

ST NICHOLAS. Plain two-stage tower in Forest Marble rubble, the lower stage C14 – see the double-chamfered tower arch dying into the imposts. Late C14 the elaborately moulded S porch doorway and shafted chancel arch. Restored 1883–4 by *W. J. Willcox*, who in 1888 added the N aisle. – FONT. Massive C11–C12 tub, tapered beneath a ring. – PULPIT. A rare C15 piece, of stone, the angled front with blind tracery.

Below the church, CHURCH FARMHOUSE, dated 1673, and MANOR FARMHOUSE, early C19, with large barn and two-storey granary.

LATTIFORD HOUSE, ¾ m. E. Edwardian Georgian, in that the house of *c.* 1800 burnt and was rebuilt with red-tiled hipped roofs in 1902. Of that date the enclosed Ionic porch, E side bays and NE ballroom.

HORNBLOTTON

A Victorian miniature, just the church and rectory.

ST PETER. Rebuilt in 1872–4 by *T. G. Jackson*, for the Rev. Godfrey Thring (cf. Alford). A really important little church to learn what the generation after the High Victorians wished a country church to be like. Jackson was a pupil of Scott, but follows Street in leaving correct Gothic, be it English Dec or Early French, for a softer more vernacular eclecticism.* The church looks more Sussex than Somerset, with its tile-hung belfry separated by a narrow band of oak bell-openings from the short broach spire. Colour and texture are handled with artistry: Lias plinth, ochre marlstone walls, dressings of paler Doulting stone. Stone tiles at the eaves soften the transition

---

* cf. Street's precisely contemporary West Lutton, Yorks.

from the walls to the red tile roofs. The details of composition also deserve study, the w door squeezed between buttresses, the vestry nestled into the chancel. Geometrical to Early Dec detail, much as Street would have done: sturdy porch responds, the triple trefoils of the nave s window tracery.

The impact of the interior comes from the colour, but it is worth considering the architecture first, for Jackson makes much of small spaces. A handsomely moulded triple w arcade opens to the rib-vaulted tower between tiny lean-to chambers, the piers with foliage capitals. The windows in these three spaces are tiny. By contrast the nave feels high and open, under a sturdy collar-truss roof with kingposts, arch-braced at both levels. The chancel arch echoes the tower arch on a larger scale. The chancel is enclosed by a panelled rather than open roof. Sgraffito plasterwork lines every wall, even the recesses of the tower and vestry. Two colours only, white incised to reveal strawberry red, the extent of cutting determining which colour dominates. It is the first such major scheme after F. W. Moody's pioneer work at the South Kensington Museum, and was done by Moody pupils, *Francis Wormleighton* and *Owen Gibbons*, to *Jackson*'s designs. Figures on the cross-walls; ornament on the side walls, divided by an inscription band. The ornament prefigures Aesthetic Movement taste of the 1880s, showing two distinct influences, Renaissance classicism and William Morris. In the nave a primary scatter of little red suns on white, then red predominates over the windows, with lush foliage and passion-flower. In the chancel apple trees, briar roses, and (in the window reveals) birds on laurel sprigs. All this is very Morris. The cross-wall figures, however, are Renaissance classical: Jeremiah and Isaiah over the w door, Moses (twice) over the tower arch, Annunciation over the chancel arch.

FURNISHINGS. Superb Cosmati-style chancel PAVEMENTS, made by *Powell's*, of exotic marbles, tile mosaic and tile borders. – REREDOS. Gothic, alabaster framing Iberian-style blue-and-white tiles of the Evangelists and passion-flowers around a dramatic red cross. – WOODWORK of superb quality in C17 rather than Gothic style: pulpit, lectern, stalls and vestry door, inlaid in ebony, satinwood and holly, with lovely birds etc. Plainer PEWS. – FONT. C12. Tapered with a roll-moulded rim and base. – STAINED GLASS. By *Powell's* to *Jackson* designs, 1873–4. Five-light Crucifixion and angels in muted grey-green, E. Five little W windows in three styles, two classicizing, one Morrisian, two Gothic. Pretty leading in the nave windows. – MONUMENT. Elizabeth Dymond †1730 (vestry). Broken pediment and urn.

In the churchyard, the W end of the previous, 'small, mean' church (Glynne).

HORNBLOTTON HOUSE. A large gabled rectory of 1848 by *F. C. Penrose*. Garden front remodelled by *Jackson* in 1881 with canted bays, and a recessed stair window in the Anglo-Renaissance of Jackson's Oxford buildings.

HORSINGTON

ST JOHN THE BAPTIST. Plain medieval W tower with a bell-stage of 1738 by *John Clewett* of Wincanton.* C14 W window brought from Stowell. The rest is of 1884–5 by *W. J. Willcox*. Complicated Dec tracery and over-elaborate detail – see the chancel arch and double chancel S opening. – FONT. Perp. Octagonal, with crudely carved angels beneath quatrefoils (cf. Axbridge, Doulting (both N) and Mark). C17 cover. – PULPIT. 1887. Delicate scrolled ironwork. – TOWER SCREEN. 1903–4. Carved by a class at North Curry. Gothic, entwined with tendrils aspiring to the Crown of Life. – REREDOS. 1920, by *George Kruger Gray*. Painted gesso relief with attractive red-painted wings. – STAINED GLASS. Two excellent windows by *Kempe*: the E, 1885, and S aisle fifth, 1886. By *Kempe & Co.*, the S aisle first, 1908, and third, 1923. – MONUMENTS. Alicia Dodington †1745. Pedimented grey marble. – Rev. Anthony Wickham †1767. Coloured marbles, by *T. Paty & Sons*. – Rev. John Wickham †1783. Beautifully carved urn girdled with seashells. 'His penetrating genius led him to explore with success the secret wonders of Nature.' – Mary Reaston (by the pulpit). Neoclassical female of *Coade* stone, 1826. – T. H. M. Bailward. Pretty painted Gothic panel, probably by *Kruger Gray*, 1920.

PRIMARY SCHOOL, Lower Road. 1857, by *Henry Hall*.

HORSINGTON HOUSE, by the church. Large, ashlar-faced, of 1839, Late Georgian style. Three storeys, divided 1–3–1 bays by broad piers, with cornice and parapet. The ground-floor windows look Edwardian. On the drive, a C14–C15 CROSS, the shaft figure under an eroded canopy. Neat pyramid-roofed LODGE, a square within a square, early C19, despite the 1887 date. THE GRANGE, set back SW, was the rectory. Mid-C18 five-bay front, the central window enriched with scrolls. Pedimented doorway probably added with the well-matched addition of 1856. HORSINGTON MANOR is early C18, a plain three-storeyed block of five-by-five bays with bolection-moulded architraves. Parapets were changed to balustrades and a Victorian front addition made symmetrical in 2005–6 by *James Fox*. C18 staircase. On the main road, MANOR FARM, of 1875–7. By *R. H. Shout*, and resembling his model farm at Chiselborough (q.v.). The hip-roofed house has eaves gablets and patterned cast-iron glazing. The extensive outbuildings were largely stables.

HORTON

ST PETER. 1899. Arched windows, the E roundel added 1911. – STAINED GLASS. E window, *c*. 1912, deep colours. W window, 1938, by *Wippell & Co*.

---

* In the ringing chamber a reset medieval grotesque.

By the crossroads, the METHODIST CHURCH, 1858, plain Gothic, and the former SCHOOL, 1877, by *Paull & Bickerdike*, similar to Ilminster Board School. E of the village, HORTON HOUSE, the late C15 house of the Balch family. Good battlemented storeyed porch. Parts of a C15 roof and framed ceilings. Windows of *c.* 1900. At HORTON CROSS, 1 m. E, HORTON MANOR has an eight-bay late C18 front of sash windows in architraves, possibly a refacing. HORTON CROSS FARM- HOUSE is early C17, mullion-windowed. Panelled room with decorated plaster frieze and beam.

WHITNEY FARM, 1 m. S. The pyramidal thatched outbuilding was for mixing clay for the Donyatt potteries, *c.* 1800.

HUISH CHAMPFLOWER

ST PETER. Roughcast Perp W tower of three stages with red sandstone diagonal buttresses and small two-light bell-openings. Each side has small statue niches, two below the bell-opening and one in the middle stage. Polygonal SE stair-tower. The rest of the church is of red sandstone, over-renewed in 1875–80, but with a most interesting N aisle for which money was left in 1534. Splendidly over-large E window of six lights, with very refined early C15 tracery of ogee-headed lights gathered in twos, the centre pair with panel tracery. This is said to come from Barlinch Priory, which is not improbable as a stone window is known to have gone from there to Morebath church, Devon, in 1537. The large N windows are typically early C16, under flat or Tudor-arched heads. Polygonal rood-stair turret. The Barlinch story is supported by the four-bay arcade not being of the 1530s. The handsome piers, unlike anything else in the region, have a square core with chamfered angles and on each face a pair of sturdy shafts. Two piers have capitals of an upright leaf pattern, C13–C14, consonant with the double-chamfered arches, and three have a thin band of foliage scroll, presumably from the re-erection.*

FURNISHINGS. FONT. C12. Narrow Ham stone tub tapered to a base roll moulding. C17 COVER. – LECTERN. Oak eagle. C15–C16, but the wings C19. – COMMUNION RAIL. Pretty Early Georgian work with thin balusters, one fluted to every two twisted. – PULPIT. Panelled, Late Georgian. – ORGAN. Handsome Late Georgian mahogany case. – STAINED GLASS. In the aisle E window remains of an early C15 Tree of Jesse, the best medieval glass of the region. Figures in the tracery and the tops of four lights. E window, after 1872, by *Clayton & Bell*. – MONUMENTS. Mary Willis †1742. Grey and white marble with panelled piers, a white heart startlingly above. – Richard and

---

* The screen at Bicknoller supposedly came from this aisle in 1726.

Sarah Darch †1808. Matching memorials with draped urn and scrolled sides.

COOMBE PARK, 1 m. W. A three-storey house of 2–3–2 bays, built *c*. 1830. Stuccoed centre with stone quoins and bands. Prebendary Hancock added two-storey ashlar bays to the wings in the 1890s, and possibly the whole top floor.

WEST COOMBE FARM, ¾ m. WNW. C17, remodelled in 1711 with a good shell-hood over the door.

HUISH EPISCOPI

ST MARY. The fame of the church is due to its W tower of *c*. 1500, 100 ft (30.5 metres) tall. It is an elaboration of those at Isle Abbots and Kingston St Mary (qq.v.) to a design of harmonious proportion enriched by profuse, delicate but still subordinate ornament. Blue Lias with Ham stone dressings. Buttresses with three tiers of diagonally set pinnacles on tall thin shafts. They are not actually set back, an illusion created by a square fillet in the angles, the fillet also with set-offs and small pinnacles. W doorway with leaf spandrels (one a green man) between shafts with pinnacles and under a quatrefoil frieze. This frieze is then the principal horizontal motif, recurring three times, under each upper stage and the crown. The stages are a big four-light W window, then a three-light transomed window flanked by elaborate niches on shafts, and then twin two-light bell-openings, also transomed, flanked by pinnacled shafts. The windows of the two upper stages are infilled with pierced stonework. Finally the splendid crown, the battlements with pierced quatrefoils in lozenges under merlons with pierced arcading. Slim outriders to the tall angle pinnacles, the outriders on the external angles flying free off corbels below the crown. The N and S sides have statue niches at the level of the W window. Panelled and shafted tower arch inside.

The rest probably evolved from an early church with crossing tower, but is now very much of the C15. However, the big lean-to porch has a C14 arch and within is a good Late Norman S doorway, reddened by fire. Two orders of shafts, the inner shafts spiral-decorated with pellets, capitals with mitre-like leaves and zigzag abaci. Tympanum of joggled voussoirs under lozenge diaper (cf. Milborne Port). Both arches have bold chevron, as also the outer jambs. Restored nailhead hoodmould. Notable plank DOOR with scrolled iron straps. The N transept N window is of *c*. 1310–20. Three lights under two trefoils and an elongated quatrefoil. The trefoils are wilfully deprived of the steadying quality they would possess in the Geometrical style. Instead of being encircled, a flowing line divides them to make a vesica around the quatrefoil, leaving outer spaces to be filled by two mouchettes. The S transept is subsumed into a two-bay late C15 S chapel by a western addition of Ham stone. This has a segmental-pointed window with tracery unusual in Somerset, ogee-headed lights in an angular matrix. Doulting stone battlements with big lion masks. *Benjamin Ferrey* rebuilt the chancel and N transept in 1872–3. The chancel and transept arches are broad with no curve to the heads at all, on typical Perp four-hollow shafted piers with polygonal capitals. These ungainly triangular forms may be early C15, copied for the extra chapel bay. C15 framed ceiling to the chapel.

FURNISHINGS. TOWER SCREEN. C15, brought from Enmore in 1873, much restored. – FONT. Perp. Octagonal, with quatrefoils. Ogee-headed stem panels splayed out to the underside. – PULPIT. 1625. Typical arched panels. Overall arabesque decoration similar to the Kingsdon pulpit by *William Squier*. – CARVING. S chapel W. C13 quatrefoil roundel, a tiny Christ Crucified. – ROYAL ARMS. 1672. – STAINED GLASS. E window, 1876, good Late Gothic style. Similar finely drawn nave N window, 1870. S chapel E, 1904, by *Morris & Co*. Nativity, with the Magi and many angels, spread across four lights. Typical of *Burne-Jones*'s later style. Chancel S, by the same firm, 1930, tired. N transept N, by *O'Connor*, 1871. Painterly figures on an oval of blue radiating turquoise and gold. N transept E, 1883, by *Mayer & Co*. Densely rich.

LYCHGATE. Oak, 1899, by *R. W. Paul*.

HUISH EPISCOPI SCHOOL, 1940, by *A. J. Toomer*. Spreading symmetrical sub-Georgian. Sixth-form addition, 2009–10, by *Mark Richmond Architects*.

Opposite the church is the WAR MEMORIAL, *c.* 1921, three grey-and-white Lias curved-headed features linked by grey curved wall. The pyramid-roofed VICARAGE of 1828 has notable C15 stonework from the previous parsonage, built into the lean-to and outbuilding. Three panels carved with quatrefoils and devices; the monogram TR may relate to a vicar from 1512. Just W, HUISH FARMHOUSE, mansard-roofed with trellis porch, *c.* 1800. Towards Muchelney, POUND COTTAGE, thatched, began as a C15 hall house. BICKNELL'S BRIDGE, 1829, crosses the Yeo with an elegant arch. Towards Langport, HUISH HOUSE, 1883, shows a compendium of Domestic Revival motifs. Brick, mostly tile-hung, the main bay canted, jettied and pargetted. Towards Long Sutton, the ROSE AND CROWN, thatched and hip-roofed, with Regency Gothic windows.

KELWAY'S, Somerton Road, ¾ m. N. An industrial complex for Kelway's Royal Nurseries, established 1851, specialists in gladioli. Five buildings, the front three hip-roofed, the stonework progressing presumably in date from squared to crazed, the last with glazed gablets and ground floor originally open. Taller warehouse ranges behind. BROOKLAND, just E, was built for James Kelway's son, 1886. Rock-faced White Lias with galleried hall.

WEARNE, I m. N. WEARNE HOUSE, 1729, has a Venetian window barely evolved from mullioned windows. Its flattened arch matches the doorhead. WEARNE WYCHE, Pict's Hill, is a good

Gothic house in White Lias of 1875, by *George Nattress*, later of Philadelphia. Tiny Gothic arches cap the chimneys and a Ham stone triple arch and oriel mark the entrance. The game larder, s, shelters a small C15 carving from Muchelney.

HURST *see* BOWER HINTON

ILCHESTER

Ilchester was a Roman town, the most important in the county after Bath. Its name was Lendiniae or Lindinis. It was important still in medieval times, having four parish churches says Leland (1542), ten says Gerard (1632). There was also a Dominican friary founded before 1261 and an Augustinian nunnery founded before 1281. Across the River Yeo, Northover was a separate settlement, probably an Anglo-Saxon minster. Ilchester was effectively the county town, holding the county gaol from 1166 until 1843 (except 1280–1371 when it was at Somerton) and the county assizes. After brief early C19 turnpike prosperity Ilchester was missed by both canal and railway. It retained its famously corrupt parliamentary seats until 1832.

ST MARY MAJOR, Church Street. Lias and Ham stone. Massive C13 W tower, octagonal on a square base with angle buttresses, like Somerton. Lancet bell-openings and plain parapet. Low double-chamfered tower arch on moulded corbels, one with dogtooth ornament. Some painted scroll on the arch. C13 nave and chancel, probably a generation earlier than the tower. A long-demolished s aisle was replaced in 1880, brutally overlarge, by *Wilson, Willcox & Wilson* of Bath. Its arcade is modelled on the short circular C13 pier found immured and now in the churchyard. The chancel has a renewed E window of early plate-traceried form. A chamfered pointed arch encloses three lancets beneath two quatrefoils and an octofoil. Its inside is the best E.E. work of the region: a deep double roll moulding on shafts with big shaft-rings and stiff-leaf capitals. Ungainly C16 windows to the N chapel and chancel, straight-headed, but with ogee lights within a four-centred arch and leaves in the spandrels. The chapel was probably an early C16 chantry of some status, for it has the cones of a fan-vault of one and a half bays and a panelled arch. Did it collapse or is it incomplete? Also two thickly canopied niches. Perp chancel arch. – FONT. C14? Octagonal on a tapered stem. – PULPIT. C17. More ornate than usual, with arches treated in perspective and a vigorous frieze of fruit. – WALL PAINTING. Behind the pulpit, two C13 outline figures in three-quarters profile. – COFFIN-LID. In the tower. C12 double lid with differing raised crosses. – MONUMENT. Mary Raymond †1639. Alabaster frame with Noah's dove in the spandrels.

ST ANDREW, Northover (Churches Conservation Trust). Plain w tower of eroding Blue Lias (repaired by *John Schofield*, 1986). Diagonal buttresses at the foot; parapet and square NE stair-tower. The tower looks early but must post-date the C14 fragments randomly reused. Chamfered tower arch dying into the sides. Perp nave and chancel confused by work in 1821 by *Joseph Beard* and 1878 by *Charles Benson*. Stiff tracery to the E and W windows. The roofs and probably the chancel and transept arches are Benson's. – FONT. Plain octagonal bowl, earlier than the Perp panelled stem.

PERAMBULATION. The triangular MARKET PLACE marks the parting of the Roman road to Dorchester from the Fosse Way. The MARKET CROSS, 1795, by *Thomas Trask*, is a larger version of the Pinnacle at Martock (q.v.), similarly on the medieval base. Tuscan column with overscaled entablature, pedestal sundial, ball and vane. Modest Georgian buildings surround the square, predominantly of Blue Lias. On the S side the roughcast BULL INN, dated 1730, adjoins the hip-roofed, five-bay TOWN HALL of 1812–16. Inside, a barrel-ceilinged assembly room.* On the W side a Late Georgian row including THE ELMS, ashlar-fronted, and CASTLE FARMHOUSE, a three-storey former coaching inn. Its outbuildings cover the site of the Augustinian nunnery. On the E, the ILCHESTER ARMS, Late Georgian, three-storeyed, of brick and Ham stone.

Behind the Town Hall, on HIGH STREET, the MUSEUM occupies a three-storey early C19 house. The long early C19 brick terrace opposite may be connected with Ilchester's politics (*see* Ilchester Mead, below). MANOR HOUSE, a tall rendered late C16 house has triple gables more typical of the Bristol region. Reserved-chamfer mullions, C18 doorway, and Venetian window. C17 panelled room with pilasters with tobacco-leaf capitals, and C18 fielded-panelled room, both with moulded fireplaces of *c*. 1600. The pedimented COACHHOUSE, of brick and Ham stone, has early C18 cross-windows. The SCHOOL, 1878, adjoins the friary site. ALMSHOUSE LANE runs behind plain Lias ALMSHOUSES of 1810 by *Joseph Beard*. On CHURCH STREET, to the r., the RECTORY, 1842, by *John Sarell* of Montacute, ashlar-fronted and hip-roofed. Typical parsonage plan with no front door. By the churchyard, a Gothic NATIONAL SCHOOL, 1837, and further up, a Gothic METHODIST CHAPEL, 1850, with Y-tracery, altered 1861.

NORTHOVER. ILCHESTER BRIDGE, widened in 1797 and 1932, may encase the medieval bridge. Two channels, so two sets of plain arches, divided by a solid piece. On this stood the gaol until 1599, when it was moved to the Northover bank. Notorious in the C18 and early C19, ILCHESTER GAOL was closed in 1843. Some walling and a hip-roofed C19 bakehouse and laundry remain. NORTHOVER HOUSE, originally C17, was

---

*The C13 Ilchester Mace in the Museum of Somerset is the oldest staff of office in England. The head is of alloy. On it, separated by twisted shafts, are three kings and an angel, above a cryptic inscription: Ie su de drverie. Ne me dunet mie.

expensively remodelled in Bath stone in 1802–4, early for the deep-eaved roof and enclosed porch. DARLINGTON HOUSE, 1835, with similar roof, was stuccoed, originally an inn. Opposite Northover church, the thatched OLD VICARAGE has cast-iron Gothick windows. Across the roundabout, at HAINBURY FARM, an unexpectedly formal mid-C19 farmhouse with quoins and steep hipped roof. Lofted BARN with large arched openings. At HAINBURY MILL, a long early C19 brick-fronted range is attached to the roofless mill. The water now turns an 8-metre Archimedes-screw turbine, 2009.

ROMAN REMAINS. There is nothing to see of Roman Lendiniae except in the museum but it was an important town, perhaps sharing with Dorchester (Dorset) the administration of the area of the Iron Age tribe of the Durotriges. It was surrounded by earthwork defences and then, in the early C4, by stone walls with large gatehouses on the principal roads. Also at this time parts of the interior appear to have been taken over by large town houses, many with expensive mosaics. This wealth is also seen in the profusion of villas in the surrounding countryside, but these represent a decline in commercial activity in the town. The roads into the town were lined, as was usual, with cemeteries. Some of these were used into the C5, indicating continued occupation somewhere, perhaps at South Cadbury. The church at Northover may have originated as a cemetery chapel in this period.

ILCHESTER MEAD, ½ m. SW. The Lincolnshire Tory Sir William Manners bought Ilchester borough in 1802 for £52,000 to control the parliamentary seats, but, still finding electoral opposition, demolished half of the town's houses to disenfranchise the householders. Lord Darlington (cf. Milborne Port) built these two long terraces, forty-five houses in all, in 1819–20 to rehouse them, in the Whig interest. A ROMAN VILLA W of the main road with mosaic floors of the C3–C4 was excavated 1967–73.

PILL BRIDGE, 2 m. W. Narrow triple-arched C17 packhorse bridge, now serenely isolated, but formerly a quay at the limit of navigation on the River Yeo.

SOCK DENNIS, 1 m. SSW. A lost parish. An outbuilding has a C15 doorway perhaps from the church. The farmhouse, dated 1723, was rebuilt *c.* 1820 by *Joseph Beard* with a Portland stone porch. Spectacular cantilevered staircase right to the attic, unusually in Ham stone.

ILMINSTER

An Anglo-Saxon minster town, later market town, on the old Exeter road. Prosperous in the C19 primarily from shirt-collar making. Much of the town is of the ochre stone from Moolham, to the SE.

ILMINSTER

St Mary. An impressive, large and consistently designed church. All Perp, culminating in its crossing tower inspired by that of Wells Cathedral, a firm and a clear composition, rich yet sober, mostly of Ham stone. Each face is a grid of square-headed panels, two tiers of three, between four piers, the outer piers inset from the angles. These give strong vertical emphasis, having low-relief gablets instead of set-offs, and pinnacles carried through the battlements. Bigger corner pinnacles give strength to the angles. Each panel has long two-light tracery with a transom, the bell-openings pierced with quatrefoils, the lower stage mostly blank. Refined NW stair-turret, the angles ribbed, with ogee spirelet.

The church, 112 ft (34 metres) long, is of a piece apart from the N transept and some grey stone in the chancel from the previous building. All embattled except for the gables, and formerly with more finials than now. Consistent Perp tracery, generally tall three-light windows, five-light main ones. The S porch is shallow-gabled, faced in blank panelling against which a crocketed ogee gable crowns the doorway. Plain embattled N porch. A low embattled vestry projects from the E end of the chancel (cf. Kingsbury Episcopi, Langport). The N transept, the most splendid part of the church, was probably built by bequest of Sir William Wadham †1452. It is a glasshouse, like the Crewkerne N transept. Only the panelled buttresses seem to remain of solid wall, rising to crocketed pinnacles. The windows are transomed and four-centred, beneath a parapet with a frieze of shields in crocketed frames, more Dec than Perp. The N window breaks through the parapet beneath a crocketed gable with pinnacle. The tracery, with seven radiating mouchettes, like a fanciful design of c. 1300. Is this sophisticated Perp revivalism?

Renewed stonework shows that the aisles were raised in a major alteration of 1824–5 by *William Burges* of Exeter. He rebuilt the upper part of the nave, replacing five clerestory windows with three broad ones. The reason for this can be seen inside. He changed a five-bay arcade to three by removing alternate piers, this to allow broader galleries (taken out 1902). The remaining piers are standard Perp. Burgess's plaster ceiling went in 1934 for a Somerset-type roof by *Caröe & Passmore*. The tall crossing has four panelled arches and a good fan-vault. The arches from the aisles to the transepts match those of the nave. Large transverse-arched squints into the chancel. Below the S transept roof four angel corbels bear emblems of the Passion; also two grotesques. The N transept roof has exaggerated cusping, surely C17 not C15. The chancel roof is a copy by *J. D. Sedding*, 1882, on original wall-shafts. Two C15 vestry doors at the E end, overwhelmed by the large stone REREDOS of 1912 by *F. B. Bond*. This has tiered statues and reliefs framed in undercut vine, latest Gothic style. Marble floor by *Sedding*. – FONT. Perp, octagonal, with large pointed quatrefoils and underside leaves. Panelled stem, one face extended to the wall. – PULPIT. C17. Panelled with paired

Ilminster, St Mary.
Brass to Nicholas and Dorothy Wadham †1609 and 1618

fluted columns; cf. Winsham, Donyatt. – SCREEN, N transept. Of c. 1700, re-set from the N aisle. Panelled below two tiers of C17 vertically symmetrical balusters. Jacobean panels over the doorway. – WEST GALLERY. 1902, by *C. E. Ponting*. Not attractive. – ROYAL ARMS. 1824. – CHANDELIERS. Two large, two smaller, 1762, by *Thomas Bayley*. – WEST DOORS. Engraved glass by *Tracey Sheppard*, 1999. – STAINED GLASS. E window by *Burlison & Grylls*, c. 1888. N transept E by *Christopher Webb*, 1964. S transept W, 2007, by *John Reyntiens*. Ascending leaves and triangles. Nave windows of c. 1900, one signed *Heaton, Butler & Bayne*. – MONUMENTS. Sir William Wadham †1452 and his mother. Large tomb-chest unusually richly adorned. Undercut vine cornice. Ten niches each side with nodding ogee arches, divided by piers carrying tiny niches. At the W end, three arches over a remarkable seated Christ between small kneeling figures of Sir William and his mother. Purbeck marble slab with two brass figures, 3 ft 6 in. (110 cm.) long, he in armour, she in widow's dress, each under a triple crocketed gable. – Nicholas Wadham †1609 and Dorothy Wadham †1618, the founders of Wadham College, Oxford. Big alabaster tomb-chest of *c.* 1610 attributed to *Nicholas Johnston* (GF). Black plaques and black slab with two 4-ft (122-cm.) brass figures, late and good examples, he in armour, she in gown and head-dress. Alabaster back wall with splendid strapwork heraldry framed by black-shafted Corinthian columns and a deep cornice with soffit rosettes. Heraldry above. Restored 1689, then 1899, by *T. G. Jackson*. – Humphrey Walrond †1580. Finely detailed alabaster. Heraldry in a broad pedimented aedicule with black-shafted columns, carrying heraldic cartouches.

Outside, WAR MEMORIAL. Crucifix in Portland stone, 1917, by *F. B. Bond*.

METHODIST CHURCH, West Street. 1887, by *Alexander Lauder*. Big and bold like all his chapels, with a tower and spire over the r. of three porches. Two large Dec three-light windows and a septfoil rose encompassed in a single surround. Gothic gallery on iron columns. Contemporary HALL adjacent.

ARTS CENTRE, East Street. The Old Meeting, built for Unitarians in 1719. To this belongs the main structure. But how much more? The ashlar pedimented centre is C18 but the two large four-centred windows are probably of 1851, also the pedimented doorcases each side. An impressive two-storey gallery colonnade of stone on the back wall looks mid-C18. SCHOOL-ROOM of 1846 behind. – STAINED GLASS. One main window has good 1920s glass by *Margaret Blake* (cf. Crewkerne Unitarian Church).

LIBRARY, Ditton Street. 1889, by *James Hine* of Plymouth. Given as a reading room by J.W. Shepherd of Dowlish Ford Mills. Moolham stone with Doulting stone dressings, free C17 style.

GREENFLYTE SCHOOL, Wharf Lane. The Boys' Grammar School of 1878 by *J. M. Allen*. Gothic, with Allen's insistent banding. Calmer W range, 1894, by *Price & Wooler* of Weston-super-Mare, with attractive roof ventilators.

SWANMEAD SCHOOL, Ditton Street. Large secondary school of 1939 by *A. J. Toomer*, county architect. Brick, stripped Georgian, like Ansford and Huish Episcopi (qq.v.).

PERAMBULATION. The elongated MARKET SQUARE is especially pleasing in the view down from the E. The square MARKET, hip-roofed and open on all sides, has depressed arches between Tuscan columns. Called newly built in 1813, but surely the columns are reused? On the N side a curved-cornered Regency building in ashlar, two-storeyed, then, much taller, Nos. 3–5, built for collar-makers in 1916, the dressings of the artificial 'Minster Stone' that the builder, W. A. Hutch-ings, pioneered here. OLD BANK BUILDING, tall, with mullion-and-transom windows and gablets, is dated 1849 on the cast-iron gateway. On the S side a mixed row dominated by the NATWEST BANK (formerly Stuckey's), c. 1875, three-storeyed, eclectic in its motifs, with a big curved gable. On the W, a more consistent three-storey ashlar-fronted row ending with the nine-bay GEORGE HOTEL, the principal coaching inn. Mid- to late C18 pedimented doorway and architraves, early C19 top floor, but some C17 beams inside. Rear wing with Venetian window and early C19 assembly room. SILVER STREET runs W to the church, with mixed, mostly Georgian, buildings. Nos. 1–3 have Soanean incised pilasters, c. 1830. LEICESTER HOUSE has an early C20 draper's shopfront with cheerful drapes. Set back is Greenflyte School (p. 377). SOMERSET HOUSE and SILVER STREET HOUSE have good open-pedimented doorways, a feature of Ilminster. Another on No. 45, which has chapel-like windows spanning both floors.

Around the CHURCHYARD are the most rewarding houses. On the W, THE CHANTRY was a mid-C15 chantry house, one of four associated with the church. Pointed doorway and two lateral chimneys, but Early Georgian windows. Front range in well-cut Moolham stone, of three rooms with cross-passage. The passage partitions are reassembled, but have pieces of fine workmanship with shields, fleurons and some surviving colour. Parlour with stone fireplace and moulded framed ceiling. The hall was probably always on the first floor and heated. Partitions continue into the roof. Above the parlour was a bedchamber-cum-oratory with N fireplace and an E window flanked by a fine image bracket on a twisted stem, l., and a piscina, r. A broken-off second bracket has red, white and blue colour. The roof has fine moulded arch-braced collar-trusses, with two-tier wind-bracing, cusped over the hall. C15 chamfered collar-trusses over the NE rear wing, a C17 jointed cruck over the SE wing.

Opposite, facing the churchyard, CROSS HOUSE was probably medieval. The long front with parapet has bolection-moulded windows of c. 1700. It adjoins the former GRAMMAR SCHOOL, founded by Humphrey Walrond in 1549 in chantry houses released at the Reformation. The schoolroom was built in 1586. The near-symmetrical façade with three large four-light transomed schoolroom windows is much restored, the gabled wings refaced in the C19. The r. wing, another chantry house, has a C15 wind-braced roof and early C16 framed ceiling. To the r., the former VICARAGE, Late Georgian, three-bay with open-pediment doorcase. Reused C15 rear doorway.

N up COURT BARTON is the thatched ABBOT'S COURT, C17, raised in the C19. A MASONIC LODGE is attached, with reused C18 doorcase. Now NW to the main road, here called HIGH STREET. The BELL INN has renewed mullions. NORTH STREET returns to the square past Nos. 13–19, a curving whitewashed thatched row of c. 1700. The former NATIONAL

School, 1853 by *J. M. Allen*, is still Early Victorian in its symmetry. Inscribed parapet with bellcote. North Street House is early C18, the front stuccoed with a curved-pedimented doorcase. Bolection-moulded panelled room.

From the square, Ditton Street runs s. No. 1 has a three-storey, five-bay Georgian front in painted brick. Frampton House opposite was a Victorian collar-works. Further down, Ditton Lea, Late Georgian, three-bay, enhanced by wings with double-curved parapets. Past the library (p. 377), Onchon House, stuccoed, early C19, and Ditton House, five-bay, early C18. Regency staircase. Then the former Board School, 1877, by *Paull & Bickerdike* of London, looser than the standard type, with half-hipped gables. Adjoining is Swanmead School (p. 377). Returning to the square and up East Street, after the Arts Centre (p. 377) are modest C18 to C19 houses up to the main road. Here is the disused drive to Dillington House (q.v.), with twin battlemented lodges with canted fronts and Y-tracery windows, *c.* 1830. The Dillington agent's house, Orchards, 1901, on Townsend, is strong-boned with big chimneys, the garden front twice stepped forward from a recessed centre.

Finally the main road w of High Street is West Street. On the n side, Nos. 8–10, Regency, with pilastered upper floors. To the s, down Brewery Lane, a plain warehouse from the brewery founded 1840, and Summerlands, a mid-C19 stuccoed brewer's house. Back on West Street, after the Methodist church (p. 377), Station Road runs downhill with detached villas, several Georgian. The Shrubbery was rebuilt for the Shepherds of Dowlish Ford Mills, *c.* 1900. The Hermitage is C17, with C18 leaded casement windows. Further out is the former station (Westcombe Industrial Estate) on the GWR Chard branch of 1866. Brick and stone, with typical overhanging hipped roof. Also a goods shed, in red and yellow brick.

Dowlish Ford Mills, 1 m. s. Three-storey early C19 silk mill, converted to flax and hemp spinning in the 1840s, then extended for Hutchings & Shepherd who made twine for carpets. In line, the original mill, an engine house and twenty-one-bay weaving shed. Mill pond in front. Just ne, New Buildings, *c.* 1873, an unusually good row of ten mill-workers' houses, porches and dormers in counterpoint.

ILTON

St Peter. The tower stands in an 'early' position, over the s porch. Plain and rendered. A tiny w lancet and a pair on the s may be C12–C13. Perp bell-lights, flat parapet. There was a timber spire. C14 cusped ogee-headed niche within. Perp nave and n aisle, earlier s transept and chancel, but the evidence confused by *J. M. Allen* in 1860. He added the ne chapel and rebuilt the chancel, reusing early C14 two-light side windows. The E window is his and the similar S transept S window. The transept E two-light window looks of c. 1300, with boldly cusped rere-arch. Standard Perp N arcade with matching chancel and transept arches. In the transept C14 TOMB-RECESS with open cusping, and ogee-cusped PISCINA. Larger C14 chancel PISCINA, crocketed, a head with upraised arm beneath. – FONT. Retooled Perp. – PULPIT. Mid-C17. Large panels and fluted frieze. – GLASS. Chancel stained glass by *O'Connor*, 1860. SW, engraved glass by *Laurence Whistler*, 1966. – MONUMENTS. A once lovely small alabaster effigy of a lady of the Wadham family, c. 1475. – Nicholas Wadham †1508. Little brass of a solemn swaddled infant. Lettered plaque and part of another to his mother †1557. – Anne Fenwick †1859. Sumptuous tomb-chest in a recess. Dark marble top.

The church and surprisingly large former VICARAGE (1874, by *Ewan Christian*) lie E of a triangular green. DRAKE'S FARM-HOUSE is C17–C18, partly Ham stone, partly Blue Lias. ILTON COURT, SW, has a cross-wing with C17 mullions. Opposite the METHODIST CHAPEL, 1874, a lane runs W to the WADHAM ALMSHOUSES, 1606, spoilt in 1964. Single-storeyed with four big projecting chimney-breasts. The thatch, dormers, mullioned windows and doorways have all gone. The lane crosses the derelict CHARD CANAL, 1840–2, to finish S of the moated site of MERRIFIELD, mansion of the Wadhams, founders of Wadham College, Oxford (*see also* Ilminster church). The AIRFIELD, just N, opened in 1944. On the main road are WHETSTONE'S ALMSHOUSES, 1634–6. Two-storeyed with projecting wings, three-light mullioned windows and paired Tudor-arched doors. A Gothic triplet marks the former chapel in one wing.

ASHFORD, 1¼ m. NNE. ASHFORD HOUSE, 1703, is one of the best early brick façades of the region, charmingly irregular with overall unity. Blind arches interrupt a nogged string course and stair lights interrupt the upper floor level. Similar arches over reused mullioned windows behind. In ASHFORD FARMHOUSE a cusped truss marks a C15 hall. ASHFORD MILL, SE, is Late Georgian, three-storeyed, behind an altered earlier house.

ROWLAND'S, 1 m. SW. A large mid- to late C16 house on the hall and cross-passage plan rebuilt for Sir Henry Cuffe, executed 1601, as secretary to the Earl of Essex. The core is the porch, cross-passage and hall, with the parlour to the l. slightly later and the kitchen to the r. slightly earlier. This last is connected to an altered L-plan rear range that may be the original C15 house on the site. Tall four-light mullioned windows with four-centred heads to the lights, the hall window longer and transomed. Storeyed and buttressed porch. Three doors open r. from the cross-passage: to a mast stair and to the kitchen, whose framed ceiling shows that it began as a parlour. Fine panelled C16 partition l. into the hall, under a jettied gallery, now plastered over. The handsome double-height hall has Queen Elizabeth's arms in a big plaster overmantel lozenge (cf. Poundisford Park) and raised-letter text with delightful spelling beneath a scrolled frieze. Early C19 heraldic glass brought from Jordans (Broadway). The parlour beyond has a moulded framed ceiling, originally sub-panelled. Staircase behind by *Raymond Erith*, 1970–2, when the house became the Speke family seat, replacing Jordans. Also by Erith the roof and hipped dormers. ROWLAND'S MILL, SE, is early, *c.* 1700, and unusually decorative with the brick blind arches set in squared stonework. House and mill share the domestic-looking building. Machinery and external waterwheel of 1851. Repaired 1995 by *Philip Hughes*.

INWOOD see HENSTRIDGE

ISLE ABBOTS

Also known as Ile Abbots. In the watery moors of the River Ile.

ST MARY. Outstanding among Somerset churches both for beauty and completeness. The W tower is early C16 – see the initials of Abbot Broke of Muchelney. It is 81 ft (25 metres) high, and belongs in that finest group of Somerset Perp towers that includes almost identical ones at Kingston St Mary and Staple Fitzpaine, the slightly varied Huish Episcopi, and the larger ones at St James, Taunton, and Bishop's Lydeard. Their characteristics are buttresses apparently set back but actually on the angles, with a false corner between and diagonal splays back to the tower faces. The buttresses have two tiers of applied pinnacles and carry large diagonally set pinnacles framing the corners of the bell-stage, while the corner itself is taken up, and turned diagonal, to carry the crowning pinnacles. The loveliness of the series comes from this complicated diffusion of the angles and the lacy crown of pierced battlements. The top pinnacles sit square a little uneasily above the angled corners (only Bishop's Lydeard sets the pinnacles diagonally), with flying outriders, and each side has a small middle pinnacle. Wiry figures, mostly animals, and a piper NW, decorate the cornice below battlements pierced with quatrefoils below merlons with pierced arcading. Higher octagonal NE stair-turret with battlements and pinnacles. The W doorway has the usual big leaves in the spandrels beneath a large transomed four-light W window. Above this follows a transomed two-light window with pierced baffles. The bell-stage has a similar pair on each side flanked and divided by pinnacled shafts. The W face is notably all of Ham stone, the others mostly Lias.

But the tower of Isle Abbots has certain points that give it a singular classicity. Six statue niches are placed at three levels on the W front: one each side of the doorway, one each side of the springing of the big window, and one each side of the second-stage window. They roughly align with the outer shafts of the bell-openings so there is a firmness of positions established which is so often lacking in parish church design, including that of Somerset. Some points of detail must be added. There are also niches on the other sides flanking the second-stage window. The window has one curious motif: in addition to hoodmoulds on square stops, there are at their foot moulds of the same kind (functionally useless) and they have diagonally set square stops. The s side has another niche in the lowest stage. The final distinguishing feature of the tower is that most of the niches are still filled with original STATUES, four on the W, three on the S, two on the E and one on the N, an unrivalled survival. They are not defaced and alas serve to prove that the strictly sculptural value of such Late Perp sculpture in England was a rule low. Notable on the W, the Virgin Mary, and Christ stepping from the tomb. Traces of colour were found in conservation by *Sally Strachey*, 2006. The tower top was rebuilt in 1875–6 by *Benjamin Ferrey*, very carefully.

The other piece of external display at Isle Abbots is the N aisle, short and compact, of four bays, with four-light windows under four-centred arches and with a pinnacled battlemented parapet pierced with quatrefoils below cusped saltire crosses. The S side is less splendid, except for the S porch which has similar battlements pierced with two tiers of quatrefoils. All this is also early C16. But further study of details reveals even before one enters the church that it is by no means all of one date. The chancel clearly is of *c.* 1300: see the E window, a group of five stepped lancet lights under a broad two-centred arch, and also the lovely N and S windows, which are groups of three stepped and cusped lancets with three quatrefoiled circles above. The tracery is of the bar, no longer the plate, variety. There is also a small N doorway with a continuous double chamfer. Now the same type of doorway is used on the S of the nave and also as the outer entry into the porch, so the porch was only made more splendid later. It is indeed quite easy to see inside that the fine fan-vault with its pendant is a late medieval addition. C13–C14 roll-moulded niche. Cut into the doorway a damaged stoup of *c.* 1500. Good oak DOOR. Then the nave S windows. One of them is a group of three cusped and stepped lancet lights under a big Perp hoodmould, and the other is a two-light Dec window. It looks then as if the church was complete by *c.* 1300, the C14 made only small alterations, and major work was left to just after 1500.

On entering through the S doorway one is at once transported into an atmosphere of great purity and lucidity, perhaps due more to the fine harmony of honey-coloured stone and whitewash than to architecture. The nave is separated from the aisle by an arcade of depressed four-centred arches on piers of the familiar Perp type of four shafts and four wave mouldings in the diagonals. The capitals are bands of foliage. NE rood stair and squint. Thin wall-shafts between the aisle windows. Panelled chancel arch. Tower arch with double wave mould.

Panelled barrel roofs in the nave and chancel, the latter cruder with heavy chamfered ribs. Framed and sub-panelled aisle roof.

The chancel has something peculiarly perfect in its proportions. The designer certainly intended to do something special here, or he would not have produced his unique piscina and sedilia. The PISCINA is set in five-bay Ham stone panelling in two tiers divided by chamfered piers, with caps and finials at both levels. The outer bays have two levels of shafted trefoiled panels under crocketed gables, and the double-width centre has a depressed pointed arch over the piscina beneath a panel with conjoined gables. Then the SEDILIA. The three seats have curved backs (as in tub chairs, only very low), decorated by shallow cusped arcading, and ending in short shafts. The back is panelled with cinquefoil-cusped arches with panelled spandrels, on attached shafts, the arches renewed in a different stone but stylistically in keeping. On the E wall an octofoil panel for a consecration cross. Three similar panels are on the outside wall.

FURNISHINGS. FONT. Square, crude Ham stone version of the widely exported C12 Purbeck fonts. The sides are carved. On the E a beast on its back carved in the primeval way of, say, the Luppitt font in Devon. On the S, plant forms and perhaps a bird. On the other two, rather random pointed arcading. Round shaft with detached colonnettes. – SCREEN. C15, retaining much original colour but missing the coving and the lower panels. Two-light sections with tracery spread over each pair. The lower panels would presumably have been as on the double doors. – PULPIT. C17. Smaller, neater and perhaps later than most. – BENCH-ENDS. C15–C16. Straight-headed with simple tracery. – TOWER SCREEN. Made up of C17 vertically symmetrical balusters, perhaps from the communion rail. ORGANS. A mid-C19 chamber organ and a barrel-organ of c. 1835, by *Henry Bryceson*. – COFFIN. A massive medieval sarcophagus dug up in the churchyard. – STAINED GLASS. C14 fragments in the chancel window heads.

The short village street is aligned on the church. MONKS THATCH is C16 with mullioned windows, plank partition and a smoke-hood. An excursion SE towards the river passes MANOR FARM, with mid-C19 Lias buildings for the Duchy of Cornwall, to end at PITT'S COTTAGE, colourwashed, dated 1583. Framed ceiling inside, and jointed crucks suggesting an earlier hall. S of the street, BROMES HOUSE, of Lias, and thatched, has a storeyed S porch dated 1627, and a cross-wing with jointed crucks. Plaster friezes upstairs, one with strange bald bearded heads. Chapel Road runs S past the plain BAPTIST CHAPEL, remodelled 1874, the former SCHOOL, 1875, in White Lias, and several C16–C17 thatched houses. Further out, BADBURY HOUSE has late C17 stone cross-windows inserted in the ground floor. Earlier moulded fireplace and jointed crucks. A lane runs W to WOODLANDS FARMHOUSE, C17 in two halves, Ham stone to the r. with moulded doorway and one stone cross-window, and Blue Lias with earlier mullions to the l. C18 timber-framed BARN.

ISLE BREWERS

Also known as Ile Brewers. On low land by the River Ile.

ALL SAINTS. 1861, by *C. E. Giles*. Built for the Rev. Joseph Wolff, son of a German rabbi, orientalist, Catholic convert, Anglican missionary, famously at Bokhara 1843–5, and finally vicar here 1846–62. A strong design with square S porch-tower broached to an octagon under a short octagonal spire in two colours of tiles. Rather exotic, but it would be fanciful to see Central Europe in it. – FONT. C12 bowl, retooled, the base with cable moulding. – STAINED GLASS. E window, 1861. The travails of St Peter in grisaille roundels. By *Mary Miles* of the Rectory, Bingham, Notts., mother of the painter Frank Miles.

Wolff's SCHOOLROOM, 1852, is SE of the church and his VICARAGE, 1847, by *Richard Carver*, down a drive S; both Tudor Gothic. The medieval church was near the river, abandoned for flooding.

BUSHFURLONG FARMHOUSE, I m. NE. Long Ham stone front with early C18 mullions, to an earlier house. EARNSHILL FARM, beyond, has an C18 hip-roofed brick barn, like those of the 1760s on the Burton Pynsent estate (Curry Rivel).

IVYTHORN MANOR see STREET

KEINTON MANDEVILLE

A village of Blue Lias stone, quarried here.

ST MARY MAGDALENE. E.E. chancel, shown by the single E lancet and two N ones with trefoiled rere-arches. Nave and simple W tower of *c.* 1830. N aisle with Y-tracery windows added 1841, the arcade removed 1903. – FONT. C12, circular, retooled. – ROYAL ARMS. 1719. – MONUMENT. Dauncey family to 1786. Lias, prettily incised.

On the main road, towards the E end, the former THREE OLD CASTLES, a long C18 inn, and KEINTON HOUSE, with large early C19 shop windows. Queen Street runs S to the church. Some garden walls of Keinton slabs. The METHODIST CHAPEL, 1848, has a windowless gable with Gothic doorway. MANOR FARM BARN has C15 jointed-cruck trusses with tiered wind-braces. By the church, the former RECTORY, 1836, with asymmetrical pedimental gables.

KILTON

ST NICHOLAS. Red sandstone, thoroughly redone by *John Norton* in 1862–3. Tower and chancel rebuilt. C15 nave wagon roof and wave-moulded chancel arch. – FONT. C15. Gawky but splendid, with original colour. Pointed quatrefoils over scroll-bearing angels. Stem with a leaf in each panel. – PULPIT. C19, reusing a C15–C16 leaf-scroll cornice. – MONUMENT. Charles Stennings †1592. Brass with long inscription: 'for lernd he was and tooke degree in Oxford schooles as there can showe'.

ST ANDREW, Lilstock. The chancel of the C15 church became a mortuary chapel when the rest was demolished in 1881. Perp hoodmoulded E window and shafted chancel arch. – MONUMENT. Joane Popham †1713. Lias slab ornately incised with rustic pilasters and urns.

LILSTOCK BEACH. A port developed by the Aclands of Fairfield after 1820. It had customs officers and warehouses and received coal and pleasure steamers. Little but boulders remains.

KILVE

The parish stretches from the Quantocks to the sea, the village on the A39, the church towards the coast.

ST MARY. White roughcast. Stocky W tower of as late as 1637, with square NE stair-turret. The rest, apart from the C14 porch, is C15, restored in 1861. Flat-headed N windows with some original hoodmould heads. Gabled S projection with a two-light pulpit window, originally a rood-stair turret – see the blocked door within. Simple nave wagon roof with bosses and decorated wall-plate. Perp chancel arch. Cusped PISCINA. The fragmentary arcade to the N vestry may indicate the lost chantry chapel to Simon de Furneaux, founded in 1329. One and a half double-chamfered arches. – FONT. Norman bowl with fluted stem and cable-moulded base. – PULPIT. Early C18. Fielded panels dotted with rosettes. – BENCHES. C16. Plain moulded square ends. – RAILS. Early C18. – SCREEN. Just one four-light C15 section, loose, in the vestry. The ogee reticulated tracery is unusual in Somerset. Leaves in the spandrels. – STALLS. Reused panelling dated 1687. – ROYAL ARMS. 1660. – STAINED GLASS. Chancel S window, medieval fragments. Nave S window, 1930, by *Christopher Webb*. – MONUMENTS. John Cunditt †1690. Rustic Baroque, arched with alabaster pilasters, and scrolls randomly around. – Cunditt daughters, †1723 and 1739. Painted wood. – Henry Sweeting †1785, by *Thomas Paty & Sons*. White on yellow marble.

THE CHANTRY, N of the church. A C13 manor house of the de Furneaux family that may have housed a short-lived college of priests for the chantry founded in 1329. The white-rendered farmhouse replaces the hall. The large E cross-wing, burnt out in 1848, is the significant survival. Eroding Lias stone. Pointed openings of a solar each end, the S end with a remnant of plate tracery over a pointed doorway. Two C14 E projections, the SE one with first-floor chapel, the large E window shafted inside, the NE one with angle buttresses.

KILVE COURT, in the village. 1782–5, for Henry Sweeting. A substantial three-storey house of five by three bays, clearly intended for stucco. Cornice and parapet. Open-pedimented doorway with a Venetian window above and a Diocletian lunette above that, all uncommonly well detailed. Staircase under a domed lantern with surrounding plasterwork of foliage and grapes. Neoclassical plaster friezes and one chimneypiece plaque of peasants and donkey. Internal porch by *Clough Williams-Ellis*, 1920.

THATCHINGS, Hilltop Lane. 1937, by *Norman Jewson*. Showing the 1930s just as capable of overdoing the thatched cottage as the 1830s.

KILVE PILL. The brick tower encasing an iron pipe remains from a pioneering extraction of oil from shale, 1924.

KINGSBURY EPISCOPI

On the edge of the Southern Levels, on a stone frontier: Blue Lias, Ham stone and marlstone all present.

ST MARTIN. Of Blue Lias with Ham stone, but the proud W tower, 99 ft (30 metres) high, all of Ham stone. The tower of c. 1500, a companion piece to that of Huish Episcopi, is very ornate. Pevsner thought it even a little overdone. Set-back buttresses with two sets of attached pinnacles on long shafts which carry a third at bell-stage level. NE stair-turret. Deep-set W door under a large transomed five-light window. The second stage has an unusually large four-light window each side, with a transom. The bell-stage has twin long two-light transomed openings, flanked typically by shafts with pinnacles, making a set of five with the larger ones on the buttresses. These do not reach the battlements, so horizontal line is maintained. The decoration consists of quatrefoil friezes, statue niches, and rich pierced battlements. Four friezes, interrupted by the buttresses, mark the three stages. Additionally there is a frieze above the W door and another dividing the ground stage of the S side. The canopied niches are as follows. On the bottom stage, a pair flanking the W door; three on the S side, one below and two above the frieze, the upper two on shafts with angels (between four heraldic shields); and one on the N side. At the second stage, on every side except the N, two niches on long shafts flank the big window. These upper niches still have their STATUES, not outstanding sculpture, but more animated than at Isle Abbots, the sculptor particularly taken with crossed legs. Additionally at the SW corner two tiny relief figures. The second-stage and bell-stage openings have traceried heads and pierced baffles. The battlements are pierced with lozenge quatrefoils and arcading in the merlons (cf. Isle Abbots), and have angle pinnacles with detached outriders (cf. Huish Episcopi and Taunton), and intermediate pinnacles.

The body of the church is externally Perp. Nave clerestory of pointed two-light windows. The aisles have three-light windows, gargoyles and parapets in Ham stone, embattled on the richer s where the aisle continues as a SE chapel. The storeyed S porch has battlements following the gable, the centre merlon shaped, with a Crucifixion relief. However, the double-chamfered arch of the porch indicates an earlier church, as do the external tomb-recess in the first bay of the S aisle and a heavy buttress before the SE chapel. The chancel and N chapel are of Ham stone, Late Perp, tall and gloriously lit. The chancel has pierced quatrefoil parapets carried across the steep E gable (also indicating an earlier church). Broad four-centred-arched five-light windows, one each to N and S and one at the E with transomed ogee tracery. The E window is shorter because (as at Langport, North Petherton and Ilminster) there is an E vestry, also with pierced parapet. The N chapel, structurally plainer, has earlier banded masonry on the E. The N and E windows are special even by Somerset Perp standards, transomed, elaborated with capitals to mullions subtly syncopated major and minor, the N window spectacularly large. Octagonal stair-tower in the angle to the N aisle.

The interior is large and of great interest. Its memorable features are at the ends. At the E beyond a complete Perp screen, the chancel and N chapel veritable glasshouses, to be seen on a fine morning. The surprise at the W end is that the tower besides its usual tall panelled arch has E buttresses inside the nave, as at Martock. That must have been decided on for reasons of structural security and then a virtue was made of a necessity. Two tiers of niches are placed on the buttresses and a second panelled arch is struck from one to the other. The tower has a fan-vault, not uncommon around 1500, but the account of the restoration of 1845–9 (by *Maurice Davis*) states that a 'groined arch was placed in the tower ... for a ringing-loft'. So this is wholly new. The account also says that the nave was 'pulled down and, with its pillars, rebuilt', a lesson in how easy it is to be fooled when detail is carefully replaced. The arcades look early C14 with double-chamfered arches on typical octagonal piers with moulded capitals, rather short for the distance they are from each other across a notably wide nave. The last arch is wider, evidence of lost transepts. Boarded C19 nave roof with frilly cusping. The chancel is of fine erect proportions. Chancel arch and two-bay arcades Late Perp, four-centred-arched, the piers shafted with foliage capitals in bands. The N chapel is a high and luminous, if empty, space, under an original framed ceiling. Chancel roof of 1845–9. The painted decoration on the E wall is late C19. Lovely colour on the Perp vestry doorway, one spandrel carved with a Tudor rose. In the SE chapel a roll-moulded cusped C14 PISCINA.

FURNISHINGS. FONT. Ham stone, C13–C14, remarkably sculptural. Three heavy octagons diminish downward divided by a moulding and a shelf. Base with a scalloped band. C19 spired Gothic COVER. – SCREEN. Five bays, tall pointed four-light sections divided vertically by a middle mullion reaching up to an angel (as at High Ham), and horizontally by a transom. Delicate sub-arched two-light tracery each side of the mullion. Thin clustered shafts between. The ribbed coving is restored, but two leaf friezes are original. – PULPIT, PEWS and STALLS. 1845–9. Linenfold. – STAINED GLASS. In the N transept canopies and heraldry datable to c. 1450. Smaller fragments elsewhere. Some particularly lovely heads in the S chapel E window, remnants of the 'beautiful' glass noted by Collinson in 1791. – E window, brash, c. 1870.

METHODIST CHAPEL. 1900, by *Alexander Lauder* (plans 1893). Ham stone, Gothic, with staircase wings and sawtooth side gables. The predecessor of 1852, Lias with Y-tracery windows, faces Church Street.

CHIMNEY COTTAGE, W of the church, with its spectacularly leaning Ham stone chimney, was perhaps the priest's house. Late C15 large haunched fireplace. Moulded framed ceiling. Further W, the OLD POST OFFICE, Lias and thatch, externally C18. The Ham stone WYNDHAM ARMS is Victorianized but has a C16 moulded beam within. Beyond the chapel is a small green with an octagonal C18 LOCK-UP, and further N, brick TOLL HOUSE of 1824. W of the lock-up, WEST END FARMHOUSE, picturesquely irregular, C16–C17, the cross-wing with dormer gables, and WEST END COTTAGE, C17, with a timber-framed S end. S from the inn, a good sequence: red brick C19 farm buildings and house at MANOR HOUSE; C18 brick and thatch at MYRTLE COTTAGE; and, the best, HOME FARMHOUSE, early C18, ashlar, with framed mullioned windows and C19 veranda. Its railed forecourt is matched across the road, making ample what is a narrow setting. Brick service wing with throughway to a hip-roofed ashlar STABLE with lunettes and arched doorway, late C18.

STEMBRIDGE, 1 m. SW. STEMBRIDGE HOUSE is a large mullion-windowed farmhouse, the regularity and continuous hoodmoulds giving away the late date, 1700. The PRIMARY SCHOOL, 1877, has twin Gothic wings, the centre altered 1906.

BURROW HILL, ¾ m. W. Its single tree is visible from afar. Large farmhouses testify to profitable farming. NW is BURROW FARM, 1890, rock-faced and pyramid-roofed, for the Portman estate. W is HIGHER BURROW FARMHOUSE, a long ashlar late C17 front with drip-courses stepped over each window. BURROW HILL FARM, NW, has a C16–C17 house opposite a very long BARN, mostly open-fronted, with some C16 jointed crucks. In the S end are four medieval stone woolly lions, perhaps from Muchelney. LOWER BURROW FARMHOUSE, N, has a long mullion-windowed front, c. 1700, and PONDCLOSE FARMHOUSE, nearby, has early C18 framed mullions.

KINGSDON

ALL SAINTS. Blue Lias. Dominated by a sturdy late C15 W tower, of four relatively short stages. Set-back buttresses, banded in Ham stone, terminating in little pinnacles (like Langport) at the bell-stage. Twin widely spaced two-light bell-openings with pierced baffles, between shafts that finish at a string course below ashlar battlements. Polygonal NE stair-turret. Panelled tower arch. The rest is cruciform and generally Perp, although the N transept is the base of a C13–C14 tower that was remodelled with handsome Perp windows when the new tower was built. Matching Perp arches with a fat shaft: to the old tower, chancel, s transept and s porch. C14 E window with reticulated tracery, copied in the rebuilding by *Giles & Robinson*, 1867–9. – FONT. Bulbous C12 bowl, coved beneath. – PULPIT. 1627, by *William Squier*. Arched panels with rich arabesques. – N TRANSEPT SCREEN. Reused C15 panels, probably bench-ends. – STAINED GLASS. Rich E window, *c.* 1870, perhaps by *Clayton & Bell*. – MONUMENTS. Cross-legged knight, *c.* 1330, in mail with surcoat, and helm beneath his head. – Brass to John Dotin †1561, 'medicus et astrologus'.

Intricate village layout of Blue Lias HOUSES; 'the inhabitants themselves scarcely know the way about it', Edmund Rack noted in the 1780s.

KINGSDON MANOR. Built by Charles Moody *c.* 1830, altered after 1864 for William Neal. Blue Lias and Ham stone. Five-bay centrepiece between pedimented two-bay wings. Elegant Greek Ionic colonnade across the centre, which has a balustraded attic storey that may be an addition.

SPRINGFIELD HOUSE, ½ m. SSW. Mid-C19 estate farmhouse for Kingsdon Manor. Pyramid-roofed, stuccoed.

CATSGORE, ½ m. W. At least thirty-seven Roman buildings were excavated along the road that led NNW from Ilchester. The settlement seems to have developed from three farmsteads and may be associated with a large ROMAN VILLA on the hillside a short distance away.

KINGSTONE

ST JOHN AND ALL SAINTS. Mostly Perp, of Moolham stone, but the central tower suggests that this is a remodelling of a C14 or earlier church. A previous nave roof-line is visible on the tower, and the chancel has C14 S windows. The short embattled nave and central tower are rebuilt with some ambition, mostly in ashlar. There are no transepts. The battlements run flat over a large W window and doorway enriched with fleurons all around the arch and leaves in the spandrels. Tracery with vertical mullions. Typical Perp tower detail, set-back buttresses continuing as diagonal shafts through the battlements.

Two-light bell-openings with pierced baffles. Pierced baffles also to a square S window below. Higher SE stair-turret. Luminous nave, the tower arches triple-shafted, not panelled. Ceilings of 1885. – FONT. C12 bowl, tapered to octagonal. – STAINED GLASS. E and S windows, 1924, by *Christopher Webb*. C15 fragments.

KINGSTONE FARMHOUSE was the medieval rectory. T-plan, C15–C16, the cross-wing with particularly big marlstone blocks and a wind-braced roof. Converted C15 TITHE BARN with large buttresses and pointed-arched doorway. Behind the church, MANOR COTTAGE, thatched, with C18 mullioned windows. Going W, past a small TOLL HOUSE, WAKEHILL, *c*. 1830, stuccoed villa with Gothic verandas.

KINGSTON ST MARY

ST MARY. The church is not big, but its W tower stands out so beautifully against the hillside that it remains one of the most memorable of a district rich in towers. The design is almost identical to those at Isle Abbots and Staple Fitzpaine, and similar to that at Huish Episcopi, so late C15. Mixed local red sandstones, the buttresses and lower part of the W front faced in buff North Curry sandstone, the windows and parapet of Ham stone. Angle buttresses with applied pinnacles, the illusion of the buttresses being set back created by a corner insert, also pinnacled. Tall, diagonally set pinnacles crown the buttresses against the bell-stage. Here three thin pinnacled shafts flank paired two-light bell-openings with transoms and pierced baffles. Fine crown of pierced battlements (quatrefoils under arcaded merlons), large corner pinnacles surrounded by little detached outriders, and smaller intermediate pinnacles. Finally the spired and pinnacled NE stair-turret. The stage below the belfry has one similar two-light window each side, between niches with angel corbels on shafts. W doorway with big leaves in the spandrels, between fine niches. Perp shafted tower arch. The S aisle and porch have pierced quatrefoil parapets, except the narrower W bay. The porch is ashlar-fronted with three niches above a big four-centred archway, and has inside a fine fan-vault of *c*. 1500 and S doorway like the W doorway. The aisle windows are of 1876 by *J. H. Spencer*, replacing square-headed ones. Plainer N aisle without parapet. Very large five-light E window.

The interior after this is a surprise, for the four-bay arcades are C13 with circular piers and double-chamfered arches, of pale sandstone. No chancel arch, just a Victorian timber arch on corbels. Perp arcade to the SE chapel, of three bays, two of standard four-hollow section, the third of an earlier wave profile and of the pale sandstone, perhaps cut through the chancel wall. N of the chancel, a single Perp arch with leaf capitals. The

KINGSTON ST MARY

SE (Hestercombe) chapel was widened with part of the S aisle perhaps to accommodate the Warre tomb after 1381. A Perp arch divides it from the W end of the aisle, the Tetton pew, still at the original width. Renewed panelled wagon roofs. – FONT. Late Perp. Octagonal, with quatrefoils in panels and on the underside. – BENCHES. A large set, one dated 1522. Square-headed with motifs of close tracery, fleshy leaves and plants. Two show a rosary, one shows oxen and yokes. – PULPIT. 1742. Panelled with carved festoons and cornice; cf. Bradford on Tone, Wellington and Woodlands. – CANDELABRA. 1733. Splendid, three-tier, by *Thomas Bayley*. – STAINED GLASS. E window by *Christopher Webb*, 1923. N aisle third, c. 1880, rich colours. – MONUMENTS. Very large tomb-chest, probably Sir John Warre †1381. Reticulated and cusped sides with shield panels. Simpler ogee tracery at each end. Massive Purbeck slab with neither brass nor effigy. – Thomas Dyke †1672 and Thomas Dyke †1689, brass plates, the former with a speaking skull: 'Farewell fond world...'. – Thomas Camplin †1716. Fine coloured marbles with curved pediment and urn. – John and Margaret Bampfylde. Elegant, in coloured marbles, scroll-sided. Erected in 1786 to his parents, by Coplestone Bampfylde of Hestercombe †1791. His plainer tablet by *Greenway* of Bristol.

p. 38

In the churchyard, several CHEST TOMBS, the best S of the porch. The latest is to Mervyn Herbert †1929.

The village is in a hollow SW of the church. At the foot of Church Lane, the large gabled OLD PARSONAGE, 1872, by *J. A. Clark* of Bristol. Going W, just up Lodes Lane, the MANOR HOUSE, built in the mid C16 for the Knight family who remodelled it in 1702. L-plan, with a hip-roofed storeyed porch. Bolection-moulded doorway. In the angle l. two-light windows (arched lights) of the former spiral staircase, otherwise Georgian sashes to the main front. On the cross-wing, cross-windows and ovals of 1702. Of that date, the handsome panelled E room and the staircase with strong turned balusters, thick ramped rail and finely carved tread-ends. Over the stairs, an oval ceiling panel and cornice of lushly modelled fruit. Down the main street: BOBBETTS, late medieval, with a C17 cross-wing, THE CONIES, mid-C19 stuccoed row with bracket eaves, and QUANTOCK COTTAGE, late medieval to C17. Towards Taunton, THE GRANGE, remodelled in 1862 by *G. G. Scott*. The muddled road elevation with terrible tower (it has lost a pyramid roof) hardly marks a good architect, but the ashlar front with bi-colour voussoirs is better. Truncated octagonal chimneys.

TAINFIELD HOUSE, 1 m. S. Stuccoed, early C19, for the Chapman family. The centre is recessed such that the eaves overhang a narrow semicircular bow. Older farmhouse behind.

TETTON HOUSE, 2 m. NW. Regency Revival of 1924–7 by *H. S. Goodhart-Rendel*, created for Mervyn Herbert from something much smaller, of c. 1800. Orange roughcast with contrasting white woodwork. Three-storey front of 3–3–3 bays with parapets and an applied pediment. White ground-floor colonnade, partly enclosed for a centre room. The W side is two-storeyed between higher ends with lunettes over two-storey curved bays. In the middle a neo-Regency tempietto, or half a one, tent-roofed below, and with caryatids to the narrow domed upper floor. Ashlar-lined stair hall with coffered ceiling. Two-storey octagonal LODGE, sw, by *Goodhart-Rendel*.

PYRLAND HALL (King's Hall School), 1½ m. SSE. Built in 1758 for Sir William Yea, but the plain three-storey cube with single-storey wings advanced to clasp an Ionic colonnade looks late C18. The hall has a broadly spaced Ionic screen (with Gothick frieze) to an imperial staircase.

YARFORD, 1 m. w. A small ROMAN VILLA was excavated in 2004, one of the westernmost in England. A fine mosaic occupied a dining room with views across the vale, on a site that had been occupied since the Iron Age.

KINGWESTON

ALL SAINTS. 1851–5 by *C. E. Giles*, his first major work, a serious one, in late C13 style. Rebuilt for Francis Dickinson, who consulted leading Ecclesiologists. Steep-roofed nave and chancel and a s porch-tower, very bare below but blossoming in an octagonal spire over an octagonal bell-stage with big gabled openings (modelled on Lostwithiel, Cornwall, at the suggestion of Benjamin Webb). Reused Norman s doorway. An arch of two rings of chevron on columns with decorated scalloped capitals frames a latticed inner arch with pellets (cf. Barton St David). The ashlar-lined interior shows typical Victorian hierarchy. The chancel arch with foliage corbels and dwarf timber screen announces a richer chancel. The density of leaf-carving (in the Southwell style) becomes quite manic in the corbels and the sedilia, where angel wings spread against net-like foliage. Most sumptuous, in marble of dried-blood hue, the sanctuary steps and the ALTAR, of two slabs separated by twisted columns. – FONT. Bulbous C12 bowl, coved below. – STAINED GLASS. Chancel, 1906–12, by *Clayton & Bell*. w, 1916, by *Powell's*. Saints of the allied nations. – MEMORIALS. C13 grave-slab with double cross (nave floor). – Rev. R. Collinson †1811. Elegant oval. – William Dickinson †1844. Slab with inlaid brass cross.

KINGWESTON HOUSE. A large plain mansion remodelled in 1824–5 by *William Wilkins* for the Dickinsons, Jamaica plantation owners. Blue Lias with just an ashlar band and cornice. On the E side a heavy ashlar Greek Doric porch with two columns between two pillars. On the s side two slight parapet breaks mark the centre. The w side has a canted centrepiece. Wilkins remodelled a pedimented Georgian house rebuilt in 1785–8 by *Samuel Heal* of Bridgwater, for which *Henry Holland* had been consulted in 1783. Interiors remodelled by *Wilkins*. Greek-key ornament in the corridor and stair hall, the latter

Kingweston House.
Engraving, 1829

with circular lantern and cantilevered stairs. The central s room has an oval ceiling on squinches. Early C19 cruciform thatched NORTH LODGE.

The principal interest of the village is the estate buildings of Caleb Dickinson (†1783). E of the house, opposed STABLES and COACHHOUSES, each with a gabled through-arch, the N one dated 1765. Pretty quatrefoil gable vents, and quatrefoil loft-lights to the S stables. These have an added SE range with oval lights. Barns with similar centrepieces are at HOME FARM and behind Nos. 15–16, where the barn, dated 1772, is part of a small-scale farmyard. More impressive are the shared buildings of MIDDLE FARM and LOWER FARM, c. 1781. The great barn has a hip-roofed lofted S end. Beyond are equally high lofted stables and, at right angles, a lofted coachhouse and open-fronted barn. Lower Farmhouse was then a coaching inn. Also for the estate, a small SCHOOL, c. 1844, with pretty iron lattice windows, a hip-roofed RECTORY (Dower House), c. 1835, with older half-hip-roofed barn, and numerous cottages, e.g. Nos. 17–18, mid-C19, with iron windows, and Nos. 19–24 (on the main road), earlier and contrastingly plain.

SUNDIAL, in woods ¾ m. WSW. Mid-C18 cube on a Ham stone column and medieval base.

KITTISFORD

ST NICHOLAS. Perp three-stage W tower, rendered except for the set-back buttresses. Plain battlements. High double-chamfered red sandstone tower arch. The rest was over-restored in 1875 by *Edmund Ferrey*. The square N chapel, dated 1659, displays the last of Gothic, flat-headed windows with clumsy cusping, the E window under a cornice on brackets instead of a hoodmould. The porch opens unusually into the W end of the S aisle. This has, uniquely for Somerset (but cf. Nymet Rowland, Devon), a two-bay arcade entirely of timber, the piers of standard four-hollow section with linked capitals, the arches four-centred. Typical C17 round arch to the N chapel, with capitals and keystone. – FONT. Perp, octagonal. Five traceried panels, three sides uncarved. Panelled underside and stem. – PULPIT. 1610. With shallow decoration and top strap-work panels, not the familiar blank arches. – STAINED GLASS. E window, 1876. Fine Crucifixion by *Lavers, Barraud & Westlake*. – MONUMENT. Two detached 2-ft (60-cm.) brass figures, Richard Bluett of Cothay †1524, in armour, and Agnes, his wife, with large roses at her belt.

NEWHOUSE FARM opposite the church is of *c.* 1600. An ovolo-moulded timber stair light in the end gable. On the hillside, N, is the large former rectory, KITTISFORD HOUSE. Externally Georgian, four-plus-three bays, stripped of stucco. Some C17 beams.

KITTISFORD BARTON, ½ m. N. Late medieval to early C17. Roughcast, with a gabled porch and some timber mullions. The hall fireplace has a reset plaster surround (from upstairs). Vine-trail jambs and a long top with big strapwork framing the arms of Tristram Wood and Helen Drake. In the parlour, early C18 bolection-moulded panelling hides an early C17 arcaded frieze.

KNOWLE ST GILES

No village, the church now a house.

ST GILES. Nave of 1837–40 by *James Lockyer*. Lancet style, with bellcote. Rather better chancel, 1849, by *J. M. Allen*. S of the church, a TOMB-CHEST with Perp blank arches and shields.

MANOR FARMHOUSE, 1 m. W. Altered, but with a late C16 canted two-storey bay with Tudor-arched lights to mullioned windows. At the railway bridge just N, remnants of the 1940 STOP LINE defences, concrete blocks, and an anti-tank gun emplacement facing N. PILLBOX in the valley below.

LAMYATT

ST MARY AND ST JOHN. Late C13 W tower of two plain stages. No W door. Flat parapet. Above the W lancet is a block with two faces, male and female, typical of *c.* 1300, the top of a semi-effigial grave-slab. Low tower arch of two chamfers, the inner one dying into the sides. Perp nave with a C15–C16 porch on each side. Equally unusually, both have ribbed vaults, the s vault with an octagonal centre. Nave roof with moulded tie-beams, embellished in 1888–90 when the chancel was rebuilt by *C. S. Adye* of Bradford on Avon. Panelled chancel arch. – FONT. Norman. Tapering to the ground, with a big cable moulding marking the foot of the bowl. – BENCH-ENDS. 1911. With tracery and a St Christopher, for Christopher Welch. He also gave the bronze eagle LECTERN, 1891 (copying the Balliol College one of 1636, minus the crown), and STAINED GLASS, 1907, by *Powell's*, nave s. – MONUMENT. Abraham Andrews †1807. Weeping woman and urn, and a large cherub head. By *Reeves & Son*.

On the lower road, the former RECTORY by *Jesse Gane*, 1833, with triple gablets and hoodmoulded windows. Opposite, the tiny former SCHOOL, 1829, with Y-tracery windows. At the lower end, WELCH COTTAGES, 1906, an Arts and Crafts Gothic pair, distinguished by a shapely ashlar central chimney. Above the village, LAMYATT LODGE, ashlar-fronted and hip-roofed, *c.* 1830, stands neatly overlooking the huge view.

CREECH HILL. Excavation in 1973 found a C3–C4 ROMAN TEMPLE, comprising a square *cella* within a lean-to ambulatory and with a sunken room off the s side. A rectangular building to the N, aligned E–W, and a cemetery may represent Christian takeover of a pagan site in the C4–C5, as at Brean Down (q.v.).

LANGFORD BUDVILLE

ST PETER. Red sandstone, Perp, and mostly early C16. In 1509 John Peryn of Wellington left three farthings to the building of the W tower (and those at Hillfarrance and West Buckland). The handsome plain three-stage tower has a polygonal SE stair-turret, set-back buttresses, and battlements. s aisle and porch ornamented with pierced quatrefoil parapets and thin pinnacles. The aisle has three-light windows. The porch archway oddly has zigzag on Perp capitals. The niche above sprouts a pinnacle. N aisle of 1866 by *John Hayward*, reusing the N windows. The S arcade has piers of standard four-hollow section but above the capitals are leaf bands, not as elsewhere in Somerset conjoined capitals but more in the place of an abacus.* On the eastern column, a needle and thread beneath the band. The arches are finely moulded; similar arch to the SE chapel. Wagon roofs, that of the nave with embellished eastern panels over the former rood screen.

---

* F. B. Bond suggested a mid-C16 Marian date for such debased detail.

FURNISHINGS. FONT. Late Perp. Octagonal with various devices in panels and a panelled underside. Strange panelled stem with thin buttresses, matching the porch niche. – STAINED GLASS. Much by *Hardman*; chancel and W windows 1880s, N aisle after 1875. 3E window, 1877, by *J. F. Bentley* for *Lavers, Barraud & Westlake*, to the American architect John Haviland †1852, 'inventor of radiating prisons', portrayed in a tabard, with sideburns. – MONUMENTS. William Bacon †1663 and Captain George Bacon †1690. Both rustic Baroque with cherubs on broken pediments. – W. B. Wade †1806, by *Thomas King* of Bath. White marble, two semi-draped females by an urn, on a large grey oval.

Across the road, SPRINGWOOD, the former vicarage, 1865, by *Hayward*, stone, rambling. W of the church, the thatched C17 OLD VICARAGE and mullion-windowed SCHOOL of 1851. Further W, LANGFORD COURT, long and stuccoed, with a storeyed porch. Late medieval smoke-blackened roof and early C18 panelled room.

HARPFORD BRIDGE, 1 m. SSW. Triple-arched. Probably late medieval, the S arch rebuilt 1852. Just S, a CANAL BRIDGE of 1832.

CHIPLEY, ¾ m. NE. An avenue aligns on the site of the long-demolished house of the Clarkes, built in 1681 probably by *William Taylor*. It was of brick with hip-roofed single-bay wings. CHIPLEY PARK was the stables, late C17 brick with outer gables. The converted hip-roofed BARN is timber-framed and aisled, C16–C17 probably. FURSDONS, just W, has a late medieval smoke-blackened roof. C17 storeyed porch and framed ceiling. The large storeyed BARN dated 1856 was built for the Nynehead estate.

BINDON HOUSE, 1 m. NNW. Late Georgian stuccoed villa with twin semicircular bows, given a festive skyline of Jacobean gables in 1878 by *Thomas Nicholson* of Hereford, these curved in plan too.

LANGPORT

Sited where the River Parrett is pinched between low hills, Langport prospered from its river traffic until the railway era. The town began on The Hill, the hilltop around the church, as an Anglo-Saxon *burh* where Athelstan had a mint. The centre shifted to the foot of the hill, linked to the river by a causeway, along which houses were built with medieval burgage plots behind. This became Bow Street, burnt by retreating Royalists in 1645. At the end were warehouses of the river trade, dominated from the late C18 to mid C19 by the firm of Stuckey & Bagehot, from which emerged Stuckey's Bank. Watery moors still closely encompass the lower town. The North Moor is crossed by the GWR's ten-arch blue-brick RAILWAY VIADUCT of 1903–5. Mixed building materials, predominantly Blue Lias but also the distinctive White Lias from Bowden Hill nearby, Ham stone, occasionally Doulting stone, red brick after the early C18, and stucco.

ALL SAINTS (Churches Conservation Trust). Long a chapelry of Huish Episcopi, but by no means modest, the hilltop tower prominent over the Muchelney levels. Nothing visible earlier than the C15 except for one remarkable piece, a Late Norman lintel dating probably from about 1190–1200 above the s door. It has a slightly pitched top and contains a Paschal Lamb in a circle supported by two angels in the Romanesque tradition, each with one wing following the circle. Small flanking figures, a female and a bishop. They could, if better preserved, be compared to the figures of the Glastonbury Lady Chapel portals.

The tower, aisled nave and N transept are outshone by the chancel and outer s chapel that have particularly handsome Ham stone detail similar to Curry Rivel. The chapel, called new in 1499, and probably the chancel, were built for John Heron (†1501), portreeve and merchant. The tower, in Blue Lias, is a poor relation of Long Sutton (q.v.). Buttresses of Doulting stone are connected diagonally across the angle of the tower, capped with squat finials below the bell-stage. W front faced in Ham stone to above the big five-light window. Higher SE stair-turret. The upper stages are relatively crude, especially the tracery, but some or all was rebuilt in 1833. The middle stage has shallow niches each side of a two-light window, blind to the N and E, pierced and transomed to the W. The bell-stage has three similar each side, the centre one again pierced and transomed. Four thin dividing shafts stop short of the battlements. Langport tower is later than that at Long Sutton, as it has a fine fan-vault instead of a lierne one, so c. 1500. The portcullis of Lady Margaret Beaufort (†1509) may confirm this. Oddly this makes the tower contemporary with Heron's eastern works, however different in treatment.

Embattled aisles with standard tracery and lively grotesques, the N transept clearly added, but with similar tracery. C19 s porch. Within, a re-set C15 niche and late C15 DOOR uncommonly fully carved, with tracery and big leaves around the head. Heron's work is distinguished by deep plinths, Ham stone battlements, more animated grotesques and refined tracery. The two-bay s chapel has richly cusped four-light windows with ogee heads to the lights. The chancel side windows are longer and more sumptuous, of four lights with transom. Below the transom, the quatrefoil spandrels typical of the Muchelney (and Cleeve Abbey) style. The E window is very large, five lights. Embattled E vestry, as at North Petherton, Ilminster and Kingsbury Episcopi. Restorations 1833 (tower), 1845 (nave roof), 1867 (chancel) by *C. E. Giles*, and 1877 (nave) by *Foster & Wood*. Repairs by *William Weir*, 1911, and *Philip Hughes*, 1996.

The arcades are not high and there is no clerestory. Slim piers of standard four-hollow type with small round capitals.

Similar chancel arch, renewed after fire in 1845 destroyed the nave roof. The E respond of the S arcade has two handsome canopied niches, and the E pier of the N arcade a small corbel head. Broader four-centred arch to the N transept, and similar two-bay arcade to the S chapel. The chancel is bathed in light after the lowish nave. SEDILIA by *J. D. Sedding*, 1887, also the densely canopied REREDOS with sculpture by *G. W. Seale*. Fine C15 framed roofs in the chancel, S chapel and N transept, with rich foliage bosses and undercut borders. Fire-blackened roof at the E end of the N aisle. – FONT. Octagonal, Perp, with heavy quatrefoils. – PULPIT. Early C18, fielded-panelled, with a little fruit down the angles. – PAINTING. Mourning over the dead Christ, after Correggio, by *Reuben Sayers*, 1863. – STAINED GLASS. The E window contains more late medieval glass than most Somerset churches, reassembled in 1867 by *Clayton & Bell*. Ten small figures in two tiers, Heron arms in the tracery. Rich colours, but the effect remains pale as surrounded by white quarries with yellow ornament. S chapel. Two S windows, 1865, typically bright (the r. one by *Alexander Gibbs*), the E one later, ethereal Late Gothic, beautifully drawn. S aisle E, 1868, by *O'Connor*. N aisle fifth, aqueous colours, by *Powell's*, 1904. W window, 1877, to Walter Bagehot, the economist (buried in the churchyard). Five figures in the rich colours of Burne-Jones, but a fiercer drawing style. By *H. A. Kennedy*, who should be better known. – MONUMENTS. Several of Lias imitating slate, intricately etched like bookplates, e.g. Mary Michell †1756. – Under the tower, eight Stuckey infants, to 1826. Poignant roundel of roses and a sickle, by *C. H. Smith*.

HANGING CHAPEL. See Perambulation.

ST JOSEPH (R.C.), The Hill. 1929. Utilitarian apart from the stark white apsidal tower over the altar, added 1965.

CONGREGATIONAL CHAPEL, Bow Street. 1828–9, with a brick Gothic front of 1874. Brick manse of 1850.

TOWN HALL, Cheapside. An attractive market house dated 1733 (weathervane). Square, under a steep pyramid roof with lantern. Three Ham stone arches front and back, on square piers; Tuscan columns within. Upper floor of brick with Ham

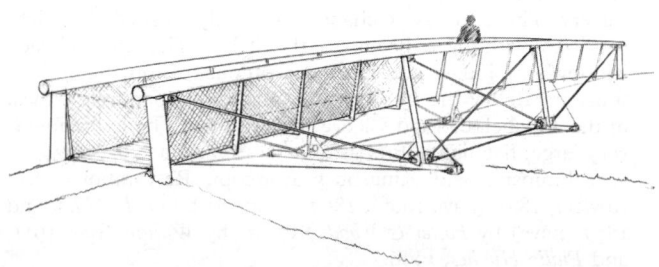

Langport, Cocklemoor Bridge.
Drawing by R. La Trobe-Bateman, *c.* 2004

stone quoins and architraves. Cast-iron GATES, 1840. Attached are a brick two-storey READING ROOM, 1833, and diminutive ashlar-fronted REGISTER OFFICE, 1838. This, probably by *Richard Carver*, is carried on iron bars over the Catchwater waterway that once divided the town (visible from the garden behind).

PRIMARY SCHOOL, North Street. 1876, by *Henry Hall*. An ample Gothic composition in White Lias with flèche. Three gables for the three divisions, a fourth the teacher's house.

GREAT BOW BRIDGE. 1839–41, by *William Gravatt*. Three handsome elliptical arches in Blue Lias. Contemporary LOCK and keeper's cottage, ¼ m. N, part of the scheme to extend navigability up to Westport (Hambridge).

COCKLEMOOR BRIDGE. 2006, by *Richard La Trobe-Bateman*. Steel. Tubular bowed rails carry the footway, ingeniously tied beneath.

EARTHWORKS. The C10 Burghal Hidage for Wessex suggests defences fairly close around the hilltop probably including the scarp NW from the Hanging Chapel, presumably the E gate. But there are prominent escarpments also behind the houses W and SW, and a dog-leg from North Street to the NW corner of the playing field must be ancient as it forms the parish boundary. The 300-yd (275-metre) bank at the edge of the playing field may be a Civil War defence.

PERAMBULATION. Opposite the church are three-storey service ranges of Hill House, the Stuckey family house, with the R.C. church (*see* above) attached. HILL HOUSE (St Gildas Centre) itself is an early C19 villa in ornamental grounds, reached from Priest Lane. Stuccoed with broad bows and a recessed Doric porch in Ham stone. Across Priest Lane, the STABLE COURT has brick elliptical arches within and a Tudorish stuccoed front. Two ESTATE COTTAGES flank the church, *c.* 1860, in contrasted colours of Lias. To the E along The Hill, the red brick Late Georgian OLD RECTORY, originally a Stuckey dower house. Good cast-iron trellis porch, one of several in Langport. The Hill is closed to the E by a large medieval TOWN GATE, the only one in Somerset, never apparently defensive as with neither corresponding walls nor rebate for a gate. Its long pointed tunnel vault, C13–C14, supports the HANGING CHAPEL, a small chapel possibly for the chantry recorded in 1344. The wave-moulded W door looks late C14. The rest was renewed after 1891 when it became the Masonic Hall. Perp square-headed S window and pointed PISCINA visible inside. The arched E window looks post-medieval, the tracery C19. C18 graffiti in the reveal. Through the archway appears Huish Episcopi church tower, only ¼ m. downhill. Just outside the gate, THE GATEWAY overlooks the moor. Stuccoed five-bay Regency front, with a bowed central tented veranda carrying flat piers as a screen in front of the upper window. The rear part is older Georgian. The OLD SCHOOL was a pair of teachers' houses for a demolished National School of 1827. Gothic cast-iron windows.

w from the church, THE GATEHOUSE faces w, down the hill. Brick C19 confection with narrow cast-iron windows and a stone carriage arch. On The Hill, ANNANDALE, on the N side, looks Early Victorian, with deep eaves and heavy arched porch. THE GRAMMAR HOUSE, on the S, was the Grammar School, on a very restricted site. Mid-C19 Blue Lias house to the street, hip-roofed brick rear, and a utilitarian mid-C19 brick schoolroom behind. At the foot, HILL HOUSE, late C18, red brick with swept parapet, has a pedimented stone doorcase of 1994, with rabbits. Bow-ended rear wing with parapet.

Until 1770 the market cross stood at the foot, the junction with Cheapside and North Street, now overlooked by the ashlar Regency front of the POST OFFICE. Timber Doric-columned porch. Across the road, a Late Georgian curved corner to Cheapside in brick and Ham stone. Facing up North Street, the three-storey former LLOYDS BANK, roughcast, with late C18 segment-headed windows. NORTH STREET has a row of early C19 houses on the E side, VICTORIA HOUSE with the best of the town's cast-iron trellis porches. Set back opposite is the SURGERY, 1998, by *HBS* of Highbridge. Brick, octagonal, with radiating consulting rooms. Before the primary school (p. 399), COPPERS, 1904, a mullion-windowed former police station, probably by *W. J. Willcox*.

The buildings of CHEAPSIDE, the core of the town, look coeval with the Town Hall of 1733, but mansard roofs suggest a date range into the late C18. On the S side, two substantial Lias fronts. First, the LANGPORT ARMS hotel. The five l. bays reface the late C16 Swan Inn (moulded framed ceiling). The three r. bays are of 1826–8 by *Richard Carver*, also the heavy columned porch. BANK CHAMBERS, adjoining, was where Stuckey's Bank was founded in the 1770s. The mansard roof suggests that it was built around that date. The NATWEST BANK was added as Stuckey's head office in 1875. Ham stone three-bay front with first-floor paired pilasters. Opposite, an attractive mixed row. The low TUDOR HOUSE has curved-headed windows and pedimented doorway, but also a mansard roof, so may well be of 1775, the reputed date. Contemporary with the Town Hall are the hip-roofed three-storey GREENSLADE, TAYLOR, HUNT premises – see the quoins, eaves cornice and thick glazing bars. Staircase with thin turned balusters. Plainer, slightly later, five-bay adjoining premises with Victorian shopfronts. VIRGINIA HOUSE, gable-ended to the street, is late C17 with C18 sash windows and pedimented doorcase. Diminutive Late Georgian dividing staircase inside. Opposite the Town Hall (p. 398), White Lias GATEPIERS of the former pig market, 1855, announce the SHOPPING PRECINCT of 1970. On the E side, a curved-pedimented DRINKING FOUNTAIN, 1905, by *George Oatley*.

BOW STREET, more irregular, has points of interest mostly on the S side. The low MARKET HOUSE of 1733, with curved-headed windows and coved eaves, contrasts in every respect with ENSOR HOUSE of similar date. Much taller, of brick, with

Gibbsian rustication to every window and thin angle piers, all in White Lias. The ground floor once matched. Further down, MANOR HOUSE, early C19, mansard-roofed, has another iron trellis porch. Then a trio displaying the difficult White Lias used as ashlar. They illustrate the evolving taste of the early to mid C19. BLAKE HOUSE has the Late Georgian cornice and parapet, ARLINGTON HOUSE the overhanging eaves of the 1830s, and the third is prettily Victorian Italianate with contrasted Blue Lias detail. *William Atyeo*, stonemason, signs one of them. BOW HOUSE is late C19 commercial, in brick and stone, arcaded below. Warehouse behind. The courts off Bow Street had industrial uses connected with the river. In BEARD'S YARD, N, a broad brick and stone front, arcaded with three cast-iron roundels above, was an early C19 iron foundry, of *Richard Down*, later architect in Bridgwater. By the bridge (p. 399) is GREAT BOW WHARF. The Late Georgian warehouse was possibly the centre of Stuckey & Bagehot trading. Brick, hip-roofed with later additions. MILL HOUSE opposite looks early C19. The warehouse was carefully restored 2003–8 as a focus for a small housing development by *Stride Treglown Architects*, in two differing short terraces. One row of monopitch-roofed 'eco-houses' with a glazed sloping front behind wooden brises-soleil, the other of more conventional 'town houses' over garages.

Across the river, WESTOVER was industrial after the railway arrived in 1853. The road rises over the former tracks, necessitating an intriguing folding iron bridge to reach first-floor public rooms of the late C19 RAILWAY HOTEL (Westover House). On the hilltop above, appropriately echoing the Stuckey house on the opposite hill, is the Bagehot house, HURD'S HILL. The newborn Walter Bagehot allegedly attended a foundation-laying in 1826. Stuccoed hip-roofed villa now disguised by a rather American two-storey colonnade added before 1900, of square Ham stone piers, with outer pediments. POUND COTTAGE, just W, began as a C15 hall house. Smoke-blackened crucks in the E cross-wing.

LEIGH HOUSE *see* WINSHAM

LEIGHLAND

ST GILES. Rebuilt 1861–2, by *C. E. Giles*. Red sandstone. Lancets and W bellcote. Fleshy floral carving on the chancel arch. Medieval TILES around the font, probably from Cleeve Abbey.
LEIGHLAND HOUSE has wooden cross-windows of *c*. 1700.
LEIGH BARTON, 1 m. SW. Four-bay rendered front of 1811 with a good columned stone doorcase. The house was a grange of Cleeve Abbey, owned by the Poyntz family from *c*. 1600. They were recusants, keeping a chapel in the rear wing of 1627 and

maintaining a chaplain until 1767. Philip Powel, chaplain here 1624–42, was executed at Tyburn in 1646. Array of large C18 OUTBUILDINGS, the barn with a polygonal horse-engine house.

LILSTOCK see KILTON

LIMINGTON

ST MARY. C14 W tower with diagonal buttresses carried up to large gargoyles under a parapet. A swirled roundel above each of the bell-openings, which are small, of two lights with pierced baffles. Polygonal N stair-turret. The body of the church is also C14 but a blocked N doorway could be Norman. The adjacent window is early C14, of two cusped lights under a sexfoil (with cinquefoiled rere-arch). C14 also one nave S window and the double-chamfered arches of the porch and S doorway. The most interesting feature is the N transept, a chantry chapel founded in 1329 by Sir Richard Gyvernay. This has good flowing tracery to the three-light N window, raised high above a middle buttress, with a trefoiled niche above. Roofed in great slabs of Ham stone over a pointed tunnel vault of chamfered close-spaced ribs. The transept is entered by a doorway next to a double-chamfered arch that dies into the sides, that might be expected to shelter the founder's tomb. His monument (*see* below), however, is probably that in the big N tomb-recess with cinquefoiled open cusping on shafts. Pointed altar recess E. The chancel and tower arches are also double-chamfered, the latter on massive grotesque corbels that look early C14. Complicated nave roof of 1882, by *Thomas Gordon*. Flanking the chancel arch are uneven recesses, probably for side altars. Perp chancel windows renewed by *Benjamin Ferrey*, 1870. C14 chancel PISCINA.

FURNISHINGS. FONT. C15, octagonal, panelled all over. – PULPIT. Early C18, panelled. – STALLS. C15 with fleur-de-lys finials and intricate water-flower, datable from the arms of William, Lord Harington, †1460. Linenfold backs. Linenfold also to the base of a cut-down SCREEN. – REREDOS. 1870. – STAINED GLASS. A good set by *Clayton & Bell*, the chancel 1870–2, the N chapel slightly later. – MONUMENTS. In the l. altar recess, broken Blue Lias COFFIN-LIDS with C13 foliated crosses. – In the chapel, the effigy of a knight in the N recess, in exceptionally detailed armour, half-turned and cross-legged, may be Sir Richard Gyvernay, *c*. 1330. The effigy of a lady on the floor may be his wife. The eroded double effigies under the arch, carved of one block and sharing a bolster, may be his daughter and son-in-law, Matilda and Henry Power, *c*. 1345. He is in civilian dress with a sword, cross-legged in prayer, she wears a wimple. – Under the tower, C18 incised Lias plaques, one with a painted head protruding.

Outside the E end, a MEMORIAL urn to George Swayne †1795.

N of the church, LIMINGTON HOUSE. Hip-roofed of 1837, the N front of creamy ashlar with balconies of cast-iron tapered columns and tall ashlar porch. Older pieces behind, the SE range with later C17 mullions and a C16 framed ceiling. Early C19 LODGE, with horizontally sliding sashes, faces down the village street. Below the church, the ashlar-fronted former RECTORY, of 1838 by *James Baron Beard* of Langport. Twin canted bays and a pillared side-wall porch. The earlier house remains behind. It had a cross-wing with a medieval window, possibly the one now re-set in the roadside STABLES. The former SCHOOL opposite, of 1834, has a Gothic centrepiece with far-from-Gothic hoodmould cherubs. Further S, a pretty early C19 shop window on the OLD POST OFFICE. HIGHER FARMHOUSE has an added front range (dated 1779) with beaded-mullioned windows. Converted C18 barns. On the Ilchester road, HIGH BARN was a brewery. Handsome three-storey ashlar-fronted house of *c.* 1820. The brick W end has Gothick windows, one essaying a Venetian triplet. Brewery buildings behind.

LONG LOAD

4020

CHRIST CHURCH (disused). 1854–6, by *C. E. Giles*. Quite large, with Geometrical tracery and a NE spirelet. C17 PULPIT

LOAD BRIDGE. Four C15 pointed double-chamfered arches. Central arch enlarged for navigation when the bridge was widened in 1814.

N of the church, MANOR FARMHOUSE with mullioned windows below C18 casements. BERRY FARMHOUSE has a N end of Ham stone ashlar and a Regency shop window. DAY'S HOUSE, all Ham stone, has ovolo-moulded mullions despite the late date, 1717. Gothic SCHOOL of 1865. Over the bridge, in the OLD DAIRY HOUSE, a late C15 fireplace, over-large for the house, with a green man in the cornice.

LONG SUTTON

4020

HOLY TRINITY. A big Perp church, called 'lately rebuilt and made new' in 1493. Lias and Ham stone. Dominant W tower, taller and more impressive than Langport's (q.v.), but similar, with set-back buttresses connected diagonally across the angles and ending in squat pinnacles at the foot of the bell-openings.

w doorway with leaf spandrels between eroded niches, under a five-light window with a transom interlaced by the arch-heads meeting reversed arch-heads above. Niches flank the window head, then a short blank stage gives elevation to the upper stages. First a two-light window flanked by niches, then the tall three-windowed bell-stage, each centre light with pierced baffles, that on the w face dated 1622, the outer ones blind. Two-light tracery. Thin shafts flanking and between the bell-lights, the inner ones carried from the string below through the battlements to end in small finials, a stronger design than at Langport. The angle pinnacles continue the diagonals between the buttresses. So there is plenty of ingenuity in the design. The s side, which has the polygonal stair-turret, is bare of any decoration, except for one niche, until the bell-stage is reached. Panelled tower arch inside and a lierne star-vault.

Fine array of battlements also to the aisles which continue as single-bay chancel chapels, to the nave clerestory, and to the s rood stair, but not to the chancel and porches. The porches are clearly added but can hardly be much later. The N porch has an ogee-canopied niche. Fine tracery with ogee-headed lights, three-light generally, the side window of each chapel four-light and the main E window five-light. All three E windows are transomed. Two-light clerestory windows. C15–C16 DOOR, N. Tall and luminous nave interior. Four-bay arcades with shafted piers of four-hollow section. Panelled arches to the chancel and to each chancel chapel. Fine Somerset nave roof, the tie-beams with angels supporting short kingposts and angels also under each sub-principal truss. Panelled enrichment at the E end. In the chancel, a ceiled wagon roof and fairly coarse triple SEDILIA.

FURNISHINGS. FONT. Perp, octagonal and large. Two quatrefoils in lozenges each face. Painted C17 cover. – SCREEN. In three parts, possibly trisected, as Sir Stephen Glynne noted it 'across the whole breadth' in 1834; brightly painted in 1866. Early C16. Four-light sections, the three mullions reaching up into the apex of the arch, with delicate tracery between. The fan-vaulted coving appears to be C19. – PULPIT. Exceptional Perp work, of a type more characteristic of Devon. Painted wood, as early as the 1450s if the monograms are correctly interpreted. Bands of carving form an octagonal base to a drum of twelve narrow panels each with statuette (replaced 1910) under a nodding-ogee canopy. Pinnacled shafts between. Panelled octagonal stem. – FRAGMENTS. In the s aisle E, two fine early C14 heads, from a double tomb, and two pieces of Norman chevron. N aisle E, piscina from a C12 corbel with carved foliage. – STAINED GLASS. E window, 1866, single Christ figure; contemporary side windows with the Devonshire arms. S aisle, 1869, by *O'Connor*, crowded and colourful. – MONUMENTS. Elizabeth Banbury †1716. Time and Death lurk behind the Corinthian columns. – Elizabeth Banbury †1729. Beautifully lettered slab (N wall).

Outside, the eroded base of a C15 CHURCHYARD CROSS with corner posts, as at Charlton Mackrell.

FRIENDS' MEETING HOUSE, Langport Road. 1717. Blue Lias, under a hipped roof edged in stone tiles. Long sides each with a doorway and two windows. Original thick glazing bars. The string course and the oak door frames are still moulded in the C17 manner. Inside, an atmosphere of peace and neatness with plain scrubbed benches in the original arrangement. Over the entrance passage, a gallery enclosed by fielded panelling, with sliding shutters, for female meetings.

COURT HOUSE, just W of the meeting house. An important medieval survival, early C14, altered in the C16 and 1658, and carefully repaired in 1932 by *Powys & Macgregor*. Irregular five-bay E front. The porch arch looks early C17 and the mullioned windows with Tudor lights look late C16, but match those on the N end dated 1658, so all the work could be old-fashioned of 1658. To the rear, a two-storey gabled projection with diagonal buttresses was probably the original porch. The massive lateral chimney to the l. marks the hall, which was floored in the C16. It retains its magnificent roof, tree-ring-dated to 1328. Base crucks with arched-braced collars carry upper crucks and crown-posts braced in four directions. Long wind-braces and massive purlins, set square. Closed S end truss of the aisled type with tall vertical posts. Cross-passage to the S with a pointed S doorway, blocked by a C16 stone staircase. But the S end was storeyed before then. The l. half of the courtyard outbuilding is a C17 DOVECOTE.

SUTTON HOSEY MANOR, N of the main road. Colourwashed Regency front in a railed forecourt with gatepiers, but the house is C16–C17 with some timber framing inside. The tall gabled DOVECOTE is a late C18 reuse of a medieval building, a pointed-arched E window visible within.

MANOR HOUSE, S of the green. In origin late C15. The N front has a lean-to porch, cut down, with a Jacobean arch (very like that on Court House). Irregular cross-wings, mullioned windows and some early C18 curved-headed sashes. The S front has distinct halves, the l. early C19, the r. C16 with Tudor-arched door and two bays of mullioned windows with Tudor lights. Victorian Gothic STABLE to the N, and substantial early C19 lofted COACHHOUSE, NE.

The churchyard is at the corner of a generous green dominated by the broad, three-gabled DEVONSHIRE ARMS HOTEL, *c.* 1868, at the N end. Equally Victorian SCHOOL, 1871, at the S end. SCHOOL HOUSE on the W side was the previous school, 1840. On the E side, STUCKEY HOUSE, brick-fronted, dated 1782. The village is extended, scattered with C16–C18 houses and cottages, e.g. along Shute Lane running NW to the Friends' meeting house (*see* above) on the main road. Just E is STEPHEN'S COTTAGES, a Gothic trio, to an unusual if ungainly Y-plan, *c.* 1870.

KNOLE, 1 m. E. A particularly attractive hamlet below Knole Hill. C16–C18 houses, mostly thatched, interspersed with hip-roofed mid-C19 cottages associated with dairy farming at Plot Dairy Farm (Ilchester estate) and, spectacularly, BINEHAM COURT, ½ m. E, of 1850 (Devonshire estate). L-plan lodges guard the foot of a hill crowned by a four-sided farmyard, the house occupying one full side, with a triple-gabled centrepiece.

UPTON, 1 m. NW. C16–C17 mullion-windowed houses on the main road and the lane N. UPTON BRIDGE FARM, c. 1870 (Devonshire estate), has a farmhouse very like the Devonshire Arms. Off Limepits Lane, an impressive pair of mid-C19 LIMEKILNS.

LOPEN

A centre of twine manufacture in the C19.

ALL SAINTS. Small, the chancel C14–C15 with a two-light E window. Windows with intersecting tracery and added N transept of 1834 by *John Patch* of Crewkerne. A Norman window head is reused in the porch. Pre-Victorian interior with plastered barrel ceilings and WEST GALLERY. C15 chancel wagon roof. – FONT. C13. Octagonal, retooled. – SCREEN. 1951, by *A. F. Erridge*. – MOSAIC. A small panel copied from the Roman villa (*see* below), 2002, by *Nick Durnan*. – STAINED GLASS. E window by *Joseph Bell*, 1874. – MONUMENT. George Sampson †1724. Incised Lias, nicely coloured.

Around the church a Late Georgian to Early Victorian sequence: CHURCH FARMHOUSE, vernacular, thatched, with a reused Medieval window in the Sunday School room behind, KNAPP COTTAGE, formal, with quoins and parapet, and LOPEN HOUSE, hip-roofed, with a pyramid-roofed belvedere. On the main road, CROSSTREE HOUSE, large and thatched, late C18. SHORE'S FARMHOUSE, raised in the C18, has C17 ground-floor mullioned windows. Down Frog Street, APPLE HAY, dated 1747, is still mullioned. S of the village, BRIDGE FARMHOUSE was a medieval hall house. C16 framed ceiling. Opposite was found in 2001 a ROMAN VILLA of corridor type with one spectacularly large C4 mosaic, a complex geometric design with some possible Christian symbolism. The mosaic has been reburied.

LOTTISHAM

ST MARY. By *T. G. Jackson*, 1876. Built for the Things of Alford, like Hornblotton (q.v.) and as pretty externally, if much less expensive. Of the same ochre marlstone, the shingled roofs replaced in dull tile. Nave and chancel with a pyramid-capped wooden bellcote over the nave E end. Dec and Perp detail. No chancel arch, but open timber roofs interestingly handled. In the nave a mixture of collar- and kingpost trusses. Two of the latter, coupled, on double-curved braces, do duty for a chancel arch. In the chancel a seven-sided rafter roof. – FONT. 1876. Octagonal and sculptural. Tapering bowl and stem divided by a moulding. Gothic COVER. – FURNISHINGS. Elegant woodwork pierced with delicate tracery, e.g. in the pulpit, the pierced roundels of the stalls almost Islamic. The pews have fielded-panelled backs and little hinged seats attached. Pretty leadwork in the windows. – STAINED GLASS. E window, 1931.

LOTTISHAM MANOR, ½ m. SE. An ostensibly C17 stone front between unequal projecting wings conceals a substantial late C14 hall. Broad jointed-cruck trusses with arch-braced collars and large wind-braces. C17 and C18 panelling downstairs.

LOVINGTON

ST THOMAS À BECKET. Much restored in 1862 by *Paull & Robinson* of Cardiff, who added the N aisle. C14 W tower with big diagonal buttresses and narrow second-stage lancet, S. Tower arch on shafts with traceried polygonal capitals. Perp bell stage with flat parapet. The rest is also Perp. S doorway with big fleurons. Ogee niche above. Moulded and shafted chancel arch. Unrestored plaster chancel ceiling. AUMBRY in a most curious stone surround. Above the door are three cusped panels under a cross of three big leaves, each like a spearhead. Similar tiny finials cap the outer shafts. C14? – FONT. Re-tooled C12, with rosettes in a raised band. – BENCHES. C15–C16, with poppyheads and three-tier motifs: foliage, tracery, quatrefoils. – STAINED GLASS. S window with medieval fragments. E window, 1867.

Two farms by the church. In front of CHURCH FARM, a pyramid-roofed early C18 SUMMERHOUSE. Irregular additions mask an early C18 house. The fielded-panelled parlour has a competent mid-C18 overmantel painting, a landscape with hunters. Large C18 BARN. CHARITY FARM, with early C18 mullioned windows, also has an overmantel painting, showing the house in C18 formal gardens (also garden-wall bee boles, which survive). The paintings and summerhouse reveal a sophisticated context for these vernacular farmhouses. Just E, very Victorian gabled former RECTORY, 1860, by *H. J. Paull*.

N of the railway, the former BIBLE CHRISTIAN CHAPEL, 1896, like a schoolroom. The PRIMARY SCHOOL has a stark schoolroom of 1840 attached to a mullion-windowed house. On the main road, the thatched OLD RECTORY was an early C16 hall house, with smoke-blackened jointed-cruck trusses. BRUE FARMHOUSE was a late C18 turnpike-road inn. Handsome ashlar, with double steps to a pedimented doorway, and half-hipped mansard roof. Just N, LOVINGTON MILL makes an extremely pretty group as seen from the bridge over the Brue. The mill has depressed arches, one the spillway, the lower arch with mid-C19 wheel. Three-storey, three-bay late C18 mill house with ashlar architraves and pedimented doorway.

LOW HAM

Low Ham was never a parish nor really a village. The houses are dispersed on two parallel lanes, the church at the SE, under Hext Hill.

CHURCH. As one approaches a queer feeling grows that there is something incongruous about the church which makes it all the more fascinating. First of all it stands not in a churchyard but pat in a field by a farmyard. Secondly it is remarkably compact in its proportions, the tower not high, the nave not long, and the clerestory tall (three-bay aisles, two-bay chancel). The tower is Somerset Perp standard, but the tracery of the windows, while clearly Gothic, will not fit precisely with anything of any Gothic date. The answer to all this is that the church was built for Sir Edward Hext (†1623) who bought the estate in 1588. It must have been structurally finished at Hext's death as his tomb is within. But the family suffered in the Civil War, and evidence, including a lost inscription in the E window glass, offers conflicting consecration dates of 1669 and 1690, for his grandsons George Stawell (†1669) and Ralph, 1st Lord Stawell (†1689). George's initials are on the chancel N door. The Gothic shades in correctness from the acceptable tower to tracery that will not fit precisely with anything of any Gothic date, its motifs Perp blended with the playful forms of the early C14. Most remarkable is the three-light E window, its head an eight-pointed star encircled by quatrefoils, clasped by fern-like forms.

Inside, the elements derive more clearly from the Late Perp, the arcades shafted, if with unusually deep hollows, the chancel and tower arches double-shafted. Victorian roofs, but original stone corbels in the aisles. – SCREEN. Instructive that there is one. Three bays with busy, rather coarse four-light tracery bisected by a centre mullion, under a vine-trail cornice and cresting. No rood loft of course. The side traceries are hinged to open like shutters. It may be late C16 but the inscription 'My sonne feare God and the Kinge, and meddle not with them that ar given to change' is a Stuart favourite, and the doll-like angels look C17. – PULPIT. From Muchelney. C17, octagonal, with arabesque panels. – BENCH-ENDS. C17, with blank arches. – ROYAL ARMS. C17. – TOWER SCREEN. Caen stone, very Gothic. Ejected in 1889 (together with the pulpit now at Muchelney) from the Lord Mayor's Chapel, Bristol.

Made in 1823 by the accomplished carver, *Thomas Clarke*; probably designed by *William Edkins*, the Theatre Royal scene-painter. Double doors in a high doorway, riotously crocketed and ogee-crested, between densely cusped and finialled side pieces with small glass panels of the four Evangelists, by *David Evans*. – STAINED GLASS. E window, *c.* 1690. Not really stained, but a Baroque transparency. The Cross, ribboned with texts, between the Virgin and St John. C15 fragments patch missing bottom pieces. Later C19 glass in the chancel and tower. – MONUMENTS. Sir Edward Hext †1623, and wife †1633. Two well-carved recumbent effigies, both in old-fashioned ruffs, he in armour, his head on a plumed helmet. Fierce C17 railings threaded through thick horizontals. – Ralph, 1st Lord Stawell, †1689, and John, 2nd Lord Stawell, †1692. Marble, of high quality, attributed to *William Stanton* (GF). White curtains looped to dark-shafted Corinthian columns reveal the upper inscription on black; heraldry in the curved pediment and a military trophy below. On the base, putti lift a drape from the second inscription. The iron railing by contrast is a splendid barbaric piece of cable-twined spearheads and scrolls, the Stawell crest a crude cut-out.

Almost nothing survives of the great MANSION begun by John, Lord Stawell, in 1689 and left unfinished at his death in 1692, apart from the gateway removed to Hazlegrove House (q.v.). Stawell spent some £10,000 – more, for example, Colvin notes, than the cost of either Calke Abbey, Derbys., or Buckingham House, London. Described in 1779 as 'vast piles of a stately ruin', it then still contained painted ceilings. The graded hillside S of the church was planned and partly laid out by *Jacques Bobart* as terraces and a canal, over the gardens of the late C16 Hext mansion, which probably stood at the top of the hill. The terraces are bounded on the E by a massive late C17 WALL. The field beyond contains fan-shaped markings, perhaps from gardens of the Hext era. The Stawell house stood at the foot, its S end central to the terraces. The big C19 FARM BUILDINGS opposite the church reuse C17 mullioned windows.

THE OLD MANOR, W of the church, has Late Georgian windows at the front, but has been turned round, for at the back is a big gabled porch with C17 oak doorway, and mullion windows. It is however a six-bay late C15 house, floored from the outset, the roof open to the first floor. Moulded framed ceiling (tree-ring-dated 1481) in the central room, divided by a framed partition from small E rooms. Good early C17 panelling. The lane N passes DAIRY HOUSE FARM, *c.* 1600, with big cross-wing and hoodmoulded mullioned windows, and DOBBINS, thatched, with Late Georgian sashes. At the upper end, CONGREGATIONAL CHAPEL, 1884. The triplet of arched windows contains, unusually, stained glass. On the parallel Long Street, W, NEW MANOR, 1877, an elaborate Victorian farmhouse with mullion windows, with a spirelet on a narrow half-timbered central oriel. A turret at the rear SE.

ROMAN VILLA, ¼ m. SE. A large villa set around a courtyard appears to have been built *c.* A.D. 340 and is best known for the 14-ft (4.25-metre) square mosaic found in its extensive bath house. The mosaic tells the story of Aeneas in five panels, showing him sailing to Carthage, meeting Dido, the pair out hunting, the pair embracing, and Dido abandoned. Lifted in 1953, it now forms the centrepiece of the Museum of Somerset, Taunton.

RIFLE RANGE, ½ m. W. Second World War period, still with target frames, marker gallery and butts.

LUCCOMBE

ST MARY. Predominantly Perp, apart from the E.E. chancel with small side lancets and triple-lancet E window. C15 nave and W tower, the S aisle coming last, *c.* 1530. The three-stage tower is tall and spare, as at Watchet and Winsford (qq.v.). Diagonal buttresses right to the top, two-light bell-openings, and battlements with quatrefoil panels. Higher square SE stair-turret. Tall shafted and moulded tower arch. The aisle has some of the elegant tracery of the region, especially the four-light E window with quatrefoil spandrels below the transom, as at Selworthy. Simpler flat-headed W window with similar spandrels. Another such window is reused in the NE vestry. Four-bay arcade with piers of the four-wave type. Polygonal capitals mostly, but two piers with finely carved bands of vine-trail with shields. No chancel arch, just a slight break in the wagon roofs. These resemble the C16 aisle roof at Selworthy: carved wall-plates, big bosses, mostly foliage, also male and female heads. In the chancel and aisle the framing itself is carved. Trefoil-headed C13 PISCINA and SEDILE, altered. The sedile had column shafts. Perp aisle PISCINA. – FONT. Retooled Perp, with pointed quatrefoils. Panelled underside and panelled stem. By the font a detached C15 stone PANEL, with quatrefoils and original colour; from a reredos? – TOMB-CHEST. Early C16. Square panels with big leaves in two tiers divided by a scrolled-foliage moulding. The adjacent C13 TILES of Cleeve Abbey type were found near the porch. – SCREEN. 1896. Dado only, with a little reused tracery. – PULPIT. Mid-C17. Two tiers divided by a band of oval cabochons, as at Watchet. – STALLS. 1896, by *Edmund Buckle*. Overblown Jacobean, the panels reused. – STAINED GLASS. E window, 1899, subtly coloured Crucifixion. By *Powell's*, who also made the nave N window, 1912. Large pale flowers in the S windows in the Arts and Crafts taste, 1890s, as at Porlock. Old fragments in the SE window. – MONUMENTS. William Harrison †1615. In front of the chancel step. Small brass portrait, in ruff, knee-breeches and long cloak. – Richard Worth †1637 and Maria †1649. Local alabaster. A broken pediment on Ionic columns. – Rev. Henry

Byam †1669. Bolection-moulded alabaster frame. – Elizabeth Stawell †1731. Broken pediment on pilasters, in coloured marbles. – Rev. R. F. Gould †1839. Grecian, with amphorae.

CHURCHYARD CROSS. C15, on octagonal steps, complete apart from the cross-head.

Luccombe is one of the prettiest of Somerset villages. The COTTAGES were embellished by the Holnicote estate in the early C19 and are unified by the estate's yellow limewash. Stoney Street, S of the churchyard, has an especially pretty thatched pair at the lower end. KETNOR was a C15 hall house, tree-ring-dated to 1437, a lateral chimney and circular stack of *c.* 1600 prominent on the front. CHURCH GATE COTTAGE, C17, was made picturesque with a curved E end when the schoolroom was added at the other end, after 1800. OAKAPPLE COTTAGE has a heavy oak doorway and lateral stack. STADDONS, an L-plan group of three single-storey houses for the elderly, 1990, by *Timothy Harbinson* of *Percy Thomas Partnership*, fits in without pastiche. Several more lateral chimneys further up, notably THE COTTAGE at the top. Facing up Stoney Street are contrasting ESTATE COTTAGES of 1900–2, red sandstone with red tiles. Yellow limewash resumes with CHURCH VIEW, dated 1680, the roof raised in the C19. Going N are a tiny former SCHOOL, 1881, with fish-scale tiles, and the large gabled former RECTORY, 1844, by *Robert Birmingham*, the Holnicote agent. Going S, WYCHANGER COTTAGE is prettily improved, its hip-roofed front projection broken by a triangular-headed window. WYCHANGER was a manor house of *c.* 1600. The E cross-wing was given Georgian Gothic glazing, but the adjoining storeyed porch retains heavy oak doorways. All this is thatched. The main range was rebuilt in the C19.

CHAPEL CROSS, ½ m. WNW. Foundations of a rectangular chapel, possibly C14.

HORNER, 1 m. NW. HORNER MILL dates from 1839, three and two storeys, with an overshot wheel. Further on, a COTTAGE ROW with lateral stacks in front and behind. The segmental-arched PACKHORSE BRIDGE, reputedly medieval, is probably C17.

WEST LUCCOMBE, 1½ m. NW. Another PACKHORSE BRIDGE, here more probably medieval, with a pointed arch. BURROWHAYES FARMHOUSE has a late medieval moulded ogee-headed oak doorway next to an oak four-light window with ogee-headed lights, the spandrels with foliage initialled WS. C16 lateral stack. Twelve-panel hall ceiling, the dais end enriched with mouldings.

LUFTON

ST PETER AND ST PAUL. 1865–6, by *Benjamin Ferrey*. Small. Nave and chancel, with W bellcote corbelled out on very

Victorian heads and flowers. – FONT. C11–C12. Heavy tub with a middle cable moulding and rim of crosses in indented circles. – STAINED GLASS. E window by *Kempe & Co.*, 1912. – MONUMENTS. John Hodges †1608. Incised floor slab. – By the font, a C13 Lias slab with raised thin cross.

LUFTON MANOR, NE of the church. 1900, by *Evelyn Hellicar*. A large red brick hip-roofed house in Queen Anne style. An ashlar loggia between the wings on one side. On the other a vernacular classical centrepiece.

ROMAN VILLA, 1 m. N. Discovered by wartime ploughing. Excavation revealed a C4 house of the corridor type, a series of rooms linked by a veranda, facing a gravelled yard with a further block projecting back. Many of the rooms had mosaics, but the main interest was the very elaborate bath house. This comprised six rooms with hypocaust heating system and large octagonal plunge pool.

LUXBOROUGH

ST MARY. The W tower rears to a High Victorian saddleback top of the 1860s by *C. E. Giles*, characteristically steeper than what it replaced. The tower is C13–C14 with heavy buttresses set low, and paired tiny bell-lights, like Wootton Courtenay. Small Dec two-light W window. Unmoulded tower arch. The rest was much altered between 1890 and 1900 by *Samson & Cottam*. The chancel was C13 – see the renewed lancets. Perp E window. Arcade and roofs of 1900. – FONT. C13–C14. Octagonal, with an inset band and tapered underside. – STAINED GLASS. E window, 1900, by *Powell's*. NE window by *Frankie Pollak*, 2002, marine colours.

CHARGOT HOUSE, 1 m. SE. The plain hip-roofed house built for John Lethbridge in 1826 was given a Tudor character in the 1840s perhaps by *Richard Carver*. Added bays to the front and W end and added SE corner porch. C18 staircase from Withiel Florey.

ESTATE COTTAGES. The Lethbridge estate built unusual hip-roofed and thatched pairs of cottages with staircases in a rounded centrepiece. Examples scattered around the parish are at Churchtown (Westcott Cross Cottage), Kingsbridge (Nos. 20–21), Couple Cross and Lypefoot.

In Chargot Wood, the LANGHAM HILL and BEARLAND WOOD MINES, sunk for iron ore. Foundations of the Langham Hill engine house, 1866, over a 650-ft (198-metre) shaft. The engine house was re-erected at Burrow Farm (Brendon Hill) in 1878, after the ore ran out. At Bearland, the round CHIMNEY, 1860, ventilated a shaft to an unsuccessful adit.

LYDEARD ST LAWRENCE

ST LAWRENCE. Mostly Perp. Severe four-stage red sandstone W tower with diagonal buttresses, battlements with pinnacles, and higher polygonal NE stair-turret, also pinnacled. Three-light bell-openings with blind traceried heads over pierced baffles. Three sides have small two-light windows below, also with pierced baffles. The nave has large Perp S windows, two three-light, one of four lights, and a porch with quatrefoil-pierced side battlements and gable parapet. The N aisle and tall N porch were added at much the same time, just after 1500. Of some grandeur, faced in buff sandstone, gabled, with large windows and a polygonal rood-stair turret. Battlements with quatre-foiled merlons, the turret also battlemented with pinnacles. Mid-C14 chancel with reticulated tracery in the E window, flowing tracery in the S window, and cusped Y-tracery in the N window, all renewed in the restoration of 1869–70 by *C. E. Giles*. Broad nave with N arcade on piers of standard four-hollow section. Interesting band capitals, each differently carved. The W respond has a fox and goose, the first pier has angels typical of the Taunton area, the second entwined leaves, and the third plaitwork. The chancel arch dies into the sides. The chancel N arch is of double-depth with angel busts carrying long scrolls. C14 PISCINA, ogee-arched within a pointed arch, the spandrels pierced. Its hoodmould rests on headstops, at different heights because of the proximity of the handsome C14 triple SEDILIA. These have stepped seats and are shafted with ogee arches and spandrel panels. Open wagon roofs of 1869–70.

FURNISHINGS. FONT. Allegedly up-ended because John Venn of Pyleigh, regicide, had been baptized here. The foot is indeed a large octagonal C12 bowl. But the present shallow bowl looks like a different C12 font cut down. – ROOD SCREEN. Early C16, in two five-bay parts, missing the coving and loft. Much restored in 1903. In place of coving the spandrels of the nave screen have lively Jacobean painting, and there is similar on the back of the aisle screen. Close-traceried base panels and a little original barber-pole paintwork. – PULPIT. 1605. Broad, ambitious piece, with the usual short blank arches, in two tiers separated by a band of plant-scroll, and topped by similar motifs between big consoles. There was apparently more below. – BENCHES. Three backs and one frontal, C15–C16 with close tracery, one with linenfold, between robustly carved muntins. Moulded square-headed ends with tracery, some entwined plants, a big Tudor rose. – Good STALLS presumably of 1870, also RAILS and carved stone REREDOS. – STAINED GLASS. E window, 1906, by *Herbert Davis*. N window medieval fragments. NE, probably by *Christopher Webb*, 1944. – MONUMENT. Doctor Goodwin †1628. Crude, scrolled sides, top with crossed bones and skull.

The VILLAGE descends N from the church and brick SCHOOL of 1876–7, with farmhouses at right angles to the road. At the lower end, MIDDLE THATCH, C17, with a long rendered front. Further on the road rises between red sandstone outbuildings of two farms, REED'S COURT, the farmhouse C16–C17 with moulded framed ceiling, and KNIGHT'S with a half-hip-roofed C19 BARN on an arcaded basement.

LOWER TARR FARMHOUSE, 2 m. SW. C16, with broad jointed-cruck trusses. Fine ground-floor fireplaces, the hall with moulded jambs and bressumer, the kitchen with a full-width bressumer carried over bacon-curing and corn-drying chambers. Upstairs room with plaster motifs, stags and fleurs-de-lys. In the rear wing, a big plaster overmantel panel dated 1691, the motifs still Jacobean. Winged horses at a globular urn, also stags and fleurs-de-lys. The stags reappear in the friezes.

LYMPSHAM

ST CHRISTOPHER. Handsome Perp four-stage W tower of Blue Lias, with ashlar set-back buttresses and bell-stage. The stair-turret is barely expressed, giving each side equal weight. Four-light W window beneath two stages each with a good canopied niche. The corresponding stages on the N and S sides each have a two-light window. Rich bell-stage of twin bell-openings (like Blagdon (N)) with a diagonal shaft between, matched by finials above the buttresses. These are set against ashlar piers that carry square corner pinnacles with slim outriders. Pierced arcaded parapets, broken by a slim intermediate pinnacle on a squatting beast. Panelled tower arch. Late C15 four-bay N aisle with buttresses, finials, and parapet pierced with cusped lozenges. Similar Perp windows to the nave S, the parapet here with finials and blind trefoils. C19 S porch. The roughcast chancel was rebuilt by three successive Stephensons, rectors almost continuously from 1809 to 1912. Blocked Y-tracery windows of 1820, replaced in 1908–9 by *E. H. Sedding* as a memorial to Prebendary J. H. Stephenson, who re-roofed the chancel in 1845, the date probably of the large pinnacled SE vestry.

The four-bay arcade must be late C15, despite the piers of four-wave section, not usual in this part of Somerset. Shafts with round capitals. Much-renewed wagon roof in the nave, on stone heads, and a fine panelled aisle roof, the panels divided Union Jack fashion. Among the bosses, a green man, and Passion implements. The aisle has wall-shafts on leaf corbels and a restored niche with spired triple-arched canopy. The inscription states 'renovata' and 'ornata' in 1845, but work had begun earlier. WEST GALLERY of 1836, over contemporary CHURCHWARDEN'S PEWS and TOWER SCREEN. Everywhere are painted TEXTS, a particular Stephenson pleasure. The chancel has a pretty pointed tunnel vault of plaster, Late Georgian in character, but of 1845. The stone corbel heads, originally Evangelists, were replaced with Stephenson portraits in

1908–9, the date of the marble pavement. The comfortable VESTRY is a Stephenson shrine, with their ancestry on brass plates in Gothic wall panels, panelled ceiling, stained glass, and their heraldry on the fireplace.

FURNISHINGS. FONT. C12 bowl on a stem with a thin zigzag. Spurred base. – PULPIT. 1845, oak, by *Thomas Cox*, the Stephenson steward. Contemporary low CHANCEL SCREEN and RAILS. – SCULPTURE. Eroded C13–C14 Crucifixion relief in the N aisle E wall. – PEWS. 1891–2. Traceried, still with doors. – ROYAL ARMS. Hanoverian. – CHANDELIER. Three-tier, by *John Bayley* of Bridgwater, 1744. – STAINED GLASS. E window by *O'Connor*, 1863. Suffer the Little Children, depicted without any medievalizing. The figures include numerous Stephensons. Bright early to mid-C19 coloured glass in the W window and nave window heads. In the NW window two early C19 roundels, the Church upon a Rock and St Christopher. – MONUMENTS. Mostly Stephensons, mostly Gothic, the largest the Rev. J. A. Stephenson †1837, by *Henry Wood*.

MANOR HOUSE. Opposite the church. Exceedingly pretty in the fanciful Gothic taste of the early C19, though the façade may be as late as the 1840s. The Rev. J. A. Stephenson rebuilt the house *c.* 1815–19, but his son, the Rev. J. H. Stephenson, there from 1844, may be responsible for the Bath stone front. This has frilly pierced battlements, Gothic string courses and windows with ogee-headed lights (the mullions free of sash windows behind). Particularly fancy are the porch and full-height bay. The bay has cusped lights, bands of shields or quatrefoils, stepped battlements and crocketed finials. The porch has a cusped ogee arch and corner piers. There are of course mottos and heraldry. Ashlar conservatory at the S end with pointed windows and an even more fanciful parapet, with pinnacles. The stuccoed rear has two octagonal towers, a thin one for the staircase and a large one central to a parallel rear

Lympsham, Manor House and church.
Engraving by W. Willis, *c.* 1840

range. The windows have the narrow marginal panes typical of the 1840s, but some at least of this side was illustrated in 1829.

Inside, much delightful plaster detail. Gothic wooden doorcases but a classical cornice and rose in the hall, into which the narrow circular cantilevered stone staircase debouches in a serpentine flourish. Cast-iron balusters. The flanking rooms have Gothic cornices typical of *Richard Carver* around 1820 (cf. Chapel Cleeve Manor, Old Cleeve, and St Audries, West Quantoxhead). A pendant rose in the drawing room, also Gothic niches and pelmets. A similar pendant at the top of the staircase. In the larger tower, a panelled octagonal chapel with fireplace and later C19 stained glass. Simple pulpit beneath a lid in the ceiling, presumably to allow invalids to hear.* Adjoining the tower, Stephenson's first-floor library has plaster leaves of icing-sugar delicacy outlining ceiling ribs and a brightly painted heraldic fireplace.

In the gardens an octagonal spired MEMORIAL, intended as a gatepier (the other in the village). In a grove, a little pyramid-roofed PRIVY, vaulted with grinning heads at each corner. Not Gothic at all are the hip-roofed STABLES, with stucco quoins and voussoirs.

The Stephenson imprint on the VILLAGE is ubiquitous. The Gothic buildings of grey Mendip limestone with octagonal brick chimneys date from 1863 onward. They were designed by *J. H. Stephenson* with his steward *Thomas Cox*. The style continues into the 1890s without concession to changing taste. Some are remodellings, like CHURCH FARM, NE of the church. Most prominent, facing down Church Road, is the MANOR HALL, 1873–5, a large and very Gothic village hall of five bays. Acutely gabled centrepiece with a rose window over a typical motto: 'The Fear of the Lord is the Begining [*sic*] of Wisdom.' Traceried W end bay window. Inside, a high roof with Stephenson heraldry and a Gothic fireplace recessed in a high panelled arch. Behind, part of the same gift, is the SCHOOL, extended 1895. Down Rectory Road are SCHOOL HOUSE, for the teacher, 1888, a roughcast Edwardian former RECTORY, 1903, by *E. H. Sedding*, and RECTORY FARM, the largest Stephenson estate farmhouse, dated 1866, battlemented with a storeyed porch. HOLM FARM, 1863, like a Victorian vicarage, was the home farm. Similar is MANOR COTTAGE, 1867, behind the manor grounds. S of the church are SYCAMORE HOUSE, 1873, and the early C19 OLD FORGE, roughcast, with cast-iron lattice windows. The 'Lympsham Parish Stables' were added for churchgoers. On the corner of South Road is the other spired gatepier of the manor, inscribed 'Fear God, Love one another'. Down South Road, THE COTTAGE, and SOUTH FARM, 1868, are Stephenson works, and on West Road, MANOR LODGE. The former METHODIST CHAPEL, 1902, is distinctly similar, with a pyramid-roofed tower. Outliers on the Brean road are the almshouse-like MILLFIELD COTTAGES, 1869, and HOPE FARM, 1868, in brick.

---

* The story that Stephenson was lowered through it to officiate is surely untrue.

LYNG see EAST LYNG

LYTES CARY
1 m. S of Charlton Mackrell

Lytes Cary is a mixed building, with parts of the C14, C15, C16, C18 and C20, yet all parts blend to perfection with one another and with the gentle landscape that surrounds them. The Lyte family had a house here before 1343 and remained until 1755. Their house, around three sides of a court, decayed; the N service range was largely rebuilt as a farmhouse in the later C18. The house was restored and re-created in 1907–12 for Sir Walter Jenner, 2nd Bt, by *C. E. Ponting*, who closed the court with a new W range. The formal gardens, a series of chambers and walks enclosed by yew hedges, are of Jenner's time. The house passed to the National Trust on his death in 1948.

The E front has first an C18 part on the r., higher and straighter than the rest, then the mid-C15 hall in the centre, with C16 gabled porch and bay, and finally the low chapel projects on the l. The CHAPEL probably dates from just before 1343, when a chaplain was instituted, and was free-standing before the mid C15. It has a three-light E window with reticulated tracery, and two-light N and S windows, straight-headed but also with reticulated tracery. The pointed-arched N doorway has tiny carved-head stops. Inside, a damaged, sharply pointed cusped piscina on the S wall, but the character otherwise is C17 as the chapel was remodelled with family piety in 1631 by Thomas Lyte. His are the roof of thin arch-braced collar-trusses and the painted heraldic frieze below the wall-plate. Two painted plaques each side of the altar record his work. The S plaque reproduces figures of William le Lyte †c. 1316 and wife, copied from a then-extant window in Charlton Mackrell church. On the W wall, a squint to the mid-C15 cross-wing. – SCREEN. Dated 1631, possibly an early C20 compilation. A round arch between panelling topped with a thin arcade, whose balusters, like those of the COMMUNION RAIL, are vertically symmetrical. – WALL PAINTING. In the upper jambs of the side windows mysterious C18 fragments, on the N two hands shaking 'Farewell Adiew'; on the S a negro head and a skull. – STAINED GLASS. E window, 1838, by *Thomas Willement*, from Charlton Mackrell, installed here in 1912. Densely drawn in silver and gold on a rich blue. The scenes are convincingly C13 style, the lettering with a modern freedom. W window, 1912. Restored late medieval Virgin feeding the infant Jesus.

The HALL is ascribed to the mid C15, but windows, porch and matching bay belong to the mid 1520s, for John Lyte. The porch is two-storeyed with a handsome oriel on the upper floor. The bay has just such an oriel on its upper storey, and the windows of the oriels, the bay, and the hall, both to the front and the rear, are all mullioned with four-centred heads to each light. The main hall windows are large and of three

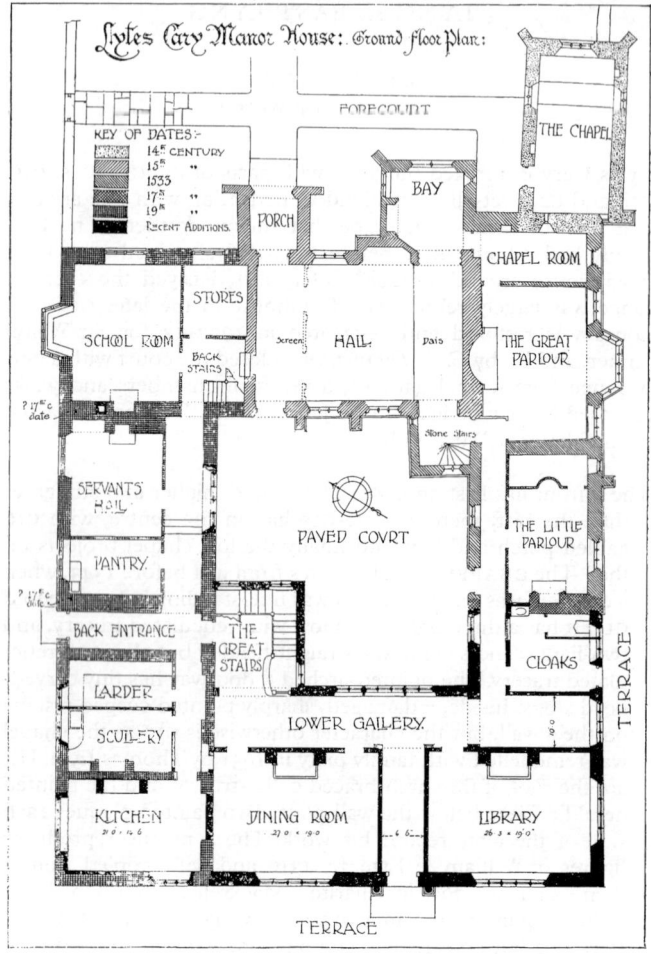

Lytes Cary, ground-floor plan showing enlargement.
Drawing by C. E. Ponting, 1909

lights. The hall has an impressive C15 roof with a finely quatrefoiled wall-plate, arched braces supporting collar-beams, and three tiers of large cusped wind-braces. Shield-bearing angels support each truss, and the collars have central pendants. The galleried screen and the linenfold panelling, unobtrusive but appropriate, are by *Ponting*. The broad fireplace on the front wall is C15 with cusped spandrels. In the rear windows, C16 heraldic GLASS, original to the house, retrieved in the C20 from Angersleigh church (q.v.). At the S or dais end, a panelled arch each side, with blind tracery. The mouldings of each arch differ, suggesting that this early C16 work was in phases. The w arch opens to the spiral staircase to the solar, in a square projection into the courtyard. The E arch opens to the hall-bay. This is not the typical oriel, but a low semi-private room with its own fireplace, an indication of the growing desire for family privacy. Slots in the arch show that the room was screened from the hall. The arrangement is found also at Gaulden Manor, Tolland (q.v.).

The S cross-wing was rebuilt in the 1530s with a new S wall and an extension to the W. The new work is eminently interesting, in some ways remarkably advanced for its date. The windows are, it is true, still of the same type as those of the hall, but the bay window is set symmetrically in relation to the windows on either side. The bay is crowned by a parapet with the typical Somerset pierced frieze of quatrefoils below crenellations, the quatrefoils with badges and initials of John Lyte and Edith Horsey, his wife. The arch to the bay on each floor inside is again panelled with blind ogee tracery. The ground-floor GREAT PARLOUR has early C17 panelling and a timber lobby, with fluted pilasters. To the E, the narrow CHAPEL ROOM with the squint to the chapel. Above the parlour is the GREAT CHAMBER. This has a three-sided plaster ceiling with thin ribs forming four-pointed stars in overlapping octagons, each star with a shield. This type of pattern one does not expect to find before the time of Elizabeth I, but did indeed begin under Henry VIII (cf. the screen at King's College Chapel, Cambridge, and the Great Watching Chamber at Hampton Court). Tudor royal arms loom large above the bed and the shields have the Lyte swans and Horsey horses, which make 1558 (when John Lyte passed the house to his son) an end date, early still, but less exceptional than the 1530s. The panelling is C17, apart from the earlier linenfold of the lobby. To the W on both floors, the C16 smaller parlour and chamber above, each reached by a corridor looking N into the courtyard. Both rooms were altered in the early C18. Ashlar bolection-moulded chimneypieces. In the LITTLE PARLOUR, a shelved shell niche.

The LATER ADDITIONS are markedly taller. N of the porch, a steep-roofed two-bay range with brick relieving arches over leaded casements. This forms a cross-wing to a similar long N range with dormers. It all looks C18, large for a farmhouse, but without architectural elaboration. *Ponting*'s W FRONT is manorial in a restrained C17 style, with mullion-and-transom windows and artisan-classical doorcase. Both dining room and drawing room are panelled in late C17 style. One of two tall Corinthian doorcases in the dining room comes from *Wren*'s St Benet, Gracechurch Street, London, of 1681–9, demolished 1867. The other woodwork, with much Grinling Gibbons-style carving by *Angell* of Bath, shows the quality of early C20 imitation. Two lacquered Chinoiserie doors upstairs illustrate the range.

The E front faces a topiaried garden aligned on a circular dovecote in the field beyond, a beautiful and timeless view that is wholly C20. The dovecote is in fact a PUMP HOUSE, 1934, by *Rolfe & Peto* of Bath. To the N of the house are FARM BUILD-INGS. Two unusual late C18 cowsheds with five brick arches on one face answered by ten narrow ones on the back. Cruciform early C19 barn. At the foot of the drive, GATEPIERS with splendid early C18 Ham stone urns, imported, or copies.

MAPERTON

Source of the iron-rich limestone used locally.

ST PETER AND ST PAUL. On a bluff above Maperton House. Small Perp W tower, the rest of 1869 by *Henry Hall*. In the porch an Anglo-Saxon CARVING, a panel of interlace of asymmetrical design, as in the initials of manuscripts. Also two C13 corbel heads. The porch hints at Hall's liking for naturalistic foliage, let loose in the chancel – see the chancel arch shafts, the roof corbels and the window imposts. E wall and arcaded reredos bright with TILES. – FONT. C13, rimmed octagon, on a round shaft. – PILLAR PISCINA. Late C12, with fluted and carved capital. – ROYAL ARMS. Painted, 1738. – STAINED GLASS. E window, rich colours, 1869, by *Holiday* for *Powell's*. Other glass by *Powell's*, 1869–85. – MONUMENT. John Davidge †1792. Marble cherub head, weeping.

MAPERTON HOUSE. The early C19 Neoclassical ashlar front may be by *Charles Harcourt Masters*. Seven bays with giant pilasters at the angles and paired each side of the broad centre bay. This has an attic storey and tripartite windows. Similar pilasters at the W end frame a two-storey canted bay. C17 origins are visible in two E gables and a basement mullioned window. Large additions, probably by *Henry Hall*, 1876, including the conservatory that curves SE with pilasters and ashlar apse. Tall lofted STABLES with cupola of 1876.

MARK

HOLY CROSS. A large handsome Perp church of Blue Lias. The W tower is tall for its three stages. It is of Blue Lias banded in a buff stone, used to face the buttresses. These are set back and end in diagonally placed shafts with finials that are conjoined against each corner of the bell-stage (a feature of e.g. Cheddar, Banwell, Winscombe (all N) and Weare). From this a diagonal pier rises through the parapet to each corner pinnacle. The tower angles also develop pinnacles that finish just into the bell-stage. On the second stage is a two-light window on three sides, between two niches on the N, the show side. On the E side a niche alone. Then the bell-stage has three close-set two-light windows on each side, the middle one blind below a transom, the outer ones entirely blind. Diagonally set shafts with pinnacles divide and flank the bell-lights. Parapet pierced with quatrefoils in lozenges. Generously moulded tower arch without capitals. The late C15 N aisle makes a fine picture, one seven-bay composition with the porch of equal height and an octagonal rood-stair turret before the final bay. Parapets as on the tower, broken by finials on buttresses between big four-light windows. On the porch another canopied niche, the base with two fine lions, and, inside, a good framed ceiling. The two-bay S aisle is treated much less conspicuously, with plain battlements and two-light windows. The porch included in the first bay is clearly older, remodelled to fit. Two bays of the nave to the W of the aisle, the l. bay with an early C19 gallery window. Perp chancel windows in older stonework.

Now inside. The church recorded as new in 1268 has left little trace. The double-chamfered chancel arch is C13–C14, and there is a chamfered window head at the end of the S aisle of similar date. There is an instructive difference between the low two-bay S aisle and the later six-bay N aisle. The S arcade is C14, with piers of four-hollow type, but the shafts have fillets and three-sided capitals with abaci. The N arcade piers are slimmer and of standard four-wave section with small capitals decorated with small fleurons. Panelled C15 arches from the chancel to the chapels, but the W arches of the chapels correspond to the different aisle patterns. Wagon roof in the nave on carved and painted wooden heads, C14–C15, including reputedly King Alfred, his queen and Guthrum. Edward VII, Alexandra and Bishop Kennion were added in the restoration of 1904 by *Edmund Sedding*. Good C15 panelled aisle roof, with traceried sub-panels and spread-winged angels, as at Brent Knoll. Bosses including Tudor roses and a fine face. In the chancel, marble paving and ceiling of 1904.

FURNISHINGS. FONT. C15, octagonal with small quatrefoils in pairs above angel busts all around the curved underside (like Axbridge and Doulting, both N). One angel carries a child. Shafted and panelled stem. C17 COVER. – SCREENS. Two, across the nave and N aisle. Damaged Perp, garishly painted, with three-light tracery. The nave screen is patched with C17 panels, one dated 1634. – PULPIT. Early C17. Two tiers of the familiar short blank arches. The lower tier has tall flowers on the angles. – S DOOR. Probably early C16. Traceried with, unusually, many small encircled quatrefoils. – BENCHES. Two heavy benches with roundel terminals, undatable. – SCULPTURE. Wooden Renaissance-style figures of the Evangelists, about 2 ft 6 in. (76 cm.) high, each seated in the act of writing. They are Flemish of 1524 from the cathedral at Bruges that was destroyed in 1794. Brought here in 1879 by the Rev. Frederic du Sautoy. – CANDELABRA. 1758. Two-tier. – ROYAL ARMS. 1660. – STAINED GLASS. In the NW window, four panels, each with a re-set pair of C15 saints. Tracery shields including the arms of Glastonbury Abbey and John Gunthorpe, Dean of

Wells from 1472 to 1498, giving a date for the aisle. Two s aisle windows of *c.* 1860. – MONUMENTS. Under the pier of the s arcade, a C13 slab with incised cross. – John Gilling †1793. Incised Lias in a rustic Adam style.

The two large terracotta LIONS incongruously outside the porch are from the *Royal Pottery*, Weston-super-Mare, 1880. The C15 MARKET CROSS came to the churchyard probably in 1750, when the shaft was given its plain finial. Gothic cast-iron CHURCHYARD GATES, 1848, made at the Mark Foundry.

Around the churchyard, the former SCHOOLROOM, 1833, brick with a Georgian Gothic window, MOUNT PLEASANT, dated 1797, and the PACK HORSE INN, externally Victorian but the rear wing C17. Towards Blackford, the former VICARAGE, 1860s, Lias, with ashlar quoins and architraves, and MARK HOUSE, *c.* 1805, brick, three-storeyed with tripartite sash windows and a delicate metal fanlight. Towards Burnham, a Gothic former BAPTIST CHAPEL, 1866, by *Hans Price*, and THE ELMS, a C17–C18 farmhouse. Then the road bends around a field, where good views open of the church tower. At the NW corner, a short cast-iron BRIDGE, dated 1824, by *Richard Down* of Bridgwater.

The Causeway then runs straight westward across the flat landscape, scattered with C18 brick farmhouses typical of the region. In WEST MARK, the SCHOOL, 1875, in polychrome brick, with cast-iron windows. WESLEY MEWS was the Methodist chapel of 1797, painted brick with mansard roof. Barrel ceiling and panelled gallery. Good brick farmhouses at LAUREL FARM, in the village, and Southwick, to the s. SOUTHWICK HOUSE is larger than most, with diaper patterning in the brick, probably mid-C18.

MARSTON BIGOT

The former estate of the Boyle family, Earls of Cork and Orrery.

ST LEONARD. Previously in front of the house, the church was moved in 1787. Rebuilt as a plain Gothic box to which a w tower with arched bell-lights was added in 1809. The nave windows and the tower door were Normanized in 1844–5 by *Edward Davis* of Bath, when he added an extravagantly neo-Norman cruciform chancel for the Rev. Richard Boyle. Neo-Norman plaster vaults in the tower and chancel, neo-Norman GALLERY, PULPIT, FONT and MEMORIALS, all in stone, and rather less convincing neo-Norman WOODWORK, even the organ case. The C18 nave roof was embellished *c.* 1860 when a N transept was added as the family pew. – STAINED GLASS. The E window incorporates interesting Continental panels. On the l. a late C15 Flemish Annunciation similar to a panel in the Lord Mayor's Chapel, Bristol. In the centre, three pieces

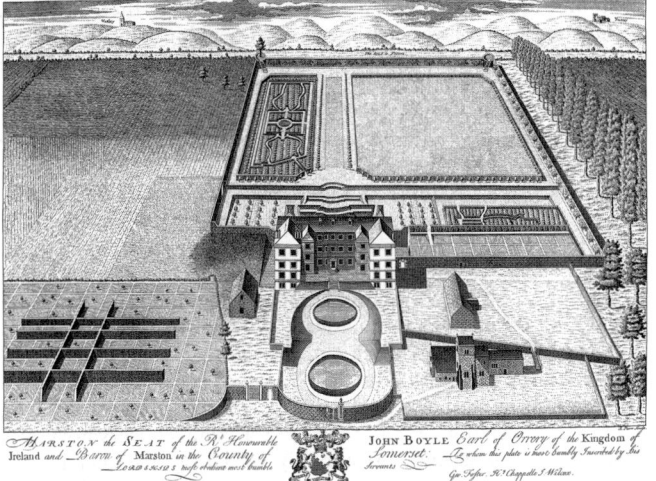

Marston Bigot, Marston House.
Engraving by R. Parr, 1739

probably from Mariawald Abbey, Germany, c. 1500: the spies carrying grapes, a prophet, and Jacob and Leah amid camels. A panel of the attempted seduction of St Bernard, c. 1525, is one of sixty-four from Altenberg Abbey near Cologne (nineteen others are in St Mary, Shrewsbury). On the r. a late C16 Rhenish piece, Christ's blood as the Fountain of Life. Nave glass of 1845–57 by *Thomas Willement*, designed by the rector's wife, *Eleanor Boyle* (the illustrator E. V. B.). The N windows stand out from Willement's normal work for their complicated imagery and lush vegetation. – MONUMENTS. Louisa Boyle †1826. Excellent Neoclassical relief, the dead girl on a couch surrounded by her disconsolate family, in Grecian dress. By *Sir Richard Westmacott* (who made her monument in Frome church). – Emily, Countess of Cork, †1912. Jade cross on mother-of-pearl framed in alabaster.

MARSTON HOUSE. The extended ashlar façade overlooks a landscaped park with a stretch of water in the distance, a perfect Georgian picture, although the story is more complicated and the architecture better at a distance. A Jacobean house with cross-wings enclosing stair-towers was built for John Symes (cf. Poundisford Park). Bought in 1641 by Richard Boyle, Earl of Cork, it became the principal seat of the Earls of Cork and Orrery until 1906. The Symes house may not have been symmetrical, as it was reputedly made so with a wing after 1713 for the 4th Earl of Orrery. By the time it was first illustrated in 1739 the house was in outline as now, with hipped roofs behind parapets. The present details date, however, from 1750–2, by an otherwise unknown London architect, *James*

Scott, with the 5th Earl's heir, *Charles Boyle*, then aged 21. Balustrades replaced parapets, sash windows in architraves with keystones replaced leaded windows, and a terrace obscured the basement. In 1776 *Samuel Wyatt* lengthened the front to 365 ft (111 metres) in twenty-seven bays, with low wings of 3–1–3–1 bays, pedimented accents dividing dissimilar sections. The W wing had private rooms, the E wing kitchen and offices. Alterations in 1800–1 included a corridor behind Wyatt's E range. In 1820 an Ionic loggia was added to the centre with pilastered porches in the re-entrant angles, probably by *Jeffry Wyatt (Wyatville)*. In 1857–8 the 9th Earl reversed the house, adding a monumental entrance hall and staircase by *C. E. Davis*, a young relative of Edward Davis. C. E. Davis also built or rebuilt stables E of Samuel Wyatt's E wing before 1864 and remodelled Wyatt's W range after 1866 for a billiard room and ballroom, losing the overall symmetry by removing the outer pavilion. Finally, in 1872 a giant conservatory was added to the W end, presumably by Davis. Derelict by the 1970s, the house was rescued by John and Angela Yeoman, owners of nearby stone quarries, and repaired by *Geoffrey Butcher* of Warminster, 1984–90.

Davis's single-storey entrance hall with a tall pedimented doorway fronts his three-storey stair hall, externally sober Neo-Georgian. A giant lantern lights the entrance hall, carried on four arches stretching from trios of columns. The front and back arches are elliptical, the back one apparently carrying several storeys of masonry. Neo-Elizabethan wooden chimneypieces under the side windows were replaced by classical stone ones after 1984. Spectacular stone stairs worthy of a Continental opera house. One flight descends to the basement between cantilevered flights to a rear landing. Above these float two more cantilevered flights and another landing, their access concealed behind the side walls. Opulent cast-iron balusters to the flights, Rococo wrought-iron on the landings, generically C18, wholly Victorian.

Reversing the house has made a basement of the principal rooms, the stairs descending to a passage behind them added by *Davis*. The original rooms are mostly plain, simplified since Collinson described them in 1791. The drawing room in the W cross-wing has an Adamesque ceiling of 1801 of no particular quality, but the square chamber off it has similar ornament better used in a shallow cross-vault. *Samuel Wyatt*'s LIBRARY, just W, is the best surviving room. White and gold bookcases in serpentine curves are framed in thin fluted columns. Fluted frieze, and fluted chimneypiece under a pedimented picture-frame overmantel. Davis's BILLIARD ROOM adjoins, notable for pull-down maps recessed in the panelling. His lavish BALLROOM has a high coved ceiling and ornament of all periods: cornice with lush fruit, Rococo festoons in the wall panels, strapwork in the ceiling. It opens to the CONSERVATORY, of even greater height, its curved glass and giant pedimented elliptical arches facing W and S reminiscent of railway architecture.

The PARK was landscaped for the 7th Earl in the 1770s. Formal gardens depicted in 1739, on which *Stephen Switzer* was employed *c.* 1720–40, have gone apart from terracing (built in 1733) above the house and a rockwork GROTTO above that, of 1743, by *James Scott*. Domed ICE HOUSE nearby, by Weighbridge Lodge. E of the house, at HOME FARM, a huge late C18 WALLED GARDEN extends behind a substantial hip-roofed house, intended for the head gardener. In front is LADY CORK'S BATH, *c.* 1740, a small pool backed by an open-pedimented entry to a now-roofless chamber. Low rockwork walls flank the pool. MARSTON POND, the 20-acre lake, was created by the 8th Earl, *c.* 1825. Three lodges were added, probably by *Edward Davis*, in the 1830s. CHURCH LODGE, 1834, once thatched, and WEIGHBRIDGE LODGE, two-storeyed, are cottage-style; MARSTON LODGE is pyramid-roofed. On the main road just W, PARK COTTAGE, the late C18 Marston Inn, later the steward's house.

To the SW is the OLD RECTORY, 1836–9 by *Edward Davis*, an intriguing villa in a stripped Italianate style. A loose agglomeration turns on a pyramid-roofed lantern. Venetian first-floor loggia without mouldings, on the garden front. This loggia feature is used by Davis at Oakwood, Bath, 1833. Grecian plasterwork and an impressive stair hall with an Ionic screen to a cantilevered stone stair. S of the park, MARSTON MAINS, a model farm on Scottish principles of *c.* 1860. In Lower Marston, the former SCHOOL, 1857, by *C. E. Davis*, is fanciful Gothic, the little house with an octagonal roof. Outside, ELEANOR'S WELL, a Gothic well-head, 1852. By *Eleanor Boyle* (cf. the church windows), whose books paid for the water supply.

THE GRANGE, Tytherington. Long C17 farmhouse with a newel stair in a rear stair-tower. Dated 1661 with initials of Robert Bisse in plasterwork upstairs. Attached early C18 barn at right angles.

MARSTON MAGNA

ST MARY. The chancel is Norman, see the broad clasping buttresses, herringbone masonry on the N side, and two narrow N windows, the second visible inside. Above the chancel arch are two re-set C11 or C12 window heads. The E end has a restored triplet of small C13 lancets. Perp W tower with Ham stone SE stair-turret. Battlements and W window decorated with roses. The tower arch looks C14 but may be later, double-chamfered on broad half-octagonal piers. The nave, S porch and N chantry chapel are C14–C15 – see the wave-moulded doorways. The position of the N and S doorways close to the W end makes it likely that the nave extended further W and that its W bay was replaced by the tower. There is, however, no change of style between nave and tower. Luminous interior, carefully restored in 1902 by *C. E. Ponting*. His is the tie-beam nave roof. Wave-moulded chancel arch without capitals. The N chapel arch also wave-moulded, but on thick shafts with joined rounded capitals. The adjoining door was external, indicating that the chapel is added. In the chapel, a GALLERY reached from a mural stair. It rests on a simple Perp SCREEN. Also C15 WALL PAINTING on the N wall, of the murder of Becket, and a canopied niche. – FONT. Very good C12. Tapered and fluted, each scallop with carving, under a ring of pellets. Late C20 beaten metal cover. – PULPIT. Nice plain C18 piece with ogee tester. – PEWS and poppyhead STALLS by *Ponting*. – STAINED GLASS. Some C15 bits in one nave S and two chancel windows.

The long MANOR HOUSE has four- and five-light ovolo-moulded mullion windows irregularly grouped under hoodmoulds. A rear sundial is dated 1613. Elegant moulded C17 beams, W, chamfered framed ceilings centre and E. At the E some timber framing indicates a re-cased earlier house. The narrow E tower may have been its garderobe. On the main road, WICKHAM FARM, with a Georgian upper floor over C17 mullioned windows and Tudor-arched doorway. MARSTON COURT to the S has an early C17 N range attached to a mullion-windowed house of 1927 with battlemented pieces. NE of the church, the former SCHOOL, 1841, with porch bellcote, at right angles to its Georgian Gothic predecessor. Further N is a brick Gothic METHODIST CHAPEL, 1882, dwarfed by twin porches. On the Rimpton road, STUDLEYS FARMHOUSE, thatched with C17 mullioned windows. On the S side, an L-plan C18 WATER MILL in brick and stone. Further out, MARSTON HOUSE has a late C18 five-bay front of White Lias with Ham stone pedimented doorcase and architraves.

MOATED SITE, S of the church. Moated earthworks probably of a manor house of *c.* 1300. They appear to have been reused as a formal garden for Marston Court (*see* above), across Garston Lane.

NETHER ADBER, ¾ m. SW. The site of the DESERTED MEDIEVAL VILLAGE extends over two fields. Manor house, chapel and fishponds lay in the northern field, damaged by agricultural improvement. In the southern field large hollows show the lines of streets meeting at a triangular green. Overgrown walls of some of the latest houses around the green are also clear. By the mid C16 only one person was recorded here.

MARTOCK

A small town with particularly good buildings of Ham stone, testimony to rich agriculture. Described in 1633 as 'seated in the fattest place of the Earth of this Countie'.

MARTOCK

ALL SAINTS. One of the loveliest of Somerset churches, on account of the splendid Perp work on the nave. The earliest surviving element is the chancel of c. 1300 with five stepped E lancets each under its own hoodmould outside, but all under one rere-arch inside. Small lancet in the gable. Short buttresses at the angles. The rest is Perp, but the ghost of a large cruciform C13 church can be discerned, probably with a crossing tower. The W tower is big if not special in design. Two-light paired bell-openings and battlements with big corner pinnacles. Set-back buttresses reach the top of the bell-stage. The stair clasped between the NW buttresses. No link to the pinnacles. W door between triangular shafts, not integrated with the very large transomed five-light W window. Much bare wall to the sides. A two-light window on the S beneath the bell-stage. The beauty of Martock is the lacy pierced embattled parapet of the early C16 clerestory rising above plainer battlements of the C15 aisles and chancel chapels, all with finely traceried four-light Perp windows. Octagonal rood turret, N side. The S porch could be late C14. Contrastingly severe, storeyed, with a small two-light parvise window and cusped niche. Inside a star-vault enriched with bosses resting on head corbels. A wide bay marks the former transepts. The chancel chapels have pinnacles as on the tower. The chancel then projects two bays beyond with Perp side windows, but a steep roof to the C13 pitch.

The interior is remarkably airy and spacious. Six-bay arcades, not too high, the piers of standard four-hollow section. Spandrels with blank tracery, an East Anglian motif unique in Somerset. They are divided by panelled shafts on angel corbels up to a cornice with angel bosses. Above, between the clerestory windows, are elaborate canopied niches, intended for statues but painted in the C17 with figures of the Apostles. More angels support brackets to the ceiling. Dated 1513 on a detached panel, the ceiling is of the best type developed in Somerset. Of moderate pitch, with embattled tie-beams carrying kingposts. Angels face out in both directions from the middle of each tie-beam and tracery fills the side spaces. Slight intermediate trusses carry big pendants. The panelling is the glory of the ceiling: each bay has four panels on each slope, divided by a massive moulded purlin, each panel subdivided into sixteen, 736 in all, in six different patterns. An elaborately panelled W arch comes forward into the nave. Its sides are the eastern buttresses of the tower (cf. Kingsbury Episcopi), ornamented with tiers of statue niches. The roof-line before the clerestory addition is visible. The aisles have wall-shafts. In the S aisle a tomb-recess. Above the chancel arch, rough older masonry and two statue niches. The chancel chapels have two-bay arcades, a little lower than those of the nave but of the same detail. Chancel roof of *Ewan Christian*'s 1883 restoration. In 1860–1 *Benjamin Ferrey* removed a huge classical reredos to reopen the E windows.

FURNISHINGS. FONT. Perp, octagonal, with paired cusped vesica shapes. Underside panels continuous with the stem. – PULPIT. Stone, 1883. – SCREENS. SE chapel, 1919, by *F. B. Bond*. Tower, 1980s, by *Gerald Beech*. – SCULPTURE. St Thomas, N aisle, 2004, by *Tom Clark*, charming Eric Gill style. – STAINED GLASS. E window, 1872, very good, probably by *Clayton & Bell*. Some C15 fragments in the NE vestry. – MONUMENTS. S aisle. Eroded early C14 effigy of a lady. – John Rice †1747. Columned with curved pediment. – Robert Chaffey †1845. Broken column for a truncated life, by *Lewis* of Cheltenham. – Wood family to 1788. Grey and white marble, with draped urn. – N aisle. Harriott Leighton †1782. Amply draped urn. – William Cole †1781. Mourner and urn, over-ambitious for the sculptor. – NE vestry. Rev. T. Bowyer †1763. Encomium of his piety.

The large churchyard has two arched C17 GATEWAYS with obelisks, dated 1625 and 1627, and a Celtic cross WAR MEMORIAL, a quirky late work by *Henry Wilson*, 1921. – Two C13 grave-slabs by the tower S wall.

METHODIST CHAPEL, North Street. 1886, by *Alexander Lauder*. Eccentric Gothic, especially the needle spire ringed with gargoyles. It is a reduced version of his South Petherton chapel of 1881–2 (q.v.).

TREASURER'S HOUSE (National Trust), opposite the church. So called because the Treasurer of Wells held the rectory. As an important official he would rarely have been resident. The precinct was walled, with an entrance arch of which one jamb remains next to the two-centred pedestrian archway. A gatehouse is mentioned in 1479. The house consists of a large hall range at right angles to an apparently earlier storeyed cross-wing, the whole mid-C13 to mid-C14. Work on a new hall is recorded in 1293–4 but the hall looks later than that. Its long transomed N window of two cinquefoil-cusped lights and a quatrefoil may be mid-C14. The windows on the E and W sides are similarly transomed with cusped lights, but have flat heads and incised spandrels. All have cinquefoiled rere-arches. Handsome late C15 roof of moulded arch-braced collar-trusses with tiered wind-bracing in alternate patterns. Unusually a doorway leads straight from the hall into the garden, next to that at the end of the screens passage. The lack of heating, there being neither fireplace nor smoke-blackening, suggests intermittent, official, use. Perhaps there was another hall in the wing. Two brattished Perp consoles for lamps.

The cross-wing is of *c.* 1250–60 – see the plate-traceried W window of two trefoil-cusped lights and a quatrefoil. This lit a first-floor solar of which only the W bay remains open. But this is a wonderful survival. The W wall is painted as masonry, with a Crucifixion with the Virgin and St John in characteristic poses of the C13. The masonry lines sprout tiny roses and harebells and a vine-trail follows the roof-line. The window mullion has bosses pierced for shutter-rods. Remarkably the windows were glazed. Another Perp lamp console. On the S

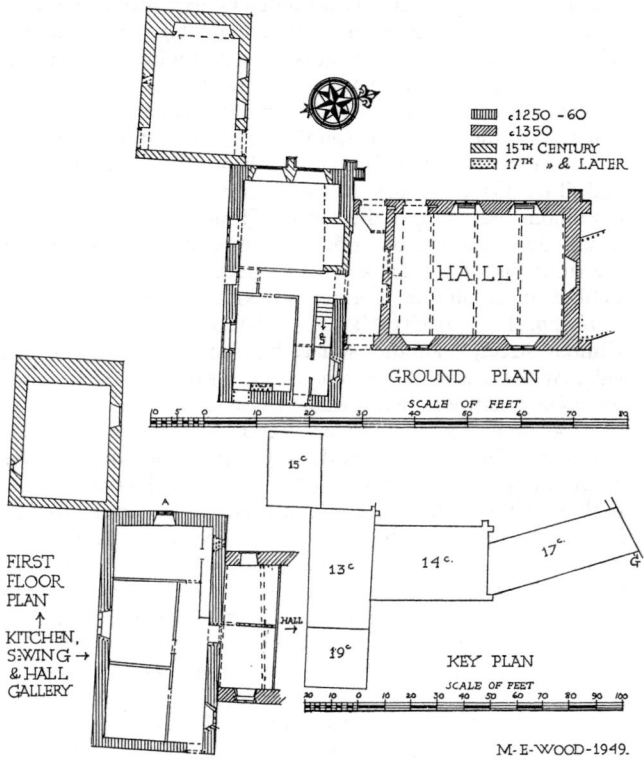

Martock, The Treasurer's House.
Plan drawn by Margaret Wood, 1949

wall a blocked doorway which opened to a wing or perhaps a garderobe. In the late C15 the roof was replaced and the floor raised, a parlour being inserted below with moulded framed ceiling and two cusped and mullioned W windows. Nearly detached SW kitchen with C15 triangular doorheads and window heads; massive Tudor-arched fireplace.

PERAMBULATION. The churchyard lies at the bend of CHURCH STREET opposite the Treasurer's House. S of the church, ASHLAR HOUSE has a five-bay early C18 front with curved-pedimented doorcase and channelled outer pilasters. Contemporary staircase. W down Pound Lane, on a moated site, was what may have been the medieval manor house. A gabled piece remains with corner garderobe turret and corbelled side chimney (1659 datestone) attached to the modern MOAT HOUSE. Across Church Street from Ashlar House, PATTENDEN was the vicarage, c. 1820, square, hip-roofed, with the side entry common to early C19 parsonages. COURT HOUSE, on the W side, a particularly splendid late C15 church house, became the Grammar School in 1661, commemorated by a plaque: 'Schola Trilinguis Trin-unideo Gloria' and the name of God in Hebrew, Greek and Latin. Eight bays of mullioned windows with four-centred lights. Low ground floor. N parlour with four-centred-arched fireplace and C15 moulded framed ceiling, s kitchen with full-width chimney beam. Stair on the rear wall to the first floor, spiral stair to the loft at the N end. C17 collar-trusses. The Gothic woodwork is a modern insertion. THE GRANGE has an ashlar front of *c.* 1760–80 with modillions like those of the Market House and a striking rusticated doorcase. The outer bays are the ends of rear wings, for the house is of U-plan and C17 (mullioned rear windows). Behind it is another former VICARAGE, 1874, by *Ewan Christian*. The DOCTOR'S OLD HOUSE, on the E side of Church Street, is another square hip-roofed early to mid-C19 villa. At the s end of Church Street, BRIDGE HOUSE has a hip-roofed centre between lean-to sides and corner chimneys like footstool legs. The curved E end has Venetian windows, one above the other. These look Georgian but the site was empty in 1839. WATER STREET runs W past BROOKLANDS, mullion-windowed, of *c.* 1700, and No. 55, Victorian Tudor, built for the owner of the three-storey glove factory at the end. This is now HURSTBOW HOUSE, early C19.

Returning to the churchyard, the street widens northward to become the typical market place of a little town. On the E side, the former SCHOOL, 1846, Perp Gothic with cast-iron windows, and the GEORGE INN, an early C19 refronting of a C16 building. Early C18 assembly room behind. The GOSPEL HALL, 1893, and PUBLIC HALL, 1888, both by *William Sparrow*, local engineer, follow. THE PHARMACY, three-storey and hip-roofed, *c.* 1850, fronts THE CHANTRY, a low range with a C14 pointed-arched doorway inside and wind-braced collar-trusses. It was possibly the priest's house of a chantry established in 1325. After a C17 row, the MANOR HOUSE, a tall L-plan house with steep dormer gables more typical of North Somerset, one dated 1679. Much C19 rebuilding. Outbuildings interestingly adapted. The service range now has early C19 deep eaves and cast-iron lattice windows. An early C18 lofted stable behind became the fire station, and a range with matching cross-windows is now a house. On the W side of the street, CHURCH LODGE, large and stately with coved eaves, was probably rebuilt for himself by *William Wadman*, *c.* 1830, from a C16–C17 house partly surviving to the l. Coachhouse and stables to the N before KNUSTON LODGE, Late Georgian, three bays. The medieval market place is marked by the base of the market cross, now carrying the PINNACLE, a fluted Roman Doric column with a cube sundial dated 1741. It stands in front of a neat ashlar MARKET HOUSE, called newly built in the 1780s, typically with a meeting room over an arcaded market. Elliptical arches, first-floor Venetian window at the s end, and modillion cornice. Community office inserted 2007–9 by *Benjamin & Beauchamp* of Wedmore. One side faces the WHITE HART, a three-storey ashlar-fronted coaching inn, rebuilt 1827, the rounded POST OFFICE added for the London mail.

Beyond a small triangular green, EAST STREET has intermittent early farmhouses. MOOLHAM, of fine ashlar, has late C17 mullioned windows. BYRON HOUSE, also mullioned, was extended E in the 1770s, seamlessly. YEWS FARM began as an early C14 hall house, of the width and nearly the height of the present house (one smoke-blackened full cruck and wind-bracing). Centrepiece of a C17 canted bay under a corbelled gable, typical of the region. Early C17 framed ceiling. Opposite, MARFLEET HOUSE, an early to mid-C19 hip-roofed villa. At the far end, in fields, MADEY MILL is C17, with an internal C19 waterwheel.

Now N from the Market House. Horribly encompassed amid the Ashfield Park houses is ASHFIELD, a large ashlar villa of c. 1845, Grecian thickened to Victorian Italianate. Bowed centrepiece between wings with giant panelled pilasters. Bowed veranda on matching panelled piers. Painful N front, with a well-detailed Greek entrance (columns *in antis* under an elliptical arch) set in an off-centre tower with panelled pilasters and a pediment set against a heavy attic. On NORTH STREET, MOORLANDS HOUSE is more purely Greek, c. 1820–30, square, with Doric columns in a beautifully worked entrance niche. ROWLEYS is C17 with a continuous hoodmould. C19 terraces with some earlier survivors run N past the Methodist chapel (p. 428). To the W on COAT ROAD, the RAILWAY HOTEL, built after the opening of the line to Yeovil, 1853. The form, a centre block between parallel ranges, echoes that of Bridge House. Just E is NEWTOWN, early council housing of c. 1914 by *Petter & Warren*. First with shallow hipped roofs, as at West Coker (q.v.), then two cottage terraces behind of their earliest, Montacute, type. They also designed the hip-roofed houses of the 1920s on the S side. A formal group of this type is STEPPES CRESCENT, E of North Street.

STAPLETON, 1 m. N. Two substantial houses. STAPLETON FARMHOUSE, thatched with mullioned windows, has a chimney dated 1688. The canted bay with corbelled gable is typical of Bower Hinton (q.v.), whence indeed it came in the C20. C16 chamfered-framed ceiling, but jointed crucks from a C15 hall house. In the corner of a BARN opposite, a piece of a C14–C15 cross-head. STAPLETON MANOR is ashlar-faced and hip-roofed of 1825.

COAT, 1 m. NW. A hamlet of good Ham stone C17 farmhouses. COAT FARMHOUSE has a Regency front but is otherwise mullion-windowed. LITTLE COAT HOUSE has a long, irregular mullioned front, and COAT HOUSE has wings extending forward and back. MANOR FARMHOUSE has another of the canted gabled bays (cf. Stapleton Farmhouse). GREYSTONE HOUSE has a late C17 continuous drip-course.

ROMAN PILLAR. A 4-ft (1.2-metre) pillar now in the Museum of Somerset was found at Venn Bridge, 1 m. WSW. Inscribed to Severus II, Emperor 306–7, it may have been a boundary stone.

MAUNSEL HOUSE see ST MICHAEL CHURCH

MEARE

A low island in the levels of the River Brue. Just N was a large lake, drained after the C16, the circumference of which was reportedly five miles. The lake was in the keeping of the abbots of Glastonbury, whose summer palace was between the church and the house of their water-bailiff.

ST MARY AND ALL SAINTS. Dedicated in 1323, a date that may refer to the present chancel and W tower. The chancel especially is interesting with its three-light E window, the tracery of which has decidedly no longer the poise of the Geometrical, but does not yet introduce flowing or ogee forms either. Three lancet lights of which the middle is lower, and above them a spheric lozenge subdivided into two trefoils. The other chancel windows are two-light, two with a spheric triangle in plate tracery, and one, now internal, with more flowing tracery. The chancel roof, like a secular hall roof (and very like the chancel at Street), has tie-beam and queenpost principals, arch-braced-collar sub-principals, and cusped wind-braces. The tower is unbuttressed, and the broad wave-and-roll mouldings of its arch look early C14. An ashlar C15 octagonal S stair-turret partly covers one bell-light. Ashlar battlements. Of the C14 nave the heavily moulded S doorway remains, and, re-set in the porch, a DOOR with the most florid ironwork in the county, large and flowing fronds issuing out of a kind of cuff (similar ironwork at Sharpham Park, q.v.).* The aisles and clerestory are late C15, added under Abbot Selwood (†1493) and Abbot Bere (†1524). Selwood's initials appear on the SE aisle parapet. The detail is good, though the aisle parapets, pierced in cusped lozenges, are otherwise largely removed. Three-light windows with finely cusped ogee-headed lights. Clerestory with three-light windows and plain parapet. Three-bay arcades of the usual details, slightly different N and S. Robust moulded framed nave roof, the ridge beam particularly large, with two bosses, one a rose. Arched braces on shield-bearing angel corbels, a SE one with Abbot Bere's arms. Similar angels with original colour carry the aisle roofs. One shield in the S aisle exceptionally names the carpenter, '*John Jacman* made ye rof'. Broad and lower chancel arch on angel capitals, offset to the r. for a squint. Ogee-cusped PISCINA, interestingly canted back in its surround. Vestry of 1823.

---

* Long proposed as C14, but Jane Geddes has suggested the late C15.

FURNISHINGS. FONT. Early C14. A series of deep, heavy mouldings on the octagonal bowl and base, much more indented than the similar Westonzoyland font. – PULPIT. A rare C15 stone one. Blind two-light tracery with ogee heads and small spandrel leaves. Fleurons in the frieze. – POOR-BOX. Resting on an unrelated C16 square oak stand, panelled between twisted shafts. – CHANDELIER. 1777. Brass, two-tier, Bridgwater-made. – ROYAL ARMS. 1840. – STAINED GLASS. Medieval fragments in the N aisle tracery. Chancel side windows, c. 1871, by *C. A. Gibbs*. SE, 1887, signed *E. Frampton*. – MONUMENTS. William Moore †1688 and Anthony Elliott †1707. Lias floor slabs.

In the churchyard, the C15 VILLAGE CROSS, moved here in 1887.

INDEPENDENT CHAPEL, Church Path. 1861–2. Polychrome brick Gothic chapel and house with hefty detail. Punched rose window over a porch with large leaf capitals.

SCHOOL, 1840, opposite the church. Blue Lias, two-storeyed, with an acutely gabled bellcote on the eaves. Further back, a polychrome brick GIRLS' SCHOOL by *Joseph Day* of Glastonbury, 1876. W of the church, the WAR MEMORIAL, 1921, is still Victorian Gothic. Church Path runs W to the chapel (above). On the main road beyond, THE LAKES, stuccoed and hiproofed, the former rectory of 1826. THE ROWANS is similar, but in Blue Lias. Then GREAT HOUSE, a three-storey villa typical of Bath, *c.* 1820, ashlar-fronted with cornice and parapet, divided by bands and pilaster strips. Iron trellis porch. MEARE MANOR is mostly late C19 Gothic, but the W end with an unmoulded Venetian window on each floor is early C19.

MANOR FARM, E of the church. A summer palace of the Glastonbury abbots, built *c.* 1325 for Abbot Adam de Sodbury. Lias and roughcast. L-shaped now, but presumably once larger, as the agricultural buildings to the W include a good moulded pointed doorway, *in situ* or reused. Principal rooms on the first floor, early for this transition. A hall in the N–S range may have had a private chamber at the S end. The front E–W range contained the chapel, indicated by the buttresses, three blocked

Meare, Manor Farm, from the north east.
Engraving after A. Nesbitt, 1859

pointed windows E of the storeyed porch, and a large E window, blocked for a corbelled chimney. The porch may be early C17, of a date with mullion windows inserted in both floors. The finial figure of an abbot and the head of the porch upper window are reused. The main roofs are replaced, a hipped SW corner substituting for the S gable of the hall range.

The chapel became a chamber in the C15, with a big lateral chimney on the N wall and handsome fireplace with shields in octofoils. (C14 wall painting of repetitive rosettes.) A pointed doorway with moulded over-arch leads into the hall. Although the roof is changed this remains an impressive room, 60 ft (18 metres) long, of five bays, with tall and exceptionally beautiful two-light windows, two to the E, one, blocked, to the W, and a much longer N end one with a transom. All have cinquefoil-cusped rere-arches and ogee-headed lights. The mullions have bosses pierced for shutter-rods (cf. the Treasurer's House, Martock). In the second bay is a particularly fine hooded chimneypiece, the hood not flat-faced but canted, carried on jowled uprights between lamp brackets. These are round capitals on delicate leaf sprays. The position makes it uncertain if the fireplace served the hall or a S chamber. If the latter, the remaining hall would have been unheated; if the former, the hall was exceptionally grand, with a fireplace below a S dais and outside stairs at the NW corner for general access. The ground floors are not vaulted and there is no obvious C14 kitchen, so the use remains uncertain. A blocked pointed arch and a wider segmental-pointed arch link the two ground floors.

FISH HOUSE. Gloriously alone in a field. A compact medieval house for the bailiff who managed the fishery, built, like Manor Farm, by Abbot Adam de Sodbury (1323–54). It is mentioned in 1344. A plain oblong, three rooms on the ground floor, not vaulted, and unconnected with the upper floor, which was reached by outside stairs. Both floors were heated. First-floor hall and bedchamber each indicated by a gable-end two-light Dec window. These are, as at Manor Farm, precursors of C15 first-floor halls. The bedchamber had a garderobe turret, known from C19 illustrations, as is the lost roof of arch-braced collar-trusses with wind-braces. Plain ashlar fireplace on the S wall. Kitchen fireplace below and twin doorways to the buttery and pantry.

LAKE VILLAGES, ½ m. WNW. Nothing remains visible of two excavated villages. They differed from that at Glastonbury, being built in a significantly drier but still boggy location, and not appearing to have supported any permanent settlement. Clay was imported to make floors on the raised bog surface, and some timber for temporary shelters. The site appears to have specialized in the production of woven braids and is one of the few places in Europe where Iron Age glass production is known. Beads made at Meare have been found as far away as the north of Scotland. Founded about a hundred years before Glastonbury, *c.* 300 B.C., both sites seem to have been abandoned *c.* 50 B.C. as the water level rose.

WESTHAY, 1½ m. w. On the junction, CROSS FARMHOUSE, externally nondescript, was an early C16 hall house. Giant leaves are painted on the early C17 screen. Large moulded fireplace.

MERRIOTT

ALL SAINTS. It is the tower that is remarkable, its sides subtly incurved, unadorned, and finished with a parapet. This is so untypical of Somerset as to give rise to the suggestion that the tower is incomplete. But it is hard to imagine a bell-stage above those sloping upper walls. Rennie Mackintosh imitated the distinctive shape at Queen's Cross Church, Glasgow, 1897. Probably late C14 despite the double-chamfer tower arch. Perp w doorway with high-relief spandrel leaves beneath a deep-set w window. The octagonal stair-turret with battlemented and pinnacled crown adds a welcome flourish, set centrally on the show s side, as at Wellington. Ashlar embattled aisles with spacious three-light Perp windows. Embattled s porch with a pinnacled niche. In the porch a C14 cinquefoiled niche beneath a square plaque with encircled and intensely cusped six-pointed star. Good and quite tall Perp arcades on standard (four-hollow) piers. The fourth bay is a good copy by *Benjamin Ferrey*, 1861–2, who added a triple-roofed E end in High Victorian taste, the arcade columns ringed by Purbeck marble shafts with naturalistic capitals. Ferrey's nave trusses have giant traceried circles. – FONT and PULPIT. 1861. – LECTERN. 1883. High Victorian Gothic, oak and brass. – CHANDELIER. 1793. – CARVINGS. A remarkable C12 relief of birds fighting beneath a sheep and a comet. Also a primitive Crucifixion carved on to the head of a churchyard cross. – STAINED GLASS. E window, 1861, by *Lavers & Barraud*. The similar NE window and more striking SE with emerald greens perhaps also by then. – MONUMENTS. Patrick Roche †1712. Rustic cartouche by *Parsons* of Tetbury. – Three in good marble pedimented frames: Robert England †1742, Mary Rodbard †1733, and Mary Rodbard †1745.

Opposite the church, former VICARAGE, mostly 1852, by *Maurice Davis*, and modest TITHE BARN, partly old (see the chamfered jambs), recast as the church hall. Plain Tudor CHURCH SCHOOL, 1834, and Gothic BOARD SCHOOL, 1876, with complex unmoulded tracery. Going E, the KINGS ARMS is C17, mullioned, with a shallow two-storey bay. On Lower Street, to the s, a small gabled late C18 LOCK-UP, stone-roofed, with a tiny barred window over the iron-studded door. MERRIOTT HOUSE, set back, has a mid-C19 ashlar front with parapet. C18 brick STABLE. Opposite the lane to Tail Mill (below), an Italianate former CONGREGATIONAL CHAPEL, 1878, and Tudor-style INSTITUTE, 1884, for the mill employees. Several houses beyond show how late classical conventions came to the villages. No. 69, dated 1729, is entirely in the convention of the previous century, but on the ground floor with a continuous drip-course that rises over the doorhead. THE GIRDLERS opposite, dated 1766, still has mullioned horizontal windows, now framed in C18 architraves. BANBURY FARMHOUSE has ovolo-moulded mullions, but elongated, i.e. after 1700. MANOR FARMHOUSE, 1663, the earliest dated house, is entirely Jacobean in its motifs, featuring the canted bay with corbelled gable found around Martock. No. 28 has early C19 flush mullions. For Georgian sash windows one must look at the Regency brick front of No. 14 and at MOORLANDS FARMHOUSE, across the main road, which is refronted.

MOORLANDS, ¼ m. W. 1852. Tudor Gothic. Multiple gables, battlements, and multiple octagonal chimneys. Much carving: tiny knights on the gable shoulders and finial beasts flying metal flags marked C (for Mr Cuff, the owner). Thin porch-tower with a triangular oriel, fancy gargoyles etc. The architect, surprisingly, was *G. G. Scott*.

SHUTTEROAKS, 1 m. SW. Late C17, with stone cross-windows on both floors.

MERRIOTT COURT (Marks Barn), 1 m. SSW. 1891, by *Charles Kirk* of Sleaford. Framed by gables, a little bleak. Plate-glass sash windows in roll-moulded surrounds.

TAIL MILL, ¾ m. SE. Richard Hayward, sailcloth maker, came here *c.* 1825. He introduced steam power as early as 1836, gas lighting by 1844, and employed 132 by 1851. Big seven-bay four-floor warehouse at the S. Single-storey mill at right angles raised on a basement with iron pillars. The tall arch marks the site of the beam-engine. Single-storey weaving sheds.

LOWER SEVERALLS FARMHOUSE, 1½ m. SE. Long mullion-windowed C17 front with a first-floor oriel.

MID LAMBROOK

MIDDLE LAMBROOK MEETING. Ashlar-fronted chapel dated 1729. Two large arched windows with mullions and transom between segment-headed doorways. Interior of evocative simplicity, with crowded woodwork. Three-sided gallery fronted in large painted-grained panels over fielded-panelled box pews and small pulpit. Splendid clock of 1734. Worn stone stairs to the gallery, which has crude benches. THE COTTAGE, just S, C16–C17, has unusually long windows, a seven-light stone-mullioned one below an eight-light wooden casement.

MANOR HOUSE. The principal feature is a lavish two-storey Perp porch with diagonal buttresses, moulded doorway, three-light windows, and a parapet pierced with quatrefoils that rises slightly, following the pitch of the roof. It stands central to a large and much-restored house. Renewed mullioned windows with curved-headed lights as on the porch. Rear wing continued as an impressively high C19 lofted barn.

MIDDLE CHINNOCK

ST MARGARET. Low Perp W tower, battlemented, with short and broad battlemented N stair-turret. The W doorway hoodmould has tiny angel figures. Tower arch of three thin continuous ribs. The cruciform church is C19 apart from the S porch and doorway. Transepts added in 1837, everything redone 1867–87 by *J. M. Allen*: nave roof 1871, chancel 1874, transepts 1887. The porch has half-octagonal C14 piers and an extraordinary hollowed C17 SUNDIAL (cf. Tintinhull). The W bench within incorporates a cusped canopy over an eroded bust of a priest. Ham stone, C13–C14, inserted here perhaps as a mark of humility. The elaborate if inartistic Norman S doorway has vertical chevron to the jambs and vertical beaded chevron across the lintel, under a fish-scale tympanum with interlaced beaded ribbon under the arch. Outer order of fat chevron. Norman fragments in the N walls. – FONT. C12. Tapered, with a beaded wavy band, a leaf in each undulation (cf. Stocklinch Ottersey). – PULPIT. C18. Fielded panels. – ROYAL ARMS. 1660.

One downhill street. The OLD RECTORY, with C17 mullioned windows, was enlarged before 1800. TWINDOWN MEAD on the roadside is extremely pretty, thatched, with mullioned windows and small stone oriel, C16. CHINNOCK HOUSE opposite is square and hip-roofed, 1830s, with large sash windows. The lovely MANOR FARMHOUSE has been reduced, but the early C17 r. part was never more than a single room on each floor. Diagonal chimneys bestride the S gable. The front has an off-centre gable, a cornice with Jacobean fluting, and ovolo-ogee mullions. Solid oak spiral staircase in a rear stair-tower. The lower l. block was C16 – see the buttress and different mullions – but was rebuilt with a Late Georgian hipped roof.

MIDDLEZOY

The middle of the three Zoyland villages.

HOLY CROSS. Blue Lias. Perp W tower of the more elaborate type, very like that at Lyng, and similar to the richer one at Westonzoyland. Angle buttresses connected by a diagonal fillet end in tall diagonally set shafts with pinnacles. Battlements with pierced quatrefoils and pinnacles set diagonally at the angles. Higher polygonal NE stair-turret. Three stages: W window of four lights, then a two-light window with pierced baffles between niches, and then twin two-light bell-openings with pierced baffles, flanked by three thin shafts with pinnacles. Inside, the tower arch is tall and panelled with small angel busts at the springing of the arch. A fan-vault was begun but not continued. The outer buttresses are caught up by two larger angel busts.

The nave N windows, the N transept and the W bay of the S aisle are Perp. But the chancel and the rest of the aisle are C13 to early C14. The earliest part seems to be the aisle. The masonry is banded in greenish sandstone, the buttresses are gabled. Both S windows are C13, plate-traceried, two-light, with differing roundels. In the r. window a twelve-petal flower, in the other a quatrefoil. The r. window has a shafted reveal. The aisle E window with reticulated tracery of *c.* 1330 appears inserted (reused inside out). Double-chamfered S doorway, under a plainly trefoiled niche of *c.* 1300. The big porch is early too, from the banded masonry, chamfered doorway and a roundel above, although the roof is C15.

The chancel has (renewed) N and S windows with typical tracery of *c.* 1300, two lancet lights with trefoils above them and a quatrefoil under the main arch. E window of the same type, but of four lights, each delicately cinquefoil-cusped with a trefoil above, leaving room for a quatrefoil above each pair and a culminating large seven-foiled shape. This is tracery of quality and excellently preserved. The S side has notably fine headstops in grey Lias. Chamfered rere-arches inside and also a cusped PISCINA, with the top cusp slightly ogee-shaped. C15 panelled chancel arch and restored C15 chancel roof.

Perp arcade of five bays with standard four-hollow shafted piers. Arch to the NE chapel of the same design. Ceiled wagon roof in the nave, the celure above the former rood emphasized by pendants, instead of bosses. Little angels along the wall-plate. The S aisle has a crudely made lean-to roof. One reused boldly cusped piece with a carved head on the cusp suggests that the aisle had a steep roof, flattened in the C15–C16 or as late as 1732 (date on the lead). Three corbel heads of *c.* 1300. Ogee-headed PISCINA. Repairs 1839–48, restored 1863–4 by *Charles Knowles*.

FURNISHINGS. FONT. Octagonal, Perp, with square quatre-foils. Panelled underside and stem. C17 flat COVER with acorn. – ROOD SCREEN. Of *c.* 1500, similar to the screen at High Ham. Tall, of four-light sections divided by a thick centre mullion up to the apex of the arch. Vertical mullions also divide the resulting two-light tracery. Transom bar with fleurons and the barley rebus of Richard Bere, Abbot of Glastonbury 1493–1524. Blind tracery to the dado panels. The coving is not preserved. Fragments of cornice on the back have the crowned olive-tree rebus of Oliver King, Bishop of Bath and Wells 1495–1503. – TOWER SCREEN. 1679. Utilitarian. Plank-and-muntin below, vertically symmetrical balusters above. – PULPIT. 1606. The usual blank arches in two tiers. – BENCH-ENDS. A very extensive early C16 series, largely with inventive flowing tracery. Also a vine emerging from a dog's mouth, a Tudor rose, and two original poppyhead ends, one with a skirted saint. – STALLS. 1905, including one C15–C16 stall with a MISERICORD of a dragon with a serpent in its mouth. – STAINED GLASS. s aisle. An early C16 female saint, perhaps Dorothy, with scimitar. E window. Lush painterly Last Supper, 1868, by *O'Connor.* – MONUMENTS. A C13 slab with incised cross is reused in the N doorstep. – Good series of C17–C18 Lias floor slabs, including one to Louis, Chevalier de Misiers, †1685, a French officer killed with the royal army at Sedgemoor. – Lias wall monuments: Anne Wallis †1697, with 'an acrostick' of her maiden name; Mary Jeanes †1801, with rustic attempt at an Adam urn.

THORNGROVE HOUSE, ¾ m. WSW. Late Georgian brick five-bay house with parapet and stone dressings. Two curved ground-floor bays with stone cornices (the r. one altered).

MIDELNEY see DRAYTON

MILBORNE PORT

6010

A Saxon *burh*, later overtaken by nearby Sherborne, Dorset. By the late C18 a notorious 'rotten borough'. In the C19 it was a glove-making centre.

ST JOHN THE EVANGELIST. The church is remarkable for its Saxo-Norman overlap, and remarkable too for the height and length of the C11 work. It contains unmistakable Norman work in immediate conjunction with characteristic Anglo-Saxon features. These features are clearest in the blind ornament of the upper walls of the chancel.* The s wall has two tiers of pilasters, the upper ones spaced twice as close, with trapezoid capitals under the moulded eaves. Such tiers are familiar from other Anglo-Saxon churches. The E wall has none of this, but may have been cut back. The N wall (inside the vestry) has the cornices and one pilaster strip. The tall proportions of the chancel are characteristically Anglo-Saxon, but the breadth is unusual. The w front, demolished in 1869, had triangular 'arches', an even more revealing Anglo-Saxon motif. So the whole church was of Anglo-Saxon type. But the chancel has the remains of an arched window on each side, the N one visible only inside, which, with their fat roll mouldings and sturdy shafts with foliage or cushion capitals, cannot possibly be pre-Norman, and the distinguishing character of the crossing tower and transepts is indeed Early Norman.

---

* Jerry Sampson notes as characteristically Anglo-Saxon rather than Norman the use of Bath stone (probably from Bradford-on-Avon, Wilts.).

How are we to account for a church which in its entire length demonstrates Anglo-Saxon work, yet with such forceful Early Norman detail? Probably the building period overlapped 1066. Anglo-Saxon masons may have absorbed Norman motifs, or Norman masons inserted transepts and a crossing tower into an Anglo-Saxon church. The broad tower is Norman in all but its top stage – see the remains of arcading on the N, and the powerful piers and arches inside. These have three orders of strong columns on massive drum bases, each pair of bases different. Some of the capitals are stone, some plaster repairs of 1842, and they are more a band than proper capitals. The E ones have livelier carving and abaci, the others crude leaf and fleur-de-lys motifs. Depressed N and S arches with fat rolls carved *in situ* (an Anglo-Saxon technique). The W and E arches were replaced in the late C14, pointed and wave-moulded, suggesting structural problems. This is confirmed by earlier internal buttressing on the N and a massive external SE buttress. The S transept was rebuilt in 1843 apart from its most interesting feature, the stair-turret in the angle to the nave. This is faced with small square slabs set diamond-wise, like the *opus reticulatum* found in monastic buildings at Westminster Abbey of *c*. 1065 and later. Billet-moulded string course. The thickly shafted Norman window on the transept W side must be reused, since it is not there in Buckler's 1839 view. The nave was two bays shorter before 1867. The tall S doorway, although much reconstructed, is original in its inner order and tympanum. The two extravagantly maned lions are quite different in character to the other C11 work, akin to the Stoke-sub-Hamdon tympanum. On the r. capital, an armed man confronts a griffin. The outer order was crudely replaced in 1843. It is possible that it carried a gable with a Christ figure amid carved paterae as at Lullington (N). The paterae in the chancel with crosses and doves may be these reused.

C13 work includes the chancel S lancet with trefoiled rere-arch, the pair of lancets set low to the W, and, rather later, the S transept two-light S window with a foiled circle and cinque-foiled rere-arch. Perp alterations include the inserted chancel windows and the chancel N aisle with two-bay arcade. The NE vestry preserves small C11 windows, surely reused. Also the nave was refenestrated and the tower raised, with a battlemented and pinnacled top. Two-light bell-openings with pierced baffles. The nave, N aisle and N transept were rebuilt in 1867–9 by *Henry Hall*, and the nave lengthened. The detail is lavish, over-rich for the medieval work, with fussy roofs on shafts from angel corbels. Hall reused the Perp W doorway. The Perp roof-line is visible inside on the nave E wall. Good C15 panelled tower ceiling. Chancel rafter roof (C18?) exposed in 1908 by *Walter Tapper*, who added the handsome painted CANOPY. Two large mutilated Perp niches in the chancel E wall.

FURNISHINGS. FONT. C12. Purbeck marble, originally square, hacked to octagonal. Shallow blank arcading as at

Templecombe. Crude stem of Beer stone, of uncertain date. C17 COVER. – ROOD SCREEN. Perp, the coving reduced. Twelve square-headed lights, but the mullions intersect delicate tracery of three four-light arches. – ROYAL ARMS. 1662. Hanging, painted both sides. – STATUES. In the E niches, by *John Skelton*, 1972. – STAINED GLASS. E window by *W. Bainbridge Reynolds*, 1910, rich Late Gothic. Nave, a good series by *Clayton & Bell*, 1869, except the acid-coloured NW one, probably by *O'Connor*. – MONUMENTS. Eroded female effigy, S transept, c. 1300. – Various to the Medlycotts of Ven, including James †1731, pedimented with obelisk top, and Sir William †1835, large, Gothic, by *Humphrey Hopper*.

In the churchyard, the MORTUARY CHAPEL, 1869, reuses two canopied C15 niches that flanked the church W door, a C14 corbel and C17 doorway. Small reused roundel in the rear gable. – CHURCHYARD CROSS, 1921, with good tabernacle head.

PERAMBULATION. The Anglo-Saxon minster precinct was probably the rectangle S of the main road, bordered on two sides by a stream and on the E by the estate of Ven House (*see below*). The ancient vicarage until 1869 enclosed the churchyard on the W. Brick VICARAGE, SW, 1937, by *Anthony Medlycott*, stripped Georgian. CANON COURT, just S, asymmetrical Tudor of the early to mid C19, was an estate farmhouse of Lord Anglesey. The Anglesey interest was political, Milborne having two parliamentary seats until 1832 but few voting householders. In 1819–21 the Earl of Darlington attempted to build up the Whig vote with eighty houses at Newtown (*see* p. 443). Lord Anglesey responded by spending £15,000 on houses before Darlington gave up in 1824. The Anglesey election houses, randomly scattered, are of the Late Georgian norm, with leaded casement windows. E of the churchyard, the former CONGREGATIONAL CHAPEL, 1844, off Church Street. Y-tracery windows and panelled galleries. Schoolroom of 1850. South Street is mostly Late Georgian, Nos. 65–67, dated 1821, adjoining a neo-Tudor FIRE-ENGINE HOUSE. Just N, a moulded C15–C16 doorway and the head of a C15 three-light window above it appear reused, perhaps a Ven estate folly. Thimble Lane connects to a little square opposite the early C19 QUEEN'S HEAD. Lofted stable with lunettes dated 1835. Beyond, Nos. 31–45 EAST STREET are Medlycott estate houses of c. 1830. Three blocks of five, the centre houses larger with a pedimental gable. Their connection with the vote is unclear. A message may be in the patriotic emblems on YARD HOUSE opposite. London Road runs E to Ven House (*see below*).

Returning W along HIGH STREET, the small early C18 TOWN HALL, of three bays by one, with forceful giant pilasters and triglyphs for capitals. Windows in architraves over an arcaded market storey, since blocked up. In the next terrace, the so-called GUILDHALL has a Norman doorway, presumably reused, in a small front with wooden cross-windows of c. 1700. Segmental arch with a moulding indented like teeth.

Gaping chevron on the angle of each jamb. The TIPPLING PHILOSOPHER, opposite, was rebuilt in 1797 for Lord Anglesey. On the s side of the main road, massive buttresses frame the BALL COURT, twin fives courts built in 1847 by the Medlycotts. By the turn to the church, the medieval VILLAGE CROSS. Further E, the unusually lavish OLD VICARAGE, 1871–2, and equally lavish former SCHOOL, 1863–4, were built for the Medlycotts by *Henry Hall*. The school shows Hall at his flashy best, a Gothic loggia between gables and below three giant stone dormers, overtopped from the rear by a slim tower, to which Hall added the clock stage in 1878. The nearby SHELTER, 1869, is the reused porch of the medieval vicarage. C15 arch and 1662 datestone.

N of the main road were tanneries for the glove industry, cleared for housing in 2009. The former METHODIST CHAPEL, 1864–6, by *Alexander Lauder*, crowns the hill to the N. Gothic, of startling mixed motifs. A huge rose window crowded with quatrefoils, and an octagonal spirelet on one shoulder. MANSE, 1871, by *Lauder*, also idiosyncratic. To the E NORTH STREET runs s to the main road past a three-storey former GLOVE FACTORY, 1858. On the W side, No. 160, a jettied C15 timber-framed house like those in Bruton, preserving the oak ground-floor front. C16 fireplace and framed ceiling. Wind-braced roof. CROSS HOUSE, C18, was altered in the 1860s for the Ensors, glove makers, with large dormers and diminutive Gothic bay window.

VEN HOUSE, ½ m. E. The Medlycotts bought the estate in 1696 for the political interest and were duly returned to Parliament for a century. The house was built *c.* 1725 for James Medlycott, by *Nathaniel Ireson*. Like Crowcombe Court (q.v.), begun in 1725, the house derives from Buckingham House, London, 1702, and represents a type familiar in the Home Counties and the Midlands, but rare in Somerset: a brick block with a stone giant order and cornice beneath a balustraded attic storey. The two seven-bay fronts are divided by Corinthian pilasters at the angles and the angles of the three centre bays. The pilasters carry a deep cornice into which intrude the keystones of the first-floor architraves. The attic has stone piers, balustrades and urns. Brick aprons under the main windows. Basement, disguised on the s by a broad terrace. On the N front, to the forecourt, the doorway (re-set on a porch of 1836) has a swan-neck pediment on attached columns. The s doorway has a curved pediment on pilasters. Differing ends, the W of 1–3–1 bays with some stone dressing, the E of six bays with none.

The interior was planned for display. Before 1836 the two-storey hall and stair hall beyond occupied the whole centre. Heavy stone fireplaces with the Medlycott eagle between pediment scrolls face each other across the splendid HALL. Mid-height panelling and pedimented centrepieces on Ionic pilasters on three sides. The fourth side opened to the stair hall but is now panelled with matching pilasters beneath a gallery that curves out elegantly at each end. Four Ionic columns, the middle two stepped back, carry the gallery on entablature blocks. Dentil cornice and finely turned balusters. Rococo scrolls frame a large ceiling painting of Time bearing naked Truth skyward away from Anger and Envy, by *G.-B. Cipriani* after Poussin, later C18. A large two-arm staircase beyond the hall was removed in 1836–7 by *Decimus Burton*. His narrow cantilevered stone staircase is to the E, replacing the servants' staircase. Burton floored the stair hall, making a new S room with a richly Rococo ceiling on a deep acanthus frieze. The rooms each side have C18 modillion cornices (as does the NE room). In the SE room some Rococo ceiling decoration. The sumptuous marble fireplaces may be brought in: bolection-moulded SE and SW, mid-C18 in the S room, with scrolled frieze and cherub-and-goat plaque on red marble. Two good 1730s rooms on the W side, the middle room fielded-panelled with pilastered Doric centrepieces on each side and another bolection fireplace. The NW room, also panelled, has a fine mid-C18 fireplace with Aesop's stork and fox. Most remarkable, for its early Chinoiserie, is the extremely delicate Rococo ceiling with birds and a tiny swinging Chinaman.

Burton's external additions are admirable. His Corinthian three-bay CONSERVATORY faces E down the S terrace, linked to the house by a glazed arcade. He altered the basement-level E service court, screening it with one of the two triumphal-arch PAVILIONS in brick with stone pilasters that frame the N approach, linked to the house by quadrant walls.

Formal GARDENS were laid out by *Richard Grange, c.* 1735. His S terrace terminated in square pavilions and overlooked a canal. The TERRACE and two tall PIERS with urns remain. The garden between with Neptune STATUE in a pool is late C20, as also the arcaded PAVILION in the walled E garden. A woodland walk follows the stream E with evidence of the C18 arrangement, a stone-lined channel, and a damaged ornamental bridge.

LITTLE VEN, towards the town, was the dower house, square, roughcast Late Georgian with hipped roofs. Edwardian E addition.

BOWLING GREEN, ½ m. W. 1914, by *Guy Dawber*. Beautifully detailed Cotswold vernacular. H-plan with central storeyed porch and bolection-moulded pedimented doorway. Stair window in the r. gable. Panelled hall in the centre; SW room with fine plaster overmantel by *George Bankart*. Dawber did STABLES well, here a small brick courtyard with a double-gabled stone house on the corner.

CRACKMORE LODGE, ½ m. W. Two early C19 lodges to Sherborne Castle, each an elongated hexagon with grid windows echoing those of the castle.

NEWTOWN, ½ m. NW. Lord Darlington's development (*see* above) of 1819–22, on a paddle-shaped plan. It was reputedly badly built and has an *ad hoc* character, reinforced by alteration and infill. The houses are thatched (the thatchers' vote was important) and have an undulating irregularity of gables, hips and canted projections.

MILBORNE WICK, 1 m. NNW. Gothic MISSION ROOM, 1891, by *Hall*, the roof projecting over the bell. Opposite a half-hip-roofed C18 MILL. To the NW, BRADLEY HEAD FARM has a particularly attractive farmyard group, early C19 to 1858. MILBORNE WICK HOUSE, NE, is C17 with broad steps to a porch, large for the house. Across the stream, a cruciform BARN with some C16 trusses.

WATERLOO CRESCENT, 2 m. N. 1820, for Lord Anglesey, hero of Waterloo. Eight houses in a low vernacular curve. A similar crescent is at Compton Pauncefoot (q.v.).

MILTON CLEVEDON

ST JAMES. W tower of 1790, of ashlar from the newly demolished Bruton Abbey (q.v.). Typical Georgian Gothic Y-tracery (cf. East Coker) and a pierced parapet. Perp nave with S transept and porch conjoined with gable parapets. In 1865 *E. B. Lamb* added a matching N transept and rebuilt a chancel of 1780. Victorian interior, the roofs all *Lamb*'s, the PULPIT and FONT carved by the *Rev. Sydney Selwyn*. The previous FONT, a tapered bowl with nailhead rim and water-lily underside, looks C12–C13. Strange C17 inscription, 'He that drinketh of this water shall thirst again.' – STAINED GLASS. E and S transept windows, 1865. Good N transept window, 1996, by *Tom Denny*. Tree of Life, in opaque autumnal colours. C15–C16 fragments above. – MONUMENTS. Effigy of a priest with chalice, *c.* 1325, horribly recarved by *Selwyn*. – Susannah Strangways †1718. Unexpectedly metropolitan. A curtained baldacchino over a gadrooned urn in a niche, framed in fluted pilasters carrying a bisected curved pediment. – Robert Welch †1824. Grecian, by *Joseph Harris* of Bath.

The church stands by the farmyard of MANOR FARM, largely C19, with big farm buildings and L-plan farmhouse. Well-detailed Gothic former SCHOOL, 1876, extended with paired glazed gables by *Nigel Begg*, 2005.

MILVERTON

A former market town on the old main road to Barnstaple, prosperous from weaving until the C19.

ST MICHAEL. A stately red sandstone church, externally mostly Perp, with broad gabled aisles and tall W tower. The tower, unlike the normal Somerset type, is without horizontal division or elaborate decoration. Diagonal buttresses, battlements with plain pinnacles, and a higher square SE stair-turret. Small two-light late C14 bell-openings with pierced baffles. But the structure is older, oddly angled to the church. Crude reused heads around the battlements echo much larger corbel heads inside, which carry the inner order of the double-chamfered tower arch. These look C13. C13 also the double-chamfered doorhead at the W end of the S aisle and perhaps the double-chamfered doorway within, into the nave. The double-chamfered nave arcades on octagonal piers are early C14 – see their moulded caps and bases (traces of original colour). A plinth of a Norman chancel S wall is visible below floor level in the SE chapel, and foundations of a pier by the adjoining chancel arch. In 1849–50 *John Hayward* replaced the entire S arcade, both ends of the N arcade, the chancel arch, chapel arches, and all the roofs. He extended the N aisle at each end to balance the S one, and inserted the aisle W galleries.

FURNISHINGS. FONT. Norman. Large, circular, with a rim of saltire crosses and a cable moulding at the bottom. – PULPIT. 1928, by *W. D. Caröe*, reusing good arched panels from the C17 pulpit. – ROOD SCREEN. 1903, by *Harry Hems*. Incorporating C16 panels similar to the bench-ends, including a wyvern and unicorn; one panel dated 1540. – STALLS. Two frontals depicting the twelve Apostles, stocky animated figures. Mid-C16, the three without scrolls C17–C18. – BENCHES. Uncommonly many, square-headed ends as well as complete fronts and backs. They date from *c.* 1540 and include the arms of Henry VIII, much Renaissance foliage, several kneeling figures, faces in roundels or lozenges, the spies carrying the bunch of grapes, a man drinking, and a holy-water sprinkler. – STAINED GLASS. E window, 1951, by *Christopher Webb*. Nave S fourth, 1877, by *Hardman*, rich Late Gothic style. Much by *John Toms* of Wellington, 1849–50, mostly patterned. Chancel S, 1850, interesting angular figures, artist unknown. – MONUMENTS. William Davison †1777. Draped urn, signed *Robert Withers*. – John Cridland †1793. Finely done with reeded angles, by *Edward Kendall*. – Catherine Spurway †1845. Neoclassical seated female in profile. By *Patrick Macdowell*.

Eroded base of a late C15 CHURCHYARD CROSS, octagonal with corner piers.

THE OLD HOUSE, E of the churchyard. An extremely interesting late medieval house belonging to the Archdeacons of Taunton, remodelled in the early C16. This was where their Milverton estate was administered, the principal room being probably a courtroom. Red sandstone, not large: a hall and buttery under an upper chamber (or two) with off-centre storeyed porch and rear stair-tower. Parallel NE range in late C17 brick on older foundations. NW service wing of 1880–3, by *Ewan Christian*. The porch has diagonal buttresses, tall pointed archway and small upper windows in red sandstone, all late C15. Massive oak inner doorway with double roll moulding and triangular leaf patterns in the spandrels. Original door. The other windows are early C16, Ham stone, with four-centred lights. One-bay buttery to the l., three-bay hall to the r. beneath a large gabled upper window lighting the principal chamber, lit also by a similar E window. The stair-tower has small red sandstone windows of the first phase, so the house was storeyed from the outset.

A heavily moulded framed ceiling survives over the hall dais and (concealed) over the cross-passage. Over the dais was found in 2010 a full-width PAINTING on plaster of Henry VIII, flanked by drapery striped in blue and yellow, an astonishing image, astonishingly well preserved. The king, enthroned and crowned, with orb and sceptre, wears a fur-trimmed damask cloak. He is dated to the 1540s by comparison with other images. The frieze is scrolled like that at Cothay, with a homily in English, and two small figures, one a cleric identified as John Redman, Archdeacon 1541–51. On the N wall, the panelled stone arch of the dais oriel. The oriel has gone but the side doorway remains, to a narrow barrel-vaulted passage behind the hall fireplace, off which opens the staircase. Four-centred arches to the under-stair and enclosed staircase, under a cambered framed ceiling. The chamber roof has arch-braced jointed crucks and wind-braces but no smoke-blackening. The buttery has a heavy oak Tudor-arched door frame and high beamed ceiling.

PERAMBULATION. The church stands on an eminence between Fore Street and North Street. W of the churchyard, BELL HOUSE, externally Georgian with added single-bay wings, hides a three-sided Elizabethan chamber ceiling of thin-ribbed four-petal forms with rosettes and fleurs-de-lys. St Michael's Hill runs up to NORTH STREET which has the best houses, an uncommonly pleasant, mostly Georgian sequence on the N side, fronting a cobbled pavement. On the corner of Mill Lane, IVY COTTAGE is C16–C17, with chimney gable to the street. Mill Lane runs down to the TOWN MILL, a picturesque limewashed range called newly erected in 1823. Mid-C19 internal waterwheel. The house, at right angles, has a C16 reserved-chamfer doorcase. To the E on North Street after Ivy Cottage, a good Georgian group in squared sandstone, including THE RECESS with pedimented doorcase. At the crossroads, WAYSIDE HOUSE, roughcast with Georgian sashes, rising to three storeys. Opposite, ROCKLYN is C16–C17 with a carved oak oriel on the cross-wing. Plastered framed ceiling with ovals. From the crossroads SILVER STREET curves back S and W past the stone Gothic METHODIST CHAPEL, 1849–50, to become FORE STREET. Another cobbled pavement, and a stuccoed former CONGREGATIONAL CHAPEL, 1821, set back behind a square hip-roofed MANSE. On the S side, three early C19 houses with pointed sashes in alternate bays. Above Fore Street stands THE FORT, a large red sandstone Elizabethan house backing on to the churchyard. Standard E-plan of gabled storeyed porch and gabled cross-wings, with gabled stair-towers in the angles. The detail is early C19 apart from the doorway. Both

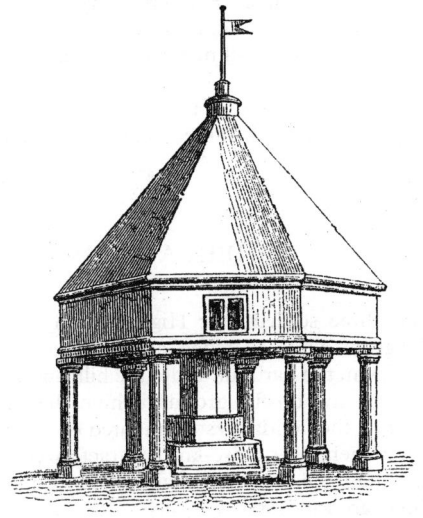

Milverton, former market cross.
Engraving, 1877

cross-wings have first-floor plaster barrel ceilings, as does
LITTLE FORT, a lower W range. Here the tympanum has delicate floral panels flanking a shield on strapwork.
A market cross formerly stood at the W end of Fore Street, whence SAND STREET runs S. In SWAN HOUSE, a twelve-panel framed ceiling, plastered in the C17, two panels with ovals. At the S end, the former SCHOOL: two buildings, one stone-and-brick Gothic, 1872, the other, larger, of 1831–5, by *Richard Carver*, in red sandstone with tall square-headed windows in half-hip-roofed wings. Across the road, NETHERFIELD, a doll's-house brick front with Venetian lower windows, cornice, and ramped parapet. The detail is Late Georgian, but a house of 1708–9 may have been remodelled. The late C20 PRIMARY SCHOOL is in the grounds of OLANDS HOUSE, a stuccoed five-bay villa with overhanging hipped roof, *c.* 1840.

MILVERTON COURT, ½ m. W. C17, rendered, with central storeyed porch. Good mid-C17 staircase with thick turned balusters.

SPRING GROVE HOUSE, 1½ m. WSW. White Regency villa of five by four bays, with cornice, parapet and encompassing veranda on panelled flat piers. Set in a charming landscaped PARK with a canal following the contour, crossed by a bridge with wrought-iron gates.

LOVELYNCH FARMHOUSE, 1 m. SW. Limewashed, with ovolo-moulded stone-mullion windows and central storeyed porch, dated 1605. Two ornamented plaster overmantels, one with a fish in strapwork, one (upstairs) with painted heraldry and rose trail above a decorated plaster chimneypiece.

GARNIVAL'S WEEK, ¾ m. E. Rendered farmhouse concealing fragments of a very early hall, part of a base-cruck truss with wind-braces and an end-wall frame with aisle posts, tree-ring-dated to 1287.

PRESTON BOWYER. 1 m. ENE. THE CHANTRY is late C15, with a C16 nine-panel moulded framed ceiling, sub-panelled.

MINEHEAD

Minehead was three settlements: Higher Town, a typical West Somerset village of white thatched cottages below the hillside church; Quay Town, the harbour under the hill; and Lower Town, the commercial centre on flat ground behind the bay. All three were enveloped by the holiday resort initiated by the railway after 1872. Modern Minehead is loose-knit, characterized by detached and semi-detached villas rather than grand terraces, and its public buildings are modest.

Minehead's wealth derived before tourism from fishing and maritime trade, mostly with Ireland. Defoe in 1722 found the port prosperous, trading even across the Atlantic, but trade had collapsed by 1791. C16–C17 cottages survive in numbers in the Higher Town, and some along the road to the Quay. Their virtual absence in the Lower Town is due to a fire in 1791. By the time that rebuilding began, Minehead was being suggested as a resort. A directory of 1794 says: 'A number of persons of fashion have been induced to visit it as a bathing place.' But few did so before the railway arrived, coinciding with an improving landlord, G. F. Luttrell, who inherited in 1867. Minehead's visual character is therefore Late Victorian and Edwardian. Substantial houses, detached, in pairs and rarely in terraces, show Minehead as a select resort and retirement place. But the railway made it also a popular resort, enhanced after 1901 by a 700-ft (210-metre) pier at which day-passengers disembarked. Since Billy Butlin established his holiday camp in 1962 the hotels and large houses have gradually become flats or care homes, to their architectural detriment as plastic replaces wooden detail.

CHURCHES AND PUBLIC BUILDINGS

ST MICHAEL. A typical dedication for churches on rocks or hills. It stands high, with superb views towards Dunster and over the bay. Mostly Perp. Tall W tower, akin to that at Watchet, of Blue Lias with red sandstone set-back buttresses, ashlar battlements with blind cusping and squat square pinnacles. Polygonal SE stair-turret, unusually on the E face. Tall transomed three-light bell-openings and four-light transomed W window. In a canopied recess on the S side, God holds the Crucified Christ, and on the E side, an interesting relief combining St Michael and the Virgin of the Misericord. He weighs souls while she shelters little humans under her mantle. The tower arch has two bold wave mouldings and moulded continuous capitals like the crossing arches of Dunster, so the tower is perhaps also the work of *John Marys*, which would give a mid-C15 date.

Single-roofed nave and chancel with a N aisle of equal length and a short additional NE chapel, giving a triple-gabled E end. Typically, the prominent S side is enriched. To the l. of the porch are battlements ornamented with crowned 'M's and roses in quatrefoils, and good grotesques. Older masonry shows in the low first buttress and the chamfered C13–C14 porch doorway. Beyond the porch the battlements are plain, but the tracery is more interesting. The large four-light window has the transom and cusped ogee-headed lights with quatrefoil spandrels known from Cleeve Abbey and Selworthy, here treated with less depth. The battlemented square rood-stair turret is unusually well lit. On the upper level a big square-headed transomed two-light window and a single light on each side wall. Similar cusped ogee heads and quatrefoil spandrels. Three small single lights at the lower level. The chancel is Perp, over-restored in 1883–9 by *J. P. St Aubyn*. The aisle E window has the interesting tracery of the nave, and is dated: stiff hoodmould angels carry shields, one with the Five Wounds, the other marked 1529. The NE chapel has conventional Perp windows.

Broad undivided nave and chancel and undivided N aisle, both under *St Aubyn*'s muscular roofs. Eight bays of double-chamfered arches on slim octagonal piers, as in Devon, probably late C14. Under the last arch, a late C15 TOMB in the Easter sepulchre position, the effigy (*see* below) rather earlier. Tomb-chest with eight empty niches under a vaulted canopy framed by paired piers with attached pinnacles. Five ogee crocketed gables overhang the recess, with little angel bosses. Cornice with fleurons, panelled frieze and straight cresting. A fine, quiet design. The pointed arch to the outer chapel is, exceptionally, of massive pieces of oak, very rustic in this context, especially compared with the well-detailed wagon roof. The rood stair has a C15–C16 traceried DOOR.

FURNISHINGS. FONT. One of the more remarkable of Somerset. Early Perp, octagonal, with figures seated on the moulding at the foot of the bowl, their legs hanging over. Christ emerging from the tomb is one. It is a great pity that they are not better preserved. Narrow niches around the stem between pinnacled shafts. Low-relief figures in the niches, including Evangelists. – ROOD SCREEN. A fine example of just after 1500, of the same workshop as Carhampton, Dunster, Timberscombe and Withycombe. Eleven bays right across, each section of four lights with subdivided arches and delicate tracery, outlined in the leaf scroll that identifies the workshop. Ribbed panelled coving with carved bosses under four layers of sharply carved foliage. Blind tracery to the dado. – PULPIT. Early to mid-C17, like Timberscombe. A band of oval cabochons between panels subdivided in the Jacobean way. – REREDOS. 1888, by *Powell's*. Tile mosaic, Crucifixion against

p. 450

Minehead, St Michael, rood screen.
Engraving after E. B. Nevinson, 1882

dark red and gold. – COMMUNION TABLE. N chapel. Early C17, with massively bulbous carved legs. Between the front legs, two half-draped angels. – CANDELABRA. 1727. Brass, two-tier. – LECTERN. 1903, by *Nelson Dawson*. Wrought iron and brass, Arts and Crafts. – ROYAL ARMS. Three: Charles II, Anne, George II. – COMMANDMENT BOARDS. 1634–7. Eight round-headed panels, formerly the reredos, the outer two painted with Moses and Aaron. – CLOCK-JACK. On the screen. A mannikin that held a hammer to strike the hours. His painted clothes look C18. – CHEST. With finely carved panels including the arms of England and of Bishop Fitzjames of London, vicar here 1485–97.* – STAINED GLASS. E window in deep rich colours, 1903, by *Henry Holiday*. By *Holiday* also the similar chancel S window, 1906. N aisle E, by *Kempe*, 1902, an opportunity to contrast Kempe's intense detail with Holiday's intense colour. Nave S, Arts and Crafts, 1914, by *Mary Hutchinson*, assistant to Christopher Whall. – MONUMENTS. Effigy of a priest holding a chalice, two angels by his head. Possibly Richard of Bruton, vicar 1401–6. – Brass of a lady of *c.* 1440. 28-in. (71-cm.) figure with high headgear. Parts of the canopied setting survive in a Purbeck marble slab appropriated in the C17 by the Quirke family.

---

* He owned the great treasure of Minehead, the illuminated MISSAL in the wall-case adjoining.

CHURCHYARD CROSS. C15, on octagonal steps too small for it.

ST ANDREW, Wellington Square. 1877–80 by *G. E. Street*. Red sandstone nave and chancel, with well-detailed tracery in the style of 1300–50. A rose window over a buttress between tall two-light windows on the (ritual) W front, and a splendidly large E window. Double-chamfered arcades, the outer chamfer ended in a kind of label, the inner continued into octagonal piers without capitals. Low clerestory. Nave roof with plain hammerbeams and arched braces, divided from the chancel by wooden boarding instead of an arch. – FURNISHINGS by *Street*. – STAINED GLASS. Excellent E window by *Kempe*, 1888. In an addition of 2004, two re-set windows by *Christopher Webb*, 1938.

ST MICHAEL, Church Street, Alcombe. Nave of 1902–3 by *C. H. Samson* (intended to run further W). Chancel and N transept of 1937 to designs of 1925 by *Samson & Colthurst*. The moulded pointed doorway of the N porch is C15, from the W end of Dunster church, removed when the Norman portal was restored. Dark aisled nave and light chancel with panelled roof.

SACRED HEART (R.C.), Townsend Road. Church and presbytery by *Canon A. J. C. Scoles*, 1896, nicely grouped. Gabled aisle added by Scoles in 1900, the arcade on octagonal columns. Carved stone PULPIT, RAILS, and two elaborate stone ALTARS. – STAINED GLASS. By *Hardman*, 1899–1907.

Behind, in Selbourne Place, the former CONVENT rears high. 1910–11 by *A. L. Cox*. Red sandstone, with a cross-wing of which the Gothic chapel occupies the top floor.

BAPTIST CHAPEL, Park Street. 1831. Stuccoed, with arched windows and dentilled eaves, the front obscured by the manse. Altered in 1902 by *F. W. Roberts*.

METHODIST CHURCH, The Avenue. A complex group by *Foster & Wood* of Bristol. The Gothic chapel of 1875–6 became the aisle to a much larger one of 1885–6, composed with long narrow windows in a drum apse and a rounded NW stair-turret. Broad interior with notched timber roof trusses. Banded stone arcade piers, alternately round and octagonal. – SUNDAY SCHOOL, 1904–5, with a stone lean-to against a brick and tile-hung gable.

FRIENDS' MEETING HOUSE. *See* Perambulation 1.

UNITED REFORMED CHURCH. *See* Perambulation 1.

MARKET HOUSE. *See* Perambulation 1.

POLICE STATION and former MAGISTRATES' COURT, Townsend Road. 1936, by *A. J. Toomer*, County Architect. Stripped classical. Brown brick. Big fifteen-bay front of sash windows, split by a narrow ashlar recess with cinema-Greek square columns.

RAILWAY STATION, Esplanade. 1872–4, terminus of the Minehead Railway. Immaculately preserved by the West Somerset Railway. Original r. half with a big half-hipped porch between paired arched windows. Extended in matching style as late as the 1920s. GOODS SHED of 1872–4. TURNTABLE from Pwllheli installed in 2008, also the curving gull-wing car park canopy and café, by *Stone & Partners*.

COMMUNITY HOSPITAL, off Seaward Way. 2010–11, by *David Kent Architects* of Bath. A good design, echoing Thirties Modern. White, with green copper. Courtyard SCULPTURE, a sphere of glass-tipped spikes over a spiked garden, by *Wolfgang Buttress*, 2010.

WEST SOMERSET COMMUNITY COLLEGE, Alcombe. 1955–8, by *Godfrey Morgan* of *Somerset County Architects*. Typical brown brick secondary school of the era.

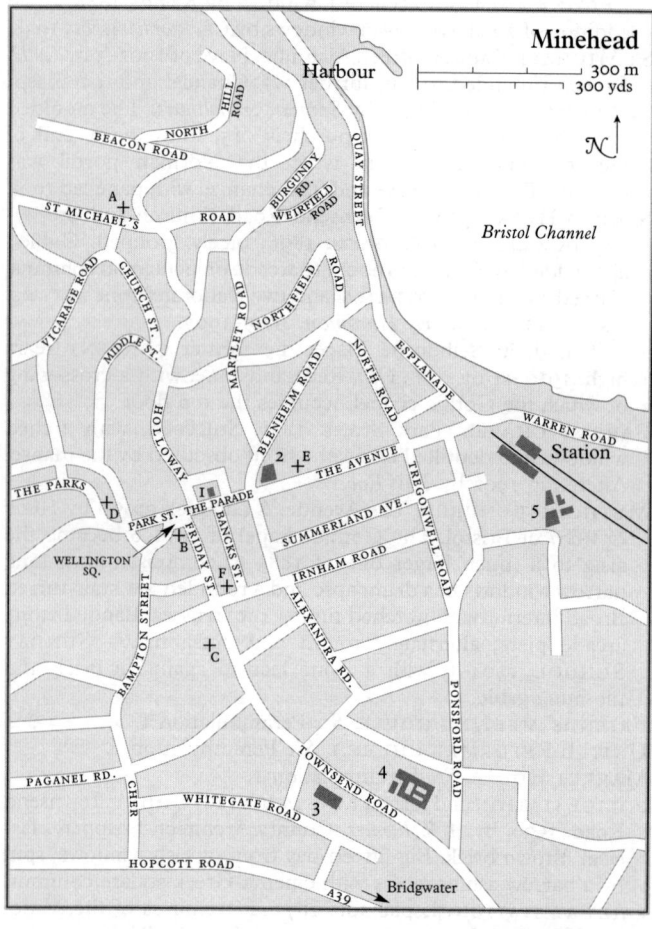

A	St Michael	1	Market House
B	St Andrew	2	Town Hall
C	Sacred Heart (R.C.)	3	Police Station
D	Baptist church	4	Middle School
E	Methodist church	5	Minehead Eye
F	United Reformed church		

MIDDLE SCHOOL, Ponsford Road. 1926–9, by *A. J. Toomer*. Red brick Neo-Georgian, the centre a cramped country house with an ashlar colonnade between hip-roofed wings.

MINEHEAD EYE, Mart Road. 2009–10, by *Mark Kingsley Architects* of Frome. A skateboarding hall with gallery café. Industrial box of black brick under an upper level clad in polycarbonate, illuminated at night. Monopitch-roofed INDUSTRIAL UNITS just N of a similar aesthetic, in grey brick.

PERAMBULATIONS

1. Town centre

WELLINGTON SQUARE more or less marks the medieval centre. In front of St Andrew's church (p. 451) is the STATUE of Queen Anne, a fine marble piece attributed to *Francis Bird*, showing great skill in the detail of the clothes. It was given to the town in 1719 by Sir Jacob Bancks, Swedish officer in the Royal Navy, M.P. for Minehead through marriage to a Luttrell widow. Previously in the parish church, it was sited here in 1894 under a pleasing Anglo-Baroque half-rotunda by *H. Dare Bryan*. On the W side, the large red sandstone DUKE OF WELLINGTON INN, rebuilt 1893, and the HSBC BANK, stuccoed commercial of 1873. This, with unremarkable stuccoed terraces in Park Street and on the corner of Friday Street and upper end of The Parade, represents the beginning of G. F. Luttrell's redevelopment of the centre, probably by *C. H. Samson*. PARK STREET is interrupted by the gabled brick former BANK, 1887, of Fox, Fowler.

THE PARADE achieves civic dignity by virtue of its width. On the N side, the cheerful MARKET HOUSE of 1902 by *W. J. Tamlyn*, principal architect of Edwardian Minehead. Banded brick and stone with a diagonally placed clock turret. Freely detailed, with a shaped gable (missing its shell-top), some mullioned windows and a Baroque doorway. The adjoining NATWEST BANK, 1901–3 by *George Oatley*, for Stuckey's Bank, is stately Anglo-Baroque of Ham stone, with a first-floor colonnade and curved corner. Opposite it, on the corner of Bancks Street, No. 8 was the predecessor Stuckey's branch, of 1869 by *J. P. St Aubyn*. Red sandstone with Gothic trefoiled window heads. BANCKS STREET is a minor civic centre. On the E side, two red sandstone fronts by *F. W. Roberts*, the MASONIC HALL, 1896, and the CHURCH INSTITUTE, 1895, less florid. The gabled FRIENDS' MEETING HOUSE was built for Plymouth Brethren in 1903. Opposite, the former READING ROOM, 1905 by *Tamlyn*, and the LIBRARY, reticent and flat-roofed, 1960–2, by *Somerset County Architects*. The UNITED REFORMED CHURCH, 1904 by *Roberts*, with a pretty domed lantern, was the schoolroom for an intended Congregational church. Opposite, a good roughcast and red-tiled pair, Nos. 17–19, by *A. L. Cox*, 1909, with corner shopfront.

Returning to THE PARADE, Nos. 10–12, on the Bancks Street corner, of sandstone with grouped narrow arched windows, are by *Samson*, 1875. In much lighter style, Nos. 16–20, 1893, with five bargeboarded gables and little oriels between ashlar piers, and the block opposite, Nos. 13–20, 1895–6, with good small-scale Renaissance detail, are by *St Aubyn* or his nephew, *F. W. St Aubyn*. MARKET HOUSE LANE runs back to Holloway Street, past plain rendered ALMSHOUSES (much rebuilt) founded by Robert Quirke in 1630. An eroded C15 CROSS indicates the medieval market.

2. *Higher Town and North Hill*

Higher Town is reached by HOLLOWAY, rightly so called, as it cuts deeply through red sandstone. At the foot, Nos. 1–3, three-storeyed with a fancy gable and oriel, 1899, an early work of *W. J. Tamlyn*, and the QUEEN'S HEAD, 1883, enlarged 1893 by *Basil Cottam*, lower and quieter, in buff sandstone. The old hill village begins with thatched cottages opposite the sandstone STABLES of Clanville, a demolished house of 1882 by *J. P. St Aubyn*, whose grounds crown the first outcrop. Facing downhill, the Gothic former SCHOOL, 1866, by *St Aubyn*. On MIDDLE STREET, No. 1, C16–C17 with a stocky lateral chimney. Nos. 3–7, a simple three-storey terrace, was the workhouse of 1820, built or adapted by *William Horn*. A little thatched group beyond, including No. 14 with roof timbers tree-ring-dated astonishingly to 1315. CHURCH STREET climbs with thatched cottages on the W side to join VICARAGE ROAD below Church Steps. Nos. 20–22, white and thatched, are C16, with lateral stacks front and rear. (Downhill is the plain stuccoed VICARAGE by *Richard Carver*, 1831, extended 1861.) The ascent of CHURCH STEPS is a visual delight – the whitewashed cottages, cobbled steps and the church tower slowly revealed. No. 1, C16–C17, has oak-mullioned windows, a lateral chimney and heavy oak doorway. No. 2, opposite, is C17 with a broad lateral chimney breast. No. 6, thatched, with a lateral chimney, was a C16 hall house. The path splits prettily just below the church. The old village ended E of the church with the row called THE CROSS.

Victorian development of North Hill began W of the church with CLEVELAND, 1877, by *Foster & Wood*, for Thomas Lomas, owner of a chemical works on the bay. Of red sandstone and brick with a great deal of timber, it is colourful in the way of the firm's Foster's Almshouses, Bristol. Balconies link to the storeyed timbered porch. North Hill above and E of the church was released for building in 1901. Church Road ascends to BEACON ROAD where FARLEIGH and BEVERLEIGH, by *Frank Tugwell* of Scarborough, 1906, are among the best houses, a Voysey-influenced pair, roughcast with dissimilar outer gables. ROSSCLERE, 1915 by *J. Kingsley Cole* of London, is more American in its long proportions, brick over roughcast. Interesting play of roof hips. Lastly, against open country, THE BEACON, 1903–4, by *Tamlyn*, is large and eclectic, out of control at the w end. NORTH HILL ROAD climbs yet higher to NORTHMOOR, 1902, by *Tamlyn*, more controlled, with an octagonal corner and two-storey veranda.

Beacon Road runs E to zigzag down to BURGUNDY ROAD. The red sandstone castle here is ELGIN TOWER, 1887, built for J. C. Kennedy, originally from Elgin, probably by *Matthews & Mackenzie* of Elgin. All battlements and crow-stepped gables, Victorian Scotland perfectly transposed. A stately interior from hallway with coffered ceiling to a double staircase under a great-hall roof. Opposite, BRIDGEWAY, 1965 by *Steel & Coleman*. Well-designed Modern, with garage and entrance above a glass-fronted living room projecting over the garden. From the large Celtic-cross WAR MEMORIAL, 1921 by *Roberts & Willman*, ST MICHAEL'S ROAD returns to the church with villas by *Tamlyn* except MARSTON LODGE, 1902, by *Cox*, and SHUTE FARM, altered C16–C17, with a lateral chimney. E of the war memorial, on WEIRFIELD ROAD, CARTREF, 1906, shows *Tamlyn* at his most entertaining, with a lacy two-storey wooden porch under a bellcast pyramid roof. MOUNT ROYAL, a bulky stone pair by *F.W. Roberts* with two-storey ironwork, looks twenty years older than its date, 1902. Finally NORTH-WOOD, 1908 by *T. H. Andrew*, is coarsely Georgian, red brick with a colonnade between hip-roofed wings. A footpath descends past CHANNEL HOUSE, 1901 by *Roberts*, up-to-date here, roughcast with Voysey-style sloping buttresses. On NORTHFIELD ROAD, three houses by *Tamlyn* on the N side, the middle one, SOUTHLANDS, 1907, his own. Brick, full of lively timber detail. MARTLET ROAD, climbing from the centre, has on the W side three gabled stone villas by *Samson*: WYNDHAM HOUSE, 1880, WYNDCOTT, 1888 and 1899, and HIGHLANDS, 1879. In the grounds of Highlands, THE OBSERVATORY, 2007–8, by *Paul Brookes*, timber-fronted with sedum roofs. Above Highlands on BALLFIELD ROAD and BALL PATH behind, several pretty inter-war houses with roofs of small Delabole slates by *Edwin Gunn*. DELABOLE, 1926, was Gunn's own house, with a slate-hung and red sandstone porch. From here Holloway descends to The Parade.

3. The Avenue and seafront

THE AVENUE continues The Parade, not with terraces but with pairs of 1880s gabled houses of red sandstone or Hangman Grit boulders, their front gardens lost to commerce. The architect was probably *J. P. St Aubyn*. On the N side, the former TOWN HALL, by *St Aubyn*, 1888–9. Red sandstone Gothic with large Ham stone windows, flat-headed and rather Venetian, except the gabled centre where twin pointed windows open to a stone balcony. It had a very large first-floor public hall. The Methodist church (p. 451) adjoins. Opposite, a battered medieval survival, THE PRIORY, probably the Luttrell courtroom, later their estate office. The gable has a C15–C16 oak two-light window, the W side a heavy oak doorway. Further down, the REGAL CINEMA, 1934 by *Andrew Mather*, in buff brick with green pantiles and an Art Deco corner tower. The interior is subdivided. The area S of The Avenue was built up in 1900–10; on TREGONWELL ROAD are varied boarding houses, mostly by *W.J. Tamlyn*. The BEACH HOTEL, 1874–5 by *C. H. Samson*, terminates The Avenue, opposite the station (p. 451) which it was built to serve. Plain curved front of painted brick. Behind the station, a short attempt at seaside cheer, the STRAND CAFÉ, 1915, and QUEEN'S HALL, 1913–15, by *Tamlyn*. MARINE COURT stretches E, a sprawling development of 1990–2004 with pyramid- and octagonal-roofed accents, by *Clarke Renner* of London. The huge white tensile roof beyond, 1998, by *S&P Architects*, covers the main attractions of BUTLIN'S holiday camp.

Across from the Beach Hotel, Nos. 1–4 THE ESPLANADE, 1874, were four exceptionally big boarding houses, probably by *St Aubyn*. Red sandstone with ashlar cornice and pedimented dormers. Minehead's grand hotel follows, the former HOTEL METROPOLE, 1893, of red stone, with three gabled accents. W piece with copper-domed corner by *T. H. Andrew*, 1910–12. Here the public seafront ended. Across Blenheim Road, QUAY STREET curves around to the harbour. Houses on the seaward side were cleared in 1914–20. The COASTGUARD HOUSES, 1877, by *St Aubyn*, stand almshouse-like around a garden, five gabled cottages in a row, the master's house separate. The QUAY INN, roughcast with battered chimneys, is by *F.W. Roberts*, 1902. Mixed and altered houses follow the curve, some thatched, some three-storey Georgian. The HARBOUR quay may incorporate George Luttrell's quay of 1610–16. The roughcast SHIP AGROUND was the Pier Hotel of 1900–1, contemporary with the new pier (dem. 1940). The small gabled warehouse adjoining was given by Robert Quirke to support his almshouses in 1630. The ground floor became ST PETER'S CHURCH, for mariners, in 1910. Behind the hotel, a red sandstone LIFEBOAT HOUSE, 1901, by *W.T. Douglass*, the RNLI engineer.

BLENHEIM ROAD returns to the centre. Opposite the coastguard houses, three large roughcast houses by *Frank Tugwell*, 1905, much altered. Overlooking BLENHEIM GARDENS, 1925, are terraces, two by *Tamlyn*, 1900, and two longer rows in stone of 1896 and 1870. The latter, with trefoiled window heads, is by *St Aubyn*, the first tourist development towards the sea.

4. The west, south and east

From Wellington Square, Park Street leads to THE PARKS, an indication of aspirations before the seaside was appreciated. After the Baptist chapel (p. 451), three short terraces built by the Acland estate *c.* 1855 face the landscaped course of a stream, one in stone, two in stucco. Between the first two, MENTONE VILLA, Gothic of 1879–80, emphatically shows that the future was not in terraces. As late as 1902 Minehead finished with the third terrace. Villas now stretch out along the Porlock road. Among the larger ones on the slope, LOWER CLEEVE, by *F. W. Roberts*, 1903, roughcast with battered chimneys, THE PARKS HOUSE, 1926, by *Roberts & Willman*, hip-roofed in red sandstone, and LITTLE STOKE, roughcast with roofs of Delabole slates, by *Edwin Gunn*, c. 1930.

Returning to Park Street, the former POST OFFICE, Parkhouse Road, of 1913, by *F. C. R. Palmer*, stone neo-Tudor. Behind, a three-storey former TELEPHONE EXCHANGE, 1932, by the *Office of Works*. Brick, Neo-Georgian, with an industrial twist. Up Park Terrace, the red brick BAGLEY'S BAKERY, by *W. J. Tamlyn*, c. 1910. It faces up BAMPTON STREET, the only Lower Town street with an older character, albeit very battered. Roughcast terraced houses, the largest BAMPTON HOUSE, early c18, and BLAKE HOUSE, three-storeyed, c17. Nos. 38–44 are thatched, c18. Selbourne Place runs E past the former convent (p. 451) to TOWNSEND ROAD, the continuation of Friday Street. TOWNSEND HOUSE was rebuilt in 1764, stuccoed, provincial Georgian, with a pedimental gable over an attic oval and first-floor niche. Opposite, IRNHAM LODGE and two similar villas on Irnham Road, 1900–2 by *W. K. Lucas* of London. Tile-hung gables over roughcast and stone. After the R.C. church (p. 451), BLAIR LODGE (Minehead First School), 1884, probably by *J. P. St Aubyn*. Sandstone, with mullion-and-transom stair windows in the front gable.

KILDARE LODGE, next, of 1905–6, by *Barry Parker* of *Parker & Unwin*, is the most interesting Arts and Crafts house in the region. White roughcast under a single roof anchored on raking corner buttresses. These are from Voysey, but the house has a more concentrated massing than usual with Voysey. Receding arches frame the deep-set porch. At the l. corner, a narrow full-height curved window is matched by two on the S end wall that rise sheer under a weatherboarded gable. Some cosy touches such as the front seat-recess into which intrudes a little three-sided window. Flowing interiors, slightly impaired by fire regulation. Stairs in the angle to the rear wing rise to a curved landing with a little oriel overlooking the hall, a tall room lit by the three tall windows, but not large. Corner inglenook, a small room in itself, with good detail in wood and metal.

Up WHITEGATE ROAD, two good houses on the r. OWL'S MEAD, 1920s, has a roof of silvery slates overhanging a square bay. A hipped dormer neatly extends the main roof-line. *Edwin Gunn* probably designed it. GREENHAVEN, c. 1910, is manorial, sandstone, with stone mullions and a moulded entrance arch. Back on Townsend Road, further out are the police station and middle school (pp. 451 and 453).

5. Alcombe and the southern fringe

Townsend Road continues to ALCOMBE. On the main road (A39), a large two-storey VILLAGE HALL, 1925–6, by *Roberts*

& Willman, roughcast over stone, the central gable framed by stone chimneys. Further E, THE TERRACE, a stuccoed row of *c*. 1797, with triple sash windows. It may be connected with the forty houses built to manipulate the vote by John Langston M.P. Opposite the village hall, CHURCH STREET runs past Alcombe church (p. 451) to MANOR ROAD. Nos. 20–22, whitewashed and thatched, are dated 1665 but certainly earlier. C17 plaster friezes and ceiling ornament in No. 22. GROVE PLACE, *c*. 1860, opposite, comprises two rows of workers' cottages meeting at a small chapel. W of Church Street is QUARRY CLOSE, well-designed council housing by *Gunn & Fry*, 1944–6, on the hillside. On COMBELAND ROAD, towards Dunster, a thatched L-plan group, of THE LODGE, C17, and THE HERMITAGE, C18, opposite, a stuccoed former METHODIST CHAPEL of 1850.

ELLICOMBE MANOR, Ellicombe. C16–C17, with a charming early C18 front made by adding a second cross-wing and sash windows. The centre has small-paned sashes and a decorative gablet.

RAVENSCOURT (now Callens Edge etc.), Hopcott Road, opposite Cher. 1904–6, by *Barry Parker*, much altered after a fire. Roughcast and originally thatched (now roofed in green tiles), an L-plan house was diagonally opposite an L-plan stable. The house was extended W in 1908, and an addition of 1946–50 cut between the stable and house. A timber loggia is the most telling surviving feature.

PERITON MEAD, Periton Road, opposite Parkhouse Road. A Cotswold manor house in buff sandstone with Ham stone-mullioned windows. Built in 1920–2 by *P. Morley Horder* for C. S. Orwin, agricultural economist, encasing an existing house. Symmetrical façades. The W front, recessed between wings, is more formal with parapets and coped gables. The E front has gables and a low centre with a hip-roofed dormer.

NORTH HILL. Several prehistoric barrows and defended enclosures. North Hill was a tank training area in the Second World War. Most of the bunkers have been cleared but the road, some earthworks and other structures remain, including part of a radar station. Almost nothing remains of the Cold War radar station built with much controversy, including design advice from the Royal Fine Art Commission, in 1953. Above the cliffs, slight remains of the C15 BURGUNDY CHAPEL, 1¼ m. WNW, much overgrown, and 1 m. further, on a high spur, EAST MYNE CAMP (Furzebury Brake), a small oval Iron Age ringwork, about 80 yds (73 metres) across, the rampart now about 8 ft (2.4 metres) high.

MISTERTON

ST LEONARD. Rebuilt 1840 by *Kempthorne*. Plain lancet style, quite large with a W gallery. – FONT. C12, circular, coved below.

– ROYAL ARMS. 1695. – STAINED GLASS. E window, 1907, by *Maurice Drake*.

By the church, THE OLD COURT. Late C16 with a cross-wing to the l. C17 addition to the r. with a tiny two-light Dec window from the old church. Long C18 stable running forward. Restored in 1905 for Major Crossley, a relation of *Harold Peto*, who may have designed the topiaried garden. The MANOR HOUSE was rebuilt after 1756 for Thomas Hallett as a five-bay double-pile house. N front distinguished by contrasted colours, ochre stone with dressings in white Beer stone. Giant Ionic angle pilasters, doorway with Ionic columns, and an eared window above. C17 service wing, enlarged in 1878 probably by *Henry Parsons*, the Portman estate steward, who lived here. To the E, MANOR FARMHOUSE has a late C17 five-bay mullion-windowed front with central storeyed porch. On the main road, ESTATE HOUSE was the estate office, 1879, presumably by *Parsons*. Towards the E end, a large mullion-and-transom-windowed SCHOOL, 1873–4, by *George Pearce*. Set back behind, the former VICARAGE, 1859, by *J. M. Allen*, hip-roofed, deep-eaved.

HENLEY MANOR, 1 m. W. Stark on a hilltop. The long, irregular three-storey, N-facing range is the earliest part, possibly late medieval, with hoodmoulded C16–C17 windows. A large gable projects towards the l. Behind, a five-bay ashlar wing with C17–C18 cross-windows faces E; built for Sir Andrew Henley or his successor in 1700, Lord Poulett. A detached parallel C17 range with dormer gables may have been lodgings built for Robert Henley (†1656). Interiors altered, panelling removed to Hinton House (*see* Hinton St George).

MONKSILVER

ALL SAINTS. A medieval possession of Goldcliff Priory, Monmouthshire. Red sandstone. Plain three-stage W tower, the lower stages perhaps C14 (see the Dec two-light W window). Perp bell-stage with top-heavy battlements and small single-light bell-openings, for which the polygonal S stair-turret was added. One small Norman window on the chancel N side. As so often in this region, there is a showy C15–C16 aisle, here on the S. Ashlar, embattled, with quatrefoiled merlons, pinnacles over the buttresses, and good squatting beasts and grotesque heads on the cornice. Embattled octagonal rood-stair turret. Nicely detailed three-light windows, one made straight-headed by piercing the spandrels of the two-centred arch. The porch is, unusually, inset in the western bay. Panelled pointed archway. Inside, a three-light window to the aisle and a panelled ceiling matching the aisle ceiling. Broad nave wagon roof with undercut foliage wall-plate. Tiny stone corbels beneath, aligned with the ribs. Flat aisle ceiling with diagonal-cross panels, also with an undercut wall-plate. Arcade piers of standard four-hollow section with polygonal capitals. N of the aisle E window a broad bracket for a statue, carved with an angel with outstretched arms holding a scroll. Perp chancel arch, wider on the l. than the chancel, which was perhaps intended to be rebuilt to the new width. In the chancel N recess, what may be a C15 EASTER SEPULCHRE, a tomb-chest without any identification. Seven panels of florid crocketed finials over small paired cusped lancets, the panels divided by thin buttresses. Chancel roof of the restoration by *J. P. Harrison* of Oxford, 1844–6.

FURNISHINGS. FONT. Perp, octagonal, with shields or lozenges on quatrefoils, the underside panels continuous with the stem. – ROOD SCREEN. C15–C16, much repaired, and perhaps brought in. Six bays, the narrow l. one the entrance to the pulpit. Twin two-light tracery in square-headed panels, i.e. not the Dunster–Minehead type. Finials against each upright. – BENCHES. C16. Straight-headed, without Renaissance elements in the carving, the foliage with a fondness for twisted stems. Also a stag, a leaping fish with a ram, and a green man. Good frontals and a continuous run of narrow traceried panels along the S side of the pews, cut into the arcade shafts. On one panel, a dog bites a fox. – PULPIT. Reached through the chancel wall. C15–C16, narrow, octagonal, with long panels of delicate close tracery. Leaf-scroll angles and thick vine-trail cornice. – LECTERN. Wooden late medieval eagle, one of two in Somerset (cf. East Brent). – POOR-BOX. 1634. – STAINED GLASS. E window, *c.* 1846. Scenes in C16 style, perhaps by *Wailes*, the lamb on the Last Supper plate worth noticing. In the aisle window heads, symbols (Passion, Evangelists) in yellow on grey, perhaps 1840s.

CHURCHYARD CROSS. 1863, by *John Seymour* of Taunton. Unaccountably commended by Pooley in his book on Somerset crosses.

By the Notley Arms, the handsome hip-roofed STABLES, 1860, incorporated a village hall upstairs. Built by the Notleys of Combe Sydenham. Opposite, COURT HALL, with a C16 stone Tudor-arched doorway. Sensitive extensions each end by *Louise Crossman*, 2009. HALF MOON COTTAGE, thatched and roughcast, was a late medieval hall house. Stair projection by the N fireplace, which has a curing chamber on the other side. On the lane SW, WAYSIDE has similar C16 stone doorways to that of Court Hall, one each end of the cross-passage. On the back lane to the E, CRIDDLE'S FARMHOUSE, thatched, with wooden cross-windows of *c.* 1700 under slightly cambered heads.

COMMUNITY HALL, SE of the village. 1990, by *Jeremy & Caroline Gould*. Strikingly modern for a village hall. Monopitch-roofed. The lean-to against the high wall contains the entrance, kitchen etc.

COMBE SYDENHAM. *See* p. 217.

MONTACUTE

The village of beautifully honey-coloured stone cottages laps S and W of the grounds of Montacute House, overlooked from the W by the conical 'mons acutus', St Michael's Hill, outlier of Ham Hill whence came the stone. Montacute was a Norman borough, founded on the Saxon village of Bishopston.

ST CATHERINE. The pride of Montacute church is its late C15 W tower. Four quatrefoil friezes mark the main divisions on the prominent W and N sides. Set-back buttresses continue as diagonal shafts against the bell-stage with beasts at cornice level and lion masks between them on the tower angles. Two-light bell-openings with transom and pierced baffles. Battlemented crown, originally with three pinnacles at each corner. Polygonal NW stair-turret. The W window is exceptionally large, of four lights with a transom, and the W doorway has traceried spandrels between diagonally set shafts with pinnacles. The tower arch is panelled with ogee tracery. All this has elements of the Shepton Beauchamp tower. The aisleless nave has Perp windows. Of about the same date is the curious chamber inserted between the N porch and the N transept. This has a panelled W arch and panelled pointed vault. But the church is older, and the evidence survived a restoration that was close to rebuilding in 1870–1, by *Henry Hall*. The oldest part is the Norman chancel arch, of three orders. The arches are plain, two on nook-shafts with simple capitals. In the nave N wall is a re-set Norman arch, just voussoirs ornamented with lozenges overlaid with beaded circles. The transepts and chancel are of *c.* 1300, the transept arches double-chamfered on triple shafts (the N ones with fillets) and round moulded capitals (the SE ones with nailhead). The transept and chancel windows are of three lights with foiled circles in the heads, renewed, but pointing to the same date. There is no evidence for a crossing tower. The tall storeyed porch has a double-chamfered arch but the ogee-canopied niche and star-vault suggest the later C14.

An expensive and ebullient Victorian character is dominant within. *Hall* put in open roofs on carved angels and inserted an organ loft into the porch chamber, with a gallery on crouching musician corbels (which are new, except the very primitive harp-player which he found). Access to the loft is from the chamber E of the porch, which Hall opened to the N transept. In the S transept a cusped PISCINA of *c.* 1300, and a C15 floral corbel on the E window mullion. In the chancel E wall are black-letter INSCRIPTIONS in English. Two of these replace statues in ornate canopied niches; the third, of 1543, frames the reredos.

FURNISHINGS by *Hall*, expensive and complete, notably the brass-railed PULPIT on a marble-shafted base, the REREDOS of naturalistic carving and *Minton* tiles, and the brass LECTERN on a block of brown Devonshire marble. – FONT. Octagonal, Early Perp, tapered below and panelled all over. – STAINED GLASS. Chancel glass by *Clayton & Bell*, 1870. – MONUMENTS. The N transept became the Phelips Chapel, though nothing commemorates Sir Edward, builder of Montacute House. – David Phelips †1484 and wife. Two poor effigies, he armoured, she in gown and head-dress. Possibly early C17 to consolidate the Phelips ancestry, which was obscure. – Matching lady (reputedly Bridget Phelips †1508), in ruff and gown. – Thomas Phelips †1588 and wife †1598. Two effigies in a panelled stone recess fronted by a depressed arch between Corinthian columns, topped by heraldry. Probably by *William Arnold*. The Berkeley tomb at Bruton is similar. – Sir Edward Phelips †1690. Very large and splendidly architectural, in coloured marbles, probably of the 1720s. A giant pedimented aedicule on pairs of Ionic pilasters frames a trapezoid sarcophagus with gadrooned lid, against a pink obelisk.

The churchyard has an eroded CROSS with a low-relief figure under a crocketed pinnacle. A kneeling donor on the other side. Also the probable base of a C14–C15 PULPIT, panelled like the font. By the tower S side, a medieval stone COFFIN. The four-centred arched GATEWAY has traces of Gothic lettering, probably C16.

BAPTIST CHURCH, South Street. 1879, by *Morgan H. Davies* of London. The gable has a big rose but no door. This is in a gabled turret whose upper level was the gallery entry, reached by a Gothic staircase that rises diagonally, and theatrically, across the front.

PRIMARY SCHOOL, Ladies Walk. 2006, by *Graham Whiteley* of *Somerset County Architects*. Loosely grouped, gabled, with a Gothic touch in the long triangular-headed windows.

MONTACUTE PRIORY, SW of the church. Founded *c.* 1078 as a Cluniac house, but nothing of the C12 remains, indeed nothing but the gatehouse range remains of the whole priory. A church, refectory, cloister and other buildings are mentioned in 1304, in bad condition. The gatehouse range is early C16, from the initials of Thomas Chard, prior 1514–32, and indicates the wealth of the house even then. The show façade is to the S, although the approach was from the N and the church and cloister stood probably to the E. The gateway itself is embattled, with a handsome oriel on both faces over a high four-centred moulded and shafted archway. The oriels are mullioned with four-centred lights and have friezes of quatrefoils with emblems above and below. On the S are flanking stair-turrets, the l. one to the tower chamber, the lower r. one to the eastern range. The two side ranges are embattled, the western one of just one bay, the eastern one of three divided by buttresses. This range has quatrefoils in the battlements and mullion-and-transom windows, the lower ones of three lights in deep reveals. Within the archway a two-bay tierceron vault with fine bosses, and an E doorway with Chard's initials. Handsome C16 fireplace, the lintel panelled in a precursor of strapwork. The

ABBEY FARM barns are C18 to C19, converted. The square DOVECOTE in the field to the SE is probably C17, with C18 brick nesting boxes.

PERAMBULATION. W of the church is the SCHOOL, 1847, Tudor-style, battlemented with central gable and bellcote. The lane runs S to the priory (*see* above). BISHOPSTON runs N. Notable at either end are the OLD VICARAGE, five bays, mullioned, 1715, and the thatched and extremely attractive MONKS HOUSE. This has C17 cross-mullioned windows in two ashlar dormers, but the house was originally a late C15 two-bay hall. A fine C15 moulded fireplace with haunched jambs stands oddly outside the hall, next to a partition with C16 painted decoration. The partition is a C20 import. The fireplace may have come from the priory. No. 6 SMITH'S ROW, C16–C17, has a mullioned bay window. (Good fireplaces inside, one with a bishop's head.) N past the Montacute House gates (*see* below) is PARK HOUSE, 1828, hip-roofed and square, a later vicarage.

MIDDLE STREET runs E from the church with mixed small houses. No. 11, with mullion windows with arched lights, has a medieval roof. THE BOROUGH, now a large square with varied two-storey houses, was the centre of a C12 planned town from which streets ran N, S and W. The drive to Montacute House replaces the N street, of which only one range of buildings remains, probably built for the priory. The N end, No. 1, has two windows with cusped ogee lights of *c.* 1400 below, and one slightly later window above, originally in a gable. The S half, THE CHANTRY, ends in a two-storey bay window with a Renaissance relief of naked figures in funny pointed hats. They hold a shield with the initials of Robert Shirburn, prior 1532–9. The square has a little tripod FOUNTAIN, by *A. R. Powys*, 1902. Powys, an Arts and Crafts architect whose father was vicar here, was instrumental through the SPAB in bringing Montacute House to the National Trust.* On the E side, the PHELIPS ARMS has stepped Late Georgian sashes. The S side is a consistent late C17 mullion-windowed row. The W side is mixed, C16 to Early Victorian. No. 27, on the corner, has a moulded C16 fireplace. On SOUTH STREET Nos. 1 and 2 are Late Georgian, detached, before the chapel (*see* above). Nos. 7–9, much altered, have a C15 window in the S gable. At the S end, TOWNSEND runs W to FULLFOOT TERRACE, 1912, by *Petter & Warren*. Possibly the first rural council houses in Britain, consequent on the 1909 Housing Act. Twelve houses, costing £162 each, in two Ham stone terraces. More cottage-like than later housing of this type, with attic dormers. Small-paned casements have been removed.

MONTACUTE HOUSE (National Trust). There are those to whom Montacute remains the most lovable of Elizabethan houses. The reasons deserve consideration. The house is built of Ham stone, whose warmth of colour, varying from a soft biscuit to

---

* Powys's siblings included the authors J.C. and T.F. Powys.

a tanned tone, is unmatched. It is large yet not overpowering. It is neither as bleakly direct as Hardwick nor as flamboyant as Wollaton. And it still has in front of its garden façade a forecourt more complete than most, with balustraded side walls crowned by obelisks, each punctuated by a transparent rotunda and terminated at two summerhouses or plaisances. It is through this forecourt that the house was and should be approached.

The house was built between about 1595 and 1601 for Sir Edward Phelips M.P. †1614, lawyer and later Speaker of the House of Commons and Master of the Rolls. His family owned the house until 1931, when it was bought by Ernest Cook and presented to the National Trust, their second country house (cf. Barrington Court), but with no furniture and no endowment. The overall plan is an H, except that the E façade has a storeyed central porch, and the house is wholly symmetrical. Symmetry links Montacute to Longleat, of the 1570s, and separates it from Somerset contemporaries such as North Cadbury Court. Montacute is above all an outward-looking show house, of a height (92 ft/28 metres) that still astonishes. The double curves of the outer gables give it an especial flamboyance, and although there is a high degree of repetition in the design, there is more syncopation than in the repeated vertical elements of Longleat. Montacute does not have Longleat's classical repertoire of pilasters and entablatures. Its more naïve classicism appears in chimneys disguised as columns (also a feature of Longleat) and cornices that differ on each floor (and revert to drip-courses off the main façade).

The architect was almost certainly *William Arnold*, whom Phelips recommended to Dorothy Wadham for her Oxford college in 1609. Certain external features tie Montacute to a group of houses across Somerset, Dorset and Wiltshire with which *Arnold* may have been, or in the case of Cranborne House, Dorset, definitely was involved. These are the rusticated arched main doorway, the paired shell-headed niches in the plinth, and the dish roundels in the first-floor sill-zone of the porch and bay windows. These roundels are decorative, not settings for classical busts as at Longleat or Cranborne. The shell niches reappear widely, at Cranborne, at Wayford Manor, Somerset, and at Lulworth Castle, Dorset. It should however be said that Arnold was a mason whose responsibility for design cannot be known. A plan like Montacute's and an elevation with Montacute's shaped gables exist by Arnold's contemporary *John Thorpe*.

The EAST FRONT rises three full storeys with additionally attics in the cross-wings. The large mullioned windows are, as at Longleat, double-transomed on the main floors and single-transomed on the second floor. The porch bay matches, under a semicircular gable flanked by obelisks. Between the porch and the outer wings are five closely spaced bays, the middle one emphasized with a semicircular gable echoing that of the porch, over a second-floor window wider than those to either side, this over a two-storey bay window capped by a low curved pediment. The balustrades that flank the gables match those of the forecourt, with obelisks. Between the upper windows are eight shell niches with statues, a ninth in the porch gable. They are the Nine Worthies, in Roman armour, from Flemish engravings. The wings project by one bay. Their inner faces have similar balustrades and a slightly different curved gable backed by a pair of column chimneys with pierced domical caps. Each wing finishes in a large shaped gable with curves and double curves, embellished again with obelisks. In each gable a mullioned window, over a second-floor window and two-storey bay window matching the middle bay of the intermediate ranges.

The N and S sides are simpler and imposingly sheer. The curved gables backed by column chimneys of the inner faces are here repeated, flanking a central shaped gable like those of the wings. The principal motif is at first surprising: a tall semicircular oriel with three transoms high up, in the middle of the second floor. The justification is that they mark the ends of the Long Gallery which runs all the way from N to S, 172 ft (52.4 metres) long.

The WEST FRONT was the rear of the Elizabethan house with wings thickened for two staircases. It became the main front when a new W drive was made in 1786. Then the façade was remodelled with a two-storey corridor between the staircases, a typical later rearrangement of the inconvenient interconnecting house plans of the C16 and C17. Here the character is unexpected because Edward Phelips ornamented his addition with pieces he purchased from Clifton Maybank, near Yeovil, just in Dorset. These pieces belong to an earlier period than Montacute, and their reuse is a sign of the Gothicism of the late C18. For Gothic the elements are, though the date is *c.* 1546 and characteristic motifs of the Italian Renaissance appear. From the corner of the house still standing in Dorset it does appear that the Montacute façade is essentially the old one, and not Georgian with retrieved elements grafted on. Three wide bays, the porch in the projecting centre, with mullion-and-transom windows and a parapet of pointed quatrefoils. Octagonal shafts in four stages flank the outer windows and form the angles of the centre. They display four types of fluting, a compendium of Gothic mouldings, have Perp panels at parapet level, and are capped by twisted finials carrying heraldic beasts. Such finials appear at Melbury House, Dorset, and Barrington Court and Brympton House, Somerset, all early to mid-C16. Renaissance motifs appear on the porch bay, first in miniature on the capitals of the Gothic four-centred doorway. Above is a large square panel between diagonal shafts. The square frames a lozenge with Phelips's arms of 1786. The outer triangles within the square have Renaissance ornament, the upper two dense foliage around knotwork roundels with initials (Horsey of Clifton Maybank), the lower two athletic cherub supporters. The flanking diagonal shafts are not

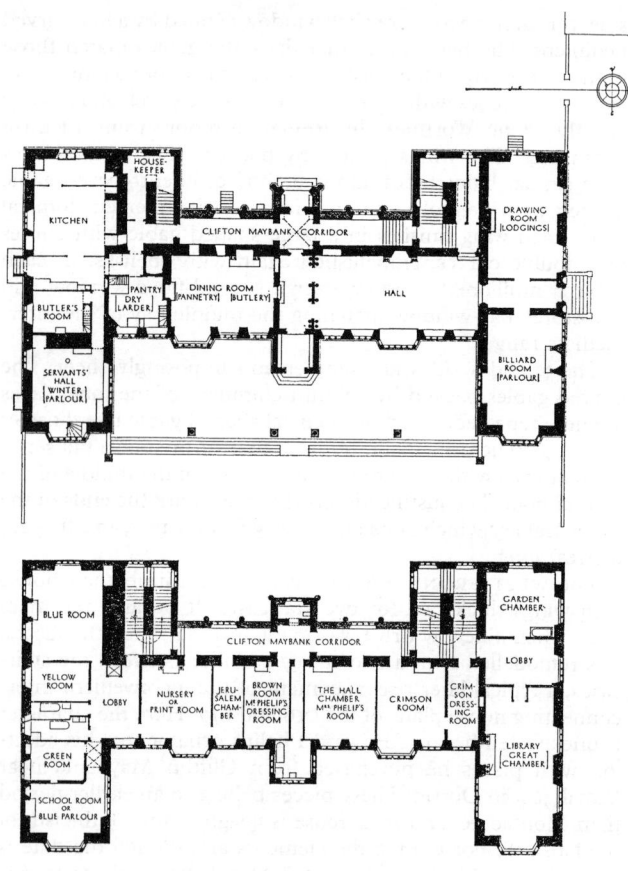

Montacute House.
Ground-floor and first-floor plans

treated in the Gothic tradition but with Renaissance candelabra; however, they revert to Gothic as they continue upward through a band of ogee Gothic ornament with shields and rosettes, and finish Renaissance again in capitals and standing putti flanking the upper window. The greater scale of Montacute leaves a full storey above and behind. This has shouldered plain gables with obelisks, the centre projected, the two intermediate gables carrying tall diagonal chimneys, and balustrades between. The wings have the shaped gables of the E front, but are widened for the stairs. String courses scramble uncomfortably over the stair windows, one infelicitous aspect of the design.

INTERIOR. The arrangement of the principal rooms is between the medieval and modern. The porch leads in the medieval way into the screens passage, to the r. of which lies the hall and to the l. of which were butteries. But in the post-medieval way the hall is no longer the principal room nor even the banqueting chamber, but a low-ceilinged antechamber. Where the dais would have been, an arch opens to the cross-wing with private rooms, parlour and bedroom perhaps. In the other cross-wing beyond the butteries were the kitchen and offices. In the angles to the rear are the staircases, linked since 1786 by the rear corridor. The NW stair is the principal one since banqueting happened in the Great Chamber upstairs (an astonishingly inconvenient distance from the kitchen).

The HALL is dominated by the screen of Ham stone, twin-arched with paired columns, the capitals in white stone of extreme delicacy and oddity. The ram's-head volutes originate in a design by Vredeman de Vries. White modillions in the frieze confirm that colour contrast was part of the design. The heavy strapwork cresting is particularly undisciplined, the centrepiece with rams' heads, human faces, festoons and nude supporters. The fireplace has coupled Tuscan columns and a triglyph frieze. The fish-like creatures in the narrow plaster frieze reappear at Nettlecombe Court, 1599 (q.v.), one of several parallels sufficient to attribute the plasterwork to *Robert Eaton* of Stogursey. Heraldic stained glass, c. 1600. At the far end is a large and surprising plaster panel. It shows a husband beaten with a shoe by his wife for helping himself to beer while minding the baby, this espied by a villager, resulting in a Skimmington ride, the man being paraded round the village on a pole, but not unhappily, as he plays the flute. What can have made Phelips choose this for his house? Sophistication and naïvety are often side by side in Elizabethan and Jacobean decoration.

A short passage divides the NE parlour and NW drawing room. The PARLOUR has a strapwork plaster frieze with animals and Phelips shields. The panelling, with typical Jacobean arched dado panels, was in the room above in 1834. The gargantuan Ham stone chimneypiece of two orders of columns and heavy strapwork ornament reappears across three counties (Wayford Manor, Somerset; Wolfeton House, Dorset; The Hall, Bradford on Avon, and Stockton House, both Wilts.), suggesting the range of *Arnold*'s employment. The DRAWING ROOM shows nothing of the C17, being re-created in 1961 around a later C18 marble chimneypiece with Lord Radnor's arms rescued from Coleshill, Berks.

The DINING ROOM, S of the screens passage, has a complicated history. The buttery with corridor behind was made into a 'common parlour' in 1787, but the part with the bay window was another room until Lord Curzon, tenant from 1915 to 1925, united the two, leaving the parlour fireplace uncomfortably off-centre. This fireplace must have been assembled in 1787 from elements original to the house. The chimneypiece has paired columns and a diamond-block frieze. Above is a plaster overmantel dated 1599 with heraldry in a strapwork surround. This is flanked by fancy woodwork topped by little obelisks. Capping it all is an early C18 plaster cartouche with

Montacute House, hall screen.
Engraving by Laing, 1848

a female portrait. The panelling is early C17, amplified by Curzon. To create the 1787 parlour a substantial room must have been dismantled, perhaps the NW one. Behind, the barrel-vaulted CORRIDOR of 1786 connects the two large oblong stone STAIRCASES, each around a solid core, the NW staircase with Montacute niches, the SW one narrower. The KITCHEN, SW, is large and plain with N wall fireplace.

On the FIRST FLOOR another corridor of 1786 runs behind previously interconnecting rooms. The principal room is to the NE, the Great Chamber that became the LIBRARY after 1875. It has the most elaborate of *Arnold*'s chimneypieces, of white Portland stone in two levels of coupled columns. There is large and strident strapwork at both levels, the overmantel between shell niches. These had standing nudes, removed by the Victorians. A small naked lady remains in the centre, similar to tiny figures on the Berkeley tomb at Bruton. The overall design is virtually repeated at Stockton House. The Jacobean-style ceiling and panelling are replacements probably of 1876 for the panelling now downstairs. The deep plaster frieze is original, its motifs in squares typifying the first-floor plasterwork. The ornate draught-porch, individually the most elaborate woodwork in the house, is original, though moved from the parlour below. The stained glass with Phelips heraldry has dates of 1598 and 1599. The SW room (LORD CURZON'S ROOM) has C17 panelling and a naïve plaster overmantel of King David at prayer, framed in strapwork with poised cherubs. The CRIMSON BEDROOM and its antechamber (probably originally one withdrawing room) have a square-panel frieze in which appears a small panel of the Judgment of Paris, on strapwork studded with lion masks, flanked by perched nudes. The overmantel of the next room, the HALL CHAMBER, has the Phelips arms on strapwork, with fruit, and caryatids very like *Eaton*'s overmantel at Combe Florey. Beyond are two single-bay rooms and a two-bay room with narrow frieze and columned fireplace. In the S cross-wing, the OAK PARLOUR (SE) was fitted up for Lady Curzon, *c.* 1920. Square-panel frieze apparently copied from the library, and ceiling plasterwork copied from the Reindeer Inn, Banbury, Oxon. Upstairs, the splendid LONG GALLERY runs the full length. Well-lit by virtue of the narrowness of the house, it is plain with a deep-coved early C19 ceiling.

GARDENS. The E FORECOURT, originally paved, is one with the façade. There have been changes: the house terrace has lost balustrades, though six free-standing columns remain, their stone finials replaced by lanterns. The side walls and pavilions form a magical enclosure, a fantasy of the castle forecourt. The walls carry balustrades (of vertically symmetrical balusters) between piers crowned by obelisks and are each punctuated by a purely decorative (inaccessible) columned rotunda with an open crown of ogee ribs carrying a pierced finial. Three rather than four ribs make the profile interestingly variable. The two PAVILIONS are fantastical palaces, their ogee slate roofs bordered by fancy battlements and obelisks, and topped by another hollow finial. They are two-storeyed, the ground floor subsidiary to upper banqueting rooms, but floors and stairs have gone. On each side a semicircular centre bay with side-lights echoes the long gallery oriels. The balustrade between the pavilions, with obelisks, gatepiers and cast-iron gates, is a C19 rearrangement. Originally there was a central gatehouse and an outer walled garden. Now a lime avenue stretches into the distance.

The N garden is of raised walks around a lawn. A 'faire Banqueting house built and arched with freestone' was once on the E walk. Pilastered ORANGERY of 1848, with obelisks, on the W terrace, perhaps by *Lewis Vulliamy*. Brick-lined ICE HOUSE under the NW bastion. The garden was embellished in 1892–4 by *Reginald Blomfield*, with terrace balustrades and central pond. On the W side a serpentine drive of 1786 was regularized in 1851–2 to run straight to re-set GATEPIERS

topped with stone flaming braziers. C19 cast-iron gates. To the
SE, behind the service court, a triple-arched LOGGIA terminates a garden walk. It has Montacute detail, even shell niches
inside, but the centrepiece is dated 1588 beneath arms of
William and Joan Strode of Barrington who married in 1621.
It must be an assemblage, but by whom?*

The SERVICE COURT, never grand, was reduced in 1853 to
three monopitch-roofed ranges. Some C16–C17 mullioned
windows and four-centred doorways, one old enough to predate the house. The STABLE COURT W of the drive seems to
be of the 1860s. Three-sided with a gabled throughway. The
several Montacute niches may be copies but the 1598 arms and
C17 cartouche are reused. At the same time the SOUTH LODGE
was reconstructed in imitation of the forecourt pavilions, and
the gable-fronted ODCOMBE LODGE, ¾ m. SE, rebuilt.

ST MICHAEL'S HILL, ¼ m. W. Here was found *c.* 1035 the Holy
Cross for which Harold founded Waltham Abbey, Essex. The
Normans placed a fort on top, recorded as attacked in 1086.
It seems to have been of stone, and there was a stone-vaulted
chapel into the C17. Impressive earthworks still ring the hill,
now crowned by a plain circular TOWER of 1760. It contains
a spiral staircase to a flat-topped conical belvedere. The top,
reached by outside ladder, carried a colossal 50-ft (15-metre)
flagpole for signalling.

MOORLAND

ST PETER AND ST JOHN. 1843–4, by *Benjamin Ferrey*. Rather
good in its simplicity. A single tall vessel, in greenish red rubble
contrasted with grey buttresses and Ham stone Perp windows.
Barn-like roof, of queenpost trusses made Gothic with arched
pieces.

NORTHMOOR PUMPING STATION. 1868, for a steam-driven
pump. The high base of the chimney remains. New station of
1941 behind.

MOORLINCH

ST MARY. Blue Lias. The lower stage of the low, unbuttressed W
tower belongs to the late C13 – see the S lancet and the W
window of three stepped lancet lights, with beautifully cinquefoiled rere-arch. Unchamfered pointed tower arch. Short
battlemented Perp bell-stage. Unaisled nave, and chancel. The
chancel has on each side a Dec two-light window and a square-

---

* It appears on the 1886 map.

headed Perp two-light, all in moulded reveals. Perp E window under C14 plaques: a saltire cross between Lamb of God and eagle roundels, a rose in the apex. Also numerous consecration crosses. The nave has indications of a blocked S arch, otherwise flat-headed Perp windows. But the S porch has a C12–C13 doorway with a fat outer roll and triple-roll inner order, this with lozenges as found in Norman chevron moulding. It must be reused. C14 pointed-arched doorway within, with good oak traceried DOOR. C15 plastered wagon roofs. Early C19 WEST GALLERY. Under it, early C18 panelling and door into the tower, which has vertiginous early C18 stairs to the bell-stage. C14 chancel arch on wave-moulded piers with big polygonal capitals. PISCINA resembling a C13–C14 polygonal capital between tiny outriders. Mid-C19 chancel FITTINGS and tiled floor. – FONT. Norman, re-tooled, with a cable moulding. – PULPIT. Perp, C15. Traceried panels, deep carved cornice, and sloping parapet with 'Qui ex Deo est verba' in large Gothic lettering. – DESK. Pieces from a Perp rood screen. – BENCHES. C16. Moulded square ends with thick tracery, leaves, and a shield with initials. Frontal with traceried panels. – WALL PAINTING. Creed on the N wall, 1636, and a piece on the W wall. – ROYAL ARMS. George III. – ORGAN. Early C19, by *James Davis* of London. Gothic mahogany case. – STAINED GLASS. Chancel, two windows with C15–C16 fragments including a lovely censing angel. Two with bright glass of the 1840s. E window by *O'Connor*, 1871. – MONUMENTS. Effigy of a lady, stiffly carved with elaborate square head-dress, *c.* 1375. – Durston family to 1688. Lias, with cow-head in a wreath amid lively scrollwork.

The view over Sedgemoor from the churchyard is not easily forgotten. Fragmentary CHURCHYARD CROSS, and another by the village hall. Just below, the substantial former VICARAGE, 1802–3, by *James Collibear* of Ashcott. Three bays with parapet and segmental-arched centre window. E of the church, PILGRIM'S REST, with a good four-centred-arched moulded doorway and front buttresses. It was probably the C15–C16 church house. Downhill, MOORLINCH FARMHOUSE, remodelled in the C19, is early C17 – see the broad arched doorway and mullioned window above.

MUCHELNEY

4020

An extraordinary place: the name means big island, but its rise above the moor is barely perceptible. In the C12 it was inaccessible in winter. The church tower visible from afar is at the centre of a little group of buildings associated with Muchelney Abbey.

MUCHELNEY ABBEY. Forged C13 documents have the foundation in 693 by Ine of Wessex. It certainly existed in 762, then

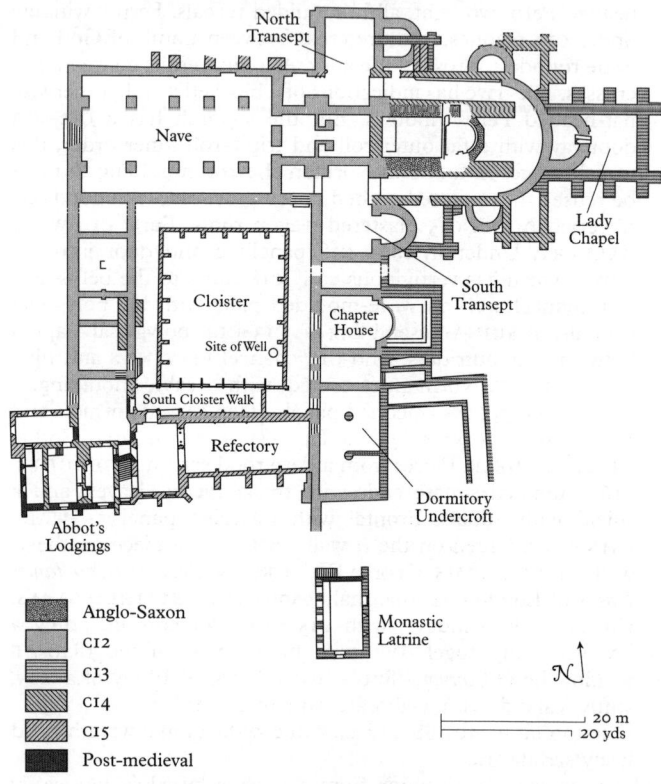

Muchelney Abbey.
Plan

nothing more is heard until a (forged but probable) refoundation charter by Athelstan in 939. It became Benedictine shortly thereafter. Following dissolution in 1538 the church was levelled and lost until excavation began in 1873; the Anglo-Saxon church was uncovered in 1948–52.

The ABBEY CHURCH as rebuilt in the early C12 had a broad apsed chancel with ambulatory, off which were three small half-round chapels, one E, the others N and S, rather than, as would have been done in France, NE and SE. There was a crossing, no doubt with a tower, transepts each with a half-round E chapel, and an aisled six-bay nave, its E bay filled by the pulpitum. The excavated fragments illuminate a sequence of rebuilding. At the core, beneath the presbytery, is the tiny C10 church, apsed with a porticus each side. This was enlarged before being demolished for the C12 work. In the mid C13 the presbytery was remodelled, flat-ended, with new side chapels, the transept chapels were rebuilt square, and a buttressed Lady

Chapel was added, giving an overall length of 260 ft (79.2 metres). The presbytery was vaulted in the C14. Then in the late C15 the crossing piers were re-cased, the surviving NW base showing panelling as in the parish church. It is suggested that the nave and aisles were then rebuilt entirely.

The abbey buildings are to the S. The plan of the cloister and the ranges on its four sides is exposed. There was a C12 cloister, rebuilt at least in part with fine fan-vaulting c. 1500, as survives in the storeyed S walk. Off the E cloister was as usual the dormitory or dorter above the chapter house and day room. The foundations indicate that the chapter house, originally apsed, was lengthened in the C13. Two pillars in the day room indicate a C13 vault. Still standing to the S is the end of the C13 REREDORTER, or lavatory range. Narrower than the dorter to which it was attached, it survived, truncated, as a farm building with half-hipped thatched roof. The first-floor lavatories discharged into a water course through the five pointed openings at the foot of the W wall.* L-plan foundations behind the day room may have been a walk connected to an infirmary. Off the W cloister may have been the abbot's hall.

Most of the remaining buildings are on the S side: the S cloister walk with rooms for the abbot above, and the major portion of the abbot's lodging behind, with the remnant of the refectory W and the kitchens E. The kitchens are early C14, but the rest was rebuilt after 1475. The CLOISTER preserves five of its six bays, a formal façade with large sub-arched and transomed four-light windows divided by buttresses, the bases of diagonal shafts suggesting battlements to the upper floor. Two two-light upper windows, flat-headed with cusped ogee-headed lights, introduce the most characteristic detail of late medieval Muchelney, little foiled circles in the spandrels. These are found nearby on the Priest's House (below) and at Langport and Curry Rivel churches, and appear also at Cleeve Abbey in the late C15 and in numerous West Somerset churches. Backing on to the cloister are remains of the REFECTORY: two and a half bays (of four) of the inner N wall. The tall five-light cusped panelling divided by shafted piers presumably matched windows in the lost S wall. The heads, missing because the refectory was taller than the cloister range, were probably flat and cusped, as at Forde Abbey, Dorset.

W of the refectory, roofed N–S, is the principal part of the ABBOT'S LODGING, a two-storey block linked to small chambers over the cloister. It survived as a farmhouse. The most interesting thing about this range is the way in which the S gable is formed into an orderly façade. Buttresses establish vertical coordination, the two-light windows are vertically aligned, and across the gable runs a band of crenellation to give horizontal finish. The windows are of the Muchelney type, transomed to the upper chamber. The ground-floor room was the ANTE-CHAMBER to the refectory, reached from the cloister via an

---

* It is also suggested that these openings were vents.

ashlar-panelled short passageway. The moulded beams have been tree-ring-dated to the late C15, but the cloister doors to the early C15, i.e. before the abbot's lodging and cloister rebuild. The CLOISTER itself shows high-quality work of *c.* 1500. Thin triple shafts carried fan-vaults, of which only the springing, a delicate dagger with pendant, survives. This detail conforms to the last of the Sherborne Abbey vaults, early C16. The window tracery is repeated as blind panelling in the SW corner, which has doorways W to the lost W range and S to the refectory antechamber. The adjacent S bay has a hand-washing recess.

W of the antechamber, the early C14 KITCHEN RANGE, roofed E–W, contains the inserted stone stair to the abbot's quarters. This turns r. through a late C15 doorway into the GREAT CHAMBER above the antechamber, a handsome room, with the windows, framed ceiling and an angel corbel on the S wall. In addition it possesses one of the most sumptuous pre-Reformation fireplaces in the country. Shafts flank a deep lintel with frieze of large enriched quatrefoils under running vine-trail, the cornice enriched with ivy trail. Above, a big plastered rectangle between shafts rising to excellently carved stone lions, couchant, facing outward. The plaster may have held a painted panel or tapestry. Amid some stained-glass canopy work, the initials TB for Thomas Broke, abbot 1505–22. The linenfold benching is much restored. Of the three small rooms over the S cloister the middle one is richest, with the traceried windows, a panelled barrel roof with traces of painted pomegranate trail, and faint early C16 painted wall hanging. The E room has a wind-braced roof, apparently reused, and faint damask wall painting. The W room has a late medieval fireplace and pointed door.*

Returning to the ground floor, the S wall of the KITCHEN was rebuilt several feet further in after the Dissolution, as indicated by the asymmetry of the roof. Two re-set carved lions on the outside are C15, similar to those in the Great Chamber. This was a most impressive space when built in the early C14, with an open hearth and high roof of close-set arch-braced collar-trusses, with upper crucks, and tiered wind-bracing. As early as *c.* 1400 the room was subdivided by back-to-back fireplaces with enormous lintels of joggled stones. Blocked high two-light W window. From the kitchen, a NW RANGE (tree-ring-dated to 1513–33) is reached. It was probably linked to the abbot's lodgings via the lost great hall. Ground floor with cambered beams. The upper room was of high status with a four-light W window, framed ceiling and deep-lintelled Tudor-arched fireplace. Good early C16 S door, to a possible strongroom against the kitchen W gable, in which are displayed several Norman capitals found in excavation.

ST PETER AND ST PAUL. The parish church immediately adjoins the abbey, as was often the case in the Middle Ages (cf.

---

* A 'Great Oak Door' and window from Muchelney went to the McGeary Snider House, Philadelphia, in 1924.

Westminster Abbey). There is no more than 3 ft (0.9 metres) between the transept of the abbey and the s chapel of the church. Recorded in Domesday, the church is now wholly late C15. Tall handsome W tower of Blue Lias and Ham stone, articulated with string courses. Set-back buttresses connected diagonally; battlements, polygonal SE stair-turret, and pinnacles. Very large transomed five-light window above the W doorway. The next stage has on each side a blind two-light window flanked by canopied niches. This also on the N side ground floor. Quite small paired two-light bell-openings, set between three diagonal shafts which carry through the battlements to pinnacles. This is a stronger design than shafts finished below the parapet (cf. Langport, Westonzoyland) and better than the similar arrangement at Long Sutton, as here the outer shafts continue the buttresses and their pinnacles join the angle pinnacles in a cluster of three. Another indication of the comparative richness of Muchelney is that the bell-stage hoodmoulds continue as string courses around the shafts and buttresses, echoed (though not around the buttresses) on the lower stages and on the chancel E wall. Lion masks flank the shafts below the parapet. Hooded stoup by the W door. The tower has a panelled high arch and fine fan-vault with big bosses very like Shepton Beauchamp. The gartered Daubeney arms give a date between 1487 and 1507.

As the church is approached from the N, this side is treated more richly – battlements with blind quatrefoils, hoodmoulds with headstops, and polygonal capitals to the aisle mullions. The two-storeyed porch is embattled also, with lively ape grotesques, and leaf capitals to the doorway shafts. Within, a good star-vault and N doorway with keeled moulding. Twin chancel chapels, the N one battlemented as is also the eastern chancel bay, enriched with pinnacles, grotesques and hoodmoulds. Three-light side windows and handsome ogee-traceried five-light E window. The three-bay nave arcades, not high, have wave-moulded shafted piers. The wagon roof of the nave has lovable rustic PAINTINGS of angels in Elizabethan dress of extreme *décolletage*. The cotton-wool clouds suggest an early C17 date. The N doorway has a reused late C14 grave-slab in its head. Porch stair to the l. C19 S vestry under a little organ loft. Panelled and shafted C15 arches to the chancel and SE chapel. C15 triple SEDILIA with damaged canopies. The SE chapel has a small reused C15 REREDOS of five niches.

FURNISHINGS. FONT. C15, octagonal with short posts on the diagonals. Four carved panels, three kneeling figures, and a strange Crucifixion, Christ metamorphosed into a tree, the figures moon-faced. – PULPIT. Ejected from the Lord Mayor's Chapel, Bristol, in 1889, with the screen now at Low Ham. The latter was made in 1823 by *Thomas Clarke*, so presumably this also. Notably careful Gothic, in Caen stone. – TILES. C13–C14, from the Abbey Lady Chapel. Among the designs, the elephant and castle. Two exceptionally rare C13 concentric roundels, before the altar and before the font. – BOX PEWS.

1849. – BARREL ORGAN. In a charming painted Gothic case. By *Gray & Davison*, c. 1840. – ROYAL ARMS. George III. – PAINTING. C19 copy of Van Dyck. – STAINED GLASS. Chancel, 1849. The side windows include C17 Flemish roundels and the E window lovely C15 tracery figures. – C15–C16 incised CROSS-SLAB (nave floor).

In the churchyard, a large C16 Perp CHEST TOMB with blind tracery.

PRIEST'S HOUSE (National Trust). A rare and delightful survival, in essence the house requested in 1308, embellished in the C15. Small, but with screens passage, hall, and storeyed ends, just as in a large mansion. A hoodmoulded pointed C14 doorway with iron entwined-serpent knocker marks the passage. The hall to the r. has a four-light transomed late C15 window front and rear, the ogee lights and blind quatrefoils as on the Abbot's Lodging (*see* p. 473). To the r. was an inner room with bedroom above, the one with an early C16 four-light window, the other lit by a small C14 cusped two-light front window and a longer transomed E window. W of the passage was the kitchen with solar over. Both upper rooms would have been accessed by lost turret staircases. In the passage, pointed stone doorways to the W and N, but a Tudor-arched oak doorway E into the hall. An early C16 fireplace with enormous Ham stone lintel was inserted into the hall, against the passage, at the same time as the tall windows. These were subsequently partly blocked by an inserted C17 floor. The E room was remodelled in the early C16 with a framed ceiling and fireplace, the inner wall moved to take in the space beneath the upper-room jetty. Upstairs, the C14 roof has full cruck trusses and lower tier wind-braces. Two smoke-blacked bays to the hall, the second partly obscured by the chimney, and a third to the solar. The boarding behind the rafters dates from repair by *John Schofield*, 1990–3.* The initial rescue in 1911 was due to the infant National Trust, and the repair to the SPAB, in the hands of *Ernest Barnsley* with *Norman Jewson*. In two phases, first the repair, then the fittings. A single curving slab props the back wall under a tile lintel – a perfect illustration of SPAB visible repair. The fittings, models of Arts and Crafts sensitivity, include the staircase, oak doors, dresser and cupboards. *Barnsley* added the thatched NW scullery.

On the triangular green, the CROSS, rebuilt *c.* 1845, on a medieval panelled base. The tiny two-room thatched ALMONRY COTTAGE by the Priest's House is C18, carefully extended behind, 2005, by *Sir Anthony Denny*. Behind, THE TOLL, *c.* 1824, a painted-brick Gothic toll house. To the W was the abbey almonry, replaced 1902 by ALMONRY FARMHOUSE, which has a small C15 relief over the door. The ALMONRY BARN, SW, has a C16 four-centred-arched doorway.

---

* John Schofield notes the experimental nature of the C14 carpentry, purlins jointed to the wind-braces not the trusses.

LOWER MUCHELNEY, ¼ m. s. An attractive street of mullion-windowed and thatched houses links two roads. Mostly of Blue Lias, like TUDOR HOUSE. But MANOR HOUSE, E, and SCHOOL FARMHOUSE, W, are of C18 red brick. Manor House is perhaps all C18, though the central chimney suggests an older core. School Farmhouse is a refacing. It had a C15–C16 wind-braced roof. Contrasted C19 estate cottages: on the N, a pinched terrace of six narrow houses with fragments from the abbey, on the S, MANOR COTTAGES, 1874, very Victorian in crazed White Lias with patterned roof tiles and a little timber. The former SCHOOL, 1872, is careful Gothic, the Priest's House window prominently copied. COURT HOUSE, further W, has an intriguing W front with irregular C16–C17 mullioned windows and buttresses. In the S end, a pointed plaster vault with thin transverse ribs looks early C19. SE wing of 1874 including bits from the abbey.

MUCHELNEY HAM, 1 m. SE. NORTH HAM FARMHOUSE is thatched, with the barn in line, C17 Ham stone below, C18 Lias above. MUCHELNEY HAM FARMHOUSE is C17, ashlar fronted with ovolo-moulded mullions.

THORNEY, 1 m. S. Several thatched and mullion-windowed houses, the best, THORNEY WEST, late C17 with linked hood-moulds. THORNEY EAST (Gothic House), 1850, is Victorian Tudor. Further S is THORNEY MILL, on the River Parrett, 1823, compact, three-storeyed, with a 14-ft (4.27-metre) double-width wheel of 1866 on the E end.

MUDFORD

5010

ST MARY. An E window with Dec reticulated tracery. Otherwise Perp and handsome in detail and proportion. The W tower has set-back buttresses, battlements, and pinnacles at the corners and corbelled out in the middle of each side. A quatrefoil frieze (cf. Chilton Cantelo) is broken by long two-light bell-openings on three sides, but runs below the W opening. The second stage has on the W side a defaced but once fine Crucifixion, apparently reused, with C15–C16 angels added at the upper ends of the cross. Deep-set three-light W window and doorway with foliage spandrels. Polygonal NE stair-turret. Panelled tower arch. The nave and porch are embattled, the chancel not; all with big gargoyles, regular buttresses of Ham stone banded in Lias, and regular three-light windows with supermullions (as at Ashington). The low N transept looks C17 – see the flat-headed windows. The arch within, and the wide chancel arch, are classical, so perhaps later C17. The porch roof, with crude bosses, is dated 1685. Cinquefoil E niche. Harmonious light interior with C15 wagon roofs. Angel corbel with cresting in one S window. – FONT. Perp, octagonal, decorated all over, including a band of cresting (cf. St John, Yeovil). – Very complete C17 FURNISHINGS, similar to those at Ashington, the PULPIT with large flowers and improbable leaves, the BOX PEWS and STALLS with shell tops. – SCREEN. C15. Just the base. Narrow panels with ogee tracery and delicate foliage. – RAILS. Early C18, turned balusters. – STAINED GLASS. E window by *Powell's*, 1919.

The former VICARAGE, 1860, by *Charles Benson*, is red brick, hip-roofed. W of the church, PARSONAGE FARM has substantial Late Georgian brick outbuildings with arched openings. On the main road, the former SCHOOL, 1847, by *Thomas Stent*, has an exaggerated bellcote. TRINITY HOUSE, white-rendered and thatched, C18, may be cob-walled. The OLD DAIRY HOUSE is mid- to late C17, with a broad cross-wing and moulded mullions. Early C18 N addition. Nos. 1–2 AMHERST are typical Goodford estate cottages (*see* Chilton Cantelo), 1860s.

MANOR HOUSE, Up Mudford. 1 m. SSE. Early C17. Ham stone with mullioned windows and a showy cross-wing rising an extra storey, the gable corbelled from a broad canted bay.

WEST MUDFORD, ½ m. NW. Two farms. OLD FARMHOUSE is red brick with stone mullions, mid-C18. Two-storey hip-roofed GRANARY of brick and plaster. WEST FARMHOUSE has later C17 mullioned windows in front, long C18 ones on the rear wing.

MUDFORD SOCK, 1 m. WSW. A Goodford estate hamlet. Hip-roofed brick farmhouse, brick terrace (1870) and characteristic striped brick houses, one dated 1867.

NAISH PRIORY *see* NORTH COKER

NETHER STOWEY

A medieval borough, once with a market cross at the intersection of its three streets. The church and Stowey Court are E of the village, across the by-pass.

ST MARY. Red and buff sandstones. The rather thin three-stage tower is Perp, with diagonal buttresses and higher square NE turret. Moulded pointed W doorway in varied stones. The rest was rebuilt in 1849–51 by *Carver & Giles*, Dec, as the Ecclesiologists preferred, showing Giles modernizing Carver. – FONT. Perp, with pointed quatrefoils, and quatefoils on the coved underside. – ROYAL ARMS. Queen Anne, excellently carved. – Two wooden MITRES on brackets in the chancel commemorate vicars who became bishops, Majendie (Chester 1800) and Fisher (Exeter 1803). – STAINED GLASS. E window by *Ward & Hughes*, 1886; NE, 1877, by *H. Hughes*; NW, 1853, by *Joseph Bell*. – MONUMENTS. Rev. William Griffin †1696. Sumptuous if small, of Watchet alabaster. Wreathed oval between columns under a scrolled pediment. – Christiana Topp †1747. Broad open-pedimented plaque, white on mottled yellow. – Thomas Poole †1837, Coleridge's benefactor. Listing his good works.

STOWEY COURT. Leland mentions works abandoned at the execution of the 7th Lord Audley in 1497, but the L-plan rendered house is mostly Elizabethan, for the 11th Baron, with a re-set doorway dated 1588. Mullion-and-transom windows of the C16 reserved-chamfer type. Gabled dormers. Heavily renewed in 1981–3. The E courtyard has two C15–C16 four-centred-arched gateways in the S wall and a doorway to the churchyard. On the N side a single-storey range with brick tunnel vault. Was it a raised walk or has an upper storey gone? There were gardens and medieval fishponds to the N. The range ends against a tall early C18 SUMMERHOUSE facing the main gateway. Stone with brick dressings, the blind upper storey with two statue niches and a central roundel. On the SW corner of the front garden, a handsome brick GAZEBO of c. 1740 overlooks the road. Square with an ogee slated roof. Stone stairs from the garden to an ashlar Palladian entrance, the doorway arch-headed with triple keystone between sidelights with entablatures on panelled pilasters. The other faces each have two sash windows.

PERAMBULATION. Where the three streets meet, a market cross of 1759 was replaced in 1862 by the Gothic CLOCK TOWER of 1862, set to one side. Red sandstone with a timber bellcote on the roof. CASTLE STREET curves SW, widening to accommodate a stream. A feature here and elsewhere are prettily cobbled pavements. The one large house is POOLE HOUSE, home of Coleridge's friend Tom Poole until 1802. Seven bays, c. 1760, of squared red sandstone with ashlar band and keystones. Poole's barrel-ceilinged 'book-room' survives upstairs. Behind is the hip-roofed late C18 BARK HOUSE of his tannery. The LIBRARY occupies the pioneering school founded by Poole in 1812, enlarged 1925. Below the castle (*see* below), CASTLE HILL HOUSE, hip-roofed behind a parapet, is a Late Georgian remodelling of a C16–C17 house. LIME STREET runs W from the centre with modest houses. The heavy doorcase on No. 12 marks the Savings Bank founded by Poole in 1817. At the end, COLERIDGE'S COTTAGE (National Trust) is neater than the damp thatched house that Coleridge rented in 1797–9, as it was raised and refronted shortly afterwards. Evocative small rooms, restored in 2011.

Finally ST MARY STREET runs E. On the S side, two early to mid-C19 stuccoed houses: THE CLOCK HOUSE, with an almost windowless front, and OAKFORD HOUSE, 1843, showing Early Victorian asymmetry, the sash windows with hoodmoulds. Opposite, three houses of squared red sandstone: No. 7, mid-C19; No. 9, diminutive, with tall early C18 small-paned windows, refacing an older house; and THE OLD HOUSE, early to mid-C18, with chequered brick window heads and band. Altered for Poole in 1802. Next, a little two-storey Georgian Gothic TOLL HOUSE, and No. 21, with segment-headed C18 stone architraves. At the former VICARAGE, a

Regency r. half and Victorian l. half hide the C17 house. Plaster love-heart inside dated 1681 with the initials of the Rev. William Griffin and his wife. STOWEY HOUSE, opposite, is early C17, with cross-wings and gabled porch. Two thin-rib plaster ceilings, the hall of eight-pointed stars, the parlour of leaf-like pointed ovals. Turned staircase balusters, flat wavy ones to the attic.

STOWEY CASTLE, Castle Hill. A spectacular circular motte overlooking the Bristol Channel. Deep ditches separate it from two baileys. Broad foundations of a small square keep on top. Built in the early C12 by Alfred d'Espaigne, the castle was held from the C14 by the powerful Lords Audley, but not apparently re-fortified. Abandoned for Stowey Court by the later C15.

DOWSBOROUGH CAMP, 2 m. w. An Iron Age hillfort on Dowsborough or Danesborough Hill, an isolated summit of the Quantocks. An oval measuring some 340 by 170 yds (310 by 155 metres), encircled by a bank and ditch. Outside the ditch is a counterscarp bank on all sides but parts of N and W. Two of the entrances appear to be original. That at the NW is a simple causeway and gap but that at the E is more complex. The entrance way leads between ramparts and continues as a passage between two flanking structures which include circular probable guardhouses. There is a mound inside the NW entrance, either an earlier barrow or later fire beacon.

NETTLECOMBE

The church stands so close to the Elizabethan mansion that not even a hedge separates the two. The village was removed to Woodford when the park was landscaped in the 1790s.

ST MARY. Red sandstone. Three-stage Perp W tower with diagonal buttresses, two-light bell-openings, and battlements. Octagonal stair-tower on the NW corner. Tower arch of unusual section: ogee, hollow, and one hollow dying in. The rest of the church was much renewed in 1858–70 by *C. E. Giles*, who added (or replaced) clerestory windows, rebuilt the chancel and refaced the S aisle, changing the window tracery. The S aisle, possibly rebuilt after 1440, has the most remarkable feature of the church, two large C13–C14 tomb-recesses so deep that they project as a pair of gables. Nave SE rood-stair turret. N aisle and porch of *c*. 1536. Square-headed windows and N door with leaf spandrels. The NE (Trevelyan) chapel looks later, from the round-headed lights, but was building in 1531–4. Arcades of three bays, the N of pale sandstone, the S of Ham stone, both with piers of standard four-hollow section and emphatically carved leaf-band capitals. The S should be the earlier one, but the distinction is hard to see. Victorian chancel arch. The NE Chapel has a two-bay arcade with double shafts to each opening and plain round capitals. The s aisle was the Ralegh Chapel, endowed in 1440. C15 wagon roof. Ralegh and Clare heraldry on medieval TILES re-set in Georgian paving. Both TOMB-RECESSES have pointed tunnel vaults on three arches starting from big corbels. The inner and rear ribs are chamfered, and the front arch is moulded with a hoodmould. They differ in date, though not by long. The earlier is the eastern one with half-octagonal shafts and moulded capitals to the front arch, and inner and rear arches on head corbels of *c.* 1300. The hoodmould has renewed foliage stops, and a fine small king's head at the apex. The younger arch runs through without capitals, and the hoodmould is unadorned. The big head corbels inside are mid- to late C14 in costume and in style. The cross-legged knight in the eastern recess wears mail and dates from *c.* 1300, the shield with the Ralegh arms. The knight and lady in the other recess are possibly Sir John Ralegh (†1372) and his first wife (†1360), he with hands in prayer and head resting on a large helm. Her effigy is smaller, with a dog by her side, and another under her feet.

FURNISHINGS. FONT. Octagonal, and quite uncommon in its sculpture. Seven scenes represent the Sacraments, and Christ in Glory faces w. Thirty-nine Sacrament fonts are known, all in East Anglia except Farningham (Kent) and here. The date seems to be *c.* 1460–70. The crowded scenes are not especially fine but a few are well preserved. On the underside are angel busts. – PULPIT. Entered via the rood stair. Early to mid-C18, panelled, with handsomely carved borders etc. (cf. Carhampton). – BENCHES. Some early C16, with tracery and plants, also one Renaissance profile head. A frontal of narrow traceried panels in the Trevelyan Chapel. – TOWER SCREEN. C19, reusing six late medieval quatrefoil panels. – STAINED GLASS. E window, 1935, sweet Virgin and Child, by *Martin Travers* (by whom also the red and gold reredos panel). SE window by *Wailes*, 1848. Trevelyan Chapel, late medieval figures re-set in the late C17. Of the three N saints, St George and St Peter are misidentified. The four in the E window include St Urith relabelled to honour a Trevelyan wife. – MONUMENTS. Lady Trevelyan †1697. Corinthian columns and a cornice arched over the heraldry. Two cherubs flat-out on top. – John Oatway †1798, by *King* of Bath. Mourning female by an urn. – Joan Wolseley †1943. A fine small bronze Madonna and Child, by *Ernest Gillick*.

CHURCHYARD CROSS. C15 base and shaft.

NETTLECOMBE COURT. Owned by the Trevelyans from Cornwall from 1453. A lease in 1531 to John Sydenham was made on condition of building a new great hall 'as the olde hall is now'. But the gabled red sandstone mansion is basically Elizabethan, dated 1599 on the porch. Sydenham's Great Hall may be incorporated in the kitchen cross-wing on the N. Whether the centre (the cross-passage and the Elizabethan Great Hall) is on medieval footings is uncertain. The plan, with stair projections in the rear angles and private apartments in the s cross-wing, is typically Elizabethan. A small dining room was added between the staircases in 1641 for George Trevelyan. In 1703–4 Sir John Trevelyan, 2nd Baronet, remodelled the s cross-wing from three storeys to two, facing it in brick with stone dressings. He also rebuilt the adjacent stair-tower and added a small piece on the r. end for a study and closet. The decoration of the stair hall dates from 1733. The s cross-wing was altered again in 1787–8 by *Samuel Heal* of Bridgwater, the dressings scraped off and the front stuccoed (since removed) with a new Ionic porch. In the 1820s the N service range was rebuilt, perhaps by *Richard Carver*. Other C19 alterations include a new secondary stair in 1880.

Nearly symmetrical five-gabled E front. Two narrow gables project furthest, those of the porch and the hall-bay. The two-bay centre gable between them is recessed further than the two-bay cross-wings. Double-height ovolo-moulded windows in Ham stone with two transoms light the hall, two three-light windows in the centre and one five-light in the adjacent hall-bay. The second-floor windows are simply mullioned. The cross-wing gables have altered windows, C18 sashes to the r., blind windows to the l. All the windows have hoodmoulds. All the gables are shouldered, with little obelisks on pedestals. The porch doorway has a four-centred arch, old-fashioned for 1599, albeit under a cornice on consoles. Early C20 heraldry above. Depressed-arched inner doorway. Red brick S side of two storeys and nine close-spaced bays, the two periods of alteration evident from differing brickwork since the stucco was removed. Of 1703–4 are the stone plinth, quoins, and traces of architraves, of 1787–8 the long sash windows and pedimented Ionic porch. Late C19 central gable.

INTERIORS. The extraordinary feature of Nettlecombe is the plasterwork, not just that it is sumptuous, but that it includes work from 1600 through to 1788. The cross-passage has a late C18 ceiling imitating the Jacobean, with flat quatrefoils in panels. The GREAT HALL contains one of the most splendid ceilings in Somerset, of c. 1600, with broad flat ribs and three heavy pendants. The ribs outline kite shapes and interlocking diagonal squares, and are ornamented where they radiate from the centre pendant. Also there are floral scrolls in the panels. The pendants are each of two spheres, the middle pendant larger and ornamented with fleshy fruit typical of the *Robert Eaton* school. The whole ceiling is very slightly coved, on a scrolled frieze matching one at Montacute, with flowers and fish-like creatures. Large Tudor-arched stone fireplace, under a very high overmantel of strapwork around a panel with Trevelyan/Chichester arms between crude female figures. Tiny hunting figures scurry above the upper strapwork, and above that is a row of shields between small figures. Early C18 large-field panelling to mid-height. Over the cross-passage, a panelled GALLERY with a very early country-house organ of 1666, the case Late Georgian.

In line with the cross-passage is the second STAIRCASE of 1880, imitating the earlier stair. Tudor-arched doorway s into the SMALL DINING ROOM (Guard Room). Plasterwork of 1641, dated on the overmantel. This has Trevelyan/Strode heraldry on strapwork. The four panels of the ceiling each have a wreath in a geometric pattern of squares (as at Gaulden Manor, Tolland) between beams plastered in the new Inigo Jones style, on classical consoles. But the classicism is minimal; the deep frieze has a strange angular pattern of opposed flat leaves. In the panelled BEDCHAMBER above, a Jonesian ceiling oval of laurel frames the Trevelyan crest of a swimming horse, but the spandrel scrolls end in animal heads and there is a vine-trail border. Similar oval ceilings are at Gaulden Manor, Poundisford Park, and Bournes (Wiveliscombe). The overmantel has Strode/Wyndham heraldry on strapwork between pendant fruit. It harks back to *Robert Eaton*, but with consoles instead of caryatid figures.

The main STAIRCASE was remodelled around 1704. Of that date the very tall pair of thirty-nine pane windows with thick glazing bars. The staircase itself, of square open-well type with relatively slim bulbous balusters and carved tread-ends, looks later, perhaps of 1733. Inlaid marquetry monograms on the half-landings. Dado panelling, marble floor, and mahogany doors in fruit-carved frames (like the pulpit in the church). Exceptionally for the region the plasterwork is Rococo, and in the Chinese taste (i.e. later than the staircase), mid-C18 probably. Charming, light and delicate motifs, very thin with much space left bare. In the ceiling centre an eagle or phoenix in a roundel. Amid the surrounding scrolls are demi-figures under Chinese parasols. In the cove, foliage and festoons with three-quarter profile heads (not Chinese) and grotesques in the corners. Amid the wall decoration, little Chinese buildings, a pheasant under a parasol, lion masks and pendant Chinese bells. Inset C19 roundel bust of Pauline, Lady Trevelyan, friend of Ruskin. The two rooms of the s front were remodelled by *Samuel Heal* in 1787-8. In the DRAWING ROOM, W, a nice Adam-style ceiling, fluted doorcase, and handsome white marble chimneypiece with flutings inlaid in red, and Neoclassical urns. In the DINING ROOM, E, a Neoclassical frieze, a screen of Ionic columns across one end, and an Ionic chimneypiece of marble and pink granite.

To the N of the cross-passage, the front room of the kitchen cross-wing was re-fitted as a PARLOUR in 1704. The nine-panel framed ceiling was plastered and the panels ornamented with acanthus rosettes in circles of laurel, crossed branches of oak and laurel in the corner panels. The addition of 1704 on the NE corner has one small room on each floor with much more ornate ceilings, by the same hand as at Fitzhead Court, Stockland Lovell (Fiddington), and No. 1 High Street, Wiveliscombe, probably the North Devon plasterer *John Abbott Jun*. Notably scowling cherubs. In the ground-floor STUDY a misshapen cherub encircled by palm sprays, within a circle of high-relief flowers and foliage, itself within a bolection moulding. Spandrels of scrolled acanthus and laurel. In the panelled CLOSET above, a quatrefoiled square is bordered in even more three-dimensional leaves. Cherub heads in the corners of the square and very naturalistic circled laurel branches in the centre. Rich acanthus spandrels. The adjacent bedroom has a moulded Tudor-arched fireplace, the monolithic lintel apparently of Watchet alabaster. Behind the parlour, the KITCHEN. A moulded Tudor-arched fireplace of great width on the inner wall may be that of the 1530s Great Hall. Moulded arched cross-passage doorways. Attached L-plan SERVICE RANGE, raised and remodelled in the early C19. Ground-floor cross-windows and the remains of four tall narrow doorways with shell motifs in blind arched heads, probably of 1704.

N of the house, the STABLE COURT, dated 1792. Plain two-storey front with pedimented archway to a single-storey courtyard. Behind the stable court, a long red sandstone BARN, c. 1700, altered in the C19 as the estate sawmill. The E end, prominent from the drive, was made into a Tudor-style gardener's house, c. 1820, by *Richard Carver*. In the orchard above, a tiny STUDIO, 1989, by *David Lea*, like a narrow upturned boat, with pointed glazed ends and thatched roof. The structure is of woodland thinnings, hooped, latticed and plastered.

The PARK stretches S. It was already landscaped in a view of 1787. *John Veitch* made improvements including the ha-ha in 1792. Sir John, 2nd Baronet, laid down a formal canal in the 1690s and embellished the stream with five cascades. The canal has gone; the cascades were altered c. 1828.

COMBE, 1 m. S. Beautifully set at the head of the park. The spreading white house was built c. 1794–5 as a dower house, but became the rectory. Economical in detail. The entrance front has a four-bay centre with a pediment over the centre two. The door and side-lights are framed by an ashlar pediment on four pilasters. L-plan service ranges each side. At the back, a plain five-bay hip-roofed block faces down the combe, set forward of pedimental gables on the service ranges. Altered inside in the mid C20 for Boise Penrose, who removed the staircase, leaving a top-lit central hall with a Neo-Georgian balcony. Imported Georgian features include mahogany doors from Bruton Street (Westminster), a wooden chimneypiece from Bloomsbury, and a yellow-and-white marble one from Tower Hill, all London; and a handsome Neoclassical chimneypiece, also yellow-and-white, from Malshanger House, Hants.

WOODFORD, ¾ m. NE. Sir John Trevelyan, 4th Baronet, moved the village in the 1790s, but the cottages here are rather later, mostly by *James Babbage*, the Nettlecombe agent. At the S end a pair of 1824 with canted bays and slightly Tudor glazing; opposite a rather more Tudor one of 1852, with a cottage row of 1865 behind. Then Woodford House, the agent's house, c. 1860, and a U-shaped block of four. At YARDE, to the N, the large former SCHOOL, 1819–21, by *Carver*. Georgian Gothic, stuccoed, with stepped gables and a triple-arched porch.

Huish Barton, ¾ m. N. A plain two-storey brick farmhouse with some late C17 brickwork and Georgian sash windows. What is notable is the rear room, on the scale of a separate house. Brick front with four long wooden cross-windows, the heads cambered, over four short basement windows. Large end chimneys and hip-roofed side porches. Built for George Musgrave of Combe Sydenham in 1698, dated with his monogram on a large plaster plaque inside. The ceiling plasterwork has gone. There were wreaths in panels, as at Nettlecombe Court. Was it a manorial courtroom? Opposite, a Late Georgian BANK BARN on eight basement arches, attached to a slightly later three-storey range.

Colton Farm, 1 m. s. Late Georgian estate farm, with a hip-roofed BANK BARN dated 1806. Single-storeyed to the farmhouse with a big attached horse-engine house, two-storeyed towards the yard. This has open-fronted sheds on round piers. At the SE corner a mill with overshot wheel.

Chidgley, 1 m. SW. CHIDGLEY FARMHOUSE is Tudor style, probably by *Richard Carver*, for the Nettlecombe estate, 1820s. CHIDGLEY HILL FARMHOUSE, thatched, L-plan, has a framed ceiling and a beam dated 1583. A little N, a small stuccoed LODGE, 1820, by *Carver*.

NEWTON SURMAVILLE

1 m. SE of Yeovil

The gabled house of Ham stone, set so beautifully in the valley of the River Yeo, is a smaller and more harmonious version of the Late Elizabethan North Cadbury Court (q.v.). It was built between 1608 and 1612 for the octogenarian Robert Harbin of Gillingham, Dorset. The N front has three gables separated by two matching but not identical features, the porch and the hall-bay. Both are two-storeyed with balustrade and corner obelisks. The porch, r., is of ashlar with a round arch and the arms of a 1647 Harbin marriage under a mullion-and-transom window. The hall-bay is identical in its upper part, but has rubble walling and the upper window repeated on the ground floor. Under the gables are neatly reducing windows, five-light, four-light, and three-light to the attics, the main ones with transoms. Two string courses. Sober regularity is subverted in the fantastical Jacobean way by the chimneys: single diagonal shafts, capped as at Longleat and Montacute with pierced domes, here crested with golf-ball spheres.

The house was carefully repaired and extended by George Harbin, owner from 1837 to 1885. The E front, remarkable in its contrast of solid and void, is mostly his, of *c.* 1850. Three large chimney-breasts carrying obelisks and tall single diagonal chimneys separate narrow balustraded window bays. Only the r. chimney-breast existed in 1840; the central one, pierced at the base by a doorway, serves no purpose. SE addition, for a library, with an oriel based on Montacute Priory, of 1875. Handsome C18 gatepiers to the N forecourt.

The interiors are largely Victorian, overlaying original and mid-C18 work. The single-storey hall has a Georgian cornice and arched niche, an altered C17 fireplace, dated 1885, and reused Jacobean panelling. Reused panelling also in the NW room and a C19 ceiling. In one corner a fragment of original frieze. The thin-ribbed ceiling of the NE drawing room could be genuine, as the mask bosses resemble work at Combe Florey, but the oak overmantel with gadrooned panels and female demi-figures is almost certainly imported. George Harbin added a corridor behind the front rooms on both floors and rebuilt the corner staircase slightly further out. The dining room, E, has large-field C18 panelling. Neo-Jacobean fireplace, overmantel and ribbed ceiling with pendants. Another neo-Jacobean thin-ribbed ceiling in the room over the hall. Moulded C17 fireplace and panelled oak overmantel. In the room over the dining room, a genuine C17 plaster overmantel with the Harbin arms.

Up the valley, the Ham-stone COACHHOUSE, 1870, its arches perhaps reused from the coachhouse of 1711. Mullion-windowed C19 stables adjoining.

THE ROUND HOUSE, Summer House Hill. Belvedere of 1745, built for Swayne Harbin. A sophisticated design, not octagonal because the diagonal faces are quadrant-curved. Cornices over each floor, blind attic panels, octagonal roof. Corniced doorcase with rusticated pilasters. Multiple keystones to the windows. Low two-storey single-bay wings in contrasting Yeovil stone.

NORTH BARROW

ST NICHOLAS. Perp three-stage W tower, the rest of 1860 by *Henry Perry* of Crewkerne, neatly done. The tower arch is C14, wave-moulded on piers with moulded capitals. – FONT. Misshapen polygon with angle rolls, chamfered below. Is it C12? Harvey Pridham thought it C15–C16.

RECTORY. 1871, by *William Clarke* of Bruton. Gabled, of Cary stone.

NORTH CADBURY

Church and house form an uncommonly fine picture.

ST MICHAEL. Rebuilt on a grand scale as a collegiate church by Lady Elizabeth Botreaux; called 'de novo aedificata' in 1417.

The college survived to the Reformation though never with the intended seven priests and four clerks. The W tower is earlier, completed before 1407. It stands some 70 ft (21 metres) high, severe apart from the W doorway and three-light window. Diagonal buttresses with many set-offs, plain upper stages, two-light bell-openings, and battlements with higher stair-turret. Pinnacles were removed and the turret capped in 1906. Although large, the tower is not spectacular, whereas the collegiate church is. Uncommonly clean lines, as the parapets, uninterrupted by finials or grotesques, run straight across nave and chancel, and are similar over the aisles and porches. Large three-light aisle and chancel windows of matching design separated by buttresses. Panel tracery. Plain three-light clerestory windows. The chancel is clearly built for a college of priests, the windows set high for their stalls. Five-light E window. The porch doorways have crocketed ogee heads set against two tiers of panelling under little upper windows which flank a statue niche (cf. Castle Cary). Lierne vaults within of different designs and pointed doorways with the thinnest of shafts.

Inside, tall arcades of five bays on shafted piers of four-wave section, the capitals and abaci not confined to the shafts but taken round the waves as well. Roof of Somerset type, of moderate pitch with tie-beams and short kingposts; arch-braced from angel corbels. Tower arch on simple shafts with round capitals ornamented with tiny leaves. The chancel arch has triple shafts, like those of the arcades but in two tiers, with a break at the level of the lost screen. The chancel is splendidly lit, the E wall bright with renewed colour. Two tall C15 niches here with flat canopies of crocketed ogee work. *John Norton* replaced the roof in 1866. C15 vestry, with two lines of black-letter ALPHABET, presumably for teaching.

FURNISHINGS. FONT. Early Perp, octagonal, on a stem with fat angle shafts. Low-relief quatrefoils and leaves. – BENCHES. An extraordinarily complete set of 1538, with linenfold frontals and dorsals. The ends have polygonal finials and curved-sided carved panels of great variety. They include Renaissance scroll, heads in profile, women nose-to-nose, a flute player, a cat with mousetrap, tortoises, a man whipping a horse, a windmill, and a church with crossing tower. Pevsner thought the technique 'inadequate or caricaturing', but the detail is charming. – REREDOS. By *Norton*, 1866. The Four Evangelists replaced with bronze ones by *Lyn Constable Maxwell*, 2005. Nearby on the N wall is the medieval ALTAR SLAB. – STAINED GLASS. E window by *Clayton & Bell*, 1876. Rich, but with much white. W window. Good small C15 figures, from the mansion. – MONUMENTS. William, 1st Lord Botreaux, †1391 and his wife †1433 (moved from the chancel steps). Defaced half-size effigies with a daintily vaulted canopy that does not fit. He wears a bascinet, she a horned head-dress. The chest has standing angels with shields, and at the E end a Virgin between kneeling donors, of good quality. The other end retains much original colour. – Two Jacobean tomb-chests without effigies. One is to

Sir Francis Hastings †1610 or his wife †1596. He wrote the sixteen-verse encomium on brass to her. The other, dated 1611, is to Frances Ewens, identified by the shield above. – Rev. Thomas Iliff †1712. Two small urns. – James Bennett †1815. Greek horned cup, signed *T. Ashton*.

Large war memorial CHURCHYARD CROSS, 1920. On a nearby wall, bronze CRUCIFIXION, by *John Robinson*, 2000, between the Saved and Damned, represented by ascending or descending paired figures.

NORTH CADBURY COURT. The great house that adjoins the churchyard appears wholly Elizabethan, but the W cross-wing immures a substantial house of *c.* 1300, built for the de Moels family. Their heiress married William de Botreaux (†1349), the Earls of Huntingdon succeeded the Botreaux, and the mansion was built in 1586–92 for Sir Francis Hastings, M.P. and Puritan pamphleteer, brother of the 3rd Earl. The C16 house faced N to a storeyed gatehouse, and had a rear court between L-plan wings with paired S gables. The Newmans, owners from the 1680s, replaced the gatehouse with two sets of gatepiers, built stables between them in 1715, and added a low NE service range. Later in the C18 they reconstructed the outer S wings, removing the gables and the floors, re-creating them as plain two-storey ashlar-fronted ranges. Finally, *c.* 1790, the rear courtyard was infilled with a bow-fronted ballroom, necessitating a new NW staircase and creating a single Georgian S front. The Bennett family followed from 1793 to 1910. Two Regency rooms remain from their period. *Melville Seth-Ward* then restored the house for Sir Archibald Langman in 1912–16, re-creating Elizabethan interiors.

The N façade resembles Newton Surmaville (q.v.) in its row of gables and balanced porch and hall-bay. Near-symmetrical, of six bays not exactly aligned with four gables. The outer gables mark the cross-wings. These have large eight-light double-transomed windows, indicating first-floor rooms with lower floors than those of the rooms over the hall. Here there are four-light transomed windows. The storeyed porch and hall-bay have matching cresting. The porch is narrower, with a renewed arched doorway under a four-light window; the bay has a grid of glazing on two floors with angle pilasters. Both cresting and pilasters echo late C16 detail at Longleat. Georgian infill at each end of the N front: a lean-to stair hall NW and kitchens NE. Low pedimented five-bay E outbuilding at right angles. In a contrast worthy of a Pugin cartoon, the S front shows nothing of the Elizabethan except blocked windows in the end walls. But the origins dictate the form – the centre cramped, the wings slightly irregular. Orange-brown ashlar with coved cornice and parapet. The bowed centre with iron balcony is distinctly better than the wings. The roofs were steep over the wings, low over the centre, until linked with an unhappy mansard in 1914.

INTERIOR. Like Montacute, there were service rooms and kitchen in the E cross-wing and private rooms in the W one.

But here the cross-wings are of L-plan, the outer ends possibly lodgings. Stair-towers were in the angles of the S courtyard. The HALL is neo-Elizabethan of 1912–16, the heraldic glass in the hall-bay original. Blocked S window from a former stair-tower. The grand neo-Elizabethan double-height STAIR HALL beyond destroyed any medieval evidence at the N end of the W cross-wing. Oak stairs, huge plaster pendant copied from Chelvey Court (N). The chamber over the hall has a C16 fireplace but the Elizabethan ceiling looks early C20. W of the stair hall is an apsed late C18 cantilevered stone staircase, the principal stair between 1790 and 1914. A small first-floor W room has a rare Georgian sunken bath, marble-lined. An early C20 attic stair reaches the splendid medieval ROOF, tree-ring-dated to c. 1300. Base-cruck trusses span 23 ft (7 metres), with massive arched braces to collars carrying crown-posts braced in four directions (cf. the Court House, Long Sutton). Two trusses were moved to open the cross-wing to an Elizabethan long gallery, in the attic of the hall range, since subdivided. The width of the cross-wing equals that of the widest C14 houses. The length, height and lack of smoke-blackening suggest a magnificent first-floor solar, 46 ft (14 metres) long and 23 ft (7 metres) wide, but much is puzzling, including how the room was heated.

Large, rather bare Georgian S rooms. The central BALL-ROOM shows good Adam detail: a triglyph frieze with paterae, and yellow marble consoled chimneypiece; but the Adamesque colonnade at the back of the room is early C20. Two early C18 fielded-panelled rooms with bolection-moulded doorways survive – ground floor NE and first floor S, E of the centre. Top-lit landing with C20 columns.

Two sets of GATEPIERS – the inner early C18, the outer late C17, with ball finials on fish-scale caps. Between the sets, long two-storey STABLES, dated 1715, with mullioned windows over cross-mullioned ones. Two reused doorheads, one dated 1607. Opposite the drive, on the corner of High Street, HALL COTTAGE, thatched, with a blocked C16 E doorway. A full-cruck truss inside, tree-ring-dated to 1344, is possibly reused (jointed crucks were dated to 1441). C16 S cross-wing with early C19 schoolroom at the W end. High Street runs N, bending W at a triple-gabled pair of c. 1845, to finish at the colourwashed CATASH INN, 1799, on Cary Road. To the N, THE DAIRY HOUSE, of banded stone with C16 reserved-chamfer mullions, and the gabled SCHOOL of 1873–5, by *Henry Hall*. Behind, a former WESLEYAN CHAPEL, 1848. Returning S from the inn, Woolston Road runs E. Former RECTORY, 1813 by *Thomas Ellis*, with a deep-eaved ashlar front with niches (not on Ellis's design) and columned porch. Bowed S window. On the N side are cottages and hall from Sir Archibald Langman's time. The VILLAGE HALL, modern-Georgian, 1930, by *A. Abbott* of Yeovil, has deep coved eaves and Cary rubble detail. E of Hall Cottage (*see* above), a varied sequence including the RED HOUSE, a square brick villa with deep eaves, and BRISTOL

House, stuccoed, Regency, with reeded angles to the two-storey bays. Further out, MANOR FARMOUSE, *c.* 1800, is mansard-roofed.

WOOLSTON, 1 m. ENE. The thatched OLD MANOR FARM must pre-date the 1770 datestone. WOOLSTON HOUSE is brick, 1840s, with square-pier ashlar porch. HIGHER FARM has a late C18 fluted pilastered doorcase. WOOLSTON MANOR FARM is a neat stuccoed box of 1835–8.

NORTH CHERITON

ST JOHN BAPTIST. Early C14 W tower with gabled NE stair-turret. Wave-moulded narrow tower arch, dying into the sides. No W door. Perp battlemented bell-stage. The rest was restored by *Foster & Wood* who added the N aisle in 1878 and rebuilt the chancel in 1886. However, the S view remains much as Buckler drew it in 1843. Victorian stonework inside, in the distinctively mottled Maperton stone. Triple-shafted C14 chancel arch. – FONT. Plain C11–C12 tapered tub. C17 scrolled COVER. – ROOD SCREEN. 1496, ejected in 1847 from Pilton, brought here in 1878 and enlarged to fill the arch. Very little is original; probably the round-arched four-light tracery with the heavy middle mullion. Carved spandrels with entangled foliage to the W, flowers E. Tiny faces in the dado tracery. – PULPIT. 1633. Two tiers of panels with typical arches, and a vine-trail frieze. – STAINED GLASS. E window by *Clayton & Bell*, 1878. S window, 1961, by *Hugh Easton*, a boyish St John.

The hip-roofed mid-C19 MANOR HOUSE sits well in the valley. Soaring war memorial CROSS, 1921. THE OLD HOUSE is C16, with a storeyed porch and moulded framed ceiling. Victorian windows. Further down, a very Victorian RECTORY, *c.* 1870, the W gable corbelled from a canted bay.

NORTH COKER

A substantial hamlet, expanded for the C18 flax industry.

HYMERFORD HOUSE. The model of a small early C15 gentry house. Hymerfords were here in 1377, and their house was built by 1461. Thatched and rendered, with two pointed two-light hall windows l. of a storeyed porch with panelled pointed doorway. Inner doorway with the Hymerford arms. Cross-passage to a similar E doorway in a lean-to porch. From the passage, two doorways to the hall, which is ceiled. N fireplace and pointed doorway into the rebuilt N end. Remnants of a jointed-cruck roof, with especially fine wall-plates embellished with quatrefoils and tiny faces. Some original colour. Moulded framed ceiling in the porch chamber.

Opposite is a pair of Coker Court ESTATE COTTAGES, 1914. Further N, HONEYSUCKLE COTTAGE, thatched, with one C17 mullioned window. The large mullion-windowed former VILLAGE HALL, 1895, was built by the owners of Coker House.

COKER HOUSE. Built c. 1855 for George Bullock, sail-maker, to evoke (if coarsely) a C16 mansion in Ham stone ashlar. Great hall with polygonal corner oriel balanced by a tall cross-wing. The service range has a reused C17 parapet with classical triglyphs alternated with hearts, also men with hammers. Reused Perp windows appear on the stable and an outbuilding over the road. LODGES, E and N, the latter dated 1887.

EAST COKER MILL, Mill Lane. Late Georgian mill and three-storey house in one. Wooden overshot wheel within.

NAISH PRIORY, 1 m. N. Not a priory, but the gatehouse and appurtenances of an early C15 mansion that presumably stood to the S. Two buildings, joined in 1899, face N on to the lane. The gatehouse, l., has a big pointed-arched doorway with richly traceried oak door, under an oriel on a coving of two fan-vaults (fancy cresting of 1899). The corresponding rear arch is panelled. A pointed and transomed two-light window in the E gable-end may mark a first-floor chapel. The block to the r., with diagonal buttresses, has a wind-braced roof with arched trusses to a very narrow first-floor hall.

PAVYOTT'S MILL, 1 m. E. A tall compact T-plan house of c. 1600. The N arm has regular mullion-and-transom windows and string courses to three storeys and attic, but the E arm, perhaps earlier, has levels so different that the strings take vertical leaps to connect the two. The S arm is plainly rendered.

HOLYWELL MILL, ½ m. W. Rebuilt as a flax mill c. 1800.

NORTH CURRY

3020

ST PETER AND ST PAUL. The church is large and in parts stately, but disjointed, because the Perp enlargement of the nave diminishes the unusually grand octagonal crossing tower. This is of North Curry sandstone, broader and richer than that at Stoke St Gregory. Of c. 1300, with big pointed bell-lights, their cusped Y-traceried divided by four transoms. Shallow piers on the angles. The quatrefoil-pierced parapet looks Victorian. Original steep roof-lines are visible on all four sides (that of the nave inside), and the lines of steeper gables appear in the end walls of the chancel and S transept. The S transept has heavy gabled buttresses and a big five-light S window of lancets with pointed trefoils in the heads. Gabled stair-turret in the angle to the chancel with one long lancet. That completes the evidence for the period c. 1300, when the church received its essential features. That there was a Norman predecessor is evident from the modest N doorway of c. 1180, with a segmental arch decorated by three layers of chevron on shafts with leaf capitals.

Now the Perp contributions, of Blue Lias with Ham stone. The nave was raised with a clerestory, the aisles rebuilt and s porch added, and the transept and chancel walls raised for large Perp windows. The parapets of the high nave and long chancel (under construction 1506) have pierced quatrefoils. The parapets are so emphatically horizontal that *John Oldrid Scott* in 1880 proposed adding pinnacles, and a lead spire to the tower. The s transept parapet is slightly gabled, with blind arcading. The aisles, s porch and N transept are embattled, the battlements running flat across gable and aisle ends, adding to the effect of assembled building blocks. Good standard Perp tracery, three-light to the four-bay aisles and clerestory, four-light to the two-bay chancel, and five-light end windows, the W window impressively large. The s side is the show side, especially the porch. Three niches over its doorway and another over the inner doorway (statues 1881, by *Harry Hems*), and a handsome early C16 fan-vault with pendant.

As one enters, the breadth and scale of the whole interior are striking. The crossing arches are triple-chamfered of c. 1300. The W piers are simply large plain masses cut diagonally and banded in Blue Lias. Blue Lias also the simple continuous capital. The E piers have been rebuilt in North Curry stone with a Lias capital band, only here there is a rich undulating contour with quasi-shafts of decidedly Perp character. There are now stone seats along these piers, not a usual arrangement in the Middle Ages. C19 wooden vault. Double-chamfered E arches to the aisles, again of c. 1300, the s aisle arch on banded chamfered piers, the N aisle arch simply dying in to the sides. The s transept windows have rere-arches in the style of c. 1300 and octagonal shafts. Cinquefoiled PISCINA in the N transept. Now the nave. Evidence of several phases. The restoration of 1881–4 by *Scott* exposed blocked clerestory windows below the Perp clerestory. Two on the N side have Dec tracery of c. 1325–50, but not matching and not relating to the present arcades. The arcades of c. 1300 were different – see the simply chamfered E responds, of North Curry stone. The present arcades are C14–C15, but not typical Perp, one continuous moulding without capitals, the moulding being two waves divided by a step. The clerestory and roofs are typical Late Perp, the framed ceilings renewed by *Scott*.

FURNISHINGS. FONT. Perp. Octagonal with quatrefoil panels. Painted Gothic COVER, 1849. – CHEST. Baulks of elm strapped with iron. Possibly of before 1200. – TEXTILE. Altar cloth with *appliqué* work, 'Johan Conock 1633', a rare survival. – CANDELABRA. Brass, 1809. – FITTINGS. Much from *Scott*'s restoration that is good. ORGAN with painted pipes, stone PULPIT, STALLS, and simple PEWS. And the ironwork of the outer DOORS deserves a look. – CHANCEL PANELLING.

1929–31, by *W. D. Caröe*, carved by *Maude Berthon*. – REREDOS. 1917, by *F. Bligh Bond*. – STAINED GLASS. Much by *Burlison & Grylls*: the E window, 1881, in C15 style, the chancel side windows, more C16 in style, and both S transept windows. Probably also the N transept N window, after 1914. Fine W window, 1881, by *Heaton, Butler & Bayne*. – MONUMENTS. Effigy of a bearded civilian (chancel) *c.* 1360, identified in a fold of the gown as Toma of Sloo (Slough Court, Stoke St Gregory). – Tomb-chest (N aisle), *c.* 1500, with three shields in cusped panels separated by little canopied niches with four small mourners. On top a cadaver with shroud, stiffly carved.

CHURCHYARD CROSS. C15 base, the rest by *Edmund Buckle*, 1891. – LYCHGATE, 1930, by *Caröe*. A playful work of pleasing materials, North Curry sandstone and stone roof tiles.

BAPTIST CHAPEL, Windmill Hill. 1825. Square, stuccoed, and hip-roofed. Three-sided gallery in long panels.

The large churchyard overlooks Curry Moor and the River Tone. To the E, in its own grounds, MANOR HOUSE, stuccoed and hip-roofed, of *c.* 1815. Church Road runs S, tree-lined to Queen Square. By the lychgate, GWYON HOUSE envelops in Victorian stucco a Late Georgian house whose first-floor windows and stone-columned doorcase survive. On the E side, FOSSE COTTAGE has reused C15 doorways and some mullion windows. CALMADY HOUSE, *c.* 1785, shows fine brickwork with stone cornice and open-pedimented doorcase. The OLD VICARAGE, low and roughcast between gabled wings, was a C15–C16 hall house. Queen Square is irregular, around a triangular green. WHATLEY HOUSE, SW, is Late Georgian brick, raised on a basement, with pedimented doorway. THE OLD BREWERY, N, *c.* 1700, also brick, with wooden cross-windows. Malthouse attached. Queen Square opens to the main road at the JUBILEE MEMORIAL, 1897, by *Edmund Buckle*, laden with secular Trinitarian symbolism. Open-arched, triangular, with emblems of England, Scotland and Ireland, 'tria juncto in uno', topped with the Victoria Cross. Facing the square, No. 2 has an early C19 stuccoed front with inset arched and columned porch. W on Windmill Hill, the METHODIST CHAPEL, 1833, a brick hip-roofed box with long arched windows. Panelled end gallery and pulpit. Opposite, VICTORIA TERRACE, four houses, still Late Georgian despite the name. Further out is the Baptist chapel (*see* above). On Stoke Road, E of the Jubilee Memorial, ANGEL HOUSE, formerly an inn. Late Georgian brick refronting of a long C17 house. Set back further on, MANOR FARMHOUSE, a tall front with ovolo-moulded mullioned windows, some under relieving arches. Left-hand window dated 1570, early for this moulding. Mid-C19 deep-eaved roof. One good Tudor-arched fireplace.

KNAPP, 1 m. W. Source of the North Curry sandstone. The RISING SUN has a moulded framed C15–C16 ceiling. Just above, MANOR FARMHOUSE, long and thatched, partly faced in squared sandstone, was a late medieval hall house. Further w, KNAPP FARMHOUSE and BIRDS FARMHOUSE, externally altered, are of similar type, with C16 framed ceilings.

NORTH NEWTON

ST PETER. Rebuilt particularly brutally in rock-faced red sandstone, 1883–5, by *E. H. Harbottle* of Exeter. This is an enormous pity as it was one of the few C17 churches of the county, of 1635–7 for Sir Thomas Wroth of Petherton Park. It had a barrel ceiling with typical C17 thin-rib plasterwork. Some woodwork was kept, and the plain thin tower with renewed mullion windows. The lower masonry may be medieval, but the broad s stair projection is C17, for a solid oak winding stair with moulded doorway. The interest is the remaining C17 WOODWORK. Five-bay SCREEN of two rounded arches each side of a broader doorway. The females attached to the (renewed) uprights are Faith, Hope, Charity, and the Virgin Mary (the child Jesus holding an apple). Arabesque frieze with consoles. The original W DOOR is re-set in the N transept. Six panels in a leaf-scroll framework, the middle panels with tracery, the arched upper ones with delightful reliefs of the Wise and Foolish Virgins. They are carrying dustpan-like lamps, and look appropriately smug or disappointed. The PULPIT, dated 1637, has three tiers of panels with cabochon type ornament in carved frames. Lozenges at the top, oval bosses in the middle tier. Also some reused PANELLING.

CHURCH FARMHOUSE, E of the church, is rendered, C16–C17. Further E an attractive stretch of CANAL, 1823–6, runs up to KING'S LOCK and STANDARDS LOCK. W of the church, NEWTON HOUSE, externally altered, has a C17 thin-rib plaster motif on one ceiling. At the centre, the SCHOOL, 1877, and large red sandstone former VICARAGE, 1880. Down Brook Street are STEPS FARMHOUSE, with late C17 timber mullions, and GREAT HOUSE FARMHOUSE, slightly later, with wooden cross-windows. Grand urns on the gatepiers.

IMPENS FARMHOUSE, ½ m. N. C16–C17, mostly rebuilt in the C19. The W cross-wing contains close-studded timber framing and a wonderfully preserved panelled room of 1649. On the overmantel four half-clothed demi-figures, and in the frieze comical opposed figures. A plaster frieze uses uncommon motifs: opposed winged figures support little cherub faces in roundels of drapery. Thin-rib ceiling, four-lobed motif growing from kite shapes. Also cherub roundels.

WEST NEWTON MANOR, 1½ m. SW. Altered C14 house, possibly an aisled hall. The rubble stone front has C17 oak-mullioned windows, the upper ones in dormers. Late Victorian chimneys. Dated 1622 on the storeyed porch, with initials of Henry Cheeke. Several massive octagonal posts inside, some cut to carry beams, may be aisle-posts.

NORTHOVER see ILCHESTER

NORTH PERROTT

ST MARTIN. Cruciform, with a tower over the crossing, apparently all Perp, but in fact a plain early C13 tower similar to South Perrott (Dorset). Perp two-light bell-openings, square-headed with pierced baffles. Perp octagonal stair-tower. The crossing arches are re-cut. They have thick Perp shafts with leaf capitals between ribbed and panelled hollows. The rest is very late, rebuilt with parapets and coarse uncusped tracery for Henry Daubeney, Earl of Bridgwater, disgraced 1541. Broad four-light windows and squat five-light W window above a barrel-vaulted porch. Nave roof on vivid head corbels. NE additions, 1909, by *W. D. Caröe*. – FONT. Hexagonal, C13. Retooled. – PULPIT. 1909, by *Caröe*. Delicate tracery. – PANELS. Painted gesso, the Annunciation and the Angel at the Tomb, possibly C17 Spanish. – REREDOS. Leonardo's Last Supper in painted marble. 1850s, by *Richard Westmacott Jun.* – STAINED GLASS. Good transept windows, 1896, the N one crowded with angels. – MONUMENT. William Hoskins †1813. By *Sir Richard Westmacott*. Greek sarcophagus with lion masks.

The former VICARAGE, 1799, has tripartite front windows and a false door in carved stone. On the main road, cottage terraces, a neo-Jacobean LODGE to the manor, 1880s, and the mullion-windowed C17 MANOR FARMHOUSE.

NORTH PERROTT MANOR, ¼ m. W. 1878, for H. W. Hoskyns, attributed to *T. H. Wyatt*, without clear evidence (*Wyatt & Brandon* made designs in the 1840s). Ham stone, Jacobean, in the freer manner of the late C19. Entrance front in three parts: storeyed porch, l., against asymmetrical gables, central stair-block with a hipped roof, and L-plan service range. On the S front, triple gables divided by a loggia from an Edwardian W addition.

NORTH PETHERTON

A large main road village that was a market town and site of an Anglo-Saxon minster.

ST MARY. Entirely Perp of c. 1500–30. The tower, even among Somerset towers, is a *tour de force*. It is 109 ft (33.2 metres) high, of pinky-grey sandstones with ample dressings and entire top stage of Ham stone. Set-back buttresses decorated by three tiers of extremely tall pinnacles. The high first stage is faced on the W side in Ham stone for effect. Doorway flanked by niches, one with a fragmentary seated figure, then a quatrefoil frieze under the large four-light transomed W window which is sub-arched and traceried also below the transom. The unifying motif of the tower is a central diagonally set pier rising from ground to crown, interrupted for the second-stage window, then becoming the mullion between the bell-lights, a notably sophisticated design. On the w it starts only above the window, on the N it rises between statue niches, and on the s the polygonal SE stair-turret, confined to this lowest stage, causes some irregularity. The pier passes through three quatrefoil friezes, the lowest below the statue niches. The second stage each side has a single tall three-light transomed window with pierced baffles. A pot-bellied figure, known as Samson, on the corbel of the N frieze, is re-set from under the pulpit. The two large transomed bell-openings match the window below. The mullion between is echoed by pairs of outer shafts and all five are continued upward as framework for a row of panels, traceried to match the baffles. The central shaft alone continues beyond, to a gargoyle below the battlements, and this carries one of the little outriders of the central pinnacle. Similar outriders to the larger angle pinnacles, all the pinnacles crocketed. The battlements are pierced with quatrefoils. The stopping of the stair-tower so low allows all four faces their full glory.

The rest of the church, of the same rubble, is embattled in Ham stone. Nave with clerestory, five-bay aisles with central porches, single-bay slightly higher chancel chapels, the chancel projecting a further two bays. The windows are Perp, all transomed, without the refinement of Langport or Curry Rivel. The chancel windows are larger, four-light on the chapels and the E window a splendidly broad five lights. Three-light clerestory windows. The aisle and chancel battlements have panelled diagonally set bases for finials. An ogee central merlon caps the porches. The storeyed s porch is served by a C17 stair on the W. Polygonal NE rood-stair turret. At the E end an embattled sacristy (as at Langport and Ilminster). The most striking feature of the interior is the tower arch, as high as nave and clerestory, and panelled. In the tower is a fan-vault. Five-bay arcades, rather thin, with standard four-hollow piers. Circular capitals to the shafts with small rosettes. Chancel arch and arches from the aisles to the chapels of the same type, and from the chancel to each chapel, here with angels as the E responds. Moulded framed roofs of low pitch on stone angel corbels, without the exuberant carpentry of e.g. Westonzoyland. In the S aisle a re-set C13 trefoil-headed recess. The chancel is divided by wall-piers; the roof is of 1884 by *J. H. Spencer*. Good carved DOOR into the sacristy, C15–C16.

FURNISHINGS. FONT. Perp, like Nether Stowey. Octagonal, with pointed quatrefoils. Panelled underside and stem. – PULPIT. Perp, early C15, much restored. Fine traceried panels in two tiers between thin shafts. – SCREENS. 1909–12. Right across the nave and aisles, with complicated ogee tracery and vaulted cove. By *Charles Baker King*. By him also the chancel STALLS, SEDILIA and PANELLING, 1914. Superb in their way, if a little mechanical. – GALLERY. The parvise of the s porch

NORTH PETHERTON

was opened to the aisle in 1623, with contemporary pews. Enlarged with a Gothic front on deep corbels, perhaps in *Richard Carver*'s restoration of 1838–9. A C17 figure of Father Time balances a skull on his head. – BENCH-ENDS. C19, reusing C17 ends with typical Jacobean arch, framing a flower. Others are reused above the C19 tower screen. Front bench-ends dated 1596 and 1629. – ROYAL ARMS. Charles II. – STAINED GLASS. NE window by *Kempe*, 1896, one of his best. There is much poetry in the verdure behind the Nativity and the choir of angels above. W window, *c.* 1890, probably by *Clayton & Bell*. Chancel N by *Henry Holiday*, 1917–18. The figures after Burne-Jones, in lovely colours. E and adjoining chancel windows, *c.* 1886, probably by *Frederick Drake*. – MONUMENTS. Eleanor Poulet †1413 (S aisle). Purbeck stone floor slab indented for a lost canopied brass. – Several incised Lias floor slabs, that to Katherine Morley †1652 with brass depicting her kneeling at a prie-dieu. – Henry Gatchell †1724. Finely engraved Lias, an urn on top. – C. B. Portman †1915. Small and rich. Green marble, white tile mosaic and mother-of-pearl.

Base of a C15 CHURCHYARD CROSS on two high steps. Octagonal with quatrefoil panels and attached angle shafts.

CONGREGATIONAL CHAPEL, Fore Street. 1869, by *Edwin Down*. Urban-scaled, in the Lombard style favoured for chapels of this time. Blue Lias with a triple-arched central feature on each floor.

CEMETERY, Old Road. 1856, by *Charles Knowles*. Very Gothic, two chapels disguised as one, the Anglican with a badly proportioned SW tower and spire, the Nonconformist at right-angles across the E end. Although under the one roof, the chapels are separated by a full-height tiny gap, which says much about Victorian attitudes.

PRIMARY SCHOOL, 1877, by *J. H. Spencer*. A long red sandstone range with three gabled features and large plate-traceried Gothic windows in buff brick.

SOMERSET AUCTION CENTRE, 1 m. NE. 2007. An integrated livestock market. A large monopitch-roofed hall with, at one end, three tall polygonal half-cylinders against the back wall, containing auction rings. The livestock is brought in from pens behind. On the front are offices and a conical-roofed café. Just S, ROBERT WISEMAN DAIRY, 2006, by *Stone & Partners*, a very large blue and grey box, with curved-topped extrusions, the N one fully glazed.

VILLAGE. Spoilt by traffic. Little shows of the market place nor of the 'good houses' mentioned by Collinson in 1791. The churchyard gives a welcome green space. On the E side, the former SWAN INN is roughcast with a C17 porch. S of the churchyard, THE MINSTER was the vicarage until 1804. Much altered. The garden front is curiously arranged: taller outer blocks frame a diminutive two-bay centre, roughcast, with long early C19 Gothic windows. To the E is the school (*see* above). To the W, DOWER HOUSE, deep-eaved, with veranda, early

C19, and No. 1 Church Walk, C16, with two stone-mullioned windows. On the main road, No. 83 was the next vicarage, called 'newly-built' in 1804, enlarged 1834. Five-bay brick front with two moulded ashlar bands. The market place was W of the church, where is now the pink brick COMMUNITY HALL, 1986, by *Stone & Partners*. By the North Newton turn, the former RECTORY HOUSE (Woodlee and Boringdon House), is stuccoed, early C19. Bracket eaves and recessed arched windows echoed by an inset columned and arched porch.

PETHERTON PARK, 1 m. E. The royal deer park at Petherton is recorded from Anglo-Saxon times. The Alfred Jewel (now in the Ashmolean Museum) was found in 1693 probably near the forester's lodge (Parker's Field). Chaucer was forester (probably non-resident) 1391–1400. A late C16 house in the centre of the park was replaced *c*. 1700 for Sir Thomas Wroth. The plain rendered eleven-bay front, relieved only by a well-carved shell-hood, is in part the result of bomb damage. The rear, with hip-roofed projecting wings and another shell-hood, displays fine early brickwork, a moulded band and gauged window heads. Large-field panelling in several rooms, including a tall ballroom in the NE wing, raised on a brick-vaulted semi-basement. Some reused C17 panelling dated 1601 and 1633. Open-well staircase to an arcaded landing, the balustrade replaced.

SHOVEL HOUSE, ½ m. SW. A brick early C19 five-bay villa with deep eaves. Single-bay wings with ramped parapets. The enclosed porch has a cast-iron railing, more 1840s than 1820s. Delicate trellised rear veranda between curved-fronted conservatories. The lofted COACHHOUSE has reused pieces supposedly from West Monkton church: corbel heads, a lion, a C16 plaque marked H8R.

BOOMER FARMHOUSE, ¾ m. W. S façade of the 1740s proudly facing down the approach. Five bays with ashlar quoins and cornice, the parapet panelled, and a taller projecting centre with an attic window above the cornice, and stone pediment. Gibbsian rustication to the entrance arch. The rainwater heads with the Catford arms are dated 1681, and inside it is clear that an earlier house was refaced. Fielded panelling and staircase of the 1740s, also a fragmentary late C17 plaster frieze.

WOOLMERSDON HOUSE, ¾ m. NW. Stuccoed, of 1820–2, with typical deep eaves, one end completely rounded.

THE CHANTRY, Rhode. 1¼ m. NW. Early C17 roughcast front with mullioned ground-floor windows. A plaster heart dated 1655 in an upper room.

NORTH WOOTTON

ST PETER. Blue Lias. Small undivided W tower. The base is early C14. No W door. Double-chamfered tower arch. C15–C16 battlemented bell-stage. Polygonal SE stair-turret. The rest is externally Perp. S porch with shafted doorway, pedimented sundial of 1767, and C17 painted text inside. C15 rood stair. Chancel rebuilt in 1867–9, keeping the C13–C14 double-chamfered chancel arch. Neat organ chamber added by *E. Buckle*, 1890. – FONT. Norman bowl and stem in one, bent like a tree trunk. The dividing moulding changes from cable to chevron. – PULPIT. C19, incorporating C15–C16 traceried square panels. – BENCHES. C16, mostly plain, some traceried ends and two with Jacobean ornament. – STALLS. C16, with poppyhead ends. – PAINTING. Copy of Botticelli's circular Virgin and Child (National Gallery, London) by *T. M. Rooke*, a former assistant of Burne-Jones. – ROYAL ARMS. 1826. – STAINED GLASS. E window, 1902, by *H. V. Milner*. Good clear drawing. – MONUMENT. Phippen family, *c.* 1770. Incised Lias, three arched panels.

S of the church, a former BAPTIST CHAPEL, 1830, with two typical Y-traceried windows remaining. It adjoins CHAPEL FARMHOUSE, partly C17. Garden front with two bays of mullioned windows carrying hoodmoulds. Towards Pilton, TYLER'S HOUSE, the former vicarage, by *Ewan Christian*, 1869.

WORMINSTER CROSS, 1½ m. NNE. C15 wayside cross on steps. Octagonal shaft and capital.

NORTON FITZWARREN

ALL SAINTS. Proud, severe W tower of eroding North Curry sandstone. Perp, with set-back buttresses. Three stages divided by string courses, a third under the battlements, each with big grotesques at the corners, and those of the polygonal NE stair-turret. Two-light bell-openings with transom. On the S side a statue niche. The triple-chamfered tower arch looks much earlier, but as at Hillfarrance may be C15–C16. The N aisle has been raised for a good Perp roof on Tudor-arched trusses, but the arcade is late C13 or early C14. Octagonal piers with plain capitals and double-chamfered arches. Window tracery and NE chapel and chancel of the restoration by *C. E. Giles*, 1865. Broad C19 barrel nave roof. Stencil decoration of the chancel roof remains from a complete painted scheme. *Giles*'s REREDOS commands attention for the blood-red cross on shining white. – FONT. C13. Massive, octagonal. – SCREENS. A very fine pair in the Devon style, datable from the name of Raphe Harris †1509, churchwarden. The five-bay rood screen has two- and four-light sections with ogee lights, the four-light sections with a thick central mullion running up to the apex. Ribbed coving and exceptional plant-trail friezes. The lowest illustrates graphically if incomprehensibly the legend of the dragon of Norton Camp, with hunting dogs, oxen ploughing, the dragon eating a naked man, and naked men being cheerfully obscene. Matching three-bay N screen, without representational elements. – BENCH-ENDS. C16. Square-topped with rich tracery bordered in leaf scroll as at Trull. – STAINED GLASS. E window, 1860s, by *Clayton & Bell*. S, signed *Warrington*, c. 1865. – MONUMENT. James Prowse †1672. Alabaster, thickly festooned and bordered in flowers, with curved pediment.

NORTON CAMP. A circular hillfort about 150 yds (140 metres) across on the hill behind the church. Its substantial ramparts up to 15 ft (4.6 metres) high are of Late Bronze Age to Iron Age date. A hoard of Bronze Age metalwork was found during excavations in 1970 and the hilltop has also produced Palaeolithic handaxes. Evidence of use in the C3 to C4 A.D. Aerial photographs show that the interior was subdivided into smaller enclosures.

NORTON COURT, below the church. Of c. 1600, altered for the Victorian owners of the adjacent brewery. Good balustraded porch. Ovolo-moulded mullions behind. The rear wing has a Jacobean thin-rib ceiling of kite shapes with rosettes and fleurs-de-lys.

On the main road, a large yellow-brick Gothic VILLAGE HALL, 1896–7, former SCHOOL, 1872, by *J. H. Spencer*, and the CONGREGATIONAL CHURCH of 1821. Stuccoed asymmetrical twin-gabled front: three-bay chapel with arched windows, and narrower manse reusing the original pedimented chapel doorway.

LANGFORD, ¾ m. N. GIFFORDS FARMHOUSE was a C16 hall house with lateral chimney. Full-height timber-framed partitions and two intermediate cusped trusses. FARTHINGS and CASTLE COTTAGE are altered late medieval.

NORTON MANOR, Norton Manor Camp (Royal Marines), 1 m. NW. 1842–3, by *Henry Roberts*, for C. N. Welman. Quite large in an unexciting Tudor style of buff brick with diaper patterning. Shallow gables, mullion-and-transom windows. STABLES of 1890.

MONTY'S COURT, 1 m. W. Tudor-style, c. 1840, by *Richard Carver*, for General Sir John Slade. More lively than Norton Manor. Symmetrical E front with an ashlar porch between gables. Asymmetrical garden front. Stables dated 1838.

NORTON-SUB-HAMDON

Under the western slope of Ham or Hamdon Hill, a village whose recorded tradition of stonemasonry goes from William of Norton, recruited to build the castles in North Wales in 1278, to the very successful stone- and wood-carving workshops of *Charles Trask*, who owned the quarries around 1900.

ST MARY. An uncommonly perfect church, perfect on its slight eminence with a view towards Ham Hill and perfect also in its display of Perp pride. The only objection that could be made is that the nave and chancel are a little too short to be a match for the proud 98-ft (30-metre) high tower. The church is ascribed to c. 1480–1500. The five-stage tower has set-back buttresses rising to the top stage, where they continue as shafts to end in delicate pinnacles above the battlements. That gives one pair of pinnacles close to each corner. Also a central pinnacle on each side, each with a small outrider in front rising from the middle gargoyle. The bell-openings are very long, through two stages (cf. Crewkerne, Hinton St George and Shepton Beauchamp), and narrow, of two lights with ogee tracery both above and below a transom. The transom does not align with the string course. A hexagonal NE stair-turret rises higher, also pinnacled. Low, rich W doorway with foliage spandrels under a quatrefoil frieze. Very tall four-light W window with ogee lights above and below a transom, and sub-arched tracery. Much spare space between it and the bell-openings, and on the sides. The S side has two small canopied niches. The baffle tracery of the bell-openings changes subtly in the top lights, the first sign of *Henry Wilson*'s 1894 restoration after lightning burnt out the tower. W DOORS with tiny Arts and Crafts animals, designed by *Wilson*, made in 1906–7 by *Arthur Parkin* of *Trask & Co.*

The rest of the church is a single unified design like Cannington (q.v.), tall with stone-tiled roofs, the nave roof continuing over battlemented four-bay aisles, a matching fifth bay overlapping the chancel which projects one bay further. Handsome four-light windows with sub-arched tracery, divided by buttresses carrying diagonal finials over particularly animated gargoyles. The chancel has a higher parapet, and that height is emphasised by a transomed E window as long as the W one. The SOUTH PORCH must be reused C14. Its barrel vault has transverse ribs, as at Closworth.*

The interior is wonderfully lofty, 50 ft (15 metres) high, with tall slim arcades and no clerestory. Enormously high tower arch, with shafts and traceried panels. Equally high chancel arch, shafted to match the arcades, so with caps at two levels. The piers are standard four-hollow with rounded capitals. The single arches to the chancel chapels match those of the nave, as do those at the E end of the aisles. These have Perp stone SCREENS, the N one original, the S one C19. Wagon roofs to the nave and chancel on shield-bearing figures. Panelled low-pitched aisle roofs on wall-shafts and head corbels. Intermediate trusses with pendants and wooden supporters. C15 canopied niche over the S door, and two on the chancel E wall. These flank a stone panelled REREDOS from *Arthur Blomfield*'s restoration of 1862. Ogee PISCINA. – FONTS. One, of 1894, is among the finest Arts and Crafts work in the country and one of *Wilson*'s best designs, a tapered cylinder of pink alabaster,

---

* Some C12 stones are inside the bell-chamber.

spirally fluted, suggestive of moving water with wonderful spiky fish as feet. The fish echo Wilson's font at Welbeck Abbey, Notts., but this is altogether more monumental. Made by *Trask & Co.*, carved by *Richard Gillman*. Lovely wooden COVER, a shallow-domed temple of eight arches ornamented with plant forms and mice, and tiny fish around the dome. Plain octagonal original font, C13–C14. – TOWER SCREEN. Also by *Wilson*, made by *Trask & Co.*, 1894. Arts and Crafts woodwork at its best. Six narrow square-headed lights with plant-like tracery above and a line of spear-like plants below. The plain cove has a carved band below. – CHANCEL SCREEN. 1880, by *Blomfield*. Iron, High Victorian in its sharp scrollwork, highlighted in red and gold. – PULPIT. 1890. Scrolled iron, altogether more delicate than the screen, but presumably by *Blomfield* as it commemorates a Blomfield vicar. – STAINED GLASS. Numerous figures of c. 1500 in the window tracery. E window, 1861, scenes from Christ's life, by *William Wailes*. Chancel S, 1875, by *Heaton, Butler & Bayne*. Chancel N, 1922, by *A. K. Nicholson*. Notable S chapel E window, 1904, by *Wilson* for Trask's golden wedding, made by *Shrigley & Hunt*. Our Lady of Pity, amid an idealized family (Vita, Caritas and Labor), sweetly serious. W window, 1895, patterned glass by *Wilson*.

In the churchyard, MEMORIAL to Charles Trask †1907, probably by *Wilson*. Between the Ham stone shaft and cross, a grey Lias roundel of a dove encircled by a ring-monster. The circular DOVECOTE remains from a medieval manorial site. Recorded in 1555, it has 1762 and 1785 inscribed. The stone-tiled roof has an ogee stone hat on C18 balusters.

PRIMARY SCHOOL. 1996–7, by *Graham Whiteley* of *Somerset County Architects*. Rendered and red-tiled, with a hint of Arts and Crafts Gothic.

By the churchyard, the former SCHOOL, 1863, with Kentish split cusps to stepped lancets. Trask lived at COURTFIELD, an early C18 five-bay house with architraved mullion windows. Late Victorian cross-wing. Kitchen addition, 2007–8, by *Designsçape Architects* of Bath. Great Street curves E with stone-mullioned and thatched houses, notably CHURCH ROW with a long C17 hoodmould. TUDOR COTTAGE and THATCHINGS, externally different, may have been the medieval church house. They share a C15 wind-braced roof. On the S side, a good row including MANOR FARMHOUSE, with a C16 lateral chimney and some reserved-chamfer mullions, and COURT FARMHOUSE, thatched, late C17, with regularly ordered windows under continuous hoodmoulds. Further W, MANOR HOUSE has a three-storey front of C17 mullioned windows, irregularly disposed. Late Georgian rear wing with a heavy pilastered porch of c. 1840. Small late C18 SUMMERHOUSE of five close-spaced arches with centre pediment. COACHHOUSE across the road, also late C18, with double coach arches under a pediment, between stable wings. In the adjacent walled garden is a modern house of brick and glass, THE HERB GARDEN, 2003, by *Justin Paterson* of *Boon Brown*. Flat-roofed, the bedroom floor with deep eaves set back on a glass-fronted ground floor behind a sunken walkway.

Higher Street runs s past KNAPP FARM, Late Georgian, the long BARN with distinctive flattened arches. SHEPHERDS COTTAGE is late C17, mullion-windowed in five close-spaced bays. Little Street returns E to join Great Street at PILL BRIDGE (two tiny medieval arches). From the LORD NELSON INN, C17 and C18, Rectory Lane runs N. On the l., the mullion-windowed rear of HOMEFIELD, with a chimney gable and two-storey s end. C17 moulded fireplaces and staircase with turned balusters. The OLD RECTORY had a five-bay mid-C18 front of narrow sashes. The two r. bays are covered by a heavy mansard-roofed early C19 addition, but the original stonework apparently reused on the side. Fielded-panelled s room. MILL HOUSE has C18 mullioned windows. Behind is MILL GREEN, 2010–11, by *Tom Gascoyne* of *Orme Architecture*. Single-storeyed, Ham stone and glass. Three parallel flat-roofed blocks. The taller centre contains the living space. Bedrooms one side, service rooms the other. Sedum roofs, boarded eaves, projected at the s for shade.

LITTLE NORTON MILL, Little Norton. Tiny watermill dated 1782 with complete and working C19 machinery and overshot wheel.

NYNEHEAD

ALL SAINTS. Red sandstone. Mostly Perp, with Victorian embellishment for the Sanfords of Nynehead Court. Probably of c. 1300 the base of the undifferentiated W tower with its double-chamfered W doorway and chamfered tower arch. Perp the upper part of the tower, the rendered gabled s aisle and big porch, and the N transept. But the jambs of the N transept arch look also of c. 1300. John Wyke left money towards building the aisle in 1410. The porch has a wagon roof. Wave-moulded s doorway. In 1869 the chancel was remodelled, the N transept extended as the Sanford Chapel, and the NE organ chamber added, by *William Ayshford Sanford*. He was a competent amateur who had designed Gothic schools in Perth, Australia, while Colonial Secretary there, 1852–3. Rose windows to both chapel and organ chamber. Nave N wall rebuilt by *F. B. Bond*, 1912.

The three-bay arcade has standard Perp piers of four hollows and shafts with capitals. Similar SE chapel and chancel arches. The chancel is richly Victorian inside with triple arcade to the organ chamber, roses along the wall-plate, and decidedly botanical capitals and corbels. The PISCINA is however C13. C15 wagon roofs in nave and aisle, the aisle taller with bull's-eye bosses (as in the porch), the nave mostly renewed, with original bosses including three gurning faces.

FURNISHINGS. The Rev. John Sanford (†1855) moved to Florence and collected Italian SCULPTURE. He gave two

C15–C16 *della Robbia* ceramics, a lovely Virgin kneeling before the Child, attributed to *Luca*, and a Virgin and Child, attributed to *Andrea*.* – FONT. Octagonal, Early Perp. Heavily panelled on the sides, underside and stem. – ROOD SCREEN. C15–C16, of the Carhampton and Dunster type. Five bays, the outer ones half-width, outlined in leaf scroll. Inner bays of four lights, sub-arched, with tiny shields in the tracery and octagonal column mullions. Ribbed coving with traceried panels and carved bosses, one with the Wyke arms. The plant-trail cornices on the front came from Hillfarrance (more on the organ case), but the E cornice may be original. – RAILS. C18 turned balusters. – ALTAR and REREDOS. 1871. Very Victorian; the communion table of 'Ceylon sacredwood and Macassar ebony', the reredos matching in marble and granite. Low-relief central panel, painted della Robbia blue, by *Seymour* of Taunton, *opus sectile* tile side panels by *Henry Holiday*, among the earliest of this technique, for *Powell's*, 1871. To each side much larger *opus sectile* panels, by *Powell's*, 1881. – STATUE. Elijah. Late C19, by *W. J. Giles* of Wellington. – STAINED GLASS. A great deal. Fading E window, 1869, by *Heaton, Butler & Bayne*. Chancel S, Faith and Hope, early C19 panels; Faith after Sir Joshua Reynolds's New College, Oxford, window of 1780. Charity, opposite, is also early C19. The very Roman Catholic image, St Thomas of Villanueva giving alms, is from a painting by Antonio Balestra, popularized in an C18 engraving by Domenico Cunego.† S aisle first, colourful Tudor royal arms, *c.* 1550, from where? Inserted 1851. SW, and second and third S windows, 1858–9, by *John Toms*. SE, 1860s, fourteen saints by *Frederick Drake*. In the tracery, one medieval St Margaret and some good copies. W window, 1887, by *Powell's*. Aesthetic Movement influence. Two N windows with fine portrait roundels, 1912, also by *Powell's*. In the Sanford Chapel heraldic glass from 1638 to 1869.

MONUMENTS. Sanctuary. Richard Wyke †1590. Arched plaque recording seventeen children by one wife. – SE chapel. Edward Clarke †1679 and Elizabeth Clarke †1667, erected during his lifetime. Kneeling figures facing each other across a prayer-desk, a riot of heraldry above. Reactionary for *c.* 1670. The monument was made at Milverton for £25. – John Locke †1704. Lias. Unnamed and undated, with a verse. The philosopher (not buried here) was a friend of Edward Clarke. – S aisle. Gustavus Venner, 1719. Alabaster frame with scrolls and skull. – Sanford Chapel. Henrietta Sanford †1837. The centrepiece, and a most dramatic one. On a Grecian pedestal, a kneeling marble (male) angel in the style of Canova, by *Aristodemo Costoli* of Florence, 1840. – John Sanford †1711. Ionic columns and scroll pediment, 1717. – William Sanford, 1720. Long Baroque cartouche with weeping cherub head. – William A.

---

* A tabernacle attributed to Mino da Fiesole has been sold to the National Museum of Wales.
† Kindly identified by Duncan Bull, Rijksmuseum.

Sanford †1833. Marble with well-carved oak and laurel. Rev. John Sanford †1855. Portrait bust by *Costoli*, 1835.

In the churchyard, the base of a fine C15 CROSS, octagonal with shields, square piers on the diagonals. Also an eroded red stone C15 DOLE TABLE, like a tomb-chest, but solid.

NYNEHEAD COURT, by the church. The house was rebuilt by John Sanford *c.* 1675, a date appearing inside, but moulded stone doorways to the front and back mark the former cross-passage of the C14–C15 house of the Wykes. John Sanford replaced the hall with a four-bay N piece and the cross-wing with a projecting three-bay S block, perhaps to designs by *William Taylor*. He kept, in a slightly recessed bay, the cross-passage between the two. The new work is stuccoed over brick (visible at the back), of two storeys with quoins, broad sash windows in architraves with keystones, and bracketed eaves cornices to steeped hipped roofs. It was an early example of the classical style in Somerset. The N block survives intact but the S block was raised a storey *c.* 1800. A hip-roofed C19 single-bay projection, NE, balances the façade. Over the medieval entrance, a leaded timber Venetian window in a square frame, more typical of the vernacular classicism of the late C17. When the S block was raised a long arch-headed stair light was inserted in the r. bay. The four-bay S side was blandly rendered and extended W by three bays.

In the hall, the depressed pointed rear doorway is medieval, with mid-C19 heraldic glass. A broad stone doorway with curved pediment dated 1675 opens into the N range. Oddly it looks as if it should be external. In the S range are the staircase, dining room and drawing room. Late C17 oak stairs with thick rail and turned balusters. Dining room with C18 panelling in large panels with fielded dado, and good mid-C18 timber chimneypiece with scrolled sides and fruit festoon. The drawing room added at the W end is Regency in character. Fine marble chimneypiece: low-relief semi-draped maidens facing outward extend a riband over a central cherub plaque. In the room over the dining room an overmantel with Martin Sanford's arms, dated 1633.

N of the house, a large brick-lined ICE HOUSE, 1803. S of the house, mid-C19 parterres. The curved wall to the church has curved brick buttresses. The PARK falls away to the river, diverted and widened after 1810 to pass under a handsome triple-arched BRIDGE of 1815–17 by *Thomas Lee*, faced in North Curry sandstone. The drive continued under a CANAL AQUEDUCT of 1833–4 and RAILWAY BRIDGE of 1842–4, both in sandstone ashlar, the price of permission to cross the park. The aqueduct, by *James Green*, is just W of a ruined BOAT-LIFT, the last of the seven on his stretch of the Grand Western Canal. Boats were lifted in water-filled iron caissons held in balance. The bridge, by *Brunel*, is effectively a short tunnel as the railway crosses at a skew, with a lodge built into the S end.

CANAL AQUEDUCT. Over the Tone. 1833, by *James Green*. Stone-faced shallow arch and cast-iron trough.

OAKE

St Bartholomew. Red sandstone, generally Perp but the S tower earlier in its lower stage. Battlemented upper stage, slightly wider. Nave, chancel and SE chapel. The most interesting feature is a fine six-light N window with Perp tracery in two three-light arches, said to have come from Taunton Priory and to have been bought for Oake after the Dissolution. Outer shafts with little heads. The ferramenta being inside, the window must be reversed. The arcade to the chapel, of two bays with rough octagonal piers and double-chamfered arches, looks early C14, but the chapel is otherwise Perp. C15–C16 SW porch, replacing the tower porch, with a quatrefoil parapet, surprising for so modest a church. The initials IP may represent John Peryn (cf. Hillfarrance and West Buckland). The doorway capitals resemble those of the N window. Is it also reused? – FONT. Ham stone bowl, C11–C12, on what may be an upturned red sandstone bowl. – PULPIT. Early C17, with angle arabesques and plant-pattern panels. – STAINED GLASS. C15–C16 figures in the N window.

Blagrove's Farm, ½ m. NW. A showy, muddled C17–C18 design in brick. Two storeys, raised on a basement. Four long arched ground-floor windows joined by an impost band and central corniced stone doorcase. Between the outer windows are rounded stair projections. But the arched window heads are blind and the stair projections hold no stairs, so this is all display. Bolection-moulded panelled room; rear staircase with flat balusters.

OARE

A green valley just behind a wall of hills. Behind this, only a mile away, is the sea.

St Mary. Perp nave and chancel, to which a plain two-stage Victorian tower and a chancel were added. Single-light windows on the old chancel, the E window reused on the N side of the new chancel. Domestic nave S windows. Pointed oak N doorway (cf. Stoke Pero). Rustic Georgian interior, mostly intact. Plastered vaults perhaps over wagon roofs. Some bosses re-fixed over the chancel. Exceptional C14 PISCINA, a male head clasped by hands. – FONT. C11–C12. Crudely tapered bowl. – FITTINGS. Late Georgian BOX PEWS, SQUIRE'S PEW, PULPIT and DESK, all fielded-panelled. Also painted ROYAL ARMS and four COMMANDMENT BOARDS. Victorian STALLS and SCREEN. – MONUMENTS. A rustic set including incised Lias ones to Peter Spure †1749 and Dorcas Spurry †1772, hers with colour and a comical trumpeting angel. Also a painted wooden one to Nicholas Snow †1791, with classical aspirations. – Nicholas

Snow †1914, by *Countess Gleichen*. Bad. – R. D. Blackmore †1900. Replica of the Exeter Cathedral memorial. *Lorna Doone* is partly set in Oare, where Blackmore's father had been rector.

OARE MANOR. Stone, gabled, C19, with E cross-wing of the 1930s. The W end includes a C17 farmhouse.

YENWORTHY FARM, 1 m. N. Mid-C19 Glenthorne estate farm (see Countisbury, Devon). Gabled farmhouse with pretty iron windows. A beam inside is dated 1628. BANK BARN with mill-wheel.

MALMSMEAD BRIDGE, ¾ m. W. Twin-arched, C17, on the county boundary.

ODCOMBE

Two villages. The upper one, on the Ham Hill ridge, has the church.

ST PETER AND ST PAUL. The church makes a good picture, cruciform with a central tower, but was all but rebuilt in 1874 by *Arthur Blomfield*, who added transepts, extended the nave and replaced the chancel. The tower is original, the bell-stage Perp, with two-light openings, battlements and pinnacles. The S porch has an exceptional C15–C16 stone vault, carried on hanging cornices over quatrefoil friezes. Shield-bearing figures support four-centred-arched transverse ribs between traceried panels. Reused Perp W doorway and some windows. Blomfield's nave roof is partly on Perp cornices, and the two original crossing arches are triple-shafted with conjoined capitals, late C14. SE rood stair. In the chancel a C14 ogee PISCINA with points on the cusps. – FONT. C12, Purbeck marble, square, with shallow arcading (cf. Milborne Port). C14–C15 base. Traceried C15 lid. – REREDOS. 1883, by *T. G. Jackson*. Sumptuous, of alabaster and much gold mosaic. – ROYAL ARMS. 1852. Lively naïve painting. – STAINED GLASS. E window, 1971, by *Christine Arnatt*. Concentric circles of blue and reds. – Saints from Hewish (N), 1864, by *O'Connor*.

S of the church, the SCHOOL, 1831, with intersecting tracery, extended in 1887. Further S, a terrace and MANOR FARMHOUSE have mid-C19 Tudor detail. The former RECTORY is early C18, hip-roofed, with a seven-bay front of stone cross-windows, and two cornices. At the rear a canted early C19 castellated centrepiece between gables.

LOWER ODCOMBE has a closely built street of Ham stone houses. At the N end, TOWNSEND is formal with early C17 mullioned windows. Further on are the thatched C18 MASONS ARMS and WESTOVER, a neat Regency villa. THE PRIORY, thatched and mullioned, in squared stone, was the Odcombe Inn. The OLD DAIRY HOUSE has C18 mullions. Artistic late C19 railings, by *J. B. Petter* of Yeovil.

OLD CLEEVE

ST ANDREW. A fine four-square Perp W tower mainly of pinkish sandstone. Money was left in a will of 1533 by John Tucker, who also left 'to the byldynge of the tower' his 'tokers shers'. Set-back buttresses, battlements, tiny pinnacles, polygonal NE stair-tower. W doorway, then a quatrefoil frieze below the tall four-light W window. Another quatrefoil frieze below the upper half which has a broad three-light blank window on each side. Above these three-light bell-openings with pierced baffles. On the S side one statue niche. Tall wave-moulded tower arch.

The body of the church is mostly C15, except for some herringbone masonry in the N wall of the nave and a blocked C13 N doorway. Also a jamb of a blocked window in the chancel S wall. Mid-C15 S aisle with parapet and porch. The plain S transept is probably earlier, of local sandstone, in contrast to the Blue Lias of the aisle and porch. Flat-headed windows to both aisle and transept with the unusual tracery found at Watchet, the lights with little shouldered heads (the transept S window is a C19 copy). Quite different three-light SW window, transomed, Perp. The porch floor is cobbled with the date 1614 and a big heart in white. Arcade of four bays with piers of four-wave section, the shafts with clumsy capitals. Those facing the nave are wider, with a little label in the centre. Four-centred arches with very little curve. Similar arches to the S transept and chancel. By the chancel arch, a squint with cusping inside. Broad wagon roof in the nave with good bosses and little wall-plate angels. Lean-to roof in the S aisle with vine-trail wall-plate. The panelled chancel roof with angels is good C19 work, prettily painted.

FURNISHINGS. FONT. Octagonal, Perp. Big pointed quatrefoil on each side; angels on the underside. C16 ogee COVER with blank tracery, the oldest in Somerset. – LECTERN. A remarkable Arts and Crafts piece, 1911, by *Ramsden & Carr*. Eagle of brass with bedraggled wings on a tall stand of sheet metal. – CANDELABRA. Brass, 1770, by *Thomas Bayley* of Bridgwater, one of his largest. – TILES. Medieval tiles around the font and in a N wall panel, similar to those at Cleeve Abbey. Good C19 tiles in the nave and richer ones in the chancel. – TOWER SCREEN. 1974. Wrought-iron, with giant angels above in an aluminium strip, distinctive work by *Rachel Reckitt*. Let down by the painted figures on the panels. – STAINED GLASS. E window, 1952, by *Sir Ninian Comper*. Chancel S, 1898, by *Kempe*. S aisle E, *c.* 1897, Burne-Jones style but probably by *Henry Holiday*, who made the S aisle W window, 1905. N window 2000, by *Frankie Pollak*. With fish. W window, *c.* 1860, to victims of the Cawnpore Massacre. – MONUMENTS. Effigy of a civilian of *c.* 1390 under a coarsely made ogee recess with heads at the top and l. At his feet a cat holding a mouse in her paws. – Mary Whitlocke †1715. Cherubs unveil an oval plaque.

Large C15 CHURCHYARD CROSS with tabernacle head of 1916. By the lychgate, a SCHOOLROOM of 1811 with two brick lancets.

LYSAGHT HALL. Arts and Crafts-inspired village hall of 1923. Buttressed stone. Probably by *F. Gabbutt* of Bridgwater, who designed the roughcast additions in 1926–8.

The village climbs to the church from two directions, both with the pretty white thatched cottages typical of the region. On the NW descent the early C19 former VICARAGE, stuccoed, three-storeyed with a deep-eaved roof.

BINHAM GRANGE, ½ m. NW. A grange of Cleeve Abbey, remodelled in 1624 for Robert Boteler. Blue Lias, with a storeyed and gabled porch in red sandstone. Timber oriel over the moulded arched doorway. Hip-roofed C16 rear SW wing. A lost stair-turret in the angle has left a C16 Tudor-arched opening on the W wall, made, unusually, of local alabaster. The present winding oak stair is C17, in a hip-roofed projection on the rear of the main range. C17 arched doorways from the cross-passage into the SE room. This has a framed ceiling and a C16 alabaster Tudor-arched rear doorway. A third alabaster doorway is in the passage behind. In the first-floor centre room a crowded C17 plaster overmantel, perhaps by *Robert Eaton* of Stogursey. It shows, between female caryatids, the Triumph of Time from Petrarch's *Trionfi*. Little figures of all ages accompany the winged old man on a chariot drawn by deer.

CHAPEL CLEEVE, 1 m. N. A chapel of St Mary was built here after a landslip destroyed its predecessor at Blue Anchor in 1452. A guesthouse for pilgrims was attached, and this remains at the back of a large Tudorbethan country house of two periods. The five SE bays, built for John Halliday in 1818–23 by *Richard Carver*, were greatly extended westward in 1912–14 for G. S. Lysaght, by *F. W. Roberts*. Rendered, with stone mullion-and-transom windows. *Carver*'s house has parapets and a central shouldered gable. The front doorway was removed and the windows redone in 1912–14 so that the whole is harmonious. The addition to the l. comprises a storeyed porch with an oriel and a three-bay link to a broad W range containing reception rooms.

Carver's front rooms have good Regency Gothic plasterwork. The former entrance hall with an octagonal dome opens to an apsidal stair hall with iron-railed stair under a rich ceiling with an oval lantern. *Roberts*'s addition is lavishly fitted with Jacobean-style panelling and excellent plasterwork, ceilings and overmantels, in early C17 style. These are by *George Bankart* and are significantly richer and more delicate than genuine ones. The reception rooms flow into each other, a sumptuous rear long gallery linking back to Carver's house, with an oak staircase on the N. The drawing room overmantel is genuine Jacobean, the heraldry not from Somerset.

The rear NE piece is a substantial late medieval building of Blue Lias. A first-floor hall runs N–S with a solar wing running E. Its N wall continues eastward with a large four-centred archway, perhaps to the chapel courtyard. The hall has a two-light gable window with transom, over three segmental-pointed windows, one blocked. The solar wing has one ground-floor two-light window of the elegant local type with quatrefoil spandrels, and a pair of segmental-pointed openings. Above are two cinquefoil-cusped single lights and a gabled dormer with ogee two-light tracery. A good haunched N fireplace survives in the first-floor hall, moulded, four-centred-arched, under a shelf interrupted by four corbels. Remnants of the wind-braced three-bay hall roof and two-bay solar roof.

SOUTH LODGE, early C19. Thatched, rounded, with a veranda.

ORCHARD PORTMAN

The church, behind Taunton Racecourse, once faced the great house of the Portmans.

ST MICHAEL. Covered in unsightly cement except the N face of the three-stage W tower. Money was bequeathed for the tower in 1521 and 1532. Polygonal NE stair-turret. Perp nave and chancel. In the blocked N porch a renewed Norman doorway of two orders, the inner with chevron and pellets, the outer with layered chevron at right angles. Chevron too on the jambs. A two-bay C15 S chapel was replaced by a porch in the 1840s, in turn replaced by a gabled Portman Chapel, 1910, by *Ernest Trepplin*, the Portman agent. – FONT. C11–C12. Unadorned massive cylinder. – STAINED GLASS. E window and Portman Chapel S, 1910–11, by *Arthur Dix*. N window 1911, by *Powell's*. – MONUMENT. Humphredus e Collibus (Colles) †1693. Brass recording his fighting at Tangiers in 1662*.

ORCHARD HOUSE has entirely gone. It was built *c.* 1540–50 for Sir William Portman (†1557), Lord Chief Justice. Of interest for its remarkable sobriety. Three-storey battlemented ranges with grid windows faced each other, linked by a lower W range. An earlier nine-gabled range was behind the S range. The main house went in 1785, the rest in 1843. Mullion windows may be reused in the twin-gabled OLD RECTORY E of the church.

ORCHARD WYNDHAM *see* WILLITON

OTHERY

ST MICHAEL. Blue Lias. A cruciform church around a tall crossing tower that must in its lower stage be C13–C14 – see the

---

* The Portman funeral helms are in the Museum of Somerset, Taunton.

cusped two-light windows. Two Perp stages above, slightly receding, between spreading diagonal buttresses added when the tower was heightened in the early C16. The SE buttress is pierced to allow sight of a lowside chancel window. The second stage has a single Perp niche on each face, with statues (Saints Mary, John and Michael, and enthroned Christ) happily preserved, but not of particular quality. The tall bell-stage is memorable for the single giant Tudor-arched four-light window that fills each side, transomed, and blind apart from the middle upper lights, which have pierced baffles. NE polygonal stair-turret with spirelet. The design has grand aspirations, in effect making a lantern or cage of the top stage. It is unlike anything in Somerset, but something similar but smaller appears at Thornbury, Glos.

Unusual for Somerset too the length of the aisleless nave. Mostly Perp windows, but the simple chamfered N doorway and cinquefoil-cusped rere-arch of one S window are indicative of a C13 date. C14 S doorway with good traceried DOOR. The church was much rebuilt between 1847 and 1861, initially by *Benjamin Ferrey*, possibly succeeded in the 1850s by *John Norton*. The S side and both ends were refaced and the roofs replaced. The chancel is late C13 – see the two-light S window with sexfoil head. The transepts should be C14 (see the crossing arches), but the N transept windows are C15 and the S transept detail is C19.

The crossing piers have the Perp shaft-and-hollow section, but with mouldings so broad and the capitals so simple that a date not too late in the C14 must be assumed. The same goes for the robust pointed arches, but these may replace older piers and arches. The splayed wall each side of the nave arch relates to the diagonal buttresses. Both are pierced with pointed arches, the S one blocked, the N now serving for access to the pulpit. Both seem related to stair-turrets, of which a fragment is visible on the S transept W wall. The present tower stair may once have been reached from the N arch. Under the tower, statue niches of 1854–5. Very Victorian chancel re-fitting of 1850–7. Roof on stone corbels (some giant heads, some with the minute naturalistic carving of *Henry Davis*), the wall-plate with spread-winged angels. Heavily cusped and crocketed SCREEN, poppyhead STALLS with angel ends, ornate canopied stone SEDILE, and splendid *Minton* TILES.

OTHER FURNISHINGS. FONT. C14. Shallow octagonal bowl with paired square panels of tiny leaves. Traceried stem. – PULPIT. 1852. Stone, the wine-glass stem and flying stair notably exhibitionist. – BENCHES. A confusing collection because of the interventions by the antiquary William Stradling of Chilton Polden in 1848–50. Some are C15–C16, with moulded square ends, thick tracery and fleshy leaves, a pelican with barley (for Abbot Bere of Glastonbury). Poppyheads to the frontals. In the S transept several poppyhead ends initialled TP with monstrous beasts. Many are Victorian, e.g. all the NE block, by *William Halliday*, Stradling's carpenter. Halliday copied originals, including some with small figures (St Margaret, St Michael) that seem of separate provenance. – STAINED GLASS. S transept, medieval fragments and three lovely C15 roundels of Doctors of the Church. E window, 1856, by *Hardman*; chancel N, 1857, by *William Holland*. – MONUMENT. Rev. John Shipton †1864, marble, Gothic, signed *W. Farmer*.

In the churchyard a plain NATIONAL SCHOOL, 1827. Opposite, the former VICARAGE, 1828, refronted in stone with canted bay windows, 1855, by *Norton*. The church is on the old straight road through; the present main road curves to the S. LITTLE ENGLAND FARMHOUSE, off to the SE, encases a C15 open hall. C16 framed ceiling.

OTTERFORD

Isolated church above the lakes of Otterhead House, demolished 1952.

ST LEONARD. C14–C15 battlemented W tower with NE stair-turret. Of chert with dressings of pale stone. The rest is Perp, much restored with new N aisle in 1860–1 by *Thomas Hargreaves* of Taunton. The panelled chancel arch and chancel roof with transverse ribs are C15. – FONT. Perp, octagonal with big quatrefoil roundels. Panelled underside.

WHATLEY, 2 m. SE. Two thatched farmhouses, LOWER WHATLEY, late medieval with a full cruck, and HIGHER WHATLEY, C17, with cross-wing and C18 mullions.

ROBIN HOOD'S BUTTS, Brown Down. Three large Bronze Age round barrows W of the B3170. Five more at School Farmhouse, close-spaced in line.

OTTERHAMPTON

Just the church, farm, and rectory of 1802.

ALL SAINTS (Churches Conservation Trust). Perp W tower with diagonal buttresses and polygonal NE stair-tower. Tower arch on capitals with underside roses where shafts seem intended. Perp nave and chancel. In the porch a cusped pointed niche. C14 ogee-headed niches flank the chancel arch, also a moulded round-headed one in the N pier. Plastered barrel ceilings and COMMANDMENT BOARDS (1805) give the interior a Late Georgian character. – FONT. Early Norman cylinder with a base rim decorated with two rows of saltire crosses. C17 COVER. – SCREEN. Small, C15–C16. Three square-headed bays with Tudor-arched four-light tracery. Crocketed ogee dado panels.

– ROYAL ARMS. George VI. – COMMUNION RAILS. C17. Vertically symmetrical balusters and leaf-scroll ornament to the rail.
HILL HOUSE, ½ m. SE. Visible from afar. Built for the Evered family *c.* 1780. A large rendered villa of five bays, with parapet and open pediment. The detail is good: ashlar pilasters frame the doorway and side-lights, under an entablature linked by scrolls to a corniced first-floor architrave. Bowed ends. The back half is castellated, a late C18 conceit. Stair hall with columned screens on each level. Drawing room with an Adam-style ceiling.

OVER STOWEY

ST PETER AND ST PAUL. Red and buff sandstone. Perp W tower with diagonal buttresses, square NE stair-turret, two-light bell-openings, and similar S window beneath. Tall shafted tower arch. The rest, nave, chancel and big gabled N aisle, feels Victorian, the estate church for Quantock Lodge. Altered by *Richard Carver*, 1840; *C. E. Giles*, 1857 (chancel); and *Basil Cottam*, 1902 (chancel extension) and 1908. Chamfered C14 chancel arch. Renewed C15–C16 arcade of three bays with uncarved band capitals. Chancel mosaic FLOOR of 1902. – FONT. Perp. Octagonal, with underside quatrefoils. – BENCHES. Several C16 with leaf-scroll borders. Plant forms, both wiry and fleshy, and tracery. – CANDELABRA. Brass, two-tier, by *Street & Pyke* of Bridgwater, 1775. – VICTORIAN FITTINGS: Gothic oak PULPIT and STALLS, stone REREDOS (after 1875), and brass CORONAE. – STAINED GLASS. Chancel windows by *Hardman*, 1857; W window, 1872 by *Clayton & Bell*. But the interest is two of 1873 by *William Morris*: Mary Magdalene and the Angel at the Tomb, NE, and musician angels, NW, their simplicity moving and original. More typical of later *Morris & Co.*, four three-light windows, 1906, 1908, and two of 1922, mostly reusing *Burne-Jones* figure designs. – MONUMENT. Thomas and James Rich †1813 and 1815, by *John Wood* of Bristol. Bachelor farmers. A draped sarcophagus above, and a very engaging 'trophy' below, of plough, harrows and other tools of the field.
The stuccoed former VICARAGE, dated 1786 on a rainwater head, has segmental-headed windows of Early Georgian type. William Holland, diarist vicar, lived here 1799–1818. PARSONAGE FARMHOUSE, refronted in 1816, was the medieval church house. Inside, a framed ceiling and sweet early C17 plaster relief of Adam and Eve. Opposite, a pretty hip-roofed oak LYCH-GATE, 1887, to the cemetery. CROFT FARMHOUSE, beyond, has a pyramid-roofed GAZEBO at the corner of the front garden.
QUANTOCK LODGE, Aley. 1857–60, by *Henry Clutton*, for Henry Labouchère, Secretary of State for the Colonies (created Lord Taunton in 1859). Built new on 5,000 acres, it represents the aspirations and wealth of the Victorian banking classes

(Labouchère was of the Baring family). The land cost £135,000, the buildings £40,000, of which £16,000 was for the house. Immediately notable is the green colour, volcanic tufa from Cockercombe. Neo-Tudor with a little French Gothic. The complicated NE front builds up in shouldered gables to an octagonal turret carrying an ogee-domed lantern. Both garden fronts lost battlements after 1950, and the symmetrical SW front is badly denatured. It had three sets of triple-shafted chimneys on the wall face above battlemented parapets. Good Gothic interiors: the high vaulted porch, the hall, an early example of informal planning, long and low with secluded window seats, and the arcaded stair hall. Fine naturalistic carving to doorways, windows and fireplaces. Towering French Late Gothic chimney-breast in the stair hall, improbably including a Neoclassical marble plaque. In the SW rooms a mixture of C17 and C18 motifs. Square CAMELIA HOUSES face each other across the SW garden, with grid windows and ogee-headed Gothic doorways, and a curved-ended bastion closes the garden at the foot of a hillside avenue. Hemispherical FOUNTAIN beneath.

The STABLE COURT, to the NW, has a cross-gabled corner carrying a tiled cone tiered in dove entries under a Chinese-hat lantern. No dovecote at all, it is entirely decorative. The style suggests the hand of *William Burges*, Clutton's partner until 1856. Two stable ranges have gone, also a spired lantern from the SW roof. Some distance away, *Clutton*'s sculptural GATE-HOUSE spans the main drive. Memorable colours: green with golden Ham stone outside, red sandstone within the barrel-vaulted throughway. Flamboyant heraldry.

PEPPERHILL FARM, ½ m. SW, 1857, was the dairy farm. A green octagonal DAIRY, paved in *Minton* tile, adjoins a large red farmhouse with typical *Clutton* hip-roofed porch. At ALEY FARM, the home farm, a large C19 barn overlooks a high-walled yard.

MARSH MILLS, ¼ m. E. Roughcast irregular house of the Poole family, older than the early C19 windows. Barrel-vaulted plaster ceiling upstairs. The adjoining SILK MILL of 1812–16 is neatly formal, hip-roofed, with an ashlar band under the eaves. Water entered at the first-floor corner.

ADSCOMBE, ½ m. S. Foundations of a late C13 chapel.

PLAINSFIELD COURT, 1½ m. SSE. Late C19 brick-framed windows, but a C15 wind-braced roof and C16 sixteen-panel framed ceiling inside. In the r. cross-wing an overmantel dated 1665, with the Blake arms.

OVER STRATTON
s of South Petherton

The ROYAL OAK is thatched C17–C18. At the S end of the village STRATTON FARMHOUSE, externally C17, has C16 jointed crucks and timber-framed smoke-hoods. OLD HARP HOUSE has C17 mullions and a continuous dripmould. Towards Wigborough, TOLLER VIEW, 2010, by *Boon Brown*, with gridded timber glazing, topped by a glazed look-out.

YEABRIDGE HOUSE, ¾ m. NE. Substantial Early Victorian ashlar villa, asymmetrical under deep-eaved hipped roofs. Extensive C19 outbuildings, less impressive since conversion.

BRIDGE HOUSE, 1¼ m. NE. Of the severe Gothic house built for William Blake by *W. B. Gingell*, 1859–60, fragments remain amid static caravans, and LODGES on the A303. Just S, OLD BRIDGE, built *c.* 1580, remodelled after 1700, with typical early C18 mullioned windows. Four-bay main range with a storeyed porch. S cross-wing with cross-windows and a long central stair light. The Bridge estate farm was at FLAXDRAYTON HOUSE, C17, altered after fire in the C18. Full basement storey to the rear, overlooking a steam-powered farmyard of 1860 with tall brick chimney. Across the road, BRIDGE FARMHOUSE and COTTAGES, *c.* 1860.

WIGBOROUGH MANOR, 1 m. E. A fine Ham stone mansion with mullion or mullion-and-transom windows built in 1585 by Henry Compton. It would have been of E-plan with stair-towers in the angles, like Barrington Court (q.v.), but the N cross-wing and angle turret were never built. Tree-ring dating confirms 1585 for the roof, so the ovolo mullions, generally a C17 form, must be Elizabethan here. Four-storeyed gabled porch with the hall to the l. The gabled angle turret contains neither stair nor hall-bay, but a small study, as e.g. at Lytes Cary. The parlour cross-wing projects to the l. Over the porch a cornice on little Elizabethan brackets and a plaque with early strapwork. Massive external rear chimney-breast. Scar of a garderobe on the S end. Enclosed gallery over the screens passage. The hall has a moulded Tudor-arched stone fireplace, and the N end kitchen a wide stone one. The little study has panelling dated 1585 and a thin-rib plaster ceiling. The SE parlour has plasterwork of *c.* 1630 for Sir Thomas Hele that is much more elaborate in a very rustic way. The ceiling has delightful motifs, some mythical, amid flowers within curved and straight ribs. The unusually deep frieze also has special motifs (e.g. two figures at a well) in strapwork cartouches. The overmantel is particularly coarse, with Hele heraldry between one-armed female terms. SW staircase around a solid core. Thin-ribbed first-floor SE ceiling.

Large C18–C19 BARNS, one piece dated 1765.

PAWLETT

ST JOHN BAPTIST. Lime-rendered white. Battlemented W tower with C16 W doorway. Square stair-turret stopped against the bell-stage with a pyramid roof under a carved head. The rest is cruciform with low unequal transepts, probably C13, although the cusped and uncusped lancets are not reliable, indeed the triple E lancet is in brick walling. Later C14 S porch. Notable Norman S doorway, without columns, but the inner responds each with two incised motifs. The arch has an inner moulding of uneven fat lozenges enclosing rosettes, a second of chevron at right angles, and an outer of beasts and some beakheads, a great rarity in Somerset. On the nave pretty Victorian iron gutters.

The interior is memorable for its plastered ceilings and C17 fittings. Simple barrel roofs with thin timbers, perhaps 'ye sealing' erected in 1728. The chancel roof has pretty borders in C17 style, of 1915, by *E. H. Sedding*. Broad four-centred C15–C16 chancel arch. – ROYAL ARMS. 1708. – FONT. Ham stone bowl, retooled, but the stem and base apparently an upturned Norman font with scalloped bowl. Octagonal Jacobean COVER. – SCREEN. C15–C16. Six ogee-headed lights each side, and a good cornice with undercut vine frieze. The loft has gone. – C17 FITTINGS, some reassembled, include the PULPIT, with typical arched panels, and a DESK with big patterned lozenges, similar to the BOX PEWS and STALLS. Also sturdy three-sided RAILS around a COMMUNION TABLE of 1678. – STAINED GLASS. E window, 1875.

Below the church, stuccoed former VICARAGE, 1806. 1 m. W, a large corrugated-iron HANGAR, 1940, that housed a practice balloon. The path opposite led to a ferry across the Parrett to Combwich, long a principal route westward.

PENDOMER

ST ROCH. Small Perp church in brown Forest Marble rubble. Plain unbuttressed W tower, probably early C14. Two stages with renewed narrow lancets to both levels. The rest is a single vessel, much rebuilt in 1870. Undivided interior, with Victorian roof. Two C15 tie-beams. The outstanding feature is the boldly cusped N wall TOMB-RECESS. Two of the four outsized cusps terminate in broken angels, one bearing the soul of the deceased. Above the recess a battlemented cornice is borne by two smocked figures each leaning on a pinnacled pier. They stand casually, one foot raised, and one uses just one hand to carry the cornice. The Ham stone EFFIGY is of a cross-legged knight, probably Sir John Dummer †1320. Hauberk and coif of mail, surcoat, gauntlets and knee plates. His head rests on a helm with eye slits. Cusped PISCINA, chancel S. – FONT. C12, circular, with a big ring. – In the blocked S doorway a late C14 LEDGER SLAB. – STAINED GLASS. Later C15 fragments. E window, 2003, by *Stewart Bowman*.

MANOR HOUSE. Backing on to the churchyard. Early C16 in squared Ham stone, a long four bays with pointed-arched doorway and triple mullioned windows with arched lights. BRYANTS FARMHOUSE, just E, has a C16 lateral chimney with

Pendomer, St Roch, monument probably to Sir John Dummer †1320. Engraving, 1871

long oak lintel over two fireplaces separated by a narrow stone pier. On the OLD SCHOOL an early C16 STATUE of St Roch.

PENDOMER HOUSE, 1 m. SE, overlooking a big view. A large rectory of 1857 by *J. M. Allen*, with mullion-and-transom windows.

PENSELWOOD

ST MICHAEL. Low battlemented Perp W tower of Greensand stone, with diagonal buttresses and polygonal N stair. The rest was rebuilt in 1805 reusing at least the Perp chancel S windows, and again in 1848–9 by *Jesse Gane* who added the gabled N aisle. Built into the S porch gable is the head of an early C15 churchyard cross. The Virgin and two donors face out, a damaged Crucifixion faces inward. Restored C12 S doorway with carving in the spirit of the Milborne Port tympanum, much redone. The ridged lintel shows an encircled Paschal Lamb (particularly poorly observed) between much livelier affronted beasts, a lion and lioness. Staring crowned heads support the lintel. Above is a bare tympanum under a chevron arch. Outer roll moulding on nook-shafts with scallop capitals. The N arcade is *Gane*'s, quite good. The roof reuses three C15 BOSSES from Stavordale Priory. – FONT. C12. Square, with exaggerated scallops like drapery. – ROYAL ARMS. Hanoverian. – BENCH-ENDS. Illustrating medieval tasks. 1927, carved by *Clemency Angell*. – TILES. On the E wall. Late C19 embossed. – STAINED GLASS. Nave S, C15 fragments. Also one of 1872, rather classicizing figures, by *H. E. Wooldridge* for *Powell's*. Chancel N, 1924, by *Comper*. – MONUMENTS. William Biging †1802. Extremely old-fashioned draped cartouche. – Also to the Bigings, a rustic one of *c.* 1800 in coloured marbles, signed *C. Clewett*, Wincanton.

By the church, the former SCHOOL, 1847.

PEN PITS, ¾ m. E. The Greensand was quarried for quern stones from the Iron Age onwards, leaving an area of 700 acres covered in circular depressions. These are the infilled remains of conical shafts up to 10 ft (3 metres) deep that were dug to extract the stones. Now wooded, they provide the setting for the best Modern Movement house of the region, built for the composer Arthur Bliss and his American wife, Trudy, in 1934–5 by *Peter Harland*. White-painted rendered brick and glass on a steel frame. The logic of the plan can be read from the outside. The solid W end contains the living room with entrance and stairs behind and main bedroom above. The rest is for outdoor living, two levels backed by shallow ranges – bathrooms and bedroom above, kitchen below. The lower terrace, a loggia behind two steel posts, is smaller because the dining room intrudes to the l. Its curved front window shares the same long rectangular frame as the living-room windows, interlocking the two parts of the composition. Two rooftop cubes (chimney and water tank) add interest and carry masts for radio wires. Nautical ladders link the levels. Bright secondary colours: red steel windows, black tiles within the window recess, blue flower-basin in the loggia, blue nautical railings above. Corbusian rear porch of two slabs, and a box-like NE garage.

In the woods is Bliss's MUSIC ROOM, 1935, a weatherboarded cube projecting over one of the pits. Cabin-like plyboard interior.

FOREST LODGE, ½ m. W. 1821. Hip-roofed villa in squared Greensand, re-roofed in 1929 after a fire. LODGE with intricate cast-iron windows.

KENWALCH'S CASTLE, 1½ m. NNW. An Iron Age hillfort cut by a lane. It is roughly oblong, 240 yds (220 metres) long and 120 yds (110 metres) wide. Large rampart, particularly on the S, rising up to 20 ft (6 metres) above the ditch. The name, from Cenwealh, the Anglo-Saxon king who defeated the Britons at Peonnan in 658, was coined by later antiquaries, as was the alternative, Vespasian's Camp. There are several Norman castles in the area, including BALLANDS CASTLE, a square earthwork enclosure with a motte, and another in Cockroad Wood with a motte and two baileys.

PILTON

ST JOHN BAPTIST. Beautifully placed down a dip from the main road and across a narrow valley from the tithe barn (*see* p. 521). Large and a little abrupt in its appearance, because both nave and chancel have a clerestory but there is neither a S aisle nor chancel chapels. The clerestories are the result of an expensive overhaul for Thomas Boleyn and Thomas Overay, successive precentors of Wells, 1451–93. Overay's arms are on the chancel gable. The architectural history begins with the S doorway, copied from a damaged Norman original in the restoration of 1871 (by *A. E. Gough* of London). An arch with two orders of chevron on heavy columns with scalloped capitals. The doorway probably pre-dates the N arcade, of five chamfered arches on octagonal piers with trumpet-scallop capitals. The trumpet scallops look like work of *c.* 1180–90 but the octagonal piers suggest a later date, contemporary with the roll-moulded C13 N doorway and the base of the tower. The tower has two small lancets and a low double-chamfered tower arch, moulded on the E face. Strong angle buttresses added perhaps at the same time as the plain bell-stage of 1506. Two-light bell-openings, battlements and corner pinnacles on thin diagonal buttresses. The NE stair-turret starts square and finishes octagonal, with a spirelet. Perp four-centred-arched W window beneath a stone clock face of 1602.

The narrow two-light windows of the N aisle may be C13, with tracery inserted at the same time as the large Perp windows of the eastern bay. This replaced a transept or chapel, suggested by the slight break before the fifth arch of the arcade. Perp panelled parapet. In the chancel nothing external survives of earlier date. Two lower windows on each side, under three clerestory windows, the irregularity showing that an older chancel was remodelled. Large five-light E window. The four-centred-arched clerestory windows have supermullions. Between the windows diagonal piers on good squatting beasts rise to finials through a parapet of pierced quatrefoils. The nave clerestory is battlemented on the S side with similar windows, shafts and pinnacles. Gabled and pinnacled S porch of 1523 faced in ashlar. Canopied niche over the doorway. Perp roof inside on stone corbels: heads and angel busts. The parapets and porch closely resemble work at West Pennard.

High and light interior with roofs of the C15–C16 Somerset type, full of angels. The nave tie-beams start from wall-posts on stone angels, and are ornamented with fleurons. There are angels against the kingposts, and on the wall-plate under each intermediate truss. Similar N aisle roof. One angel corbel is still painted. In the NE chapel, a Dec recess with ballflower in one arch moulding. The C13–C14 Lias coffin-lid is unrelated. In the lozenge centre of the foliated cross is a bearded face, perhaps of Christ. Also in the chapel an angel corbel set low, with original colour, a cusped ogee PISCINA, and a squint passage to the chancel. Where the passage emerges, a stone angel finishes the chancel window reveal. The four-centred chancel arch is low enough to suggest an earlier arch refashioned. Panelled jambs and panelled arch, the arch starting with three angel busts on either side. Panelled chancel ceiling with six spread-winged angels each side, on stone angel corbels. Bench SEDILE in the SE window, with quatrefoil front, squat lions at each end, and angels stopping the window reveal. Elaborate cusped ogee PISCINA with foliage spandrels and a little vault.

FURNISHINGS. FONT. C17. Octagonal with arched panels. – PARCLOSE SCREENS (NE chapel). Screens are mentioned in the churchwardens' accounts between 1498 and 1508. The two screens resemble each other, except that the W screen has robust Renaissance motifs in the dado and the cushion-like doorway spandrels, surely later than 1508. Each screen has three four-light sections, of square-headed lights with delicate tracery, as at West Pennard, and a good undercut frieze. The S screen mullions have been cut.* – COPE. Given c. 1492 by Richard Pomeroy, custos of Wells Cathedral. Very faded. The motifs are familiar, the Assumption of the Virgin and Cherubim. Ornaments from another piece are on new cloth over the NE altar. – CANDELABRA. 1749 by R. Rice of Bristol. – COMMUNION RAIL. C18, with delicate twisted balusters. – STAINED GLASS. Late C15 glass in the chancel side windows: Thomas Overay and St Andrew, with beasts or Evangelist symbols in the tracery. Fragments in the NE chapel include a head of Christ. Chancel S W, 1871, by *Horwood Bros*, and perhaps the E, Nativity in a giant eight-pointed star. Nave S, 1907, the first work of *Margaret Chilton*. A throwback to painterly glass of the early C19, in ludicrously large pieces, but a rare sensibility shines through. Also a Resurrection, 1874, good colours, by *James Bell*. Chancel N, 1926, by *Christopher Webb*. – MONUMENTS. Mary Huntley †1738. Exuberantly carved, especially the cherub heads beneath. – Thomas Clerk †1817 and Dorothy Clerk †1847. Full-blown tomb-recess, mid-C19 Perp.

In the churchyard, two eroded EFFIGIES, a late C13 civilian and early C14 lady. Drain-holes show that her effigy was intended to be outside, as many were.

METHODIST CHAPEL, Top Street. Gothic of *c.* 1840. Four-light window with intersecting tracery over a later C19 double porch.

EBENEZER CHAPEL, Pylle Road. 1839. Originally Bible Christian. Hip-roofed with arched openings and Georgian Gothic glazing.

Above the church is the former VICARAGE, 1866, by *Ewan Christian*, gabled with mullion-and-transom windows. On the main road, the three-storey PILTON STORES, formerly the Swan Inn. Georgian, but with marks of older windows. Opposite the

---

* The C15 chancel screen from Pilton, reconstructed at North Cheriton, resembles neither.

church, the CHURCH HOUSE, 1892, with cinquefoil-cusped windows, reputedly reproduces a Glastonbury Abbey hostelry on the site. Below the church are MONKS MILL, a Late Georgian Gothic cottage, and the manor grounds.

PILTON MANOR may be identifiable with an ill-recorded house of the abbots of Glastonbury. The E front is restrained Georgian, of five bays, for Edward Andrews, *c.* 1754. Central Venetian window and thick glazing bars. Late C18 castellation and pinnacles hint at the vigorous Gothicizing to the SW rear wing, where three large tripartite windows face S and another W, under similar battlements. Also a false stair-turret. The stepped lancets have no archaeological justification, but the relieving arches over two S windows and the W one show that this is a remodelling. A rear stair gable with early C16 windows adjoins a short NW wing with C17 mullioned windows. Cornerstones show that the latter came first, so the stair windows must be reused. Inside, a medieval depressed arch into the back of the front range could mark a hall oriel. Other medieval remnants are under the rear range, principally a doorway and vaulted chamber at right angles to the range. Just 18 by 13 ft (5.5 by 4 metres), it has four-centred transverse arches. Enough remains to indicate an L-plan medieval house, perhaps with two halls. The principal Georgian interiors are a mid-C18 panelled SE room and two tall Georgian Gothic rooms in the rear wing, the triple windows embellished with panelling etc. Outside are Georgian pointed-arched garden gateways, and Georgian outbuildings ending in a square medieval DOVECOTE, the cruck trusses tree-ring-dated to 1441–6.

The BRIDGE over the Pilton Stream has a part-blocked pointed medieval arch. On top of the S slope is a magnificent C14 TITHE BARN of Glastonbury Abbey. Cruciform, 120 ft (36.6 metres) long, of nine bays – two bays longer than the Glastonbury barn. As at Glastonbury, there are Evangelist symbols on the four gables. Big projecting porches, cross-loops between side buttresses, and a big mid-buttress at each end beneath a cusped two-light window. The roof burnt in 1963 was replaced in 2003 by *Peter McCurdy* with *Caroe & Partners*. The two-tier cruck trusses with a square-set purlin echo the Glastonbury and West Bradley barns. Plain tiles substitute for thatch. The restoration was initiated by Michael Eavis, founder of the Glastonbury Festival held on Worthy Farm S of the village since 1970. THE BRIDGE, the gabled stone house by the barn, was built for Eavis in 2010. CUMHILL FARMHOUSE, E of the barn, has a C15–C16 Tudor-arched doorway. Down Bread Street, MALT HOUSE was a C15 hall house, with unusual cusped braces to a cruck truss. Beyond the Pylle road, on Lower Street, GABLE HOUSE has a compact mid-C17 front with twin dormer gables. At PYLLE HOUSE, asymmetry in the handsome corniced Georgian front shows that an older house (dated 1629) is refaced. One fielded-panelled room. Georgian Gothic lofted STABLE. From Gable House, a lane runs down to BEALE'S HOUSE, C16–C17, triple-gabled with later windows. GREY GABLES, thatched, with a cross-wing and three dormer gables, is dated 1671, but has two-tier cruck trusses from a medieval hall and a moulded Tudor-arched fireplace. C17 stairs with pierced flat balusters.

EAST TOWN, ¾ m. E. Along the Pilton Stream are WELLANDS, dated 1664, with a rear stair gable, EAST TOWN FARMHOUSE, a C17 mill, but dated 1747, and CHANTERS HOUSE, a large stuccoed villa of *c.* 1840, with deep-eaved hipped roof and triple casement windows.

EAST COMPTON HOUSE, 2 m. ENE. Late Georgian double-pile house of three bays, ashlar-fronted, with cornice and parapet.

BURFORD HOUSE, ¾ m. NNE. 1853, neo-Jacobean, with extensive stables etc. For the Clerks of Westholme. BURFORD FARM, behind, C17, has a two-storey square bay with ovolo mullions on the cross-wing.

WEST COMPTON, I m. NNE. MANOR HOUSE was a C15 open hall with cruck trusses, remodelled with early C17 ovolo mullions and gables. Cross-gabled SW corner added *c.* 1680 for James Bisse. Framed C16 ceiling with late C17 plaster ovals, one corner cut for an elaborate early C17 staircase. Pierced finials and pendants, and heavy carved balusters cut to the slope. WEST COMPTON HOUSE, behind pineapple gatepiers, is mid-C18, for the next Bisse generation. Whitewashed with ashlar dressings, cornice and parapet. Seven close-spaced bays without a window over the doorway, which has a hood on consoles under a scroll-sided panel. Full-length vaulted basement. A good C18 staircase was sold in the 1980s. C17 rear wing. KNOWLE FARMHOUSE, ¾ m. ENE, was a C15 hall house with wind-braced cruck roof. Painted text of 1648.

WESTHOLME HOUSE, ¾ m. NW. A small Georgian estate, the ashlar mansion proud above a lake fed by a prettily landscaped stream. Five-bay, three-storey W front with cornice, parapet, and central Venetian window. Partridge Smith bought a 'mansion house' in 1768 from Stephen Stone of Perridge House, possibly new-built as a speculation. The porch and attic centre window (originally oval) were altered when Thomas Clerk enlarged the house *c.* 1798. He added to the rear to create a three-bay S front with tripartite French windows, each with a depressed central arch. Good open-well staircase of alternate fluted and twisted balusters, *c.* 1768, under an elegant oval glazed dome of *c.* 1800. Also of *c.* 1800, the SW room with coloured marble chimneypiece and the near-circular anteroom. Service range with a bell dated 1776 in a timber cupola. The oval light in the COACHHOUSE may be from the W front. Italianate LODGE, dated 1847. Contemporary drive with a balustraded bridge. Matching balustraded garden TERRACES. Below the lodge, JACOB'S WELL, in a rockwork grotto with niches. WESTHOLME COTTAGE, SW, was a Victorian dower house, steep-gabled, echoing the local vernacular.

PERRIDGE HOUSE, ¾ m. W. A confusing medley. The S garden front, on high basements, has a two-bay centre with cornice, parapet, and long Tudor-arched sash windows, apparently early C19 infill between C17 cross-wings. Interiors of 1909 and 2009–12.

PITCOMBE

ST LEONARD. Slim Perp w tower with diagonal buttresses and grotesque gargoyles. Primitive flat faces terminate the w window sill. Panelled tower arch. The rest is by *G. E. Street*, 1857–8, in ochre stone, Dec to Perp style, for the Hobhouses of Hadspen. The way the vestry lifts over the N aisle shows Street's sure handling of form. Quatrefoil arcade piers with a broad fillet, similar chancel arches. – FONT. C12 bowl shaved hexagonally, on a ring base. – BENCH-ENDS. Some C15–C16, traceried. – STAINED GLASS. E window, 1858, by *O'Connor*. w window, C15 fragments including cherubim. – MONUMENTS. Sarah Hobhouse †1792 and Sarah Hobhouse †1810, the latter signed *John Bacon Jun.*

CHURCHYARD CROSS, C14–C15. The base is circular and moulded, with most unusual lion spurs. – HEADSTONE to Henry Hobhouse †1937, lettered by *Eric Gill*. – LYCHGATE, 1858, by *Street*.

WOODLEAZE, with a round turret, was a Hadspen lodge with coachhouse for church use, 1860s. The attractive SCHOOL, 1864, is a Hobhouse memorial. The Somerset & Dorset Railway VIADUCT of 1862 overwhelms the village to the N.

BRUTON GIRLS' SCHOOL, ½ m. N. 1900, by *Arthur Pictor*. In the Board School mode, with generous arched windows in twin gables. Extended W, 1912, by *Pictor*, who surprisingly also designed the hip-roofed Thirties-Modern DAY SCHOOL behind, 1936–8. Additions from 1978 by *Ronald Vallis* and successors. The best is CUMBERLEGE HOUSE, 1980–1, brick with gambrel roof, by *Pamela Lea*. The former VICARAGE, 1860–1, by *Ewan Christian*, SE, is now a boarding house.

COLE, ¾ m. NNW. COLE MANOR is L-plan with some C17 mullioned windows. Mill behind, with an internal C19 wheel. The water has powered a turbine since 2007. MANOR HOUSE opposite, with corniced mullioned windows and basket-arched door hood, is datable by similar detail on COLE FARMHOUSE further W, of 1766.

PITMINSTER

ST MARY AND ST ANDREW. Utterly plain square w tower of *c*. 1300, buttressed by lean-to chambers. It is broached to a C14 octagonal bell-stage with small pointed two-light openings, parapet and lead-covered spire, somewhat as at South

Petherton. Double-chamfered tower arch. The chamfered arch and shafted doorway of the N porch are also of *c.* 1300. Perp aisles and chancel chapels, the N one with quatrefoil parapet. Analysis is confused by *J. M. Allen*, who in 1869–70 rebuilt the N aisle and S porch, raised the S rood-stair turret, and refenestrated the clerestory. The N arcade is entirely Victorian (Glynne in 1855 saw obtuse Perp arches), to match the S one. This has early C14 responds and double-chamfered arches, although the piers are Victorian. These are circular with attached shafts facing E and W, and clustered thin shafts N and S. In the NW chapel three re-set C13–C14 corbel heads. Perp side arches to the chancel, with angels holding scrolls as capitals. – FONT. Beer stone. Unusually good early C14, octagonal, on a base of equal width. Panels with quatrefoils and also sculpture, St George on horseback and St James with two donors. The base has niches between shafts under a band of excellent foliage. – PULPIT. From the Bluecoat School, Frome, or the predecessor almshouses of 1621. Handsome, with tiers of carved panels, mainly strapwork and cartouches under a tester with pendant and radiating fluting. – BENCH-ENDS. C19, a few C16 pieces reframed. – STAINED GLASS. NE, 1894 (with C15 angels in the tracery lights), and W, 1905, both by *Kempe*. E, 1988, by *Jane Gray*. NW, 1949, by *Christopher Webb*. – MONUMENTS. Three, with effigies, to the Colles of Barton Grange, Corfe. In the NW chapel, Humphry †1570, in black civilian dress, repainted. In the chancel, John †1608 and Anne, on two tiers, he in armour. Alabaster tomb-chest with six kneeling children (little adults). Repainted. Opposite, John †1627 and Elizabeth †1634. Somerset alabaster. Similar but altogether less stiffly carved, he in armour, she with a baby at her feet, and four charming kneeling girls on the tomb-chest. Comparable with Sir John Bluett †1634 at Holcombe Rogus, Devon.

N of the churchyard, the bargeboarded former VICARAGE, 1840, by *Richard Carver*. Former SCHOOL of similar date. A little NE, CHURCH ROW was an early C19 row of cottages for the poor, the upper floor lit only from behind.

FULWOOD, 1 m. NW. Former CONGREGATIONAL CHAPEL of *c.* 1820. Stuccoed two-storey front with arched windows. FULWOOD FARM was a late medieval hall house, the N crosswing showing C17 brick. To the W, WATER TREATMENT WORKS, 1991–3, by *Graham Carruthers Partnership*.

PITNEY

Two halves represent two medieval manors, the church and Pitney House at the West End.

ST JOHN BAPTIST. A small, mostly Victorian, Blue Lias church, the chancel rebuilt in 1853, the nave in 1874–5 by *Charles*

Knowles. The W tower is C14 below – see the square stair-turret, W window with flowing tracery, and chamfered tower arch – and C15 above (two-light bell-openings with pierced baffles). The S transept is Perp with good Ham stone battlements and S window tracery. Thoroughly Victorian inside, lined in White Lias, but the chancel arch matches the tower arch and the squint looks C14 (tunnel vault with three single-chamfered ribs). Reused chancel roof bosses including a green man, possibly C14. – FONT. Octagonal, C14, with rosettes beneath. The plinth has sheep-head spurs. – PULPIT. Restored C17, arch-panelled. Surplus panels on the lectern. – STAINED GLASS. S transept S, 1977, by *J. E. Nuttgens*.*

PITNEY HOUSE. 1810. Square hip-roofed Regency house of immaculately squared White Lias. The three-bay front has large triple sashes and a broad porch on Ham stone Greek Doric columns.

N of the church, the gabled OLD RECTORY, 1856, by *Richard Carver*. The medieval predecessor had a Muchelney-type hall window which Carver copied on the rear wall. OLD COURT, thatched, was a C15 hall house. At East End, EAST END FARMHOUSE was another. ESTATE FARMHOUSE, large, dated 1694, has timber-mullioned windows.

ROMAN VILLAS. Two are known from C19 excavations. One had several figured mosaics. The largest depicted Bacchus surrounded by male and female figures, another featured the Phoenician prince Cadmus surprised by a snake.

PIXTON PARK *see* DULVERTON

PODIMORE

5020

Formerly Podimore Milton. Still rural, despite the nearby Yeovilton air station.

ST PETER. Blue Lias. An early C14 church of nave and chancel and a slim W tower which turns octagonal above the lowest stage, like that at Bishop's Hull. Lancets to the three octagonal stages, Dec W window. Double-chamfered tower arch on moulded corbels. The octagon is carried on double-chamfered squinches. Dec windows in the nave and chancel. C16 E window. The narrow single-chamfered chancel arch could be C13. It keeps some red-and-white lattice decoration. Colour also on the rood-stair door. Nave roof by *Slater & Carpenter*, 1871, with some reused bosses. Two plain E niches probably C15, found 2008. – FONT. Retooled C11–C12 bowl. – C16

---

*The Anglo-Scandinavian Pitney Brooch (British Museum) was found in the churchyard in 1898.

square-ended BENCHES and panelled PULPIT. – COMMUNION RAIL. Probably after 1660, with slim vertically symmetrical turned balusters. – STAINED GLASS. E window fragments including the barley rebus of Abbot Bere of Glastonbury. Churchyard and TABLE TOMB to John Swadel †1593. Bold lettering.

A symmetrical C19 row faces the stuccoed hip-roofed former rectory, REEDLEY HOUSE, 1830s. LOWER FARMHOUSE, at the N end of the village, has C16–C17 stone mullions to the cross-wing and narrow adjoining gable. Framed ceiling.

BRIDGEHAMPTON, I m. SE. COURTRY FARMHOUSE has the framed mullioned windows of the early C18. SPECKINGTON MANOR, SW, is C16, refronted in the C19. Tudor-arched fireplace in the wing.

8040 inset

PORLOCK

Three settlements behind Porlock Bay: the small town on the main road, West Porlock and Porlock Weir. Scattered with the hotels and villas of Exmoor tourism and hunting.

ST DUBRICIUS. St Dubricius is Dyfrig, C5–C6 apostle of Herefordshire and SE Wales. The church is substantial and much of it dates from the late C13. Red sandstone rubble, once roughcast. Low heavy W tower with long W lancet and chamfered tower arch. Big shingled medieval spire, the top missing since c. 1700. The rest has two undivided roofs, over the nave and chancel and over the S aisle. Storeyed C15 N porch, and a N organ chamber. This is by *J. D. Sedding*, 1890, in chequered red and buff; Sedding at his most advanced, atypical of his Somerset work. Restored C13 triple-lancet E window and C13 N and S doorways, the S doorway re-set in a C14 S aisle. Otherwise Perp two-light windows. Early C14 five-bay arcade of double-chamfered arches on octagonal piers with very elementarily shaped capitals. Roofs of 1890–1 with some C15 wall-plate and bosses reused. In the aisle are two C14 tomb-recesses with moulded arches and hoodmoulds. In the chancel a C13 roll-moulded trefoil-headed PISCINA and C15 doorway to an E sacristy.

FURNISHINGS. FONT. Octagonal, Perp, with large shields in cusped panels; fleurons on the underside. Panelled stem, moulded base with shields. COVER by *W. H. Randoll Blacking*, 1939. – FRAGMENT, W wall, of an Anglo-Saxon cross-shaft, with interlace decoration. – REREDOS. 1931, by *Blacking*. Two tiers, the lower with statuettes on black, the upper a gilded triptych painted by *Christopher Webb*. – STALLS. 1895, by *Sedding*. Complex plant motifs and spade-like finials, as at Wincanton. – PULPIT. 1901, by *Edmund Buckle*. Open-fronted. – TOWER SCREEN. 1939, by *Blacking*. – STAINED GLASS. Good E window, after 1872. Nine Arts and Crafts windows of 1890

with large pale flowers outlined by the leading (cf. Luccombe).
– MONUMENTS. Cross-legged knight, badly defaced, possibly
Simon Fitz-Roges, late C13. The legs are shortened to fit the
recess. – Sir John Harington †1418 and wife †1471, made
c. 1460. A major piece. On a tomb-chest with ogee arcading,
two fine alabaster effigies, he in plate armour with wreathed
helmet resting on a helm supported by angels, she with splendid horned head-dress on a tasselled cushion, supported by
angels, with the Courtenay boar at her feet. The canopy has a
four-centred arch frilled with cusping, the soffit panelled, with
fleurons around the arch and spandrel tracery. Cornice and
cresting missing, the tomb apparently moved. – Two Perp
tomb-chests commissioned by Alice Hensley in 1527, her husband's in the chancel, hers in the porch (originally in the churchyard), both ornamented with big quatrefoils, his more elaborate.
Both display the Five Wounds in the central quatrefoil.

CHURCHYARD CROSS. C15 on two octagonal steps, the head
C19.

ST NICHOLAS, Porlock Weir. 1877. Corrugated iron. A flower in
the E window glass, like the parish church windows of 1890.
– PULPIT made of two faces of a Georgian one.

METHODIST CHURCH, High Street. 1926–7 by *W. J. Tamlyn* of
Minehead. Red sandstone with Bath stone in the Free Gothic
favoured by Nonconformists around 1900. The bedpost battlements of the porch especially evoke the Art Nouveau.

PRIMARY SCHOOL, Parsons Street. 1992–3, by *Somerset County
Architects*. Low and spreading, white roughcast with hipped
roofs.

PERAMBULATION. The winding HIGH STREET has C16–C17
cottages amid much that is Late Victorian and Edwardian. The
view from the churchyard is prettily filled by the long thatched
former ROSE & CROWN with two lateral chimneys. By the
churchyard, THE CHANTRY, probably built for the Harington
chantry established c. 1474, is altered. An oak doorway and
cinquefoil-cusped window (in the end wall) remain. Going N,
the former CASTLE HOTEL, 1890, radiates Domestic Revival
cheerfulness with half-timber and red tiles borrowed from the
Home Counties. The terraced SHOPS opposite, 1910, are
similar, with half-timbered dormers and timber oriels. Old
survivals are CHIMNEY COTTAGE and MYRTLE COTTAGE,
both with lateral chimneys, that on Myrtle Cottage dated 1604.
Another lateral chimney, here circular, adorns the SHIP INN
around the corner, thatched, and very picturesque. Roughcast
VILLAGE HALL, 1925, Voysey-style, by *Roberts & Willman*, the
r. half original. Here begins the four-mile TOLL ROAD cut in
the 1840s by the Porlock Manor estate to by-pass Porlock Hill.
Returning, the library and information centre occupy the
SCHOOL of 1876.

E of the church, High Street is more closely built, the main
accents Victorian to Edwardian. At the E end is DOVERY
MANOR, a small C15 manor house, restored in 1893–4 by
Edmund Buckle. The hall window is surprisingly grand, showing

Porlock, the Ship Inn.
Drawing by J. Crowther, 1901

both types of local tracery, the upper lights with the shouldered cusped heads of Watchet and Old Cleeve; the lower lights the quatrefoil spandrels of Cleeve Abbey and Selworthy. Haunched fireplace on the back wall and a moulded framed ceiling. Winding stone stair to an upper chamber with arch-braced roof. The cross-wing, largely reconstructed, has a garderobe side projection. Up Doverhay, THE GABLES and DOVERHAY HOUSE, C17, thatched, were in the later C19 given exaggerated dormers and leaded Gothic windows.

PARSONS STREET runs S from the church. The OLD RECTORY is older than its seven-bay Early Georgian front. C16 framed ceiling and early C18 staircase. Cross-wing of 1874 by *Edward Ashworth*. In the grounds, the primary school (*see* above). Up Hawkcombe are Victorian and Edwardian villas. GLEN CLOSE, 1890s, prominent on the E slope, has a steeply hipped roof with tall brick chimneys. At the upper end, THE HUNTING LODGE (originally Windrush), 1905 by *John Lomas*, a painter not an architect. Low and square, under a spreading hipped roof. Roughcast with first-floor half-timbering and corner oriel. Arts and Crafts interiors with simple dark panelling, the hall overlooked by an internal balcony. It was noticed in Germany, by Hermann Muthesius in *Landhaus und Garten*, 1907.

On Bossington Lane, E of the village, are more villas. The largest is NEW PLACE, 1890–2, by *Edmund Buckle* for Sir Charles Chadwyck-Healey, barrister. Startling free Tudor in rock-faced stone, with mullioned windows and magnificent circular chimneys. Chimneys like cannon clasp the garden-front gable.

Double-height hall with strapwork rails. In the dining room an extraordinary leather FRIEZE, 1897, of hunters amid twisted trees. A plaque gives the details: designed by *Anne Baker*, made by *Philip Burgess* and *John French*, all of Porlock, a remarkable Arts and Crafts endeavour. A thatched yellow-washed LODGE spans the former drive. Further up, MIDDLE CROFT, 1923, by *Worthington & Sons* of Manchester, red sandstone with an off-centre gable and hipped dormers, and MERRYFIELD, thatched with tall stone chimneys, by *Stone & Francis*, 1926. On the parallel Minehead road, DOVERHAY PLACE spreads amply, red, white and black, skirted with verandas, *c.* 1895. HACKETTY WAY, ¼ m. SE, was a hunting lodge for F.C. Clifford, 1913–15. Rock-faced red sandstone, poised between baronial and suburban. The front has a cornice, parapet and curved bays like bastions; the rear is hip-roofed. Circular chimneys.

W towards Porlock Weir, GREENCOMBE, 1934, is notable for the woodland garden created by *Joan Loraine*. A circular wooden CHAPEL, 2000–1, designed with the *Rev. Dan Olive*, shelters 'Our Lady of the Secret', carved by *Tom Preater* from sweet chestnut. At West Porlock, above the road, WEST PORLOCK HOUSE, 1922, rendered with red-tile roofs, a stone chimney perched on a roof hip after Lutyens.

PORLOCK WEIR has whitewashed cottages behind the boulder beach, picturesque, if more workaday than Clovelly or Mevagissey. Lock gates enclose an inner harbour next to simple Georgian stone STORES and OFFICE with hip-roofed dormers. Across the lock, the pretty cottage row on TURKEY ISLAND was once all thatched, the l. cottage a storehouse. On the shingle, two PILLBOXES, 1940, studded with beach stones for camouflage. The ANCHOR HOTEL was enlarged at each end for the holiday trade, the double-gabled E addition by *A. Bromley* of Folkestone, 1902. THE SHIP is two separate long C17 whitewashed ranges with lateral chimneys, the front one thatched, the back one dated 1651 and 1920. Towards Porlock, the best group, GIBRALTAR COTTAGES, backs on to the strand with an array of lateral chimneys. Whitewashed fronts, with a taller house at one end. This seashore road supplanted in 1894 the hillside route past a C17–C18 cottage row at LANE HEAD and St Nicholas's church (*see* p. 527). CHAPEL KNAP, a villa of 1890, has as its porch the tiny wagon-roofed chancel of a C15 chapel of St Olave.

WORTHY, NW of Lane Head, was the Lovelace domain. Byron's daughter Ada married in 1835 Lord King, *1st Earl of Lovelace* from 1837. The Kings had built a small house at Ashley Combe *c.* 1799, which the Lovelaces turned into an Italian villa with steeply terraced gardens, paths and tunnels, designed by the earl, an engineer of some repute. In 1837 the toll road to Culbone was constructed. Cottages were added, even after Lady Lovelace died in 1852 and Lord Lovelace turned to altering Horsley Towers, Surrey. Another phase began after his death in 1893. The 2nd Earl (†1906) and his countess, Mary (†1941) had employed C. F. A. Voysey in Surrey and

Leicestershire in 1895–6 and Voysey himself taught *Lady Lovelace* architecture. The Voysey-style work here, at Culbone, and at Bratton, is by her. She extended WORTHY MANOR in 1911–14. The C16 house has a lateral chimney and massive rounded oak doorway in a catslide porch. Plank screen inside. Lady Lovelace's wing is roughcast, hip-roofed, with tall chimneys, their gabled tops almost her signature. She altered the STABLES to the E. The thatched GATEWAY LODGE announced Ashley Combe itself. Two-storeyed with brick detail to the tall through arch, arcaded eaves, and paired arched windows. Probably by the *1st Earl*, *c.* 1840, though the eaves arcading looks forward to Horsley Towers in the 1850s. Engaging play of curves; the front is concave while the cottage behind bellies amply. w extension probably by *Lady Lovelace*. Terraces on the r. remain from ASHLEY COMBE, demolished 1974. Below the lodge are former STABLES, altered in 1901 with Voysey-style battered chimneys, by *Lady Lovelace* presumably.

STONE CIRCLE, Porlock Allotment, 3 m. WSW. In contrast to Dartmoor, Exmoor has only two stone circles and these of very small stones. This had twenty-one when first reported in 1928, only fourteen in 1989 and only ten twenty years later. It presumably dates from the Bronze Age. A significant Mesolithic site at Hawkcombe Head, ½ m. N, suggests the importance of this area in early prehistory.

POUNDISFORD
Pitminster

The Bishop of Winchester's deer park is still legible on the map, surrounded by a bank three miles in circumference. Excavation when it was cut by the M5 showed that it was 23 ft (7 metres) wide and 6½ ft (2 metres) high, with a roadway along the 13-ft (4-metre) wide top. In 1534 the chase was divided and a lease granted for the part that is now Poundisford Lodge to Roger Hill. The other half, now Poundisford Park, came into the hands of Roger's brother William, by family tradition around the time of Roger's death in 1546. The Hills were a merchant family. Their two houses stand relatively close to each other on the eastern edge of the park, and represent a very interesting stage in the mid C16, the move in English architecture to formal Renaissance house plans. The two share a great deal: both are rendered with deep-set mullion windows with depressed-arched lights, of H-plan, with the hall between cross-wings, but only Poundisford Park is formalized to external symmetry.

POUNDISFORD LODGE. There was a house here when Roger Hill took the lease, of which some structure may remain. His house should date from after 1534 but the only dated feature is an overmantel of 1590. The H-plan gives an E front between slightly projected cross-wing gables, the centre with gabled dormers flanking a central chimney. So already here is the urge to symmetry developed at Poundisford Park and more so at Barrington Court in the later 1550s. But here there is still much casual asymmetry: non-matching cross-wings, and the first-floor rhythm of 1–2–2–1-light windows not replicated below, where the door is in the third bay and the hoodmoulds of the outer windows are cut by the cross-wings. The side of the N cross-wing has symmetrical first-floor windows and chimneys (the ground floor is behind an early C19 addition), but the side of the S cross-wing is much more random despite two dormer gables. A massive chimney-breast, r., marks the kitchen, and on the l. are early C19 additions. On the rear the cross-wings project much further and are again non-matching. The centre was built out probably in the early C19 for the Helyar family, the typical solution for easing circulation. First-floor sash windows, and a Ham stone quatrefoil parapet that is surely reused C15.

So symmetry is confined to the centre of the E front and the N cross-wing. This raises the possibility of alteration as late as 1590, as the cross-wing contains the generous Elizabethan rooms with the dated plasterwork. The NW parlour has a thin-rib ceiling of concave-sided lozenges with scrolled floral terminals. The typical Elizabethan frieze oddly overlays C18 wall-lining above a panelled dado, contemporary with the fine wooden chimneypiece of *c.* 1760 (female head between festoons). This may merely suggest lost panelling, or that the frieze was repositioned in the C18 work. Broad C18 dog-leg staircase with column-on-vase balusters. The NE room has Georgian panelling and a veined marble chimneypiece of *c.* 1740. In the early C19 addition, the W room has a shallow domed square ceiling. Both upper rooms of the cross-wing are exceptionally fine Elizabethan chambers with barrel ceilings made more sumptuous with ornament in the tympana. Both have thin-rib patterns of kite-shaped petals, radiating from a central foliage rose in the E room, and a pendant in the W one. The petals intersect with square and concave lozenges, and intersected lozenges ornament the lunettes. Both rooms have Tudor-arched fireplaces under rich plaster overmantels, attributed to *Robert Eaton* of Stogursey. The E room overmantel, dated 1590, has the initials of William and Elizabeth Symes (Elizabeth being Roger Hill's granddaughter) and high-relief fruit in a strapwork cartouche, between scrolls on which sit naked men (cf. Montacute and West Coker). Two walls have C17 panelling, the others large Late Georgian panels. In the W room the overmantel has a strapwork cartouche with similar fruit around a rustic classical scene (a robed figure carries a basket of flowers to Apollo with sunburst hair and lyre, a castle behind the first, the sun overhead). Cornice supported by American Indian caryatids. The lunettes here are enriched with a Tudor rose and a fleur-de-lys, both crowned. The walls have early C18 large-field panels.

The rest of the house has less to offer. Plain hall altered in the early C19, when a Tudor-arched arcade replaced the back wall. The cross-passage has disappeared, as has any dais end. There is no sign of the double-height hall which one would expect in Somerset before the 1590s. In the S cross-wing, a kitchen with heavy beams, and a small room with original fireplace, late C17 panelling and C18 shelf recess.

To the SE, a service court with free-standing early C19 servants' hall in roughcast brick at right angles to a roofless rubble range whose N end has reused C15–C16 mullion windows. Backing on to the road, a tall mid-C18 SUMMERHOUSE in roughcast brick. The pyramid roof is simplified from its original splayed form. Staircase with column-on-vase balusters. N of the drive, an enclosed STABLE COURT, two big parallel ranges and a brick barn at the back. The front gables are faced in chert, as also the pedimented Gothick screen between them, all early C19.

POUNDISFORD PARK. Larger and more evolved than Poundisford Lodge, although the assumption that it was built shortly after 1546 cannot be substantiated. The only reliable date is from the hall, which has initials from William Hill's second marriage in 1570. Its symmetry in plan is more advanced than at Poundisford Lodge, but externally it lacks Renaissance detail almost entirely, and displays the same buttresses and windows. The plan is an H with projections in the inner angles. The hall and cross-passage are compacted to a tight three bays with gabled storeyed projections (porch and oriel both front and back) that frame the hall window on the rear and the hall chimney on the S front. Cross-wings project considerably on the S, and barely on the N. The N front, an array of five gables, the outer ones broad, the central one stepped back, is entirely symmetrical apart from the doorway. The symmetry of the S front is less obvious, as the central recession is disguised by an irregularly fenestrated stair across the back of the chimney and an C18 attic passage above. The cross-wings have gabled dormers facing inward. Their outer faces have large gabled garderobe towers and none of the symmetry of the main fronts, but they do match; the E side is partly disguised by a NE addition made for Isaac Welman after 1737.

The SCREENS PASSAGE introduces the thin-rib plaster ceilings and moulded friezes that characterize the interiors. The oak screen has heavy half-round banded door frames, like cannons, that look mid-C16. The HALL itself is an impressive double-height room, like those at Barrington and Rowland's, Ilton (qq.v.). The splendid ceiling of ribs forming patterns of elongated hexagons, and no fewer than fifteen pendants, must date from after 1570, according to the initials, and the evidence points to a Late Elizabethan date. The ceiling in the gatehouse at Combe Florey, 1593, is to the same basic pattern, without pendants, and the royal arms on the W wall match those at Rowland's, assumed to be late C16. Densely patterned scrolled frieze at each end. The hall chimney-breast incorporates a winding stair to the gallery and E cross-wing, old-fashioned by comparison with the twin staircases in the angles at Barrington and Montacute. But the fireplace moulding is of earlier type than any other in the house, perhaps representing a start in the late 1540s. Both hall-bays and both porches have thin-rib plaster, each slightly different. The gallery above the screen was closed off with a plaster wall, presumably after 1570, with a picturesque little oriel window opening into the hall.

The main STAIRCASE is central to the W cross-wing, rising around a solid core with solid oak treads. Oak four-centred-arched doorway at the foot. The NW room is called the JUSTICE ROOM: the small N door may have been to allow direct access to those attending the court. It has a late C16 fireplace with delicately carved spandrels (matched in the Queen's Room above, and on the N porch). But the ceiling is of a style very different from the hall, reflecting the innovations of Inigo Jones and John Webb that appear in the region c. 1640. Concentric ovals frame the Hill crest, Noah's dove; first a foliage scroll, then the Jonesian bay leaf, then an outer oval with scroll, and finally foliage, fruit and flowers in the spandrels. The combination of scroll within a wreath occurs at Gaulden Manor (Tolland) c. 1640 and, with more artistry, at Forde Abbey, Dorset, c. 1650. The Poundisford work is closest to the former. The equivalent NE room has mid-C18 panelling. It is an anteroom to the DINING ROOM added shortly after 1737, but with decoration of c. 1750–60. Ionic screen, modillion cornice and delicately carved wooden chimneypiece, bought reportedly in London from *Samuel Norman*. Above is a relatively plain bedchamber and a panelled closet.

There is thin-rib plasterwork in the two principal first-floor chambers, the KING'S ROOM, NW, and QUEEN'S ROOM, SW, and also the HALL GALLERY, with scrolled friezes. These friezes reappear at Holcombe Court, Devon, and Haddon Hall, Derbys., evidence of itinerant plasterers. Closets over the hall-bays. Some reused medieval tiles in the lobby to the S closet. Surprisingly the plasterwork extends to the ATTIC, the central chamber over the hall and the NE chamber. On balance it would seem that the 1570s is the likely date for the plasterwork, none of which closely resembles the 1590 work at Poundisford Lodge. The E staircase dates from alterations of 1928, for A. W. Vivian-Neal, by *Anthony Methuen*.

E of the house a cobbled SERVICE COURT. The long E range of barn, stable and coachhouses is dated 1717 on the S end. Reused medieval quatrefoil plaques. W of the house, a very pretty red brick SUMMERHOUSE, with moulded-brick open-pediment doorway and pyramid roof splayed out on brackets. The moulded brickwork dates it to the late C17, but inside is a plaster frieze of fish-tailed beasts found also in the King's Room, inexplicable unless the moulds had survived from the earlier work.

POUNDISFORD FARMHOUSE, opposite Poundisford Lodge. Roughcast cob and brick, irregular. A medieval hall with jointed-cruck roof and traces of a timber-framed front wall. A window with timber reticulated tracery is unparalleled, early C14, or retrograde C15.

HAYGRASS HOUSE, 1 m. NE. Handsome Early Victorian villa, hip-roofed, with an advanced hip-roofed central bay, and deep bracketed eaves. Heavy paired columns flank the doorway.

PRESTON PLUCKNETT

Overwhelmed by Yeovil's westward expansion.

ST JAMES. Perp W tower with battlements and single two-light bell-openings. Wave-moulded tower arch, late C14, later than the cruciform church. This must be early C14 – see the typical two-light windows and reticulated E window, all replaced in *R. H. Shout*'s restoration of 1862. His S doorway shows an elephantine High Victorianism otherwise held in check. Impressive wagon roof, the moulded ribs continued in moulded stone to corbel heads, all C19 apart from six exquisite late C13 heads of grey Lias in the chancel. Their presence is a puzzle, as Glynne did not mention them in 1849. Low double-chamfered transept arches on good C14 corbels – male and female heads S; hare and cat (or dog) N. – FONT. 1862. Copying the ejected early C14 original now in St Andrew, Yeovil. – CARVING. C15 Crucifixion from the churchyard cross. – PULPIT. 1862. Stone, cut down. – STAINED GLASS. 1862. Bright patterned glass with insets.

ABBEY MANOR. A notable group of manor house and barn, built *c*. 1420 by John Stourton (cf. Stavordale Priory), of Yeovil stone, like the church. Stourton's will mentions a chapel, now lost. The site was moated to the S. The house has a long W front with the great hall at the S end. A cross-wing beyond has been removed, giving undue dominance to the N service range. The hall is much rebuilt, its roof returned to its original height in the 1920s, restoring the pointed head to the long dais window. It has been floored and its roof is modern. The handsome storeyed porch has a transomed two-light window over a two-centred doorway with shield spandrels, outlined in roll moulding. C15 door. Ham stone vault on head corbels with ridge and diagonal ribs and swirled central boss. Similar inner doorway; another at the rear of the screens passage. The service range is two-storeyed with mostly later mullioned windows, the kitchen to the l. The first bay had the great chamber above the buttery, once gabled, in counterpoint to the S cross-wing. Its pointed transomed rear window survives. Also a fine fireplace with frieze of three traceried or quatrefoil panels. Fireplace and panels are outlined in heavy roll mouldings, the verticals continued to capitals in the cornice (similar fireplace in the King's House, Salisbury). Pointed doorway with original door. The kitchen, originally full-height, was lit by single lights (one survives blocked). Exceptional N end-turret chimney, octagonal, two-stage (originally three) with cusped upper vents, serving a full-width timber-lintel fireplace, now blocked. Tudor-arched stone E wall fireplace. An angle buttress shows that the N outbuilding is added, its C15 doorway presumably reused.

The splendid stone BARN is 114 ft (34.7 metres) long. Ten bays. Buttresses and long cross-shaped slits on the S side, bays six and seven filled by the porch with a tall segmental-pointed doorway, double-chamfered, without capitals. The N porch is simpler, with an oak lintel. Roof of jointed-cruck trusses with wind-braces and four rows of purlins.

HOUNDSTONE HOUSE, ¾ m. W. Formal front of Ham stone ashlar with mullioned windows and curved-pedimented enclosed porch, *c.* 1700.

PUCKINGTON

ST ANDREW. Perp W tower of Ham stone, with set-back buttresses ending at the bell-stage with squat pinnacles (cf. Langport). Battlements (missing corner pinnacles) and two-light bell-openings. Similar blind windows below, and a big four-light transomed W window. Doorway in a square-headed frame with triangular shafts. The rest of the church is of local marlstone, heavily restored in 1857. Perp nave. The S transept is rebuilt. Its windows imitate genuine ones on the C13 chancel, particularly the two-light N window with bar tracery. Renewed E window of three stepped lights with three cinquefoiled circles. Tall panelled tower arch. Incised axe on the tower-stair doorway. C19 chancel arch. Fine C14 stepped triple SEDILIA with linked hoodmoulds (cf. Shepton Beauchamp) and cusped PISCINA. – FONT. Norman, circular, with middle cable moulding and rim triangles. – PULPIT. C17. Panelled, with fluted frieze. – MONUMENT. Rev. James Ilston †1693. Lias floor slab, extravagantly incised.

By the church, MANOR FARMHOUSE, formerly the rectory. 1853, by *Maurice Davis*. Ashlar, Italianate. Below is the former SCHOOL, 1862. The main road runs S with C17 thatched cottages. To the N, BAKERS FARMHOUSE was raised in brick in the early C18, with blind arches like those of Ashford House, Ilton.

ILFORD BRIDGE FARMHOUSE, ½ m. SW. Elongated thatched house, C17–C18. The brick-fronted part was a courtroom. Late C17 Speke arms in plaster on the ceiling.

PURITON

ST MICHAEL. Blue Lias. Unbuttressed W tower of thrice-receding girth. Early C13 lower stages – see the narrow lancets and broad rectangular stair projection. Low double-chamfered tower arch on moulded brackets, typical of their date. Perp bell-stage with battlements and pyramid roof. Perp also the N aisle, S windows (in older walling), and tall S porch with nicely wave-moulded arch. In the porch a stair to a lost gallery, and a framed ceiling, on heavy billet-moulded wall-plates, presumably reused. Standard four-bay Perp arcade; framed aisle ceiling. Broad C14 double-chamfered chancel arch. Chancel of 1877. – FONT. C14, octagonal, coved beneath. – SCREEN. C15–C16, missing the loft. Five bays, with pointed three-light tracery cut from planks. Crude foliage to the sills. Traces of colour. – STAINED GLASS. NE window, 1965, by *Paul Jefferies*. Good blue-grey tones. – MONUMENT. W. M. Greenhill †1808. Mourning female.

PURITON MANOR, stuccoed, without character, has a triple-arched early C19 gateway in Tudor style, with the Greenhill arms. Ungainly Victorian Lias tower over the stables.

ROYAL ORDNANCE FACTORY, 1 m. NE. A large site, now disused, built up in the late 1930s to manufacture the new RDX explosive. The HUNTSPILL RIVER, dug to provide a reservoir and water supply, was disguised by its design as a large land drain.

DUNBALL WHARF, 1 m. SW. Wharf of 1844 on the River Parrett.

DOWN END CASTLE, 1 m. W. Earthworks of a C12 motte-and-bailey castle.

PYLLE

ST THOMAS À BECKET. Three-stage W tower with diagonal buttresses and ashlar NE stair-turret with spirelet, probably added with the Perp bell-stage. Two-light bell-openings with pierced baffles. Two-light intermediate windows with different tracery and baffles may mark the C14 bell-stage, of a date with the triple-chamfered tower arch. The rest was rebuilt in 1868 for the Portman estate. The predecessor had a Norman chancel arch and Perp clerestory. Reused angel corbels in the chancel. – FONT. Early Norman tapered bowl with a curious wandering thin line beneath triangles that suggest scallops. – FITTINGS. C20 pieces by the *Somerset Guild of Craftsmen*, the ironwork better than the woodwork. *Lt-Col. J. A. Garton* of Pylle Manor, who founded the guild in 1933, made the chandeliers. – STAINED GLASS. E window, 1868, by *R. T. Bayne* of *Heaton, Butler & Bayne*. Good colours and expressive faces. – MONUMENT. Lady Burland †1779. By *T. King*.

PYLLE MANOR. Rebuilt for Edward Berkeley (†1707) or his son Maurice (†1715). Five-bay double-pile house with stone cross-windows in moulded architraves, those on the ground floor with pulvinated friezes under a full-width cornice. Doorway in the fifth bay. Channelled angle piers. The hipped roof and timber eaves cornice look C19. Staircase with turned balusters and column newels. A C19 E wing incorporates Berkeley heraldry of 1609. The W wing is partly C17, truncated at the W where a C20 timber-framed gable was inserted by *Lt-Col. Garton*. Early C18 COACHHOUSE of five narrow arches, the l. two paired. The roof was originally hipped. Outside the gates, mid-C18 lofted STABLES resembling two three-bay houses, each with a roundel over a pedimented doorway and two-light mullioned windows.

PYRLAND HALL see KINGSTON ST MARY

QUANTOCK LODGE see OVER STOWEY

QUEEN CAMEL

5020

So called because Eleanor of Castile held the manor.

ST BARNABAS. A stately Perp church with a high, severe W tower, aisled and clerestoried nave, and chancel. The tower, 96 ft (29.3 metres) high, of an exceptional five stages, has no openings on the N and S sides below the bell-lights. On the W side, the doorway, three-light window and a statue niche occupy the lower two stages and a narrow two-light window the third. Two-light bell-openings and plain battlements. Big set-back buttresses, stepped five times. They carry pinnacled shafts which appear in pairs at the battlement corners. The NW stair-turret grows neatly between the buttresses (cf. Martock). Straight joints to the aisles and the line of a nave roof within tell of major reconstruction in the late C15, when the clerestory was added and the aisles altered. So the tower must be early C15. By that time the church was already aisled, with relatively low octagonal piers, probably mid-C14. The S piers have banded capitals, the N ones are simpler, but three have plant decoration (vine, rose, oak). Two S piers have small image niches. But the piers carry arches wave-moulded like the tower arch, and the W arches are narrowed to accommodate the tower buttressing, suggesting that the arcades were adjusted in the early C15. The aisles are of differing widths, with Late Perp square-headed windows, the S aisle E window particularly lavish. One S window is pointed-arched, C14, of two lights, of a date with a Dec tomb-recess within. Ham stone flat parapets to the aisles and clerestory, which has pointed-arched three-light windows. In the chancel angle, an octagonal rood-stair turret. The big pedimented S porch on Tuscan columns of c. 1840 narrowly survived *J. L. Pearson*'s restoration of 1887. Chancel richly remodelled in the late C15. Three-light windows with ogee-headed panel tracery. The fleurons and gargoyles (mostly defaced) of the eaves and the beasts on the buttresses were designed for an ornate parapet, either not built or removed. The long E window has below the transom the unconventional shouldered tracery found at St John, Glastonbury, and in West Somerset. Crocketed niche above.

The nave roof is of late C15 Somerset type, with decorated tie-beams, short kingposts, and spandrel tracery. The tie-beams rest on short braces on stone angel corbels, the sub-principals begin with wooden figures, and the E bay is sub-panelled. C15 aisle roofs too, on good carved corbels, the N roof with traces of colour. In the N aisle a shallow C15 ogee-headed recess, decorated with fleurons and a finial. In the S aisle a big Dec TOMB-RECESS with big open cinquefoil cusping, the two surviving cusps enriched by heads. Panelled chancel arch of c. 1500, contemporary with the existing rood screen. The arch is wider than the chancel, to disguise which the chancel corners are moulded with delicate inset canopies. C15 wagon roof with carved supporters and many bosses – plant forms and animals from the bestiary (phoenix, amphisbaena, syren, griffin, basilisk, aspidochelone, unicorn, elephant, etc.). The PISCINA and single SEDILE, early C15, have thickly decorated canopies with tiny vaults. Of 1887 the TILE FLOORS and elegant brass RAILINGS. Stone REREDOS, 1906, infilled in tile mosaic by *Powell's*, who added flanking tiles in 1907. Lovely William Morris patterns in matt colours.

OTHER FURNISHINGS. FONT. Late Perp, of unusual design. Octagonal, with shields on quatrefoils under a leaf-scroll frieze. At the diagonals four pillars rise from the floor, each with a defaced figure under a nodding arch.* Cover of scaly serpents, 1958. – ROOD SCREEN. Of the Devon type, c. 1500, with broad, luxuriantly decorated cornice on ribbed coving. Five bays each of six lights with broad transom, the mullions running up to the arch. Crocketed ogee lower panels. Some original colour. – PULPIT. Timber, of the same period, less ornate than that at Long Sutton but similarly ringed with nodding canopies (for missing statues) between pinnacles, all crocketed. – LECTERN. 1889. Eagle on an improbable timber rock pillar. – PEWS. 1887, reusing C15 panels, not from bench-ends. – EMBROIDERY. A frontal with much silver thread, C18, inscribed with IHS, Mary and Joseph; i.e. English, presumably Roman Catholic. – PANELLING. C17, from the Mildmay family pew and the tower. – STAINED GLASS. E window, 1887, by *Clayton & Bell*. S aisle E by the same, 1869, finely drawn. C15 fragments in one N aisle window. – MONUMENTS. Humphrey Mildmay †1690, black-and-white, with heraldry between urns. The inscription records his wounds for Charles I. – Edith Mildmay †1772, more elegant in detail than composition. Trapezoid on a gadrooned coloured background between Ionic columns and under an Adamesque urn. – Paulet Mildmay †1845. Small, very Gothic, by *William Osmond* of Salisbury.

---

* Similar fonts are at Bradford Abbas and Winterborne Whitechurch, both Dorset.

PRIMARY SCHOOL, opposite the church. 1872, by *Henry Hall*. Entirely symmetrical and forcefully Gothic, two porches clasping a central gable with bellcote.

Church Path is aligned charmingly on the church tower, with cottages on each side. At the W end, LAVENDERS and GATEHOUSE, C17 with N cross-wing. High Street runs S, with houses in both colours of Lias. Much was rebuilt after a fire in 1639. On the E side, a high wall with C18 gadrooned urns on C19 piers encloses THE COACH HOUSE, a barn altered to serve as a coachhouse to MORVEN. Morven has Lias walls and stone C17 windows with hoodmoulds, the mullions removed for Georgian small panes, probably when the brick parapet was added. Brick SE addition with Regency deep eaves. The ovolo-moulded mullion-and-transom windows of CAMELOT HOUSE suggest some importance. It was indeed the C17 Great House, altered as an inn from 1744. On the W, a mixed row before the stuccoed mid-C19 former VICARAGE. Further up, QUEEN CAMEL COTTAGE, C17, with a dripmould lifted over the doorway. HENSHALLBROOK FARMHOUSE is earlier, with C15 wind-braced roof. RECTORY FARMHOUSE, opposite, has C16 origins, the oldest part with banded stonework. Finally QUEEN CAMEL HOUSE. This looks Edwardian, with shaped brick chimneys, but is of 1812, remodelled 1911, restored 1921 after a fire.

EYEWELL HOUSE, ¾ m. WNW. 1926–7, by *Sir Guy Dawber*. Formal Neo-Georgian, only five bays wide, with big hipped roof and tall chimneystacks.

RIDGE, Gason's Lane. 1923, by *A. C. Martin*. Late Arts and Crafts, rendered with irregular gables.

WALES, 1 m. W. Twin-arched BRIDGE. To its S, WALES HOUSE, tidied in the C19 with columned porch. To the W, the thatched OLD WALES FARMHOUSE has tall later C17 proportions with mullion windows. VINE COTTAGE, thatched, is late C15 with a raised cruck truss, C16 framed ceiling, and tree-trunk newel stair.

RADDINGTON

ST MICHAEL. Alone on a hillside, approached down a field. Small unbuttressed W tower, plastered, without significant external detail. The triangular tower arch looks early C14. Small plastered nave, embattled on the S up to a rough square rood turret. Square-headed red sandstone Perp window. Pretty C19 porch with timber-framed gable. It protects a C15 DOOR, in a two-centred-arched oak doorway of two massive baulks. Original ironwork, the top strap a firework of foliage. The chancel looks early C15, with pointed two-light windows in grey stone, the E end originally battlemented. A wonderful interior, gently touched by restoration. Fragments of C17 WALL PAINTING, mainly texts framed in swags. Perp wagon roof with carved bosses to the nave. Some re-set medieval FLOOR TILES. No chancel arch, but a beam supporting a plastered tympanum, a rare survival. C19 chancel roof. s wall, early C15 PISCINA with trefoil arch and lancet spandrels. – ROOD SCREEN. Early C15. Five square-headed bays, each with pointed three-light panel tracery and ogee-headed lights. Foliage and a rose in the spandrels, florets on the head beam. The coving has gone, so the front beam (with fine vine-trail between spiral-painted rolls) is deposited on the head beam. Carefully repaired in 1992 by *Hugh Harrison* and *Elizabeth Cheadle* to reveal much original colour under early C19 painted graining (still surviving on the back). – FONT. Octagonal, C12–C13. Three trefoil-headed arches per side, shallow, as on Purbeck marble fonts. Crude ogee-domed C17 COVER. – BOX PEWS and PULPIT. Early to mid-C19. By the pulpit a reused panel dated 1713. – COMMANDMENT BOARDS. Early C19. – ROYAL ARMS. 1852.

REDLYNCH

From 1672 to 1912 the estate of the Fox-Strangways family, Earls of Ilchester from 1756. The mansion has gone, but its service ranges overlook the landscape like twin country houses.

ST PETER. Probably of 1750 by *Nathaniel Ireson*, although marked on landscape proposals of 1738. Like a meeting house. Five bays, hip-roofed, the doorway between arched windows, and bare wall above the band. Diminutive added bellcote, E (bell dated 1820). Porch and vestry of 1916 by *John Egerton Thorpe* of Oxford. Deep coved ceiling. Ionic pedimented REREDOS with garlanded cherub heads over arched panels. Ilchester ARMS in Rococo plaster, post-1756, with the earl's coronet. Neat FURNISHINGS by *Thorpe*, the pulpit and chancel seat recessed into the wall and a CINERARIUM in the w wall.

REDLYNCH. The mansion of Sir John Fitzjames, Chief Justice in the 1530s, was replaced in 1708 for Sir Stephen Fox, promoter of the Royal Hospital, Chelsea. This house, by *Thomas Fort*, seems to have been unfinished, for it was greatly extended for Fox's son (later the 1st Earl) in 1725–30, apparently by *Nathaniel Ireson*. That work continued into the mid 1750s, with chimneypieces by *Henry Flitcroft*. The mansion was demolished in 1913. It faced W down a terrace backed by large twin service ranges of 1740–6 by *Ireson*. These remain, converted into flats. Both of 2–7–2 bays, with parapets and ashlar-framed windows, the lower ones heavily keyed. The W stable range has a clock turret. The E range became a house for the 5th Earl in 1901, converted by *Edwin Lutyens*. It burnt in 1914 and was rebuilt in 1915–16 for Frederick Pepper by *John Egerton Thorpe*. Little of Lutyens remains. His E front was Surrey-vernacular, three hipped roofs over oak-mullioned two-storey bays. The Gibbsian W porch is his, moved from the S front. The nearby garden archway matches but could be by Thorpe; the iron gate comes from Lutyens's porch. On the slope above is a late C18 ORANGERY, plain brick with long windows. The hip-roofed SUMMER-ROOM to the E is early C20, crudely detailed, but the pedimental ends (one dated 1742) suggest Lutyens. – Cruciform EAST LODGE. By *Thorpe*?

To the W, THE PAVILION, 2007, by *Bertram & Fell*, ostentatiously mid-Georgian, of brick with a cupola. Single-storeyed to the front; the rear spills incoherently. Of the PARK, planned in 1738 by *Edward Grant*, little but the lake survives. A serpentine walk ran S to plantations and the lake (1741), a Chinese seat (1756) and a temple (1762). The castellated TOWERS GATE, 1 m. WSW, is possibly by *Henry Flitcroft*, 1754–5. A Gothic arch between round turrets with Y-tracery windows under large quatrefoils. Down the drive, THE AVIARIES is a Palladian villa built as a tearoom from which to view the menagerie, *c.* 1755, perhaps by *Flitcroft*. Pyramid-roofed, raised on a basement. The N centrepiece is pedimented, the S one a canted ashlar bay with canted Venetian window and octagon glazing. The main room has a semi-dome in the bay.

DISCOVE HOUSE, ½ m. W. Exceptionally long for a thatched house, 140 ft (42.7 metres), with storeyed S porch (and stair-tower). C16, Georgianized with a pedimented rear doorcase and additions each end. The original W room has simplified C16 linenfold panelling. The room added beyond is elegant mid-C18 with gadrooned doorcases and dado, and good chimneypiece.

MONKSMEAD, ½ m. N. Mid-C18, brick, three-sided, the wings with pilasters and long windows. Supposedly a schoolhouse.

RIMPTON

6020

ST MARY. Chancel of the late C13 – datable from the three-light E window of cusped lancets and acutely pointed cusped side lancets. Moulded rere-arches inside. Early C14 S porch and doorway with double-chamfered arches (original S DOOR). Battlemented nave and S transept rebuilt after 1508 by Richard Fox, newly appointed Bishop of Winchester. The battlements run flat across the transept, which has a three-light window with supermullions. The base of the plain W tower may be C13, although the narrow tower arch is Perp. Mark of a steeper nave roof. Polygonal stair-tower starting as a diagonal square. Matching Perp shafted arches to the chancel and transepts. N transept added in 1877 by *Henry Hall*, who replaced the roofs. – FONT. Octagonal, Perp, with crude panels. C17 scrolled COVER. – PULPIT. Early C17, with much pattern decoration. – BENCH-ENDS. From Corton Denham. Early C16, with pentagonal finials and coarse tracery. Also an owl amid foliage, and a dog on a shield. – MONUMENTS. James Andrews †1778. Incised Lias, with Father Time. – In the vestry a damaged C13 cross-slab.

MANOR HOUSE, W of the church. A property of the Bishops of Winchester from the C11 to 1864. Windows mainly C17 with ovolo mullions but the cross-wing has a C16 window and an angle buttress on the W wall at the original corner. C17 plank screen; jointed-cruck trusses. The OLD RECTORY is C18, altered 1867 by *Hall*. Modest SCHOOL of 1843. At the S end, THE COIGN, C16, thatched, with jointed crucks. At the N end, LOWER FARMHOUSE, with late C17 stone cross-windows.

ROADWATER

A long ribbon in the valley of the Washford River.

ST LUKE. Combined church and schoolroom of 1875–6. Schoolroom windows on the side, church lancets on the end. Church room added 1906.

METHODIST CHAPEL. 1907. Gothic gable front of crazed rubble.

VILLAGE HALL, 1928, by *Norman Reckitt*. A late Arts and Crafts work, somewhat Alpine, of crazed rubble with little hipped tops to the chimneys.

At the S end, in Watersmeet Close, is the hip-roofed former STATION, 1864, of the West Somerset Mineral Railway (*see* Brendon Hill). Just S is OATWAY COTTAGE, C16–C17, long and thatched, with a stair gable and lateral chimney on the W. Further out, the VALIANT SOLDIER has a cheerful metal inn sign of the 1950s by *Rachel Reckitt*. N of the church, a three-storey Victorian terrace screens the derelict C18–C19 MANOR MILLS, the gable-end with loading doors. Opposite, SINGER INSTRUMENTS has a neat grey metal and glass factory by *Louise Crossman*, 2011.

CLITSOME FARMHOUSE, NE of Lower Roadwater. Tall early C18 brick farmhouse with a three-storeyed porch in stone, a C17 type.

ST PANCRAS CHAPEL, 1 m. NNE. Cottage formed from a C14–C15 chapel associated with a holy well. Single-chamfered S doorway. Arch-braced roof with remnants of wind-braces. The small slot window in the W wall may indicate an anchorite's cell.

ROCKWELL GREEN

ALL SAINTS. 1888–90, by *J. H. Spencer*, the porch-tower with shingled spire of 1907–8. Rock-faced red sandstone, E.E. to

Dec. Interior unexpectedly of polychrome brick (cf. St Andrew, Taunton). – Elaborate FONT and PULPIT by *W. J. Giles* of Wellington. – REREDOS. *Opus sectile*, by *Powell's*, 1890. – STAINED GLASS. Mostly by *Mayer & Co.* of Munich, in lush colours. The one English design (NW) in comparison looks very English indeed.

Behind the church, two WATER TOWERS compete with the spire, one of 1886 by *Edwin Howard*, brick, neo-medieval with conical cap, the other skeletal concrete of 1935. In Westford is *Howard*'s PUMPING STATION, 1885, two-colour brick with paired arched windows. Of the Elworthy Bros' Westford Mills, around which the settlement grew, there remains little: a brick and stone READING ROOM, 1885, probably by *Howard*, a stuccoed hip-roofed manager's house, and the earliest mill, three-storeyed, stone, roofless.

WELLINGTON CEMETERY. 1875. Typically Gothic lodge and cast-iron gates.

RODHUISH

ST BARTHOLOMEW. A delightful little white chapel with a pyramid-roofed W turret. C15–C16, altered in 1826. Of that date the nave barrel roof, stripped of plaster, and W gallery. No chancel arch. Restored in 1924 by *Norman Reckitt*, whose family continued to beautify it through the C20. EMBROIDERIES by *Beatrice Reckitt*, his wife, and SCULPTURE by his daughter *Rachel Reckitt*: the wooden angels on the riddel-posts, 1961, and, after she discovered the Horrobin forge at Roadwater, the wrought-iron and aluminium-strip Jacob wrestling with the angel, 1973. Much IRONWORK by *James Horrobin*. Retooled C12 circular FONT, from Carhampton.

CROYDON HALL, 1 m. SSE. The long plain house between gables illustrated in a photograph of 1880 was altered after 1901 for himself by *Cyril Tubbs*, architect to the London Necropolis Company, and, after 1909, for Count Konrad von Hochberg, cousin of the Kaiser. Hochberg added Italian gardens, Tubbs perhaps the two semicircular bays facing the gardens.

GOLSONCOTT HOUSE, 1 m. SE. 1912, for Count von Hochberg's private secretary, by *W. J. Parker* of London. An Arts and Crafts house of sweeping tiled roofs over roughcast, with accents in stone and half-timber. Obtuse-angled entrance front, hinged at a half-round tower under an oversailing timber-framed gable. Garden loggia between a large jettied gable in half-timber and tile and a much smaller hip-roofed roughcast bay. *Norman Reckitt*, owner from 1923, added the half-timbered N end and the half-hipped W gable. This overlooks a canal garden designed by *Beatrice Reckitt*, by whom also the front terraces. Hip-roofed STABLES, 1923, by *Norman Reckitt*.

ESCOTT FARMHOUSE, 1 m. E. Roughcast Early Georgian six-bay front range with a big shell-hood. C17 behind. Cobbled path dated 1739.

ROWLAND'S see ILTON

RUISHTON

ST GEORGE. Associated with Taunton Priory. The W tower is ambitious, a condensed variant of those at Huish Episcopi and Kingsbury Episcopi, though less delicate in detail. Money was left in 1533, but work was apparently given up and the tower finished without battlements. Lias with Ham stone dressings. Four stages, the top two relatively short. Paired two-light bell-openings with quatrefoil-pierced baffles between thin diagonal shafts. A similar window below, between canopied niches. The second stage has quatrefoil bands above and below. Set-back buttresses carry big diagonal pinnacles against the bell-stage. W doorway with a hoodmould on angel busts under another quatrefoil frieze. Four-light W window. The tower arch is panelled, between thin shafts. Ham stone C15 S porch attached to an earlier S chapel. Within the porch are remains of a Late Norman doorway. One shaft with trumpet-scallop capital, the other side just the capital, a single scallop outlined with pellets. Fragment of chevron arch. The narrow nave and chancel are older than their Perp windows – see the irregular N wall buttressing and rood stair with tiny Dec two-light window. The S chapel with plain parapet is C13 – see the Geometric E window tracery of three multifoil circles, shafted within. Perp S windows. At the SW corner a re-set CARVING of a bishop, possibly Norman. Inside, C14–C15 wagon roofs, chancel arch and two-bay arcade to the chapel, the pier with wave mouldings and shafts with polygonal capitals. The chancel is not in line with the nave, leaving room for a squint to the r., flat-headed with twin cusped lights. – FONT. Early Perp, of unusual design. Octagonal with big square piers at the diagonals, as at Queen Camel. Elliptical quatrefoils on four sides; leaf-scroll rim. The piers carry thickly crocketed gables. – PULPIT. 1920. The Georgian predecessor is at Thornfalcon. – REREDOS. C19, flanked by C15–C16 traceried panels. – ROYAL ARMS. Lively cartouche of *c.* 1700. – STAINED GLASS. Mostly by *Clayton & Bell*, the E windows *c.* 1872. First S, 1871, by *Lavers, Barraud & Westlake*. – MONUMENTS. Elizabeth Strong †1769. Brass with tiny urns. – John Arundell †1784. Tondo by *Jones, Dunn & Drewett* of Bristol. Conventional mourning woman and urn. – C. Proctor Anderdon †1824, by *Thomas King*. Similar, with broken column. – H. Murray-Anderdon †1922. Prettily painted Gothic Calvary.

CHURCHYARD CROSS. C15. Octagonal base with eroded reliefs. Attached shafts on the diagonal faces. Section of shaft with an angel corbel.

Hints of a medieval square plan to the village S of the church. Early C19 stuccoed hip-roofed VICARAGE. Red sandstone former SCHOOL, 1861, by *William White*. On the main road, suburban houses of prosperous Taunton. RUISHTON COURT is tile-hung, with intricate ironwork to the verandas. 1898–9, by *Henry Spiller*, Taunton contractor. Built for Creech St Michael paper manufacturers. WOODLANDS CASTLE, stuccoed Tudor of *c.* 1833, by *Richard Carver*, encases a villa of *c.* 1800. The BLACKBROOK INN, roughcast, with a pretty bowed projection, is Late Georgian.

CHARD CANAL, ¼ m. NE. 1836–42, *Sydney Hall*, engineer. An embankment carries the derelict canal across the flood plain to an AQUEDUCT over the Tone. Four brick arches, two broad, two narrow, faced in Lias. Upstream, fine five-arch RAILWAY BRIDGE, 1863, by *Francis Fox*, for the GWR Chard branch that killed the canal. Rock-faced stone with ashlar dressings, the arches skewed.

RUMWELL see BISHOP'S HULL

RUNNINGTON

ST PETER. Red sandstone. Small, with small Perp W tower. Late Perp square-headed nave windows. Porch and chancel of *c.* 1840. Even so small a church possessed a rood loft, whose staircase survives. Framed barrel ceiling to the nave. – FONT. Perp, with rosettes in big quatrefoils.

ST AUDRIES see WEST QUANTOXHEAD

ST MICHAEL CHURCH

ST MICHAEL. Very small single vessel. The end walls rebuilt *c.* 1500 in Blue Lias with Perp windows. Gabled chapels of 1868 on each side. Utterly plain C17 N tower of red sandstone under a pyramid roof. Curved plaster ceiling, probably of 1794. – FONT. C13. Plain octagon, tapered to a misshapen octagonal stem. – MONUMENT. Elizabeth Bacon †1668. Slab painted with Jacobean twin-arched design.

MAUNSEL HOUSE. The house of the Maunsels, here until 1631, remains at the core of the present irregular house of red sandstone. The E front is a large late medieval hall house, extended by three bays to the N after 1772 for John Slade. The windows were given hoodmoulds by *Richard Carver* for General Sir John Slade in 1827–8, when a parallel NW piece was added for the dining room. This added a second gable to the N end. The third gable, with a spired bellcote, is part of an L-plan addition of 1868. Returning to the E front, the four-bay original piece has two first-floor C16 mullion windows from when the hall was floored, and a blocked two-light window at mid-height to the r. representing a storeyed upper end. C19 porch to the l. The rebuilt triple stack at the S end relates to a lower two-storey piece on the SE corner with one medieval cusped two-light window.

Inside the porch a Georgian ashlar doorway. The hall has a four-panel C16 framed ceiling, plastered in the C17. Early C19 elliptical arches on the back wall, one to a full-height contemporary staircase. But the stair projection is late C16 – see the stone cross-window – as is the hip-roofed wing to the l. of the stair projection, with a similar window. This lights a bedroom with a plastered four-panel ceiling like that of the hall. Similar ceiling to the bedroom over the hall, part of the same alterations. In the attic the hall roof survives, probably early C15, the moulded arch-braced trusses close-spaced with frilly cusped wind-braces. A pointed hollow-chamfered C14 doorway leads from the hall into the SE room. *Carver*'s dining room has panelled pilasters and a scrolled plaster frieze. L-plan NW room of 1868 with Victorian panelling and big Norman-to-Gothic fireplace. Above it, the impressive Victorian billiard room, with a six-sided rafter roof. Derelict by the 1980s, Maunsel was bought back by Sir Benjamin Slade, 7th Baronet, and restored with *Donald Insall Associates*. Their single-storey kitchen on the W side, 2006, with splayed hipped roof and flèche, echoes the Victorian work.

Two OUTBUILDINGS at right angles, one of cob, have leaded cross-windows of *c.* 1700. A vane on the house dated 1703 with the initials of Thomas Bacon indicates work at this period.

MAUNSEL LOCKS. Two locks and brick bridges of the Bridgwater and Taunton Canal of 1823–7. *James Hollinsworth*, engineer.

SAMPFORD ARUNDEL

HOLY CROSS. Slender unbuttressed W tower, mostly of chert. No W door. This and the unmoulded tower arch point to a C13 date for the short lower stage. Plain Perp upper stage. The rest virtually rebuilt in 1867, the aisles under one roof. The only medieval feature is a small pointed RECESS in the N aisle. Over a sunken box, rebated for a lid, two hands hold a cup-shaped casket under a little crocketed ogee canopy, its finial a chalice. It was probably the heart burial of a priest, C14. –

MONUMENTS. Christopher Baker †1729. Fine Baroque. A fictive curtain in a curved-headed pilastered frame. – Maria Browne †1828 and Colonel Browne †1833, one with urn, the other military, both by *William Pistell* of London. – STAINED GLASS. Mostly 1876, the SE window signed *H. Hughes*.

SAMPFORD BRETT

ST GEORGE. The immediate impression derives from a gauche remodelling in 1835 for the 4th Earl of Egremont, but the church is C13–C14. The unbuttressed battlemented S tower has small bell-openings and a large S doorway, the double-chamfered arch dying into the jambs. The N transept, lengthened in the C15, reuses a late C13 N window of two trefoiled pointed lights and a plate-tracery quatrefoil. Chancel lancets of 1835, apparently echoing C13 originals. The Perp E window is reused. Of 1835 the S transept, SE vestry and the bald W triple windows. Tracery in the middle one of 1967 by *W. E. Marsden*, replacing tracery that Pevsner found 'monstrously ignorant'.

The whitewashed interior is sweetly romantic. The C15 nave wagon roof with high-quality bosses (foliage and some mythical beasts) rests on plaster cherub heads with wings like spaniel ears. The plaster arches to the transepts and chancel have multiple little shafts and tiny vine leaf capitals. Rope-like vine-trail frames the chancel window heads. Filling the church is a most complete assemblage of carved WOODWORK. Some can only be of the 1830s, like the huge acanthus leaves on a Gothic post for the LECTERN, or the COMMUNION TABLE with fruit climbing the legs. More sober, the PULPIT, with traceried panels. Old woodwork is notable in several low movable BENCHES. But the PEWS are a challenge. The arrangement is Late Georgian, raised on pedestals, the back rows stepped up. The bench-ends have good close tracery and wiry plant motifs typical of the region (cf. Broomfield, Bicknoller), but the leaf-scroll frames are not integral and the backs have unmedieval panels. It must be skilful reframing of genuine C16 work. One quite different W bench-end shows a female in Stuart dress, lush fruit and two small piping cherubs. – FONT. Panelled stem splayed out as if for a missing bowl. Early C19 rather than C15? – ROYAL ARMS. Charles II. – MONUMENTS. Vestry. Eroded late C13 effigy of a cross-legged knight, of Ham stone, probably Sir William Brett. – Zacharias Windhams †1627. Good alabaster-framed plaque with little obelisks and a heraldic panel.

The broad village street is aligned on the church. WOODBURNES is C16, with a moulded Tudor-arched doorway and lateral chimney. The apparently Late Georgian OLD RECTORY encases a late medieval wind-braced roof. In the NE wing a C16 nine-panel ceiling, the framing, unusually, carved with vine-trail. Late C19 Acland-Hood estate cottages at Nos. 4–6.

WOOLSTON, ¾ m. ESE. WOOLSTON GRANGE was reconstructed in 1911 by *Horace Farquharson* in a severe late C17 style. Wooden cross-windows and an off-centre hip-roofed storeyed porch. The garden front has gables and dormers, the roofs swept low. Two framed ceilings, one probably imported. Stables with a pyramid-roofed corner. MANOR FARMHOUSE, C17, has Jacobean carving on the timber oriel of the gable-end. Further W are the BARTHOLOMEW THOMAS ALMSHOUSES, 1904 by *T. H. Andrew* of Minehead, rather fussy. Roughcast with half-hip-roofed wings, timber oriels and a veranda with glazed gablets.

CAPTON, 1 m. SW. Hamlet of thatched cottages of the red sandstone quarried here. CAPTON HOUSE looks neo-Tudor of the early to mid-C19, but the core is C17. CAPTON FARM has hip-roofed Georgian outbuildings and a farmhouse dated 1809.

SANDHILL PARK *see* ASH PRIORS

SEAVINGTON ST MARY

ST MARY (Churches Conservation Trust). C13 originally – see the chamfered S doorway and roll-moulded chancel arch. This was originally flanked by blind arches for side altars, of which one remains. Otherwise mostly Perp, restored in 1880–1 by *Henry Hall*. Battlemented tower, the squat bell-stage with C16 square-headed lights. NE stair-tower. Shafted tower arch. Limewashed interior repaired in 1998 by *John Schofield*, who uncovered the nave wagon roof. – FONT. Early Norman tub, re-tooled. – STAINED GLASS. E window, 1934, by *A. K. Nicholson*. – MONUMENT. Arthur Russell, killed in 1824 by Ashantees.

SEAVINGTON ST MICHAEL

ST MICHAEL. Small, with bellcote fronting a slate-hung turret. Remodelled with Perp windows and nave parapet with mask gargoyles. C14 wave-moulded N porch. Late Georgian interior with barrel nave ceiling of 1825. WEST GALLERY of 1841 by *Maurice Davis*. Perp panelled chancel arch flanked by rood-loft corbels, a man with his tongue out and a woman with head-dress of *c.* 1350–75. C14 cinquefoiled nave PISCINA; trefoiled chancel one. – FONT. C12. Tub with lower roll. – ROYAL ARMS. Charles II. – EFFIGY. Civilian, *c.* 1330, eroded. – STAINED GLASS. Two tiny C15 figures, SW. Early C19 dove, W.

SEAVINGTON HOUSE, on the main road, is three-storeyed, ashlar, *c.* 1820. Down Upton Lane, NW, COURT FARMHOUSE,

1702, mullion-windowed with stepped drip-course, and the OLD RECTORY. Not built as a rectory, but a fine hip-roofed house of *c.* 1740–50. Five-bay ashlar fronts, the E with pedimented Doric doorcase between corniced windows, the S longer, with pilastered arched stair light.

SELWORTHY

ALL SAINTS. Prominently white against the hillside. Save for the lower parts of the short unbuttressed W tower, which are C14 (double-chamfered tower arch), this is a Perp church and one remarkably lavish for its remote position. The glory of the church is its S aisle, dated 1538 on the capital of the W respond, and probably built for the Steynings of Holnicote. Four bays, embattled on the S front. The porch has a two-light window over a fine doorway with a panelled arch and thin shafts. DOOR with linenfold panels. Two large four-light transomed windows are of that elegant yet by no means exuberant series that begins at Cleeve Abbey and includes Luccombe, Timberscombe and West Lynch. Characteristic are the little quatrefoil spandrels beneath the transom. The aisle E window is of the same type, as is that of the N aisle, which otherwise has earlier and plainer tracery. Lean-to N rood-stair turret. The chancel E window is also probably a little earlier. Note the knobs on the cusps.

Remarkably airy interior with tall slim piers and large windows. Four-bay arcades on piers of four-wave section with polygonal capitals. But in the S arcade two piers have very crisply modelled leaf bands and the respond capitals are ornamented with leaf scroll or rose. Broader, four-centred fourth arch on each side, to the chancel. No chancel arch. Wagon roofs, those to the nave and chancel renewed in 1874, the big square bosses mostly if not all C19. The N aisle roof is C15, repaired by *J. D. Sedding* in 1891. The S aisle roof is one of a local group of which the entire framing is carved (cf. Luccombe and Watchet). Elegant foliage bosses, a matching set on each rib, except the central rib, which has the face of Christ and Passion symbols. Carved wall-plates each with seventeen angels holding shields (cf. Watchet). In the chancel, pointed niches flank the E window. – WEST GALLERY. Dated 1750. Oak, heavily classical, triple-arched with fluted Doric pilasters and triglyph frieze. – ACLAND PEW. A little Gothic pavilion of 1804 corbelled out from the porch chamber. Three-sided panelled front with clustered shafts carrying an ogee roof.

OTHER FURNISHINGS. FONT. Re-tooled C12–C13 bowl, flared out at the rim. Good linenfold COVER, as at Porlock, presumably by *Randoll Blacking*, 1930s. – PULPIT. Early C16, oak, much restored, with narrow traceried panels. C17 HOURGLASS. Hexagonal C17 TESTER. – WOODWORK. C15–C16 BENCH-ENDS in the N aisle, alternating with others of *c.* 1900, carved by one of those talented Arts and Crafts local groups, here directed by *Sidney Burgess*. The group carved roof bosses in the N aisle in 1891, probably some STALLS, certainly the extremely competent READING DESKS, 1898, and, presumably, the remarkable REREDOS, 1900, with sinuous plants and lettering. The angel panels in embossed leather are by *Philip Burgess* of Porlock (cf. New Place, Porlock). – COMMUNION RAIL. C18. Slim turned balusters. – PANEL. NW end. Two planks stencilled with red and white roses, perhaps from a C16 rood screen. – STAINED GLASS. E window by *Clayton & Bell*, 1890. Some old fragments in the N aisle E window. Two N windows by *Christopher Webb*, 1958 and 1956, clearly indebted to *Comper*, who made the rather better adjacent window in 1924. – MONUMENTS. Perp tomb-chest in the chancel, with a band of pointed quatrefoils. – Philip Stenynges †1589. Lettered brass in Latin and English. – Rev. W. Fleete †1617. Lettered brass: 'London my birth; my bringinge upp Winton & Oxon had, Where taught I was with Wickham's flock among ye grave & sad.' – Charles Staynings, 1701. Curved pediment between flaming urns, on Corinthian columns. – William Blackford †1730. Large and handsome, of contrasted marbles. Corinthian pilasters carry a curly pediment bedecked with flowers. Triple cherub heads at the foot. – Charles and Dudley Dyke Acland †1837 by *Sir Francis Chantrey*, and Charles Dyke Acland †1828, also by *Chantrey*. A near-identical pair with profile portrait medallions on draped Grecian altars.

CHURCHYARD CROSS. C15, on octagonal steps. Complete, apart from the head.

Like the other Acland estate villages Selworthy is memorable for the yellow-washed cottages rebuilt or embellished in the long tenure of Sir Thomas Dyke Acland, 10th Baronet (1794–1871), mainly *c.* 1810–50. Typically, roofs were raised, lateral chimneys rebuilt with tapering circular shafts and pretty wooden windows inserted with ogee-headed lights. The cottages were thatched, but many were tiled in the C20. Behind the church, ZEALS is a C15–C16 hall house with a lateral chimney of *c.* 1600 and early C19 circular stacks. Formerly thatched. E of the church, CHURCH COTTAGES, a stone Victorian pair, have triple niches for bee-skeps. The WAR MEMORIAL CROSS, 1921, stands above SELWORTHY GREEN, laid out by Sir Thomas Dyke Acland in 1828. The five buildings so prettily disposed around the steeply sloping green are partly remodelled and partly new to create an ideal hamlet, similar to Blaise Hamlet, Bristol. The top cottage is remodelled, the adjacent single-storey one is of 1828. On the slope, PERIWINKLE COTTAGE is remodelled, the storeyed porch added, the C15 five-light oak window reused. IVY'S COTTAGE, ridiculously Picturesque with corner doors in cylindrical bulges, is new, while the pair opposite with the lateral stack is C16–C17, with Acland windows. Across the road is a substantial late C14 TITHE BARN, now a house. Six bays, buttressed, with a curious blocked pointed window whose hoodmould carvings may represent tithes: a pig, sheep, and sheaf of corn. Perp two-light end window. The rambling OLD RECTORY behind has C15–C16 corner buttresses to both the main range and cross-wing, but was remodelled after 1780. The roughcast front has Acland windows, the rear a three-sided stair projection. Downhill on the r. two altered C17 pairs with lateral chimneys flank SELWORTHY COTTAGE. This is entirely of c. 1828–9, determinedly Picturesque, with false jettying and no fewer than three circular chimneys.

HOLNICOTE HOUSE, ½ m. SW. The centre of the Exmoor estates of the Aclands of Killerton (Devon) was never particularly grand. A gatehouse remains of the medieval manor of the Steynings, a stable block survives of the Queen Anne house of William Blackford, burnt in 1779, and cellars remains of the late C18 thatched 'cottage' of Sir Thomas Dyke Acland, 7th Bart, burnt in 1851. The present house, of 1859–61, also cottage-like, is by *Robert Birmingham*, the Holnicote agent. It was thatched until burnt in 1941. Contrasting rear addition, 1873–4, in sandstone, gabled like a vicarage. The previous Acland house was on the present lawn, the swimming pool marking a cellar. To the SE, the late medieval GATEHOUSE faces N, between a cottage and outbuildings. Heavy oak-framed gateway and original oak doors, beneath a cusped oak two-light window. Another window, narrower and simpler, faces S. Winding stone stairs to a chamber with fireplace and two-bay jointed-cruck roof. There must have been a courtyard of buildings to the S, as at Bratton Court (q.v.). The attached GATEHOUSE COTTAGE is C16–C17 with a big W chimney. To the N is a long range of BARNS, partly C17. Blackford's house was further SE, near his large hip-roofed STABLE. Curved-headed windows on two floors.

Plain C19 LODGES along the main road. The main road formerly passed through BUDDLE HILL, N of the drive, between a lodge and two rows of yellow-washed cottages in a pretty group by a stream. The half-hipped roofs of porch and gable-end are typical Acland cottage additions. The lodge is Late Georgian picturesque: thatched, cruciform, with Gothic glazing. W of Holnicote, PILES MILL, a long C16–C17 house with the C19 mill behind with an overshot waterwheel. At BRANDISH STREET, across the main road, altered C16–C17 cottages and an estate FARM. Behind the Late Georgian barn, a conical thatched HORSE-ENGINE HOUSE.

EAST LYNCH FARM, ¾ m. ESE. Prominent on the hillside, a yellow Victorian farmhouse and an impressive Victorian BANK BARN, with brick arches. The thatched COTTAGE behind has a full cruck truss visible in the E outbuilding, tree-ring-dated to 1314, among the earliest in Somerset.

BURY CASTLE, Selworthy Hill. A sub-rectangular Iron Age defended enclosure, c. 70 by 50 yds (64 by 46 metres). An outwork provided better visibility to the NW. Near the top road, a MEMORIAL SEAT, 1878, under a hipped stone roof. It has inscriptions in all four recesses to the 10th Baronet (†1871), who on Sunday walks instilled in his family the 'love of Nature and of Christian poetry'. Christian poems by Keble and Heber.

SHANKS HOUSE see CUCKLINGTON

SHAPWICK

ST MARY. Unusual in that the building dates are known, 1329–31, replacing a church on another site. Unbuttressed central tower of that time, on low E and W arches with double chamfers continued in the piers without a break. Short Perp bell-stage, the square NW stair-turret turning octagonal. Battlements of 1860–1 by *G. G. Scott*. There were never transepts (cf. Dowlish Wake, Kingstone). Dec two-light windows generally, three-light E window with cusped lights. Large five-light Perp W window, transomed with supermullions. Broad C15 nave barrel roof of arch-braced rafters. Chancel lined in ashlar and re-roofed by *Scott*. – FONT. Early C14. Large, octagonal, with heavy upper and lower mouldings, as at Meare and Westonzoyland. Heavily moulded stem. – PULPIT. Stone, C15. Traceried panels, pinnacled angle shafts, and leaves in the cornice. – RAILS. Disused C17 set. – IRONWORK. Ornate wrought-iron behind the altar, 1895. – STAINED GLASS. Mostly of 1861. Chancel windows by *Alexander Gibbs*, nave S windows possibly by *Powell's*. Notably bright W window 1863, possibly by *Gibbs*. – MONUMENTS. Jane Bull †1657. Rich alabaster aedicule with curved pediment on black Corinthian columns. To each side cherubs on half-pediments. – Henry Bull †1691. Extravagant pilastered aedicule, with big broken curved pediment. On the pilasters skulls and bones. – Thomas Strangways †1766. Lias, large, with a flaming vase on the pediment. – Lt-Col. Isaac Eaton †1789. A female amid banners in the tympanum, under a coloured marble urn draped in white. – William Cator and T. H. Graham. Two memorials with urns to friends killed by privateers, 1800.

A spacious village of Blue Lias houses. Uphill from the church is the former SCHOOL, 1840s, Tudor Gothic, probably by *Richard Carver*, five bays between gabled porches. Downhill are Shapwick Manor and Shapwick House (*see* below). SW of the church, FORSTERS, a late C15 hall house with E end solar. Large early C16 hall fireplace with moulded shelf. Upstairs, plaster fleurs-de-lys and floral-scroll frieze of C17 type, but dated 1712.

SHAPWICK MANOR. A manor of Glastonbury Abbey, rebuilt for William Bull after 1622, altered for the Strangways family in the early C19. Not especially grand. The storeyed porch in the fourth bay is original, otherwise the mullioned windows, gables over each bay, and the addition r. of the porch are early C19. Long C16 to early C17 rear range. One mid-C18 panelled room with a good carved wood chimneypiece. In front of the house, a SCREEN WALL with vertically symmetrical balusters and obelisks, typical of the early C17, and a central gabled archway with ball finial. The long STABLE RANGE had a vane dated 1691. Cross-windows and a pretty octagonal clock turret.

Arcaded stalls inside. To the S, a circular medieval DOVECOTE with buttresses, much repaired.

SHAPWICK HOUSE. Another manor of Glastonbury Abbey. Tall H-plan house with storeyed central porch remodelled in the early to mid C17 for Sir Henry Rolle, Lord Chief Justice 1649–55. It incorporates a late medieval first-floor hall and E cross-wing with roofs tree-ring-dated to 1489. For Rolle the W cross-wing was added, the hall floored for a long gallery, and the whole fenestrated with ovolo-moulded mullions. Collinson's view of 1791 shows an off-centre three-storey gable and a porch against the W cross-wing. These were removed, the remaining mullion windows of the S front were changed to sashes, and a bald two-storey brick piece was added between the rear wings, probably after 1806. Mullions remain on the E side and rear. The present storeyed porch came after 1860. Georgian interiors: black-and-white paved hall, good late C18 open-well staircase, a Regency marble chimneypiece in the SE parlour, with sleeping cherub, and Regency cornice to the dining room between the rear wings. In the SW room, a large C17 kitchen fireplace. Picturesque W service wing with C17 dormer gables and C19 lantern. It incorporates the medieval kitchen, the roof tree-ring-dated to 1428. To the SE, a rare hexagonal DOVECOTE, c. 1630, lined with nesting boxes. A short hexagonal column in the middle provides a few more; 1,080 in all.

NORTHBROOK FARMHOUSE, 1 m. NE. Brick and Bath stone pedimented front to an estate farmhouse, 'new built' in 1785.

SHAPWICK HEATH. The modern road follows the route of the Early Neolithic SWEET TRACK across the wetlands to Westhay. The track comprised planks supported on wooden posts driven diagonally to form an X-shape and has been dated to the spring of 3806 B.C. Later trackways have also been found

Shapwick House.
Engraving by T. Bonnor, 1791

preserved in the peat in this area, such as the Bronze Age ABBOT'S WAY, linking what were formerly islands in a swamp.
ROMAN VILLA. A hoard of 9,238 Roman silver coins was found in 1998 E of Shapwick. They appeared to have been buried below a large but not luxurious villa.

SHARPHAM PARK

1 m. N of Walton

An eminently interesting house historically in that it was a residence of the abbots of Glastonbury, where the last abbot, Richard Whiting, was arrested. It was also the birthplace of Sir Edward Dyer (†1607), the poet, and, in 1707 of Henry Fielding, the novelist. A manor house built c. 1512 by Abbot Bere replaced what Leland called 'a poor lodge' in a deer park. In 1540 it had a 'little hall', parlour, chapel, buttery and cellar, beneath eight rooms. The works for Dyer and his successors are unrecorded, but a handsome open-well staircase of 1726 taken to the Victoria and Albert Museum from Glastonbury may have originated in the large parts of Sharpham demolished between 1799 and 1826.

The present HOUSE is more confusing than enlightening. The rear range may represent the original hall, with a cross-wing now the r. gable of the E front. Next to it, slightly set back, a C19 gabled porch, then, further back, a gable with Late Georgian sash windows. On the cross-wing a Georgian pedimented doorway on pilasters (now a window). On the porch, three re-set early C16 plaques with the abbey arms, a portcullis and Abbot Bere's pelican. The door, also reused, has the elaborate ironwork found at Meare church, there formerly dated to the C14, but reassigned by Jane Geddes to the C15–C16. The rear has C19 stone-mullioned windows with iron latticed glazing, and several more plaques. S service range rebuilt with twin-gabled E front in 1991–3 by *Roger Saul*, the owner. Inside, the principal indication of medieval status is the remnant of a traceried pointed window in the S gable, now internal, suggesting a first-floor hall. Heavy beams below and a moulded C16 fireplace in the N room. The medieval window is at the N end of a new great hall by Roger Saul, with a screen and gallery reusing C16–C17 woodwork. To the SE, a seven-bay STABLE dated 1701, with ovolo-moulded cross-windows. The roof pitch has been lowered.

SHEPTON BEAUCHAMP

ST MICHAEL. Fine Perp W tower of Ham stone, similar to Norton-sub-Hamdon and Hinton St George, indeed sharing masons' marks with them. Their characteristic is a single long bell-opening of two lights carried down through two top stages. A string course divides the upper half (with unusual pierced infill) from the blank lower half, both with ogee-headed lights. Set-back buttresses continue as triangular shafts through the upper stages and battlements to diagonally set pinnacles, now missing, two at each corner and one central on each side, corbelled from a crouching beast. Higher NE stair-turret. Quatrefoil frieze at the foot of the second stage, broken for a canopied W niche with rather poor statue of a bishop-saint. Tall four-light transomed W window with sub-arched ogee tracery. W door with carved spandrels and quatrefoil frieze, between pinnacled triangular shafts. Another canopied niche low on the S side. Tall panelled tower arch to the nave. Lavish fan-vault with big bosses and circular bell-hole. The vault resembles that at Muchelney even to the inclusion of Lord Daubeney's gartered arms, post-1487. The tower replaces one of just after 1300 in the N transept position. Much survives of the C14 church. Chancel with particularly handsome, if renewed, Dec side windows with curved-sided triangles in the tracery. E window of three lights with a wheel of four mouchettes. Perp alterations to the aisles with parapets and square-headed windows, and tall embattled Perp N chapel with three-light windows. The vaulted N porch with strange triangular transverse arches has Perp doorway mouldings. There is another important layer to this church, a High Anglican restoration for the Rev. James Coles in 1865 by *G. E. Street*. He endeavoured to take the church back from Perp to Dec, evidenced by clerestory roundels replacing Perp windows, the rebuilt S aisle with steep-gabled S porch and the steep-gabled N vestry. Re-set C14 porch STATUE; reused roll-moulded early C14 S doorway.

Inside, the octagonal arcade piers and double-chamfered arches are early C14 on the N (S arcade replaced 1865). Similar arches survive of the lost N tower, one ending the N arcade, the other to the NE chapel. *Street*'s nave roof has strong tie-beams with braced crown-posts. His also the chancel arch and colourful chancel roof with trefoiled half-circles on the wall-plate. Good early C14 sequence of PISCINA, three SEDILIA and S doorway under linked hoodmoulds (cf. Puckington). The sedilia piers are prettily pierced, with a curved-sided triangle and a cinquefoiled circle. – FONT. C12. Bulbous bowl ringed above and below. – FURNISHINGS by *Street*. Stone octofoil PULPIT, low chancel SCREEN with iron railing, and carved REREDOS. Also Gothic STALLS. – ROOD BEAM. 1930, by *Herbert Read*. – STAINED GLASS. Interesting compendium: excellent chancel set by *Clayton & Bell*, c. 1870; three delicate S aisle windows, 1888–97, designed by *J. F. Bentley*, architect (one depicts the Ugandan martyrs); S aisle E, 1880s, by *Philip Westlake*; N aisle E, 1923, Comper style.

CHURCHYARD CROSS to James Coles †1872. Shaft with canopied statue.

The main street runs S from a triangle in front of the C17–C18 DUKE OF YORK pub. On the E side is the churchyard. On the W, STEPHENS, C17, with ovolo-moulded mullions, the S end dated 1752. Set back is the former RECTORY, 1873, by *Richard Drew*, built for Stuckey Coles to house a community of clerics, hence larger and more Gothic than usual. A circular stair tourelle and projecting chapel to the l. Drew was Butterfield's pupil, which shows in the half-hipped side dormers. Next, James Coles's Gothic SCHOOL, 1856 by *J. M. Allen*, extended 1909. The lantern was originally central. ROSE COTTAGE, *c.* 1860, rambling, built for Coles's daughter. Opposite, SALISBURY HOUSE, thatched, possibly the C15 church house. Further down, MARTLETS, stone and rendered cob, early C17. On the l., a curved-headed early C19 FIVES WALL with ball finials, as at Stoke-sub-Hamdon, in a former pub yard. Down Robin's Lane, PAULLS has C16 jointed crucks. THE OLD THATCH facing the churchyard was a C15–C16 hall house. On the Lambrook road, ST MICHAELS, an earlier rectory, externally unremarkable, but with C16 moulded arch-braced roof trusses and early C18 parlour panelling. From 1886 it housed a penitentiary for fallen girls, indicative of the high-minded Coles era.

SHEPTON HOUSE, ½ m. SW. Victorian Tudor, 1850, a wedding present to Coles from his banker father-in-law, Vincent Stuckey. Probably by *Maurice Davis* of Langport. Complete with kitchen and stable courtyards. Drawing-room ceiling in cusped squares, after Pugin, who would have hated the marble Gothic chimneypiece. Just S, MOUNTFIELDS, an ashlar deep-eaved villa with columned porch, 'lately built' in 1838.

LITTLEFIELDS, 1 m. ESE. Large farmhouse of *c.* 1700, mullion-windowed, with continuous drip-courses.

SHEPTON MONTAGUE

ST PETER, ½ m. E of the village. Sturdy Perp S porch-tower of two stages with diagonal buttresses, the small uncusped bell-openings perhaps C17. Doorway carefully lettered 'Port Esynd Thomas', unexplained. The church was gutted by fire in 1964, and the C13 chancel subsequently demolished. Some Norman fragments then found are re-set in the E wall, and some corbel heads in the low wall beyond. Light interior with low-pitched roof and W gallery by *Kenneth Wiltshire*, 1966. – ROYAL ARMS. 1967. – STAINED GLASS. N window, 1928.

Panelled base of a C15 CHURCHYARD CROSS.

SHERFORD see TAUNTON

SIMONSBATH

There was only one house here for two centuries from 1654, that of the lessee of the Royal Forest of Exmoor. The village grew after John Knight, Worcestershire ironmaster, created a very large but ultimately unprofitable agricultural estate from 1818, enclosing moorland with some 29 miles of walls and banks.

ST LUKE. 1855–6. Nave, chancel and bellcote in a simple lancet Gothic, the W end slate-hung after the stone crumbled. High interior with cusped nave trusses and tall shafted chancel arch. – STAINED GLASS. E window, 1922, by *Maurice Drake* of Exeter. – Below is the rendered gabled VICARAGE, also 1856.

SIMONSBATH HOUSE. Built in 1652–4 by James Boevey, lessee, and repaired in 1767–9 for Sir Thomas Dyke Acland, 7th Bt. It was an inn before John Knight moved here in 1830. Long and white, much altered, with a pyramid-roofed porch-tower and moulded oak doorway. (Fireplace dated 1654.) Opposite is an early C19 SAWMILL, refurbished in 1897–8 for the 3rd Earl Fortescue, who bought the estate from Sir Frederic Knight.

FARMSTEADS were built after 1841, typically with hip-roofed stuccoed farmhouses. EMMETT'S GRANGE, 2 m. SW, 1848, built for the agent, is the largest.

COW CASTLE, 2 m. SE. A hillfort on a knoll above the River Barle. The rampart is stone-faced with two entrances, but the interior is steep, with only a few places where habitation might be expected.

ROMAN LODE, Burcombe, 1¾ m. WSW. A gash in the hillside following deposits of iron ore may, as its name suggests, originate in the Roman period. A Roman iron-smelting site is known nearby at Sherracombe, Devon. There is also evidence of subsequent working and reworking of the site and others in the area.

SKILGATE

9020

ST JOHN. Unbuttressed unadorned W tower, C13–C14. The rest is of 1872, Dec style. Reused roll-moulded S doorway.

To the E, stuccoed, hip-roofed former RECTORY, *c.* 1830–40.

SOCK DENNIS *see* ILCHESTER

SOMERTON

4020

Somerton was called a 'royal town' when occupied by the Mercians in 733 and was a royal manor through the early medieval period, though the claim that it was the 'capital' of Wessex is unfounded. It was the county town by virtue of holding the shire courts and gaol from 1278 to 1366, but otherwise has been a small market town, of distinct character from being almost entirely built of local Blue Lias stone.

ST MICHAEL. A large church which is not predominantly Perp, evidenced immediately by the big octagonal tower placed on the S transept. The tower and corresponding N transept are early C13, see the triple-chamfered arches to the nave and lancet windows. The tower has a square base with a small E lancet and a larger W one (hidden by the S aisle), then the transition to octagonal is made by the most primitive, plain, large broaches. Lancet in the S gable. Blocked lancets in the octagon, which must have been raised *c.* 1500 with two-light bell-openings with pierced baffles and battlements. The N transept has a blocked W lancet. The two-light N window is later, of *c.* 1300, with delicately cusped Y-tracery and an elongated trefoil in each head. The unusual width of the nave was established by the transepts, but the detail of nave and aisles seems to be mid-C14. The aisles have reticulated and other tracery and a richly moulded S doorway. W window of five lights with flowing tracery. The last phase, *c.* 1500, saw the raising of the nave roof with an embattled clerestory of three-light windows with four-centred arches, and the rebuilding of the three-bay chancel, with a large five-light E window. N vestry of 1770. S porch of the restoration in 1889 by *George Vialls*.

The four-bay arcades have octagonal piers with plain moulded capitals and double-chamfered arches. The very wide proportions make the piers appear short, a discrepancy that must have been worse before the clerestory was built. Splendid Late Perp roof of the best Somerset qualities (cf. Martock), datable if a barrel ('tun') indicates John Preston, vicar 1494–1511. Moderate pitch, alternate tie-beams decorated with vine-trail and castellation, kingposts on angel figures, and, instead of tracery, wonderful dragons in the spandrels. The end bays are elaborated with pendants on the intermediate beams and the wall-plates are decorated too. The roof itself is framed, with leaf bosses and 640 identical quatrefoil panels. The C13 arch into the tower dies into the imposts as does the N transept arch. Under the tower a tall recess, E, a tomb-recess, S, and stair doorway, NW, all single-chamfered. Also a trefoiled PISCINA. The broad chancel arch has C14 double wave mouldings dying into the nave walls. C19 chancel ceiling on C16–C17 plaster cornices of opposed fish-tailed beasts.

FURNISHINGS. COMMUNION TABLE. Made in Langport, 1626. The hugely bulbous legs are charmingly carved: Adam and Eve, Adam ploughing, and Noah as carpenter. – CHANCEL PANELLING. Early C17, brought in. Arcading divided by small female demi-figures of Virtues, displaying a mirror, a chicken and a viol. Amid foliage above are Adam and Eve. – PULPIT. 1615. Large and delicately coloured. Arched panels, floral frieze and cornice. – CANDELABRA. Two of 1782, 'To Gods Glory and the Honor of the Church of England'.* – BENCH-ENDS. C15, the tops bifurcated; tracery and some thick leaf carving.

---

*Words which inspired John Betjeman to undertake his guide to English parish churches.

SOMERTON

– FONT. Octagonal, C19. Cover of C17 pieces. – STAINED GLASS. E window and one N aisle, 1918–19, by *Jones & Willis*, old-fashioned. – W window, c. 1880, cherubim, powers etc., Late Gothic style. – MONUMENTS. Eroded female effigy, c. 1300 (tower). – John Withed †1679, floor slab with woolly lions (nave). – Thomas Rooke †1764, pedimented, with winged skull (chancel). – Harbin Arnold †1782, three colours of marble (chancel). – Two reliefs of mourning females (nave), one seated and Grecian to John Pinney †1818, by *Francis Chantrey*, 1827, the other sprawled and Romantic to the Hall family, 1860s, by *Robert Physick*. – Two Pinney memorials (tower), 1860s, a very Victorian etched brass in the W lancet and a well-carved Gothic plaque with brass insets. – F. N. Pretor-Pinney †1909, Edwardian tile mosaic (S aisle). – Rev. L. Jackson †1950, by *George Pace*, incised slate (chancel).

ST DUNSTAN (R.C.), West Street. 1967. Square and pyramid-roofed, lit from long windows near the corners and a cylindrical lantern.

METHODIST CHURCH, West Street. 1845–6. Facing a long forecourt. Gothic, with simple Y-traceried windows. Painted end gallery.

CONGREGATIONAL CHURCH (United Reformed), West Street. The Gothic front of 1865 is greatly higher than the chapel of 1822, very evident in the side views. Gallery with leaf-pattern ironwork. Adjacent hall, 1875.

PERAMBULATION. Somerton MARKET PLACE is one of the most happily grouped urban pictures in Somerset. The church lies back from the N side, and the irregular square has plenty that is attractive. The size is disguised by an island site with houses and two public buildings, the stone-tiled MARKET CROSS of 1673, octagonal about a central pier, with segmental arches and battlements, and the mullion-windowed TOWN HALL. Originating in 1596, this has been much altered, in 1716–19 and in the late C19. Long transomed E and NE windows indicate that the E end was not floored, probably a court room. The mullions are unmoulded, i.e. C18. The W end projection was the town lock-up. On the S side, the WHITE HART INN has Late Georgian sashes but the l. bay is an altered C15 crosswing, identifiable from a tiny stair light in the E wall. Moulded framed ceiling and jointed-cruck roof. The GLOBE INN has early C19 multi-paned sash windows and parapet, but is older. It adjoined a large late medieval house called (without cause) Somerton Castle, demolished in 1842. The house had transomed hall windows and a Perp battlemented porch, which was re-erected at Chilton Polden (q.v.). On the site is SELWOOD HOUSE, with Ham stone windows and pilastered doorcase. No. 2 looks slightly earlier, a broad three-storey front with an enclosed Ionic porch. On the E side, THE OLD BELL and FREEMAN HOUSE show Georgian windows on C16–C17 structures.

On the W side, behind the MEMORIAL HALL of 1901 (by *W. J. Willcox*), MANOR HOUSE has a stone-mullioned front that

'Somerton Castle'.
Drawing by J. C. Buckler, 1830

looks later C17 but is essentially C16. Broad rear stair gable. Inside, a moulded four-centred doorway downstairs and a first-floor parlour with some early decorated plasterwork, an overmantel with mid-C16 heraldry over an early C16 haunched fireplace. Ribbed ceiling of curvilinear crosses in diagonal squares. On the N side, after the churchyard gates, a row including MARKET HOUSE, a good C17 front with two oriels and attic gables. On the island site, the stuccoed earlier C19 LANGLER HOUSE with columned porch turns a rounded corner towards Broad Street. TUDOR HOUSE, to the S, with mullioned windows and an oriel in Ham stone, was once dated 1616. Late C19 dormers.

BROAD STREET, broad indeed and tree-lined, was the beast market. On the E side, the former RED LION, the most ambitious of the Somerton inns, under construction in 1768. The long five-bay front has tripartite windows and a centrepiece with giant Ham stone pilasters carrying an open pediment (formerly with Lord Ilchester's arms) over a Venetian window and a depressed-arched throughway. The NATWEST BANK stands out architecturally for its formal five-bay front of 1708. Lias with painted ashlar dressings: quoins, bolection-moulded doorcase and channelled window jambs. NARROW HOUSE, adjoining, was a solicitor's office. The gable-end was the public entrance, embellished with a pedimented doorway between side-lights and a false pediment to the attic. Thick glazing bars suggest an early to mid-C18 date. Fielded panelling in the office conceals document shelves. CRAIGMORE has early C18 mullioned windows and a curved-headed two-light window in the middle. The curved-pedimented doorcase is more up-to-date.

MEDWYN and STOCKERS HOUSE have early C19 glazing. They were divided in 1815 from a C16–C17 L-plan house, evidenced by the Tudor-arched doorway. Tudor-arched fireplaces in Stockers House, and a big elliptical-arched voussoired one in Medwyn. This also has an Elizabethan plaster frieze upstairs like those in the church chancel, similar beasts but naked women. The plain three-storey building opposite was a shirt-collar factory, employing over 100 women in 1868.

COW SQUARE, NW, retains the livestock market name but is, unusually for the region, a little residential square about an oval lawn. Coronation cast-iron TROUGH by the *Coalbrookdale Foundry*, 1902. The OLD HALL, on the W end, double-pile and mansard-roofed with an enclosed Ionic porch, looks mid- to late C18. On the N side, HOPEFIELD, mid-C18, four bays, with an older service wing, and the principal house, DONISTHORPE, behind C18 wrought-iron forecourt gates. Said to date from 1770, but surely earlier. Broad seven-bay front with a curved-headed centre window. Stair with thick ramped rail and balusters in threes. Behind the Old Hall, the OLD VICARAGE incorporates a late medieval first-floor hall; only the W gable visible externally, and a pointed-arched doorway and a framed ceiling within. The arch-braced roof, wind-braced in three tiers, is concealed. S block of 1787 with stair hall and drawing room. Additions E and N of 1867 by *Charles Knowles*. On opposite corners of NORTH STREET are CORNER HOUSE, a Regency three-storey former inn, and the SCOTT-GOULD ALMSHOUSES, 1866, two-storeyed with mullioned windows and gables. NEW STREET, the medieval road in from the E, has on the S side some altered C17 houses and the OLD MANSE, mid-C18, prettily formal with parapet. On the N side, the SOMERTON HOTEL was the New Inn, Late Georgian, with multiple paired sashes. The OLD SCHOOL, 1875, was a Quaker meeting house. T-plan with bi-colour voussoirs. COCKSPURS, a toll house, divided roads to Yeovil and Bath. Returning to NORTH STREET, on the l. heading N is JENNINGS HOUSE, C17, mullion-windowed with dormer gables. At the N end, in its own grounds, stands THE LYNCH, a well-designed villa of c. 1812, under a deep-eaved roof with a big glazed lantern. Three bays. The entrance bay projects slightly with a parapet and porch. On each side, elegant radially fluted arches frame floor-length Venetian windows. Neatly planned interior with cantilevered stone stairs.

Back in the Market Place, the COURTHOUSE, SW, was a mid-C19 police station, the gabled courtroom added in 1876 by *A. Whitehead*. On WEST STREET, the two chapels (p. 559) are on opposite sides. LEAVER'S COURT, N, is a rare timber-framed front, jettied between stone walls, probably C15. The UNICORN HOTEL has mullioned windows and an asymmetrically placed two-storeyed porch with an early C17 arch, but is earlier. Chamfered framed ceiling and roof of arch-braced jointed crucks, not smoke-blackened, probably early C16. On the S, the single-storey HEXT ALMSHOUSES, 1626. Eight one-room houses each with door and two-light window, rhythmically divided by four pairs of niche seats, plain versions of the niches at Montacute. Further out, to the l. on SUTTON ROAD, the half-hip-roofed former ZION CHAPEL, Bible Christian, 1841. Off the Langport Road, on WEST END to the l., BALLACREE, thatched and mullion-windowed, of *c.* 1500, much extended. Moulded framed C16 hall ceiling and reused early linenfold panelling from Devon. The barn, converted in 1938 by the craftsman-builder *Ralph Fry*, has a massive fireplace from Dorset.

Back towards the Market Place, from West Street PESTERS LANE runs SE to CRANE FARM. Unremarkable exterior (with attached cruciform barn), but in the rear range two raised-cruck trusses, tree-ring-dated to 1338. PARSONAGE HILL climbs N to the OLD PARSONAGE, *c.* 1620. Long façade with mullioned windows and central storeyed porch, once battlemented, with a canted oriel. The N room has C17 panelling (possibly from Medwyn, Broad Street), and an unusual overmantel with *trompe l'œil* Elizabethan architecture flanked by female figures. Just N, a long buttressed TITHE BARN, rebuilt in 1759 by *Nathaniel Ireson*. In MOUNT HEY, opposite, five monopitch-roofed houses, 1968–70, by *Steel & Coleman*.

SOMERTON COURT, ½ m. SE. A large seven-bay house with mullioned windows and a central three-storey porch dated 1641. There were gables and gabled dormers before a Regency-Romantic transformation, with battlements each side of the porch now raised to a toy-fort tower with a rose window, thin angle turrets and battlements. Early C19 cantilevered stone stair.

SOMERTON RANDLE, 1 m. E. Called newly built in 1789, for the Howe family, here since 1662, the house was sold in 1798 to John Pinney, Bristol merchant, extremely wealthy from West Indian sugar plantations on Nevis. Three-bay N front, the projecting pedimented centre with a Venetian window over a four-column Tuscan porch. Slightly irregular seven-bay S front. So far unexceptional, but the well-planned four-room ground floor contains the best late C18 decoration in the county, surely done for Pinney by Bristol plasterers. In the entrance hall, a generous open-well cantilevered stair with wrought-iron leaf-and-scroll standards and inlaid handrail. Oval ceiling on pendentives. Three rooms lead off, each with Neoclassical plasterwork of extreme delicacy and a fine marble chimneypiece. The dining room, E, more masculine, has plaster wall panels and a Neoclassical frieze. The square morning room, S, and the full-width drawing room, W, are both richer and more delicate. In the former, Soaneian lunettes and pendentives bring the square to a circle, the plaster in wreaths of wonderfully naturalistic leaves. The latter has a deep cove to a three-part ceiling, a segmented circle in a square, with urns and festoons, between two rectangles. All restrained and classical, but in a Rococo touch a spray of wheat breaks from each rectangle. The chimneypiece jambs finish in triple goat feet.

Two C18 SE service ranges face each other. The W range has arched windows over a semi-basement with pedimented doorcase. The plain E range has a blocked throughway and columned N porch, marking the estate office. A dramatic Victorian STABLE BLOCK, 1860–2, spans the E drive, the arch under a hipped roof pushed off-centre by an outlandish Italianate tower with ogee slated dome. The way that the clock stage (turret-clock of 1863) juggles planes defies description. The architect was almost certainly *E. B. Lamb*.

The house was called SOMERTON ERLEIGH until the Pinney family took the name to a new house on the hill to the S, of 1972–4 by *Stout & Litchfield*. Blue Lias, single-storeyed about a small courtyard. The multiple monopitch roofs with two prominent chimneys or vents compose like a miniature Italian hilltop village. SOMERTON MILL, by the main road, was rebuilt *c.* 1786. The house with curved-headed mullion windows looks earlier. It abuts the upper part of the gabled mill. Internal overshot wheel dated 1869. Lean-to with brick chimney added in 1860 for a steam engine. Uphill S, THE GRANGE, dated 1863, with storeyed porch. This was the Pinney residence by the late C19. SOMERTON COURT FARM beyond may be the farm John Pinney built in 1799. Three-bay farmhouse and barn with arched entry.

RAILWAY. The GWR line of 1903–6 (*A. W. Armstrong*, engineer) cuts a deep gash through the town before crossing the River Cary on a five-arch VIADUCT. Further E the SKEW BRIDGE spans the Castle Cary road, not as a true skew but multiple staggered arches.

SOUTH BARROW

ST PETER. Plain two-stage Perp W tower of Blue Lias. Diagonal buttresses with many set-offs, two-light bell-openings with pierced baffles, and ashlar battlements. Gabled square N stair-turret. Shafted tower arch. The rest was unattractively rebuilt in 1882 by *Henry Parsons*. – FONT. Massive octagonal bowl chamfered below. Inscribed RM 1584, but it fits the C12–C13 Purbeck marble stem, round with four half-shafts. – PULPIT. Early C17, with flat Jacobean ornament. – COMMUNION RAILS. C17, the balusters vertically symmetrical. – BENCHES. C15–C16. Simple tracery below ornamented panels. Frontals with finials. – STAINED GLASS. E window, 2000, by *Laura Gilroy*. – MEMORIALS. Richard Morice. C16 brass with an acrostic in Gothic script, in English. He may be the RM of the font.

PISGAH METHODIST CHAPEL, Chapel Lane. Chapel of 1857 attached to a three-storey house of 1860. Late Georgian in style apart from the rock-faced stonework of the house, and the chapel entrance being on the gable-end. Simple painted panelled gallery.

MANOR FARMHOUSE, N of the church. Early C17, with ovolo-moulded mullioned windows. Decorated plaster to an upper room: a frieze of winged horses and curvilinear thin-rib ceiling with Tudor-rose sprays.

SOUTH BREWHAM

ST JOHN BAPTIST. The lower half of the S tower is C13 – see the double-chamfered doorway. Two layers of bell-stage, Perp and C19. C13 chamfered arch within, infilled with a depressed-arched S doorway with reused Norman imposts. Perp N aisle with standard piers (four hollows). Matching S arcade of 1826–7. C15 nave roof. Restoration by *Henry Hall*, 1883–4. – FONT. C19. Also a C14 octagonal bowl from Bruton. – COMMUNION RAIL. Early C18. – STAINED GLASS. Panels of *c.* 1858 from Clandown (N). – MONUMENTS. Edward Court †1639. Heraldry on strapwork. – Balch family. Two monuments, *c.* 1800, with affixed iron cherub heads. – Two late C17 brasses, one signed *Guliet Cockey*, Wincanton.

CHURCHYARD CROSS. C15 octagonal pillar with a capital.

Above the church, a Gothic SCHOOL, 1863, by *William Clarke* of Bruton. In the village below, STREET FARMHOUSE, late C17 with a hip-roofed cross-wing.

ALFRED'S TOWER, 2 m. ESE. 1769–72 by *Henry Flitcroft* for Henry Hoare of Stourhead, across the Wiltshire boundary. Triangular brick tower of 131 ft (40 metres), colossal and sublime, like Victorian engineering. Four stages, with ashlar string courses and battlements. Three round angle turrets, one of them carried higher to contain the stairs to the top platform, this with a conical cap. Georgian Gothic pointed doorway, trefoiled plaque above, and canopied niche for Alfred's twice life-size statue. The inscription reads: 'Alfred the Great A.D. 879 on this summit erected his standard against the Danish Invaders. To Him we owe the origin of Juries The Establishment of a Militia the Creation of a Naval Force. Alfred the light of a benighted age was a Philosopher and a Christian The Father of his People The Founder of the English Monarchy and Liberty.' The project was conceived in 1762 to honour George III as a British rather than Hanoverian monarch.

CARDS FARMHOUSE, 1 m. S. Dated 1605 and 1647. Three-storey front with reserved-chamfer mullioned windows. Georgian doorcase beneath a C17 bare-breasted maiden. Three-gabled rear, the middle gable an insertion in front of the moulded C17 rear doorway. Also a reused Perp doorway.

COLINSHAYS, 1 m. W. A rambling house with generally Tudor detail, illustrated in 1825, early for the type.

The parish has an unusual pattern of scattered farms. E of North Brewham, JERRARDS FARMHOUSE is late C18 with open-pediment doorcase. A similar doorcase to BREWHAM HOUSE, a Late Georgian villa. COOKS FARMHOUSE, SW of Border, is early C17, with a wooden winding stair and four-centred-arched fireplace. CANNWOOD HOUSE, NE of Border, 1760, has parallel hip-roofed three-storey ranges in brick with mullioned windows. At BREWHAM LODGE was the Stourhead brickyard. Diapered brick farmhouse of 1848. NW of North Brewham, at BATT'S FARM, is a buttressed C16 BARN.

SOUTH CADBURY

ST THOMAS À BECKET. Beneath Cadbury Castle. Nice Perp W tower of squared Cary stone with higher NE stair-turret, similar to Charlton Musgrove. Diagonal buttresses, two-light bell-openings, battlements and pinnacles. Perp N porch between square-headed windows. The S aisle was extended in 1835 by *William Wadman* of Martock, and the chancel rebuilt, apparently accurately, in 1873–5 by *Henry Hall*. The three-bay arcade seems to be late C13 or early C14: double-chamfered arches on quatrefoil piers with moulded capitals. Single-shaft responds each with two layered shaft-rings. The tower arch on shafts with round capitals and octagonal bases is Perp, earlier than the panelled chancel arch. Four-sided nave roof in panels with angel brackets and leaf bosses. In 1874 the splay of an original S aisle window and a PISCINA (made from a C13 memorial) were discovered, the splay with a C15 PAINTING of a bishop. – FURNISHINGS. Mostly 1870–5, including the stone Crucifixion REREDOS by *Thomas Earp*, 1870. – STAINED GLASS. By *Clayton & Bell* the E window, 1874, and probably also one S aisle window.

Opposite the church, SOUTH CADBURY HOUSE, a substantial mid-C18 rectory. Two fronts of sash windows in keystoned architraves, the S side ending in a hip-roofed cross-wing with a canted bay. Further S, MANOR FARMHOUSE, thatched, dated 1687. Partly of good squared stone, with four-light stone-mullioned windows downstairs. The rest, with timber mullions, may be earlier.

CHAPEL CROSS, N of the A303. Early C15 wayside chapel, with a house added to the W. Thatched, with banded stonework and cinquefoil-cusped single-light windows. Leper squint in the E wall. Pointed wagon-roof with ribs ending in a little delicate tracery.

CADBURY CASTLE. The ramparts are much hidden by trees, but this is the most impressive hillfort in Somerset. Settlement is known from the Neolithic and Bronze Ages as well as the Iron Age, when the four encircling banks were constructed. Occupation appears to have continued until about twenty years after the Roman conquest, when some form of military action took place. The hilltop was reoccupied in the C5–C6, when a timber and stone wall some ¾ m. long was built around the top with at least one gateway tower. Pottery from the eastern Mediterranean shows international links at this time. 'Cadnan' and Glastonbury are the only two places in SW England named on the Hereford Mappa Mundi of *c.* 1300, which may suggest that the identification of Cadbury Castle with King Arthur's Camelot was current by that time. The hillfort was occupied for a final time in the early C11, when a mortared wall was constructed and coins were minted for Æthelred †1016.*

SOUTH CHERITON

The village runs E on to Horsington Marsh. It has a Nonconformist character, with its 'UNSECTARIAN TEMPERANCE HALL', 1887, Gothic METHODIST CHAPEL, 1844, and CONGREGATIONAL CHAPEL, 1886. On the main road, the two-storey TOLL HOUSE, 1824, still has its toll board. CHERITON HOUSE, mid-C18, has heavy voussoirs suggesting *Nathaniel Ireson*. In the cellar, a C17 moulded doorway.

SOUTH PETHERTON

A small town of complicated plan, largely built of ochre-coloured stone. The church is at the highest point. An Anglo-Saxon minster and mint here support traditional association with Ine, King of Wessex *c.* 688–726. South Petherton, together with Montacute, had a significant bronze-casting industry in the C17 and C18 producing skillets and cauldrons, often decorated with mottoes.

ST PETER AND ST PAUL. A spreading cruciform building crowned by a fine, tall octagonal crossing tower. Despite thorough Perp remodelling, perhaps for Abbot Gilbert of Bruton *c.* 1525, the church is essentially mid- to late C13. External signs include the small lancets of the lower part of the tower, two chancel side windows with bar tracery (quatrefoiled circles), the low E buttresses, and the S porch. Mid-C14 N transept with reticulated N and straight-headed reticulated E window. This transept is the only embattled part (apart from the tower). The rest has plain parapets from the Perp remodelling, when large windows were inserted, the principal ones transomed. Added then were the storeyed N porch and the tall bell-stage of the tower, which gives the church such character. Two-light

---

* At Milsom's Corner, W of the hillfort, was discovered a sheet bronze shield (now in the Museum of Somerset) dating to about 1000 B.C. The metal, beaten to less than 1 mm. thick, had a pattern of close-spaced concentric ridges, each crowned with a line of dots. Obviously symbolic, as suggested by its being placed face down in a ditch and stabbed three times, perhaps a ritual 'killing' of the object.

openings with latticed baffles, far-projecting gargoyles and battlements. Spike of 1717.

Four-bay nave arcades on standard Perp shafted piers. No clerestory. Aisles with wall-shafts. Roofs of 1860, by *Hickes & Isaac* of Bath. The s porch has a lovely C13 pointed vault with keeled diagonal and ridge ribs meeting at a ribbed hexagon, the six small bosses with delicate stiff-leaf and two heads. Two C12 zodiac CORBELS, Leo and Sagittarius (also the two zodiacal signs on the Stoke-sub-Hamdon tympanum). The crossing arches to E and W are triple-chamfered on three orders of columns with coved round capitals. Between the shafts are chamfers which terminate between the capitals with bar stops under tiny pointed trefoils. One would date the arches c. 1300 if it were not for the fine rib-vault which rests on corbels with the signs of the Evangelists, the head of St John's angel of a type more like c. 1250. Plain triple-chamfered N and S arches dying into the piers. Perp corbel heads and angels in the s transept. Perp polygonal corbels under the high chancel roof (by *A. W. Blomfield*, 1882). The two C13 chancel side windows are shafted with stiff-leaf capitals (one on the N particularly fine, one on the s with three charming heads). The E window is also shafted, showing that it was of equal size to the present four-light Perp window. Restored C13 PISCINA, gabled, cinquefoil-cusped.

FURNISHINGS. FONT. 1860. – PULPIT. Stone, 1882. – PAINTING. Nave E, Sanctus angels, 1900, by *Jones & Willis*, hard to like. A Doom found in 1860 could not be saved. – ROYAL ARMS. Elizabeth II. – BENEFACTION BOARDS. 1738. – STALLS. A Gothic set, 1935, by *Sir George Oatley*, commemorates Thomas Coke (1747–1814), Wesleyan missionary, formerly a curate here. RAILS. 1882. Wrought-iron with brass flowers. – SCULPTURE. Fragments in the N squint include a C14 Crucifixion, perhaps from a churchyard cross and part of a painted carved figure. – E wall, Saints Peter and Paul, bronzed resin, by *Avril Vellacott*, 1974. – STAINED GLASS. Fine W window, 1875, by *Clayton & Bell*, in their densely worked later style. Theirs probably the E window, 1882. Two-light chancel windows by *Hardman*, 1876 and 1880. Chancel N, sombre blue and silver, 1912, by *A. K. Nicholson*. N aisle W, 2000, by *Joanna Dover*, spiralled angels. s aisle W, 2012 by *John Yeo*, bells. – MONUMENTS. s transept. Sir Philip de Albini (Daubeney) †1294. Doulting stone effigy excavated at Pitway, 1929. Bareheaded knight in mail and surcoat. – Sir Giles Daubeney †1446 and his first wife, Joan. A large low Perp tomb-chest with quatrefoils and corner figures, the Purbeck marble top inlaid with brasses. He is in plate armour, she with wide head-dress, under crocketed ogee canopies. On the floor, a small brass of Mary, his second wife, †1442. – Henry Compton of Wigborough †1628. Painted stone. Bad thin elongated figures kneel at a prie-dieu under a hoop canopy. Damaged in 1860. – N transept. Elizabeth Ayshe †1677, William Ayshe †1657 and Hannah Sandys †1658. Large and coarse but splendid. Ionic columns and a broken pediment in Somerset alabaster frame three black-clad figures kneeling in line against a three-bay arcade. In two of the bays white-robed children stare outward. – William Sandys †1679. Copper, delicately engraved with musical instruments and lengthy verse: 'Rebellion he did openly abhor,/ Though guilded with the name of Civil War./ Rome's impositions, and Scotch Covenant/ He did dislike, and therefore was no Saint./ But prayers of our Church he more admir'd/ Than theirs that madly think themselves inspir'd.' – Emanuel Sandys †1655. Lias with relief heraldry. – Samuel Cabell †1699 and wife †1724. Baroque, finely carved in grey and white. Heavy curved top with reclining cherubs, skull below.

War memorial CHURCHYARD CROSS, 1921. Plain two-storey SCHOOL, 1828, windows altered 1866.

ST MICHAEL (R.C.), Lightgate Road. 1961. Boarded walls. Later stone W wall with laminated STAINED GLASS roundel by *John Reyntiens*, 2009.

COKE MEMORIAL CHURCH (Methodist), Palmer Street. 1881–2, by *Alexander Lauder*. Muscular Gothic. The needle spire with coat-peg gargoyles must derive from the parish church tower. It was evidently admired as Lauder repeated it, smaller, at Martock. Contemporary triple-gabled MANSE.

SOUTH PETHERTON HOSPITAL, Pitway. 2009–10, by *David Kent Architects* of Bath. Twenty-four-bed community hospital. Long two-storey range, boarded above.

MANOR HOUSE, Silver Street. A seat of the Daubeneys from the C13, fancifully known as King Ine's Palace in the C19. It had a hall with storeyed lower end and a late C15 solar cross-wing. In 1863 *Joseph Chapman* of Frome floored the hall and

South Petherton, Manor House, before alteration.
Engraving, 1888

destroyed the wind-braced roof in a remodelling denounced to *The Builder*. A splendid late C15 battlemented two-storey oriel fronts the cross-wing, ornamented between the floors with shields, one belted with Lord Daubeney's garter awarded in 1487. Two- and three-light windows, the lower ones ogee-traceried with quatrefoil tracery in the spandrels (the Muchelney type), and the upper pointed with complex tracery. The surviving hall details are late C15: doorway with thin shafts and leaf spandrels, lateral chimney, and a cross-window with Muchelney tracery. The mullion inside has bosses for shutter-rods. *Chapman* regularized the front with three gables (copying windows from the solar) over cross-windows (copying the original one). He added a turret porch to the cross-wing and some pretty leaded glazing. The haunched hall fireplace is covered in Victorian botanical carving. Reused C17 stair balusters, with flat-topped newel finials. An outbuilding has a tall two-light window assembled from two originals.

PERAMBULATION. Below the churchyard is the Market Square, filled by an arcaded MARKET HALL, 1843, by *Maurice Davis*, and the much bigger hip-roofed BLAKE HALL, 1911, whose heavy detail suggests *C. B. Benson*. On the N side, MARKET HOUSE has mullioned windows but a Georgian eaves cornice. Going N up St James's Street, an ascending sequence from the low thatched C16–C18 (Nos. 31–37) to the tall Victorian commercial (the POST OFFICE), with encaustic tile bands. Opposite, Nos. 40–44, C15–C16, much refaced in the 1890s, was the rectorial manor house. The OLD COURT HOUSE was probably the manorial court. Early C18 ashlar r. part with long first-floor windows, at right angles to a C15–C16 range altered at the same time. Gable-end two-storey bay with sash windows and paired C16 spiral chimneys. Inside, one early Gothic doorway, and two panelled rooms. One has late C17 oak panelling, the other an early C18 office, the panels concealing shelves.

From the Methodist church (p. 568), Palmer Street runs SW past LAMB COTTAGE, C16–C17, thatched, and THE FARMHOUSE, with mullioned windows of *c.* 1700. Early C18 COACHHOUSE opposite. Crown Lane returns E past a monumental C19 FIVES WALL, curved-topped with ball finials (cf. Shepton Beauchamp, Stoke-sub-Hamdon). On West Street, the SURGERY faces the churchyard. Long mullion-windowed front of *c.* 1700. On the corner opposite, THE OLD HOUSE, mid-C18, has a Late Georgian single-storey addition with elegant double bow to the garden. Further out, the former VICARAGE, 1841, by *Maurice Davis*, L-plan, deep-eaved with sash windows, incorporates three early C16 shields from the rectory barn: Abbot Gilbert of Bruton and two Mohun family.

Now from the Market Place SE down St James's Street. The BREWERS ARMS, 1622, has dormer gables. ST JAMES'S HOUSE, to the r., is C17 remodelled *c.* 1790 with pedimented doorcase. At the foot, the DAVID HALL was the Congregational church of 1862–3. Rock-faced Gothic with pinnacles and five-light window. In a Gothic group, also the MANSE, 1868, with cast-iron window columns, and large SUNDAY SCHOOL, 1882. On South Street, KNAP HOUSE is ashlar-fronted late C18, between C19 additions, the bowed r. end more of a screen than integral. WEST HAYES, ostensibly a Late Georgian villa with Ionic porch, is dated 1743 and was clearly one with the mullioned C17 house adjoining. Regency interiors. SOUTH STREET FARM, 1700, is substantial, with continuous hoodmoulds. At the far end, COLES FARM, a neat early C19 brick box with centre pediment. Coles Lane runs E up to the CEMETERY, 1867, by *J. M. Allen*, with near-matching chapels (a bellcote for the Anglicans). On Hayes End are the Gothic SCHOOL, 1879, and HAYES END MANOR, externally C17 but originating as a C15 hall house. C16 moulded framed ceiling. Two impressive outbuildings, a three-floor GRANARY and a very large FLAX BARN, 1803, with gambrel roof, have been converted as part of a retirement complex, 1986, by *Sidell Gibson*.

HOLBROOK PARK, Stoodham. Self-build project of timber-framed houses based on Walter Segal plans, 1996–7 by *David Innes-Wilkin*. Boarded, balconied on two floors.

PETHERTON BRIDGE, 1 m. E on the A303. Affixed to the ugly modern bridge is an eroded C14 double effigy from the triple-arched previous bridge, probably the donors. Civilian and wife on a single block of Ham stone, legless, as if kneeling.

COMPTON DURVILLE MANOR, 1 m. WNW. C17, mullion-windowed with storeyed porch. N cross-wing of 1926–7 with a second-floor chapel. Buildings opposite for an Anglican Franciscan community, 1963–4, by *Roydon Cooper Associates*. Bell-turret, 1828, from Sandpit Mill, Broadwindsor, Dorset.

BARCROFT HALL, 1 m. N. 1987–8, by *Shrimpton & Salmon* of Ludlow. Large and not quite Early Georgian in brick and Ham stone.

SPARGROVE see WESTCOMBE

SPARKFORD

ST MARY MAGDALENE. Perp W tower and chancel; nave rebuilt 1824 by *Thomas Ellis* of Sherborne. C15 tower niche with incurved finials. Typical early C19 Y-tracery to the nave and two S projections – a chapel (with reused C16 side windows) and a vestry. C15 tower arch with single shafts, chancel arch with triple ones. – FONT. Octagonal, C13–C14. – PULPIT. C17, with long feathers at the angles, as at Ansford. – STALLS. Reused C15–C16 bench-ends. – SCULPTURE. Crucifixion, 1953, by *William Thornton*. Bronze nail-like forms. – STAINED GLASS. E window, 1910, and S chapel E, *c.* 1920, both by *A. K. Nicholson*. S chapel W, Flemish C17 panel.

On the old main road, the SPARKFORD INN, C17, with an early C19 stuccoed front. Just N, THE ROUNDHOUSE, thatched, C18, the r. half an unexplained big drum. HOME FARMHOUSE has C17 ovolo-moulded mullions. Over the railway, the two-storey early C19 OCTAGON is also unexplained; not a toll house. S towards the church, the former RECTORY, Ainstey Drive, 1838, by *Maurice Davis*, is symmetrical neo-Tudor. MANOR FARMHOUSE is mid-C17, T-plan, with timber mullions.

SPARKFORD HALL, N of the A303. 1840s, for the squire-vicar Henry Bennett. Finely tooled Lias with ashlar detail elegantly done. Four-bay front, square-pillar side porch.

HAZLEGROVE HOUSE. See p. 349.

SPAXTON

ST MARGARET. Perp three-stage tower for which John Hill left money in 1434. Mixed red and buff sandstones, the lower stage on the W and the diagonal buttresses faced in the buff local ashlar. Pointed two-light bell-openings, and blind flat-headed two-light windows in the second stage. Elongated heads terminate the hoodmoulds of the W door and window. A great deal of evidence of an earlier church. A Norman or earlier nave is identified by herringbone masonry in the N wall, and the chancel has a C13 E window (renewed), three lights with three roundels, all uncusped. Also two small plate-traceried windows of *c.* 1300 in the nave and N chapel, of two cusped ogee lights with a pointed quatrefoil. The S aisle is a showpiece, typical of the region, and typically late, probably of 1536. Buff ashlar with large four-light windows, gable parapets, and quatrefoil-pierced battlements over lively carved beasts. Storeyed porch with a corner stair-turret. Three-bay arcade on standard shafted four-hollow piers, but the two-bay arcade to the SE chapel has capitals overlaid by a band of leaf scroll. Broad late C14 wave-moulded chancel arch. Tall shafted tower arch. C15–C16 wagon roofs on egg-and-dart cornices left from C18 plaster ceilings.

FURNISHINGS. FONT. C14, octagonal, tapered below. – BENCHES. Mostly C16, characterized by Renaissance ornament without religious imagery. A group in the S aisle W, dated 1536, includes a finely detailed bird with outstretched wings, initialled IB. These resemble work at Barwick. The main group, dated 1561, includes profile heads, and one exceptional depiction of a fuller at work. – POSTS. Two C17 Ionic columns covered in vine-trail, formerly gallery posts, as at East Brent. – ROYAL ARMS. Carved. Later C17. – STAINED GLASS. SE window, 1898, by *A. L. Moore*, richly coloured. W, SW, and two N windows, by *Hardman*, early C20. – MONUMENTS. Knight and his lady, either John Hill †1434, who willed his burial here or his son †1456. A handsome canopied tomb between chancel and N chapel. Two effigies, he in plate armour of mid-C15 type, she with angels at her pillow, on a tomb-chest with shields in panels that are cusped and pointed at head and foot. Four-centred canopy arch with foliage spandrels, thick cusping and sub-cusping (better preserved on the N) and cornice under an attic of shields in crocketed ogee panels. Panelled and cusped soffit – Mary York †1729. Lias, incised with rare skill. Scrolled pediment and putti holding emblems of mortality. – Rev. W. Yorke †1817. Oval between detached Ionic columns, by *J. Wood* of Bristol.

CHURCHYARD CROSS. C15, notably intact. Tabernacle head carved with the Crucifixion on both faces and a canopied figure on each narrow side, all in shallow relief. Also a shield with weaver's shuttles.

COURT FARM, N of the church. Manor house of the Hill family from 1395, an oratory recorded in 1408, a hall with parlour and chamber in 1423, a gatehouse in 1662. Two hall ranges at right angles, both with pointed doorways to cross-passages. The W range has Georgian front windows. At the back, a lateral chimney marks the hall and the gable to the r. with two-light Perp window may be a hall oriel. Stonework shows that both chimney and gable are added. A second cross-passage, with blocked Tudor-arched doorways, just N of the first, separates a possible service end, raised and given cusped two-light windows to both floors in the C15. The N range has three similar first-floor S windows, and a cross-passage at the extreme r., but no evidence of a lost building beyond that. Both ranges have smoke-blackened jointed-cruck roofs, neither of particular quality. Cusped braces reused in the main roof indicate that something grander has gone. BARN to the E, with another jointed-cruck roof, with wind-braces. Blocked mullion windows on two levels suggest a domestic use originally.

The COTTAGES W of the churchyard were the C15 church house. PEART HALL was the rectory. Large hip-roofed, five-bay Regency front range added to a C16 house, remodelled in the C18. NE of the church, at SPLATT MILL, the house is C15–C16 with jointed crucks and a moulded framed ceiling. This has a painted C16–C17 frieze of foliage scroll with half-naked angels holding roundels with shields. Upstairs a biblical text dated 1690.

FOUR FORKS, ½ m. E. The interest here is the Agapemone, the religious community founded after 1840 by the Rev. Henry Prince, curate at Charlinch, self-proclaimed immortal. Continued after his death by the Rev. Hugh Smyth-Pigott, who declared himself Messiah in 1902. The community survived until 1958. Buildings of 1846, by *William Cobbe*, engineer (converted while surveying the Bristol & Exeter Railway). Lancet-Gothic CHAPEL, formerly with a large lion on the gable. Early C20 Arts and Crafts glazing. The HOUSE has neo-Tudor ashlar bays. The Reading architect *Joseph Morris*, an Agapemonite, retired here and designed the rearmost addition, 1888, in red sandstone, like a Victorian vicarage. His daughter, *Violet Morris*, pioneer woman architect, designed houses for the community.

These were roughcast with the battered buttresses and chimneys typical of Voysey. THE EAST GATE, 1905, for her parents, was followed by THE WEST GATE, 1908, THE NORTH GATE, 1915, and, across the crossroads, THE LARCHES, 1921. The East Gate has the best detail, the door pierced with hearts, the staircase with tall flat newels and spatula balusters carved by *Olive Morris*, Violet's sister, in Celtic style.

LONGTHORNS, ¾ m. E of Four Forks. Late C19 stucco villa with a small Italianate belvedere tower.

Two nearby houses illustrate repair in the SPAB tradition, both begun in the 1990s, both altered medieval hall houses. CLERK'S COTTAGE, S of Four Forks, repaired from ruin by *Cyril Harriss*, was an early C15 hall with jointed crucks and square-set ridge. A plank partition with traces of C16 painted decoration carries the jettied floor of the W solar. C16 rear wing, with jointed crucks. PEACOCK COTTAGE, Pightley, repaired by *Paul Richold*, has a limewashed front with C17 oak first-floor mullions; the original, steeper roof at the back. C16 framed ceiling, and C17 plaster friezes of fish-tailed beasts and delicate flowers.

STAPLE FITZPAINE

ST PETER. Ornate Perp W tower, almost identical to Kingston St Mary and Isle Abbots. Blue Lias, with Ham stone angle buttresses decorated with two tiers of attached pinnacles and tall, diagonally set pinnacles at bell-stage level. A corner insert, this also with pinnacles, gives the illusion that the buttresses are set back. Finally there are big angle pinnacles with thin outriders and smaller diagonally set intermediate pinnacles, rising through pierced battlements. Fine set of thin-legged beasts. W window of four lights over a doorway flanked by niches, and niches on busts of angels flanking a middle-stage two-light transomed window. Two similar bell-openings above, between three thin shafts carrying pinnacles. Pierced baffles. Polygonal NE stair-turret, ringed with pinnacles and spired. Tall moulded tower arch. The church itself after this display seems modest. Externally it is Perp with aisles. But the story is more complicated. The S aisle is of 1841, copying the N, and the N aisle has reused fragments, two small figures under canopies (St Michael and Christ) at the angles and a cusped ogee stoup. And there is a good Norman S doorway. Pale stone, without columns, the inner arch with chevron, the outer with varied jelly-mould roundels alternated with diaper. Abaci with corner heads, a scallop shell, a beast and a bird. Norman fragments also in the back of the chamfered early C14 chancel arch. Three-bay arcades of standard Perp elements (piers of four-hollow type), plus a very narrow fourth bay. Wagon roofs with wall-plate angels. In the N aisle NE corner a Perp canopied niche on a grotesque corbel. In the adjoining window jamb, a little canopied niche. – FONT. Perp, octagonal. – ROOD SCREEN. Four-light sections with depressed pointed arches. Surely mid-C19, matching the PULPIT and DESK. A medieval screen was brought from Bickenhall in 1849. Perhaps this is the VESTRY SCREEN, of two four-light traceried sections. – STAINED GLASS. Chancel windows of *c.* 1851. – MONUMENT. Rachael Portman †1632. Kneeling painted figure (from Bickenhall).

CHURCHYARD CROSS. 1894. With well-carved tabernacle head. Medieval base.

A very small VILLAGE. THE MANOR, s of the church, is large and Tudor Gothic of 1840 with numerous octagonal chimneys, for a wealthy Portman rector. The PORTMAN ALMSHOUSES, NE, date from 1643. Symmetrical, with mullioned windows and four dormer gables.

PERRY HALL FARM, ½ m. SE. L-plan, thatched. The front range a C14–C15 hall house with one arch-braced true cruck truss, at 22 ft (6.7 metres) the widest in Somerset after the Mells tithe barn (N).

STAPLEGROVE

2020

ST JOHN. An unadorned s porch-tower, the doorway C13 with continuous double chamfer. Perp small bell-lights. The rest was remodelled by *C. E. Giles* in 1857. Only the N aisle W window looks pre-Victorian. *Giles* replaced the arcade and extended the nave one bay W. The plain pointed chancel arch and plain rounded arch to the SE chapel could be C13. – FONT. 1857. Minutely carved by *Henry Davis*. – PULPIT. Oak, 1909, by *Arthur Parkin* of *Trask & Co*. A bravura piece with foliage columns, influenced by Henry Wilson. Some similar BENCH-ENDS. – IRONWORK. Tree of Life, 1973, by *James Horrobin*. Designed by *Robin Shirley-Smith*. – STAINED GLASS. W window, archangels, by *Kempe*, 1897. E window by *A. L. Moore*, 1906. S window by *Henry Haig*, 2000, semi-abstract aspiring flames. – MONUMENTS. James Minifie †1725. Careful Palladian. – Rev. James Minifie †1789. Plaque and urn on yellow, by *Thomas King*.

NE of the church, POMEROY'S FARMHOUSE, stuccoed and hip-roofed, and the former RECTORY, 1809, similar but larger, with canted bays and columned doorcase. NORWOOD and STEADING HAY have matching mid-C19 bargeboards and verandas, but Norwood is structurally C17. STAPLEGROVE MANOR looks Edwardian from a remodelling in 1908 by *F. W. Roberts*, roughcast with gabled bays. One end rides on a colonnade with curved-pedimented doorway. On the Minehead road, STAPLEGROVE HOUSE, a hip-roofed square villa, 'newly built' in 1828, and STAPLEGROVE ELM (Nuffield Hospital), a villa of 1837, by *Richard Carver*, with an elegant recessed Ionic porch, pediment, and deep eaves.

YARDE FARMHOUSE, 1 m. NW. Long late C17 brick house with a storeyed porch. Framed hall ceiling with rustic cherub-head and leaf motifs in the plaster panels. Deep-coved parlour ceiling with bolection-moulded panel.

STAVORDALE PRIORY
Charlton Musgrove

Augustinian priory founded in the early C13, oddly just three miles from the priory at Bruton. The church was rebuilt by John Stourton before 1443. It survived, as a farmhouse in the chancel, a barn in the nave, before restoration by *Thomas Collcutt* in 1904–5 as a country house for the shopfitter Frederick Sage. The cloister to the N had gone. *Collcutt* added a range on the site of the E cloister to link to a small C14 reredorter. Restored from 1995 by *Keith Leaman* for Sir Cameron Mackintosh.

Four-bay nave and four-bay buttressed chancel. A broad C14 S arch marks a demolished porch-tower. The nave has renewed Perp tracery and a small E bellcote. Disturbed NW masonry at the join of the lost cloister. *Collcutt* kept the chancel as he found it, floored, with inserted early C18 bead-moulded cross-windows. *Leaman* restored tracery to the E window. On the N side is the glory of Stavordale, the early C16 Jesus Chapel added by Lord Zouche, a Yorkist, who retired here after Bosworth. Segmental-pointed E and N windows, fine tracery with supermullions to the E window, C18 infill in the N one. Lively animals on the buttresses. *Collcutt's* wing wisely attempts no rivalry; tall, with strong unadorned chimneys.

Much survives inside despite the inserted floors, C16 in the chancel, 1904 in the nave. The nave roof is ceiled, above cambered tie-beams bracketed from stone corbels. It was still open in 1785. Moulded C15 S piscina. The panelled and shafted chancel arch has leaf capitals. Its mouldings stop high to allow for a screen. The chancel roof, fully visible, has similar tie-beams on magnificent stone shield-bearing angels (except at each end where there are carved heads). On the ground floor are a pointed recess with C13 foliated capitals on the S wall (possibly re-assembled) and two polygonal C15 corbels on carved heads on the E wall, for statues. On the N is a damaged Perp tomb-recess, originally between piers with finials. Also a pointed doorway, probably to the sacristy – see the stoup outside. Subtly indistinct neo-medieval painting by *Fleur Kelly*. Then an elaborate square-headed doorway (monogrammed Z) by a tall panelled four-centred arch to the JESUS CHAPEL. The fine carving of the doorway and arch introduces that of the chapel itself, with some lovely minor detail and a fan-vault of one and a half bays, the cones on tiny angels. The W wall has two-tier stone panelling, shield-bearing angels beneath glazed panels lighting *Collcutt*'s stair hall. His staircase has a curved panelled ceiling. The C14 REREDORTER uses the local Greensand stone hardly found elsewhere in the priory. The offset E window and drain arch, and N ventilation slots, indicate first-floor lavatories.

To the W, new BUILDINGS and SWIMMING POOL by *Leaman*.

STAWELL

ST FRANCIS. Blue Lias. The broad squat W tower is unfinished. The base with diagonal buttresses, square NE turret, and plain chamfered tower arch is C13–C14, the three-light W window a Perp insertion. The second stage was finished with a steep gable perhaps in 1610 (date on the E side). The rest, a single vessel, is C13. It was aisled on the N side, the blocked three-bay arcade visible inside. Broad double-chamfered arches on round piers with moulded capitals. In the chancel one lancet window each side and a three-light E window of cusped lancets, all renewed in 1874. Perp S porch. – FONT. C15. Shallow, octagonal, with square quatrefoils. – MONUMENT. Ann Dawbin †1814. Urn above an oval plaque, by *Henry Wood*.

THE MANOR, W of the church, 1735. Stuccoed, four bays, with curved-headed windows. Panelled ground-floor rooms. The OLD APPLE STORE, a small energy-saving development, 2008–10, by *Malcolm McCall*, executed by *O2i Design*, is conventional to the street, but two houses behind have green roofs and balconied timber garden fronts. E of the church, the mansard-roofed OLD MANOR HOUSE, *c.* 1800, of brick, and a very Gothic rock-faced former SCHOOL, 1872.

FORD FARMHOUSE, ½ m. NNW. Square hip-roofed house with three-bay fronts and mid-C18 Gibbsian doorcase.

STAWLEY

ST MICHAEL. Behind a farm on a hillside. Roughcast three-stage Perp W tower with polygonal NE turret. Above the W doorway a quatrefoil frieze of Ham stone with shields. The central scrolled inscription reads 'Pray for the sowle of Henry Howe and Agnes his wyffe AD 1523', the first words reversed with the twist of the scroll. Also the Poulett arms. Tall chamfered tower arch. On the nave N wall some early herringbone masonry. The S doorway is late C14, but the DOOR itself with bifurcated iron straps looks earlier, even C13. A cusped C14 lancet to the l. and Perp two-light of red sandstone to the r. The plain pointed chancel doorway and adjoining paired lancets may be C13. C15–C16 wagon roofs. The delight of Stawley is the Late Georgian FITTINGS: panelled PULPIT with ogee tester; high panelled PEWS and panelled dados; turned and alternately fluted

COMMUNION RAILS; painted ROYAL ARMS (1795); and Commandment, Creed and Lord's Prayer BOARDS (1819 and 1826). – FONT. C13, octagonal, chamfered below, on a broached octagonal stem.

Scattered farmhouses. HILL FARMHOUSE, ¾ m. s, is L-plan, late C16, with lateral chimney and framed ceiling. N, on a lane into the Tone valley, are BURROW FARMHOUSE, colourwashed, C16–C17, BENNETTS, early C17, red sandstone, and CARDS FARMHOUSE with C16 jointed crucks, rebuilt from ruin. HAGLEY BRIDGE FARMHOUSE, 1 m. N, is late C16, L-plan, partly of cob, with a lateral chimney and framed ceiling.

STEART

A windswept spit projecting into Bridgwater Bay.

ST ANDREW. 1882. A little brick chapel, red and buff without, buff and red within, the interior charming in its simplicity.

STOCKLAND BRISTOL

ST MARY MAGDALENE. 1865–7, by *Oswald Arthur* of Plymouth. Blue Lias with Bath dressings. Cruciform, with a W tower. Dec detail, with the angularity favoured in the 1860s (cf. Combwich). – FONT. Early Perp. Octagonal bowl with pointed quatrefoils. Underside foliage and shields. – SCREEN. C15–C16. Four-light tracery, undercut foliage along the rail, and crocketed ogee base panels. Outer panels and cornice by *Bligh Bond*, 1920. – PULPIT. 1867. Massive. – STAINED GLASS. E window, 1867, by *Clayton & Bell*, excellent, with much red and blue. W window, 1882, perhaps by *F. Drake*.

Thomas Daniel of Stoodleigh, Devon, built the church and STOCKLAND MANOR, 1860, for his son, the vicar. The house is Victorian Tudor, large, with arrays of octagonal chimneys and mullion-and-transom windows. The son built the attractive SCHOOL, 1880, and VICARAGE, 1883, the school with flèche and tile-hung gables, the vicarage Gothic, informally composed.

ROGERS FARMHOUSE, at the E end of the village, has plasterwork dated 1675.

STOCKLINCH

Two churches, Stocklinch Magdalen, in the village, and Stocklinch Ottersey, beautifully alone on a slope to the E.

STOCKLINCH

ST MARY MAGDALEN. Small and pretty. Perp nave, Dec chancel. W bellcote for three bells, the openings adapted for large ringing-wheels. Three-light E window with simple flowing tracery. Perp s porch with monolithic four-centred-arched doorhead and sundial dated 1612. Perp nave roof and shafted chancel arch. Earlier corbel heads above. Ogee-cusped chancel PISCINA. – WEST GALLERY. Mid-C18, coloured blue, with King David painted on the arched centre panel. – FONT. C12, not round but sixteen-sided. – PULPIT. Altered C18 three-decker with tester. Reading desk fixed to a box pew. – PEWS. 1908, by *Rupert Austin.* – ROYAL ARMS. George I. Formerly on tympanum boarding in the chancel arch. – COMMUNION RAILS. Early C17. Vertically symmetrical balusters.

ST MARY, Stocklinch Ottersey (Churches Conservation Trust). Modest Perp w tower with battlements and short polygonal N stair. Shafted tower arch. The nave is C14 – from the wave-moulded s doorway. Porch with stone-slab roof. Large s transept of *c.* 1300 with remarkable Dec s window, traceried in cusped kite shapes and triangles. Dec side windows. In the E wall a good C13 grave-slab with raised cross. Chancel rebuilt by *J. M. Allen,* 1856. Narrow whitewashed interior. Early C14 s tomb-recess with roses instead of points to the cusps. Panelled C15 chancel arch built across the transept arcade, indicating an undivided earlier church. Double-chamfered transept arches on an octagonal pier and king and queen corbels. From the transept, a large quatrefoil once opened to the nave. Shafted window reveals in the transept, the s one with bold open cusping. Ogee PISCINA with carved head below. – FONT. C12, tapered, with band of delicate leaf scroll, like Middle Chinnock. – ROYAL ARMS. 1664. – STAINED GLASS. E window, 1882, and one transept window, 1891, by *Ward & Hughes.* Two by *Morris & Co.*, 1911 and 1921, still to *Burne-Jones* designs. – MONUMENT. Eroded late C13 effigy of a lady.

Below Stocklinch Ottersey church, STOCKLINCH MANOR is stuccoed Victorian with verandas. The VILLAGE has several late medieval houses typically with jointed crucks and inserted smoke-hoods. The lane E ends at one, UNDERHILL, with chamfered framed ceiling. Going W, STOCKLINCH GROVE, dated 1653, is grander, mullion-windowed with gabled porch. C17 plaster vine frieze upstairs. Early C18 panelled rear room. By Stocklinch Magdalen church, MANNINGS, with post-and-truss framing exposed at one end, and a large smoke-hood. At the N end on Stoney Lane, MAGDALEN COTTAGE, with heavy oak door frame; BRAKES COTTAGE, partly rendered over cob, a C14–C15 cruck exposed at one end; and JOHNSON'S ORCHARD, of longhouse type, with three C14 full crucks. Lastly THE CHANTRY, with post-and-truss framing one end. Chamfered framed ceiling.

ATHERSTONE FARM, ½ m. s. Mullion-windowed C17 farmhouse by a large farm courtyard, partly thatched C18, partly C19. An estate farm of Dillington.

STOFORD
SE of Barwick

A medieval borough that declined by the C17 after the London road passed to Yeovil. On the N side of the green, THE GUILDHALL, recorded as building in 1353. Two-centred-arched doorway with big hoodmould. Mullioned and hoodmoulded windows of C16–C17 type. On the S, STOFORD FARMHOUSE, mid-C19, mullioned. STOFORD BRIDGE, small, of two arches with a high cutwater, is mentioned in the C16 by Leland.

YEOVIL JUNCTION STATION, ½ m. NE. Opened 1860, the third of the four stations that Yeovil achieved in eight years. Platform building with canopies, 1907–9, for the London & South Western Railway. The brick shed of 1864 was for goods transfer from GWR broad gauge to narrow gauge.

STOGUMBER

ST MARY. A large and complicated church, equally interesting in its architectural history and its furnishings. Mostly of red sandstone, the N aisle of the buff sandstone ashlar. The rather plain SW tower comes first, probably early C14 (see the two tower arches). To the nave a big arch with a continuous triple chamfer and to the aisle a double chamfer. Diagonal buttresses up to the bell-stage, two-light C14 ground-floor windows on both W and S. The W window is partly covered by a square stair-turret. It serves a battlemented Perp bell-stage with two-light openings (longer, with transoms, N and S). The S porch is also early C14, and embattled. Only the first arch remains of a contemporary S arcade, to go with a nave which no longer exists. Octagonal red sandstone pier and W respond, flared out to the plainest capitals. The next two bays are C15, in different stone with standard four-hollow piers and small circular capitals to the shafts. Contrasting square-headed aisle windows, the eastern one (re-set in a C19 organ chamber) with a variant on the odd tracery of Watchet and Old Cleeve. At much the same time (C15) a substantial SE chapel was added for the Sydenhams of Combe Sydenham. Three bays, taller and quite distinct, although not especially rich, despite having battlements and pinnacles. Big three-light windows, one of the three on the S and the E window blocked by later monuments. The chancel was expensively renewed in 1873–5 by *J. D. Sedding*, for the Rowcliffes of Halsway Manor.

The N aisle is the last part of the church, notably finer than the Sydenham Chapel, one of those showpiece aisles added *c.* 1500 to churches in this part of Somerset (cf. Bishop's Lydeard, Bicknoller, Watchet). The especial prominence may be because it faces the village square, or because it included the chapel of the Stradlings of Halsway. A fine seven-bay display, the battlements with quatrefoils and good cornice beasts, some carrying diagonal shafts and pinnacles. Tall gabled porch with two large three-light windows each side, then an octagonal rood-stair turret, and two matching windows to the chapel.

Now back to the interior. The N arcade is of five bays with piers of the four-wave section and capitals with well-carved bands of leaves. Each is different, one with Passion emblems on shields. The two-bay NE chapel arcade has similar piers and capitals, but because the arcade was cut through thick wall, the piers are stretched such that narrow W–E arches could be opened in the wall thickness. The band capitals are correspondingly stretched to run right around. In the E respond a green man. Under the arcade may have been the Easter sepulchre and founder's tomb, or the founder could have occupied the simple N tomb-recess. Good continuous wagon roof. Broad wagon roof in the nave, with good bosses, but that in the Sydenham Chapel very economical. The chancel arch matches the S arcade, and the three-bay arcade to the Sydenham Chapel is similar. Good wrought-iron C19 RAILINGS in the chapel arches. The chancel is a rich later Victorian piece, the walls stencilled in a Morrisian damask pattern, dark blue and gold, and the roof more cheerfully in red and white. *Sedding* was the designer, *G. W. Seale* carved the lavish stone REREDOS, where Christ ascends through the frame between marble columns and alabaster sides, and the vicar, the *Rev. Edward Jones*, stencilled the walls. Encaustic TILES on the E wall and floors.

OTHER FURNISHINGS. FONT. Octagonal, Late Perp, with shields or fleurons in quatrefoils. The panelling of the stem is carried on to the underside (cf. Timberscombe). – PULPIT. Stone, c. 1500, on a thin stem, but entirely recut. Cusped panels and diagonal angle shafts. The foliage carving below resembles the N arcade capitals. – BENCHES. Numerous, C16, the ends mostly carved with close tracery. Trevelyan arms on one. – DOOR to the rood stair. Small and closely traceried with some foliage decoration. Original ironwork, especially an excellent door handle. – CANDELABRA. Brass, spectacularly large, by *Thomas Bayley*, 1770 (cf. Old Cleeve). – STAINED GLASS. By *Clayton & Bell* the E window, c. 1865, and the NE chapel and W window of 1875 and later, showing the firm's transition from C14 to Late Gothic styles. Medieval fragments in some N windows. – MONUMENTS. Margery Wyndham †1585. In the NE tomb-recess. Small brass figure. – Sir George Sydenham †1597, in pride of place, between the Sydenham Chapel and chancel. A contrast of quality, not unusual at this period. The effigies, he in armour raised up above two uncomfortably squeezed wives, are hardly fine work, nor the little relief of three swaddled babies with a kneeling woman. And the inscription, 'Sir Gorge Sidnum' is no error, as repeated both sides. Yet the canopy is both monumental and finely detailed. Three pairs of half-fluted Corinthian columns on each side carry twin arches, these connected by finely coffered vaults. Poor-quality heraldry and sculpture on top. – George Musgrave †1721. Lias slab, with flamboyant incised heraldry. – Thomas Musgrave †1723 and George Musgrave †1724. Large and handsome. A double-curved pediment and pilasters frame twin long panels framed in grey marble, with heraldry above. Skull and palm branches beneath. – Thomas Rich of Hartrow, 1731. Baroque, of high quality, in varied marbles. Double-curved pediment on which recline putti. The side volutes, decorated with acanthus, are overgrown with lovely oak leaves and acorns. – Thomas Musgrave †1766. In coloured marbles with well-carved small detail, an urn above.

CHURCHYARD CROSS. C14 base and thick shaft, with a terrible Victorian top.

The church in its large churchyard crowns a little hill. Behind the churchyard, HALL FARM BARN, with heavy C16 jointed-cruck trusses. In front of the church, the WHITE HORSE INN includes at the r. a pyramid-roofed former MARKET of *c.* 1800. It had an upstairs assembly room. On High Street, the OLD VICARAGE is late medieval with a pointed-arched doorway, and incorporates a three-bay roof of arched-braced jointed crucks. Regency wing at right angles. The outbuilding behind, perhaps a medieval kitchen, became the church house in the C16, the large fireplace adapted for brewing. On the lower road, THE ALMONRY was almshouses for six widows, founded by Sir George Sydenham. A single-storey row of *c.* 1600 with six red sandstone two-light windows alternated with depressed-arched doorways. Further down, set back, is a hip-roofed BAPTIST CHAPEL, rebuilt in 1869, the front partly obscured by the slightly earlier manse. WICK HOUSE, adjoining, has a good early C19 trellis veranda. On the hillside further s, OLD WAY HOUSE, thatched, with a central hip-roofed stair projection, dated 1635. On the Vellow road, JAMES BARTON is recorded from 1510, thatched and roughcast. Jointed-cruck trusses and an inserted framed ceiling.

STATION, 1 m. E. 1862. Sweetly small, red sandstone, for the West Somerset Railway.

VELLOW, 1 m. N. Hamlet of red sandstone rows, several thatched, backing on to an impressive quarry face. Slightly s, by another quarry, a large early C19 LIMEKILN. S again, at right angles to the road, THE CHANTRY, a thatched cottage, formerly the chapel of Our Lady Sweetwell, licensed in 1542. On the N side a Tudor-arched doorway and two-light window. Wagon roof with moulded ribs and wall-plate.

STOGURSEY

A small borough founded before 1225, the name the Englished form of Stoke Courcy.

St Andrew. Given by William de Falaise II to the Abbey of Lonlay in Normandy, between 1100 and 1107. Stogursey was until 1414 a Benedictine priory, a cell of Lonlay and mother church of at least one further cell, Black Abbey at Ards, Co. Down, in 1183. The implication of the gift is that a church was already built. The style of the crossing makes a date not many years before 1100 likely. To this original cruciform church was added a Late Norman chancel and chancel aisles. The priory was suppressed with the alien priories in 1414, the lands and revenues being given to the royal foundation of Eton College in 1440. The nave was rebuilt *c.* 1500 apart from the Norman w doorway, and the transepts and chancel aisles remodelled. The external detail is almost all renewed, in 1823–4 by *Richard Carver* and 1864–5 by *John Norton*. White roughcast, with a broad rectangular crossing tower and copper-clad spire. Neo-Norman bell-openings by *Norton*, who added the tower parapet. The spire was probably an addition of the C13–C14, since rebuilt. The chancel E end is neo-Norman, by *Norton*, replacing Perp work.

The church given to Lonlay was already ambitious in size, but with a short one-bay chancel and three staggered apses, two attached to the transepts and one at the E end. This plan occurs with modifications at Muchelney Abbey, also at Melbourne (Derbys.) and Old Shoreham (Sussex), but is more common in Normandy and France and especially in C11 Germany. The length of the nave may be original unless the Norman w doorway is re-set. The crossing remains in fine completeness: four broad and strong arches on sturdy attached columns. The arches are single-stepped but the western faces of the nave and chancel arches are moulded with a multiple roll moulding, possibly altered when the chancel aisles were built. Their outer arches, a kind of ridge-and-furrow under a billet hood-moulding to the nave and an incised zigzag to the chancel arch, hardly accord with *c.* 1090. Above the chancel arch a Norman window now looking into the chancel. The capitals ought to be studied one by one. They are all different, decidedly Early Norman in character, and have stunted volutes. Otherwise there are upright leaves of various kinds, in one, two or three rows, including classical anthemion. Also there are ill-conceived lions, addorsed winged creatures and a green man. Only the chancel arch capitals are of Ham stone. They could be copies of 1864–5. Herringbone masonry is exposed in the upper chambers, so the whole tower is Early Norman. The transepts are now roofed in line with the later chancel chapels. Traces of the former N transept roof against the tower N side. In the tower W face a curious splayed doorway.

The outlines of the apses E of the transepts and the original chancel apse, found in excavation, are marked out in the paving. They were removed late in the C12 when the chancel was lengthened and given aisles. Their floor level is much higher than that of the crossing and must have been still higher – see the pedestals under the arcades. So there must have been a broad central flight of steps, something more often found on the Continent than in England. The arcades each have a circular central pier rather fatter than the responds, the piers apparently renewed, and many-scalloped capitals. The arches display all the exuberant chevron decoration of the latest stage of Norman as found at Glastonbury Abbey, across western England and at St Davids Cathedral, Pembrokeshire. The chevron is at right angles, at an angle of 45 degrees, and in two kinds of sawtooth. A dogtooth hoodmould terminates in little heads. The most likely date is 1180 or 1185; for work started at Glastonbury in 1184 and at Wells a little earlier, and that is decidedly one step in advance of Stogursey. The E end, of 1865, has much marble shafting, to the windows, reredos, piscina and sedilia. Arcaded reredos inlaid in coloured marbles, with Evangelist heads in roundels above. The chancel aisles were remodelled *c.* 1500 with Perp windows and arches from the transepts. The S aisle became the chapel of the Verneys and subsequent owners of Fairfield. The N aisle had two chapels and an added two-storey vestry. The second chapel is now the organ chamber. Roofs of 1865, with neo-Norman detail over the chancel. The TRANSEPTS, of the initial phase, were remodelled with the chancel chapels in the C15, and re-roofed in 1865. In the W wall of the N transept the remains of a small Norman doorway. The small S transept doorway, partly Norman although Perp externally, probably communicated with the monastic buildings. The NAVE is Perp apart from the heavily renewed Norman W doorway, with mouldings similar to the eastern crossing arch. Plainly traceried Perp five-light W window and large three-light N and S windows, these renewed by *Carver*. On the N side is a large porch. Inside, the pulpit stands in a panelled recess, probably a tomb-recess, next to the rood stair. Roof of 1865 with angels, the corner ones C15–C16.

FURNISHINGS. FONTS. Two Norman monoliths. The Stogursey font, a red cylinder, has four strange masks, very elementary in the carving, between a band of cable and a rim of saltire crosses. The font from Lilstock (*see* Kilton) is slightly later. A band of incised chevron between simple mouldings, over heavy spiral fluting. – PULPIT. 1940s, of Jacobean parts. It replaces a stone neo-Norman pulpit, for which the Jacobean one, now at West Huntspill (q.v.), was ejected. – BENCH-ENDS. A particularly good set, with more Renaissance ornament than usual but also medieval close-knit tracery and wiry plants. Several birds: a pelican and double-eagle on one; another, uniquely, shows a spoonbill with an eel in its bill. On another a little man in a loincloth holds aloft a branch, standing on a Renaissance baluster. The initials IS ES and SE may refer to *Isabell & Elizabeth Symons*, who with *Robert Evered* were paid for making benches in 1534–9. – BANNERS. Two Late Georgian Friendly Society banners, one with 'God save the King' and Hanoverian arms, the other 'God speed the plough' and Ceres. – CANDELABRA. 1732, three-tier, by *John Bayley* of Bridgwater.

– FOSSIL. In the N transept floor, an Ichthyosaurus. – STAINED GLASS. E window, 1866, by *Lavers & Barraud*, superb colours. W window, 1871, possibly by *Burlison & Grylls*. C16 style, the Creation to Jonah. – MONUMENTS. S chapel. William de Verney †1333. Stiff effigy holding a heart. – John de Verney †1461. A fine piece, of Beer stone. Effigy in plate armour, his bare head resting on his helm. Tomb-chest with six shallow niches each side, divided by cusped panels. The niches have small characterful figures in contemporary dress. At the W end a queen, at the E St John. – Col. Peregrine Palmer †1684. Good cartouche with cherubs' heads and flowers, a favourite type of the Gibbons period. – Nathaniel Palmer †1717. Standing monument of two mourning cherubs by an obelisk garnished with flowers. – Sir Thomas Wroth †1721. Excellent standing monument. Made after 1737, probably by *Henry Cheere* (Matthew Craske). An open-pedimented niche frames a beautifully carved cherub and Rococo shield on a scroll-pedimented yellow marble pedestal. A brown marble urn each side.

BURTON BAPTIST CHAPEL, 1 m. NW. 1833. Square, pyramid-roofed with arched windows and Georgian Gothic glazing.

STOGURSEY CASTLE, ¼ m. S (Landmark Trust). Held by William de Falaise in 1086 and by the de Courcys until 1194, the castle is first mentioned when a chapel is recorded in 1204. Its military history is scant. Hugh de Neville was ordered to re-fortify in 1233. Records of repairs indicate how much has gone: in 1304 to bridges, in 1473–4 to the kitchen chimney and roofs of the hall and chamber, and in the 1490s to two towers which were re-roofed. A new one which was added at this date was in decay in 1538.

What remains is exceptionally pretty. The yellow-washed thatched cottage reflected in the moat stands on the remains of twin E gatehouse towers. The moat is spanned by a twin-arched medieval bridge and a modern replacement for the drawbridge. The water encircles a roughly circular raised site without buildings inside, but with substantial remains of the curtain wall and the base of a round W tower (shown in the Buck drawing of 1733). Evidence has been found of buildings against the curtain, but not of a keep. The curtain was apparently polygonal, which would have made a fine show, but has been rebuilt less formally at the NW. It is possible that there is C12 masonry below C13 work, but very little is datable. To the S and E are earthworks of the inner bailey, and earthworks over the stream to the E enclose a larger outer bailey. The HOUSE probably dates from a lease of 1583. T-plan, running back from the gatehouse arch (the jambs visible inside) with a wing incorporating the N tower. Renovated in 1981–5 by *John Schofield* of *Architecton*. E of the castle is the TOWN MILL, mostly C18 with C19 machinery and overshot wheel, on a medieval site.

VILLAGE. Church Street runs W from the church. No. 3 was the vicarage recorded in 1487. Cross-passage unusually at one end. High Street was the medieval market place, originally much larger, the S side all infill. Little of note apart from Nos. 8–10, thatched, on the corner of Lime Street. Among the encroachments the large Victorian ACLAND-HOOD ARMS. The western limit is marked by the stump of the C15 MARKET CROSS. Opposite it on the N, STOKE HOUSE is Late Georgian, with an open-pediment doorway. OLD CROSS HOUSE, on the S side, is Regency stucco with deep bracketed eaves and hoodmoulds. This echoes the more humble CROSS COTTAGES nearby on St Andrew's Road, roughcast with similar eaves, but the r. cottage encases a C15–C16 house. Facing up St Andrew's Road is ST ANDREW'S WELL. A Victorian red sandstone Gothic arch screens earlier work built for Lord Egmont after 1757, a Blue Lias pointed arch between enclosed well-heads. At the W end of the High Street, the red sandstone former VICARAGE, 1910, by *Samson & Cottam*. This replaces one by *John Norton*, 1869, who designed the very Gothic PRIMARY SCHOOL adjoining, 1860–1. Much more elaborate than usual, as Sir Peregrine Fuller-Palmer-Acland of Fairfield built it in thanks for the recovery of his last surviving child. Red sandstone, with gables, chimneys, a spired tower and a flèche. Teacher's house attached.

SHURTON, 1 m. N. SHURTON COURT is late C18, three-storeyed, stuccoed, with a Venetian window over a doorway with an open pediment on attached columns. At the angles, one Ionic pilaster under a taller one, a clumsy detail. Medieval to C17 rear range. SHURTON LODGE, early C18, has two naïve overmantel paintings, a rural scene with country house, and a busy urban riverside.

STEYNING MANOR, 1 m. E. Early C17, for the Burland family. Unremarkable pink-washed roughcast exterior, but the plan is advanced, for it is the Renaissance double-pile with a central staircase in the back half. Three-gabled front with renewed wooden mullion-and-transom windows, the upper ones breaking the eaves, and a central storeyed porch. Tudor-arched oak doorway. Inside, the cross-passage is thrown into the hall. This has high-relief plasterwork of around 1700, probably by the same hand as at Stockland Lovell (Fiddington), Nettlecombe Court and Fitzhead Court. Low ceiling with beams clad in undercut acanthus on the sides and highly realistic flower and fruit beneath. Overmantel cartouche with moustachioed heads, sweeping acanthus scrolls each side, and small floating cherubs. Cherub heads over the three doors; over one window two ravens perch on festooned drapes. Half-panelling of Jacobean type, but a wide bolection-moulded fireplace of *c.* 1700. Bolection-moulded doorway into the parlour, which has early C18 panelling and another bolection-moulded fireplace, under an overmantel painting of an ideal landscape with ruins and a port. Early C17 thin-rib plaster ceiling. Similar ceilings also in two bedrooms. The staircase has a balustered screen at the top under a spiked beam, an unusual degree of security.

Across the rear courtyard is a small C14–C15 end-entry HOUSE, extended in the C16 with a kitchen and winding stair of solid treads.

Stoke Pero church, before restoration.
Drawing by J. Crowther, 1901

STOKE PERO

Save for the farm below, the church stands alone in its fold of Exmoor, the most solitary church in Somerset.

CHURCH. Short W tower of heavy squared blocks. Only one stage and a bit, but intended to go higher – see the way that the saddleback roof cuts the NE stair-turret. Round tower arch on the simplest imposts with heavy cornerstones. It looks Norman, though so remote a locality makes a much later date likely. Nave and chancel in one, rebuilt except for the porch in 1897–8 by *Edmund Buckle*. Heavy N doorway of oak, a two-centred arch. Three small S windows may be reused Perp. Simple interior with a wagon roof. – FONT. Re-tooled late C12 bowl on a rough octagonal stem. – BENCHES. Plain moulded square ends, probably C18, still in the local tradition.

CHURCH FARMHOUSE. C16–C17, L-plan, with a full-height porch. The roughcast cross-wing against the churchyard has a big lateral chimney.

CLOUTSHAM FARM, 1 m. E. The Swiss-chalet embellishment dates from 1869, for Sir Thomas Dyke Acland. The rest was thatched until a fire in 1916.

STOKE ST GREGORY

ST GREGORY. The church, although much of its finest work is Perp, belongs to an earlier type, with transepts and crossing.

And its crossing and crossing tower are indeed its earliest parts, c. 1300. The tower is octagonal. The lower stage has shafts at the angles and double-chamfered cusped single lights with hoodmoulds linked across the shafts. Statues inserted 1886. The bell-stage is Perp (two-light bell-openings with transom), embattled and crowned by a pretty little recessed lead spire. Of the same date as the lower tower windows or only a little later are two small ogee-headed E windows in the S transept. The Perp contribution is the rebuilding of the nave with clerestory, aisles and S porch, the remodelling of the transepts, and the raising of the tower. Quatrefoiled pierced parapets to the aisles, transepts and porch. Windows of three and four lights, two-light to the clerestory. Fine five-light W window, very large, with ogee-headed lights above and below the transom. The transepts have four-light main windows, the N tracery refined. The clumsy S tracery is the latest in the church, with two transoms, one interlaced. An almost-detached short square battlemented turret, C15, gives external access to the crossing tower. C15 canopied niche over the S door. The chancel is lower, altogether modest, and much restored in 1886–7 by *J. H. Spencer*. Windows of the C15–C16 Muchelney Abbey type with quatrefoil spandrels.

Inside, the nave is light, the arcades tall and slim, of four bays with piers of standard section and small capitals to the shafts. The line of the previous roof is visible against the tower. The crossing arrangement is sturdy and impressive. Triple-chamfered and even quadruple-chamfered arches and then again triple-chamfered squinches (an unusual sight in England) to lead from the square to the octagon. The piers are just solid pieces of walling set diagonally, but the bases have complex mouldings. All this looks c. 1300 and hardly later. Double Perp arches from aisles to the transepts, showing that they are cut through older walls. The inner S arch has little angel corbels. In the transept three defaced C15 niches, the little E windows dividing them.

FURNISHINGS. FONT. C14. Strangely clumsy but bold in design. Octagonal, with cusped lozenges bent over most but not all the angles. The ensuing lower triangles, also cusped, give a zigzag underside. Stem of earlier type. – PULPIT. Early C17, richly patterned. Figures in shell-headed arches: an Archangel holding the soul of Adam, Charity, Hope, Faith and Father Time. Naïve fruity style. The lower panels have plants springing from the appropriate emblem – dove, anchor etc. – BENCHES. A large set of square-ended C15–C16 bench-ends, bordered in leaf scroll with varied tracery, one Tudor rose. – ROYAL ARMS. Hanoverian, the frame marked VR. – PAINTING. King David, C18, naïve, from the former gallery. – SCREEN. N transept. Made up c. 1958 of C16–C17 pieces. Several Wise Virgins displaying dustpan-like lamps (cf. North Newton), some linenfold, and four angel-busts with shields, two dated: 1595 and 1628. – STAINED GLASS. E window, bright colours, c. 1845. N aisle, four lights, 1932–3, by *Morris & Co.*

s of the churchyard, a small early C19 hip-roofed SCHOOLROOM with two Gothic doors. Just W, JESSAMINE HOUSE was possibly the late medieval church house. Brick Gothic SCHOOL, 1857, by *C. E. Giles*. Little else in the village.

SLOUGH COURT, ½ m. N. A very remarkable survival of a small Early Tudor manor house on a moated site. John of Slough had an oratory here in 1337. Over the moat, a buttressed gateway, marked IM, with Montague heraldry, over a depressed arch. The house, across what must have been a forecourt, is of Blue Lias, the oldest part banded in Ham stone. Broad two-storeyed porch with lozenge band over the entry and tiny stair lights on the corner, a quatrefoil on the side wall. Two bays to the l., the first the chimney-breast to the hall, with a small single light under the eaves, then a rendered bay with a three-light window each floor. The bay to the r. of the porch was rebuilt in the C19, with the wing behind. Three-light windows with four-centred-arched lights and hoodmoulds. The hall, a ground-floor room with a heavy moulded framed ceiling, has its original screen of planks and muntins. The most remarkable feature is that despite the smallness of the room the dais end had a bay window on each side, the back one fairly complete, the front one fragmentary. They have panelled arches between thin shafts. Traces of the spiral staircase also remain.

Further E, DYKES FARMHOUSE, L-plan, mostly roughcast. An altered late medieval hall house with cross-wing of 1638. CHURLEY FARMHOUSE, faced in C19 red brick, has a C16 chamfered framed ceiling. W from Slough Lane, the BAPTIST CHAPEL, 1895, round-arched, in the Lombard style. Continuous cast-iron gallery railing. Under Windmill Hill, WOODHOUSE FARMHOUSE, cob-walled and thatched, with five-light C17 stone-mullioned windows.

STOKE ST MARY

ST MARY. Plain two-stage C13 W tower with low diagonal buttresses and small W lancet. Vigorously moulded low tower arch (a chamfer and a bold roll). The rest is mostly roughcast, remodelled in 1864 with a new S aisle, the tracery copying a reused C14 window. The nave ceiling is still plastered. The chancel arch may reuse C13 shafts and capitals. – STAINED GLASS. Three S windows by *Patrick Reyntiens*, 2000–3, each a different dominant colour, busily worked in black.

Opposite the church, APLENS, roughcast and thatched, C16–C17, by the drive to Stoke House (*see* below). Along the village street, FYRSE COTTAGE, dated 1658, thatched, and the stuccoed Gothic METHODIST CHAPEL, 1825. At STOKE FARM, a hip-roofed barn with Georgian Gothic blind openings. Further out, HIGHER BROUGHTON FARM encases some very early timber, tree-ring-dated 1267–99. The W bay survives, comprising the end cruck of a hipped roof and a closed partition with arched braces and posts, derived from aisled-hall construction.

STOKE HOUSE. Overlooking a huge view. Plain stucco of 1810, somewhat colonial, with a timber arcaded veranda on a basement arcade.

STOKE COURT, 1 m. S. The W half is early C17. Two full-height canted bays with mullioned windows, and a gabled storeyed porch against a C19 E cross-wing. To the E, a three-bay hip-roofed addition of c. 1700 has channelled rustication to the windows and angle piers. Georgian staircase in the older part.

STOKE-SUB-HAMDON

Known also as Stoke-under-Ham, the village lies indeed below Hamdon Hill or Ham Hill (see p. 344), the source of the famous golden stone. The village stretches nearly three miles in two distinct parts. East Stoke, with the church, is rural, while West Stoke expanded with the C19 glove industry. But it also has the more interesting houses, having originated around a long-vanished castle.

ST MARY. An uncommonly varied assortment of parts and motifs, diverse styles overlapping each other in pleasant disorder. Cruciform, with a tower over the N transept and a storeyed porch adjoining. C11–C12 nave and chancel – see the chancel corbel table, chancel arch, nave doorways, and three small arched windows (two nave, one chancel). The corbels are a lexicon of primitive shapes, also two sheila-na-gigs (S) and a hare (N). The N doorway in the porch is remarkable and complete. The tympanum is exceptional, more Anglo-Saxon than Norman: the Tree of Life in the middle, with three big birds, to the l. a centaur archer whose surprising presence is attested by the inscription SAGITARIUS, to the r. a dog-like animal labelled LEO. Above it a small Lamb with the Cross. Why just two signs of the zodiac? Perhaps they were to stand for Summer and Winter.* The doorway has colonnettes, one shaft polygonal with saltire crosses, the other fish-scaled. The capitals have volutes. The outer arch, visible from above, has two orders of flat chevron and an outer billet moulding. Of the S doorway only shafts with fluted capitals remain. One shaft is spiral-fluted, the other fish-scaled. The small arched windows have monolithic heads with flattened cable or chevron ornament. Above the nave N window a man in trews (St George?) attacks a dragon with spear and sword. Again, more Saxon than Norman. Inside, the deep reveals run right to the wall face, the nave N window reveal with painted fictive masonry. The chancel

---

*The same two signs appear on corbels at South Petherton.

Stoke-sub-Hamdon, St Mary, interior.
Engraving, 1853

arch is of three orders, much renewed in 1862 (inner columns entirely new). The outer shafts have fish-scale and chevron decoration and volute capitals. A lozenge pattern covers the abaci. The arches have thick rolls, one order of billet and one of flat chevron. Above, a damaged C12 string course.

The next building period is represented by the tower, whose base is the N transept, with a double-chamfered arch to the nave. The tower base has a rib-vault, which from the Transitional details of the capital-shaped corbels in the corners can hardly be later than 1190. A rib-vault of that date is a rarity in a parish church in Somerset but occurs at the Glastonbury Lady Chapel. The capitals with swirling trumpet flutes and leaves of a rare grace are comparable to work there. E wall pointed altar recess. The upper stages of the tower are C13 – see the coupled-lancet bell-openings with a roll moulding all round. The stair projection on the E side resembles a chimney-breast. A strange canopy low on the nave N wall, with lively leaf cresting, is C13 also. Much more was done *c.* 1300. To this period belong the numerous cusped lancets of different length and arrangement. The nave has one large cinquefoil-cusped lancet on each side, overlying the Norman windows. The chancel has them on each side, not quite matching, on the S mostly uncusped, on the N with hoodmoulds. The first on each side is a low-side window, extended beneath a transom for ventilation (retaining the wooden shutter). The middle ones are similar but not extended, and the eastern ones are of two lights with trefoiled shafted rere-arches. The S transept, a complete and well-proportioned addition of this period, has an even row of four on each side, spaced so that the reveals meet under linked hoodmoulds, an elegant arrangement, and one S window. The transept arch is double-chamfered, on fat triple shafts with round capitals. The N porch overlaps the adjacent nave window and is early C14 – see the heavy rib-vault on head corbels. The arch is simply rebated. In the r. jamb is the doorway to the parvise above, which has a mid-C14 reticulated three-light window. Of similar date the matching five-light nave w window. Finally in the C15 came the gargoyles and battlements of the tower and its three-light lower window, also the E window of four lights with sub-arched tracery and the large nave S window with panel tracery, inserted when the nave was raised and battlemented. The previous wall height shows on the S from the remaining original render. Restorations: chancel arch, 1862, by *Benjamin Ferrey*; S transept, 1877, by *Edmund Ferrey*; nave roof and N transept, 1914–15, by *C. E. Ponting*.

Inside are various elements contemporary with the architecture. Of *c.* 1300 the double PISCINA with a large cusped arch placed curiously across the chancel SE corner, the similar cusped shelf recess in the S transept, here shafted, and the adjoining cusped tomb-recess. A stoup cut into the transept arch must be later. The tower stair became in the late C14 the rood stair, with plain chamfered openings to the nave. DOOR with notable scrolled ironwork. Of *c.* 1500 the fine panelled nave ceiling, sub-panelled in the eastern bays. Of post-Reformation date are the C17 black-letter INSCRIPTIONS in coloured cartouches, two series superimposed. Twin organ cases and W vestry, 1915, by *Ponting*. Chancel ceiling, 1950s, by *John Macgregor*.

OTHER FURNISHINGS. FONT. C12, heavy tub (cf. Lufton and Hardington Mandeville) with cables at middle and bottom, the middle one paired with a lozenge string. – PULPIT. Early C17, with arched and strapwork panels. Fixed nearby is an HOURGLASS. – TOWER SCREEN. Stone, Perp, with segmental-pointed arches. Reputedly from the castle chapel at West Stoke. It was the chancel screen until removed by *Benjamin Ferrey*. Installed here by *Ponting*, who also brought inside a quatre-foiled C15 table tomb for use as ALTAR. – SCULPTURE. Loose in the porch chamber, a well carved head of a king, with original colour. – COMMUNION RAIL. C17. Turned balusters. – BENCH-ENDS. Some early C16 with Perp panelling, quatre-foils and roses. – STAINED GLASS. S transept. Good set by *Heaton, Butler & Bayne*, 1877. C15 fragments above the E window (1949, by *Bell* of Bristol). – MONUMENTS. Early C14 Ham stone effigy, a priest, possibly Reginald de Monkton †1307, in the S transept tomb-recess. – Thomas Strode †1595. Ham stone effigy in plate armour, on a tomb-chest beneath an arched canopy with cornice on pilasters. – John Strode †1725. Lias plaque with flamboyant painted heraldry. – Robert and Susanna Chaffey, mid-C18, marble with heraldry. Commissioned by their son Thomas, master mason to the king in Jamaica and Portsmouth Dockyard. – Three Regency draped urns: the Bean family *c.* 1797, by *Francis Lancashire*; John Bondfield *c.* 1806, good swirled urn on a pedestal, and the Rev. C. Tatchell †1820.

CHURCHYARD CROSS. C15 head with Crucifixion and Virgin Mary back-to-back. Retrieved from a Chaffey house in Bristol and re-set here on an Arts and Crafts shaft of 1911 from the *Trask* workshop. Numerous fine CHEST TOMBS of Ham stone. C17 churchyard GATEWAY.

CONGREGATIONAL CHURCH, North Street. 1865–6, by *R. C. Bennett* of Weymouth. Pevsner though it hideous with its attenuated corner spirelet and curly flying buttresses, but its lively unconventionality may now be appreciated. Note the tracery of the seven-light window. It has a basement schoolroom. Another schoolroom added behind in 1875. Behind that, a detached infants' schoolroom. Large Gothic MANSE, *c.* 1868, with columned windows and elaborate porch. The complex reflects the investment of the Southcombe family, glove manufacturers, who lived at Brock's Mount, a large, now-demolished, Victorian villa adjoining.

METHODIST CHURCH, West Street. 1909, by *Latrobe & Weston* of Bristol. Gothic, as simplified by the Arts and Crafts movement. Square-shouldered with a half-timbered porch. Tiny squares of STAINED GLASS in the windows.

STANCHESTER SCHOOL, East Stoke. 1939–40 by *A. J. Toomer*, County Architect. A large secondary school in stripped Georgian style (cf. Ansford, Huish Episcopi).

THE PRIORY (National Trust), North Street. A remarkable house, built for a provost and four priests endowed in 1304 by Lord Beauchamp to serve his chantry in the castle. Repaired, probably rebuilt, after 1444. C16–C17 alterations for the Strode family. The hall faces N over a farmyard. Storeyed porch to the l. with pointed archway and single light above. A six-light ground-floor window with depressed-arched heads marks the insertion *c.* 1600 of a floor into the hall. Any W service range there may have been has gone. The cross-range at the E end, backing on to the street, is substantially altered. There was a heated room below a dormitory linked to a small first-floor chapel. Bellcote at the N end over a Perp single-light window, oddly offset. A formerly detached kitchen at the S end is marked by a lower roof and pointed garden doorway. The final gable was of a bakery or brewhouse.

The N porch opens to a screens passage with moulded pointed doorways at each end and a good ogee-headed doorway to the dormitory stairs, E. The hall has been stripped to the bare shell with minimal repair (by *Burrough & Hannam*, 1966). The plain roof is wind-braced with jointed-cruck trusses. A large SW projection, an early dais bay, was floored *c.* 1600, hence the windows and fireplaces on two levels. Enough remains to show an original full-height S window. Ogee piscina. The chapel has an ogee piscina combined with a squint from the dormitory. The parlour has panelling dated 1585 and a C17 fireplace.

A high entrance wall with broad arch and blocked pointed pedestrian entry joins the chapel to an outbuilding with medieval rear buttresses, altered to a STABLE in the C18. Across the yard, a large thatched BARN with gabled off-centre porch. Late medieval, the roof C18. Another BARN, burnt in 1969, and a roofless circular DOVECOTE are in line W of the hall. Both have medieval buttresses.

VILLAGE. The church is in East Stoke, S of the main road. On Windsor Lane N of the main road, EAST STOKE FARMHOUSE is C17, made thoroughly Victorian after a fire in 1890. The little gable obelisks reappear on AVALON, mullion-windowed, C17. EAST STOKE COTTAGE, dated 1696, has flush mullioned windows of early C18 type. EAST STOKE HOUSE, just E in its own grounds, has an ashlar W front of c. 1760–70 with channelled piers and pedimented doorway. Long ashlar S front with restless symmetrical Early Victorian detail: Greek porch, niches, canted bays. Coachhouse dated 1846. Georgian lofted stable. Further E is Stanchester School (q.v.). Returning W along the main road, the High Street of the main village has C19 terraces interspersed with earlier houses. No. 45, 1674, has one of the two-storey canted bays under a corbelled gable typical of the Martock area. No. 35 had prominent C17 gables before the wall was built up between. TANYBRYN is mid-C18 with flush mullioned windows, given elegance by added wings with swept parapets. Naïve C19 Ionic porch. THE OLD BAKERY is early C18, its windows mullioned with architraves. Doorcase with pulvinated frieze. PRANKETTS, 1695, is thatched with three dormer gables, the lower windows under a single hoodmould.

From the centre, North Street descends past The Priory and Congregational church (*see* above). Down Castle Street to the E, the PRIMARY SCHOOL by *Charles Benson*, 1875, extended 1901. Beyond, in Pound Lane, unusually thick garden walls mark the precinct of the CASTLE, a late C13 fortified manor of the Beauchamp family. It had a chapel which Leland describes as filled with effigies, heraldic glass and tiles. Back on North Street, THE GABLES has an animated five-bay front of c. 1600. Three gabled projections, the centre one over an arched porch, the outer ones with canted bays under corbelled gables. Plaster ceiling with thin curved ribs scrolled into berry fruits and roses. Also a vine frieze. Early C18 SE addition. NORTH STREET FARMHOUSE is an ashlar-fronted early C19 villa with columned doorcase. DAIRY COTTAGE resembles a picturesque early C19 lodge, mullion-windowed with a steep hipped thatched roof. CASTLE FARMHOUSE has C17 mullion windows, a Georgian pedimented doorway and a Victorian porch.

Returning to the centre, the main road becomes West Street. The long FLEUR DE LYS inn is very much altered. It was the church house of 1544, but the two handsome Gothic doorways look late C15, with foliage spandrels. The r. one was moved from the back. Behind is a Late Georgian FIVES WALL with a curved top and ball finials. Angle buttresses echo the church towers against which the game was played until banned in 1754. Opposite is the former CHURCH SCHOOL, 1831, Tudor-style. Behind that, PRIORY COURT, the first factory of the Southcombe family, called the Spats Factory, reduced by a storey in 1948. The main Southcombe GLOVE FACTORY, 1870s and later, is NW, down Langlands. Further out is the Methodist church (*see* p. 592).

STOKE TRISTER

ST ANDREW. 1841, by *George Follett* of Cucklington. Better than usual for the date. Sturdy W tower. Nave and chancel with Y-tracery. Light interior with broad chancel arch. – Original PULPIT and COMMANDMENT BOARDS. – STAINED GLASS. 1895, by *Clayton & Bell*.

MANOR HOUSE, to the E, by the site of the medieval church. The long six-bay E range has one SE and one front buttress that suggest early work. A C16 drawing shows a great hall still with smoke-vent and lower l. range. This was presumably raised shortly afterwards, with a large S end chimney. Some mullioned windows with four-centred-arched lights. Moulded framed ceiling.

STOLFORD

NE of Stogursey. The mudflats of Bridgwater Bay preserve the remains of FISH TRAPS and the posts of fixed nets.

ST PETER. The temporary church erected at West Quantoxhead, 1853, re-erected here in 1866. Weatherboarded timber frame with leaded casements and a slim NW bell-turret with a pyramid cap. – Perp FONT from Stogursey.

A scatter of farms and cottages shelter behind the sea walls. STOLFORD FARM, of pink-washed rubble, is an early three-room and cross-passage house of *c*. 1500, the roof subsequently raised.

STOWELL

ST MARY MAGDALENE. Modest Perp W tower, the bell-stage of 1748 with simple arched openings. Wave-moulded triple-shafted tower arch. Everything else of 1913 by *F. Bligh Bond*, the broad E window and shallow S gable typically early C20. Norman S doorway, based on fragments. Pleasant interior, the chancel ceiling panelled and coloured, the stone PULPIT let into the N wall. Simple oak SCREEN, backed by STALLS with chickens on the two bench-ends, dated 1670 and 1913. – FONT. C12. Octagonal, on a haunched base. – STAINED GLASS. E window, 1915, by *Alice Erskine*. Strangely amateur Crucifixion against aqueous green with sinuous plants.

STOWELL FARMHOUSE has a Victorian Gothic front, but the massive S chimney remains from a C15–C16 house, and two N end windows may be reused doorways.* STOWELL HOUSE, 1870, by *Silas Hoskins* of Castle Cary, was the rectory. Hip-roofed with an off-centre gable and emphatic quoins. CLARE FARMHOUSE, below, is late C17. Upper centre window in a good C18 pedimented frame.

WILKINTHROOP, ½ m. NNE. 1909. Edwardian manorial, with mullioned windows.

STOWELL HILL, ¾ m. NNE. By *Guy Dawber*, 1923–4. Spreading stone house in vernacular Georgian style, near-symmetrical between hip-roofed wings. Simple casements and a narrow square-shouldered centrepiece. Weatherboarded STABLE COURT about a tall tile-hung water tower with belvedere, reminiscent of early Lutyens.

STREET

4030

Named for a causeway skirting the marshes. Street developed from 1825 with the C. & J. Clark company. The Clarks were farmers, then tanners, and eventually shoemakers with a world-wide business. Their Quaker ethos gives Street a different character from other Somerset towns, with modest public buildings and extensive workers' housing provided by the company. Blue Lias was quarried here, and almost everything is built of it. The chief period of Clark building, from the 1880s to the 1920s, under W. S. Clark (1839–1925), features three architects: *George Skipper* of Norwich, 1885–90, replaced by Clark's nephew *William Reynolds*, 1890–1906, followed by Clark's son-in-law, *S. T. Clothier*, who was also responsible for the early municipal housing. Because it was overlaid on the older settlement, Street is more of a patchwork than similar company towns like Bournville or New Earswick.

HOLY TRINITY. A Celtic site called Lantokay, where Gildas, the historian, probably established a church in the mid C6. The church is mostly early C14, with C19 additions (N aisle of 1834 by *John Ralphs* of Warminster, nave roof and S vestry of 1843 by *Benjamin Ferrey*). Chancel with reticulated E window tracery, and two-light side windows with trefoils in the heads, which look slightly earlier. Unbuttressed W tower with wave-moulded C14 tower arch on piers with double-hollow mouldings and plain banded capitals. Short C16 bell-stage with parapet. Late C14 nave two-light windows, one reused in the C19 N aisle, others copied from it. Interior cleared in a reordering of 2003 by *Chedburn Dudley*. Of that date the fine etched glass DOORS

---

* A C15 window is at Horsington church.

by *Martin Donlin*. Fussy nave roof of 1843, based on the C14 chancel roof. This resembles that at Meare, more domestic than ecclesiastical. Queenpost trusses infilled with a pointed arch, and another pointed arch, reversed, over the collar. Two tiers of cusped wind-braces. The chancel arch resembles the tower arch. C14 PISCINA and SEDILIA, with cusped and crocketed ogee heads and diagonally set pinnacles. Under the piscina, ballflower decoration and two little supporting figures. – FONT. Early C14. Octagonal with mouldings, coved beneath. – STAINED GLASS. E window, 1951, and two others by *Rachel Montmorency*. – MONUMENTS. Margaret Dyer, chancel floor. Lettered brass: 'died in childbed, 1583, aged 24 years and 5 months, mar. 10 years saving 5 weeks, left 3 sons and 2 daus., one son more buried.' – Edward Brown †1808. Draped urn, by *Reeves & Son*. – Thomas Petvin †1809. Lias oval, signed *Isaac Petvin*.

MISSION CHURCH, Vestry Close. 1990, by *Douglas Smith*. Staggered walls for concealed lighting, under pointless boarded gables. The church rooms reuse the spirelet from the corrugated-iron church of 1897.

FRIENDS' MEETING HOUSE, High Street. 1850, by *J. F. Cotterell* of Bath, Quaker relative of the Clarks. Uncommonly stately. Squared Blue Lias. Hip-roofed, six bays, with large windows set high and an ashlar pedimented porch in the third bay. A lantern marks the meeting room in the l. three bays, which enlarges to five bays by retracting partitions into the roof and floor. Vestry and schoolrooms in the r. end bay. In the graveyard, uniform small headstones, Clarks undistinguished from the rest.

BAPTIST CHAPEL, Glaston Road. 1890 by *H. Hawkins* of Glastonbury. Gothic with plate tracery.

METHODIST CHAPEL, Leigh Road. 1893, by *Hawkins & Alves*. A big Geometrical four-light end window, porches at right angles. Side windows of quite another style, mullioned and transomed. Large schoolrooms behind, 1895–6.

UNITED REFORMED CHURCH, High Street. 1853. Gable front with rock-faced outer piers and a broad curved-headed window, not Gothic. Manse of 1866 adjoining, schoolroom of 1884 behind, extended 1899.

CIVIC BUILDINGS, Leigh Road. *See* Perambulation 1.

STRODE COLLEGE, THEATRE, and CRISPIN SCHOOL. 1960–3, by *Dennis Tabert* of *Somerset County Architects*. The logic of the similar six-storey curtain-walled blocks separated by the theatre has been lost in additions. The theatre was realigned in 1997 to face the street with a new entrance block by *Steel, Coleman & Davis*.

MILLFIELD SCHOOL. See p. 601.

ELMHURST JUNIOR SCHOOL, Elmhurst Lane. Cyrus Clark's house of 1856, by *J. F. Cotterell*, a large unadorned villa of rock-faced Lias, became the Grammar School. School hall by *Clothier*, 1929, hip-roofed, Neo-Georgian, linked to the house by a veranda corridor.

HINDHAYES INFANTS SCHOOL, Leigh Road. 1928, by *S. T. Clothier*. Whitewashed brick in an attractive minimal Georgian style. Courtyard plan centred on a hipped-roofed hall. The Clarks took Clothier to see the through-ventilated 'veranda schools' developed from 1911 in Derbyshire. The classrooms open fully to verandas on both sides. Neat red brick addition, 2000, by *Matthew Lloyd Architects*.

BROOKSIDE PRIMARY SCHOOL, Brooks Road. 2010, by *Somerset County Architects*. Cheerful two-storey front block under an asymmetrical overhanging roof. Tall windows in pinkish red render, with, inevitably, boarding elsewhere.

GREENBANK OPEN-AIR POOL, Wilfrid Street. 1936–7. A Clark gift. Formally planned in a modest way: the rectangular pool with a semicircular children's pool on an axis to a low flat-roofed white building. This comprises just two kiosks flanking a throughway, advanced for rural England. *Bancroft Clark*, of the family, was much involved, with *Jack Stock*, of Clark's building department. Portrait roundel of Alice Clark †1934, by *Henry Parr*. Restored by *Jeremy & Caroline Gould*, 2003.

THE GRANGE, Clarks Village. On the site of a Glastonbury Abbey grange, owned by the Strode family from 1628. Plenty of C17 evidence, but confused. The two storeys of mullion-and-transom windows on the s side are renewed, but blocked ones in the paired w gables and on the N are reliable. Some C17 doorways, the N one under the pointed window of a stair hall inserted *c.* 1800. This staircase was soon supplanted by one in a new front block across the E end. Typically Late Georgian, with panelled parapet, ground-floor over-arched Venetian windows and doorway, and first-floor tripartite sash windows. Nicely detailed ashlar embellishments added before 1829, a curved porch and ten-bay Roman Doric colonnade bowed out in the centre. Restored 2010–12 by *Feilden Clegg Bradley Studios* for the Clark archives. GRANGE BARN was a large nine-bay late C17 lofted stable, the l. two bays demolished. Original stable entries within the throughway.

PERAMBULATIONS

1. From the church to Leigh Road

The church is at the N edge of the town. Just E is the former BOWLINGREEN MILL, where leather-board was made from the 1870s. Twelve-bay stone front by *Reynolds*, 1891 and 1906. A walnut avenue runs E from the mill to CLARK'S FOLLY, the columned Late Georgian porch of Westcombe House (at Westcombe, dem. 1956), re-erected here by Stephen Clark. CHURCH ROAD curves past Strode College (*see* above) to THE CROSS, the crossroads of the pre-industrial village. Here is the Late Georgian STREET INN, of six bays, with parapet. W down GRANGE ROAD is one of the most coherent areas of Clark workers' housing. Designed by *Reynolds*. The form established in Wilfrid Road (*see* below), of terraces broken up by gables, is here varied with semi-detached houses. On Grange Road two terraces of 1898 face four semi-detached pairs, the outer pair of 1896, the inner pair of 1892–3. These are set diagonally at the top of BRUTASCHE TERRACE, 1892–3, two opposed terraces running N. At the end, the wooden TOLL GATES from the Glastonbury road toll house. Beyond Grange Road, a further pair (1892) and row of three (1895), before the factory rear lodge. Returning to The Cross, HIGH STREET runs SW. Early buildings include, in a terrace, GOSS HOUSE, c. 1810, by *William Goss*, carpenter, with three little canted bays under deep eaves, and, opposite the Friends' meeting house (*see* p. 596), MULLIONS, late C16, with a plank partition and moulded Tudor-arched fireplace. The BEAR HOTEL, opposite the Clark factory, was a (teetotal) coffee house and hotel of 1894, by *Reynolds*. Picturesque in the Domestic Revival manner. Taller addition behind.

The CLARK FACTORY is now the company headquarters. The gable to the l. of the front is the original factory of 1829, that to the r. the three-storey house of Alfred Clark, 1857, united over an archway by *Reynolds* in 1898. The tall CLOCK TOWER is by *Skipper*, 1887, the corbelled top with steep tiled roof modelled allegedly on a tower at Thun, Switzerland. Behind is the equally tall WATER TOWER, 1897, by *Reynolds*. The factory buildings tend towards large windows and sawtooth roofs for good lighting. The towers flank the longest range, a tall four storeys, late C19. To the r., the square-plan MORE LIGHT BUILDING, 1933, by *Jack Stock*, introduces the modernism espoused by Bancroft Clark, who chose Goethe's dying words to name it. Large metal windows, sans serif lettering. Behind is the NEW ROOM, 1897, by *Reynolds*, an open-plan workshop, under five parallel roofs. Within the main factory is preserved the STEAM ENGINE of 1910 that powered and heated the works. Beyond the High Street entrance are NETHERLEIGH, the plain three-bay house of James Clark, 1835, with a rock-faced addition of 1855–6 by *Samuel Pollard*, and GREENBANK, a modest farmhouse enlarged for W. S. Clark, who lived here 1866–89.

WILFRID ROAD, running SE from High Street, displays the most generous Clark housing. Opposite the Greenbank Pool (*see* above), WILFRID TERRACE, by *Skipper*, 1885, establishes the pattern of gabled accents with Ham stone-mullioned windows punctuating terraces with simpler wooden casements. COBDEN TERRACE, by *Skipper*, 1889, after the pool, is the longest and most ornamental; too ornamental for Mrs Clark, who disliked the cupola. Hence LAWSON TERRACE, 1891, by *Reynolds*, is slightly simpler.* SW of the pool at right angles to the High Street, STRODE COTTAGES are two short rows by *Reynolds*, one dated 1886, influenced by *Skipper*, the second simpler. Back on the High Street, the plain three-storey TEMPERANCE HOTEL, 1847, was a Clark promotion.

---

* The terraces are named for Sir Wilfrid Lawson and Jane Cobden who spoke in favour of women's suffrage at Leeds with Helen Clark in 1883.

The civic buildings of LEIGH ROAD are mostly Clark gifts. On the corner with High Street, the CRISPIN HALL, 1885, by *Skipper*, the most exuberant, named for the patron saint of shoemakers. Mullion-windowed with picturesque detail, red tile roofs and a spired lantern. An octagonal stair-turret divides the front meeting rooms from the public hall. The former GYMNASIUM, 1890, behind, with a half-hipped roof, was *Skipper*'s last commission at Street. The CRISPIN CENTRE, shops of 1979 by *Alec French*, is fortunately reticent. Good TILE PANEL of Somerset buildings, 1979, by *Philippa Threlfall*. Opposite the Crispin Hall, the LIBRARY of 1924 by *Clothier*. Quite well done, with pedimented centre and differing cross-wings to suggest a C17–C18 evolution. The E wing housed the librarian. After the Crispin Hall, two gabled buildings of 1887 with mullion-and-transom windows, the VESTRY ROOM, by *Skipper*, and homely POLICE STATION, by *W. J. Willcox*. After the Methodist chapel (*see* p. 596), the TECHNICAL SCHOOL, 1899, by *Reynolds*, also with mullion-and-transom windows, in the gable-end clumsily united vertically. Opposite, the former CINEMA, 1920, by *Clothier*, red brick. The combination of C17 and C18 detail works uneasily compared to his library, or his STRODE SCHOOL opposite. This is of 1925, built for after-work education for young employees. A Venetian window to the school, mullioned windows to the teacher's house. The back of HINDHAYES, 1807, closes the street, appropriately as this was the farmhouse where Cyrus and James Clark were born. BARN to the l. in Hindhayes Lane, opposite THE VINES, a small Late Georgian house with large SURGERY behind, 1997–8 by *Jeremy & Caroline Gould*. Silver brick, with red roofs and glass-box roof-lights. Beyond Hindhayes is Hindhayes School (*see* p. 597).

2. North and west of the High Street

From the High Street, opposite Leigh Road, FARM ROAD runs N through CLARKS VILLAGE, a shopping development of 1993 on former Clark industrial land, by *Brewer, Smith & Brewer*. Some factory buildings are reused. New buildings in Blue Lias and red brick. Further on, Nos. 25–39 are two weatherboarded bungalow rows, 1920s, a type not found elsewhere in Street. STREET FARM is three-bay Late Georgian, c. 1830. BARN CLOSE lines the former rear drive to The Grange (p. 597) with the first terraces to use brick, of 1913 by *Clothier*. SOUTH-LEAZE ORCHARD runs W to WOODSBATCH, a small group of Clark housing, by *Reynolds*, 1892, truncated by the by-pass. ORCHARD ROAD runs back to High Street past LAURA TERRACE, a long, unadorned terraced row of 1890. Nos. 2–12, similarly plain, 1860, by *Samuel Pollard*, was for Clark outworkers, financed by a loan company the firm set up.

The junction of Orchard Road with HIGH STREET was a little civic centre before the development of Leigh Road, with the

United Reformed church (p. 596), a VESTRY ROOM of 1860, and large BRITISH SCHOOL, 1858–9, by *Pollard*. This was extended E in 1876 and behind in 1892 (by *Reynolds*) to take 1,150 children. Further W are intermittent terraces, e.g. Nos. 171–189. It is worth persevering to the ICON development, West End, of 2007–9 by *Feilden Clegg Bradley Studios*. Although modified in erection, it remains almost the only interesting C21 housing in the region. No single houses or pairs, but terraces grouped in a stylish urban layout. Clad in cream render or red brick, with varying amounts of boarding, there are both flat and pitched roofs. The smaller terraces have an undulating rhythm, the houses divided by a first-floor outdoor room over each garage, a clever addition to otherwise minimal space. Paving gives primacy to pedestrians and cyclists. LIME TREE SQUARE, gravelled, with trees and picnic tables, is backed by four-storey flats on two sides, brick three-storey houses on the W, and low two-storey houses on the N between boarded three-storey end houses. Two-storey terraces form the bulk of the development. The surprise is the generous open space, a small wildlife area stretching E, then a really large open lawn with trees, bordered by terraces. To the N, through to the by-pass, is a second development from 2011, a poor echo of the original. Back on West End, a short row just W echoes the adjacent C19 terraces.

3. The slope to the south

From the High Street, opposite Orchard Road, VESTRY ROAD climbs to the double-gabled RECTORY, 1897, by *Reynolds*, and the mission church (p. 596). In MERRIMAN ROAD, two terraces and a pair between of 1911–12, by *Clothier*, probably the first municipal housing in Somerset. Generous by later standards. Stone, with red roofs and white woodwork, the roofs swept down over veranda porches. Later council houses are simpler: MERRIMAN GARDENS, 1920–1, stone with brick dressings, then brick entirely, and mostly by *Clothier*. Much further uphill, in OVERLEIGH, E of Ivythorn Road, two houses enlarged for the Clarks. WHITEKNIGHTS was a farmhouse of 1878, extended by *Clothier* in 1910, roughcast, gabled, and rather muddled. OVERLEIGH HOUSE, a large Lias villa of 1829–30 with high parapets, has two-storey square bays of 1904 and 1930. At the top of SLUGG HILL, HILL HOUSE, 1961, by *Ray Moxley*, for another Clark generation. Two-storey glazed front under an overhanging roof on slim concrete posts. These are the uprights of H-beams carrying the structure. Open ground floor with inbuilt fittings. Stair cantilevered from the wall, returning on a cranked concrete beam. Finally, on IVYTHORN HILL, THE CHALET, 1914, built by Quaker sisters for recuperating factory workers. Swiss of course, the balconies originally more rustic. A youth hostel since 1931.

OUTER STREET

WESTWAY is the by-pass of 1969 (planned by *Alison & Peter Smithson*). CLARKS DISTRIBUTION CENTRE, 2005, by *Atkins, Walters & Webster* of Bristol, an enormous warehouse, covers 8 acres. Clad in sky-blue and curved-roofed, the size surprisingly does not overwhelm. Offices on the corner. Opposite, outside the Sainsbury supermarket, SCULPTURE, Spirit of the Trees, by *Eve Body*, 2003, triple seated mytho-poetic figure. Further E, GRANGE AVENUE was the last significant Clark development, semi-detached pairs in rendered brick or blockwork. *Godfrey Samuel* designed the first seven, Nos. 1–27, in 1935, with pitched roofs, longer at the back.* The rest is by *Jack Stock*, 1937 onwards. Plain pairs, interesting mainly for their staggered layout. At the entrance to the main car parks, two large steel SCULPTURES, Diamond and Steps, by *Phillip King*, 1975, mark 150 years of Clarks.

MILLFIELD SCHOOL, Butleigh Road. The house of W. S. Clark became a private school in 1935. Despite fairly intense development between the house and the road, something of the park remains. The air of a well-funded American campus is relatively recent, enhanced by the very generous SCULPTURE Collection (thirty pieces by 2012). For the first decades, under Robert Meyer, the school leased the estate and made do with temporary buildings. From the 1970s the school buildings were mostly by *Higgison, Brown & Stuckey (HBS)* of Highbridge, renamed *Leading Environmental Design (LED)*.

On Butleigh Road, a small LODGE, 1899. The large MEYER THEATRE, 1994–5, by *Neville Conder*, divides two loose quadrangles. Symmetrical E front of some monumentality, in brick and ashlar, the centrepiece a canted glazed foyer on ashlar piers. Glazed corners. Attached three-sided classroom courtyard. The lawn behind is fronted on the N by the LIBRARY, 1977–80, red brick, by *Jeremy & Caroline Gould*. A distinguished design in two parts, a low front range of reception, offices and classrooms, the library behind with seven almost windowless monopitch bays facing N. Opposite is a long split-level DINING HALL by *David Kent Architects (DKA)* of Bath, 2000–1. Brick, with curved glazed E end. A balcony under tent awnings faces S over playing fields. Tall stainless-steel WATER SCULPTURE inside by *William Pye*, 2001. On the W are science buildings of the 1970s by *HBS*, since re-clad and re-roofed. CHEMISTRY, behind, 2008–9 by *LED*, has the motifs of the time: partly boarded, with a glass-fronted entrance and curved rendered stair-tower. Brises-soleil to Somerton Road.

E of the theatre, the lawn is bounded on the S by parallel teaching blocks of 1966 (by *Nealon Tanner* of Bristol) notable only for being placed diagonally. Added top floors. Opposite the theatre stands the lavish MUSIC SCHOOL, 2005–6, by *DKA*. Red brick modelled with inset bands and applied stone

---

* In 1934 Samuel, then with *Tecton*, had proposed for another site flat-roofed concrete houses, rejected as too expensive.

reliefs of musical instruments (by *Stephen Hitchin*). On the N side a rendered stair-tower divides a full-height plate-glass foyer from three-storey teaching rooms. Fine auditorium fitted in pale wood. On the other side of a quadrangle, the ARTS CENTRE, 1990–2, by *Jeremy & Caroline Gould*. This rises in a long monopitch from a minimal presence on the quad to a two-storey glass wall of N-facing studios. A top-lit foyer divides the art gallery from the studios. The DESIGN SCHOOL, E of the quad, occupies a dining hall of 1975, converted in 2005.

To the S is MILLFIELD HOUSE, W. S. Clark's residence. 1889, by *Skipper*, in cheerful Domestic Revival style: Ham stone dressings, red roofs, tall red chimneys. Cramped stair hall, but ample panelled SE drawing room. William Clark liked mottoes: 'Essayez' in the library, 'Repos Ailleurs' in the study. The CHAPEL behind was built as a summerhouse in 1882 before Clark built the rest. Boarded upper floor, chalet-style.

Below the house, lawn merges with the cricket field to the E. Neat glass-box PAVILION of 2005. Screened by trees is the residential lower campus. The form of the BOARDING HOUSES, by *HBS*, was established in the 1970s (Keen's Elm and Acacia), and continued with Martin's, 1998. In 2002 eight more were added around the Junior Field. Two-storeyed, each with a pyramid-roofed common room, they are conventional without especial personality. To the W, a SWIMMING POOL, 1994–5, in an enormous glass-fronted shed, by *HBS*. By the Somerton Road entrance, a STAFF HOUSE of 2012, by *Collier Reading* of Glastonbury. Twin roofs flare outward from a curved-topped glass stair-tower, a surfeit of fashionable motifs.

IVYTHORN MANOR, 1½ S. C15 and C16–C17, much altered in the C20. A main E–W range with a parallel two-storeyed porch on the N side. NW kitchen wing at right angles. In 1834 Buckler illustrated C16–C17 buildings on the N side of the courtyard, now gone. Six-light mullioned windows in the E gable, C16–C17, but the hoodmould angels look C15. The porch has features of *c.* 1500: four-centred-arched outer doorway, oak inner doorway, and cusped single-light side window. The monogram of Abbot Selwood must be inserted, Ivythorn not being connected with Glastonbury Abbey. Moulded C16 fireplaces inside and a framed ceiling (partly modern). Also a resited stone inscribed JP 1578. Two-storey gabled bay on the S of 1971, for Robert Boscawen M.P., by *William Bertram*. The kitchen wing was refronted and enlarged in 1938. C16 full-width kitchen fireplace, the bressumer on ashlar jambs. In the garden, NE, a rectangular DOVECOTE may be C16. To the SW, a battlemented tower and gateway of 1904.

STRINGSTON

ST MARY. Externally Victorian, clad in uniform cement from a restoration in 1879, when a tiled broach spire was added to the

W tower of 1765. The porch has a moulded Perp arch and a PILLAR STOUP within. Simple panelled nave roof, partly C15–C16. Shafted Perp chancel arch. Some original carved wall-plate in the chancel roof. – FONT. Octagonal, Perp, with pointed quatrefoils. – BENCHES. One dated 1602, still late medieval in form. Some with occupants' initials or the names of tenements, e.g. 'For a hos of Ser Tomas Pamer'. – MONUMENTS. Several to the St Albyns of Alfoxton (Holford), death dates 1708 to 1791, that to John St Albyn †1766 by *Ford* of Bath. Fine relief of a disconsolate woman clutching an urn. Flaming urns flank the indispensable obelisk above. – STAINED GLASS. Chancel windows by *John Baker*, 1992.

Good C15 CHURCHYARD CROSS with an eroding pierced tabernacle head (similar to Spaxton), the Crucifixion backed by the Virgin and Child, a bishop and a knight on the narrow sides. – Railed CHEST TOMB to John Prior †1618 with a rhyming epitaph.

PRIOR'S FARMHOUSE, just NE. Magnificently overdone plasterwork in the ground-floor room, covering a framed ceiling. Four panels with floral ornament, the beams and frieze with fish-tailed creatures and vases in a style still entirely Elizabethan. Yet the overmantel with its naïve ornament is dated 1658 (initials of George and Jane Prior). The same initials and the date 1641 upstairs, and a decorated fireplace surround.

PLUD FARMHOUSE, ¼ m. E. Notable also for C17 plasterwork. In the parlour the ceiling panels have thin-rib designs with flowers etc. On the wall the initials of John Prior and the date 1622. In the room above, the overmantel shows the Sacrifice of Isaac between figures of Hope and Mercy, dated 1641.

SUTTON BINGHAM

The RESERVOIR of 1951–5 wraps around the low hill with the church and manor house.

ALL SAINTS. A tiny church without even a bellcote. In the W gable are two cusped niches of *c*. 1300 for bells over a C14 two-light window. But the nave is C12 – see the narrow arched light on each side (deep-splayed within) and the much renewed N doorway. Ridged lintel, roll-moulded arch, and hoodmould with intermittent nailhead. The blocked arched S doorway is too plain to date. The two eastern nave windows – a narrow N lancet and a cusped single S light of *c*. 1300 – have chamfered rere-arches. Sumptuous Late Norman chancel arch of three orders, on a sturdy inner shaft and two nook-shafts. The inner shaft has fluted capitals, the others geometrical decoration, one with a bit of leaf. The arch has an order of chevron between rolls and a hoodmould with intermittent nailhead. Plain eastern face. The arch-braced collar trusses of the nave roof were revealed in 1956. Single-roofed in old pictures, the chancel is now differentiated in its roof and has rendered walls. One restored N lancet and two S windows of *c.* 1300 like the nave S windows. All three have broad pointed trefoiled rere-arches. The small E window has renewed bar tracery (two-light with an encircled quatrefoil) – that is, late C13.

The most important thing about the church, however, is the WALL PAINTINGS. They are probably of *c.* 1300, but some friezes below may be C12. In the nave a fine large Death of the Virgin. In the chancel, a large Coronation of the Virgin, and single figures, bishops and saints, on the walls and in the window splays. Fictive masonry on the chancel arch. Some C17 black-letter text over the arch facing the nave. – FONT. Norman, circular, with one cable moulding. – STAINED GLASS. E and W, *c.* 1882, perhaps by *Hardman.* S window, 1918.

In the churchyard, an octagonal C15 CROSS-SHAFT with moulded cap, standing on a tomb-like slab.

SUTTON BINGHAM MANOR. Early C17 (detached datestone of 1608), extended 1887 and 1927. Gabled, with mullioned windows. U-plan. The N front and E cross-wing with storeyed E porch are C17. Victorian Gothic staircase. In the W room a C17 oak overmantel of two panels between Ionic columns.

SUTTON MALLET

CHURCH (Churches Conservation Trust). A chapelry of Moorlinch. 1827, by *Richard Carver*, except for the short unbuttressed W tower. This, however, was thickened (by *Carver* probably) in 1832–3, with a giant pointed W arch to carry a new top stage. C16 mullioned W window and bell-lights, now absurdly low under Carver's top, which has shallow-gabled parapets. The rest of the church is a preaching box with minimal Tudor detail, hoodmoulded nave windows and a thin ashlar porch. Five-sided apse with reused Perp E window. Originally roughcast. Typical broad interior with a simple WEST GALLERY, high BOX PEWS and a three-decker PULPIT, all of pine. In the apse reused C17 RAILS.

SUTTON FARMHOUSE, ½ m. WNW. Late medieval hall house with a wind-braced roof. Enlarged with two wings on the front.

SUTTON MONTIS

HOLY TRINITY. All of ochre stone with a squat W tower overlooking a grand view. The unbuttressed tower with lean-to S stair-turret could be C13 – see the slot-like coupled bell-openings and Lias tower arch on the plainest imposts, though both are too plain to be definitive. Perp W window. Battlements with Georgian obelisks. There was rebuilding in 1805, including perhaps the Y-traceried N windows. But the two three-light nave s windows are C15–C16, flat-headed with ogee-headed lights. Absurdly contrasting Late Georgian pedimented porch between them, with Tuscan columns. The chancel is late C13 – see the two-light side windows with foiled circles in the heads. Hoodmoulds with headstops, heads also to the gable kneelers. E window of 1862.

Norman chancel arch with five-layer chevron, the middle layer with pellets. Inset columns with renewed capitals, one with anthemion. Chancel rere-arches on slender shafts with moulded capitals. Nave ceiling and FURNISHINGS from *F. Bligh Bond*'s restoration of 1913. – FONT. Perp, re-tooled. – PULPIT. C17, with arabesques and concave lozenges. Panelled back and early C18 ogee-domed tester. – ROYAL ARMS. 1805. – MEMORIALS. Cicely Spreat †1921. Solemn angel in a grey vine-carved frame. – STAINED GLASS. Patterned chancel glass of 1862. W window, 2000. Subtle colours, by *John Hayward*.

ABBEY HOUSE, NW of the church, was a C15 priest's house. Diagonal buttress and first-floor traceried two-light window at the W end. Other windows flat-headed, some with Tudor lights. Storeyed S porch. The lateral N chimney serves C15 fireplaces in both W rooms. Wind-braced roof. Opposite the church, PARSONAGE FARM is early C17, ashlar-fronted with ovolo-moulded mullions. GOLDSBOROUGH FARMHOUSE has similar windows (two with king mullions). Up Rectory Hill, the OLD RECTORY is mid-C18, two-plus-five bays. Continuing S, the former SCHOOL, 1840s, like a miniature medieval hall and cross-wing, and BLANDFORD HOUSE, *c.* 1800, Cary ashlar with pedimented doorcase. SUTTON MONTIS HOUSE has a plain Late Georgian centre between taller additions, early C19 and Edwardian. The latter, a large house on its own, has Voysey-style detail. HOME FARMHOUSE, 1889, typical of the Portman estate, is pyramid-roofed and strikingly coloured, grey and red. SUTTON FARMHOUSE, hip-roofed, five bays, reputedly dates from the 1830s despite typically early C18 bolection-moulded architraves and corniced lower windows.

PADDOCK HOUSE, ¼ m. E. 1913–14 by *Kingsley Jupp* of Beaminster. Rough ochre stone, of E-plan with interestingly minimal detail. Contemporary cottages.

SWELL

Just the manor house and church, like a private chapel.

ST CATHERINE. Small and perfect mid-C15 Perp. Roughcast apart from the W wall of White Lias. Deep-set windows of Ham stone. A Victorian bellcote has gone. Porch arch unexpectedly of Beer stone, with C16–C17 graffiti. Norman S doorway with two orders of colonnettes under a latticed arch (cf. Barton St David and Kingweston) with minutely detailed pellets. The capitals are scalloped with small motifs. A lovely, luminous and invisibly restored interior of white walls, golden stone and grey flagstones under barrel ceilings. C15 nave ceiling, C17 ceiling in the chancel. Panelled chancel arch. Defaced E wall niches. Trefoiled PISCINA, the small scalloped bowl reused C13. – FONT. C13? Octagonal, scraped. – PULPIT. 1634. Arabesque panels between turned colonnettes. Matching LECTERN. – COMMUNION RAIL. C17. Turned balusters. – BENCHES. Plain, probably C16. – STAINED GLASS. Quite a collection of C15–C16 fragments. An angel with the Beauchamp shield in the E window.

SWELL MANOR. An Early Tudor manor house altered in the C18. Startlingly white render with Ham stone detail. Cross-wings flank a hall with a two-centred cross-passage doorway to the r. of three tall square-headed windows. The doorway has big leaves in the spandrels, and the hall windows have depressed or four-centred arched heads. The cross-wings have diagonal buttresses and C18 hipped roofs, the W cross-wing a big six-light transomed parlour window. Original and C18 windows in the long NE rear wing. (Cross-passage and screen; parts of a late C15 hall roof with carved detail.) In the farmyard, a large brick gabled GRANARY.

SYDENHAM MANOR *see* BRIDGWATER

TARR STEPS
3 m. SW of Winsford

CLAPPER BRIDGE over the River Barle, the longest in Britain at 180 ft (55 metres), and the image of the Exmoor region. Seventeen spans formed from great slabs up to 8 ft (2.4 metres) long rest on piers of flat stones, with leaning slabs as cutwaters. Repeatedly washed away and reassembled. Often called prehistoric; recent opinion inclines to a medieval date.

TATWORTH

ST JOHN EVANGELIST. 1850–1, by *Charles Pinch*. E.E. style with spired W bellcote. Tall bare interior. WEST GALLERY, 1860.
PARROCK'S LODGE. 1801. Reduced by a storey. Creamy ashlar. 1–3–1 bays, and pavilions with plaques of *Coade*(?) stone. Within the later porch a broad doorway with delicate elliptical fanlight. Plaster-vaulted hall and tightly curved cantilevered staircase. Gothick STABLES.

s from the church, LONG HADDON incorporates a C15 hall house. W of the school, the thatched OLD CHAPEL, rebuilt c. 1836, includes a headless W lancet from a C14–C15 chapel that stood nearby. Post Office Lane curves to SPRINGFIELD, roughcast, disguising another C15 hall house. Mid-C18 panelled room. The long MANOR HOUSE has C15–C16 jointed crucks.

PERRY STREET LACE FACTORY, ¾ m. SE. Mostly demolished. The mid-C19 stuccoed OFFICE remains, fronted like a chapel.

CHARDSTOCK HOUSE, 1 m. NW. Early C19 stuccoed villa under a broad hipped roof. Grecian columned porch.

MANOR FARMHOUSE, Forton, ½ m. NE. Large lateral chimney on a C15 hall. Upstairs, mid-C17 biblical texts painted on sloping ceiling panels.

TAUNTON

2020

The county town, in the vale of the River Tone. There was an Anglo-Saxon settlement on the castle site with a minster church, and Wilton church, outside the centre, retains traces of Anglo-Saxon work. By the C10 Taunton was the centre of the manor of the Bishops of Winchester. The bishops' castle dominated the medieval history of the vale. Taunton also had an Augustinian priory and two large parish churches. A market town, it was the county seat from 1843 when the gaol and assizes moved from Ilchester. Consolidation as county centre was followed by the foundation of middle-class schools, with no fewer than three large Gothic schools built by Wesleyans (1846), Anglicans (1867–9) and Congregationalists (1867–70). Victorian middle-class housing along the radial arteries; working-class housing concentrated N and E of the centre. The built character has been determined by the local brick, brown shaded with pink, giving way to yellow and red in the later C19. The town expanded with council and private estates from the 1920s, accelerating after 1945. Its industrial base grew with the canals to Bridgwater (1827) and Tiverton (1835) and the early arrival of the railway (1842). The principal industry was textiles, silk in the early C19 giving way to shirt-making, and shirt collars by the later C19. There was also iron-founding, and brewing was important.

CHURCHES AND CHAPELS

ST MARY MAGDALENE, Church Square. Here more than anywhere one is puzzled by the contrast of scale and care between tower and body of the church. The church is big, and its double aisles are certainly an effort to do the exceptional. Yet much more would have been needed for an interior to stand up to the pomp and circumstance of the 163-ft (50-metre) tower. This was rebuilt from the ground in 1858–62 by *Benjamin Ferrey* and *George Gilbert Scott*, in red Williton sandstone with

35, p. 30

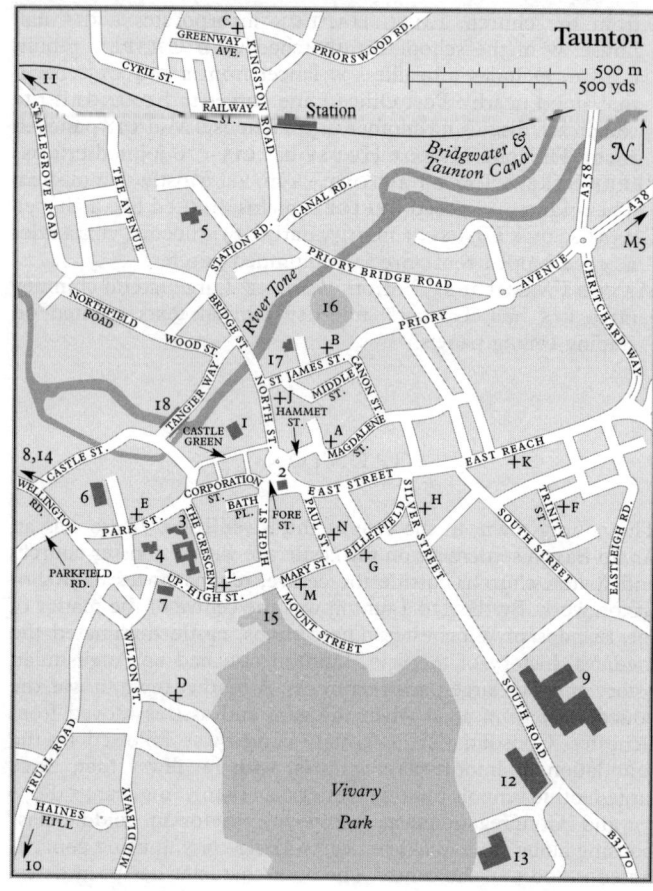

A St Mary Magdalene
B St James
C St Andrew
D St George, Wilton
E St John
F Holy Trinity
G St George (R.C.)
H Baptist church
J Congregational church
K Octagon Chapel
L Temple Methodist Church
M Unitarian chapel
N United Reformed church

1 Taunton Castle
2 Market House
3 County Offices
4 Shire Hall
5 Deane House
6 Magistrates' Court
7 Police Station
8 Somerset College
9 King's College
10 Queen's College
11 Taunton School
12 Richard Huish College
13 Bishop Fox School
14 Musgrove Park Hospital
15 Vivary Park
16 County Cricket Ground
17 Brewhouse Theatre
18 New Tone Bridge

Ham stone dressings (carving by *R. Boulton*). The job was apparently done extremely carefully, without visual damage. The design is brought out to perfection by the Hammet Street approach, an C18 idea of course, quite alien to medieval conceptions. But it is only from a greater distance that one realizes to the full how capricious the contour of the tower is, with the pinnacles standing distant from the wall below the battlements, and with the whole crown projecting so that it would be top-heavy if air were not let through the filigree battlements and filigree top pinnacles. The effect is of looking through lace, yet with all its fancies it is still very much English Perp in that all major lines are kept straight, with nothing of the flowing and swelling which France or Germany or Spain would have indulged in at the time. This effect is not typical of Somerset but derives from Gloucester Cathedral of the 1450s, via St Stephen, Bristol, of the 1470s, and Dundry (N) of 1484. The date here can be determined by wills offering money for the building dating from 1488 to 1514.

Now in detail. The tower has set-back buttresses with attached pinnacles on three tiers and then the already mentioned very big and tall detached pinnacles set diagonally. They reach up to the bell-openings. The w front has a doorway with big spandrels filled by defaced scenes of the legend of the Magdalene, almost the only original stonework. A canopied stoup on each side. Above is a transomed five-light window. Doorway and window are flanked by statue niches. Then follows what is unique at Taunton: three tiers of twin three-light windows with transoms and pierced baffles, all the windows flanked by shafts and pinnacles. So instead of a contrast between bare wall and a blossoming out into open and ornamented forms at the bell-stage, Taunton prefers an even display of its riches. The first tiers are of about the same size, the bell-stage a good deal taller. Below each tier runs a quatre-foil frieze. The transoms of the windows in the two top tiers are enriched by demi-figures of angels. Furthermore, the lower tiers of windows carry crocketed ogee gables, while above the bell-openings the whole wall is blank panelling, and then yet another quatrefoil frieze prepares for the crown. This consists of very large battlements pierced in two-storeyed arcading. At the angles stand uncommonly tall pinnacles. They have four little storeys and then a crocketed spirelet. Once again, all this is pierced. Finally, to accompany battlements and pinnacles there are, corbelled out from the corners and the middle of the sides, yet thinner wholly detached shafts with pinnacles. On the s there are three niches at the level of the w window niches, on the N only two, because here the stair-turret rises – but not, as is the Somerset custom, higher than the crown.

The rest of the exterior is easily described. The aisles are of six bays, with five-light end windows and three-light side windows. The nave clerestory has four-centred four-light windows. The N side is the oldest part, although externally Perp. Less important than the s side, it has a plain parapet and is of rough rubble (two E bays of 1912 in red sandstone). The s side has Ham stone facing to the first three bays, that is porch and flanking bays, with particularly elaborate Perp tracery, i.e. a subsidiary centre of display. Rubble stone and narrower windows to the next three bays. The rich porch, dated 1508, is of two storeys with finials on its buttresses, NW stair-turret, and three canopied niches above the doorway, the middle one for three figures (C19 Crucifixion with thieves) on a candelabra-like support. Star-vault inside and doorway with the Five Wounds on one spandrel shield. The parapet of pierced quatrefoils continues over the whole aisle (copied in the C19 on the chancel), whereas the nave parapet is of pierced triangles. Thin parapet finials, many missing. The tall four-bay chancel has diagonal E buttresses with finials and a big seven-light window. SE chapel with plain parapet. A NE addition (1992, by *Martin Stancliffe*) screens a double gable, the clearest external indication of the peculiarity of double aisles inside.

INTERIOR. There are indeed two arcades of six bays on each side, the inner aisles much narrower than the outer. The arcade between the N aisles is the only conspicuous survival of the church before the present one. It dates from the late C13. The piers are circular with four attached shafts, the capitals are of simple moulded form, and the arches double-chamfered. Carved head responds, a king and a bishop. The rest is Perp, and the surprise is that no more is done to distinguish this large parish church from others in the county. The piers have the standard shaft-and-hollow section. In one of them is a large canopied niche. The capitals are handsome, with angel busts, and there are also angel busts in the capitals of the high, panelled tower arch. Higher still a fine fan-vault. Between the arcade arches thin shafts rise to yet more angels carrying canopied niches (statues of 1871) between the clerestory windows (cf. Martock). The canopies carry the braces of the fine Somerset ROOF. Of moderate pitch and panelled, it has the usual decorated cambered tie-beams, kingposts, and a little tracery. Gilded angels against the kingposts and on the wall-plates, here supporting arched intermediate trusses. The inner aisles have narrow framed roofs on angel corbels. The outer s arcade matches the nave arcades. Chancel altered in 1869–70 by *G. E. Street*, contemporary with his reredos. Raised arcades, clerestory windows, new sedilia and piscina. The low-pitched ceiling was restored with painted decoration by *A. Stansell*. Street's chancel wall and fine gates were removed in 1980. SE chapel re-fitted 1912, by *F. W. Roberts*, with screens and painted decoration.

FURNISHINGS. FONT. 1843, by *Benjamin Ferrey*, with a tall spired COVER. – PULPIT. 1867, by *Ferrey*. Lavish with canopied saints between green marble shafts. – REREDOS. By *Street*, 1869–70, carved by *Thomas Earp*. Stone, elaborate, and delicately coloured. Relief of the Agony in the Garden. – TOWER SCREEN. 1843, by *Ferrey*. – ROYAL ARMS. 1637. – GLASS DOORS. 2008. Engraved by *Tracey Sheppard*. – STAINED GLASS.

w window, 1862, splendidly coloured Last Judgment, by *Alexander Gibbs*. Chancel glass 1887 by *Clayton & Bell*. S aisle E, 1912, by *A. L. Moore*, miscellaneous notables. SE chapel S, two painted saints, by *William Ray* of Taunton. They look C18 but are of 1843. Compare the figures from the E window of 1843 by *Wailes*, re-set in the S aisle second window and N sixth. Medieval fragments in the N aisle and clerestory.

MONUMENTS. Thomas More †1576 (w end). The back of a dismantled altar tomb. Five panels containing shields around the full heraldic achievement. – Richard Huish †1612 (S aisle). Perhaps Victorian Jacobean? – John Young †1629 (SW corner), 'who repayring to this town to recover his health met with deth'. – Frances Lechland †1631 (N aisle). Exuberant heraldry, the shelf below marbled with painted strapwork. – Robert Gray †1638 (N aisle), founder of the almshouses. Painted life-size standing figure under an open curved pediment on big Ionic columns, of Somerset alabaster. 'Taunton bore him, London bred him, Piety trained him, Virtue led him.' – Bernard Smith †1696 (SE chapel). Engraved brass with cherubs between little aedicules. – William Courtenay, 1719 (w end), Baroque cartouche. – Mary Treble †1721 (NW corner). Incised Lias, painted black, red and gold. – Numerous Late Georgian memorials with typical urns, some mourning women, e.g. Sarah Dare, by *King* of Bath, 1808; Mary Norris, 1837, by *John Hinchliffe*. An unsigned memorial to Lt John Bliss †1828 (N aisle) shows dramatically his sinking ship.

ALL SAINTS, Halcon. 1952, by *Stone & Partners*. Left incomplete, fronted c. 1980 with abstract STAINED GLASS by *Henry Haig*.

HOLY TRINITY, Trinity Street. 1840–2, by *Richard Carver*. White Lias, and very white, in an original if decidedly pro archaeological Gothic. It cost £7,000. Sheer gabled buttresses emphasize the height of the 90-ft (27.4-metre) tower. It formerly had big pinnacles. Broad battlemented nave with narrow windows between gabled buttresses. Short chancel. Period interior: galleries on quatrefoil iron columns under an impressive open roof with tie-beams and much thin tracery. – ORGAN. 1846. By *Henry Willis*. Painted Gothic case. – PULPIT and FONT. 1881. – REREDOS. Carved stone, by *Bligh Bond*, 1916. – STAINED GLASS. Dispersed panels of the E window of 1858. Old-fashioned painterly style.

ST JAMES, St James's Street. Close to the site of Taunton Priory. Smaller than the Magdalene, though its tower is still impressive at 120 ft (36.6 metres). Like the Magdalene tower it was taken down and re-erected, in 1870–5 by *J. H. Spencer*. It closely resembles the slightly smaller towers at Bishop's Lydeard and Isle Abbots, the latter dated to the early C16. All three create the illusion of set-back buttresses by adding a square fillet in the angles. Buttresses with tiers of applied pinnacles, carrying tall diagonally set pinnacles against the bell-stage. The fillets have applied finials at different levels, in counterpoint. The crown, with pierced parapet and merlons, is not quite authentic, as *Spencer* added intermediate pinnacles, corner outriders and the top to the NE stair-turret.* The intermediate stages have one two-light window on each side (the third stage embellished with niches on the show S side) while the bell-stage has twin three-light windows, a more typical hierarchy than the overall sumptuousness of the Magdalene. Niches flank the W doorway. The body of the church is Perp, heavily rebuilt. There were arcades, but the S aisle was no more than a passage until widened in 1837–8 by *Richard Carver*. He kept the porch, adding the incongruous rose window. The eastern parts were rebuilt in 1884–5 by *Edmund Ferrey*, reusing the E window. Five-bay arcades, the N arcade slightly higher and with a double-width fifth arch, suggesting a transept. The corresponding S arch was altered to match by Carver. Standard piers with four hollows and the usual thin round capitals. The tower has a fan-vault, the tall moulded arch without capitals. C19 boarded roofs with tie-beams.

FURNISHINGS. FONT. C15. One of the most adorned in the county. Octagonal, with three saints under arcading each side, except one with the Crucifixion with the Virgin and Magdalen. The naïve figures are much restored. – PULPIT. 1633. Panelled with lozenge motifs, the narrow top panels with improbable mermaids. – SCREENS to S chapel. 1924, by *W. D. Caröe*. Burmese coco-wood; exhibited at the British Empire Exhibition. – ROYAL ARMS. Victorian. – STAINED GLASS. E window, 1860, by *Clayton & Bell*. Lovely Gothic drawing and vivid colours. W window, small scenes, 1875, by *Heaton, Butler & Bayne*. Four S aisle windows, 1886–91, signed *Swaine Bourne*. S chapel S, early C19 heraldry. – MONUMENTS. Maria Wyndham †1719. Corinthian pilasters. – Elizabeth Corfield †1811. By *Mark Long*. Woman and urn, copying one by *King* in St Mary Magdalene. – Lt-Col. Yea, killed 1855 at Sebastopol. With two standing fusiliers. By *T. Gaffin*.

The CHURCHYARD has iron Gothic GATES and railings of c. 1820. Red brick ALMSHOUSES to the E, 1897–8, by *Spencer*. Brown brick Tudorish former SCHOOL, N, 1828.

ST ANDREW, Kingston Road. 1879–81, by *J. H. Spencer*. The Rev. F. J. Smith (*see* St John, below) gave it as a church for the railway district in gratitude for Britain avoiding involvement in the Balkan conflict of 1876–8. Enveloped in S and E additions of 1892 by *Edmund Buckle*. Pinched between is Spencer's thin S tower with broach spire. All of Westleigh stone. Remarkable polychrome brick interior, Buckle echoing Spencer, save that Spencer's arcade piers are brick. Three arcades create a darkly complex space. Byzantinesque capitals in the chancel addition, with tiny carved scenes. Anglo-Catholic FITTINGS: lustrous green bowl FONT, 1912 (carved by *Messrs Bridgeman* of Lichfield); ROOD SCREEN, 1920. – Good STAINED GLASS, much by *Lavers & Westlake*, after 1893, including the

---

* The red Williton sandstone may also be inauthentic, as the brown stones reused on Mitre House, Park Street, are alleged to be from here.

spectacular Te Deum E window. SW window, 1881, by *Hardman*, the original E window. Railway window, 2002, by *Clare Maryan Green*.

ST GEORGE, Wilton. Much rebuilt. Although the church appears Perp it goes back very much further. Evidence of an aisleless church in the W wall each side of the tower: traces of Saxon long-and-short work to the l. and quoins to the r. The interior reveals that the church was already aisled in the late C13. Five-bay arcades of circular piers with four attached shafts, just as the outer N arcade at St Mary Magdalene (above). But the arches are C15–C16, four-centred. The previous tower was C13, unbuttressed and quite plain. C15–C16 S doorway, arched with leaf spandrels. *Richard Carver* extended the nave and rebuilt the chancel in 1837, and replaced the tower in 1853. *J. H. Spencer* added the S porch, 1870, the triple window above the chancel arch, 1884, and the reredos, 1887. Sanctuary embellished in 1903 by *Samson & Cottam*, in alabaster, marble, and tile mosaic. – ROYAL ARMS. 1787. – PULPIT. 1907, by *Dudley Forsyth*. An extraordinary thing of coloured marbles with mosaic and bronze. – STAINED GLASS. E window, colourful and over-detailed, 1890s. Nave E, 1884 by *Clayton & Bell*. SE, Annunciation, in rich blues and turquoise, 1962, by *Paul Jefferies*. – MONUMENTS. Sir Benjamin Hammet †1800. Grecian, the tapering relief of the soul ascending above a recumbent youth and eagle quintessentially Romantic. By *Sir Richard Westmacott*. – Early C19 plaques by the *Long* family. – Outside, a curious early C19 MEMORIAL, a tapered stone pedestal, the plinth hollowed for a tiny sarcophagus.

ST JOHN EVANGELIST, Park Street. 1858–63, by *G. G. Scott*. Muscular E.E., not in any local tradition, and a significant work of Scott's maturity. Of coloured local stones with a great deal of Ham stone. It cost the Rev. F. J. Smith (vicar of Holy Trinity) £12,000 and was intended to serve a poor district. Big SE tower with a spire. The tower has diapering of Ham stone over the bell-lights, and the spire is emphatically banded. At the foot are statues under spired tabernacles and four lucarnes. Triple-gabled W front with triple lancets beneath cinquefoil roundels. Splendid interior with much lively leaf carving – see the arcades of alternate round and shafted piers, especially the two-tier capitals of the latter. Concentrated shafting and capitals to the chancel arch and especially the tower arch. Stencilled roofs. – FONT and PULPIT, both massive and shafted, by *Scott*. – SCREEN. 1891–2. A little-known but major Arts and Crafts work by *J. D. Sedding*, or probably his partner, *Henry Wilson*, made by *Henry Longden* of Sheffield. A stark iron grid infilled with scrolls, alleviated with gold: a silhouette frieze of animals going to the ark, and over the archway, the Heavenly Jerusalem. Of the same scheme, the marble PAVING and the STALLS, a lively bestiary carved by *Trask* of Norton-sub-Hamdon. – ALTAR. 1964, by *Alan Rome*. Gilded gesso with vesica panel of Christ. – ORGAN. 1864, by *Henry Willis*. – STAINED GLASS. E and W windows by *Hardman*, 1863, the colours clear and radiant. Baptistery windows by *Dudley Forsyth*, 1914, good of their kind.

ST MICHAEL, Comeytrowe Centre, Galmington. 1987, by *Stephen Bartleet* of *Stone & Partners*. Barn-like with a gambrel roof. The hip-roofed ends are meeting rooms, and a square central church is lit from the gablets.

ST PETER, Eastwick Road. 1956, by *Michael Torrens*. Brick with concrete trusses.

ST GEORGE (R.C.), Billet Street. 1858–60, by *Benjamin Bucknall*. Purple Monkton stone. The tower (added 1875) proudly faces down the street, as at St Mary Magdalene. Its resemblance to Somerset towers is incidental: Bucknall intended a tall spire, and the tracery is flowing rather than Perp. Long pierced bell-openings divided by a transom, designed for tubular bells. Large W window. High aisled interior with clerestory, the capitals left uncarved except on the chancel arch. – PULPIT. Gothic, on marble-shafted base. – REREDOS with statuary, gables and spires, probably by *C. F. Hansom*. Similar SIDE ALTARS. – STATIONS OF THE CROSS. 1977, by *Tom Preater* of Taunton. – STAINED GLASS. E window, *c.* 1860, with six large canopied figures. W window, 2009, by *Patrick Reyntiens*. Christ in Majesty on glowing blues, greens and yellows.

Tudor-style brick PRESBYTERY by *Bucknall*. PARISH CENTRE, 1991, and former SCHOOL, 1870, beyond. Behind is the present SCHOOL, pyramid-roofed, by *Shirley-Smith & Gibson*, 1966.

ST TERESA (R.C.) Eastwick Road, Priorswood. 1958–60 by *Eric Francis*. A striking church, between Georgian and Swedish Modern. Red brick, steep-roofed. The tapering S tower carries a glazed octagon under a flèche like a radio mast. Broad nave lit from dormers, with transverse arches on scrolled brackets. Passage aisles. – Monumental octagonal FONT with festive scrolled cover.

BAPTIST CHURCH, Silver Street. 1814, hip-roofed, of red brick. Refronted twice, latterly in stucco, 1870, by *J. H. Smith*, Borough Surveyor, in that debased round-arched Italian Trecento style called Lombard, popular with Nonconformists. Mid-C19 curved-ended gallery on iron columns.

CONGREGATIONAL CHURCH, North Street. 1843, by *James Pollard*. Eroding lancet Gothic front of red sandstone and Ham stone. It had twin pencil finials. Church-like interior with stone arcades, the galleries set behind.

OCTAGON CHAPEL, East Reach. 1965 by *Steel, Coleman & Davis*. Yellow brick octagon, faintly echoing Wesley's Octagon (*see* Middle Street) where the Open Brethren had been since 1892.

QUAKER MEETING HOUSE, Bath Place. 1816. Plain brick. Hipped roof.

TEMPLE METHODIST CHURCH, Upper High Street. Brown brick, Gothic. The gable of the chapel of 1846 by *James Wilson* remains between turrets, but in 1868–9 *Samuel Shewbrooks* rebuilt everything else. The new church is parallel to the road, with a schoolroom across the E end. Large interior, arcaded on impressively tall cast-iron columns with naturalistic capitals. Broad galleries set back. – PULPIT, by *Benjamin Ferrey*, 1842, from St Mary Magdalene.

UNITARIAN CHAPEL, Mary Street. 1721. The five-bay stuccoed front of 1881 (by *J. H. Spencer*) replaces one with twin scrolled-pediment doorways. The interior is the best surviving Nonconformist auditorium in the county. Two massively disproportionate fluted Corinthian pillars of timber prop the ceiling. From three sides panelled galleries face the PULPIT, itself panelled with undercut decoration. Diminutive pedimented pulpit-back. – Fine three-tier CANDELABRA, 1728, on a complicated iron hanger. – MONUMENTS. John Noble †1733. With flaming urns, by *Esau Osborn*. – Bartholomew Rosseloty †1824. Grecian.

Attached SCHOOLS, 1886, in the then fashionable Norman Shaw style. Red brick with a little purple sandstone, Queen Anne sash windows and a corner tower with square dome and cupola.

UNITED REFORMED CHURCH, Paul Street. The Paul's Meeting of 1672, rebuilt in 1797 as a five-bay brick box. It had parapet urns and three doorways. Now there are outer porches of 1877. Large square interior with Victorian galleries and pulpit. – MONUMENTS. Rev. Immanuel Harford †1706. Small Baroque cartouche. – John Westcott, 'serge-maker', †1781. Lively winged cherub head.

TAUNTON CASTLE

The castle and Taunton Deane estate of the Bishops of Winchester originated in C8 grants of land. The bishops' hall became a castle probably in the early C12, and was strengthened by Bishop Henry of Blois during the wars of 1139–54. The first mention of stone is of repairs to turrets in 1264. The keep probably stood on a mound E of the triangular inner ward. The NW wall and W end of the inner ward display characteristic C12 flat buttresses. The S side was probably walled at the same time, for which the prime piece of evidence is a re-set Norman beakhead arch in Castle House. The NW range contained the Great Hall, the short W block the bishop's chamber or camera, and the S range the chapel, gatehouse and lodgings. Remodellings are recorded in 1207 for Bishop des Roches, 1246–50 for Bishop Raleigh, and in the late C15 for bishops Waynflete and Langton.

More administrative centre than great fortress, Taunton was nevertheless sufficiently a castle to be besieged in 1451 and sufficiently garrisoned in 1497 for the Constable to end Perkin Warbeck's uprising. Decayed in the C16, it was repaired by Bishop Horne in 1578. The S range was a prison by the early C17, but the castle was 'much ruinated' by 1635. Hastily fortified, it held out for Parliament under heavy siege in 1644–5. Parliament ordered it rendered indefensible in 1651, and Charles II ordered demolition in 1662. But it was intact enough for Judge Jeffreys to try 526 rebels in three days in 1685, presumably in the hall.

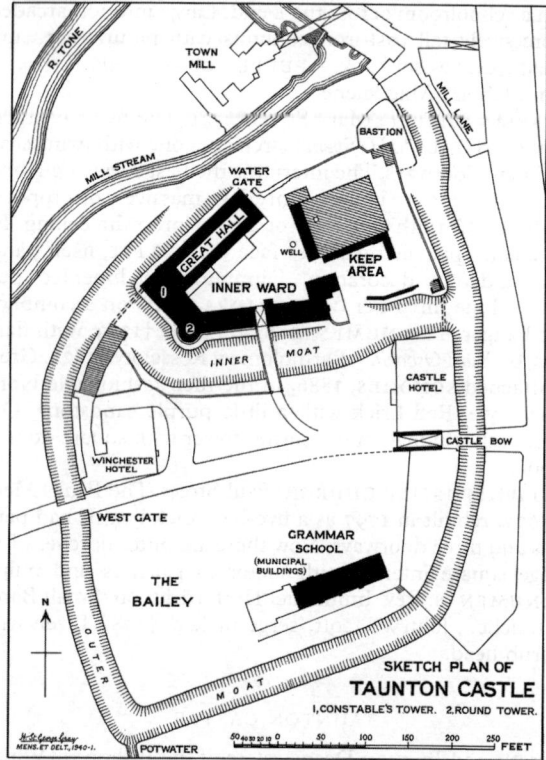

Taunton Castle.
Plan

The apartments E of the gatehouse were refashioned *c.* 1700 as Castle House. In 1786 Sir Benjamin Hammet initiated radical rebuilding for the Assize Courts: courtrooms in the great hall, judges' lodgings in the W and S ranges. This work, still in progress *c.* 1816, is marked by Georgian Gothic windows and chert rubble facing. The courts moved out in 1858 and the castle was rescued by the Somerset Archaeological and Natural History Society in 1874. The society used *J. H. Spencer* for repairs before 1911, and made two substantial later additions: galleries in front of the Great Hall in 1931–2 and the Wyndham Galleries in 1934. The county took over the museum in 1958. The Wyndham Galleries were subsequently enlarged as the military museum, and the whole complex was refurbished in 2007–13.

From North Street, the OUTER WARD, now Castle Green, is reached through CASTLE BOW, the eastern gateway, a substantial vaulted structure some 50 ft (15.2 metres) long, with double-chamfered C13 arches. The upper storeys with Georgian Gothic windows were added *c.* 1816 with the adjoining

Castle Hotel. CASTLE GREEN, long a car park, was brought back to civic use in 2011–12 by *LDA Design*, paved with a raised lawn. The castle sits low on the N side, behind a dry moat. The line of the southern ramparts is the arc from the Castle Hotel along the backs of the Corporation Street buildings, to the Winchester Arms and Castle Lodge on the W. Outer walls of cob and thatch are recorded, also a stone W gatehouse, all gone. The Winchester Arms and Castle Hotel were near-matching castellated buildings of 1816, built in harmony with Hammet's alterations to the castle. The smaller WINCHESTER ARMS remains as built, two-storeyed, with Georgian Gothic windows. The CASTLE HOTEL was similar, between three-storey ends (one end over the Castle Bow), but was raised after 1930 to four storeys and the pointed windows changed, except on the ends. At the NW corner, CASTLE LODGE has a curving late C17 N front, of brick, with a raised band from which labels frame the ground-floor window heads. Mid-C18 staircase. FOOTBRIDGE, W of the castle, skirting the moat, of 2011–12, by *Flint & Neill*, engineers, with *Moxon Architects*. Designed for minimal physical and visual impact, the balustrades and outer parts of the footway are of plate glass, illuminated to striking nocturnal effect. Just W of it, the brick WYNDHAM HALL, 1927, by *F. W. Roberts*, incorporates a C16 oak doorway from the Post Office site.

The surviving castle buildings are around the S and N sides and short W end of the roughly triangular INNER WARD. A dry moat on the S and W. The Pipe Rolls refer to a great tower and turrets at Taunton. This may be the missing KEEP, which was probably to the E in the garden of the Castle Hotel. A platform found in 1924–9 has impressive chamfered stonework on the W and S sides, and a SE projection. But the stonework looks more like revetment than the foundations of a massive structure. Because the site slopes down from Castle Green, the S RANGE of the castle looks low. Its battlements and chert facing are late C18. The GATEHOUSE, however, was not altered. It has a plain chamfered segmental-pointed S arch of the C13–C14, with portcullis slot within. The upper part was rebuilt in 1495–6 by Bishop Langton, whose arms are over the arch. The parapet has eroded arms of Henry VII, who received Warbeck's submission here in 1497. The face to the courtyard is all late C15, apart from the NE stair-turret, refaced in 1886. Straight joints at first-floor level W of the gatehouse indicate an infill bay, called the 'Bridehowse' or lock-up in 1638. C16 mullioned windows. In this piece and above the gate itself are small rooms used for the administration of the manor. Large Lias quoins W of the infill may indicate C13 work. Here was the first-floor chapel, which Hammet remodelled for the justices' dining room. The outside has Hammet's Gothic windows and chert refacing. Mullioned windows below by *Spencer*, 1874 and 1910. To the courtyard the dining room is windowless, but Hammet lit the room below with reused C16 mullion windows. To the r. a reused four-light Perp window lights the stair hall, over a pointed doorway and C13 lancet. The first-floor quatrefoil on the outside is also a Hammet insertion. The SW TOWER, invisible within the court, is externally all Hammet's, with pointed windows to the two circular rooms. Hammet's Adamesque decoration survives in both rooms. Simple Gothic cornices, curved panelled doors. The staircase behind, partly later C18, gives access also to the judges' dining room, named the ADAM ROOM for the delicate wooden chimneypiece, attributed to the *Adam* brothers. Plaster barrel vault, in panels, radial fluting in the tympana. The deep embrasures of the curtain wall are echoed in arcading on the inner wall. Above is, in part, a late C15 wagon roof, perhaps that of the chapel.

N of the tower is the keep-like battlemented block of the bishops' apartment or CAMERA. Rectangular, with square NE turret. The C12 building was raised and also extended southward in the mid C13, perhaps over an existing porch. This S bay has a Hammet window on each floor on the outer face and a Victorian neo-Norman museum entry to the courtyard. The narrow rectangular window above is one of four that lit the chamber, the reveals of the others visible inside. C12 flat buttresses on the outside to the ground floor, higher at the NW corner. The undercroft barrel vault is a C13 insertion doubling the thickness of the curtain wall, as shown by a small W loop that no longer penetrates right through. The vault is plastered. The jambs of the S doorway of the C12 undercroft remain, now internal. Three Hammet first-floor windows to the outside, W, and a larger ground-floor one on the N end. Above this two long C13 lancets, one renewed. In the first-floor chamber are segmental-pointed embrasures of the four E windows, and arched ones for the two N lancets. Hammet's windows on both floors are blocked for museum purposes.

The NW RANGE, the Great Hall, under its long low-pitched roof of 1816, is disappointing. The hall, almost featureless now, began as a C12 first-floor hall raised on an undercroft, but was altered to a ground-floor hall in the mid C13 and narrowed by rebuilding the S wall further in. The crease of the C13 roof remains on the W wall. The hall was extended E in the C16–C17, of which date the pair of large oak mullion-and-transom windows in the E wall. The N wall is mostly C12 (see the buttresses). The massive thickness reduces at eaves level of the medieval hall. Above this four large mullion-and-transom windows of C16–C17 type, rising as catslide dormers forward of a thin upper wall. One window was inserted in 1863, the others are shown in early C19 views. All have smaller bottom lights as if used upside down. On the courtyard side are oval lights of *c.* 1700 and a blocked square-headed C16 doorway. The hip-roofed courtyard addition of 1931–2, by *Stone & Francis*, in the style of 1700, replaces a Jury Room of *c.* 1800 on an open columned ground floor. Between the hall and the Wyndham Galleries, the new MUSEUM entrance, 2010–11, by *Feilden Clegg Bradley*, flat-roofed, plate glass, the front turned towards the gatehouse. In the same programme, single-storey pieces each side of the 1931–2 range were rebuilt. Otherwise the very extensive works were internal or repairs. The WYNDHAM GALLERIES to the E, by *Sir George Oatley*, 1933–4, had a hipped roof before 1974, when it was raised with a flat roof. During refurbishment, 2009, the curtain wall was traced beneath this building.

Finally E of the gatehouse, behind the S wall, is CASTLE HOUSE, probably a late C15 lodgings range remodelled *c.* 1700, as shown by mullioned windows with four-centred lights above timber cross-windows. The timber shell-hood may be reused as it does not fit the width of the doorway. The taller cross-wing was added *c.* 1700, its back wall on the footings of the eastern wall of the inner ward. A hip-roofed NE addition is C18. The first-floor chamber has a handsome roof of arch-braced trusses, tree-ring-dated to 1483. The roof continues beyond the timber-framed E wall, indicating a suite of rooms. Moulded stone S fireplace. By the fireplace, at floor level, the head of a doorway of C12 voussoirs decorated with beakheads, a type very rare in Somerset. A doorway here is inexplicable in the context of the castle curtain wall. Investigation during the repairs in 2012–13 by *Robert Battersby* for the Somerset Building Preservation Trust failed to explain it. The room below has panelling of *c.* 1700 and beams of *c.* 1483, so the range was always floored. No structural division to the cross-wing, which has a principal staircase with thick ramped rails. Reused moulded stonework to the doorway to the NE addition.

Just N of Castle House, one bay of the timber-framed ST JAMES'S ALMSHOUSES, late C15, dismantled 1897 and thrice re-erected, lastly by *Paul Quinn*, 2009. Substantial post-and-truss frame with tension-braces and jettied first floor.

PUBLIC BUILDINGS

MARKET HOUSE, The Parade. 1770–2 by *Coplestone Warre Bampfylde* of Hestercombe, an amateur of wealth and influence. Red brick, larger than its good proportions initially suggest. Three-storey, five-bay front with a painted stone rusticated doorway connected to a pedimented window above. Remarkable cruciform arcaded markets on each side were demolished in 1930 for unremarkable two-storey attachments by *H. S. W. Stone*. *Professor Charles Reilly* was consultant. He may have suggested stretching an ashlar pediment across all five bays, replacing a parapet and clock turret, a successful intervention.

COUNTY OFFICES, The Crescent. A large formal composition by *Vincent Harris*, 1932–5. Two hip-roofed wings at right angles connected by a nine-bay concave-curved range. Buff brick with Portland stone dressings, akin to Harris's Bristol Council House of 1933. Pevsner disliked its 'meaningless aedicules with columns and pediments' and its failure to relate to the Shire Hall in a 'large campus composition'. But Harris's aedicules (one each side of the curved range) make monumental what is essentially an office block, and, as the Shire Hall faced the gaol, Harris chose to face the town. Barrel-vaulted ashlar-lined entrance hall (disused). RAILINGS of red Somerset dragons clutching sceptres like ice-creams.

Behind, a quietly careful quadrangle of 1962–4, by *Goodwin & Tatum* of London, to which they added an eight-storey slab in 1968–9. The quadrangle is raised on pilotis and has good landscaping, with a moat placed asymmetrically across the courtyard. The later addition is darker, slate-clad, and well-proportioned, the mass broken by an inset fourth floor.

SHIRE HALL, Shuttern. 1855–8, by *W. B. Moffatt*, Gilbert Scott's former partner. Large irregular Early Tudor group of courts and judges' lodgings. It cost £28,000. Moffatt was prolix with bays, turrets, etc., but the underlying symmetry marks him as less inventive than Scott. Broad central porch beneath a very large square bay window, mildly unbalanced by a turret. Twin rear gables with giant traceried windows mark the courtrooms. Two flamboyant roof lanterns have gone, one over each part. Inside were three high chambers, the entrance hall, since floored for the County Council meeting room, and hammer-beam-roofed courtrooms, reached up a dividing stair with iron rails. Since 1860 the hall has housed the 'Somerset Valhalla', BUSTS of notables including Pym, Blake, Locke, Speke, etc.

DEANE HOUSE, Belvedere Road. 1987. Offices of Taunton Deane Borough Council. Coloured brick with hipped roofs. The offices, car parks, and SWIMMING POOL of 1976, cover the grounds of FLOOK HOUSE. Badly treated, stuccoed, with C18 to Victorian detail. A lost SE range had a strapwork overmantel dated 1652.

MAGISTRATES' COURTS, St John's Road. 1992, by *Somerset County Architects*, project architect *Graham Whiteley*. A cramped site. Red brick, steep-gabled in Victorian reference, decorated in contrasting blue brick. Entrances understated to invisibility.

POLICE STATION, Shuttern. Brown brick, 1940, by *Somerset County Architects*. It replaces the forebuilding of TAUNTON GAOL. The grim former prison by *Richard Carver*, 1843, largely survives. A twenty-five-bay, three-storey cell block (original cell windows to the W half) runs behind the octagonal observation tower that formerly commanded exercise yards and a demolished four-storey block running s.

LIBRARY, Paul Street. Reused supermarket under a multi-storey car park of 1973. Notable only for *Philip Thomason*'s terracotta dragon, 1996.

SOMERSET COLLEGE OF ARTS AND TECHNOLOGY, Wellington Road. The front buildings, box shapes clad in silver and blue metal, of 2005, by *LHC Architects* of Exeter, are flashy compared to the ART SCHOOL, 1972, by *Somerset County Architects* (project architects *Peter Hirst* and *Derek Rutherford*). This is a locally rare example of Brutalism, the aesthetic deliberately harsh. Dark brown brick layered with board-marked concrete. Hard-wearing interiors – concrete floors and ceilings, painted brick walls – planned to maximize natural light. To the NE, the GENESIS BUILDING, by *Architype*, 2006, displays sustainable building technologies. To a glazed hall are attached 'pods' of wood, earth, straw and clay, more didactic than practical.

KING'S COLLEGE, South Road. 1867–9, by *C. E. Giles*, for the Grammar School. Re-founded in 1880 by Canon Woodard as one of his middle-class schools. Purple Monkton stone. The main block is hip-roofed with plate tracery and Ruskinian naturalistic carving. Central tower with steep pavilion roof and flèche. The big schoolroom projects on the l., with plate-traceried end window and apex niche. A rear NE quadrangle has *Giles*'s dining hall on the E, a good Tudor cloistral range, 1899–1901, on the W, by *Walter Tower*, and on the N, the CHAPEL begun in 1903, also by *Tower*. The promoters of the chapel sought (as at Lancing, Sussex) to bind their successors by laying out the whole length and beginning at both ends, with the W half (roofed temporarily in 1908) and a SE chapel. These remained separate until *H. S. W. Stone* added the E half in 1936. The W front shows the initial ambition with its fine stone doorway and neat stair-turret, but the window is capped flat as the intended height was never achieved. Whitewashed interior under a modern low-pitched roof, the great length giving a barn-like calm. – CRUCIFIX by *Kempe*, 1907, carved by *Zwinck* of Oberammergau. – Quadrangle CROSS by *Tower*, 1920. – WAR MEMORIAL panel in the cloister by *Kempe & Co*. HEADMASTER'S HOUSE, SW, 1926–7, by *Tower*, manorial and surprisingly large (it bankrupted the school). Behind it, LIBRARY, 2010–11, by *Mitchell Taylor* of Bath, of burnt misshapen bricks of an interesting texture. Three gables fold over at the ends of parallel roof-lights.

QUEEN'S COLLEGE, Trull Road. 1846–7, by *James Wilson*, for the Wesleyan Collegiate Institution. North Curry sandstone with Bath stone. Symmetrical Early Tudor with mighty central tower and projecting wings, as Wilson pioneered at Cheltenham College, 1840, and repeated at Kingswood School, Bath, 1850–2. A potent type for the British public school, followed twice in Taunton alone. The tower has a complex angular two-storey oriel and the wings have large three-tier mullioned windows under Star of David roundels. To the NE, a brick JUNIOR SCHOOL, 1880, going Gothic on the skyline.

TAUNTON SCHOOL, Staplegrove Road. Founded in 1847 by Congregationalists. The new building of 1867–70 is grandly near-symmetrical, with central pyramid-roofed tower and projecting dining-room and schoolroom wings, like Queen's and King's, writ larger. By *Joseph James*, a favoured Congregationalist architect. Gothic of course, in grey Westleigh stone. Attached to the r., a low LIBRARY, 1911–12, by *Frank Wills*. To the E, SCIENCE BUILDING, in fine ashlar, 1923–5, by *Vincent Harris*. Stripped Tudor blocks on each side of a war memorial entrance hall, excellently carved by *Read* of Exeter. Purple sandstone CHAPEL, 1906–7, by *Wills*. Its E.E. detail and apsed cruciform plan look forty years older, but are wholeheartedly done. Complete stained glass by *Powell's*, 1906–21. Mosaic apse decoration. By the entrance, FAIRWATER, the predecessor house. Seven-bay Regency stucco front. The rear, of brick, preserves a mid-C18 rusticated doorcase. PREPARATORY SCHOOL, 1910–11, by *F. W. Roberts*, with half-timbered gables, extended 1928. Roberts did much else in the early to mid C20, mostly in buff brick.

RICHARD HUISH COLLEGE, South Road. 1961–3, by *Somerset County Architects* (project architect *Dennis Tabert*). Two-storeyed, concrete-framed, flat-roofed ranges, logically laid out, the classroom block at right angles to an entrance range with hall behind. In a different vein, the curved MUSIC SCHOOL, 2002, by *NVB Architects*.

BISHOP FOX COMMUNITY SCHOOL, off South Road. 1993–4, by *Somerset County Architects* (*Gerald Fogwill* project architect). A much softer aesthetic than Richard Huish College. Hip-roofed pavilions of coloured brick around a courtyard, fronted by an octagonal assembly hall. Car park GATES by *James Horrobin*.

MUSGROVE PARK HOSPITAL, Wellington Road. Very large hip-roofed main buildings of 1987–95 in orange brick. JUBILEE BUILDING, 2012–14, by *BDP* (Bristol office). Much glass, and wall cladding of coloured ceramic panels. Near the main building, wrought-iron BUS SHELTER by *James Horrobin*.

RAILWAY STATION. The Bristol & Exeter station of 1842 survives on the S side, simple two-storeyed brick, between altered single-storey wings. Contemporary former RAILWAY HOTEL opposite. There were two stations end-to-end on the same side until 1868. The N side was rebuilt in 1931–2.

NEW TONE BRIDGE, Castle Street. 2007–11, by *Flint & Neill*, engineers, with *Moxon Architects*. Twin openwork arches support the deck on angled stainless steel ties. Walkways cantilevered on each side. Appalling hard landscaping of the approaches.

VIVARY PARK. Laid out 1894–5. The ornate Victorian cast-iron GATES facing High Street are by Messrs *Macfarlane* of Glasgow, 1895, who supplied the BANDSTAND and the hilarious tiered FOUNTAIN, 1907.* WAR MEMORIAL, 1921–2, by *Ivor Shellard*, Borough Surveyor. Portland stone domed canopy over a granite stele recording the names.

COUNTY CRICKET GROUND, St James's Street. Laid out 1881. Large balconied brick PAVILION, 1981, by *Marshman Warren Taylor*, much modified 2009 by *LED*. Across the W end, PEGASUS COURT, curving flats of 2009, by *Armstrong Burton*. For the Museum see Perambulation 2.

BREWHOUSE THEATRE, Coal Orchard. 1976–7 by *Norman Branson* with *Somerset County Architects*. Small, clad in dark brick, the auditorium hexagonal. Attached, the Late Georgian OLD BREWERY HOUSE, red brick with an arched doorway.

---

* A matching one is in the Princess Gardens, Torquay.

Taunton, Market House and New Market.
Drawing by E. Turle, 1829

BRIDGWATER & TAUNTON CANAL, Canal Road. The canal of 1822–6 leaves the River Tone at Firepool Lock. The brick WATER TOWER of 1877 serviced the successor railway. It stands on two LIMEKILNS that burnt stone brought here via the Chard Canal of 1842.

PERAMBULATIONS

1. The Parade, High Street, The Crescent and Corporation Street

The hub of the town is THE PARADE, a triangular island with the former Market House (*see* p. 619) at the junction of three broad streets (North Street, East Street and High Street). A fourth, Corporation Street, was cut through in 1893–4. In front of the Market House, BURMA WAR MEMORIAL, a Celtic cross of 1889, moved here in 1934.* The three sides are called FORE STREET. The W and NE sides are now without interest, apart from the palazzo-style former STUCKEY'S BANK on the corner of Corporation Street. The five r. bays are of 1857 by *Giles*, copied with rounded corner in 1906–7 by *George Oatley*, when the branch briefly became Stuckey's head office. From the same side two classical public buildings have gone – the New Market (Ionic, by *William Burgess* of Exeter, 1821, dem. 1963) and the Corn Exchange (Greek Doric, 1853, dem. 1937). On the S side is the best surviving group of timber-framed town houses in Somerset, evoking the gable-fronted streets of pre-Georgian times. No. 17, low and gabled, and No. 16, a storey higher, with a jettied overhang, are C16–C17. No. 15, much larger, was owned from the C15 by the Portmans, whose fortune began as Taunton merchants. It has a bi-coloured double-chamfered stone

---

* It replaced a Gothic memorial by *C. E. Giles*, 1867, echoing a High Cross lost in 1770.

doorway to one side but is otherwise entirely timber-framed, in square panels with quadrant corner pieces. Three overhangs, two oriels, one of nine lights. Richly carved bressumers. This towering front, dated 1578, is only a refacing of an early C14 hall. Massive beams in the low shop are propped by bulbous Elizabethan columns. Behind is the impressive hall, open to the roof, tree-ring-dated to 1323–4. Two bays with cusped intermediate trusses, and massive central base cruck with crown-post. Heavy wind-braces. Three-storey C17 brick rear wall, then a low timber-framed two-storey range with jointed crucks. Nos. 13–14 are low and twin-gabled with three nicely irregular gabled oriels. No. 12, Victorian stucco, has a C16 rubble side wall. Nos. 10–11 are Late Georgian with recessed arched first-floor windows. No. 7, a late C19 palazzo of Ham stone, was the Wiltshire & Dorset Bank. The Ham stone Corinthian pilasters of Nos. 5–6 are of 1982, by *Alec French Partnership*, screening a shopping arcade. No. 4 stands out: purple stone, Ruskinian Gothic with colourful polychromy. Of 1865, probably by *Giles*. It was an earlier Wiltshire & Dorset Bank.

HIGH STREET has lost many of the buildings Pevsner noted in 1958, but is at least closed to traffic. On the corner, No. 1, 1977–9, by *Whicheloe Macfarlane*, has character, echoing a half-timbered predecessor. White panels framed in aggregate-faced concrete with gridded wooden first-floor windows. Opposite, confusingly still numbered with Fore Street, No. 21, cheerful Edwardian, stuccoed, with an octagonal corner turret, formerly the Prudential Insurance. No. 18, Victorian, bestrides the entry to Bath Place. At the back are the best plaster ceilings in Taunton, for this is a refronted C16–C17 town house. Ground floor with a thin-ribbed pattern of kite shapes and diagonal squares with centre pendant. 1627 date over the door. In the room above (access from Bath Place), thicker, more curvaceous ribs frame four shields (heraldry related to William Lechland, *c.* 1582). Deep frieze of roses and fruit over square panels with floral ornament (cf. Montacute). Remarkable overmantel of courtroom themes. Two conventionally dressed ladies, Justice and Hope, each unexpectedly exposing one leg, flank a strapwork panel of the Sacrifice of Isaac. An earlier arch-braced roof above. There seem to have been three distinct blocks to the house: the rearmost, l. of the Bath Place entrance, has mostly been taken down, but a C17 room with moulded framed ceiling and plaster rosettes remains. C16 oak doorway with traceried spandrels in the throughway to BATH PLACE, a charming enclave, too narrow for cars. A good minor stuccoed sequence on the S side, the former PUBLIC HALL, 1838–9, with centre pediment, and Nos. 1–12, a little earlier, two matching blocks separated by a lower piece. Attractive shopfronts. On the N side, small houses in small gardens, the best No. 26, red brick, with delicate balcony on a columned porch. Further on, the Quaker meeting house (*see* p. 614). Back on HIGH STREET, on the W side, Nos. 54–55, 1894, three floors of plate glass, gabled. At the end, No. 34 is a truncated five-bay

Georgian house. Red brick, ashlar voussoirs and good pedimented Tuscan doorway.

Across the road, Vivary Park (*see* p. 622) marks the limit of the old urban area. The relief road of 1958–60 widened the perimeter streets and traffic has blighted them ever since. On UPPER HIGH STREET, by the park gates, the stuccoed former SAVINGS BANK, 1831, by *Richard Carver*. Further W, Temple Methodist Church (*see* p. 614) and KINGLAKE HOUSE, a six-bay Late Georgian brick pair on the corner of THE CRESCENT. This was an extra-urban development of 1807 promoted by William Kinglake, banker. Two terraces were built, facing W over parkland that became the setting for the Shire Hall and County Offices (*see* p. 620). The curve of the crescent is so shallow as to be hardly noticeable. There was to have been more N of the park. Brownish brick in the style of Late Georgian Exeter, each house two-bay with no more decoration than an arched doorway. At the S end of The Crescent, the stuccoed MASONIC HALL, the former R.C. church of 1822. Remarkably monumental on a small scale. A large pedimented Ionic doorway set in bare wall, with Ionic angle pilasters and cornice but no pediment. Ionic pilasters to the side elevation (cornice missing). Pilasters also inside linked with swags under a curved ceiling. The reredos with paired columns survives, now inscribed 'Audi, vide, tace'. Two houses went for TELEPHONE HOUSE, 1938–41, Neo-Georgian regional headquarters with a thick-set ashlar Tuscan porch. At the N end, UNISON HOUSE, mid-C19, with ashlar quoins and bracket cornice.

CORPORATION STREET returns E, following the line of the castle outer moat. On the S side, CASTLEMOAT PLACE, 2009–10, flats framed in white, the balconied attic clad in grey metal. On the N, the former GAUMONT CINEMA, 1932, by *W. Benslyn*. Very large, of brown brick in jazz-modern forms. A Ham stone 'proscenium arch' frames the façade, the nude with cherub carved by *Newbury Trent*. Colourful Art Deco interior with wall motifs like tiered fountains. The former TECHNICAL INSTITUTE, 1898 by *C. H. Samson*, of Westleigh stone, mullion-windowed, is enlivened by a tower with ogee dome and lantern. The former GRAMMAR SCHOOL (Registry Office) was built by Bishop Fox in 1521–2. Schoolroom with high roof of close-spaced arch-braced collar-trusses and three tiers of windbraces. Four large C16 mullion-and-transom windows, the lights depressed-arched, and small central doorway. The W half was originally the master's house (with arch-braced roof). Unattractive dormer windows and lantern of 1897, when the building was municipal offices. Cross-passage partitions survive. Extended twice to the W, the municipal stair hall, 1897, and square mullion-windowed tower, 1902–5. Back on the S side, the former COLLEGE OF ART, 1907, by *Samson & Cottam*, contrastingly classical, but with turn-of-the-century freedom. A Bath stone superstructure of giant pilasters and columned central recess (artist cherubs in the pediment) rides on a monumental basement in rock-faced Westleigh stone. No front door. Next door, the former LIBRARY, 1904, by *Little & Goodson* of London, also shows individuality, here neo-Tudor. Deep purple sandstone. The angular details (lozenges in the parapet, unmoulded corbelling) come from Lethaby. Parallel reading rooms with open timber roofs. Plaster barrel ceiling across the end. On the corner of Fore Street, BRIDGWATER HOUSE, c. 1960, by *Robin Shirley-Smith*, with heraldic tiles, inserted into a curved Neo-Georgian range of 1949, by *Michael Torrens*.

2. *North Street, Hammet Street, Canon Street, St James's Street*

NORTH STREET is heavily rebuilt. On the W side CASTLE BOW leads to Castle Green (*see* Taunton Castle, above). On the High Street corner, the giant arcaded front of BURTON'S, 1930, and some minor Late Georgian accents before DEBENHAMS (originally Chapman's), in the style of the Great West Road but of 1963–8, at the other end. Halfway down the W side, down MILL LANE, INA COTTAGE, late C17, brick, Gothicized in 1875 as an entrance to the castle. The passageway has an ogee-traceried window (reused?) and two stiff-leaf corbels, the back wall a comical octagonal brick tower. On the E side of North Street, LLOYDS BANK, 1960, by *Trehearne & Norman, Preston & Partners*, is smoothly horizontal, with overhanging granite-clad upper floors. Fussy ashlar detail to Hammet Street. No. 50 was the National Provincial Bank, 1912, by *C. H. Brodie*, the bank surveyor. Ashlar with urns, Edwardian Queen Anne. Larger and coarser, the brick and stone POST OFFICE, 1911, by *John Rutherford* of the *Office of Works*. Two low gable fronts beyond hint at the previous C17 scale. At the N end, the BRIDGE of 1895, with thickly decorated cast-iron railings by the *Phoenix Foundry*, Chard.

Now back to Lloyds Bank, and E into HAMMET STREET, laid out in 1788 by Sir Benjamin Hammet, Alderman of the City of London, M.P. for Taunton, and Keeper of the Castle. Hammet had been involved in development in the City of London in 1767–70 (America Square, Circus and Crescent, with George Dance Jun. as architect). The purpose at Taunton was to house 'genteel families out of trade', whose votes might be useful. It frames the tower of St Mary Magdalene (*see* p. 607) which until then had been obscured by small irregular streets. The effect obtained is splendid and, as has already been said, wholly of the Age of Enlightenment. The terraced houses are large, of five bays, and of brick, with cornices, Tuscan open-pediment doorways and dividing piers. On CHURCH SQUARE, three-bay returns and a pair of houses to the N. N of the churchyard, the low brick VICARAGE, C17, altered. S of the churchyard, on MAGDALENE STREET, the large former CENTRAL SCHOOL, 1866, by *Benjamin Ferrey*, plate-traceried Gothic. Further E are the former HUISH HOMES, almshouses of 1868, by *C. E. Giles*. Attractively irregular Gothic in red sandstone with Ham stone dressings and varied roofs.

CANON STREET runs N from the end of Magdalene Street. Scattered early C19 three-storey brick houses. No. 19, low with exposed sash boxes, is early C18. MIDDLE STREET, opening off the W side, has a plain but good Late Georgian terrace, ST JAMES'S PLACE, that ends with two taller houses framing the former OCTAGON CHAPEL, built in 1776–8 under the direction of John Wesley, who preached at its opening. Red brick, with two tiers of windows, arched and circular. The panelled gallery on four sides survived office conversion. More Georgian houses further down Middle Street: No. 11, at right angles to the street, with late C18 brickwork and open-pediment doorcase, and MELVILLE HOUSE, early C18, plain, square, three-storeyed. The brickwork is distorted because the Town Ditch runs beneath. Panelled rooms and panelled staircase. On the N side, a fancy gabled YMCA GYMNASIUM, 1896. SOMERSET HOUSE, on the corner, was the Register Office, 1836–7, by *Richard Carver*. Stuccoed Tudor, with a gable facing down the street.

Now back to Canon Street, to the scant remains of TAUNTON PRIORY, an important Augustinian house founded c. 1120. It had twenty-six canons in 1377. Of the church, rebuilt between 1277 and 1337, foundations of a corner of an aisled nave have been found. Facing Middle Street is the remaining one of two stuccoed Regency Gothic lodges to Priory House (stuccoed, early C19, dem.) that succeeded the priory. In the roadside wall some reused tracery. At the corner with PRIORY AVENUE, the large red former MALTINGS, 1901, by *W. Bradford*, with characteristic twin kiln roofs, stands just W of the priory church site. Opposite, PRIORY LODGE is clearly part of the Regency arrangements, a neat battlemented three-bay Gothick villa. Behind is the PRIORY BARN (Cricket Club Museum), the only standing medieval remnant. Little can be deduced except that the red sandstone cornerstones at both corners of the SW end are the moulded jambs of giant arches, suggesting that the building was one side of a gatehouse range. In the gable-end, two Ham stone windows with late C13 plate tracery and a small cusped arch above. These must be reused if the gable was within a gateway. The adjoining part of the SE front has a C15–C16 Tudor-arched doorway in red sandstone, beneath a loading doorway with a peaked hood of Ham stone, also perhaps reused. The r. half has no medieval features. ST JAMES STREET returns to North Street past the Cricket Ground (*see* p. 622) and St James's church (*see* p. 611). On the S side are THE COURTYARD, 1882, a warehouse for Chapman's department store, nicely detailed in red brick, and brick terraces dated 1866. Minor Late Georgian houses opposite. The Brewhouse Theatre (*see* p. 622) is behind, near the river bank.

3. East Street, East Reach, Silver Street, Billetfield and Mary Street

Now down EAST STREET from the centre. On the S side, the triangular block of CHEAPSIDE, 1822, is typical if undistinguished Regency urban improvement. Stuccoed, four-storeyed, with a bowed E end. The former COUNTY HOTEL, to the E, was updated shortly afterwards, in stucco with Soanean pilasters. Columned porch of 1856. The stuccoed houses beyond are now façades to a shopping development of 1996–7. A larger shopping development, of 1984–5, beyond Billet Street, fossilizes the little gable of the C17 SWAN INN and the Late Georgian stuccoed PHOENIX HOTEL, with Soanean piers. Further on, No. 48 is mid-C18, brick, with pedimented doorway. GRAY'S ALMSHOUSES are a relief after this battered commercial street. A long two-storey brick front dated 1635 with nine chimneys on the eaves, each with two diagonally placed shafts. This date would make the almshouses the earliest brick building in Somerset by more than forty years, which prompts questions. The almshouses, built for ten women, with a chapel under a schoolroom at the W end, were extended westward for six men, perhaps in 1696 – see the date on the cupola. It may be that the older almshouses were refronted in brick with the extension. Two rear gables contain open-well stairs. The chapel is low, square, benched on four sides, with minimal pulpit and reading desk. Low ceiling painted with a clouded night sky. Opposite, the OLD COUNCIL HOUSE, mid-C19, combines Soanean pilasters with elongated Victorian windows.

SILVER STREET runs S past the Baptist church (see p. 614). On the W side, MANSFIELD HOUSE, stately Late Georgian in brown brick. Three-storeyed, with narrow pedimented centre. The pedimented porch bisects a narrow courtyard flanked by two-storey wings. On BILLETFIELD, part of the inner ring road, running W, two red brick Gothic houses by *Henry Davis*, 1868, face each other, SALISBURY HOUSE and Nos. 11–13. The latter, elaborated with a corner turret, was Davis's own house. The former is on the corner of BILLET STREET, with the R.C. church (see p. 614) at the S end. The ring road continues as MARY STREET after the United Reformed church (see p. 615). The N side went for road widening and the horrible former Ministry of Agriculture offices, QUANTOCK HOUSE, 1964. The S side remains intact. No. 18 is Late Georgian, stuccoed, with a slightly projected centre. No. 19, early C17 behind a low Regency front, was the pub for the Mary Street Brewery, of which a red brick late C19 aerated-water factory survives. Behind this, No. 20, *c.* 1800, hip-roofed with an Ionic porch, was the brewer's house. MARY STREET HOUSE is another good Late Georgian town house. Three-storeyed, brown brick, with a porch of four thin Tuscan columns. Delicate staircase. It faces THE LAWN, stuccoed, with an open-pedimented doorway. Beyond are the Unitarian chapel (see p. 615) and Vivary Park (see p. 622).

OUTER TAUNTON

1. *South of the centre: Mount Street, Wilton and Trull Road*

Vivary Park is the end of a green lung running into Taunton from open fields. Long may it remain. On its E side, the backs of houses on MOUNT STREET overlook the park. Notable are Nos. 21–22A, a hip-roofed row with Georgian Gothic windows and trellis veranda, and ASHFIELD HOUSE, dated 1794 at the back, but the two-storey verandas are surely later. Dwarfing them is the gatehouse of the former JELLALABAD BARRACKS, 1879–81, built under the Cardwell army reforms. *Major Henry Seddon* oversaw the programme. *Thomas Berry* and *Major Crozier* were here responsible. Massive, of red brick, with corner towers, the scale exaggerated by the narrow street. The front is defended by musketry slots. The main barracks have gone but the OFFICER'S MESS remains by MOUNT HOUSE (stuccoed Late Georgian and Victorian) further down, and two smaller BARRACKS with Gothic gabled ends. MOUNT TERRACE beyond is two-storeyed, stuccoed, late 1820s.

WILTON HOUSE, W of Vivary Park, of whose grounds the park was formed, is dated 1705, although it was called 'new built' in a lease from Hammet of 1781. The upswept parapet is a Queen Anne motif but the good Corinthian stone doorcase is later and the cantilevered staircase with scroll railings later still.

WILTON, across the park, remains a village. Below the church (*see* p. 613), FONS GEORGE HOUSE, rendered, with bargeboarded cross-wings, 1840s, must be by *Richard Carver*. The deep-eaved OLD VICARAGE, *c.* 1800, has iron balconies. On Wilton Street, the three-storeyed ORCHARD HOUSE combines Late Georgian brickwork with Victorian bracketed eaves. The VIVARY ARMS is C17, from the beams and rear door. ST GEORGE'S TERRACE, 1896, displays patterned brickwork more elaborate than most. Carved animal heads between the doorways.

Further S (r. off Middle Way) is HAINES HILL, an Early Victorian suburb laid out by *Carver* in 1846–7. The stuccoed houses vary from Italianate through bargeboarded-cottage to Tudor Gothic. On the N, five semi-detached pairs, Nos. 23–25 Italianate with outer pediments, the others, Nos. 7–21, cottage-style or Tudor. Around the circular green are three single houses: No. 20, with Italian belvedere tower, No. 18, Tudor, and No. 16, hip-roofed, brown brick. On the corner to TRULL ROAD, MOUNTSWOOD is *Carver* again, for himself, 1852, brown brick, bargeboarded. S on Trull Road, also by *Carver* is HAINES HILL TERRACE, Trull Road, 1857, showing Carver pioneering the red and yellow brick of late C19 Taunton. No. 72, brick with steep stone-tiled roofs and tall chimneys, is by *Eric Francis*, 1930s. SHERFORD ROAD runs W to Sherford. Off the N side, in HIGHLANDS, are four flat-roofed white Modernist houses of the 1930s, No. 1, 1935, by *Stone & Francis*.

SHERFORD is still a village, winding into fields. SHERFORD HOUSE, roughcast and painted brick, has a cross-wing and small storeyed porch. Early C17, enlarged in the late C17. Upstairs, plaster overmantel dated 1679, wholly in the style of the early C17. Two arches on stubby balusters frame flower vases, between three little female figures. Across the fields is CUTLIFF FARM, brick, both house and outbuildings late C17.

Back on TRULL ROAD, continuing S, Nos. 82–84, bleakly triple-gabled pair in yellow brick, 1870s, and Nos. 86–98 (*Thomas Penny*, builder), 1880s, asymmetrical deep-eaved houses in red and yellow, one dated 1882. Beyond Queen's College (*see* p. 621), WILDOAK HOUSE, early C19, stuccoed, with a barrack-like brick wing of 1877, intended as a boarding house for the college. Returning N, opposite Haines Hill are Nos. 62–64, an overblown pair, and HOVELAND TERRACE, two fussy blocks linked in the C20, all 1870s. Opposite, No. 33, by *Francis*, 1937, asymmetrical under a hipped roof. The road then descends, narrow and sunken, through trees remaining from the grounds of two large early C19 villas. WHEATLEIGH HOUSE (Wheatleigh Close), *c.* 1817–20, stuccoed, has an ashlar Ionic colonnade on the ground floor, both attached and detached, carrying uneasily a central columned bow window. BELMONT (Belmont Drive), 1823, is more thoroughly Greek, of Bath stone, with giant panelled pilasters. On the garden front a first-floor recess with square piers, reminiscent of H. E. Goodridge at Bath. Further down, LOWLANDS, 1834, stuccoed with bargeboards, was *Carver*'s own house before Mountswood. At the bottom, OSBORNE HOUSE, Late Georgian, roughcast, faces WILTON GROVE, 1830s, with a stuccoed pilastered front. Trull Road joins the inner ring road just W of the Shire Hall (*see* p. 620).

2. West of the centre: Park Street, Wellington Road and Galmington

PARK STREET runs W from Corporation Street. Opposite the County Offices (*see* p. 619), PAUL'S HOUSE is a large square villa of *c.* 1800, three-storeyed and deep-eaved. To this MITRE HOUSE was added in 1871 for the Convent of Perpetual Adoration, by *J. F. Bentley*. A model Gothic composition with top-floor chapel marked by narrow triple lancets (lovely stained-glass angels, 1873, by *Bentley*, with *Lavers & Westlake*) and subtle side composition of gable, polygonal stair, and lean-to roof beneath lateral chimneys. The stone came from St James's church tower. The linked slabs of BEDFORD HOUSE, 1960,* by *Reginald Gallanaugh*, interpose before St John's church (*see* p. 613) and the Magistrates' Courts (*see* p. 620). Next, a sequence of 1856–60, by *C. E. Giles*, with the builder *Henry Davis*. Nos. 26–30, red brick, four-gabled, and Nos. 21–25, brick and stone, are sober by comparison with Nos. 16–20, a showcase of Somerset geology. Two tones of brown, layered and accented in red, grey, and copper-green. Gables with side turrets frame the row, which has corbelled eaves, canted bays and Gothic porches. Lastly CANNFIELD HOUSE, 1857, acutely Gothic in red brick, takes the corner. Stone oriels with fantastically minute carving by *Davis*.

On WELLINGTON ROAD, PARK TERRACE ends in Italianate pyramid roofs. BATH HOUSE, Bath-stone, Regency-style,

---

* SCULPTURE outside, Agriculture by *José Manuel Alberdi*, 1960.

three-storeyed, stood alone in 1840. WELLINGTON TERRACE, stuccoed with pedimented ends, was just complete in 1847 when taken for the Dissenters' College, predecessor of Taunton School. The row beyond was the dining room and schoolroom, 1847–8, by *William Shewbrooks*. Embellished with doorcases and hip-roofed dormers after 1870, when converted to houses. Nos. 70–72, a stuccoed 1840s pair with trellis veranda between pedimented ends, look like *Richard Carver*'s work. After Somerset College (*see* p. 620), the CEMETERY, 1854, by *Edward Ashworth*, with Gothic ARCHWAY and LODGE (the chapels have gone). To the S is Musgrove Park Hospital (*see* p. 622).

A return may be made S through GALMINGTON, once a rural hamlet. Little notable apart from the PRIMARY SCHOOL, 1972, by *Robert Willis*, of pyramid-roofed brick pavilions, the composition obscured by additions. Nearby is Galmington church (*see* p. 614). Off Galmington Road, the tiny pointed-arched RAMSHORN BRIDGE (Hoveland Crescent) may be medieval. Stepped cobbled paving. Parkfield Road returns to Wellington Road. Up Barton Close, MUSGROVE MANOR is C16 with two chamfered framed ceilings. Refronted in Tudor style, probably by *Carver*, c. 1850.

3. North of the centre: North Town, north-west up Staplegrove Road, and north-east

Over the Tone Bridge, BRIDGE STREET has some Late Georgian brick, too broken up to make a picture. The COAL ORCHARD, 1937, horizontally striped *moderne*, was builders' merchants' offices. On the W side, No. 43, 1860, is High Victorian Gothic with cusped lancets and an oriel in stone. An excursion up STATION ROAD has little to offer: a pedimented brick BAPTIST CHAPEL, 1874–5, in Albemarle Street, and No. 70, GURD'S menswear shop, a Victorian gable front with a lively Gothic shopfront under a semicircular oriel.

STAPLEGROVE ROAD, running NW from Bridge Street, begins with YARDE HOUSE, a well-finished mid-C19 brick pair with ashlar dressings. Some modest terraces follow, and then villas, the largest, BLORENGE, with Jacobean gables. No. 88 belonged to *Charles Samson*, architect. Behind it he built a half-timbered BILLIARD ROOM, c. 1880, with pretty leaded glazing and stained-glass roundels of the Seasons. No. 100 was the Girls' Grammar School, 1904–5, by *Samson & Cottam*, brick and roughcast with a cupola. Down ELM GROVE is a compact Victorian suburb begun in 1880, yellow brick with a little red, and the bracketed eaves typical of late C19 Taunton. Three-storey terraces on Elm Grove, two-storey on Linden Grove and Birch Grove, and semi-detached villas on THE AVENUE. The largest, HATFIELD, 1899, with coved eaves and Late Victorian detail, was probably designed for himself by the contractor *Henry Spiller*. The former St James's VICARAGE, Linden Grove, is by *Samson*, 1892.

Back on Staplegrove Road, the lodge remains of ST JAMES'S
CEMETERY, 1876–7, by *John Bevan* of Bristol. Over the railway
is Taunton School (*see* p. 621). N of Greenway Road and Priorswood Road are large areas of post-war housing in Wellsprings,
Lyngford and Priorswood. Above Wellsprings Road, two groups
which reflect post-war material shortages: metal-clad, steel-
framed BISF (British Iron and Steel Federation) houses,
1947–8, around QUANTOCK ROAD, and mansard-roofed
concrete 'Cornish Unit' houses, 1953, around BAGBOROUGH
ROAD.

LYNGFORD HOUSE, Lyngford Lane. Built after 1831 for John
Allen in far from archaeological Tudor. Ashlar three-sided
centrepiece between rubble square turrets, set diagonally,
intended for stucco, and Tudor outer windows. Octagonal stair
hall.

4. South-east and east of the centre: South Road, Trinity and East Reach

SOUTH ROAD continues Silver Street. SILVER STREET HOUSE,
stuccoed, 2-3-2 bays with a pedimented centre, is mid-C18,
from the rusticated doorway. The former FRANCISCAN
CONVENT began in 1772 as the general hospital by *Stowey &
Jones* of Exeter to an ambitious square plan around a circular
light well. Abandoned unfinished in 1790, it was sold to nuns
in 1807. The main block in pinkish brick is the E half of the
intended hospital, the central bow replaced by a bow-ended
refectory range of 1853 by *Charles Hansom*, in matching Late
Georgian style. Original front door re-set to the r. The nuns
added a NW wing with chapel over a schoolroom in 1808–11.
Hansom re-windowed the chapel in 1849–50, adding a chancel
and side chapel on an undercroft. He enclosed the front lawn
as a burial ground with a charming brick CLOISTER, 1859–60.
Inside, a Puginian BRASS to Helen Luck †1851, by *Hardman*,
showing a priest and child. Large wings SW (with square
lantern) and NE, 1853 and 1864, by *Hansom*, continuing the
Late Georgian style. Interiors lost in conversion to flats.*

Further down South Road are King's College, Richard Huish
College and Bishop Fox's School (*see* p. 622). Richard Huish
College occupies the grounds of ELMFIELD, *c.* 1863, brown
brick Italianate. When King's College was built on the former
racecourse in 1867, the rest of the site was laid out for villas.
Their styles change from one to the next, or even within a
single villa: No. 79 has Italian pediments, Gothic colonnettes,
and Jacobean quoins. Nos. 85–87, notably large, have twin
Italian towers. Nos. 93–115, six pairs, subtly vary one design
with steep-roofed canted bays. N of King's College, Holway
Avenue runs E to SOUTH STREET, the edge of a modest Early
Victorian suburb around Holy Trinity church (*see* p. 611)

---

*The chapel had painted decoration by *Charles Weld*, 1851.

prompted by the building of the workhouse in 1837–9. On TRINITY ROAD, E off South Street the yellow-brick RECTORY, 1889, by *George Strawbridge*, and the three-storey front range of the WORKHOUSE, with a pediment. The rest has gone. It was to *Sampson Kempthorne*'s hexagonal plan, built by *Richard Carver*, 1837.

E from the top of South Street, EAST REACH, Taunton's eastern approach, keeps some battered Late Georgian brick houses. The former TAUNTON AND SOMERSET HOSPITAL began as a three-storey brick building on a high basement, 1810–12, by *John White & Son* of London. In 1839–43 *Carver* added an overhanging roof, two-storey wings, and heavy pillared porch. Early Victorian sans serif lettering. The yellow brick former NURSING INSTITUTION, 1887–8, by *J. H. Spencer*, is pedimented with undisciplined detail, e.g. the heavy doorcase not quite reaching the ground. Beyond the modern road junction to the E, a formal suburban layout centres on ST MARGARET'S, a humble building with thatched roof carried over an open front. A medieval leper hospital rebuilt after fire *c.* 1510 by Abbot Bere of Glastonbury (initials on a shield behind), it became almshouses in 1612. Of that date the simple Tudor-arched oak doorways. Carefully repaired in 2003–4 by *Architecton* for the Somerset Building Preservation Trust. The encircling brick Neo-Georgian terraces of LEYCROFT, *c.* 1932, probably by *H. S. W. Stone*, are over-self-conscious for so modest a monument, but assured in a garden-suburb way. The large red brick Neo-Georgian building just E on HAMILTON ROAD was a TELEPHONE REPEATER STATION of 1927. N of Hamilton Road, HALCON, council housing for Taunton Borough Council, begun 1935, is formally laid out around concentric central roads. To the N, along the A358, the HYDROGRAPHIC OFFICE, with flat-roofed buildings of 1939–40, and CREECH CASTLE, remodelled in 1849, a toy fort, battlemented, with a thin square turret.

Close to the motorway, in Heron Gate business park, the HANKRIDGE ARMS, a large late C16 farmhouse rescued as a pub. Restored by *Mackenzie Wheeler*, 1992. Substantial timbers inside: moulded cross-passage partitions and two framed ceilings. Upstairs, a triple-arched Jacobean plaster overmantel, as at Ashe Farm, Thornfalcon.

TEMPLECOMBE

7020

The railway divides Abbas Combe, with the church, from Temple Combe, the names reflecting medieval ownership by Shaftesbury Abbey and the Knights Templar.

ST MARY. S porch-tower with simple Perp detail. The position shows that it is earlier, the plain arched inner doorway possibly C12. Perp W doorway and window. The chapel E of the tower may be C16 – see the broad shafted arch to the nave. But everything is much rebuilt – N aisle added in 1834, chancel 1864–5 by *F. C. Penrose*. C16 panelled nave roof. Cusped PISCINA in the chapel. – FONT. Early Norman, square, Purbeck marble, with shallow blank arches (cf. Milborne Port). Ornate Gothic cover, 1897, carved by *Gertrude Fox*. – A few C17 BENCHES. – PAINTING. Christ's head in a lozenge frame, perhaps C13, i.e. of the Templar era.

TEMPLECOMBE STATION. Signal box, 1938 (Southern Railway), in the streamlined modern of the arterial roads.

Below the church, CHURCH GARTH, a formal five-bay front with hollow-moulded mullioned windows, *c.* 1700. Across the main road, HILL HOUSE, with a large pedimented timber doorcase framing a doorway with broad fanlight, late C18.

MANOR FARM, ½ m. s. Site of the preceptory of the Knights Templar, given to the Knights Hospitaller after 1312. The house has C17 ovolo-moulded mullioned windows and rear stair-tower under a low early C19 roof, but is older – see the SW stub wall and reserved-chamfer mullions in the NW bay. Some older fragments inside: a moulded stair lintel, an inexplicably curved cross-wall, and Agnus Dei and Tudor rose spandrels in a partition to the rear range. Stair window glass, 1986, by *Stewart Bowman*. The long rear range has C17 detail except for two windows with Tudor lights. Both chimneys, however, are large for domestic use, the W one inserted into a deep smoke-blackened cavity, the E one with an impressive 20-ft (6-metre) lintel. There was a chapel to the E. C19 drawings show a pointed doorway and two two-light windows, modest for such a site.

TETTON HOUSE *see* KINGSTON ST MARY

THEALE

CHRIST CHURCH. 1826–8, an early and economical work of *Richard Carver*. Grey render with four projecting corner pieces, as at Wiveliscombe. The W ones contain gallery stairs, the E ones are there for symmetry. Four-centred-arched windows with wooden Y-tracery and a canted ashlar W porch with similar arches. Instead of a chancel, a curved bow window projects, like that of a house, with wooden tracery. Sparse interior with a WEST GALLERY. – FONT. Later C20, by *Gerald Beech*. – ROYAL ARMS. Hanoverian.

The village runs W for a mile to Great House. An early C19 group around the OLD VICARAGE (1826) includes THEALE HOUSE, with parapet and Gothic stair window, and NORTHLEIGH and MAX GATE, both stuccoed.

GREAT HOUSE. Dated 1670 on iron roof finials. Nearly square, with five-bay façades under hipped roofs on deep coved eaves.

Wooden cross-windows on both floors, but the panelled doors to the E and S fronts still Jacobean in style. For this house is advanced in form and plan but old-fashioned in detail, especially the splendid staircase, the finest of its type in the county. It rises to the attic in a square open well and has newel posts with big openwork finials. Below the handrail are openwork panels: scrolls frame fleur-de-lys roundels, or become primitive dragons, altogether more rustic than the openwork foliage of e.g. Forde Abbey, Dorset. On the staircase wall are two unexplained wall paintings, the head of a Roman emperor, and a church interior in the Dutch taste, vaulted, with many columns in perspective. A black-clad gentleman stands behind a red-robed priest. Elaborately carved doorcase to the SE room and moulded stone fireplace. Forecourt WALLS pierced with roundels. Five-bay STABLE with cross-windows.

THORNE COFFIN

ST ANDREW. Small nave with simple, possibly C17, bellcote and (renewed) Dec ogee tracery. Porch dated 1613. Chancel mostly of the 1893 restoration by *Evelyn Hellicar*. – PULPIT. 1624. Large panels. – FONT and LECTERN. Both stone balusters – C17? – SCREEN. 1919. Intriguingly rectilinear in a Japanese, not Gothic, way.

W of the church, the OLD RECTORY, 1853, by *George Truefitt* of London. Material from the Governor's House, Ilchester Prison, was reused. Lias with sparse Ham stone banding. Below the church, BRAMBLE COTTAGE has C17 ovolo moulded mullions. THORNE HOUSE was reconstructed by *T. G. Jackson* around an existing house, 1878–88. Neo-Jacobean, the entrance front with shaped gables and storeyed porch, asymmetrical, the garden front symmetrical with curved pediments on the gables, obelisks, attached columns etc. MANOR FARMHOUSE, mid-C18, contrasts Yeovil and Ham stones.

THORNE ST MARGARET

ST MARGARET. Simple two-stage Perp W tower. Square bell-lights, the S one with curious tracery. The rest of 1865 by *C. E. Giles*. Inside, a C12 doorhead with chevron, re-cut to ogee in the C14. – FONT. C12. Bowl on a circular shaft. – VESTRY SCREEN. Four bays of thickly detailed C16 tracery. – BRASS. John Worth, *c.* 1600, a small bearded gowned figure.

MANOR FARMHOUSE, ¼ m. SW. Long C16 house more typical of Devon. Big bolection-moulded porch, *c.* 1700, under prettily patterned slate-hanging.

WELLISFORD, ¾ m. N. HIGHER WELLISFORD, a tall rendered farmhouse, began as a C15–C16 hall house, the jetty into the hall surviving. Late C17 cross-windows. WELLISFORD MANOR is brick of *c.* 1700, but the Queen Anne detail is mostly early C20. Late C18 roughcast rear elevation with twin bows.

THORNFALCON

HOLY CROSS. Early Perp. White-rendered. w tower with thin set-back buttresses, two-light bell-openings with ogee-headed lights, and battlements. Polygonal NE stair-turret. W doorway with a hoodmould accentuated by five animals' heads. C14 chamfered tower arch on polygonal shafts with polygonal capitals. Nave windows with thin rere-arches on angels or well-carved heads. Small rood light each side, set high. Chancel arch with thin clustered shafts. Panelled roofs, the nave wall-plate dated 1652. – FONT. C13. Unadorned octagon, tapered beneath. – PULPIT. Georgian, from Ruishton. Ionic pilasters folded at the angles. – BENCH-ENDS. Twice dated 1542. Mostly tracery bordered in leaf scroll (cf. Trull). Others by a Thornfalcon woodworking group, 1890–1911. – STAINED GLASS. E and W windows *c.* 1854, the E very naïve.

By the church THORNFALCON HOUSE, stuccoed Late Georgian, the former rectory. On Thorn Lane, MANOR FARMHOUSE, thatched, early C18, is the best local display of the North Curry sandstone, here used as ashlar. Further W, COURT HOUSE, remodelled in Victorian Tudor style (with a bad modern storeyed porch), incorporates a late medieval hall-house. Notable early C15 hall fireplace with panels of flowing ogee tracery with shields and rosettes. C16 moulded framed ceilings.

ASHE FARMHOUSE, 1 m. S Early C17 with later cross-wing. Upstairs, a thickly ornamented triple-arched plaster overmantel, like that at the Hankridge Arms, Taunton.

THURLBEAR

ST THOMAS (Churches Conservation Trust). The church from outside, apart from its beautiful position, promises little. The W tower is Perp, its eroding Lias much patched in repair by *John Schofield*, 1989. Early C16 W window with thick tracery; capitals to the mullions. The church itself, attractively colour-washed, has Perp aisle windows and S porch, and neo-Norman chancel windows of 1861. These hint at the real interest of the church. One window head is genuine, as are the internal splays. A thin N column-buttress of purple sandstone is Anglo-Saxon, indicating a pre-Conquest minster church, the chancel perhaps vaulted (tufa fragments). The nave was rebuilt with aisles hardly later than c. 1110. A Norman aisled village church is a rarity. Rarer still, these aisles were never widened to satisfy later medieval taste. Four unmoulded arches each side, on circular piers. Scalloped capitals, slightly varied, and flat bases with angle spurs. Originally there were low aisle roofs, the line visible inside, and narrow clerestory windows. Late C13 corbel tables in the aisles under the present overall roof. Curious triple-vesica vents from aisle to nave, perhaps to clear smoke from side altars. Only piers remain of the notably broad chancel arch, the N pier with late medieval colour. C13 recess to the r., C15 rood stair, l. Moulded C15 tower arch. – FONT. C12 bowl, rimmed below. – STAINED GLASS. E and W windows, 1861, the latter, possibly by *Clayton & Bell*, to Elizabeth Barrett Browning's sister.

CHURCHYARD CROSS. C15, with restored head.

Across the road, lavish tile-hung former RECTORY, 1887, for a Portman rector. SCHOOL of 1872. CHURCH FARMHOUSE may be medieval. C16 oriel one end.

THURLOXTON

ST GILES. Plain little building of red sandstone. Two-stage W tower with diagonal buttresses and polygonal NE stair projection to the lower part only. Late, probably C16, square-headed bell-lights. The tower appears to be added to the nave, but its W window has Dec tracery (renewed). So does the E window. Otherwise the church has C15–C16 windows and a porch arch of after 1600. Cross-gabled N aisle of 1868, the arcade on thin round columns of brick. C15–C16 panelled barrel nave roof. No chancel arch. – Exceptional WOODWORK of c. 1634 (date on the pulpit). The pretty SCREEN has fluted Ionic piers and three frilled arches. Central entrance, reading desks in the side arches, over the usual short blank arches. The screen abuts a splendidly elevated PULPIT. Two tiers of panels, the lower with narrow arches. Above are four relief figures, a crowned man with sword (Faith), and three crowned women, Hope, Charity (spoon-feeding a baby), and Love (in petticoats, bare-breasted, with a child). An angel carries the book-rest, carved with rose and thistle. The back-panelling survives but not the tester. The BOX PEWS are probably contemporary. – FONT. Early Norman. Plain tapered bowl of Ham stone on a painted cylinder. Conical C17 COVER with crockets. – ROYAL ARMS. George II. On the tower ceiling.

MANOR HOUSE, NW of the church. A hip-roofed villa, mid- to late C19, built for T. C. Colthurst, Bridgwater brickmaker. Terracotta quoins and edge-on brickwork, usually a sign of penury (rat-trap bond), here done for effect.

LEVERSDOWN HOUSE, ¾ m. SE. Hip-roofed Regency, nicely detailed. Shallow arches over tripartite sashes and a central inset porch with ashlar columns.

TIMBERSCOMBE

ST PETROCK. Dedicated to the C6 Welsh saint celebrated in Cornwall, Devon and Brittany. Red sandstone, mostly Perp. w tower of 1701, made Perp by *J. D. Sedding* in 1881–2. Early C16 s aisle with the pretty tracery of the Cleeve Abbey region, with quatrefoil spandrels to cusped ogee-headed lights. Flat-headed side windows, the E window transomed as at Selworthy and Luccombe. Four-bay arcade of four-centred arches, not high. Piers of standard four-hollow section with small polygonal capitals, except one pier with a banded capital carved with vine-trail and shields (as at Luccombe). Cusped ogee PISCINA with shelf. Roofs renewed by *Sedding*, keeping bosses and the chancel wall-plate.

FURNISHINGS. FONT. Octagonal, Perp, with fleurons or shields in quatrefoils. The stem panels continue on the underside (cf. Stogumber). Re-set medieval TILES at the foot. – ROOD SCREEN. The outstanding feature, if much renewed. C15–C16, with all the delicacy of the local type (Carhampton, Dunster, etc.). Five bays of four-light sections with leaf-scroll borders, the tracery sub-arched and ogee-cusped. Ribbed panelled coving to a cornice of four fine foliage strips. The dado has the pretty spandrels of the windows, but with rosettes. – PULPIT. Early to mid-C17. Band of oval cabochons between Jacobean-type panels (cf. Minehead). – BENCHES. Some plain C16 square ends, copied in 1882. – ROOD-STAIR DOOR. Perp, with original metalwork. – N DOOR. C17, with good ironwork. – WALL PAINTING. King David, post-Reformation, with black-letter text. – STAINED GLASS. E window by *Clayton & Bell*, N window by *Wailes & Strang*, both 1882. Medieval fragments in the SE window.

CHURCHYARD CROSS. C15 with a late C19 Crucifixion.

Behind the former vicarage, good modern-vernacular housing, VICARAGE COURT, 1987–8, by *Peterjohn Smyth* of *Percy Thomas Partnership*. GREAT HOUSE, ENE of the church, is early to mid-C18. Close-spaced five-bay, three-storey front with segmental-headed windows, harshly rendered. Staircase with alternate twisted and column balusters.

BICKHAM MANOR, ¼ m. SW. C18 remodelling of a medieval and C17 house. Long E front with sash windows. To the W, cross-wings frame a broad gable, all three gables with oval attic lights above sash windows. Narrow staircase with C18 Chinese Chippendale rail and dog gate. Large farm buildings including a C19 BANK BARN.

COWBRIDGE MILL, ¼ m. N. U-plan with a three-storey house. Called 'newly-erected' in 1809. Restored 1995–2012 with a new stone-clad FORGE, 2010–11, by *Owen Rush*, owner.

CROYDON HOUSE, 1 m. S. Remarkable that the Siderfin family chose to build on this remote site in the later C17, and also that they chose the newly fashionable brick, previously unknown in this region. Financial difficulties in 1700 halted work with one wing and only part of the centre complete. An exemplary restoration in 2000–10 by *John & Pippa Prideaux* (owners) with *Nick Mahlich* and *Louise Crossman*, added two bays (on old foundations) so that the main range is now properly symmetrical. In most respects a typical Restoration house with wooden cross-windows, shell-hood doorway and hipped roofs on a heavy wooden cornice, it has very untypical painted symbols between the cornice modillions. Such decoration is recorded at Clarendon House, London, 1664–9, demolished 1683. A date after 1680 seems probable here. Large-field panelling in several rooms, and a panelled archway between hall and stair hall. Closed-string staircase with stout turned balusters. Some remarkable painted graining upstairs on shutters and elsewhere.

Monopitch-roofed service range cut into the hillisde. Pyramid-roofed GRANARY at the corner of the front garden. Among the farm buildings, a BANK BARN with two doorways may be C17.

KNOWLE MANOR, ¾ m. NNE. 1878, by *J. D. Sedding*. Compact hip-roofed country house in the Northern Renaissance idiom of T. G. Jackson. Red sandstone, animated by three Bath stone accents under little shell pediments: a three-storey porch and two-storey bays against the outer gables. Despite some good detail a rather static design.

Altered STABLES by *Sedding*, partly slate-hung. BANK BARN dated 1828. SOUTH LODGE by *Sedding*, with half-timber under a jettied roughcast upper floor. Early C19 WEST LODGE, with pointed windows.

TINTINHULL

ST MARGARET. Mostly mid-C13, a relatively rare date in the county. Nave and chancel with corbelled eaves and heavy buttresses, slightly earlier than the N tower. Rather bare tower, with angle buttresses at the foot and slot-like paired lancet bell-openings at the third stage under the original parapet. A second bell-stage added in 1516 was designed to match, with triple lancets and parapet. Octagonal N stair-turret of 1516. Stone-tiled chancel with late C14 two-light windows inserted in C13 settings. Nave with low parapets. One narrow square-headed late C14 S window, the other windows C15. Perp S porch with a ribbed tunnel vault, the middle rib on wall-shafts. On top a hollowed SUNDIAL (cf. Middle Chinnock) perhaps of 1634. E window from the restoration by *A. W. Hansell*, 1884–6. W vestry, 1951–2, by *Alban Caröe*. Enough survives within to show a mid-C13 church with lancets in reveals linked by a roll-moulded sill course rising around the doorways. There were also continuous hoodmoulds (almost all lost). One C13 N window survives, blocked when the tower was added. Shafted reveal with round caps and bases. Shafted C13 reveals also in the chancel, the splays widened for the C14 windows. Chancel arch on short shafts on large corbel heads of a king and a bishop. Base wall of an early C14 chancel screen. Ornate C13 double PISCINA with two pointed-trefoiled arches on Lias shafts, reconstructed.

FURNISHINGS. FONT. Early Perp. Octagonal, each side with three rosettes over two quatrefoils. – PULPIT. 1623, with back and tester. Large flowers in arched panels. – BENCH-ENDS. 1511–13. With heavy quatrefoils or flowers, as at Rimpton. Some C17–C18 hinged servants' seats. – TILES. C13–C14. In the sanctuary step. Shields of England, France and De Clare. – STAINED GLASS. E window, 1930, by *F. C. Eden*. Well-drawn figures on a clear ground. – MONUMENTS. Chancel floor: John Heth, rector, †1464. Brass, small demi-figure 18 in. (46 cm.) long. – Thomas Napper †1694. Large Ham stone frame with Corinthian columns. Heraldry and scrolls above. – Martha Manason †1721. Open pediment on columns of yellow marble. Unexceptional but for *Roubiliac*'s signature. He made it *c.* 1750 to a design by *Martha Fursman*, whose husband erected it. – Sarah Napper †1752. Baroque, in coloured marbles. – John Priddle †1773. Chinese hat pediment. – Andrew Napper †1784. Obelisk plaque in grey and white.

In the churchyard, a pedimented structure preserves the doorhead of the 'STONYNG DOOR' made in 1518 with stone from Montacute Castle. The Latin texts suggest that it came from the chapel there. – WAR MEMORIAL. Cross, 1920, by *Ninian Comper*, with tabernacle head.

TINTINHULL COURT. The large L-plan house began as the C15 parsonage. Originally hall, cross-passage and storeyed N end; but before the 1530s the Prior of Montacute built a S crosswing, floored the hall, and added an oriel bay in the angle. The present character is largely C17, for the Napper family. They re-roofed and re-windowed the original range in the 1620s and the cross-wing in 1679. Both have cross-mullioned windows. The back has cross-mullions of 1739 and a C17 gabled stair-tower, this in the angle to a kitchen wing rebuilt in 1777. Early C17 arched doorway to the cross-passage. C18 ashlar wall with arched doorway into the hall. The hall was made into a parlour in 1739 with fielded panelling, shell niche, and ceiling with lozenge centrepiece and scroll border. Moulded C16 arch to the oriel. Its handsome framed ceiling with rose bosses was lifted a storey in 1927 for stairs, the stairs being neatly replaced 2003. Drawing room, S, with painted panelling and bolection-moulded detail of 1679. Dining room, N, with a massive C16 fireplace. In the stair-tower a tight open-well C17 staircase with turned balusters and acorn finials. An avenue running W (since replanted) is shown on C18 maps.

TINTINHULL HOUSE (National Trust), Farm Street. Remodelled for Andrew Napper *c.* 1722 from an L-plan house dated 1630, his new front refacing on the r. the C17 cross-wing. Lovely in its Ham stone ashlar and stone tiles, this five-bay front has a pediment on giant pilasters, accentuating the three middle bays, and channelled outer piers. Stone cross-windows in architraves, Baroque pediment bullseye, and channelled basement with giant voussoirs. A little old-fashioned in the cross-windows and proportions (the upper windows leave no room for an entablature). Simple C18 interiors: stone-flagged hall, dining room (SW) with shell niche, and panelled drawing room (NW) with mouldings and chimneypiece of the 1740s. The N sash windows may have been inserted then. Staircase of three slim balusters per tread, the tread-ends panelled and scrolled. C17 NE fireplace. Small forecourt behind eagle GATEPIERS, the origin of the famous enclosed GARDENS. These were begun in the early C20 but are principally due to *Phyllis Reiss*, after 1933.

The Court and church are off the upper end of the dumb-bell shaped centre of the village. On the upper green, FRANCIS HOUSE, 1603, with ovolo-mullioned windows. Nine-panel framed ceiling. On the lower green, the seven-bay DOWER HOUSE, built for Honour Napper in 1685. Much of the character is of 1935 by *Charles Pullen*, farmer and owner. He inserted mullioned windows and created interiors with magpie exuberance: stone fireplaces styled between C17 and Arts and Crafts, woodwork from Frampton Court, Dorset, a C16 moulded beam. He bought the pedimented C18 courtyard ARCH, provenance unknown. Just NE is LAMB FARM, an extended end-entry house, with a framed ceiling, one fireplace dated 1602. COLLEGE FARMHOUSE, NW, was similar, extended to the W. Further up Queen Street, WALTERS FARMHOUSE, with mid-C17 mullioned windows, is early C16 at the W end – see the jointed cruck and full-width fireplace beam. Late C16 partition and framed ceiling to the E. Attached Baptist chapel, 1869. Down Vicarage Street, S, LEACH'S FARMHOUSE is mullion-windowed, later C17. On the Yeovil road, the asymmetrical VICARAGE, 1871. Strong minimal Gothic detail.

TIVINGTON

ST LEONARD. A C15 chapel of Selworthy that became cottages in the C16, with an E end addition and lateral chimneys. Restored in 1896, it is charmingly rustic with its thatch half-hipped over the W door. Flat-headed two-light N windows flank the chimney inserted into the chapel. Renewed arch-braced rafter roof, blocked E window. – READING DESK. 1896. Made from box pews from Selworthy. – BENCHES. Straight-headed moulded ends in the Somerset tradition, although made for Milverton church as late as 1850.

A hamlet of scattered thatched cottages and farmhouses, many yellow-washed and altered in the early C19 for the Holnicote estate. In the valley below the church, WILSDEN, partly cob-walled, was a late medieval hall house. Lateral stack in the angle to the cross-wing. GREENHILLS is prettily compact with a big front chimney. N from the church, DWARF'S COTTAGE has a circular lateral chimney next to an oak doorway in a broad porch, and KNAPP HOUSE a lateral stack next to a cross-wing that was the original house, tree-ring-dated 1508. Oak-mullioned windows. TIVINGTON FARM, C17, has Holnicote estate windows and circular stacks. The rear wing has oak-mullioned windows in what was a storeyed porch. At TIVINGTON KNOWLE, ½ m. s, an unusual pair of C18 single-cell COTTAGES, joined corner to corner.

BLACKFORD DOVECOTE (National Trust), ¾ m. W. Big, circular, and probably C15, roofed in receding flat stones up to a circular hole (cf. Toomer Farm, Henstridge).

TOLLAND

ST JOHN BAPTIST. Squat roughcast W tower, the very short bell-stage Perp, the base C13–C14, from the small s lancet and double-chamfered tower arch. Gabled N aisle with C14 arcade of double-chamfered arches on two octagonal piers with very plain capitals. Rood-stair turret on the s side. Two High Victorian E windows from the restoration by *C. E. Giles*, 1871. – FONT. Large C12 bowl. – Victorian ashlar PULPIT, low SCREEN and REREDOS. – On the altar step, some medieval TILES. – On the back of the PEWS, two C15–C16 panelled dorsals with carved muntins, one panel with rabbit, dog and horn. – STAINED GLASS. By *Kempe & Co.* the E window, 1911, chancel S, 1920, and two N windows, 1920 and 1931. – MONUMENT. Hammond family to 1790. Oval beneath a draped urn.

C15 CHURCHYARD CROSS.

GAULDEN MANOR, 1 m. SE. A manor of Taunton Priory, rebuilt by John Turberville *c.* 1640. Plain rubble stone, once roughcast, with a storeyed porch. Hall to the r. and lower service wing to the l. of the porch. The hall, reflecting the date, is a low-ceilinged room in a square block, the back half containing the staircase and two small chambers. The porch has moulded square-headed doorways, the inner one with the inverted wine-glass stop found also inside. The cross-passage opens r. into the hall, a long room with impressive PLASTERWORK, transitional between the Jacobean and the style of Inigo Jones. The principal ceiling motifs are three big garlanded roundels, the middle one framing a heavy pendant, the others crude reliefs: King David with his harp and the Angel of Judgment hovering over the skeleton. Scrolls with Latin texts issue from both king and angel. The ceiling resembles post-1650 work at Bournes (Wiveliscombe) and Coalharbour (Creech St Michael), but here must be just pre-Civil War, from the strapwork behind the garlands. Also, the iconography of the broad frieze suggests a Laudian rather than Puritan or Restoration context. The frieze, of leaf scroll, has plaques with symbolic emblems on shields (mirror, tower, spectacles) and some sacred scenes (Virgin and Child, Lamb of God, John the Baptist beheaded, Adam and Eve). Also beasts (lions, bear, fox and man, monkey and bird), probably didactic too, and Latin mottos. Lavish plaster overmantel with Latin and French mottos and Turberville heraldry on strapwork between two females (Peace and Plenty). To the r. of the fireplace, an arcaded plaster valance over a panelled carved screen opens to a small withdrawing room. Plastered four-panel ceiling ornamented with linear patterns. The frieze has three cartouches (naked woman, cherub and angel). To the l. of the hall fireplace, oak doorways of differing heights open to a study and the enclosed staircase. Thick flat balusters to the return flight. First-floor plaster overmantel with Turberville and Willoughby arms (marriage of 1639) on strapwork between fish-tailed beasts. In the service range, a large kitchen fireplace backs on to the passage.

Joined to the house by a raised granary, a C17 OUTBUILDING with a long fireplace beam.

TREBOROUGH

High on the Brendon Hills, source of the slate once widely used.

ST PETER. Harshly roughcast. Ungainly s tower with angle pilasters, early to mid-C19. It had battlements, replaced by an early C20 pyramid roof. Altered Perp nave and chancel. One C15–C16 nave window on each side has the pretty quatrefoil spandrels of Timberscombe etc. – FONT. Late Perp, octagonal, with foliage panels over large demi-angels. – PISCINA. A good minor Perp piece. Ogee niche with spandrel rosettes, small polygonal bowl with fleurons, and a thin wall-shaft. – ALTAR. Victorian slate.
CHURCHYARD CROSS. C15, restored.

In the little village, SCHOOL HOUSE and TREBOROUGH FARM are hung with local slate. The quarries are to the NE, with LIMEKILNS on the lane.

TRISCOMBE HOUSE *see* WEST BAGBOROUGH

TRUDOXHILL

ST LAWRENCE. 1898 by *E. Lingen Barker*. Small mission church.
CONGREGATIONAL CHAPEL. Converted in 1717 from a house dated 1699. Mullioned windows on two floors, but a single interior with a C19 end gallery.

MILLARDS HILL HOUSE, ½ m. s. Rebuilt in 1820 for the Earl of Cork. Handsome ashlar front of two full-height canted bays with balustrading in the parapet. Front rooms with contemporary detail. A Neoclassical marble chimneypiece in a rear room looks earlier.

TRULL

ALL SAINTS. Modest late C13 tower – see the three stepped W lancet lights, the absence of a W doorway, and the triple-chamfered arch dying into the imposts. Perp bell-lights, battlements, and short polygonal S stair-tower. The rest of the church is also Perp. S side embellished with battlements over aisle and porch. Arcades of standard four-hollow section with shafts and capitals, the S arcade the earlier. Here the abaci form a continuous strip, while on the N side the capitals are individuated to let the hollows run continuously into the arches. The capitals are rather tall and funnel-shaped. No chancel arch, just a cambered beam with plain plaster above where probably the Doom was painted over the screen. Framed ceilings to the aisles and tower.

The importance of this church is the WOODWORK. Three early C16 SCREENS across the nave and aisles. The centre is a fine example of the Devon type despite missing the tracery. Openings framed in the leaf scroll typical of the Carhampton–Dunster group. Thin shafts with angel capitals carry a ribbed vault, the panels all relief-carved with foliage and some Renaissance faces. Exceptionally rich cornice in undercut bands. Base panelled with ogee tracery above quatrefoils. The back is picked out in pretty colours; C18? The aisle screens are much lighter. Each has four three-light traceried sections with a convex leaf cornice and a base with the simplest, parchemin-type linenfold. On the N side over the door are the names of the donors. Blue and red remaining colour. – PULPIT. Of exceptional rarity, a wooden pulpit with undamaged figures of saints. Small angels hold on to the crocketed gables above the five figures (St John and the four Doctors of the Church). They have draperies falling in angular folds and probably belong to c. 1500. Their faces are all of one type, and there is nothing of the consummate skill or power of characterization of contemporary German woodcarving. Back made up of reused carved panels. – BENCH-ENDS. A large and interesting selection of c. 1530–40. The date 1560 and name of *Simon Werman* (here spelled Warman) are inscribed over finely pleated linenfold panelling on the back wall. Amid the bench-end motifs are the initials S and W, and the leaf-scroll border that probably identifies Werman's workshop (e.g. Hatch Beauchamp, Bishop's Hull). Apart from the Instruments of the Passion, big leaves, plants, tracery, Renaissance vases and profiles, there is a dispersed little procession – a boy with a processional cross, a man with a taper, a chorister with surplice and book, a server with maniple and casket, and a priest in a cope, all very rustic. – STAINED GLASS. Two unusually complete C15 windows, the E showing the Crucifixion with the Virgin and St John, and Evangelist symbols above, the chancel S particularly good with Saints Michael, Margaret and George. The figures stand on pedestals. Also one N window, much restored. SE, 1865, by *Horwood Bros* of Mells. S aisle fourth, 1876, by *Lavers, Barraud & Westlake*. NW windows by *Kempe*, 1899, and *Kempe & Co.*, 1913. – MONUMENTS. John Baker †1677. Painted, very rustic, the inscription above a draped altar and between scrolls, some capped with angel heads. – Robert Lucas †1722. Well carved, with fluted pilasters and broken curved pediment.

War memorial CHURCHYARD CROSS, 1920, with tabernacle head.

NW of the churchyard, CHANTRY COTTAGE was probably a C15 priest's house, possibly originally timber-framed. Moulded framed ceiling. At the E end of Church Road, EASTBROOK HOUSE, C16, disguised in Victorian stucco and half-timber, is less interesting than its Puginian Gothic GATEHOUSE range of *c*. 1860, perhaps by *C. E. Giles*. Chert-faced, the throughway vaulted in brick. Contemporary estate houses opposite, Nos. 57–59, with shared eight-shaft chimney. W of the church, on the main road, KINGS GATCHELL, L-plan, externally Victorian, with plasterwork upstairs, the arms of James I with lively lion and unicorn under typical arcading. W down Dipford Road, GATCHELL COTTAGES were a C15 hall house with a C16 lateral fireplace, cob-walled under roughcast. Jettied timber-framed gable to the cross-wing. TRULL GREEN FARM, L-plan and thatched, was probably a hall house raised in the C16, to which the SE wing, dated 1637, was added. Good moulded oak doorway. S of Trull, beyond Staplehay, CANONSGROVE, 1827, one of the best of the C19 villas around Taunton. Deep eaves and open pediment, the ashlar ground floor showing an Early Victorian richness. E of Staplehay, AMBERD FARMHOUSE, thatched, has late medieval origins. AMBERD HOUSE, of 2–1–2 bays with an open-pedimented doorcase, is probably Early Victorian. Victorian gable on each side.

CHILLISWOOD, 1 m. W. Medieval, remodelled in the late C16. Stuccoed S front of *c*. 1835 between Tudor-style stone archways. Re-set 1594 plaque. The front wall was moved outward. Inside is a mast stair with octagonal finial, and plank partitions. A narrow range running back at a slight angle has a lateral chimney-breast indicating possibly an open hall. C16 oak-mullioned windows. Jointed-cruck roof. At the N end a smoke-chamber accessed from outside. A short NW cross-wing with exposed timber-framing links to a former BARN, also with jointed-cruck trusses. C18–C19 polygonal HORSE-ENGINE HOUSE.

HAMWOOD FARMHOUSE, 1 m. SW. Remnant of a late C17 house of brick with ovolo-moulded mullion windows. Heraldic cartouche (Baker arms) and Tudor-arched E doorway. The roofs have been lowered. Other Tudor-arched doorways amid outbuildings.

CUTSEY FARM, 2 m. SW. A large group of brick model farm buildings (all converted), c. 1860, by *John Watson* of Torquay. Fodder was mixed in the three-storey centrepiece and distributed at loft level to the cattle sheds.

UPTON

ST JAMES. 1867, by *C. F. Edwards* of Axminster. Harsh Early Dec style with a bargeboarded porch and nave E bellcote. – FONT. Broken C13 bowl with an inset ring and coved underside.

OLD CHURCH, 1 m. WNW, at Upton Farm. Only the W tower remains, with footings of the rest. The tower is plain of three stages, with a parapet sloped to triangular corners. It looks C18 but the tower arch has panelled C15 jambs. Infilled with a moulded C14 doorway and two-light E window from the demolished parts.

HADDON LODGE, ½ m. W. On a disused driveway to Pixton Park (Dulverton). Stuccoed triangular lodge of c. 1800 for Lady Harriet Acland. Two-storeyed, with battlemented hexagonal turrets.

UPTON NOBLE

ST MARY MAGDALENE. C13 S porch-tower, saddleback-roofed, sturdy and unadorned, with a chamfered doorway. Round-arched roll-moulded S doorway, C12–C13. Perp SE chapel attached, with Perp arch inside. *R. J. Withers* rebuilt the nave and chancel in 1878, longer at each end. Barrel roofs and fat column-shafts to the chancel arch. – FONT. Early Norman bowl with a roll moulding. – SCULPTURE. C12–C13 small stone Crucifixion, the cross encircled.* – STAINED GLASS. E window, 1878, by *Clayton & Bell*.

LYCHGATE by *Withers*.

UPTON NOBLE MANOR, at the lower edge of the village, is probably C16, enlarged in the early C17. Cramped Jacobean stair with tall square finials and pierced pendants. Two handsome stone fireplaces in the cross-wing are surprisingly classical, one with a heavy broken pediment on consoles, the other corniced. A lane runs S to LOVEL HOUSE, a good hip-roofed five-bay house of c. 1700 with stone cross-windows.

---

* Possibly C11; see the uncrossed legs and the splayed ends of the cross. B. and M. Gittos.

Ground-floor architraves with pulvinated friezes. Above the village, HIGHER FARM, dated 1711 over a bolection-moulded doorway.

BELLERICA FARM, ¾ m. E. L-plan. Georgian to Victorian windows. Remains of a C15 wind-braced roof. C16 framed ceiling.

VEN HOUSE see MILBORNE PORT

WALFORD HOUSE see WEST MONKTON

WALTON

4030

HOLY TRINITY. Plain NE tower of 1836 by *John Ralphs* of Warminster, with a pyramid roof of 1886. The rest of 1865–6, by the otherwise unknown *Rev. J. F. Turner*.* A creditable design in Blue Lias with varied Dec tracery. The interior was banded in brick, unfortunately painted over. Good carved detail, ballflower to the chancel arch, naturalistic corbels etc., by *John Seymour* of Taunton. – FONT. Massive, with rounded diapered angles on marble shafts. – STAINED GLASS. Bright glass by *Lavers & Barraud* in the chancel and nave second window, 1866, and W window, slightly later (Elijah particularly dramatic). Aisle windows, rather softer, 1871–4, by *Lavers, Barraud & Westlake*. – MONUMENT. Effigy of a priest, his feet on a lion, *c*. 1300.

THE OLD PARSONAGE, by the church. Late C15, replacing a rectory built in 1252. Attractive but not entirely credible, as windows and other pieces were introduced from a demolition in Wiltshire in 1938. The long N–S range has a first-floor hall with NE garderobe, the hall marked by square-headed three-light windows, one on the E, the other transomed on the N end. They have the typical ogee lights and spandrel quatrefoils found at Muchelney Abbey. A short range attached to the NW corner by a spiral staircase contained a first-floor parlour with a similar E window and a canted N end bay, the tracery here introduced after 1938. The W side of the main range has a variety of one- and two-light windows.

Towards Street, the former SCHOOL of 1836 stands opposite WALTON HOUSE, a large rectory of 1821, by *Hugh Adams* of Glastonbury. Coarsely detailed. The gables are an early departure from standard Late Georgian.

WALTON MILL, ¾ m. S. Prominent white windmill tower of *c*. 1793, converted in 1929.

IVYTHORN FARM, 1 m. SSE. Pyramid-roofed Longleat estate farmhouse of *c*. 1830. Brick chimney for a steam-sterilizing plant.

---

*The attribution to *John Norton* is a confusion with Walton near Clevedon.

WAMBROOK

Part of Dorset until 1896.

St Mary. Mostly of chert. Perp three-stage w tower with set-back buttresses and octagonal NE stair-turret. Two-light bell-openings. Larger blind N window beneath with quatrefoil infill. w doorway under a quatrefoil frieze. Nave with square-headed C16 windows and opposed porches, the s one prettily roofed in 1929 by *Herbert Read*. Norman s doorway, segmental-arched on block capitals. Chancel, 1892, by *G. H. Gordon*. – Font. C13. Massive octagon tapered beneath a middle band. – Pulpit. Reused linenfold panels. – Royal Arms. 1703. – Some C15–C16 bench-ends with heavy tracery.

At Higher Wambrook, ½ m. N, Wambrook Farm. Gothic buildings of *c.* 1840–50. Notably angular brick granary. Bartletts, downhill E, and Drake's Farmhouse, N, are thatched, C15–C16.

Weston Farm, 1 m. N. Tall farmhouse of chequered stone and chert with an off-centre storeyed porch dated 1672. This marks alterations (see the blocked upper window of the porch) to a house dated 1583 on the rear wing. The first-floor leaded casements set low in the wall suggest lost attic windows, perhaps in gables. The rear wing has remarkably long mullioned windows, a seven-light over a nine-light, with ovolo-moulded mullions, early for this type. These light rooms with exceptional early C17 plasterwork. The parlour has four panels between moulded beams. Thick curvilinear ribs enclose strange beasts, datable to after 1614 from the heraldry. The beasts relate to those at Hinton House (Hinton St George), Wigborough Manor (Over Stratton) and Whitestaunton Manor. The room above has a three-sided ceiling, the centre with charming spiral trails (acorn and mulberry) radiating from a roundel. Unique in Somerset, such plant-trail appears at Rashleigh Barton, Devon. Chapel Cottage, NW, is an altered C15 chapel, still with its wagon roof.

Lancin Farmhouse, ½ m. W. Picturesquely thatched early C15 cruck-framed hall. Low end tree-ring-dated 1533.

WANSTROW

St Mary. s tower of 1810 with typical Y-tracery. The rest is attractively stone-tiled. Two-bay Perp SE chapel, enlarged in 1504, the E window with supermullions, the s windows square-headed. Nave and chancel rebuilt in 1875–6 by *Ferrey & Son*. Victorian interior, apart from an early C16 arch in the s chapel. – Royal Arms. 1810.

Manor House, opposite the church. C17, but the pretty castellated and mullion-windowed front is early C18. Three-bay centre between hip-roofed cross-wings of uneven widths. Five-bay rear addition, not much later, with sash windows in architraves with keystones. Early C18 staircase with column newels.

ALICE STREET FARMHOUSE, 1 m. NE. Neatly compact early C17 front. Storeyed porch and five three-light mullion-and-transom windows.

WASHFORD

ST MARY. 1909–10, by *Samson & Cottam*. Red sandstone mission chapel, with lancets. Boarded roofs on deep curved trusses.
On the main road, a former METHODIST CHAPEL, 1824–8, red sandstone, with a later octagonal stair-turret. Behind the primary school, THE CROFT, thatched, C16–C17, has a good plaster frieze of scrolls and fruit. W of the village, the well-preserved STATION on the Minehead Railway of 1872–4.

BBC TRANSMITTING STATION, 1 m. E. 1932–3, by *M. T. Tudbery*, the BBC engineer. An existing design by *L. R. Guthrie* of *Wimperis, Simpson & Guthrie*, for the London regional station (Brookmans Park, Herts.), was broadly followed here and at the other three regional transmitter stations at Huddersfield, Falkirk and Droitwich. A heavy square modern-classical building of concrete imitating stone, the front block with the BBC arms and a granite doorway. Behind is a high square transmitter hall, top-lit from an octagonal roof-light. Rear ranges held the generators, battery store and emergency diesel engines. Contemporary twin 500-ft (152-metre) masts. Mostly decommissioned in 1983.

WATCHET

An Anglo-Saxon settlement, named in the Burghal Hidage of 919, and the site of a mint. It was repeatedly raided by Vikings in the C10. A medieval borough developed behind the harbour, which was protected by a pier from 1708. The buildings are mostly rendered over beach stones and indeed ships' ballast, with some brick and red sandstone. Lime was a principal export well into the C19. From 1857 ore from the Brendon Hills was shipped to South Wales ironworks. Paper has been made in the valley below the church since the mid C18.

ST DECUMAN, on the hill outside the town. The same saint is commemorated at Rhoscrowther, Pembs. The church is one of the largest in the district, and with the exception of the chancel is all Perp. The chancel is of the C13, rendered, with a three-light E window of lancets stepped beneath three circles with thin tracery, two trefoiled and one quatrefoiled, showing early development from plate tracery to bar tracery. Crude headstops. Inside it is shafted. The single N lancet is also shafted inside, under a pointed trefoiled rere-arch. Also inside, a damaged C13 piscina with remains of shafting.

Now the late medieval work. Big three-stage W tower of squared purple-grey sandstone, resembling that at Winsford in the set-back buttresses almost up to the battlements and higher polygonal NE stair-turret, and the battlements. Four-centred-arched W doorway, four-light W window, and large three-light bell-openings, each with a transom and pierced baffles. On the S side a low-relief saint in a canopied niche. The N aisle is a typical show piece of the late C15, of squared sandstone, embattled, with quatrefoils in the crenellations and an embattled rood-stair turret. Four-centred-arched three-light windows with supermullions. The S aisle is more modest, mid-C15, white-rendered, built in two halves. The eastern half has the mannered tracery found also at Old Cleeve, thickly cusped, with oddly shouldered heads to the lights. Two three-light S windows, one with transom, and a longer E window, also transomed. The western half has conventional tracery, one three-light window each side of the porch. The porch floor is of slates placed on end, in a handsome chessboard pattern.

The tall tower arch has a wave and a hollow moulding. Arcades of four bays, a rudimentary chancel arch, and one much broader arch each side from the chancel to each side chapel. Piers of four-hollow section in the N arcade, and four-wave section in the S. On the N most of the piers have the charming enrichment of small shallow niches for images. Four statuettes survive on one pier (Doctors of the Church), and two more on the eastern respond (St George and St Anthony). The sculptural quality is low. Each chapel arch matches those of its corresponding arcade. Very good wagon roofs, with angels all along carved wall-plates, and carved bosses. They are mostly of foliage; one boss in the chancel shows a serpent. In the N aisle the entire roof framing is carved, as at Luccombe and Selworthy. Marble sanctuary PAVING by *J. P. St Aubyn*, 1886.

FURNISHINGS. FONT. Perp, octagonal, with big angel busts against the underside. Panelled buttressed stem. – SCREENS. C15–C16, very much renewed. The five-bay nave screen has sub-arched four-light tracery. Dado with crocketed ogee panels and original colour. The three-bay screen to the S aisle may be a little earlier, of six-light tracery divided by a heavy central mullion. Dado also with some colour. Marks of a rood stair some way to the W show the original position. A parclose screen to the chancel has three-light sections of delicately traceried square-headed lights. – PULPIT. Early C17, similar to Luccombe. Two tiers of panels divided by a band of oval cabochons. Tester with acorn pendants. – COMMUNION RAIL. Early C17. Sturdy, vertically symmetrical balusters. – WYNDHAM PEW. 1688. Fielded-panelled with excellent scrolled foliage. – TILES. An exceptionally large collection of

C13 tiles similar to those at Cleeve Abbey, many of them heraldic. The chancel floor between the stalls is wholly tiled. Also some framed on the N wall. – STAINED GLASS. E window, 1886, beautifully drawn, probably by *Westlake*. Good early C20 heraldic glass, chancel N and SE chapel S. Several anaemic sub-Comper windows, by *Cuthbert Atchley*, 1935–40.

MONUMENTS. Mostly in the Wyndham Chapel. Sir John Wyndham †1574. Interesting because in spite of its date it has no hints whatever of the Renaissance. Tomb-chest with shields in three square panels, of undetermined ornamental forms rather than the usual Perp quatrefoils. Perp pinnacled shafts between. Two finely detailed small brasses on top, 2½ ft (80 cm.) long, he in armour, she in a ruff and divided head-dress. Until 1972 the tomb had a stone canopy. Four amorphous piers carried a round-arched canopy with Gothic panelling inside. A large, striking demi-figure of an angel was above that against an attic with buttresses and shields. – Florence Wyndham †1596 and John †1572 (chapel E wall). Two 4-ft (1.2-metre) brass figures on a black wall slab, he in armour. Enamelled heraldry. – Edmund Wyndham †1616 (chancel floor). Single brass figure in armour. – Henry and George Wyndham †1613 and †1624. Sumptuous wall monument of local alabaster and marble with two typical C17 painted figures, both kneeling facing E. Columned frame with a broken pediment. – Sir John Wyndham †1645 and his wife †1633 (chapel E wall). On a big black wall slab of Tournai marble, two highly unusual relief portraits in brass, in scrolled frames. Bills confirm that it was made in London by *Nicholas Stone*, 1634–7. – Sir William Wyndham †1683. A marble monument good enough for Westminster Abbey, attributed to *James Hardy* (GF). Two putti hold a shield in front of a curvaceous dark sarcophagus on white console brackets. Above, a scrolled pediment carries a great flaming vase between flaming urns. A flowing drape on the pedestal has the inscription. – Charles Kinaird †1723 (N aisle). Bulging cartouche with draped heraldry. – George Wyndham †1845. Gothic tomb-chest with painted shields in traceried panels, the top a great slab of Purbeck marble. *Minton* tiles to the step.

CHURCHYARD CROSS, of red sandstone from Capton, on a high stepped base. N of the churchyard, the former VICARAGE, 1833, with a deep-eaved hipped roof and red sandstone addition by *Samson & Cottam*, 1885. On the slope W of the churchyard, a HOLY WELL in a stone-lined chamber.

METHODIST CHAPEL, Harbour Street. 1870–1 by *Robert Williams*, one of the chapel trustees, after they had 'resolved to go no further' with *Alexander Lauder*. Substantial Gothic, of Williton red sandstone with Bath dressings, divided by sheer red-and-buff buttresses. Raised on a basement hall.

The HARBOUR is enclosed by two piers rebuilt in 1902–3 (*W. T. Douglass*, engineer), in concrete, after a storm had all but destroyed the predecessors of 1861–3 by *James Abernethy*. Marina of 2001 in the E half. On the W pier a small cast-iron

LIGHTHOUSE from *George Hennet*'s foundry, Bridgwater, 1862. On The Esplanade at the back, bronze STATUES of seafarers, the Ancient Mariner, 2003, and Yankee Jack, 2008, both by *A. B. Herriot* of Penicuik. At the E end of the harbour, the sandstone lifeboat house of 1875, given a new façade as the LIBRARY in 1953. At the W end is the small two-storey MARKET HOUSE of 1819–20. Rendered, with depressed-arched openings of stone. Hipped roof with a louvred lantern. Swain Street runs S, with the best of the houses. On the W side, THE GEORGIAN HOUSE, handsome brick of four bays, with stone quoins and a Gibbsian rusticated doorcase, *c.* 1730–40. Dining-room fireplace between curved-headed alcoves. Further up, No. 12, Victorian coloured brick, with keystone lumps of local alabaster. The modest later C19 TOWN COUNCIL CHAMBER is attached to an equally modest late C18 stuccoed house. THE BANK HOUSE opposite has a formal three-bay Late Georgian stuccoed front. On the upper floor is a central niche. At the top, the excellently preserved STATION of 1862 for the West Somerset Railway. This stands at right angles to the line, as Watchet was the terminus until the railway was extended to Minehead in 1872–4. The GOODS SHED has become the Boat Museum. Facing down Swain Street from above the railway line is the former BAPTIST CHAPEL of 1824. Stuccoed, with arched windows on two floors under a rather exotic double-curved gable.

From the Market House, Market Street runs W. A hip-roofed house beyond the Washford River was the STATION of the West Somerset Mineral Railway of 1857–64 (cf. Brendon Hill). Upstream, by a narrow twin-arched BRIDGE, the last thatched houses, the C17 WATERLOO COTTAGES. Beyond, the disused early to late C19 industrial buildings of TOWN MILLS.

KENTSFORD FARM, ½ m. W. Medieval, rebuilt *c.* 1600 for the Wyndhams of Orchard Wyndham, altered in the late C17. Roughcast with a hip-roofed cross-wing to the l. and porch with a Jacobean arched doorway. Mixed mullion, mullion-and-transom, and sash windows. In the wing at the back, an early C17 plaster ceiling with double ribs and floral sprays. Just W, a low two-arched PACKHORSE BRIDGE.

DAW'S CASTLE, on the cliffs to the W. Incoherent earthwork. Excavation suggests that this is the site of the Anglo-Saxon *burh*, built as a defence against the Danes. The surrounding earthwork bank and ditch are lost to coastal erosion on the seaward side.

WAYFORD

ST MICHAEL. Low and pebbledashed, with its bells in a box behind the bellcote. Georgian mullioned windows for the gallery and pulpit. Chancel rebuilt in 1846 retaining two C13 s lancets with trefoiled rere-arches. The interior has a barn-like charm. Early to mid-C19 roof, tall posts supporting the bells, and timber arcade to a N aisle added with notable sympathy by *George & Yeates* in 1906. Good C13 double PISCINA, of cusped arches with shelves under a big quatrefoil. – FONT. C14. Heavy octagonal bowl. – PULPIT. Late Georgian, hexagonal. – BOX PEWS. 1840s. – ROYAL ARMS. George III. – CREED and LORD'S PRAYER, on boards, 1795. – MONUMENTS. Azariah Pinney †1760, elegant, in coloured marbles. – John Pinney M.P. †1762. Grey and white with heraldry against a black obelisk. Sarah Pinney †1818, Grecian with draped urn, by *Samuel Gibbs* of Axminster.

WAYFORD MANOR. Rebuilt *c.* 1602 (date on the library chimneypiece), for Giles Daubeney. The regular E-plan W front with gabled projecting wings is due to the addition of a N wing matching the S one, by *George & Yeates* in 1902–5. The storeyed and hip-roofed porch has a handsome group of three prettily decorated arches on Tuscan columns, very similar to the porch at Cranborne Manor, Dorset. The six shell-headed niches within compare with those at Montacute, all of which suggests *William Arnold* as designer. Mullion and mullion-and-transom windows, the latter of six lights overlooking the forecourt. The S side has a hip-roofed stair-tower. Conservatory and arcaded loggia of 1902. In the hall a ribbed plaster ceiling of 1902. The library ceiling, however, is original. Thin ribs, curved and straight, outline a pattern familiar in Somerset (and all over England) with decoration of rosettes, floral finials and leaf bosses. Good heavy fireplace with coupled Corinthian columns and an overmantel with strap cartouche framed in a heavy egg-and-dart moulding between niches. The library fireplace at Montacute is almost identical. Another plaster ceiling in the small first-floor S chamber. Rear courtyard prettily framed by an L-plan service range. The E part of this range was probably a late medieval priest's house. Jointed-cruck truss. At the N end a cusped ogee light and an eroded armorial plaque of *c.* 1602. Lovely stepped gardens laid out by *Harold Peto* for his sister Helen Baker, 1900–10.

CLAPTON MILL, 1 m. E. Tall three-storey mill, late C18, remodelled 1867. Of that date the broad 21-ft (6.4-metre) wheel served by an overhead iron trough.

WEARE

ST GREGORY. Perp W tower. Unusually it is banded, in Dundry stone and Blue Lias, with set-back buttresses of pale limestone. The buttresses finish in conjoined finials against the corners of the bell-stage, a local feature (cf. Cheddar, Winscombe, Banwell (all N), Mark). Cusped lattice parapet with corner and intermediate pinnacles. Triple two-light bell-openings, the outer ones blind. Not separated by shafts, as they are on the similar towers. Blind two-light window to the third stage on each side. Four-light w window between canopied niches. NE stair-turret, barely expressed externally. Wave-moulded tower arch. The rest of the church has C15–C16 flat-headed windows, some reused in the N aisle of 1846. Tall round-arched s doorway, the door latch dated 1705. Interior stripped of plaster. Nave roof and N arcade of 1846; chancel roof of 1901, by *E. H. Sedding*.

FITTINGS. What makes Weare special is the Arts and Crafts work introduced from 1901 by *E. H. Sedding*, the craftsmanship good enough to be by the *Trask* firm (cf. Norton-sub-Hamdon). The COMMUNION RAILS are walls of pale green marble pierced with stylized tracery and ending in large kneeling angels; the tracery and angels of alabaster, the coping of dark marble. Lavishly carved STALLS and DESKS, the desks with carving relating to St Gregory, the stall fronts traceried. All have large branching tree finials covered in fruit and flowers. On the LECTERN, made after 1908, decoration slides into excess. Also PANELLING with a crested frieze, and a coloured marble FLOOR. – FONT. Norman, near-square, with lovely wavy fluting beneath. – PULPIT. 1617. Plainer than usual. Blank arches over rectangular panels. – PEWS. C16. A set with thin finials, like those at Badgworth. – STAINED GLASS. N aisle tracery, glass of *c.* 1500, with initials IB, and Passion implements. – MONUMENTS. John Bedbere, *c.* 1505, 18-in. (46-cm.) brass showing him gowned with a purse. – Robert Hooper †1729. Rustic thin broken pediment on Draycott marble piers. Signed *William Sweet*.

In the churchyard a C15 CROSS, with a good tabernacle head of 1930 by *Caröe*. Early C19 SCHOOLROOM with iron lattice windows.

Just W, HENMOORE HOUSE, hip-roofed, early C19. Opposite, former VICARAGE, remodelled in Victorian parsonage style, 1870, by *E. G. Bompas* of Bristol.

WEDMORE

Site of a Saxon royal estate and probably of a minster church. Here Guthrum submitted to King Alfred in 878. Later a manor of the Deans of Wells.

ST MARY. A grand church with crossing tower, at first sight entirely Perp. But the s doorway is an extremely good piece of *c.* 1200, so much in the style of Wells that one can presume Wells workmen. Two orders of colonnettes with excellent *mouvementé* stiff-leaf capitals. Finely moulded arch. Of the same time probably the crossing piers and arches. The piers are altered, but the low arches with their two slight chamfers are good evidence. An early C13 date for the chancel is discernible from the exposed upper parts of slender blocked windows inside, apparently rows of lancets that must have made a fine show. The two-light E window of the SE chapel is of *c.* 1300 but resited (cusped lights and a spherical triangle above; pointed cinquefoiled rere-arch on keeled shafts).

The rest is Perp. Upper parts of the crossing tower with set-back buttresses. Two-light windows below triple two-light bell-openings, the outer ones blind. Parapet with arcading and no pinnacles, like Yeovil. So the tower is late C14 and perhaps by *William Wynford*. Inside, however, are squinches for a spire, a feature not associated with Wynford. Higher octagonal NW stair-turret. The W front is quite monumental, all Perp, but the nave clearly older and remodelled (no plinth). Four-light W window and four-light aisle windows, these under sloping parapets with blind arcading of cusped-headed panels. The same parapet continues all along the S side except for the S transept gable: two-bay aisle, the porch, two-bay S chapel, and single-bay SE chapel, giving notably horizontal lines, again as at Yeovil. The three-storey porch is a special and impressive feature, almost a subsidiary tower. The top floor, with canopied niche to the front and windows to the sides, is reached from a corner stair-turret. The front continues in a very multiform way: first the S chapel in line with the porch, then three steps back for the S transept, SE chapel, and chancel. The S chapel, a chantry founded in 1449, is almost all window; the transept has large S and E windows; and the SE chapel has a late flat-headed S window and the C13 E window already referred to. The chancel projects by one bay, without a parapet. Exceptionally large five-light E window. On the N side the treatment is simpler, but also with a transept and a chancel chapel.

The nave is spacious and light, despite having no clerestory. The arcades are of five bays, with very fragile piers (of four-hollow section) and four-centred arches. The capitals differ from side to side. The N arcade details continue in the arches of the N transept and NE chapel, so these are contemporary, while the S transept and SE chapel arches are of a more robust C14 type, with banded capitals. Two tall arches without capitals open to the S chantry chapel, which has a good panelled ceiling with traces of colour. The stone corbels include two dolphins. Cusped PISCINA. A W door between small windows opens to the porch, but the window above shows that the porch predates the chapel. The aisle roofs have moulded cambered beams on carved stone corbels. The nave roof is thinner, possibly C17, with posts on tie-beams, arch-braced off similar corbels. Similar transept roofs. Chancel chapel ceilings as in the S chapel, the NE ceiling with C15 angels painted in the panels. In the S aisle a good canopied niche. Under the tower a handsome inserted fan-vault of *c.* 1500. In the chancel a cinquefoil cusped PISCINA. Restoration, 1880–1, by *Edmund Ferrey*.

FURNISHINGS. FONT. Perp. Plain octagon, moulded beneath. Panelled stem. – PULPIT. Large, C17, with blank arches filled by plants (the thistle prominent) under a frieze of tablets surrounded by plant-scroll or strapwork. – DOORS. S door with very lively scrolled ends to the hinges and straps, apparently medieval, but dated 1677. Similar N door. – WALL PAINTING. Above the pulpit. Of *c.* 1520, a very large St Christopher with tiny ships and a mermaid at his feet. It was painted over one of the same subject, of which the head of the Child Christ is visible and seems to be mid-C15. – CANDELABRA. One given in 1779, two in 1856. – ROYAL ARMS. Large, Hanoverian. – STAINED GLASS. E window, 1888, and W window, 1890, by *Clayton & Bell*. A panel in the latter shows Queen Victoria *en famille*. By contrast, two brash windows by *Mayer & Co.*, 1892, like oil paintings, in chancel and SE chapel.

MONUMENTS. Grave-slab of *c.* 1300, with male head and relief cross. – Thomas Hodges †1585. C17 brass cartouche, relating his death at the siege of Antwerp. Only his heart came back: 'Here lyes his wounded heart for whome/ One kingdom was two small a roome/ Two kingdoms therefore have thought good to part/ So stout a body and so brave a heart.' – George Hodges †1634. Small brass figure in cavalier dress. Both brasses attributed to *Edward Marshall* (GF). – Ann Hodges †1684. Rustic columned frame to a plaque with Halloween skulls. – Boulting family to 1689. Baroque, with curved pediment and black-shafted columns. Cherub heads beneath, tied by drapery to a skull wreathed in green laurel. – William Boulting †1726. Handsome; white marble on grey, the pediment broken for a flaming urn. – William Boulting †1755. Superb standing monument on a bow-fronted pedestal. A bird withdraws a sumptuous drape from a tall urn. Little flaming urns on each side, all against a grey obelisk. The Phelips memorial at Yeovil is similar. – Ann Rishton †1765. White marble on grey, pedimented. – Gabriel Stone †1815. By *Thomas King*; in a triptych with matching later memorials. – John Barrow †1853. Marble, Gothic, with small angels, by *Tyley*.

In the churchyard, C15 CROSS with two-tier low-relief canopies on the shaft. – WAR MEMORIAL CROSS, 1921, by *A. J. Pictor* of Bruton.

BAPTIST CHAPEL, Grant's Lane. 1840s. Rendered, with big four-centred-arched windows into which are gathered cast-iron latticed lancets.

METHODIST CHAPEL, Sand Road. A simple hip-roofed chapel of 1817, with late C19 cement pilasters and window surrounds. Porch of 1902. Late C19 gallery.

PERAMBULATION. The MANOR HOUSE, Late Georgian to Victorian stucco, has Gothic windows facing S over the churchyard. A medieval to C16 house is encased. On CHURCH STREET, the stuccoed OLD VICARAGE. Scant medieval remains in the L-plan part, which has a Venetian window. A pleasant mixed row runs E. Late Georgian shopfront at the OLD POST OFFICE. On the opposite side, the GEORGE INN, older than its early to mid-C19 Tudor Gothic face. Then in very

Victorian contrast, the Ruskinian Gothic ASSEMBLY ROOMS, 1866, with bi-colour window heads, and the stuccoed former TONKIN STORE, not much earlier, Italianate, three-storeyed, with deep eaves and arcaded windows. It had a rear belvedere tower (dem.). Tonkin's house, r., has bargeboarded gables.

THE BOROUGH, site of the market granted in 1255, runs S. The C14–C15 MARKET CROSS, with octagonal shaft and eroded tabernacle head, survives in the garden of CROSS HOUSE, 1880. Opposite, a white-rendered cottage with iron Georgian Gothic windows. At the top, GRANT'S LANE runs W. Opposite the Baptist chapel (*see* above), a hip-roofed early C19 villa with iron veranda. At the end, on the corner of Sand Road, THE HALL, a three-storey, three-bay Late Georgian villa, stuccoed with ashlar dividing piers, cornice and pedimented doorcase. Down GLANVILLE ROAD, ELMSETT COURT is late C18 beneath Victorian Italianate stucco. Hip-roofed, three-storeyed, with an exceedingly uncomfortable four-storey porch-tower.

PILCORN STREET runs W from the church, past RUSTIC PORCH, whitewashed rubble, late C16, and THE GRANGE, *c.* 1830, deep-eaved, stuccoed, with a Roman Doric porch. Further out, WEST END curves SE, a rural suburb from the C17. WESTOVERS, 1680, compact, gabled, and mullion-windowed, was a hospital built for John Westover, surgeon, surely a very early example. Westover lived at PORCH HOUSE. Late C17 large roughcast porch room with wooden mullion windows, carried on two stone columns. C18 iron casements elsewhere. WESTHOLME has a long six-bay front with iron casements. Further up is MULBERRY HOUSE, handsome late C18. Five bays with ashlar cornice, parapet and pedimented Roman Doric doorcase. Cast-iron glazing bars. GOG'S HOUSE, a large four-bay villa of *c.* 1840, has typical deep eaves. Trellised iron porch. Behind is BROOK FARM, *c.* 1800, roughcast, with parapet and pedimented doorway. SAND ROAD returns past the Methodist chapel (*see* above).

CHEDDAR ROAD runs N from The Borough. THE SWAN is stuccoed, early to mid-C19, with an enclosed porch. HOLDENHURST, stuccoed, with parapet, cornice and pedimented doorcase, is earlier than its bay windows and pretty glazing of *c.* 1840. (Stable dated 1839 and early C19 grotto.) The large Gothic VILLAGE HALL was built as church schoolrooms *c.* 1880. Another ½ m. out, the former BOARD SCHOOL stands alone. 1876–9, by *J. H. Spencer*, a long Gothic front with three gables.

SAND HOUSE, 1 m. S. 1774, designed for himself by *William White*, surveyor. Three-bay rendered front with quoins and pedimented doorcase. Urns on the parapet. The side elevation has been extended, to six bays. Carved Indian woodwork inside, introduced after 1929 by the 13th Earl of Carnwath. SAND HALL, further W, is a square mid-C19 ashlar villa.

STOUGHTON CROSS, 1½ m. NNW. C15 wayside CROSS, the head missing.

WELLINGTON

Market town on the old road to Exeter. The buildings are mostly C18 to C19 and of brick, dark red supplanted by brighter late C19 bricks from the nearby Poole brickworks, where not obscured by paint or render. Prosperity came in the late C18, due to the Fox family, Quaker clothiers and bankers whose mills at Tonedale were on a very large scale. There were other textile mills, and also iron foundries.

ST JOHN BAPTIST. The best part of the church is its proud Perp tower of red sandstone with much Ham stone. Tall (104 ft/31.7 metres), sturdy, and with the stair-turret rising high and centrally placed for show on the s side (cf. Totnes, Devon, also Hillfarrance and West Buckland). Set-back buttresses rise to groups of three pinnacles on each corner, and there are intermediate pinnacles and pinnacles on the stair-turret. w door between diagonal shafts and defaced niches, beneath a very tall four-light transomed window. Miniature two-light windows flank the stair-turret, with transom and pierced baffles. Above, on all sides, are similar two-light bell-openings. Lively gargoyles.

Nave with clerestory, a rarity as far W as this. Embattled aisles continued as two-bay chapels. All Perp, the windows mostly renewed. Of an older church, the porch doorways (*see below*) and part of the sw wall. The N aisle was rebuilt when the aisles and chancel were extended by *C. E. Giles* in 1848. The chancel is datable to *c.* 1300 from the reused three-light E window with three encircled quatrefoils, shafted inside. The porch has curious Transitional detail: a big double roll clumsily suited to the capitals, and a single roll on the inner doorway that accords neither with the wave-moulded arch nor with the shafts, whose feet look like inverted Norman capitals. The bracket dated 1577 may refer to the porch roof.

White and bare interior, much of the stained glass having been swept away in 1938 and the Victorian furnishings in 1986. Soaring tower arch, panelled and shafted; clumsier panelled chancel arch. Tall nave with four-bay arcades on slim shafted piers of standard four-hollow section. Framed wagon ceiling. In the E window of the s aisle a tiny 'lily crucifix' carved on the central mullion below the tracery; two ogee niches in the jambs. Two small niches also in the N arcade piers. Only the responds of the chancel arcades are original. Fine early C14 PISCINA with cinquefoiled arch, the shafts on two heads, a king and a monk/monkey. Cinquefoiled tomb-recess opposite, over an early C14 EFFIGY of a priest, named as Richard in the faint inscription, one of the earliest anywhere to be in English.*
– FONT. 1848. Splendid ogee-domed COVER on gold columns, by *Randoll Blacking*, 1957. – PULPIT. Probably of 1728 and by

---

* A stone reredos of *c.* 1380 with many small figures in tiers and a Crucifixion at the top, found in 1848, is in the Museum of Somerset.

Robert Culverwell. Similar to those Kingston St Mary and Woodlands; spoilt by applied Gothic panels. It stood higher with a tester before 1848 and was pushed aside in 1986. – ROYAL ARMS. Cast-iron, 1848. – Mid-C19 WEST GALLERIES in the aisles. – STAINED GLASS. E window, harshly coloured, by *Francis Skeat*, 1981. Two s windows by *Kempe*, 1901 and 1907, female saints. – MONUMENTS. Sir John Popham †1607, the Chief Justice who presided over the trials of Raleigh and Guy Fawkes, and wife. Stateliest of Somerset's Jacobean monuments, with the triumphal-arch canopy on eight Corinthian columns of contemporary monuments in Westminster Abbey to Queen Elizabeth and Mary, Queen of Scots, but of inferior workmanship. All painted. Coffered arch soffit, heraldic achievements and obelisks on top. High tomb-chest with recumbent effigies. The kneeling figures are Popham's parents, son and daughter-in-law, six daughters, three maidservants, and thirteen grandchildren.

ST JOHN FISHER (R.C.), Mantle Street. Originally the Popham Almshouses, as rebuilt in 1833 by *Charles Bailey*, the Nynehead agent. Tudor style, red sandstone. The three-bay sides were originally two-storeyed with chimneys on dormer gables. The chimneys have gone and long windows in the l. range mark the church inserted in 1936–7 by *John Willman*. The centre gable has lost a pierced parapet.

BAPTIST CHAPEL, South Street. 1833, by *Richard Carver*. Stuccoed, with tall arched windows and flat bracketed eaves. The detail just on the point of going Victorian-Italianate. Long side along the street. On the front, lunettes above an enclosed porch with good early C19 lettering over attached Tuscan columns. Interior of 1876–7. Attached SCHOOLS by *Samuel Pollard* of Taunton, 1864–5, extended 1907.

CONGREGATIONAL CHAPEL (United Reformed), Fore Street. 1860–1, by *Samuel Pollard*. Large and Gothic, of chert, with ashlar pinnacles and spiky tracery.

FRIENDS' MEETING HOUSE, High Street. *See* Perambulation.

METHODIST CHAPEL, Station Road. 1899, by *F. W. Roberts*. Red brick with a little stone. Four-lancet window and chamfered angle turrets with finials.

CEMETERY. *See* Rockwell Green.

WELLINGTON SCHOOL, South Street. Founded in 1837 in a Late Georgian brick house (SCHOOL HOUSE), to which a storey was added with the Gothic schoolroom to the l. in 1880. Similar TECHNICAL SCHOOL to the r., 1893. All this by *Edwin Howard*, the Technical School extended in 1908 by *Ernest Howard*. The buildings overlooking the playing fields reflect grander C20 aspirations. Three principal buildings, all brick, a hip-roofed seven-bay GREAT HALL, 1924, stripped Georgian, a Perp Gothic CHAPEL, 1928–31, both by *Charles Biddulph-Pinchard*, separated by single-storey CLASSROOMS with Jacobean gables, 1932, by *Ernest Howard*. The chapel interior is light, colourfully painted, and with notably good Gothic woodwork made at the school, the fine carving by *Francis Hunt*.

Julian Hannam added DUKE'S BUILDING, 1982–3, behind the chapel, and CORNER BUILDING, 1986, beyond the hall, both square brick pavilions. Along the N edge, NORTHSIDE was the Royal Jubilee Warehouse, 1887 by *Edwin Howard*, for mail-order clothing, extended 1903 and 1910. The Ham stone porch carries the royal arms in red sandstone. Additions 1991–2 by *Stone & Partners*. Across South Street, the JUNIOR SCHOOL, with deep-eaved pyramid roof, 1998–9, the curved-roofed SPORTS CENTRE, 2001–2, and ALAN ROGERS CENTRE, 2008–9, all by *Stone & Partners*.

WELLINGTON PARK, Beech Grove. 1902–3. Laid out by *F. W. Meyer*. Charming Arts and Crafts COTTAGE, roughcast and pantiled, with a semicircular bow and plaque with wayward lettering. Perhaps by *Samson & Cottam*.

PERAMBULATION. The staggered crossing of the broad main street with North Street and South Street makes a feature of the former TOWN HALL, 1832–3. Five by three bays, with arched openings on both floors and giant corner pilasters. Bath stone and stucco. HIGH STREET, running NE, has the best Georgian houses, if none of exceptional merit. The finest was No. 10, of 1770, set back in a forecourt, infilled in 1907 by shops (pretty Arts and Crafts balconies). Five bays, hip-roofed, three-storeyed, with stone angle piers and a cornised central architrave. Behind No. 18, the FRIENDS' MEETING HOUSE, 1845. Buff brick three-bay front with pedimental gable. Galleries on two sides. On the N side, No. 17, painted, with close-spaced segment-headed windows of early C18 type. No. 21 stands out, the brick unpainted, with a good Tuscan open-pediment doorcase. The little pellets under the cornice show that this is Late Georgian, after 1800. Similar brickwork and doorcases on Nos. 41–45 and Nos. 48–50 opposite. (Good doorways also on Nos. 7 and 35.) By the churchyard, No. 71, a neat stuccoed villa in the manner of *Richard Carver*, c. 1830. Deep bracketed eaves and pediment, Greek Doric porch. Facing the churchyard, the OLD VICARAGE, large, bald, Late Georgian, between C20 additions. Beyond are ST JOHN'S SCHOOL, 1855–6, Gothic, of chert and Bath stone, by *C. E. Giles*, and PRIORY HOUSE, stuccoed and hip-roofed, early C19. Set back opposite, DRAKE'S PLACE has two five-bay stuccoed elevations of Late Georgian character, but the central window has thick early C18 glazing bars, the date of a good panelled room inside with fluted pilasters and Baroque carving.

Returning to the Town Hall, FORE STREET runs SW. Banks provide the principal display here. In a minor key, the HSBC, opposite the Town Hall, an ashlar refacing by *Woolfall & Eccles*, 1924. Then two competing behemoths, the NATWEST, 1864, for Stuckey's Bank, probably by *Giles*, and on the other side LLOYDS, the former headquarters of Fox, Fowler & Co., 1885, the major work of *Edwin Howard*. Both are Italian palazzi of red sandstone with much limestone ashlar, the NatWest more reposeful than Howard's varied pediments and arched windows breaking into the entablature. On the S side, No. 20, an early

C19 oddity with triangle-headed windows and lozenge glazing. Further down, the former SQUIRREL HOTEL (Wellington Museum and Town Council), a roughcast Late Georgian two-storey row, refronting older work. C16 moulded framed ceiling in the museum. No. 35, opposite, Late Georgian, stuccoed, originally brick, has a broad canted centre. No. 37, altered, has the swept parapet of the early C18. By the United Reformed church (p. 659), neo-Gothic flats in keeping, 2002, by *Steel, Coleman & Davis*.

Fore Street then becomes MANTLE STREET. OLD COURT stands at the former entrance to Sir John Popham's mansion (*see* Courtland Road, below). The Late Georgian two-bay front with lower single-bay wings screens older work. Scrolled iron gatepiers. The former METHODIST SCHOOLROOM, 1875 by *Samuel Shewbrooks*, of Westleigh stone, is heavily Romanesque, the bellcote especially so. Chapel of 1851 behind. On the S side, the WELLESLEY CINEMA, 1937, by *E. Holding*, stark brick cubic front. Further down, the R.C. church (p. 659), and, on the S side, Gothic GATEPIERS marking the site of Holy Trinity church, by *Carver*, 1828–31 (dem.). On the hilltop behind, FOXDOWN HOUSE, rebuilt for the Elworthys, mill-owners, *c.* 1870, in stone with acute half-timbered gables. Further out, THE CLEVE, a dour stone villa without especial personality. Surprisingly by *Alfred Waterhouse*, for Joseph Fox, 1864, extended 1868 and 1878.

Returning to the centre, SOUTH STREET runs past the Baptist chapel (p. 659). On the E side, THE AVENUE, a handsome three-storey brick house of 1784, for Thomas Fox. It adjoins THE WILLOWS, stuccoed, five-bay, early C19. No. 30, opposite, rusticated stucco, was the Baptist manse, 1824. Minor Late Georgian houses opposite Wellington School (p. 659). Further down is WELLESLEY PARK, a suburb begun in 1887 by *Edwin Howard* and continued after 1920 by *Ernest Howard*. The earlier houses are brick, with some half-timber, one partly tile-hung. THE GRANGE, 1906, with corner turret, is stone-fronted. The houses of the 1920s are roughcast, interestingly varied. *Edwin Howard*'s WATER TOWER, Dark Lane, 1896, is comically perched on a two-storey house.

Now back, and up NORTH STREET. The small stone Gothic former REGISTER OFFICE, 1836, by *Carver*, adjoined *Carver*'s demolished workhouse. Down COURTLAND ROAD is Wellington Park (p. 660). On the way, COURTLAND TERRACE, 1858, with little bargeboarded gables, and a three-bay former POLICE STATION, 1857, marked 'Constabulary'. Playing fields cover the site of Sir John Popham's Elizabethan mansion, burnt in the Civil War. THE COURT, late C18, hip-roofed, three-storeyed and stuccoed with a modillion cornice, occupies one corner. Beyond North Street is much late C19 housing, largely by *Edwin Howard*: villas on the main road (Waterloo Road/Station Road) with artisan housing in streets behind. On STATION ROAD, the villas are on a raised pavement called High Path. No. 8, 1887, was *Howard*'s own house. Behind, on

SPRINGFIELD ROAD, terrace housing for Fox workers, 1887–97. The E side of Station Road and streets behind were by *F. W. Roberts*, 1899–1910, for the Co-operative Society. After his Methodist chapel (p. 659), SWALLOWFIELD HOUSE, a mid-C19 deep-eaved stuccoed villa with a pedimented Doric porch. *Waterhouse* altered it in 1857, not obviously. Of the former Bristol & Exeter station, a large mid-C19 red sandstone GOODS SHED survives. Tonedale begins across the railway.

TONEDALE. Thomas Fox moved his enterprise here in 1801–3. He built TONEDALE HOUSE, 1807, square, stuccoed, with bracketed eaves and central pediments, attached to the mill. The N front was soon absorbed into the mill and an E wing added to compensate. A three-storey laundry overlooking the gardens illustrates how completely private life and industry were combined. TONEDALE MILL is the finest industrial group in Somerset, an impressive record of the development of the cloth industry. Three main parts run W. The upper range was for finishing cloth. Late C19, of fifteen bays and two storeys, stone, with segmental-arched windows. Single-storey offices beyond. Behind rises the compact late C18 mill already on the site. The middle part, attached to Tonedale House, comprises Fox's mill and warehouse of 1801–3. Brick-fronted three-to-four-storey ranges at right angles. The part in the angle burnt in 1821, and was rebuilt with fireproof floors. Behind is a narrow mid-C19 beam-engine house, replaced in the late C19 by the power complex below with its tall octagonal chimney. The lower site is dominated by the most spectacular mill, built in two phases in 1861–71. Hipped roofs over red sandstone with Ham stone arched window heads in five storeys. Lunettes under the eaves. These arcaded layers give a Roman grandeur to its dereliction. Thirty bays, divided unevenly by projections for a beam engine, N, and stairs, S, the latter capped with a later brick-clad water tank. Six-bay W end overlooking fields. Lower adjacent ten-bay range, of stone, and extensive brick buildings running S.

Other Fox buildings include, on the Milverton Road, a stone INFANTS' SCHOOL, 1848, and TONE MILLS, a tightly packed works divided by the river. On BURCHILLS HILL, two parallel short mid-C19 rows with octagonal brick chimneys. Across the valley, NW of Burchill's Hill, FIVE HOUSES, early C19 factory housing around an open court, hip-roofed and stuccoed. Comically varied window shapes: segment-headed outer windows, arched windows over pointed ones in the intermediate bays, and a blind pointed centre window over a pointed doorway.

WELLINGTON MONUMENT (National Trust). 2 m. S, crowning the Blackdown Hills. An enormous triangular obelisk faced in eroding Calcareous Gritstone, on a neo-Egyptian plinth (actually a curtain wall) with projecting pedestals at the angles. It soars to 176 ft (53.6 metres) but was not so intended. *Thomas Lee* in 1817 proposed a shorter shaft with a statue of the Duke in cast iron on top, and cottages for veterans at the three corners. Abandoned unfinished, it was heightened to a conical cap in 1853–4 by *Giles* and given the slightly taller triangular cap in 1892.

WEMBDON

St George. Plain two-stage W tower with diagonal buttresses. C14 wave-moulded tower arch on corbels. Nave rebuilt after a fire by *J. M. Hay* of Bath, 1869–70. His is the harsh Dec tracery, but the non-matching arcades echo the originals. Chancel of *c.* 1300 – see the E and N window tracery, the E window in a broad shafted reveal. Georgian plaster ceiling. Victorian TILES and marble-shafted REREDOS, 1882, the gold-mosaic panels with tilework by *Powell's*. – COMMUNION TABLE. C17. Eight bulbous legs with Ionic capitals. – PAINTING. Dramatic early C17 Crucifixion. Italian. – STAINED GLASS. E window, 1890, possibly by *Clayton & Bell*. S window, 1890s, unbearably sentimental.

Victorian VILLAS, mostly of sandstone from Mount Radford quarry on Wembdon Hill.

SANDFORD MANOR, 1 m. W. Red sandstone, Elizabethan, with mullioned windows. Ashlar pedimented porch of 1570 with thin fluted columns and initials of Thomas Broughton. The S cross-wing may be earlier – see the end-wall garderobe turret. One very large chamfered fireplace and some smaller moulded ones.

WEST BAGBOROUGH

The church and Bagborough House sit beautifully under the Quantocks.

St Pancras. Red sandstone. Perp tower with diagonal buttresses, polygonal NE stair-turret, and battlements. W window with angel-stops. Tall wave-moulded tower arch. At the back two crudely carved earlier headstops. N aisle of 1838–9, the arcade of standard Perp design. S wall and porch rebuilt in 1873–4 by *Giles & Gane*, keeping the square rood-stair turret. C15 chancel arch, wave-moulded and shafted. In 1935 *Ninian Comper* added plaster panels to the Victorian nave roof to harmonize with the C15 chancel roof, part of an intervention that gives a special lustre to the interior. By *Comper* almost all the STAINED GLASS (1923–33), with a fine clarity of drawing against clear backgrounds, the ROOD BEAM with three figures, the ALTAR angels on riddel-posts, the lovely painted and crocketed FONT COVER, and the TOWER SCREEN (1925). This was carved by a class at the rectory under *Ethel Lance*. It has a pierced balcony above four good low-relief lunettes of Noah, Moses, etc. – FIGURES. At the W end, two C15 oak statues, a female and a cleric. – BENCH-ENDS. C16. Mostly foliage motifs, also Renaissance scrollwork terminating in grotesques. – ROYAL ARMS. Charles II, changed to George II. – HATCHMENTS. Popham family, C19. – MONUMENTS. Robert Kellett, †1641. Brass with varied lettering, and heraldry. – Henry Shuldham. 1806, by *Robert Pierce* of Exeter. Elegant Adam-style urn.

BAGBOROUGH HOUSE. Quintessential Regency S front, of five stuccoed bays with a handsome Bath stone colonnade of coupled Greek Ionic columns. This represents the remodelling *c.* 1820 of the house of the Pophams dated 1739 on a downpipe. Extended N with a new columned entrance to a Grecian entrance hall. The dining room to the N of this hall has unusually lavish plasterwork, Greek, enlivened with scrolls and shells. Cantilevered oval staircase with early C18 detail, in a remodelled stair hall. S of the entrance hall, a small C18 panelled room. The large three-bay saloon was created *c.* 1820 by uniting the original hall and drawing room. Kentian door frames with oak-leaf friezes, modillion cornices and pedimented overmantel. Brick early C19 STABLES with arched doorways.

LITTLE COURT, SW of the church. The former rectory, externally remodelled with an early C19 character; but the rear range is C15–C16, and ends in a solar cross-wing with wind-braced jointed-cruck roof and lively Jacobean plasterwork. Tympanum of flowers and pears, and overmantel heraldry (Rev. Edward Kellett, vicar from 1608) on a strapwork cartouche with naked figures on the scrolls, probably by *Robert Eaton* (cf. Poundisford Lodge). A mid-C19 rector's family, including the Academician *James Clarke Hook*, painted the dining room to a delightful Raphaelesque scheme with innumerable figures, views, animals, etc.

TRISCOMBE HOUSE, 2 m. NW. 1902–4, by *Ernest Newton* for Henry Cheetham of Manchester. Stuccoed, with sash windows

West Bagborough, Triscombe House.
Drawing by Ernest Newton, 1905

and parapets. Ostensibly Georgian, but essentially styleless, the broad curved door hood deriving from Lethaby and the front irregularly composed. Interiors reinstated after a fire in 2002. To the NE, neatly designed brick STABLEYARD and COTTAGES.

WEST BOWER MANOR see DURLEIGH

WEST BRADLEY

ST ANDREW. Blue Lias. Slim two-stage W tower without buttresses, the base earlier than the battlemented bell-stage with a pyramid roof. Inside the tower a chamfered C14 arch on robust shafts and a pretty star-vault. Perp nave with parapet and N rood-stair projection. Late C14 shafted arches to the S porch and chancel. Chancel mostly rebuilt in 1873, keeping C15 window types. Plain C18 nave roof tricked out with C19 mouldings. – FONT. Early Norman. Squat bowl with a broad indented band, on a spurred base.

BRADLEY HOUSE. A remarkable sight, a square three-storey block with full-height bays set diagonally at each corner. It looks like an Elizabethan conceit, but was called 'just finished' in 1726. Built for Col. William Peirs M.P., who was connected politically with the antiquarian circle around the Pelham family. The house has Late Georgian sash windows, but the ovolo-moulded stone frames indicate cross-windows to the main floors and two-light attic windows. The windows have all been lengthened. Two string courses, stepped over the windows. Chimneys on the diagonal bays, the NE bay windowless. Late Georgian interiors, apart from some four-centred-arched fireplaces that seem deliberately antiquarian. The broad single roof is C20, replacing twin spans. Two CANALS, one in front, the other a quadrant curve at a higher level to the E, remain from works undertaken in 1726 by a Dutch landscaper named *Long*.

CHAPEL COTTAGE, ¾ m. WSW. Former Bible Christian chapel of 1837. Pyramid-roofed, with cusped pointed two-light windows on two levels. Over the doorway, rustic Gothic carving, the lamb and flag.

COURT BARN (National Trust), 1 m. W. The smallest and latest of the four surviving Glastonbury Abbey tithe barns, late C14 or early C15. Only five bays, divided by buttresses, the lean-to porches with chamfered ashlar piers. The two-tier cruck trusses with arch-braced base crucks resemble on a smaller scale those of the other barns (Glastonbury, Doulting (N), Pilton). Restored in 1934 by *Ernest Bowden*. Remnant of a dovecote on the E end.

BRIDGE FARM, ¾ m. SW. A Georgian front range conceals an early C14 hall house, tree-ring-dated to 1336–42. The two-tier cruck trusses resemble those of the Glastonbury Abbey barns and Bridge Farm, Butleigh. Five bays with intermediate trusses, the upper crucks alternately cusped. Two tiers of wind-bracing.

WEST BUCKLAND

ST MARY. Three-stage W tower of after 1509, when John Peryn of Wellington left money to its building (cf. Hillfarrance). Stair-turret nearly central on the show side, as at Hillfarrance and Wellington, of pale sandstone, as are the diagonal buttresses. Ham stone W doorway. Plain two-light bell-openings with pierced baffles, battlements, and small pinnacles, the intermediate ones corbelled out and set diagonally. Impressively tall tower arch, triple-chamfered and dying into the sides. This is normally a C13–C14 motif, but here the framed ceiling and Tudor-arched stair door show that the tower is all C16. The rest of the church, of local chert, is externally Perp, with battlemented aisles. Restored in 1891 by *Edwin Howard*. Broad nave with Perp framed barrel roof, but the arcades are C13–C14 – see the octagonal piers with plain splayed capitals. The N arcade with double-chamfered arches is earlier than the S arcade, whose arches have double wave mouldings. The SE chapel has a wave-moulded arch to the chancel; the NE chapel arch is later, standard Perp. The single-chamfered chancel arch could be C13, altered almost beyond recognition. The capitals have Perp leaf moulding and the piers are cut back. – FONT. C12. Purbeck marble, square with shallow blank arches (cf. Milborne Port, Odcombe) on two sides. The other two have incomplete flat fleurons. – BENCHES. Two plain C16 ones in the SE chapel. – STAINED GLASS. E window, 1858, by *Toms* of Wellington. N window by *Morris & Co.*, 1897, the figures typically Burne-Jones, the background typically Morris.

In the churchyard two elephantine late C19 granite SARCOPHAGI on lion feet.

BUCKLAND FARMHOUSE, ¾ m. SSE. Roughcast and gabled. Two good plaster ceilings, one upstairs with thin ribs, late C16, the other, in the parlour, with broad patterned bands of *c.* 1620 outlining squares within the panels of a framed ceiling. Oak-leaf centre motif and spandrel flowers.

GERBESTONE MANOR, 1½ m. SW. The house is basically pre-Reformation (see one arched brace left of the former hall roof and two wooden doorheads on the first floor), but was modernized *c.* 1575 and *c.* 1610 with ovolo-moulded mullioned windows. In 1925 *Hubert Lidbetter* added the main staircase and pretty courtyard at the back. The façade is of Early Tudor character, with broad cross-wing gables and a lower two-storey porch attached to the l. one – just as e.g. at Cothay. The porch leads into the screens passage. Hall screen and panelling are preserved, as is the framed ceiling. Plain Tudor-arched fireplace. Next to it is the original spiral staircase to the solar. The kitchen, at first in the S wing, was moved to the N wing during the Elizabethan alterations. Thatched barn behind, converted to a SQUASH COURT by *Lidbetter*.

WEST CAMEL

ALL SAINTS. A picturesque ensemble, by river meadows. Essentially early C14. The base of the unbuttressed S tower could be C13, earlier than the short bell-stage with two-light Dec openings and corbelled parapet with large gargoyles. Squat octagonal lead spire, dated 1631 on a beam. The nave was raised in the C15 with inserted Perp windows, but the double-chamfered W and S doorways (depressed without capitals) and one S window are early C14. Similar C14 windows to the chancel N and S, with rere-arches, and a three-light E window with mid-C14 reticulated tracery and trefoiled pointed rere-arch on column shafts. The N side and N transept have uneven buttresses, and the narrow C14 transept window is curiously offset. Inside, the arches to the N transept and the tower are double-chamfered, that to the tower on corbelled capitals. Under the tower, an altar recess and small double PISCINA. In the chancel, blank pointed panels flank the E window. C13 PISCINA and elaborate triple SEDILIA of cusped arches on column shafts, renewed in 1866–7 when *Ewan Christian* restored the chancel. Carved head on the r. of the sedilia, pierced for a cord for the Lenten veil. Ornate late C15 nave roof (cf. Queen Camel) with stone angels carrying tie-beams with fleurons and rose bosses. Intermediate trusses on little figures in pillbox hats carrying shields with emblems of the Passion. – FONT. C12. Ham stone bowl with interlaced Norman arcading. Cover carved with a nesting bird, 1961. – PULPIT. A rare medieval one. Doulting stone drum with cusped panels. Initials of Andrew Grantham, rector 1471–92. – SCULPTURE. Important fragment of an early C9 Saxon cross-shaft with band-like intertwined snakes or dragons and much close interlace. – WEST GALLERY, 2006, by *Philip Hughes*. – STAINED GLASS. Pulpit window, four small C15 figures: saints and a cleric. E window, 1905, by *Powell's*. – MONUMENTS. Edward Aubery †1786, draped urn on red, by *King* of Bath. – Constantine Crowbrow †1796, coloured marbles, signed *Fisher's*, York.

MANOR FARMHOUSE, W of the church, has a narrow two-storey piece on the W end, a dovecote over a bread oven, early C18. At the OLD RECTORY a five-bay house of 1836 (by *John Thatcher* of Midsomer Norton) replaces the hall of a late medieval house of which the cross-wing remains, with pointed S doorway and C16–C17 mullions. Arch-braced collar-trusses with crown-posts. Late C15 BARN behind with jointed crucks.

West Camel, Anglo-Saxon cross.
Engravings, 1877

Circular DOVECOTE, SW, with buttresses, probably early C17. Just N, the small SCHOOL, 1837, and MANOR HOUSE, late C18, five bays, Lias with Ham stone. Down Back Street, NAISH'S FARMHOUSE, three bays, with early C18 wooden cross-windows below. On Howell Hill, prominent below the A303, are four pairs of the hoop-roofed COUNCIL HOUSES, 1928, that *Petter & Warren* designed for Yeovil Rural District Council using Maj. Nissen's curved steel trusses (*see* Introduction, p. 82, also Barwick and Yeovil).

PARSON'S STEEPLE, ¾ m. N. A gloomy folly amid trees, a tall niche hollowed in tapering rubble. Built by Henry Parsons †1794.

WEST CHINNOCK

ST MARY. Rebuilt in 1889–90, by *Charles Kirk* of Sleaford, for Richard Hayward, twine and webbing manufacturer. A late example of the High Victorian developed by Bodley and Blomfield in the 1860s, with severe saddleback tower and good C13–C14 detail. One original C13 chancel lancet. Gabled aisles with arcades on circular piers. Naturalistic foliage of high quality in the corbels and especially the REREDOS. Good too the arcaded drum PULPIT and circular FONT. – ROYAL ARMS. 1825. – STAINED GLASS. 1890 and later, by *Ward & Hughes*.

A single street, divided into Higher and Lower, scattered with thatched and mullion-windowed cottages. Overlooking the churchyard, CHURCH CLOSE, a terrace with cast-iron windows, *c.* 1844. It housed Hayward's workers. On Higher Street, No. 47 is early C15, altered, with one smoke-blackened full cruck. At the top, HIGH CROSS has a continuous dripmould stepped over the doorway, and ovolo-moulded mullions. Dated 1604, raised *c.* 1700. Below the churchyard, the two-storey Tudor-style SCHOOL, 1833. On Lower Street, MANOR FARMHOUSE, thatched, with one dormer gable, dated 1673, originated as an early C16 hall house. At the foot, BRIDGE HOUSE, 1806–10, was Hayward's house, modest Late Georgian, three bays with a hip-roofed cross-wing. BARN behind of 1815. The industrial buildings have gone.

BOW MILL, ½ m. w. Mill house with C17 mullioned windows under one roof with the mill, re-fitted in 1862, with broad waterwheel.

WEST COKER

5010

A long village on the Exeter road. From the C18 a centre of sailcloth and twine manufacture.

ST MARTIN. Squat W tower rebuilt in 1765 by *Benjamin Bastard* of Sherborne. But the lower half is medieval, with a rendered rounded stair-tower, the narrow slits glazed with horn. The rest of the church is large with gabled aisles and chapels, the S aisle by *William Wadman*, 1833–4. In 1863–4 *J. M. Allen* rebuilt the N aisle and re-windowed the S aisle. Only the Perp NE chapel with its crude panelled C16 roof remains unaltered. Both arcades are Allen's, based on a C14 N arcade with round piers. – FONT. C12, re-tooled. Vertical strips between thick rings. – PULPIT. 1626. Arched panels. – BENCH-ENDS. With large flowers, one dated 1633. – TOWER SCREEN. 1937, by *W. D. Caröe*. – STAINED GLASS. E and S aisle, colourful set of 1864 by *O'Connor*. N aisle W, 1900, by *Powell's*. N window, 2001, by *Stewart Bowman*. – MONUMENTS. Grace and Elizabeth Portman †1661 and 1636. Two kneeling matronly figures under an arch framed by paired Corinthian columns. Cornice with heraldry. – Mary Tatchell †1689. Pilasters and skull, crudely incised Lias. – John Tatchell †1693. Similar. – Moore family, *c.* 1777. Coloured marbles, pedimented under a grey obelisk. – Thomas Warry †1791. Festooned urn, by *Charles Regnart*. – John Warry †1799, similar.

CHURCHYARD CROSS, 1937, by *W. D. Caröe*. The head with the Virgin and Child.

THE MANOR, Manor Street. A beautiful manor house of Ham stone and stone tiles, even if much of the attraction is from restoration. A property of the Courtenay family, Earls of

Devon, from the C14. The present house may date from before the execution of the 14th Earl in 1461, but more probably was rebuilt after 1485, for Sir Edward Courtenay, created Earl of Devon in 1485. Sold before 1600 to Sir John Portman, who extended the house. Restored from 1873 for the Moore family; after 1907 for Sir Matthew Nathan, the first Jewish colonial governor (and Under-Secretary for Ireland during the 1916 Rising), by *Maurice Webb*. Repaired after 1984 by *Caroe & Martin*. Already in 1922 Christopher Hussey wrote that 'much of the present medievalism is recent replacement of a more or less conjectural kind'.

The hall is in the centre, facing w, with storeyed ends, and there is a NW cross-wing. SE and NE wings frame a rear courtyard. The S end has the kitchen, marked by a fine turret chimney like that at Abbey Manor, Preston Plucknett, with a chamber above. The N end has the Great Parlour, over a service room. These ends are both late C15 like the hall between them, as also the first part of the SE wing. Large gabled W porch, once dated 1600, with the Portman arms over a pointed arch outlined in block rustication. Two-light hall window to the l., flat-headed, transomed and cusped, matched by two on the rear. In the angle to the cross-wing, a square bay with a tall two-light transomed S window with a C15 pointed head. It may be an altered hall-bay, but contains a renewed spiral stair. To the r. of the porch, the chamber over the kitchen has a square-headed window with hoodmould next to a tall octagonal chimney corbelled from the wall. The turret chimney at the S end is ashlar, octagonal with cusped openings and octagonal cap. The original part of the SE wing has a tall, narrow projecting S gable, which was a DOVECOTE, identified by the alighting-shelf in the gable and a blocked door halfway up the E side. The loft extends into the main roof-space. Beyond is a full-height three-bay library, by *Maurice Webb*, 1910, its windows imitating those of the hall.

The cross-wing has a first-floor solar roofed like the Great Hall (below), but has reserved-chamfer mullions of *c.* 1600. The evidence is unreliable, as the wing was dismantled and rebuilt for Joseph Moore. The N end windows of the Great Parlour have similar reserved chamfers, suggesting alteration for Portman, for whom the NE service wing was added. The rear courtyard, open to the E, makes a harmonious show. Pointed doorways and cusped lights to both the E wall of the main range and the first part of the SE wing. Buttresses mark the three bays of the screens passage and Great Hall. The NE wing has C17 mullioned windows and a double-ridge chimney, marking a second kitchen.

The screens partition and gallery are late C19. The GREAT HALL is handsome, with a roof of arch-braced collar-trusses elaborated with decorative wind-bracing and large encircled quatrefoils, these possibly C19 enhancements. Big stone N end fireplace with a frieze of cusped quatrefoils with foliage and shields. Timber-framed S end wall. The kitchen has a vast

Tudor-arched fireplace. A four-centred-arched doorway leads from the hall into the NW cross-wing. The roof here matches the Great Hall roof, with similarly ornamented panels, but all renewed. The wall-plate has an additional frieze of particularly ornate quatrefoils. The quatrefoiled fireplaces on both floors are renewed, under late C20 plaster overmantels. These echo a genuine overmantel of *c.* 1600 in the GREAT PARLOUR. The Portman arms are balanced by two cheerful nudes similar to figures at Montacute, and probably by *Robert Eaton* of Stogursey.

PERAMBULATION. On CHURCH STREET, the OLD RECTORY, Late Georgian with a parapet, enlarged 1870. The LANES HOTEL was an earlier rectory, large, double-gabled, with fussy detail from a rebuilding by *Charles Benson*, 1875. Additions by *Boon Brown*, 2005, a minimal plate-glass dining room and a glass-fronted stair-tower. Also a bedroom block with vertical accents of glass or oak board. Opposite, the Tudor-style PAROCHIAL SCHOOL, 1850. Across the High Street, EAST STREET runs SE. The OLD DAIRY HOUSE has late C17 mullioned windows and drip-course. CROSS HOUSE, opposite, hip-roofed with C18 mullions, is dated 1754 on a C17 rear wing re-cased to match. The Rendells made sailcloth here; an outbuilding dated 1804 was presumably associated. At the former TWINE WORKS a long late C19 covered walk remains. Three low floors, two for twisting, one for finishing. Chimney of 1898. Further on, BERNERS, dated 1733, is thatched and mullioned-windowed with a curved pediment over the doorway. MARLBOROUGH has early C17 mullioned windows and a moulded doorway. The RUDDOCK ALMSHOUSES, dated 1719, a two-storey terrace, have arched doorways and windows with typical heavy square imposts and keystones. WEST COKER HOUSE, mid-C19, was enlarged with gables and finicky detail in 1892, probably by *C. B. Benson*. MANOR STREET returns past The Manor (*see* p. 669) and a Gothic METHODIST CHAPEL, 1839.

Now NE along the main road. WESTLAKE HOUSE, set back, has an ashlar cornicad front of the late C18, but early C18 mullions on the side wall and fielded panelling inside. BARTON FARMHOUSE, behind on Dibbles Lane, has C17 mullioned windows, but a pointed W window indicates the solar end of a C15 hall house. Further out N of the main road, the curious MANOR BARN, incorporates Gothic doorways and windows with four-centred arches and hoodmoulds, one window traceried. John Moore built the barn in 1764 (datestone), but these features are not Georgian Gothic. Probably they are insertions for a later John Moore, antiquary. He built WEST COKER HALL across the High Street in 1839–42. This is in a Gothic-to-C16 style, supposedly reusing pieces from Naish Priory (North Coker). Ham stone ashlar with cross-mullioned windows, except in the gabled centre where the detail is Gothic. The side porch has Perp detail, not obviously reused save perhaps the niche. Perp windows appear on the stables and cottage.

Returning SW on the main road, after Manor Street is the ROYAL GEORGE INN, with early C17 mullioned windows and Tudor-arched doorway. No. 17, ashlar-fronted with channelled piers, pedimented doorway, and, still, mullioned windows, dates probably from after 1750. Further W, Nos. 42–56 are early council houses by *Petter & Warren*, 1914–15, stone, interestingly disposed between hip-roofed ends. Opposite is the PRIMARY SCHOOL, 1875, by *Henry Hall*. After the thatched CASTLE INN, the two rows of CASTLE TERRACE, 1887, with varied gables and some tile-hanging. Were they for industrial workers? MILLBROOK HOUSE was built before 1830 for Israel Rendell, sailcloth maker. His successor, J. W. Dawe, erected the adjacent TWINE WALK in 1899. The 100-yd (91-metre) long timber shed is happily preserved. Yarn was twisted in the loft, and washed and waxed below. The early C19 MILL beyond became a flax mill and sailcloth factory. PENTLANDS, an early C19 hip-roofed villa, was called Wash House, and was connected with the bleaching of sailcloth, which was dried on the grassed terraces still apparent in the slope S of the road. BRIDGE COTTAGES, by the A30 bridge, were an C18 sailcloth factory.

WESTCOMBE
1 m. W of Batcombe

WESTCOMBE HOUSE was demolished in 1956. It had a seven-bay front with projecting end bays, remodelled after 1817 for T. H. Ernst. The columned porch is re-erected in Street (q.v.). Attractive L-plan STABLES of 1784 survive. Two symmetrical five-bay ranges, each with oval loft windows apart from a circular centre one, and pretty Gothick windows below. Converted for Hermione Hobhouse, the historian, *c.* 1970, by *Harry Graham*. Below, a spring issues from a rockwork GROTTO with tunnel passage. Oblong pool in front and pointed rockwork archway. The old drive crosses a triple-arched, ivy-covered BRIDGE.

SPARGROVE MANOR, 1 m. SW. The early C17 mansion of Edward Bisse, known from Buckler's early C19 drawing, was reduced in the 1880s. Victorian ashlar front, but elsewhere original reserved-chamfer mullion-and-transom windows. Inside, a joyously rustic late C17 bolection-moulded fireplace beneath a great festoon of foliage. Burnt in 1988, the house was restored from 1995–8 by *David Mlinaric* with *Mitch & Pené Pope*. Attractive half-hip-roofed STABLES dated 1749, the cupola reinstated after Buckler's drawing. The C17 BREWHOUSE has a twin-arched coachhouse added to one end. Traces of a medieval MOAT. Cruciform C17–C18 BARN with tie-beam trusses. SPARGROVE MILL is mid-C19, with iron-framed industrial windows.

WEST COMPTON see PILTON

WEST CRANMORE

ST BARTHOLOMEW. Good C15–C16 tower, not tall but richly adorned, and similar to the much larger tower at Bruton. Angle buttresses finish in diagonal pinnacles level with the bell-stage, while the diagonal plane between the buttresses continues to diagonally set corner pinnacles. Battlements. Polygonal NE stair-turret. Moulded w doorway and four-light w window, both with large headstops. Canopied niche above, with a statue of St Bartholomew. Two-light window on each of the other sides. Triple two-light bell-openings, the outer ones blind, between four diagonal shafts answering to the buttress pinnacles. Panelled tower-arch. Fan-vault inside the tower. Humble Perp nave and N aisle, the latter with a flat parapet. Three-bay arcade on standard four-hollow piers with round capitals; one pier with a demi-figure of an angel. Georgian plastered nave ceiling. Chancel rebuilt in 1848 with a family pew on the N.

FURNISHINGS. FONT. C13. Octagonal, with flat shields. – PULPIT. Late C17. Fielded panels and fluted frieze, but some Jacobean ornament. – BIER. Elizabethan. A rare survival. – COMMUNION RAILS. Cast-iron, Gothic. 1848. – STAINED GLASS. E window, 1862, by *Thomas Baillie*, shockingly coloured Crucifixion. W window, 1863, by *C. Clutterbuck*. – MONUMENTS. Numerous to the Strodes of Southill from the early C17. – Col. Thomas Strode †1827, Grecian. – Admiral Sir Edward Strode †1862. Flags and sword, by *Tyley*.

CHURCHYARD CROSS. C14–C15. Heavy shaft and later head.

By the church, low Tudor-style former SCHOOL, 1840, by *Jesse Gane*. Overlooking the pond, the STRODE ARMS, with early C18 mullioned windows, but earlier timbers within.

SOUTHILL HOUSE, ¾ m. SSE. Prominent hilltop house of the Strode family. Three storeys, 1–3–1 bays, refaced *c.* 1825 in ashlar. Giant Ionic pilasters over a three-bay arcaded porch. Some Greek ornament. Contemporary entrance hall with chamfered angles, but the staircase with column newel and turned balusters is mid-C18. Before refacing there were Venetian windows in the outer bays and a plain centre with pedimented doorway, that is *c.* 1760. Early C17 origins are indicated by cellar doorways and also doorways to the rear wing, one round-arched and defaced, the other Tudor-arched. Strode arms of 1611 inside, possibly imported.

CRANMORE STATION, ¼ m. SW. The East Somerset Railway station of 1858 remains at the end of the platform, by one of Messrs *Macfarlane*'s cast-iron urinals. Large VISITOR CENTRE for the present steam railway, by *James Barratini*, 1991. A clever pastiche; the goods shed (1862) from the terminus at Wells, combined with bargeboards and other detail from Lodge Hill Halt on the Cheddar Valley Line.

WEST HATCH

ST ANDREW. Rebuilt 1860–1, by *Benjamin Ferrey*, keeping the look of the Perp original. Perp W tower rebuilt faithfully, the set-back buttresses carrying pinnacles and in addition higher pinnacles in the corners, all rising through the battlements. Octagonal NE stair-turret with spirelet. Ferrey reused Perp windows in his N aisle, kept the panelled tower arch, and reset the nave wagon roof. – PULPIT. Oak, C19. The panels could be medieval. Attached Victorian oak chancel rails. – MONUMENT. Christian Sealy †1727. Incised Lias, delightfully coloured. Oval between pilasters.

GREENINGS, ½ m. ESE. Small, with ball finials on three dormer gables. Originally a late C15 hall house. C16 framed ceiling. PARK FARMHOUSE, just S, is also late C15, with an early C18 staircase.

WEST HUNTSPILL

ST PETER. An ambitious Perp church of Blue Lias with Ham stone. Sturdy four-stage W tower with set-back buttresses, two-light bell-openings with pierced baffles, and battlements. Datable to *c.* 1400 from the tall tower arch, which has responds of four-hollow section, but treated broadly. Stair-turret clasped between the SW buttresses (cf. Martock and Queen Camel). Big pointed-arched W doorway in a heavily roll-moulded frame with shield spandrels, between round shafts. Were these meant to continue upward to flank a window narrower than the broad five-light window above? Cinquefoil-cusped niches outside the shafts. Broad aisles with plain parapets and two-light windows, continued as battlemented three-bay chapels with larger three-light windows. S chapel with four-light E window; N chapel with a contemporary single-bay vestry, originally two-storeyed, with a moulded cornice and gargoyles, so of some importance. Similar parapets to the storeyed S porch and chancel S side. Large five-light E window.

The interior is roomy and dark, lightening impressively towards the E. Five-bay arcades continued seamlessly with two slightly narrower arches to the chapels. Piers of standard four-hollow section, turned red by fire in 1878, as also the carved head corbels. Lavish restoration after the fire by *Price & Wooler* of Weston-super-Mare – complicated roofs, rich tiled FLOORS (by *Minton*), carved STALLS, frothy stone REREDOS. – PULPIT. From Stogursey via the Dowry Square Chapel, Bristol. An exceptionally rich example of the typical Jacobean pulpit. Top tier of the usual blank arches, but with a flower in each panel, long feathers on the piers, and encrusted arches. Scrolled frieze with fleurs-de-lys, cornice with small demi-figures at the angles. Square lower panels with Gothic-letter texts, e.g. 'How beautiful are the feet of they that preach the Gospel of peace.' – FONT. Lozenge-patterned large bowl, 1878, reputedly designed and given by *Sir Edward Beckett* (later Lord Grimthorpe). Steep Jacobean octagonal COVER. – ROYAL ARMS. Charles II. – STAINED GLASS. Splendid E window by *Clayton & Bell*, 1880, the colours particularly subtle. S window, late Arts and Crafts, by *William Aikman*, 1933. – MONUMENT. Effigies of knight and lady in a recess, *c.* 1370. He is in plate armour with shield. The cusped arch is all renewed, with carved heads to the points.

Gothic churchyard GATES and RAILINGS made by the *Coalbrookdale Foundry*, 1898.

METHODIST CHAPEL, Bristol Road. 1851. Brick, with crocketed pinnacles.

The church stands by the former RECTORY, rebuilt in 1710 in Lias, extended in brick by *William Wilkinson* of Oxford, 1870. On the Bristol road, ILEX HOUSE is Late Georgian brick, with parapet. SWELL HOUSE (Swell Close) has late C17 Dutch gables of brick at each end, rare in Somerset, the r. gable showing earlier stonework. Stuccoed Georgian façade, the three-bay centre with mid-C18 stone-framed windows and Venetian window in the pediment.

HUNTSPILL COURT, E of the Bristol road. Built *c.* 1765 for Admiral Sir Charles Saunders, who commanded the fleet at Quebec. A sophisticated three-storey façade of chequered brick with ashlar dressings. Balustraded two-storey canted bays under Diocletian attic windows frame a centre with pedimented doorway, arched window, and curved-headed attic window, whose architrave echoes the centre light of the Diocletian windows. Plain wings, the top floor for show.

HUNTSPILL RIVER. Cut in a straight course for some five miles to the sea in 1940, primarily to supply the Puriton explosives factory.

WEST LAMBROOK

Roadside hamlet with good C16–C17 houses. LOWER FARMHOUSE and MALLOW CROSS are mullion-windowed C17, the former ashlar-fronted, steep-roofed, and earlier. WEYLANDS is older, thatched with timber-framed end gables and a wholly timber-framed short rear wing, unusual in this region. Ashlar C17 front with two dormer gables.

RODWELL MANOR, 1 m. W. Picturesque, long C17 thatched house, much restored in the C20. Elongated ground-floor mullioned windows. Framed ceiling.

NEW CROSS HOUSE, 1 m. N. Substantial square ashlar villa with parapet and columned porch. Built for a solicitor in South Petherton, it was dismantled when just completed and re-erected here in 1836, for the Portman estate.

WEST LYDFORD

St Peter. Charmingly placed with a graveyard stretching to the edge of the River Brue. Rebuilt in 1843–4 by *Benjamin Ferrey*. An early work in a notably competent Somerset Perp, no longer picturesquely Gothic and satisfied with that. It echoes but does not copy its predecessor. w tower with set-back buttresses, battlements and pinnacles. Embattled nave and gabled N aisle, with pinnacles (mostly gone). The chancel has a parapet pierced by cusped lozenges, also with pinnacles. Stone-tiled roofs. The arcade and chancel arch are standard Somerset Perp. – STAINED GLASS. E window by *Wailes*, c. 1855. – MONUMENT. Margaret Colston †1812. Yellow and white, with urn. By *Wood*.

In the churchyard eroded EFFIGY of c. 1330.

The five-arched BRIDGE SE of the church is probably C17, with upstream cutwaters. Parapets repaired in 1846, each pierced by five small arches in case of flood. Just NE, the former RECTORY, 1800. Unmoulded Venetian windows on both floors, porch of paired fluted columns. Over the bridge, BRIDGE FARM, dated 1637 inside, has ovolo-moulded mullioned windows under continuous dripmoulds. HIGHER HOUSE is thatched, C18. HIGH STREET FARM, set back, is Tudor Gothic of c. 1840, for the steward of the Colston estate. Pretty cast-iron windows.

WEST LYNCH
Selworthy

Lynch Chapel. An unusually ambitious chapel of ease, built for the Sydenham family c. 1520. A neat rectangle with diagonal buttresses, three doors, and just three windows, the three-light E window especially good (restored by *J. D. Sedding* in 1885). It has the quatrefoil spandrels below the transom typical of the region, but differs from the windows at Selworthy in having supermullions. In the N and S walls, a two-light window. The extremely attractive interior is due to work by *W. H. Randoll Blacking* in 1930, a quiet harmony of whitewash and light oak. Reused panelling from Georgian box pews from Selworthy. Over a balustraded screen, the GALLERY has C17 panels with balustrading, from Selworthy. The E window by *Christopher Webb* complements the whole, with heraldry on clear glass. Wagon roof with foliage bosses, the wall-plate angels added. Ogee-cusped PISCINA.

The chapel is in the farmyard of WEST LYNCH FARM. Thatched outbuildings, including a half-hip-roofed BARN with a horse-engine house. The long yellow-washed FARMHOUSE is a late medieval hall house, ceiled and given a large lateral chimney in the C16. Oak three-light mullion-and-transom window to the r. of the heavy oak doorway.

LYNCH HOUSE, on the hillside. A long stone house of 1911–13, by *C. H. B. Quennell* for Allan Hughes, shipping company director. In contrast to many Arts and Crafts houses the front has no picturesque flourishes; a single roof without dormers, articulated by tall stone chimneys. Regular oak windows and a triple-arched central loggia. A neatly arranged 'living-hall' is sunk below the foot of the staircase. Rear addition of 1923. Timber-clad SQUASH COURT on the hillside. The driveway was cut through the corner of the MILL and its outbuilding, which were rebuilt as staff cottages. The MALTHOUSE remains with a pyramid-roofed kiln. The miller lived at WEST LYNCH HOUSE, a long thatched C16–C17 farmhouse with lateral stack, altered after 1813.

WEST MONKTON

2020

ST AUGUSTINE. Four-stage Perp W tower, tall (88 ft/26.8 metres) and spare, as though in opposition to the fripperies of Taunton. Local slaty stone with Ham stone dressings. Set-back buttresses up to battlements without pinnacles. Polygonal NE stair-tower. Two-light bell-openings with transom, and similar second-stage S window over an image niche. Broad W doorway and three-light W window also with transom. As at Norton Fitzwarren, the triple-chamfered tower arch could indicate earlier origins, but is probably contemporary. The rest is externally Perp, four-bay nave with clerestory, embattled porch and aisles, and chancel with embattled side chapels, these last added in 1883–4, by *George Strawbridge* of Taunton. S aisle with two-light windows, N aisle and clerestory windows with three lights, the three-light ones with supermullions, not the common type. Statue bracket over the S door. There are hints of an earlier church: a roof-line above the tower arch, a probably reused plate-traceried S aisle W window, the banded chancel arch, continuously double-chamfered, and a small C14 chancel N window with pellets in the spandrels, a detail matched in the chancel PISCINA. Good C15 wagon roof with very pretty undercut carving to the wall-plate; nine angels each side. Simple standard arcades (four hollows) of four bays, but not identical. The capitals of the S arcade have rosettes, as do those of the porch.

FURNISHINGS. FONT, PULPIT and REREDOS of Beer stone, 1884. Also a fire-damaged C14 Perp FONT. – ORGAN. 1829, by *Smith* of Bristol. Painted Gothic. – N aisle SCREEN of random woodwork, some from a family pew dated 1614. – STAINED GLASS. E window, 1884, by *Clayton & Bell*. SE, 1898, by *Drake* of Exeter. Three colourful windows (two S aisle and one N) by *Heaton, Butler & Bayne*, 1880s. Also one of their gloomy later works, N aisle, †1901.* – MONUMENTS. Brass, demi-figure of a priest in academic dress, probably Henry Abyndon, rector from 1436. – George Musgrave †1693. Framed in branches, over a winged skull. – Rev. Thomas Rich †1699. Rustic Baroque with broken curved pediment. – Henry Gatchell †1726. Large, columned, with curved top. – Richard Musgrave †1727. Elegant, with fluted pilasters and triglyph frieze, like the Lucas monument, Trull. – Alexander Popham, 1767. Spiral-fluted urn in a niche, very chaste and classical, but enveloped in a Baroque drape.

HEATHFIELD SCHOOL, Monkton Heathfield. 1953, by *Somerset County Architects*. Buff brick, much enlarged. L-plan classroom block of black brick with cylindrical entrance tower, 2006, by *Boon Brown*. The school specializes in the performing arts. The TACCHI-MORRIS ARTS CENTRE, 2000, by *Kensington Taylor* of Exeter, has an auditorium between ranges at right angles, linked by a cylindrical glazed foyer with a nautical balcony. THE SPACE, 2008–9, by the same, is a smaller echo with a glazed cylinder entrance.

High garden walls give the village an enclosed character. The walls around the church relate to Court Place, a mansion demolished *c.* 1815. GLEBE COURT, just S, was built *c.* 1783 as the rectory. Mansard-roofed in pink stucco. To the SW, COURT PLACE is stuccoed, early C19. Opposite, LONG MEADOW, 1930, by *Eric Francis* for himself. Simplified well-proportioned Queen Anne, of red brick with a steeply hipped roof, set between hip-roofed pavilions. On The Street, MARLOWS is ashlar-fronted Late Georgian, with a columned porch. To the N, MONKTON HOUSE had an Italianate porch-tower, the belvedere now missing, but the garden front looks rather earlier, Greek of the 1820s. Stuccoed with ashlar cornice, bands and giant pilasters. Single-storey, single-bay wings. Top-lit stair hall with Ionic columns.

WALFORD HOUSE, 1 m. SE, above the A38. A three-storey house of *c.* 1800, roughcast above rusticated ashlar. Five-bay front with three-bay pedimented centre. The first floor has a pedimented centre window, over a Roman Doric full-width colonnade with balustrade. Matching porch on the three-bay side elevation. Simple Adam-style plasterwork to the entrance hall and stair hall. Cantilevered open-well timber staircase under a pretty oval lantern. Stuccoed LODGE with painted ashlar dressings. Small but monumental, the doorway recessed behind columns *in antis*, the end walls curved.

WESTON BAMPFYLDE

HOLY CROSS. Small W tower, C13 in its broad lower stages with a W lancet and unmoulded pointed arch to the nave. The

---

* The W window glass by *Gray & Son*, 1827, noted by Pevsner, has gone.

second stage is chamfered to carry two octagonal top stages. The battlemented bell-stage is Perp, but the one beneath with large broaches is perhaps also C13. Nave and chancel restored 1872–3 by *Edmund Ferrey*. Mostly Perp, with a wave-moulded s doorway, but an early C14 double-chamfered chancel arch on shafts with octagonal capitals. Chancel re-fitted in 1914. – FONT. C12 bowl with flat zigzag above, thick cable below. – PULPIT. Jacobean arabesques and lozenges. – LECTERN. 1909. Oak eagle on a pillar carved as rocks. – One C15 BENCH-END with intricate tracery. – SCREEN, 1912. – MONUMENT. Grace Mist †1726. Baroque cartouche with cherub heads. The text alludes to the imprisonment of her husband Nathaniel, a Jacobite publisher.

The village spreads loosely around a square field, the church NE, the former RECTORY of 1827 NW, and a little SCHOOLROOM, SE, of 1857, with latticed iron windows.

MANOR HOUSE, ¼ m. E of the church. Picturesque ensemble of mullioned windows and stone tiles, achieved by sensitive additions of 1907 to a five-bay C17 house. Good chamfered framed ceiling, otherwise typical Edwardian intervention with reused C17 panelling and new work in keeping.

WESTONZOYLAND

The northernmost of the three Zoyland villages, its elevation minimal above Sedgemoor.

ST MARY. The most splendid of Somerset Perp churches, rebuilt *c.* 1500 for Abbot Bere of Glastonbury. Blue Lias with ashlar dressings. The tower is especially memorable in the flat landscape, rising to just over 100 ft (30.5 metres). Four stages, with Doulting stone angle buttresses connected by diagonal fillets. Lower stage on the W faced in Ham stone, with plain doorway and tall four-light window. On the N and S sides this stage is entirely bare. The next two stages have a two-light window between canopied niches on each face except the N, where the octagonal NE stair-turret intervenes. One statue survives on the S. The third-stage windows have pierced baffles on the third stage. Then the bell-openings. Three in a row, each of two lights with a transom. Only the middle one is a real opening, with pierced baffles. Battlements with quatrefoils, square-set panelled pinnacles, and thin, diagonally set intermediate pinnacles. Sublimely tall panelled tower arch, opening to a fan-vault with circular bell-hole.

Clerestoried nave with aisles, porches and transepts, all Perp, and an earlier chancel. The decoration is richer on the S side, with embattled aisle, porch and transept. The clerestory is embattled on both sides. Porch and transept battlements have the ogee central merlon found at North Petherton, Curry

Rivel and Langport. The clerestory windows have four-centred arches and three-light tracery with supermullions, as at High Ham. Porch with a tall panelled arch and niche above, and a roof on angel corbels. Traceried oak DOOR. The transept S window has some unusual details in the tracery and is flanked by small niches. On one buttress the initials of Abbot Bere, on the other his pelican rebus. The N aisle has a plain parapet and low porch. The N transept is taller than the S one, and later, as it covers the corresponding clerestory window. Low chancel, not embattled, and a good deal earlier, for it has two-light Dec windows on both sides. It was being tiled in 1302–3. N vestry with asymmetrical buttress and small lancet window. In the angle to the N transept a rood stair of the restoration by *W. D. Caröe* in 1933–7.

On entering the church the nave roof is a sudden thrill, one of the finest of Somerset, comparable with those of Somerton and Martock. Of moderate pitch, with big tie-beams on short arched braces which rest on angel busts. The tie-beams have a pierced cresting carried around from the wall-plate, a decorated central boss, and a broad-winged angel on each side. These appear to carry kingposts with shafts connecting to thin arches under the ridge. On each side of the kingposts all is close tracery in two tiers. Intermediate trusses rise from spread-winged angels on the wall-plate. These trusses have no tie-beams but retain the motif of kingpost connected to the longitudinal arcading and also, by thin curved braces, to the principal rafters. The kingposts finish in a lush foliate pendant. The roof is divided into plain panels, without the decorative infill of Martock and Somerton. The panelling is slightly simpler in the wider eastern bay, where one would expect a richer celure. Nave arcades of six bays, the eastern arch wider across the transepts. Piers of standard four-hollow section with round capitals to the shafts. Framed S transept and aisle roofs with many bosses, on angel corbels. Angels fitted to the outside of each last nave pier support, uncomfortably, panelled arches into the transepts from each aisle. These arches must replace solid wall, yet the arcades suggest that aisles and transepts were planned together. In the N transept a plastered ceiling and cusped PISCINA. On the N wall a tomb-recess, square-headed with pierced spandrels. Four-centred arch with big cusps, each cinquefoil-cusped. The motifs suggest a late date; C15? Panelled and shafted chancel arch. Chancel roof of the restoration by *Giles & Robinson*, 1865. The side window reveals are shafted with small variations, octagonal or round capitals, one N window with shaft-rings; details of *c.* 1300. Vestry DOOR with early ironwork.

FURNISHINGS. FONT. Octagonal, unusually architectural, with dominant horizontals giving a layered profile. Early C14, as at Meare and Shapwick (qq.v.). – ROOD SCREEN. 1935–6, by *W. D. Caröe*. The finest piece of church woodwork of the C19 or C20 in Somerset. Caröe does not imitate, although imitation is well done in the county by such as Harry Hems,

and the carving is not mechanical, as for example at North
Petherton. Three tall bays with delicate inventive tracery and
carved transoms, fan-vaulted coving, and notably simple but
striking loft panelling. The screen was made by *Archie Osborne*
of Norton-sub-Hamdon, the excellent ROOD FIGURES carved
by *Cameron* of London. – CHANCEL FITTINGS by *Caröe*, also
the ORGAN CASE under the tower. Reused traceried panels are
incorporated in the various pieces. – PULPIT. By *Caröe*; earlier,
more commonplace, on a stone and alabaster base. – BENCHES.
C15–C16. Square-headed bench-ends with inventive tracery,
similar to Middlezoy. Frontals and dorsals with poppyhead
ends, one with the initials of Abbot Bere. – STAINED GLASS.
Medieval fragments in the N transept and chancel S, this
with Bere's initials. – MONUMENT. Effigy of a priest, praying,
c. 1300 (N transept tomb-recess).

NE of the churchyard, the former VICARAGE, stuccoed and hip-
roofed, by *Richard Carver*, 1839. Incorporated into PRIORY
HOUSE, opposite the church, a reused four-centred-arched
doorway and a similar window head above.

AIRFIELD, ½ m. E. The former RAF Weston Zoyland. The
runways of 1942–3 survive remarkably intact. Ruined control
tower to the N and other brick structures.

WESTONZOYLAND PUMPING STATION, 1½ m. SW. Brick hip-
roofed building of 1831, the first steam pumping station on the
Levels. The present engine, by *Easton & Amos* of Southwark,
1861, could raise 100 tons of water per minute. The attendant
lived above, his accommodation extended with a cottage to the
E. The huge Lancashire boiler of 1914 remains, also the workshop and associated buildings.

SEDGEMOOR BATTLEFIELD, ½ m. N. An evocatively lonely spot
overlooking flat moor. Uninspired granite MEMORIAL, 1928,
between staddle-stones engraved with battle names from four
centuries.

WEST PENNARD

ST NICHOLAS. Perp two-stage W tower with angle buttresses to
halfway up the bell-stage. A good crown embellished with
panelled battlements, panelled and crocketed corner pinnacles,
and, unusually, canopied niches (cf. Chew Stoke and Wraxall,
both N) in the centre of each side. Leaded spike and polygonal
NE stair-tower, narrowed at the bell-stage. Ashlar W face, the
doorway between canopied niches, under a broad string course
with three busts of angels. Four-light W window between more
elaborate niches, under a similar string course with angel busts.
The bell-stage has a two-light bell-opening over a smaller two-
light opening, both with pierced baffles. The ashlar facing on
the S side was for a fives wall. Star-vault inside the tower and
wave-moulded tower arch, panelled between shafts. The rest

of the church has good ashlar detail very similar to Pilton: tracery, buttresses, S porch façade, polygonal rood-stair turret and parapets. Pierced quatrefoil parapets with thin finials to the clerestory and chancel. Parapet with cusped blind arcading to the S aisle and porch. Porch with niche over the doorway and traceried Perp S DOOR within. Plain N aisle parapet. The depressed arches of the clerestory windows look C16. Arcades of four-centred arches on four-hollow piers. Polygonal capitals to the four-bay N arcade, apart from the W respond, which has a round capital. Round capitals to the five-bay S arcade, polygonal only to the E respond. The uneven spacing of the arcade suggests an altered earlier church. Chancel arch matching the N arcade. Nave wagon roof with wall-plate angels. Panelled aisle ceilings on stone angels (N) and older stone heads (S). Panelled chancel ceiling with wall-plate angels, on angel corbels. Cusped ogee PISCINA.

FURNISHINGS. SCREEN. C16. Three four-light bays, the lights square-headed with delicate tracery, as at Pilton (q.v.), under a thin carved frieze. Tudor-arched doorway with the rose and pomegranate of Henry VIII in the spandrels. Original colouring. Brass GATES from a Victorian altar rail. – FONT and PULPIT. 1852–3, of the restoration by *J. C. Buckler & Son*. – ROYAL ARMS. Hanoverian. – STAINED GLASS. An interesting collection in that much is not English. Four S aisle windows by *Ména* of Paris, otherwise unknown in Britain, dated 1842, 1851 and 1865. Flat colour like chromo-lithographs. Similar chancel N window, 1863, very Nazarene, unsigned. Much thicker in colour and line are the adjoining window by *Mayer* of Munich, 1890, and two opposite, early 1880s. E window by *O'Connor* and S aisle fourth by *Wailes*, both *c.* 1860. Medieval tracery figures in two N windows. Medieval fragments reused in the kneeling Prince Arthur, a C19 version of the Malvern Priory figure.

CHURCHYARD CROSS of *c.* 1500, with Abbot Bere of Glastonbury's initials and Passion emblems around the octagonal base. Attached piers on the diagonal faces. Truncated shaft.

SOUTHTOWN FARM, ½ m. SE. Dated 1611. Ovolo-moulded mullion windows, banded stonework, two eaves gables and a cross-wing. But inside are two C16 moulded framed ceilings, one with Tudor-rose bosses. A plaster overmantel upstairs with a fleur-de-lys in a lozenge of Renaissance batons may be mid-C16. Unusual timber-framed OUTBUILDING, possibly a C16 brewhouse.

MANOR FARM, Coxbridge, 1 m. SSW. Three gables, the outer ones projecting, of differing sizes. The l. cross-wing is C17, the rest is dated 1577 and has reserved-chamfer mullions. Elizabethan fireplace with fluted piers on over-large pedestals.

CHAPEL HOUSE, Piltown, ¾ m. NE. Former Methodist chapel. Georgian Gothic, with parapets ramped up to a small pediment; 1830s.

OLD FARM, East Town, 1 m. NW. Thatched, with windows of various dates. Originally a mid-C14 hall house. The solar is

West Pennard, churchyard cross.
Engraving, 1877

most intact, with one two-tier cruck truss (typical of Glastonbury Abbey farms), the upper cruck cusped. Restored, with a glazed link to outbuildings, 2009–10 by *Jo Hibbert*.

WESTPORT *see* HAMBRIDGE

WEST QUANTOXHEAD

A Victorian estate between the Quantocks and the sea.

ST ETHELDREDA. By the drive to St Audries, against a wall of trees, a classic Victorian picture. Rebuilt in 1853–6 by *John Norton*.* One of Norton's most expensive works, reportedly it cost £16,000. Pinkish sandstone with stone-tiled roofs. Big NW tower with a higher stair-turret crowned by a spirelet. Gabled aisles with pierced parapets, large S porch. All the detail is late C13 Geometrical. The interior is sumptuous, ashlar-lined, the arcades on monolithic quatrefoil piers of Babbacombe marble.

---

*There was a medieval church, demolished in 1853 (the screen re-erected at Exford) and a temporary wooden church, re-erected in 1866 at Stolford.

Much excellent naturalistic carving, *à la* Southwell chapter house, by *William Farmer*. He also carved the angel corbels supporting the roofs. Heavy cusped roof trusses and two tiers of huge wind-braces. Beneath the tower is a rib-vaulted baptistery, the two arches richly shafted. Similarly richly shafted chancel arch and chancel N arcade. The chancel is further enriched with an encaustic TILE FLOOR by *Minton*, featuring Fuller-Acland-Hood heraldry. – FONT. C12 bowl, with a roll rim, on a round shaft. The bowl of *Norton*'s Devonshire marble font is outside. – STALLS, PEWS and PULPIT. Oak, Gothic. – COMMUNION RAILS. Delicate brass, framed in wood, by *Hardman*, by whom probably also the brass LECTERN. – Another LECTERN, wrought-iron, by *James Horrobin*, 1996. – STAINED GLASS. Mostly of 1856. Chancel and vestry windows by *O'Connor*, the E Crucifixion typically melodramatic; patterned nave windows by *Powell's*; tower window by *Hardman*. Two by *Kempe*, the SE, 1882, conventional compared to the deep colours and minute detail of the W window, 1905. S aisle window, 1939, by *Eleanor Fortescue Brickdale*. Charming children in the lower panels.

Remains of a C15 CHURCHYARD CROSS.

ST AUDRIES. The spreading neo-Tudor mansion created for the Aclands of Fairfield was built around a house of the Malets, here from *c.* 1500 to 1736. Illustrations show it with hip-roofed cross-wings and cross-mullioned windows. The five cross-windows surviving upstairs on the N side of the N wing are bead-moulded, of *c.* 1700. The house was remodelled in Tudor Gothic style before 1860. The sequence seems to be this. *Richard Carver* was involved *c.* 1815–25, and again after the sale in 1835 to Sir Peregrine Fuller-Palmer-Acland of Fairfield. Acland gave it to his seventeen-year-old daughter on her marriage in 1849 to Sir Alexander Hood, and much was done thereafter by *John Norton*. Old photographs show the W façade remodelled with gables and a pyramid-roofed porch-tower, more 1850s than 1835. This disappeared behind a new front by *Norton* of 1870–2, part of works costing £13,000. A memorable if coarse display of red sandstone contrasting with the greyish conglomerate of the earlier work. A four-bay Great Hall is set back between a tall battlemented entrance tower and a gabled projection. The four-storey tower has a three-storey Bath stone oriel and a sheer octagonal NW stair-turret. The S elevation is principally early C19, with an off-centre octagonal turret and a big kitchen gable to the r. On the N side, projections of 1870–2 – the library, NW, and billiard room, NE – flank the original five bays (C19 ground-floor windows) and an early C19 three-bay shallow-gabled addition (dining room) to the E, by *Carver*. At the rear, an early C19 STABLE COURT with battlemented three-bay S gatehouse and plain Tudor E stable and coachhouse range, both perhaps by *Carver*. A service range between gabled wings opposite is something older, remodelled.

Such a history makes for a complicated plan. *Norton*'s GREAT HALL and the passage behind are robustly Gothic. The

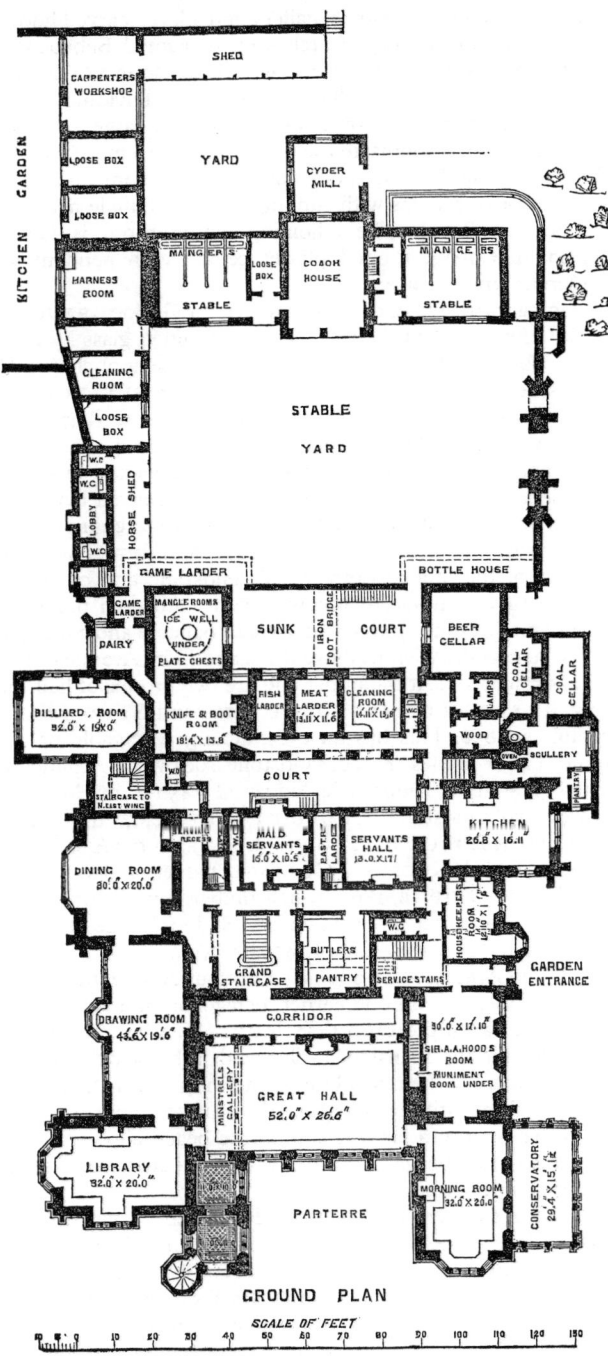

West Quantoxhead, St Audries.
Plan, 1872

hall has a wooden minstrels' gallery and a large carved hooded fireplace between pairs of arches on octagonal Babbacombe marble pillars, open to the passage. Tudoresque STAIR HALL of c. 1840 by *Carver*, infilling a rear court. Dividing stair of oak, under a ribbed coved ceiling with a large octagonal lantern. The best rooms, to the N, have early C19 marble Gothic fireplaces. The drawing room was once two rooms, hence the twin mid-C18 ceilings with sunbursts from a female head, and Rococo scrollwork. The adjoining dining room is Gothic, typical of *Carver*. Ribbed plaster ceiling with pendant and undercut vine cornice.

Facing the N side of the house is a Tudor Gothic ORANGERY, built before 1817, probably by *Carver*. Stained glass by *Christopher Webb*, 1946, from when it served as a school chapel. On the E side of the same garden is a contemporary SHELL GROTTO of rockwork with wooden Y-tracery windows. Remarkable swirling interior, the floor patterned in coloured cobbles, the walls and vault encrusted with shells, minerals and fossils.

The village between church and house was removed before the church was rebuilt. A triangle of green has the church at one corner, and the former RECTORY, 1872, and former SCHOOL, 1856–7, at the others. Both of red sandstone and by *Norton*. The rectory is mullion-windowed with a storeyed porch, the school picturesque Gothic with a lacy E bellcote and a teacher's house across the W end. Above the school, The Avenue of 1770 runs straight SW. At the upper end are two groups of half-hip-roofed ESTATE COTTAGES of the 1870s and STAPLE FARM, rebuilt c. 1830. This has an eye-catching rear gable of twin blind Tudor arches in red sandstone rockwork. Around the estate are three Tudor-style lodges of 1850–1 by *Norton* in crazed red sandstone: CHURCH LODGE below the church, WILLITON LODGE and STOWEY LODGE on the A39. On the Doniford road, KEEPER'S COTTAGE, bargeboarded, of 1857, and RYDON LODGE, 1861–2, half-timbered with entirely dissimilar ornamental brick chimneys. Rydon Lodge stands by the drive to HOME FARM, of 1855, by *Norton*. Large mullion-windowed FARMHOUSE opposite farm buildings with a picturesque DOVECOTE on one corner, octagonal on a square base. SW of the farm, the OLD GAS HOUSE, c. 1860, a coal-fired gasworks for the mansion. L-plan with a brick chimney and central louvre to the retort house. The wing ends in a little rose window. A beautifully constructed ROADWAY built in 1855–6 from the farm to a landing slip on the beach allowed coal to be landed for the gas house, the slip and lower end of the roadway since swept away.

DONIFORD, 1 m. WNW. DONIFORD FARM, rambling and roughcast, is late medieval, rewindowed in the C19. Moulded two-panel ceiling and arch-braced cruck roof with wind-braces. A rear NW room has deep C17 plaster friezes of fish-tailed beasts. Towards the beach, an impressive Victorian LIMEKILN. Round-ended battered walls, twin hemispherical brick-lined openings.

WEACOMBE HOUSE, ¾ m. s. Built for Thomas Cridland after 1757. Quite a fine show on the hillside, yellow-washed with stone Gibbsian rusticated openings, and cornice and pediment in timber. Early C19 columned porch. Entrance hall with curved angles, between front rooms with good cornices and timber chimneypieces. The curving staircase is later Georgian, under rather rustic original plasterwork of branches and cherub heads. Added Regency room to the NE. Single-storey plate-glass and timber kitchen, well fitted behind the stair projection. By *Alex Michaelis*, executed by *Marius Barran*, 2007. – Picturesque early C19 Gothic LODGE, the main part circular, inset for a veranda.

WHEATHILL

1 m. w of Lovington

ST JOHN THE BAPTIST. Now a house. Single cell with square-headed Perp single lights. Altered by restoration (1858) and conversion, the E window now not as Buckler drew it in 1846, and the bellcote gone.

PRIORY FARMHOUSE is C17, with ovolo-moulded mullioned windows. Across the railway, the long LOWER FARMHOUSE has early C18 corniced mullioned windows and a bolection-moulded doorcase. In the E outbuilding, wall-slots for a lost cruck.

WHITELACKINGTON

ST MARY. Sturdy Perp four-stage W tower. Diagonal buttresses, battlements and NW stair-turret. W door and four-light W window. Broad three-light bell-opening each side, with pierced baffles. Similar S window on the stage below. The transepts are older, the large N and S windows clearly of the early C14. They are of three lights with a large circle in the middle, divided in the N window into three trefoils and the S one into three spherical triangles. Moulded rere-arches, the S one in addition with heavy shafts. Perp aisle windows; Perp chancel, the three-light E window with supermullions. Broad spacious nave, the aisles post-dating the tower whose buttresses intrude. Panelled tower arch. Tall and broad three-bay Perp arcades extending across the transepts on thin piers. Perp chancel arch. The transepts each have a broad squint and cusped PISCINA. In the S one also a cinquefoil-cusped and gabled C14 niche.

FURNISHINGS. FONT. C14, shallow octagon, coved below. – PULPIT. 1875. Stone, with careful tracery. – PEWS. Early C19. Scrolled arm-rests. – STAINED GLASS. E window, very good, by *Kempe*, 1896. – MONUMENTS. Two eroded effigies in the S transept, a bare-headed civilian of *c.* 1350 and a damaged knight in armour of *c.* 1375. – Sir George Speke †1582. Mentioned as already prepared in his will, the monument looks twenty-five years earlier, still entirely in the flamboyant latest Perp style, with hardly more than one frieze that shows a recognition of the Renaissance. Tomb-chest with shields in cusped lozenges. Octagonal panelled shafts at each end carry a four-centred-arched canopy with leafy crockets. The shafts continue as big twisted chimney-like finials; a similar finial over the apex. Four fan-traceried pendants hang from the soffit, very exuberant. The ends, behind the polygonal shafts, are pierced tracery panels. Three shields in large lush foliage at the back. – Speke family. Plain Grecian by *John Kendall* of Exeter.* – Rev. William Gyllett †1803, by *Kendall*. – John Hanning †1807, by *J. Richards* of Exeter. Grecian, let down by incompetent sculpture. – Jessy Lee Lee †1826. Emotive mourning husband and child, unsigned. – John Brooke †1868, Raja Muda of Sarawak.

WHITELACKINGTON MANOR, next to the church. The seat of the Spekes from the mid C15 to mid C18. The present house is late C16, near-square, with three gables between parapets on the S. Two gables to each side. Later C18 and early C19 sash windows, some mullioned windows to the W. Cross-passage between arched C18 doorways on the W and E fronts, the E one in an open-pedimented doorcase. – OUTBUILDING to the W ending in a thatched horse-engine house.

On the main road, THE LODGE and THE FORGE, L-plan, thatched, with two tall gabled porches, a picturesque early C19 transformation of an earlier building. The former RECTORY is stuccoed with a deep-eaved hipped roof, 1820s. Further N are pairs of late C19 Dillington estate COTTAGES and ABRAHAMS, thatched, with Late Georgian casement windows.

EAGLEWOOD PARK. *See* Dillington House.

WHITESTAUNTON

ST ANDREW. Handsome Perp church in the creamy local sandstone. Three-stage early C16 tower with SE octagonal stair-turret and two-light bell-openings. Nave with three-light windows and S porch. The chancel, rebuilt by *Sedding*, 1877–9, stands between a narrow lean-to C15 N chapel and a gabled S chapel built under the will of John Brett †1588. This has a parapet, uncusped tracery, and a moulded arch to the chancel. Plain stone screen to the N chapel with one-light divisions. – FONT. Norman bowl, scalloped below. – SCREEN. C15–C16. Unremarkable two-light tracery and blind tracery in the lower

---

* *John Flaxman* was paid fifty guineas for a memorial in 1802–5, but it is not clear what resulted.

panels. – BENCH-ENDS. C16. Renaissance motifs, also a dog. – TILES. By the altar. C15, armorial (Staunton and Montague). – MONUMENTS. Two Perp tomb-chests, much reworked. One has Brett and other heraldry, the other C19 Elton arms. – Margaret Brett and Marie Morgane, her daughter, both †1582. Brass, Gothic lettering and painted heraldry. – Charles Elton †1900. Arts and Crafts embossed copper.

Tall, tapered C15 CHURCHYARD CROSS. Portland stone pedestal MONUMENT, Lutyens-style, to Frederick Elton †1922.

WHITESTAUNTON MANOR. Eminently picturesque, the elements arranged with casual grace. The spine is the hall roof, hipped down on the l. to the E cross-wing, the centrepiece a massive projecting lateral chimney with tall twin shafts, next to a two-storey Elizabethan battlemented porch in the angle to the W cross-wing. The E cross-wing was the solar end, partly over the cross-passage whose blocked door is visible. A cobbled hearth indicated a ground-floor hall replaced by the present first-floor hall, for John Brett †1478. Elizabethan alterations include a mullion-and-transom window lighting the hall each side, and the W cross-wing with its gable faced in squared chert (cf. Chard School, 1583). In the rear angle a gabled stair-tower. Two C15 cusped ogee windows are reused on the back wall. The Bretts, recusant exiles, sold in 1718 to the Eltons of Clevedon, non-resident until the 1840s. Around 1846 the W cross-wing was extended sympathetically to make a symmetrical garden front. In restoration for Stuart Moore by *Jo Hibbert*, 2004–11, the hall roof and much else was brought to light.

The Great Hall is over the entrance hall and kitchen, the latter with an Elizabethan rear window. E of the kitchen the medieval cross-passage. In the stair-tower are much-altered open-well stairs. The splendid hall roof (tree-ring-dated 1446–78) has moulded arch-braced collar-trusses on short hammerbeams, separated by deep wall-plates and tiers of ornamental wind-bracing to a cusped Y-tracery pattern. Tudor-arched fireplace. In the E range, the similar solar roof has uncusped wind-bracing. Also an early C17 courtroom, originally barrel-roofed and decorated. A heraldic tympanum remains, above the present ceiling.

Much survives in the W cross-wing. The first-floor NW room has a plaster frieze of exotic and mythical beasts linked by an animal-headed scroll, and a heraldic overmantel. Datable to the 1630s, it resembles work at Wigborough Manor (Over Stratton) and Weston Farm (Wambrook). It may have been moved from the courtroom. The adjoining chamber has a sixteen-panel moulded framed ceiling. The downstairs parlour has a good Tudor-arched chimneypiece with heraldry. The pilastered panelling dated 1577 is apparently reused. In the C19 S room, the ornate Renaissance chimneypiece is imported, provenance unknown. Datable to 1547–9 from the ducal arms of Lord Protector Somerset. Paired Ionic columns, entablature, and overmantel heraldry between splendid male and female demi-figures supporting a cornice.

The outbuilding range to the E comprises a C17 lofted STABLE with two reused C15 doorways, an early C19 coach-house, and an exceptionally large early C18 DOVECOTE, the pyramid roof from a later remodelling as a granary. In the GARDENS a stream crossed by a rockwork bridge emerges from a HOLY WELL dedicated to St Agnes. The Roman foundations exposed in the water garden were presumed to be a villa, but are of a ROMAN BATH HOUSE. Excavation has failed to find any further buildings.

In the village the OLD RECTORY, c. 1835, with mullion-and-transom windows. A C15–C16 moulded haunched fireplace in an older attached range.

HOWLEY FARMHOUSE, 1 m. SW. C16, roughcast and thatched with central chimney gable. C16 half-hip-roofed BARN with jointed crucks.

WIGBOROUGH MANOR see OVER STRATTON

WILLETT see ELWORTHY

WILLITON

A small town at the intersection of main roads to Taunton, Bridgwater and Minehead, now the administrative centre for West Somerset.

ST PETER. The triple-gabled building looks Victorian on account of the N aisle and W front of 1856–9 by *C. E. Giles*. His wooden spirelet has been replaced by a bellcote. But the nave and chancel are late medieval and flat-headed C16 windows are re-set in the S aisle of 1810. C15–C16 W doorway. Plastered round pillars to the Georgian S arcade. – FONT. Octagonal, of Watchet alabaster, 1666, by *John Miller* of Watchet. – STAINED GLASS. E window, 1907, by *Powell's*.

Across the road, remains of a C15 CHURCHYARD CROSS.

METHODIST CHAPEL, Tower Hill. 1883, by *Robert Curwen*. Large, Dec Gothic. Red sandstone with Ham stone. Built with the hall and manse.

DISTRICT COUNCIL OFFICES, Fore Street. 2007–8, by *Pick Everard*. Brick and render with monopitch roofs and glazed corner entrance.

DANESFIELD SCHOOL, North Road. 1954–7, by *Somerset County Architects*. Curtain walling and buff brick.

PERAMBULATION. On the junction of main roads, the long stuccoed former EGREMONT HOTEL of c. 1820–30. Opposite, the NATWEST BANK (originally Stuckey's Bank), 1867–9, red sandstone, Italianate. Beside the bank are fragments of two C15 MARKET CROSSES that stood at either end of Fore Street. To the W is the forceful Gothic POLICE STATION, 1858, by *John Norton* (cf. Dunster). Red sandstone, E-plan with a pyramid-roofed porch-tower. 'Williton' was chiselled off in 1940 to confuse invaders. BRIDGE STREET runs S, past the former SCHOOL, 1872–4 by *C. E. Giles*. BRIDGE FARMHOUSE is partly C17 with C19 bargeboards. Undershot waterwheel of 1890. To the W, the church (*see above*) sits well with two rows of COTTAGES. The nearer row was the church house, rebuilt in 1591. Pointed medieval N doorway. A gabled Victorian LODGE beyond marks the drive to Orchard Wyndham (*see below*). On the hill above, EASTFIELD was a dower house. Early C19, U-plan, with deep-eaved hipped roofs. The three-storey ORCHARD MILL is Late Georgian, with a house in the r. half and a 16-ft (4.9-metre) overshot wheel of 1871 on the other end. Bridge Street turns SE, past altered C17–C18 thatched cottages, to HIGH STREET. A detour past the Methodist chapel (*see above*) up TOWER HILL finds on the N side BROWNWICH HOUSE, 1923 by *Welch & Hollis* of London. Arts and Crafts Georgian in red brick under a big hipped roof. Gabled centre with an oriel. The return to the centre is via High Street.

FORE STREET runs N from the junction. The Gothic red sandstone building on the W is probably by *J. P. St Aubyn* (cf. his bank of 1869 in Minehead). LONG STREET is the Bridgwater road, with scattered C16–C18 thatched houses. Nos. 13–17 are dated 1624. ARDEN COTTAGE, remodelled 1814–18, was a C15 hall house. It has smoke-blackened jointed crucks. HONEYSUCKLE COTTAGE, although dated 1607 and 1677, has a similar C15 roof. Traces of painted decoration on a partition. Further out is the former WORKHOUSE (now Sir Gilbert Scott Court). By *Scott & Moffatt*, 1837–40, to the classical design they used also at Bideford (Devon), Flax Bourton (N) and Witham (Essex). Octagonal four-storey centre accommodating the master and matron, with pedimented angle projections for observation of the exercise yards. Three-storey wings for men (W) and women (E). Gatehouse range of two colours of sandstone with an impressive pedimented central archway. The chapel was in the r. pavilion. Beyond is the STATION of the West Somerset Railway, 1862, beautifully preserved with its GOODS SHED. Ancillary structures include the wooden PLATFORM SHELTER, 1874, and brick SIGNAL BOX, 1875. Imported since the line was rescued in 1976, an iron FOOTBRIDGE from Trowbridge, Wilts., and a hoop-topped WORKSHOP of 1899, from Swindon, Wilts.

ORCHARD WYNDHAM, ¾ m. SW. The medieval house of the Orchard family passed to the Sydenhams of Combe Sydenham in 1448, and to John Wyndham of Felbrigg, Norfolk, in 1528. A C14 hall is enveloped between two small courtyards (one subsequently infilled) added by John Sydenham II, owner 1493–1521. The N courtyard had a new hall on the N side, and the S courtyard a new kitchen on the S. A cross-wing projected NW of the new hall. In the mid C16 the side of the N hall was advanced to align with the cross-wing, the new N front was given mullion-and-transom windows, and the hall itself was perhaps floored. Around 1680 the hall became again of double height with a barrel ceiling and a new central doorway. In the early C18 Sir William Wyndham M.P. (briefly Chancellor of the Exchequer in 1713) filled in the northern courtyard as a stair hall, with a drawing room to the w. Sir William's son inherited Petworth, Sussex, in 1750, as 2nd Earl of Egremont. Thereafter Orchard Wyndham was neglected. The 3rd Earl demolished a large NW piece before 1816. The 4th Earl did not inherit Petworth in 1837 and instead commissioned an enormous Neoclassical house from *J. T. Knowles* for Blackdown Hill opposite Orchard Wyndham, to be called Egremont Castle. This was not built. Knowles designed instead a somewhat smaller house for Egremont at Silverton, Devon. Orchard Wyndham was repaired in 1839–40, probably by *Richard Carver*, and the N front rearranged. After the 4th Earl died in 1845 little more was done. His widow added bargeboards to the W side.

The N front is the single architectural statement and not a grand one. Five bays with a straight parapet. Renewed mullion-and-transom windows on each side of a very large C19 Tudor-arched window, over an undersized porch. The front was stuccoed, but the outer bays have been stripped, to the disadvantage of appearance. But this has revealed details of the medieval cross-wing: a blocked doorway and part of a ground-floor window with the typical West Somerset quatrefoil spandrel of *c.* 1500. The low stuccoed NE wing was remodelled from coachhouses. A NW wing disappeared in the 3rd Earl's demolitions.

The other fronts are utterly informal. The long W side begins with the chimney of the N front, clearly once internal, next to the early C18 drawing-room block, red sandstone, four bays, unevenly spaced. The lower piece to the r. is medieval, the gable marking the solar end of the earliest hall (frame of a C15–C16 window), the rest a C15 cross-wing extended in the C16. Queen Anne sash windows and Victorian bargeboards. The S side is marked by the kitchen chimney gable. The long E side has C16–C17 mullioned windows and early C19 sash windows.

The new HALL on the N has a roof akin to the late C15 roof at John Halle's house, Salisbury. Moulded arch-braced collar-trusses in eight close-spaced bays with moulded purlins. It was originally more ornate, with false hammerbeams and complex cusped wind-braces. Until the 1950s the roof was hidden by the late C17 barrel ceiling. The half-height pine panelling with bolection-moulded panels and pulvinated frieze is late C17. Early C18 stone chimneypiece. Deep window bays indicate how far the front wall was moved in the C16. The opening at the E end of the S wall, now into the stair hall, has moulded jambs of the former hall oriel. Similar late C17 panelling with pulvinated frieze in the LIBRARY, NW. Plastered crossed beams here may conceal a framed ceiling contemporary with the moulded C15–C16 fireplace, as this was originally the parlour under the solar. Upstairs, a good wind-braced roof is concealed by a C16 thin-rib ceiling. Plain Late Georgian MORNING ROOM, NE, formerly the library, with a C15–C16 Tudor-arched S doorway. The STAIR HALL in the former courtyard has an early C19 square lantern. Bulbous balusters to the early C18 staircase and landing, with carved tread-ends and a ramped rail. The DRAWING ROOM, also early C18, has plain large-field panelling. Lush neo-Rococo chimneypiece of white marble with enormous scrolls, of the 1830s by *J. E. Carew*, the Irish-born sculptor patronized by the 3rd Earl at Petworth.

Upstairs, at the E end of the original hall, is the PEACOCK ROOM, part of a C15–C16 NE range with a concealed wind-braced roof. Furnished *c.* 1600 with panelling under a lively plaster frieze of men in pointy hats, naked figures riding dragons, birds and fishes. C19 thin-rib ceiling. A blocked S window shows that the E side of the S courtyard was the last to be enclosed, in the C17. The SE corner room of the kitchen range, THE SOLAR, had linenfold panelling, now at Wadham College, Oxford. Ribbed mid-C16 ceiling decorated with fleurs-de-lys and wreathed Wyndham–Sydenham heraldry, such plasterwork early for Somerset.

Opposite the E side are a roughcast, hip-roofed BAILIFF'S HOUSE, C18–C19, and an Early Victorian ICE HOUSE, built against a bank, with a square SUMMERHOUSE on top. Early C19 FARM to the S, with parallel red sandstone ranges including a bank barn. To the SW is the hip-roofed GARDEN HOUSE of 1725, fronted in brick. Three bays and apparently two-storeyed, it contains a banqueting room with bolection-moulded fireplace. The Long Walk SW to Black Down and the wood on the hill with radiating paths were planted at the same period. An undulating wall of sandstone blocks called the GIANT'S CAVE on the N edge of the wood, and MOTHER SHIPTON'S STONE nearby, a tall slab carved with designs copied from Roman grave markers, are probably late C18. The SW drive emerges at STREAM LODGE, a C17–C18 pink-washed thatched farmhouse. STREAM FARMHOUSE, with C19 bargeboards, is dated 1619. Nine-panel framed ceiling.

BATTLEGORE, ½ m. N, W of the Watchet road. Earthworks, difficult to detect, related to a mound or barrow at their centre. Probably Bronze Age.

WILTON *see* TAUNTON

WINCANTON

The town rises eastward from the River Cale, along the old main road to London, from which came its prosperity. A

Wincanton, St Peter and St Paul, before rebuilding.
Drawing by J. Buckler, 1844

predominantly Georgian centre, the result partly of destructive fires, notably in 1707. The materials are a mixture of local yellowish rubble stone, ashlar, stucco and brick.

ST PETER AND ST PAUL. Mostly of 1887–9 by *J. D. Sedding*, with a thin Perp W tower, raised by a stage in 1793. The church was rebuilt with a new clerestoried nave, chancel and N aisle. The original nave and S aisle were kept but remodelled to eradicate Georgian work, the nave and chancel having been altered in 1748 by *Nathaniel Ireson* and the S aisle rebuilt in 1735 by *John Clewett*. Only a pedimented S doorway remains of all this. Sedding's church is Perp, mechanically detailed apart from the N porch of 1891, with the Crucifixion and saints on a grid of tracery. A storeyed organ chamber animates the NE corner. The interior, consequent on retaining much of the old church, has effectively two naves with chancels, and outer aisles. The three arcades have similar four-hollow shafted piers, the southern two presumably C15, thoroughly redone.

FURNISHINGS. STALLS, PULPIT, and linenfold PEWS of 1890, by *Sedding*. The stalls have plant-form arm-rests, as at Porlock. Intricate S chancel SCREEN of 1921 by *G. H. Shackle*. – ROYAL ARMS. 1664. – SCULPTURE. N porch. Late medieval relief of St Eloi re-attaching the horse's leg. – STAINED GLASS. E window by *Clayton & Bell*, 1891. N aisle window by *Morris & Co.*, 1921, awful. Much better the war memorial window by *Powell's*, S. – MONUMENTS. J. L. Churchey †1716. Curved-headed marble. – Philip Bennet †1725. More rustic, with sweetly coloured cherub faces. – Messiter family. By *Reeves & Son*, early C19. Large pedimented double memorial.

In the churchyard an eroded MONUMENT of 1772 to *Nathaniel Ireson* †1769, builder, architect and potter, who came to Wincanton from Stourhead in 1726. He carved his own statue, decapitated now, the base with old-fashioned symbols of mortality. – GATE SCREEN, 1818, with elegant urns on piers.

ST LUKE AND ST TERESA (R.C.), South Street. 1907–8 by *Scoles & Raymond*. Austere lancet Gothic. Battlemented thin towers frame a tall gable with quintuple lancets under a seven-lobed roundel. Long and tall interior with clerestory and arcades on octagonal piers. The apse is screened by a Gothic HIGH ALTAR of 1913 by *Percy Lamb* of London, the altar fronted in *opus sectile* tilework. Behind is the gaunt former PRIORY, 1888–9 by *Scoles*, the second post-Reformation Carmelite priory in Britain. Three storeys, stone, with gabled wings.

PERAMBULATION. CHURCH STREET climbs E from the church to the Market Place. The MASONIC HALL may have begun as a silk mill *c.* 1800. No. 7, nondescript externally, is a C15 hall house with a cruck-framed wind-braced roof, tree-ring-dated to 1430. Solar to the E; the former hall to the W, now with a rich C16 moulded framed ceiling. Mullion-windowed stair-tower in the rear angle. The MARKET PLACE comprises two triangular widenings. At the lower end, No. 5, Late Georgian, is notable for its flat roof, a curious Wincanton feature, this one already there in a photograph of *c.* 1875. No. 6, 1796, stuccoed, three-storeyed, was an inn. On the N side, Nos. 7–8, 1836, curving sharply into North Street, were originally stuccoed. Another Wincanton flat roof. Opposite is the very Victorian tower of the TOWN HALL which has its main front towards South Street. Pevsner found the hall 'rather an eyesore with its ugly turret'. Its brick front with Gibbsian rustication to the arches and upper windows reproduces the Market House of 1768–9, burnt in 1877. Rebuilt 1878 by *Wilson, Willcox & Wilson* of Bath. On the N side again, a three-storeyed group: No. 9, a bank in 1806, handsome late C18, ashlar, with a central Venetian window; and the GREYHOUND HOTEL, 'new built' in 1760, clumsier, stuccoed with parapet and urns. The triple keystones are suggestive of *Ireson*'s work. Central throughway framed in timber pilasters and cornice, under a canted oriel window. No. 11, 1840s, is stuccoed, 1–2–1 bays. Then the BEAR HOTEL, dated 1720, but altered. Five bays before a tall rusticated arched throughway in a broader r. bay. C17 framed ceiling within. Both inns have scrolled wrought-iron sign brackets. Opposite is a C19 three-storey group: No. 13, *c.* 1848, stucco, with Venetian shop windows divided by thin iron shafts; LLOYDS BANK, ashlar-fronted, with another flat roof; No. 15, stuccoed, dated 1878; and Nos. 16–17, 1830s, in a six-bay painted ashlar curve into South Street.

HIGH STREET continues the Market Place upward, with mostly Georgian fronts, few particularly noteworthy. On the N side, No. 5, late C18 red brick, was Messiters Bank by 1801. No. 7, rubble stone and ashlar, was refronted *c.* 1760 for the Messiters. Attributed to *Ireson*, but a clumsy design, the pediment and windows uncomfortably aligned. C17 rear gables frame a curved C18 stair projection with a rusticated window. Pedimented SUMMERHOUSE with triglyphs matching those on the house. Opposite, the WHITE HORSE INN, dated 1733, rustic Baroque and not at all metropolitan, is possibly by *Ireson* in his early manner. Stuccoed with exceptionally heavy detail – keystones, curved pediments, rusticated doorway. Quoins to two storeys then short tapered pilasters at the corners of the attic. No. 10 is Late Georgian, rubble, with an ashlar Ionic doorcase. Nos. 18 and 20 are late C18 brick, No. 18 with a columned open-pedimented doorcase, No. 20, slightly earlier, of chequered brick, with an arched doorcase framed by Corinthian columns and pediment.

Scattered things beyond. The DOLPHIN HOTEL has Gibbsian ground-floor surrounds, suggesting *Ireson*. Only the r. half is original. No. 48, early C19, has curved-ended shop windows echoed in twin curved-ended first-floor bays. Another Wincanton flat roof. The METHODIST CHAPEL, 1916–18, is in the free Perp style popular with Nonconformists *c.* 1900. On the N side the thatched UNCLE TOM'S CABIN, *c.* 1700, so named since 1861. At the upper end, No. 69, with a late C18 pedimented doorcase, and No. 71, Late Georgian, red brick, with a diminutive two-storey bay. Up Ireson Lane, IRESON HOUSE was built by *Ireson* for himself *c.* 1726, but altered *c.* 1851 into a hip-roofed villa. The porch incorporates a corniced doorcase with diagonally set pilasters, intermittently vermiculated, surely too Baroque for 1851. The rear range has rusticated window surrounds that may also be original. Ireson made delftware pottery in the NE range from 1738. Just E of Ireson Lane, COLYTON TERRACE, 1830, has hip-roofed stuccoed villas of seaside type.

A detour down COMMON ROAD, opposite, finds BALSAM HOUSE, the early C17 house of the Lewis family. On the N, two wings with obelisk finials flank a narrow recessed stair-gable. On the S, a storeyed porch is the centrepiece with arched doorway. Ovolo-moulded mullioned windows and early C19 ground-floor sashes. At the SE corner, an almost detached (kitchen?) block, also with an obelisk finial. The interiors are largely 1930s. An arch on the front terrace may be by *Ireson*.

Returning to the Market Place and down SOUTH STREET, No. 1 is of the 1830s, ashlar, similar to Nos. 16–17 Market Place adjoining. Four bays, with a late C19 shopfront. Opposite the R.C. church (p. 695), ST AUDREY'S, a plain square villa by *John Peniston* of Salisbury, 1835–6, and OLD ST AUDREY'S, late C18 with a pedimented doorway. The former PLAZA CINEMA, 1934, by *Edward Holding*, is brick modern-Georgian, with shaved corners and tile arches and roundels.

Next door is THE DOGS, the best house of Wincanton. Although called 'recently built' when William of Orange lodged here with Richard Churchey in 1688, it is probably early to mid-C17. Roughcast with ashlar dressings. An original S range with a central storeyed porch and W cross-wing was enlarged to square in the late C17, to front E to the street. The new entrance is recessed between gables. Ovolo-moulded mullions are mixed with the earlier reserved-chamfered type. Double-height W stair window. A fascinating interior of some grandeur, refashioned after 1680 and characterized by detail at the cusp of the C17 and C18: deep cornices, pulvinated friezes, large-field panelling. The E entrance (now blocked) opened on to a grand staircase up to the attic. Pulvinated string, ball finials, twisted balusters and a particularly massive rail. Dog-gate at the foot. The SE room has a panelled overmantel with spit-rack, and the NW room large-field panelling, as does the room above. On the landing are opposed pedimented doorcases. The SW or Orange Room has panelling painted with classical landscapes with ruins in muted colours, not quite grisaille. These, fairly crudely done, are attributed to Napoleonic War prisoners but look of the early C18. The chimneypiece with pulvinated frieze encloses a moulded early C17 fireplace. Lofted C17 STABLE with reserved-chamfer mullions.

TOUT HILL HOUSE opposite, a large house of *c.* 1795, has a four-bay front with parapet and open pedimented doorcase. Open-well stone staircase. The long stable range is C17, refronted in the C18 with central Venetian window. Further down, the PRIMARY SCHOOL, 1896, by *Thomas Hudson*, with gables between gabled wings. STATION ROAD returns to the parish church past BELLEFIELD, a plain hip-roofed range of *c.* 1700 marooned outside the former Cow & Gate MILK FACTORY, of 1936, in the West London arterial road manner. From the church, SILVER STREET runs N to MILL STREET, which ascends to the Market Place past two chapels. The former CONGREGATIONAL CHAPEL, behind the round-arched schoolroom of 1859, is red brick of 1799 by *Samuel Clewett*, remodelled in 1862 in the Lombard style. The BAPTIST CHAPEL, behind Gothic schools of 1887, is stuccoed minimal classical of 1832–3, apparently by the minister, *George Day*. Three bays, the outer bays slightly canted.

NORTH STREET drops from the Market Place, past the former NATIONAL SCHOOL, 1838, bleak, two-storeyed, with Late Georgian symmetry, and the stuccoed deep-eaved ROCKHILL HOUSE, early to mid-C19. At the foot, the former POLICE STATION, 1856, by *R. H. Shout*, two L-plan houses joined by an archway, like estate lodges, with profuse angular Gothic detail.

Back to the foot of Mill Street. Across the river, three suburban houses. BATCH HOUSE is early C19, stone, with a pedimented doorcase and timber semicircular bow windows. DIAL HOUSE has a sundial dated 1690, but Georgian sash windows and cornice. Canted first-floor projection on Tuscan columns. RODBER HOUSE, of red brick of the 1730s, is possibly by *Ireson*, with a later pyramid roof. Up West Hill, WEST HILL HOUSE is early C19, hip-roofed, with quoins and columned porch. Beyond are KING ARTHUR'S SCHOOL, 1956–8 by *Somerset County Architects*, and the wave-roofed LEISURE CENTRE, 2000, by *David Lambert*.

MOORHAYES FARMHOUSE, 1½ m. NW. Long late C16 house, with a spiral staircase in a semicircular turret on the SE end gable. C18 hip-roofed addition against the SW side.

SUDDON GRANGE, 1½ m. WNW. Long six-bay house with reserved-chamfer mullions of late C16 type and a storeyed porch, this rebuilt in the early C18. C17 stair gable oddly placed behind the westernmost room, which has a framed ceiling. Good fireplace in the room above the entrance, with a reserved-chamfer moulding.* Early C19 pyramid-roofed GRANARY.

HOLBROOK HOUSE, 1½ m. W. Quite large. The Edwardian W front of 1901–4 (said to be by *Blomfield*, which one uncertain) disguises a house of the 1730s. Rendered, with parapet and ashlar dressings. The five l. bays of the E side with central Venetian window and the simpler five-bay S front are original. Circular C19 rendered DOVECOTE. Just NW, HOLBROOK FARM, 1840s. Cottage-like hip-roofed farmhouse with Gothic dormer on each side, backing on to a three-sided farmyard.

PHYSIC WELL, 1 m. ESE. One of two short-lived spas opened at Horwood after 1800. The pump room and lodgings of 1803–5 remain, the pump room in an ashlar hip-roofed villa. Waters were taken in the apsed main room with the intricate fanlight. A spiral cantilevered staircase rises to a similar upper room. Lodgings were over the coachhouse and stable range, whose big traceried end window marks the visitors' chapel.

BAYFORD, 1 m. NE. On the old London road, IVY HOUSE, early C18, steep-roofed with leaded casements. BAYFORD LODGE, in its park, NW, is late C18. Five bays, with cornice and parapet beneath an attic added in 1871.

WINSFORD

ST MARY MAGDALENE. The round-arched S doorway could be Norman, but there is no detail at all. The DOOR has heavy hinges with sleeves once thought to be typical of C13–C14 work and also decorative scrolls, but is dated by Jane Geddes to the late C15 or early C16. The chancel is C13 – see the roll-moulded triangular-headed S doorway and the small lancet windows. Late Perp E window with a transom and an ogee head to each light below it, but without the quatrefoil spandrels typical of this region. A flat-headed chancel N window has the quatrefoils, as at Exford, Exton, etc. Perp nave and aisles under one big roof (cf. Cannington and Norton-sub-Hamdon). This leaves room for two small two-light windows above the chancel arch, a great rarity in this part of England. The N aisle E window, very late Perp, is finely traceried under a depressed-arched head of most uncomfortable form. Over the S door a

---

* The Ewen family, owners in the C17, were fined as Catholics. A 'low room called the Chappell' is mentioned in 1675.

crude crocketed and vaulted niche. Nave and chancel are roughcast. The grey stone W tower is big for the district. Late Perp, of three stages, with set-back buttresses almost to the top, small two-light bell-openings, battlements and no pinnacles. Statue niche on the S side, over a two-light window with C16 arched lights. Polygonal NE stair-turret. Large four-light W window, transomed like the E one.

Inside, a tall moulded tower arch on roughly coved capitals, and a high nave wagon roof on relatively low four-bay arcades of buff and red stone. Piers of standard four-hollow section and big polygonal capitals to fat shafts, all primitively treated. The interest is that the capitals are painted grey in imitation of Lias. Chancel arch of similar type, but the capitals are brattished. The black-and-white nave paving, the simple pews, and the nave and aisle roofs date from the restoration of 1890–1 by *J. D. Sedding*, who died at Winsford rectory in 1891. Some reused bosses. Rood stair behind the pulpit. The chancel roof is mostly original, with foliage bosses and carved wall-plate. N window recess with angel corbels, sheltering a plain EASTER SEPULCHRE or chest tomb. – FONT. Circular, Norman. Coarse arcading, the shafts plaited, under a frieze of large saltire crosses or nailhead. – PULPIT. Early C17, in two tiers. The usual arches here frame unusual crowned roses. – COMMUNION RAIL. Early C17, the balusters replaced. – ORGAN. 1847, by *J. W. Walker*. Gothic case with octagonal turrets. – ROYAL ARMS. James I, 1609. One of the earliest known from a church, the texts not the Authorized Version of 1611. – STAINED GLASS. In the E window a small C14 figure of the Virgin on pretty star quarries. Much attractive patterned leadwork in the clear glazing, typical of *Sedding*.

The church is on the hillside W of the village. The Steep drops down past STEEP COTTAGE, with a lateral chimney. At the foot, a large green with thatched cottages. THORN COTTAGE and WINN COTTAGE are Late Georgian, with rounded stair-turrets on the front. The ROYAL OAK with thatch undulating over dormers and porches is mostly Late Georgian too, with an older core. Some very pretty leaded glazing in the l. projection. Uphill, KARSLAKE HOUSE has a long front of Late Georgian sash windows. N of the village, VICARAGE BRIDGE is medieval, one wide and two small pointed arches, widened in 1928. Just upstream is a two-arch PACKHORSE BRIDGE with a cobbled track, and the stuccoed former VICARAGE, a Late Georgian hip-roofed addition to an earlier house.

CARATACUS STONE, Winsford Hill, 1½ m. SW. Protected by a shelter built in 1906, is the Langestone or Longstone mentioned in C13 boundary perambulations of Exmoor Forest. The stone is 3 ft 11 in. (1.2 metres) high, with the vertical inscription CARAACI NEPUS, meaning a grandson or immediate descendant of Caratacus, not necessarily his nephew. Probably C6, but Professor Okasha would not date it any more precisely than C5–C11.

ROAD CASTLE. *See* Exford.

WINSHAM

ST STEPHEN. The plan is unusual and impressive, and the church is by no means small. Nave and inclined chancel separated by a tower which, in the absence of transepts, cannot be called a crossing tower. It is a Norman plan (cf. e.g. Iffley, Oxon) but the details are Perp (cf. Dowlish Wake and Kingsdon). In the chancel, lancets, and also Dec tracery, over-restored 1873, but credible on account of the rere-arches. The nave has an early C14 W window with modest flowing tracery, Perp W doorway and three-light Perp side windows. C15 S porch, attractively linked to a vestry of 1929 (by *G. Streatfeild*). Broad panelled C15 nave roof. The tower is plain, embattled, with a higher stair-turret. The 'crossing' arches have responds of standard four-hollow type, but the wall thins at the springing and two heads on the E side suggest that the tower is older and reworked. Chancel roof of 1873. – FONT. Perp. Octagonal with pairs of cusped ovals, panelled beneath. – PULPIT. Early C17. Elaborate, with misunderstood Ionic columns (cf. Donyatt and Aller) and fluted frieze. Large ogee C18 TESTER. – SCREEN. C15, with good detail. Six two-light square-headed sections with fragile tracery paired across the intervening mullion as Tudor arches. The top tracery also delicately crosses the mullion. Renewed cove, original vine and leaf cornice with broad-winged angels. A stag, phoenix and barrel amid the plant motifs of the dado may identify the donor. – PAINTING. An exceptional survival of the boarded tympanum that filled the arch above the screen, no longer *in situ*. Late C15 Crucifixion with the two thieves, the Virgin and Mary Magdalene. Rustic figures. – REREDOS. 1873, by *Harry Hems*. Sumptuous. Alabaster with stone reliefs on gold mosaic. – TOWER RAILS. Wrought-iron lilies, 2003, by *James Blunt*, designed by *John Bucknall*. – STAINED GLASS. E window, 1880. – MONUMENTS. Robert Henley. †1614. A small theatrical wall monument of 1639, attributed to *Humphrey Moyer* (GF). Against black, a half-visible alabaster figure emerges, in grave-clothes (cf. Rodney Stoke (N)). Trumpeting cherub in the alabaster curved pediment. – Mary Royse †1742. Elegant, white and coloured marbles.

By the church, the former VICARAGE. Early C19 stucco to the front, but the N chimney-breast shows older origins. Going N, the SCHOOL, 1850, with small-paned lancets, and startlingly chequered pink-and-white JUBILEE HALL, 1887. Restored medieval VILLAGE CROSS outside the former GEORGE INN, early C19, roughcast. Up Fore Street, several thatched C16–C18 houses, LULLINGSTONE with an oak Tudor-arched doorway. Further on, the CONGREGATIONAL CHAPEL, 1811, hip-roofed with rusticated arched windows, once stuccoed. STUCKEY HOUSE, thatched, with a storeyed porch dated 1729, was a C15 hall house. One thin full cruck truss.

LEIGH HOUSE. 1 m. W. Sizeable mansion on the E-plan, built for Henry Henley in 1617 (dated rainwater heads). Two storeys and attic, mullioned windows in the wings, mullion-and-transom in the centre. Arched doorway. Gables with obelisk finials to the porch, to the bay on each side, and central to each wing. The courtyard is faced in local grey (Calcareous Grit) stone. Typical plan, with the hall to the l. of the screens passage and twin staircases central to each cross-wing. The cross-passage opens to additions and staircase of 1877. The hall is relatively low (cf. Montacute), with Tudor-arched fireplace and panelling. Early C18 panelling closes off a SW oriel chamber. The staircases are framed around four close-set pairs of full-height posts. Turned balusters. Good panelled SE parlour with arcaded dado and pilasters, the ribbed plaster ceiling in crosses of doubled elongated hexagons with flowers. Dining room N of the cross-passage with late C18 plaster ceiling: urns and musical instruments. The best room is the first-floor MUSIC ROOM, with a shallow curved C17 ceiling densely patterned in crosses of elongated hexagons within curvilinear patterns enclosing flowers. The end-wall drop motif with lion head appears also at Montacute. Late C18 cornice. Similar, more curvilinear, patterns in the porch-bay. S bedroom with C17 panelling and floral frieze. SE bedroom with C18 fielded panelling. The NE ground-floor room was fitted c. 1950 with elaborate panelling brought from Bath, probably Continental, covered in relief ornament with urns and profile heads. Imported Italian Renaissance chimneypiece with inserted C17–C18 marble plaques.

HEY FARMHOUSE, 1 m. E. A C15 house of status. The W end, presumably a solar, has cusped mullioned two-light windows on both floors and angle buttresses, but it is not clear that the E end was a hall. Moulded four-panel ceiling to the ground floor W, chamfered beams in the E room. Wind-braced roof.

WITHAM FRIARY

Site of the first English Carthusian priory, founded 1178–9.

ST MARY, ST JOHN BAPTIST AND ALL SAINTS. The Augustinian priory of Bruton built a chapel after 1142. It was enlarged and the walls thickened to take a ribbed vault, for lay brothers of the Carthusian priory (*see* below), probably under Hugh of Avalon (St Hugh of Lincoln), the first effective prior, 1179–86.* A single apsed vessel of three bays plus a W bay added in 1876 by *William White*, replacing a tower of 1828. To *White* is due the stern Northern French character, for he added the steep single roof sweeping around the apse, the acutely gabled W bellcote, and sturdy flying buttresses. Round-headed deeply splayed windows, the western ones *White*'s. E triple lancet of

---

*The first prior returned to France, the second died, and Hugh was the third.

Witham Friary, Witham Park, elevation.
Engraving by T. White, 1771

1860. Four bays of quadripartite vaulting. Chamfered ribs without bosses, on short corbelled shafts with polygonal capitals. *White* added the first bay and restored the second. Double PISCINA with shouldered heads. C15 N rood stair. – PULPIT. C17. Typical arched panels and feather angles. Vine-leaf cornice from a C15 screen. – FONT. Installed 1459, but surely C14. Plain octagon, tapered below. – ROYAL ARMS. 1660. – ORGAN. Red-painted C19 Gothic case, from Longbridge Deverill, Wilts. – STAINED GLASS. Medieval fragments on the N, in one window pieces from Burton Hall, Leics. – Four S windows by *Ninian Comper*, 1923, delicately drawn scenes from the life of St Hugh.

By the church, the former SCHOOL, 1838, with mullioned windows under thin lunettes. MANOR FARMHOUSE, reconstructed *c.* 1850, is on the site of the monastic grange, of which the DOVECOTE with diagonal buttresses remains, opposite, converted to a READING ROOM, 1900, by *Wallace Gill*. In the village are terraced C19 ESTATE COTTAGES with brick dressings built by the Dukes of Somerset, also the hip-roofed SEYMOUR ARMS of 1864–6.

WITHAM HOUSE, ¼ m. NE. Hip-roofed former vicarage of 1832.

WEST BARN GRANGE, 1 m. SE. Early C18 five-bay ashlar front raised on a basement, with a central open pediment on consoles. Doorcase with a narrow pulvinated frieze.

WITHAM HALL FARM, 1 m. NE. Mid-C19 hip-roofed farmhouse. Across the railway is the site of the CARTHUSIAN PRIORY founded in penitence for Becket's murder. Nothing is visible, and nothing of succeeding mansions. The monastic buildings became the seat of the Hopton family from 1544 to 1697. 'Part of Witham old mansion house' on a map of 1812 may be the Hopton house. *Vitruvius Britannicus*, vol. II, 1717, illustrates a major Baroque house for Sir William Wyndham, with a cupola over an inset giant portico. This was almost certainly never built. The design is attributed to *James Gibbs*. Sketches of *c.* 1702 for altering the old house, with a similar portico, by *William Talman*, may also not have been executed. The site was sold to Alderman William Beckford in 1761 who built anew further S. His house, by *Robert Adam*, illustrated in the fifth volume of *Vitruvius Britannicus* (1771), was finished but unfurnished when Beckford died in 1770, and was rapidly dismantled.

THE HERMITAGE, 2 m. S. Gothick cottage-villa of *c.* 1830 incorporating an older house. Canted bay window each side of a two-storey polygonal porch. Cusped-headed mullioned windows. LIBRARY, 2000, for himself by *Michael Franses*, resembling a Tudor Gothic barn, in stone and brick.

WITHIEL FLOREY

ST MARY. In the Brendon Hills, alone by Castle Hill Farm. Small and roughcast, yellow-washed. The simple w tower may be C13 in its lower half: low diagonal buttresses, w lancet (renewed), low chamfered tower arch. The nave windows are C19, though the curved-headed doorway could be Norman. Porch dated 1695. Chancel rebuilt 1882. Early C19 curved nave ceiling. – FONT. C12–C13. Shallow bowl with a roll moulding above a splayed stem. – BENCHES. C19, in Somerset C16 style. – STAINED GLASS. Chancel, after 1882, by *A. L. Moore*. – MONUMENT. James Bryant †1780. Pediment on pilasters, between scrolls mutating into palm leaves.

WITHYCOMBE

ST NICHOLAS. One of those Somerset churches without Perp enlargement. All white render. Very square s porch-tower, simple as a child's drawing. This is C13 – see the outer doorway and the tiny bell-openings. So is the double-chamfered s doorway. The nave windows are Perp apart from one Dec two-light, l. of the tower. C13–C14 chancel – see the s wall lancet and blocked chamfered doorway with ogee head inside, these earlier than the Dec two-light window to the l., and the three-light reticulated E window. Interior stripped of plaster. Plain pointed chancel arch. Nave ceiling of arch-braced rafters, chancel with pointed wagon roof, the panels doubled over the sanctuary.

FURNISHINGS. FONT. Stately Norman bowl of fourteen panels between thin ribs. Cable moulding below. Circular stem with spurs. – SCREEN. C15–C16, of the local (Carhampton, Dunster, Minehead) type. Five bays, with sub-arched four-light tracery in leaf-scroll borders. Rib-vaulted loft with blind tracery in the panels, and four carved friezes. The dado panels have spandrel rosettes as at Carhampton. – BEAM. At the w end. A C14 head beam with vine-trail emerging from the heads of a king, a lion and a leper. – STATUE. St Nicholas, 1989, by *Rachel Reckitt*. Beaten metal strip with some colour, endearingly eccentric. – MONUMENTS. Two Ham stone C14 effigies with clasped hands holding hearts. Below a Perp N window which must have replaced the arch of the tomb-recess, a lady of the early C14 (similar to one at Limington). She is flanked by two exceptionally rare stone SCONCES or candleholders, of similar date but not necessarily intended for here. They have plain castellated tops on square capitals thickly ornamented with naturalistic foliage emerging from human or animal heads, and short octagonal shafts broached from square. In the s wall, under a low recess, a mid-C14 civilian, much eroded.

In the centre of the village a stone MILL, rebuilt c. 1800, overlooks a ford. At the s edge, COURT PLACE, with a long rendered front, lateral chimney and hip-roofed storeyed porch. An oratory is recorded here in 1449. Just N, COURT PLACE COTTAGES, by *Louise Crossman*, 2009, the boarded front cleverly, not slavishly, barn-like.

SANDHILL FARMHOUSE, ½ m. E. A late medieval hall house, altered in the late C16, dated 1586 on the cross-passage partition. A long s front with a central storeyed porch between a tall E cross-wing and an added SW projection. The cross-wing is late C16, with an eastward projection and oak-mullioned windows.

COMBE FARM, ¾ m. SW. Whitewashed roughcast, grown by accretion. Ground-floor plaster overmantel, dated 1629 in an oval strapwork cartouche with initials. Naked figures on the side scrolls and fat fruit relate it to *Robert Eaton* of Stogursey.

WITHYPOOL

ST ANDREW. All very rebuilt, the short W tower in 1902, the nave and chancel restored in 1885–7. The tower has older masonry in the base of the N side, a C13 foliated cross-slab reused in the NW buttress. The round tower arch with its misinterpreted Perp detail looks C17 rather than C20. Whitewashed Perp N arcade of three bays, the piers of four-hollow type, but each with a thin continuous ring instead of capitals. – FONT. Norman, the bowl with vigorous large flutings beneath a band of broad chevron. Short round stem and moulded round base. – MONUMENT. Dorothy Adams †1804. Incised Lias with some colour.

Restored C15 CHURCHYARD CROSS.

BARLE BRIDGE. Of six segmental arches divided by shallow piers, probably C17.

LANDACRE BRIDGE, 2 m. W. Five pointed arches between cutwaters. Probably medieval, recorded in 1610.

STONE CIRCLE, 1 m. SSW, at a height of 1,250 ft (380 metres). A Bronze Age stone circle with about twenty-nine stones surviving. Like other Exmoor stone monuments most of the stones are very small, with four larger ones.

WIVELISCOMBE

Hilltop market town on the old Barnstaple road, of Anglo-Saxon origin. Georgian prosperity from cloth, Victorian from brewing. Mixed building materials, red sandstone, stucco and brick.

ST ANDREW. A notably ambitious rebuilding of 1827–9 by *Richard Carver*, Gothic within classical conventions. Red sandstone, originally roughcast; a much grander version of Carver's Theale church, 1826. Four symmetrical fronts between narrow corner towers. Each face has a centrepiece: on the N a wider window, on the S a three-bay schoolroom (and wider centre window), on the E a broad canted bay, and on the W the tower. Brick-vaulted catacombs appear as a basement under the E end. The tracery is remarkably good, some of it reused Perp. The tower has set-back buttresses and battlements, the date showing in large lower windows, the doorway, and the triple-lancet bell-openings. E rose window of 1915 by *F. Bligh Bond*, in a French Rayonnant style quite different to Carver's Perp.

Broad, light interior, lit from a clerestory. Ham stone arcades of five bays of depressed four-centred arches in a simplified Somerset Perp style. Similar arch to the apse, which has a ribbed plaster vault. Framed nave ceiling. Gothic WEST GALLERY, signed by *Carver*, with Hanoverian ROYAL ARMS. A chancel re-fitting of 1872 by *Giles & Gane* was obliterated by PANELLING of 1915 with reused late medieval pieces. – FONT. C12–C13, octagonal. Edwardian spired cover from St James, Taunton. – BOX PEWS. 1829. – PULPIT and STALLS. 1967–9 by *Michael Torrens*; the pulpit twelve-sided on a concrete stalk, with reused panels. – COMMUNION RAILS. Two sets, both Continental, early C18, introduced in 1935. Curved chancel rails from a war-damaged church in Flanders. Bulbous balusters to the SE chapel. – STAINED GLASS. Medieval fragments in the Lady Chapel. Chancel, 1915, by *Alice Erskine*. Patron saints of Britain and Ireland, in striking Arts and Crafts colours. Three N windows, 1887–93, by *Clayton & Bell*. NW and SE, 1916 and 1923, by *Kempe & Co*. S aisle, 1860s glass from the chancel. – MONUMENTS. Humphrey Wyndham †1622 and wife. Of Somerset alabaster. Effigies of some quality, detached from the back, which is double-arched with Corinthian columns and a rich heraldic top. The inscription records her healing powers. – Sir William Yea †1806. Long plaque with urn, by *Robert Shout*.

CHURCHYARD CROSS. C14–C15, the shaft with an extremely eroded figure under a crocketed canopy.

The former CHURCH SCHOOL, NW of the church, has a barrack-like wing of 1842 added to a house which may be C16 (see the narrow W stair-turret). But the two-storey S bay, with C16–C17 mullion-and-transom windows, is apparently reused from a house that Buckler illustrated in 1837. This stood SE of the churchyard, on the site of an early C14 palace of Bishop Drokensford of Wells, of which only an ARCHWAY survives, between later cottages. Segmental-pointed arch with a continuous double chamfer.

ST RICHARD (R.C.), Church Street. 1967, by *Ivor Day & O'Brien*. Low asymmetrical roof on concrete trusses.

CONGREGATIONAL CHURCH, Silver Street. 1708, enlarged in 1825. Roughcast with red sandstone dressings. The doorway with its segmental arch is clearly of the first date, the arched windows of the second. Panelled gallery of 1825, and an iron-railed side gallery of 1876. The SCHOOLROOM across a narrow cobbled yard has arched Y-tracery windows on the first floor, apparently early C19, but actually of 1857.

KINGSMEAD SCHOOL, South Street. 1953, by *Leonard Mew* of *Somerset County Architects*. Unusual among Somerset schools, it was intended as a 'village college' on the Cambridgeshire model, housing also community activities. Buff brick. Flat-roofed classroom wings of uneven length flank a higher theatre block with cinema-like curved front between concave walls of patterned brickwork, and a false hipped roof. South Block, 2006, and Science Block, 2012–13, both by *Mark Richmond Architects*. Buff brick and render.

PRIMARY SCHOOL, North Street. 1875–6, by *J. H. Spencer*. Long and Gothic, nearly symmetrical between gabled wings. Extended in 1904.

PERAMBULATION. The centre is THE SQUARE, with the TOWN HALL in the centre of the long s side. This is by *Carver*, 1841–2, for Lord Ashburton. Buff brick, with arched upper windows under a deep bracketed pediment and square bellcote. The ground floor has lost a projecting colonnade and the single-storey wings are horribly altered. Down NORTH STREET, a large mullion-windowed former POLICE STATION, 1858, extended in 1899, before the primary school (*see* above). Returning to the Square, on WEST STREET, No. 5, stuccoed, has a Greek Doric porch. Further on, JONES GARAGE, 1930, is neatly done, with pedimented lunette on a hipped roof. E of the square, facing down High Street, is COURT HOUSE, a pretty composition of 1881 in the Norman Shaw style, built as the house and bank of William Hancock, brewer. Tile-hung with oak oriel windows, the Gothic woodcarving especially lively. The chamfered sandstone arch to the r. is reused medieval. Inside, a romantic Gothic stair hall galleried on two levels.

Before descending the High Street, an excursion E along SILVER STREET. Here are a well-detailed stone and half-timber former READING ROOM, 1887, by *T. W. F. Newton*, who made his career in Birmingham but came from Wiveliscombe, and the Congregational church (*see* above). The summit to the r. is crowned by the remains of HANCOCK'S BREWERY, once the largest of the region. Altered stone buildings and a bright red brick hip-roofed malting tower of 1897. No. 1 Golden Hill, *c.* 1860, was the brewery office, red sandstone, ecclesiastical, originally with a bellcote. Is the gable tracery reused? Down Golden Hill are narrow three-storey early C19 tenements, Nos. 14–24, proposed for clearance in 1974, rescued in an early conservation scheme.

HIGH STREET descends S with a good mixture of houses. No. 1, externally Early Victorian, but in the C18 the Fountain Inn, has an early C18 first-floor ceiling of two long panels with thickly detailed floral garlands, shells and cherub heads. Similar plaster at Fitzhead Court (q.v.). No. 2, opposite, painted brick, Late Georgian, was the Lion Hotel, identified by an oval plaque by *John Alder*, from an admirable scheme of 2003 identifying lost inns with plaques by local artists. No. 6, of brick, five bays, has slightly curved first-floor window heads and depressed arched doorways, early C18 rather than the supposed date of 1693. Nos. 7–9 is late C18, rubble stone. The 1804 in wooden numerals in the fanlight marks the foundation here of the Wiveliscombe Dispensary. No. 17 is early C19, three-storeyed, roughcast.

There was a T-junction at the foot of High Street before Croft Way was cut through as a by-pass. Church Street is still the main road E. SOUTH STREET continues High Street downhill. Mullion-windowed former VICARAGE, 1845–6, by *Samuel Pollard*, on the corner, and a lancet-Gothic former METHODIST CHAPEL, 1845, further down, before Kingsmead School (*see* above). CHURCH STREET begins with terraced rows. Nos. 2–4, deep-eaved, Late Georgian, was the Anchor Inn, the plaque here by *Joanna Dewfall*. Another plaque on No. 18, by *Bronwen Gwillim*. Opposite the church (*see* p. 705), BRAYNES, red sandstone with hip-roofed wings, is of *c.* 1700, the centre with its porch remodelled *c.* 1800. One room has early C18 fluted pilasters and ceiling plaster. Further E, BOURNES, with a storeyed gabled porch and C19 sash windows, is C16, associated with Bishop Gilbert Bourne †1569. Four-centred-arched back doorway and partitions inside. Rear wing with a plaster ceiling by the same hand as at Gaulden Manor, Tolland, *c.* 1640. Naïvely modelled Venus and cherub, with a riband inscribed 'Sine Cerere et Baccho friget Venus' (Without bread and wine, love freezes), in a double oval of fruit and flowers. Further out, the R.C. church (*see* p. 705) and a former STATION of the Devon & Somerset Railway, 1871, economical brick.

ABBOTSFIELD, ½ m. W. 1870–3, by *Owen Jones* for Charles Lukey Collard, of the piano-manufacturing dynasty that originated in Wiveliscombe. The strange rambling red stone house, of a single storey with attics, is planned around a stark pyramid-roofed three-storey tower. The tale that a first floor was omitted, which might explain so disappointing a design by an architect of advanced ideas, appears to be myth. Abbotsfield is just mixed in its elements and put together without much taste. Pale stone mullion-and-transom windows and odd Greek gable ornaments. The garden front has an arcaded stone loggia between gables, suggesting a grand Anglo-Indian bungalow. The near-detached SW music room and a fragment of the huge conservatory recall the musical life here. Wagner reputedly visited and Adelina Patti certainly sang here. Subdivided interiors. Matching LODGE, after 1897, i.e. not by Jones.

FORD, ½ m. NE. FORD HOUSE, 1799, for the Hancock family, is a plain three-storey block with tripartite outer windows. Bay windows of 1889. Just N, FORD FARM is C16–C17, attached to a three-storey early C19 MALTHOUSE. SE of Ford House, at CASTLE ROCKS FARM, three monumental early to mid-C19 LIMEKILNS are built into the end of Castle Hill. This is crowned by KING'S CASTLE, an Iron Age hillfort. Ramparts defended the whole crest of the hill, but they are eaten away by quarrying.

MANOR FARM, ½ m. E. Large Ashburton estate farmhouse of c. 1840, with bargeboards, probably by *Carver*. Across the fields, SSW, the rectangular earthworks of Nunnington Camp were a small ROMAN FORT, 140 by 110 yds (130 by 100 metres), dated to the C1.

WOODLANDS

ST KATHARINE, East Woodlands, on the edge of the Longleat woods. Built by Thomas, Viscount Weymouth, in 1712–14, possibly in tribute to Bishop Ken of Bath and Wells †1711. The W tower remains, with two orders of sturdy Tuscan angle pilasters carrying cornices: a piece of early C18 classicism, but not entirely classical, for the octagonal spire and Gothic corner pinnacles appear to be of the same date. *C. E. Giles* made plans in 1870 for a complete rebuilding, but only the chancel and vestry could be afforded. The nave and aisles were then rebuilt in 1879–81 by *J. L. Pearson*, modifying Giles's plans for economy. Pearson retained the tower, to which he added the neat round NE stair-turret and the intrusively neo-Jacobean bell-lights and W window. The rest of the church is well detailed and finished in late C13 to early C14 style. Pale stone banded with Greensand. Ashlar-lined interior with rafter roofs, arcades on octagonal piers, and a chancel arch on short corbelled shafts. The more expensive details are *Giles*'s: shafted E window, corner piscina, and REREDOS with painted Nativity and angels. Minton TILES of 1846–7, from Frome church. – FONT. Octagonal, with foliage crosses in quatrefoils; C14, retooled? – PULPIT. Early to mid-C18, with delicate monograms above fielded panels and floral angles. Similar pulpit at Kingston St Mary (q.v.). – SCREEN. 1871. Low stone wall. RAILINGS and GATES of 1919. – COMMUNION RAILS. Cast bronze uprights with grapes or roses, c. 1913. Probably by *Singer* of Frome. – STAINED GLASS. E window, 1877, fading but good.

Opposite the church, the Tudor-style former SCHOOL, 1835. Built by *William Brown* of Frome, apparently to a design by *Sir Jeffry Wyatville*. Further back, the OLD RECTORY is of 1856–8, by *Giles*. Picturesque, with banded fish-scale tiles and a profusion of angular Gothic forms. Porch and a stair projection at right angles; triple-gabled garden front, with triple lancets. N of the church, NEW CHURCH FARM is mansard-roofed, c. 1800.

MANOR FARM, West Woodlands. Late C16. A two-gabled, three-bay asymmetrical front with reserved-chamfer mullions and a moulded doorway. Gabled stair-tower behind.

ST ALGAR'S FARM, 1½ m. SSW. C17 and C19 gabled front, but the rear range is medieval. The wagon roof of a domestic chapel (tree-ring-dated to the 1490s) survives in part, the eastern end replaced after fire. In line are older collar-trusses of the hall.

GRANDON MANOR, 1½ m. NNE. Hip-roofed house with cross-windows, mostly of wood, a few of stone, under drip-courses. Five by two bays. Dated 1679 over the rear door and 1671 over an upstairs fireplace. The rear wing may be partly C15. (Staircase with finials and pendants to the newels and turned balusters.)

RODDENBURY CAMP, ½ m. ESE. An Iron Age hillfort on the end of a spur with impressive ramparts running across the hill. The camp is oval, 150 yds (137 metres) long and 75 yds (69 metres) wide. The interior has been disturbed by sand-digging. Below is HALES CASTLE, a circular ringwork, 40 yds (37 metres) in diameter, with traces of an attached bailey, which suggest a Norman date.

WOOKEY

ST MATTHEW. Mostly Perp, but with a late C13 three-light E window of stepped cusped lancets. The chancel was in disrepair in 1423, and there is much of the early C15 including the tower. This has ashlar diagonal buttresses, and a big sub-arched four-light W window over a doorway with thin inset shafts. Corner pinnacles and tall octagonal spirelet, this rebuilt in 1906. The S porch doorway resembles the tower arch, wave-moulded on fat shafts. Low-pitched roof over nave and aisles, without battlements. Plain two-light windows. Steep-roofed SE chapel added for the burial of Thomas Clerke †1555, brother of the Marian Bishop of Wells. It has two reused C15 S windows, but the large flat-headed four-light window is C16. Inside, wave mouldings predominate: on the tower arch, the low chancel arch and the high arcades. Two phases are discernible. The earlier phase, of the late C14, comprises the flat-faced responds of the N arcade, and the chancel arch. This work is of Chilcote stone whereas the arcades are of Doulting. The rest of the N arcade was replaced when the S arcade was built in the C15. Both arcades have shafted piers, but the N capitals echo the original responds whereas the S capitals are typical C15. The SE chapel is still Perp, although the detail is handled badly, the inner order of the arches ill-matched to the piers. Capitals left uncarved. C15 nave and aisle roofs, the nave tie-beams on timber brackets with foliage and dragons. Chancel roof of 1871–2 by *Giles & Gane*.

FURNISHINGS. FONT. C12–C13 bulbous bowl, ringed at top and bottom. C13 base. – RAILS. SE chapel. 1635. – REREDOS. 1871. Very Gothic, with incised marble panels. – ROYAL ARMS. 1837. – TOWER GALLERY. 1902. – STAINED GLASS. E window, 1871, by *Henry Holiday* for *Powell's*. In the SE chapel, E window, 1903, by *Hemming*, and two S windows, one very pretty with

C15-style Evangelists on patterned quarries, the other, C16 style, 1874, probably by *Lavers, Barraud & Westlake*. By them two N aisle windows, 1871 and 1882. – MONUMENTS. Thomas Clerke †1555. Large Perp tomb-chest with three shields in quatrefoils on each side, one in an octofoil each end. No effigy, just an inscription around an inset Purbeck marble slab. Could it be reused C15? – Julian Trym †1667. Thickly detailed, with heraldry in a broken curved pediment. – Frances Salmon †1776. Tall, open-pedimented, yellow and white. – In the tower: Peirs family to 1729. Rustic, with six moon-faced angel heads, charmingly coloured. Also two elegant Neoclassical urns by *Thomas King* to Sir Jacob Wolff †1809 and his wife †1815.

CHURCHYARD CROSS restored in 1906 by *Harry Hems*, the base C14–C15 with Passion emblems. – Granite Celtic CROSS to E. M. Alexander †1915, well detailed, by *Mossman* of Glasgow. – LYCHGATE, by *F. B. Bond*, 1915. Rather Viking. Long-roofed, with masks on the beam-ends.

The village curves pleasantly around the medieval episcopal estate, now divided between Mellifont Abbey and Court Farm (*see* below). YEW TREE FARM has thin early C15 full crucks. LITTLE COURT, further W, 2013–14, by *John Winstone*, hip-roofed and weatherboarded.

MELLIFONT ABBEY. The medieval rectory (of which a two-bay roof survives behind) was rebuilt in Georgian Gothic, at an uncertain date. According to the historian William Phelps, who lived here in the 1820s, Colonel Peirs, M.P. for Wells, built it *c.* 1730. But it was called 'late new-built' in 1783, and the name, from the Irish abbey, only appears *c.* 1800. Battlemented eight-bay W front with pointed windows and a tower that is central if the canted S end is included. Plain brick window surrounds and string courses suggest that the house was originally stuccoed, apart from the three-storey porch-tower. Here the lower stages are of red brick laid to a strange indented chequer, with banded diagonal buttresses. It evokes late medieval brick gatehouses. John Winstone points to William Kent's reworking of Wayneflete's Tower at Esher Place, Surrey, *c.* 1733, for Henry Pelham, to whom Peirs was politically connected. Pointed rusticated ground-floor arches. Above, undersized niches flank a handsome C15 stone oriel with Muchelney-type tracery of ogee-headed lights and spandrel quatrefoils, brought perhaps from Wells. The extent of imported medieval material betokens a serious Gothicism. The top stage, of stone, with brick pedimented niches and a cusped roundel, incorporates the most important medieval pieces: ten early C13 cusped spandrels depicting mermaids, mermen, fish and monkeys; also a saint. They may come from Bishop Jocelyn's residence at Court Farm (*see* below), but similar spandrels are known from Wells Cathedral, originating from the demolished cloisters of *c.* 1200–25 and the adjacent Lady Chapel. There are also reused corbels, those l. of the tower particularly lively.

The interiors, however, are consistent to one period, and the staircase points to later in the C18 than the 1730s. The front door and those in the entrance hall have timber Gothick surrounds:

pointed crocketed arches between piers with steep triangular finials, the front doorway elaborated with side-lights and stellar fanlight tracery. The narrow open-well stair has Chinese Chippendale balustrades under an octagonal dome with Gothick plasterwork. First-floor doorway like those of the hallway.

COURT FARM. Still rural, although within the village. It incorporates remnants of a favourite palace of the Bishops of Wells, built by Bishop Jocelyn (1206–46) who 'nobiliter construit capellas cum camariis de Wellys et Woky'. There was a courtyard, with Great Hall and chamber block on the W side, linked by a N cloister to a narrow E gatehouse range from which projected a chapel. Hall and chapel have largely gone, and the cloister was rebuilt as a parlour range in the late C15, not of particular quality. Plain three-light ground-floor windows with uncusped pointed lights. Ashlar porch of c. 1840. The W wall is a fragment of the Great Hall, the broken end projecting slightly being the jamb of a C13 window. A pointed doorway survives within. Both ground-floor rooms have rear-wall fireplaces. In the W room also a moulded six-panel ceiling and evidence of a NW winding stair. The narrow E cross-wing contains the outstanding survival, the chapel doorway of c. 1225, clearly the work of Jocelyn's cathedral masons. A pointed arch of three rolls frames a chamfered doorway. Nook-shafts have gone and the capitals are damaged apart from fine top moulding of two rolls of polished Blue Lias.

EAST COURT, Doctor's Hill. Stately brick house of five bays and three storeys. Parapet, cornice and ashlar band. Doorway with pediment on brackets. Although quoin pilasters suggest the first half of the C18, rainwater heads are dated 1773. The hall and staircase confirm the date. Matching single-bay, single-storey wings, the r. wing raised a storey.

BURCOTT, ¼ m. SE. Around 1860 Edward Freeman, the historian, bought SOMERLEAZE, a villa of 1794 with a three-bay front. The shallow-curved outer bays look original, the broader projecting centre early to mid-C19, with a mullion-and-transom window added presumably for Freeman. He rebuilt BURCOTT MILL in 1864 alongside the original mill of 1750, which was refaced to match. Internal wheel. Just S, BURCOTT HOUSE FARM has a tall early C17 gable with stone mullions.

FENNY CASTLE, 1½ m. SW, on the edge of the wetlands. A natural hillock, scarped to form an undocumented motte-and-bailey castle. Opposite Castle Farm, the base of a C15 WAYSIDE CROSS.

WOOKEY HOLE. See Somerset: North and Bristol.

WOOLAVINGTON

3040

ST MARY. Blue Lias, much refaced. Three-stage W tower with Perp bell-stage and C17 battlements. The tower poses several problems. On the W face is the line of a low-pitched roof, so there was a building to the W. The bottom stage has heavy angle buttresses and inside are heavy triple-chamfered arches on all four sides, those to the N and S somewhat squeezed. The E arch opens to the nave, the rest are blocked with no exterior sign of their existence. They suggest an intended cruciform church with the present nave as the chancel. But this cannot be. The arches with their continuous moulding date the tower to *c.* 1300. The roof mark on the W front is characteristic of the late medieval period and unlikely to represent a lost nave. A Norman triangular-headed N doorway in the present nave allows a date for the nave earlier than that of the tower. The chancel and N transept are roughly contemporary with the tower, from the double-chamfered chancel arch and triple lancet windows (if these are reliable). So was the project something quite different, the arches within the tower never intended to be opened? The tower at Aller is similarly arranged, and similarly inexplicable. Perp S porch, big nave S window breaking the eaves, and E window. Nave plastered barrel ceiling of 1936. In the transept a cusped C13–C14 PISCINA. – FONT. Octagonal, Perp, with pointed quatrefoils. – PULPIT. Oak. Reusing three pairs of long Perp panels, mostly tracery, some plant-scroll. – SCULPTURE. On a window sill, a fine C13–C14 Lias head of a priest from an effigy. – MONUMENT. Jeanes family, 1767. Pedimented, against an obelisk.

In Church Street, Nos. 8–10, the former VICARAGE, 1807, by *Daniel Carver* (father of Richard), with a mansard roof. W of the church, No. 4 Lower Road is dated 1734, still with mullioned windows. The near-symmetry of their arrangement and the near-continuous drip-course make the late date credible. Further on, THE GRANGE has C17 wooden mullion windows. Behind it (reached from Higher Road) is a thatched circular COCKPIT, windowless and buttressed, perhaps formed from a dovecote. There would have been a gallery inside. The village was much enlarged after 1941 for munitions workers at the Puriton factory.

WOOTTON COURTENAY

ALL SAINTS. Red sandstone. C13 tower, similar to that at Luxborough, with low diagonal buttresses and paired tiny bell-lights. The top with its saddleback roof is of 1866–7 by *Edward Ashworth*, but the corbel tables N and S are original. Unmoulded tower arch. C13 chancel, datable from the over-restored three stepped E lancets. The nave and gabled N aisle are mid-C15. Around 1530 the S side of the nave and E end of the aisle were provided with those large and elegant transomed windows with quatrefoil spandrels beneath the transom typical of the region W of Cleeve Abbey. Handsome angels and animals as hoodmould stops outside and inside. C19 S porch. Inside, a square pillar STOUP with a quatrefoil panel. The arcade piers have standard four-wave mouldings with small round capitals to the shafts. Both piers have big canopied statue niches towards the nave, an ostentatious feature (cf. St Mary Magdalene, Taunton). Ceiled wagon roofs in the nave and aisle. The aisle bosses are especially big (cf. Selworthy, Luccombe) and include the Signs of the Evangelists, St George, animals, etc. – FONT. Octagonal, Perp, with quatrefoil panels ornamented with alternate foliage and shields. Quatrefoils and shields also on the underside. – SCREEN. 1911, reputedly carved locally. If so, of remarkable skill. Similar frontals to the STALLS. – REREDOS, NE chapel. 1943. Beautifully painted in Book of Hours style, by *Christopher Webb*, for F. C. Eeles, first secretary of the Council for the Care of Churches, who also had Victorian chancel fittings removed. – STAINED GLASS. 1866–7 by *Hardman*, the NE window especially good.

The OLD RECTORY, remodelled in 1809 by *William Horn* of Minehead, has a C16 wind-braced roof. Downhill to the S, C16–C17 thatched cottages, including BRIDGE COTTAGE with two lateral chimneys on the back, and HIGHPARK with a large stone end chimney.

BURROW FARM, 1 m. S. An extended thatched farmhouse of cross-wings added to a C17 core. Across the farmyard, the cob and rubble BARN began as a C15 house. Oak-mullioned windows, the end-wall four-light window best preserved, with trefoil-headed lights. Fire-damaged *c.* 2003.

FAIRGARDEN FARMHOUSE, 1 m. SSW. An altered longhouse with late C15 smoke-blackened roof at the centre.

WOOTTON LODGE, 1 m. E. 1925–6, by *Stone & Francis*. Butterfly-plan house, of stone with render above, originally thatched, and subsequently extended. Circular terrace below, geometrically paved. CLOUDS, opposite the drive, also of 1925 by *Stone & Francis*, is contrastingly formal, Cape Dutch in style, stuccoed with a shaped central gable and steep hipped roof of silvery slates.

WRANTAGE
North Curry

One massive abutment remains of the AQUEDUCT of the 1836–42 Chard Canal (*Sydney Hall*, engineer). An inclined plane, a feature of this remarkable canal, climbed SE to the 1,800-yd (1,650-metre) CRIMSON HILL TUNNEL. Tub-boats of standard 26-ft (8-metre) length were floated into a caisson and then drawn up by the counterweight of the descending water-filled caisson. STOP LINE DEFENCES of 1940 from the portal to the summit. The CANAL INN has a C16–C17 moulded framed ceiling. WEAVER'S FARMHOUSE, just NE, is C15, with a C16 moulded framed ceiling. Moulded brattished bressumer.

LILLESDON COURT, 1 m. N. Medieval site, a chapel recorded in 1317. Early C16 mullion-windowed house, with Late Georgian pedimented doorcase and Victorian roof. Two Tudor-arched doorways inside, one blocked. Early C19 dividing stair.

NEWPORT, 1 m. NE, is a failed borough, granted a market in 1206.

WYKE CHAMPFLOWER

HOLY TRINITY. 1623–4. Attached to the back of the Manor House like a private chapel, such that the bellcote appears over the house and the church porch has a domestic room above. Three-light windows still in the Perp tradition, straight-headed to the sides, stepped at the E under an arch, all with cusped lights and hoodmoulds. The bell-turret is a miniature tower with crenellation and pinnacles. Lovely interior, carefully restored by *Martin Travers*, 1943. The flattened wagon roof has shields at the intersections of moulded ribs. Royal arms of Elizabeth and Henry VIII in the W corners. These answer to those of James I, flamboyantly painted between the shields of Wells and Canterbury on the TYMPANUM that marks off the chancel. E wall with plaques inscribed 'Domus Mea' and 'Domus Orationis'. – C17 BOX PEWS with acorns, chancel PANELLING and ALTAR TABLE. – Remarkable PULPIT, like that at Wells Cathedral, the scale and assembly suggesting that it was intended for somewhere grander. Beer stone. Strapwork piers, vigorous undercut foliage in the frieze. – FONT. By *Travers*, 1943. C17 ogee COVER. – REREDOS. A Crucifix fixed by *Travers* to a Georgian Commandment board. – STAINED GLASS. Fragments. Prince of Wales feathers and the arms of Elizabeth of Bohemia. – MONUMENT. Henry Southworth †1625, builder of the church. A fine piece, of alabaster, with black-shafted Corinthian columns and broken curved pediment.

The MANOR HOUSE has a low irregular front with late C16 recessed-chamfered mullion windows. Early C19 hip-roofed S front with Tudor detail. To the S are WYKE HOUSE, Late Georgian, ashlar-fronted, with parapet, and a late medieval BRIDGE of two narrow pointed narrow arches.

YARLINGTON

ST MARY. The squat transeptal S tower has a Perp bell-stage but is much older. A broad round arch inside may indicate that the tower replaces an C11–C12 transept. Nave rebuilt and N aisle added 1877–8 by *J. Arthur Reeve*, clearly influenced by William

Burges. Early French tracery, a rose window at the W. The chancel, all but rebuilt, was C14 – see the boldly cusped tomb-recess. Good Victorian interior, strong and not fussy. Boarded nave roof with kingposts on tie-beams. Arcade on a sturdy quatrefoil pier, and coloured chancel arch shafts. – FONT. Perp, with quatrefoils, and simple tracery on the chamfered angles. – PAINTING. King David. Early C19, from the gallery. – REREDOS. By *Powell's*, 1921. Sweet tile-mosaic Annunciation on blue. Two similar Rogers family MONUMENTS, a St George and a laurel-bordered plaque.

YARLINGTON LODGE, above the village, was the rectory. 1827–8, hip-roofed, ashlar-faced, with thin Tudor detail.

YARLINGTON HOUSE, ¾ m. SE. 1782–5 for John Rogers. E front of three broad bays with pedimented centre and parapet. Brick with elegant, sparing ashlar detail: the cornice, a sill course, and a Venetian window on each side of a Tuscan-columned doorway with rosettes between the triglyphs of the frieze. Plain five-bay S front, extended to nine bays in 1912 by *W. H. Boney* of Highgate. Delicate curving cantilevered timber staircase, top-lit.

YEOVIL

5010

Until the later C18 Yeovil was small, comprising the church enclosure (a probable Anglo-Saxon minster precinct) off the market place, from which a street ran E between converging back streets. A cattle market W of the churchyard completed the rough triangle. There were a few suburban houses. Growth from C19 glove-making and C20 engineering – aircraft from 1915, helicopters from 1948 – has expanded the town greatly N and W, the SE still enclosed by hills. The characteristic Yeovil stone is pale and friable.

CHURCHES

ST JOHN BAPTIST, Church Street. A major church of a single harmonious later C14 design, attributed to *William Wynford* from similarities to his work at New College Oxford, Windsor Castle, and Winchester College. It is in this overall unity exceptional amid Somerset churches, and in the emphasis of window over wall a radical pioneer. Robert de Sambourne (†1382), canon of Wells, rector from 1362, left money 'to the works of Yeovil church begun by me'. The church replaces one probably sited just W, of which a portion called The Chantry survived next to the tower until 1854–5, when it was reconstructed outside the churchyard (*see* p. 720). Yeovil stone with Ham stone dressings. Aisled nave and chancel of even height, and transepts each with an octagonal stair-turret on the outer eastern corner. Four-bay nave aisles, then transepts, then two-bay

25

chancel chapels before the chancel projects a further one and half bays, raised on a crypt, to a total length of 144 ft (44 metres). The width across the transepts is 80 ft (24.4 metres), the height of the W tower 92 ft (28 metres). The Early Perp date is noticeable in the use of parapets with blind arcading (N parapets plain) and in the severity of the tower with which the work finished around 1400. Large five-light windows with panel tracery fill each bay between buttresses (once pinnacled). The tracery is not fanciful; cusped and without sub-panels, except in the principal transept and eastern windows. The setting out of the church, David Martyn has shown, follows careful geometries in ground plan and elevations. The square within the circle (*ad quadratum*) and geometries developed from the triangle within the circle (*ad triangulum*) are both used. The main body of the church, its extended plan including transepts, tower and chancel, and the width and rhythm of the nave bays, correspond to the *ad triangulum* system, while the setting out of the aisles and the elevations use the *ad quadratum* technique. The central setting-out point corresponds with a demonic head carved on one of the nave roof bosses.

The four-stage tower has plenty of bare wall, strong set-back buttresses, not yet the thin later ones, a stair-turret between the NW buttresses (cf. Wells St Cuthbert (N), Martock, and Queen Camel), and a parapet with pierced arcading but without pinnacles. Large five-light W window, and on both upper stages a large two-light opening each side, all with the refinement of tiny shafts in the embrasures. The tower arch is also refined, of triple shafts with leaf capitals and a thin intermediate shaft. Restoration by *R. H. Shout* in 1859–60. Work in the 1890s (S porch renewed and vaulted; NE organ-chamber) and 1914–15 (NE vestry by *W. D. Caröe*).

The interior is high and light despite having no clerestory, a single great vessel interrupted only by the chancel arch. The arcades are uniform, five bays to the nave, two to the eastern chapels, with shafted piers of standard four-hollow section. Indeed the detail of the church is notably restrained, a framework to the great windows. One wayward detail is the way in which in each transept the descending moulding curves over the stair doorway. The roof, of striking simplicity, has ridge bosses only, including several broad faces. The framed aisle ceilings have very many bosses, mostly foliage but also faces. The oddly African devil masks in the corners are exceptional, and may relate to medieval religious plays. E end enriched in 1860 with niches, tiles, etc., and in 1897 with statues. Two apparently reused elements are the king and queen heads that supported the Lenten veil and the crocketed early C14 ogee-arched doorway to the CRYPT, double-cusped between pinnacled piers. The stairs are covered by a miniature rib-vault on tiny heads, with a comparatively massive foliage boss. Pevsner thought the crypt early C14, but a date after 1362 would better fit the history, and there are similar vaults at New College Oxford, and Windsor Castle. A crypt was necessary because the new church was pushed to the edge of the sloping site. It has a central octagonal pier with moulded capital carrying four quadripartite vaults with heavy chamfered ribs. The ribs rest on corbels with ring-moulded capitals, a C13 type, possibly reused.

FURNISHINGS. FONT. Large, octagonal, Perp, with quatrefoil frieze and cresting (cf. Mudford). – LECTERN. Brass. An important piece of c. 1450–80, from the Meuse region. Two-sided book-rest with a large finial, on a round shaft and heavy moulded base with lion feet. Engraved demi-figure of a monk, named as Frater Martinus Forester. Bought in London in 1541; the parish paid 2d. to have Forester's face erased in 1565. – STAINED GLASS. A fine series by *Hardman* of 1862: w window (to Prince Albert) E, N chapel E, S transept, and S chapel S windows. S chapel E, 1859, by *Lavers & Barraud*. N aisle, 1917, by *Henry Holiday*. Virtues over Evil, in Burne-Jones colours. – MONUMENTS. SE chapel. Gyles and Isabell Penne, c. 1519. 2-ft (61-cm.) brass figures. – Chancel. Rev. John Phelips †1766. Great ovoid urn with dove under a curved pediment. The Boulting monument at Wedmore is similar. – Rev. Robert Phelips †1855. Demi-figure, probably by *J. S. Westmacott*. – Newman family, 1790, columned with an Adamesque urn. – N transept. Harbin family, 1711. Curved pedimented Baroque with exuberant carving: fruit, urns and mourning cherubs. – Swayne Harbin †1781, obelisk type in white and grey. George Harbin †1880. Alabaster, intricate Northern Renaissance. – S transept. Three Baroque including Edward Boucher †1724 depicted in a bust; and three late C18 variants on the obelisk. – S aisle w. Thomas Hawker †1696. Cast brass.

HOLY TRINITY (Yeovil Foyer), Peter Street. 1843–6, by *Benjamin Ferrey*. E.E., with big transepts and short chancel. Aisled with hammerbeam roofs, now subdivided. – STAINED GLASS. Three E lancets, 1840s. Two robust residential wings in stone added to the S, by *Boon Brown*, 1996–7.

HOLY TRINITY, Lysander Road. 1998, by *Boon Brown*. A low and asymmetric pyramid covers church and hall. – STAINED GLASS. By *Jon Callan*. Face and hands of Christ large on blue and green. – FONT. Octagonal with ribbed tapered stem, from Trent, Dorset.

ST ANDREW, Preston Grove. 1934, by *Petter & Warren*. An interesting church, wearing tradition lightly. Mullioned windows set high. Slim bellcote. Plaster-vaulted interior with a classical chancel arch. – FONT. Early C14, from Preston Plucknett. Octagonal with crude ogee panels, the underside and base shaped for column shafts.

ST MICHAEL, St Michael's Road. 1895–7, by *J. Nicholson Johnston* of Yeovil. An expensive church (£10,000). Full-blown Somerset Perp, with a big sw tower and battlemented nave and aisles. Broad interior with five-bay arcades. – SCREEN and other woodwork by *Harry Hems* of Exeter. – STAINED GLASS. Both E windows are good, by *Kempe*, 1902. S chapel S by *Kempe & Co.*, 1915. – The lively Edwardian CHURCH HALL, 1908, by

Drake & Pizey of Bristol, takes its cue from C16 Flanders – see the cupola atop the w gable.

HOLY GHOST (R.C.), Higher Kingston. 1897–9, by *Canon Alexander Scoles*, founder and first priest. Severe E.E. Rock-faced Ham stone. Impressive interior with moulded chancel arch, two-bay r. arcade, and cusped blind arcading to the polygonal chancel. Splendid HIGH ALTAR, the Pentecost in relief over an altar and tabernacle marble, onyx and alabaster. Similar Lady Chapel altar. – Rare C13 SCULPTURE, an eroded Crucifixion, from a churchyard cross; found built into the chantry at the parish church. – Brick PRESBYTERY, by *Scoles*, 1899.

BAPTIST CHURCH, South Street. 1828–9, refronted in 1866–8 in Ham and Doulting stone. Italianate, with an inset Doric porch under an arched triplet. Matching two-storey HALL of 1866–8, extended E in 1911–12 by *Newby, Vincent & Findlay Smith* of Southampton. S end addition and interior subdivided in 2003.

UNITED REFORMED CHURCH (Congregational), Princes Street. 1878, by *T. Lewis Banks*. Ham stone, with red sandstone shafts to a stilted five-light window under a corbelled gable, i.e. North Italian Romanesque. Arcades inside of 1923.

METHODIST CHURCH, Vicarage Street. 1869–70, by *Andrew Lauder* of Barnstaple. Characterful E.E. front spreading from a five-light window to gabled porches to drum stair-towers. An asymmetrical thin spirelet has gone.

CEMETERY, Preston Road. 1860, by *R. H. Shout*. Twin chapels and a lodge. Wilful Gothic with a Moorish tinge. The chapels are cruciform: large porches face inward, polygonal apses S, and peculiar spirelets crown the crossings. Adjoining Friends' BURIAL GROUND, dated 1669 in the wall.

PUBLIC BUILDINGS

MUNICIPAL OFFICES (former), POST OFFICE and LIBRARY, King George Street. *See* Perambulation 1.

DISTRICT COUNCIL OFFICES, Lynx West Trading Estate. 1984–9, by *Jeremy & Caroline Gould* with *Sir John Burnet, Tait & Partners*. Banded red and beige brick with blue windows and green roof.

MAGISTRATES' COURT, Petter's Way. 1936–8, by *Leonard Mew* of *Somerset County Architects*. Imposing brown brick modern-Georgian, the central giant arch lined in Ham stone. POLICE HOUSES adjoining.

DIVISIONAL POLICE HEADQUARTERS, Horsey Roundabout. 1973, by *Richard Samuel* of *Somerset County Architects*. Strongly modelled five-storey block of structural pre-cast panels, raised on pilotis.

DISTRICT HOSPITAL, Higher Kingston. 1970–3, by the *Percy Thomas Partnership* (*Frederick Jennett*, project architect). Its nine-storey slab banded in brown brick looms large. Four-storey, grid-walled WOMEN'S HOSPITAL, 1968, by the same. Also the courtyard of NURSES' FLATS in brown brick opposite.

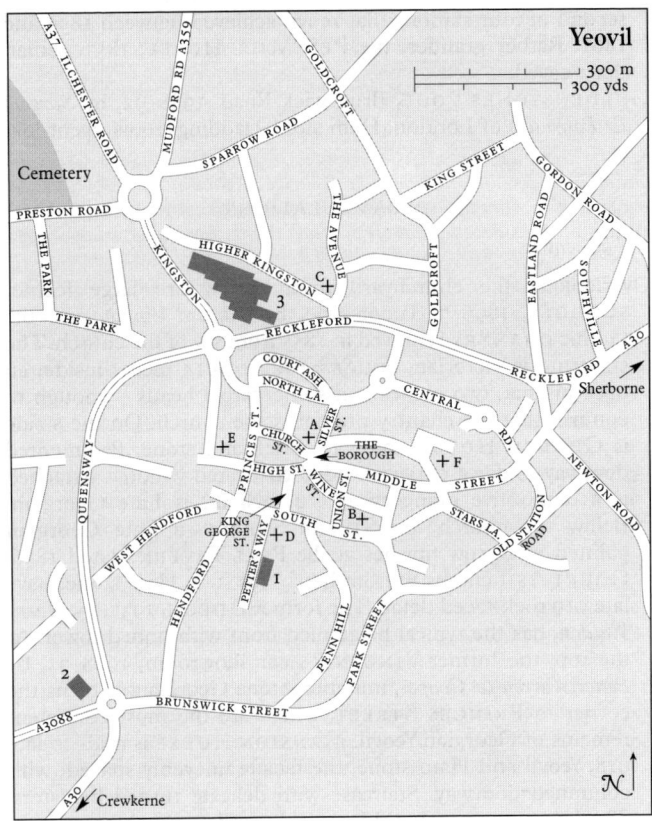

A St John
B Holy Trinity (Yeovil Foyer)
C Holy Ghost (R.C.)
D Baptist church
E United Reformed church
F Methodist church

I Magistrates' Court
2 Police Headquarters
3 District Hospital

SUMMERLANDS HOSPITAL, Preston Road. The pedimented front range remains from the workhouse by *Sampson Kempthorne*, 1837.

ST MARGARET'S HOSPICE, East Coker Road. 2002–3, by *ADP*. Brick, X-plan, behind a curving range opening on to lawns.

YEOVIL COLLEGE, Mudford Road. Curtain-walled six-storey slab of 1963, by *Somerset County Architects*. The LEONARDO BUILDING, 2007, by *ADP*, contrasts white wall with curtain-glazing.

OAKLANDS SCHOOL, Preston Grove. 2007–8, by *Somerset County Architects*. Informally grouped. Typical C21 mix of oak boarding, brick, and sedum roofs.

PEN MILL STATION, Sherborne Road. 1856, for the Great Western Railway. Stone, single-storeyed, hip-roofed. The second of four stations that Yeovil achieved between 1853 and 1861. Rather grander, the PEN MILL HOTEL, 1857, ashlar, deep-eaved.

GOLDENSTONES POOL, Brunswick Road. 1988–92, by *Sargent & Potiriadis* of London. Ham stone cladding, roofs swept low.

PERAMBULATIONS

1. *The centre*

Overlooking the churchyard from the W are large former SCHOOLS, 1896–7, Tudor-style, by *Edward Vining*, and the Gothic CHANTRY removed in 1855 from SW of the church. The structure is Victorian, but *Shout* reused C14 pieces inside, an ogee piscina, two niches and some corbel heads – enough to confirm that the chantry pre-dated the church. On the S side is CHURCH HOUSE, mid-C18, brick and stone. Pedimented doorway under a curved-headed rusticated window. Attached is a diminutive orangery. No. 4, behind, is Late Georgian. Below the church, on SILVER STREET, a Late Georgian painted brick row finishes at the PALL TAVERN, dated 1836. COURT ASH climbs W from here. Nos. 1–2, Ham stone, have late C19 rock-faced detail. The former ODEON, 1937, by *Harry Weedon*, has the typical beige tiled front with finned tower. At the top, the former VINCENT'S car showroom, 1928–31, by *Petter, Warren & Cooper*, imitation-stone Georgian. It turns the corner to PRINCES STREET, where are the most consistent remains of Georgian Yeovil. MANSION HOUSE is mid- to late C18, Yeovil and Ham stone, the façade unevenly spaced, with columned doorway. Staircase with delicate turned balusters. The lower r. range could be a little earlier. On the W side of the street, OLD SARUM HOUSE, *c.* 1730, once grand, now mostly reconstruction. No. 45 has a good curved-pedimented mid-C18 doorcase on an early C19 ashlar front. WYNDHAM HOUSE is also early C19, divided by channelled piers. Nos. 23–29, a lower row, are altered early C18. Brick upper floor except at the end house, all stone, dated 1714. Further on, the United Reformed church (*see* p. 718). Opposite, on the E side, No. 2, stuccoed with Regency pedimented windows in arches. It has lost a balcony and parapet balustrades. On the corner of High Street, the former CAPITAL & COUNTIES BANK, 1897–9, by *Nicholson Johnston*. All Ham stone, florid Northern Renaissance style, with a corner oriel.

HIGH STREET begins and ends in irregular squares. The NATWEST BANK faces E down the street. Portland stone classical in the Edwardian manner, by *Petter & Warren*, 1925. The core of the former DENNER'S store on the S side is a large painted brick emporium of 1836, pedimented with Soanean incised ornament. On the N side, the MERMAID HOTEL. Three bays, standard Late Georgian except for the l. bay, an entertaining Gothic version of the classical inn archway with a Venetian window above. The archway has coupled shafts and a trefoiled head, and the Venetian window has, perhaps uniquely, ogee-headed sides and a pointed trefoiled centre. No. 7 was the Savings Bank of 1838–9, by *George Bennett* of Yeovil. Ashlar-faced with a triangular oriel. On the s was a large classical Town Hall (1847–9 by *Thomas Stent*), burnt in 1935. By then KING GEORGE STREET had been laid out as a municipal centre with Bath stone Neo-Georgian buildings. The former MUNICIPAL OFFICES, 1926–8, by *Petter & Warren*, sixteen bays long, face the POST OFFICE, 1932, by *Harry Seccombe* of the *Office of Works*; both with lanterns, the latter daintier in detail. To complete the group, at the s end of King George Street, the large stone-faced LIBRARY, 1986–7, by *Alan Dickens* of *Somerset County Architects*, and at the N, contrasting fronts of the 1920s, the TOWN CLERK'S OFFICE, with classical urns, by *Petter & Warren*, and former TAYLOR'S store, imitation-stone Tudor, the top floor 1930s.

The heart of the town is THE BOROUGH, at the E end of High Street, around the Gothic WAR MEMORIAL (1921, by *Wilfred Childs*). LLOYDS BANK, a Ham stone palazzo built for the Wiltshire & Dorset Bank, 1856, by *Thomas Stent*, is emphatically Victorian in its overall modelling. On the s, No. 15, *c.* 1800, was a large ironmongers' premises; five-bay, painted brick. HSBC BANK (Midland Bank), by *Thomas Whinney*, 1914, with French roofs and corner cupola, introduces MIDDLE STREET. Architecturally null now; only No. 35, by *Petter & Warren*, *c.* 1910, shows personality: mottled brick and square shoulders. Halfway down is THE TRIANGLE, with the Methodist church (*see* p. 718) off to the N. SOUTH STREET returns SW by the former GAUMONT CINEMA, 1934, by *W. E. Trent*, stripped Georgian. Further up, WOBORNE'S ALMSHOUSES, 1860, by *Hickes & Isaac* of Bath, Gothic, in Yeovil stone, the chapel window clamped between turrets. Behind in Peter Street is Holy Trinity church (*see* p. 717). On UNION STREET, to the r., the TOWN HOUSE, by *Thomas Stent*, 1849, pedimented ashlar with Italianate triple arched window. WINE STREET returns to The Borough past the coarser pedimented WINE VAULTS, 1877, and No. 11, C18, remarkable for a columned brick-vaulted cellar.

From the W end of High Street, HENDFORD runs s past the barrack-like former THREE CHOUGHS HOTEL, by *Maurice Davis*, 1844, of Yeovil stone (dated 1724 on a rear building). Across South Street, FLOWERS HOUSE is late C18, also of Yeovil stone. Two substantial Georgian suburban houses further out. THE MANOR HOTEL (Hendford House), a square ashlar villa of 1776, suggests Bath with its parapet and pedimented doorcase. Contemporary staircase. The hip-roofed brick STABLE behind with mullioned windows looks early to mid-C18. MASONIC HALL of 1894 opposite. HENDFORD MANOR is mid-C18, ashlar-fronted, of seven bays, originally balustraded. Edwardian porch by *J. N. Johnston*, and probably also the Venetian window of the r. wing. Mullioned-windowed service wing in Yeovil stone, 1840. Attractive brick STABLE behind, mid-C18, with a Venetian upper window between roundels. Similar end wall. House, stables and park were to have been replaced by Neoclassical civic buildings by *Cecil Howitt*, 1938. Instead the park was messily encroached by the OCTAGON THEATRE (1974 and later) and by MALTRAVERS HOUSE, government offices of 1969, by *Roydon Cooper Associates*. The park backs on to the wooded PENN HILL, crowned by PENN HOUSE, pyramid-roofed and deep-eaved, early C19, the door neatly recessed in a coved arch. Smaller villas on the return to SOUTH STREET. After the Baptist church (*see* p. 718) and across Hendford are car parks for a supermarket that incorporates the sad façade of the NATIONAL SCHOOL, 1845–6, by *Thomas Stent*, missing its centrepiece, a bellcote between gablets.

2. *Outer Yeovil: east and north-east*

From The Triangle, MIDDLE STREET continues downhill without interest, the N side rebuilt 1967–9. South Western Terrace, r., once framed Yeovil Town Station.* On the site is a shopping development of 2002. Just W is the best surviving GLOVE FACTORY, 1872–5. Brick, three storeys, with large windows, happily retained in an encompassing development of 2010–12 by *ESHA Architects*. Middle Street continues to the former WESTERN GAZETTE, 1906, by *Oatley & Lawrence*. Office front of brick banded in stone, the deep shell-headed entry carved by *Gilbert Seale*.

Further N, on RECKLEFORD, the inner ring road, RECKLEFORD SCHOOL, 1916 by *Petter & Warren*, brick with cupola, contrasting with the Gothic BOARD SCHOOL of 1874, by *T. M. Reade* of Liverpool. Ham stone, the porches neatly turned. E of the school, up SOUTHVILLE (also in Eastville and Westville), is the earliest COUNCIL HOUSING, of which Yeovil was a pioneer; of 1912, by *Petter & Warren*. Red brick, the windows spoilt. Returning S, on EASTLAND ROAD, a roofless stone TANNERY of 1853. Back on Reckleford, heading W, the GLOVER'S ARMS has late C17 mullioned windows. The former NAUTILUS WORKS (1902, by *Petter & Warren*) on the corner of GOLDCROFT were the Petter & Co. engineering works. Some distance N, Nos. 172–174 Goldcroft are the pioneer pair of houses designed in 1925 by *Petter & Warren* with Maj. Nissen, to see if Nissen's steel-hoop truss could be useful for cheap housing (*see* Introduction, p. 82; also Barwick and West Camel). A return may be made down THE AVENUE, laid out in 1892 on land bought by Canon Scoles for his R.C. church (*see* p. 718). W of the hospital (*see* p. 718), two Late Georgian villas on the W side of KINGSTON: SWALLOWCLIFFE and KINGSTON HOUSE (Park School).

---

*Tudor style, 1860–1, possibly by *William Tite*, between matching stationmasters' houses for the LSWR and GWR.

3. West and south-west

PRESTON ROAD runs w from Kingston. s of the cemetery (see p. 718), THE PARK is Yeovil's Late Victorian suburb, centred on SIDNEY GARDENS of 1897. Brick houses with some half-timber and terracotta, mostly by *J. N. Johnston*. The largest are PARK LODGE, 1888, and at the sw corner the former GIRLS' HIGH SCHOOL, 1895, by *Johnston*, extended 1908. Little on Preston Road before the Summerlands Hospital (see p. 719). WESTFIELD ROAD, running N, is the spine of one of Yeovil's larger council estates, 1920s by *Petter & Warren*, with gabled and hip-roofed brick houses. Grove Avenue runs s to St Andrew's church (see p. 717). WESTLAND ROAD, further s off West Street, is lined by 1920s brick housing in culs de sac by *Petter & Warren*, for workers at the new Westland works. The first two, roughcast, pairs are of *c.* 1916, when a garden suburb was planned.* The WESTLAND WORKS were set up in 1915 to build military aircraft on a greenfield site. Closely packed buildings s of the airfield. The grid-walled offices in a hollow square began with the lower rear wing, 1955, by *Farmer & Dark*. Enveloped in later buildings are the ASSEMBLY SHED of 1918 for the Vimy bomber, with a 140-ft span roof and brick-walled FOUNDRY of 1917. From Westland Road, a route SE via Seaton Road, West Hendford and Horsey Lane reaches the ring road at the Police Headquarters (see p. 718).

From the Police Headquarters, HENDFORD HILL climbs SW. Early to mid-Victorian villas on the w side. On the E, two larger Late Victorian houses with turrets, INGLEWOOD, 1895, by *Johnston*, partly timbered, and BRAGGCHURCH, 1892, by *C. & C. B. Benson*. Behind, at the top of Southwoods, is a former civil defence CONTROL CENTRE, 1960–1. Three underground storeys. On DORCHESTER ROAD, a gabled lodge marks the drive to ALDON, a beautifully set house of 1829–50. Two open-pedimented wings in the Italianate of Henry Goodridge's Bath villas frame the front. The back is neo-Jacobean. The flat-topped stable turret is of the 1830s but looks of the 1930s. The Batten family made a romantic walk of the steep valley down to Yeovil, with cascades and ponds, now NINESPRINGS PARK.

YEOVIL MARSH

5010

ST ANDREW. 1870. Cusped lancets and bellcote.
Two farmhouses with C18 mullion-windowed fronts. MARSH FARMHOUSE has quoins and band. CARENTS is earlier – see

---

* ROMAN REMAINS partly under the playground were excavated in the 1920s, but it is not clear if they are of a large villa or a small village. Several mosaics were discovered.

the massive W chimney-breast. WEST FARMHOUSE of 1850 is carefully Tudor. C18 BARN.

YEOVILTON

Surprisingly unaffected by the large naval air base.

ST BARTHOLOMEW. Blue Lias. Plain three-stage Perp W tower with much uninterrupted wall. Richard Swann, rector, left money 'to the fabric of the new tower' in 1486. Diagonal buttresses, small two-light bell-openings with pierced baffles, ashlar battlements with slight crenellations and small pinnacles. Niche at the base on the N side, with St Bartholomew statue, by *Frank Taylor*, 2001. Polygonal SW stair-turret. The tower arch is double-chamfered, an indication that such forms continued rather than this being of an earlier date. The same is probably true for the double-chamfered arches dying into the sides, on the N porch and the chancel arch. The porch has reused C13 fragments, a sexfoil W and a tiny two-light E with cusped rere-arch. Otherwise the windows are Perp with delicate rosettes on the cusps and Tudor roses on some hoodmoulds. Chamfered rere-arches, again an older feature, are unlikely to be so here. C14 relief over the E window. The S porch, actually a vestry of 1871 by *Slater & Carpenter*, incorporates a strip of fire-reddened Norman fragments. Victorian roofs, the nave roof with reused bosses, two broad faces (Christ and Mary?) and a two-headed eagle. Statue bracket in the nave S wall, on a bat grotesque. In the chancel, a small carved head on each side wall may be to support the Lenten veil. C14 ogee PISCINA on a contorted figure. Interior restored from 1993 as the Fleet Air Arm memorial church. Simple FITTINGS, including scrolled CHANDELIERS and PORCH GATES made by apprentices. The medieval ALTAR SLAB is reused. – FONT. Perp, panelled all over. – STAINED GLASS. C15 fragments including Swann's initials in the tracery over the E window, otherwise by *John Yeo*, 2000. – MONUMENT. Rev. Robert Woodforde. A white marble floor slab that Parson Woodforde records his father ordering at Sherborne, 1763.

E of the church, the former SCHOOL, 1868 and 1893. The OLD RECTORY is framed by cross-wings, a C16 arrangement, with mullioned windows and curved-pedimented door of 1713. C16 beams. Opposite the church, WEST FARMHOUSE, Late Georgian, thatched. MANOR FARMHOUSE, further W, is late C17, with tall mullioned windows and drip-course. Late Georgian brick BARN behind.

RNAS YEOVILTON (HMS Heron). The Fleet Air Arm base covers a large area. Opened 1940. Original PILLBOXES at Bridgehampton; a Bessoneau HANGAR visible from there.

GLOSSARY

Numbers and letters refer to the illustrations (by John Sambrook) on pp. 734–741.

ABACUS: flat slab forming the top of a capital (3a).

ACANTHUS: classical formalized leaf ornament (4b).

ACCUMULATOR TOWER: see Hydraulic power.

ACHIEVEMENT: a complete display of armorial bearings.

ACROTERION: plinth for a statue or ornament on the apex or ends of a pediment; more usually, both the plinth and what stands on it (4a).

AEDICULE (*lit.* little building): architectural surround, consisting usually of two columns or pilasters supporting a pediment.

AGGREGATE: see Concrete.

AISLE: subsidiary space alongside the body of a building, separated from it by columns, piers, or posts.

ALMONRY: a building from which alms are dispensed to the poor.

AMBULATORY (*lit.* walkway): aisle around the sanctuary (q.v.).

ANGLE ROLL: roll moulding in the angle between two planes (1a).

ANSE DE PANIER: see Arch.

ANTAE: simplified pilasters (4a), usually applied to the ends of the enclosing walls of a portico *in antis* (q.v.).

ANTEFIXAE: ornaments projecting at regular intervals above a Greek cornice, originally to conceal the ends of roof tiles (4a).

ANTHEMION: classical ornament like a honeysuckle flower (4b).

APRON: raised panel below a window or wall monument or tablet.

APSE: semicircular or polygonal end of an apartment, especially of a chancel or chapel. In classical architecture sometimes called an *exedra* (q.v.).

ARABESQUE: non-figurative surface decoration consisting of flowing lines, foliage scrolls etc., based on geometrical patterns. Cf. Grotesque.

ARCADE: series of arches supported by piers or columns. *Blind arcade* or *arcading*: the same applied to the wall surface. *Wall arcade*: in medieval churches, a blind arcade forming a dado below windows. Also a covered shopping street.

ARCH: Shapes see 5c. *Basket arch* or *anse de panier* (basket handle): three-centred and depressed, or with a flat centre. *Nodding*: ogee arch curving forward from the wall face. *Parabolic*: shaped like a chain suspended from two level points, but inverted. Special purposes. *Chancel*: dividing chancel from nave or crossing. *Crossing*: spanning piers at a crossing (q.v.). *Relieving or discharging*: incorporated in a wall to relieve superimposed weight (5c). *Skew*: spanning responds not diametrically opposed. *Strainer*: inserted in an opening to resist inward pressure. *Transverse*: spanning a main axis (e.g. of a vaulted space). See also Jack arch, Triumphal arch.

ARCHITRAVE: formalized lintel, the lowest member of the classical entablature (3a). Also the moulded frame of a door or window (often borrowing the profile of a classical architrave). For *lugged* and *shouldered* architraves see 4b.

ARCUATED: dependent structurally on the arch principle. Cf. Trabeated.

ARK: chest or cupboard housing the

tables of Jewish law in a synagogue.
ARRIS: sharp edge where two surfaces meet at an angle (3a).
ASHLAR: masonry of large blocks wrought to even faces and square edges (6d).
ASTRAGAL: classical moulding of semicircular section (3f).
ASTYLAR: with no columns or similar vertical features.
ATLANTES: *see* Caryatids.
ATRIUM (plural: atria): inner court of a Roman or C20 house; in a multi-storey building, a toplit covered court rising through all storeys. Also an open court in front of a church.
ATTACHED COLUMN: *see* Engaged column.
ATTIC: small top storey within a roof. Also the storey above the main entablature of a classical façade.
AUMBRY: recess or cupboard to hold sacred vessels for the Mass.

BAILEY: *see* Motte-and-bailey.
BALANCE BEAM: *see* Canals.
BALDACCHINO: free-standing canopy, originally fabric, over an altar. Cf. Ciborium.
BALLFLOWER: globular flower of three petals enclosing a ball (1a). Typical of the Decorated style.
BALUSTER: pillar or pedestal of bellied form. *Balusters*: vertical supports of this or any other form, for a handrail or coping, the whole being called a *balustrade* (6c). *Blind balustrade*: the same applied to the wall surface.
BARBICAN: outwork defending the entrance to a castle.
BARGEBOARDS (corruption of 'vergeboards'): boards, often carved or fretted, fixed beneath the eaves of a gable to cover and protect the rafters.
BAROQUE: style originating in Rome c.1600 and current in England c.1680–1720, characterized by dramatic massing and silhouette and the use of the giant order.
BARROW: burial mound.
BARTIZAN: corbelled turret, square or round, frequently at an angle.

BASCULE: hinged part of a lifting (or bascule) bridge.
BASE: moulded foot of a column or pilaster. For *Attic* base *see* 3b.
BASEMENT: lowest, subordinate storey; hence the lowest part of a classical elevation, below the *piano nobile* (q.v.).
BASILICA: a Roman public hall; hence an aisled building with a clerestory.
BASTION: one of a series of defensive semicircular or polygonal projections from the main wall of a fortress or city.
BATTER: intentional inward inclination of a wall face.
BATTLEMENT: defensive parapet, composed of *merlons* (solid) and *crenels* (embrasures) through which archers could shoot; sometimes called *crenellation*. Also used decoratively.
BAY: division of an elevation or interior space as defined by regular vertical features such as arches, columns, windows etc.
BAY LEAF: classical ornament of overlapping bay leaves (3f).
BAY WINDOW: window of one or more storeys projecting from the face of a building. *Canted*: with a straight front and angled sides. *Bow window*: curved. *Oriel*: rests on corbels or brackets and starts above ground level; also the bay window at the dais end of a medieval great hall.
BEAD-AND-REEL: *see* Enrichments.
BEAKHEAD: Norman ornament with a row of beaked bird or beast heads usually biting into a roll moulding (1a).
BELFRY: chamber or stage in a tower where bells are hung.
BELL CAPITAL: *see* 1b.
BELLCOTE: small gabled or roofed housing for the bell(s).
BERM: level area separating a ditch from a bank on a hill-fort or barrow.
BILLET: Norman ornament of small half-cylindrical or rectangular blocks (1a).
BLIND: *see* Arcade, Baluster, Portico.
BLOCK CAPITAL: *see* 1a.
BLOCKED: columns, etc. interrupted by regular projecting

GLOSSARY

blocks (*blocking*), as on a Gibbs surround (4b).

BLOCKING COURSE: course of stones, or equivalent, on top of a cornice and crowning the wall.

BOLECTION MOULDING: covering the joint between two different planes (6b).

BOND: the pattern of long sides (*stretchers*) and short ends (*headers*) produced on the face of a wall by laying bricks in a particular way (6e).

BOSS: knob or projection, e.g. at the intersection of ribs in a vault (2c).

BOWTELL: a term in use by the C15 for a form of roll moulding, usually three-quarters of a circle in section (also called *edge roll*).

BOW WINDOW: see Bay window.

BOX FRAME: timber-framed construction in which vertical and horizontal wall members support the roof (7). Also concrete construction where the loads are taken on cross walls; also called *cross-wall construction*.

BRACE: subsidiary member of a structural frame, curved or straight. *Bracing* is often arranged decoratively e.g. quatrefoil, herringbone (7). See also Roofs.

BRATTISHING: ornamental crest, usually formed of leaves, Tudor flowers or miniature battlements.

BRESSUMER (*lit.* breast-beam): big horizontal beam supporting the wall above, especially in a jettied building (7).

BRICK: see Bond, Cogging, Engineering, Gauged, Tumbling.

BRIDGE: *Bowstring*: with arches rising above the roadway which is suspended from them. *Clapper*: one long stone forms the roadway. *Roving*: see Canal. *Suspension*: roadway suspended from cables or chains slung between towers or pylons. *Stay-suspension* or *stay-cantilever*: supported by diagonal stays from towers or pylons. See also Bascule.

BRISES-SOLEIL: projecting fins or canopies which deflect direct sunlight from windows.

BROACH: see Spire and 1C.

BUCRANIUM: ox skull used decoratively in classical friezes.

BULL-NOSED SILL: sill displaying a pronounced convex upper moulding.

BULLSEYE WINDOW: small oval window, set horizontally (cf. Oculus). Also called *œil de bœuf*.

BUTTRESS: vertical member projecting from a wall to stabilize it or to resist the lateral thrust of an arch, roof, or vault (1c, 2c). A *flying buttress* transmits the thrust to a heavy abutment by means of an arch or half-arch (1c).

CABLE OR ROPE MOULDING: originally Norman, like twisted strands of a rope.

CAMES: see Quarries.

CAMPANILE: free-standing bell-tower.

CANALS: *Flash lock*: removable weir or similar device through which boats pass on a flush of water. Predecessor of the *pound lock*: chamber with gates at each end allowing boats to float from one level to another. *Tidal gates*: single pair of lock gates allowing vessels to pass when the tide makes a level. *Balance beam*: beam projecting horizontally for opening and closing lock gates. *Roving bridge*: carrying a towing path from one bank to the other.

CANTILEVER: horizontal projection (e.g. step, canopy) supported by a downward force behind the fulcrum.

CAPITAL: head or crowning feature of a column or pilaster; for classical types see 3; for medieval types see 1b.

CARREL: compartment designed for individual work or study.

CARTOUCHE: classical tablet with ornate frame (4b).

CARYATIDS: female figures supporting an entablature; their male counterparts are *Atlantes* (*lit.* Atlas figures).

CASEMATE: vaulted chamber, with embrasures for defence, within a castle wall or projecting from it.

CASEMENT: side-hinged window.

CASTELLATED: with battlements (q.v.).

CAST IRON: hard and brittle, cast in a mould to the required shape.

Wrought iron is ductile, strong in tension, forged into decorative patterns or forged and rolled into e.g. bars, joists, boiler plates; *mild steel* is its modern equivalent, similar but stronger.

CATSLIDE: *See* 8a.

CAVETTO: concave classical moulding of quarter-round section (3f).

CELURE OR CEILURE: enriched area of roof above rood or altar.

CEMENT: *see* Concrete.

CENOTAPH (*lit.* empty tomb): funerary monument which is not a burying place.

CENTRING: wooden support for the building of an arch or vault, removed after completion.

CHAMFER (*lit.* corner-break): surface formed by cutting off a square edge or corner. For types of chamfers and *chamfer stops see* 6a. *See also* Double chamfer.

CHANCEL: part of the E end of a church set apart for the use of the officiating clergy.

CHANTRY CHAPEL: often attached to or within a church, endowed for the celebration of Masses principally for the soul of the founder.

CHEVET (*lit.* head): French term for chancel with ambulatory and radiating chapels.

CHEVRON: V-shape used in series or double series (later) on a Norman moulding (1a). Also (especially when on a single plane) called *zigzag*.

CHOIR: the part of a cathedral, monastic or collegiate church where services are sung.

CIBORIUM: a fixed canopy over an altar, usually vaulted and supported on four columns; cf. Baldacchino. Also a canopied shrine for the reserved sacrament.

CINQUEFOIL: *see* Foil.

CIST: stone-lined or slab-built grave.

CLADDING: external covering or skin applied to a structure, especially a framed one.

CLERESTORY: uppermost storey of the nave of a church, pierced by windows. Also high-level windows in secular buildings.

CLOSER: a brick cut to complete a bond (6e).

CLUSTER BLOCK: *see* Multi-storey.

COADE STONE: ceramic artificial stone made in Lambeth 1769–c.1840 by Eleanor Coade (†1821) and her associates.

COB: walling material of clay mixed with straw. Also called *pisé*.

COFFERING: arrangement of sunken panels (coffers), square or polygonal, decorating a ceiling, vault, or arch.

COGGING: a decorative course of bricks laid diagonally (6e). Cf. Dentilation.

COLLAR: *see* Roofs and 7.

COLLEGIATE CHURCH: endowed for the support of a college of priests.

COLONNADE: range of columns supporting an entablature. Cf. Arcade.

COLONNETTE: small medieval column or shaft.

COLOSSAL ORDER: *see* Giant order.

COLUMBARIUM: shelved, niched structure to house multiple burials.

COLUMN: a classical, upright structural member of round section with a shaft, a capital, and usually a base (3a, 4a).

COLUMN FIGURE: carved figure attached to a medieval column or shaft, usually flanking a doorway.

COMMUNION TABLE: unconsecrated table used in Protestant churches for the celebration of Holy Communion.

COMPOSITE: *see* Orders.

COMPOUND PIER: grouped shafts (q.v.), or a solid core surrounded by shafts.

CONCRETE: composition of *cement* (calcined lime and clay), *aggregate* (small stones or rock chippings), sand and water. It can be poured into *formwork* or *shuttering* (temporary frame of timber or metal) on site (*in-situ* concrete), or *pre-cast* as components before construction. *Reinforced*: incorporating steel rods to take the tensile force. *Pre-stressed*: with tensioned steel rods. Finishes include the impression of boards left by formwork (*board-marked* or *shuttered*), and texturing with steel brushes (*brushed*) or hammers (*hammer-dressed*). *See also* Shell.

GLOSSARY

CONSOLE: bracket of curved outline (4b).

COPING: protective course of masonry or brickwork capping a wall (6d).

CORBEL: projecting block supporting something above. *Corbel course*: continuous course of projecting stones or bricks fulfilling the same function. *Corbel table*: series of corbels to carry a parapet or a wall-plate or wall-post (7). *Corbelling*: brick or masonry courses built out beyond one another to support a chimney-stack, window, etc.

CORINTHIAN: see Orders and 3d.

CORNICE: flat-topped ledge with moulded underside, projecting along the top of a building or feature, especially as the highest member of the classical entablature (3a). Also the decorative moulding in the angle between wall and ceiling.

CORPS-DE-LOGIS: the main building(s) as distinct from the wings or pavilions.

COTTAGE ORNÉ: an artfully rustic small house associated with the Picturesque movement.

COUNTERCHANGING: of joists on a ceiling divided by beams into compartments, when placed in opposite directions in alternate squares.

COUR D'HONNEUR: formal entrance court before a house in the French manner, usually with flanking wings and a screen wall or gates.

COURSE: continuous layer of stones, etc. in a wall (6e).

COVE: a broad concave moulding, e.g. to mask the eaves of a roof. *Coved ceiling*: with a pronounced cove joining the walls to a flat central panel smaller than the whole area of the ceiling.

CRADLE ROOF: see Wagon roof.

CREDENCE: a shelf within or beside a piscina (q.v.), or a table for the sacramental elements and vessels.

CRENELLATION: parapet with crenels (*see* Battlement).

CRINKLE-CRANKLE WALL: garden wall undulating in a series of serpentine curves.

CROCKETS: leafy hooks. *Crocketing* decorates the edges of Gothic features, such as pinnacles, canopies, etc. *Crocket capital*: see 1b.

CROSSING: central space at the junction of the nave, chancel, and transepts. *Crossing tower*: above a crossing.

CROSS-WINDOW: with one mullion and one transom (qq.v.).

CROWN-POST: see Roofs and 7.

CROWSTEPS: squared stones set like steps, e.g. on a gable (8a).

CRUCKS (*lit.* crooked): pairs of inclined timbers (*blades*), usually curved, set at bay-lengths; they support the roof timbers and, in timber buildings, also support the walls (8b). *Base*: blades rise from ground level to a tie- or collar-beam which supports the roof timbers. *Full*: blades rise from ground level to the apex of the roof, serving as the main members of a roof truss. *Jointed*: blades formed from more than one timber; the lower member may act as a wall-post; it is usually elbowed at wall-plate level and jointed just above. *Middle*: blades rise from half-way up the walls to a tie- or collar-beam. *Raised*: blades rise from half-way up the walls to the apex. *Upper*: blades supported on a tie-beam and rising to the apex.

CRYPT: underground or half-underground area, usually below the E end of a church. *Ring crypt*: corridor crypt surrounding the apse of an early medieval church, often associated with chambers for relics. Cf. Undercroft.

CUPOLA (*lit.* dome): especially a small dome on a circular or polygonal base crowning a larger dome, roof, or turret.

CURSUS: a long avenue defined by two parallel earthen banks with ditches outside.

CURTAIN WALL: a connecting wall between the towers of a castle. Also a non-load-bearing external wall applied to a C20 framed structure.

CUSP: see Tracery and 2b.

CYCLOPEAN MASONRY: large irregular polygonal stones, smooth and finely jointed.

CYMA RECTA and CYMA REVERSA: classical mouldings with double curves (3f). Cf. Ogee.

DADO: the finishing (often with panelling) of the lower part of a wall in a classical interior; in origin a formalized continuous pedestal. *Dado rail*: the moulding along the top of the dado.
DAGGER: *see* Tracery and 2b.
DALLE-DE-VERRE (*lit.* glass-slab): a late C20 stained-glass technique, setting large, thick pieces of cast glass into a frame of reinforced concrete or epoxy resin.
DEC (DECORATED): English Gothic architecture *c.* 1290 to *c.* 1350. The name is derived from the type of window tracery (q.v.) used during the period.
DEMI- or HALF-COLUMNS: engaged columns (q.v.) half of whose circumference projects from the wall.
DENTIL: small square block used in series in classical cornices (3c). *Dentilation* is produced by the projection of alternating headers along cornices or stringcourses.
DIAPER: repetitive surface decoration of lozenges or squares flat or in relief. Achieved in brickwork with bricks of two colours.
DIOCLETIAN OR THERMAL WINDOW: semicircular with two mullions, as used in the Baths of Diocletian, Rome (4b).
DISTYLE: having two columns (4a).
DOGTOOTH: E.E. ornament, consisting of a series of small pyramids formed by four stylized canine teeth meeting at a point (1a).
DORIC: *see* Orders and 3a, 3b.
DORMER: window projecting from the slope of a roof (8a).
DOUBLE CHAMFER: a chamfer applied to each of two recessed arches (1a).
DOUBLE PILE: *see* Pile.
DRAGON BEAM: *see* Jetty.
DRESSINGS: the stone or brickwork worked to a finished face about an angle, opening, or other feature.
DRIPSTONE: moulded stone projecting from a wall to protect the lower parts from water. Cf. Hood-mould, Weathering.
DRUM: circular or polygonal stage supporting a dome or cupola. Also one of the stones forming the shaft of a column (3a).
DUTCH or FLEMISH GABLE: *see* 8a.

EASTER SEPULCHRE: tomb-chest used for Easter ceremonial, within or against the N wall of a chancel.
EAVES: overhanging edge of a roof; hence *eaves cornice* in this position.
ECHINUS: ovolo moulding (q.v.) below the abacus of a Greek Doric capital (3a).
EDGE RAIL: *see* Railways.
E.E. (EARLY ENGLISH): English Gothic architecture *c.* 1190–1250.
EGG-AND-DART: *see* Enrichments and 3f.
ELEVATION: any face of a building or side of a room. In a drawing, the same or any part of it, represented in two dimensions.
EMBATTLED: with battlements.
EMBRASURE: small splayed opening in a wall or battlement (q.v.).
ENCAUSTIC TILES: earthenware tiles fired with a pattern and glaze.
EN DELIT: stone cut against the bed.
ENFILADE: reception rooms in a formal series, usually with all doorways on axis.
ENGAGED or ATTACHED COLUMN: one that partly merges into a wall or pier.
ENGINEERING BRICKS: dense bricks, originally used mostly for railway viaducts etc.
ENRICHMENTS: the carved decoration of certain classical mouldings, e.g. the ovolo (qq.v.) with *egg-and-dart*, the cyma reversa with *waterleaf*, the astragal with *bead-and-reel* (3f).
ENTABLATURE: in classical architecture, collective name for the three horizontal members (architrave, frieze, and cornice) carried by a wall or a column (3a).
ENTASIS: very slight convex deviation from a straight line, used to prevent an optical illusion of concavity.
EPITAPH: inscription on a tomb.
EXEDRA: *see* Apse.

EXTRADOS: outer curved face of an arch or vault.

EYECATCHER: decorative building terminating a vista.

FASCIA: plain horizontal band, e.g. in an architrave (3c, 3d) or on a shopfront.

FENESTRATION: the arrangement of windows in a façade.

FERETORY: site of the chief shrine of a church, behind the high altar.

FESTOON: ornamental garland, suspended from both ends. Cf. Swag.

FIBREGLASS, or glass-reinforced polyester (GRP): synthetic resin reinforced with glass fibre. GRC: glass-reinforced concrete.

FIELD: see Panelling and 6b.

FILLET: a narrow flat band running down a medieval shaft or along a roll moulding (1a). It separates larger curved mouldings in classical cornices, fluting or bases (3c).

FLAMBOYANT: the latest phase of French Gothic architecture, with flowing tracery.

FLASH LOCK: see Canals.

FLÈCHE or SPIRELET (*lit.* arrow): slender spire on the centre of a roof.

FLEURON: medieval carved flower or leaf, often rectilinear (1a).

FLUSHWORK: knapped flint used with dressed stone to form patterns.

FLUTING: series of concave grooves (flutes), their common edges sharp (arris) or blunt (fillet) (3).

FOIL (*lit.* leaf): lobe formed by the cusping of a circular or other shape in tracery (2b). *Trefoil* (three), *quatrefoil* (four), *cinquefoil* (five), and *multifoil* express the number of lobes in a shape.

FOLIATE: decorated with leaves.

FORMWORK: see Concrete.

FRAMED BUILDING: where the structure is carried by a framework – e.g. of steel, reinforced concrete, timber – instead of by load-bearing walls.

FREESTONE: stone that is cut, or can be cut, in all directions.

FRESCO: *al fresco*: painting on wet plaster. *Fresco secco*: painting on dry plaster.

FRIEZE: the middle member of the classical entablature, sometimes ornamented (3a). *Pulvinated frieze* (*lit.* cushioned): of bold convex profile (3c). Also a horizontal band of ornament.

FRONTISPIECE: in C16 and C17 buildings the central feature of doorway and windows above linked in one composition.

GABLE: For types *see* 8a. *Gablet*: small gable. *Pedimental gable*: treated like a pediment.

GADROONING: classical ribbed ornament like inverted fluting that flows into a lobed edge.

GALILEE: chapel or vestibule usually at the W end of a church enclosing the main portal(s).

GALLERY: a long room or passage; an upper storey above the aisle of a church, looking through arches to the nave; a balcony or mezzanine overlooking the main interior space of a building; or an external walkway.

GALLETING: small stones set in a mortar course.

GAMBREL ROOF: see 8a.

GARDEROBE: medieval privy.

GARGOYLE: projecting water spout often carved into human or animal shape.

GAUGED or RUBBED BRICKWORK: soft brick sawn roughly, then rubbed to a precise (gauged) surface. Mostly used for door or window openings (5c).

GAZEBO (jocular Latin, 'I shall gaze'): ornamental lookout tower or raised summer house.

GEOMETRIC: English Gothic architecture c. 1250–1310. See also Tracery. For another meaning, *see* Stairs.

GIANT or COLOSSAL ORDER: classical order (q.v.) whose height is that of two or more storeys of the building to which it is applied.

GIBBS SURROUND: C18 treatment of an opening (4b), seen particularly in the work of James Gibbs (1682–1754).

GIRDER: a large beam. *Box*: of hollow-box section. *Bowed*: with its top rising in a curve. *Plate*: of I-section, made from iron or steel plates. *Lattice*: with braced framework.

GLAZING BARS: wooden or sometimes metal bars separating and supporting window panes.

GRAFFITI: *see* Sgraffito.

GRANGE: farm owned and run by a religious order.

GRC: *see* Fibreglass.

GRISAILLE: monochrome painting on walls or glass.

GROIN: sharp edge at the meeting of two cells of a cross-vault; *see* Vault and 2c.

GROTESQUE (*lit.* grotto-esque): wall decoration adopted from Roman examples in the Renaissance. Its foliage scrolls incorporate figurative elements. Cf. Arabesque.

GROTTO: artificial cavern.

GRP: *see* Fibreglass.

GUILLOCHE: classical ornament of interlaced bands (4b).

GUNLOOP: opening for a firearm.

GUTTAE: stylized drops (3b).

HALF-TIMBERING: archaic term for timber-framing (q.v.). Sometimes used for non-structural decorative timberwork.

HALL CHURCH: medieval church with nave and aisles of approximately equal height.

HAMMERBEAM: *see* Roofs and 7.

HAMPER: in C20 architecture, a visually distinct topmost storey or storeys.

HEADER: *see* Bond and 6e.

HEADSTOP: stop (q.v.) carved with a head (5b).

HELM ROOF: *see* IC.

HENGE: ritual earthwork.

HERM (*lit.* the god Hermes): male head or bust on a pedestal.

HERRINGBONE WORK: *see* 7ii. Cf. Pitched masonry.

HEXASTYLE: *see* Portico.

HILL-FORT: Iron Age earthwork enclosed by a ditch and bank system.

HIPPED ROOF: *see* 8a.

HOODMOULD: projecting moulding above an arch or lintel to throw off water (2b, 5b). When horizontal often called a *label*. For label stop *see* Stop.

HUSK GARLAND: festoon of stylized nutshells (4b).

HYDRAULIC POWER: use of water under high pressure to work machinery. *Accumulator tower*: houses a hydraulic accumulator which accommodates fluctuations in the flow through hydraulic mains.

HYPOCAUST (*lit.* underburning): Roman underfloor heating system.

IMPOST: horizontal moulding at the springing of an arch (5c).

IMPOST BLOCK: block between abacus and capital (1b).

IN ANTIS: *see* Antae, Portico and 4a.

INDENT: shape chiselled out of a stone to receive a brass.

INDUSTRIALIZED or SYSTEM BUILDING: system of manufactured units assembled on site.

INGLENOOK (*lit.* fire-corner): recess for a hearth with provision for seating.

INTERCOLUMNATION: interval between columns.

INTERLACE: decoration in relief simulating woven or entwined stems or bands.

INTRADOS: *see* Soffit.

IONIC: *see* Orders and 3c.

JACK ARCH: shallow segmental vault springing from beams, used for fireproof floors, bridge decks, etc.

JAMB (*lit.* leg): one of the vertical sides of an opening.

JETTY: in a timber-framed building, the projection of an upper storey beyond the storey below, made by the beams and joists of the lower storey oversailing the wall; on their outer ends is placed the sill of the walling for the storey above (7). Buildings can be jettied on several sides, in which case a *dragon beam* is set diagonally at the corner to carry the joists to either side.

JOGGLE: the joining of two stones to prevent them slipping by a notch in one and a projection in the other.

KEEL MOULDING: moulding used from the late C12, in section like the keel of a ship (1a).

KEEP: principal tower of a castle.

KENTISH CUSP: *see* Tracery and 2b.

GLOSSARY

KEY PATTERN: see 4b.
KEYSTONE: central stone in an arch or vault (4b, 5c).
KINGPOST: see Roofs and 7.
KNEELER: horizontal projecting stone at the base of each side of a gable to support the inclined coping stones (8a).

LABEL: see Hoodmould and 5b.
LABEL STOP: see Stop and 5b.
LACED BRICKWORK: vertical strips of brickwork, often in a contrasting colour, linking openings on different floors.
LACING COURSE: horizontal reinforcement in timber or brick to walls of flint, cobble, etc.
LADY CHAPEL: dedicated to the Virgin Mary (Our Lady).
LANCET: slender single-light, pointed-arched window (2a).
LANTERN: circular or polygonal windowed turret crowning a roof or a dome. Also the windowed stage of a crossing tower lighting the church interior.
LANTERN CROSS: churchyard cross with lantern-shaped top.
LAVATORIUM: in a religious house, a washing place adjacent to the refectory.
LEAN-TO: see Roofs.
LESENE (*lit.* a mean thing): pilaster without base or capital. Also called *pilaster strip*.
LIERNE: see Vault and 2c.
LIGHT: compartment of a window defined by the mullions.
LINENFOLD: Tudor panelling carved with simulations of folded linen. *See also* Parchemin.
LINTEL: horizontal beam or stone bridging an opening.
LOGGIA: gallery, usually arcaded or colonnaded; sometimes free-standing.
LONG-AND-SHORT WORK: quoins consisting of stones placed with the long side alternately upright and horizontal, especially in Saxon building.
LONGHOUSE: house and byre in the same range with internal access between them.
LOUVRE: roof opening, often protected by a raised timber structure, to allow the smoke from a central hearth to escape.
LOWSIDE WINDOW: set lower than the others in a chancel side wall, usually towards its W end.
LUCAM: projecting housing for hoist pulley on upper storey of warehouses, mills, etc., for raising goods to loading doors.
LUCARNE (*lit.* dormer): small gabled opening in a roof or spire.
LUGGED ARCHITRAVE: see 4b.
LUNETTE: semicircular window or blind panel.
LYCHGATE (*lit.* corpse-gate): roofed gateway entrance to a churchyard for the reception of a coffin.
LYNCHET: long terraced strip of soil on the downward side of prehistoric and medieval fields, accumulated because of continual ploughing along the contours.

MACHICOLATIONS (*lit.* mashing devices): series of openings between the corbels that support a projecting parapet through which missiles can be dropped. Used decoratively in post-medieval buildings.
MANOMETER or STANDPIPE TOWER: containing a column of water to regulate pressure in water mains.
MANSARD: see 8a.
MATHEMATICAL TILES: facing tiles with the appearance of brick, most often applied to timber-framed walls.
MAUSOLEUM: monumental building or chamber usually intended for the burial of members of one family.
MEGALITHIC TOMB: massive stone-built Neolithic burial chamber covered by an earth or stone mound.
MERLON: see Battlement.
METOPES: spaces between the triglyphs in a Doric frieze (3b).
MEZZANINE: low storey between two higher ones.
MILD STEEL: see Cast iron.
MISERICORD (*lit.* mercy): shelf on a carved bracket placed on the underside of a hinged choir stall seat to support an occupant when standing.

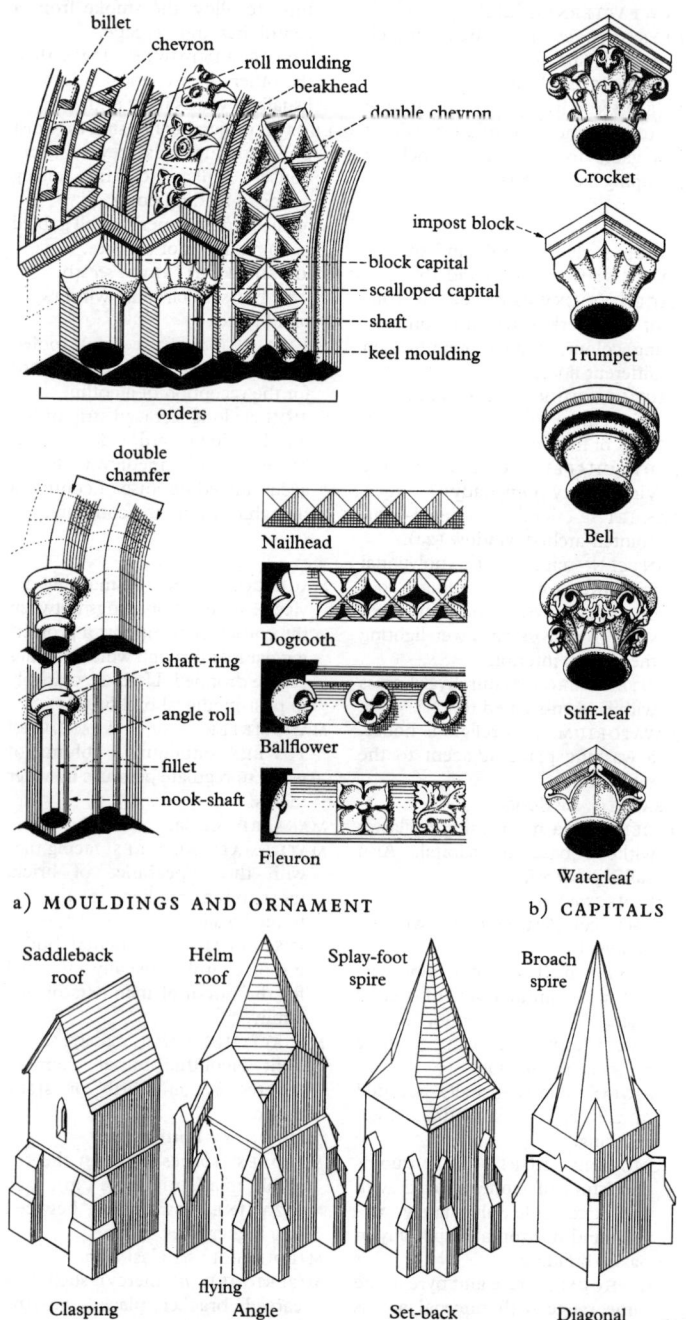

FIGURE 1: MEDIEVAL

a) PLATE TRACERY

b) BAR TRACERY

c) VAULTS

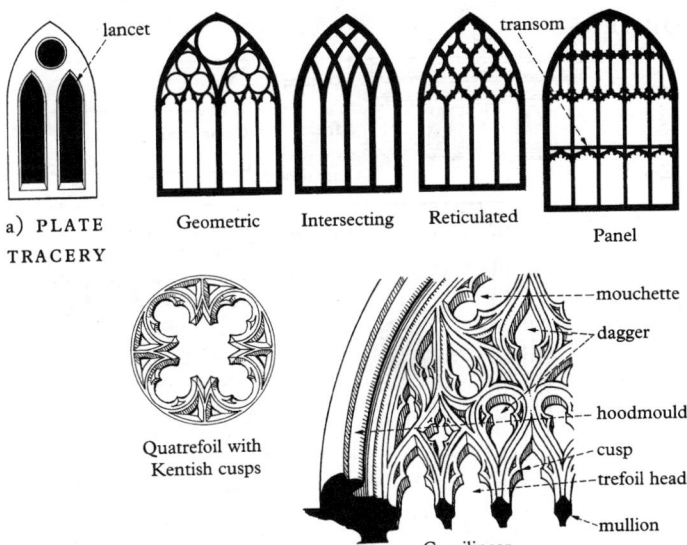

FIGURE 2: MEDIEVAL

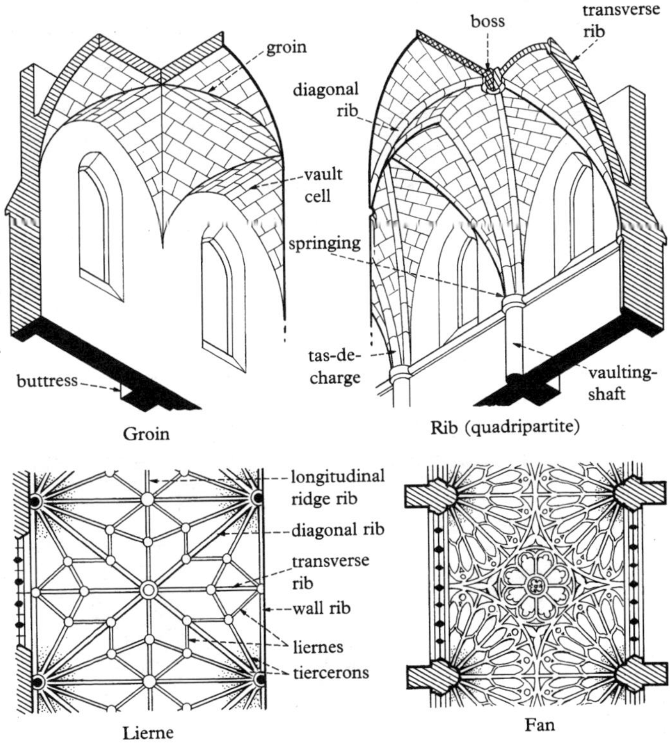

GLOSSARY

ORDERS

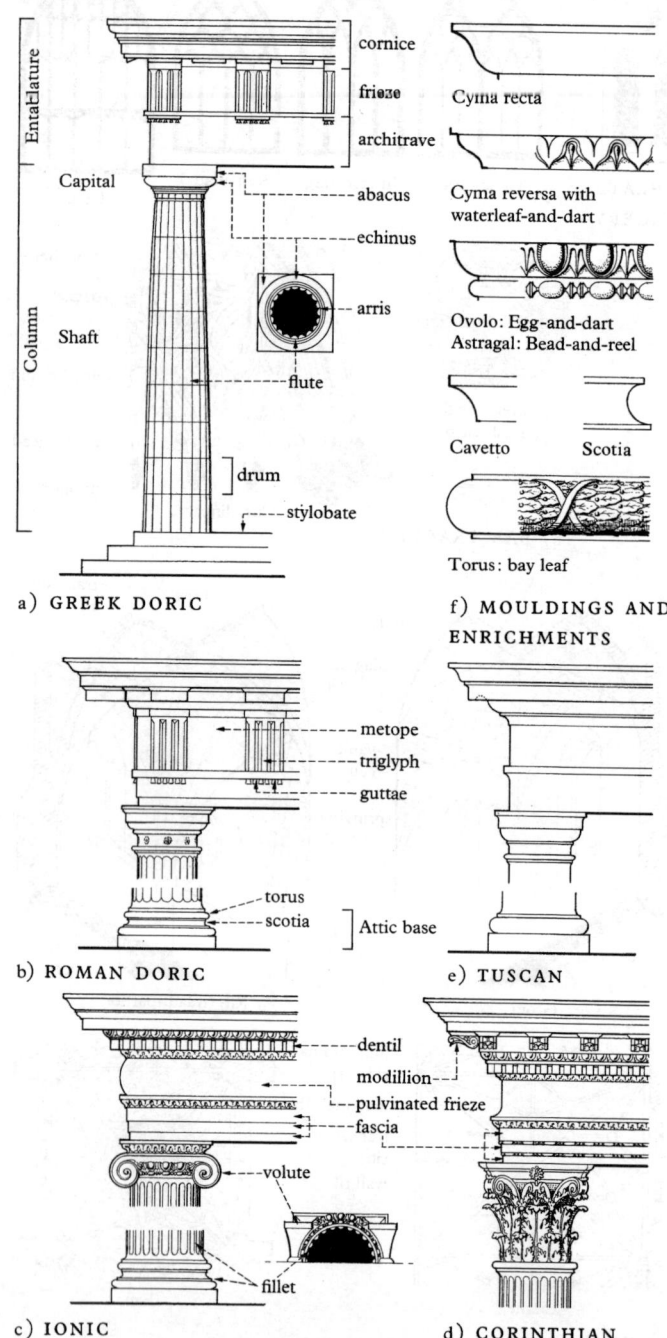

FIGURE 3: CLASSICAL

FIGURE 4: CLASSICAL

738 GLOSSARY

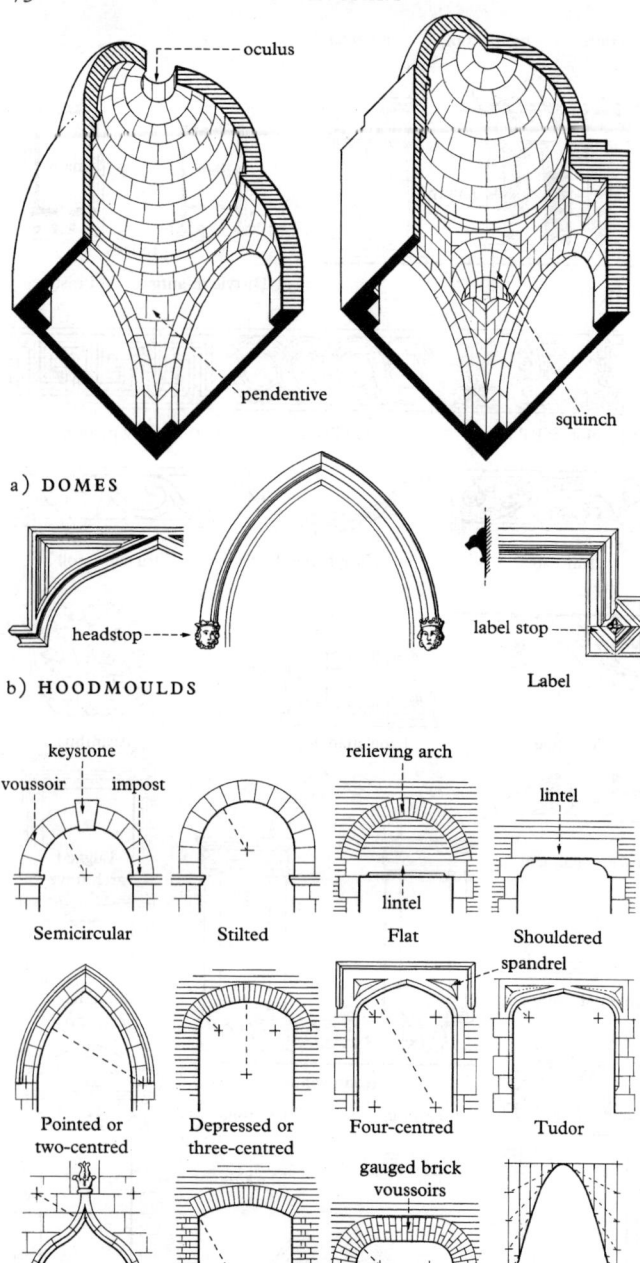

a) DOMES

b) HOODMOULDS

c) ARCHES

FIGURE 5: CONSTRUCTION

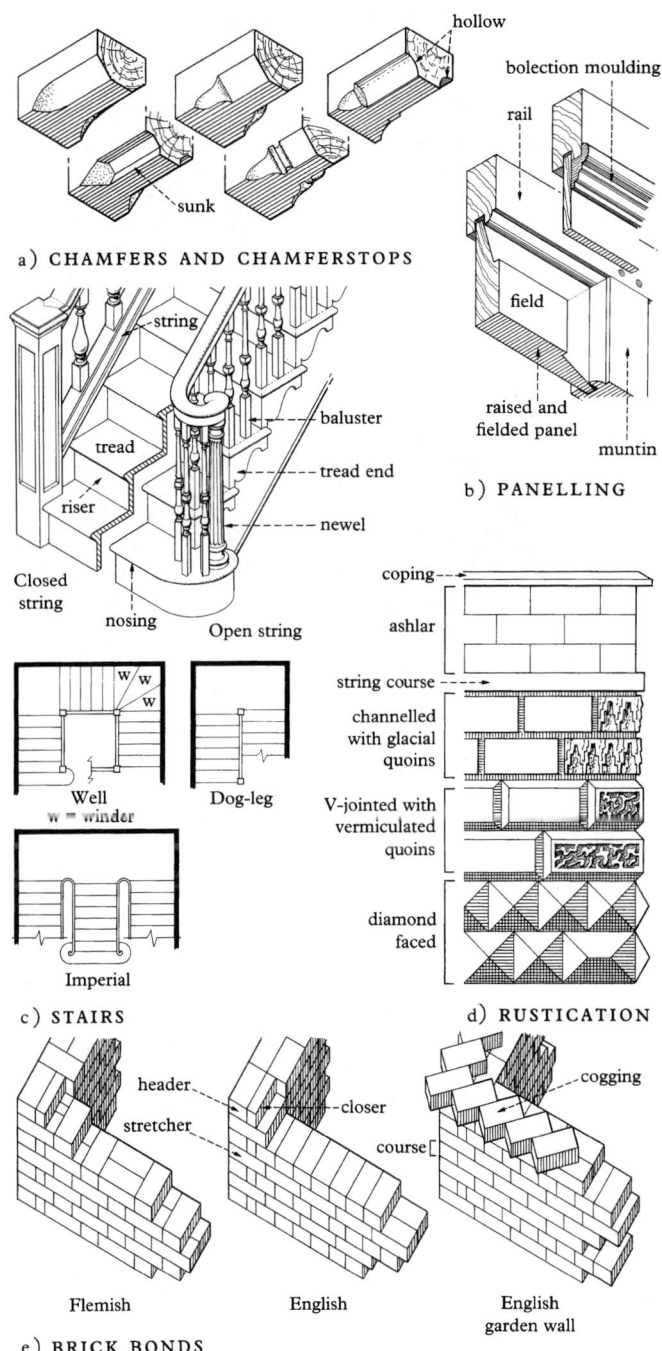

FIGURE 6: CONSTRUCTION

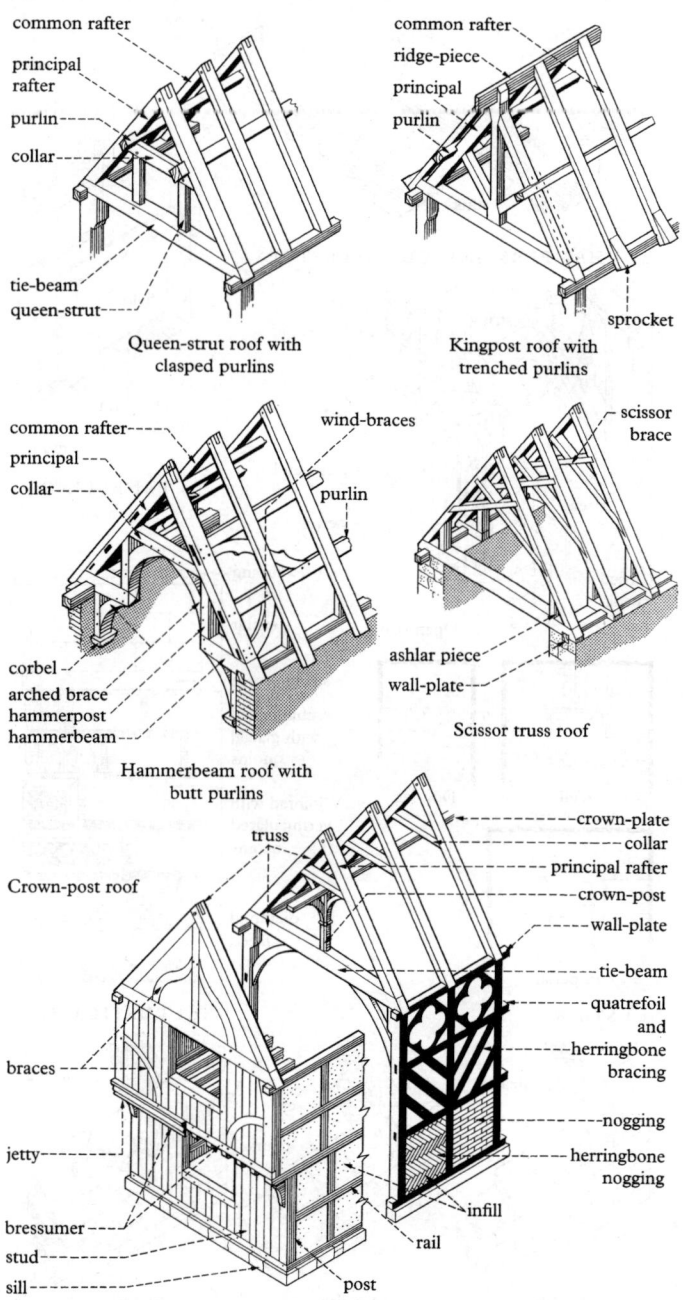

FIGURE 7: ROOFS AND TIMBER-FRAMING

GLOSSARY

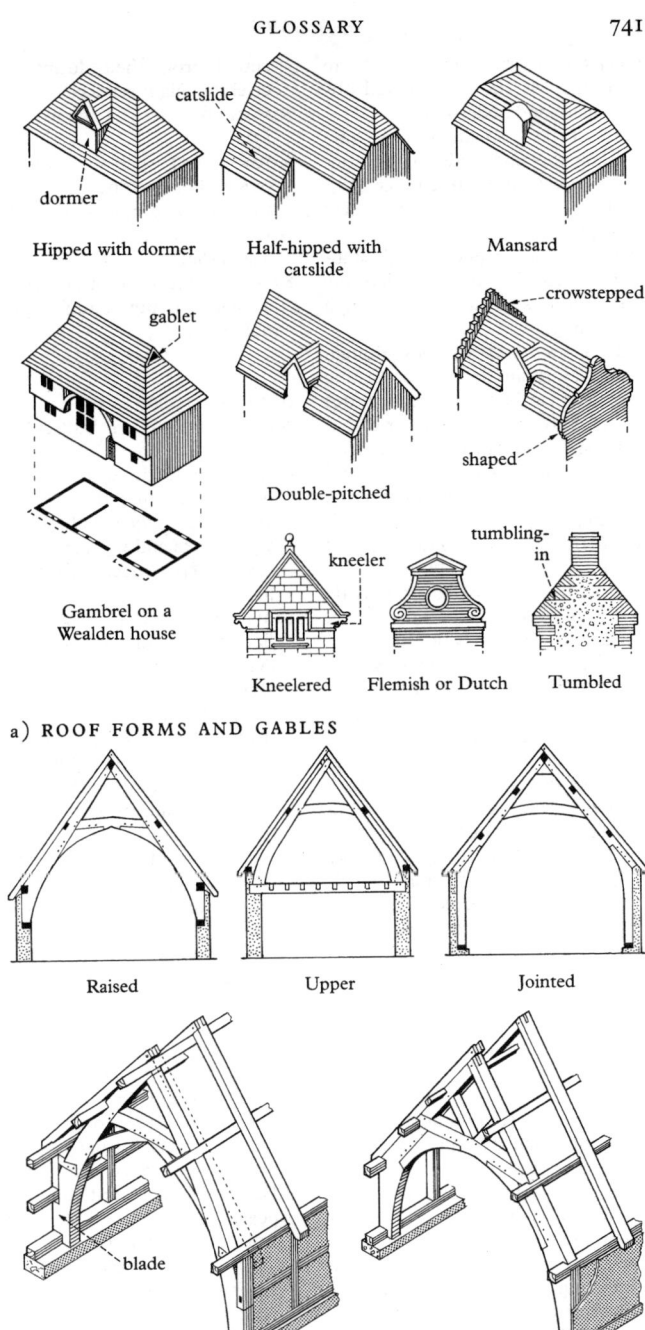

a) ROOF FORMS AND GABLES

b) CRUCK FRAMES

FIGURE 8: ROOFS AND TIMBER-FRAMING

MIXER-COURTS: forecourts to groups of houses shared by vehicles and pedestrians.

MODILLIONS: small consoles (q.v.) along the underside of a Corinthian or Composite cornice (3d). Often used along an eaves cornice.

MODULE: a predetermined standard size for co-ordinating the dimensions of components of a building.

MOTTE-AND-BAILEY: post-Roman and Norman defence consisting of an earthen mound (motte) topped by a wooden tower within a bailey, an enclosure defended by a ditch and palisade, and also, sometimes, by an internal bank.

MOUCHETTE: see Tracery and 2b.

MOULDING: shaped ornamental strip of continuous section; see e.g. Cavetto, Cyma, Ovolo, Roll.

MULLION: vertical member between window lights (2b).

MULTI-STOREY: five or more storeys. Multi-storey flats may form a *cluster block*, with individual blocks of flats grouped round a service core; a *point block*, with flats fanning out from a service core; or a *slab block*, with flats approached by corridors or galleries from service cores at intervals or towers at the ends (plan also used for offices, hotels etc.). *Tower block* is a generic term for any very high multi-storey building.

MUNTIN: see Panelling and 6b.

NAILHEAD: E.E. ornament consisting of small pyramids regularly repeated (1a).

NARTHEX: enclosed vestibule or covered porch at the main entrance to a church.

NAVE: the body of a church w of the crossing or chancel often flanked by aisles (q.v.).

NEWEL: central or corner post of a staircase (6c). Newel stair: see Stairs.

NIGHT STAIR: stair by which religious entered the transept of their church from their dormitory to celebrate night services.

NOGGING: see Timber-framing (7).

NOOK-SHAFT: shaft set in the angle of a wall or opening (1a).

NORMAN: see Romanesque.

NOSING: projection of the tread of a step (6c).

NUTMEG: medieval ornament with a chain of tiny triangles placed obliquely.

OCULUS: circular opening.

ŒIL DE BŒUF: see Bullseye window.

OGEE: double curve, bending first one way and then the other, as in an *ogee* or *ogival arch* (5c). Cf. Cyma recta and Cyma reversa.

OPUS SECTILE: decorative mosaic-like facing.

OPUS SIGNINUM: composition flooring of Roman origin.

ORATORY: a private chapel in a church or a house. Also a church of the Oratorian Order.

ORDER: one of a series of recessed arches and jambs forming a splayed medieval opening, e.g. a doorway or arcade arch (1a).

ORDERS: the formalized versions of the post-and-lintel system in classical architecture. The main orders are *Doric*, *Ionic*, and *Corinthian*. They are Greek in origin but occur in Roman versions. Tuscan is a simple version of Roman Doric. Though each order has its own conventions (3), there are many minor variations. The *Composite* capital combines Ionic volutes with Corinthian foliage. *Superimposed orders*: orders on successive levels, usually in the upward sequence of Tuscan, Doric, Ionic, Corinthian, Composite.

ORIEL: see Bay window.

OVERDOOR: painting or relief above an internal door. Also called a *sopraporta*.

OVERTHROW: decorative fixed arch between two gatepiers or above a wrought-iron gate.

OVOLO: wide convex moulding (3f).

PALIMPSEST: of a brass: where a metal plate has been reused by turning over the engraving on the back; of a wall painting: where one overlaps and partly obscures an earlier one.

PALLADIAN: following the examples and principles of Andrea Palladio (1508–80).

PALMETTE: classical ornament like a palm shoot (4b).

PANELLING: wooden lining to interior walls, made up of vertical members (*muntins*) and horizontals (*rails*) framing panels: also called *wainscot*. *Raised and fielded*: with the central area of the panel (*field*) raised up (6b).

PANTILE: roof tile of S section.

PARAPET: wall for protection at any sudden drop, e.g. at the wall-head of a castle where it protects the *parapet walk* or wall-walk. Also used to conceal a roof.

PARCLOSE: see Screen.

PARGETTING (*lit.* plastering): exterior plaster decoration, either in relief or incised.

PARLOUR: in a religious house, a room where the religious could talk to visitors; in a medieval house, the semi-private living room below the solar (q.v.).

PARTERRE: level space in a garden laid out with low, formal beds.

PATERA (*lit.* plate): round or oval ornament in shallow relief.

PAVILION: ornamental building for occasional use; or projecting subdivision of a larger building, often at an angle or terminating a wing.

PEBBLEDASHING: see Rendering.

PEDESTAL: a tall block carrying a classical order, statue, vase, etc.

PEDIMENT: a formalized gable derived from that of a classical temple; also used over doors, windows, etc. For variations see 4b.

PENDENTIVE: spandrel between adjacent arches, supporting a drum, dome or vault and consequently formed as part of a hemisphere (5a).

PENTHOUSE: subsidiary structure with a lean-to roof. Also a separately roofed structure on top of a C20 multi-storey block.

PERIPTERAL: see Peristyle.

PERISTYLE: a colonnade all round the exterior of a classical building, as in a temple which is then said to be *peripteral*.

PERP (PERPENDICULAR): English Gothic architecture *c.* 1335–50 to *c.* 1530. The name is derived from the upright tracery panels then used (*see* Tracery and 2a).

PERRON: external stair to a doorway, usually of double-curved plan.

PEW: loosely, seating for the laity outside the chancel; strictly, an enclosed seat. *Box pew*: with equal high sides and a door.

PIANO NOBILE: principal floor of a classical building above a ground floor or basement and with a lesser storey overhead.

PIAZZA: formal urban open space surrounded by buildings.

PIER: large masonry or brick support, often for an arch. *See also* Compound pier.

PILASTER: flat representation of a classical column in shallow relief. *Pilaster strip: see* Lesene.

PILE: row of rooms. *Double pile*: two rows thick.

PILLAR: free-standing upright member of any section, not conforming to one of the orders (q.v.).

PILLAR PISCINA: see Piscina.

PILOTIS: C20 French term for pillars or stilts that support a building above an open ground floor.

PISCINA: basin for washing Mass vessels, provided with a drain; set in or against the wall to the S of an altar or free-standing (*pillar piscina*).

PISÉ: see Cob.

PITCHED MASONRY: laid on the diagonal, often alternately with opposing courses (*pitched and counterpitched* or *herringbone*).

PLATBAND: flat horizontal moulding between storeys. Cf. stringcourse.

PLATE RAIL: see Railways.

PLATEWAY: see Railways.

PLINTH: projecting courses at the

foot of a wall or column, generally chamfered or moulded at the top.

PODIUM: a continuous raised platform supporting a building; or a large block of two or three storeys beneath a multi-storey block of smaller area.

POINT BLOCK: see Multi-storey.

POINTING: exposed mortar jointing of masonry or brickwork. Types include *flush*, *recessed* and *tuck* (with a narrow channel filled with finer, whiter mortar).

POPPYHEAD: carved ornament of leaves and flowers as a finial for a bench end or stall.

PORTAL FRAME: C20 frame comprising two uprights rigidly connected to a beam or pair of rafters.

PORTCULLIS: gate constructed to rise and fall in vertical grooves at the entry to a castle.

PORTICO: a porch with the roof and frequently a pediment supported by a row of columns (4a). A portico *in antis* has columns on the same plane as the front of the building. A *prostyle* porch has columns standing free. Porticoes are described by the number of front columns, e.g. tetrastyle (four), hexastyle (six). The space within the temple is the *naos*, that within the portico the *pronaos*. *Blind portico*: the front features of a portico applied to a wall.

PORTICUS (plural: porticūs): subsidiary cell opening from the main body of a pre-Conquest church.

POST: upright support in a structure (7).

POSTERN: small gateway at the back of a building or to the side of a larger entrance door or gate.

POUND LOCK: see Canals.

PRESBYTERY: the part of a church lying E of the choir where the main altar is placed; or a priest's residence.

PRINCIPAL: see Roofs and 7.

PRONAOS: see Portico and 4a.

PROSTYLE: see Portico and 4a.

PULPIT: raised and enclosed platform for the preaching of sermons. *Three-decker*: with reading desk below and clerk's desk below that. *Two-decker*: as above, minus the clerk's desk.

PULPITUM: stone screen in a major church dividing choir from nave.

PULVINATED: see Frieze and 3c.

PURLIN: see Roofs and 7.

PUTHOLES or PUTLOG HOLES: in the wall to receive putlogs, the horizontal timbers which support scaffolding boards; sometimes not filled after construction is complete.

PUTTO (plural: putti): small naked boy.

QUARRIES: square (or diamond) panes of glass supported by lead strips (*cames*); square floor slabs or tiles.

QUATREFOIL: see Foil and 2b.

QUEEN-STRUT: see Roofs and 7.

QUIRK: sharp groove to one side of a convex medieval moulding.

QUOINS: dressed stones at the angles of a building (6d).

RADBURN SYSTEM: vehicle and pedestrian segregation in residential developments, based on that used at Radburn, New Jersey, USA, by Wright and Stein, 1928–30.

RADIATING CHAPELS: projecting radially from an ambulatory or an apse (see Chevet).

RAFTER: see Roofs and 7.

RAGGLE: groove cut in masonry, especially to receive the edge of a roof-covering.

RAGULY: ragged (in heraldry). Also applied to funerary sculpture, e.g. *cross raguly*: with a notched outline.

RAIL: see Panelling and 6b; also 7.

RAILWAYS: *Edge rail*: on which flanged wheels can run. *Plate rail*: L-section rail for plain unflanged wheels. *Plateway*: early railway using plate rails.

RAISED AND FIELDED: see Panelling and 6b.

RAKE: slope or pitch.

RAMPART: defensive outer wall of stone or earth. *Rampart walk*: path along the inner face.

REBATE: rectangular section cut out of a masonry edge to receive a shutter, door, window, etc.

GLOSSARY

REBUS: a heraldic pun, e.g. a fiery cock for Cockburn.

REEDING: series of convex mouldings, the reverse of fluting (q.v.). Cf. Gadrooning.

RENDERING: the covering of outside walls with a uniform surface or skin for protection from the weather. *Limewashing*: thin layer of lime plaster. *Pebbledashing*: where aggregate is thrown at the wet plastered wall for a textured effect. *Roughcast*: plaster mixed with a coarse aggregate such as gravel. *Stucco*: fine lime plaster worked to a smooth surface. *Cement rendering*: a cheaper substitute for stucco, usually with a grainy texture.

REPOUSSÉ: relief designs in metalwork, formed by beating it from the back.

REREDORTER (*lit.* behind the dormitory): latrines in a medieval religious house.

REREDOS: painted and/or sculptured screen behind and above an altar. Cf. Retable.

RESPOND: half-pier or half-column bonded into a wall and carrying one end of an arch. It usually terminates an arcade.

RETABLE: painted or carved panel standing on or at the back of an altar, usually attached to it.

RETROCHOIR: in a major church, the area between the high altar and E chapel.

REVEAL: the plane of a jamb, between the wall and the frame of a door or window.

RIB-VAULT: see Vault and 2c.

RINCEAU: classical ornament of leafy scrolls (4b).

RISER: vertical face of a step (6c).

ROACH: a rough-textured form of Portland stone, with small cavities and fossil shells.

ROCK-FACED: masonry cleft to produce a rugged appearance.

ROCOCO: style current *c.* 1720 and *c.* 1760, characterized by a serpentine line and playful, scrolled decoration.

ROLL MOULDING: medieval moulding of part-circular section (1a).

ROMANESQUE: style current in the C11 and C12. In England often called Norman. *See also* Saxo-Norman.

ROOD: crucifix flanked by the Virgin and St John, usually over the entry into the chancel, on a beam (*rood beam*) or painted on the wall. The *rood screen* below often had a walkway (*rood loft*) along the top, reached by a *rood stair* in the side wall.

ROOFS: Shape. For the main external shapes (hipped, mansard, etc.) see 8a. *Helm* and *Saddleback*: see 1c. *Lean-to*: single sloping roof built against a vertical wall; lean-to is also applied to the part of the building beneath.

Construction. *See* 7.

Single-framed roof: with no main trusses. The rafters may be fixed to the wall-plate or ridge, or longitudinal timber may be absent altogether.

Double-framed roof: with longitudinal members, such as purlins, and usually divided into bays by principals and principal rafters. Other types are named after their main structural components, e.g. *hammerbeam*, *crown-post* (*see* Elements below and 7).

Elements. *See* 7.

Ashlar piece: a short vertical timber connecting inner wall-plate or timber pad to a rafter.

Braces: subsidiary timbers set diagonally to strengthen the frame. *Arched braces*: curved pair forming an arch, connecting wall or post below with tie- or collar-beam above. *Passing braces*: long straight braces passing across other members of the truss. *Scissor braces*: pair crossing diagonally between pairs of rafters or principals. *Wind-braces*: short, usually curved braces connecting side purlins with principals; sometimes decorated with cusping.

Collar or *collar-beam*: horizontal transverse timber connecting a pair of rafter or cruck blades (q.v.), set between apex and the wall-plate.

Crown-post: a vertical timber set centrally on a tie-beam and supporting a collar purlin braced to it longitudinally. In an open truss

lateral braces may rise to the collar-beam; in a closed truss they may descend to the tie-beam.
Hammerbeams: horizontal brackets projecting at wall-plate level like an interrupted tie-beam; the inner ends carry *hammerposts*, vertical timbers which support a purlin and are braced to a collar-beam above.
Kingpost: vertical timber set centrally on a tie- or collar-beam, rising to the apex of the roof to support a ridge-piece (cf. Strut).
Plate: longitudinal timber set square to the ground. *Wall-plate*: plate along the top of a wall which receives the ends of the rafters; cf. Purlin.
Principals: pair of inclined lateral timbers of a truss. Usually they support side purlins and mark the main bay divisions.
Purlin: horizontal longitudinal timber. *Collar purlin* or *crown plate*: central timber which carries collar-beams and is supported by crown-posts. *Side purlins*: pairs of timbers placed some way up the slope of the roof, which carry common rafters. *Butt* or *tenoned purlins* are tenoned into either side of the principals. *Through purlins* pass through or past the principal; they include *clasped purlins*, which rest on queenposts or are carried in the angle between principals and collar, and *trenched purlins* trenched into the backs of principals.
Queen-strut: paired vertical, or near-vertical, timbers placed symmetrically on a tie-beam to support side purlins.
Rafters: inclined lateral timbers supporting the roof covering. *Common rafters*: regularly spaced uniform rafters placed along the length of a roof or between principals. *Principal rafters*: rafters which also act as principals.
Ridge, ridge-piece: horizontal longitudinal timber at the apex supporting the ends of the rafters.
Sprocket: short timber placed on the back and at the foot of a rafter to form projecting eaves.
Strut: vertical or oblique timber between two members of a truss, not directly supporting longitudinal timbers.
Tie-beam: main horizontal transverse timber which carries the feet of the principals at wall level.
Truss: rigid framework of timbers at bay intervals, carrying the longitudinal roof timbers which support the common rafters.
Closed truss: with the spaces between the timbers filled, to form an internal partition.
See also Cruck, Wagon roof.

ROPE MOULDING: see Cable moulding.

ROSE WINDOW: circular window with tracery radiating from the centre. Cf. Wheel window.

ROTUNDA: building or room circular in plan.

ROUGHCAST: see Rendering.

ROVING BRIDGE: see Canals.

RUBBED BRICKWORK: see Gauged brickwork.

RUBBLE: masonry whose stones are wholly or partly in a rough state. *Coursed*: coursed stones with rough faces. *Random*: uncoursed stones in a random pattern. *Snecked*: with courses broken by smaller stones (snecks).

RUSTICATION: see 6d. Exaggerated treatment of masonry to give an effect of strength. The joints are usually recessed by V-section chamfering or square-section channelling (*channelled rustication*). *Banded rustication* has only the horizontal joints emphasized. The faces may be flat, but can be *diamond-faced*, like shallow pyramids, *vermiculated*, with a stylized texture like worm-casts, and *glacial* (frost-work), like icicles or stalactites.

SACRISTY: room in a church for sacred vessels and vestments.

SADDLEBACK ROOF: *see* 1C.

SALTIRE CROSS: with diagonal limbs.

SANCTUARY: area around the main altar of a church. Cf. Presbytery.

SANGHA: residence of Buddhist monks or nuns.

SARCOPHAGUS: coffin of stone or other durable material.

SAXO-NORMAN: transitional Romanesque style combining Anglo-Saxon and Norman features, current *c.* 1060–1100.

SCAGLIOLA: composition imitating marble.

SCALLOPED CAPITAL: *see* 1a.

SCOTIA: a hollow classical moulding, especially between tori (q.v.) on a column base (3b, 3f).

SCREEN: in a medieval church, usually at the entry to the chancel; *see* Rood (screen) and Pulpitum. A *parclose screen* separates a chapel from the rest of the church.

SCREENS or SCREENS PASSAGE: screened-off entrance passage between great hall and service rooms.

SECTION: two-dimensional representation of a building, moulding, etc., revealed by cutting across it.

SEDILIA (singular: sedile): seats for the priests (usually three) on the S side of the chancel.

SET-OFF: *see* Weathering.

SETTS: squared stones, usually of granite, used for paving or flooring.

SGRAFFITO: decoration scratched, often in plaster, to reveal a pattern in another colour beneath. *Graffiti*: scratched drawing or writing.

SHAFT: vertical member of round or polygonal section (1a, 3a). *Shaft-ring*: at the junction of shafts set *en delit* (q.v.) or attached to a pier or wall (1a).

SHEILA-NA-GIG: female fertility figure, usually with legs apart.

SHELL: thin, self-supporting roofing membrane of timber or concrete.

SHOULDERED ARCHITRAVE: *see* 4b.

SHUTTERING: *see* Concrete.

SILL: horizontal member at the bottom of a window or door frame; or at the base of a timber-framed wall into which posts and studs are tenoned (7).

SLAB BLOCK: *see* Multi-storey.

SLATE-HANGING: covering of overlapping slates on a wall. *Tile-hanging* is similar.

SLYPE: covered way or passage leading E from the cloisters between transept and chapter house.

SNECKED: *see* Rubble.

SOFFIT (*lit.* ceiling): underside of an arch (also called *intrados*), lintel, etc. *Soffit roll*: medieval roll moulding on a soffit.

SOLAR: private upper chamber in a medieval house, accessible from the high end of the great hall.

SOPRAPORTA: *see* Overdoor.

SOUNDING-BOARD: *see* Tester.

SPANDRELS: roughly triangular spaces between an arch and its containing rectangle, or between adjacent arches (5c). Also non-structural panels under the windows in a curtain-walled building.

SPERE: a fixed structure screening the lower end of the great hall from the screens passage. *Spere-truss*: roof truss incorporated in the spere.

SPIRE: tall pyramidal or conical feature crowning a tower or turret. *Broach*: starting from a square base, then carried into an octagonal section by means of triangular faces; and *splayed-foot*: variation of the broach form, found principally in the south-east, in which the four cardinal faces are splayed out near their base, to cover the corners, while oblique (or intermediate) faces taper away to a point (1c). *Needle spire*: thin spire rising from the centre of a tower roof, well inside the parapet: when of timber and lead often called a *spike*.

SPIRELET: *see* Flèche.

SPLAY: of an opening when it is wider on one face of a wall than the other.

SPRING or SPRINGING: level at which an arch or vault rises from its supports. *Springers*: the first stones of an arch or vaulting rib above the spring (2c).

SQUINCH: arch or series of arches thrown across an interior angle of a square or rectangular structure to support a circular or polygonal superstructure, especially a dome or spire (5a).

SQUINT: an aperture in a wall or through a pier usually to allow a view of an altar.

STAIRS: *see* 6c. *Dog-leg stair*: parallel flights rising alternately in opposite directions, without an open well. *Flying stair*: cantilevered from the walls of a stairwell, without newels; sometimes called a *Geometric* stair when the inner edge describes a curve. *Newel stair*: ascending round a central supporting newel (q.v.); called a *spiral stair* or *vice* when in a circular shaft, a *winder* when in a rectangular compartment. (Winder also applies to the steps on the turn.) *Well stair*: with flights round a square open well framed by newel posts. See also Perron.

STALL: fixed seat in the choir or chancel for the clergy or choir (cf. Pew). Usually with arm rests, and often framed together.

STANCHION: upright structural member, of iron, steel or reinforced concrete.

STANDPIPE TOWER: *see* Manometer.

STEAM ENGINES: *Atmospheric*: worked by the vacuum created when low-pressure steam is condensed in the cylinder, as developed by Thomas Newcomen. *Beam engine*: with a large pivoted beam moved in an oscillating fashion by the piston. It may drive a flywheel or be *non-rotative*. *Watt* and *Cornish*: single-cylinder; *compound*: two cylinders; *triple expansion*: three cylinders.

STEEPLE: tower together with a spire, lantern, or belfry.

STIFF-LEAF: type of E.E. foliage decoration. *Stiff-leaf capital see* 1b.

STOP: plain or decorated terminal to mouldings or chamfers, or at the end of hoodmoulds and labels (*label stop*), or stringcourses (5b, 6a); *see also* Headstop.

STOUP: vessel for holy water, usually near a door.

STRAINER: *see* Arch.

STRAPWORK: late C16 and C17 decoration, like interlaced leather straps.

STRETCHER: *see* Bond and 6e.

STRING: *see* 6c. Sloping member holding the ends of the treads and risers of a staircase. *Closed string*: a broad string covering the ends of the treads and risers. *Open string*: cut into the shape of the treads and risers.

STRINGCOURSE: horizontal course or moulding projecting from the surface of a wall (6d).

STUCCO: *see* Rendering.

STUDS: subsidiary vertical timbers of a timber-framed wall or partition (7).

STUPA: Buddhist shrine, circular in plan.

STYLOBATE: top of the solid platform on which a colonnade stands (3a).

SUSPENSION BRIDGE: *see* Bridge.

SWAG: like a festoon (q.v.), but representing cloth.

SYSTEM BUILDING: *see* Industrialized building.

TABERNACLE: canopied structure to contain the reserved sacrament or a relic; or architectural frame for an image or statue.

TABLE TOMB: memorial slab raised on free-standing legs.

TAS-DE-CHARGE: the lower courses of a vault or arch which are laid horizontally (2c).

TERM: pedestal or pilaster tapering downward, usually with the upper part of a human figure growing out of it.

TERRACOTTA: moulded and fired clay ornament or cladding.

TESSELLATED PAVEMENT: mosaic flooring, particularly Roman, made of *tesserae*, i.e. cubes of glass, stone, or brick.

TESTER: flat canopy over a tomb or pulpit, where it is also called a *sounding-board*.

TESTER TOMB: tomb-chest with effigies beneath a tester, either free-standing (tester with four or more columns), or attached to a wall (*half-tester*) with columns on one side only.

TETRASTYLE: *see* Portico.

THERMAL WINDOW: *see* Diocletian window.

THREE-DECKER PULPIT: *see* Pulpit.

TIDAL GATES: *see* Canals.

TIE-BEAM: *see* Roofs and 7.

TIERCERON: *see* Vault and 2c.

TILE-HANGING: *see* Slate-hanging.

TIMBER-FRAMING: *see* 7. Method of construction where the structural frame is built of interlocking timbers. The spaces are filled with non-structural material, e.g. *infill* of wattle and daub, lath and plaster, brickwork (known as *nogging*), etc. and may be covered by plaster, weatherboarding (q.v.), or tiles.

TOMB-CHEST: chest-shaped tomb, usually of stone. Cf. Table tomb, Tester tomb.

TORUS (plural: tori): large convex moulding usually used on a column base (3b, 3f).

TOUCH: soft black marble quarried near Tournai.

TOURELLE: turret corbelled out from the wall.

TOWER BLOCK: see Multi-storey.

TRABEATED: depends structurally on the use of the post and lintel. Cf. Arcuated.

TRACERY: openwork pattern of masonry or timber in the upper part of an opening. *Blind tracery* is tracery applied to a solid wall.
Plate tracery, introduced *c.* 1200, is the earliest form, in which shapes are cut through solid masonry (2a).
Bar tracery was introduced into England *c.* 1250. The pattern is formed by intersecting moulded ribwork continued from the mullions. It was especially elaborate during the Decorated period (q.v.). Tracery shapes can include circles, *daggers* (elongated ogee-ended lozenges), *mouchettes* (like daggers but with curved sides) and upright rectangular *panels*. They often have *cusps*, projecting points defining lobes or *foils* (q.v.) within the main shape: *Kentish* or *split-cusps* are forked (2b).
Types of bar tracery (*see* 2b) include *geometric(al)*: *c.* 1250–1310, chiefly circles, often foiled; *Y-tracery*: *c.* 1300, with mullions branching into a Y-shape; *intersecting*: *c.* 1300, formed by interlocking mullions; *reticulated*: early C14, net-like pattern of ogee-ended lozenges; *curvilinear*: C14, with uninterrupted flowing curves; *panel*: Perp, with straight-sided panels, often cusped at the top and bottom.

TRANSEPT: transverse portion of a church.

TRANSITIONAL: generally used for the phase between Romanesque and Early English (*c.* 1175–*c.* 1200).

TRANSOM: horizontal member separating window lights (2b).

TREAD: horizontal part of a step. The *tread end* may be carved on a staircase (6c).

TREFOIL: see Foil.

TRIFORIUM: middle storey of a church treated as an arcaded wall passage or blind arcade, its height corresponding to that of the aisle roof.

TRIGLYPHS (*lit.* three-grooved tablets): stylized beam-ends in the Doric frieze, with metopes between (3b).

TRIUMPHAL ARCH: influential type of Imperial Roman monument.

TROPHY: sculptured or painted group of arms or armour.

TRUMEAU: central stone mullion supporting the tympanum of a wide doorway. *Trumeau figure*: carved figure attached to it (cf. Column figure).

TRUMPET CAPITAL: see 1b.

TRUSS: braced framework, spanning between supports. *See also* Roofs and 7.

TUMBLING or TUMBLING-IN: courses of brickwork laid at right-angles to a slope, e.g. of a gable, forming triangles by tapering into horizontal courses (8a).

TUSCAN: *see* Orders and 3e.

TWO-DECKER PULPIT: *see* Pulpit.

TYMPANUM: the surface between a lintel and the arch above it or within a pediment (4a).

UNDERCROFT: usually describes the vaulted room(s), beneath the main room(s) of a medieval house. Cf. Crypt.

VAULT: arched stone roof (sometimes imitated in timber or plaster). For types see 2c.
Tunnel or *barrel vault*: continuous semicircular or pointed arch, often of rubble masonry.

Groin-vault: tunnel vaults intersecting at right angles. *Groins* are the curved lines of the intersections.

Rib-vault: masonry framework of intersecting arches (ribs) supporting *vault cells*, used in Gothic architecture. *Wall rib* or *wall arch*: between wall and vault cell. *Transverse rib*: spans between two walls to divide a vault into bays. *Quadripartite rib-vault*: each bay has two pairs of diagonal ribs dividing the vault into four triangular cells. *Sexpartite rib-vault*: most often used over paired bays, has an extra pair of ribs springing from between the bays. More elaborate vaults may include *ridge ribs* along the crown of a vault or bisecting the bays; *tiercerons*: extra decorative ribs springing from the corners of a bay; and *liernes*: short decorative ribs in the crown of a vault, not linked to any springing point. A *stellar* or *star* vault has liernes in star formation.

Fan-vault: form of barrel vault used in the Perp period, made up of halved concave masonry cones decorated with blind tracery.

VAULTING SHAFT: shaft leading up to the spring or springing (q.v.) of a vault (2c).

VENETIAN or SERLIAN WINDOW: derived from Serlio (4b). The motif is used for other openings.

VERMICULATION: *see* Rustication and 6d.

VESICA: oval with pointed ends.

VICE: *see* Stair.

VILLA: originally a Roman country house or farm. The term was revived in England in the C18 under the influence of Palladio and used especially for smaller, compact country houses. In the later C19 it was debased to describe any suburban house.

VITRIFIED: bricks or tiles fired to a darkened glassy surface.

VITRUVIAN SCROLL: classical running ornament of curly waves (4b).

VOLUTES: spiral scrolls. They occur on Ionic capitals (3c). *Angle volute*: pair of volutes, turned outwards to meet at the corner of a capital.

VOUSSOIRS: wedge-shaped stones forming an arch (5c).

WAGON ROOF: with the appearance of the inside of a wagon tilt; often ceiled. Also called *cradle roof*.

WAINSCOT: *see* Panelling.

WALL MONUMENT: attached to the wall and often standing on the floor. *Wall tablets* are smaller with the inscription as the major element.

WALL-PLATE: *see* Roofs and 7.

WALL-WALK: *see* Parapet.

WARMING ROOM: room in a religious house where a fire burned for comfort.

WATERHOLDING BASE: early Gothic base with upper and lower mouldings separated by a deep hollow.

WATERLEAF: *see* Enrichments and 3f.

WATERLEAF CAPITAL: Late Romanesque and Transitional type of capital (1b).

WATER WHEELS: described by the way water is fed on to the wheel. *Breastshot*: mid-height, falling and passing beneath. *Overshot*: over the top. *Pitchback*: on the top but falling backwards. *Undershot*: turned by the momentum of the water passing beneath. In a *water turbine*, water is fed under pressure through a vaned wheel within a casing.

WEALDEN HOUSE: type of medieval timber-framed house with a central open hall flanked by bays of two storeys, roofed in line; the end bays are jettied to the front, but the eaves are continuous (8a).

WEATHERBOARDING: wall cladding of overlapping horizontal boards.

WEATHERING or SET-OFF: inclined, projecting surface to keep water away from the wall below.

WEEPERS: figures in niches along the sides of some medieval tombs. Also called mourners.

WHEEL WINDOW: circular, with radiating shafts like spokes. Cf. Rose window.

WROUGHT IRON: *see* Cast iron.

INDEX OF ARCHITECTS, ARTISTS, PATRONS AND RESIDENTS

Names of architects and artists working in the area covered by this volume are given in *italic*. Entries for partnerships and group practices are listed after entries for a single name.

Also indexed here are names/titles of families and individuals (not of bodies or commercial firms) recorded in this volume as having commissioned architectural work or owned, lived in, or visited properties in the area. The index includes monuments to members of such families and other individuals where they are of particular interest.

Abbott family (plasterers) 55, 62, 364–5
Abbott, A. 489
Abbott, John Jun. 272, 304, 483
Abbott, John Sen. 364
Abbott, Richard 365
Abernethy, James 651
Acanthus Clews Architects 156
Acland family 61, 265, 385, 456, 550–1, 684
Acland, Lady Harriet 646
Acland, John *see* Palmer-Acland, Sir John
Acland, Sir Thomas Dyke, 7th Bart 300, 551, 557
Acland, Sir Thomas Dyke, 9th Bart 266
Acland, Sir Thomas Dyke, 10th Bart 550, 551, 586
Acland-Hood family 82, 547
Adair, Alexander 127
Adam brothers 618
Adam, Robert 58, 342, 702
Adams, Hugh 326, 647
Adams, Holden & Pearson 365
ADP 85, 719
Adye, C. S. 395
Æthelred, King 566
Aikman, William 675
Alder, John 707
Aldhelm, St 14, 153
Alfred, King 15, 93, 170, 288, 564, 654
Allen, James 202
Allen, James Mountford 68–9, 70, 71, 76, 104, 186, 189, 214, 235, 236, 237, 238, 252, 256, 351, 377, 379, 394, 437, 459, 517, 524, 556, 570, 578, 669

Allen, John 632
Alves, Harold 82, 326, 328
Ames family 155
Anderdon family 351, 544
Andrew, T. H. 69, 77, 455, 456, 548
Andrews, Edward 521
Angel, John 83, 144
Angell (carver, fl. *c*. 1910) 419
Angell, Clemency 518
Anglesey, 1st Marquess of 221, 441, 442, 444
Angus, Mark 198
Anne, Queen 57, 364, 153
Anton, Günther 282
Architecton 196, 353, 584, 633
Architype 621
ARCO2 357
Arkwright, Arabella 226
Armstrong, A. W. 563
Armstrong Burton 622
Arnatt, Christine 507
Arnold, William 46, 48, 49, 155, 271, 462, 464, 467, 468, 653
Arthur, King 13–14, 130, 306, 307, 308, 566
Arthur, Oswald 70, 577
Artima, Baldassare 53, 361, Pl. 82
Ashburton, 3rd Baron 706, 708
Ashe, James 113
Ashton, Thomas 488
Ashworth, Edward 78, 198, 263, 264, 301, 350, 528, 631, 712
Aston, Edward 254
Atchley, Cuthbert 96, 651
Athelstan, King 396, 472
Atkins, Walters & Webster 601
Atyeo, William 401
Audley, Barons 480
Audley, 7th Baron 479

INDEX OF ARCHITECTS, ETC.

Audley, 11th Baron 479
Austin, James 322
Austin, Rupert 578
Austin, William 103
Ayshe, Elizabeth and William 53, 567

Babbage, James 484
Bacon, John Jun. 523
Bacon, Percy 234
Bacon, Thomas 546
Bagehot family 401
Bagehot, Walter 398, 401
Bailey, Arthur 186
Bailey, Charles 659
Baillie, Thomas 72, 673
Baily, J. 97
Baker family 646
Baker, Anne 529, Pl. 120
Baker, Helen 653
Baker, John 603
Baker King, Charles 72, 496
Balch family 369
Balston, Michael 245
Bampfylde, Coplestone Warre 61, 341, 353–5, 391, 619
Bancks, Sir Jacob 453
Bankart, George 76, 443, 509
Banks, T. Lewis 73, 718
Baring family 514
Barkentin & Krall 172
Barker, E. Lingen 643
Barlow, Brother Louis 321
Barnsley, Ernest 476
Barran, Marius 332, 687
Barratini, James 673
Barrington family 252
Barry, Edward Middleton 243–4
Bartleet, Stephen 614
Bastard, Benjamin 669
Bastard, John 350
Batten family 723
Battersby, Robert 619
Bayley, John 65, 415, 583
Bayley, Thomas 65, 168, 376, 391, 508, 580
Bayley & Street 174
Bayne, Robert Turnill 72, 202, 536, Pl. 106
BDP (Bristol office) 85, 622
Beard, James Baron 97, 403
Beard, Joseph 321, 373, 374
Beauchamp family 209, 268, 347, 593, 606
Beauchamp, Lord 592
Beaufort, Cardinal Henry 339
Beaufort, Lady Margaret 397
Beaverbrook, Lord 238
Beckett, Sir Edward see Grimthorpe, Lord
Beckford, Alderman William 58, 702
Beckford, William 352

Beech, Gerald 428, 634
Beech Tyldesley 310
Beer, Robert 335
Begg, Nigel 85, 332, 444
Bell, Charles 75, 184
Bell, James 520
Bell, Joseph 93, 126, 195, 198, 282, 347, 406, 478, 591
Bell, Reginald 300
Bellamy, Thomas 202
Benjamin & Beauchamp 85, 160, 430
Bennett family 488
Bennett, George 721
Bennett, Henry 571
Bennett, Robert Christie 73, 592
Benslyn, W.T. 83, 625
Benson, Charles 68, 373, 478, 593, 671
Benson, Charles Bernard 68, 96, 161, 235, 569, 671
Benson, H. C. 122
Benson, C. & C. B. 158, 183, 723
Bentley, John Francis 73, 105, 396, 555, 630
Bere, Abbot Richard 40, 154n., 308, 312, 314, 316, 320, 326, 432, 438, 511, 526, 554, 633, 679, 680, 681, 682
Berkeley family 48, 153, 155–6, 157, 158, 159, 537
Berkeley, John, 5th Baron 155, 160
Berkeley, Sir Charles 154
Berkeley, Edward 536
Berkeley, Sir Maurice (d. 1581) 46, 155, 462, 468, Pl. 75
Berkeley, Maurice (d. 1715) 536
Bernard, James 244, 294
Berry, P. R.. 252
Berry, Thomas 629
Berthon, Maude 493
Bertram, William 602
Bertram & Fell 541
Besil family 171
Betere, John 133
Betjeman, (Sir) John 558n.
Bettscomb, Edward 236
Bevan, John 632
Bewsey, J. C. 175, 360
Biddulph-Pinchard, Charles H. 83, 221, 659
Biging family 518
Billo, Francis 268
Bird, Francis 57, 453
Bird, Peter 178, 342
Bird, Robert 237
Birmingham, Robert 411, 551
Bisse family 112–13, 522
Bisse, Edward 672
Bisse, James 111, 112, 522
Bisse, Dr Philip 113
Bisse, Robert 425

INDEX OF ARCHITECTS, ETC. 753

Blackford, William 550, 551
Blackmore, R. D. 507
Blackmore, Samuel 347
Blake family 514
Blake, Margaret 234, 377
Blake, Admiral Robert 78, 140
Blake, William 515
Blensdorf, Ernst 155, 156, 319
Bligh Bond, F. see Bond, F. Bligh
Bliss, Sir Arthur and Lady 82, 518
Blomfield 698
Blomfield, (Sir) Arthur W. 70, 72, 201, 202, 501–2, 507, 567
Blomfield, (Sir) Reginald 469
Blommart, Lt-Gen. Daniel 294
Blore, Edward 172
Bluett family 42, 224, 226, 334
Bluett, Richard 224, 226, 394
Blunt, James 700
Board, John 81, 142
Bobart, Jacques 409
Bobbett family 231
Body, Eve 345, 601
Boevey, James 557
Boleyn, Thomas 519
Bompas, Edward G. 654
Bond, Frederick Bligh 71, 83, 123, 149, 200, 203, 204, 234, 309, 319, 325, 327, 375, 377, 395n., 428, 493, 503, 577, 594, 605, 611, 705, 710
Boney, W. H. 715
Bonville family 255
Boon Brown 85, 96, 502, 515, 671, 678, 717
Boscawen, Robert 602
Boteler family 206, 509
Boteler, Robert 509
Botreaux family 487–8
Botreaux, Lady Elizabeth 486
Botreaux, William, 1st Baron 487
Botreaux, William de 488
Boulting, William 656, 717
Boulton, Richard 609
Bourne, Bishop Gilbert 707
Bourne, Swaine 612
Bowden, Ernest 665
Bowen, John 57, 137, Pl. 98
Bower, Stephen Dykes see Dykes Bower, Stephen
Bowman, Stewart 516, 634, 669
Bowyer, Edmund 219
Boyd, John 183, 184
Boyle family *see* Cork and Orrery, Earls of
Boyle, Charles 424
Boyle, Eleanor 71, 423, 425
Boyle, Richard (C17) *see* Cork, 1st Earl of
Boyle, Rev. Richard (C19) 422
Bracebridge, Edward L. 204
Bradford, W. 627

Bradney, Stephen de 114
Brakspear, (Sir) Harold 82, 224–5
Brakspear, William Hayward 133, 135
Branson, Norman 622
Bratton (de) family 127
Brett family 689
Brett, John (C15) 689
Brett, John (C16) 688
Brewer, William (fl. 1200) 132
Brewer, William (d. 1618) 53, 188
Brewer, Smith & Brewer 599
Breynton, Abbot John 315
Brickdale, Eleanor Fortescue 684
Bridgeman, Messrs 612
Bridgwater, Henry Daubeney, Earl of 105, 495
Bridport, Admiral Alexander Hood, 1st Viscount 58, 66, 239
Bridport, Mary, Viscountess (d. 1831) 239
Bridport, Mary, Viscountess (d. 1884) 73, 239
Brierley, Michael 112
Broderip, Edmund 224
Brodie, C. H. 626
Brodripp family 331
Broke, Abbot Thomas 381, 474
Bromley, A. 529
Brookes, Paul 455
Broughton, Thomas 663
Brown, Lancelot (Capability) 61, 253, Pl. 94
Brown, John 69, 136
Brown, John William 241
Brown, William 708
Brunel, Isambard Kingdom 89, 138, 146, 166, 280, 348, 505
Bryan, H. Dare 453
Bryant, Abraham 182, 184
Bryceson, Henry 293, 383
Brymer, Archdeacon 195, 196
Buckfast Abbey 264
Buckle, Edmund 71, 76, 109, 220, 246, 262, 332, 351, 410, 493, 499, 526, 528, 586, 612
Buckler, John 40, 87, 113, 134, 149, 162, 163, 182, 195, 259, 266n, 270, 293, 299n. 320, 327, 440, 490, 560, 602, 672, 687, 694, 705
Buckler, John Chessell 172
Buckler (J. C.) & Son 172, 682
Bucknall, Benjamin 73, 614
Bucknall, John 168, 700
Bull, William 146, 552
Bullock, George 491
Buncombe family 331
Burges, William 70, 514, 714–15
Burgess, Philip 529, 550
Burgess, Sidney 550
Burgess, William 97, 375, 623
Burgin, Victor 159
Burland family 585

INDEX OF ARCHITECTS, ETC.

Burlison & Grylls 71, 347, 376, 493, 584
Burne-Jones, (Sir) Edward 72, 151, 152, 371, 398, 497, 499, 508, 513, 578, 666, 717
Burnet (Sir John), Tait & Partners 718
Burrough & Hannam 592
Burton, Decimus 443
Burton, Wilf 332
Buss, A. E. 360
Butcher, Geoffrey 424
Butler family 255
Butlin, Billy 448
Butterfield, William 70, 305–6, 556
Buttress, Wolfgang 452
Byron, (Augusta) Ada *see* Lovelace, 1st Countess of

Callan, Jon 717
Camel, John 37, 320, Pl. 53
Cameron (carver, fl. 1935–6) 681
Campbell, Colen 58, 347
Cannon family 303, 304
Capes, Rev. Moore 136
Capronnier, J.-B. 71, 221, 223
Carantoc, St 14, 181
Caratacus 14, 699
Carent family 351, 352
Carent, William and Margaret 37, 351
Carew family 241
Carew, J. E. 63, 162, 693
Carew, Thomas 241, 242
Carnarvon, 2nd Earl of 265
Carnarvon, 4th Earl of 152
Carnwath, 13th Earl of 657
Caröe, Alban 102, 639
Caröe, W. D. 70, 71, 83, 132, 135, 173, 198, 216, 220, 309, 311, 317, 445, 493, 495, 612, 654, 669, 680–1, 716
Caroe & Martin 670
Caröe & Passmore 200, 375
Caroe & Partners 85, 136, 178, 342–3, 521
Carpenter & Ingelow 201
Carter, Johnson & Co. 199
Cartwright, Francis 340
Carver, Daniel 68, 712
Carver, Richard 57, 59, 60, 62–3, 64, 68, 69, 73, 74, 76, 77, 78, 95, 114, 118–19, 123, 137, 141, 147, 167, 170, 171, 189, 191, 224, 229, 254, 282, 294, 304, 347, 348, 384, 399, 400, 412, 416, 447, 454, 478, 482, 484, 485, 497, 500, 509, 513, 524, 525, 545, 546, 552, 574, 582–3, 604, 611, 612, 613, 620, 625, 627, 629, 630, 631, 633, 634, 659, 660, 661, 684–6, 692, 705, 706, 708, Pl. 96

Carver & Giles 478
Casentini & Co. 168, 282
Catford family 498
Catling, Charlotte Skene 85, 336
Cawcy, Diacinto 53, 361, Pl. 82
Cely-Trevilian family 82, 262
Cenwealh, King 14, 307, 518
Chadwyck-Healey, Sir Charles 528
Chaffey family 591
Chambers, (Sir) William 283
Chandos, 1st Duke of 56, 68, 133, 143, 145
Chantrey, (Sir) Francis 66, 550, 559
Chapman family 391
Chapman, Joseph 568–9
Chard, Thomas 462
Charles II, King 273
Chatham, 1st Earl of *see* Pitt, William the Elder
Chaucer, Geoffrey 498
Cheadle, Elizabeth 540
Chedburn Dudley 595
Cheeke, Henry 494
Cheere, (Sir) Henry 65, 584
Cheetham, Henry 664
Chichester family 482
Childs, Wilfred 721
Chilton, Margaret 72, 520
Chinnock, Abbot John 40, 308, 315
Christian, Ewan 98, 167, 220, 324, 380, 427, 430, 445, 499, 520, 523, 667
Churchey, Richard 696
Churchouse, Thomas 284
Cipriani, Giovanni Battista 443
Clare (de) family 210, 268, 481, 640
Clark family 69, 78, 81, 82, 83, 85, 595, 596, 597, 598, 599, 600, 601
Clark, Alfred 598
Clark, Bancroft 597, 598
Clark, Cyrus 596, 599
Clark, Helen 77, 598n.
Clark, James Adams 391
Clark, James 598, 599
Clark, Philip Lindsey 321
Clark, Stephen 597
Clark, Tom 428
Clark, William Stephens 69, 75, 77, 595, 598, 601, 602
Clark, William 183
Clarke family 396
Clarke, Edward 504
Clarke, Geoffrey 119
Clarke, Joseph 227
Clarke, Thomas (carver, fl. 1823) 65, 409, 475
Clarke, Thomas (Greenham Hall) 334
Clarke, William 486, 564
Clarke Renner 456
Clayton & Bell 71, 72, 93, 100, 101, 136, 155, 167, 168, 194, 204, 215,

INDEX OF ARCHITECTS, ETC.

227, 241, 245, 254, 268, 269, 293, 300, 320, 330, 360, 369, 389, 392, 398, 402, 428, 441, 461, 487, 490, 497, 500, 513, 544, 550, 555, 565, 567, 577, 580, 594, 611, 612, 613, 637, 638, 646, 656, 663, 675, 677, 694, 705
Clerk family 522
Clerk, Thomas 522
Clerke, Thomas 46, 709, 710
Clewett, C. 518
Clewett, John 368, 694
Clewett, Samuel 697
Clifford family 175, 176
Clifford, F.C. 529
Clifford of Chudleigh, 1st Baron 176
Clifton, William 105
Clothier, Samuel Thompson 69, 82, 595, 596, 597, 599, 600
Clutterbuck, Charles 222, 673
Clutton, Henry 74, 513–14
Coade (stone) 355, 360, 368, 606
Coalbrookdale Foundry 561, 675
Cobbe, William 572
Cobden, Jane 598n.
Cock, John 349
Cockey, Guliet 564
Cogan family 190
Coke, Thomas 567
Coker family 279
Cole, J. Kingsley 454
Coleridge, Samuel Taylor 91, 248, 479
Coles family 555–6
Coles, Gerald 126
Coles, Rev. James 555–6
Coles, John 122
Coles, Stuckey 556
Collard, Charles Lukey 707
Collcutt, Thomas E. 76, 575–6
Colles family 222, 524
Colles, Humphrey (d. 1693) 510
Colles, Humphrey (C16) 222
Colles, Humphry (d. 1570) 524
Colles, John (d. 1608) 52–3, 524
Colles, John (d. 1627) 53, 524, Pl. 77
Collibear, James 471
Collier Reading 602
Collingridge, Bishop 176
Collins, John 347
Colthurst, T. C. 637
Colthurst, William B. 147
Colwyn Foulkes, S. see Foulkes, S. Colwyn
Combe, Richard 343
Comper, (Sir) J. Ninian 83, 121, 227, 508, 518, 550, 640, 663, 702
Compton, Henry 515, 567
Conder, Neville 84, 601
Conock, Johan 492

Constable, W. H. 285
Cook, Ernest 464
Cook, Sir Francis 225
Cook, James 147
Cooke, P. C. 326
Cooper, Reginald 224
Cork, Richard Boyle, 1st Earl of (d. 1643) 423
Cork and Orrery, Earls of 58, 305, 422–3
  see also Boyle family
Cork and Orrery, 7th Earl of (d. 1798) 425
Cork and Orrery, 8th Earl of (d. 1856) 425, 644
Costoli, Aristodemo 73, 504, 505, Pl. 103
Cothay (de) family 224
Cottam, A. Basil 68, 77, 80, 141, 142, 144, 145, 147, 148, 178, 179, 454, 513
Cotterell, J. Francis 74, 596
Cottrell, William 96
Couling, Andy 235
Courcy (de) family 584
Courcy, Robert de 16, 174
Courtenay family 42, 283, 527, 669–70
  see also Devon, Earls of
Courtenay, Sir Peter 93
Cox, Arthur L. 69, 73, 77, 451, 453, 455
Cox, Thomas 415, 416
Crickmay, George R. 238, 244
Cridland, Francis 180
Cridland, Thomas 687
Crombie, James 131–2
Crosse family 151
Crosse, Andrew (C17) 151
Crosse, Andrew (C19) 151
Crossley, Major Alwyne 459
Crossley, Sarah 253
Crossman, Louise 264, 294, 460, 542, 639, 704
Crotch, William 119
Crowe, (Dame) Sylvia 150
Crozier, Major 629
Cuff, Mr 436
Cuffe family 260
Cuffe, Sir Henry 380
Culverwell, James 137
Culverwell, Robert 659
Curwen, Robert 74, 189, 217, 690
Curzon, George, 1st Marquess 467–8, 469
Cyngar, St 14, 101

Dalton, Rev. Nathaniel 245
Dampier, Edward 97
Daniel, Thomas 577
Darlington, William Vane, 3rd Earl of 374, 441, 443

Daubeney family 105, 475, 555, 567, 569
Daubeney, Giles Daubeney, Baron (d. 1507) 43, 475, 555, 569
Daubeney, Sir Giles (d. 1446) 37, 567
Daubeney, Giles (fl. 1602) 653
Daubeney, Henry *see* Bridgwater, Earl of
Davey, Jeff 138, 234
David, St 14, 307
Davies, Mr 128
Davies, Archibald John 168, 320
Davies, Rev. David 169
Davies, Morgan H. 73, 462
Davis, Charles Edward 75, 79, 197, 424, 425
Davis, Edward 69, 76, 422, 424, 425
Davis, Henry 77, 113, 166, 187, 333, 511, 574, 628, 630
Davis, Herbert 413
Davis, James (Frome, fl. 1845–51) 76, 158, 184
Davis, James (organ-builder, 1762–1827) 471
Davis, Maurice 69, 188, 194, 262, 361, 387, 435, 535, 548, 556, 569, 571, 721
Dawber, (Sir) E. Guy 443, 539, 595
Dawe, J. W. 672
Dawson, Nelson 450
Day, George 697
Day, Joseph 79, 332, 433
Day (Ivor) & O'Brien 705
Dean, Ptolemy 335
Decuman, St 14
Deering, Samuel 265
Defoe, Daniel 56, 137, 448
della Robbia *see* Robbia
Denebaud family 362
Denison, Archdeacon 281
Denny, Sir Anthony 476
Denny, Tom 444
Designscape Architects 502
Devereux Architects 322
Devon, Earls of *see* Courtenay family
Devon, Thomas Courtenay, 14th Earl of 670
Devon, Sir Edward Courtenay, 1st Earl of 670
Dewfall, Joanna 707
Dickens, Alan 157, 721
Dickinson family 392
Dickinson, Caleb 393
Dickinson, Francis 392
Dinsley, W. Hugill 137
Dix, Arthur J. 258, 510
Dixon, Joseph 283
Dixon, William F. 155
DKA 84, 85, 329
see also Kent (David) Architects

DLA 114
Dodesham, William 42, 178
Dodington family 259, 260
Donlin, Martin 596
Donne, Charles 184
Donne, J. S. 184
Douglass, W. T. 456, 651
Dovell, Abbot William 212
Dover, Joanna 567
Down, Edwin 68, 73, 78, 97, 137, 142, 145, 146, 147, 168, 169, 497, Pl. 108
Down, Evan R. 68, 175
Down, Richard 68, 260, 365, 401, 422
Down & Son 147, 293
Drake, Frederick 497, 504, 577
Drake, Helen 394
Drake, Maurice 459, 557
Drake & Pizey 718
Drake (Frederick) & Son 188, 677
Drayton, George 281, Pl. 69
Drew, Richard 76, 556
Drokensford, Bishop John 209, 705
Drury, Alfred 73, 239
Dubricius, St *see* Dyfrig, St
Dummer, Sir John 516–17
Dunstan, St 15, 103, 307, 310
Durnan, Nick 406
Dyer, Sir Edward 554
Dyer, John 357
Dyfrig/Dubricius, St 14, 526
Dyke, R. 357
Dykes Bower, Stephen 252

Earp, Thomas 71, 166, 565, 610
Easton, Hugh 126, 221, 490
Easton, Josiah 127
Easton & Amos 170, 288, 681
Eastwood, Arthur E. 94
Eaton, Robert 48, 124, 215, 292, 467, 469, 482, 483, 509, 531, 664, 671, 704
Eavis, Michael 521
Edalatpur, Seyed 329
Eden, Frederick C. 83, 640
Edgar, King 15, 307, 308
Edinburgh Weavers 321
Edkins, William 409
Edmund, King 15, 307
Edmund of Cornwall 210
Edmund Ironside, King 15, 307
Edward I, King 308
Edward the Elder, King 15
Edwards, Charles F. 646
Edwards, E. Henry 202
Edwards, J. Ralph 143
Eeles, Francis C. 713
Egmont, John Perceval, 2nd Earl of 59, 295–6, 585
Egremont, Charles Wyndham, 2nd Earl of 692

INDEX OF ARCHITECTS, ETC.

Egremont, George Wyndham, 3rd Earl of 692, 693
Egremont, George Wyndham, 4th Earl of 547, 692
Eleanor of Castile, Queen 308, 537
Eliot family 283
Eliot, Thomas Stearns 283
Elizabeth I, Queen 360
Ellis, Thomas 489, 570
Else, Richard 142
Elsworth, George 299
Elton family 689
Elworthy family 661
Embleton, Neil 254
Ensor family 442
Erith, Raymond 381
Ernst, Captain 112
Ernst, T. H. 672
Erridge, A.F. 406
Erskine, Alice 72, 126, 337, 594, 705
Esdaile, E. J. 227, 229
ESHA Architects 722
Espaigne, Alfred d' 480
Evans, Charles 156–7
Evans, David 409
E. V.B. *see* Boyle, Eleanor
Evered family 513
Evered, Robert 583
Every family 226
Every, William 224
Ewen family 698n.
Eyles, Francis 343

Falconer, Thomas 289
Falk, G. 365
Fane family 162
Fane, Francis 162, 165
Fane, Lady Georgiana 162, 166
Farewell, George 52, 119
Farmer, William 71, 512, 684
Farmer & Dark 723
Farquharson, Horace 76, 152, 548
Feilden Clegg Bradley 618
Feilden Clegg Bradley Studios 85, 597, 600
Feilden Clegg Design 235
Fellowes Prynne, G. H. 168
Felton (surveyor, fl. 1788) 363
Ferrey, Benjamin 69, 70, 71, 166, 167, 182, 204, 222, 248, 261, 287, 295, 303, 320, 323, 343, 352, 371, 382, 402, 411, 427, 435, 470, 511, 591, 595, 607, 610, 615, 626, 674, 676, 717
Ferrey, Edmund 394, 591, 612, 655, 679
Ferrey (Benjamin) & Son 101, 648
Field, Richard 293
Fielding, Henry 554
Finden, John 60, 63, 221
Fineberg, Paul 159

Fish, Margery 286
Fisher, Bishop 478
Fisher (York, sculptors) 667
FitzGeldewin, Bishop Savaric 16
Fitzjames, Bishop Richard 154n., 156, 158, 450
Fitzjames, Sir John 540
Flaxman, John 688n.
Fletcher, Henry M. 263
Flint & Neill 617, 622
Flitcroft, Henry 61, 540, 541, 564, Pl. 93
Foden, John 326
Fogwill, Gerald 622
Follett, George 594
Forbes, J. Edwin 82, 106–8
Forbes & Tate 106
Ford (Bath, sculptors) 65, 603
Ford, John Jun. 96, 112
Ford, John Sen. 112, 182, 253, 258
Forester, Frater Martinus 717
Forsyth, J. Dudley 71, 72, 73, 136, 613, 614
Forsyth, James 166, 167
Fort, Thomas 143, 540
Fortescue, 3rd Earl 557
Foster & Wood 74, 75, 124, 357, 397, 451, 454, 490
Foulkes, S. Colwyn 91, 206
Fownes Luttrell family *see* Luttrell family
Fox family 75, 81, 658, 661
Fox, Francis 166, 545
Fox, Gertrude 634
Fox, James 368
Fox, Joseph 661
Fox, Bishop Richard 541, 625
Fox, Sir Stephen 540
Fox, Thomas 67, 661, 662
Fox-Strangways family 540
Frampton, Edward 433
Francis, Eric 82, 85, 614, 629, 630, 678
Franses, Michael 703
Fraunceis family 215
Fraunceis, John 215
Fraunceis, William 215
Freeman, Edward 711
French, Alec 599
French, John 529
French (Alec) Partnership 624
Fromond, Abbot 308, 313
Fry, Harold 334
Fry, Ralph 562
Fuller-Acland-Hood, Lady Isabella 301
Fuller-Acland-Hood family 684
Fuller-Palmer-Acland, Sir Peregrine 301, 585, 684
Furneaux (de) family 385
Furneaux, Simon de 385
Fursman, Martha 640

758 INDEX OF ARCHITECTS, ETC.

Gabbutt, Frederick 509
Gabie, Neville 191
Gaffin, Thomas 612
Gahagan, Lucius 172, 239
Gallanaugh, Reginald 630
Gallannaugh, Roger 159
Gane, Jesse 69, 112, 290, 297–8, 395, 517–18, 673
Gane, John 112
Garton, Lt-Col. James A. 536, 537
Gascoyne, Tom 503
Gatehouse family 103
Gaye, Howard 233–4
George III, King 564
George (Sir Ernest) & Alfred Yeates 653
Gibberd, (Sir) Frederick 85, 358
Gibbons, Grinling 53, 167–8
Gibbons, Owen 367
Gibbs, Alexander 72, 121, 347, 357, 398, 552, 611
Gibbs, Charles A. 360, 433
Gibbs, James 57, 702
Gibbs, Philip 348
Gibbs, Samuel 65, 234, 653
Gibbs (Alexander) & Co. 234
Gibbs & Howard 199
Giffard, Bishop William 16
Gifford, Col. J.W. 192
Gilbert, Abbot William 154n., 566, 569
Gildas 595
Giles, Charles Edmund 68, 69, 70, 71, 77, 78, 79, 95, 109, 113, 114, 121, 150, 180, 187, 195, 196, 222, 250, 252, 254, 299–300, 304, 333, 358, 384, 392, 397, 401, 403, 412, 413, 478, 480, 499, 513, 574, 588, 621, 623, 624, 626, 630, 635, 642, 645, 658, 660, 663, 690, 691, 708
Giles, William J. 337, 504, 543
Giles & Gane 663, 705, 709
Giles & Gough 79, 236
Giles, Gough & Trollope 224
Giles & Robinson 389, 680
Gill, Eric 152, 264, 310, 333, 428, 523
Gill, Wallace 702
Gillick, Ernest 481
Gillman, Richard 502
Gilroy, Laura 563
Gingell, William B. 515
Gleichen, Countess Feodora 507
Godolphin, William 53, 155
Golding, William A. 183
Goodford family 202, 478
Goodford, Rev. Charles 201
Goodhart-Rendel, Harry S. 391–2
Goodridge, Henry Edmund 61, 173, 630, 723
Goodwin & Tatum 84, 620
Gordon, G. Hamilton 648

Gordon, Thomas 402
Goss, William 598
Goudge, Edward 55, 272
Gough, A. E. 519
Gould, Jeremy & Caroline 84, 460, 597, 599, 601, 602, 718
Gould, Kate 240
Graham family 224
Graham, Harry 672
Graham Carruthers Partnership 192, 279, 524
Grandisson, Bishop John 209
Grange, Richard 443
Grant, Edward 541
Grantham, Andrew 667
Gravatt, William 67, 344, 399, Pl. 116
Gray, George Kruger 368
Gray, Jane 524
Gray, Robert 53, 611
Gray & Davison 476
Gray & Son 678n.
Green, Clare Maryan 613
Green, James 67, 505
Green, James Baker 70, 223, 353
Greenfield, Guy 85, 264
Greenhill family 536
Greenhill, Benjamin 114
Greenway 391
Gregory, Thomas 142
Grenville, Rev. George Neville 172
Greswell, Charles 117
Griffin, Rev. William 479, 480
Grimshaw Architects 359
Grimthorpe, Sir Edward Beckett, 1st Baron 675
Grobham, Sir Richard 122
Grueber, Rev. Charles 343
Grundy, Thomas 239
Grylls, Chinks 264
Guest family 352
Guest, Thomas Merthyr 351, 352
Guinevere, Queen 14, 308
Gunn, Edwin 82, 455, 457
Gunn, Rev. John 188, 191
Gunn & Fry 84, 458
Gunthorpe, Dean John 257, 258, 421–2
Guthrie, Leonard Rome 649
Guthrum, King 15, 93, 654
Gwillim, Bronwen 707
Gyvernay, Sir Richard 24, 402

Habershon & Brock 175
Haig, Henry 574, 611
Hales, Sir Philip 179
Hall family 559
Hall, Henry 70, 72, 75, 76, 79, 184, 350, 352, 353, 368, 399, 420, 440, 442, 444, 461, 489, 539, 541, 542, 548, 564, 565, 672
Hall, Sydney 545, 713

INDEX OF ARCHITECTS, ETC.

Hallett, Thomas 459
Halliday, John 509
Halliday, William 203, 511
Halswell family 330–1, 339
Halswell, Sir Nicholas 52, 330
Hammet, Sir Benjamin 60, 613, 616–18, 626, 629
Hancock family 707
Hancock, Rev. John 345–6
Hancock, Prebendary Frederick 370
Hancock, William 706
Hannam, Julian 660
Hansell, A. W. 639
Hansom, Charles F. 73, 614, 632
Harbin family 65, 485–6, 717, Pl. 84
Harbin, George 485–6
Harbin, Robert 485
Harbin, Swayne 486
Harbinson, Timothy 411
Harbottle, E. H. 494
Harcourt Masters see Masters, Charles Harcourt
Hardman (John) & Co. 71, 72, 114, 137, 172, 186, 223, 234, 283, 396, 445, 451, 512, 513, 567, 571, 604, 613, 632, 684, 713, 717
Hardwick, Philip Charles 116
Hardy, James 53, 651
Hargreaves, Thomas 512
Harington family 527
Harington, Sir John 37, 527, Pl. 52
Harington, William, Lord 402
Harland, Peter 82, 518
Harris, John 336
Harris, Joseph 444
Harris, Raphe 499
Harris, E. Vincent 83, 186, 189, 619–20, 621, Pl. 125
Harrison, Hugh 540
Harrison, James Park 149, 460
Harriss, Cyril 573
Harvey, Henry 144
Hassell (Exeter, architect) 265
Hastings, Sir Francis 488
Haviland, John 396
Hawkins, Henry 596
Hawkins & Alves 596
Hay, John Mountford 663
Hayward, John (Exeter, architect) 395–6, 445
Hayward, John (glass-stainer) 123, 605
Hayward, Richard 436, 668, 669
HBS 329, 400
see also Higgison, Brown & Stuckey
Heal, Samuel 392, 482, 483
Hearst, William Randolph 350
Heathcoat Amory, Henry 152
Heaton, Butler & Bayne 112, 113, 202, 376, 493, 502, 504, 536, 591, 612, 677

Hele, Sir Thomas 515
Hellicar, Evelyn 412, 635
Helyar family 283, 531
Helyar, Archdeacon William 283
Hemming, Alfred O. 279, 352, 709
Hems, Harry 189, 234, 241, 268, 445, 492, 680, 700, 710, 717
Henley, Sir Andrew 459
Henley, Henry 700
Henley, Robert 459
Hennet, George 652
Henry II, King 308, 311
Henry VII, King 617
Henry VIII, King 43, 46, 446, Pl. 61
Henry of Blois, Bishop of Winchester 308, 310, 615
Hensley, Alice 527
Henton, Prior John 159
Hepworth, A. Jackson 85, 327
Herbert, Mrs Mary 264
Herbert, Aubrey 152
Herbert, Mervyn 391
Herlewin, Abbot 307
Heron, John 397, 398
Herriot, Alan B. 652
Hervey family 350
Hext, Sir Edward 46, 53, 408, 409
Hibbert, Jo 683, 689
Hickes & Isaac 567, 721
Higgison, Brown & Stuckey (HBS) 601, 602
see also HBS; Leading Environmental Design
Hill family 530, 533, 571, 572
Hill, John 571
Hill, Roger 530, 531
Hill, William 530, 532
Hinchliffe, John 611
Hine, James 377
Hirst, Peter 620, Pl. 126
Hitchin, Stephen 602
Hoare, Henry 61, 341, 342, 355, 564
Hoare, Prince 162
Hobhouse family 335, 523
Hobhouse, Henry 335
Hobhouse, Hermione 672
Hobhouse, Niall 335–6
Hochberg, Count Konrad von 543
Hody family 332
Hody, Sir William 42, 332
Holden, Charles 82, 117
Holding, Edward 191, 661, 696
Holiday, Henry 72, 152, 420, 450, 497, 504, 508, 709, 717
Holland, Henry 392
Holland, Rev. William 513
Holland, William 512
Hollingbery, Richard 160
Hollinsworth, James 231, 546
Holloway, Benjamin 56, 143
Holt, William 132
Hone, Evie 264

Hood family 172, 173, 239, 321
Hood, Admiral Alexander (d. 1814) see Bridport, 1st Viscount
Hood, Sir Alexander (d. 1892) 684
Hood, Vice-Admiral Sir Samuel Hood 172, 173–4
Hook, James Clarke 664
Hopkins, Rice 130
Hopper, Humphrey 222, 346, 441
Hopton family 257, 258, 299, 702
Horder, P. Morley 82, 458
Horn, William 454, 713
Horne, Bishop 615
Horner family 212–13
Horner, Sir George 213
Horrobin, James 241, 543, 574, 622, 684
Horsey family 419, 465
Horwood Bros 289, 305, 520, 645
Hoskins, Gareth 146
Hoskins, Silas 595
Hoskyns, Henry W. 495
Hoskyns-Abrahall, Rev. John 156
Howard, Cecil de B. 152
Howard, Edwin 69, 77, 80, 543, 659, 660, 661, 666
Howard, Ernest 659, 661
Howard, Frank Ernest 357
Howe family 562
Howe, Henry and Agnes 576
Howitt, Cecil 141, 722
Hudson, Thomas 697
Hugh of Lincoln, St 700
Hugh de Neville 584
Hughes, Allan 677
Hughes, Henry 478, 547
Hughes, Philip 107, 381, 397, 667
Hughes (Philip) Associates 213
Huish, Frederick 329
Hunt family 221
Hunt, Francis 659
Hunt, John Hubert 221
Huntingdon, Earls of 488
Hutchings, Thomas 137, 144
Hutchings, William A. 378
Hutchinson, Mary 72, 450
Huxley-Jones, T. B. 357
Hymerford family 490

Ilchester, Earls of 540, 560
Ilchester, Stephen Fox-Strangways, 1st Earl of 540
Ilchester, William Fox-Strangways, 4th Earl of 205
Ilchester, Henry Fox-Strangways, 5th Earl of 540
Ilett, Philip 66, 170
Ine, King of Wessex 14, 15, 153, 307, 471, 566, 568
Innes-Wilkin, David 570
Insall (Donald) Associates 160, 348, 546

Ireson, Nathaniel 56, 57–8, 62, 64, 154, 155, 183, 242, 245, 442, 540, 562, 566, 694, 695, 696, 697, Pl. 90

Jackson, (Sir) Thomas Graham 70, 75, 92, 109, 298, 366–7, 377, 406, 507, 635, 639, Pls. 102, 104
Jacman, John 432
James II, King 167
James, Joseph 78–9, 621
Jeanes, James 295, 296
Jebb, Philip 187
Jefferies, Paul 536, 613
Jeffreys, Judge George 615
Jekyll, Gertrude 108, 353
Jenner, Sir Walter 417
Jennett, Frederick 718
Jennings family 253
Jennings, Marmaduke 52, 252
Jennings, Robert (d. 1593) 46, 252
Jennings, Robert (d. 1630) 52, 252
Jervois, (Sir) William 129
Jewson, Norman 82, 386, 476
Jocelyn, Bishop 711
John of Slough 588
Johnson, Gerard 360
Johnson, John 343
Johnson, Matthew Wharton 252
Johnston, Joseph Nicholson 68, 71, 77, 80, 96, 717, 720, 721, 723
Johnston, Nicholas 53, 377
Jones, Rev. Edward 580
Jones, Inigo 54, 55, 163, 363, 483, 533, 642
Jones, Owen 75, 707
Jones & Co. (sculptors, fl. c. 1792) 230
Jones, Dunn & Drewett 544
Jones & Willis 559, 567
Joseph of Arimathea 306, 308, 312
Joy, William 316
Jupp, C. Kingsley 605
Juyner, Abbot David 39, 206, 210

Keene, Henry 61, 64, 330, 342
Kellett, Rev. Edward 664
Kelly, Captain 305
Kelly, Fleur 316, 575
Kelway family 371
Kemeys Tynte family see Tynte
Kempe, Charles Eamer 72, 97, 102, 105, 150, 175, 221, 287, 291, 368, 450, 451, 497, 508, 524, 574, 621, 645, 659, 684, 688, 717
Kempe & Co. 95, 167, 252, 291, 356, 368, 412, 621, 642, 645, 705, 717
Kempshed, John 234
Kempthorne, Sampson 96, 145, 345, 458, 633, 719
Ken, Bishop Thomas 708

INDEX OF ARCHITECTS, ETC.

Kendall, Edward 445
Kendall, John 688
Kennedy, Hugh Arthur 72, 398, Pl. 107
Kennedy, J. C. 455
Kensington Taylor 85, 678
Kent, William 58, 59, 62, 63, 243, 347, 355, 710
Kent (David) Architects 452, 568, 601
  see also DKA
King (Bath, sculptors) 65, 112, 151, 175, 481, 529, 611, 612, 667
King, Charles Baker, see Baker King, Charles
King, Oliver, Bishop of Bath and Wells 438
King, Phillip 601
King, Thomas 122, 149, 206, 289, 396, 536, 544, 656, 710
King, Walker, Bishop of Rochester 168
Kinglake, William 625
Kingsley (Mark) Architects 453
Kingsmill of Ballybeg, Sir Francis 52, 136
Kirk, Charles 75, 436, 668
Knight family 391
Knight, Sir Frederic 557
Knight, John 557
Knight, Bishop William 46
Knowles, Charles 68, 70, 74, 77, 137–8, 176, 179, 199, 219, 224, 279, 331, 438, 497, 524–5, 561
Knowles, James Thomas 692
Kruger Gray, George see Gray, George Kruger
Kuitca, Guillermo 160

Labouchère, Henry see Taunton, Lord
Laffan, G.B. 142
Lamb, Edward Buckton 172, 173, 444, 563
Lamb, Percy 695
Lambert, David 697
Lancashire, Francis 591
Lance, Ethel 663
Lance, Rev. John 166–7
Lance, Madalina 73, 166, 167
Langman, Sir Archibald 488, 489
Langston, John 458
Langton, Bishop Thomas 615, 617
Laplace, Luis 160
Lassen, Michael 168
La Trobe-Bateman, Richard 399
Latrobe & Weston 592
Laud, Archbishop William 51
Lauder, Alexander 74, 168, 377, 388, 428, 442, 568, 651, 718, Pl. 109
Lavers & Barraud 72, 95, 198, 227, 303, 333, 347, 435, 584, 647, 717

Lavers, Barraud & Westlake 72, 249, 300, 303, 320, 330, 394, 396, 544, 645, 647, 710
Lavers & Westlake 71, 103, 612, 630
Lawray Architects 156
Lawson, Sir Wilfrid 598n.
LDA Design 617
Lea, David 484
Lea, Pamela 523
Leading Environmental Design (LED) 601, 622
Leaman, Keith 575–6
Lechland, William 624
LED see Leading Environmental Design
Lee, John Lee 254
Lee, Thomas 505, 662
Leir family 197, 259
Leland, John 14, 174, 270, 318, 372, 479, 554, 579, 593
Lennox-Boyd, Arabella 294
Le Sueur, Hubert 53, 156
Lethbridge family 100, 122, 412
Lethbridge, John 412
Lewis (Cheltenham, sculptors) 428
Lewis family 696
LHC Architects 85, 620
Lidbetter, Hubert 82, 666–7
Lincoln, William de Roumare, Earl of 16, 206
Linscombe, Henry 283
Little & Goodson 78, 626
Llewellyn Harker 256
Lloyd (Matthew) Architects 597
Locke, John (d. 1704) 504
Locke, John (fl. 1859) 265
Lockyer, James 394
Lomas, John 77, 528
Lomas, Thomas 454
Long (family, sculptors) 65, 613
Long (Dutch landscaper) 665
Long, Mark 612
Longden, Henry 613
Loraine, Joan 529
Lotys family 278
Lovel family 183
Lovelace, 1st Countess of (née Augusta Ada Byron) 529
Lovelace, Mary, 2nd Countess of 76, 128, 247–8, 529–30
Lovelace, William King, 1st Earl of (former Lord King) 247, 529, 530
Lovelace, Ralph King-Milbanke, 2nd Earl of 247, 529
Lucas, Robert 645, 678
Lucas, William King 457
Luttrell family 42, 69, 124, 266, 267, 269, 270, 276, 291, 453, 455
Luttrell, Lady Elizabeth 37, 269
Luttrell, Col. Francis 271
Luttrell, George Fownes 206, 448, 453

Luttrell, George (d. 1629) 52, 124, 269, 271, 274, 276, 291, 456
Luttrell, Henry Fownes 274, 275, 278
Luttrell, Margaret 274
Lutyens, (Sir) Edwin 76, 83, 152, 348n., 353–5, 529, 540–1, 595, 689, Pls. 121, 123
Lyle, Col. Arthur 82, 106–8
Lysaght, Gerald S. 509
Lyte family 417–19
Lyte, John 417–19
Lyte, Thomas (fl. 1631) 42, 417
Lyte, Thomas (fl. 1726) 196
Lyte, William le 417

MacBean, Timothy 157
McCall, Malcolm 576
McCurdy, Peter 521
MacDermott, Edward 248
Macdowell, Patrick 72, 445
Macfarlane (Walter) & Co. 78, 622, 673
Macgregor, John 591
Mackenzie Wheeler 159, 633
Mackintosh, Sir Cameron 575
Mackintosh, David 334–5
Maddicks, Thomas 145
Mahlich, Nick 639
Majendie, Bishop Henry 478
Malet family 332, 684
Mancon Project Management 156
Manners, George Phillips 69, 115, 132, 229, 285, 332
Manners, Sir William 374
Marsden, William E. 547
Marsh, Thomas 359
Marshall, Edward 656
Marshman Warren Taylor 622
Martin family 289
Martin, Arthur C. 539
Marys, John 33, 267, 449
Masters, Charles Harcourt 197, 219, 420
Mather, Andrew 456
Matthews & Mackenzie 455
Maunsel family 42, 545
Mawer, Richard 213
Maxwell, Lyn Constable 487
Mayer & Co. 371, 543, 656, 682
Medici, Cosimo de' (Cosimo III of Tuscany) 361
Medlycott family 441–2
Medlycott, Anthony 441
Medlycott, James 442
Ména (Paris, glass-stainers) 72, 682
Merefield family 234, 235–6, 355
Merer, Mark 196
Merer, Stanley 159
Meriet/Merriet (de) family 215
Merrick, Frederick 321, 324, 327
Merrick, John 327

Merriett *see* Meriet/Merriett (de) family
Messiter family 694, 695
Methuen, Anthony 533
Mew, Leonard 286, 706, 718
Meyer, F.W. 660
Meyer, Robert 329, 601
Michaelis, Alex 687
Michell, Mary 65, 398
Mildmay family 538
Mildmay, Carew Hervey 349
Mildmay, Humphrey 57, 349
Mildmay, Sir Walter 349–50
Miles, Mary 72, 282, 384
Miller, John 690
Miller, Sanderson 58, 347
Milne, Oswald 266
Milner, Henry Victor 499
Minton 71, 72, 195, 196, 238, 274, 281, 461, 511, 514, 651, 674, 684, 708
Mitchell, Chris 270
Mitchell, William 339
Mitchell Taylor Workshop 84, 621
Mlinaric, David 672
Moels (de) family 488
Moffatt, William Bonython 77–8, 620
Mohun (de) family 209, 270, 569
see also William de Mohun
Monington, Abbot Walter 24–5, 308, 313–14, 315
Montagu family 209
Montague family 588, 689
Montmorency, Rachel 596
Moody, Charles 389
Moody, Terence 136
Moore family 669, 670, 671
Moore, A. L. 230, 571, 574, 611, 703
Moore, Christopher 72, 331
Moore, James P. 186
Moore, John (C18) 671
Moore, John (C19) 671
Moore, Joseph 670
Moore, Stuart 689
Moore, Temple 76, 283–4
Moore (A. L.) & Son 189
Morgan, Godfrey 452
Morgans, Morgan 130
Morland family 85, 327, 328
Morris, Elizabeth 65, 258
Morris, Joseph 572
Morris, Olive 573
Morris, Violet 76, 572, 573
Morris, William 513, 666
Morris & Co. 72, 151, 152, 187, 285n., 371, 513, 578, 587, 666, 694
Mortain, Robert, Count of 185
Mortain, William, Count of 16
Moss, Rev. J. J. 287
Mossman (Glasgow, sculptor) 710
Moxley, Ray 85, 600

Moxon Architects 617, 622
Moyer, Humphrey 53, 700
Moysey, Archdeacon C. A. 113
Murch, Edward 125, 136, 231
Musgrave family 581, 678
Musgrave, George 217, 485, 581

Napier, Gerard Berkeley 289
Napper family 640
Napper, Andrew 640
Napper, Honour 641
Nathan, Sir Matthew 670
Nattress, George 74, 235, 255, 372
Neal, William 389
Nealon Tanner 601
Nelson, Rev. William Nelson, 1st Earl 66, 239, Pl. 97
Nelson, Joseph 168
Neville, Mrs (painter, fl. 1920s) 193
Neville, Claude 193
Neville-Grenville family 103
Newbolt, Sir Henry 91
Newby, Vincent & Findlay Smith 718
Newman family 110, 488, 717
Newton, Ernest 664
Newton, T. W. F. 706
Nicholls, Francis 234
Nicholls, Ralph 137
Nicholson, A. K. 112, 234, 502, 548, 567, 570
Nicholson, Thomas 192, 396
Nicolson, Harold 224
Nissen, Major P. N. 668, 722
Nollekens, Joseph 66, 331
Norman, Samuel 533
North, John William 338
Norton, John 69, 74, 75, 76, 78, 79, 93, 132, 278, 303, 356, 357, 365, 384, 487, 511–12, 582, 585, 647n., 683–4, 686, 691, Pl. 101
Notley family 460
Notley, George 217
Nuttgens, J. E. 525
NVB Architects 84, 112, 138, 622

Oatley, (Sir) George 80, 141, 240, 400, 453, 567, 619, 623
Oatley & Lawrence 722
O'Connor (glass-stainers) 71, 92, 166, 182, 214, 217, 238, 261, 282, 288, 298, 371, 380, 398, 404, 415, 439, 441, 471, 507, 523, 669, 682, 684
Odda 180
Office of Works 83, 326, 457, 626, 721
Olive, Rev. Dan 529
Orchard family 691
Orme Architecture 85, 328, 503
Orrery, Charles Boyle, 4th Earl of 423
Orwin, C. S. 458

Osborn, Esau 615
Osborne, Archie 681
Osborne, James 188
Osmond, William 156, 538
O2i Design 220, 576
Oudolf, Piet 160
Overay, Thomas 519, 520
Owen, Evan 223

Pace, George G. 559
Page, E. Godfrey 78, 138
Paget, John Moore 285
Palmer, F. C. R. 457
Palmer, Philip 186
Palmer, Sir Thomas (C16) 302
Palmer, Thomas (C18) 302, 603
Palmer, William 301, 302
Palmer-Acland, Sir John (former John Acland) 301
Palmerston, Henry Temple, 2nd Viscount 355
Parker, Barry 77, 457, 458, Pl. 122
Parker, Thomas 57, 65, 241, 242–3, Pl. 89
Parker, W. J. 543
Parker & Unwin 77, 147, 457
Parkin, Arthur 501, 574
Parr, Francis 78, 138
Parr, Henry 597
Parry, James 142
Parsons 435
Parsons, George 125–6
Parsons, Henry (C18) 668
Parsons, Henry (C19) 149, 459, 563
Parsons, Samuel 91
Patch, John 234, 236, 237, 406
Patch, William 98
Patehull, William 135
Paterson, Justin 502
Patrick, St 14, 307
Patti, Adelina 707
Paty, James Sen. 298
Paty (Thomas) & Sons 65, 136, 188, 298, 368, 385
Paul, Roland W. 371
Paulet/Paulett family 331
Paulet, Sir Amyas and Sir Hugh 46, 356, 360
Paulet, William 362
Paull, Henry J. 407
Paull & Bickerdike 369, 379
Paull & Robinson 407
Pauncefoot family 221
Pauncefoot, Sir Walter 221
Paxton, Richard 85, 329
Peacham, Henry 364
Pearce, Edward 55, 273, Pl. 81
Pearce, George 345, 459
Pearson, John Loughborough 70, 537, 708
Peirs, Col. William 59, 665, 710
Pelham family 59, 665, 710

Peniston, John 64, 177, 696
Pennethorne, James 60, 254, Pl. 99
Penny, Thomas (C18) 162, 197
Penny, Thomas (C19) 630
Penoyre & Prasad 146
Penrose, Boise 484
Penrose, Francis Cranmer 75, 92, 173, 182, 252, 367, 634, Pl. 111
Penruddocke, Charles 129
Pepper, Frederick 540
Perceval family 146
Perceval, John *see* Egmont, 2nd Earl of
Perceval, Theophilus 160
Periam family 172–3, 321
Periam, John 100
Perriam, James 173
Perry, Henry 282, 486
Peryn, John 358, 395, 506, 666
Peto, Harold 253, 459, 653
Petter, James B. 507
Petter & Warren 82, 83, 110, 431, 463, 668, 672, 717, 720, 721, 722, 723, Pl. 124
Petter, Warren & Cooper 720
Petvin, Isaac 596
Phelips family 462, 464
Phelips, Caroline 244
Phelips, Sir Edward (d. 1614) 462, 464, 467
Phelips, Sir Edward (d. 1690) 65, 462
Phelips, Edward (d. 1797) 465
Phelips, Rev. Robert 656, 717
Phelips, Thomas 46, 462
Phelps, Richard 61, 244, 275
Phelps, Rev. William 710
Phillips (Niall) Architects 85, 256, Pl. 127
Phoenix Foundry 626
Physick, E. J. 72, 361
Physick, Robert 559
Pick Everard 690
Pickthall, Mark 159
Pictor, Arthur J. 83, 156, 158, 160, 335, 523, 656
Pierce, Robert 663
Pinch, Charles 606
Pinch, John 202
Pinney family 559, 563, 653
Pinney, John 62, 562, 563
Pistell, William 547
Pitt, Stephen 238
Pitt, William the Elder (1st Earl of Chatham) 64, 217, 253–4
Pleydell-Bouverie family 175
Pollak, Frankie 412, 508
Pollard (family) 68
Pollard, George 229
Pollard, James 73, 614
Pollard, Samuel 73, 598, 599–600, 659, 707

Pollitzer, Sally 112
Pomeroy, F. W. 78, 142
Pomeroy, Richard 520
Ponting, C. E. 76, 337, 376, 417–19, 426, 591
Poole family 514
Poole, J. R. 179
Poole, Rev. John 295
Poole, Thomas 479
Pope, Richard 267
Pope, Mitch & Pené 672
Popham family 124, 664, 678
Popham, Sir John 52, 659, 661, Pl. 76
Porch family 329
Porch, Albert 329
Portman family 223, 282, 346, 355, 388, 510, 536, 574, 605, 623, 669, 670–1, 675
Portman, Edward, 1st Viscount 353
Portman, the Hon. Edward 353, 355
Portman, Sir John 670
Portman, Sir William 510
Potter & Hare 85, 119
Poulett family 54, 204, 359–61, 363, 576
Poulett, John, 1st Baron 53, 54, 361, 365, Pl. 82
Poulett, John, 1st Earl 66, 361, 459
Poulett, John, 4th Earl 60, 363
Poulett, Anne, M.P. 136, 361
Poulett, Elizabeth 164
Powel, Philip 402
Powell family 252
Powell, E. Turner 76, 305
Powell, Samuel 252
Powell's 71, 72, 92, 100, 121, 152, 161, 167, 175, 182, 186, 197, 199, 201, 215, 227, 239, 241, 254, 283, 300, 320, 367, 392, 395, 398, 410, 412, 420, 449, 478, 504, 510, 518, 538, 543, 552, 622, 663, 667, 669, 684, 690, 694, 709, 715
Powys family 463
Powys, A. R. 463
Powys & Macgregor 405
Poynings, Prioress Alianor 177
Poynton Bradbury Wynter Cole 234
Poyntz family 401
Prat, Richard Periam 327
Preater, Tom 174, 175, 529, 614
Preston, John 558
Price, Cedric 336
Price, Hans 422
Price & Wooler 71, 129, 377, 674
Prideaux, John & Pippa 639
Prince, Rev. Henry 572
Prior, George and Jane 603
Prior, John 603
Prowse, Thomas 58, 61, 342, 347, Pls. 91, 95

Prynne, G. H. Fellowes see Fellowes Prynne, G. H.
Pugin, A. W. N. 72, 172, 556
Pullen, Charles 641
Pye, William 601
Pym, John 179
Pyne family 249
Pyne, John 53, 249
Pyne, Thomas 249
Pynsent, Sir William 253

Quellin, Arnold 53, 167, Pl. 83
Quennell, C. H. B. 76, 677
Quicke, Rev. C. P. 96
Quinn, Paul 619
Quirke family 450
Quirke, Robert 454, 456

Radford, C. A. Ralegh 309
Radford, Joseph 283
Ralegh family 209, 481
Raleigh, Bishop 615
Ralphs, John 595, 647
Ramsden & Carr 72, 508
Randoll Blacking, W. H. 83, 117, 155, 181, 526, 549, 658, 676
Rawle, George 244
Ray, William 611
Read, Herbert 318–19, 555, 621, 648
Reade, T. M. 722
Reckitt, Beatrice 543
Reckitt, Norman 542, 543
Reckitt, Rachel 181, 508, 542, 543, 703
Redman, Archdeacon John 446
Reed, George 169
Reeve, J. Arthur 70, 714
Reeves/Reeves & Son (Bath, sculptors) 65, 112, 136, 151, 395, 596, 694
Reeves, John Fry 327, 329
Regnart, Charles 669
Reilly, Professor Charles 619
Reiss, Phyllis 641
Rendel, Palmer & Tritton 160
Rendell family 671–2
Rendell, Israel 672
Rennie, John 67
Reskymer, Prioress Alice 151
Reynold de Mohun 270
Reynolds, W. Bainbridge 72, 441
Reynolds, William 69, 77, 595, 597, 598, 599, 600
Reyntiens, John 376, 568
Reyntiens, Patrick 256, 588, 614
Rice, R. 520
Richard, King of the Romans 210
Richards, J. 688
Richardson, (Sir) Albert 264
Richmond (Mark) Architects 371, 706
Richold, Paul 196, 573
Ricketts, Wayne 316

Robb, Alastair and Mary Anne 227
Robbia, Andrea della 504
Robbia, Luca della 504
Robert de Courcy see Courcy, Robert de
Roberts, Frederick William 68, 69, 76, 77, 293, 451, 453, 455, 456, 457, 509, 574, 610, 617, 622, 659, 662
Roberts, Henry 74, 500
Roberts & Willman 83, 455, 457, 527
Robins, Francis 241
Robinson, Arnold 116
Robinson, Geoffrey 116
Robinson, John 156, 488
Roches, Bishop Peter des 615
Rodbard, William 298
Rofe, Kennard & Lapworth 150
Rofe & Raffety 206
Rogers family 176, 715
Rogers, Edward 176
Rogers, Harold 155
Rogers, John 715
Rolfe & Peto 420
Rolle, Sir Henry 553
Rolt, Tim 256, Pl. 127
Rome, Alan 155, 613
Rooke, T. M. 499
Rope, Margaret 117
Roth, Björn & Oddur 160
Roubiliac, L. F. 640
Rousseau, Jacques 350
Rowcliffe family 338, 579
Royal Pottery 422
Royal Windsor Stained Glass Works 155
Roydon Cooper Associates 570, 722
Rush, Owen 638
Rutherford, Derek 620, Pl. 126
Rutherford, John 626
Ryder Architecture 85, 138
Rysbrack, Michael 66, 331, 361

Sage, Frederick 575
St Albyn family 365, 603
St Aubyn, F. W. 454
St Aubyn, James Piers 69, 76, 78, 80, 180, 253, 278, 449, 453, 454, 455, 456, 457, 650, 691
St Audries, Alexander Fuller-Acland-Hood, 2nd Baron 301
St Barbe family 99
St Barbe, Sir John 99, 264
St Vigor, Abbot William de 310
Salvin, Anthony 75, 271–4, Pl. 113
Sambourne, Robert de 715
Samson, Charles H. 68, 69, 151, 451, 453, 454, 455, 456, 625, 631
Samson & Colthurst 82, 141, 144, 148, 169, 200, 451
Samson & Cottam 132, 135, 137, 144, 287, 412, 585, 613, 625, 631, 649, 651, 660

INDEX OF ARCHITECTS, ETC.

Samuel, Godfrey 601
Samuel, Richard 718
Sanderson, John 347
Sandford Fawcett, E. A. 279
Sandys family 567, 568
Sanford family 72, 503, 504–5
Sanford, Henrietta 504, Pl. 103
Sanford, John (C17) 505
Sanford, Rev. John (d. 1855) 337, 503, 505
Sanford, Martin 505
Sanford, William Ayshford 503
Sarell, John 373
Sargent & Potiriadis 720
Saul, Roger 554
Saunders, Admiral Sir Charles 675
Sautoy, Rev. Frederic du 421
Sayers, Reuben 398
Schaell, Rev. Andreas 357
Scheemakers, Peter 156
Schofield, John 373, 476, 548, 584, 636
Scoles, Rev. Alexander J. C. 73, 136–7, 169, 451, 695, 717, 722
Scoles, John Joseph 137
Scoles & Raymond 695
Scott, (Sir) George Gilbert 70, 75, 78, 319, 326, 347, 391, 436, 552, 607, 613, 620
Scott, James 423–4, 425
Scott, John Oldrid 71, 492
Scott Brownrigg 84, 138
Scott & Moffatt 76, 78, 101, 691, Pl. 110
Seale, Gilbert W. 398, 580, 722
Seccombe, Harry E. 83, 326, 721
Sedding, Edmund Harold 71, 416, 421, 516, 654
Sedding, John Dando 70, 71, 93, 98, 117, 188, 193, 233, 241, 320, 338, 375, 398, 414, 526, 549, 579–80, 613, 638, 639, 676, 688, 694, 699
Seddon, Major Henry 629
Segal, Walter 570
Selwood, Abbot John 97, 257, 281, 329, 356, 432, 602
Selwyn, Rev. Sydney 444
Seth-Ward, Melville 488
Severnside Architects 156
Seward, Derek 253
Sexey, Hugh 157
Seymour family 347
Seymour, Jane (d. *c*. 1565) 304
Seymour, John 460, 504, 647
Shackle, G. H. 694
Sharp, Thomas 84
Shellard, Ivor 622
Shepherd family 379
Shepherd, J.W. 377
Shepherd, Edward 143
Sheppard, Tracey 376, 610
Sherborn, C. 181

Shewbrooks family 68
Shewbrooks, Samuel 74, 277, 282, 614, 661
Shewbrooks, William 293, 631
Shirburn, Prior Robert 463
Shirley-Smith, Robin 574, 626
Shirley-Smith & Gibson 614
Shirley-Smith, Gibson & Rigler 138
Shout, Robert H. 74, 75, 78, 110, 205, 368, 534, 697, 705, 716, 718, 720
Shrigley & Hunt 502
Shrimpton & Salmon 570
Sidell Gibson 570
Siderfin family 638
Sidnell, Michael 269
Silley, George M. 80, 325
Silverton, Richard 151
Singer (J.W.) & Sons 106, 283, 708
Skeat, Francis 659
Skelton, John 441
Skipper, George J. 69, 75, 77, 78, 79, 81, 123, 156, 595, 598, 599, 602, Pl. 114
Slade, Sir Benjamin, 7th Bart 546
Slade, John (fl. 1772) 546
Slade, General Sir John (d. 1859) 500, 546
Slater, William 149, 194
Slater & Carpenter 154, 525, 724
Smallcorn, Lewis 334
Smith, John 677
Smith, C. H. 398
Smith, Douglas 596
Smith, Rev. F. J. 612, 613
Smith, Grace 337
Smith, James Henry 614
Smith, Partridge 522
Smith, Susan 337
Smith, Rev. Sydney 215
Smith, William 202
Smith Gamblin 138, 139
Smith (C.) & Son 361
Smithson, Alison & Peter 601
Smyth, Peterjohn 638
Smyth, Thomas 54, 363
Smyth, William 317
Smyth-Pigott, Rev. Hugh 572
Soane, (Sir) John 58, 60, 66, 69, 239–40, 335–6, 364, 628
Sodbury, Abbot Adam de 308, 316, 328, 433–4
Somerset, Dukes of 702
Somerset, John 53, 132
Somerset County Architect's Department/Somerset County Architects 84, 138, 139, 157, 169, 224, 234, 264, 286, 326, 356, 357, 452, 453, 462, 502, 527, 596, 597, 620, 622, 678, 690, 697, 706, 718, 719, 721, Pl. 126
Somerset Guild of Craftsmen 536

Somerville, John, 15th Lord 303
Soppitt, James 129
Southcombe family 592, 593
Southworth, Henry 714
S&P Architects 456
Sparrow, William 430
Speke family 255, 261, 381, 688
Speke, Sir George 46, 688
Speke, John Hanning 73, 261
Speke, William 148
Spence, William 331
Spencer, John Houghton 68, 70, 71, 100, 115, 119, 170, 330, 351, 390, 496, 497, 500, 542, 587, 611–12, 613, 615, 616, 617, 633, 657, 706
Spiller (family) 68
Spiller, Henry 545, 631
Spire, Joseph 323
Squier, William 371, 389
Stallwood, Spencer Slingsby 71, 199
Stancliffe, Martin 610
Stansell, Alfred 166, 181, 610
Stanton, William 54, 157, 409
Staunton family 689
Stawell family 227–8, 409
Stawell, Ralph, 1st Lord 54, 408, 409
Stawell, John, 2nd Lord 54, 350, 409
Stawell, George 408
Stawell, Sir John (d. 1603) 52, 227, 228
Stawell, Sir John (d. 1662) 227, 228
Stawell, Sir Matthew de 24, 227
Steel & Coleman 455, 562
Steel, Coleman & Davis 596, 614, 661
Stent, Thomas 68, 80, 478, 721, 722
Stephenson family 72, 75, 414–16
Stephenson, Rev. J. A. 415, 416
Stephenson, Rev. J. H. 75, 414, 415, 416
Steyning family 549–51
Stillington, Bishop 257
Stock, Jack 597, 598, 601
Stocking, Thomas 343
Stone, Andrew 348
Stone, H. S. W. 83, 127, 349, 619, 621, 633
Stone, John 153, 170, 265
Stone, Nicholas 53, 651, Pl. 78
Stone, Stephen 522
Stone & Francis 82, 529, 618, 629, 713
Stone & Partners 136, 326, 451, 497, 498, 611, 614, 660
Stourton family 161, 162
Stourton, John 42, 162, 534, 575
Stout & Lichfield 85, 563
Stowey & Jones 632
Strachey, Sally 332, 382
Stradling family 199, 338–9, 579

Stradling, Sir Edward 339
Stradling, William 61, 62, 202, 203, 511
Strange, Hugh 336
Strangways family 193, 196, 444, 552
Strawbridge, George 633, 677
Streatfeild, G.E.S. 700
Street, G. E. 70, 71, 72, 187, 188, 266–9, 277, 366–7, 451, 523, 555, 610
Street & Pyke 513
Stride Treglown Architects 401
Strode family 107, 483, 591, 592, 597, 673
Strode, Sir Thomas 46, 591
Strode, William (d. 1666) 107, 470
Strode, William (d. 1697) 107
Stuckey family 398, 399, 401
Stuckey, Vincent 556
Sturdy, Philip 146, 304
Suffling, E. R. 181
Sully family 147n.
Sully, Abbot Henry de 308
Swann, Richard 724
Sweet, William 654
Sweet-Escott, Rev. Thomas 294
Sweeting, Henry 385, 386
Sweetland, William 166
Switzer, Stephen 61, 425
Sydenham family 42, 152, 162, 217, 265, 579, 676, 691, 693
Sydenham, Sir George 46, 217, 218, 580, 581
Sydenham, Humphrey 99, 264
Sydenham, Sir John V (d. 1625) 52, 162
Sydenham, Sir John Posthumus (d. 1696) 54, 161–2, 164, 217
Sydenham, John II (d. 1534) 162, 481, 691
Sydenham, Walter 161
Symes family 48, 189, 423, 531
Symes, John 423
Symes, William (fl. 1671) 189
Symes, William and Elizabeth (fl. 1590) 531
Symons, Isabell & Elizabeth 583

Tabert, Dennis 596, 622
Talkes, Dan 256, Pl. 127
Talman, William 702
Tamlyn, W. J. 69, 77, 78, 453, 454, 455, 456, 457, 527
Tapper, Walter 440
Taunton, Henry Labouchère, 1st Lord 74, 513–14
Taylor, Frank 724
Taylor, J. J. 278
Taylor, W. C. 188
Taylor, William 54, 339, 353, 396, 505, Pl. 80

Taylor (Stephen) Architects 336
Tecton 601n.
Tegetmeier, Denis 152
Thatcher, John 667
Theed, William 361
Thomas, Brian 262–3
Thomas, P. Hartland 123
Thomas (Percy) Partnership 85, 254, 411, 638, 718
Thomason, Philip 343, 620
Thornhill, Sir James 268, 271
Thornton, William 570
Thorpe, John 464
Thorpe, John Egerton 540–1
Threlfall, Philippa 138, 599
Thring family 92, 406
Thring, Rev. Godfrey 366
Thring, John 92
Tite, (Sir) William 81, 235, 722n.
Toma of Sloo 493
Toms, John 97, 113, 126, 149, 206, 445, 504, 666
Tonkin, John 657
Toomer, A. J. 82, 96, 157, 371, 377, 451, 453, 592
Torrens, Michael 614, 626, 705
Tower, Walter 621
Trask, Charles 262, 500, 501–2
Trask, Thomas 373
Trask & Co. 501–2, 574, 592, 613, 654
Travers, Martin 83, 117, 200, 262, 282, 481, 714
Trehearne & Norman, Preston & Partners 626
Tremayle, Sir Thomas 179
Trent, Newbury 625
Trent, William E. 721
Trepplin, Ernest 510
Trevelyan family 481–3
Trevelyan, George 482
Trevelyan, Sir John, 2nd Bart 482, 484
Trevelyan, Sir John, 4th Bart 484
Trevelyan, Pauline, Lady 483
Trevilian family 252, 253, 263
Tristram, E. W. 226
Truefitt, George 635
Tubbs, Cyril 543
Tucker, John 508
Tudbery, M. T. 649
Tugwell, Frank 454, 456
Turberville family 643
Turberville, John 642
Turner, Rev. J. F. 647
Turstin, Abbot 307–8
Tyler, William 241
Tyley 65, 92, 148, 361, 656, 673
Tynte, Sir Charles Kemeys 61, 331, 341, 342, 355
Tynte, Sir Halswell 339
Tynte, Rev. Sir John 66, 331

Ubbe 180
Unwin, Raymond 147n.
Urtiaco (de) 251

Vallis, Ronald 156, 573
Valpy & Gibbs 118
Vaughan-Lee family 255
Veitch, John 484
Veitch, Lt Robert 129
Vellacott, Avril 567
Venn, John 413
Venning, Virginia 174
Vermeylen, François 244
Vernai *see* Verney
Verney (de) family 42, 583, 584
Verney, Elizabeth 301
Verney, Robert 301
Verney, William (C15) 301
Verney, William de (C14) 358, 584
Vialls, George 237, 558
Vickery, Thomas 340
Victoria, Queen 656
Vining, Edward 720
Vivian-Neal, A. W. 533
Voysey, C. F. A. 76, 144, 147, 247, 248, 529–30
Vulliamy, Lewis 469

Wadham family 376–7, 380
Wadham, Nicholas and Dorothy 53, 376–7, 464
Wadham, Sir William 37, 375, 376–7
Wadman, William 430, 565, 669
Wagner, Richard 707
Wailes, William 97, 347, 460, 481, 502, 611, 676, 682
Wailes & Strang 131, 175, 638
Wainwright, C. & J. 290
Waleys, Nicholas 26, 133
Walker, Fred 338
Walker, J. W. 349, 699
Walker, Leonard 283
Waller, Son & Wood 335
Walrond family 261
Walrond, Humphrey 46, 377, 378
Walsh family 249
Walsh, John (Cathanger Manor) 304
Walsh, John 342
Walton, Richard and Alice 103
Warbeck, Perkin 615, 617
Ward, Guy 139
Ward & Hughes 95, 262, 357, 478, 578, 668
Ward & Nixon 172
Ware, Peter 168
Warman, Simon *see* Werman, Simon
Warre family 353
Warre, Sir John 391
Warrington, William 206, 215, 350, 500

INDEX OF ARCHITECTS, ETC.

Waterhouse, Alfred 75, 661, 662
Watson, John 646
Watson, R. A. 279
Watts, Elizabeth 245
Waugh, Evelyn 215
Waynflete, Bishop 615
Webb, Christopher 83, 117, 234, 376, 385, 390, 391, 413, 445, 451, 520, 524, 526, 550, 676, 686, 713
Webb, Maurice 76, 670
Weedon, Harry 720
Weir, William 397
Welch, Christopher 395
Welch & Hollis 691
Weld, Charles 632n.
Wellington, Arthur Wellesley, 1st Duke of 662
Wells, Thomas 261
Welman, C. N. 500
Welman, Isaac 532
Werman (or *Warman*), *Simon* 119, 151, 347, 644
Wesley, John 627
Westlake, Nathaniel 651
Westlake, Philip 555
Westmacott, J. S. 717
Westmacott, (Sir) Richard 66, 239, 241, 361, 423, 495, 613, Pl. 97
Westmacott, Richard Jun. 495
Westmorland, Earls of 162
Westover, John 657
Weymouth, Thomas Thynne, 1st Viscount 708
Wheelwright, Robert 346
Whicheloe Macfarlane 624
Whinney, Thomas B. 80, 721
Whistler, Laurence 252, 380
White, William 70, 216, 545, 700–1
White, William (surveyor, fl. 1774) 657
White (John) & Son 633
Whitehead, Arthur 561
Whiteley, Graham 462, 502, 620
Whiting, Abbot Richard 308, 319, 328, 554
Wilkins, William 58, 392
Wilkinson, Horace 136
Wilkinson, William 675
Willcox, W. J. 197, 366, 368, 400, 559, 599
Willement, Thomas 72, 417, 423
William III, King (William of Orange) 696
William de Falaise 584
William de Falaise II 16, 582
William of Malmesbury 14, 307
William de Mohun 16, 153, 266
William of Norton 500
William de Roumare *see* Lincoln, Earl of
William de Say 104
Williams, Henry 189

Williams, Robert 651
Williams-Ellis, (Sir) Clough 240, 386
Williamson, F. 239
Willis, Henry 135, 611, 613
Willis, Robert 631
Willman, John H. H. 83, 321, 659
Willoughby family 643
Wills, (Sir) Frank W. 79, 188, 266, 621
Wills, Sir Frederick 265
Wills, John 191
Wilson, Henry 71, 72, 262, 428, 501–2, 574, 613, Pl. 119
Wilson, James 74, 78, 169, 351, 614, 621, Pl. 112
Wilson & Fuller 259
Wilson, Willcox & Ames 110
Wilson, Willcox & Wilson 372, 695
Wiltshire, Kenneth 556
Wimperis, Simpson & Guthrie 649
Winde, William 272
Winstone, John 710
Winter family 100
Winter, Charles 122
Winter, John (Ash Priors) 100
Winter, John (Combe Florey) 216
Wippell & Co. 148, 205, 368
Withers, R. J. 646
Withers, Robert 445
Witz, Konrad 319
Wolff, Rev. Joseph 384
Wood (Bristol, sculptors) 65, 295, 676
Wood, Henry 224, 415, 576
Wood, John 513, 572
Wood, Tristram 394
Woodard, Canon 621
Woodforde, Rev. James (Parson) 96, 724
Woodforde, Rev. Robert 724
Woodward, Julia 106
Woodyer, Henry 72, 212–13
Wooldridge, H. E. 518
Woolfall & Eccles 660
Wordsworth, William and Dorothy 365
Wormleighton, Francis 367
Worthington, (Sir) Hubert 237
Worthington (Thomas) & Sons 529
Wratten, John 252
Wren, Sir Christopher 54, 107, 167, 354, 419
Wright, Thomas 341, 342
Wroth, Sir Thomas (d. 1672) 494
Wroth, Sir Thomas (d. 1721) 65, 498, 584
Wulfric 16, 346
Wyatt, James 60, 63, 364
Wyatt, (Sir) Jeffry (Wyatville) 58, 60, 68, 359, 364, 424, 708
Wyatt, Samuel 58, 424

Wyatt, Thomas Henry 75, 265, 285, 495
Wyatt & Brandon 495
Wyke family 504, 505
Wyke, John 503
Wyndham family 483, 651, 652, 693
Wyndham, Humphrey 52, 705
Wyndham, Sir John (d. 1574) 46, 651, 691
Wyndham, Sir John (d. 1645) 53, 651, Pl. 78
Wyndham, Sir William 1st Bart 53, 651

Wyndham, Sir William 3rd Bart 57, 692, 702
Wynford, William 25, 30, 655, 715

Yea, Robert 229
Yea, Sir William 392, 705
Yeo, John 72, 567
Yeoman, John and Angela 424
YRM 359

Zouche, Lord 40, 575
Zwinck (Oberammergau, carver) 621

INDEX OF PLACES

Principal references are in **bold** type; demolished buildings are shown in *italic*.

The area covered by this volume is described on p. xvi

Abbas Combe *see* Templecombe
Abbey (The) *see* Charlton Adam
Abbotsfield *see* Wiveliscombe
Abbot's Way **554**
Aisholt **91**
Alcombe *see* Minehead
Alford **91–2**
 Alford House 75, 91, **92**
 All Saints 34, 39, **92**
Alfoxton Park *see* Holford
Alfred's Tower *see* South Brewham
Alhampton **93**
Aller **93–4**
 Old Rectory 35, 40, **94**
 St Andrew 15, 17, 33, 72, **93–4**, 195, 260, 700, 712
 toll house 66, **94**
Allerford **94–5**
Allerton *see* Chapel Allerton
Angersleigh **94–5**
 St Michael **94–5**, 418
Ansford **95–6**
 Ansford School 82, **96**, 377, 592
 St Andrew 6, **95–6**, 570
Ash **96**
Ashbrittle **96–7**
Ashcott **97**
 All Saints 72, **97**
Ashford *see* Charlinch; Ilton
Ashill **97–8**
 St Mary 17, 18, **97–8**, 115
Ashington **98–9**
 St Vincent 34, 52, **98–9**, 161, 201, 264, 477–8
Ashley Combe *see* Porlock
Ash Priors **99–100**
 Sandhill Park 57, 61, **100**
Ashton windmill *see* Chapel Allerton
Athelney *see* East Lyng

Babcary **101**
 Holy Cross 6, **101**
 Old Rectory 76, **101**

Badgworth **101–2**
 St Congar 14, 37, 39, 51, 72, **101–2**, 654
Bagborough House *see* West Bagborough
Baltonsborough 15, **103**
 Moravian chapel 74, **103**
 St Dunstan 37, **103**, 172
Barford House *see* Enmore
Barlinch Priory **104**
 St Nicholas Priory 16, 21, 45, **96**, **104**, 369
Barrington **104–8**
 Barrington Court 47, 48, 82, **105–8**, 163, 249, 255, 286, 334, 465, 515, 531, 532, 533, Pl. 59
 Eason House 55, **105**
 St Mary 21, 23, **104–5**
Barrow Court *see* Galhampton
Barton Grange *see* Corfe
Barton St David **108–9**
 Breadstone House 54, **109**
 St David 17, 21, **108–9**, 392, 606
Barwick **109–11**
 Barwick House 62, 75, **110–11**
 council houses 82, **110**, 668
 St Mary Magdalene 24, 39, **109–10**, 204, 571
Batcombe **111–13**
 St Mary 6, 25, 26, 27, 30–1, 32, 65, **111–12**
Bathealton **113**
 St Bartholomew 70, **113**
Bathpool **113–14**
 Hyde **113–14**
Battleborough *see* Brent Knoll
Bawdrip **114–15**
 Knowle Hall 60, 63, **114**
 Morrison Distribution Centre 85, **114–15**
 St Michael 6, 21, **114–15**, Pl. 16
Bayford *see* Wincanton
Beercrocombe **114**
 St James 98, **114**

Berrow **115–16**
  St Mary **115–16**, 129
Bickenhall **116**, 574
Bickham Manor *see* Timberscombe
Bicknoller 3, **116–18**
  Great Hillcroft 82, **117–18**, 365
  St George 32, 34, 35, 38, **116–17**, 240, 369n., 547, 579
Biddisham **118**
  St John Baptist 19, **118**
Binham Grange *see* Old Cleeve
Bishop's Hull **118–20**
  Manor House 47, **119–20**
  Rumwell **120**
  St Peter and St Paul 21, 36, 52, 64, **118–19**, 347, 525, 644
  Taunton Deane Crematorium 85, **119**
Bishop's Lydeard 4, **120–2**
  St Mary 4, 27, 28, 29, 30–1, 35, 36, 37, 38, 51, 83, 100, **120–1**, 198, 227, 240, 381, 579, 611, Pls. 47, 48
  station 81, **122**
Blackford (nr Sparkford) 6, **123**
  St Michael 17, 64, **123**
Blackford (nr Tivington) *see* Tivington
Blackford (nr Wedmore) **123**
  Holy Trinity **123**, Pl. 96
  Hugh Sexey School 79, **123**
Blackmore Farm *see* Cannington
Blue Anchor 4, **124**
  chapel **212**, **509**
Bossington 71, **124**
  cottages 50, **124**
Bower Hinton **125–6**
  Hirsts Farmhouse and Bower House 99, **125**
  Parrett Works 81, **125–6**, Pl. 117
Bradford on Tone **126–7**
  Heatherton Park 83, **127**
  St Giles 32, 65, 72, **126–7**, 391
Bradley House *see* West Bradley
Bratton **127–8**
  Bratton Court 41, 43, **127–8**, 551
  Lady Lovelace cottages 76, **128**, 530
Bratton Seymour **128–9**
  St Nicholas 15, 17, **128**
Breadstone House *see* Barton St David
Brean **129**
  Brean Down 11, **129**, 395
  Brean Down Fort 78, **129**
  St Bridget 115, **129**
Brendon Hill **130**
  Langham Hill engine house **130**, 412
  West Somerset Mineral Railway 81, **130**

Brent Knoll 2, 12, **130–2**
  Battleborough 130, **132**
  Manor House 74, **132**
  Methodist (Bible Christian) chapel 74, **132**
  St Michael 6, 17, 24, 35, 36, 39, 51, 53, **130–2**, 213, 281, 421, Pl. 45
Bridgwater 1, 3, 7, 8, 44–5, 56, 68, 84, **132–48**
  Castle 40–1, 56, 132–3, **142–3**, *144*
  churches etc. **133–7**
    Baptist church 73, **137**, Pl. 108
    Christ Church Unitarian Chapel 64, **137**
    Franciscan friary 16, 132, 140
    Holy Trinity 85, **136**, *147*
    Methodist church, Eastover 74, **137**
    Methodist church, King Street (former) 74, **137**
    St John Baptist 69, **136**
    St John's Hospital, Eastover 16, 132, 135
    St Joseph (R.C.) 73, **136–7**
    St Mary 21, 22, 23, 26, 38, 52, 65, 83, **133–6**, 176, Pls. 17, 74
  industry 81, 133, **145–6**
    brickworks 81, **138**
    British Cellophane 133, 146, 279
    glass kiln 68, 145
  outer areas **146–8**
    Eastover *16, 132, 135*, **137**, **142**, 146
    Huntworth 145
    Newtown 82, **148**
    Sydenham 133, **146**
    Westfield **137**, **147**; point block 84, 133, **147**
  public buildings 84, **137–46**
    Blake Museum 45, **145**
    Blake statue 78, **142**
    Bridgwater College 84, **138**
    Bridgwater Docks and canal 56, 67, 80, 81, 133, **145–6**
    Castle *see above*
    Chilton Trinity School 84, **138**
    Corn Exchange *see* Market Hall *below*
    County Court (former) 78, **142**
    Library 78, **138**
    Magistrates' Court 78, **138**
    Market Hall and Corn Exchange 77, **137–8**, Pl. 98
    Regional Police Headquarters 85, **138**
    Robert Blake School 84, **138**

INDEX OF PLACES

schools 84, **138–9**, **145**
Somerset Brick and Tile
  Museum 81, **138**
station and bridges 81, 133,
  138, 146
Town bridges 66, *141*, **142**
Town Hall 57, 77, **137**
war memorial 83, **144**
workhouse 78, **145**
streets and houses 8, 45, 77, 80,
  82, 84, 132–3, **140–8**
  Castle House 81, **142**
  Castle Street 8, 56, 59, 133,
    142, **143–4**, Pl. 86
  King Square 56, **144**
  Lions, The 56, **143**
  quays 133, **142–3**, **144–5**
  Rosary House 75, **147**
  St Mary Street 45, **140–1**
  Stuckey's Bank (former) 80,
    141
  Sydenham Manor 146
  Westfield point block 84, 133,
    147
Bridgwater and Taunton Canal 67,
  80
  Bathpool and Hyde **113**
  Bridgwater 67, 80, **145–6**
  Creech St Michael **231**
  North Newton **494**
  St Michael Church (Maunsel
    Locks) **546**
  Taunton **623**
Bristol & Exeter Railway 80, 81, 572
  Brean 129
  Bridgwater 81, **138**
  Brympton D'Evercy **166**
  Durston **280**
  Taunton 81, **622**
  Wellington **662**
Broad Hinton *see* Bower Hinton
Broadway **148–9**
  Every's Almshouses 50, **148**
  Jordans 62, **148–9**, 381
  meeting house (former) **148**,
    234
  St Aldhelm and St Eadburga 38,
    148
Brompton Ralph **149**
  St Mary 32, **149**
Brompton Regis (formerly King's
  Brompton) **150**
  St Mary 35, **150**
Broomfield **150–1**
  St Mary and All Saints 35,
    150–1, 547
Brushford **151–3**
  Dulverton station (former) **152**,
    263
  Hele Manor 76, **152–3**
  St Nicholas 19, 38, 72, 83, **151–2**,
    Pl. 123

Bruton 2, 44, 56, **153–60**
  churches etc. **153–6**, **159**
    Bruton Priory, later Abbey 16,
      45, *48*, *153*, *156*, **158–9**, 174,
      444
    St Mary 19, 27, 28, 29, 36,
      46, 52, 53, 64, 83, **153–6**,
      468, 564, Pls. 36, 75, 87
    Union Chapel (former silk
      factory) 67, **159**
  Durslade Farm 85, **160**
  Gant's Mill 67, **160**
  Godminster Manor 59, **160**
  public buildings **156–8**
    Bow Bridge 45, **158**
    Bruton School for Girls 84,
      523
    King's School 50, 79, 83, 84,
      154, **156**, 349
    primary school 83, **157**
    Sexey's Hospital 50, 51, **157**,
      Pl. 65
    Sexey's School 84, 123, **156–7**
  streets and houses 45, **157–60**,
    442
    Bruton Abbey (lost Berkeley
      mansion) *48*, *153*, *157*, *159*
    Dovecote, The 48, **157**
    High Street 45, **158–9**
    Priory, The (possible Priory
      courthouse) 16, 45, **159**
Brympton D'Evercy 42, **160–6**
  Brympton House 42, 43, 47, 54,
    55, 106, 160, **162–6**, 465, Pl. 58
  Chantry, The 44, **165–6**
  St Andrew 22, 23, 52, 98, **161–2**,
    201
Buckland St Mary **166–7**
  Buckland House (rectory) 76,
    167
  St Mary 69, 71, 73, **166–7**
Burnham-on-Sea 57, 77, **167–70**
  churches etc. **167–8**
    Baptist chapel 73, **168**
    Methodist chapel 74, **168**
    R.C. priory (former) 73, **169**
    St Andrew 53, 65, **167–8**, 282,
      Pl. 82
  Daviesville 57, *169*
  railway 80, *169*
Burrowbridge **170–1**
  bridge 66, **170**
  Burrow Mump (King Alfred's
    camp) 2, **170**
  Ebenezer Baptist chapel 73, **170**
  pumping stations 81, **170–1**
Burtle **171**
  priory 16, *171*
Burton Pynsent *see* Curry Rivel
Bury **171**
  Bury Castle **171**
Bury Castle *see* Bury; Selworthy

INDEX OF PLACES

Butleigh **171–4**
    Bridge Farm 44, **173**, 666
    Higher Hill Farm 63, **173**
    Hood Monument 61, **173–4**, 220
    St Leonard 72, **171–2**
    Wootton House, Butleigh
        Wootton **173**, 174

Cadbury Castle *see* South Cadbury
Cannington *13*, **174–80**
    Blackmore Farm 42, **179–80**,
        Pl. 57
    Cannington Court 40, 55, **176–7**
    chapel 64, 175, 176, **177**
    Cannington priory 16, 46, *174*,
        176–7, 215
    Gurney Manor 42, **178–9**, Pl. 56
    St Mary 28, 72, **174–5**, 501, 698
Carhampton **180–1**
    St Carantoc 14, 181
    St John the Baptist 38, 65, 117,
        152, 175, **180–1**, 216, 268, 300,
        337, 449, 481, 504, 543, 638,
        644, 703, Pl. 49
Castle Cary 2, 6, 56, 81, **181–4**
    Castle 40–1, 183
    churches **182**, 184
        All Saints 24, 69, 112, **182**,
            487
        Methodist chapel 74, **182**
    industry 68, 81, 181, **183**
    lock-up 57, **183**
    Market House **182–3**, Pl. 111
    primary school 79, **184**
    streets and houses 182, **183–4**
        Cumnock Terrace 77, **184**
        Florida House 75, **184**
        Lower Cockhill Farmhouse
            44, **184**
        vicarage (former) 76, **184**
Castle Neroche 40–1, **185**
Catcott **185–6**
Cathanger *see* Fivehead
Chaffcombe **186–7**
Chapel Allerton **187**
    Allerton church 51, 70, **187**
    Ashton windmill 67, **187**
Chapel Cleeve *see* Old Cleeve
Chard 2, 7, **187–92**
    churches **187–9**, 191
        Baptist chapel 73, **188–9**
        St Mary the Virgin 34, **187–8**
    industry 67–8, 187, **191**, 192
        Boden Mill **191**, Pl. 115
    public buildings **189**
        Chard Joint Station 80, 81, **192**
        Chard School 7, 48, **189**, 689
        toll house 66, **191**
        Town Hall 57, **189**
    Snowdon Hill 7, 66, **191**
    streets and houses **189–92**
        Court House 48, **189–90**

Chard Canal 67, 80, 192, 623
    Beercrocombe **115**
    Chard **192**
    Creech St Michael **231**
    Ilton **380**
    Ruishton **545**
    Wrantage **713**
Charlinch **192**
Charlton Adam **192–3**
    The Abbey **193**
Charlton Horethorne **194–5**
    Manor Farmhouse **194**, 197
    St Peter and St Paul 21, 22, 23,
        194
Charlton Mackrell 4, **195–7**
    Charlton House 59, **196**
    Manor Farm 63, **196**
    St Mary 23, 39, 72, **195**, 405,
        417
    school 79, **196**
Charlton Musgrove **197**
    Roundhill Grange 59, **197**
    St John, Barrow Lane **197**
    St Stephen 65, **197**
Cheddon Fitzpaine **198**, 355
    St Mary 36, 83, **198**
Chedzoy 10, **198–200**
    St Mary 21, 28, 46, 71, 111,
        198–9
Chesterblade **200**
    St Mary 17, 18, **200**
Chillington **200**
    St James 71, **200**
Chilthorne Domer **201**
    St Mary 52, 98, 161, **201**
Chilton Cantelo **201–2**
    Chilton House 75, **202**
    estate cottages 75, **202**, 478
    St James 70, 72, **201–2**, 477,
        Pl. 106
Chilton Polden **202–3**
    Tower House 61, 62, **202–3**
Chilton Trinity **203**
    Holy Trinity 51, **203**
Chipstable **204**
    All Saints 32, **204**
Chiselborough **204–5**
    Manor Farm **205**, 368
    St Peter and St Paul 26, **204**
Churchinford *see* Churchstanton
Churchstanton **205**
    Churchinford **205**
        Baptist chapel 73, **205**
    St Peter and St Paul 36, **205**,
        Pl. 40
Clapton *see* Wayford
Clatworthy **206**
Cleeve Abbey 16, 21, 24, 35, 36,
    39–40, 41, 45, 104, 175, **206–12**,
    240, 267, 324, 397, 410, 449, 473,
    508, 528, 549, 638, 651, 712, Pls.
    15, 30

Cleveland *see* Minehead
Cloford **212–13**
  Cloford Manor 49, **213**
  St Mary 53, 72, **212–13**
Closworth **214**
  All Saints 32, **214**, 501
Coker Court *see* East Coker
Combe Florey **214–16**
  gatehouse 48, **215**, 469, 486, 532
  St Peter and St Paul 4, 32, 36, 38, **214–15**
Combe St Nicholas **216–17**
  St Nicholas 38, 65, 117, **216–17**, 337
  Wadeford House **217**, 253n.
Combe Sydenham 42, **217–18**
Combwich **219**, 516
  Beere Manor 42, **219**, 577
  St Peter 70, **219**
Compton Castle *see* Compton Pauncefoot
Compton Dundon **219–21**
  Castlebrook Barn 44, **220**
  medieval parsonage 40
  St Andrew 23, **219–20**, 320
Compton Durville *see* South Petherton
Compton Pauncefoot 6, **221–2**
  Compton Castle 60, 61, 62, 63, **221–2**
  Crescent, The **221**, 444
  St Mary 26, **221**
Corfe **222–3**
  St Nicholas 69, **222**
Corton Denham 2, **223**
  St Andrew 70, 71, **223**, 541
Cossington **223–4**
Cotford St Luke **224**
Cothay Manor 41, 42, 43, 44, 82, **224–7**, 333–4, 446, 666
Cothelstone **227–9**
  Cothelstone House 61, 229
  Cothelstone Manor 48, **227–8**, 305
  St Thomas of Canterbury 24, 52, **227**
  Stoneage Barton 13
  Terhill 229
Court Farm *see* Wookey
Court House *see* East Quantoxhead; Long Sutton; Thornfalcon
Coxley **229**
Cranmore Hall *see* East Cranmore
Cranmore Station *see* West Cranmore
Creech Hill *see* Lamyatt
Creech St Michael **230–1**
  Coalharbour **231**, 642
  paper mills 81, **231**
  St Michael 65, **230**
Crewkerne 2, 5, 56, 69, **231–8**
  churches **231–4**

    Baptist church 73, **234**
    St Bartholomew 17, 19, 25, 26, 31, 33, 37, **231–4**, 318, 375, 501, Pl. 33
    Unitarian chapel 64, **234**, 377
  industry 68, 81, 231, **237**
  public buildings **234–5**
    cemetery 74, **235**
    Chubb's almshouses 50, **237**
    Crewkerne Grammar School 79, **236**
    railway station (Misterton) 81, **235**
  streets and houses 56, **235–8**
    Severalls Park 82, **237**
    Stuckey's Bank (former) 80, **237**
Cricket Malherbie **238–9**
  St Mary Magdalene 70, 71, **238**
Cricket St Thomas **239–40**
  Cricket House 58, **239–40**
  St Thomas 65, 73, **239**, Pl. 97
Crimson Hill Tunnel *see* Wrantage
Crowcombe **240–4**
  Church House 40, **242**
  Crowcombe Court 8, 57, 61, 62, 63, 65, **242–4**, 245, 338n., 442, Pls. 89, 90
  Holy Ghost 32, 35, 37, 39, 65, **240–2**, Pl. 43
Croydon Hall *see* Rodhuish
Croydon House *see* Timberscombe
Cucklington **244–6**
  St Lawrence 7, 21, **244–5**
  Shanks House 62, 63, **245**
Cudworth **246**
  St Michael 21, **246**
Culbone **246–8**
  Lillycombe (Lady Lovelace) 76, **248**, 530
  St Beuno 38, **246–7**
Curland **248**
Curry Mallet **248–50**
  St James 52, 53, **248–9**
Curry Rivel **250–4**
  Burton Pynsent 61, 64, 217, **253**, 384
  Congregational chapel 73, **252**
  Midelney Place 82, **253**, 263
  Pynsent Column 61, **253–4**, Pl. 94
  St Andrew 5, 24, 31, 33, 35, 38, 39, 46, 52, **250–2**, 397, 473, 496, 679
Cutcombe **254**
  St John 72, **254**

Devon and Somerset Railway 80
  Brushford (former Dulverton station) **152**
  Chipstable (Waterrow) **204**
  Wiveliscombe **707**

INDEX OF PLACES

Dillington House 60, 61, 63, 85, **254–6**, 379, 688, Pl. 99
  Hyde, The (conference centre) 85, **256**, Pl. 127
Dinnington **256**
  Roman villa 12, **256**
Ditcheat **256–9**
  Priory, The 48–9, 75, **258–9**
  St Mary Magdalene 17, 23, 33, 39, 49, 65, 112, **256–8**
Dodington **259–60**
  Dodington Hall 41, 49, **259–60**
Donyatt **260–1**, 369
  St Mary 28, 51, **260**, 376, 700
Dowlish Ford *see* Ilminster
Dowlish Wake **261–2**
  St Andrew 5, 15, 17, 73, **261**, 552, 700
  West Dowlish church 261
Dowsborough Camp *see* Nether Stowey
Drayton **262–3**
  Midelney Manor 82, 253, **263**
  Red House, The 55, **263**
  St Catherine 15, 37, 83, **262–3**
Dulverton 3, **263–6**
  All Saints 3, 72, 99, **263–4**
  Barle Bridge 45, **265**
  Congregational church 73, **265**
  crepe mill 67, **264–5**
  Exmoor House (former workhouse) 78, **264**
  Exmoor Medical Centre 85, **264**
  Pixton Park 59, 171, **265**, 646
  station *see* Brushford
Dundon *see* Compton Dundon
Dunster 24, 42, **266–78**
  Bats Castle **278**
  Conygar Tower 61, 266, **275**
  Dunster Castle 7, 40–1, 48, 55, 61, 62, 63, 75, 266, **270–5**, 291, 340, Pls. 79, 81, 113
    castle mill 67, **275**
    chapel 268, **271**
    stables 55, **274**
  Dunster Priory 16, 40, 266, 268, **269–70**
    Old Priory 41, 43, **269**;
      dovecote 44, **269**
  police station 78, **278**, 691
  St George 17, 22, 33, 35, 36, 37, 38, 40, 46, 52, 70, 71, 72, 117, 167, 175, 181, 216, **266–9**, 300, 337, 449, 451, 460, 504, 638, 644, 703
  streets and houses **275–8**
    Luttrell Arms 45, 49, 274, **276**
    Nunnery, The 7, 45, **277**
    Old Manor 41, **278**
    vicarage 76, **278**
    Yarn Market 50, **275–6**

Durleigh **279**
  West Bower Manor 44, **279**, Pl. 27
Durston **279–80**
  Minchin Buckland Preceptory 16, 151, 280

Earnshill House *see* Hambridge
Eason House *see* Barrington
East Brent **280–2**
  St Mary 26, 32, 35, 39, 51, 52, 131, **280–2**, 460, 571, Pl. 69
East Chinnock **282**
  St Mary 24, 201, **282**
East Coker **283–4**
  Coker Court 41, 42, 43, 49, 63, 76, **283–4**
  Helyar Almshouses 50, **284**
  medieval parsonage 40
  St Michael 15, 21, 64, **283**, 444
East Cranmore **285**
  Cranmore Hall (now All Hallows School) 75, **285**
East Huntspill **285–6**
  All Saints 69, **285**
East Lambrook **286**
  St James 19, **286**
East Lydford **287**
East Lyng 15, **287–8**
  Athelney 15, **288**
  fort 15, 288
  St Bartholomew 5, 28, 38, 39, 110, **287–8**, 437
East Pennard **288–90**
  All Saints 19, 34, 65, **288–9**
  Pennard House **289–90**
East Quantoxhead **290–3**
  Court House 42, 48, 49, 274, **291–3**
  St Mary 46, **290–1**, Pl. 4
East Somerset Railway 80
East Stoke *see* Stoke-sub-Hamdon
Edington **293**
  Edington House 63, **293**
  St George 19, **293**
Elworthy **293–4**
  Hartrow Manor 59, 149, **294**
  Old Rectory 76, **294**
  St Martin 52, 149, **293–4**
  Willett House 59, **294**
  Willett Tower 61, 216, 244, **294**
Enmore **295–6**
  Barford House 59, **296**
  Enmore Castle 59–60, **295–6**
  St Michael 17, 32, 33, 51, **295**
Evercreech 8, 56, 69, 80, **297–9**
  St Peter 6, 30, 34, **297–8**
Exebridge *see* Brushford
Exford 7, **299–300**
  St Mary Magdalene **299–300**, 683n., 698

INDEX OF PLACES

Exton **300–1**
  St Peter 299, **300–1**, 698

Fairfield 41, 47, 62, 63, 82, **301–2**, 303, 583, Pl. 62
Fiddington **302–3**
  Roobies Farm 63, **303**
  St Martin 72, **302–3**
  Stockland Lovell 62, 272, **303**, 483, 585
Fitzhead **303–4**
  Fitzhead Court 62, **303–4**, 483, 585, 706
Fivehead **304–5**
  Cathanger Manor 48, 228, **304–5**
  Langford Manor 55, **304**
Ford *see* Wiveliscombe
Fosse Way 12, 373

Galhampton **305**
  Barrow Court 76, **305**
  toll house 66, **305**
Galmington *see* Taunton (outer areas)
Gare Hill **305–6**
  St Michael 70, **305**
Gaulden Manor *see* Tolland
Gerbestone Manor *see* West Buckland
Glastonbury 4, 8, 13–14, 45, 56, 84, **306–30**, 566
  churches etc. **317–21**
    Abbey *see below*
    cemetery 172, **321**
    Methodist church 74, **321**
    pilgrimage chapels **327**
    St Benedict 33, **320**
    St John Baptist 25, 26, 27, 29, 33, 35, 37, 65, **317–20**, 538, Pls. 38, 53
    St Margaret's Chapel **324**
    St Mary (R.C.) 83, **321**
    St Mary Magdalene's Hospital *see* public buildings (Magdalene Almshouses) *below*
    St Michael, Glastonbury Tor **328–9**
  Glastonbury Abbey 6, 13–14, 15, 16, 19–21, 24–5, 31, 39, 40, 45, 131, 154, 256, **306–17**, 326–7, 329, 583, Pl. 13
    Abbey Gatehouse 40, **316–17**, 321
    Abbot's Kitchen 23, 129, **316**, Pl. 23
    barn (Abbey Farm) 44, 173, **321–2**, 521, 665–6, Pl. 20
    cloisters and chapter house 40, 308, 310, 313, **315**
    hospitium (George and Pilgrim Hotel) 45, 80, **324–5**, Pl. 55
    Lady Chapel (St Mary's Chapel) 18, 19–21, 40, 307, 308–9, **310–13**, 314, 397, 590, Pls. 11, 12
    vetusta ecclesia and *Anglo-Saxon church* 20, 306, **307–8**, 309, 310
  Glastonbury Tor 2, **328–9**, Pl. 1
  industry **328**
    Baily & Co. 81, **328**
    Clark, Son & Morland works 81, 83, **328**
  outlying buildings **328–30**
    Edgarley House (now Millfield Preparatory School) **329**
    Glastonbury Lake Village 11, **329–30**
    Ponter's Ball 174, **330**
  public buildings 84, **321–7**
    Abbey Farm (Somerset Rural Life Museum) 44, 173, **321–2**, 521, 665–6, Pl. 20
    Magdalene Almshouses and St Mary Magdalene's Hospital 40, **323–4**
    Millfield Preparatory School **329**
    Post Office 83, **326**
    pump room (former) 57, **323**
    Town Hall 57, **321**
    war memorial 83, **325**
    West Mendip Hospital 85, **322**
  streets and houses 8, 45, 306, 317, **322–30**
    George and Pilgrim Hotel 45, 80, **324–5**, Pl. 55
    Newtown 82, **326**
    Northload Street 319, **324**
    Stuckey's Bank (former) 80, **323**
    Tribunal, The 43, 45, 173, **325**
    Upper Crannel Farm 85, **329**
    Wick Hollow 85, **327**
    Wiltshire & Dorset Bank (former) 80, **325**
Glastonbury Canal 67, 80, 327
  Highbridge 356
Glastonbury Tor *see* Glastonbury
Goathurst **330–1**
  St Edward 32, 51, 52, 53, 64, 65–6, 72, **330–1**
Godminster Manor *see* Bruton
Godney **332**
  Holy Trinity 69, 229, **332**
  school 79, **332**
  Temple Cross House 85, **332**
Golsoncott *see* Rodhuish
Gothelney Hall 42, **332–3**
Grand Western Canal 67
  Nynehead **505**

Great Western Railway (GWR) 80, 81
  Chard Joint Station **192**
  Chard line 81
    Donyatt **260–1**
    Hatch Beauchamp 81, **348**
    Ilminster 81, **379**
    Ruishton **545**
  Langport viaduct 81, **396**
  Somerton **563**
  Yeovil:
    Pen Mill **719–20**
    Stoford **579**
    Yeovil Town 722
Greenham **333–4**
  Greenham Barton 42, **333–4**
Greinton **334–5**
Gurney Manor *see* Cannington
GWR *see* Great Western Railway

Hadspen 6, **335–6**
  Hadspen House 58, **335–6**
  Shatwell 85, **336**
Halse **336–7**
  St James 22, 38, 72, 117, **336–7**
Halsway **338–9**
  Halsway Manor 244, **338–9**, 579
Halswell House 54, 55, 61, 272, 331, **339–43**, Pls. 80, 95
  Mill Wood 61, **342**
  Robin Hood's Hut 61, **342**
Hambridge **343–4**
  Earnshill House 8, 58, 62, 63, **343–4**
  St James 4, 69, 72, **343**
  Westport 67, 81, **344**, 399
Ham Hill 5, 6, 7, 11, **344–5**, Pl. 5
Hardington Mandeville **345**
  St Mary the Virgin **345**, 591
Hartrow Manor *see* Elworthy
Haselbury Plucknett **345–6**
  Haselbury Bridge 45, **346**
  Wulfric's cell 16, **346**
Hatch Beauchamp **346–9**
  Hatch Court 58, 61, 62, 63, 346, **347–8**, Pl. 91
  St John Baptist 28, 64, 119n., **346–7**, 644, Pl. 46
  station (former) 81, **348**
Hawkcombe Head *see* Porlock
Hawkridge **349**
Haydon *see* Henlade
Hazlegrove House 57, 63, **349–50**, 409
Heatherton Park *see* Bradford-on-Tone
Heathfield **350–1**
Heathfield School *see* West Monkton
Hele Manor *see* Brushford; South Petherton

Henlade **351**
  Haydon House 8, 55, **351**
  Henlade House (Mount Somerset Hotel) 63, **351**
Henley *see* High Ham
Henley Manor *see* Misterton
Henstridge **351–2**
  Inwood 61, 75, **352**
  Toomer Farm 44, **352**, 642
  Yenston Priory 16, 37, **352**
Henton **352**
  Christ Church 69, **352**
Hestercombe **353–5**
  Hestercombe House 61, 75, 76, 341, **353–5**, Pl. 121
Hewish **355**
Highbridge 60, 67, **356**
  St John Evangelist 69, **356**
Higher Broughton *see* Stoke St Mary
High Ham **356–8**
  Old Rectory 76, **357**
  St Andrew 33, 38, 46, **356–7**, 388, 680
  Stembridge Tower Mill 67, 187, **358**
Hillfarrance **358**
  Holy Cross 26, 32, **358**, 395, 499, 504, 658, 666
Hill House *see* Otterhampton
Hinkley Point **358–9**
  nuclear reactors 85, **358–9**
Hinton House *see* Hinton St George
Hinton St George **359–65**
  Hinton House 48, 54, 55, 58, 60, 63, 163, 164, **362–5**, 459, 648, Pl. 66
  rectory (former) 76, **361**
  St George 31, 33, 34, 46, 53, 65–6, 72, 233, 250, **359–61**, 501, 554, Pl. 82
Holford **365–6**
  Alfoxton Park **365**
  Willoughby Cleeve 82, 117, **365**
Holnicote House *see* Selworthy
Holton **366**
  St Nicholas 5, 37, **366**
Hornblotton **366–7**
  St Peter 70, 71, **366–7**, 406, Pls. 102, 104
Horsey *see* Bawdrip
Horsington **368**
  Horsington House 59, **368**
  St John the Baptist 37, 64, 65, 72, **368**, 595n.
Horton **368–9**
Horwood *see* Wincanton
Huish Barton *see* Nettlecombe
Huish Champflower **369–70**
  St Peter 21, 32, 117, **369–70**
Huish Episcopi 29, **370–2**
  Huish Episcopi School 82, 96, **371**, 377, 592

Rose and Crown inn 61, **371**
St Mary 5, 17, 25, 26, 27, 28, 30–1, **370–1**, 381, 386, 387, 390, 399, 544
Huntspill Court *see* West Huntspill
Huntspill River 2
  East Huntspill **286**
  Puriton **536**
  West Huntspill **675**
Hurst *see* Bower Hinton
Hyde *see* Bathpool
Hymerford House *see* North Coker

Ilchester **372–4**
  churches etc. **372–3**
    Dominican friary 16, 372
    Methodist chapel 74, **373**
    St Andrew, Northover 13, **373**, 374
    St Mary Major 21, 51, 256, **372**
    Whitehall Augustinian nunnery 16, 372, 373
  Northover 372, **373–4**
  public buildings 67, 372, **373–4**
    gaol 78, 372, **373**, 673
    market cross 57, **373**
  Roman town 12–13, 344, 372, 373, **374**, 389
  Sock Dennis **374**
  streets and houses 373
    Ilchester Mead 373, **374**
    rectory 76, **373**
Ile Abbots *see* Isle Abbots
Ile Brewers *see* Isle Brewers
Ilminster 5, 7, 14, 236, **374–9**
  churches etc. **375–7**
    Chantry 16, 42, **378**
    Methodist church 74, **377**
    St Mary 5, 17, 25, 26, 31, 33, 37, 46, 51, 53, 65, 233, 318, **375–7**, 387, 397, 496, Pl. 34
    Unitarian meeting house (now Arts Centre) 64, **377**
  Dowlish Ford Mills 81, 377, **379**
  public buildings 67, 344, **378–9**
    Grammar School 50, **378**
    market 57, **377**
    National School, 79, **378–9**
    station (former) 81, **379**
Ilton **379–81**
  almshouses 50, **380**
  Ashford House 55, **380**, 535
  Rowland's 47, 48, **380–1**, 532
  Rowland's Mill 67, **381**
Inwood *see* Henstridge
Isle Abbots **381–3**
  St Mary 5, 19, 22, 23, 25, 26, 27, 28, 29, 30, 32, 33, 46, 120, 166, 214, 251, 359, 370, **381–3**, 386–7, 390, 573, 611

Isle Brewers **384**
  All Saints 70, 72, **384**
Ivythorn Manor *see* Street

Jordans *see* Broadway

Keinton Mandeville 4, **384**
  St Mary Magdalene 21, 108, **384**
Kilton **384–5**
  St Andrew, Lilstock **385**, 583
  St Nicholas 37, **384–5**
Kilve **385–6**
  Chantry, The 16, **385–6**
  Kilve Court 59, **386**
  St Mary 51, **385**
  Thatchings 82, **386**
King's Brompton *see* Brompton Regis
Kingsbury Episcopi **386–8**
  Chimney Cottage 43, **388**
  lock-up 57, **388**
  Methodist chapel 74, **388**
  St Martin 24, 28, 29, 30, 32, 38, 233, 375, **386–8**, 397, 427, 544
  toll house 66, **388**
Kingsdon **389**
  All Saints 25, 28, 193, 371, **389**, 700
King's Sedgemoor Drain 2, 94, 170, Pl. 2
Kingstone **389–90**
  St John and All Saints 17, 25, **389–90**, 552
Kingston St Mary **390–2**
  St Mary 21, 25, 26, 28, 33, 38, 39, 65, 120, 126, 181, 359, 370, 381, **390–1**, 573, 659, 708
Kingweston **392–3**
  All Saints 17, 70, 108, **392**, 606
  Kingweston House 58, 62, **392–3**
Kittisford **393–4**
  St Nicholas 32, 36, 51, **393–4**
Knapp *see* North Curry
Knowl *see* Long Sutton
Knowle Hall *see* Bawdrip
Knowle Manor *see* Timberscombe
Knowle St Giles **394**

Lamyatt **394–5**
  Creech Hill 129, **395**
  St Mary and St John 33, **394–5**
Langford Budville **395–6**
  St Peter 122, **395–6**
Langford Manor *see* Fivehead
Langport 4, 15, 69, 80, **396–401**, 558
  All Saints 17, 28, 33, 35, 36, 39, 65, 72, 154, 203, 233, 250, 375, 387, 389, **397–8**, 403, 404, 473, 475, 496, 679, Pl. 107

Langport *cont.*
  public buildings 67, 396,
      398–401
      Great Bow Bridge 67, **399**,
        Pl. 116
      Market House and Town
        Hall 57, **398–9**, **400**
      primary school 79, **399**
      viaduct 81, **396**
      warehouses 56, 396, **401**
    streets and houses 56, 396–7,
        399–401
      Hurd's Hill 252, **401**
      Westover **401**
Leigh House *see* Winsham
Leighland **401–2**
  St Giles 39, **401**
Lillycombe *see* Culbone
Lilstock *see* Kilton
Limington **402–3**
  St Mary 23, 24, 33, **402–3**, 703
London & South Western Railway
    (LSWR) 80, 81
  Crewkerne 81, **235**
  Yeovil Junction (Stoford) 80, **579**
  Yeovil Town 722
Long Load 67, 70, **403**
Long Sutton **403–6**
  Court House 41, **405**, 489
  Friends' Meeting House 64, **405**,
    Pl. 85
  Holy Trinity 27, 28, 33, 38, 182,
    397, **403–5**, 475, 538
Lopen **406**
  Roman villa 12, **406**
Lottisham **406–7**
  St Mary 70, **406–7**
Lovington **407–8**
  St Thomas à Becket 101, **407**
Lower Cockhill *see* Castle Cary
Low Ham **408–10**
  church 46, 53, 54, 65, 66, 245,
    408–9, Pl. 71
  Roman villa 12, **410**
  Lord Stawell's mansion 350, **409**
LSWR *see* London & South Western
  Railway
Luccombe **410–11**
  St Mary 22, 25, 26, 32, 33, 34,
    35, 36, 51, **410–11**, 527, 549,
    638, 650, 713
Lufton **411–12**
  St Peter and St Paul **411–12**, 591
Luxborough **412**
  Langham Hill Mine 130, **412**
  St Mary **412**, 712
Lydeard St Lawrence **413–14**
  St Lawrence 35, 51, 150, **413**
Lympsham 75, **414–16**
  Manor House 75, **415–16**
  St Christopher 28, 35, 65, 71–2,
    414–15

Lynch Chapel *see* West Lynch
Lynch House *see* West Lynch
Lyng *see* East Lyng
Lytes Cary 41, 42, 43, 47, 48, 72,
  76, 160, **417–20**, 515, Pl. 54

Maperton 6, 8, **420**
Mark **420–2**
  Holy Cross 28, 35, 36, 37, 38,
    368, **420–2**, 653
Marston Bigot **422–5**
  Marston House 58, 61, 75,
    423–5
  Old Rectory 76, **425**
  St Leonard 65, 69, 71, **422–3**
  school 79, **425**
Marston House *see* Marston Bigot
Marston Magna **425–6**
  St Mary 19, **425–6**
Martock 49, 255, **426–32**
  All Saints 5, 22, 27, 29, 33, 36,
    65, 154, 387, **427–8**, 537, 558,
    610, 674, 680, 716, Pl. 39
  Market House and Pinnacle 57,
    373, **430**
  Methodist chapel 74, **428**, 568
  streets and houses 82, 125,
    429–31, 593
    Court House 40, **429–30**
    Stapleton Farmhouse 99,
      431, 436
    Treasurer's House 41, 226,
      428–9, 434
Maunsel House *see* St Michael
  Church
Meare **432–5**
  Fish House 42, **434**, Pl. 19
  lake villages 11, 330, **434**
  Manor Farm (summer palace)
    42, 43, 257, 432, **433–4**
  St Mary and All Saints 23, 24,
    29, 39, 65, 97, **432–3**, 552, 554,
    596, 680, Pl. 22
  schools 79, **433**
  Westhay 10, **435**
Mellifont Abbey *see* Wookey
Merriott **435–6**
  All Saints 32, 34, 65, **435**
  Congregational chapel (former)
    73, **435**
  lock-up 57, **435**
  Merriott Court 75, **436**
  Moorlands 75–6, **436**
  sailcloth factory 68, **436**
Mid Lambrook **436–7**
  Middle Lambrook Meeting 64,
    148, 234, **436**
Middle Chinnock **437**
  St Margaret 17, **437**, 578, 639
Middlezoy **437–9**
  Holy Cross 22, 28, 38, 39, 51,
    287, **437–9**, 681

Midelney *see* Drayton
Midelney Place *see* Curry Rivel
Milborne Port **439–41**
  public buildings **441–2**
    Guildhall 18, **441–2**
    school 79, **442**
    Town Hall 57, **441**
  St John the Evangelist 6, 15, 17, 19, 70, 72, 152, 370, **439–41**, 507, 517, 634, 666, Pls. 7, 8
  streets and houses **441–4**
    Newtown 441, **443–4**
    Old Vicarage 76, **442**
    Ven House 8, 57, 62, 63, 441, **442–3**
    Waterloo Crescent 221, **444**
Millfield *see* Street
Milton *see* Ash
Milton Clevedon **444**
  St James 64, **444**
Milverton **444–8**
  Old House, The 43, 226, **445–6**, Pl. 61
  St Michael 21, 22, 39, 72, 204, **444–5**, 641
Minchin Buckland *see* Durston
Minehead 1, 3, 8, 45, 56, 57, 69, **448–58**
  Alcombe **451**, **452**, **457–8**
  churches **448–53**
    Baptist chapel 73, **451**
    Methodist church 74, **451**
    Sacred Heart and convent (R.C.) 73, **451**
    St Andrew 70, 72, **451**
    St Michael 32, 33, 35, 37, 38, 51, 52, 72, 117, 152, 167, 181, 216, 267, 300, **448–51**, 460, 638, 703
  North Hill **458**
  public buildings 448, **451–3**
    Queen Anne statue 57, **453**
    Community Hospital 85, **452**
    harbour 56, **456**
    Lido 83
    Market House 78, **453**
    middle school 82, **453**
    pier 56, 448, 456
    police station and Magistrates' Court 83, **451**
    railway station 80, 81, 448, **451**
    Town Hall (former) 78, **455**
    war memorial 83, **455**
  streets and houses 56, 77, 80, 82, 448, **453–8**
    Cleveland 75, **454**
    Elgin Tower 75, **455**
    Kildare Lodge 77, **457**, Pl. 122
    Middle Street 44, **454**
    Parade, The 80, **453**, 455
    Periton Mead 82, **458**

Quarry Close estate 84, **458**
Stuckey's Bank branches (former) 80, **453**, 691
Minehead Railway *see* West Somerset Railway
Misterton **458–9**
  Henley Manor 364, **459**
  railway station *see* Crewkerne
Monksilver **459–60**
  All Saints 34, 38, **459–60**
Montacute 7, **461–70**, 566
  castle 40, 41, 640
  churches etc. **461–2**
    Baptist church 73, **462**
    Montacute Priory 16, 40, **462–3**, 486, Pl. 31
    St Catherine 22, 27, 33, 46, 65, 70, 72, **461–2**, 562
  Montacute House 47–8, 49, 106, 163, 165, 292, 305, **463–70**, 482, 485, 488, 531, 533, 624, 701, Pl. 64
    gardens and forecourt 48, 61, 354, 464, **469–70**
    library fireplace 46, 48, 49, 82, **468–9**, 653
    plasterwork 48–9, 292, **467**, **469**, 482, 531, 671
    porch from Clifton Maybank 46–7, **465**, Pl. 60
  St Michael's Hill **470**
  village 82, 461, **463**
    council houses 431, **463**
    Monks House 43, **463**
Monty's Court *see* Norton Fitzwarren
Moorland **470**
  St Peter and St John 69, **470**
Moorlinch 187, **470–1**
  St Mary 38, **470–1**
Muchelney **471–7**
  Muchelney Abbey 15, 16, 18, 35, 39, 40, 45, 174, 175, 204, 211, 240, 250, 372, 388, 408, **471–4**, 475, 582
    Abbot's Lodging 35, 40, 43, **473–4**, 476; fireplace in Great Chamber 40, 43, **474**, Pl. 29
  St Peter and St Paul 24, 33, 37, 39, 51, 65, 174, 251, 408, **474–6**, 555, Pls. 44, 70
  Thorney **477**
    mill 67, **477**
  village **476–7**
    Priest's House 42, 43, 473, **476**, 477, Pl. 28
    Toll, The 66, **476**
Mudford **477–8**
  St Mary 34, 51, 52, 99, 201, **477–8**, 717
  school 79, **478**

Naish Priory see North Coker
Nether Stowey **478–80**
  St Mary 69, **478–9**, 496
  Stowey Castle 40–1, **480**
  Stowey Court **479**, 480
Nettlecombe **480–5**
  Huish Barton 8, **485**
  Nettlecombe Court 47, 48, 55, 62, 63, 272, 303, 304, 467, **481–4**, 485, 585, Pl. 67
  St Mary 37, 65, 83, 181, **480–1**
  Woodford 480, **484**
New Cut 356
Newton Surmaville 47, 61, **485–6**, 488
North Barrow **486**
North Cadbury **486–90**
  North Cadbury Court 41, 47, 464, 485, **488–9**, Pl. 63
  St Michael 25, 27, 33, 34, 36, 37, 39, 182, **486–8**
  school 79, **489**
North Cheriton **490**
  St John Baptist **490**, 520n.
North Coker **490–1**
  Hymerford House 42, 43, **490–1**
  Naish Priory 44, **491**, 671
North Curry 368, **491–4**
  Knapp 4, **493–4**
  Nonconformist chapels 73, **493**
  priory 16
  St Peter and St Paul 21, 29, 37, 71, 83, 251, **491–3**
North Newton **494**
  St Peter 51, 52, **494**, 587
Northover see Ilchester
North Perrott **495**
  North Perrott Manor 75, **495**
  St Martin 387, **495**
North Petherton **495–8**
  cemetery 74, **497**
  Congregational chapel 73, **497**
  Petherton Park 55, **498**
  St Mary 5, 27, 28, 29, 31, 33, 36, 38, 72, 318, 397, **495–7**, 679, 681
North Wootton **498–9**
Norton Fitzwarren 8, **499–500**
  All Saints 4, 38, 233, **499–500**, 677, Pl. 50
  Monty's Court 74, **500**
  Norton Camp 11, 499, **500**
  Norton Manor 74, **500**
Norton Manor see Norton Fitzwarren
Norton-sub-Hamdon **500–3**
  Little Norton Mill 67, **503**
  St Mary 5, 31, 33, 71, 72, 214, 250, 359, **500–2**, 554, 680, 698, Pl. 119
    dovecote 44, **502**
  streets and houses **502–3**
    Herb Garden, The 85, **502**
    Mill Green 85, **503**
Nynehead **503–5**
  All Saints 66, 71–2, 73, **503–5**, Pls. 103, 105
  canal boat-lift 67, **505**
  Nynehead Court 54, **505**

Oake **506**
Oare **506–7**
  St Mary 65, **506–7**
Odcombe **507**
  St Peter and St Paul 33, 70, **507**, 666
Old Cleeve **508–10**
  Binham Grange 49, 124, **509**, Pl. 68
  Chapel Cleeve 60, 62–3, 76, 416, **509–10**
  St Andrew 33, 35, 36, 37, 39, 52, 65, 72, 319, **508–9**, 528, 579, 580, 650
Orchard Portman **510**
  Orchard House 48, 353, 510
Orchard Wyndham see Williton
Othery **510–12**
  St Michael 39, **510–12**
Otterford **512**
  St Leonard 32, **512**
Otterhampton **512–13**
  All Saints 38, **512–13**
  Hill House 59, 62, **513**
Over Stowey **513–14**
  Quantock Lodge 74, 75, **513–14**
  St Peter and St Paul 72, **513**
Over Stratton **514–15**
  Wigborough Manor 48, 190, **515**, 648, 689

Parrett Navigation 67, **344**
Patcombe see Halswell House
Pawlett **515–16**
  St John Baptist 17, 38, 71, **515–16**
Pendomer **516–17**
  Pendomer House (rectory) 76, **517**
  St Roch 5, 24, 201, **516**
Penselwood 14, **517–18**
  Pen Pits 82, **518**
  St Michael 17–18, **517–18**
Petherton Park see North Petherton
Pilton **519–23**
  Ebenezer (Bible Christian) chapel 74, **520**
  Pilton Manor 44, 59, 60, **521**
  St John Baptist 19, 21, 29, 38, 72, 257, 490, **519–20**, 682
  tithe barn 44, 321, **521**, 665, 666
  West Compton 49, **522**
  Westholme House 59, 63, **522**

Pitcombe **523**
  St Leonard 70, **523**
Pitminster 14, **523–4**
  St Mary and St Andrew 21, 24, 51, 52–3, **523–4**, Pl. 77
Pitney **524–5**
  medieval parsonage 40, **525**
Pixton Park *see* Dulverton
Podimore 11, **525–6**
  St Peter 21, 118, **525–6**
Porlock 1, 3, 24, 71, **526–30**
  churches **526–7**
    Methodist church 74, **527**
    St Dubricius 14, 21, 22, 37, 83, 300, 410, **526–7**, 549, 694, Pl. 52
  Hawkcombe Head 9, **530**
  Porlock Weir 124, **529**
  streets and houses 128, **527–30**
    Ashley Combe 75, **530**
    Chantry, The 16, **527**
    Dovery Manor 35, **527–8**
    Hunting Lodge, The 77, **528**
    Merryfield 82, **529**
    New Place 76, **528–9**, 550, Pl. 120
    Worthy Manor 76, **530**
Post Track 10
Poundisford **530–4**
  Poundisford Lodge 47, 48, 292, **530–2**, 533, 664
  Poundisford Park 47, 48, 228, 231, 381, 483, 530, 531, **532–3**
Preston Plucknett **534–5**
  Abbey Manor 5, 42, 43, 44, **534–5**, 670
  St James 5, **534**, 717
Puckington **535**
  St Andrew 22, **535**, 555
Puriton 286, **535–6**
  Royal Ordnance Factory 286, **536**, 675, 712
  St Michael **535–6**
Pylle **536–7**
Pyrland Hall *see* Kingston St Mary

Quantock Lodge *see* Over Stowey
Queen Camel 4, **537–9**
  primary school 79, **539**
  St Barnabas 27, 28, 36, 38, 72, 182, **537–8**, 544, 667, 674, 716

Raddington **539–40**
  St Michael 52, **539–40**
Redlynch **540–1**
  Redlynch 57–8, 61, **540–1**
  St Peter 64, **540**
Rimpton **541–2**
  St Mary 22, 34, 51, **541–2**, 640
Road Castle *see* Exford
Roadwater **542**, 543
  St Pancras Chapel 16, **542**

Rockwell Green **542–3**
  All Saints 70, **542–3**
Rodhuish **543–4**
  Escott Farmhouse 55, **544**
Roobies Farm *see* Fiddington
Roundhill Grange *see* Charlton Musgrove
Rowland's *see* Ilton
Ruishton **544–5**
  St George 25, 28, 198, **544–5**, 636
Rumwell *see* Bishop's Hull
Runnington **545**
  St Peter 32, **545**

St Audries *see* West Quantoxhead
St Michael Church **545–6**
  Maunsel House 41, 42, 60, **545–6**
  St Michael 203, **545**
Saltmoor *see* Burrowbridge
Sampford Arundel **546–7**
Sampford Brett **547–8**
  Woolston 76, **548**
Sandhill Park *see* Ash Priors
Seavington St Mary **548**
Seavington St Michael 5, **548–9**
Sedgemoor *see* Westonzoyland
Selworthy **549–51**
  All Saints 35, 36, 65, 66, 72, 410, 449, 528, **549–50**, 638, 641, 650, 676, 713
  estate cottages 61, **550–1**
    Selworthy Green 61, **550**, Pl. 100
  Holnicote House 43, 94, 124, 128, 411, **551**, 641, 642
Shanks House *see* Cucklington
Shapwick **552–4**
  St Mary 53, 70, **552**, 680
  Shapwick Manor 44, **552–3**
  Sweet Track 10, **553–4**
Sharpham Park 432, **554**
Shatwell *see* Hadspen
Shepton Beauchamp **554–6**
  fives wall **556**, 569
  rectory (former) 76, **556**
  St Michael 5, 31, 33, 70, 71, 99n., 233, 250, 359, 475, 501, 535, **554–5**
Shepton Montague **556**
Sherford *see* Taunton (outer areas)
Simonsbath 3, **556–7**
Skilgate **557**
Slough Court *see* Stoke St Gregory
Snowdon Hill *see* Chard
Sock Dennis *see* Ilchester
Somerset Central Railway 80, 169
Somerset & Dorset Railway 80, 114, 356
  Evercreech **299**
  Pitcombe **523**

Somerton 4, 45, 372, **557–63**
  public buildings 557, **559–63**
    Hext Almshouses 50, **561–2**
    market cross 50, 323, **559**
    railway viaduct and bridge 81, **563**
    Town Hall 50, **559**
    St Michael 21, 22, 36, 52, 65, 66, 252, 372, **558–9**, 680, Pls. 42, 72
  streets and houses 56, 557, **559–63**
    Market Place 56, **559**, Pl. 3
    Medwyn **561**, 562
    Old Parsonage 49, **562**
    Old Vicarage 40, **561**
    Somerton Castle 203, 559–60
    Somerton Erleigh 85, **563**
    Somerton Randle 59, 62, 63, **562–3**
    West Street 45, **561**
South Barrow **563–4**
South Brent *see* Brent Knoll
South Brewham **564–5**
  Alfred's Tower 2, 61, 342, **564**, Pl. 93
South Cadbury **565–6**
  Cadbury Castle 10, 11, 12, 13, 14, 374, **565–6**
  Milsom's Corner **566n.**
  St Thomas à Becket 21, 197, **565**
South Cheriton **566**
  toll house 66, **566**
Southern Railway **634**
Southill House *see* West Cranmore
South Petherton 10, **566–70**, 675
  churches **566–8**
    Coke Memorial Methodist Church 74, 428, **568**, Pl. 109
    Congregational church and Sunday School 74, **569–70**
    St Peter and St Paul 21, 22, 24, 25, 37, 53, 523–4, **566–8**, 589n.
  Hele Manor 125
  South Petherton Hospital 85, **568**
  streets and houses **569–70**
    Manor House 43, **568–9**
    South Street Farm 54, **570**
Sowy River **94, 170**
Spargrove *see* Westcombe
Sparkford 350, **570–1**
  St Mary Magdalene 51, 95, 345, **570**
Spaxton **571–3**
  Agapemonite houses and chapel 74, 76, **572–3**
  St Margaret 4, 27, 32, 33, 35, 39, 52, 110, 150, 281, **571–2**, 603

Staple Fitzpaine **573–4**
  St Peter 17, 28, 116n., 120, 381, 390, **573–4**
Staplegrove **574–5**
Stavordale Priory 16, 40, 42, 46, 76, 518, 534, **575–6**, Pl. 32
Stawell **576**
Stawley **576–7**
  St Michael 65, **576–7**
Steart **577**
Steyning Manor *see* Stogursey
Stockland Bristol **577**
  St Mary Magdalene 70, **577**
  Stockland Manor 75, **577**
Stockland Lovell *see* Fiddington
Stockland Manor *see* Stockland Bristol
Stocklinch **577–8**
  St Mary Magdalen 65, **578**
  St Mary, Stocklinch Ottersey 23, 437, **578**, Pl. 18
Stocklinch Ottersey *see* Stocklinch
Stoford **579**
  Yeovil Junction Station **579**
Stogumber 4, **579–81**
  Almonry, The (almshouses) 50, **581**
  St Mary 34, 35, 46, 65, 71, **579–81**, 638
Stogursey **581–5**
  primary school 79, **585**
  priory 16, 582
  St Andrew 17, 18, 19, 65, 70, 203, **582–4**
    pulpit and font from 51, 583, **594**, 674–5
  Steyning Manor 55, **585**
  Stogursey Castle 40–1, **584**
Stoke Pero **586**
  church 506, **586**
Stoke St Gregory **586–8**
  St Gregory 21, 24, 51, 491, **586–7**, Pl. 73
  Slough Court 42, 493, **588**
Stoke St Mary **588–9**
  Higher Broughton 44, **588–9**
Stoke-sub-Hamdon 344, **589–94**
  castle 589, 591, 593
  Congregational church 73, **592**
  fives wall 556, 569, **593**
  glove works 81, 589, **593–4**
  Priory, The 16, **592–3**
  St Mary 17, 22, 23, 24, 36, 46, 345, 440, 567, **589–92**, Pl. 9
Stoke Trister **594**
Stoke-under-Ham *see* Stoke-sub-Hamdon
Stolford **594**
  St Peter **594**, 683n.
Stowell **594–5**
  St Mary Magdalene 71, 72, 127, 368, **594**

Stowey Castle *see* Nether Stowey
Stowey Court *see* Nether Stowey
Street 4, 69, 84, **595–602**
   churches **595–6**
      Friends' Meeting House 74, **596**
      Holy Trinity 432, **595–6**
      Lantokay 14, 595
      Methodist chapel and schoolrooms 74, **596**
   Clark company buildings 81, 595, 598
      Clark Factory **598**
      Clark's Folly (from Westcombe) **597**
      Clarks Village (shopping development) 597, **599**
      Distribution Centre 85, **601**
      More Light Building 83, **598**
   outer areas **601–22**
   public buildings 77, 78, 84, **596–7**, **599–600**
      British School 79, **600**
      Crispin Hall 78, **599**
      Greenbank Open-air Pool 83, **597**, 598
      Hindhayes Infants School 82, 157, **597**, 599
      Millfield School 75, 84, 329, **601–2**
      Strode College, Theatre, and Crispin School **596**
      Technical School 78, **599**
      Vestry Room and police station 78, **599**
   streets and houses 77, 82, 595, **597–602**
      Hill House 85, **600**
      Icon development 85, **600**
      Ivythorn Manor 43, **602**
      workers' housing 77, **597–601**; Cobden Terrace **598**, Pl. 114
Stringston **602–3**
Sutton Bingham **603–4**
   All Saints 17, 22, 39, **603–4**
Sutton Mallet **604**
   church 64, **604**
Sutton Montis **604–5**
   Holy Trinity 17, **604–5**
Sweet Track 10, **553–4**
Swell **605–6**
   St Catherine 17, **605–6**
   Swell Manor 43, **606**
Sydenham Manor *see* Bridgwater

Tarr Steps 45, **606**
Tatworth **606–7**
Taunton 1, 3, 4, 44–5, 56, 68, 84, **607–33**
   Castle 17, 40–1, 60, 607, **615–19**, Pl. 92
   Castle House 17, 42, 615, 616, **619**
   churches etc. **607–15**, **631**
      Baptist church 73, **614**
      Convent of Perpetual Adoration (former) 73, **630**
      Franciscan convent (former) 73, **632**
      Holy Trinity 69, 71, 77, **611**, 632
      Masonic Hall (former R.C. church) 64, **625**
      Octagon Chapel (former; C18) 64, 614, **627**
      Octagon Chapel (C20) **614**
      St Andrew 3, 70, 71, 543, **612–13**
      St George, Wilton 15, 21, 72, 607, **613**
      St George (R.C.) 73, **614**
      St James 5, 26, 28, 30, 33, 37, 120, 381, **611–12**, 630, 705
      St John Evangelist 70, 71, 72, **613–14**
      St Mary Magdalene 4, 5, 21, 25, 26, 27, 28, 29, 30, 33, 34, 35, 36, 37, 53, 56, 70, 72, 73, 119, 126, 198, 318, 387, **607–11**, 613, 614, 615, 626, 677, 713, Pl. 35
      St Teresa (R.C.) 85, **614**
      Taunton Deane Crematorium *see* Bishop's Hull
      Taunton Priory 14, 16, 45, 506, 607, 611, 627
      Temple Methodist Church 74, **614–15**
      Unitarian chapel and schools 64, 74, **615**
   outer areas **628–33**
      Galmington **614**, **631**
      Wilton 68, 607, **613**, **629**
   public buildings 77–8, 84, 607, **619–33**
      Art School 84, **620**
      Bishop Fox Community School 84, **622**
      canals 67, 607, **623**
      College of Art 78, **625**
      County Offices 83, 84, **619–20**, Pl. 125
      Gaumont cinema (former) 83, **625**
      Grammar School (former; now Registry Office) 45, 78, **625**
      Gray's Almshouses 8, 50, 611, **628**
      Jellalabad Barracks (former) 78, **629**
      King's College 78–9, 84, 127, **621**, 632

Taunton, public buildings *cont.*
　Library (former) 78, **626**
　Magistrates' Courts 84, **620**
　Market House 56, 57, **619**
　Musgrove Park Hospital 85, **622**
　Queen's College 4, 78, **621**, Pl. 112
　railway station and hotel 81, 607, **622**
　Richard Huish College 84, **622**, 632
　Shire Hall 77–8, 619, **620**
　Somerset College of Arts and Technology 84–5, **620–1**, Pl. 126
　Taunton Castle *see* Castle *above*
　Taunton Gaol (former) 78, 607, **620**
　Taunton School 3, 78–9, 83, **621–2**, 631
　Technical Institute 78, **625**
　Town Ditch **627**
　Vivary Park 78, **622**, 628–9
　workhouse 78, 145, 633
streets and houses 45, 56, 76–7, 84, 607, **623–33**
　Corporation Street 78, **625**
　Crescent, The 56, **625**
　Elm Grove 77, **631**
　Fore Street 45, **623–4**, 626; No. 4 and No. 7: 80, **624**; No. 15: 45, 48, **623–4**; No. 18: 48, 276n., **624**
　Halcon 82, **633**
　Hammet Street 56, **626**, Pl. 35
　Hankridge Arms **633**, 636
　Highlands 82, **629**
　High Street **624–5**
　Mitre House 612n., **630**
　Parade, The 56, **623**
　Park Street 77, 612n., **630**
　South Road 77, **632**
　Trull Road 77, **629–30**
　Wiltshire & Dorset Banks (former) 80, **624**
Templecombe **633–4**
　Manor Farm 16, **634**
　St Mary 19, 152, 441, **633–4**
Terhill *see* Cothelstone
Tetton House *see* Kingston St Mary
Theale **634–5**
　Christ Church 64, **634**, 705
　Great House 49, 55, **634–5**
Thorne Coffin **635**
　Thorne House 75, **635**
Thorne St Margaret **635–6**
Thorney *see* Muchelney
Thornfalcon **636**
　Ashe Farmhouse 231, 633, **636**
　Court House 43, **636**
　Holy Cross 544, **636**
Thurlbear **636–7**
　St Thomas 17, 18, **636–7**, Pl. 10
Thurloxton **637**
　St Giles 51, 52, **637**
Timberscombe **638–9**
　Bickham Manor 63, **638**
　Croydon House 55, **638–9**
　St Petrock 35, 36, 38, 39, 51, 268, 300, 449, 549, 580, **638**, 643
Tintinhull **639–41**
　St Margaret 33, 51, 83, 437, **639–40**
　Tintinhull House 59, **640–1**, Pl. 88
Tivington **641–2**
　Blackford Dovecote 44, 352n., **642**
Tolland **642–3**
　Gaulden Manor 55, 231, 419, 483, 533, **642–3**, 707
Treborough 3, 7, **643**
　St Peter 37, **643**
Triscombe House *see* West Bagborough
Trudoxhill **643–4**
Trull **644–6**
　All Saints 38, 39, 117, 119, 215, 230, 303, 500, 636, **644–5**, 678, Pl. 51

Upton **646**
Upton Noble **646–7**

Vellow *see* Stogumber
Ven House *see* Milborne Port

Wadeford *see* Combe St Nicholas
Wales *see* Queen Camel
Walford House *see* West Monkton
Walton **647**
　Old Parsonage 35, 76, **647**
Wambrook **648**
　St Mary 18, **648**
　Weston Farm 364, **648**, 689
Wanstrow **648–9**
Washford **649**
Watchet 1, 4, 15, 52, 56, 81, **649–52**
　harbour and piers 56, 649, **651–2**
　Methodist chapel 74, **651**
　St Decuman 14, 22, 25, 26, 32, 35, 36, 37, 39, 46, 51, 52, 53, 116, 300, 319, 410, 448, 508, 528, 549, 579, **649–51**, Pl. 78
　West Somerset Mineral Railway station 81, **652**
　West Somerset Railway station 80, **652**
Wayford **652–3**
　Wayford Manor 46, 48, 49, 464, 467, **653**

Weare **653-4**
  St Gregory 6, 71, 101, 420, **653-4**
Wedmore 4, 15, **654-7**
  St Mary 4, 21, 25, 26, 28, 33, 36, 39, 51, 65, 101, 172, **654-6**, Pl. 24
Wellington 3, 8, 69, **658-63**
  churches **658-9**
    Baptist chapel 73, **659**
    Congregational chapel (United Reformed) 73, **659**
    Friends' Meeting House 74, **660**
    Holy Trinity 64, *661*
    St John Baptist 28, 32, 35, 37, 52, 65, 96, 126, 391, 435, **658-9**, 666, Pl. 76
  public buildings **659-62**
    Town Hall 57, **660**
    Wellington School 83, 84, **659-60**
  streets and houses 75, **660-2**
    Fox, Fowler Bank (former) 80, **660**
    Station Road 77, **661-2**
    Stuckey's Bank (former) 80, **660**
    Wellesley Park 77, **661**
  Tonedale Mill 67, 75, 81, 86, **662**, Pl. 118
  Wellington Monument 7, 61-2, **662-3**
Wembdon **663**
West Bagborough **663-5**
  Bagborough House 62, 663, **664**
  St Pancras 32, 83, **663-4**
West Bower Manor *see* Durleigh
West Bradley **665-6**
  Bradley House 59, **665**
  Court Barn 44, 321, 521, **665**
West Buckland **666-7**
  Gerbestone Manor 82, **666-7**
  St Mary 19, 26, 32, 72, 126, 395, 658, **666**
West Camel **667-8**
  All Saints 19, 23, 36, 37, **667-8**
    cross-shaft 15, **667-8**
  council houses, Howell Hill 82, **668**, Pl. 124
  Old Rectory 40, **667**
West Charlton *see* Charlton Mackrell
West Chinnock **668-9**
West Coker 68, **669-72**
  council houses 82, 431, **672**
  Manor, The 41, 42, 44, 48, 76, 292, 531, **669-71**
  St Martin 52, **669**
  twine works 81, **671**
  West Coker Hall 74, **671**, **672**

Westcombe **672**
  Spargrove chapel 112
  Spargrove Manor **672**
  Westcombe House 597, *672*
West Compton *see* Pilton
West Cranmore **673**
  St Bartholomew 28, 72, **673**
West Dowlish *see* Dowlish Wake
West Hatch **674**
Westhay *see* Meare
Westholme House *see* Pilton
West Huntspill **674-5**
  Huntspill Court 59, **675**
  St Peter 27, 71, **674-5**
    Stogursey pulpit 51, 583, **674**
West Lambrook **675**
West Lydford **676**
  St Peter 69, **676**
West Lynch **676-7**
  Lynch Chapel 83, 549, **676**
  Lynch House 76, **677**
West Monkton **677-8**
  Heathfield School 85, **678**
  Long Meadow 82, **678**
  St Augustine 28, 36, 498, **677-8**
  Walford House 61, **678**
Weston Bampfylde **678-9**
  Holy Cross 21, **678-9**
Westonzoyland 9, 10, 203, **679-81**
  pumping station 81, **681**
  St Mary 6, 24, 26, 27, 28, 33, 36, 83, 154, 287, 433, 437, 475, 496, 552, **679-81**, Pls. 37, 41
Westover *see* Langport
West Pennard **681-3**
  St Nicholas 29, 33, 72, 519, 520, **681-3**
Westport *see* Hambridge
Westport Canal 67, 81, **344**
West Quantoxhead 1, **683-7**
  St Audries 60, 62, 74, 75, 82, 301, 416, **684-6**
  St Etheldreda 69, 71, **683-4**, 686, Pl. 101
    medieval church 299-300, *683n.*
    temporary church 594, 683n.
  school 79, **686**
West Somerset Mineral Railway 81
  Brendon Hill 81, **130**
  Roadwater **542**
  Watchet 81, *652*
West Somerset Railway/Minehead Railway 80, 81, 451
  Bishop's Lydeard 122
  Blue Anchor 124
  Dunster 278
  Minehead 451
  Stogumber 581
  Washford 649
  Watchet 80, **652**
  Williton **691**
West Stoke *see* Stoke-sub-Hamdon

Wheathill **687**
Whitelackington **687–8**
  St Mary 23, 46, 66, **687–8**
Whitestaunton **688–90**
  St Andrew 7, 19, 32, **688–9**
  Whitestaunton Manor 42, 48, 190, 364, 648, **689–90**
Wigborough Manor *see* Over Stratton
Willett *see* Elworthy
Williton 4, **690–3**
  Methodist chapel 74, **690**
  Orchard Mill 67, **691**
  Orchard Wyndham 41, 42, 57, 61, 63, **691–3**
  police station 78, **691**
  St Peter 52, 293, **690**
  workhouse (former) 78, **691**, Pl. 110
Willoughby Cleeve *see* Holford
Wilton *see* Taunton (churches *and* outer areas)
Wiltshire, Somerset & Weymouth Railway 80
Wincanton 6, 56, **693–8**
  churches etc. **694–5, 697**
    Methodist chapel 74, **696**
    St Luke and St Teresa (R.C.) and former priory 73, **695**
    St Peter and St Paul 64, 70, **695–6**
  Horwood spa buildings 57, **698**
  police station (former) 78, **697**
  streets and houses 56, 694, **695–8**
    Dogs, The 63, **696–7**
    High Street 56, **695–6**
Winsford **698–9**
  Caratacus Stone 14, **699**, Pl. 6
  St Mary Magdalene 19, 26, 32, 410, 650, **698–9**
Winsham **700–1**
  St Stephen 23, 25, 51, 53, 260, 261, 376, **700**
Witcombe *see* Ash
Witcombe *see* Ham Hill
Witham Friary **701–2**
  Carthusian priory 16, 21, 46, **701**, 702
  dovecote 44, **702**
  St Mary, St John Baptist and All Saints 21, 51, 70, **701–2**, Pl. 14
  Witham Park 46, 57–8, **702**
Withiel Florey 412, **703**
Withycombe 3, 7, **703–4**
  St Nicholas 38, 181, 449, **703–4**, Pl. 21
Withypool **704**
  Landacre Bridge 45, **704**
  St Andrew 19, **704**

Wiveliscombe 56, **704–8**
  Kingsmead School 84, **706**
  St Andrew 52, 64, 72, **705**
  station (former) 80, **707**
  streets and houses 704, **706–7**
    Abbotsfield 75, **707**
    Bournes 55, 231, 483, 642, **707**
    High Street 483, **706**
Woodford *see* Nettlecombe
Woodlands **708–9**
  St Katharine 64, 65, 70, 391, 659, **708**
Wookey **709–11**
  Court Farm 41, 710, **711**
  Mellifont Abbey 59, 63, **710–11**
  St Matthew 46, **709–10**
Woolavington **711–12**
  St Mary 93, **711–12**
  vicarage (former) 68, **712**
Woolston *see* Sampford Brett
Wootton Courtenay **712–13**
  All Saints 412, **712–13**
  Stone & Francis houses 82, **713**
Worthy *see* Porlock
Wrantage **713–14**
  Chard Canal and Crimson Hill Tunnel 67, **713**
Wyke Champflower **714**
  Holy Trinity 50, 51, 83, **714**

Yarlington **714–15**
  St Mary 70, **714–15**
Yenston *see* Henstridge
Yeovil 2, 5, 45, 68, 84, **715–23**
  churches etc. **715–18**
    Baptist church 73, **718**
    cemetery 74, **718**
    chantry 715, 718, 720
    Holy Ghost (R.C.) and presbytery 73, **718**, 722
    Holy Trinity, Lysander Road **717**
    Holy Trinity (Yeovil Foyer), Peter Street **717**
    Methodist church 74, **718**
    minster 14, 715
    St Andrew 83, 534, **717**
    St John Baptist 5, 25, 26, 27, 28, 29, 32, 34, 35, 39, 65, 72, 110, 477, 655, 656, **715–17**, Pls. 25, 26, 84
    St Michael 70–1, **717–18**
    United Reformed (former Congregational) church 73, **718**
  industry 81, 715, **722–3**
  glove factories 81, **722**
  Nautilus Works (former) 81, **722**
  tannery 81, **722**
  Westland Works 81, **723**

public buildings 84, **718–20**
  Divisional Police
    Headquarters 84, **718**
  Library 84, **721**
  Magistrates' Court 83, **718**
  Municipal Offices 83, 84, **721**
  Post Office 83, **721**
  stations 80, **579**, **719–20**, *722*
  Town Hall 77, *166*, *721*
  workhouse (former) 78, 145, **719**
  Yeovil College 84, **719**
streets and houses 82, 84, **720–3**
  Britannia Inn 96
  Capital & Counties Bank
    (former) 80, **720**
  Manor Hotel (Hendford
    House) 59, **721**
  Midland Bank (former) 80, **721**
  Park, The (suburb) 77, **723**
  Petter & Warren housing 82, **722–3**
  Wiltshire & Dorset Bank
    (former) 80, **721**
Yeovil Junction *see* Stoford
Yeovil Marsh **723–4**
Yeovilton **724**